Greece

THE ROUGH GUIDE

There are more than one hundred Rough Guide titles
covering destinations from Amsterdam to Zimbabwe

Forthcoming titles include
Bangkok • Brussels • Florence • Japan

Rough Guide Reference Series
Classical Music • European Football • The Internet • Jazz
Opera • Reggae • Rock Music • World Music

Rough Guide Phrasebooks
Czech • Egyptian Arabic • French • German • Greek
Hindi & Urdu • Hungarian • Indonesian • Italian • Japanese
Mandarin Chinese • Mexican Spanish • Polish • Portuguese
Russian • Spanish • Swahili • Thai • Turkish • Vietnamese

Rough Guides on the Internet
http://www.roughguides.com

ROUGH GUIDE CREDITS

Text editor: Helena Smith
Series editor: Mark Ellingham
Editorial: Martin Dunford, Jonathan Buckley, Samantha Cook, Jo Mead, Kate Berens, Amanda Tomlin, Ann-Marie Shaw, Paul Gray, Sarah Dallas, Chris Schüler, Julia Kelly, Helena Smith, Caroline Osborne, Kieran Falconer, Judith Bamber, Olivia Eccleshall, Orla Duane (UK); Andrew Rosenberg (US)
Picture research: Eleanor Hill

Production: Susanne Hillen, Andy Hilliard, Judy Pang, Link Hall, Nicola Williamson, Helen Ostick
Cartography: Melissa Flack, Maxine Burke
Online editors: Alan Spicer (UK); Geronimo Madrid (US)
Finance: John Fisher, Celia Crowley, Catherine Gillespie
Marketing & Publicity: Richard Trillo, Simon Carloss, Niki Smith (UK); Jean-Marie Kelly, SoRelle Braun (US)
Administration: Tania Hummel, Alexander Mark Rogers

ACKNOWLEDGEMENTS

Marc Dubin thanks Christina, Ritsa and Thanos in Athens, for years of support; the Della family in Ioannina; Kostas and Madelon Vassiliou in Kípi, Zagoria; Kiveli Petropoulou in Thessaloníki; Persephone Papayriakou, Manolis and Maria on Thássos; the Papasotiriou family on Límnos; George & Barbara Ballis, Jennifer Yiannakou and Melinda on Lésvos; Markos Kostalas on Khíos; Alexis and Dhionysia Zikas on Kós; Christine Sakelaridhes Khálki and Baz Ward for Tílos updates; Bruce Bastin at Interstate Music, for discographic material; Andrew Stoddart at Hellenic Bookservice, for the thorough bibliographic search; Theodhore Spordhilis for restaurant tips on Khios; and Terena at Horiatopoulos Tours on Sámos.

Nick Edwards thanks Yiannis Karapapas for political insight and brotherly hospitality in Athens, Richard Hartle for sorting out Pátra, Martin Burne for expert chauffering, Murray Kane in Athens, Geraldine Cassidy on Kéa, Maria Koureli on Mílos, Vassilis Tzavaras on Mílos and elsewhere, Anne Collins, Vassilis, Melissa and Ruth on Síros, Catherine McLaughlin on Ándros, Kent Goulden on Kalamáta and Sean Sutton and Annalisa Trapani in Spárti.

John Gill thanks Helena Smith and Jonathan Buckley for editing the text into its final shape, and Iannis Tranakas,

whose filoxenía revived my filellinísmos when it was evaporating in the heat; Stephan Jaskulowski for vital editorial contributions; Lia Mathioudaki and the Corfu NTOG for help beyond the call of duty; Judith Mackrell and Mitzi Rogers for hospitality and help; Towering Inferno for sharing a secret; Mrs Pat Stubbs, for shelter; the Vassilas and Petrou families of Paxos for their friendship over the years; Maria Gazi and brother Yioryios of Nidhrí, for their kindness; Yioryios Moraitis of Kioni, who introduced me to the virtual Ionian via his website; Mr Messaris and Mrs Vassilikis of the Argostóli NTOG for their many favours; Barbara Salisbury, for spotting the *Arekia* taverna in Zákynthos; and KTEL staff and drivers everywhere – in particular the St Exuperys of the Argostóli–Fiskárdho road.

John Hartle thanks Fanis Gavalas on Iráklia, Kathleen Gika on Íos and Sharon Turner on Tínos.

The editor thanks Rosemary Morlin for proofreading, and MicroMap (Romsey, Hants) for cartography. At the Rough Guides thanks go to Jonathan Buckley for help and support; to Susanne Hillen, Maxine Burke, Dave Abram, Nicola Williamson, Helen Ostick and, most especially, to Judy Pang for her patience and efficiency.

PUBLISHING INFORMATION

This seventh edition published February 1998 by Rough Guides Ltd, 62–70 Shorts Gardens, London WC2H 9AB. Reprinted in November 1998.
Distributed by the Penguin Group:
Penguin Books Ltd, 27 Wrights Lane, London W8 5TZ
Penguin Books USA Inc., 375 Hudson Street, New York 10014, USA
Penguin Books Australia Ltd, 487 Maroondah Highway, PO Box 257, Ringwood, Victoria 3134, Australia
Penguin Books Canada Ltd, 10 Alcorn Avenue, Toronto, Ontario, Canada M4V 1E4
Penguin Books (NZ) Ltd, 182–190 Wairau Road, Auckland 10, New Zealand
Typeset in Linotron Univers and Century Old Style to an original design by Andrew Oliver.
Printed in England by Clays Ltd, St Ives PLC
Illustrations in Part One and Part Three by Edward Briant.
Illustration on p.1 by Henry Iles and on p.767 by Jane Strother.

Greece

THE ROUGH GUIDE

written and researched by

Mark Ellingham, Marc Dubin, Natania Jansz and John Fisher

with additional contributions by

John Chapple, Nick Edwards, Geoff Garvey, John Gill, John Hartle, Diana Louis and Julia Tweed

THE ROUGH GUIDES

TRAVEL GUIDES • PHRASEBOOKS • MUSIC AND REFERENCE GUIDES

 We set out to do something different when the first Rough Guide was published in 1982. Mark Ellingham, just out of university, was travelling in Greece. He brought along the popular guides of the day, but found they were all lacking in some way. They were either strong on ruins and museums but went on for pages without mentioning a beach or taverna. Or they were so conscious of the need to save money that they lost sight of Greece's cultural and historical significance. Also, none of the books told him anything about Greece's contemporary life – its politics, its culture, its people, and how they lived.

So with no job in prospect, Mark decided to write his own guidebook, one which aimed to provide practical information that was second to none, detailing the best beaches and the hottest clubs and restaurants, while also giving hard-hitting accounts of every sight, both famous and obscure, and providing up-to-the-minute information on contemporary culture. It was a guide that encouraged independent travellers to find the best of Greece, and was a great success, getting shortlisted for the Thomas Cook travel guide award, and encouraging Mark, along with three friends, to expand the series.

The Rough Guide list grew rapidly and the letters flooded in, indicating a much broader readership than had been anticipated, but one which uniformly appreciated the Rough Guide mix of practical detail and humour, irreverence and enthusiasm. Things haven't changed. The same four friends who began the series are still the caretakers of the Rough Guide mission today: to provide the most reliable, up-to-date and entertaining information to independent-minded travellers of all ages, on all budgets.

We now publish 100 titles and have offices in London and New York. The travel guides are written and researched by a dedicated team of more than 100 authors, based in Britain, Europe, the USA and Australia. We have also created a unique series of phrasebooks to accompany the travel series, along with an acclaimed series of music guides, and a best-selling pocket guide to the Internet and World Wide Web. We also publish comprehensive travel information on our web site:

and http://www.roughguides.com

HELP US UPDATE

We've gone to a lot of effort to ensure that this new edition of The Rough Guide to Greece is accurate and up-to-date. However, things change – places get "discovered", opening hours are notoriously fickle, restaurants and rooms raise prices or lower standards, extra buses are laid on or off. If you feel we've got it wrong or left something out, we'd like to know, and if you can remember the address, the price, the time, the phone number, so much the better.

We'll credit all contributions, and send a copy of the next edition (or any other Rough Guide if you prefer) for the best letters. Please mark letters: "Rough Guide Greece Update" and send to:
Rough Guides, 62–70 Shorts Gardens, London WC2H 9AB, or Rough Guides, 375 Hudson St, 9th floor, New York NY 10014.
Or send email to: mail@roughguides.co.uk
Online updates about this book can be found on Rough Guides' website at http://www.roughguides.com

THE AUTHORS OF THE ROUGH GUIDE TO GREECE

Mark Ellingham and Natania Jansz wrote the original edition of this book – the first ever Rough Guide – in 1981. They couldn't believe their good fortune in being paid by a publisher to spend time roaming around Classical ruins and medieval castles, and island-hopping in the Aegean. Mark continued writing Rough Guides and still works for the company as Series Editor. He is currently spending most of his time developing publication of the guides on the Internet but would be happier roaming the ruins, etc. Natania divides her time between Clinical Psychology and writing; she has edited the Rough Guide special, More Women Travel. Natania and Mark have a toddler, Miles, who rates Greek food (and sand) high on his list of life's good things.

John Fisher has also been involved with Rough Guides from the start. One of the original authors of the Greek guide, he has since written numerous other Rough Guide titles including the Rough Guide to Crete. Between travels, John can usually be found chained to a desk at Rough Guide HQ in London. He lives in south London with his wife and two young sons.

Marc Dubin first arrived in Greece in 1978, able to ask only for yoghurts, and the loo, in the local tongue. Since 1981 he has returned yearly, thereby acquiring fluency in Greek, and from 1989 onwards has lived part-time on the island of Sámos, where he recently restored an old cottage. Marc writes regularly for various publications on topics as diverse as Greek cuisine, music and backcountry trekking. When not in Greece, he lives in London or ranges across the Mediterranean in the course of updating his other Rough Guides: Turkey, Cyprus, and the Pyrenees.

READER'S LETTERS

We'd like to thank the readers of previous editions, who took time to write in with comments and suggestions. For this edition, we were helped by letters from:

Loretta Alborghetti, Helen Alice, David Authers, Jim Bainbridge, Christine and Marshall Becker, Rev and Mrs R. J. Blakeway-Phillips, Monica Bradley, Michael Davies, Sonia Barr, Richard Bunting and Penny Dykes, Nigel Burtt, Cathy and Steven Butler, Peter Ceulemans, Fiona Collingwood, M. Colman, Alison-Louise Conn, Marie Demetriou, Bridget Deutsch, David and Yvette Dickinsin, Constantine Dimaros, David Edwards, Arnulf Elvevold, Marit Erikksson, Norman Foot, Mike Gerrard, Emma Gervasio, Michael Graubart, Barbara Goulden, C.J. Hardy, R.J. Hartley, Nicholas Harvey, Kathy and Martyn Heald, R.A. Hine, Andrew Humphrey, Howard Huws, Suzanne Ince, Zane Katsikis, Sue Kennedy, Udo Kock, Paul Lawlor, Andreas Loizou, Kevin McCarthy, Michael O'Hare and Sally Manders, R.E. Miller, Stephen Minta, Ainsley Monaghan and Esther Sakine, Mr Nielsen, Dr Ian Parker, Zena L. Polin, Christopher Price, Paul K. Rawcliffe, Caroline Read, Julian Richards, Chritos Rigas, David and Wendy Rumsey, Philip Ryan, Dennis Samuels, Carola Scupham, Henrietta Seymour, Christopher Stocks, Brian Storey, Ann Thomas, Pippa Todd, Steven White, Leslie Whitehouse, Adrian Whittaker and Deena Omar, Bill Wier, Christine Winter and David Wright, and Carolyn Smith.

CONTENTS

Introduction xi

PART THREE THE ISLANDS 411

PART FOUR · CONTEXTS 765

LIST OF MAPS

MAP SYMBOLS

Railway		Cave
Road		Viewpoint
Minor road		Refuge
Path		Campsite
Ferry route		Hotel
Waterway		Restaurant
Chapter division boundary		Airport
International boundary		Lighthouse
Mosque		Information office
Synagogue		Post office
County church		Telephone
Monastery or convent		Metro station
Castle		Bus stop
Ruins		Building
Peak		Church
Mountains		Christian cemetery
Marshland		Park
Waterfall		National park
Ancient site		Pedestrianised area
		Beach

INTRODUCTION

With well over a hundred inhabited islands and a territory that stretches from the Mediterranean to the Balkans, Greece has interest enough to fill months of travel. The **historic sites** span four millennia, encompassing the legendary and renowned, such as Mycenae, Olympia, Delphi and the Parthenon, and the obscure, where a visit can still seem like a personal discovery. The **beaches** are parcelled out along a convoluted coastline equal to France's in length, and they range from those of islands where the boat calls twice a week to resorts as cosmopolitan as any in the Mediterranean. Perhaps less expected by visitors, the country's mountainous interior offers some of the best and least exploited **hiking** in Europe.

Modern Greece is the sum of an extraordinary diversity of **influences**. Romans, Arabs, French, Venetians, Slavs, Albanians, Turks, Italians, to say nothing of the great Byzantine empire, have been and gone since the time of Alexander the Great. All have left their mark: the Byzantines in countless churches and monasteries and in ghost towns like Mystra; the Venetians in impregnable fortifications at Náfplio, Monemvassía and Methóni in the Peloponnese; and other Latin powers, such as the Knights of Saint John and the Genoese, in magnificent castles throughout the eastern Aegean. Most obvious of all is the heritage of four hundred years of Ottoman Turkish rule which, while universally derided, exercised an inestimable influence on music, cuisine, language and way of life. The contributions, and continued existence, of substantial minorities – Vlachs, Muslims, Jews, Gypsies – have also helped to forge the Hellenic identity.

All of this has been instrumental in the formation of the character of the people, which embodies a powerful and hard to define strain of **Greekness** that has kept alive the people's sense of themselves throughout their turbulent history. With no ruling class to impose a superior model of taste or to patronize the arts, the last few centuries of Greek peasants, fishermen and shepherds have created a vigorous and truly popular culture, which is manifest in a thousand instinctively tasteful ways, ranging from songs and dances, costumes, embroidery, woven bags and rugs, and furniture, to the white cubist houses of popular image.

Of course there are formal cultural activities as well: **museums** that shouldn't be missed, in Athens, Thessaloníki and Iráklion; compelling buildings like the **monasteries** of the Metéora and Mount Áthos; **castles** such as those in the Dodecanese, Lésvos, central Greece and the Peloponnese; as well, of course, as the great **ancient sites** dating from Mycenaean, Minoan, Classical, Macedonian and Roman times. The country hosts some excellent summer **festivals** too, bringing international theatre groups and orchestras to perform in ancient theatres at Epidaurus, Dodona and Athens – magical settings in themselves.

But the call to cultural duty should never be too overwhelming on a Greek holiday. The **hedonistic pleasures** of languor and warmth – always going lightly dressed, swimming in the sea without a hint of a shiver, talking and drinking under the stars – are just as appealing. But despite recent improvements to the tourism "product", Greece is still essentially a land for simple sybarites, not for those who crave the five-star treatment of super-soft beds, faultless plumbing, exquisite cuisine and attentive service. Except at the top of the range, hotel accommodation tends to be plain, rented rooms can be box-like and stuffy, campsites often offer the minimum of facilities, and the food at its best is fresh and uncomplicated.

The Greek people

To begin to get an understanding of the Greek people, it is important to realize just how recent and profound were the events that created the **modern state** and national

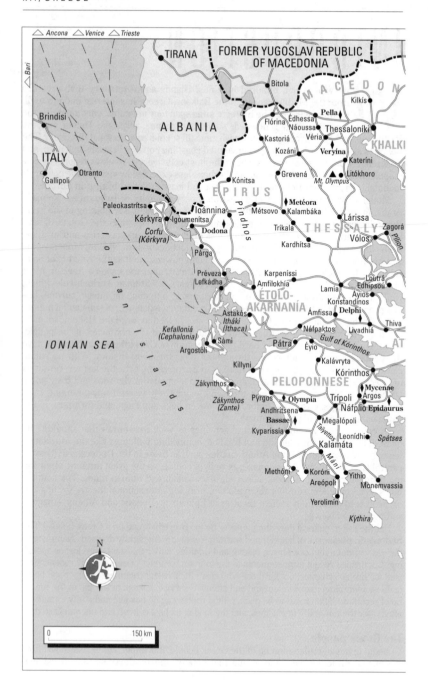

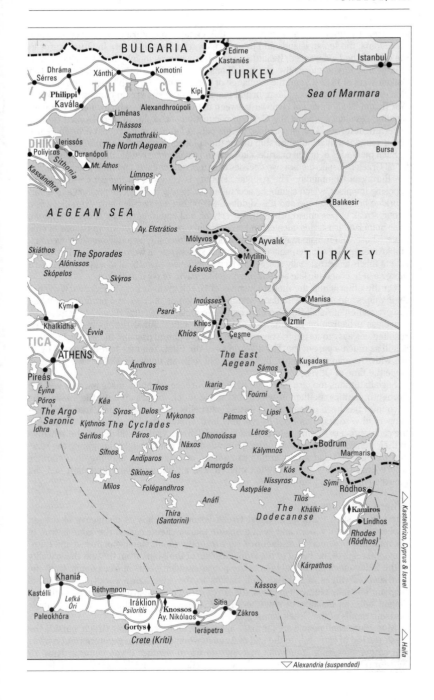

character. Up until the early decades of this century many parts of Greece – Crete, Macedonia, the Ionian islands and the entire eastern Aegean – were in Ottoman (or in the case of the Dodecanese, Italian) hands. Meanwhile, as many ethnic Greeks lived in Asia Minor, Egypt and in the north Balkans as in the recently forged kingdom. The Balkan Wars of 1912–13 and the exchange of "Greek" and "Turkish" populations in 1923 changed everything in a sudden, brutal manner. Worse still was to come during World War II, and its aftermath of civil war between the Communists – who formed the core of wartime resistance against the German occupation – and the western-backed rightist government forces. The viciousness of this period found a more recent echo in nearly seven years of military dictatorship under the colonels' junta between 1967 and 1974.

Such memories of brutal misrule, diaspora and catastrophe remain uncomfortably close for all Greeks, despite the last two decades of democratic stability and their integration into the European Community. The resultant identity is complex, an uneasy coexistence of opposing impulses, which cannot be accounted for merely by Greece's position as a natural bridge between Europe and the Middle East. Within a generally extrovert outlook is a strong streak of pessimism, while the poverty of, and enduring paucity of opportunity in, their homeland frustrates talented and resourceful Greeks, many of whom choose to emigrate. Those who remain may have been lulled, until recently, by a civil-service-driven full-employment policy which resulted in the lowest jobless rate in western Europe. The downside of this is an occasionally staggering lack of initiative, but official attempts to impose a more austere economic line are still often met by waves of popular strikes.

On the other hand, the meticulousness of Greek craftworkers is legendary, even if their values and skills took a back seat to the demands of crisis and profiteering when the evacuation of Asia Minor and the rapid depopulation of rural villages prompted the graceless urbanization of Athens and the other cities. Amid the sophistication that resulted, it's easy to forget the nearness of the agricultural past and the fact that Greece is still as much a part of the Third World as of the First. You may find that buses operate with Germanic efficiency, but ferries sail with an unpredictability little changed since the time of Odysseus.

Social attitudes too, are in a state of flux as Greece adapts to mass tourism and the twentieth century, neither of which had made much impact up until the 1960s. The encounter has been painful and at times destructive, as a largely rural, traditional and conservative society has been irrevocably lost. Though the Greeks are adaptable and the cash registers ring happily, at least in tourist areas, visitors still need to be sensitive in their behaviour towards the older generation. The mind boggles imagining the reaction of the black-clad grandparents to nudism, or even scanty clothing, in a country where until recently the Orthodox church was all but an established faith and the guardian of national identity.

Where and when to go

There is no such thing as a typical Greek island; each has its distinctive character, appearance, history, flora and even a unique tourist clientele. And the same is true of the mainland provinces. **Landscapes** vary from the mountainous northwest and rainy, shaggy forests of the Pílion to the stony deserts of the Máni, from the soft theatricality of the Peloponnesian coastal hills to the poplar-studded plains of Macedonia, from the pine-scented ridges of Skiáthos and Sámos to the wind-blown rocks of the central Aegean. The inky plume of cypress, the silver green of olive groves, the blue outline of distant hills, an expanse of shimmering sea: these are the enduring and unfailingly pleasing motifs of the Greek landscape.

Most places and people are far more agreeable, and recognizably Greek, outside the **peak period** of early July to the end of August, when soaring temperatures and crowds can be overpowering. You won't miss out on warm weather if you come in **June** or **September**, excellent times everywhere but particularly amid the Sporades and Ionian or east Aegean islands. In **October** you might hit a stormy spell, especially in western Greece or in the mountains, but for most of that month the "summer of Áyios Dhimítrios" (the Greek equivalent of Indian summer) prevails, and the Dodecanese and Crete are pleasant. Autumn in general is beautiful; the light is softer, the sea often balmier than the air, and the colours subtler.

December to **March** are the coldest and least reliable months, though there are many fine days of perfect crystal visibility, and the glorious lowland flowers begin to bloom very early in spring. The more northerly latitudes and high altitudes of course endure far colder and wetter conditions, with the mountains themselves under snow from November to May. The most dependable **winter weather** is to be found in the Dodecanese, immediately around Rhodes, or in the southeastern parts of Crete. As spring slowly warms up, **April** is still uncertain, though fine for visiting the Dodecanese; by **May** the weather is more generally predictable, and Crete, the Peloponnese, the Ionian islands and the Cyclades are perhaps at their best, even if the sea is still a little cool for swimming.

Other factors that can affect the timing of your Greek travels are mainly concerned with the level of tourism. Standards of service invariably slip under the high-season pressures, and room rates are at their highest in July and August. If you can only visit in high season, then you'll do well to plan your itinerary a little away from the beaten track. Explore the less obvious parts of the Peloponnese or the northern mainland for example; or island-hop with an eye for the more obscure – the places where ferries call less than once a day and where there's no airport.

Out of season, especially between November and March, you may have to wrestle with uncertain ferry schedules to the islands, and often fairly skeletal facilities when you arrive. However, you will find reasonable service on all the main routes and at least one hotel open in the port or main town. On the mainland, out-of-season travel poses no special difficulties except, of course, in mountain villages cut off by snow.

AVERAGE TEMPERATURES AND RAINFALL

	Jan			March			May			July			Sept			Nov		
	°F		Rain	°F		Rain	°F		Rain	°F		Rain	°F	Rain		°F		Rain
	Max	Min	days	Max	Min	days	Max	Min	days	Max	Min	days	Max	Min	days	Max	Min	days
Athens	54	44	13	60	46	10	76	60	9	90	72	2	84	66	4	65	52	12
Crete (Haniá)	60	46	17	64	48	11	76	56	5	86	68	0	82	64	3	70	54	10
Cyclades (Mýkonos)	58	50	14	62	52	8	72	62	5	82	72	0.5	78	68	1	66	58	9
North Greece (Khalkidhikí)	50	36	7	59	44	9	77	58	10	90	70	4	83	64	5	60	47	9
Ionian (Corfu)	56	44	13	62	46	10	74	58	6	88	70	2	82	64	5	66	52	12
Dodecanese (Rhodes)	58	50	15	62	48	7	74	58	2	86	70	0	82	72	1	68	60	7
Sporades (Skiáthos)	55	45	12	58	47	10	71	58	3	82	71	0	75	64	8	62	53	12
East Aegean (Lésvos)	54	42	11	60	46	7	76	60	6	88	70	2	82	66	2	64	50	9

GETTING THERE FROM BRITAIN

It's close on 2000 miles from London to Athens, so for most visitors flying is the only viable option. There are direct flights to a variety of Greek destinations from all the major British airports. Flying time is around three and a half hours and the cost of charter flights is reasonable – sample return fares to Athens from London in midsummer start from around £160 (Manchester £180, Glasgow £200), but there are always bargains to be had. Easter is also classed as high season, but outside these periods flights can be snapped up for as little as £120 return. Costs can often be highly competitive, too, if you buy a flight as part of an all-in package: see pp.6–7 for details of holiday operators.

Road or **rail** alternatives take a minimum of three days but are obviously worth considering if you plan to visit Greece as part of an extended trip through Europe. The most popular route is down through Italy, then across to Greece by ferry, an alternative being to take a ferry from Croatia. The old overland route through the former Yugoslavia is still impractical, but a much longer route is possible via Hungary, Romania and Bulgaria.

BY PLANE

Most of the cheaper flights from Britain to Greece are **charters**, which are sold either with a package holiday or as a flight-only option. The flights have fixed and unchangeable outward and return dates, and often a maximum stay of one month.

For longer stays or more flexibility, or if you're travelling out of season (when few charters are available), you'll need a **scheduled** flight. As with charters, these are offered under a wide variety of fares, and are again often sold off at discount by agents. Useful sources for discounted flights are the classified ads in the travel sections of newspapers like the *Independent*, *Guardian*, *Observer* and *Sunday Times*. Teletext is also worth checking, while your local travel agent shouldn't be overlooked.

Although **Athens** remains the prime destination for cheap fares, there are also **direct flights** from Britain to **Thessaloníki, Kalamáta, Kavála** and **Préveza** on the Greek mainland, and to the islands of **Crete, Rhodes, Corfu, Lésvos, Páros, Zákynthos, Kefalloniá, Skiáthos, Sámos** and **Kós**. And with any flight to Athens, you can buy a **domestic connecting flight** (on the national carrier, Olympic) to one of three dozen or so additional Greek mainland and island airports.

CHARTER FLIGHTS

Travel agents throughout Britain sell **charter flights** to Greece, which usually operate from May to October; late-night departures and early-morning arrivals are common. Even the high street chains frequently promote "flight-only" deals, or discount all-inclusive holidays, when their parent companies need to offload their seat allocations. In any case, phone around for a range of offers. Charter airlines include GB Airways, Excalibur and Monarch, but you can only book tickets on these through travel agents.

The greatest variety of **flight destinations** tend to be from London Gatwick and Manchester. In summer, if you book in advance, you should have a choice of most of the dozen Greek regional airports listed above. Flying from elsewhere in Britain (Birmingham, Cardiff, Glasgow or Newcastle), or looking for last-minute discounts, you'll find options more limited, most commonly to Athens, Corfu, Rhodes and Crete.

It's worth noting that **non-EU nationals** who buy charter tickets to Greece must buy a return ticket, to return after no fewer than three days and no more than four weeks, and must accompany it with an **accommodation voucher** for at least the first few nights of their stay – check that the ticket satisfies these conditions or you could be refused entry. In practice, the "accommodation voucher" has become a formality; it has to name an existing hotel but you're not expected to use it (and probably won't be able to if you try).

The other important condition regards travel to **Turkey** (or any other neighbouring country). If you travel to Greece on a charter flight, you may visit another country only as a day trip; if you stay overnight, you will invalidate your ticket. This rule is justified by the Greek authorities because they subsidize charter airline landing fees, and are

therefore reluctant to see tourists spending their money outside Greece. Whether you buy that excuse or not, there is no way around it, since the Turkish authorities clearly stamp all passports, and the Greeks usually check them. The package industry on the east Aegean and Dodecanese islands bordering Turkey, however, does sometimes prevail upon customs officials to back-date re-entry stamps when bad weather strands their tour groups overnight in Anatolia.

Student/youth charters are allowed to be sold as one-way flights only. By combining two one-way charters you can, therefore, stay for over a month. Student/youth charter tickets are available to anyone under 26, and to all card-carrying full-time students under 32.

Finally, remember that **reconfirmation** of return charter flights is vital and should be done at least 72 hours before departure.

SCHEDULED FLIGHTS

The advantages of scheduled flights are that they can be pre-booked well in advance, have longer ticket validities and involve none of the above restrictions on charters. However, many of the cheaper APEX and SuperAPEX fares do have an advance-purchase and/or minimum-stay requirements, so check conditions carefully. Scheduled flights also usually operate during the day.

As with charters, discount fares on scheduled flights are available from most high-street travel **agents**, as well as from a number of specialist flight and student/youth agencies. Most discount scheduled fares have an advance-purchase requirement

The biggest choice of scheduled flights is with the Greek national carrier **Olympic Airways**, and **British Airways**; both fly direct from London Heathrow to Athens (Olympic three times daily, BA twice daily) and also to Thessaloníki (Olympic four times a week, BA once daily). **Virgin Airways** also has a daily service (twice daily in summer) to Athens. All these airlines offer a range of special fares and even in July and August can come up with deals as low as £160 return; more realistically, though, you'll pay around £250–325 return for a scheduled flight. You'll also be able to book onward connections to domestic Greek airports; flights from British regional airports route through Heathrow in the first instance.

East European airways like BSA, Balkan, Malev and LOT can be cheaper – £120 one way, £240 return for much of the year – but nearly always involve delays, with connections in (respectively) Prague, Sofia, Budapest and Warsaw. It is not always possible to book discount fares direct from these airlines, and you'll often pay no more by going through an agent (see box).

PACKAGES AND TOURS

Virtually every British **tour operator** includes Greece in its programme, though with many of the larger groups you'll find choices limited to the established resorts – notably the islands of Rhodes, Kós, Crete, Skiáthos, Zákynthos and

Corfu, plus Toló and the Khalkidhi on the mainland. If you buy one of these at a last-minute discount, you may find it costs little more than a flight – and you can use the accommodation offered as much or as little as you want. For a rather more low-key and genuinely "Greek" resort, however, it's better to book your holiday through one of the smaller **specialist agencies** listed below.

BY TRAIN

Travelling by **train** from Britain to Greece takes around three and a half days and fares work out more expensive than flights. However, with a regular ticket stopovers are possible – in France, Switzerland and Italy – while with an InterRail or Eurail train pass you can take in Greece as part of a wider rail trip around Europe.

ROUTES

The most practical route from Britain takes in France, Switzerland and Italy before crossing on the ferry from Bari or Brindisi to Pátra (Patras). Book seats well in advance, especially in summer (for ferry information, see the box on p.9).

Until the outbreak of civil war, the route through **former Yugoslavia** was the most popular; this is still problematic, and probably best avoided. A more rambling alternative from Budapest runs via **Bucharest** and **Sofia** to **Thessaloníki**, which is advised as your first stop since Athens is nearly nine hours further on the train.

TICKETS AND PASSES

Regular train tickets from Britain to Greece are not good value. London to Athens costs at least £380 return. If you are **under 26**, you can get a

---

RAIL TICKET OFFICES

Eurotrain, 52 Grosvenor Gardens, London SW1 (☎0171/730 3402).

International Rail Centre, Victoria Station, London SW1 (☎0990/848848).

Wasteels, Victoria Station, London SW1 (☎0171/834 7066).

BUS TICKET OFFICES

National Express Eurolines, 52 Grosvenor Gardens, London SW1 (☎0990/808080).

SPECIALIST PACKAGE OPERATORS

VILLA OR VILLAGE ACCOMMODATION
These companies are all fairly small-scale operations, offering competitively priced packages with flights and often using more traditional village accommodation. They make an effort to offer islands without over-developed tourist resorts and, increasingly, unspoiled mainland destinations.

Argo Travel, 100 Wigmore St, London W1H 9DR (☎0171/331 7070).
Attractive properties in the Cyclades, Spétses, Póros, Sámos and Lésvos.

CV Travel, 43 Cadogan St, London SW3 2PR (☎0171/581 0851 or 0171/584 8803).
Quality villas on Corfu and Paxí.

Corfu à la Carte, The Whitehouse, Bucklebury Alley, Cold Ash, Newbury, Berks RH16 9NN (☎01635/201140).
Selected beach and rural cottages on Corfu, Paxí, Skópelos, Sími and Skiáthos.

Direct Travel, Oxford House, 182 Upper Richmond Rd, Putney, London SW15 2SH (☎0181/785 4000).
Moderately priced studios and villas at mainland Parga and on Crete, Lefkádha, Zákynthos, Lésvos, Khálki and Rhodes.

Elysian Holidays, 16 High Street, Tenterden, Kent TN30 6AP (☎01580/766599, fax 765416).
Small company recently expanded from Volissós, Khíos to include Pátmos, Sýros and Évvia.

Grecofile/Filoxenia, Sourdock Hill, Barkisland, Halifax, West Yorkshire HX4 0AG (☎01422/375999).
Tailor-made itineraries and specialist packages to unspoiled areas.

Greek Islands Club, 66 High St, Walton-on-Thames, Surrey KT12 1BU (☎01932/220477).
Holidays on the Ionian islands, Skiáthos, Skópelos, Alónissos, Santórini, Mýkonos, Páros, Siros, Crete, Ídhra and Spétses.

Greek Sun Holidays, 1 Bank St, Sevenoaks, Kent TN13 1UW (☎01732/740317).
Offer a variety of packages, including fly-drive, on a wide range of islands and on the Pílion peninsula.

Laskarina Holidays, St Marys Gate, Wirksworth, Derbyshire DE4 4DQ (☎01629/822203).
Top-end villas and apartments on Lipsi, Tilos, Kalimnos, Leros, Sými, Khálki, Alónissos, Skópelos and Spetses; consistently high marks for service.

Simply Crete, Chiswick Gate, 598–608 Chiswick High Rd, London W4 5RT (☎0181/995 9323).
Simply Ionian, same address and phone number.
High-quality apartments, villas and small hotels on Crete and Ionian islands.

Skiathos Travel, 4 Holmesdale Rd, Kew Gardens, Richmond, Surrey TW9 3J2 (☎0181/940 5157).
Packages to the Sporades; some flight-only deals.

Sunvil Holidays, Sunvil House, 7–8 Upper Square, Old Isleworth, Middlesex TW7 7BJ (☎0181/568 4499 or 0181/847 4748).
Ionian islands, Sporades, Cyclades, Limnos, Khíos, Crete, Peloponnese, Epirus and the Pílion.

Voyages Ilena, Old Garden House, The Lanterns, Bridge Lane, London SW11 3AD (☎0171/924 4440).
Mainland specialists.

BIJ ticket, discounting these fares by around 25 percent; these are available through Eurotrain and Wasteels (see box on p.5 for addresses). Both regular and BIJ tickets have two months' return validity, or can be purchased as one ways, and the Italy routes include the ferry crossing. The tickets also allow for stopovers, so long as you stick to the route prescribed.

Better value by far is to buy an **InterRail pass**, available to anyone resident in Europe for six months. You can buy it from British Rail (or any travel agent), and the pass offers unlimited travel on a zonal basis on up to 25 European rail net-

works. The only extras you pay are supplements on certain express trains, plus half-price fares in Britain (or the country of issue) and on the cross-Channel ferries. The pass includes the ferry from Brindisi in southern Italy to Pátra in Greece. There are several types: to reach Greece from the UK you'll need a pass valid for at least two zones (£209 for a month), though if you're intending to travel further in Europe you might invest in an all-zone card for £275; Greece is zoned with Italy, Turkey and Slovenia.

Finally, anyone over 60 and holding a British Rail Senior Citizen Railcard, can buy a **Rail**

HIKING TOURS

All the operators below run trekking groups, which generally consist of ten to fifteen people, plus an experienced guide. The walks tend to be day-hikes from one or more bases, or point-to-point treks staying in village accommodation en route; camping is not usually involved.

Explore Worldwide, 1 Frederick St, Aldershot, Hampshire GU11 1LQ (☎01252/344161).
Organized hikes in Peloponnese, Évvia, Crete, Tinos, Páros and Náxos. They describe these as easy to moderate treks. They also organize caique sailing.

Ramblers Holidays, Longcroft House, Fretherne Rd, Welwyn Garden City, Herts AL8 6PQ (☎01707/331133).
Walking tours on the Pílion and Olympus, Delphi, Évvia, the Mani, Crete, Sámos, Patmos, Khíos, Rhodes and Corfu.

Robinson Holidays, Ogdhóïs Merarkhías 10, 45 445 Ioánnina (fax 30/651/25 071).
Píndhos and north Greece specialists, with extremely knowledgeable, multi-lingual group-leading.

Sherpa Expeditions, 131a Heston Rd, Hounslow, Middlesex TW5 0RD (☎0181/577 2717).
Good range of tours concentrated on the mainland.

Trekking Hellas, Filellinon 7, 105 57 Athens (☎30/1/33 10 323).
The most extensive Greece-wide programme, covering the Píndhos, Taïyettos, the Pílion, western Crete and central Greece; also canyoning and rafting.

Waymark Holidays, 44 Windsor Rd, Slough SL1 2EJ (☎01753/516477).
Spring and autumn walking holidays on Sámos, Náxos and Mílos; tougher hikes in the Píndhos and Peloponnese.

NATURE AND WILDLIFE

Marengo Guided Walks, 17 Bernard Crescent, Hunstanton PE36 6ER (☎01485/532710).
Spring and autumn botanical outings in northern Lésvos, Thássos, Sámos and southern Crete, led by a trained botanist.

Peregrine Holidays, 40/41 South Parade, Summertown, Oxford OX2 7JP (☎01865/511642).
Natural history tours on Corfu and Crete; the emphasis on each tour is on wildlife, though combined with visits to archeological sites.

SAILING

Dinghy sailing, yachting and windsurfing holidays based on small flotillas of four- to six-berth yachts. Prices start at around £350 per person per week off-season: all levels of experience. Sailing holidays can be flotilla- or shore-based. If you're a confident sailor and can muster a group of people, it's possible simply to charter a yacht from a broker; the Greek National Tourist Organization has lists of companies.

The Moorings, Bradstowe House, Middle Wall, Whitstable, Kent CT5 1BF (☎01227/776 677).
Operates charters out of Athens, Corfu and Kós.

Sunsail The Port House, Port Solent, Portsmouth, Hampshire PO6 4TH (☎01705/210345).
Tuition in dinghy sailing, yachting and windsurfing. Clubs include Lefkadha, Kefallonia and the Sporades.

MIND AND BODY

Skyros Centre, 92 Prince of Wales Rd, London NW5 3NE (☎0171/267 4424).
Holistic health, fitness and "personal growth" holidays on the island of Skíros, as well as

---

Europe Senior Card (£5 for a year). This gives up to 30 percent reductions on rail fares throughout Europe and 30 percent off sea crossings.

BY BUS

With charter flights at such competitive rates, it's hard to find good reasons for wanting to spend three or four days on a bus to Greece. However, it's still a considerably cheaper option than taking the train.

Olympic Bus offers low-cost fares (£100–120 return) but National Express Eurolines (bookable through any National Express office; see box above) has a more reliable reputation, better buses, and higher prices (£200–220 return). These days, other operators are thin on the ground, but even so it pays to be very wary about going for the cheapest company unless you've heard something about them. There have been a string of accidents in recent years with operators flouting the terms of their licence, and horror stories abound of drivers getting lost or their coaches being refused entry.

The **route** is either Belgium, Germany and Austria, or via France and Italy and then a ferry across to Greece. Stops of about twenty minutes are made every five or six hours, with the odd longer break for roadside café meals.

BY CAR

If you have the time and inclination, **driving to Greece** can be a pleasant proposition. Realistically, though, it's really only worth considering if you have at least a month to spare, are going to stay in Greece for an extended period, or want to take advantage of various stopovers en route.

It's important to plan ahead. The **Automobile Association** (AA) provides a comprehensive service offering general advice on all facets of driving to Greece and the names and addresses of useful contact organizations. Their European Routes Service (contact AA on ☎01256/20123 or your local branch) can arrange a detailed print-out of a route to follow. Driving licence, vehicle registration documents and insurance are essential; a green card is recommended.

The most popular **route** is down through France and Italy to catch one of the Adriatic ferries. A much longer alternative through Eastern Europe (Hungary, Romania and Bulgaria) is just about feasible, and there is the option of taking a car on the ferry from Croatia.

LE SHUTTLE AND THE FERRIES

Le Shuttle operates trains 24 hours a day, carrying cars, motorcycles, buses and their passengers, and taking 35 minutes between Folkestone and Calais. At peak times, services operate every 15 minutes, making advance bookings unnecessary; during the night, services still run hourly. Through trains connect London with Paris in just over three hours. Return fares from May to August cost around £280–310 per vehicle (passengers included), with discounts in the low season; passenger fares from London to Paris cost £95–155 return, depending on when you book.

The alternative **cross-Channel** options for most travellers are the **ferry** or **hovercraft** links between Dover and Calais or Boulogne (the quickest and cheapest routes), Ramsgate and Dunkerque, or Newhaven and Dieppe.

Ferry **prices** vary according to the time of year and, for motorists, the size of your car. The Dover–Calais/Boulogne runs, for example, start at about £180 return low season, £220 return high season for a car with up to five passengers. **Foot**

CROSS-CHANNEL INFORMATION

Hoverspeed, (☎01304/240101). To Boulogne and Calais.

Le Shuttle, Customer Services Centre Information and ticket sales (☎01303/271100).

P&O European Ferries, Dover (☎01304/203388); Portsmouth (☎01705/772244); London (☎0990/980980). To Calais

Sally Line, (☎01843/595522). To Dunkerque.

Stena Sealink Line, Ashford (☎01233/647047). To Calais and Dieppe.

---

passengers should be able to cross for about £50 return year round; taking a **motorbike** costs from £80–90 return.

VIA ITALY

Heading for western Greece or the Ionian islands, it has always made most sense to drive **via Italy** – and whatever your final destination, taking a ferry on the final leg makes for a more relaxed journey. Initial routes down to Italy through **France** and **Switzerland** are very much a question of personal taste. One of the most direct is Calais–Reims–Geneva–Milan and then down the Adriatic coast to the Italian port of your choice. Even on the quickest autoroutes (with their accompanying tolls), the journey will involve two overnight stops.

Once in Italy, there's a choice of five **ports**. Regular car and passenger ferries link **Ancona**, **Bari** and **Brindisi** with **Igoumenítsa** (the port of Epirus in western Greece) and/or **Pátra** (at the northwest tip of the Peloponnese and the closest port to Athens). Most sail via the island of **Corfu**, and a few link other Ionian islands en route to Pátra; you can stop over at no extra charge if you get these stops specified on your ticket. Generally, these ferries run year round, but services are greatly reduced out of season. Ferries also sail – less frequently – from **Trieste** and **Venice**. For more details see the box on p.9.

Note that crossing to Igoumenítsa is substantially cheaper than to Pátra; the cheapest of all the crossings are from Brindisi to Igoumenítsa. However, drivers will discover that the extra cost in Italian fuel – around double the British price – offsets the routes' savings over those from Bari or Ancona; the shipping companies are well aware of this and set their prices accordingly.

In summer, it is essential to **book tickets** a few days ahead, especially in the peak July–August season. During the winter you can usually just turn up at the main ports (Ancona, Bari, Brindisi, Igoumenítsa/Corfu), but it's still wise to book in advance, certainly if you are taking a car or want a cabin. A few phone calls before leaving are, in any case, advisable, as the range of fares and operators (from Brindisi especially) is considerable; if you do just turn up at

FERRIES FROM ITALY

Note: all timings are approximate.

From Ancona Marlines, Strintzis, ANEK and Minoan to Igoumenítsa (23–25hr) and Pátra (30hr); daily or nearly so year round. Strintzis, Minoan and ANEK via Corfu and/or Igoumenítsa; Marlines only via Igoumenítsa. Most sailings 8–10pm, but there are a number of afternoon departures. Superfast is just that, direct to Pátra in 21hr almost daily year round; Minoan offers high speed craft on the same line at 22hr. Most departures in the afternoon, but a few in the late evening.

From Bari Ventouris to Pátra direct (20hr), nearly daily departures year round, July–Aug calls alternate days at Kefallonía; to Igoumenítsa (12hr) slightly less frequent; Marlines to Igoumenítsa (13hr) daily in season, 4 weekly out. All sailings 7–11pm.

From Brindisi Adriatica to Corfu, Igoumenítsa (11hr) and Pátra (20hr) year round; direct to Pátra (17hr) summer only. Fraglines to Corfu/Igoumenítsa (11hr) almost daily March–Oct; Agoudimos to Igoumenítsa most days March–late Oct (10hr); Adria to Igoumenítsa (9hr) daily June–Sept. Hellenic Mediterranean Lines to Corfu/Igoumenítsa (11hr), 3–7 weekly March–Oct; Kefallonía (13–15hr), alternate days June–Sept; Itháki, Paxí and Zákynthos, variable mid July–early Sept; Strintzis almost daily March–Oct to Corfu and/or Igoumenítsa (9–10hr); Minoan to Corfu/Igoumenítsa, 4–7 weekly year round (11hr). Most ferries leave Brindisi 9–11pm, but Minoan, Strintzis and (occasionally) Hellenic Mediterranean offer 9–10am departures. There's always at least one daily boat in winter, except between Christmas and New Year's Eve.

From Trieste ANEK to Igoumenítsa , Corfu and Pátra (33–35hr). One weekly in winter, four weekly in summer, departing variable hours.

From Venice Strintzis, Fri–Sat only to Corfu, Igoumenítsa and Pátra (37hr); Minoan to same ports 3–7 weekly (37hr); twice weekly May–Sept calls at Kefallonía also. Departures about 5pm.

SAMPLE FARES

Prices below are one-way high/low season fares; port taxes (£3–5 per person in each direction) are not included. Note that substantial reductions apply on most lines for both InterRail or Eurail pass-holders, and for those under 26. Slight discounts are usually available on return fares. Many companies now allow you to sleep in your van on board; ask about reduced "camping" fares.

Igoumenítsa from Bari or Brindisi: deck class £18–£32/£13–£15; car from £21–£35/£13–£17.

Pátra from Bari or Brindisi: deck class £30–£32/£15–£23; car from £35–£46/£17–£23.

Pátra from Ancona: deck class £34–£50/£27–£36; car from £65–£75/£34–£38.

Pátra from Venice: deck class £42/£31; car from £76/£37.

Pátra from Trieste: deck class £40/£29; car from £71/£35.

UK AGENTS

For details of local agents in Greece, see the respective listings for Pátra and Igoumenítsa. The following are UK agents for advance bookings:

Serena Holidays, 40 Kenway Rd, London SW5 (☎0171/373 6548).

For Adriatica Lines.

Viamare Travel Ltd, Graphic House, 2 Sumatra Rd, London NW6 (☎0171/431 4560).

Agents for Agoudimos, ANEK, Fragline, Jadrolinija, Marlines, Medlink, Strintzis, Superfast, Ventourist, Vergina. Also for Salamis and Poseidon Lines, which route Pireás–Rhodes or Crete–Limassol–Haifa.

FERRIES FROM CROATIA

Rijeka–Split–Korcula–Dubrovnik–Bari–Igoumenítsa: Jadrolinija: Saturday (38hr from Rijeka, 28hr from Split, 20hr from Dubrovnik) returning Wednesday.

Rijeka–Zadar–Split–Stari Grad–Korcula–Dubrovnik–Igoumenítsa: Jadrolinija: Tuesday (36hr from Rijeka, 24hr from Split, 14hr from Dubrovnik) returning Saturday.

SAMPLE FARES

Igoumenítsa from Rijeka or Zadar: deck class £36/£27; car from £50/£30.

Igoumenítsa from Split, Stari Grad, Korcula or Dubrovnik: deck class £27/£20; car from £47/£28.

AGENTS

Viamare Travel (see above) is the agent for Jadrolinija on its Bari–Igoumenítsa crossing but not for Croatia–Greece or internal Croatian services. The Igoumenítsa agent for Jadrolinija is Katsios, Ethnikis Andistasis 54; ☎0665/22 409.

---

the port, spend some time shopping around the agencies.

VIA HUNGARY, ROMANIA AND BULGARIA

Avoiding former Yugoslavia involves a pretty substantial diversion through Hungary, Romania and Bulgaria. This is not a drive to contemplate unless you actively want to see some of the countries en route – it's too exhausting and too problematic. However, it's all easier than it was, with visas easier to obtain at the borders, if you haven't fixed them in advance.

From **Budapest**, the quickest route **through Romania** is via Timisoara, then to head towards Sofia in Bulgaria and on across the Rila mountains to the border at Kulata. Once at the Greek border, it's a three- to four-hour drive to Thessaloníki or Kavála. Bear in mind that road conditions are often poor and border crossings difficult. Contact the respective embassies and the AA for more advice.

GETTING THERE FROM IRELAND

Summer charters operate from Dublin and Belfast to Athens and there are additional services to Mýkonos, Rhodes, Crete and Corfu. A high-season charter from Dublin to Athens costs upwards of IR£200 return, while a week's package on one of the above islands costs from IR£440 per person for two weeks.

Year-round **scheduled services** with Aer Lingus and British Airways operate from both Dublin and Belfast via Heathrow to Athens, but you'll find them pricey compared to charters. Youth and student fares are offered by USIT (see below for address).

Travelling to London in the first place to pick up a cheap charter from there may save you a little money, but on the whole it's rarely worth the time and effort. For the record, budget flights to London are offered by British Midland, Aer Lingus and Ryan Air; while buying a Eurotrain boat and train ticket may also slightly undercut plane fares.

FLIGHT AGENTS IN IRELAND

Balkan Tours, 37 Ann St, Belfast BT1 4EB (☎01232/246795).
Direct charter flights.

Joe Walsh Tours, 8–11 Baggot St, Dublin (☎01/676 3053).
General budget fares agent.

Thomas Cook, 118 Grafton St, Dublin (☎01/677 1721).
Mainstream package holiday and flight agent, with occasional discount offers.

Trailfinders, 4/5 Dawson Street, Dublin 2 (☎01/677 7888).

USIT Branches at: Aston Quay, O'Connell Bridge, Dublin 2 (☎01/679 8833); 10–11 Market Parade, Cork (☎021/270 900); Fountain Centre, College St, Belfast (☎01232/324073).
Student and youth specialist.

AIRLINES
Aer Lingus, 41 Upper O'Connell St, Dublin (☎01/844 4777); 46–48 Castle St, Belfast (☎01232/314844); 2 Academy St, Cork (☎021/274331).

British Airways, 9 Fountain Centre, College St, Belfast (☎0345/222111); in Dublin, contact Aer Lingus.

GETTING THERE FROM NORTH AMERICA

Only a few carriers fly directly to Greece from North America, so most North Americans travel to a gateway European city, and pick up a connecting flight on from there with an associated airline. If you have time, you may well discover that it's cheaper to arrange the final Greece-bound leg of the journey yourself, in which case your only criterion will be finding a suitable and good-value North America–Europe flight; for

details of onward flights from the UK, see "Getting There from Britain" above.

The **Greek national airline**, Olympic Airways, only flies out of New York (JFK), Boston, Montreal and Toronto, though the airline can offer reasonably priced add-on flights within Greece, especially to the Greek islands, leaving from the same Athens terminal that you will fly into.

Another option to consider is picking up a flight to Europe and making your way to Greece by train, in which case a **Eurail Pass** makes a reasonable investment – all the details are covered below. For details of train routes, see "Getting There from Britain".

SHOPPING FOR TICKETS

Discount ticket outlets – advertised in the Sunday travel sections of major newspapers – come in several forms. **Consolidators** buy up blocks of tickets that airlines don't think they'll be able to sell at their published fares, and unload them at a discount. Many advertise fares on a one-way basis, enabling you to fly into one city and out from another without penalty. Consolidators normally don't impose advance purchase requirements (although in busy times you should book ahead just to be sure of getting a ticket), but they do often charge very stiff fees for date changes. **Discount agents** also deal in blocks of tickets offloaded by the airlines, but they typically offer a range of other travel-related services like insur-

---

AIRLINES IN NORTH AMERICA

Air Canada (Canada, call directory inquiries, ☎1-800/555-1212, for local toll-free number; US toll-free number is ☎1-800/776-3000).

Air France (US, ☎1-800/237-2747; Canada, ☎1-800/667-2747).

Alitalia (☎1-800/223-5730).

British Airways (US, ☎1-800/247-9297; Canada, ☎1-800/668-1059).

Canadian Airlines (Canada, ☎1-800/665-1177; US, ☎1-800/426-7000).

Czech Airlines (☎1-800/223-2365; 212/765-6022; Montreal ☎ 1-800/561 5171; Toronto ☎1-800/641-0641).

Delta Airlines (☎1-800/241-4141).

Iberia (US, ☎1-800/772-4642; Canada, ☎1-800/423-7421).

KLM (US, ☎1-800/374-7747; Canada, ☎1-800/361-5073).

LOT Polish Airlines (☎1-800/223-0593).

Lufthansa (☎1-800/645-3880).

Olympic Airways (☎1-800/223-1226; 212/838-3600).

Sabena (☎1-800/955-2000).

Swissair (☎1-800/221-4750).

United Airlines (☎1-800/538-2929).

ance, rail passes, youth and student ID cards, car rentals and tours. These agencies tend to be most worthwhile for students and under-26s, who can benefit from special fares and deals. **Travel clubs** are another option – most charge an annual membership fee, which may be worth it for their discounts on air tickets and car rental. Some agencies specialize in **charter flights**, which may be even cheaper than anything avail-

able on a scheduled flight, but again there's a trade-off: departure dates are fixed, and withdrawal penalties are high (check the refund policy). Student/youth fares can sometimes save you money, though again the best deals are usually those offered by seat consolidators advertising in Sunday newspaper travel sections.

Don't automatically assume that tickets purchased through a travel specialist will be cheap-

DISCOUNT TRAVEL COMPANIES

Air Brokers International, 323 Geary St, Suite 411, San Francisco, CA 94102 (☎1-800/883-3273).
Consolidator.

Air Courier Association, 191 University Boulevard, Suite 300, Denver, CO 80206 (☎303/278-8810).
Courier flight broker.

Airhitch, 2472 Broadway, Suite 200, New York, NY 10025 (☎212/864-2000).
Standby-seat broker. For a set price, they guarantee to get you on a flight as close to your preferred destination as possible, within a week.

Council Travel, Head Office: 205 East 42nd St, New York, NY 10017 (☎1-800/226-8624; 1-888 COUNCIL; 212/822-2700).
Student travel organization with sixty branches in the US.

Educational Travel Center, 438 North Frances St, Madison, WI 53703 (☎1-800/747-5551).
Student/youth discount agent.

Encore Travel Club, 4501 Forbes Blvd, Lanham, MD 20706 (☎1-800/444-9800).
Discount travel club.

Interworld Travel, 800 Douglass Rd, Miami, FL 33134 (☎305/443-4929).
Consolidator.

Last Minute Travel Club, 132 Brookline Ave, Boston, MA 02215 (☎1-800/LAST MIN).
Travel club specializing in standby deals.

Moment's Notice, 425 Madison Ave, New York, NY 10017 (☎212/486-0503).
Discount travel club.

New Frontiers/Nouvelles Frontières, Head Offices: 12 East 33rd St, New York, NY 10016 (☎1-800/366-6387; 212/779-0600); 1001 Sherbrook East, Suite 720, Montreal, Quebec H2L 1L3 (☎514/526-8444).
French discount travel firm. Other branches in LA, San Francisco and Québec City.

Now Voyager, 74 Varick St, Suite 307, New York, NY 10013 (☎212/431-1616).
Courier flight broker.

STA Travel, Head Office: 48 East 11th St, New York, NY 10003 (☎1-800/777-0112).
Worldwide specialist in independent travel with branches in the Los Angeles, San Francisco and Boston areas.

TFI Tours International, Head Office: 34 West 32nd St, New York, NY 10001 (☎1-800/745-8000).
Consolidator; other offices in Las Vegas, San Francisco, Los Angeles and Miami.

Travac, Head Office: 989 6th Ave, New York NY 10018 (☎1-800/872-8800).
Consolidator and charter broker; has another branch in Orlando.

Travel Avenue, 10 South Riverside, Suite 1404, Chicago, IL 60606 (☎1-800/333-3335).
Discount travel agent.

Travel Cuts, Head Office: 187 College St, Toronto, Ontario M5T 1P7 (☎1-800/667-2887; 1-888/238-2887; 416/979-2406).
Canadian student travel organization with branches all over the country.

Travelers Advantage, 3033 South Parker Rd, Suite 900, Aurora, CO 80014 (☎1-800/548-1116).
Discount travel club.

UniTravel, 1177 North Warson Rd, St Louis, MO 63132 (☎1-800/325-2222).
Consolidator.

Worldtek Travel, 111 Water St, New Haven, CT 06511 (☎1-800/243-1723).
Discount travel agency.

Worldwide Discount Travel Club, 1674 Meridian Ave, Miami Beach, FL 33139 (☎305/534-2082).
Discount travel club.

est – once you get a quote, check with the airlines and you may turn up an even better deal. In addition, exercise caution and never deal with a company that demands cash up front or refuses to accept payment by credit card.

For destinations not handled by discounters – which applies to most regional airports – you'll have to deal with airlines' published fares. The cheapest of these is an **APEX** (Advance Purchase Excursion) ticket. This carries certain restrictions. For instance, you may be expected to book – and pay – at least 21 days before departure, keep to a minimum/maximum limit on your stay, and be liable to penalties if you change your schedule. On transatlantic routes there are also winter **Super APEX** tickets, sometimes known as "Eurosavers" – slightly cheaper than ordinary Apex, they limit your stay to between 7 and 21 days. Some airlines also issue **Special APEX** tickets to those under 24, often extending the maximum stay to a year.

Note that fares are heavily dependent on **season**, and are highest from June–September; they drop either side of this, and you'll get the best deals during the low season, November–February (excluding Christmas). Note that flying on weekends ordinarily adds $50 or so to the round-trip fare; price ranges quoted in the sections below assume midweek travel.

FLIGHTS FROM THE USA

The twice-weekly non-stop flights to Athens out of **New York** and **Boston** on Olympic start at around US$760 round trip in winter, rising to around $1080 in summer for a maximum thirty-day stay with seven-day advance purchase. Delta has a daily direct service from New York to Athens for the same APEX fare; likewise United, Swissair, Sabena and Iberia although their flights are via European gateway cities. And United also flies to Athens from Washington DC for a high/low season rate of around $1140/$820.

As with the service from the Eastern cities, the stiff competition between the different airlines dictates that fares to Athens from the Midwest or West Coast are virtually identical: high/low season fares on Olympic, Delta, United, Iberia and so on start at $1180/$860 from Chicago or $1330/$1010 from LA, San Francisco or Seattle. With little else to choose between the major carriers, you might look into the stopover time at the different European gateway cities, as

---

EUROPEAN CONNECTIONS

There are direct flights to:

Thessaloníki from Amsterdam, Brussels, Copenhagen, Dusseldorf, Frankfurt, London, Munich, Stuttgart, Vienna, Zurich.

Corfu from Amsterdam, Dusseldorf, Frankfurt, Geneva, London, Milan, Stuttgart.

---

these can sometimes be overnight; check with your ticket agent.

At the time of writing, LOT Polish Airlines have a special deal on their round-trip low season APEX fares from the US to Athens via Warsaw ($596 from New York, $656 from Chicago, $846 from LA). Since it's possible that similar offers may be made in the future (including comparative reductions on their high season fares), it's certainly worth contacting them.

FLIGHTS FROM CANADA

As with the US, air fares from **Canada** to **Athens** vary tremendously depending upon where you start your journey. Olympic fly non-stop out of Montreal and Toronto twice a week for a scheduled fare of CDN$1268 round trip in winter or CDN$1751 in summer.

KLM operates several flights a week to Athens via Amsterdam, from Toronto, Montreal, Vancouver and Edmonton. From Toronto, expect to pay around CDN$1050 in low season, CDN$1750 in high season; and from Vancouver CDN$1470 (low) or CDN$2170 (high). Travellers from Montreal can also try the European carriers Air France, Alitalia, British Airways, Iberia, Lufthansa and Swissair all of which operate several flights a week to Athens via major European cities. One unlikely source for good deals is Czech Airlines, which flies out of Montreal to Athens via Prague for CDN$840 (low) or CDN$1240 (high).

Finally, Air Canada flying in conjunction with European carriers, quote the following low/high season fares to Athens: from Toronto/Montreal around CDN$1150/CDN$1485, and from Vancouver around CDN$1570/CDN$1860.

RAIL PASSES

A **Eurail Pass** is not likely to pay for itself if you're planning to stick to Greece, though it's

SPECIALIST TOUR OPERATORS

USA

Adriatic Tours, 691 West 10th St, San Pedro, CA 90731 (☎1-800/262-1718).
City highlights tours and cruise vacations.

Archeological Tours, 271 Madison Ave, New York, NY 10016 (☎212/986-3054).
Specialist archeological tours.

Astro Tours, 2359 East Main St, Columbus, OH 43209 (☎1-800/543-7717; 614/237-7798).
Cruise packages to the Greek islands.

Brendan Tours, 15137 Califa St, Van Nuys, CA 91411 (☎1-800/421-8446).
City highlights, cruise packages and car rental.

Caravan Tours Inc, 401 North Michigan Ave, Suite 2800, Chicago, IL 60611 (☎1-800/621-8338).
All kinds of packages covering the entire country.

Classic Adventures, PO Box 153, Hamlin, NY 14464-0153 (☎1-800/777-8090).
Trekking, biking and walking tours in June and September, covering archeological sites and coastal trips.

Classic Holidays, 350 Park St, Suite 204, North Reading, MA 01864 (☎1-800/752-5055).
Packages from 8 to 21 days, group tours and cruises.

Cloud Tours Inc, 645 Fifth Ave, New York, NY 10022 (☎1-800/223-7880).
Affordable escorted tours and Mediterranean cruises.

Different Strokes Tours, 1841 Broadway, New York, NY 10023 (☎1-800/668 3301).
Customized tours for gay/lesbian travellers.

Educational Tours and Cruises, 9 Irving St, Medford, MA 02155 (☎1-800/275-4109).
Custom-designed tours to Greece and the islands, specializing in art, history, food and wine, ancient drama, painting and birdwatching.

Elderhostel, 75 Federal St, Boston, MA 02110 (☎617/426-8056)
Educational and activity programmes for senior travellers (companions may be younger).

Globus and Cosmos Tours, 5301 South Federal Circle, Littleton, CO 80123 (☎1-800/221-0090).
Offers a variety of city and island packages.

Guaranteed Travel, 83 South St, Morristown, NJ 07963 (☎201/540-1770).
Specializes in "Greece-Your-Way" independent travel.

Hellenic Adventures, 4150 Harriet Ave South, Minneapolis, MN 55409 (☎1-800/851-6349; 612/827-0937).
A vast range of small group and independent tours: cultural, historical, horseback riding, hiking, wilderness, culinary and family oriented.

Homeric Tours, 55 East 59th St, New York, NY 10017 (☎1-800/223-5570).
All-inclusive tours from 9–23 days, as well as cruises and charter flights.

Insight International Tours, 745 Atlantic Ave, Suite 720, Boston, MA 02111 (☎1-800/582-8380).
General Greek vacations.

ST Cultural Tours, 225 West 34th St, New York, NY 10122 (☎1-800/833-2111; 212/563-1202).
A wide range of package and independent educational tours.

Triaena Travel, 850 Seventh Ave, New York, NY 10019 (☎1-800/223-1273; 212/245-3700).
Packages, cruises, apartments and villas.

Valef Yachts, Box 391, Ambler, PA 19002 (☎1-800/223-3845; 215/641-1624).
Yachting trips and charters.

CANADA

Adventures Abroad, 20800 Westminter Highway; Suite 2148, Richmond, BC V6V 2W3 (☎1-800/665-3998; 604/303-1099).
General operator, offering group and individual tours and cruises.

Auratours, 1470 Peel St, Suite 252, Montreal, Quebec H3A 1TL (☎1-800/363-0323).
General operator, offering group and individual tours and cruises.

Chat Tours, 241 Bedford Rd, Toronto, Ontario M5R 2K9 (☎1-800/268-1180).
Motorcoach and sea tours, and cruises.

Worldwide Adventures, 36 Finch Ave West, Toronto, Ontario M2N 2G9 (☎1-800/387-1483; 416/221-3000).
General operator, offering group and individual tours and cruises.

worth considering if you plan to travel to Greece across Europe from elsewhere. The pass, which must be purchased before arrival in Europe, allows unlimited free train travel in Greece and sixteen other countries. The **Eurail Youthpass** (for under-26s) costs US$365 for 15 days, $587 for one month or $832 for two months; if you're 26 or over you'll have to buy a **first-class pass**, available in 15-day ($522), 21-day ($678), one-month ($838), two-month ($1188) and three-month ($1468) increments.

This, too, comes in under-26/first-class versions: ten days, $431/$616 and fifteen days, $568/$812. If you're travelling in a group of two or more, you might also want to consider the **Eurail Saverpass**. This costs $444 for fifteen consecutive days, $576 for 21; $712 for a month; $1010 for two months or $1248 for three. And there's also a **Flexi Saverpass** at $524 for ten days or $690 for fifteen.

A further alternative is to attempt to buy an InterRail Pass in Europe (see "Getting There from Britain") – most agents don't check residential

> ### RAIL CONTACTS IN NORTH AMERICA
>
> **CIT Tours**, 9501 W Devon Ave, Suite 502, Rosemont, IL 60018 (☎1-800/223-7987).
>
> **DER Tours/GermanRail**, 9501 W Divon Ave, Suite 400, Rosemont, IL 60018 (☎1-800/421-2929).
>
> **Online Travel**, 9501 W Devon Ave, Suite 502, Rosemont, IL 60018 (☎1-800/660-5300)
>
> **Rail Europe**, 226 Westchester Ave, White Plains, NY 10604 (☎1-800/438-7245).
>
> **ScanTours**, 3439 Wade St, Los Angeles, CA 90066 (☎1-800/223-7226).

qualifications, but once you're in Europe it'll be too late to buy a Eurail Pass if you have problems. You can purchase Eurail passes from one of the agents listed above.

North Americans are also eligible to purchase more specific passes valid for travel in Greece only, for details of which see "Getting around", p.31.

GETTING THERE FROM AUSTRALIA & NEW ZEALAND

It's fairly easy to track down flights from Australia to Athens, less so from New Zealand, but given the prices and most people's travel plans, you'll probably do better looking for some kind of Round-the-World ticket that includes Greece. If London is your first destination in Europe, and you've picked up a reasonably good deal on a flight there, it's probably best to wait until you reach the UK before arranging your onward travel to Greece; see "Getting there from Britain" for all the details.

Fares are seasonally adjusted with low season from mid January–end February, October–November; high season mid–end May, June–August, December–January and shoulder seasons the rest of the year. Tickets purchased direct from the airlines tend to be expensive; travel agents offer much better deals on fares and have the latest information on limited specials, round-the-world fares and stopovers. The best discounts are through **Flight Centres** and **STA**, who can also advise on visa regulations.

FLIGHTS FROM AUSTRALIA

Cheapest fares to Athens **from Australia** are with Olympic Airways from A$1700 low season, while Alitalia via Rome, Aeroflot via Moscow and Thai Airways via Bangkok all start

AGENTS AND AIRLINES IN AUSTRALIA AND NEW ZEALAND

DISCOUNT TRAVEL AGENTS

Anywhere Travel, 345 Anzac Parade, Kingsford, Sydney (☎02/9663 0411).

Brisbane Discount Travel, 260 Queen St, Brisbane (☎07/3229 9211).

Budget Travel, 16 Fort St, Auckland, plus branches around the city (☎09/366 0061 and 0800/808 040).

Destinations Unlimited, 3 Milford Rd, Auckland (☎09/373 4033).

Flight Centres Australia: 82 Elizabeth St, Sydney, plus branches nationwide (☎13 1600), 205 Queen St, Auckland (☎09/309 6171), plus branches nationwide. *Good discounts on fares.*

Northern Gateway, 22 Cavenagh St, Darwin (☎08/8941 1394).

STA Travel, Australia: 702 Harris St, Ultimo, Sydney; 256 Flinders St, Melbourne; other offices in state capitals and major universities (nearest branch ☎13 1776, fastfare telesales ☎1300/360 960); 10 High St, Auckland (☎09/309 0458, fastfare telesales ☎09/366 6673), plus branches in Wellington, Christchurch, Dunedin, Palmerston North, Hamilton and at major universities. World Wide Web site: *www.statravelaus.com.au*, email: *traveller@statravelaus.com.au*. *Fare discounts for students and under 26s.*

Thomas Cook, Australia: 175 Pitt St, Sydney; 257 Collins St, Melbourne; plus branches in other state capitals (local branch ☎13 1771; Thomas Cook Direct telesales ☎1800/063 913); 96 Anzac Ave, Auckland (☎09/379 3920). *Travellers cheques, bus and rail passes.*

SPECIALIST AGENTS

Adventure World, 73 Walker St, North Sydney (☎02/956 7766); 8 Victoria Ave, Perth (☎09/221 2300). *Agents for a vast array of international adventure travel companies that operate trips to mainland Greece and islands.*

Australians Studying Abroad, 1/970 High St, Armadale, Melbourne (☎03/9509 1955 and 1800/645 755). *Study tours exploring Greek culture and art.*

Grecian Mediterranean Holidays, 49 Ventnor Ave, West Perth (☎09/321 3930). *A good selection of mainland and island holidays.*

Grecian Tours Travel, 237a Lonsdale St, Melbourne (☎03/663 3711). *Offers a variety of accommodation, and sightseeing tours.*

House of Holidays, 298 Clayton Rd, Clayton, Victoria (☎03/543 5800). *Greek specialist with a wide selection of holidays.*

Kompas Holidays, 71 Grey St, Brisbane (☎07/3846 4006 and 1800/269 968); 115 Pitt St, Sydney (☎02/231 1277). *City stopovers, sightseeing tours, cruises, traditional accommodation and yacht charter. Booking through travel agents only.*

Kyrenia Travel Services, 92 Goulburn St, Sydney (☎02/9283 2144). *Mainland and island accommodation, land tours and island hopping.*

Peregrine Adventures, 258 Lonsdale St, Melbourne (☎03/9663 8611), plus offices in Brisbane, Sydney, Adelaide and Perth. *Walking and cycling trips, visiting historical towns and monuments.*

Travel Market,11th floor, 141 Queen St, Brisbane (☎07/3210 0323). *Individually tailored holidays in the Greek Islands, for a range of budgets.*

AIRLINES

☎0800 numbers are toll free, but apply only if dialled outside the city in the address.

Aeroflot, Australia (☎02/9262 2233). *Twice weekly flights from Sydney to Athens via transfers in Moscow and Bangkok.*

British Airways, Australia (☎02/9258 3300); New Zealand (☎09/356 8690). *Daily flights to London from major Australasian cities: code share with Qantas to offer their "Global Explorer" RTW fare.*

Garuda, Australia (☎02/334 9944 or 1-800/800 873); New Zealand (☎09/366 1855). *Several flights weekly from Australian and New Zealand cities to London, Frankfurt and Amsterdam via either a transfer or stopover in Denpasar/Jakarta.*

Olympic Airways S.A., Australia (☎02/9251 2044); no NZ office. *Twice weekly flights to Athens from Sydney and Melbourne, with onward connections to other Greek destinations.*

Qantas Australia (☎13 1211); New Zealand (☎09/357 8900 and 0800/808 767). *Daily flights to London from major Australasian cities: code share with British Airways to offer their "Global Explorer" RTW fare.*

Singapore Airlines, Australia (☎13 1011); New Zealand (☎09/379 3209). *Daily flights to Athens from Brisbane, Sydney, Melbourne, Perth and Auckland via Singapore.*

Thai Airways Australia (☎13 1960); New Zealand (☎09/377 3886). *Three flights a week to Athens via either a transfer or stopover in Bangkok from Brisbane, Sydney, Perth, Melbourne, Perth and Auckland.*

around A$1850. In addition Singapore Airlines have a good connecting service to Athens from $1899. Qantas and British Airways offer a free return flight within Europe for A$2499–3099 which differs only slightly from their "Global Explorer" Pass A$2599–3199, a **Round-the-World** fare that allows six stopovers worldwide wherever these two airlines fly to (except South America). Also worth considering is Garuda's A$1550 fare from Sydney, Brisbane or Cairns via Jakarta or Denpasar to various European cities, from where you could pick up a cheap onward flight or continue **overland** to Athens. **Departure tax** from Athens, sometimes added to the ticket at the time of purchase, is $33.

FLIGHTS FROM NEW ZEALAND

From New Zealand, the best deals to Athens are with Thai Airlines via Bangkok from $2399, and Singapore Airlines via Singapore and Alitalia via Rome, both for around NZ$2499. United Airlines fly via Los Angeles, Washington and Paris starting at NZ$2599, and there's a very versatile offer with Lufthansa for $2899, who can route you through anywhere that Air New Zealand or Qantas fly – including Los Angeles, Singapore, Sydney, Hong Kong or Tokyo – for a stopover. British Airways/Qantas can get you to Europe, but not Athens, for $2699, so again you're better off with their Global Explorer Pass (see p.17) from NZ$3089. **Departure tax** from Athens is $42.

TRAVELLERS WITH DISABILITIES

It is all too easy to wax lyrical over the attractions of Greece: the stepped, narrow alleys, the ease of travel by bus and ferry, the thrill of clambering around the great archeological sites. It is almost impossible, on the other hand, for the able-bodied travel writer to see these attractions as potential hazards for anyone who has difficulty in walking, is wheelchair-bound or suffers from some other disability.

However, don't be discouraged. It is possible to enjoy an inexpensive and trauma-free holiday in Greece if some time is devoted to gathering **information** before arrival. Much existing or readily available information is out of date – you should always try to double-check. A number of addresses of contact organizations are published below. The Greek National Tourist Office is a good first step as long as you have specific questions to put to them; they publish a useful questionnaire which you could send to hotels or owners of apartment/villa accommodation.

PLANNING A HOLIDAY

There are **organized tours** and **holidays** specifically for people with disabilities; many companies in Britain will advise on the suitability of holidays or villas advertised in their brochures. If you want to be more independent, it's perfectly possible, provided that you do not leave home with the vague hope that things will turn out all right, and

that "people will help out" when you need assistance. This cannot be relied on. You must either be completely confident that you can manage alone, or travel with an able-bodied friend (or two).

It's important to become an authority on where you must be self-reliant and where you may expect help, especially regarding transport and accommodation. For example, to get between the terminals at Athens airport, you will have to fight for a taxi; it is not the duty of the airline staff to find you one.

It is also vital to **be honest** – with travel agencies, insurance companies, companions and, above all, with yourself. Know your limits and make sure others know them. If you do not use a wheelchair all the time but your walking capabilities are limited, remember that you are likely to need to cover greater distances while travelling (often over tougher terrain and in hotter weather) than you are used to. If you use a wheelchair, have it serviced before you go, and carry a repair kit.

Read your travel **insurance** small print carefully to make sure that people with a pre-existing medical condition are not excluded. And use your travel agent to make your journey simpler: **airlines** or bus companies can cope better if they are expecting you, with a wheelchair provided at airports and staff primed to help. A **medical certificate** of your fitness to travel, provided by your doctor, is also extremely useful; some airlines or insurance companies may insist on it.

USEFUL CONTACTS

National Tourist Organization of Greece: See p.29 for addresses. Offers general advice on terrain and climate. They have nothing specific for disabled visitors except a brief list of hotels which may be suitable.

GREECE
Association Hermes, Patriárkhou Grigoríou tou Pémptou 13, 165 42 Aryiroúpolis, Athens (☎01/99 61 887).
Can advise disabled visitors to Greece.

Lavinia Tours, Egnatía 101, 541 10 Thessaloníki (☎031/240 041).
Evyenia Stravropoulou will advise disabled visitors and has tested many parts of Greece in her wheelchair. She also organizes tours within Greece.

UK
Holiday Care Service, 2nd floor, Imperial Buildings, Victoria Rd, Horley, Surrey RH6 7PZ (☎01293/774535).
Publishes a fact sheet, and also runs a useful "Holiday Helpers" service for disabled travellers.

Mobility International, 228 Borough High St, London SE1 1JX (☎0171/403 5688).
Issues a quarterly newsletter on developments in disabled travel.

Opus 23, Sourdock Hill, Barkisland, Halifax, West Yorkshire HX4 0AG (☎01422/375999).
Part of Grecofile; will advise on and arrange independent holidays, or trips for those with carers.

RADAR, 12 City Forum, 250 City Rd, London EC1V 8AF (☎0171/250 3222).
They publish fact sheets and an annual guide to international travel for the disabled.

Tripscope, The Courtyard, Evelyn Rd, London W4 5JL (☎0181/994 9294).
Transport advice to most countries for all disabilities.

NORTH AMERICA
Directions Unlimited, 720 North Bedford Rd, Bedford Hills, NY 10507 (☎1-800/533-5343).
Tour operator specializing in custom tours for people with disabilities.

Jewish Rehabilitation Hospital, 3205 Place Alton Goldbloom, Montreal, PQ H7V 1R2 (☎514/688-9550, ext 226).
Guidebooks and travel information.

Mobility International USA, PO Box 10767, Eugene, OR 97440 (Voice & TDD: ☎503/343-1284). *Information and referral services, access guides, tours and exchange programmes. Annual membership $20 (includes quarterly newsletter).*

Society for the Advancement of Travel for the Handicapped (SATH), 347 5th Ave, New York, NY 10016 (☎212/447-7284).
Non-profit travel-industry referral service that passes queries on to its members as appropriate; allow plenty of time for a response.

Travel Information Service, Moss Rehabilitation Hospital, 1200 West Tabor Rd, Philadelphia, PA 19141 (☎215/456-9600).
Telephone information and referral service.

Twin Peaks Press, Box 129, Vancouver, WA 98666 (☎206/694-2462 or ☎1-800/637-2256).
Publisher of the *Directory of Travel Agencies for the Disabled* ($19.95), listing more than 370 agencies worldwide; *Travel for the Disabled* ($14.95); and the *Directory of Accessible Van Rentals and Wheelchair Vagabond* ($9.95), loaded with personal tips.

AUSTRALIA AND NEW ZEALAND
ACROD (Australian Council for Rehabilitation of the Disabled), PO Box 60, Curtin, ACT 2605 (☎02/6282 4333).

Disabled Persons Assembly, 173–175 Victoria

Make a **list** of all the facilities that will make your life easier while you are away. You may want a ground-floor room, or access to a large elevator; you may have special dietary requirements, or need level ground to enable you to reach shops, beaches, bars and places of interest. You should also keep track of all your other special needs, making sure, for example, that you have extra supplies of drugs – carried with you if you fly – and a prescription including the generic name in case of emergency. Carry spares of any kind of drug, clothing or equipment that might be hard to find in Greece; if there's an association representing people with your disability, contact them early in the planning process.

VISAS AND RED TAPE

UK and all other EU nationals need only a valid passport for entry to Greece; you are no longer stamped in on arrival or out upon departure, and in theory at least enjoy uniform civil rights with Greek citizens. US, Australian, New Zealand, Canadian and most non-EU Europeans receive mandatory entry and exit stamps in their passports and can stay, as tourists, for ninety days.

If you are planning to **travel overland**, you should check current visa requirements for Hungary, Romania and Bulgaria, Slovenia and Croatia at their closest consulates; transit visas for most of these territories are at present issued at the borders, though at a higher price than if obtained in advance at a local consulate.

VISA EXTENSIONS

If you wish to stay in Greece for longer than three months, you should officially apply for an **extension**. This can be done in the larger cities like Athens, Thessaloníki, Pátra, Rhodes and Iráklio through the Ipiresía Allodhapón (Aliens' Bureau); prepare yourself for concerted bureaucracy. In remoter locations you visit the local police station, where staff are apt to be more cooperative.

Unless you are of Greek descent, visitors from **non-EU** countries are currently allowed only one six-month extension to a tourist visa, which costs 11,000dr. In theory, **EU nationals** are allowed to stay indefinitely but, at the time of writing, must still present themselves every six months or every year, according to whether they have a non-employment resident visa or a work permit; the first extension is free, but you will be charged for subsequent extensions. In all cases, the procedure should be set in motion a couple of weeks before your time runs out and, if you don't have a work permit, you will be required to present pink, personalized bank **exchange receipts** (see "Costs, Money and Banks: Currency Regulations" below) totalling at least 500,000dr for the preceding three months, as proof that you have sufficient funds to support yourself without working. Possession of unexpired credit cards, a Greek savings account passbook or travellers' cheques can to some extent substitute for the pink receipts.

Certain individuals get around the law by leaving Greece every three months and re-entering a few days later, ideally via a different frontier post, for a new tourist stamp. However, with the recent flood of Albanian and ex-Yugoslavian refugees into the country, and a smaller influx of east Europeans looking for work, security and immigration personnel don't always look very kindly on this practice.

If you **overstay** your time and then leave under your own power – ie are not deported – you'll be given a 22,000dr spot fine upon departure, effectively a double-priced retroactive visa extension – no excuses will be entertained except perhaps a doctor's certificate stating you were immobilized in hospital. It cannot be overemphasized just how exigent Greek immigration officials often are on this issue.

CUSTOMS REGULATIONS

For EU citizens travelling between EU countries, limits on goods already taxed have been relaxed enormously. However, **duty-free allowances** are as follows: 200 cigarettes or 50 cigars, two litres of still table wine or one litre of spirits, and 50ml of perfume.

Exporting **antiquities** without a permit is a serious offence; **drug smuggling**, it goes without saying, incurs severe penalties.

GREEK EMBASSIES ABROAD

Australia 9 Turrana St, Yarralumla, Canberra, ACT 2600 (☎02/6273-3011).

Britain 1a Holland Park, London W11 3TP (☎0171/221 6467).

Canada 76–80 Maclaren St, Ottawa, ON K2P 0K6 (☎613/238-6271).

Ireland 1 Upper Pembroke St, Dublin 2 (☎01/767254).

New Zealand 5–7 Willis St, PO Box 27157, Wellington (☎04/473 7775).

USA 2221 Massachusetts Ave NW, Washington DC 20008 (☎202/939-5800).

INSURANCE

British and other EU nationals are officially entitled to free medical care in Greece (see "Health" p.22) upon presentation of an E111 form, available from most post offices. "Free", however, means admittance only to the lowest grade of state hospital (known as a *yenikó nosokomío*), and does not include nursing care or the cost of medications. In practice, hospital staff tend to greet E111s with uncomprehending looks, and you may have to request reimbursal by the NHS upon your return home. If you need prolonged medical care, you should make use of private treatment, which is expensive.

Some form of **travel insurance**, therefore, is advisable – and essential for **North Americans** and **Australasians**, whose countries have no formal health care agreements with Greece (other than allowing for free emergency trauma treatment). For medical claims, keep receipts, including those from pharmacies. You will have to pay for all private medical care on the spot (insurance claims can be processed if you have hospital treatment) but it can all be (eventually) claimed back. Travel insurance usually provides cover for the loss of baggage, money and tickets, too. If you're thinking of renting a moped or motorbike in Greece, make sure the policy covers motorbike accidents, which most don't without a supplemental payment.

EUROPEAN COVER

In Britain, there are a number of low-cost **specialist insurance companies** including Endsleigh, 97–107 Southampton Row, London WC1 (☎0171/436 4451), Campus Travel, 52 Grosvenor Gardens, London SW1 (☎0171/730 3402), and Columbus, 17 Devonshire Square, London EC2 (☎0171/375 0111). At all of these you can buy two weeks' basic cover in Greece for around £20; £30 for a month.

Most **banks** and **credit card** issuers also offer some sort of vacation insurance, often automatic if you pay for the holiday with a card. In these circumstances, it's vital to check what the policy actually covers – usually only death and/or dismemberment.

NORTH AMERICAN COVER

Before buying an insurance policy, check that you're not already covered. **Canadians** are usually covered for medical mishaps overseas by their provincial health plans. Holders of official student/teacher/youth cards are entitled to accident coverage and hospital in-patient benefits. **Students** will often find that their student health coverage extends during the vacations and for one term beyond the date of last enrolment. Bank and credit cards (particularly American Express) often have certain levels of medical or other insurance included, and travel insurance may also be included if you use a major credit or charge card to pay for your trip. **Homeowners'** or **renters'** insurance often covers theft or loss of documents, money and valuables while overseas, though conditions and maximum amounts vary from company to company.

After exhausting the possibilities above, you might want to contact a specialist **travel insurance** company; your travel agent can usually recommend one, or see the box on p.22. Policies are comprehensive (accidents, illnesses, delayed or lost luggage, cancelled flights, etc), but maximum payouts tend to be meagre. Premiums vary, so shop around. The best deals are usually to be had through student/youth travel agencies. The policy offered by STA, for instance, comes with or with-

TRAVEL INSURANCE COMPANIES IN NORTH AMERICA

Access America, PO Box 90310, Richmond, VA 23230 (☎1-800/284-8300).

Carefree Travel Insurance, PO Box 9366, 100 Garden City Plaza, Garden City NY 11530 (☎1-800/323-3149).

Travel Assistance International, 1133 15th St NW, Suite 400, Washington, DC 20005 (☎1-800/821-2828).

Travel Guard, 1145 Clark St, Stevens Point, WI 54481 (☎1-800/826-1300).

Travel Insurance Services, 2930 Camino Diablo, Suite 300, Walnut Creek, CA 94596 (☎1-800/937-1387).

out medical cover. Rates are $110/$85 for one month, $165/$120 for two, and rise by $55/$35 for each extra month.

Most North American travel policies apply only to items lost, stolen or damaged while in the custody of an identifiable, responsible third party – hotel porter, airline, luggage consignment, etc. Even in these cases you will have to contact the local police within a certain time limit to have a complete report made out so that your insurer can process the claim. Note also that very few insurers will arrange on-the-spot payments in the event of a major expense or loss; you will usually be **reimbursed** only after going home.

COVER FOR AUSTRALIA AND NEW ZEALAND

Travel insurance is available from most **travel agents** (see p.17) or direct from **insurance companies**, for periods ranging from a few days to a year or even longer. Most policies are similar in premium and coverage – but if you plan to indulge in **high-risk activities** such as mountaineering, bungee jumping or scuba diving, check the policy carefully to make sure you'll be covered.

A typical policy for Greece will cost: A$100/NZ$110 for two weeks, A$170/NZ$190 for one month, A$250/NZ$275 for two months. Try Cover More, 9/32 Walker St, North Sydney (☎02/9202 8000 and 1800/251 881), and Ready Plan, 141 Walker St, Dandenong, Melbourne (☎03/9791 5077 and 1800/337 462); 10/ 63 Albert St, Auckland (☎09/379 3208).

INSURANCE REPORTS

In all cases of loss or theft of goods, you will have to contact the local police to have a **report** made out so that your insurer can process the claim. This can occasionally be a tricky business in Greece, since many officials simply won't accept that anything could be stolen on their turf, or at least don't want to take responsibility for it. Moreover, there have been enough fraudulent claims in recent years to make the police justifiably wary. Be persistent, and if necessary enlist the support of the local **tourist police** or tourist office.

HEALTH

There are no required inoculations for Greece, though it's wise to have a typhoid-cholera booster, and to ensure that you are up to date on tetanus and polio. Don't forget to take out travel insurance (see "Insurance" p.21), so that you're covered in case of serious illness or accidents.

The **water** is safe pretty much everywhere, though you will come across shortages or brackish supplies on some of the drier or more remote islands. Bottled water is widely available if you're cautious.

SPECIFIC HAZARDS

The main health problems experienced by visitors have to do with over-exposure to the sun, and the odd nasty from the sea. To combat the former, don't spend too long in the sun, wear a hat plus loose, long sleeves, and drink plenty of fluids in the hot months to avoid any danger of **sunstroke**; remember that even hazy sun can burn. For sea-wear, a pair of goggles for swimming and footwear for walking over wet rocks are useful.

HAZARDS OF THE DEEP

In the sea, you may have the bad luck to meet an armada of **jellyfish**, especially in late summer; they come in various colours and sizes ranging from purple "pizzas" to invisible, minute creatures. Various over-the-counter remedies are sold in resort pharmacies; baking soda or ammonia also help to lessen the sting. The welts and burning usually subside of their own accord within a few hours; there are no deadly man-of-war species in Greek waters.

Less vicious but more common are black, spiky **sea urchins**, which infest rocky shorelines year-round; if you step on or graze one, a needle (you can crudely sterilize it by heat from a cigarette lighter) and olive oil are effective for removing spines; if you don't extract them, they'll fester.

The worst maritime danger – fortunately very rare – seems to be the **weever fish** (*dhrakéna*), which buries itself in tidal zone sand with just its poisonous dorsal and gill spines protruding. If you tread on one the sudden pain is unmistakably excruciating, and the **venom** is exceptionally potent. Consequences can range up to permanent paralysis of the affected area, so the imperative first aid is to immerse your foot in water as hot as you can stand. This serves to degrade the toxin and relieve the swelling of joints and attendant pain.

Somewhat more common are **stingrays** (Greek names include *platý, selákhi, vátos* or *trígona*), who mainly frequent bays with sandy bottoms where they can camouflage themselves. Though shy, they can give you a nasty lash with their tail if trodden on, so shuffle your feet a bit when entering the water.

SANDFLIES, MOSQUITOES AND SNAKES

If you are sleeping on or near a **beach**, it's wise to use insect repellent, either lotion or wrist/ankle bands, and/or a tent with a screen to guard against **sandflies**. Their bites are potentially dangerous, carrying visceral leishmaniasis, a rare parasitic infection characterized by chronic fever, listlessness and weight loss.

Mosquitoes (*kounóupia*) are less worrying – in Greece they don't carry anything worse than a vicious bite – but they can be infuriating. The best solution is to burn pyrethrum incense coils (*spíres* or *fidhákia* in Greek); these are widely and cheaply available, though smelly. Better if you can get them are the small electrical devices (trade name Vape Net) which vaporize an odourless insecticide

tablet; many "rooms" proprietors supply them routinely. Insect repellents such as Autan are available from most general stores and kiosks.

Adders (*okhiés*) and **scorpions** (*skorpí*) are found in Greece, though both are shy; just take care when climbing over dry-stone walls where snakes like to sun themselves, and don't put hands/feet in places, like shoes, where you haven't looked first.

PHARMACIES AND DRUGS

For **minor complaints** it's enough to go to the local **farmakío**. Greek pharmacists are highly trained and dispense a number of medicines which elsewhere could only be prescribed by a doctor. In the larger towns there'll usually be one who speaks good English. Pharmacies are generally closed in the evenings and on Saturday mornings, but are supposed to have a sign on their door referring you to the nearest open alternative.

Homeopathic and **herbal** remedies are quite widely available, with homeopathic pharmacies in many of the larger towns. There is a large homeopathic centre in Athens at Nikosthénous 8, Platía Plastíra, Pangráti (☎70 98 199); the Centre of Homeopathic Medicine is at Perikléous 1, Maroússi (☎80 52 671). Others are identified by the characteristic green cross sign.

If you regularly use any form of **prescription drug** you should bring along a copy of the prescription together with the generic name of the drug – this will help should you need to replace it, and will also avoid possible problems with customs officials. In this context, it's worth being aware that codeine is banned in Greece. If you import any, you just might find yourself in serious trouble, so check labels carefully; it's the core ingredient of Panadeine, Veganin, Sopadeine, Codis and Empirin-Codeine, to name just a few common compounds.

Contraceptive pills are more readily available every year, but don't count on local availability, except in the large towns; unfortunately abortion is still the principal form of birth control. **Condoms**, however, are inexpensive and ubiquitous – just ask for *profylaktiká* (the more slangy *plastiká* or slightly vulgar *kapótes* are even better understood) at any pharmacy or corner *períptero* (kiosk); the pill, too, can be obtained over-the-counter from larger *farmakía*.

Lastly, **hay fever** sufferers should be prepared for the early Greek pollen season, at its height from April to June. Pharmacists stock tablets and creams, but it's cheaper to come prepared. Commercial antihistamines like Triludan are difficult to find in smaller towns, and local brands can cost upwards of £10/$16 for a pack of ten.

DOCTORS AND HOSPITALS

You'll find English-speaking **doctors** in any of the bigger towns or resorts; the tourist police (☎171 in Athens), travel agents, hotel staff or even your consulate should be able to come up with some names if you have any difficulty.

For an **ambulance**, phone ☎166. In **emergencies**, treatment is given free in **state hospitals** – for cuts, broken bones, etc – though you will only get the most basic level of nursing care. Greek families routinely take in food and bedding for relatives, so as a tourist you'll be at a severe disadvantage. Somewhat better are the ordinary state-run outpatient clinics (*yatría*) attached to most public hospitals and also found in rural locales. These operate on a first-come, first-served basis, so go early; usual hours are 8am to noon.

Don't forget to obtain **receipts** for the cost of all drugs and medical treatment; without them, you won't be able to claim back the money on your travel insurance.

POLICE, TROUBLE AND HARASSMENT

> In an emergency, dial ☎100 for the police and ☎171 for the tourist police; in a medical emergency, dial ☎166 for an ambulance.

As in the past, Greece remains one of Europe's safest countries, with a low crime rate and a deserved reputation for honesty. If you leave a bag or wallet at a café, you'll most likely find it scrupulously looked after, pending your return. Similarly, Greeks are relaxed about leaving possessions unlocked or unattended on the beach, in rooms or on campsites.

However, in recent years there has been a large increase in **theft** and **crimes** (perpetrated largely by Albanian refugees) in the cities and resorts, so it's wise to lock things up and treat Greece like any other European destination. Below are a few pointer offences that might get you into trouble locally, and some advice on **sex-**

ual harassment – all too much a fact of life given the classically Mediterranean machismo of the culture.

SPECIFIC OFFENCES

The most common causes of a brush with authority are nude bathing or sunbathing, and camping outside an authorized site.

Nude bathing is legal on only a very few beaches (on Mýkonos, for example), and is deeply offensive to the more traditional Greeks – exercise considerable sensitivity to local feeling and the kind of place you're in. It is, for example, very bad etiquette to swim or sunbathe nude within sight of a church. Generally, if a beach has become fairly established for nudity, or is well secluded, it's highly unlikely that the police will come charging in. Where they do get bothered is if they feel a place is turning into a "hippie beach" or nudity is getting too overt on mainstream tourist stretches. Most of the time, the only action will be a warning, but you can officially be arrested straight off – facing up to three days in jail and a stiff fine.

Topless (sun)bathing for women is technically legal nationwide, but specific locales often opt

---

CONSUMER PROTECTION ON HOLIDAY

In a tourist industry as developed as in Greece there are inevitably a number of cowboys and shady characters amongst the taxi-drivers, hoteliers and car rental agencies. **EKPIZO**, the **Greek Consumers' Association**, has established a "Legal Information and Assistance for Tourists" programme, to be run yearly from June to September. Their main branch is in Athens (☎01/330 4444), with offices also in Vólos, Pátra, Crete and Kavála. EKPIZO issues a pamphlet about holidaymakers' rights, available in airports and tourist offices. They are always prepared to pursue serious cases, by friendly persuasion, or court action if necessary.

out of the "liberation" by posting signs to that effect, which should be heeded.

Very similar guidelines apply to **camping rough** – though for this you're still less likely to incur anything more than a warning to move on. The only real risk of arrest is if you are told to move on and fail to do so. In either of the above cases, even if the police do take any action against you, it's more likely to be a brief spell in their cells than any official prosecution.

Incidentally, any sort of **disrespect** towards the Greek state or Orthodox Church in general, or Greek civil servants in particular, may be construed as offences in the most literal sense, so it's best to keep your comments on how things work (or not) to yourself. Every year a few foreign louts find themselves in deep trouble over a drunken indiscretion.

Drug offences are treated as major crimes, particularly since there's a growing local use and addiction problem. The maximum penalty for "causing the use of drugs by someone under 18", for example, is life imprisonment and at least a 10-million drachma fine. Theory is by no means practice, but foreigners caught in possession of small amounts of grass do get long jail sentences, if there's evidence that they've been supplying others.

If you get arrested for any offence, you have a right to contact your **consulate** who will arrange a lawyer for your defence. Beyond this, there is

little they can, or in most cases will, do. Details of consulates in Athens and Thessaloníki appear in their respective "Listings" sections.

SEXUAL HARASSMENT

Many women travel independently in Greece without being harassed or feeling intimidated. Greek **machismo**, however, is strong, if less upfront than in, for example, southern Italy. Most of the hassle you are likely to get is from a small minority of Greeks, known as *kamákia* (fish harpoons) who migrate to the main resorts and towns in summer in pursuit of "liberated, fun-loving" tourists.

Indigenous Greeks, who become increasingly protective of you as you become more of a fixture in any one place, treat these outsiders with contempt. Their obvious stake-outs are beach bars and discos. Words worth remembering as unambiguous response include "*pápsteh*" (stop it), "*afístemeh*" (leave me alone) and "*fíyeteh*" (go away), the latter intensified if followed by "*dhrómo!*" (road, as in "Hit the road!").

Hitching is not advisable for lone women travellers, but **camping** is generally not a problem, though away from recognized sites it is often wise to attach yourself to a local family by making arrangements to use nearby private land. In the more remote mountains and inland areas you may feel more uncomfortable travelling alone. The intensely traditional Greeks may have trouble understanding why you are unaccompanied, and might not welcome your presence in their exclusively male *kafenía* – often the only place where you can get a drink. Travelling with a man, you're more likely to be treated as a *xéni*, a word meaning both (female) stranger and guest.

Men need to be aware of one long-established racket in Athens. Near Sýndagma, you'll be approached by dubious gents offering to take you for a drink in a nearby bar. This is invariably staffed with hostesses (not really hookers) who convince you to treat them to drinks. At the end of the day you'll be landed with an outrageous bill, some of which goes for the hostess's "commission"; physical threats are brought to bear on reluctant payers.

COSTS, BANKS AND MONEY

The costs of living in Greece have spiralled during the years of EU membership: the days of renting a house for a few thousand drachmas a week are long gone, and food prices at corner shops now differ little from those of other member countries. However, outside the established resorts, travel in the country remains reasonably priced, with the cost of restaurant meals, accommodation and public transport less expensive than anywhere in northern or western Europe except Portugal.

Prices depend on where and when you go. The cities and tourist resorts are usually more expensive and costs increase in July, August and at Easter. **Solo travellers** invariably spend more than if they were sharing food and rooms. An additional frustration is the relative lack of single rooms. **Students** with an International Student Identity Card (ISIC) can get fifty percent discount off admission fees at most archeological sites and museums. Those over 65 can rely on site-admission discounts of twenty-five to thirty percent. These, and other occasional discounts, tend to be more readily available to EU nationals. A FIYTO card (available to non-students) has fewer benefits. Both cards are available from student/youth travel agencies.

SOME BASIC COSTS

In most places you can get by on a **budget** of £20–24/US\$32–38.50 a day, which will get you a share of a double room in basic accommodation, breakfast, picnic lunch, a ferry or bus ride and a simple taverna meal. Camping would cut costs marginally. On £29–32/\$46–51 a day you could live quite well, and share the cost of renting a motorbike or a small car.

Domestic Aegean **ferries**, a main unavoidable expense, are quite reasonably priced, helped by government subsidies to preserve island communities. A deck-class ticket from Pireás, the port of Athens, to Crete or Sámos, both twelve-to-fourteen-hour trips, costs about £12/US\$18. For half the cost, there are dozens of closer islands in reach.

Long-distance **buses** now cost nearly the same as their equivalents elsewhere in Europe, but city services are still very cheap, as are **trains** – for example Athens–Thessaloníki, the longest single journey you're likely to make, is just £10/US\$15 second class.

The simplest double **room** can generally be had for £11–17/\$17.50–27 a night, depending on the location and the plumbing arrangements. Organized **campsites** cost little more than £2/US\$3.25 per person, with similar charges per tent and perhaps 25 percent more for a camper van. With discretion you can camp for free in the more remote, rural areas, though note the warning under "Police, Trouble and Harassment".

A very basic taverna **meal** with local wine costs around £6/US\$10 a head. Add a better bottle of wine, seafood, or more careful cooking, and it could be up to £10/US\$16 a head; you'll rarely pay more than that. Sharing seafood, Greek salads and dips is a good way to keep costs down in the better restaurants, but even in the most developed of resorts with inflated "international" menus you'll usually be able to find a more earthy but decent taverna where the locals eat.

CURRENCY

The Greek currency is the **drachma** (*dhrakhmí*), and the exchange rate is currently around 460dr to the pound sterling: 280dr to the US dollar.

The most common **notes** in circulation are those of 100, 200, 500, 1000, 5000 and 10,000 drachmas (*dhrahmés*), while **coins** come in denominations of 5, 10, 20, 50 and 100dr; you might come across 1dr and 2dr coins, and 50dr bills, too, though they're rarely used these days. In practice, shopkeepers rarely bother with differences of under 10dr – whether in your favour or theirs.

BANKS AND EXCHANGE

Greek **banks** are normally open Mon–Thurs 8.30am–2pm, Fri 8.30am–1.30pm. Certain branches in the major cities and tourist centres are open extra hours in the evenings and on Saturday mornings for exchanging money, while outside these hours larger hotels and travel agencies can often provide this service, albeit sometimes with hefty commissions. Always take your passport with you as proof of identity and be prepared for at least one long line: usually you have to line up once to have the transaction approved and again to pick up the cash.

The safest and easiest way to carry money is as **travellers' cheques**. These can be obtained from banks (even if you don't have an account) or from offices of Thomas Cook and American Express; you'll pay a commission of between one and two percent. When exchanging money in Greece using travellers' cheques, a flat-rate **commission** of 400–800dr is charged, so it's not a good idea to change really small amounts. You can cash the cheques at most banks and post offices.

Small-denomination foreign bank notes are also extremely useful. Since the freeing up of all remaining currency controls in 1994, a number of authorized **bureaux** for exchanging foreign cash have emerged in Athens and other major tourist centres. When changing small amounts, choose those that charge a percentage commission (usually one percent) rather than a high flat minimum.

Alternatively, most British banks can issue current account holders with a **Eurocheque** card and chequebook, with which you can pay for things in some shops and withdraw drachmas from cash machines or Greek banks. An annual fee is payable for this service, plus a two percent processing charge on the debit facility (subject to a minimum), but usually there's no commission on straightforward transactions. The current limit is 45,000dr per cheque.

Exchanging money at the **post office** has some considerable advantages in Greece. You miss out on the queues at banks. Also, small islands and villages without banks almost all have a post office. Commissions levied for both cheques and cash tend, at about 300dr per

transaction, to be much lower than at banks. If you have a UK-based Girobank account, you can use your chequebook to get money at remote post offices.

Finally, there is no need to change foreign currency into drachmas **before arrival** unless you're coming in at some ungodly hour to one of the remoter land or sea frontier posts, or on a Sunday. Airport arrival lounges will always have an exchange booth for passengers on incoming international flights.

CREDIT CARDS AND CASH DISPENSERS

Major credit cards are not accepted by the cheaper hotels and tavernas, but they're useful – indeed almost essential – for renting cars, for example, for buying Olympic Airways tickets, and for souvenirs.

If you run short of money, you can get an over-the-counter cash advance on a **credit card**, but be warned that the minimum amount is 15,000dr. The Emborikí Trápeza (Commercial Bank) handles Visa, and the Ethnikí Trápeza (National Bank) services Mastercard customers. However, there is usually a two percent credit card charge, often unfavourable rates and always interminable delays while transaction approval is sought by telex.

It is far easier to use the small but growing network of Greek **cash dispensers** – don't forget the PIN numbers for your various debit and credit cards. The most useful and well distributed are those of the National Bank/Ethniki Trapeza, which take Cirrus and Mastercard; the Commercial Bank/Emboriki Trapeza, which accepts Plus and Visa; and the Trápeza Písteos/Credit Bank, which accepts Visa and American Express. In the larger airports the Commercial and National banks often have cash dispensers in the arrivals hall.

EMERGENCY CASH

All told, learning and using the PIN numbers for your various cards is the quickest and least expensive way of securing moderate amounts of emergency funds from home. But in an emergency, you can arrange to have **money sent** from abroad to a bank in Greece. Receiving funds via telex takes a minimum of three days and often up to six days, so be prepared for delays. From the UK, a bank charge of three percent, or minimum £17, maximum £35, is levied. Bank drafts can also be sent, with higher commission rates.

Funds can also be sent via Western Union Money Transfer (☎0800/833833 in the UK, 1-800/325-6000 in North America). Fees depend on the destination and the amount being transferred, but as examples, wiring £400–500 should cost around £37, while $1000 will cost around $75. The funds should be available for collection at Western Union's local representative (often Trapeza Ergasías/Ergo Bank) within minutes of being sent. The American Express MoneyGram (☎1-800/543-4080 in North America) is now only available to American Express cardholders.

CURRENCY REGULATIONS

Since 1994, Greek currency restrictions no longer apply to Greek nationals and other EU-member cit-

izens, and the drachma is freely convertible. Arcane rules may still apply to arrivals from North America, Australia or non-EU European countries, but you'd have to be extremely unlucky to fall foul of them.

If, however, you have any reason to believe that you'll be acquiring large quantities of drachmas – from work or sale of goods – declare everything on arrival, then request (and save) pink, personalized **receipts** for each exchange transaction. Otherwise you may find that you can only re-exchange a small sum of drachmas on departure; even at the best of times many banks stock a limited range of foreign notes – your best bet is often the exchange booth in airport arrivals (*not* departures). These pink receipts are also essential for obtaining a visa extension (see "Visas and Red Tape" p.20).

INFORMATION AND MAPS

The National Tourist Organization of Greece (Ellinikós Organismós Tourismoú, or EOT; GNTO abroad) maintains offices in most European capitals, plus major cities in North America and Australia (see box opposite for addresses). It publishes an impressive array of free, glossy, regional pamphlets, which are good for getting an idea of where you want to go, even if the actual text should be taken with an occasional pinch of salt. Also available from the EOT are a reasonable fold-out map of Greece and a large number of brochures on special interests and festivals.

TOURIST OFFICES

In Greece, you will find **EOT offices** in most of the larger towns and resorts. The principal Athens office is at 2 Ameríkas Street, just up from Stadíou. Here, in addition to the usual leaflets, you can pick up weekly **schedules** for the inter-island **ferries** – not 100 percent reliable, but useful as a guideline. The EOT staff are themselves very helpful for advice on **ferry**, **bus**, and **train** departures as well as new opening hours for sites and museums, and occasionally can give assistance with accommodation.

Where there is no EOT office, you can get information (and often a range of leaflets) from municipally run tourist offices or from the **Tourist Police**. The latter are basically a branch (often just a single delegate) of the local police. They can sometimes provide you with lists of rooms to let, which they regulate.

MAPS

Maps are an endless source of confusion and sometimes outright disinformation in Greece. Each cartographic company seems to have its own peculiar system of transcribing Greek letters into English – and these, as often as not, do not match the transliterations on the road signs.

The most reliable **road maps** of Greece are the two *Geo Center* maps "Greece and the

Islands" and "Greek Islands/Aegean Sea", which together cover the country at a scale of 1:300,000. The single-sided fold-up *Freytag-Berndt* 1:650,000, with an index, is very nearly as good. Despite recent revisions and updating, *Michelin #980* remains a third choice. All these are widely available in Britain and North America, though less easily in Greece; see the list of map outlets below. *Freytag-Berndt* also publishes a series of more detailed maps on various regions of Greece, such as the Peloponnese and the Cyclades; these are best bought overseas from specialist outlets, though in Greece they are re-jacketed and distributed by Efstathiadis.

Maps of **individual islands** are more easily available on the spot, and while most are wildly inaccurate or obsolete, with strange hieroglyphic symbology, a rare few are reliable and up-to-date.

The most useful map of **Athens**, with a decent index, is the *Falkplan* – available from most specialist outlets. If you can read Greek, and plan to stay for some time in the city, the *Athina-Pireás Proastia Alpha-Omega* street atlas, published by Kapranidhis and Fotis, is invaluable. It has a complete index, down to the tiniest alley – of which there are many – and also shows cinemas and the outlines of important buildings.

HIKING/TOPOGRAPHICAL MAPS

Hiking/topographical maps, subject to uneven quality and availability, are gradually improving. Road Editions (41 Ilia Iliou St, 117 43 Athens ☎ 92 96 541) have produced a series of maps with the cooperation of the **Army Geographical Service** (*Yeografikí Ipiresía Stratoú*); these are available in Athens. The Greek mountaineering magazine **Korfes** publishes 1:50,000 maps of select alpine areas, with Roman-alphabet lettering appearing on a few sheets. More than sixty maps are in print, and a new one is issued every other month as a centrefold in the magazine – though some are revisions or previous titles. To get back issues you may need to visit the magazine's office at Platía Kentrikí 16, Ahharnés, Athens (☎24 61 528), although the more central bookstore Iy Folia tou Vivliou (see p.121) also has an extensive back catalogue.

The *Korfes* maps are, unfortunately, unreliable in the matter of trails and new roads, but extremely accurate for natural features and village position, based as they are on the older maps of the Army Geographical Service. If you want to obtain these for islands, and mainland areas not covered by *Korfes*, visit the YIS at Evelpídhon 4, north of Aréos Park in Athens, on Monday, Wednesday or Friday from 8am to noon only. All foreigners must leave their passport with the gate guard; EU citizens may proceed directly to the sales hall, where efficient, computerized transactions take just a few minutes. Other nationals will probably have to go upstairs for an interview; if you don't speak reasonably good Greek, it's best to have a Greek friend get them for you.

As of writing, maps covering Crete, the Dodecanese, the east Aegean, Skýros, most of Corfu and much of Epirus, Macedonia and Thrace are still off-limits to all foreigners, as well as

MAP OUTLETS

UK
London
National Map Centre, 22–24 Caxton St, SW1H
0QU (☎0171/222 2466); Stanfords, 12–14 Long
Acre, WC2E 9LP (☎0171/836 1321); Daunt Books,
83 Marylebone High Street, London W1M 3DE
(☎0171/224 2295); The Travel Bookshop, 13–15
Blenheim Crescent, London W11 2EE (☎0171/229
5260).

Glasgow
John Smith and Sons, 57–61 St Vincent St
(☎0141/221 7472).

Maps by mail or phone order are available from
Stanfords (☎0171/836 1321).

USA
Chicago
Rand McNally, 444 N Michigan Ave, IL 60611
(☎312/321-1751).

New York
The Complete Traveler Bookstore, 199 Madison
Ave, NY 10016 (☎212/685-9007); Rand McNally,
150 East 52nd St, NY 10022 (☎212/758-7488);
Traveler's Bookstore, 22 West 52nd St, NY 10019
(☎212/664-0995).

San Francisco
The Complete Traveler Bookstore, 3207 Fillmore
St, CA 92123 (☎415/923-1511); Rand McNally,
595 Market St, CA 94105 (☎415/777-3131).

Santa Barbara
Map Link Inc., 30 S La Patera Lane, Unit 5, Santa
Barbara CA 93107 (☎805/692 6777 or fax 962
0884).

Seattle
Elliot Bay Book Company, 101 S Main St, WA
98104 (☎206/624-6600).

Washington DC
The Map Store Inc., 1636 Ist NW, Washington,
DC 20006 (☎ 202/628-2608).

Note: Rand McNally now has more than twenty
stores across the US; call ☎1-800/333-0136 (ext
2111) for the address of your nearest store, or for
direct mail maps.

CANADA
Montreal
Ulysses Travel Bookshop, 4176 St-Denis
(☎514/843-9447).

Toronto
Open Air Books and Maps, 25 Toronto St, M5R
2C1 (☎416/363-0719).

Vancouver
World Wide Books and Maps, 736a Granville St
V6Z 1G3 (☎604/687-3320).

AUSTRALIA
Sydney
Travel Bookshop, 20 Bridge St (☎02/9241 3554).

Melbourne
Bowyangs, 372 Little Bourke St (☎03/9670 4383).

Adelaide
The Map Shop, 16a Peel St (☎08/8231 2033).

Perth
Perth Map Centre, 891 Hay St (☎08/9322 5733).

NEW ZEALAND
Auckland
Specialty Maps, 58 Albert St (☎09/307 2217).

Greeks. With matters unsettled across the
Balkans, previous plans to lift such restrictions
have been shelved indefinitely. A German company, **Harms**, has released a series of five maps
at 1:80,000 scale which cover Crete from west to
east and show, partly accurately, many hiking
routes – invaluable until and unless the YIS
declassifies this area.

GETTING AROUND

The standard means of land transport in Greece is the bus. Train networks are usually slow and limited, though service on the northern mainland lines is improving. Buses, however, cover just about every route on the mainland – albeit infrequently on minor roads – and provide basic connections on the islands. The best way to supplement buses is to rent a moped, motorbike or car, especially on the islands, where in any substantial town or resort you can find a rental outlet.

Inter-island travel of course means taking **ferries**. These again are extensive, and will eventually get you to any of the 166 inhabited isles. Planes are expensive, at three to four times the cost of a deck-class ferry ticket and almost twice as much as first or cabin class.

BUSES

Bus services on the **major routes**, both on the mainland and islands, are highly efficient and frequent. On **secondary roads** they're less regular, with long gaps, but even the most remote villages will be connected – at least on weekdays – by a school or market bus to the provincial capital. As these often leave shortly after dawn, an alarm clock can be a useful travel aid. Coming in the opposite direction, these local buses usually leave the provincial capital at about 2pm. On the **islands** there are usually buses to connect the port and main town for ferry arrivals or departures.

The network is nationally run by a single syndicate known as the **KTEL** (*Kratikó Tamío Ellinikón Leoforíon*). However, even in medium-sized towns there can be several scattered terminals for services in different directions, so make sure you have the right station for your departure. Some sample one-way fares from

Athens are: Thessaloníki (7000dr), Pátra (3000dr) and Delphi (2500dr).

Buses are amazingly **prompt** as a rule, so be there in plenty of time for scheduled departures. For the major, inter-city lines such as Athens–Pátra, ticketing is computerized, with assigned seating, and such buses often get fully booked. On smaller rural/island routes, it's generally first-come, first-served with some standing allowed, and tickets dispensed on the spot by a *ispráktoros* or conductor.

A few long-distance and international routes are also served by express buses operated by **OSE**, the State Railway Organization. These always leave from the train station and can be useful supplements to regular mainline services.

TRAINS

The Greek railway network, run by **OSE**, is limited to the mainland, and with a few exceptions trains are slower than the equivalent buses. However, they're also much cheaper – nearly fifty percent less on non-express services, even more if you buy a return ticket – and some of the lines are enjoyable in themselves. The best, a real treat, is the rack-and-pinion line between Diakoftó and Kalávryta in the **Peloponnese** (see p.241).

Timetables are sporadically available during May or June and printed in Greek only; the best place to obtain them are the OSE offices in Athens at Sína 6, or in Thessaloníki at Aristotélous 18, or the main train stations in these cities. Always check the station schedule boards, since with the once-yearly printing changes often crop up in the interim. Trains tend to leave promptly at the outset, though on the more circuitous lines they're invariably late by the end of the journey.

If you're starting a journey at the initial station of a run you can (at no extra cost) **reserve a seat**; a carriage and seat number will be written on the back of your ticket. At most intermediate points, it's first-come, first-served.

There are two basic classes: first and second. **First class** may be worth the extra money, insomuch as the cars may be emptier and the seats more comfortable. Since 1993 an express category, the **Intercity**, has been inaugurated on certain routes between Alexandhroúpoli, Thessaloníki, Vólos, Athens, Pátra, Korinthos and Kalamata – wagons are relatively sleek, with stiff

Belgrade △   △ Belgrade   △ Sofia △ Sofia

GREECE: TRAINS

0   100 km

supplements charged depending on distance travelled, and much faster than the bus if the
timetable is adhered to. There is also one nightly
sleeper in each direction between Athens and
Thessaloníki, again with fairly hefty surcharges.
Note that any kind of ticket issued on board a
train carries a fifty percent surcharge.

InterRail and **Eurail** Pass holders (see appropriate "Getting There" sections) can use their
pass in Greece but must secure reservations like
everyone else, and pay express **supplements** on
a few lines. InterRail passes and Eurotrain tickets
are available in Greece through the International
Student and Youth Travel Service (ISYTS), Níkis
11, 2nd floor, Athens, or at Wasteels, Xenofóndos
14, 6th floor, Athens.

You probably won't get sufficient value out of
your InterRail or Eurail pass if you just intend to
use it to travel in Greece. However, there are a
couple of specific passes just for use in Greece,
which are worth considering, and are best bought
within the country. Such tourist passes allow
unlimited travel on the Greek network for 10, 20
or 30 days in the a month.

North Americans can buy the Greek Rail
pass, valid any three days in a month for first
class travel ($86) or five days in a month ($120).
There's also a Greek Flexi Rail and Flight Pass
which entitles the holder to three days first class
rail and two days air travel (on Olympic) within a
month. The price is $202 for adults, $108 for children aged 4–11, with an option to purchase three

extra air days at $66/$33 each day. Both these passes must be purchased prior to departure and are available from Online Travel (see p.16).

FERRIES

Ferries are of use primarily for travel to and between islands, though you may also want to make use of the routes between Athens and Monemvassía in the Peloponnese. There are three different varieties of vessel: medium-sized to large **ordinary ferries** (which operate the main services), **hydrofoils** (run by the Ceres "Flying Dolphins" and Dodecanese Hydrofoils, among several companies), and local **kaïkia** (small boats which do short hops and excursions in season). Costs are very reasonable on the longer journeys, though proportionately more expensive for shorter, inter-island connections. Short-haul lines with monopolies – for example Alexandhroúpoli–Samothráki and Kými–Skýros – are invariably overpriced.

We've indicated most of the **ferry connections**, both on the maps (see p.412–413 for a general picture) and in the "Travel Details" at the end of each chapter. Don't take our listings as exhaustive or wholly reliable, however, as schedules are notoriously erratic, and be aware that we have given details essentially for departures between June and September. **Out-of-season** departure frequencies are severely reduced, with many islands connected only once or twice a week. However, in spring or autumn those ferries that do operate are often compelled by the transport ministry to call at extra islands, making possible some interesting connections.

The most reliable, up-to-date information is available from the local **port police** (*limenarkhío*), which maintains offices at Pireás (☎01/42 26 000) and on or near the harbours of all fair-sized islands. Smaller places may only have a *limenikós stathmós* (marine post), often just a single room with a VHF radio. Their officers rarely speak much English, but keep complete schedules posted – and, meteorological report in hand, are the final arbiters of whether a ship will sail or not in stormy weather conditions. *Apagorevtikó*, or obligatory halt of all seaborne traffic, is applied for weather in excess of Force 7 on the Beaufort scale.

REGULAR FERRIES

On most ferry routes, your only consideration will be getting a boat that leaves on the day, and for the island, that you want. However, when sailing from **Pireás**, the port of Athens, to the Cyclades or Dodecanese islands, you should have quite a range of choice and may want to bear in mind a few of the factors below.

Most importantly, bear in mind that **routes** taken and the speed of the boats vary enormously. A journey from Pireás to Thíra (Santoríni), for instance, can take anything from nine to fourteen hours. Before buying a ticket it's wise to establish how many stops there'll be before your ticket, and the estimated time of arrival. Many agents act just for one specific boat (they'll blithely tell you that theirs is the only available service), so you may have to ask around to uncover alternatives. Especially in high season, early arrival is critical in getting what may be a very limited stock of accommodation.

The boats themselves have improved somewhat recently, with a fair number of elderly rust-buckets consigned to the scrap heap or dumped overseas – just about the only ferry you might want to avoid if you have the choice are the odiferous *Áyios Rafael*, in the north Aegean. You will more often than not be surprised to encounter a former English Channel or Scandinavian fjord ferry, rechristened and enjoying a new (and final) lease of life in the Aegean.

Regular ferry **tickets** are, in general, best bought on the day of departure, unless you need to reserve a cabin berth or space for a car. Buying tickets in advance will tie you down to a particular ferry at a particular time – and innumerable factors can make you regret that. Most obviously there's bad weather, which, particularly off-season, can play havoc with the schedules, causing some small boats to remain at anchor and others to alter their routes drastically. There are only three periods of the year – March 23–25, the week before and after Easter, and mid-August – when ferries need to be booked at least a couple of days in advance. Following cases in 1996 of captains loading ferries to double their rated capacity, obligatory, computerized advance ticketing was to be universally introduced as from 1997 – and in the end this didn't happen. The larger, reputable companies such as ANEK and DANE have been computerized for some years anyway. Until further notice, you can still buy a ticket once on board with no penalty, despite what travel agents may tell you. Ticket prices for each route are currently set by the transport ministry and should not differ among ships or agencies.

The cheapest class of ticket, which you'll probably automatically be sold, is **deck class**, variously called *tríti* or *gámma*. This gives you the run of most boats except for the upper-class restaurant and bar. On the shorter, summer journeys the best place to be, in any case, is on deck – space best staked out as soon as you get on board. However, boats acquired recently seem, with their glaring overhead lights and moulded-plastic bucket seats, expressly designed to frustrate those attempting to sleep on deck. In such cases it's well worth the few thousand extra drachmas for a **cabin bunk**, especially if you can share with friends. Class consciousness has increased of late, so deck-class passengers will find themselves firmly locked out of second-class facilities at night to prevent them from crashing on the plush sofas. First-class cabin facilities usually cost scarcely less than a plane flight and are not terrific value – the only difference between first and second being the presence of a bathroom in the cabin. Most cabins, incidentally, are apt to be overheated, stuffy and windowless.

Occasionally, with non-computerized companies, you will be sold a cabin berth at an intermediate port only to find that they are "full" when the boat arrives. Pursers will usually not refund you the difference between a cabin and third-class. Your first- or second-class fare entitles you to a bunk, and this is clearly stated (in Greek) on the verso of your ticket. Make a scene if necessary until you are accommodated – there are almost always cabins in the bilge, set aside for the crew but generally unused, where you can sleep.

Motorbikes and **cars** get issued extra tickets, in the latter case up to four times the passenger fare. This obviously limits the number of islands you'll want to drag a car to – it's really only worth it for the larger ones like Crete, Rhodes, Khíos, Lésvos, Sámos or Kefalloniá. Even with these, unless you're planning a stay of more than four days, you may find it cheaper to leave your car in Pireás and rent another on arrival.

Most ferries sell a limited range of **food**, though it tends to be overpriced and mediocre in quality. Honourable exceptions are the decent, reasonable meals served on the ferries to Crete, and the DANE Dodecanese ferries. On the short hops in the Argo-Saronic, Cyclades and Sporades, it is well worth stocking up with your own provisions.

HYDROFOILS

Hydrofoils – more commonly known as *dhelfínia* (after the Ceres "Flying Dolphins") – are roughly twice as fast (and at least twice as expensive) as ordinary ferries. They're a useful alternative to regular ferries if you are pushed for time; networks seems to be growing each year, so it's worth asking about services, even if they are not mentioned in this guide. Their drawback is that they were originally designed for cruising on placid Russian or Polish rivers, and are quite literally out of their depth on the Aegean; thus they are extremely sensitive to bad weather, and not for the seasick-prone. Most of these services don't operate – or are heavily reduced – from October to June and are prone to arbitrary cancellation if not enough passengers turn up.

At present, hydrofoils operate among the **Argo-Saronic islands** close to Athens, down the east coast of the **Peloponnese** to Monemvassía and Kýthira, among the **northern Sporades** (Évvia, Skýros, Skiáthos, Skópelos and Alónissos), between Thessaloníki and certain resorts on **Khalkidhikí**, between Kavála and **Thássos**, among certain of the **Cyclades** (Ándros, Tínos, Mýkonos, Páros, Náxos, Amorgós, the minor islets, Íos, Thíra – and Crete), and in the **Dodecanese** among Rhodes, Kós, Kálymnos, Léros and Pátmos, with occasional forays up to Sámos or over to Tílos and Níssiros. The principal **mainland ports** are Zea and Flísvos marinas in Pireás, Rafína, Vólos, Áyios Konstandínos, Thessaloníki and Alexandhroúpoli.

Schedules and **tickets** for the Ceres company, which operates the far-flung "Flying Dolphin" lines, are available in Athens from Filellínon 3, off Platía Sýndagma (☎01/32 44 600); in Pireás from Ceres Hydrofoils, Aktí Themistokléous 8 (☎01/42 80 001, fax 42 83 526); in Vólos from Tsoulos, Andonopoúlou 9–11 (☎0421/39 786); and in Thessaloníki from Kriti Travel, Íonos Dhragoúmi 1 (☎031/547 454). The main offices of Mamidhakis–Dodecanese Hydrofoils are Platía Kíprou 6, Ródhos (☎0241/24 000) or Goúnari 2, Pireás (☎42 24 980).

KAÏKIA AND OTHER SMALL FERRIES

In season **kaïkia** (caiques) and small ferries of a few hundred tonnes' displacement sail between adjacent islands and to a few of the more obscure ones. These can be extremely useful and often very pleasant, but are no cheaper than mainline services. Indeed if they are technically **tourist agency charters**, and not passenger lines controlled by the transport ministry, they tend to be quite expensive, with pressure to buy return fares (one-ways almost always available). We have tried to detail the more regular links in the text, though many, inevitably, depend on the whims of local boat-owners. The only firm information is to be had on the quayside. Kaïkia and small ferries, despite appearances, have a good safety record; indeed it's the larger, overloaded car-ferries that have in the past run into trouble.

MOTORBIKES, MOPEDS AND BIKES

The cult of the **motorcycle** is highly developed in Greece, presided over by a jealous deity apparently requiring regular human sacrifice. Accidents among both foreign and local bikers are routine occurrences, with annual fatalities edging into two figures on the busier islands. Some package companies have even taken to warning clients in print against renting them, not incidentally to make more money on group excursions, but with caution and common sense – and an eye to increasingly enforced regulations.

Many tourists come to grief on rutted dirt tracks or astride mechanically dodgy machines. In other cases **accidents** are due to attempts to cut corners, in all senses, by riding two to an underpowered scooter simply not designed to propel such a load. Don't be tempted by this apparent economy – you won't regret getting two separate mopeds, or one powerful 125cc bike to share – and remember that you're likely to be charged an exorbitant sum for any repairs if you crash. Above all, make sure your **travel insurance policy** covers motorcycle accidents.

One worthwhile precaution is to wear a **crash helmet** (*kránio*); most rental outfits will offer you one, and some will make you sign a waiver of liability if you refuse it. Helmet-wearing is in fact required by law, and more and more riders are having to comply as police set up roadblocks to catch offenders. Reputable establishments demand a full motorcycle driving licence for any engine over 75cc, and you will usually have to leave your passport as security.

Mopeds and small motor scooters, known in Greek as **papákia** (little ducks) after their characteristic noise, are good transport for all but the hilliest islands. They're available for rent on many islands and in a few of the popular mainland resorts. Motorcycles and scooters cost around 4000dr a day and upwards, mopeds about 3000dr. All rates can be reduced with bargaining outside of peak season, or if you negotiate for a longer period of rental.

Before riding off, make sure you check the bike's mechanical state, since many are only cosmetically maintained and repaired. Bad brakes and worn spark plugs are the most common defects; dealers often keep the front brakes far too loose, with the commendable intention of preventing you going over the handlebars. If you break down it's your responsibility to return the machine, so take down the phone number of whoever rents it to you in case it gives out in the middle of nowhere; top agencies may offer a free retrieval service.

As far as **models** go, the three-speed Honda 50 and Suzuki Townmate and Yamaha Birdie are the favourites; gears are shifted with an easy-to-learn left-foot pedal action, and (very important) they can be push-started if the ignition fails. These can carry two, though if you have a choice, the Cub 70–90cc series gives more power at nominal extra cost. A larger Vespa scooter is more comfortable on long trips, with capacious baskets, but has less stability, especially off paved surfaces. The Suzuki Address and its clones, though also comfortable for 30km trips, is thirsty on fuel and cannot be push-started. Smaller but surprisingly powerful Piaggio Si or Monte Carlo models can take one person almost everywhere, carry two baskets or bags and are automatic action. Bungee cords (*khtapódhi* in slang) for tying down bundles are available on request.

If you intend to stay for some time in the warmer months, it's well worth considering the **purchase** of a moped or motorbike once in Greece. They are relatively inexpensive to run or repair, don't cause problems with passport stamps, can be taken on the ferries very cheaply, and can be resold easily upon departure.

CYCLING

Cycling in Greece is not such hard going as you might imagine (except in mid-summer), especially on one of the mountain bikes that are rapidly supplanting the old bone-shakers at rental outfits; they rarely cost more than 1500dr a day. You do, however, need steady nerves, as roads are generally narrow with no verges or bike lanes (except on Kós), and many Greek drivers consider bicycles a low form of life.

If you have your own mountain or touring bike, you might consider taking it along by **train** or **plane** (it's free if within your 23kg allowance). Once in Greece you should be able to take a bike for free on most of the **ferries**, in the guard's van on most trains (for a small fee – it goes on a later goods train otherwise), and with a little persuasion on the roof of **buses**. Any spare parts you might need, however, are best brought along, since most **specialist bike shops** are in Athens and Thessaloníki.

DRIVING AND CAR RENTAL

Cars have obvious advantages for getting to the more inaccessible parts of mainland Greece, but this is one of the more expensive countries in Europe to **rent a car**. If you drive **your own vehicle** to and through Greece, via EU member states, you no longer require a Green Card. In accordance with recent directives, **insurance** contracted in any EU member state is valid in any other, but in many cases this is only third party cover – the statutory legal minimum. Competition in the industry is so intense, however, that many UK insurers will throw in full, pan-European cover for free or for a nominal sum, up to sixty days; shop around if necessary.

Upon arrival with EU number plates, your EU passport should no longer get a carnet stamp, and the car is in theory free to circulate in the country until its road tax or insurance expires. Other nationalities will get a non-EU car entered in their passport; the **carnet** normally allows you to keep a vehicle in Greece for up to six months, exempt from road tax. It is difficult, though not impossible, to leave the country without the vehicle; the nearest customs post will seal it for you (while you fly back home for a family emergency, for example) but you must find a Greek national to act as your guarantor, and possibly pay storage. This person will assume ownership of the car should you ultimately abandon it.

CAR RENTAL

Car rental within Greece starts at £180/US$290 a week in high season for the smallest model, including unlimited mileage, tax and insurance. Tour operators' and local agents' brochures threaten alarming rates of £220/$350 for the same period but, except in August, no rental company expects to fetch that price for a car. Outside peak season, at the smaller **local outfits**, you can sometimes get terms of about £25/$40 per day, all inclusive, with better rates for three days or more. Shopping around in the busier resorts can yield a variation in quotes of up to fifteen percent for the same conditions over a four-to-seven-day period; the most negotiable point is whether or not kilometres in excess of 100km per day are free. Open jeeps, an increasingly popular extravagance, begin at about £35/$55 per day, rising to £55/$90 at busy times. Except in the largest cities, rental cars can be unavailable between late October and late April, since insurance policies may only be paid for the six summer months.

Note that brochure prices in Greece almost never include tax, **collision damage waiver** (CDW) and personal insurance. CDW in particular

CAR RENTAL AGENCIES

UK
Avis ☎0990/900500.
Budget ☎0800/181181.
Europcar/InterRent ☎0345/222525.
Hertz ☎0990/996699.
Holiday Autos ☎0990/300400.
Transhire ☎0171/978 1922.
Thrifty ☎ 0990/168238.

USA
Alamo ☎1-800/522-9696.
Auto Europe ☎1-800/223-5555.
Avis ☎1-800/331-1084.
Budget ☎1-800/527-0700.
Camwell Holiday Autos ☎1-800/422-7737.
Dollar ☎1-800/800-6000.

Europe by Car ☎1-800/223-1516; 212/245-1713.
Hertz ☎1-800/654-3001; in Canada ☎1-800/263-0600.
National ☎1-800/CAR RENT.
Thrifty ☎1-800/367-2277.

AUSTRALIA
Avis ☎1800/225 533.
Budget ☎13 2727.
Hertz ☎13 3039.

NEW ZEALAND
Avis ☎09/526 2847.
Budget ☎09/375 2222.
Hertz ☎09/309 0989.

is absolutely vital, as the cover included by law in the basic rental fee is inadequate, so check the fine print on your contract. Be wary of the hammering cars get on dirt tracks: damage to tyres, windscreen and the underside of the vehicle are nearly always excluded from coverage. All agencies will want either a credit card or a large cash **deposit** up front; minimum age requirements vary from 21 to 25. In theory an **International Driving Licence** is also needed, but in practice European, Australasian and North American ones are honoured.

In **peak season**, you may get a better price by booking through one of the **foreign companies** that deal with local firms than if you negotiate for rental in Greece itself; this may also be the only way to get a car at all at such times. One of the most competitive companies, which can arrange for cars to be picked up at most airports, is Holiday Autos; Transhire is another (see box for phone numbers). Most package operators can also offer car rental in Greece, though their rates are generally higher than the specialist rental agents. **In Greece**, Payless, European, Thrifty, and Just are reliable medium-sized companies with branches in many towns; all tend to be cheaper than (and just as reputable) as the biggest international operators Budget, Europcar, Hertz and Avis. Specific local recommendations are given in the guide.

In terms of available **models**, the more competitive companies tend to offer the Subaro M80 or Vivio, the Fiat Cinquecento and the Suzuki Alto 800 as A-group cars, and Opel (Vauxhall) Corsa, Nissan Micra or Fiat Uno/Punto in the B-group. The Suzuki Alto 600, Fiat Panda or Seat Marbella should be avoided if at all possible. The standard four-wheel-drive options are Suzuki jeeps, mostly open – great for bashing down rutted tracks.

DRIVING IN GREECE

Greece has the highest **accident rate** in Europe after Portugal, and many of the roads can be quite perilous – asphalt can turn into a one-lane surface or a dirt track without warning on the smaller routes, and railway crossings are rarely guarded. You're heavily reliant on the magnifying mirror at blind corners in congested villages. Uphill drivers insist on their right of way, as do those first to approach a one-lane bridge – headlights flashed at you mean the opposite of what they mean in the UK or North America, signifying that the driver is coming through or overtaking. On many of the so-called motorways, there is no proper far-right lane for slower traffic, which is expected to straddle the solid white line on the verge and allow rapid traffic to overtake.

Wearing a **seatbelt** is compulsory and children under ten are not allowed to sit in the front seats. First-aid kits are mandatory in the boot. If you are involved in any kind of accident it's illegal to drive away, and you can be held at a police station for up to 24 hours. If this happens, ring your consulate immediately, in order to get a lawyer (you have this right). Don't make a statement to anyone who doesn't speak, and write, very good English.

There are a limited number of **express highways** between Pátra, Athens, Vólos and Thessaloníki, on which tolls are levied – currently between 400dr and 700dr at each sporadically placed gate. They're nearly twice as quick as the old roads, and well worth using.

Tourists with proof of AA/RAC or similar membership are given free road assistance from ELPA, the Greek equivalent, which runs **breakdown services** based in Athens, Pátra, Lárissa, Vólos, Ioánnina, Corfu, Trípoli, Crete and Thessaloníki, plus many smaller, loosely affiliated garages. In an **emergency** ring their road assistance service on ☎104, anywhere in the country. Many car rental companies have an agreement with ELPA's competitors, Hellas Service and Express Service, but they're prohibitively expensive to summon on your own – it costs over 25,000dr to enrol you as an "instant member" in their scheme.

RUNNING A VEHICLE

Petrol/gasoline currently costs 225–240dr a litre for unleaded (*amólyvdhi*) or super. It is easy to run out of fuel after dark or on weekends in both rural and urban Greece; most stations close at 7 or 8pm sharp, and nearly as many are shut all weekend. There will always be at least one pump per district open on a rota basis, but it's not always apparent which one it is. This is not so much of a problem on the major highways, but it is a factor everywhere else. So always fill up, or insist on full rental vehicles at the outset, and if you've brought your own car, keep a full jerrycan at all times. Filling stations run by international companies (BP, Mobil and Shell) usually take credit cards; Greek chains like EKO, Mamidhakis and Elinoil usually don't.

Incidentally, the smallest grade of **mopeds** and **scooters** consume **mix**, a red- or green-tinted fuel dispensed from a transparent cylindrical device. This contains a minimum of three-percent two-stroke oil by volume; when unavailable, you brew it up yourself by adding to super-grade fuel the necessary amount of separately bottled two-stroke oil (*ládhi dhy'o trokhón* in Greek). It's wise to err on the generous side – say five percent – or you risk the engine seizing up.

In terms of **maintenance**, the easiest models to have serviced and buy parts for in Greece are VWs, Mercedes, Ladas, Skodas and virtually all French, Italian and Japanese makes. British models are a bit more difficult, but you should be fine as long as you haven't brought anything too esoteric.

In general, both mechanics' **workshops** and **parts retailers** are clustered at the approach and exit roads of all major towns, usually prominently signposted. For the commonest makes, emergency spares like fan belts and cables are often found at surprisingly remote service stations, so don't hesitate to ask at an unlikely-looking spot. Rural mechanics are okay for quick patch-up jobs like snapped clutch cables, but for major problems it's best to limp into the nearest sizeable town to find a mechanic who is factory-trained for your make.

HITCHING

Hitching carries the usual risks and dangers, and is inadvisable for women travelling alone, but overall Greece is one of the safer countries in which to do it. It's fairly reliable, too, as a means of getting around, so long as you're not overly concerned about time; lifts are fairly frequent but tend to be short.

Hitching is easier on islands and in rural areas than as a means of getting out of big cities, whose suburbs tend to sprawl for miles. At its best, hitching is a wonderful method of getting to know the country – there's no finer way to take in the Peloponnese than from the back of a truck that looks like it has been converted from a lawn-mower – and a useful way of picking up some Greek. While you'll often get lifts from Greeks eager to display or practise their English, there will be as many where to communicate you're forced to try the language.

TAXIS

Greek **taxis**, especially Athenian ones, are among the cheapest in western Europe and well worth making use of (though see the caveats on fares on p.75).

Use of the metre is mandatory, with Tariff "1" applying within city or town limits, and Tariff "2" (double rate) applying outside them or between midnight and 5am. The flag falls at 200dr throughout the country. There are also surcharges for entering a ferry harbour (currently 100dr), leaving an airport (200dr), and per large bag (50dr). For a week or so before and after Christmas and Easter, a *filodhórima* or bonus is levied. If you summon a taxi by phone, the metre starts running from the moment the driver begins heading towards you. All of this may legitimately bump up the fare from the basic meter reading of about 1700dr per ten rural kilometres.

A special warning needs to be sounded about **unlicensed taxi-drivers** who congregate outside major trains stations, particularly Athens and Lárissa. These shady characters may offer to shuttle you several hundred kilometres for the same price as the train/KTEL bus, or less; upon arrival you will discover that the fare quoted is per person, not per vehicle, and that along the way stops are made to cram several more passengers in – who again do not share your fare. Moreover, the condition of the vehicles usually leaves a lot to be desired.

DOMESTIC FLIGHTS

Olympic Airways and its subsidiary Olympic Aviation operate most **domestic flights** within Greece. They cover a fairly wide network of islands and larger towns, though most routes are to and from Athens, or the northern capital of Thessaloníki. **Schedules** can be picked up at Olympic offices abroad (see "Getting There" sections) or through their branch offices or representatives in Greece, which are maintained in almost every town or island of any size.

Fares, including domestic airport tax of about £8.50/$14, usually work out around three to four times the cost of an equivalent bus or ferry journey, but on certain inter-island hauls poorly served by boat (Rhodes–Kastellórizo or Kárpathos–Sitía, for example), you might consider this time well bought. For obscure reasons, flights between Athens and Mílos, Kýthira, Préveza or Kalamáta are slightly better value per kilometre, so take advantage.

Although airline operation is deregulated in Greece, thus far the only **private companies** to successfully challenge the Olympic monopoly are Air Greece and Kriti Air, which run internal flights from Athens to major destinations like Corfu, Rhodes and

Crete. These generally undercut the equivalent Olympic Airlines flights by quite a margin, though departure frequencies tend to be sparse.

Island flights are often full in peak season; if they're part of your plans, **reserve** at least a week in advance. Domestic air tickets are **non-refundable** but you can change your flight details, space permitting, as late as a day before your original intended departure, without penalty.

Like ferries, flights can be **cancelled** in bad weather, since many services are on small, 30- to 68-seat turbo-prop planes that won't fly in strong winds. A flight on a Dornier puddle-jumper is recommended at least once; you fly low enough to pick out every island feature.

The small aircraft also mean that a 15-kilo domestic baggage **weight limit** is fairly strictly enforced; if, however, you've just arrived from overseas, or purchased your ticket outside Greece, you are allowed the 23-kilo standard international limit. All services operated on the domestic network are **non-smoking**.

ACCOMMODATION

There are huge numbers of beds for tourists in Greece, and most of the year you can rely on turning up pretty much anywhere and finding a room – if not in a hotel, then in a private house or block of rooms (the standard island accommodation). Only from mid-July to early September, the country's high season, are you likely to experience problems. At these times, it is worth striking off the standard tourist routes, turning up at each new place early in the day, and taking whatever is available in the hope that you will be able to exchange it for something better later on.

HOTELS

Hotels are **categorized** by the tourist police from "Luxury" down to the almost extinct "E-class", and all except the top category have to keep within set price limits. Letter ratings are supposed to correspond to facilities available, though in practice categorization can depend on such factors as location within a resort and "influence" with tourism authorities. D-class usually have attached baths, while in C-class this is mandatory, along with a bar or breakfast area. The additional presence of a pool and/or tennis court, rooftop in cities if necessary, will attract a B-class rating, while A-class hotels must have a bar, restaurant and extensive common areas. Often they, and the De Luxe outfits (essentially self-contained complexes), back onto a beach.

In terms of **food**, C-class are only required to provide the most rudimentary of continental breakfasts – you may choose not to take, or pay for it – while B-class and above will usually offer some sort of buffet breakfast including cheese, cold cuts, sausages, eggs, and so on. With some outstanding exceptions, lunch or supper at hotel restaurants will be bland and poor value.

ROOMS

The most common form of island and mainland-resort accommodation is privately let **rooms** – *dhomátia*. These are regulated and officially divided into three classes (A down to C), according to facilities. These days the bulk of them are in new, purpose-built low-rise buildings, but a few are still actually in people's homes, where you'll occasionally be treated to disarming hospitality.

Dhomátia are usually better value than hotels, and in general spotlessly clean. At their (now vanishing) simplest, you'll get a bare, concrete room, with a hook on the back of the door and toi-

ROOM PRICES

All establishments listed in this book have been **price-coded** according to the scale outlined below. The rates quoted represent the **cheapest available room** in high season; all are prices for a double room, except for category ①, which are per person rates for hostels. Out of season, rates can drop by up to 50 percent, especially if you negotiate rates for a stay of three or more nights. Single rooms, where available, cost around 70 percent of the price of a double.

Rented private rooms on the islands usually fall into the ② or ③ categories, depending on their location and facilities, and the season; a few in the ④ category are more like plush self-catering apartments. They are not generally available from late October to the beginning of April, when only hotels tend to remain open.

You should expect rooms in all ① and most ② accommodation to be without private bath, though there may a basic washbasin in the room. In the ③ category and above there are usually private facilities. Some of the cheap places will also have more expensive rooms including en suite facilities – and vice versa, especially in the case of singles tucked in less desirable corners of the building.

Prices for rooms and hotels should by law be **displayed** on the back of the door of your room, or over the reception desk. If you feel you're being overcharged at a place which is officially registered, threatening to report it to the tourist office or police – who will generally adopt your side in such cases – should be enough to elicit compliance. Small amounts over the posted price may be legitimately explained by municipal tax or out-of-date forms. Occasionally you may find that you have bargained so well, or arrived so far out of season, that you are actually paying less than you're supposed to.

① 1400–2000dr	③ 6000–8000dr	⑤ 12,000–16,000dr
② 4000–6000dr	④ 8000–12,000dr	⑥ 16,000dr and upwards

let facilities (cold water only) outside in the courtyard. At the fancier end of the scale, they are modern, fully furnished places with an en-suite, marble-clad bathroom and a fully equipped kitchen shared by the guests. Between these two extremes you may find that there's choice of rooms at various prices (they'll usually show you the most expensive first). Price and quality are not necessarily directly linked: always ask to see the room before agreeing to take it and settling on the price.

Hot water is more reliably provided by a **thermosífono** (electric boiler) than by rooftop solar units, which tend to run out or cool off by sunset; "rooms" proprietors either jealously guard the boiler controls or entrust you with its workings. The "I" position is usually on, with a glow-light indicator on the tank; never leave the switch on while bathing, you risk electric shock and/or burning out the heating element.

Areas to look for rooms, and suggestions for the best options, are again included in the guide. But as often as not, the rooms find you: owners descend on ferry or bus arrivals to fill any space they have, sometimes waving photos of the premises. In smaller places you'll often see rooms advertised – sometimes in German (*zimmer*); the Greek signs to look out for are "Enikiazómena

Dhomátia" or "Enikiázonteh Dhomátia". In the more developed resorts where package clients predominate, *dhomátia* owners will often demand that you stay at least three days, or even a week.

If you are stranded, or arrive very late in a remote mountain or island **village** with no apparent tourist facilities whatsoever, you may very well find that you are invited to spend the night in someone's home. This should not be counted on, but things work out more often than not. The most polite course is to have a meal or drink at the taverna/kafenío and then, especially in summer, enquire as to the possibility of sleeping either in the vacant schoolhouse or in a spare room at the *kinotikó grafío* (community records office).

In **winter**, from November to early April, private rooms are closed pretty much across the board to keep the hotels in business. There's no point in traipsing about hoping to find exceptions – most rooms owners obey the system very strictly. If they don't, the owners will find you themselves and, watching out for hotel rivals, guide you back to their place.

It has become standard practice for rooms proprietors to ask to keep your **passport** – ostensibly "for the tourist police", but in reality to prevent you skipping out with an unpaid bill. Some owners may be satisfied with just taking down the details, as in hotels, and they'll almost always return documents once you get to know them, or if you need them for another purpose.

VILLAS AND LONG-TERM RENTALS

The easiest – and usually most economical – way to arrange a **villa rental** is through one of the package holiday companies detailed on pp.6–7. They represent some superb places, from simple to luxury, and costs can be very reasonable, especially if shared between four or more people. On the islands, a few local travel agents arrange villa rentals, though these are mostly places the overseas companies gave a miss on or couldn't fill. Out of season, you can sometimes get a good deal on villa or apartment rental for a month or more by asking around locally, though in these days of EU convergence and the increasing desirability of Greece as a year-round residence, "good deal" means anything under 45,000 for a large studio (*garsonieera*) or small one-bedroom flat.

YOUTH HOSTELS

Greece is not exactly packed with **youth hostels** (*xenón neótitos* in the singular) but those that there are tend to be fairly easy-going affairs: slightly run-down and a far cry from similar north-European institutions. Competition from unoffi-cial "student hostels" (see below) and low-budget rooms means that they are not as cost-effective as elsewhere in Europe. It's best to have a valid IYHF card (see box below for national organizations), but you can usually buy one on the spot, or maybe just pay a little extra for your bed. Charges for a dormitory bed are around £3–5/US$5–8 a night; most hostels have a curfew at 11pm or midnight and many places only open in spring and summer.

Hostels on the **mainland** include: Athens, Náfplio, Mycenae, Olympia, Pátra, Delphi, and Thessaloníki. On the islands you'll find them only on Thíra (3) and Crete (4). Not all of these are officially recognized by the IYHF.

A number of alternatives to official youth hostels exist, particularly in Athens. These inexpensive dormitory-style **student hostels** are open to anyone but can be rather insalubrious. Some offer **roofspace**, providing a mattress and a pleasantly cool night under the stars.

MONASTERIES

Greek **monasteries** and **convents** have a tradition of putting up travellers (of the appropriate sex). On the mainland, this is still a customary – if steadily decreasing – practice, used mostly by villagers on pilgrimage; on the islands, far less so. However, you should always ask locally before

---

YOUTH HOSTEL ASSOCIATIONS

AUSTRALIA
Australian Youth Hostels Association, Level 3, 10 Mallett St, Camperdown, NSW (☎02/565 1325).

CANADA
Hostelling International/Canadian Hostelling Association, Room 400, 205 Catherine St, Ottawa, Ontario K2P 1C3 (☎613/237-7884 or ☎1-800/663-5777).

ENGLAND AND WALES
Youth Hostel Association (YHA), Trevelyan House, 8 St Stephen's Hill, St Alban's, Herts AL1 2DY (☎01727/855215). London shop and information office: 14 Southampton St, London WC2 7HY (☎0171/836 1036).

IRELAND
An Oige, 61 Mountjoy Square, Dublin 7 (☎01/830 4555).

NEW ZEALAND
Youth Hostels Association of New Zealand, PO Box 436, Christchurch 1 (☎03/799-970).

NORTHERN IRELAND
Youth Hostel Association of Northern Ireland, 56 Bradbury Place, Belfast, BT7 (☎01232/324733).

SCOTLAND
Scottish Youth Hostel Association, 7 Glebe Crescent, Stirling, FK8 2JA (☎01786/451181).

USA
Hostelling International-American Youth Hostels (HI-AYH), PO Box 37613, Washington DC 20013-7613 (☎202/783-6161).

heading out to a monastery or convent for the night. Also, dress modestly – shorts for men and women, and short skirts are total anathema – and try to arrive early in the evening, not later than 8pm or sunset (whichever is earlier).

For **men**, the most exciting monastic experience is a visit to the "Monks' Republic" of **Mount Áthos** (see p.386), on the Khalkidhikí peninsula, near Thessaloníki. This is a far from casual travel option, involving a fair amount of advance planning and bureaucratic procedure to obtain a permit.

CAMPING

Official campsites range from ramshackle compounds on the islands to highly organized and rather soulless complexes run by the EOT (Greek Tourist Organisation). Cheap, casual places cost from £2/US$3.50 a night per person, as much again for a tent and perhaps £3/$5 for a camper van; at the larger sites, though, it's not impossible for two persons and one tent to add up almost to the price of a basic room. The Greek Camping Association, Solonós 102, 106 80 Athens (☎01/36 21 560), publishes a booklet covering most officially recognized Greek campsites and the facilities they offer; it's available from EOT offices.

Generally, you don't have to worry about leaving tents or **baggage** unattended at campsites; Greeks are very honest. The main risk, sadly, comes from other campers, and from Albanians camping rough.

Camping rough – outside authorized campsites – is such an established element of Greek travel that few people realize that it's officially illegal. Since 1977, however, it has been forbidden by a law originally promulgated to harass Gypsies, and increasingly the regulations are enforced.

If you do camp rough, it is vital to exercise sensitivity and discretion. Obviously the police crack down on people camping (and littering) on or near popular tourist **beaches**, particularly when a large community of campers develops. Off the beaten track, however, and particularly in **rural inland areas**, nobody is very bothered. During high season, when everything – even campsites – may be full, attitudes towards freelance camping are more relaxed, even in the most touristy places. At such times the best strategy is to find a sympathetic taverna willing to guard small valuables and let you use their facilities in exchange for regular patronage.

EATING AND DRINKING

Greeks spend a lot of time socializing outside their homes, and sharing a meal is one of the chief ways of doing it. The atmosphere is always relaxed and informal, and pretensions (and expense-account prices) are rare outside of the more chi-chi parts of Athens and major resorts. Greeks are not prodigious drinkers – what tippling they do is mainly to accompany food – though in the resorts a whole range of bars and pubs have sprung up, principally to cater to tourists.

BREAKFAST, PICNIC FARE AND SNACKS

Greeks don't generally eat **breakfast** and the only egg-and-bacon kind of places are in resorts where foreigners congregate; they can be quite good value (1100–1600dr), especially where there's competition. More indigenous alternatives include yoghurts at a *galaktopolío* (milk bar), or cheese pies and pretzel rings from a street stall (see "Snacks" below).

Picnic fare is good, cheap and easily available at bakeries and *manávika* (fruit-and-veg stalls). **Bread**, alas, is often of minimal nutritional value and inedible within a day of purchase. It's well worth paying the bit extra at the bakery (*foúrnos*) for *olikís* (wholemeal), *sikalísio* (rye), *oktásporo* (eight-grain), or even *enneásporo* (nine-grain), the latter types commonly baked where Germans or Scandinavians are about. When buying **olives**, go for the fat Kalamáta or Ámfissa ones; they're more expensive, but tastier. **Fétta cheese** is ubiquitous – often, ironically, imported from Holland or Denmark, though local batches are usually better and not much dearer. The goat's-milk variety can be very dry and salty, so it's wise to taste before buying. If you have access to a fridge, dunking the cheese overnight in a plastic container with water will solve both problems. Another palatable cheese is the expensive gruyère-type *graviéra*.

Despite EU membership, and growing personal incomes and exotic tastes, Greece imports very little garden produce from abroad, aside from bananas. **Fruit** in particular is relatively expensive and available only by locale and season, though in the more cosmopolitan spots it's possible to find such far-away delicacies as avocados (Cretan ones are excellent). Reliable picnic fruits include *yiarmádhes*, giant peaches appearing in August and September, and *krystália*, tiny hard green pears which ripen a month later and are heavenly. Greece also has a booming kiwi industry, and while the first crop in October coincides with the end of the tourist season, the harvest carries over into the following May. Salad **vegetables** are more reasonably priced; besides the enormous, red-ripe tomatoes (June–Sept), there is a bewildering array of spring greens, including rocket, dill, enormous spring onions and Kos lettuce. Useful expressions in the market include *éna tétarto* (250g) and *misó kiló* (500g).

SNACKS

Traditional **snacks** can be one of the distinctive pleasures of Greek eating, though increasingly edged out by an obsession with *tóst* (toasted sandwiches) and other western junk food at nationwide chains such as *Goody's* (burgers), *Roma Pizza* and *Theios Vanias* (baked pastries) – somewhat the less insipid for being home-grown. However, small independently produced **kebabs** (*souvlákia*) are widely available, and in most larger towns and resorts you'll find *yíros* – doner kebab with chips-and-sauce garnish in thick, doughy pitta bread that's closer to an Indian *nan*.

Other common snacks include *tyrópites* (cheese pies) and *spanokópita* (spinach pies), which can usually be found at the baker's, as can *kouloúria* (crispy baked pretzel rings sprinkled with sesame seeds) and *voutímata* (biscuits heavy on molasses, cinnamon and butter).

RESTAURANTS

Greek cuisine and **restaurants** are simple and straightforward. There's no snobbery about eating out; everyone does it and it's still reasonably priced – 2800–3600dr per person for a substantial meal with house wine.

In choosing a restaurant, the best strategy is to go where the Greeks go. And they go late: 2pm to 3pm for **lunch**, 9pm to 11pm for **dinner**. You can eat earlier, but you're likely to get indifferent service and cuisine if you frequent establishments catering to the tourist schedule. Chic appearance is not a good guide to quality; often the more ramshackle, traditional outfits represent the best value. One good omen is the waiter bringing a carafe of refrigerated water, unbidden, rather than pushing you to buy bottled stuff.

In Athens and resort areas, it's wise to keep a wary eye on the **waiters**, who are inclined to urge you into ordering more than you want and then bring things you haven't ordered. They often don't actually write anything down and may work out the bill by examining your empty plates. Although cash-register receipts are now legally required in all establishments, these are often only for the grand total, and any itemized tabs, will be in totally illegible Greek scribble. Where prices are printed on menus, you'll be paying the right-hand (higher) of the two columns, inclusive of all taxes and usually service charge, although a small tip (150–200dr) is standard practice for the lad who lays the table, brings the bread and water, and so on. **Bread** costs extra, but consumption is not obligatory; so much Greek bread is inedible sawdust that there's no point in paying for it.

Children are always welcome, day or night, at family tavernas, and Greeks anyway don't mind if they play tag between the tables or chase the **cats** – mendicant packs of whom you should not feed, as signs often warn you.

ESTIATÓRIA

There are two basic types of restaurant: the **estiatório** and the **taverna**. Distinctions between the two are slight, though the former is more com-

A FOOD AND DRINK GLOSSARY

Basics

Alát	Salt	Méli	Honey
Avgá	Eggs	Neró	Water
(Khorís) ládhi	(Without) oil	O logariazmós	The bill
Khortofágos	Vegetarian	Psári(a)	Fish
Katálogo/lísta	Menu	Psomí	Bread
Kréas	Meat	Olikís	Wholemeal
Lakhaniká	Vegetables		bread

Sikalísio	Rye bread
Thalassiná	Seafood
Tyrí	Cheese
Yiaoúrti	Yoghurt
Zákhari	Sugar

Cooking terms

Akhnistó	Steamed	Sto foúrno	Baked
Pastó	Marinated in salt	Tiganitó	Pan-fried
Psitó	Roasted	Tis óras	Grilled/fried to order
Saganáki	Rich red sauce	Yakhní	Stewed in oil and tomato sauce
Skáras	Grilled	Yemistá	Stuffed (squid, vegetables, etc)
Sti soúvla	Spit roasted		

Soups and starters

Avgolémono	Egg and lemon soup	Krítamo	Rock samphire
Dolmádhes	Stuffed vine leaves	Mavromátika	Black-eyed peas
Fasoládha	Bean soup	Melitzanosaláta	Aubergine/eggplant dip
Florínes	Canned red Macedonian peppers	Revithokeftédhes	Chickpea (garbanzo) patties
		Skordhaliá	Garlic dip
Kápari	Pickled caper leaves	Soúpa	Soup
Kopanistí, Khtypití, tyrosaláta	Spicy cheese purée	Taramosaláta	Cod roe paté
		Tzatzíki	Yoghurt and cucumber dip

Vegetables

Angináres	Artichokes	Koukiá	Broad fava beans
Angoúri	Cucumber	Maroúli	Lettuce
Ánitho	Dill	Melitzána	Aubergine/eggplant
Bámies	Okra, ladies' fingers	Papoutsákia	Stuffed aubergine/eggplant
Bouréki, bourekákia	Courgette/zucchini, potato and cheese pie	Patátes	Potatoes
		Piperiés	Peppers
Briám	Ratatouille	Pligoúri, pinigoúri	Bulgur wheat
Domátes	Tomatoes	Radhíkia	Wild chicory
Fakés	Lentils	Rízi/Piláfi	Rice (usually with sáltsa – sauce)
Fasolákia	French beans		
Khoriátiki (saláta)	Greek salad (with olives, fétta etc)	Rókka	Rocket greens
		Saláta	Salad
Khórta	Greens (usually wild)	Spanáki	Spinach
Kolokithákia	Courgette/zucchini	Yígandes	White haricot beans

Fish and seafood

Astakós	Aegean lobster	Gópa	Bogue
Atherína	Sand smelt	Kalamarákia	Baby squid
Bakaliáros	Cod	Karavídhes	Crayfish
Barboúni	Red mullet	Kalamária	Squid
Fangrí	Common bream	Kefalás	Bream
Galéos	Dogfish, hound shark	Koliós	Club mackerel
Garídhes	Shrimp, prawns	Koutsomoúra	Goatfish (small barboúni)
Gávros	Mild anchovy	Kydhónia	Cherrystone clams
Glóssa	Sole	Lakérdha	Light-fleshed premium tuna

Marídhes	Whitebait	*Sinagrídha*	Dentex
Melanoúri	Saddled bream	*Skathári*	Black bream
Mýdhia	Mussels	*Skoumbrí*	Atlantic mackerel
Okhtapódhi	Octopus	*Soupiá*	Cuttlefish
Platýs	Skate, ray	*Tsipoúra*	Gilt-head bream
Sardhélles	Sardines	*Vátos*	Skate, ray
Sargós	White bream	*Xifías*	Swordfish
Selákhi	Skate, ray		

Meat and meat-based dishes

Arní	Lamb	*Moussakás*	Aubergine, potato and meat pie with bechamel topping
Biftéki	Hamburger		
Brizóla	Pork or beef chop	*Païdhákia*	Lamb rib chops
Keftédhes	Meatballs	*Pastítsio*	Macaroni baked with meat
Khirinó	Pork	*Patsás*	Tripe and trotter soup
Kokorétsi	Liver/offal roullade, spit-roasted	*Salingária*	Garden snails
		Sikóti	Liver
Kopsídhia	Lamb shoulder chops	*Soutzoukákia*	Mincemeat rissoles/beef patties
Kotópoulo	Chicken		
Kounélli	Rabbit	*Stifádho*	Meat stew with tomato
Loukánika	Spicy homemade sausages	*Youvétsi*	Baked clay casserole of meat and short pasta
Moskhári	Veal		

Sweets and dessert

Baklavás	Honey and nut pastry	*Karydhópita*	Walnut cake
Bougátsa	Salt or sweet cream pie served warm with sugar and cinammon	*Kréma*	Custard
		Loukoumádhes	Dough fritters in honey syrup and sesame seeds
Galaktobóureko	Custard pie	*Pagotó*	Ice cream
Halvás	Sweetmeat, sesame or semolina	*Pastélli*	Sesame and honey bar
		Rizógalo	Rice pudding

Fruit and nuts

Akhládhia	Big pears	*Kerásia*	Cherries	*Pepóni*	Melon
Aktinídha	Kiwis	*Krystália*	Miniature pears	*Portokália*	Oranges
Fistíkia	Pistachio nuts	*Kydhóni*	Quince	*Rodhákino*	Peach
Fráoules	Strawberries	*Lemóni*	Lemon	*Sýka*	(Dried) figs
Karpoúzi	Watermelon	*Míla*	Apples	*Stafýlia*	Grapes

Cheese

Féta	Salty, white cheese	*Kasséri*	Medium-sharp cheese
Graviéra	Gruyère-type hard cheese	*Mizíthra*	Sweet cream cheese
Katsikísio	Goat cheese	*Próvio*	Sheep cheese

Drinks

Bíra	Beer	*Limonádha*	Lemonade
Boukáli	Bottle	*Metalikó neró*	Mineral water
Gála	Milk	*Portokaládha*	Orangeade
Galakakáo	Chocolate milk	*Potíri*	Glass
Gazóza	Generic fizzy drink	*Rosé/Kokkinélli*	Rosé
Kafés	Coffee	*Stinyássas!*	Cheers!
Krasí	Wine	*Tsaï*	Tea
Áspro	White	*Tsaï vounoú*	"Mountain" (sage) tea
Kókkino/mávro	Red		
Kokkinélli/rozé	Rosé		

monly found in towns and tends to have the slightly more complicated dishes termed **mayireftá** (literally, "cooked").

An estiatório will generally feature a variety of such oven-baked **casserole** dishes: *moussakás*, *pastítsio*, stews like *kokinistó* and *stifádho*, *yemistá* (stuffed tomatoes or peppers), the oily vegetable casseroles called *ladherá*, and oven-baked meat and fish. Usually you go into the kitchen and point at the desired steam trays to choose these dishes.

Batches are cooked in the morning and then left to stand, which is why this *mayireftá* food is often **lukewarm** or even cold. Greeks don't mind this (most actually believe that hot food is bad for you), and dishes like *yemistá* are actually enhanced by being allowed to cool off and stand in their own juice. Similarly, you have to specify if you want your food with little or no oil (*khorís ládhi*), but once again you will be considered a little strange since Greeks regard olive oil as essential to digestion (and indeed it is one of the least pernicious oils to ingest in large quantities).

Desserts (*epidhórpia* in formal Greek) of the pudding-and-pie variety don't exist at estiatória, and yoghurt or cheese only occasionally. Fruit, however, is always available in season; watermelon, melon and grapes are the summer standards. Autumn treats worth asking after include *kydhóni* or *akhládhi sto foúrno*, baked quince or pear with some sort of syrup or nut topping.

TAVERNAS

Tavernas range from the glitzy and fashionable to rough-and-ready cabins set up under a reed canopy, behind a beach. Really primitive ones have a very limited (often unwritten) menu, but the more established will offer some of the main *mayireftá* dishes mentioned above as well as standard taverna fare. This essentially means mezédhes (hors d'oeuvres) and *tis óras* (meat and fish fried or grilled to order).

Since the idea of courses is foreign to Greek cuisine, starters, main dishes and **salads** often arrive together unless you request otherwise. The best thing is to order a selection of *mezédhes* and salads to share, in true Greek fashion. Waiters encourage you to take the *khoriátiki* salad – the so-called Greek salad, with *fétta* cheese – because it is the most expensive one. If you only want tomato, or tomato and cucumber, ask for *domatosaláta* or *angourodomáta*. *Lákhano* (cab-

bage) and *maroúli* (lettuce) are the typical winter and spring salads.

The most interesting **starters** are *tzatzíki* (yoghurt, garlic and cucumber dip), *melitzanosaláta* (aubergine/eggplant dip), *kolokithákia tiganitá* (courgette/zucchini slices fried in batter) or *melitzánes tiganités* (aubergine/eggplant slices fried in batter), *yígandes* (white haricot beans in vinaigrette or hot tomato sauce), *tyropitákia* or *spanakópittes* (small cheese and spinach pies), *okhtapódhi xydháto* (octopus vinaigrette) and *mavromátika* (black-eyed peas).

Among **meats**, *souvláki* (shish kebab) and *brizóles* (chops) are reliable choices. In both cases, pork (*khirinó*) is usually better and cheaper than veal (*moskharísio*). The best *souvláki*, though not often available, is lamb (*arnísio*). At **psistariés** (grills), meaty lamb shoulder chops (*kopsídha*) are more substantial than the scrawny rib chops called *païdhákia*; roast lamb (*arní psitó*) and roast kid (*katsíki*) are **estiatório** fare. *Keftédhes* (meatballs), *biftékia* (a sort of hamburger) and the spicy sausages called *loukánika* are cheap and good. *Kotópoulo* (chicken) is also usually a safe bet.

Seaside tavernas also offer **fish**, though the choicer varieties, such as *barboúnia* (red mullet), *fangrí* (sea bream), *tsípoura* (gilt-head bream) and *lavráki* (sea bass) are expensive, and less tasty, if farmed. The price is usually quoted by the kilo, which should not be much more than double the street market rate, so that if squid is 2500dr/kilo at the fishmonger's, that sum should fetch you two 250gm portions. The standard procedure is to go to the glass cooler and pick your own. The cheapest widely available fish are *gópes* (bogue) and *marídhes* (tiny whitebait, eaten head and all, rolled in salt and sprinkled with lemon).

Cheaper **seafood** (*thalassiná*) such as *kalamarákia* (fried baby squid) and *okhtapódhi* (octopus) are a summer staple of most seaside tavernas, and occasionally *mýdhia* (mussels), *kydhónia* (cherrystone clams) and *garídhes* (small prawns) will be on offer at reasonable prices. Keep an eye, however, on freshness – mussels in particular are a common cause of stomach upsets or even mild poisoning.

Summer visitors get a relatively poor choice of fish, much of it frozen: net-trawling is prohibited from late May to late October, when only lamplure, trident and multi-hook line methods are allowed. During these warmer months, such few fish as are caught tend to be smaller and dry-tasting, and are served with butter sauce.

As in estiatória, traditional tavernas offer fruit rather than sticky desserts, though nowadays these too are often available, along with coffee, in places frequented by foreigners.

SPECIALIST TAVERNAS – AND VEGETARIANS

Some tavernas specialize in a particular type of food: psarotavérnes, for example, feature fish, and psistariés serve spit-roasted lamb, pork or goat (generically termed *kondosoúvli*), grilled chicken (*kotópoulo skáras*) or *kokorétsi* (grilled offal roulade) – often plunked straight on your table on a mat of waxed paper. A handful of other tavernas offer **game** (*kiníqi*): rabbit, quail or turtle dove in the autumn. In the mountains of the north where there are rivers, trout, pike and freshwater crayfish are to be found in some eating places.

If you are **vegetarian**, you may be in for a hard time, and will often have to assemble a meal from various mezédhes. Even the standbys of yoghurt with honey, *tzatzíki* and Greek salad begin to pall after a while, and many of the supposed "vegetable" dishes on menus are cooked in stock or have pieces of meat added to liven them up. Wholly or largely vegetarian restaurants slowly on the increase in touristy areas; this guide highlights them where appropriate.

WINES

Both estiatória and tavernas will usually offer you a choice of bottled **wines**, and many have their own house variety: kept in barrels, sold in bulk by the quarter-, half- or full litre, and served either in glass flagons or brightly coloured tin "monkey-cups" called *kantária*. Not as many tavernas stock their own wine as once did, but it's worth asking whether they have wine *varelísio* (barrelled) or *khíma* (in bulk). Non-resinated wine is frequently more than decent. **Retsína** – pine-resinated wine, a slightly acquired taste – is also usually better straight from the barrel, though the bottled *Yeoryiadhi* brand from Thessaloníki is excellent.

Among the more common bottled wines, Cambas, Boutari Lac des Roches, the Rhodian CAIR products, and the Cretan Logado are good inexpensive whites, while Boutari Nemea is perhaps the best mid-range red. If you want something better but still moderately priced, Tsantali Agioritiko makes an excellent white or red; Boutari has a fine Special Reserve red; the Macedonian Carras does both excellent whites and reds. In addition, there are various small, pre-mium wineries whose products are currently fashionable: Hatzimikhali, Athanasiadhi, Skouras and Lazaridhi, for which you can expect to pay in excess of 4500dr a bottle.

CAFÉS, CAKE SHOPS AND BARS

The Greek eating and drinking experience encompasses a variety of other places beyond restaurants. Most importantly, there is the institution of the **kafenío**, found in every town, village and hamlet in the country. In addition, you'll come across **ouzerís**, **zakharoplastía** and **barákia**.

THE KAFENÍO

The **kafenío** (plural, kafenía) is the traditional Greek coffee shop or café. Although its main business is Greek coffee – prepared *skéto* or *pikró* (unsweetened), *métrio* (medium) or *glykó* (sweet) – it also serves spirits such as *oúzo* (aniseed-based spirit), brandy (Metaxa or Botrys brand, in three grades), beer, tea (either mountain sage tea or British-style) and soft drinks. Another refreshing drink sold in cafés is *kafés frappé*, a sort of iced instant coffee with or without milk and sugar – uniquely Greek despite its French-sounding name. Like Greek coffee, it is always accompanied by a welcome glass of cold water. Standard fizzy soft drinks are also sold in kafenía.

Usually the only edibles available are *glyká koutalioú* (sticky, syrupy preserves of quince, grape, fig, citrus fruit or cherry), and the old-fashioned *ipovrýkhio*, which is a piece of mastic submerged in a glass of water like a submarine, which is what the word means in Greek.

Like tavernas, kafenía range from the plastic and sophisticated to the old-fashioned, spit-on-the-floor variety, with marble or brightly painted wood tables and straw-bottomed chairs. An important institution everywhere in Greece, they form the pivot of life in the country villages. You get the impression that many men spend most of their waking hours there. Greek women are rarely to be seen in the more traditional places – and foreign women may sometimes feel uneasy or unwelcome in these establishments. Even in holiday resorts, you will find there is at least one café that the local men have reserved for themselves.

Some kafenía close at siesta time, but many remain open from early in the morning until late at night. The chief socializing time is 6–8pm, immediately after the *mikró ípno* or siesta. This is the time to take your pre-dinner oúzo, as the sun begins to sink and the air cools down.

OÚZO, MEZÉDHES AND OUZERÍ

Oúzo and the similar *tsípouro* (mainland) and *tsikoudhiá* (Crete), are simply **spirits** of up to 48 percent alcohol, distilled from grape-mash residue left over from wine-making, and then flavoured with herbs such as anise or fennel. There are nearly a score of brands, with the best reckoned to be from Lésvos, Sámos and Tírnavos on the mainland; the bad ones are spiked with molasses or neat alcohol to "fortify" them. Mini (after the mini-skirted lass on the label), is a common, very dry variety.

When you order, you will be served two glasses: one with the oúzo, and one full of water, to be tipped into your oúzo until it turns a milky white. You can drink it straight, but its strong, burning taste is hardly refreshing.

Until the 1980s, every oúzo you ordered was automatically accompanied by a small plate of **mezédhes**, on the house: bits of cheese, cucumber, tomato, a few olives, sometimes octopus or even a couple of small fish. Unfortunately these days you have to ask, and pay, for them.

Though confined to the better resorts and select neighbourhoods of the bigger cities, one kind of drinking establishment specializes in oúzo and mezédhes. These are called an **ouzerí** (same in the Greek plural) or *ouzádhiko – tsipourádhiko* in the north – and are well worth trying for the marvellous variety of mezédhes they serve (though of late numbers of mediocre tavernas have appropriated the name). At the genuine article, several plates of mezédhes plus drinks will effectively substitute for a more involved meal at a taverna (though it usually works out to be more expensive, if you have a healthy appetite). Faced with the often bewilderingly varied menu, you might opt for the *pikilía* (medley) available in several sizes, the largest usually heavy on seafood.

SWEETS AND BREAKFAST

Similar to the kafenío is the **zakharoplastío**. A cross between a café and patisserie, it serves coffee, alcohol, yoghurt and honey, and sticky cakes. The better establishments offer an amazing variety of pastries, cream and chocolate confections, honey-soaked Middle Eastern sweets like *baklavás*, *kataïfi* (honey-drenched "shredded wheat"), *loukoumádhes* (deep-fried batter puffs dusted with cinnamon and dipped in syrup); *galaktoboúreko* (custard pie), and so on.

If you want a stronger slant towards dairy products and away from pure sugar, seek out a *galaktopolío*, where you'll often find *rizógalo* (**rice pudding** – better than English canned variety), *kréma* (custard) and locally made *yiaoúrti* (yoghurt), best if it's *próvio* (from sheep's milk).

Ice cream, sold principally at the *gelaterie* which have swept over Greece of late (Dhodhoni is a posh chain), can be very good and almost indistinguishable from Italian prototypes. A scoop (*baláki*) costs 200–300dr; you'll be asked if you want it in a cup (*kypelláki*) or a cone (*khonáki*), and whether you want toppings like *santí* (whipped cream). By contrast, the mass-produced Delta or Evga brands are pretty average. A sign reading *pagotó politikó* or *kaïmáki* means that the shop concerned makes its own Turkish-style ice cream – as good as or better than the usual Italian – and the proprietors are probably of Asia Minor or Constantinopolitan descent.

Both *zakharoplastía* and *galaktopolía* are more family-oriented places than the kafenío, and many also serve a basic **continental breakfast** of *méli mé voútyro* (honey poured over a pat of butter) or jam (all kinds are called *marmeládha* in Greek; ask for *portokáli* – orange – if you want proper marmalade) with fresh bread or *friganiés* (melba-toast-type slivers). You are also more likely to find proper (*evropaïkó*) tea and non-Greek coffee. Nescafé has become the generic term for all instant coffee, regardless of brand; in resorts smart proprietors have taken to offering filter coffee, dubbed *gallikós* (French).

BARS – AND BEER

Bars (*barákia* in the plural), once confined to towns, cities and holiday resorts, are now found all over Greece, especially in pedestrian areas. They range from clones of Parisian cafés or Spanish bodegas to seaside cocktail bars, or imitation English "pabs" (sic), with videos running all day. At their most sophisticated, however, in the largest cities and resorts, they can hold their own against close equivalents in Spain or London; they are well-executed theme venues in ex-industrial premises or Neoclassical houses, with western (currently techno) soundtracks.

Formerly operating from mid-afternoon to dawn, most *barákia* now shut by 2 or 3am, depending on the municipality; during 1994 they were required by the Ministry of Public Order to make an admission/cover charge which included the first drink. Met with a wave of street demos and other mass civil disobedience, this decree is presently in abeyance but could be revived at any time.

For this and other reasons, drinks are invariably more expensive than at a café. *Barákia* are, however, the most likely to stock a **range of beers**, which in Greece are 98 percent foreign label made under licence, since the indigenous Fix brewery closed in 1984. A new brand appeared in 1996 – Pils Hellas, akin to Heineken, but less bitter; Mythos, in light green bottles, is a good newish lager. Kronenberg and Kaiser are available, the former in both light and dark vari-

eties; since 1993 a tidal wave of even pricier, imported German beers such as Bitburger and Warstein has washed over the bigger resorts. Amstel and Henninger are the two ubiquitous cheapies, rather bland but inoffensive. A possible compromise in both palate and expense is the sharper-tasting Heineken, universally referred to as a "*prássini*" by bar and taverna staff after its green bottle.

Incidentally, try not to be stuck with the one-third litre cans, vastly more expensive (and more of a rubbish problem) than the returnable half-litre bottles.

COMMUNICATIONS

POSTAL SERVICES

Post offices are open Monday to Friday from 7.30am to 2pm, though certain main branches have hours through the evening and on Saturday morning. They exchange money in addition to handling mail.

Airmail letters from the mainland take three to six days to reach the rest of Europe, five to ten days to get to North America, and a bit longer for Australia and New Zealand. Allow an extra day or two when sending from an island without an airport. Aerograms are slightly faster, while for a modest fee (about 500dr) you can use **express service** (*katepígonda*). **Registered** (*sistiméno*) delivery is also available, but it is quite slow unless coupled with express service. If you are

sending large parcels home, note that these should and often can only be dealt with in large provincial or county capitals. This way your bundle will be in Athens, and on an international flight, within a day.

For a simple letter or card, a **stamp** (*grammatósima*) can also be purchased at a *períptero* (corner kiosk). However, the proprietors charge ten percent commission and never seem to know the current international rates. Ordinary **post boxes** are bright yellow, express boxes dark red; if you are confronted by two slots, "Esoterikó" is for domestic mail, "Exoterikó" for overseas.

RECEIVING MAIL

The **poste restante/general delivery** system is reasonably efficient, especially at the post offices of larger towns. Mail should be marked *poste restante*, with your surname underlined, and addressed to the main post office of whichever town you choose. It will be held for a month and you'll need your passport to collect it.

PHONES

Making calls is relatively straightforward, though **OTE** (*Organismós Tiliepikinoníon tis Elládhos*, the state-run telecom) provides some of the worst service in the EU – at about the highest rates. **Call boxes**, invariably sited at the noisiest street corners, work only with phone cards (in three sizes: 100, 500 and 1000 units), bought from kiosks, OTE offices and newsagents. Not surprisingly, the largest ones represent the best value.

If you won't be around long enough to use up a phone card, it's probably easier to make local calls from a *períptero*, or **street kiosk**. Here the phone may be connected to a meter (if not, there'll be a sign saying *móno topikó*, "local only"), and you pay after you have made the call. Local, one-unit calls are cheap enough (20dr for six minutes), but long-distance ones add up quickly (see below). There are a growing number of digital (*psifiakó*) exchanges, but most are still pulse-analogue (*palmikó*); when dialling long distance on the latter, you must wait for a characteristic series of six electrical crunches after the country or Greek area code before proceeding. Other options for calling include **counter coin phones** in bars and hotel lobbies; these take 10-, 20-, 50- and 100-drachma coins and, unlike the street phone boxes, can be rung back. Most of them are made in northern Europe and bear instructions in English. Avoid making long-distance calls from a hotel-room phone, as a fifty percent surcharge will be slapped onto the already steep rates.

For **international** (*exoterikó*) calls, it's better to use either card phones or visit the nearest OTE office, where there may be a digital booth reserved for overseas calls only; make your call and pay afterwards. **Reverse charge** (collect) or person-to-person calls can also be made here, though connections are not always immediate; be prepared to wait.

Increasingly, however, OTE offices are less and less in the business of providing metered calls, with most booths converted to cardphones and opening hours shortened. In the biggest cities there will be at least one branch open 24 hours, while elsewhere schedules are more commonly 7am–10pm or even 8am–3pm. In a few resorts there are OTE Portakabin booths keeping odd but useful schedules like 2–10pm. Outgoing **faxes** can also be sent from OTE offices, post offices and some travel agencies – at a price. Receiving a fax may also incur a small charge.

Calls will **cost**, very approximately, £2 for three minutes to all EU countries and most of the rest of Europe, or US$5 for the same time to North America or Australasia. **Cheap rates**, such as they are, apply from 3pm to 5pm and 9pm to 8am daily, plus all weekend, for calls within Greece; overseas off-peak periods are variable, but for Europe fall between 10pm and 8am.

For details of **phone codes** and **useful numbers**, see the box below.

PHONING GREECE FROM ABROAD

Dial the international access code (given below) + 30 (country code) + area code (minus initial 0, see below) + number.

Australia ☎0011 New Zealand ☎00 Canada ☎011 UK ☎00 Ireland ☎010 USA ☎011

PHONING ABROAD FROM GREECE

Dial the country code (given below) + area code (minus initial 0) + number

| Australia ☎0061 | New Zealand ☎0064 | Canada ☎001 |
| UK ☎0044 | Ireland ☎00353 | USA ☎001 |

GREEK PHONE CODES

Athens ☎01	Corfu ☎0661	Iráklion ☎081	Kós ☎0242
Mobiles ☎093 & ☎094	Mýkonos ☎0289	Páros ☎0284	Pátra ☎061
Rhodes ☎0241	Santoríni ☎0286	Skiáthos ☎0427	Thessaloníki ☎031
Zákynthos ☎0695			

USEFUL TELEPHONE NUMBERS

Operator ☎131 (Athens only)	Operator ☎132 (Domestic)	Operator ☎161 (International)
Medical emergencies ☎166	Police emergency ☎100	Speaking clock ☎141
Tourist police ☎171	Fire brigade, urban ☎199	Forest fires ☎191
ELPA road assistance ☎104		

British Telecom, as well as North American long-distance companies like AT&T, MCI and Sprint all enable their customers to make **credit-card calls** from Greece, but only back to the home country. There are now a few local-dial numbers with some providers, such as BT, which enable you to connect to the international network for the price of a one-unit call, and then charge the call to your home number – usually cheaper than the alternatives.

Mobile users should note that only GSM phones will work in Greece, over one of two networks. The Greeks, incidentally, are very keen on them, and they've become a fashion accessory among certain classes.

THE MEDIA

British newspapers are fairly widely available in Greece for 450–600dr, 800–900dr for Sunday editions. You'll find day-old copies of *The Independent* and *The Guardian*'s European edition, plus some of the tabloids, in all the resorts as well as in major towns. **American** and **international** alternatives include the turgid *USA Today* and the more readable *International Herald Tribune*; *Time* and *Newsweek* are also widely available.

Among monthly **magazines**, the late lamented *Athenian* folded in 1997 after 23 years, with a successor, *Atlantis*, rising less than phoenix-like from the ashes. Slightly better is the expensive, glossy *Odyssey*, produced by and for wealthy diaspora Greeks and little different from an in-flight magazine.

GREEK PUBLICATIONS

Currently the only local **English-language** Greek newspaper is the *Athens News* (250dr, daily except Mon), in colour with full Athens cinema schedules, features and Balkan news, available in most resorts.

Many Greek papers are funded by **political groups**, which tends to decrease the already low quality of Greek dailies. Among these, only the centrist *Kathemerini* – whose former proprietor Helen Vlakhos attained heroic status for her defiance of the junta – approaches the standards of a major European newspaper. *Eleftherotypia*, once a PASOK mouthpiece, now aspires to more independence and has links with the UK's *Guardian*; *Avriani* has taken its place in the PASOK cheerleading section. *Ta Nea* is mostly known for its extensive small ads. On the **Left**, *Avyi* is the Eurocommunist form with literary leanings, while *Rizospastis* acts is the organ for the KKE (unreconstructed Communists). *Ethnos* became notorious some years back by receiving covert KGB funding to act as disinformation bulletin. At the opposite end of the political spectrum, *Apoyevmatini* generally supports the **centre-right** *Néa Dhimokratía* party, while *Estia*'s no-photo format and reactionary politics are both stuck somewhere at the turn of the century. The **ultra-nationalist** lunatic fringe is staked out by *Stokhos* ("Our Goal: Greater Greece. Our Capital: Constantinople").

Among **magazines** which are not merely translations of overseas titles, *Takhydhromos* is the respectable news-and-features weekly; *Ena* is a more sensationalist, *Klik* a crass rip-off of *The Face*, and *To Pondiki* (The Mouse) a satirical weekly revue in the same vein as Britain's *Private Eye* – its famous covers are spot-on and accessible to anyone with minimal Greek. More specialized niches are occupied by low-circulation titles such as *Adhesmatos Typos* (a slightly rightist, muckraking journal) and *Andi*, somewhat in the mould of Britain's *New Statesman and Society*.

RADIO

If you have a **radio**, playing dial roulette can be rewarding. Greek music programmes are always accessible (if variable in quality) despite the language barrier, and with recent challenges to the government's former monopoly of wavelengths, regional stations have mushroomed; the airwaves are now positively cluttered, as every town sets up its own studio and transmitter.

The **BBC World Service** can be picked up on short-wave frequencies throughout Greece, the most common ones are 15.07 and 12.09Mhz.

TV

Greece's two central, government-controlled **TV stations**, ET1 and ET2, nowadays lag behind private channels – Mega-Channel, New Channel,

Antenna, Star and Seven-X – in the ratings. Programming on all stations tends to be a mix of soaps (especially Italian, Spanish and Latin-American), gameshows, westerns, B-movies and sports. All foreign films and serials are broadcast in their original language, with Greek subtitles. Except for Seven-X, which begins at 7pm, and Mega (a 24-hour channel), the main channels broadcast from breakfast time until the small hours.

Numerous **cable** and **satellite channels** are received, including Sky, CNN, MTV, Super Channel and French Canal Cinque and Italian Rai Due. The range available depends on the area (and hotel) you're in.

OPENING HOURS AND PUBLIC HOLIDAYS

It is virtually impossible to generalize about Greek opening hours, except to say that they change constantly. The traditional timetable starts at a relatively civilized hour, with shops opening between 8.30am and 9.30am, and runs through until lunchtime, when there is a long break for the hottest part of the day. Things (except banks) may then reopen in the mid- to late afternoon.

Tourist areas tend to adopt a slightly more northern timetable, with certain shops and offices, as well as the most important archeological sites and museums, usually open throughout the day.

BUSINESS AND SHOPPING HOURS

Most **government agencies** are open to the public from 8am to 2pm. In general, however, you'd be optimistic to show up after 1pm expecting to be served the same day. **Private businesses**, or service providers are apt to operate on a 9am–6pm schedule. If someone is actually selling something, then they are more likely to follow a split shift as detailed below.

Shopping hours during the hottest months are theoretically Monday, Wednesday and Saturday from approximately 9am to 2.30pm, and Tuesday, Thursday and Friday from 8.30am to 2pm and 6 to 9pm. During the cooler months with shorter daylight hours, the morning schedule shifts slightly forward, the evening trade thirty minutes or even a full hour back. However, there are so many **exceptions** to these rules by virtue of holidays and professional idiosyncrasy that you can't count on getting anything done except from Monday to Friday, between 9.30am and 1pm. It's worth noting that **delis** and **butchers** are not allowed to sell fresh meat during the afternoon (though some flout this rule); similarly **fishmongers** are only open in the morning, as are **pharmacies**, which additionally are shut on Saturday.

All of the above opening hours will be regularly thrown out of sync by the numerous **public holidays** and **festivals**. The most important, when almost everything will be closed, are listed in the box below.

ANCIENT SITES AND MONASTERIES

All the major **ancient sites** are now fenced off and, like most **museums**, charge admission fees ranging from a token 400dr to a whopping 2000dr,

---

PUBLIC HOLIDAYS

January 1	May 1
January 6	Whit Monday (50 days after Easter; see below)
March 25	August 15
First Monday of Lent (Feb or March; see below)	October 28
Easter weekend (April or May; see below)	December 25–26

VARIABLE RELIGIOUS FEASTS

	Lent Monday	Easter Sunday	Whit Monday
1998	March 2	April 19	June 8
1999	Feb 22	April 11	May 31

with an average fee of around 800dr. At most of them reductions of twenty five to thirty percent apply to senior citizens, and fifty percent to students with proper identification. In addition, entrance to all state-run sites and museums is **free** to all EC nationals on Sundays and public holidays outside of peak season – non-EU nationals are unlikely to be detected as such unless they go out of the way to advertise the fact.

Opening hours vary from site to site. As far as possible, individual times are quoted in the text, but bear in mind that these change with exasperating frequency, and at smaller sites may be subject to the whim of a local keeper. The times quoted are generally summer hours, which operate from around late April to the end of September. Reckon on similar days but later opening and earlier closing in winter.

Smaller sites generally close for a long lunch and **siesta** (even where they're not supposed to),

as do **monasteries**. The latter are generally open from 9am to 1pm and 5 to 8pm (3.30 to 6.30pm in winter) for limited visits. Most monasteries impose a fairly strict dress code for visitors; no shorts on either sex, with women expected to cover their arms and wear skirts; the necessary wraps are sometimes provided on the spot.

It's free to take **photos** of open-air sites, though museum photography and the use of videos or tripods anywhere requires an extra fee and written permit. This usually has to be arranged in writing from the nearest Department of Antiquities (*Eforía Arkhaiotíton*). It's also worth knowing that Classical studies students can get a free annual pass to all Greek museums and sites by presenting themselves at the office on the rear corner (Tossítsa/Bouboulínas) of the National Archeological Museum in Athens – take documentation, two passport-sized photographs and be prepared to say you're a teacher.

FESTIVALS AND CULTURAL EVENTS

Many of the big Greek popular festivals have a religious basis so they're observed in accordance with the Orthodox calendar. Give or take a few saints, this is similar to the regular Catholic liturgical year, except for Easter, which can fall as much as three weeks to either side of the Western festival. Other festivals are cultural in nature, with the highlight for most people being to catch a performance of Classical drama in one of

the country's ancient theatres. There's also a full programme of cinema and modern theatre, at its best in Athens, but with something on offer in even the smallest town at some point during the year.

EASTER

Easter is by far the most important festival of the Greek year – infinitely more so than Christmas – and taken much more seriously than it is anywhere in Western Europe. From Wednesday of Holy Week until the following Monday, the state radio and TV networks are given over solely to religious programmes.

The **festival** is an excellent time to be in Greece, both for its beautiful religious ceremonies and for the days of feasting and celebration that follow. The mountainous island of **Ídhra** with its alleged 360 churches and monasteries is the prime Easter resort, but unless you plan well in advance you have no hope of finding accommodation at that time. Probably the best idea is to make for a medium-sized village where, in most cases, you'll be accepted into the community's celebration. Other famous Easter celebrations are held at Corfu, Pyrgí on Khíos, Ólymbos on Kárpathos and Pátmos.

The first great public ceremony takes place on **Good Friday** evening as the Descent from the Cross is lamented in church. At dusk the *Epitáfios*, Christ's funeral bier, lavishly decorated by the women of the parish, leaves the sanctuary and is paraded solemnly through the streets. In many places, Crete especially, this is accompanied by the burning of effigies of Judas Iscariot.

Late **Saturday** evening sees the climax in a majestic *Anástasis* mass to celebrate Christ's triumphant return. At the stroke of midnight all the lights in every crowded church are extinguished, and the congregation plunged into the darkness which envelops Christ as He passes through the underworld. Then there's a faint glimmer of light behind the altar screen before the priest appears, holding aloft a lighted taper and chanting "*Avtó to Fós . . .* " (This is the Light of the World). Stepping down to the level of the parishioners, he touches his flame to the unlit candle of the nearest worshipper intoning "*Dévthe, lévethe Fós*" (Come, take the Light). Those at the front of the congregation and on the aisles do the same for their neighbours until the entire church is ablaze with burning candles and the miracle re-affirmed.

Even the most committed agnostic is likely to find this moving. The traditional greeting, as fireworks explode all around you in the street, is "*Khristós Anésti*" (Christ is risen), to which the response is "*Alithós Anésti*" (Truly He is Risen). In the week up to Easter Sunday you should wish people a Happy Easter: "*Kaló Páskha*"; on or after the day, you say "*Khrónia Pollá*" (Many Happy Returns).

Worshippers then take the burning **candles** home through the streets, and it brings good fortune to the house if they arrive still burning. On reaching the front door it is common practice to make the sign of the cross on the lintel with the flame, leaving a black smudge visible for the rest of the year. The Lenten fast is traditionally broken early on Sunday morning with a meal of *mayerítsa*, a soup made from lamb tripe, rice and lemon. The rest of the lamb will be roasted on spits for Sunday lunch, and festivities often take place through the rest of the day.

The Greek equivalent of **Easter eggs** are hard-boiled eggs (painted red on Holy Thursday), which are baked into twisted, sweet bread-loaves (*tsouréki*) or distributed on Easter Sunday. People rap their eggs against their friends' eggs, and the owner of the last uncracked egg is considered lucky.

THE FESTIVAL CALENDAR

Most of the other Greek festivals are celebrations of one or another of a multitude of **saints**; the most important are detailed on pp.54–56. A village or church bearing the saint's name is a sure sign of celebrations – sometimes right across the town or island, sometimes quiet, local and consisting of little more than a special liturgy and banners adorning the chapel in question. Saints' days are also celebrated as name days; if you learn that it's an acquaintance's name day, you wish them "*Khrónia Pollá* " (Many Happy Returns). Also detailed on pp.55–56 are a few more **secular** holidays, most enjoyable of which are the pre-Lenten carnivals.

In addition to the specific dates mentioned, there are literally scores of **local festivals**, or **paniyíria**, celebrating the patron saint of the main village church. With hundreds of possible name-saints' days (calendars list two or three, often arcane, for each day) you're unlikely to travel around Greece for long without stumbling on something.

It is important to remember the concept of the **paramoní**, or **eve of the festival**. Most of the events listed below are celebrated on the night before, so if you show up on the morning of the date given you will very probably have missed any music, dancing or drinking.

January 1

New Year's Day (Protokhroniá) in Greece is the feast day of Áyios Vassílios, and is celebrated with church services and the baking of a special loaf, *vassilópitta*, in which a coin is embedded, bringing its finder good luck throughout the year. The traditional New Year greeting is "Kalí Khroniá".

January 6

Epiphany (Ayía Theofánia, Fóta for short), when the kalikántzari (hobgoblins) who run riot on earth during the twelve days of Christmas are rebanished to the nether world by various rites of the Church. The most important of these is the blessing of baptismal fonts and all outdoor bodies of water. At lakeside, river and seaside locations, the priest traditionally casts a crucifix into the deep, with local youths competing for the privilege of recovering it.

January 8

The **Yinekokratía** of certain villages in Thrace is a festival where St Domenica (Dhomníka in

Greek), patroness of midwives, is celebrated by men and women reversing roles for the day: the women populate the cafés while the men do the domestic chores.

Pre-Lenten carnivals

These – known in Greek as Apokriátika – span three weeks, climaxing during the seventh weekend before Easter. **Pátra Carnival**, with a chariot parade and costume parties, is one of the largest and most outrageous in the Mediterranean, with events from January 17 until "Clean Monday", the last day of Lent; on the last Sunday before Lent there's a grand parade, with the city's large **gay population** in conspicuous participation. Interesting, too, are the boúles or masked revels which take place around Macedonia (particularly at Náoussa), Thrace (Xánthi) and the outrageous **Goat Dance** on Skýros in the Sporades. The Ionian islands, especially Kefalloniá, are also good for Carnival, while Athenians "celebrate" by going around hitting each other on the head with plastic hammers. In Thebes, a mock shepherd wedding occurs, while most places celebrate with colourful pageants reflecting local traditions.

March 25

Independence Day and the feast of the **Annunciation** (Evangelismós in Greek) is both a religious and a national holiday, with on the one hand military parades and dancing to celebrate the beginning of the revolt against Turkish rule in 1821, and on the other church services to honour the news being given to Mary that she was to become the Mother of Christ. There are major festivities on Tínos, Ídhra (Hydra) and many other places, particularly near any monastery or church named Evangelístria or Evangelismós, whose name-day celebration it is.

April 23

The feast of Saint George (Áyios Yeóryios), the patron of shepherds, is a big rural celebration, with much feasting and dancing at associated shrines and towns. Good venues include Arákhova, near Delphi, and the island of Skýros, for which George is patron saint. If April 23 falls before Easter, ie during Lent, the festivities are postponed until the Monday after Easter.

May 1

May Day is the great urban holiday when towns-

people traditionally make for the countryside for picnics, returning with bunches of wild flowers. Wreaths are hung on their doorways or balconies until they are burned on Midsummer's eve. There are also large demonstrations by the Left, claiming the Ergatikí Protomayiá (Working-Class First of May) as their own.

May 21

The feast of Áyios Konstandínos (Saint Constantine) and his mother, Ayía Eléni (Saint Helen), the first Orthodox Byzantine rulers. There are firewalking ceremonies in certain Macedonian villages, and elsewhere the day is celebrated rather more conventionally as being the name day for two of the more popular Christian names in Greece.

June 29

The feast of Áyios Pétros and Áyios Pávlos (Peter and Paul). Widely celebrated name days.

July 17

The feast of Ayía Marína is a big event in rural areas, as she's an important protector of crops. The eponymous port on Léros will also be en fête. Between this celebration and mid-September there are religious festivals every few days, and between these, secular holidays and the heat, most business comes to a standstill.

July 18–20

The feast of Profítis Ilías (the Prophet Elijah) is widely celebrated at the countless hill- or mountain-top shrines of Profítis Ilías. The most famous is on Mount Taïyettos, near Spárti.

July 26

The feast of Ayiá Paraskeví, with big village festivals, especially in Epirus.

August 6

The feast of the Metamórfosis (Transfiguration) provides another excuse for celebrations, particularly at Khristós village on Ikaría.

August 15

The Apokímisis tis Panayías (Assumption of the Blessed Virgin Mary). As at Easter, this is a day when people traditionally return to their home village, and in most places there will be no accommodation available on any terms. Even some Greeks will resort to sleeping in the streets.

There is a great pilgrimage to Tínos, and major festivities at Páros, at Ayiássos on Lésvos, and at Ólymbos on Kárpathos.

August 29
Feast of the Beheading of John the Baptist (Áyios Ioánnis Pródhromos).

September 8
The Yénisis tis Panayías (Birth of the Virgin Mary) sees special services in churches dedicated to the event (with major festivals 24hr beforehand), and a double cause for rejoicing on Spétses where they also celebrate the anniversary of the Battle of the Straits of Spétses, which took place on September 8, 1822. A re-enactment of the battle takes place in the harbour, followed by fireworks and feasting well into the night.

September 14
A last major summer festival, the **Ípsosis tou Stavroú** (Exaltation of the Cross), keenly observed on Khálki.

September 26
Feast of Saint John the Evangelist (Áyios Ioánnis O Thelógos).

October 26
The Feast of Áyios Dhimítrios (Saint Demetrius), is another popular name-day, particularly celebrated in Thessaloníki, of which he is the patron saint. New wine is traditionally tapped on this day, a good excuse for general inebriation.

October 28
Ókhi Day, the year's major patriotic shindig – a national holiday with parades, folk-dancing and feasting to commemorate Metaxas's apocryphal one-word reply to Mussolini's 1940 ultimatum: "Okhi!" (No!).

November 8
Another popular name-day, **the feast of the Archangels Michael and Gabriel** (Mikhaïl and Gavriïl, or Taxiárkhon), with rites at the numerous rural monasteries and chapels named after them – particularly on Sými and Lésvos.

December 6
The feast of Áyios Nikólaos (Saint Nicholas), the patron of seafarers, who has many chapels dedicated to him.

December 25
A much less festive occasion than Greek Easter, **Christmas** (Khristoúyenna) is still an important religious feast celebrating the birth of Christ, and in recent years it has started to take on more of the trappings of the Western Christmas, with decorations, Christmas trees and gifts. December 26 is not Boxing Day as in England but the **Sýnaxis tis Panayías**, or Meeting of the Virgin's Entourage.

December 31
New Year's Eve (Paramoní Protokhroniá), when, as on the other twelve days of Christmas, children go door-to-door singing the traditional kálanda (carols), receiving money in return. Adults tend to sit around playing cards, often for money. The *vassilópitta* is cut at midnight (see January 1).

CULTURAL FESTIVALS

As well as religious festivals, Greece has a full range of **cultural festivals** – highlights of which include classical **drama** in ancient theatres at Athens, Epidaurus, Dodona and Philippi. A leaflet entitled "Greek Festivals", available from GNTO offices abroad, includes details of smaller, **local festivals** of music, drama and dance, which take place on a more sporadic basis.

MAJOR FESTIVALS
Athens: the **Athens Festival** (June–Sept) encompasses a wide range of performances including modern and ancient theatre, ballet, opera, jazz and classical music, held at the open-air Herodes Atticus odeion. Athens International Jazz and Blues Festival (June) puts on big-name acts at the modern open-air theatre on Lykavitós Hill. Details and tickets for events can be obtained from the Athens Festival box office (Stadhíou 4, ☎32 21 459), or at Herodes Atticus itself on the day from 6 until 9pm, when most performances start. It's worth calling in very soon after you arrive in Greece, since the more prestigious events often sell out.

Epidaurus: **Epidaurus Festival** (July–Aug) Strictly open-air performances of Classical drama in the ancient theatre.

Pátra: **International Festival** (mid-June–Sept): ancient drama, theatre and classical music up in the castle as well as the odeion.

Thessaloníki: hosts the **Dhimitría Cultural Festival** and a film festival (Oct); and Philoxenia, a large international trade and tourism exhibition (Nov).

MINOR FESTIVALS

Itháki Music Festival (July).

Ioánnina Cultural Summer (July/Aug).

Iráklion Festival (early Aug).

Kavála Festival (Aug).

Lefkádha Arts Jamboree (Aug).

Makrinítsa/Vólos Festival (Aug).

Réthymnon Renaissance Fair (Aug–Sept).

Santoríni Music Festival (Aug–Sept).

Rhodes Festival (Aug–Oct).

Sými Festival (late June–late Sept).

CINEMA AND THEATRE

Greek **cinemas** show a large number of American and British movies, always in the original soundtrack with Greek subtitles. They remain affordable, currently 1600–1800dr depending on location and plushness of facilities, and in summer a number set up outside. An **outdoor movie** (cheaper at 1500dr) is worth catching at least once for the experience alone, though it's best to opt for the early screening (about 9pm) since the sound on the 11pm show gets turned down or even off to avoid complaints of noise from adjacent residences.

    Theatre gets suspended during the summer months but from late September to May there's a lot of activity; Athens alone has scores of theatres, with playbills ranging from the classics to satirical revues (all in Greek).

SPORTS AND OUTDOOR PURSUITS

The Greek seashore offers endless scope for water sports, with windsurfing-boards for rent in most resorts and, less reliably, water-skiing and parasailing facilities. On land, the greatest attraction lies in hiking, through what is one of Europe's more impressive mountain terrains. Winter also sees possibilities for skiing at one of a dozen or so underrated centres.

    As far as spectating goes, the twin Greek obsessions are **football** (soccer) and **basketball**, with **volleyball** a close third in popularity.

WATER SPORTS

The years since the mid-1980s have seen a massive growth in the popularity of **windsurfing** in Greece. The country's bays and coves are ideal for beginners, and boards can be rented in literally hundreds of resorts. Particularly good areas, with established schools, include the islands of Lefkádha, Zákynthos, Náxos, Sámos, Lésvos, Corfu and Crete, and Methóni in the Peloponnese. You can almost always pay for an initial period of instruction, if you've not tried the sport previously. Rates are very reasonable – about £6/US$10 an hour.

    Waterskiing is available at a number of the larger resorts, and a fair few of the smaller ones

too. By the crippling rental standards of the ritzier parts of the Mediterranean it is a bargain, with twenty minutes' instruction often available for around £8–10/$13–16. At many resorts, **parasailing** (*parapént* in Greek) is also possible; rates start at £10/$16 a go.

    A combination of steady winds, appealing seascapes and numerous natural harbours have long made Greece a tremendous place for **sailing**. Holiday companies offer all sorts of packaged and tailor-made cruises (see p.6 & p.7 in "Getting There"). In Greece, boats and dinghies are rented out by the day or week at many resorts. Spring and autumn are the most pleasant and least expensive seasons; *meltémi* winds make for pretty nauseous sailing between late June and early September, and summer rates for the same craft can be three times as high as shoulder-season prices For more details, pick up the informative brochure "Sailing the Greek Sea" from GNTO offices, or contact the Hellenic Yachting Federation, Aktí Navárkhou Koundourióti 7, 185 34 Pireás (☎01/41 37 351, fax 01/41 31 119).

    Because of the potential for pilfering submerged antiquities, **scuba diving** is severely restricted, its legal practice confined to certain coasts around Attica, Crete, Kálymnos, Mýkonos, most of the Ionian islands and selected spots in northern Greece and the Peloponnese. For more information, contact the Union of Greek Diving Centres (☎01/92 29 532 or 41 18 909), or request the information sheet "Regulations Concerning Underwater Activities" from the nearest branch of the GNTO/EOT.

Greece also has lots of white water, especially in the Peloponnese and Epirus, so if you're into **river rafting** there is much potential. There are periodically articles and advice (in Greek) in the outdoors magazine *Korfes*.

SKIING

Skiing is a comparative newcomer to Greece, in part because snow conditions are unpredictable, and runs generally short. However, there are now a dozen ski centres scattered about the mountains, and what they may lack in professionalism is often made up for by a very easy-going and unpretentious *après-ski* scene. Costs are an attraction, too – much lower than in northern Europe, at around £11/US$18 a day for rental of skis and boots, plus £7/$11 a day for a lift pass. The season generally lasts from the beginning of January to the end of April, with a few extra weeks possible at either end, depending on snow conditions.

The most developed of the resorts is on **Parnassós**, the legendary mountain near Delphi. It's easily accessible from Athens; throughout the season Athenian operators run buses up to the resort, returning the same day. Avoid weekends (which can be chaos) and you may have the resort more or less to yourself. The leading operator is Klaoudatos, a big department store on Dhimarkhíou street, near Platía Omónia. In winter they devote a floor to skiing, including ski rental (though this is simpler at Parnassós itself). The resort has slopes for beginners and enough to keep most experienced skiers happy, at least for a couple of days. Its main problem is that the lifts are often closed due to high winds.

Other major **ski centres** include **Veloúkhi**, near Karpeníssi in central Greece; **Khelmós**, near Kalávryta on the Peloponnese; **Vérmion**, near Náoussa in Macedonia; nearby **Pisodhéri** near Flórina, also in Macedonia; and **Métsovo** in Epirus, which has ample other attractions besides

the skiing. **The Pílion** is another enjoyable region to ski in as part of a general holiday. Buses run to its ski centre at Khaniá from Vólos. All of these centres rent out ski equipment for casual visitors. The last two are at a lower altitude than the others, so seasons are shorter.

Further details are available from the EOT, which publishes a leaflet entitled "Ski Centres and Mountaineering Shelters".

WALKING

Greeks are just becoming used to the notion that anyone should want to **walk** for pleasure, yet if you have the time and stamina it is probably the single best way to see the country. This guide includes descriptions of a number of the more accessible mountain hikes, as well as suggestions for more casual walking.

In addition, you may want to acquire one or both of the specific Greek **hiking guidebooks**; – see *Contexts*. See also p.7 for details of hiking maps available, and p.7, p.15 and p.17 for details of companies offering walking holidays in the mountains.

FOOTBALL AND BASKETBALL

Football (soccer) is far and away the most popular sport in Greece – both in terms of participating and watching. The most important (and most heavily sponsored) teams are Panathanaïkós and AEK of Athens, Olympiakós of Pireás and PAOK of Thessaloníki. Other major teams in the provinces include Lárissa and the Cretan Ofí. If you're interested, matches (usually played on Wednesdays and Sundays) are easy enough to catch from September to May. In mid-autumn you might even see one of the Greek teams playing European competition. The Greek national team qualified for the 1994 World Cup in some style, and then proceeded to lose all their three games heavily and returned from the USA without scoring a goal.

The nation's **basketball** team is one of the continent's strongest and won the European Championship in 1987 – cheered all the way with enormous enthusiasm. At club level, many of the football teams maintain basketball squads.

FINDING WORK

EU membership notwithstanding, short-term work in Greece is always on an unofficial basis and for this reason it will generally be where you can't be seen by the police or you're badly paid – or, more often, both. The recent influx of over 300,000 Albanians, Poles, Yugoslavs, Russian Greeks and assorted other refugees from the upper Balkans has resulted in a surplus of unskilled labour and severely depressed wages. There's a little more dignity to permanent employment; as elsewhere in Europe this is largely limited to teaching English.

SHORT-TERM WORK

A few ideas to get you started – from bars to harvests. Note that **youth hostels** are a good source of information on temporary work – indeed a few may even offer you a job themselves, if you turn up at the right time.

TOURISM-RELATED WORK

Most tourists working casually in Greece find jobs in **bars** or **restaurants** around the main resorts. Women will generally find these jobs easier to obtain than men – who should generally count themselves lucky to get work washing up. "Trained" chefs, however, sometimes fare better.

If you're waiting or serving, most of your wages will probably have to come from tips but you may well be able to get a deal that includes free food and lodging; evening-only hours can be a good shift, leaving you a lot of free time. The main drawback may be the machismo and/or chauvinist attitudes of your employer. (Ads in the local press for "girl bar staff" are certainly best ignored; see "Sexual Harassment" on p.25)

Corfu, with its big British slant, is an obvious choice for bar work; Rhodes, Crete, Skiáthos, Páros, Íos and Santoríni are also promising. Start looking, if you can, around April or May; you'll get better rates at this time if you're taken on for a season.

On a similar, unofficial level you might be able to get a sales job in **tourist shops** on Corfu, Ídhra, Rhodes or Crete, or (if you've the expertise) helping out at one of the **windsurfing** schools that have sprung up all around the coast.

Perhaps the best type of tourism-related work, though, is that of courier/greeter/group co-ordi-

nator for a **package holiday company**. All you need is EU nationality and language proficiency compatible with the clientele, though knowledge of Greek is a big plus. English-only speakers are pretty well restricted to places with a big British package trade, namely Crete, Rhodes, Skiáthos and the Ionian islands.

Many such staff are recruited through ads in newspapers issued outside Greece, but it's by no means unheard of to be hired on the spot in April or May. A big plus, however you're taken on, is that you're usually guaranteed about six months of steady work, and that if things work out you may be re-employed the following season with contract and foreign-currency wages from the home company, not from the local affiliate.

Outside the tourist season there can be building/painting/signpainting work preparing for the influx; ask around at Easter time. **Yacht marinas** can also prove good hunting-grounds though less for the romantic business of crewing, than scrubbing down and repainting. Again, the best possibilities are likely to be on Rhodes, Corfu, or Kálymnos; the Zéa port at Pireás is actually the biggest marina, but non-Greek owners don't tend to rest up there for long.

SELLING AND BUSKING

You may do better by working for yourself. Travellers report rich pickings during the tourist season from **selling jewellery** on island beaches, or on boats – trinkets from Asia are especially popular with Greeks. Once you've managed to get the stuff past the customs officials (who will be sceptical, for instance, that all those trinkets are presents for friends), there rarely seem to be problems with the local police, though it probably pays to be discreet.

Busking can also be quite lucrative. Playing on the Athens metro or the city's streets, it's possible to make around 3000dr in a two-hour session. At resorts, you might just strike luckier if you've talent, and even back in Athens the western-style pubs occasionally hire foreign musicians for gigs.

AGRICULTURE

Harvesting and other **agricultural jobs** are invariably low-paid, more so now with the glutted labour pool, but they provide a winter fallback for a dwindling number of long-term travellers. It's predominantly male, Albanian work, however, with the fields often quite a rough scene. In addition some Greeks see fit to pay women a lower daily rate.

If you're still intent on doing it, the most promising course is to ask around among fellow travellers at youth hostels – at some of which you'll find employers recruiting casual labour.

The best areas, month by month are:

November–February: Oranges, in the region bounded by Mycenae, Árgos, Náfplio and Tólo. Lemons at Mystrás, near Spárti, and Kiáto on the coast by Kórinthos, after the oranges are gone. On Crete the season may continue into April or May, especially at Paleokhóra and Falásarna in the west.

March: Artichokes at Iría, near Tólo.

June: Peaches around Véria in Macedonia.

October–December: Olive harvest, most notably around Ámfissa, near Kalamáta, and on Crete.

TEACHING ENGLISH

Language schools (*frondistíria*) have expanded massively through Greece since the 1980s, and English remains by far the most popular required language. To get a job in a school you need to have a university degree (preferably in English). A **TEFL** (Teaching of English as a Foreign Language) certificate is not essential, but will increase your chances of a better job. It isn't necessary to speak Greek, but a basic knowledge is helpful.

The simplest way to get a teaching job is to apply before leaving – preferably in Britain. There are ads published weekly, particularly from June to September, in the *Guardian* newspaper (Tuesday) and in the weekly *Times Educational Supplement* (Friday). Once accepted, you should get one-way air fare from London paid (usually), accommodation found for you, and a contract of employment. The other big advantage of arranging work from abroad is that some of the red tape will be cleared up for you before you set off. A work permit isn't necessary for EU nationals, but a **residence permit** and **teacher's licence** are. You'll always be asked for a translated copy of your degree or TEFL certificate. You will also be obliged to present a medical certificate of good health.

For **non-EU citizens**, it is now very difficult to obtain a work permit to teach English legally in Greece. However, those of Greek descent will find it easier (and in fact qualify to operate their own schools). In practice, however, schools don't always follow the letter of the law, and if they like you and your qualifications, and you're around at the right time, you're likely to find a place.

One technique is to approach *frondistíria* directly – dozens are listed in the phone book for all larger towns, and many are jointly owned and will send you to an affiliate if they don't have a vacancy. Try in late August/early September, or again in January – some teachers don't last the isolation of Greek winters. Teaching is essentially a winter/spring exercise; most, though not all, schools close down from the end of May until September, operating only a few summer courses in June and July.

The current minimum gross **salary** is about 180,000dr per month (equivalent to about £400/US$600). Wage increases are indexed to approximately the rate of inflation. Often you will be paid a net salary, after a portion of the Greek income tax and IKA (social security payments) have been deducted by your employers. The average working week is about 25 hours; contracts

---

USEFUL TEACHING ORGANIZATIONS

UK

Native English Teachers (NET). Contact Susan Lancaster at 160 Littlehampton Rd, Worthing, West Sussex BN13 1QT (☎01903/218638).

Teachers in Greece (TIG), Taxílou 79, Zográfou, 157 71 Athens (☎01/77 92 587), or 53 Talbot Rd, London W2 (☎0171/243 8260).

USA

English International, 655 Sutter St, Suite 500, San Francisco, CA 94102 (☎415/749-5633).

Transworld Teachers Training Center, 683 Sutter St, San Francisco, CA 94102 (☎415/776-8071).

Both the above offer TEFL courses, job listings and guidance for finding teaching work in Greece.

generally last nine months, from September to May, with two paid holidays and bonuses.

It's general practice to supplement your income by giving **private lessons**, and for this the going rate is between 2500dr and 4000dr an hour. Many teachers finance themselves exclusively on private lessons; although you still officially need a teaching permit for this, few people experience any problems (though some schools don't like their employees to indulge, and/or may demand a cut). To obtain private students, you can advertise in the *Athens News*. *Teaching English Abroad* by Susan Griffiths (Vacation Work) also provides useful information.

Examining work is another lucrative area, and the British Council recruits examiners for sessions in May–June and November–December. Both a degree and a TEFL qualification are required; if you have them, and some experience, it's worth contacting the British Council in Athens,

at Filikís Eterías, Platía Kolonáki (☎01/36 33 211 or ☎36 42 820).

AU PAIR WORK

The popularity and scale of private English teaching also means that English-speaking women are heavily in demand as **au pairs**. As ever, such positions tend to be exploitative and low-paid, but if you can use them to your own ends – living reasonably well and learning Greek – there can be mutual benefits.

It's unwise to arrange anything until you're in Greece, so you can at least meet and talk terms with your prospective family, and in Athens you should find little difficulty fixing something up. Posts are advertised in the daily *Athens News* and a couple of specialist agencies cater for women looking for employment. Try Pioneer Tours, Níkis 11, Athens (☎01/32 24 321) or XEN (Greek YWCA), Amerikís 11, Athens (☎01/36 26 180).

DIRECTORY

BARGAINING This isn't a regular feature of life, though you'll find it possible with private rooms and some hotels out of season. Similarly, you may be able to negotiate discounted rates for vehicle rental, especially for longer periods. Services such as shoe, watch and camera repair don't have iron-clad rates, so use common sense when assessing charges (written estimates are not routine practice).

CHILDREN Kids are worshipped and indulged in Greece, perhaps to excess, and present few problems when travelling. Baby foods and nappies/diapers are ubiquitous and reasonably priced, plus concessions are offered on most forms of transport. Private rooms establishments and luxury hotels are more likely to offer some kind of babysitting service than the mid-range, C-class hotels.

DEPARTURE TAX This is levied on all international ferries – currently 1500dr per person and per car or motorbike. To non-EU states (Turkey, Egypt and Israel), it's 4000dr per person, sometimes arbitrarily levied twice, on both entry and exit. There's also an airport departure tax of £8.50 equivalent (currently 3800dr) for destinations less than 750 miles away, £17/7600dr if it's further, but this is always included in the price of the ticket – there's no collection at the airport itself.

ELECTRICITY Voltage is 220 volt AC throughout the country. Wall outlets take double round-pin plugs as in the rest of continental Europe. Three-to-two-pin adapters should be purchased beforehand in the UK, as they can be difficult to find locally; the standard five-amp model permits operation of a hair dryer. North American appliances will require both a step-down transformer and a plug adapter (easy to find in Greece).

FILMS Fuji and Agfa print films are reasonably priced and easy to have processed – you practically trip over "One Hour Foto" places in resorts; Kodachrome and Ektachrome slide films can be purchased, again at typical UK prices, in larger towns, but all processing orders are sent to Athens – wait until you get home.

GAY LIFE For men, overtly gay behaviour in public remains taboo in rural areas, and only visible at certain resorts like Ídhra, Rhodes or Mýkonos, still the most popular European gay resort after Ibiza in Spain. Erissós on Lésvos, the birthplace of Sappho, is (appropriately) an international mecca for lesbians. Homosexuality is legal over the age of 17, and (male) bisexual behaviour common but rarely admitted. Greek men are terrible flirts, but cruising them is a semiotic minefield and definitely at your own risk – references in gay guides to male cruising grounds should be treated sceptically. "Out" gay Greeks are rare, and "out" local lesbians rarer still; foreign same-sex couples will be regarded in the provinces with some bemusement but accorded the standard courtesy as foreigners. The gay movement in Greece is represented by *Akoe Amphi*, PO Box 26022, 10022 Athens (☎01/77 19 221). See also p.118 and "Listings" in Chapter One.

GREEK LANGUAGE COURSES These abound in Athens – see the city's "Listings" section for addresses.

LAUNDRIES *Plindíria* in Greek, they're beginning to crop up in most of the main resort towns; sometimes an attended service wash is available for little or no extra charge over the basic cost of 1300–1500dr per wash and dry. Otherwise, ask rooms owners for a *skáfi* (laundry trough), a bucket (*kouvás*), or the special laundry area often available; they freak out if you use bathroom washbasins, Greek plumbing and wall-mounting being what they are.

PERÍPTERA These are street-corner kiosks, or sometimes a hole-in-the-wall shopfront. They sell everything from pens to disposable razors, stationery to soap, sweets to condoms, cigarettes to plastic crucifixes – and are often open when nothing else is.

TIME As throughout the EU, Greek summer time begins at 4am on the last Sunday in March, when the clocks go forward one hour, and ends at 4am the last Sunday in October when they go back. Be alert to this, as scores of visitors miss planes, ferries, etc, every year – the change is not well publicized. Greek time is thus always two hours ahead of Britain. For North America, the difference is seven hours for Eastern Standard Time, ten hours for Pacific Standard Time, with an extra hour plus or minus for those weeks in April and October when one place is on daylight saving and the other isn't. A recorded time message (in Greek) is available by dialling ☎141.

TOILETS Public toilets are usually in parks or squares, often subterranean; otherwise try a bus station. Except in areas frequented by tourists, public toilets tend to be pretty filthy – its best to use those in restaurants and bars. Remember that throughout Greece, you drop paper in the adjacent wastebins, not in the bowl.

USEFUL THINGS TO BRING An alarm clock (for early buses and ferries), a torch (especially if you camp out), mosquito repellent, sunscreen with a high SPF (15 or above, generally unavailable in Greece), and ear plugs for noisy ferries and hotels.

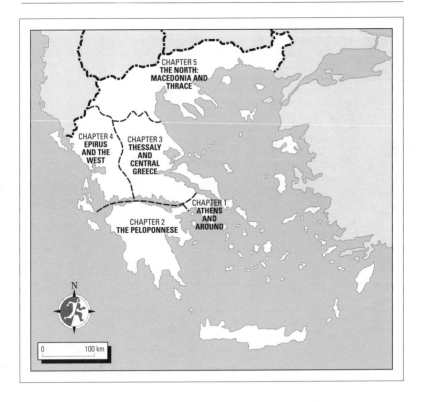

PART TWO

THE

MAINLAND

CHAPTER 5
**THE NORTH:
MACEDONIA AND
THRACE**

CHAPTER 4
**EPIRUS
AND THE
WEST**

CHAPTER 3
**THESSALY
AND
CENTRAL
GREECE**

CHAPTER 1
**ATHENS
AND
AROUND**

CHAPTER 2
THE PELOPONNESE

N

0   100 km

CHAPTER ONE

ATHENS AND AROUND

Athens is not a graceful city. It looks terrible from just about every approach, its air pollution is dire, and its traffic and postwar architecture are a disaster. For many of the four million-plus visitors who pass through each year, it can seem a dutiful stop. Their priorities usually include visits to the Acropolis and the National Archeological Museum and an evening or two amid the tavernas of Pláka,

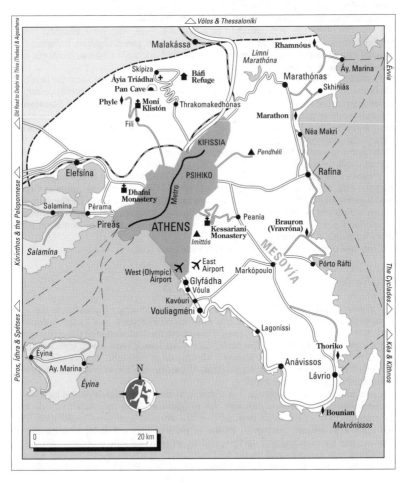

the one surviving old quarter. Most tourists then get out fast, disillusioned with such sparse evidence of the past and so little apparent charm.

Such are the basic facts – yet somehow the city has the character to transcend them. An exhausting but always stimulating mix of metropolis and backwater, First and Third World, West and East, Athens has seen its population soar from 700,000 to over four million – over a third of the nation's people – since World War II. The pace of this transformation is reflected in the city's chaotic mix of urban and rural: goats graze in yards, horsecarts are pulled along streets thick with traffic, Turkish-style bazaars vie for space with outlets for Armani and Benetton. And the city's hectic modernity is tempered with an air of intimacy and hominess; as any Greek will tell you, Athens is merely the largest village in the country.

Once you accept this, you'll find that the **ancient sites** and the **Acropolis** – supreme monument though it is – are only the most obvious of **Athens' attractions**. There are startling views to be had from the hills of **Lykavitós** and **Filopáppou**; and, around the foot of the Acropolis, the **Pláka** has scattered monuments of the Byzantine and medieval town that seemed so exotic to Byron and the Romantics. As you might expect, the city also offers the best **eating** to be found in Greece, with some beautiful cafés, garden tavernas and street markets – as well as the most varied nightlife, including traditional **music and films** in the winter months, and **open-air cinema**, **concerts** and **classical drama** in summer.

Outside Athens, the emphasis shifts more exclusively to ancient sites; the beaches along the Attic coast are functional enough escapes for Athenians, but hardly priorities if you are moving on to the islands. Of the sites, the Temple of Poseidon at **Sounion** is the most popular trip, and rightly so, with its dramatic cliff-top position above the cape. Lesser-known and less-visited are the sanctuaries at **Rhamnous** and **Brauron** (Vravróna), both rewarding ruins with beaches nearby. The committed might also take in the burial mound at **Marathon** – though this is more Classical pilgrimage than sightseeing – and the Sanctuary of Demeter at **Eleusis** (Elefsína).

Walkers may want to head for the **mountains – Párnitha**, most compellingly – that ring the city, where springtime hikes reveal some of the astonishing range of Greek wild flowers. Hedonists, however, will already be making escape plans for **the islands**, which are served by ferries and hydrofoils from the Athenian port-suburb (and heavy industrial centre) of **Pireás** (Piraeus) and, more selectively, from the two other Attic ferry terminals at **Rafína** and **Lávrio**.

Coverage of the ports and sights of Attica starts on p.125.

ATHENS

For visitors, **ATHENS** (Athiná in modern Greek) has stunning highlights in the vestiges of the ancient, Classical Greek city, most famously represented by the **Acropolis** and its surrounding archeological sites. These form the first section of the guide to the city's sights in this chapter – "The Acropolis and Ancient Athens" – and, if it's your first trip to the city, they're likely to occupy a fair amount of your time. An essential accompaniment is the **National Archeological Museum**: the finest collection of Greek antiquities anywhere in the world.

Even on a brief visit, however, it is a shame to see Athens purely as the location of ancient sites and museums. Although the **neighbourhoods** may lack the style and monuments of most European capitals, they are worth at least some exploration. The old nineteenth-century quarter of **Pláka**, in particular, is a delight, with its mix of Turkish and Greek-island architecture, and an array of odd little museums devoted to traditional arts, ceramics and music. Just to its north, the **bazaar** area, around Athinás and Eólou, retains an almost Middle Eastern atmosphere in its life and trade, while the

National Gardens, elegant **Kolonáki** and the hill of **Lykavitós** offer respite from the maelstrom. Further afield, but still well within the limits of Greater Athens, are the monasteries of **Kessarianí** and **Dhafní**, the latter with Byzantine mosaics the equal of any in Greece.

Some history
Athens has been inhabited continuously for over 7000 years. Its *acropolis*, supplied with spring water, commanding views of all seaward approaches, and encircled by protective mountains on its landward side, was a natural choice for prehistoric settlement and for the Mycenaeans, who established a palace-fortress on the rock. Its development into a city-state and artistic centre continued apace under the Dorians, Phoenicians and various dynastic rulers, reaching its apotheosis in the fifth century BC. This was the **Classical period**, when the Athenians, having launched themselves into an experiment in radical democracy, celebrated their success with a flourish of art, architecture, literature and philosophy that has influenced Western culture ever since. (An account of the Classical period is given with the main sites of Ancient Athens on pp.79–81; Roman history is outlined on p.94.)

The discontinuity from ancient to medieval Athens was due, essentially, to the emergence of **Christianity**. Having survived with little change through years of Roman rule, the city lost its pivotal role in the Roman-Greek world after the division of the Roman empire into Eastern and Western halves, and the establishment of Byzantium (Constantinople) as capital of the Eastern – **Byzantine** – empire. There, a new Christian sensibility soon outshone the prevailing ethic of Athens, where schools of philosophy continued to teach a pagan Neoplatonism. In 529 these schools were finally closed by Justinian I, and the city's temples, including the Parthenon, were reconsecrated as churches.

Athens featured rarely in the chronicles of the time, enjoying a brief revival under the foreign powers of the Middle Ages: in the aftermath of the piratical Fourth Crusade, Athens – together with the Peloponnese and much of Central Greece – passed into the hands of the **Franks**. At the Acropolis they established a ducal court (of some magnificence, according to contemporary accounts) and for a century Athens was back in the mainstream of Europe. Frankish control, however, was based on little more than a provincial aristocracy. In 1311 their forces battled **Catalan** mercenaries, who had a stronghold in Thebes, and were driven to oblivion in a swamp. The Catalans, having set up their own duchy, in turn gave way to **Florentines** and, briefly, **Venetians**, before the arrival in 1456 of **Sultan Mehmet II**, the Turkish conqueror of Constantinople.

Turkish Athens was never much more than a garrison town. The links with the West, which had preserved a sense of continuity with the Classical and Roman city, were severed, and the flood of visitors was reduced to a trickle of French and Italian ambassadors to the Sublime Porte, and the occasional traveller or painter. The town does not seem to have been oppressed by Ottoman rule, however: the Greeks enjoyed some autonomy, and both Jesuit and Capuchin monasteries continued to thrive. Although the Acropolis became the home of the Turkish governor and the Parthenon was used as a mosque, life in the village-like quarters around the Acropolis drifted back to a semi-rural existence. Similarly, the great port of **Pireás**, still partially enclosed within its ancient walls, was left to serve just a few dozen fishing boats.

Four centuries of Ottoman occupation, followed until, in 1821, in common with the inhabitants of a score of other towns across the country, the Greeks of Athens rose in **rebellion**. They occupied the Turkish quarters of the lower town – the current Pláka – and laid siege to the Acropolis. The Turks withdrew, but five years later were back to reoccupy the Acropolis fortifications, while the Greeks evacuated to the countryside. When the Ottoman garrison finally left in 1834, and the Bavarian architects of the new German-born monarchy moved in, Athens was arguably at its nadir.

For all the claims of its ancient past, and despite the city's natural advantages, Athens was not the first-choice capital of modern Greece. That honour went instead to Náfplio in the Peloponnese, where the **War of Independence** was masterminded by Capodistrias and where the first Greek National Assembly met in 1828. Had Capodistrias not been assassinated, in 1831, the capital would most likely have remained in the Peloponnese; if not at Náfplio, then at Trípoli, Corinth or Pátra, all much more established and sizeable towns. But following Capodistrias's death, the "Great Powers" of Western Europe intervened, inflicting on the Greeks a king of their own choosing – **Otho**, son of Ludwig I of Bavaria – and, in 1834, transferring the capital and court to Athens. The reasoning was almost purely symbolic and sentimental: Athens was not only insignificant in terms of population and physical extent but was then at the edge of the territories of the new Greek state, which was yet to include Northern Thessaly, Epirus and Macedonia, or any of the islands beyond the Cyclades or Sporades.

The **nineteenth-century development** of Athens was a gradual and fairly controlled process. While the archeologists stripped away all the Turkish and Frankish embellishments from the Acropolis, a modest city took shape along the lines of the Bavarians' Neoclassical grid. **Pireás**, meanwhile, grew into a port again, though until this century its activities continued to be dwarfed by the main Greek shipping centres on the islands of Síros and Ídhra (Hydra).

The first mass expansion of both municipalities came suddenly, in 1923, as the result of the tragic Greek–Turkish war in **Asia Minor**. The peace treaty that resolved the war entailed the exchange of Greek and Turkish ethnic populations, their identity being determined solely on the basis of religion. A million and a half Greeks, mostly from the age-old settlements along the Asia Minor coast, but also many Turkish-speaking peoples from the communities of inland Anatolia, arrived in Greece as refugees. Over half of them settled in Athens, Pireás and the neighbouring villages, changing at a stroke the whole make-up of the capital. Their integration and survival is one of the great events of the city's history, and has left its mark on the Athens of today. The web of suburbs that straddle the metro line from Athens to Pireás, and sprawl out into the hills, bear nostalgic names of their refugees' origins – Néa Smýrni (New Smyrna), Néa Iónia, Néa Filadhélfia – as do many streets. Originally, these neighbourhoods were exactly that: refugee villages with populations primarily from one or another Anatolian town, built in ramshackle fashion, often with a single water source for two dozen families.

The merging of these shanty-suburbs and their populations with the established communities of Athens and Pireás dominated the years leading up to **World War II**. With the war, however, new concerns emerged. Athens was hit hard by German occupation: during the winter of 1941–2 there were an estimated 2000 deaths from starvation each day. In late 1944, when the Germans finally left (Allied policy was to tie them down in the Balkans), the capital saw the first skirmishes of **civil war**, with British forces being ordered to fight against their former Greek allies in the Communist-dominated resistance army, ELAS. Physical evidence of the ensuing month-long battle, the *Dhekemvrianá*, can still be seen in a handful of bullet-pocked walls. From 1946 to 1949 Athens was a virtual island in the civil war, with road approaches to the Peloponnese and the north only tenuously kept open.

But during the 1950s, after the civil war, the city started to expand rapidly. A massive **industrial investment** programme – financed largely by the Americans, who had won Greece for their sphere of influence – took place, and the capital saw huge **immigration** from the war-torn, impoverished countryside. The open spaces between the old refugee suburbs began to fill and, by the late 1960s, Greater Athens covered a continuous area from the slopes of mounts Pendéli and Párnitha down to Pireás and Elefsína.

On a visual level, much of the modern city is unremittingly ugly, since old buildings were demolished wholesale in the name of quick-buck development, particularly during the colonels' junta of 1967–74 (see p.778). Only now are planning and preservation

ATHENS AND ITS ENVIRONMENT

The enormous and rapid population increase and attendant industrial development that characterized the postwar period had a disastrous effect on the **environment** of Athens. With a third of the Greek population, half the country's industry and over two-thirds of its cars crammed into Greater Athens, the capital has found itself with one of the world's worst **pollution** problems. A noxious cloud, the *néfos*, trapped by the circle of mountains and aerial inversion layers, can frequently be seen hovering over the city. Despite what your burning eyes and throat may tell you, some improvement in the situation has been registered in recent decades, though not in the critical pollutant nitrogen dioxide. Moreover, the level of pollution still aggravates acute respiratory diseases and arguably contributed to the high death toll in the freak heat waves or *kávsones* during the summers of 1987 and 1988. Alarmingly, the *néfos* is also gnawing away at the very fabric of the ancient city, including the Parthenon marbles. As sulphur dioxide settles on the columns and statuary, it becomes a friable coating of calcium sulphate, which is washed off by the winter rains, taking a thin layer of stone with it.

Despite the severity of the situation, the main anti-pollution measure of recent years has been restrictions on the use of **private cars**. Successive governments have toyed with limitations on weekday use of vehicles in a central restricted zone, stipulating alternate days for odd- and even-numbered number plates, but their efforts are undermined by the fact that most shops, offices and businesses persist in closing for a three-hour summer siesta – making for four rush hours a day and double the amount of pollution and traffic problems. Additionally, short-sighted government taxation and duty policies mean that Athenians keep their beloved cars until they die of metal fatigue, rarely maintaining or tuning them to optimum, low-exhaust running conditions.

More far-reaching measures are at last being taken to help the city's **public transport** system rise to the challenge: the extra airport at Spata creeps slowly towards realization and, back in the heart of the city, virtually every landmark square is being excavated for the expansion of the metro system in time for the 2004 Olympic Games. The three-line metro will be complemented by a circular tram system downtown and the operation of passenger ferries between the coastal suburbs and metro stations at Pireás and Fáliro.

Furthermore, all electricity, most heating and some cooking is now fuelled by copious supplies of Russian natural gas, installed (by pipeline) in Athens in 1997. With air inversion layers prompting pollution alerts in both summer and winter, there is still a long way to go, but these policies do at least offer a ray of hope.

measures being enforced – in a last-ditch attempt to rescue the city from its engulfing **pollution** (see box above). The PASOK administration of the late 1980s endowed the city with thousands of trees, shrubs, patches of garden and an ever-growing number of pedestrian-only streets – though Athens still lags far behind Paris or London in terms of open space. There is also increasing awareness of the nineteenth-century architectural heritage – what's left of it – with many old houses being restored and repainted.

Long-term solutions are proving more elusive: priorities include decanting industry and services into the provinces to ease the stresses on the city's environment (see box above) and its ailing infrastructure, and creating a mass transport network capable of meeting the needs of a modern capital city.

Orientation, arrival and information

As a visitor, you're likely to spend most time in the central grid of Athens, a compact, walkable area. Only on arrival at, or departure from, the various far-flung stations and terminals (see below), do you have to confront the confused urban sprawl. Once in the centre, it's a simple matter to orient yourself. There are four strategic reference points:

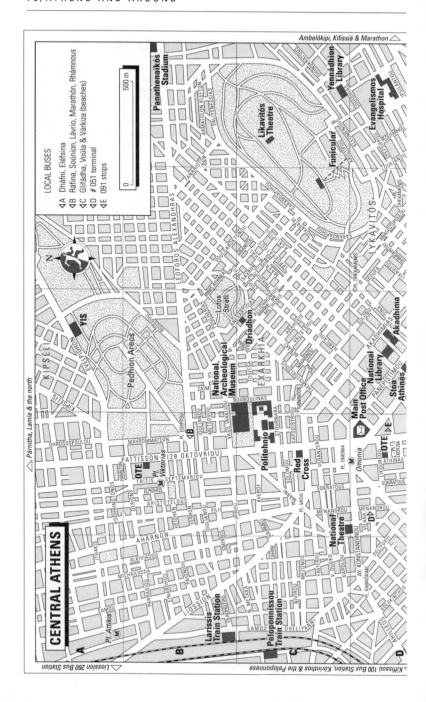

CENTRAL ATHENS

LOCAL BUSES
◁A Dháfni, Eléfsina
◁B Ráfina, Soúnion, Lávrio, Marathón, Rhámnous
◁C Glifádha, Voúla & Várkiza (beaches)
◁D # 051 terminal
◁E 091 stops

500 m

Ambelókipi, Kifissiá & Marathon △

Vennádhion Library

Evangelismos Hospital

Panathenaïkós Stadium

Likavitós Theatre

Funicular

LYKAVITÓS

YIS

Pedhíon Áreos

KIPSÉLI

Lófos Stréfi

Dríadhon

EXARKHIA

National Archeological Museum

Akadhima

National Library

Stóa Athinás

Main Post Office

PANEPISTIMIOU

AKADHIMA

Politehnío

Red Cross

BOUBOULINAS

Omonia

OTE

Pl. Viktorías

OTE

Pl. TRITIS

PATTISSON (28 OKTOVRIOU)

MAVROMMATEON

DHROSSOPOULOU

SEPTEMVRIOU

ARISTOTELOUS

AHARNON

National Theatre

Laríssis Train Station

Pelopónnissou Train Station

Pl. Attikís

△ Párnitha, Lamía & the north

Liossíon 260 Bus Station ▽

Kifissoú 100 Bus Station, Kórinthos & the Peloponnese ▽

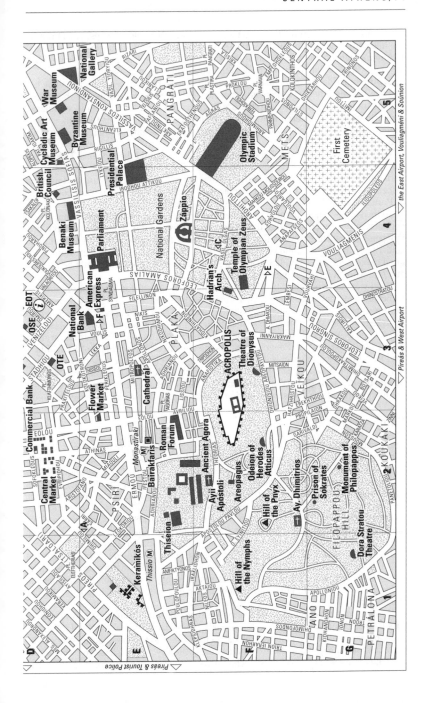

the squares of **Sýndagma** ("Syntagma" on many English-language maps) and **Omónia**, the hills of the **Acropolis** (unmistakable with its temple crown) and (to the northeast) **Lykavitós**. Once you've established these as a mental compass you shouldn't get lost for long – anyone will point you back in the direction of Sýndagma or Omónia.

Sýndagma (Platía Sindágmatos, "Constitution Square", to give it its full title) lies midway between the Acropolis and Lykavitós. With the Greek Parliament building – plus mammoth metro tunnelling and traffic diversions – on its uphill side, and banks and airline offices clustered around, it is to all intents and purposes the centre of the capital. Almost everything of daytime interest is within twenty to thirty minutes' walk of the square.

To the northeast, the ritzy **Kolonáki** quarter curls around the slopes of **Lykavitós**, with a funicular up the hillside to save you the final climb. To the east, behind the Parliament, the jungly **National Gardens** function as the city's chief lung and meeting place; beyond them are the 1896 Olympic stadium and the attractive neighbourhoods of **Pangráti** and **Méts**, both crammed with restaurants and bars.

To the southwest, up to the base of the **Acropolis**, spread the ramshackle but much-commercialized lanes of **Pláka**, the lone surviving area of the nineteenth-century, pre-independence village. Beyond the Acropolis itself lie **Filopáppou hill**, an area of parkland ringed by the neighbourhoods of **Veïkoú**, **Koukáki** and **Áno Petrálona**, also good choices for accommodation and meals. (Filopáppou Hill itself should be avoided at night, when it has a reputation for rapes and muggings.)

Northwest of Sýndagma, two broad thoroughfares, **Stadhíou** and **Panepistimíou** (officially but ineffectually renamed Venizélou), run in just under a kilometre to **Omónia** (fully, Plátia Omonías, "Concord Square"). This is an approximate Athenian equivalent of Piccadilly Circus or Times Square: more than a bit seedy, with fast-food cafés, gypsies, pickpockets and a scattering of porno shows in the backstreets around. To the northeast, beyond Panepistimíou, is the student neighbourhood of **Exárkhia**, a slightly "alternative" district, with a concentration of lively tavernas and bars there and in its extension **Neápoli**. South of Omónia, stretching down to **Ermoú** street and the **Monastiráki** bazaar district on the borders of Pláka, lies the main commercial centre, crammed with offices and shops offering everything from insurance to machine tools.

Points of arrival

Athens airport – **Ellinikón** – is 9km out of the city, southeast along the coast towards Glifádha. It has two distinct sections – **west** (*dhitikó*) and **east** (*anatolikó*) – whose separate entrances are five minutes' drive apart on either side of the perimeter fence. **Olympic Airways** flights, domestic and foreign, operate from the western terminal; all **other international flights** use the eastern, which adjoins the charter-flight terminal. Both the east and west terminals have **money exchange** facilities, open 24 hours at the eastern terminal, but only from 7am to 11pm at the western one (though there are two automatic teller machines that accept Visa, Mastercard, Cirrus and Plus); insist on some small-denomination notes for paying for your bus ticket or taxi ride.

To get into the city, the quickest and simplest way is to get a **taxi**, which, at 1500–2000dr to central Athens or Pireás, is a modest cost split two or more ways. Make sure before setting out that the meter is switched on, and visible; overcharging of tourists can be brutal. You may have fellow passengers in the cab; each drop-off will pay the full fare.

If you're willing to wait a bit, and carry your bags around, a blue-and-yellow **express bus** (see box opposite) calls at both terminals on a variable schedule around the clock, dropping you at selected points in the city centre. You should note that the wait can be up to an hour at night, and 30–40 minutes during the day. Service from the west terminal tends to be less consistent; the schedule is further cut back between October and

EXPRESS AIRPORT BUSES

Owing to the metro uproar and funding problems, **express bus services** linking the airport terminals, the centre of the city and the port of Pireás can often be disrupted, particularly between October and April.

In summer at least, the #091 from Omónia via Sýndagma to the west airport, calls at the east airport, before ending up at the west airport. The most obvious stops for the centre of town are Stadhíou, near Omónia, and Sýndagma; the Singroù 96 and Stíles stops are useful if you plan to stay in the Veíkou/Koukáki area. Heading out to the airport, it's safest to flag the buses down at the corner of Othónos and Amalías at Sýndagma, where they make a short halt. In theory, the bus runs every 30 minutes from 5.30am to 11.30pm and every hour from 11.30pm to 5.30am. In practice, especially in winter, it's easier on the nerves to take a taxi when leaving to catch a flight.

At the east airport there are three bus stops between the arrival and departure terminals, somewhat closer to the arrival terminal. The stop closest to the arrival terminal is for express bus #091 for Athens. The stop some 20m towards the departure terminal is used by express bus #091 when it is going on to the west terminal. The third bus stop, closer to the departure terminal at the east airport, is used by express bus #19 on its way to the west airport and then Pireás, about every hour between 5am and 10.20pm.

Each service has a 170dr flat fare (200dr from midnight to 5.30am).

April. The fare is currently 170dr (200dr between midnight and 5.30am); tickets can usually be bought on the bus if you have small change.

Train stations

There are two train stations, almost adjacent, a couple of hundred metres northwest of Omónia, off Dheliyáni street. The **Stathmós Laríssis** handles the main lines coming from the north (Lárissa, Thessaloníki, the Balkans, Western Europe and Turkey). The **Stathmós Peloponníssou** three blocks south, is the terminal for the narrow-gauge line circling the Peloponnese, including the stretch to Pátra (the main port for ferries from Italy and Corfu).

From either station, you are five to fifteen minutes' walk away from the concentration of hotels around Platía Viktorías and Exárkhia, both handy for the National Archeological Museum and excellent restaurants. For hotels elsewhere, the yellow trolley **bus #1** southbound passes along Sámou, one block east of the Laríssis station (to get to it from the Peloponníssou terminal, use the giant metal overpass, then detour around the metro works) and makes a strategic loop down through Omónia, along Stadhíou to Sýndagma, then down Filellínon to Hadrian's Arch (for Méts), and finally along Veïkoú to Koukáki (on the southeast side of Filopáppou hill).

Be wary of **taxis** (both official and unlicensed) at the train stations – some thrive on newly arrived tourists, shuttling them a couple of blocks for highly inflated fares.

Bus stations

Again, there are two principal terminals. Coming into Athens from Northern Greece or the Peloponnese, you'll find yourself at **Kifissoú 100**, a ten-minute bus ride from the centre. The least expensive way into town is to take city bus #051 to the corner of Zinónos/Menándhrou, just off Omónia and only a block or two from a yellow trolley-bus stop. Routes from central Greece (see p.137 for specific destinations) arrive at **Liossíon 260**, north of the train stations; to get into the centre, take the blue city bus #024 to Sýndagma.

In addition, there are international **OSE buses**, run by the railway company, which arrive at the Stathmós Peloponnísou. Private **international bus companies** arrive at,

---

FINDING AN ADDRESS

The Greek for street is **odhós** but – both when addressing letters and in speech – people usually refer only to the name of the street: Ermoú, Márkou Moussoúrou, etc. The practice is different with **platía** (square) and **leofóros** (avenue), which always appear before the name. In written addresses, the house number is written after the street name, thus: Ermoú 13. We have adopted the same practice. **Grid keys**, given in italics throughout this chapter, refer to the main Athens map on pp.70–71; for more detail on the Pláka area, see the map on p.91.

---

and leave from, a variety of locations. Most will take you to the train station or to Kifissoú 100; a few drop passengers right in the city centre.

Pireás: the ferries

If you arrive by boat at **Pireás**, the simplest access to Athens is by **metro** to the stations at Monastiráki, Omónia or Viktorías. Trains run from 6am to midnight, with fares varying from 75 to 200dr according to a zone system. For the airport, take express bus #091 (see box on p.73). **Taxis** between Pireás and central Athens should cost around 1500dr, including baggage, although rates per kilometre double at night – again, see the comments below.

There's a full account of Pireás, together with a map of the central area, showing the metro station and harbours, on pp.126–130.

Information

The main EOT tourist office (Mon–Fri 9am–7pm, Sat 9am–2pm; ☎33 10 437 or 33 10 562 or 33 10 565) is at 2 Ameríkas Street, just up from Stadiou; it dispenses ferry timetable sheets (use these as guidelines only), along with maps and pamphlets, and is also a source of information about the **Athens Festival** (see p.119).

To complement our plans and the free EOT map, the street-indexed **Falk-Plan** is a good, **large-scale map** of the city (available from the shops listed on p.121). The Historical Map of Athens produced by the Greek Ministry of Culture is well worth its 1000dr price. It has a good map of central Athens and, on the other side, a clear, large scale map of Pláka. Both maps number all the sites by period, and the museums.

If you are planning a long stay, the **Athína-Pireás Proastia** A–Ω **atlas**, co-published by Kapranidhis and Fotis, is available from kiosks and bookshops, but is in Greek only and is quite pricey at 5500dr. It does, however, show absolutely everything, including cinemas and concert venues.

City transport

Athens is served by slow but wide-ranging **buses**, and a fast but very limited **metro** system; taxis fill in the gaps. Public transport networks operate from around 5am to midnight, with a skeleton service on some of the buses in the small hours. In addition, a few of the yellow trolley buses, including the useful #1 route, run all night on Saturdays.

Buses

The **bus network** is extensive and cheap, with a flat fare of 100dr. Tickets must be bought in advance from kiosks, certain shops and newsagents, or from the limited number of booths run by bus personnel near major stops – look for the brown, red and white logo proclaiming *Isitíria edhó* (tickets here). They're sold individually or in bundles of ten, and must be cancelled in a special machine when boarding. Fare-dodgers risk an on-the-spot fine equivalent to twenty times the current fare. Cancelled tickets apply only to a particular journey and vehicle; there are no transfers. If you're staying long enough, it would be worth buying a monthly pass for 5000dr.

Buses are very crowded at peak times, unbearably hot in summer traffic jams, and chronically plagued by strikes and slow-downs; walking is often a better option. Express services run to and from the airport – see box on p.73. Other **routes**, where relevant, are detailed in the text. The most straightforward are the **yellow trolley buses**: #1 connects the Laríssis train station with Omónia, Sýndagma and Veïkoú/Koukáki; #2, #3, #4, #5 and #12 all link Sýndagma with Omónia and the National Archeological Museum on Patissíon. In addition, there are scores of **blue city buses**, all with three-digit numbers and serving an infinity of routes out into the straggling suburbs and beyond.

The metro

The single-line **metro** (75dr single-zone fare, 200dr if you go the full length of the line) runs from Pireás in the south to Kifissiá in the north; in the centre, there are stops at Thissío, Monastiráki, Omónia and Platía Viktorías. Long awaited work on the lateral extensions to the system is well under way and should be ready early in the new millennium. Metro and bus tickets are not interchangeable.

Taxis

Athenian **taxis** are the cheapest of any EU capital – fares around the city centre will rarely run above 700dr, with the airport and Pireás only 1500–2000dr – the exact amount determined by traffic and amount of luggage. All officially licensed cars are painted yellow and have a special red-on-white number plate. You can wave them down on the street, pick them up at ranks at the train station, airport or the National Gardens corner of Sýndagma, or get your hotel to phone one for you. They are most elusive during the rush hours of 1.30–2.30pm and 7.30–8.30pm.

Make sure the **meter** is switched on when you get in, with its display visible and properly zeroed; theoretically, it's illegal to quote a flat fare for a ride within city limits – the meter must be used. If it's "not working", find another taxi. Attempts at **overcharging** tourists are particularly common with small-hours arrivals at the airport; a threat to have hotel staff or the police adjudicate usually elicits cooperation, as they will very likely take your side and the police have the power to revoke a driver's operating permit.

Legitimate surcharges can considerably bump up the final bill from the total shown on the meter. Currently the flag falls at 200dr, there's an automatic 300dr supplement for entering the confines of the airport, and a 150dr surcharge for journeys involving train or ferry terminals; luggage is 50dr extra for each bag over 10 kg; the rate per kilometre doubles between midnight and 5am; and there are Easter and Christmas bonuses which seem to extend for a week or two either side of the actual date. Every taxi must have a plastic dash-mounted placard listing regular rates and extra charges in English and Greek.

On odd-numbered days of each month, only those taxis (and passenger vehicles) which have the last digit of their licence plate number odd are permitted to enter a large central grid, and vice versa on even-numbered dates; this may account for reluctance on the part of a driver to take you to your destination. The restrictions do not apply to cars with foreign registration plates or to rented cars.

To try and make ends meet on government-regulated fare limits, taxi drivers will often pick up a whole string of passengers along the way. There is no fare-sharing: each passenger (or group of passengers) pays the full fare for their journey. So if you're picked up by an already-occupied taxi, memorize the meter reading at once;

> The **telephone code** for Greater Athens and Pireás is ☎01;
> when calling from overseas, omit the zero.

you'll pay from that point on, plus the 200dr minimum. When hailing an occupied taxi, call out your destination, so the kerb-crawling driver can decide whether you suit him or not.

Accommodation

Hotels and **hostels** can be packed to the gills in midsummer – August especially – but for most of the year there are enough beds in the city to go around, and to suit most wallets and tastes. It makes sense to **phone** before turning up: if you just set out and do the rounds, you'll find somewhere, but in summer, unless you're early in the day, it's likely to be at the fourth or fifth attempt.

For cheaper places, you're on your own. Find a street kiosk (there are hundreds in Athens) and ask to use their phone; you pay 20dr per unit after you've finished making all the calls – there's no need to find coins. Virtually every hotel and hostel in the city will have an English-speaking receptionist. Once you locate a vacancy, ask to see the room before booking in – standards vary greatly even within the same building, and you can avoid occasional overcharging by checking the government-regulated room prices displayed by law on the back of the door in each room.

Our listings are grouped into four main areas. The quarters of **Pláka and Sýndagma**, despite their commercialization, are highly atmospheric – and within easy walking distance of all the main sites and the Monastiráki metro station (a useful gateway for the port of Pireás). Occasionally gritty and sleazy, the **bazaar area** is the city at its most authentic. The downside of some of the hotels in these areas is that they are subject to round-the-clock noise; if you want uninterrupted sleep, you're better off heading for one of the quieter neighbourhoods a little further out. **Veïkoú**, **Koukáki** and **Pangráti** are attractive parts of the city, and though slightly out of the way – twenty minutes' walk from Sýndagma or the heart of Pláka – compensate with excellent neighbourhood tavernas and cafés. Veïkoú and Koukáki are easiest reached from Pireás via the #9 trolley bus, whose terminus is just outside the Petrálona metro station, while Pangráti is on the #4 or #12 trolleys from Záppio. Around **Exárkhia** and **Platía Viktorías** (officially Platía Kyriákou), to the north of Omónia, you are again out of the tourist mainstream, but benefit from good-value local restaurants and the proximity of cinemas, clubs and bars. These areas now have clusters of very good-value, mid-range hotels, just a short walk away from the train stations (and metros Omónia or Viktorías).

ACCOMMODATION PRICE CODES

Throughout the book we've used the following **price codes** to denote the cheapest available room in high season; all are prices for a double room, except for category ①, which represents per person rates. Out of season, rates can drop by up to fifty percent, especially if you are staying for three or more nights. Single rooms, where available, cost around seventy percent of the price of a double.

① 1400–2000dr	④ 8000–12,000dr
② 4000–6000dr	⑤ 12,000–16,000dr
③ 6000–8000dr	⑥ 16,000dr and upwards

For more accommodation details, see pp.39–42.

The city's **campsites** are out in the suburbs, not especially cheap, and only worth using if you have a camper-van to park; phone ahead to book space in season. Camping rough in Athens is not a good idea. Police patrol many of the parks, especially those by the train stations, and muggings are commonplace. Even the train stations are no real refuge; they close when services stop and are cleared of stragglers.

Grid references (in italics) refer to the map on pp.70–71.

Pláka and Sýndagma

Adams, Kherefontos cnr Thálou, *E3* (☎32 25 381). Rather average small hotel, with some Acropolis views, in heart of Pláka. ⑤.

Acropolis House, Kódhrou 6, *E3* (☎32 22 344). A very clean, well-sited pension; all rooms have baths, though some are across the hall. Rates include breakfast. ④.

Adonis, Kódhrou 3, *E3* (☎32 49 737). A modern but unobjectionable low-rise pension across the street from *Acropolis House*, with some suites. ⑤.

Dioskouri, Pittákou 6, *F3* (☎32 48 165). This renovated pension benefits from a breakfast garden and a good locale (one block in from Leofóros Amalías); no singles or bargaining. ④.

George's Guest House, Níkis 46, *E3* (☎32 36 474). One of the most enduring of the hostel-type places, located just a block west of Sýndagma. Various-sized dorms and some doubles, but cramped bathrooms are consistently grubby and the place is not noted for its courtesy. ②.

John's Place Patróou 5, *E3* (☎32 29 719). Basic (no en suite baths) but acceptable pension. ②.

Kouros, Kódhrou 11, *E3* (☎32 27 431). Slightly faded pension, but with adequate facilities: shared baths and sinks in rooms. Located on a pedestrianized street (the continuation of Voulís – two blocks southwest of Sýndagma). ③.

Nefeli, Iperídhou 16, *E3* (☎32 28 044). Another mid-range hotel, mercifully not usually block-booked by tour groups. ④.

Phaedra, Kherefóndos 16 at the Adhrianoú junction, *F3* (☎32 27 795). Very plain and ripe for an over-haul, but clean and quiet at night – thanks to its location at the junction of two pedestrian malls. ④.

Student Inn, Kydhathinéon 18, *E3* (☎32 44 808). A former hostel, now a bona fide hotel: singles, doubles and triples with shared baths. Prone to nocturnal noise from outside, but otherwise acceptable; 1.30am curfew. ③.

Thisseus Hostel, Thisséos 10, *E3* (☎32 45 960). You don't get much more central than this – three blocks west of Sýndagma – nor much cheaper. No frills, but clean enough, and with a kitchen for guests' use. Some 3- and 4-bed rooms. ①.

XEN (YWCA), Amerikís 11, *D3* (☎36 24 291). Women-only hostel just north of Sýndagma that provides clean, relatively quiet rooms, a self-service restaurant, a small library and Greek classes. Recommended. ③.

The Bazaar area

Attalos, Athinás 29, *E2* (☎32 12 801). A bit pricey but comfortable. ⑤.

Pella Inn, Ermoú 104, *E2* (☎32 50 598). A family run hotel under new enthusiastic management. From the third floor up the views of the Acropolis and Hephaisteion are startling. ③.

Temi, Eólou 29, *E2* (☎32 13 175). Used to foreigners: book exchange, drinks, fridge, plus handy affiliated travel agency. ③.

Veïkoú, Koukáki and Pangráti

Acropolis View, Webster 10, Veïkoú, *F2* (☎92 17 303). Stone-clad, smallish hotel whose front rooms and roof café live up to its name. ⑤.

Art Gallery, Erekhthíou 5, Veïkoú, *G3* (☎92 38 376). Original paintings on the walls lend this rather over-priced pension its name. ④.

Austria, Moussón 7, Veïkoú, *G2* (☎92 35 151). Owned and staffed by Greek-Austrians, hence the name; they serve real filter coffee at breakfast. ⑥.

Marble House, cul-de-sac off A. Zínni 35, Koukáki, *G2* (☎92 34 058). Probably the best value in Koukáki, with a very helpful management. Often full, so call ahead. Most rooms with bath; also two self-catering studios. ③.

Youth Hostel #5, Damaréos 75, Pangráti, off map beyond *G5* (☎75 19 530). A bit out of the way but friendly, no curfew and in a decent, quiet neighbourhood; trolleys #2 and #11 from downtown stop just around the corner. ②.

Exárkhia and Platía Viktorías

Athenian Inn, Háritos 22, Kolonáki, *D5* (☎72 38 097). Actually in Kolonáki, adjacent to Exárkhia, this mid-range hotel is small, elegant and convenient for most of the museums around the National Gardens. ⑥.

Hostel Aphrodite, Inárdhou 12, cnr Mikhaïl Vódha 65, *B1* (☎88 10 589). Friendly and clean, this is the best deal in the area, providing hot water, a safe, a roof for sunning and free storage. A few blocks northwest of the Victoria metro station. ②.

Brazil, Fílis 62, Platía Viktorías, *B2* (☎88 14 944). Small, quiet hotel with garden. Bargain rates, depending on seasonal fluctuations. ②.

Dryades, Dhryadhón 4, off Anexartisías, Exárkhia, *C3* (☎36 20 191). A small, quiet hotel, co-managed with the *Orion*, behind the National Archeological Museum. ④.

Elli, Heïdhen 29, Platía Viktorías, *B2* (☎88 15 876). Characterful pension in refurbished Neoclassical building on a quiet tree-lined street. ③.

Exarkhion, Themistokléous 55, Platía Exárkhia, *C3* (☎36 01 256). Big 1960s high-rise hotel that's surprisingly inexpensive and well placed, if a bit noisy. ③.

Feron, Férron 43, Platía Viktorías, *B2* (☎82 32 083). Small hotel with two eight-bedded rooms and a few doubles. ③.

Museum, Bouboulínas 16, *C3* (☎36 05 611). Nicely placed, good-value hotel, right behind the National Archeological Museum and parkland. ④.

Orion, Anexartisías 5, Exárkhia, *C3* (☎36 27 362). Very quiet, well-run hotel across from the Lófos Stréfi park – a steep uphill walk. Self-service kitchen and communal area on the roof with an amazing view of central Athens. ③.

San Remo, Nisýrou 8, near Stathmó Laríssis *C1* (☎52 33 245). Small, inexpensive hostel offering clean but basic accommodation in a grubby neighbourhood. ①.

Campsites

Camping Nea Kifissia (☎80 75 579: open all year round), with a swimming pool, is in the cool, leafy suburb of Kifissiá. Take bus #528 from just north of Omónia to the final stop, from which the site is a short walk. Alternatively, you can take the metro all the way to its end in Kifissiá, flagging down the #528 from behind the station for the final stretch.

Voula Camping (☎89 52 712, 89 53 249: open all year round), on the beach but with swimming pool, bar and restaurant. Bus A2 from Sýndagma Square.

THE SITES: OPENING HOURS AND FEES

Summer opening hours for the **sites** and **museums** in Athens are included with some trepidation. They are notorious for changing without notice, from one season to another, or from one week to the next, due to staff shortages.

To be sure of admission, it's best to visit between 9am and noon, and to be wary of Monday – when many museums and sites close for the whole day. Last tickets are sold at the time given for closure, although the site may be open fifteen minutes more. For (generally) reliable and up-to-the-minute details, ask at the EOT office at 2 Amerikas Street for their printed list of opening hours.

For many years, during the off-season (from Oct–March), entrance has been free on Sundays. During the summer months some sites and museums may let students in for half price (EU students free) and there may be a reduced price if you are over 65. The response will vary from site to site, but ask.

The Acropolis and Ancient Athens

This section covers the **Acropolis** and the assorted Classical and Roman sites on its **slopes**; the hills of the **Pnyx** and **Philoppapus (Filopáppou)** over to the southwest; and the neighbouring **Ancient Agora** (marketplace) and **Keramikos** (cemetery) to the northwest. This is essentially the core of the ancient, Classical Greek city, though a few further pockets and Roman extensions are covered in the Pláka section, beginning on p.90.

Classical Athens: some history

Perhaps the most startling aspect of ancient, Classical Athens is how suddenly it emerged to the power and glory for which we remember it – and how short its heyday proved to be. In the middle of the **fifth century BC**, Athens was little more than a country town in its street layout and buildings. These comprised a scattered jumble of single-storey houses or wattled huts, intersected by narrow lanes. Sanitary conditions were notoriously lax: human waste and rubbish were dumped outside the town with an almost suicidal disregard for plague and disease. And on the rock of the Acropolis, a site reserved for the city's most sacred monuments, stood blackened ruins – temples and sanctuaries burned to the ground during the Persian invasion of 480 BC.

There was little to suggest that the city was entering a unique phase of its history in terms of power, prestige and creativity. But following the victories over the Persians at Marathon (490 BC) and Salamis (480 BC), Athens stood unchallenged for a generation.

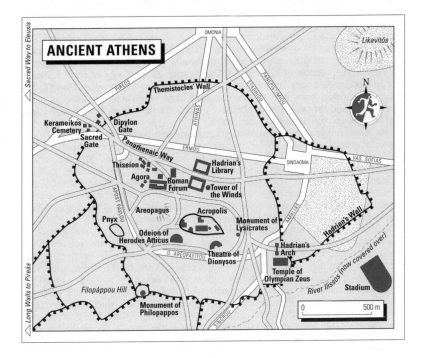

It grew rich on the export of olive oil and of silver from the mines of Attica, but above all it benefited from its control of the **Delian League**, an alliance of Greek city-states formed as insurance against Persian resurgence. The Athenians relocated the League's treasury from the island of Delos to their own acropolis, ostensibly on the grounds of safety, and with its revenues their leader **Pericles** was able to create the so-called **Golden Age** of the city. Great endowments were made for monumental construction, arts in all spheres were promoted, and – most significantly – a form of **democracy** emerged.

This democracy had its beginnings in the sixth-century BC reforms of Solon, in which the political rights of the old land-owning class had been claimed by farmer- and craftsmen-soldiers. With the emergence of Pericles the political process was radically overhauled, aided in large part by the Delian League's wealth – which enabled office-holders to be paid, thereby making it possible for the poor to play a part in government. Pericles's constitution ensured that all policies of the state were to be decided by a general assembly of Athenian male citizens – six thousand constituted a quorum. The assembly, which met outside at either the **Agora** or the **Pnyx**, elected a council of five hundred members to carry out the everyday administration of the city and a board of ten *strategoi* or generals to guide it. Pericles, one of the best known and most influential of the *strategoi*, was as vulnerable as any other to the electoral process: if sufficient numbers had cast their lot (*ostra*) against him, his citizenship would be forfeited (he would be literally ostracized); as it was, he managed to stave off such a fate and died with his popularity intact.

In line with this system of democratic participation, a new and exalted notion of the Athenian citizen emerged. This was a man who could shoulder political responsibility, take public office, and play a part in the **cultural** and **religious events** of the time. The latter assumed ever-increasing importance. The city's Panathenaic festival, honouring its protectress deity Athena, was upgraded along the lines of the Olympic Games to include drama, music and athletic contests. Athenians rose easily to the challenge. The next five decades were to witness the great dramatic works of **Aeschylus**, **Sophocles** and **Euripides**, and the comedies of **Aristophanes**. Foreigners such as **Herodotus**, considered the inventor of history, and **Anaxagoras**, the philosopher, were drawn to live in the city. And they, in turn, were surpassed by native Athenians. **Thucydides** wrote *The Peloponnesian War*, a pioneering work of documentation and analysis, while **Socrates** posed the problems of philosophy that were to exercise his follower **Plato** and to shape the discipline to the present day.

But it was the great civic **building programme** that became the most visible and powerful symbol of the age. Under the patronage of Pericles and with vast public funds made available from the Delian treasury, the architects **Iktinos**, **Mnesikles** and **Callicrates**, and the sculptor **Pheidias**, transformed the city. Their buildings, justified in part as a comprehensive job-creation scheme, included the Parthenon and Erechtheion on the Acropolis; the Thiseon (or Hephaisteion) and several *stoas* (arcades) in the Agora; a new Odeion (theatre) on the south slope of the Acropolis hill; and, outside the city, the temples at Sounion and Rhamnous.

Athenian culture flourished under democracy, but the system was not without its contradictions and failures. Only one in seven inhabitants of the city were actual citizens; the political status and civil rights that they enjoyed were denied to the many thousands of women, *metics* (foreigners) and slaves. While the lives of men became increasingly public and sociable, with meetings at the Agora or Pnyx and visits to the gymnasiums and theatres, **women** remained secluded in small and insanitary homes. Their subordination was in fact reinforced by a decree in 451 BC, which restricted their property rights, placing them under the control of fathers, husbands or guardians. At any one time, only forty women could be appointed priestesses – one of the few positions of female power. Aeschylus summed up the prevailing attitude when he declared that the mother does no more than foster the father's seed.

The city's democracy was also sullied by its **imperialist** designs and actions, which could be brutal and exploitative, although acts of mercy against rebellious allies were also documented. Atrocities included the wholesale massacre of the male population of Melos – and the building programme of Pericles itself relied on easy pickings from weaker neighbours and allies. In the *polis* of Athens the achievements of democracy could be overshadowed, too, with attacks on the very talents it had nurtured and celebrated: Aristophanes was impeached, Pheidias and Thucydides were exiled, Socrates was tried and executed.

But, historically, the fatal mistake of the Athenian democracy was allowing itself to be drawn into the **Peloponnesian War** against Sparta, its persistent rival, in 431 BC. Pericles, having roused the assembly to a pitch of patriotic fervour, died of the plague two years after war began, leaving Athens at the mercy of a series of far less capable leaders. In 415 BC a disastrous campaign in Sicily saw a third of the navy lost; in 405 BC defeat was finally accepted after the rest of the fleet was destroyed by Sparta in the Dardanelles. Demoralized, Athens succumbed to a brief period of oligarchy.

Through succeeding decades Athens was overshadowed by Thebes, though it recovered sufficiently to enter a new phase of democracy, the **age of Plato**. However, in 338 BC, nearly one and a half centuries after the original defeat of the Persians, Athens was again called to defend the Greek city-states, this time against the incursions of **Philip of Macedon**. Demosthenes, said to be as powerful an orator as Pericles, spurred the Athenians to fight, in alliance with the Thebans, at Chaironeia. There they were routed, in large part by the cavalry commanded by Philip's son, Alexander, and Athens fell under the control of the Macedonian empire.

The city continued to be favoured, particularly by **Alexander the Great**, a former pupil of Aristotle, who respected both Athenian culture and its democratic institutions. Following his death, however, came a more uncertain era, which saw periods of independence and Macedonian rule, until 146 BC when the **Romans** swept through southern Greece, subjugating it as an imperial province (see p.94).

The Acropolis

April–Sept daily 8am–6.30pm; Oct–March Mon–Fri 8am–4.30pm, Sat & Sun 8am–2.30pm; site and museum 2000dr, Oct–March free on Sun.

The **rock of the Acropolis**, with the ruins of the Parthenon rising above it, is one of the archetypal images of Western culture. A first glimpse of it above the traffic is a revelation, and yet feels utterly familiar. Pericles had intended the temple to be a spectacular landmark, a "School for Hellas" and a symbol of the city's imperial confidence – as such, it was famous throughout the ancient world. Even Pericles, however, could not have anticipated that his ruined temple would come to symbolize the emergence of Western civilization – nor that, two millennia on, it would attract some three million tourists a year.

As Donald Horne points out in *The Great Museum*, it would be hard to imagine the ruins having such a wide appeal if they had retained more of their former glory: if, for example, the Parthenon "still had a roof, and no longer appealed to the modern stereotype for outline emerging from rough stone", or if "we repainted it in its original red, blue and gold and if we reinstalled the huge, gaudy cult-figure of Athena festooned in bracelets, rings and necklaces". Yet it's hard not to feel a sense of wonder as you catch glimpses of the ancient ruins from the city below. The best of these street-level **views** are along Eólou, where the Parthenon forms the focal point of the horizon. Calmer and quieter vantage points higher up include the nearby hills of **Lykavitós**, **Ardhittós** and **Filopáppou**, where you can look on, undisturbed, from among the pine groves; a walk to one of these is highly recommended.

The main **approach** to the ruins is the path that extends above Odhós Dhioskoúron, where it joins Theorías at the northwest corner of Pláka. Two alternative options – though both perhaps better as ways down from the rock – are to make your way

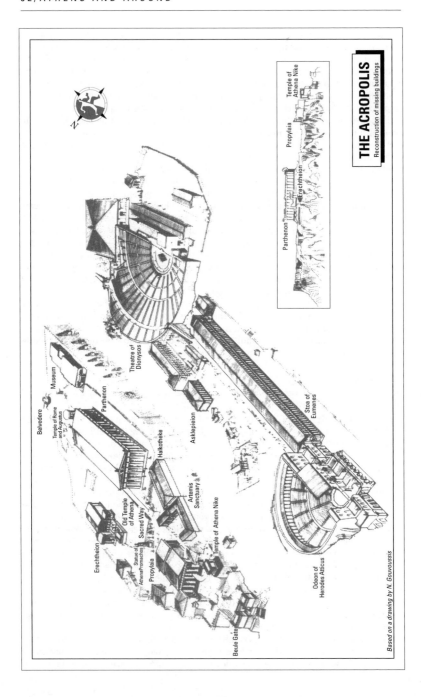

Belvedere

Museum

Temple of Rome and Augustus

Parthenon

Theatre of Dionysos

Erechtheion

Old Temple of Athena

Statue of Athena Promachos

Sacred Way

Halkotheke

Asklepieion

Stoa of Eumenes

Propylaia

Artemis Sanctuary

Temple of Athena Nike

Beule Gate

Odeon of Herodes Atticus

THE ACROPOLIS
Reconstruction of missing buildings

Parthenon

Erechtheion

Propylaia

Temple of Athena Nike

Based on a drawing by N. Gouvoussis

through the ancient Agora (entrance on Adhrianoú, *E2*; see p.89) or, from the south side of the slope, around the footpath beside the Odeion of Herodes Atticus (*F2*).

THE PROPYLAIA AND ATHENA NIKE TEMPLE

Today, as throughout its history, the Acropolis offers but one entrance – from a terrace above the Agora. Here in Classical times the Panathenaic Way extended along a steep ramp to a massive monumental double-gatehouse, the **Propylaia**; the modern path makes a more gradual, zigzagging ascent through an arched Roman entrance, the **Beule Gate**, added in the third century AD.

THE PROPYLAIA

The **Propylaia** were constructed by Mnesikles upon completion of the Parthenon, in 437 BC, and their axis and proportions aligned to balance the temple. They were built from the same Pentelic marble (from Mount Pendéli, northeast of the city), and in grandeur and architectural achievement are no mean rival to the Parthenon temple. In order to offset the difficulties of a sloping site, Mnesikles combined for the first time standard Doric columns with the taller and more delicate Ionic order. The ancient Athenians, awed by the fact that such wealth and craftsmanship should be used for a purely secular building, ranked this as their most prestigious monument.

The halls had a variety of uses, even in Classical times. To the left of the central hall (which before Venetian bombardment supported a great coffered roof, painted blue and gilded with stars), the Pinakotheke – currently in scaffolding – exhibited paintings of Homeric subjects by Polygnotus. Executed in the mid-fifth century BC, these were described 600 years later by Pausanias in his Roman-era *Guide to Greece*. There was to have been a similar wing-room to the right, but Mnesikles's design trespassed on ground sacred to the Goddess of Victory and the premises had to be adapted as a waiting room for her shrine – the Temple of Athena Nike.

TEMPLE OF ATHENA NIKE

Simple and elegant, the **Temple of Athena Nike** was begun late in the rebuilding scheme (probably due to conflict over the extent of the Propylaia's south wing) and stands on a precipitous platform overlooking the port of Pireás and the Saronic Gulf. Pausanias recounts that it was from this bastion that King Aegeus maintained a vigil for the tell-tale white sails that would indicate the safe return of his son Theseus from his mission to slay the Minotaur on Crete. Theseus, flushed with success, forgot his promise to swap the boat's black sails for white. On seeing the black sails, Aegeus assumed his son had perished and, racked with grief, plunged to his death. The temple's frieze, with more attention to realism than triumph, depicts the Athenians' victory over the Persians at Plateia.

Amazingly, the whole temple was reconstructed, from its original blocks, in the nineteenth century; the Turks had demolished the building two hundred years previously, using it as material for a gun emplacement. Recovered in this same feat of jigsaw-puzzle archeology were the reliefs from its parapet – among them *Victory Adjusting her Sandal*, the most beautiful exhibit in the Acropolis Museum.

In front of this small temple are the scant remains of a **Sanctuary of Brauronian Artemis**. Although its function remains obscure, it is known that the precinct once housed a colossal bronze representation of the Wooden Horse of Troy. More noticeable is a nearby stretch of **Mycenaean wall** (running parallel to the Propylaia) that was incorporated into the Classical design.

The Parthenon

Seen from the Propylaia, the Acropolis is today dominated by the Parthenon, set on the rock's highest ground. In Classical times, however, only the temple's pediment could be viewed through the intervening mass of statues and buildings. The ancient focus was a ten-metre-high bronze statue of *Athena Promachos* (Athena the Champion), moved to Constantinople in Byzantine times and there destroyed by a mob who believed that its beckoning hand had directed the Crusaders to the city in 1204. The statue was created by Pheidias as a symbol of the Athenians' defiance of Persia; its spear and helmet were visible to sailors approaching from Sounion.

To the right of the statue passed the Panathenaic Way, the route of the quadrennial festival in honour of the city's patroness, the goddess Athena. Following this route up

THE ACROPOLIS: PERICLES TO ELGIN – AND BEYOND

The Acropolis's natural setting, a craggy mass of limestone plateau, watered by springs and rising an abrupt hundred metres out of the plain of Attica, has made it a focus and nucleus during every phase of the city's development.

The site was one of the earliest settlements in Greece, its slopes inhabited by a **Neolithic** community around 5000 BC. In **Mycenaean** times it was fortified with Cyclopean walls (parts of which can still be seen), enclosing a royal palace and temples which fostered the cult of Athena. City and goddess were integrated by the **Dorians** and, with the union of Attic towns and villages in the ninth century BC, the Acropolis became the heart of the first Greek city-state, sheltering its principal public buildings. So it was to remain, save for an interval under the **Peisistratid tyrants** of the seventh and sixth centuries BC, who re-established a fortified residence on the rock. But when the last tyrant was overthrown in 510 BC, the Delphic Oracle ordered that the Acropolis should remain forever the **province of the gods**, unoccupied by humans.

It was in this context that the monuments visible today were built. Most of the substantial remains date from the **fifth century BC** or later; there are outlines of earlier temples and sanctuaries but these are hardly impressive, for they were burned to the ground when the Persians sacked Athens in 480 BC. For some decades, until Pericles promoted his grand plan, the temples were left in their ruined state as a reminder of the Persian action. But with that threat removed, in the wake of Athenian military supremacy and a peace treaty with the Persians in 449 BC, the walls were rebuilt and architects drew up plans for a reconstruction worthy of the city's cultural and political position.

Pericles's **rebuilding** plan was both magnificent and enormously expensive but it won the backing of the democracy, for many of whose citizens it must have created both wealth and work – paid for from the unfortunate Delian League's coffers. The work was under the general direction of the architect and sculptor **Pheidias** and it was completed in an incredibly short time. The Parthenon itself took only ten years to finish: "every architect", wrote Plutarch, "striving to surpass the magnificence of the design with the elegance of the execution".

Their monuments survived unaltered – save for some modest Roman tinkering – for close to a thousand years, until in the reign of the Emperor Justinian the temples were converted to **Christian** worship. In subsequent years the uses became secular as well as religious, and embellishments increased, gradually obscuring the Classical designs. Fifteenth-century Italian princes held court in the Propylaia, the entrance hall to the complex, and the same quarters were later used by the **Turks** as their commander's headquarters and as a powder magazine. The Parthenon underwent similar changes from Greek to Roman temple, from Byzantine church to Frankish cathedral, before several centuries of use as a Turkish mosque. The Erechtheion, with its graceful female figures, saw service as a harem. A Venetian diplomat, Hugo Favoli, described the Acropolis in 1563 as "looming beneath a swarm of glittering golden crescents", with a minaret rising from the Parthenon. For all their changes in use, however, the buildings would have resembled – very much more than today's bare ruins – the bustling and ornate ancient Acropolis, covered in sculpture and painted in bright colours.

today, you can make out grooves cut for footholds in the rock and, to either side, niches for innumerable statues and offerings.

The **Parthenon** was the first great building in Pericles's scheme. Designed by Iktinos, it utilizes all the refinements available to the Doric order of architecture to achieve an extraordinary and unequalled harmony. Its proportions maintain a universal 9:4 ratio, not only in the calculations of length to width, or width to height, but in such relationships as the distances between the columns and their diameter. Additionally, any possible appearance of disproportion is corrected by meticulous mathematics and

Sadly, such images remain only in the prints and sketches of that period: the Acropolis buildings finally fell victim to the demands of war, blown up during the successive attempts by the Venetians to oust the Turks. In 1684 the Turks demolished the temple of Athena Nike to gain a brief tactical advantage. Three years later the Venetians, laying siege to the garrison, ignited a Turkish gunpowder magazine in the Parthenon, and in the process blasted off its roof and set a **fire** that raged within its precincts for two days and nights. The apricot-tinged glow of the Parthenon marbles so admired by the Neoclassicists of the eighteenth century was one of the more aesthetic results.

Arguably surpassing this destruction, at least in the minds of modern Greeks, were the activities of Western looters at the start of the nineteenth century: the French ambassador Fauvel gathering antiquities for the Louvre, and **Lord Elgin** levering away sculptures from the Parthenon in 1801. As British Ambassador to the Porte, Elgin obtained permission from the Turks to erect scaffolding, excavate and remove stones with inscriptions. He interpreted this concession as a licence to make off with almost all of the bas-reliefs from the Parthenon's frieze, most of its pedimental structures and a caryatid from the Erechtheion – which he later sold to the British Museum. There were perhaps justifications for Elgin's action at the time – not least the Turks' tendency to use Parthenon stones in their lime kilns, and possible further ravages of war – though it was controversial even then. Byron, a more sympathetic character who roundly disparaged all this activity, visited in 1810–11, just in time to see the last of Elgin's ships loaded with the marbles. Today, however, the British Museum's continued retention of the "Elgin Marbles" (a phrase that Greek guides on the Acropolis, who portray Elgin unequivocally as a vandal, do not use) rests on legal rather than moral claims. Hopefully the British Museum will soon find a graceful pretext to back down; the long-awaited completion of the new Acropolis Museum, slated to occupy land around the Makriyánni barracks just south of the bluffs, would be a perfect opportunity, but the project – originally scheduled for completion in 1996 – seems to have stalled.

As for the Acropolis **buildings**, their fate since the Greeks regained the Acropolis after the war of independence has not been entirely happy. Almost immediately, Greek archeologists began clearing the Turkish village that had developed around the Parthenon-mosque; a Greek regent lamented in vain that they "would destroy all the picturesque additions of the Middle Ages in their zeal to lay bare the ancient monuments". Much of this early work was indeed destructive: the iron clamps and supports used to reinforce the marble structures were, contrary to ancient example, not sheathed in lead, so they have since rusted and warped, causing the stones to crack. Meanwhile, earthquakes have dislodged the foundations; generations of feet have slowly worn down surfaces; and, more recently, sulphur dioxide deposits, caused by vehicle and industrial pollution, have been turning the marble to dust.

Since a 1975 report predicted the collapse of the Parthenon, visitors have been barred from its actual precinct, and a major, long-term restoration scheme of the entire Acropolis embarked upon. Inevitably this has its frustrations, with many of the buildings scaffolded and the Acropolis at times taking on the appearance of a building site. Of late, progress has been delayed by disputes between the architect in charge of the restoration, Manolis Korres, and the committee of non-specialists which has been put over him.

craftsmanship. All seemingly straight lines are in fact slightly curved, an optical illusion known as *entasis* (intensification). The columns (their profile bowed slightly to avoid seeming concave) are slanted inwards by 6cm, while each of the steps along the sides of the temple was made to incline just 12cm over a length of 70 metres.

Built on the site of earlier archaic temples, the Parthenon was intended as a new sanctuary for Athena and a home for her cult image – a colossal wooden statue of *Athena Polias* (Athena of the City) decked in ivory and gold plate, with precious gems as eyes and sporting an ivory gorgon death's-head on her breast. Designed by Pheidias, the statue was installed in the semi-darkness of the *cella* (cult chamber), where it remained an object of prestige and wealth, if not veneration, until at least the fifth century AD. The sculpture has been lost since ancient times but its characteristics are known through numerous later copies (including a fine Roman one in the National Archeological Museum).

The name "Parthenon" means "virgins' chamber", and initially referred only to a room at the west end of the temple occupied by the priestesses of Athena. However, the temple never rivalled the Erechtheion in sanctity and its role tended to remain that of treasury and artistic showcase, devoted rather more to the new god of the *polis* than to Athena herself. Originally its columns were painted and it was decorated with the finest frieze and pedimental sculpture of the Classsical age, depicting the Panathenaic procession, the birth of Athena, and the struggles of Greeks to overcome giants, Amazons and centaurs. Of these, the best surviving examples are in the British Museum, but the greater part of the pediments, along with the central columns and the *cella*, were destroyed by the Venetian bombardment in 1687.

The Erechtheion

To the north of the Parthenon, beyond the foundations of the Old Temple of Athena, stands the **Erechtheion**, the last of the great works of Pericles to be completed. It was built over ancient sanctuaries, which in turn were predated by a Mycenaean palace. Here, in a symbolic reconciliation, both Athena and the city's old patron of Poseidon-Erechtheus were worshipped; the site, according to myth, was that on which they had contested possession of the Acropolis. The myth (which probably recalls the integration of the Mycenaeans with earlier pre-Hellenic settlers) tells how an olive tree sprang from the ground at the touch of Athena's spear, while Poseidon summoned forth a sea-water spring. The Olympian gods voted Athena the victor.

Pausanias wrote of seeing both olive tree and seawater in the temple, adding that "the extraordinary thing about this well is that when the wind blows south a sound of waves comes from it".

Today, in common with all buildings on the Acropolis, entrance is no longer permitted, but its series of elegant Ionic porticoes are worth close attention, particularly the north one with its fine decorated doorway and frieze of blue Eleusinian marble. On the south side is the famous **Porch of the Caryatids**, whose columns are transformed into the tunics of six tall maidens holding the entablature on their heads. The statues were long supposed to have been modelled on the widows of Karyai, a small city in the Peloponnese that was punished for its alliance with the Persians by the slaughter of its menfolk and the enslavement of the women. There is, though, little suggestion of grieving or humbled captives in the serene poses of the Caryatid women. Some authorities believe that they instead represent the Arrephoroi, young, high-born girls in the service of Athena. The ones in situ are now, sadly, replacements. Five of the originals are in the Acropolis Museum, a sixth was looted by Elgin, who also removed a column and other purely architectural features – pieces that become completely meaningless out of context in the British Museum and which are replaced here by casts in a different colour marble. The stunted olive tree growing in the precinct was planted by an American archeologist in 1917.

The Acropolis Museum

Placed discreetly on a level below that of the main monuments, the **Acropolis Museum** contains all of the portable objects removed from the site since 1834 (with the exception of a few bronzes displayed in the National Archeological Museum). Over recent years, as increasing amounts of stone and sculptures have been removed from the ravages of environmental pollution, the collection has grown considerably. Labelling is rudimentary at best; a supplementary guide is useful.

In the first rooms to the left of the vestibule are fragments of pedimental sculptures from the **old Temple of Athena** (seventh to sixth century BC), whose traces of paint give a good impression of the vivid colours that were used in temple decoration. Further on is the **Moschophoros**, a painted marble statue of a young man carrying a sacrificial calf, dated 570 BC and one of the earliest examples of Greek art in marble. Room 4 displays one of the chief treasures of the building, a unique collection of **Korai**, or maidens, dedicated as votive offerings to Athena at some point in the sixth century BC. Between them they represent a shift in art and fashion, from the simply contoured Doric clothing to the more elegant and voluminous Ionic designs; the figures' smiles also change subtly, becoming increasingly loose and natural.

The pieces of the **Parthenon frieze** in Room 8 were sundered from the temple by the Venetian explosion and subsequently buried, thereby escaping the clutches of Lord Elgin. They portray scenes of Athenian citizens in the Panathenaic procession; the fact that mortals featured so prominently in the decoration of the temple indicates the immense collective self-pride of the Athenians at the height of their Golden Age. This room also contains a graceful and fluid sculpture, known as **Iy Sandalízoussa**, which depicts **Athena Nike** adjusting her sandal. Finally, in the last room are four authentic and semi-eroded **caryatids** from the Erectheion, displayed behind a glass screen in a carefully rarefied atmosphere.

West and south of the Acropolis

Most visitors to the Acropolis leave by the same route they arrived – north through Pláka. For a calmer and increasingly panoramic view of the rock, it's worth taking the time to explore something of the area to the **west of the Acropolis**, punctuated by the hills of the Areopagus, Pnyx and Filopáppou, each of which had a distinct function in the life of the ancient city.

The **south slope** is rewarding, too, with its Greek and Roman theatres and the remains of *stoas* and sanctuaries. It can be approached from the Acropolis, with an entrance just above the Herodes Atticus theatre, though its main entrance is some way to the south along Leofóros Dhionissíou Areopayítou.

No less important, these sites all give access to the neighbourhoods of **Veïkoú**, **Koukáki** and **Áno Petrálona**, three of the least spoilt quarters in Athens, and with some of the city's best tavernas (see pp.113–114).

The Areopagus, Pnyx and Filopáppou Hill

Rock-hewn stairs ascend the low hill of the **Areopagus** immediately below the entrance to the Acropolis. The "Hill of Mars" was the site of the Council of Nobles and the Judicial Court under the aristocratic rule of ancient Athens. During the Classical period the court lost its powers of government to the Assembly (held on the Pnyx) but it remained the court of criminal justice, dealing primarily with cases of homicide. Aeschylus used this setting in *The Eumenides* for the trial of Orestes, who, pursued by the Furies' demand of "a life for a life", stood accused of murdering his mother Clytemnestra.

The hill was used as a campsite by the Persians during their siege of the Acropolis in 480 BC, and in the Roman era by Saint Paul, who preached the *Sermon on an*

Unknown God here, winning amongst his converts Dionysius "the Areopagite", who became the city's patron saint. Today, there are various foundation cuttings on the site, and the ruins of a church of Áyios Dhioníssios (possibly built over the court), though nothing is actually left standing. The Areopagus's historic associations apart, it is notable mainly for the views, not only of the Acropolis, but down over the Agora and towards Kerameikos – the ancient cemetery (see p.90).

Following the road or path over the flank of the Acropolis, you come out onto Leofóros Dhionissíou Areopayítou, by the Herodes Atticus theatre. Turning right, 100m or so down (and across) the avenue, a network of paths leads up **Filopáppou Hill**, also known as the "Hill of the Muses" (*Lófos Moussón*). This strategic height has played an important, if generally sorry, role in the city's history. It was from here that the shell which destroyed the roof of the Parthenon was lobbed; more recently, the colonels placed tanks on the slopes during their coup of 1967. (Avoid the area at night, as it has a reputation for rapes and muggings.)

The hill's summit is capped by a somewhat grandiose monument to a Roman senator and consul, Filopappus, who is depicted driving his chariot on its frieze. Again, it is a place above all for views. To the west is the Dora Stratou Theatre (or Filopáppou Theatre) where Greek music and dance performances (see p.119) are held. Northwest, along the main path, and following a line of truncated ancient walls, is the church of **Áyios Dhimítrios**, an unsung gingerbread gem, which has kept its original Byzantine frescoes. In the cliff face across from this to the south you can make out a kind of cave dwelling, known (more from imagination than evidence) as the **prison of Socrates**.

Further to the north, above the church, rises the **Hill of the Pnyx**, an area used in Classical Athens as the meeting place for the democratic assembly, which gathered more than forty times a year. All except the most serious political issues, such as ostracism, were aired here, the hill on the north side providing a convenient semicircular terrace from which to address the crowd. All male citizens could vote and, at least in theory, all could voice their opinions, though the assembly was harsh on inarticulate or foolish speakers. There are remains of the original walls, used to form the theatre-like court, and of *stoas* for the assembly's refreshment. The arena is today used for the *son-et-lumière* (not greatly recommended) of the Acropolis, which takes place on most summer evenings.

Beyond the Pnyx, still another hill, **Lófos Nymfón** (Hill of the Nymphs), is dominated by a nineteenth-century observatory and gardens, occasionally open to visitors.

The south slope of the Acropolis

Entrance on Leofóros Dhionissíou Areopayítou; daily 8.30am–2.45pm; 500dr.

The second-century Roman **Odeion of Herodes Atticus**, restored for performances of music and Classical drama during the summer festival (see p.119), dominates the south slope of the Acropolis hill. It is open only for shows, though; the main reason to come here otherwise is the earlier Greek sites to the east.

Pre-eminent among these is the **Theatre of Dionysos**, beside the main site entrance. One of the most evocative locations in the city, it was here that the masterpieces of Aeschylus, Sophocles, Euripides and Aristophanes were first performed. It was also the venue for the annual festival of tragic drama, where each Greek citizen would take his turn as member of the chorus. The ruins are impressive. Rebuilt in the fourth century BC, the theatre could hold some 17,000 spectators – considerably more than the Herodes Atticus's 5000–6000 seats; twenty of the theatre's sixty-four tiers of seats survive. Most notable are the great marble thrones in the front row, each inscribed with the name of an official of the festival or of an important priest; in the middle sat the Priest of Dionysos and on his right the representative of the Delphic Oracle. At the rear of the stage along the Roman *bema* (rostrum) are reliefs of episodes in the life of Dionysos flanked by two squatting Sileni, devotees of the satyrs. Sadly, all this is roped off to protect the stage-floor **mosaic** – itself a magnificent diamond of multi-coloured marble best seen from above.

Above the theatre – reached by steps, then a path to the right – looms a vast grotto, converted perhaps a millennium ago into the chapel of **Panayía Khryssospiliótissa**; it's worth a look for the setting rather than its kitsch iconography. To the west of the theatre extend the ruins of the **Asclepion**, a sanctuary devoted to the healing god Asclepius (see p.163) and built around a sacred spring. The curative centre was probably incorporated into the Byzantine church of the doctor-saints Kosmas and Damian, of which there are prominent remains. Nearer to the road lie the foundations of the Roman **Stoa of Eumenes**, a colonnade of stalls that stretched to the Herodes Atticus Odeion.

The Ancient Agora

Southeastern entrance down the path from the Areopagus; northern entrance on Adhrianoú, E2; Tues–Sun 8.30am–2.45pm; 1200dr.

The **Agora** (market) was the nexus of ancient Athenian city life. Competing for space were the various claims of administration, commerce, market and public assembly. The result was ordered chaos. Eubolus, a fourth-century poet, observed that "you will find everything sold together in the same place at Athens: figs, witnesses to summonses, bunches of grapes, turnips, pears, apples, givers of evidence, roses, medlars . . . water clocks, laws, indictments". Women, however, were not in evidence; secluded by custom, they would delegate any business in the Agora to slaves. Before shifting location to the Pnyx, the assembly also met here, and continued to do so when discussing cases of ostracism for most of the fifth and fourth centuries BC.

Originally the Agora was a rectangle, divided diagonally by the Panathenaic Way and enclosed by temples, administrative buildings, and long porticoed *stoas* (arcades of shops) where idlers and philosophers gathered to exchange views and listen to the orators. In the centre was an open space, defined by boundary stones at the beginning of the fifth century BC; considered sacred and essential to the life of the community, those accused of homicide or other serious crimes were excluded from it by law.

The site today is a confused, if extensive, jumble of ruins, dating from various stages of building between the sixth century BC and the fifth century AD. The best overview is from the Areopagus, by the southeast entrance. For some idea of what you are surveying, however, the place to head for is the **Museum**, housed in the reconstructed **Stoa of Attalos**. The stoa itself was a US$1.5 million project of the American School of Archeology in Athens. It is, in every respect bar one, an entirely faithful reconstruction of the original. What is missing is colour: in Classical times the exterior would have been painted in bright red and blue (like the Minoan palaces of Crete). Of the displays – mostly pottery from the sixth to fourth century BC, plus some early Geometric grave offerings – highlights are the red-figure dishes depicting athletes, musicians and minor deities, together with the adjacent oil flask in the form of a kneeling boy (both exhibits are in the centre of the hall).

Around the site, the most prominent ruins are of various other stoas, including the recently excavated "Painted Stoa" where **Zeno** expounded his Stoic philosophy, and those of the city's gymnasiums and council hall (*bouleuterion*). Somewhat above the general elevation, to the west, is the **Thiseon**, or Temple of Hephaistos. Because exploits of Theseus were displayed on the metopes and frieze this temple was long thought to be dedicated to Theseus. The name Thiseon lingers for the train station and the area to the southwest. The best preserved, though perhaps least admired, of all Doric temples, it lacks the curvature and "lightness" of the Parthenon's design. Dedicated to the patron of blacksmiths and metalworkers – hence its popular name – it was the first building of Pericles's programme, though not the first completed. Its remaining *metopes* depict the labours of Hercules and the exploits of Theseus, while the barrel-vaulted roof dates from the Byzantine conversion of the temple into a church of Saint George. The other bona fide church on the site – that of **Áyii Apóstoli** (the Holy Apostles), by the south entrance – is worth a glance inside for its fresco fragments, exposed during a 1950s restoration of the eleventh-century shrine.

Kerameikos (Keramikós)

Entrance at Ermoú 148, E1; Tues–Sun 8.30am–3pm; 500dr.

The Kerameikos site, encompassing the principal cemetery of ancient Athens, provides a fascinating and quiet retreat from the Acropolis. It is little visited and in addition has something of an oasis feel about it, with the lush Iridhanós channel, speckled with water lilies, flowing across it from east to west.

From the entrance can be seen the double line of the **Long Walls**, which ran to the port at Pireás; the inner wall was hastily cobbled together by the men, women and children of Athens while Themistocles was pretending to negotiate a mutual disarmament treaty with Sparta in 479 BC. The barriers are interrupted by the great **Dipylon Gate**, where travellers from Pireás, Eleusis and Boeotia entered the ancient city, and the **Sacred Gate**, used for the Eleusinian and Panathenaic processions. These followed the Sacred Way, once lined by colonnades and bronze statues, into the Agora. Between the two gates are the foundations of the **Pompeion**, where preparations for the processions were made and where the main vehicles were stored.

Branching off from the Sacred Way is the **Street of the Tombs**, begun in 394 BC and now excavated along a hundred or so metres. Both sides were reserved for the plots of wealthy Athenians. Some twenty, each containing numerous commemorative monuments, have been excavated, and their original stones, or replicas, reinstated. The flat vertical *stelai* were the main funerary monuments of the Classical world; the sarcophagus belonged to Hellenistic and Roman times. The sculpted crescent with the massive conglomerate base to the left of the path is the *Memorial of Dexileos*, the twenty-year-old son of Lysanias of Thorikos, who was killed in action at Corinth in 394 BC. The adjacent plot contains the *Monument of Dionysios of Kollytos*, in the shape of a pillar *stele* supporting a bull carved from Pentelic marble. As with any cemetery, however, it is the more humble monuments, such as the statue of a girl with a dog on the north side of the street, that connect past and present in the shared experience of loss. From the terrace overlooking the tombs, Pericles delivered his famous funeral oration dedicated to those who died in the first years of the Peloponnesian War. His propaganda coup inspired thousands more to enlist in a campaign during which one-third of the Athenian force was wiped out.

The **Oberlaender Museum**, named after the German-American manufacturer who financed it, contains an extensive collection of *stelai*, terracotta figures, vases and sculptures from the site. Among them, Room 1's *Ampharete Holding her Infant Grandchild*, and *The Boxer*, with a cauliflower ear and the thongs of a glove tied around his wrist, are remarkable in their detailed execution. The terracotta figures and vases of Room 2 include some of the earliest art objects yet found in Greece.

Pláka and Monastiráki

Pláka, with its alleys and stairs built on the Turkish plan, is the most rewarding Athenian area for daytime wanderings – not least because of its pedestrianization, with cars banished from all but a few main streets. In addition to a scattering of Roman sites and various offbeat and enjoyable museums, it offers glimpses of an

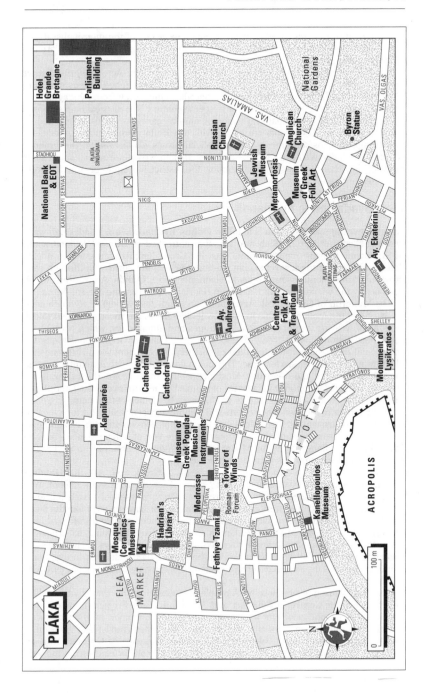

exotic past, refreshingly at odds with the concrete blocks of the metropolis. If you can, time your visit to coincide with the Sunday morning **flea market** around Monastiráki square.

Roughly delineated by Sýndagma, Odhós Ermoú and the Acropolis, the district was basically the extent of nineteenth-century, pre-independence Athens, and provided the core of the city for the next few decades. Once away from Sýndagma, the narrow winding streets are lined with nineteenth-century Neoclassical houses, some grand, some humble, with gateways opening onto verdant courtyards overlooked by wooden verandas. Tiled roofs are edged with terracotta medusa-heads, goddesses and foliage designs, ornaments known collectively as *akrokerámata*; the grander facades are decorated with pilasters and capitals and wrought-iron balconies. Poor and working class for most of this century, the district has lately been extensively gentrified and renovated.

From Sýndagma to Adhrianoú

An attractive approach to Pláka is to follow **Odhós Kydhathinéon**, a pedestrian walkway that starts near the **English and Russian churches** on Odhós Filellínon, south of Sýndagma. It leads gently downhill, past the Greek Folk Art Museum, on a leafy square with one of the few remaining old-time cafés on the corner, on through café-crowded Platía Filomoússou Eterías to Hadrian's street, **Odhós Adhrianoú**, which runs nearly the whole length of Pláka from Hadrian's Arch past the ancient Agora.

The **Museum of Greek Folk Art** (Tues–Sun 10am–2pm; 500dr), at Kydhathinéon 17, is one of the most enjoyable in the city. Its five floors are mostly devoted to collections of weaving, pottery, regional costumes and embroidery, which reveal both the sophistication and the strong Middle Eastern influence of Greek popular arts. On the second floor, the carnival tradition of northern Greece, and the all-but-vanished shadow-puppet theatre, are featured. The fourth floor dazzles with its exhibits of gold and silver jewellery and weaponry. Most compelling of all, on the third floor, is the reconstructed village room with a series of murals by the primitive artist **Theophilos** (1873–1934). Theophilos was one of the characters of turn-of-the-century Greece, dressing in War of Independence outfits and painting tavernas and cafés for a meal or a small fee. A museum of his work is on the island of Mytilini and other paintings – usually scenes from peasant life or battles during the War of Independence – survive in situ in the Peloponnese and on Mount Pílion, though they have only in the last few decades been recognized as being worth preserving.

Down and across the street from the Museum of Greek Folk Art, the **Hellenic Children's Museum**, Kydathinéon 14, *E3* (Mon, Tues & Fri, 9.30am–1.30pm, Wed 9.30am–6.30pm, Sat & Sun 10am–2pm; free) is more a playschool than a museum: chaotic but fun. It includes workrooms, playrooms and displays on stuff like the building of the new Athens metro lines, which children can enter complete with hard hats. On a similar theme, the **Museum of Greek Children's Art**, Kódrou 9, *E3* (Tues–Sat 10am–2pm, Sun 11am–2pm; closed Aug; free) has changing displays of children's art, including sculpture, but also tables and drawing materials for children to use. Some paintings are for sale, as well as a large range of eye-catching cards painted by Greek children.

Two other museums are close by. A couple of blocks to the northwest, at Angelikís Hatzimiháli 6, the **Centre of Folk Art and Tradition** (Tues–Fri 9am–1pm & 5–9pm, Sat & Sun 9am–1pm; closes for a movable month during summer; free) features costumes, cloth, musical instruments, and so forth, in another grand Pláka mansion. A short distance to the east, at Níkis 39, is the **Jewish Museum of Greece** (Mon–Fri 9am–2.30, Sun 10am–2pm; free). Displaying art and religious artefacts from the very ancient Jewish communities scattered throughout Greece, the centrepiece is the reconstructed synagogue of Pátra, dating from the 1920s, whose furnishings have been moved here en bloc and remounted.

The Monument of Lysikrates and around

At the eastern end of Pláka, Odhós Lissikrátous gives onto a small, fenced-off archeological area at one end of Odhós Tripódhon, the **Street of the Tripods**, where winners of the ancient dramatic contests dedicated their tripod-trophies to Dionysos. Here you can see the **Monument of Lysikrates**, a tall and graceful stone and marble structure from 335 BC, which stands as a surprisingly complete example of these ancient exhibits. A four-metre-high stone base supports six Corinthian columns rising up to a marble dome on which, in a flourish of acanthus leaf carvings, a winning tripod was placed. The inscription on its architrave tells us that "Lysikrates of Kikyna, son of Lysitheides was *choregos* (sponsor); the tribe of Akamantis won the victory with a chorus of boys; Theon played the flute; Lysiades of Athens trained the chorus; Evainetos was archon". The monument was incorporated into a French Capuchin convent in 1667, and tradition asserts that Byron used the convent as a study, writing part of *Childe Harold* here; at the time Athens had no inn and the convent was a regular lodging for European travellers.

The street beyond, **Výronos**, is named after the poet (*O Lórdhos Výronos* to Greeks). At its far end, facing you across the road, is the old Makriyánni police barracks, revered by Greek rightists for its stout resistance to Communist attack during December 1944. Part of it has been transformed into the so-called **Acropolis Study Centre** (daily 9am–2.30pm; free), flanked by the metro construction and containing little beyond plaster casts of the Elgin Marbles and models of the winning designs for the hypothetical **Acropolis Museum**.

Hadrian's Arch and the Temple of Olympian Zeus

Taking the other street at the Lysikrates monument crossroads, Ódhos Lýssikratoús, you emerge at the edge of Pláka near one of the most hazardous road junctions in Athens, the meeting of Dhionissíou Areopayítou, Amalías and Singroú. Across the way, facing Leofóros Amalías, stands **Hadrian's Arch**, erected by that emperor to mark the edge of the Classical city and the beginning of his own. On the near side its frieze is inscribed "This is Athens, the ancient city of Theseus", and on the other "This is the City of Hadrian and not of Theseus". Since there are few obvious signs of a Roman city, this makes little sense to today's visitor, but there are Roman remains south of the Temple of Olympian Zeus and recent excavations suggest that the Roman city occupied at least the Zapio area.

Directly behind the arch, the colossal pillars of the **Temple of Olympian Zeus** (Tues–Sun 8.30am–3pm; 500dr; entrance on Vassilíssis Olgas) dominate their surroundings. The largest temple in Greece, and according to Livy, "the only temple on earth to do justice to the god", it was dedicated by Hadrian in 131 AD, some 700 years after the tyrant Peisistratos had laid its foundations. Hadrian marked the occasion by contributing a statue of Zeus and a suitably monumental one of himself, although both have since been lost. Just fifteen of the temple's original 104 Pentelic marble pillars remain erect, though the column drums of another, which fell in 1852, litter the ground, giving a startling idea of the project's size. Almost equally impressive is the fact that in the Byzantine era, a stylite made his hermitage on the temple architrave.

From the Olympian Zeus temple, a shady route up to Sýndagma or Kolonáki leads through the Záppio and the **National Gardens** (see p.102).

Anafiótika and the Kanellópoulos Museum

Continuing straight ahead from the Kidhathinéon–Adhrianoú intersection, up **Odhós Thespídhos**, you reach the edge of the Acropolis precinct. Up to the right, the white-washed cubist houses of **Anafiótika** cheerfully proclaim an architect- free zone amid the higher slopes of the Acropolis rock. The pleasingly haphazard buildings here were erected by workers from the island of Anáfi in the southern Aegean, who were employed in the mid-nineteenth-century construction of Athens. Unable to afford land, they took advantage of a customary law to the effect that if a roof and four walls could be thrown up overnight, the premises were yours at sunrise. The houses, and the two churches that serve them, are the image of those the Cycladic islanders had left behind.

Follow Rangavá or Stratoús anticlockwise around the Acropolis rock and you will eventually emerge on Theorías, outside the eclectic **Kanellópoulos Museum** (Tues–Sun 8.30am–3pm; 500dr). Though there is nothing here that you won't see examples of in the bigger museums, this collection of treasures, exhibited in the topmost house under the Acropolis, has a calm appeal. The bulk of the ground-floor exhibits are icons but there is also Byzantine jewellery, bronze oil-lamps and crosses, and Roman funerary ornaments from Fayum. The top floor is given over entirely to Geometric, Classical and Hellenistic art, primarily pottery and votive figurines, generally of a high standard and distinguished by whimsical execution. The middle floor and the stairwells are devoted to Near Eastern and Cypriot art of various periods from the Bronze Age on, including some exquisite Persian goldwork and flamboyantly painted "Phoenician" vials.

The Roman Forum and Tower of the Winds

The western reaches of Adhrianoú, past the newly restored Neoclassical Demotic School, is largely commercial – souvenir shops and sandals – as far as the **Roman Forum** (entrance cnr Pelopídha/Eólou; Tues–Sun 8.30am–2.45pm; 500dr), a large irregularly shaped excavation site bounded by railings.

ROMAN ATHENS

When the **Romans** ousted Athens' Macedonian rulers and incorporated the city into the vast new province of Achaia in 146 BC, Athens continued to enjoy rare political privileges. Its status as a respected seat of learning and great artistic centre had already been firmly established throughout the ancient world: Cicero and Horace were educated here and Athenian sculptors and architects were supported by Roman commissions. Unlike Corinth, though, which became the administrative capital of the province, the city was endowed with relatively few imperial Roman **monuments**, Hadrian's Arch being perhaps the most obvious. Athenian magistrates, exercising a fair amount of local autonomy, tended to employ architects who would reflect the public taste for the simpler *propylaion*, gymnasium and old-fashioned theatre, albeit with a few Roman amendments.

The city's Roman **history** was shaped pre-eminently by its alliances, which often proved unfortunate. The first major onslaught occurred in 86 BC, when Sulla punished Athens for its allegiance to his rival Mithridates by burning its fortifications and looting its treasures. His successors were more lenient. Julius Caesar proffered a free pardon after Athens had sided with Pompey; and Octavian, who extended the old *agora* by building a forum, showed similar clemency when Athens harboured Brutus following the Ides of March. The most frequent visitor was the **Emperor Hadrian**, who used the occasions to bestow grandiose monuments, including his eponymous arch, a magnificent and immense library and (though it had been begun centuries before) the Temple of Olympian Zeus. A generation later **Herodes Atticus**, a Roman senator who owned extensive lands in Marathon, became the city's last major benefactor of ancient times.

The forum was built by Julius Caesar and Augustus (Octavian) as an extension of the older ancient Greek *agora* to its west. It has undergone substantial excavation in recent years, but the majority of it is now open to visitors. Its main entrance, on the west side, was through the relatively intact **Gate of Athena Archegetis**, which consisted of a Doric portico and four columns supporting an entablature and pediment. On the pilaster facing the Acropolis is engraved an edict of Hadrian announcing the rules and taxes on the sale of oil.

The Tower of the Winds

The best-preserved and easily the most intriguing of the forum ruins is the graceful octagonal structure known as the **Tower of the Winds** (Aéridhes in Greek). Designed in the first century BC by Andronikos of Kyrrhos, a Syrian astronomer, it served as a compass, sundial, weather vane and water clock – the latter powered by a stream from one of the Acropolis springs.

Each face of the tower is adorned with a relief of a figure floating through the air, personifying the eight winds. On the **north** side (facing Eólou) is Boreas blowing into a conch shell; **northwest**, Skiron holding a vessel of charcoal; **west**, Zephyros tossing flowers from his lap; **southwest**, Lips speeding the voyage of a ship; **south**, Notos upturning an urn to make a shower; **southeast**, Euros with his arm hidden in his mantle summoning a hurricane; **east**, Apiliotis carrying fruits and wheat; and **northeast**, Kaikias emptying a shield full of hailstones. Beneath each of these, it is still possible to make out the markings of eight sundials.

The semicircular tower attached to the south face was the reservoir from which water was channelled in a steady flow into a cylinder in the main tower; the time was read by the water level viewed through the open northwest door. On the top of the building a bronze Triton revolved with the winds. In Ottoman times dervishes used the tower as a *tekke* or ceremonial hall, terrifying their superstitious Orthodox neighbours with their chanting, music and exercises.

Other forum ruins – and Hadrian's library

The other forum ruins open to view are somewhat obscure. Among the more prominent Roman bits and pieces are a large public latrine, a number of shops and a stepped *propylaion* or entrance gate just below the Tower of the Winds. To the northwest is the oldest Ottoman mosque in Athens, the **Fethiye Tzami**, built in 1458. It was dedicated by Sultan Mehmet II, who conquered Constantinople in 1453 (Fethiye means Conqueror in Turkish). It now is used as an archeological warehouse.

Bordering the north end of the forum site, stretching between Áreos and Eólou, stand the surviving walls of **Hadrian's Library**, an enormous building which once enclosed a cloistered court of a hundred columns. **Odhós Áreos**, alongside, signals the beginning of the Monastiráki flea market area (see p.96). At its end, round behind the forum, are some of the quietest, prettiest and least spoiled streets in the whole of Pláka – many of them ending in steps up to the Anafiótika quarter (see p.94).

Across the street from the Tower of the Winds stands another Turkish relic – a gateway and single dome from a **Medresse**, an Islamic school. In the last years of Ottoman rule and the early years of Greek independence it was used as a prison and was notorious for its bad conditions; a plane tree in the courtyard was used for hangings. The prison was closed early in this century and torn down.

The Museum of Greek Popular Musical Instruments

Just beside the *medresse*, at Dhioyénous 1–3, is the **Museum of Greek Popular Musical Instruments** (Tues & Thurs–Sun 10am–2pm, Wed noon–8pm; free). Superbly accommodated in the rooms of a Neoclassical building, this wonderful display traces the history and distribution of virtually everything that has ever been played in Greece, including (in the basement) some not-so-obvious festival and liturgical instruments such as triangles, strikers, livestock bells and coin garlands worn by Carnival masquers. Reproductions of frescoes show the Byzantine antecedents of many instruments, and headphone sets are provided for sampling the music made by the various exhibits.

After all this plenty, it's difficult to resist the stock of the museum shop, which includes virtually the entire backlist of the Society for the Dissemination of Greek Music's excellent "Songs of . . . " series (see Contexts, p.812).

Monastiráki: the Flea Market area

The northwest districts of Pláka, along Ermoú and Mitropóleos, are noisier, busier and more geared to the Greek life of the city. Neither street lays any claim to beauty, though the bottom (west) half of **Ermoú**, with its metalworkers and other craftsmen, has an attractive workaday character. The top third, from Eólou just west of the pretty Byzantine church of the Kapnikaréa east to Sýndagma Square has been made into an attractive pedestrian mall.

Churches are also the chief feature of **Odhós Mitropóleos** (Cathedral Street). The dusty, tiny chapel of **Ayía Dhynámis** crouches surreally below the concrete piers of the Ministry of Education and Religion; the **Mitrópolis** itself, an undistinguished nineteenth-century cannibal of dozens of older buildings, carves out a square midway along; and the **old cathedral** stands alongside it, a beautiful little twelfth-century church cobbled together from plain and carved blocks, some of which are as ancient as Christendom itself.

Pandhróssou, Platía Monastirakioú and the Mosque of Tzisdarákis

From the bottom corner of the pedestrianized cathedral square, **Odhós Pandhróssou** leads the way into the **Monastiráki Flea Market** – not that its name is really justified by the rich and conventional jewellery and fur shops that pack the first section. In fact, not many genuine market shops remain at all this side of Platía Monastirakíou. With the exception of a couple of specialist icon dealers, everything is geared to the tourist. The most quirky among them is the shop of Stavros Melissinos, the "poet-sandalmaker of Athens", at Pandhróssou 89. Melissinos enjoyed a sort of fame in the 1960s, hammering out sandals for The Beatles, Jackie Onassis and the like; it is said that John Lennon sought him out specifically for his poetic musings on wine and the sea, which Melissinos continues to sell alongside the footwear.

Platía Monastirakíou, full of nut sellers, lottery sellers, fruit stalls, kiosks – and currently metro-digging paraphernalia – gets its name from the little monastery church (*monastiráki*) at its centre, possibly seventeenth century in origin and badly restored in the early twentieth century. The area around has been a marketplace since Turkish times, and maintains a number of Ottoman features. On the south side of the square, rising from the walls of Hadrian's Library and the shacks of Pandhróssou, is the eighteenth-century **Mosque of Tzisdarákis**, now minus minaret and home to the **Museum of Greek Folk Art Kyriazopoulos Ceramic Collection** (daily except Tues; 9.30am–2pm; 500dr). Donated by a Thessaloníki professor, the collection is devoted to folk sculpture and pottery, together with some decorated household items from various points in the Hellenic world.

The mosque itself, especially its striped *mihrab* (the niche indicating the direction of Mecca) is equally interesting. Above the entrance is a calligraphic inscription recording the mosque's founder and date, and a series of niches used as extra *mihrabs* for occasions when worshippers could not fit into the main hall.

West of Platía Monastirakioú: the flea market proper

West of Monastiráki square, the **flea market** caters more and more for local needs, with clothes, iron- and copperware, tools and records in **Odhós Iféstou**; old furniture, bric-a-brac and camping gear in **Platía Avyssinías**; chairs, office equipment, wood-burning stoves, mirrors, canaries and sundry other goods in **Astíngos, Ermoú** and nearby. Beside the church of **Ayíou Filípou**, there's a market in hopeless jumble-sale rejects, touted by a cast of eccentrics (especially on Sundays); of late this extends around the corner, along Adhrianoú, as far as Platía Thisíou.

The north entrance to the **Agora** (see p.89) is just south of Platía Avyssinías on Adhrianoú, across the cutting where the metro line for Pireás re-emerges into the open air after tunnelling under the city centre. Odhós Adhrianoú is here at its most appealing, with a couple of interesting antique shops, a shady kafenío above the metro tunnel, and good views of the Acropolis. Following the Agora fence around to the southwest, you'll come to another good café vantage-point on busy **Apostólou Pávlou**. On the hill above is the old **Observatory**, surrounded by a last enclave of streets untroubled by tourism or redevelopment. There's nothing of particular interest here, just a pleasant wander through the very north end of Áno Petrálona.

North from Pláka: the Bazaar, Omónia square and the National Archeological Museum

When the German Neoclassicists descended on Athens in the 1830s, the land between Pláka and present-day **Omónia square** was envisaged as a spacious European expansion of the Classical and medieval town. Time and the realities of Athens's status as a commercial capital have made a mockery of that grandiose vision: the main **bazaar area** is no less crowded and oriental than Monastiráki, while Omónia itself stubbornly retains a mix of gritty bad taste. For visitors, the focus of interest is the **National Archeological Museum**, which, with its neighbour, the **Politehnío**, fronts the student/alternative quarter of **Exárkhia**, currently the city's liveliest option for nights out.

The Bazaar: Ermoú to Omónia

A broad triangle of streets, delineated by Piréos (officially Tsaldhári) in the west and Stadhíou in the east, reaches north to its apex at Omónia square. Through the middle run **Athinás** and **Eólou streets** – the modern **bazaar**, whose stores, though stocked mainly with imported manufactured goods, still reflect their origins in their unaffected decor, unsophisticated packaging and, most strikingly, their specialization. Each street has a concentration of particular stores and wares, flouting modern marketing theory. Hence the Monastiráki end of Athinás is dedicated to tools; food stores are gathered around the central market in the middle, especially along Evripídhou; there's glass to the west; paint and brasswork to the east; and clothes in Eólou and Ayíou Márkou. Praxitélous is full of lettering merchants; Platía Klafthmónos and Aristídhou of electrical goods; and department stores cluster around Omónia. Always raucous and teeming with shoppers, *kouloúri* (bread-ring) sellers, gypsies and other vendors, the whole area is great free entertainment. Eólou is now for pedestrians only and is much more pleasant though perhaps not so dramatic to walk along than Athinás.

The best bit is the central **meat** and **seafood** market, on the corner of Athinás and Evripídhou. The building itself is a grand nineteenth-century relic, with fretted iron awnings sheltering forests of carcasses and mounds of hearts, livers and ears – no place for the squeamish. In the middle section of the hall is the fish market, with all manner of bounty from the sea squirming and glistening on the marble slabs. Across Athinás is the fruit and vegetable bazaar arrayed around a supended archeological dig. On the surrounding streets are rows of grocers, their stalls piled high with sacks of pulses, salt cod, barrels of olives and wheels of cheese.

To the north is the **flower market**, gathered around the church of Ayía Iríni on Eólou. This has stalls through the week but really comes alive with the crowds on a Sunday morning. An additional feature of **Eólou** is its views: walk it north to south, coming from Omónia, and your approach takes you towards the rock of the Acropolis, with the Erechtheion's slender columns and pediment peeking over the edge of the crag.

Around Omónia square

Omónia itself has little to offer. A continuous turmoil of people and cars, it is Athens at its sleaziest and most urban. There are sporadically functioning escalators (the only public ones in Greece) down to the **metro**, and, at the top, *períptera* selling everything from watch straps to porn. The centre is another metro building site. The palms around the perimeter are replacements for their predecessors, which were cut down in the 1950s lest foreigners think Greece "too Asiatic". Destitute Albanian refugees congregate near the square, which has recently developed a reputation for hustle and petty crime, while after dark the area is also frequented by prostitutes and their customers (the main red-light district is on nearby Sofokléous).

To the north, just beside the National Archeological Museum on Patissíon, is the **Polytekhnío**, a Neoclassical building housing the university's school of engineering and science. It was here in late 1973 that students launched their protests against the repressive regime of the colonels' junta, occupying the building and courtyards, and broadcasting calls for mass resistance from a pirate radio transmitter. Large numbers came down to demonstrate support and hand in food and medicines. The colonels' answer came on the night of November 16. Snipers were positioned in neighbouring houses and ordered to fire indiscriminately into the courtyards while a tank broke down the entrance gate. Even today nobody knows how many of the unarmed students were killed – figures range from twenty to three hundred. Although the junta's leader, Papadhopoulos, was able publicly to congratulate the officers involved before being overthrown by secret police chief Ioannidhes, a new, more urgent sense of outrage was spreading; within a year the dictatorship was toppled.

The anniversary of the massacre is invariably commemorated by a march on the US Embassy, outpost of the colonels' greatest ally; it's a bit apathetic nowadays, but still a day out for the Left. The date is also a significant one for the shadowy terrorist group *Dhekaefta Noémvri* (17 November), which has operated since the early 1980s. With just two or three low-ranking members caught to date, rumour has it that the group enjoys semi-official protection from rogue elements of the powers-that-be.

The National Archeological Museum

Mon 12.30–7pm, Tues–Fri 8am–7pm, Sat & Sun 8.30am–7pm; 2000dr.

The National Archeological Museum, Patissíon 28 (*C2/3*) is an unrivalled treasure house of Cycladic, Minoan, Mycenaean and Classical Greek art – and an essential Athens experience. Despite inadequate labelling and generally unimaginative displays, it elbows its way into the list of the world's top ten museums. To avoid disappointment, give yourself a clear morning or afternoon for a visit; better still, take in the collection – which can be overwhelming if you delve beyond the obvious highlights – in two or more separate trips.

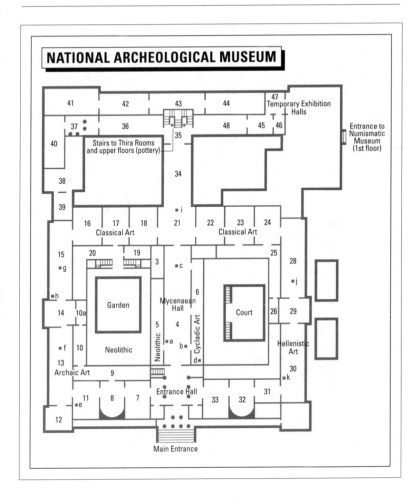

The museum's main divisions are: **prehistoric**, with Mycenae predominating; **sculpture** from the Archaic (eighth century BC) to Hellenistic (third to second centuries BC) periods; and **pottery** from the Geometric period (ninth century BC) to the end of the fourth century AD. Smaller self-contained collections include **bronzes** in Rooms 36 to 40; immensely covetable **jewellery** in Room 32; and the brilliant Minoan-style **frescoes** from Thira (Santorini) upstairs in Room 48.

Mycenaean and Cycladic art

The biggest crowd-puller is the **Mycenaean hall**, in Room 4. Schliemann's gold finds from the grave circle at Mycenae are the big attraction; as hard to get a look at on a summer's day as the Louvre's *Mona Lisa* is the so-called funerary *Mask of Agamemnon* [a] in Case 3. Despite the proof offered by modern dating techniques, which indicate that it belonged to some more ancient Achaian king, crowds are still drawn by its correspondence with the Homeric myth.

The Mycenaeans' consummate art was small-scale decoration of rings, cups, seals and inlaid daggers – requiring eye-tiring scrutiny of the packed showcases to appreciate. As well as the death masks, there's a superb golden-horned *Bull's Head* [b] in Case 18, and in Case 1 a lovely duck-shaped vase of rock crystal; in Case 3, with the "Agamemnon" mask, is a magnificent inlaid dagger. Case 8 has jewellery, daggers and a miniature golden owl and frog from Nestor's palace at Pylos; alongside, in Case 9, are baked tablets of Linear B, the earliest Greek writing.

On the left wall there are Cretan-style frescoes from Tiryns which depict chariot-borne women watching spotted hounds in pursuit of boar, and bull-vaulting reminiscent of Knossos. More finds from Tiryns, in Case 15, include a large krater with a chariot and warriors. In Case 32 [c] are the superb *Vafio* cups, with their scenes of wild bulls and long-tressed, narrow-waisted men, while in Case 33 an equally eye-catching cup is decorated with twining octopuses and dolphins. Further references to Homer abound: in the small Room 3 to the left there's a magnificent *Boar's Tusk Helmet* and an ivory lyre with sphinxes adorning the soundboard.

To the right of the Mycenaean hall, Room 6 houses a large collection of **Cycladic art** – pre-Mycenaean pieces from the Aegean islands. Many of these suggest the abstract forms of modern Cubist art – most strikingly in the much-reproduced *Man Playing a Lyre* [d]. Another unusual piece, at the opposite end of the room, is a sixteenth-century BC cylindrical vase depicting a ring of fishermen carrying fish by their tails. Room 5, to the left of the Mycenaean hall, contains **Neolithic** finds, primarily from excavations in Thessaly.

Sculpture

Most of the rest of the ground floor is occupied by **sculpture**. Beginning in Room 7, on the left of the museum's main entrance, the exhibition proceeds chronologically (and this is the best way to see it) from the Archaic through the Classical and Hellenistic periods (Rooms 7–31) to the Roman- and Egyptian-influenced periods (Rooms 41–43). The gradual development from the stiff, stylized representations of the seventh century BC towards ever freer and looser naturalism is excitingly evident as you go through these cold and rather shabby rooms.

Early highlights include the Aristion *Stele of a Young Warrior* [e], with delicately carved beard, hair and tunic-folds in Room 11, and the Croesus *kouros* (statue of an idealized youth) in Room 13 [f]; both are from the late sixth century BC. You need sharp eyes not to miss some of the less obvious delights. Behind the Croesus *kouros*, for instance, and quite untrumpeted, a statueless plinth is carved with reliefs showing, on one side, young men exercising in the gymnasium, on the other a group of amused friends setting a dog and cat to fight each other – a common enough sight in contemporary Greece.

Room 15, which heralds the **Classical art** collection, leaves you in rather less doubt as to its central focus. Right in the middle stands a mid-fifth-century BC *Statue of Poseidon* [g], dredged from the sea off Évvia in the 1920s. The god stands poised to throw his trident – weight on the front foot, athlete's body perfectly balanced, the model of idealized male beauty. A less dramatic, though no less important, piece in the same room is the *Eleusinian Relief* [h]. Highly deliberate in its composition, the relief shows the goddess of fertility, accompanied by her daughter Persephone, giving to mankind an ear of corn – symbol of the knowledge of agriculture.

Other major Classical sculptures include the *Little Jockey* (Room 21; [i]) seeming too small for his galloping horse, found in the same shipwreck as the *Poseidon*; the fourth-century BC bronze *Ephebe of Antikithira* [j]; the bronze head of a **boxer**, burly and battered, in Room 28; and the third-century BC bronze head of a *Philosopher*, with furrowed brow and unkempt hair, in Room 30. The most reproduced of all the sculptures is also in Room 30: a first-century AD statue of a naked and indulgent *Aphrodite* [k] about to rap Pan's knuckles for getting too fresh – a far cry (a long fall, some would say) from the reverent, idealizing portrayals of the gods in Classical times. Room 31 has an extraordinary bronze equestrian portrait statue of the Roman *Emperor Augustus*.

Too numerous to list, but offering fascinating glimpses of everyday life and changing styles of craftsmanship and perception of the human form, are the many **stelai** or carved gravestones found in several of the Classical rooms. Also worth a mention is Room 20, where various Roman copies of the lost Pheidias *Athena*, the original centrepiece of the Parthenon, are displayed.

Upstairs: the Thira rooms, pottery and coins

Keep a reserve of energy for the **Thíra rooms** upstairs. A visual knockout, these have been reconstructed as they were originally arranged, with their frescoes of monkeys, antelopes and flowers, and furnishings of painted wooden chairs and beds. Discovered at Akrotiri on the island of Thíra (Santórini), they date from around 1450 BC, contemporary with the flourishing Minoan civilization on Crete.

The other upper rooms are occupied by a dizzying array of **pottery**. Rooms 49 and 50 are devoted to the Geometric Period (1000–700 BC), 52 and 53 to sixth-century black-figured pottery, 54 to black- and red-figured pots, and 55 and 56 to funerary white urns and fourth-century pottery. Beautiful though many of the items are, there is absolutely nothing in the way of explanation, and this is probably the section to omit if you are running short of time or stamina.

In the south wing of the museum, entered from the first floor, is the extensive **Numismatic Collection**. This takes in over 400,000 coins, from Mycenaean times (with the Homeric double-axe motif) to Macedonian. At the time of writing this section was closed.

Exárkhia and back towards Sýndagma

Exárkhia, fifty-odd blocks squeezed between the National Archeological Museum and Stréfi hill, is perhaps the city's liveliest and most enjoyable night-time destination. Since the early 1980s it has become home to a concentration of ouzerí, nightclubs and genuine music tavernas, many relocated from the Pláka; student budgets confronting bistro prices results in the nursing of a single drink all evening.

In the early 1990s, the area was linked – in the press at least – with Athens' disaffected youth, and became synonymous with the so-called anarchists who frightened the sedate and respectable by staving in car windscreens, splattering walls with black graffiti and drug-dealing. Since then, Exárkhia has been resolutely cleaned up and gentrified, and the reality is not so extreme as Athenians – who like their city pretty savoury – would lead you to believe.

Back towards Sýndagma

Between the counter-culturality of Exárkhia and the occasional frowsiness of the bazaar, the broad busy avenues of Stadhíou, Panepistimíou and Akadhimías are lined with mainstream retailers, usually tucked into cavernous, occasionally opulent arcades that would have gained the approval of the original Bavarian planners.

Except for the blue city buses peeling off behind on Akadhimías and the metro works along Panepistimíou, the grounds of the Neoclassical **National Library** and **University** buildings, bang in the middle of all this, are an oasis of calm. The scattered buildings, designed by the Dane, Christian Hansen, deserve a look, since their garish decoration gives an alarming impression of what the Classical monuments might have looked like when their paintwork was intact. Also worth a stop if you've time are two minor but quite enjoyable museums, devoted to the city's and nation's history.

The first of these, on Platía Kolokotróni, housed the parliament from 1874 until 1935, but since 1961 has been home to the **National Historical Museum** (Tues–Sun 9am–1.30pm; 500dr). Its exhibits are predominantly Byzantine and medieval, though there is also a strong section on the War of Independence that includes Byron's sword and helmet.

The other, the **City of Athens Museum** (Mon, Wed, Fri & Sat 9am–1.30pm; 400dr) is at Paparigopoúlou 7, on Platía Klafthmónos, *D3*. This was the residence of the German-born King Otho in the 1830s before the new palace (now the Parliament, on Sýndagma) was completed in 1842. Exhibits – mainly prints, and still somewhat sparse – feature an interesting model of the city as it was in 1842, with just three hundred houses.

Sýndagma, the National Gardens and south

All roads lead to Platía Sindágmatos – **Sýndagma** (Syntagma) square – so you'll find yourself there sooner or later. Catering to tourism, with the a post office (extended hours), American Express, airline and travel offices grouped around – not to mention *McDonalds, Arby's Roast Beef* and *Wendy's* – it has convenience but not much else to recommend it.

The square

Most of the square's buildings are modern and characterless, except on the uphill (east) side where the **Voulí**, the Greek National Parliament, presides. This was built as the royal palace for Greece's first monarch, the Bavarian King Otho, who moved in in 1842. In front of it, goose-stepping **Evzónes** in tasselled caps, kilt and woolly leggings – a prettified version of traditional mountain costume – change their guard at intervals in front of the **Tomb of the Unknown Soldier**, to the rhythm of camera shutters. Hemingway, among others, impugned their masculinity but they are in fact a highly trained elite corps with rigorous height and weight requirements; formerly they were recruited almost exclusively from mountain villages.

Other flanking buildings to have survived postwar development include the vast **Hotel Grande Bretagne** – Athens' grandest. In the course of one of the more nefarious episodes of British meddling in Greek affairs, it nearly became the tomb of Winston Churchill. He had arrived on Christmas Day 1944 to sort out the *Dhekemvrianá*, the "events of December", a month of serious street-fighting between British forces and the Communist-led ELAS resistance movement, whom the British were trying to disarm. ELAS saboteurs had placed an enormous explosive charge in the drains, intending to blow up various Greek and Allied VIPs; according to whom you believe, it was either discovered in time by a kitchen employee, or removed by ELAS themselves when they realized they might get Churchill as well.

"Sýndagma" means "constitution" and the name derives from the fact that Greece's first one was proclaimed by a reluctant King Otho from a palace balcony in 1843. The square is still the principal venue for mass **demonstrations**, whether trade-union protests against government austerity programmes or "drive-in" sabotage by taxi drivers outraged at proposals to curtail their movements in the interest of cleaner air. In the run-up to elections, the major political parties stage their final campaign rallies here – a pretty intimidating sight, with around 100,000 singing, flag-waving Greeks packed into the square. At such times, overground city transport in the area comes to a halt.

The National Gardens

At the back of the Voulí, the **National Gardens** (sunrise to sunset; free) are the most refreshing acres in the whole city – not so much a flower garden as a luxuriant tangle of trees, whose shade and duck ponds provide palpable relief from the heat and smog of summer. They were originally the private palace gardens – a pet project of Queen Amalia in the 1840s; purportedly the main duty of the minuscule Greek navy in its early days was the fetching of rare plants, often the gifts of other royal houses, from remote corners of the globe.

Of late, however, the gardens have fallen on hard times: pond-cleaning and pruning are done only when funding permits, a botanical museum is closed more often than not, and a sorry excuse for a mini-zoo has become the target of criticism by environmental and animal-welfare groups. To add insult to injury, the metro project has requisitioned a large area of the gardens for air vents and site bungalows. The general air of dereliction is reinforced by the numerous cats abandoned here and fed only intermittently. Nonetheless, there are few better places in the city to read or wait for an evening ferry or plane.

The southern extension of the gardens, open 24 hours, consists of the graceful crescent-shaped grounds of the **Záppio**. This grand Neoclassical exhibition hall, another creation of the Danish architect Hansen (he of the University), was for a period the Greek State Radio headquarters but is now used mainly for press conferences and commercial exhibitions. A well shaded **café**, the *Kipos*, is up at the east (uphill) exit of the park on to Iródhou Attikoú (see "Eating and drinking", p.109, for more on these).

Iródhou Attikoú also fronts the **Presidential Palace**, the royal residence until Constantine's exile 1967, where more *evzónes* stand sentry duty. The surrounding streets, with a full complement of foreign embassies and hardly a store or taverna, are very posh and heavily policed. The centre-right party, *Néa Dhimokratía*, has its headquarters in Odhós Rigílis nearby, as does the army's Officers' Club, scene of much antidemocratic intriguing in the past.

The Olympic Stadium

A walk to the base of Iródhou Attikoú and across busy Leofóros Ardhittoú will bring you to the **Olympic Stadium**, a nineteenth-century reconstruction on Roman foundations, slotting tightly between the pine-covered spurs of Ardhittós hill; access is via the gate on Arhimídhous.

This site was originally marked out in the fourth century BC for the Panathenaic athletic contests, but in Roman times, as a grand gesture to mark the reign of the Emperor Hadrian, it was adapted for an orgy of blood sports, with thousands of wild beasts baited and slaughtered in the arena. Herodes Atticus (see p.94) later undertook to refurbish the 60,000 seats of the entire stadium; his white marble gift was to provide the city with a convenient quarry through the ensuing seventeen centuries.

The stadium's reconstruction dates from the modern revival of the Olympic Games in 1896 and to the efforts of another wealthy benefactor, the Alexandrian Greek Yiorgos Averoff. Its appearance – pristine whiteness and meticulous symmetry – must be very much as it was when first restored and reopened under the Roman senator, and indeed it's still used by local athletes. Above the stadium to the south, on the secluded **Hill of Ardhittós**, are a few scant remnants of a Temple of Fortune, again constructed by Herodes Atticus.

Méts and Pangráti

South and east of Ardhittós are the only two central neighbourhoods outside Pláka to have retained something of their traditional flavour – **Méts** and **Pangráti**. Particularly in Méts, a steep hillside quarter on the southwest side of the stadium, there are still nearly intact streets of pre-World War II houses, with tiled roofs, shuttered windows, and courtyards with spiral metal staircases and potted plants. They're a sad reminder of how beautiful this out-of-control city once was, even quite recently.

Méts and the Próto Nekrotafío

More specific attractions in **Méts** are the concentration of tavernas and bars around Márkou Moussoúrou and Arhimídhous (see p.113), and the Próto Nekrotafío (First Cemetery), at the top end of Anapáfseos (Eternal Rest) street, itself lined with shops catering to the funerary trade.

The **Próto Nekrotafío** shelters just about everybody who was anybody in twentieth-century Greek public life: the humbler tombs of singers, artists and writers are interspersed with ornate mausolea of soldiers, statesmen and "good" families, whose descendants come to picnic, stroll and tend the graves. One of the "unregarded wonders of Athenian life", Peter Levi called it: "the neoclassical marbles run riot, they reflower as rococo, they burst into sunblasts of baroque". The graveside statuary occasionally attains the status of high art, most notably in the works of Ianoulis Khalepas, a Belle Epoque sculptor from Tínos generally acknowledged to be the greatest of a school of fellow-islanders. Khalepas battled with mental illness for most of his life and died in extreme poverty in 1943; his masterpiece is the idealized **Kimiméni** (Sleeping Girl), on the right about 300 metres in.

Pangráti

Pangráti is the unremarkable but pleasant quarter to the north and east of the Stadium. Platía Plastíra, Platía Varnáva and Platía Pangratíou are the focal points, the first with a vast old-fashioned kafenío where you can sit for hours on a leafy terrace for the price of a coffee. Pangratíou, fringed by the local *álsos* or grove-park, is the rallying place for the neighbourhood's youthful posers. Several good tavernas are tucked away between (and on) Platía Varnáva and nearby Odhós Arkhimídhous, and the latter has an impressive *laikí agorá* – **street market** – every Friday.

More Pangráti eating places are down towards Leofóros Vas. Konstandínou, among the rather claustrophobic alleys opposite the **statue of Harry Truman** – repeatedly restored to his pedestal after being blown off it by leftists in reprisal for his bringing the US into the Greek civil war. The Nobel-laureate poet **George Seferis** lived not far away in Odhós Ágras, an attractive stair-street flanking the northeast wall of the Olympic Stadium.

North of Sýndagma: Kolonáki, Lykavitós and the Benáki and Cycladic Art museums

Athens is at its trendiest north of Sýndagma, and if you have money to spend, **Kolonáki** is the place to do it, catering to every Western taste from fast food to high fashion. The quarter is not especially interesting for visitors to the city – though it's a fond haunt of expatriates – but it does give access to **Lykavitós hill**, where a funicular hauls you up for some of the best views of the city. Also close by are two fine museums: one devoted to **Cycladic Art**, the other, the **Benáki**, an assembly of just about all things Greek, from Mycenaean artefacts to twentieth-century memorabilia. Here too, what is believed to be the fourth-century BC foundations of **Aristotle's Lyceum** were recently unearthed, during routine excavation work for a new Museum of Modern Art. The discovery of the Lyceum, where Aristotle taught for thirteen years and Socrates was a frequent visitor, is of immense importance to scholars.

Kolonáki

Kolonáki is the city's most chic central address and shopping area. Although no great shakes architecturally, it enjoys a superb site on the southwest-facing slopes of Lykavitós (Lycabettus), looking out over the Acropolis and National Gardens. From its summit, on one of those increasingly rare clear days, you can see the mountains of the Peloponnese. The lower limits of Kolonáki are defined by Akadhimías and Vassilísis Sofías streets, where in grand Neoclassical palaces Egypt, France and Italy have their embassies. The middle stretches of the quarter are for shopping, while the highest are purely residential.

The heart of the district is officially called Platía Filikís Eterías, but is known to all as **Kolonáki square**, after the ancient "little column" that hides in the trees on the southwest side. Other diversions include the kiosks with their stocks of foreign papers and magazines, the **British Council** on the downhill side, and numerous cafés on Patriárkhou Ioakím to the east – the principal display ground for Kolonáki's well-heeled natives. Assorted cafés and pubs nearby on pedestrianized Tsakálof, Milióni and Valaorítou are better and slightly cheaper options for snacks and drinks.

Kolonáki's streets also contain an amazing density of small, classy **shops**, with the accent firmly on **fashion** and **design**. In a half-hour walk around the neighbourhood you can view the whole gamut of consumer style. Patriárkhou Ioakím and Skoufá, with its cross-streets to the northwest, comprise the most promising area, along with the pedestrianized Voukourestíou-Valaorítou-Kriezótou block, just below Akadhimías.

For more random strolling, the highest tiers of Kolonáki are pleasant, with steep streets ending in long flights of steps, planted with oleander, jasmine and other flowering shrubs. The one **café** spot up here is at **Platía Dhexamenís**, a small and attractive square close to the Lykavitós loop road, where in summertime tables are set under the trees around the **Dhexamení**, a covered reservoir begun by the Emperor Hadrian.

Lykavitós

Not far away from Kolonáki square, at the top of Ploutárkhou, a **funicular** (Mon–Wed & Fri–Sun 8.45am–12.40am, Thurs 10.30am–12.40am, every 10min in summer, less frequent the rest of the year; 500dr) begins its ascent to the summit of **Lykavitós hill**. For the more energetic, the principal path up the hill begins by the bus stop across from the St George Lycabettus Hotel above Platía Dhexamenís and rambles through woods to the top. There's a small café half way up eyeball-to-eyeball with the Acropolis. On the summit, the chapel of **Áyios Yeóryios** dominates – a spectacular place to celebrate the saint's name-day if you're around on April 23. An expensive restaurant commands the adjacent terrace facing the Acropolis and the sea. The restaurant also operates a café on the terrace facing inland.

The road up the hill goes to the open-air **Lykavitós Theatre**, used primarily as a music venue during the Athens Summer Festival (see p.119). If you come down by the southeast slopes, you emerge near the lovely little enclave that the British and American archeological schools have created for themselves on Odhós Souidhías. Here, too, is the **Yennádhion Library**, with large collections of books on Greece and an unpublicized drawerfull of Edward Lear's watercolour sketches; good-quality and reasonably priced reproductions are on sale.

The Benáki Museum

Once it re-opens (scheduled for 1998), this overlooked **museum** at Koumbári 1/cnr Vassilísis Sofías (*D4*), should not be missed. Housing a private collection given to the state by **Emmanuel Benaki**, a collector who had grown wealthy on the Nile cotton trade, it is constantly surprising and fascinating, with exhibits ranging from Mycenaean jewellery, Greek costumes and folk artefacts to Byronia, and memorabilia of the Greek War of Independence – even a reconstructed Egyptian palace reception hall. These, together with displays of jewellery and other items from the Hélène Stathatos collection (of National Archeological Museum fame) are worth an hour or two of anyone's time.

Among the more unusual exhibits are collections of early Greek Gospels, liturgical vestments and church ornaments rescued by Greek refugees from Asia Minor in 1922; dazzling embroideries and body ornaments; and some unique historical material – on the Cretan statesman Eleftherios Venizelos, Asia Minor and the Cretan Revolution.

An additional attraction, especially if you've been dodging traffic all day, is the **rooftop café**, with good snacks and views over the nearby National Gardens. A **shop**, by the entrance, stocks a fine selection of books on Greek folk art, records of regional music and some of the best posters and postcards in the city. The nineteenth-century **Stathatos House** now functions as a wing of the museum, containing the Greek art collection of the Academy of Athens.

Goulandris Museum of Cycladic and Ancient Greek Art

For display, labelling, explanation and comfort, the small private **Goulandris Museum of Cycladic and Ancient Greek Art** (Mon, Wed–Fri 10am–4pm, Sat 10am–3pm; 600dr, free Sat) at Neofýtou Dhouká 4 (*D4*), is way ahead of anything else in Athens. The collection includes objects from the Cycladic civilization (third millennium BC), pre-Minoan Bronze Age (second millennium BC) and the period from the fall of Mycenae to the beginning of historic times around 700 BC, plus a selection of Archaic, Classical and Hellenistic pottery; you learn far more about these periods than from the corresponding sections of the National Archeological Museum.

If Cycladic art seems an esoteric field, don't be put off. The distinctive marble bowls and folded-arm figurines with their sloping wedge heads are displayed in a way that highlights their supreme purity and simplicity, and elucidates their appeal to twentieth-century artists like Moore, Picasso and Brancusi. You can also see in the figurines the remote ancestry of the Archaic style that evolved into the great sculptures of the Classical period. The exact purpose of the mostly female effigies is unknown but, given their frequent discovery in grave-barrows, it has been variously surmised that they were spirit-world guides for the deceased, substitutes for the sacrifice of servants and attendants, or representations of the Earth Goddess in her role of reclaiming yet another of her children.

Much of the top floor is devoted to a collection of painted Classical bowls, often showing two unrelated scenes on opposite sides. The curators consider the one with a depiction of revellers on one face and three men in cloaks conversing on the other to be the star exhibit, but there is not one dud. Most of the more exquisite items date from the fifth century BC – not for nothing was it referred to as a "Golden Age".

To round off the experience, there's a good **shop**, **snack bar** and shaded courtyard.

Other nearby museums

A number of other museums of somewhat more specialist interest are grouped conveniently close together near the angled intersection of Vassilísis Sofías and Vassiléos Konstandínou, close by the Benáki and Cycladic Art museums.

Byzantine Museum

The setting of the **Byzantine Museum** (Tues–Sun 8.30am–3pm; 500dr) at Vassilísis Sofías 22, *D5*, is perhaps its best feature: a peaceful, courtyarded villa that once belonged to the Duchesse de Plaisance, an extravagantly eccentric French philhellene and widow of a Napoleonic general who helped fund the War of Independence. To enjoy the exhibits – almost exclusively icons, housed in two restored side galleries – requires some prior interest, best developed by a trip to the churches at Mystra, Dhafní or Óssios Loukás. Labelling is generally Greek-only and you are told little of the development of styles, which towards the sixteenth century show an increasing post-Renaissance Italian influence, due to the presence of the Venetians in Greece. The rear hall contains marble artefacts, plus a reconstructed basilica. An annexe is currently under construction, which will hopefully mean better exposure for artefacts previously held in storage.

War Museum

The only "cultural" endowment of the 1967–74 junta, the **war museum** (Tues–Fri 9am–2pm, Sat & Sun, 9.30am–2pm; free) at Vassilísis Sofías 24 (*D5*) becomes predictably militaristic and right-wing as it approaches modern events: the Asia Minor campaign, the civil war, Greek forces in Korea, etc. Earlier times, however, are covered with a more scholarly concern and this gives an interesting insight into changes in warfare from Mycenae through to the Byzantines and Turks. Among an array of models is a fascinating series on the acropolises and castles of Greece, both Classical and medieval.

National Gallery of Art

The **National Gallery** (Mon & Wed–Fri 9am–3pm, Sun 10am–2pm; 500dr) at Vassiléos Konstandínou 50 (*E5*), has a rather disappointing core collection of Greek art from the sixteenth century to the present. One of the few modern painters to stand out is Nikos Hatzikyriakos-Ghikas (Ghika), who is well represented on the ground floor. On the mezzanine is a small group of canvases by the primitive painter Theophilos (more of whose work can be seen at the Museum of Greek Folk Art in Pláka – see p.92). Temporary exhibitions can be worth catching; keep an eye out for posters or check in *The Hellenic Times*.

The outskirts: Dhafní, Kessarianí and Kifissiá

Athens pushes its suburbs higher and wider with each year and the **monasteries of Dhafní** and **Kessarianí**, once well outside the city limits, are now approached through more or less continuous cityscape. However, each retains a definite countryside setting and makes for a good respite from the central sights.

The monasteries are easily reached by taxi or by local **city transport**. For Dhafní (9km west of the centre), take bus A16, B16 or Ã16 from Platía Elefthérias (*D1*); the monastery is to the left of the road, about twenty minutes' ride (Platía Elefthérias is popularly known as Platía Koumoundoúrou and the return buses are so marked). For Kessarianí, take blue bus #224 from Akadhimías (*D3/4*) to the last stop, from where the church is a thirty- to forty-minute climb up the lower slopes of Mount Imittós.

The northern suburb of **Kifissiá** is included in this section as an insight into wealthy Athenian life – it has long been where the rich have their villas – and for natural history students, who may want to check out the Goulandhrís Museum. Kifissiá is the most northerly stop on the metro.

Classical enthusiasts may want to continue from Dhafní to the site of **Eleusis** (see p.136), a further twenty-minute ride on the Ã16 bus route.

Dhafní

Dhafní Monastery (daily 8.30am–2.45pm; 500dr) is one of the great buildings of Byzantine architecture. Its classic Greek-cross-octagon design is a refinement of a plan first used at Óssios Loukás, on the road to Delphi (see p.253), and its mosaics are considered among the great masterpieces of the Middle Ages.

The monastic church replaced a fortified fifth-century basilica, which in turn had been adapted from the ruins of a sanctuary of Apollo – the name is derived from the *daphnai* (laurels) sacred to the god. Both the church and the fortifications which enclose it incorporate blocks from the ancient sanctuary; a porch featuring Classical columns was present up until two centuries ago, when it was hauled off among Lord Elgin's swag.

The Byzantines only occupied the building for little over a century. When the monastery was established, in 1070, the Greek Church was undergoing an intellectual revival, but the state was in terminal collapse. The following year the Normans took Bari, the last Byzantine possession in southern Italy, and the Seljuk Turks defeated the Byzantine army in Armenia – a prelude to the loss of Asia Minor and, before long, Greece itself. The fortifications and remains of a Gothic cloister show evidence of later building under the Cistercians, who replaced Dhafní's Orthodox monks after the Frankish conquest of Athens in 1204. The monastery today is unoccupied; the Cistercians were banished by the Turks, and Orthodox monks, allowed to return in the sixteenth century, were duly expelled for harbouring rebels during the War of Independence.

Inside the church, the **mosaic cycle** is remarkable for its completeness: there are scenes from the life of Christ and the Virgin, saints (a predominance of Eastern figures from Syria and elsewhere in the Levant), archangels and prophets. The greatest triumph is the *Pandokrátor* (Christ in Majesty) on the dome: lit by the sixteen windows of the drum, and set against a background of gold, this stern image directs a tremendous and piercing gaze, his finger poised on the Book of Judgement. A perfect encapsulation of the strict orthodoxy of Byzantine belief, the scene is rendered poignant by the troubled circumstances in which it was created.

Kessarianí

What it loses in a strict architectural comparison with Dhafní, **Kessarianí monastery** makes up for in its location. Although just five kilometres from the centre of the city, it is high enough up the slopes of Mount Imittós to escape the *néfos* and the noise. The sources of the river Ilissos provide for extensive gardens hereabouts, as they have since ancient times (Ovid mentions them); Athenians still come to collect water from the local fountains, though it may have become contaminated and should not be drunk.

The monastery buildings date from the eleventh century, though the frescoes in the chapel are much later – executed during the sixteenth and seventeenth centuries. In contrast to Dhafní's clerics, Kessarianí's abbot agreed to submit to Roman authority when the Franks took Athens, so the monastery remained in continuous Greek (if not quite Orthodox) occupation through the Middle Ages. Today the monastery maintains a small group of monks, who allow **visits** (Tues–Sun 8.30am–3pm; 800dr). Outside these hours you can while away the time in the well-maintained grounds, full of picnickers in summertime.

On the way up to the monastery, which is fairly obvious from the bus terminal, don't overlook the refugee neighbourhood of Kessarianí. With an attractively casual, ramshackle aspect, its streets were used as a 1920s location for the Greek movie *Rembetiko*.

Kifissiá

Kifissiá, Athens' most desirable suburb, edges up the leafy slopes of Mount Pendéli, about eight kilometres north of the city centre. A surprising 300m above sea level and a good 5°F cooler than central Athens, it appealed to the nineteenth-century bourgeoisie as a suitable site for summer residence. Their villas – Neoclassical, Swiss, Alsatian and fantasy-melange – still hold their own amid the newer concrete models.

Indeed, despite the encroachments of speculators' apartment buildings and trendy boutiques, the suburb's village-like character prevails.

The centre of the old "village" is the crossroads called Plátanos – though the mighty plane tree that gave it its name has long since fallen under the axe of the traffic planners – just at the uphill end of the gardens opposite the Kifissiá metro station. The hub is the two or three streets around Plátanos: *Varsos*, in the middle of the block up Kassaveti from Platía Platánou, an old-fashioned patisserie specializing in home-made yoghurts, jams and sticky cakes, acts as a meeting place for the whole neighbourhood.

If you want some direction to your wanderings around trees and gardens, head for the **Goulandris Natural History Museum** Sat & Sun 9am–2pm; 800dr) at Levídhou 13, fifteen minutes' walk from the metro. The collection has especially good coverage of Greek birds and butterflies and endangered species like the monk seal (*Monachus monachus*; see p.705) and sea turtle (*Caretta caretta*) and a 250,000-specimen herbarium. The museum has a café and a shop selling superb illustrated books, postcards, posters and prints.

Eating and drinking

As you'd expect in a city that houses almost half the Greek population, Athens has the best and the most varied **restaurants** and **tavernas** in the country – and most places are sources not just of good food but of a good night out.

Starting with **breakfast**, most Athenians survive on a thimbleful of coffee, but if you need a bit more to set you up for the day, you'll easily find a bakery, yoghurt shop or fruit stall. Veïkoú and Koukáki are particularly good for this, with the *Nestoras Tzatsos* bakery at Veïkoú 45, another at no. 75, and still another on pedestrianized Olimbíou, just off Platía Koukáki, offering excellent wholegrain bread and milk products. Alternatively, you could try one of the places listed under "Tea houses and patisseries" on p.114. For a regular **English breakfast**, there are several options in and around Pláka. The cheapest and friendliest place is at Níkis 26 (*E3*); a second choice is nearby at Apollonós 11; and a third is at Kydathinéon 10, near the corner of Moní Asteríou (*E3*).

Later in the day, a host of **snack** stalls and outlets get going. If your budget is low you can fill up at them exclusively, avoiding sit-down restaurants altogether. The standard **snacks** are *souvláki me píta* (kebab in pitta bread), *tyrópites* (cheese pies) and *spanakópites* (spinach pies), along with *bougátses* (cream pies) and a host of other speciality pastries. One of the best **souvláki** stands in Pláka is widely acknowledged to be *Kostas'*, at Adhrianoú 116 (*E3*), which usually has a queue. There is a *Bagel Café* at 9b Karayeóryi Servías, just below Sýndagma, while the *Aríston* around the corner at Voulís 10 has been famous for years for its good, inexpensive *tirópites*.

For **main meals**, Pláka's hills and lanes are full of character, and provide a pleasant evening setting, despite the aggressive touts and general tourist hype. But for good value and good quality, only a few of the quarter's restaurants and tavernas are these days worth a second glance. For quality Greek cooking, if you're staying any length of time in the city, it's better to strike out into the ring of **neighbourhoods** around: to Méts, Pangráti, Exárkhia/Neápoli, Veïkoú/Koukáki, Áno Petrálona, or the more upmarket Kolonáki. None of these is more than a half hour's walk, or a quicker trolley bus or taxi ride, from the centre – effort well repaid by more authentic menus, and often a livelier atmosphere.

Restaurants

The listings below are devoted mainly to **restaurant meals**, grouped according to district and divided into cheap (under 3500dr per person) and less so (over 3500dr). Note that some of our recommendations are closed in summer (usually in August), and for five days or so around Easter; this is usually due to hot, un-air-conditioned locales, or the exodus of their regular business trade. All grid listings refer to the map on pp.70–71.

Pláka

Selections here represent just about all of note that **Pláka** has to offer; most are on the periphery of the quarter, rather than on the more travelled squares and stairways. At the latter, don't be bamboozled by the touts, positioned at crucial locations to lure you over to their tavernas' tables – invariably a bad sign.

UNDER 3500DR

Damingos, Kidhathinéon 41, *F3*. Tucked away in the basement, this place has dour service, but is good value, with barrelled wine and excellent *bakaliáro skordhaliá* (cod with garlic sauce). Evenings only; closed midsummer.

Kouklis, Tripódhon 14, *F3*. Attractive split-level taverna which serves a good selection of mezédhes and good house red wines; it has a perennially popular summer terrace.

OVER 3500DR

Eden, Lissíou 12, off Mnesikléous, *E3*. The city's oldest vegetarian restaurant offers dishes you'll pine for on travels around Greece; the setting is pleasant as well, on the ground floor of an old house. Portions not huge but very tasty.

Iy Klimataria, Klepsídhras 5, *E/F2*. A hundred years old in 1998, this unpretentious and pleasant taverna has decent food, with live, unamplified music in the winter. In the summer the roof opens and the quiet shaded street becomes an oasis. There's a good combination bar and sweetshop just down the steps.

O Platanos, Dhioyénous 4, *E3*. One of the oldest tavernas in Pláka, with outdoor summer seating under the namesake tree. Serves lunch and supper. Closed Sun.

Monastiráki and the Bazaar

The shift from Pláka to the more genuinely commercial quarter of **Monastiráki** is refreshing, since the area attracts serious eaters. There is a definite character about the streets, too, at its best around the flea market.

UNDER 3500DR

Bairaktaris, Platía Monastirakioú 2, *E2*. Large old restaurant whose walls are lined with wine barrels. Straightforward menu. Daily 7am–3am.

To Monastiri, central meat market (entrance from Eolóu 80), *D2*. The best of the three restaurants here; the raw ingredients are certainly fresh, and there's *patsás* (tripe and trotter soup) if you're in need of a hangover cure. Daily 6am–10pm.

O Savvas, Mitropóleos 92, *E2*. *Souvláki* and kebab joint with a wide menu, outdoor seating under umbrellas and a rather touristy feel.

O Thanasis, Mitropóleos 69, *E2*. Reckoned to be the best *souvláki* and kebab place in this part of Athens. Always packed with locals at lunchtime.

Exárkhia/Platía Viktorías

Exárkhia is still surprisingly untrodden by tourists, considering its proximity to the centre. Its eating and drinking establishments are conveniently close to the National Archeological Museum and several recommended hotels, and exploring them gives some insight into how the student/youth/alternative crowd carries on.

UNDER 3500DR

Barba Yannis, Emmanuíl Benáki 94, Exárkhia, *C3*. Varied menu (changes daily) and good cooking in a relaxed atmosphere, aided and abetted by barrel wine. Tables outside in summer.

FOREIGN CUISINE RESTAURANTS

Healthy as it may be, you may tire of Greek food, especially during an extended visit. Unlike the rest of the country, Athens offers a fair selection, from highly chi-chi **French** places, through **Armenian** and **Arabic**, **Spanish** and **Balkan**, to **Japanese** and **Korean**. Listed below are some of the more central places, which don't require a large outlay in taxi fares to reach – others are to be found at the beach suburbs to the south. Eating in Athens is comparatively expensive: budget for 4000–6000dr per person.

Unless otherwise indicated, the places listed below are closed in summer and on Sunday, but stay open until 1.30am. Reservations are advisable.

ARMENIAN-TURKISH
Tria Asteria, Mélitos 7, Néa Smyrni, off map below *G3*, at end of #10 trolley line (☎93 58 134). Specialities include *tandir kebab* and *kionefe*, a special stuffed-filo dessert. Open in summer.

CHINESE
Dragon Palace, Andínoros 3, Pangráti, Off map past *E5* (☎72 42 795). Cantonese dishes such as Peking duck. Open in summer.
Golden Dragon, Olimbíou 27–29/Singroú 122, Koukáki, off map, below *G2/3* (☎92 32 316). A cut above average: ginger chicken, stuffed chicken wings, etc. Open in summer.
Golden Flower, Níkis 30, Sýndagma, *E3* (☎32 30 113). A regular work-a-day, and inexpensive Chinese restaurant. Open daily and in summer.

CZECH
Bohemia, Dhímou Tséliou, Ambelókipi, *A5* (☎64 26 341). Czech beers (of course); open in summer.
O Kalós Stratiótis Svejk, Roúmbesi 8a, Néos Kósmos, off map, below *G3* (☎90 18 389). Rich stew-like main courses, also duck and carp according to season. Closed Mon & Tues.

FRENCH
Prunier, Ipsilándou 63, Kolonáki, *D5* (☎72 27 379;). Central and unpretentious bistro.
Calvados, Alkmános 5, Ilísia, off map, just past *D5* (☎72 26 291). Norman cuisine.

GERMAN
Ritterburg, Formíonos 11, Pangráti, off map, past *E/F5* (☎72 38 421). Schnitzels, sausages and the like.

ITALIAN
Al Convento, Anapíron Polémou 4–6, Kolonáki, *C/D5*. (☎72 39 163). Claims to be the oldest Italian restaurant in Athens; the speciality is pasta and scallopine. Open in summer. Closed Sun.
Jimmy's Cooking, Loukianoú, Kolonáki, *D4/5* (☎72 47 283). Some more interesting main courses – not just the usual pasta variations. Closed Mon.

JAPANESE
Michiko, Kidathinéon 27, Pláka, *E3* (☎32 20 980). Touristy and expensive – but very central and surprisingly authentic. Open in summer.

KOREAN
Seoul, Evritanías 8, off Panórmou in Ambelókipi, off map beyond *A/B5* (☎69 24 669). Speciality Korean barbecue. Garden seating in summer.
Orient, Lékka 26, Sýndagma, *E3* (☎32 21 192). Also Chinese and Japanese dishes. Open in summer.

MEXICAN
Blue Velvet, Ermoú 116, Thisió, *E2* (☎32 39 047). Jazz and blues with your chilli on Friday and Sunday. Closed Mon.

SPANISH
Ispaniki Gonia, Theayénous 22, Pangráti, off map, past *E5* (☎72 31 393). Housed in an old mansion near the *Caravel Hotel*. Occasional live music. Open in summer.

Mainas, Kallidhromíou 27, Exárkhia, *C3*. Fine pizza and other main courses to eat in or take away.

Neapolis, Kallidhromíou 29, Exárkhia, *C3*. Another well-known old standby taverna with good standard fare at reasonable prices.

Ouzeri, Elpídhos 16, Platía Viktorías *B1*. Mostly seafood – a midtown rarity – and a few mezédhes with ouzo or barrel wine. Ungreasy, moderately pricey dishes for lunch and supper. Closed Sun.

Vangelis, Sakhíni, off Liossíon, *C1* (200m up from Platía Váthis), *C2*. Simply one of the friendliest and most traditional tavernas in the city. Oven casseroles and 1950s decor. Grilled food available in the evening. Open garden at the back.

OVER 3500DR

Greenery, Kodhringtónos 14, Exárkhia, *C2*. Vegetarian snack bar open for lunch and dinner. Closed Sun.

Kostoyiannis, Zaími 37, behind the National Archeological Museum, *C3*. One of the city's best restaurants – much frequented by crowds from the theatres and cinemas around. Quality mezédhes and delicacies like rabbit stew. Evenings only. Closed Sun.

Oasis, Valtetsíou 44, Exárkhia, *C3*. A wonderful taverna with seating in the garden, and a varied menu.

Rozalia, Valtetsíou 58, Exárkhia, *C3*. The best mezédhes-plus-grills taverna immediately around the platía, with highly palatable sparkling red wine and corny serenading musicians. You order from the proffered tray as the waiters thread their way through the throng. Suppers only. Garden in summer.

Neápoli

Neápoli is a long walk or short bus ride up Hariláou Trikoúpi from Exárkhia, with a concentration of calmer clubs, bars and cinemas that make it a favourite dining-out area for savvy locals. The food here is good, teetering to either side of the 3000dr divider. Mavromiháli is parallel to and one street higher up the slopes of **Lykavitós** from Hariloáu Trikoúpi.

Avthentikon, Armatólon Kléfton 20 (cnr Argyroupóleos), *B5*. Elegant and filling traditional Greek cooking, not cheap but usually packed – the most telling recommendation. Evenings only. Closed mid-summer.

Ta Bakiria, Mavromikháli 119, *C4*. Similar to *Iy Lefka* next door but marginally less expensive, and with a more imaginative menu. Atmospheric interior for wintertime and a summer garden. Closed Sun.

O Fondas, Arianítou 6, just off Mavromikháli, *C4*. Probably the most expensive of the four tavernas in this immediate area, but high-quality food.

Iy Lefka, Mavromikháli 121, *C4*. Standard taverna fare, with barrelled retsina. Summer seating in a huge garden enclosed by barrels.

O Pinaleon, Mavromikháli 152, *B4*. Rich mezédhes and meaty entrées, washed down with unresinated bulk wine and served up by a young couple from Khíos. Open Oct–mid-May.

Strefis Taverna tis Xanthis, Irínis Athinéas 5, *B3/4*. House specialities include rabbit stew and schnitzel. A pleasant old mansion with a roof garden that offers fine view across northern Athens. Mon–Sat; 9pm–2am.

Ta Tria Adhelfia, Leofóros Alexándhras 116, *B5*. Good, straightforward taverna food. Closed Sun & Aug.

Kolonáki

Kolonáki has a ritzy, upmarket reputation that puts off a lot of tourists. Nonetheless, among the boutiques are some surprising finds.

UNDER 3500DR

To Kioupi, Platía Kolonáki, *D4*. Subterranean taverna. Good standard Greek food. Closed Sun evening & Aug.

OVER 3500DR

Rodhia, Aristípou 44, near the base of the téléférique, *C5*. Elegant main courses. Open year round. Closed Sun.

Taverna Dhimokritos, Dhimokrítou 23, *D4*. A bit snooty, but a beautiful building and well prepared food from a vast menu. Open lunchtime and evenings. Closed late summer and Sundays.

Pangráti and Méts

These two neighbourhoods feature many of the city's best eating places. All the places below are a short (if generally uphill) walk across busy Ardhitoú and past the Olympic stadium, or accessible via a #4 trolley ride to Platía Plastíra. **Goúva** is an extension of Méts, just south of the First Cemetery.

UNDER 3500DR

O Ilias, cnr Stasínou/Telesílis, Pangráti, *E5*. A very good and very popular taverna. Evenings only. Tables outside in summer.

O Megaritis, Ferekídhou 2, Pangráti, *F5*. Casserole food, barrel wine, indoor/pavement seating. Open all year.

Prasino, John Kennedy 23 (cnr Vrioúlon), Pangráti, off map beyond *F5*. Caters to refugee clientele with Anatolian-style food, including brains. Tables out on pavement in summer. Closed Mon.

To Kalyvi, Empedhokléous 26, off Platía Varnáva, Pangráti, *F5*. Excellent, traditional mezédhes-type fare. Rustic decor. Closed late May–late Sept.

Vellis, Platía Varnáva/cnr Stilpónos, Pangráti *F5*. Limited choice, but a very characterful little place at the west end of the square. One of the last of a dying breed of tradesmen's wine-with-food shops. Evenings only. Indoor and outdoor seating.

OVER 3500DR

Karavitis, Arktínou 35, off Leofóros Vas. Konstandínou, Pangráti *F5*. Old-style taverna with bulk wine, mezédhes and clay-cooked main courses. Indoor and outdoor seating.

Manesis, Márkou Moussoúrou 3, Pangráti *F4*. Egyptian co-management reflected in such mezédhes as humous, tabbouli and falafel; the red house wine is excellent. Long list of daily specials. Pricey but worth it. Tables in walled garden in summer. Evenings only. Closed Sun.

O Vyrinis, Arkhimídhous 11 (off Platía Plastíra), Pangráti *F5*. Good-quality, regular-priced taverna, with its own house wine and a wide variety of mezédhes. Tables in garden in summer.

Pergoulia, Márkou Moussoúrou 16, Pangráti *F4*. Delicious, unusual mezédhes – order seven or eight and you'll have a fair-sized bill but a big meal. Closed May–Oct.

To Strateri, Platía Plíta 3, Goúva, off map below *G5*. A good, slightly upmarket psistariá. Outdoor seating in the park in summer.

Veïkoú/Koukáki

This is one of the most pleasant parts of the city in which to while away the middle of a day or round off an evening, having wandered down from the south slope of the Acropolis or Filopáppou hill. It's very much middle-class, residential Athens – uneventful and a bit early-to-bed. The districts straddle the #1, #5 and #9 trolley lines.

UNDER 3500DR

Iy Gardhinia, Zínni 29, Koukáki, *G3*. Extremely basic, inexpensive casserole food and barrel wine in a cool, cavernous setting. Lunchtime only in summer.

Ouzeri Evvia, G. Olymbíou 8, Koukáki, off map below *G2*. Hearty food as well as drink served on the pedestrian way, very reasonable and informal.

Ouzedhiko To Meltemi, Zínni 26, Koukáki, *G2/G3*. A modest-priced ouzerí that shields its customers from street traffic with banks of greenery. Offers a wide range of mezédhes dishes, but the emphasis is on seafood. Closed Sun.

O Yeros tou Morea, Arváli 4, Koukáki, *G2*. Best for lunch when the oven food and mezédhes are fresh. Full of Koukáki bachelors of all ages, who can eat here more cheaply than at home, and indulge in the bulk wine from the barrels that form the main decor. Closed Sun.

To Ikositeseroöro, Syngroú 42/44, Veïkoú, *C3*. The name means "open round-the-clock", and that's its main virtue. Fair, if rather overpriced, portions of anti-hangover food such as lamb tongues and *patsás*. At its liveliest after midnight in summer.

To Triandaokto (38), Veïkoú 38, Veïkoú, *G3*. This taverna offers large portions of simple, well-prepared food but has a limited menu. Wonderful Neméa red and Attica white wine from the barrel. Evenings only. Closed June–Aug.

OVER 3500DR

Socrates' Prison, Mitsaíon 20 (below Herodes Atticus theatre) Koukáki, *F3*. Long a justifiably popular taverna, with sidewalk tables. Closed Sun and 20 days in Aug.

Áno Petrálona

Áno Petrálona, old refugee neighbourhood on the west flank of Filopáppou Hill, is the least touristy district of central Athens. Just why is a mystery: the range of tavernas is excellent, the #9 trolley bus appears regularly, and it's a natural choice for eating after an evening at the Dora Stratou folk-dance theatre. There's a trolley stop on the Platía Amalías Merkoúri, from where the main artery of Dhimifóndos is a short stroll northwest. All of the places listed below are off our map beyond *G1*.

UNDER 3500DR

Iy Avli tou Pikiliou, Dhimifóndos 116. Despite the name (which means "Variety Courtyard"), this is a limited-menu cheap taverna with a garden.

Ikonomou (no sign displayed), cnr Tróön/Kidhandídhon. Basic home cooking served to packed pavement tables in summer.

To Koutouki, Lakíou 9. Inexpensive traditional taverna. Roof seating looks on Filopáppou Hill. Mon–Sat 8.30pm–2am.

To Monastiri, Dhimifóndos 46. Very popular, moderately priced neighbourhood place. Occasional guitar music on an informal basis after 11.30pm.

OVER 3500DR

Kharis, cnr Tróön/Kidhandídhon. Newer and smarter rival to *Ikonómou* across the way, long and interesting menu. Evenings only. Closed Aug.

T'Askimopapo, Iónon 61. A wonderful winter taverna with unusual dishes. Closed Sun and all summer.

Tea houses and patisseries

With a couple of honourable exceptions, **tea houses** and continental-style **patisseries** are a recent phenomenon in Athens. Quiet, rather consciously sophisticated places, they're essentially a reaction against the traditional and basic kafenía. Most are concentrated around the Pláka and in Kolonáki and the more upmarket suburbs. The pedestrianized streets of Milióni and Valaorítou in Kolonaki, *D4*, in particular, seem to be one uninterrupted pavement café.

De Profundis, Angelikís Hatzimihális 1, Pláka, *E3*. A trendy-looking tea house but reasonably priced: herb teas, quiches, small main courses, pastries. Mon–Fri 5pm–2am; Sat & Sun noon–2am; closed Aug.

Floca, Stóa Athinás between Panepistimíou and Koraï, *D3*. The longest-established Athenian café-patisserie – and still the best. Their *chocalatina* (cream chocolate cake) is unrivalled. City-centre branches at Leofóros Kifisías 118, Ambelókipi (off map), cnr Panepistimíou/Voukourestíou (in the arcade), *D3*, and just south of junction Veïkoú/Dhimitrakopoúlou, Veïkoú, *F3*.

Gelateria Firenze, Dhimitrakopoúlou 42, cnr Dhrákou, Veïkoú, *G3*. Athens' most extensive range of rich and wonderful Italian *gelati* – not exorbitant for the quality. Seating indoors and out.

Galaktopolio Iy Amalthea, Tripódhou 16, Pláka, *F3*. Tasteful if pricey, serving mostly crepes as well as non-alcoholic drinks.

Kipos (no sign), east gate of the National Gardens, just south of cnr Iródhou Attikoú/V. Sofías, *E4*. Overpriced ice cream, hot and cold drinks in a shaded locale.

La Chocolatiere, Skoufá, Kolonáki, *D4*. Exquisite chocolates and cakes; also light snacks, shakes and drinks, served under trees on the platía opposite. A good place to come for a present if you're invited to a Greek's name day.

La Tasse, Milióni 8, Kolonáki, *D4*. One of the most popular of the establishments on this pedestrianized lane, just north of Kolonáki square.

Oasis, west side of National Gardens, opposite cnr of Amalís and Filellínon *E4*. A unexpected haven just off the main avenue, offering ice cream and snacks in the shade.

Strofes, Akarnanís 10, Ambelókipi, off map past *A5*. Claims to serve sixty varieties of tea.

To Tristrato, cnr Dedhálou/Angélou Yéronda, Pláka, *F3*. Coffee, fruit juices, and salads, eggs, desserts, cakes. Comfortable but expensive. Daily 2pm–midnight.

Zonar's, Panepistimíou 9, *D3*. *Floca's* equally traditional rival – still much as it was described, as a haunt of Harriet and Guy Pringle and Yakimov, in Olivia Manning's *Fortunes of War*.

Ouzerí and bars

Ouzerí – also called *ouzédhika* or *mezedhopolía* – are essentially bars selling oúzo, beer and wine (occasionally just oúzo), along with mezédhes (hors d'oeuvres) to reduce the impact. A special treat, is a *pikilía* (usually 1500–2000dr), a selection of all the mezédhes available; this will probably include fried shrimp, pieces of squid, cheese, olives, tongue, cheese pies, sausage and other delicacies. Ordinarily, you should allow about 6000dr for two, with drinks. The food, while good, is on an equal footing with the drink – as in a Spanish *tapas* bar – and you never need reservations.

The listings in this section also include more Western-style – and more expensive – **bars**, which serve cocktails and the suchlike. All the places included here put their drinks on at least equal footing with their snacks; certain *ouzédhika* that put more emphasis on the food side of things are listed in the main restaurant section above.

Athinaikon, Themistokléous 2, cnr Panepistimíou, *D3*. An old ouzerí in a new location, but retaining its style – marble tables, old posters, etc. Variety of good-sized mezédhes, such as shrimp croquettes and mussels in cheese sauce. Closed Sun.

Balthazar, Vournázou 14/Tsókha 27, Ambelókipi, off map past *B5*. An "in" brasserie (the bar part is more fun) installed amid the palm-tree gardens and on the ground floor of a palatial old mansion. A long list of cocktails, plus snacks and main courses.

Dhexameni, Platía Dhexamenís, Kolonáki, *D4*. Café-ouzerí that serves drinks and snacks in summer under the trees. Shaded and moderately expensive.

Epistrofi Stin Ithaki, cnr Kolléti and Benáki, Exárkhia, *C3*. Featuring Santorini wine, this is just one of more than a dozen along Emmanuíl Benáki and its cross streets. Closed Sun.

Neon, Mitropóleos 3, *E3*. Glitzy bistro on two levels that's worth a drink (alcoholic or otherwise) just for the setting. With moderately pricey food, this is the new location of the famous original *Neon* at Omónia. Open long hours.

Salamandra, Mantzárou 3, Kolonáki, *D4*. Moderately expensive mezédhes bar, with a wide-ranging menu, in a restored Neoclassical house on a pedestrian street. Open lunchtimes and evenings; closed Sun.

Music and nightlife

Traditional **Greek music** – *rembétika* and *dhimotiká* – can, at its best, provide the city's most compelling night-time entertainment. To partake, however, you really need to visit during the winter months; from around May to October most clubs and *boîtes* close

---

LISTINGS INFORMATION

The **listings** and recommendations in this section are up-to-date at the time of going to press, but obviously venues change fast and often. Useful additional sources of information include the English-language daily *Athens News*, whose Friday edition has a complete events programme for the weekend, and the Greek-language *Athinórama* (every Thursday), the single most reliable source, with screening times for all films. The weekly *Hellenic Times* has good coverage of forthcoming art exhibitions and events, including the summer Athens Festival.

---

their doors, while the musicians head off to tour the countryside and islands. Most of the places that remain open are a tourist travesty of over-amplified and overpriced *bouzouki* noise – at their nadir, not surprisingly, in the Pláka.

As for other forms of live music, there are small, indigenous **jazz** and **rock** scenes, perennially strapped for funds and venues but worth checking out. **Classical** music performances tend to form the core of the summer Athens Festival, but with the completion in 1991 of the city's concert hall out on Vassilísis Sofías there's now a long-running winter season as well. **Discos** and **music bars** are very much in the European mould. The clubs in the city tend to close during the summer, unless they have roof terraces; Athenian youth, meanwhile, move out to a series of huge hangar-like disco-palaces in the coastal suburbs.

For **information** and knowledgeable advice on all kinds of Athens music – traditional, rock and jazz – look in at the **record shops** Philodisc, Emmanuel Benáki 9, Exárkhia, *C3*; Melody House, Mitropóleos 88, Monastiráki, *E2*; or Music Corner, Panepistimíou 36, *D3*. All of these generally display posters for the more interesting events and have tickets on sale for rock, jazz or festival concerts.

Traditional music

For an introduction to Greek **traditional** and **folk music** see Contexts, p.809. In Athens, the various styles can coexist or be heard on alternate evenings at a number of music clubs or *boîtes*. There are purely traditional music venues (such as *To Armenaki*, especially for island music from the Cyclades and Crete), where people go to dance, or to celebrate weddings and other occasions. Most gigs start pretty late – there's little point in arriving much before 10.30pm – and continue until 3 or 4am. After midnight (and a few drinks) people tend to loosen up and start dancing; at around 1am there's generally an interval, when patrons may move to other clubs down the street or across town. Prices tend to be pretty stiff, with expensive drinks (and sometimes food), plus an admission fee or a minimum consumption per set.

Rembétika

For anyone with an interest in folk sounds, **rembétika**, the old drugs-and-outcast music brought over by Asia Minor Greeks, is worth catching live. The form was revived in the late 1970s and, though the fad has waned, there are still good sounds to be heard. If possible, phone to make a reservation and check who's playing.

EXÁRKHIA/PLÁKA/BAZAAR
Boemissa, Solomoú 19, Exárkhia, *C3* (☎36 43 836). *Rembétika*, old folk songs, and music from the Cyclades – the most popular with Greeks, irrespective of their place of origin. Drinks 1000dr. Closed Mon.

Iy Palia Markiza, Próklou 41, Pangráti, *F5*. (☎75 25 074). Claims to offer *rembétika* "as you would have heard it in Smyrna and Pireás". Housed in a fine old turn-of-the-century building above Platía

Varnáva. Open Wed–Sun 11pm–5am, and occasionally 3.30–8pm; afternoon sessions are cheaper, otherwise count on 3000dr per person.

Nikhtes Mayikes, Vouliagaménis 85, Glifádha, off map (☎94 47 600). Plays host to some of the big names. Drinks at the bar 2000dr; menu 7000dr; whisky 22,000dr per bottle.

Reportaz, cnr Athanasíou Dhiákou and Syngroú, Veïkoú, *F3* (☎92 32 114). Owned by the chief editor of a Sunday newspaper, this joint is popular with journalists. Good singing and fine folk atmosphere. Drinks 1000dr.

Stoa Athanaton, Sofokléous 19 (in the old meat market), *D2* (☎32 14 362). Fronted by bouzouki veterans Hondronákos and Koúlis Skarpélis. Good taverna food; 2000dr minimum. Open 3–6pm and midnight–6am. Closed Sun.

Taximi, Isávron 29, off Kharláou Trikoúpi, Exárkhia, *C3* (☎36 39 919). Crowded salon on third floor of a Neoclassical building; no food, no cover, but reckon on 3000dr for drinks. Closed Sun, also July & Aug.

FURTHER AFIELD

Kendro Dhaskalakis, Leofóros Marathónos (☎66 77 255). Out-of-town taverna run by veteran *bouzouki* star Michalis Daskalakis. Open Wed–Sat.

Marabou, Panórmou 113, near Leofóros Alexándhras in Ambelókipi (look for a sign with a toucan), off the map past *B5*. One of the first *rembétika* revival clubs, and still one of the most popular – mobbed at weekends. For four nights of the week the music is taped, but on Friday and Saturday they feature *laterna* (hurdy-gurdy). Expensive food and drink, at around 3000–4000dr a head. No reservations. Open year-round.

To Palio Mas Spiti, Odhemissíou 9, Kessarianí (☎72 14 934), off map past *F5*. Arguably the best and most genuine of all the surviving clubs – a real neighbourhood place with decent food, reasonable drinks, no minimum charge and no amplification. The part-owner, Girogos Tzortzis, plays *baglama*, alongside a *bouzouki*-ist, guitarist and singer; excellent house band album on sale. Closed Sun and in summer.

Dhimotiká (folk) music

There's a real mix of styles at these clubs – everything from Zorba-like Cretan *santoúri* music to wailing clarinet from the mountains of Epirus, from ballroom dancing to lyrical ballads from Asia Minor. Venues are scattered throughout the city and are rather pricier than their *rembétika* equivalents; reservations are advisable.

Elatos, Trítis Septemvríou 16, nr Omónia Square, *C2* (☎52 34 262). An eclectic assortment of *dhimotiká*. Closed Wed.

Kriti, Ayíou Thomá 8, Ambelókipi, off map past *D5* (☎77 58 258). Specializes in Cretan music. Closed Mon.

To Armenaki, Patriárkhou Ioakím 1, short taxi ride from Venizélou/Távros metro station, off map past *G1* (☎34 74 716). Island music, with the classic singer Irini Konitopoulou-Legaki often putting in an appearance. Closed Mon & Tues.

Jazz and Latin

Jazz has a rather small following in Greece, but the main club, *Half-Note*, has a pleasant environment and usually good musicians. The major events take place as part of the **Bic Jazz and Blues Festival** at the end of June; information and tickets are available from the Athens Festival box office (see p.119) and select record stores. Semi-permanent venues include:

The French Quarter, Mavromikháli 78, Exárkhia, *C4*. Recorded jazz and blues only. Closed in summer.

Half-Note, Trivonianoú 17, Mets, Ambelókipi, off map beyond *A/B5* (☎64 49 236). Live jazz most nights, often provided by good musicians brought in from abroad, but closed Tuesday and for much of the summer.

La Joya, Tsókha 43, nr American Embassy, Ambelókipi, off map past *D5* (☎64 40 030). Great atmosphere. The live or taped rock, jazz and Latin accounts for of its considerable success – as does beautiful decor, adventurous food and its popularity as a venue for celebrity parties. Open until 2.30am.

Take Five, Patriárkhou Ioakím 37, Kolonáki, *D5* (☎72 40 736). Supper club with live bands. Reservations suggested. Closed Mon & Thurs.

Rock: live venues and music bars

The tiny indigenous Greek rock scene is beset by difficulties. Instruments are the most expensive in Europe, audiences the smallest, and the whole activity is still looked upon with some official disfavour. Clubs pop up and disappear like mushrooms, though there are a number of semi-permanent music bars, especially in Exárkhia (*C3*). Many of these host the occasional gig and generally have a dance floor of sorts.

Decadence, junction Poulherías/Voulgaroktónou, *B3/4*. Features indie/alternative sounds. Fairly expensive drinks.

Kittaro Retro Club, Ipírou 48, *C2*. Open Thurs–Sun; it features live bands.

Rodhon, Márni 24, Platía Váthys, *C2*. The city's most important venue for foreign and Greek rock, soul and reggae groups. Good atmosphere in a converted cinema. Closed in summer.

Stadhio, cnr Márkou Moussoúrou/Ardhittoú, Méts, *F4*. A high-tech, fashionable bar – extremely pricey, attracting rich, well-dressed young Greeks. However, there's good music, exorbitant cocktails and a terrace open to the stars and to views of the Acropolis.

Wild Rose, Panepistimíou 10 (basement), *D3*. House soundtrack for model types and wealthier students from the northern suburbs.

Discos and clubs

The music bars detailed above are probably the most enjoyable of downtown Athens's disco options. **Rave parties** do happen, with local and foreign DJs, but, as elsewhere, the business operates underground, so look out for posters or ask compulsive clubbers. Expect the unexpected at these clubs: most play recent hits, but don't be surprised if the music turns to Greek or belly-dancing music towards the end of the night. 1994 legislation compelled all clubs within Athens to shut at 2am, but it's hard to predict how long this will last. Although most Athenian clubs close during the summer, you can still find life in the fashionable clubs of Glyfádha (16km from Athens) and Kalamáki (18km), out past the airport along the east coast of Attica, where Athens youth congregate at weekends. If you join them, bear in mind that the taxi fare will be the first of several hefty bills, although admission prices usually include a free drink.

Amazon, opposite the eastern Ellenikó airport, off map (☎98 20 300). The summer face of the live *bouzouki* restaurant *Fantasia*. Drinks 1700dr. Open summer only.

Black Hole, Astéria, Glifádha, off map (☎89 46 898). The place to be seen. Drinks 2000dr.

Bouzios, Vassiléos Yeoryíou 2, Kalamáki, off map (☎98 12 004). Heavyweight clubbing spot. Spacious, glamorous and very popular with celebrities. Open year-round.

Gay venues

The gay scene is fairly discreet but Athens has a handful of clubs, especially in the Makriyánni district to either side of Singroú, with an established reputation. For further ideas, check the (brief and not entirely reliable) gay sections in the listings magazines *Athinorama* and *Exodus*.

Alekos Island, Tsakálof 42, Kolonáki, *D4*. Easy-going atmosphere, with rock/pop music. Owned by Alekos, who claims to be known around Europe.

Alexandher's, Anagnostopoúlou 44, *D4*. Relaxed, slightly middle-of-the-road gay bar in the Kolonáki district.

Café Oval, Tosítsa 4, Exárkhia *C3*. Open in the morning for coffee, drinks and refreshments. Student meeting place.

City, Korizí 4, Makriyánni, *F3/G3* border (☎92 40 740). Glamorous marble decor and quality drag show. Drinks 1500dr. Closed Mon & Tues.

Granazi, Lembéssi 20, near Syngroú, *F3/4*. Gay bar close by the transvestite cruising area.

Lambda, 15 Lembéssi & 9 Syngroú, *F3/4*. Popular, with Greek and international music, live shows and gay films.

Arts and culture

Unless your Greek is fluent, the contemporary **Greek theatre** scene is likely to be inaccessible. As with Greek music, it is essentially a winter pursuit; in summer, the only theatre tends to be satirical and (to outsiders) totally incomprehensible revues. **Dance**, however, is more accessible and includes a fine traditional Greek show, while **cinema** is un-dubbed – and out of doors in summer.

In addition, in winter months, you might catch **ballet** (and **world music** concerts) at the convenient but acoustically awful Pallas Theatre, at Voukourestíou 1; **opera** from the Greek National Opera Lyrikí Skiní, in the Olympia Theatre at Akadhimías 59; and **classical events** either in the Hall of the Friends of Music (Mégaro Mousikís), out on Leofóros Vassilísis Sofías next to the US embassy, or at the Filippos Nakas Concert Hall, at Ippokrátous 41. Also worth looking out for are events at the various **foreign cultural institutes**. Among these are the Hellenic American Union, Massalías 22 (*D3*), British Council, Platía Kolonáki 17 (*D4*), French Institute, Sína 29/Massalías 18 (*D3*), and Goethe Institute, Omírou 14–16 (*D3*).

Athens Festival

The summer **Athens Festival** has, over the years, come to encompass a broad spectrum of cultural events: most famously **ancient Greek theatre** (performed, in modern Greek, at the Herodes Atticus theatre on the south slope of the Acropolis), but also traditional and contemporary dance, classical music, jazz, traditional Greek music, and even a smattering of rock shows. The **Herodes Atticus theatre**, known popularly as the *Iródhio*, is memorable in itself on a warm summer's evening – although you should avoid the cheapest seats, or you won't see a thing. Other festival venues include the open-air Lycabettus Theatre on **Lykavitós Hill**, the **mansion of the Duchess of Plakentia** in Pendéli and (with special but expensive bus excursions) to the great ancient **theatre at Epidaurus** (see p.162).

Events are scheduled from early June until September, although the exact dates may vary each year. Programmes of performances are best picked up as soon as you arrive in the city, and for theatre, especially, you'll need to move fast to get tickets. The **festival box office** is in the arcade at Stadhíou 4 (*D4*; ☎32 21 459 or 32 23 111, ext 240; Mon–Sat 8.30am–2pm & 5–7pm, Sun 10.30am–1pm); most events are held in the Herodes Atticus Theatre, where the box office is open 5–9pm on the day of performance. Schedules of the main drama and music events are available in advance from EOT offices abroad (though they don't handle tickets). For student discounts, you must buy tickets in advance.

Dance

On the **dance** front, one worthwhile "permanent" performance is that of the **Dora Stratou Ethnic Dance Company** in their own theatre on Filopáppou hill (*G1*). Gathered on a single stage are traditional music, choreography and costumes you'd be hard put to encounter in many years' travelling around Greece. Performances are held nightly at 10.15pm (extra show Wed & Sun 8.15pm) from June to September. To reach the theatre, walk up the busy Areopayítou street, along the south flank of the Acropolis, until you see the signs. Tickets (2500–3000dr) can almost always be picked up at the door; take your own refreshments, or rely on the somewhat pricey snacks on offer.

Cinema

Athens is a great place to catch up on movies. There are literally dozens of indoor cinemas in the city, some of them very new and plush, some relics of the 1920s and 1930s, whilst in summer **outdoor** screens seem to spring up all over the place. Unless they have air conditioning or a roll-back roof, the indoor venues tend to be closed between mid-May and October.

Admission, whether at indoor or outdoor venues, is reasonable: count on 1400–1700dr for outdoor screenings, 1800dr for first-run fare at a midtown theatre. Films are always shown in the original language with Greek **subtitles** (a good way to increase your vocabulary). For **listings**, the weekly magazine *Athinorama* (every Thurs; 450dr), is the most reliable source of programme information if you can decipher Greek script. Films are divided according to category and geographical location of the cinema. English-language cinema listings – less complete – can be found in the *Athens News* or *The Hellenic Times* magazine.

Among **indoor cinemas**, a cluster showing regular English-language films can be found in three main central areas: Patissíon/Kipséli; downtown, on the three main thoroughfares connecting Omónia and Sýndagma; and Ambelókipi. The new, posh Village Center in Maroúsi (just off Kifissiá, near the Aïdhonákia amusement park) has ten theatres showing current films year round, with the added advantage that you can reserve tickets by phone (☎68 05 950). **Oldies** and **art films** tend to be shown at the Asty on Koräï downtown (*D3*); the Orfeus, Artémonos 57, (off map below *G5*, a fifteen-minute walk from Pangráti or Koukáki); the Alfaville, Mavromikháli 168, (*B4*); the Aavora, Ippokrátous 180 (*B4*); and the Studio, Stavropoúlou 33, Platía Amerikís, Kipséli (off map above *A2*). The Hadjikyriakos-Ghika Cinema Museum, at Kriezótou 3, has screenings of classic art-house films each Saturday at 6pm. Catch **horror/cult films** at the Pti-Paleh (cnr Vasilíou Yeoryíou Víta/Rizári *E5*); the Plaza, Kifissiá 118, Ambelókipi (off map); the Philip, Platía Amerikís/Thássou 11 (off map above *A2*); the Amalia, Dhrossopoúlou 197 (off map above *A2*); the Nirvana, Leofóros Alexándhras 192 (*B5*); and the Rialto, Kypsélis 54, Kypséli (off map above *A2*).

The summer **outdoor screens** are less imaginative in their selections – second-run offerings abound – though to attend simply for the film is to miss much of the point. You may in any case never hear the soundtrack above the din of Greeks cracking *passatémpo* (pumpkin seeds), drinking and conversing; at late screenings (11pm), the sound is turned right down anyway, so as not to disturb local residents. The most central and reliable outdoor venues are Sine Pari, Kydathinéon 22, Pláka (*F3*); Thissio, Apostólou Pávlou 7, under the Acropolis (*F1*); Nea Panathinea, Mavromikháli 165, Neápoli (*B4*); Zefyros, Tróön 36, Áno Petrálona, (*G1*) and the Riviera in Exárkhia, at Valtetsíou 46 (*C3*).

Markets and shops

You can buy just about anything in Athens and even on a purely visual level the city's **markets** and **bazaar** areas are worth an hour or two's wandering. Among the markets, don't miss the Athinás food halls, nor, if you're into bargain-hunting through junk, the Sunday morning **flea markets** in Monastiráki, Thissíon and Pireás. The **Athens flea**

market spreads over a half-dozen or so blocks around Monastiráki square each Sunday from around 6am until 2.30pm. In parts it is an extension of the tourist trade – the shops in this area are promoted as a "flea market" every day of the week – but there is authentic Greek (and nowadays Soviet refugee-Greek) junk, too, notably along (and off) Iféstou and Pandhróssou streets (*E2/3*). The real McCoy, most noticeable at the Thissío metro station end of Adhrianoú and the platía off Kynéttou near the church of Áyios Fílippos, is just a bag of odds and ends strewn on the ground or on a low table: dive in.

The **Pireás flea market** – at similar times on Sunday mornings – has fewer tourists and more goods. The market is concentrated on Alipédou and Skilítsi streets parallel to the railroad tracks about 500 yards from the sea (see the map on p.127). It is a venue for serious antique trading, as well as the sale of more everyday items.

In addition, many Athenian neighbourhoods have a *laikí agorá* – **street market** – on a set day of the week. Usually running from 7am to 2pm, these are inexpensive and enjoyable, selling household items and dry goods, as well as fresh fruit and vegetables. The most centrally located ones are: Hánsen in Patissíon (*A20*) on Monday; Lésvou in Kypséli (off map) and Láskou in Pangráti (off map), both on Tuesday; Xenokrátous in Kolonáki (*D5*), Tsámi Karatássou in Veïkoú (*B4*), and Arhimídhous in Méts (*F5*), all on Friday; and Plakendías in Ambelókipi (one of the largest; off map) and Allidhromíou in Exárkhia (*C3*), both on Saturday. Finally, if you're after live Greek **plants** or **herbs**, there's a Sunday-morning gathering of stalls on Vikéla street in Patissíon (off map) and plants and flowers on sale daily at the Platía Ayía Iríni near Ermoú (*E2*).

The selections below include some of the most enjoyable shops for souvenir-hunting, plus a few more functional places for those in search of books and outdoor gear.

Books

Archeological Service Bookstore, Panepistimíou 57, in stoa on left. Outlet for the high-quality if dry archeological service publications.

Compendium, Níkis 28 (upstairs), off Sýndagma, *E3*. Friendliest and best value of the English-language bookstores, featuring Penguins, Picadors, Rough Guides and other paperbacks, plus a small secondhand section.

Eleftheroudhakis, Panepistimíou 17, *D3*. Five floors of English books provide space for an extensive stock.

Estia-Kollarou, Sólonos 60, *D3*. Big Greek-language bookshop, strong on modern history, politics, folk traditions and fiction.

Iy Folia tou Vivliou (The Book Nest), Panepistimíou 25, *D4*, in the arcade and upstairs. The city's biggest selection of English-language fiction, with a good collection of recent academic work on Greece, and back issues of the *Korfes* hiking magazine.

Reymondos, Voukourestíou 18, *E4*. Good for foreign periodicals in particular.

Crafts and antiques

Greek handicrafts are not particularly cheap but the workmanship is usually very high. In addition to the stores listed below, consider those at the **National Archeological Museum**, **Benáki Museum** and **Cycladic Art Museum**, which sell excellent, original designs as well as reproductions; and the cluster of antique shops at the base of **Adhrianoú**, near the corner of Kynnéttou, which are good for Ottoman and rural Greek items like backgammon boards, hubble-bubbles, kilims, etc – the best is at Adhrianoú 25.

Athens Design Centre, Valaorítou 4, *D4*. A highly original modern potter has her base here. Prices aren't exorbitant considering the quality.

Gravoures, Kolokotróni 15, Sýndagma, *D3/E3*. Engravings and prints.

Karamichos, Voulís 31–33, *E3*. A central outlet for *flokátes*, those hairy-pile wool rugs that are still the best thing to warm up a cold stone floor.

Lalaounis, Panepistimíou 6, *D3*. Home-base outlet of the world-renowned family of goldsmiths, whose designs are superbly imaginative and very expensive.

Les Amis de Livres, Valaorítou 9, in a cul-de-sac, *D4*. Prints and engravings.

National Welfare Organization, Ipatías 6, cnr Apóllonos, Pláka, *E3*. Rugs, embroideries, copperware – traditional craft products made in remote country districts.

Stavros Melissinos, Pandhróssou 89, off Monastiráki, *E3*. The "poet-sandalmaker" of Athens – see p.96. The sandals translate better than the poems but nevertheless an inspiring (and not especially inflated) place to be cobbled.

Skyros, cnr Makriyánni/Khadzikhrístou, Veïkoú, *F3*. Traditional, if not very portable, Greek village furniture (particularly from Skíros), and more practical cushions, lamps, etc.

To Kati ti Sas, Iperídhou 23, Pláka, *E3*. Eclectic stock of craft items.

Health and speciality food

Herbs and herb teas are sold dry and fresh at most street markets and at the Athinás bazaar. Otherwise, the following central outlets are useful:

AB Vassilopoulos The three huge main stores are at Leofóros Kifissías, Psykhikó, by the east airport and above Kifissiá on the National Road (all off map), but there are several other outlets throughout the city. Gigantic supermarket stocking esoteric ingredients for just about every cuisine or diet.

Aralus, Sofokléous 17, Central Bazaar, *D2*. Fruits, nuts, wholegrain bread, pasta and so on. Also supplements and vitamins.

Kendro Fyzikis Zois keh Iyias, Panepistimíou 57, *D3*. Headquarters of the Greek Green Party, but also a tremendously well-stocked store and vegetarian snack bar with a pleasant loft where afternoon snacks are served.

To Stakhi, Mikrás Asías 61–63, Ambelókipi (off map). Well-stocked store.

Outdoor supplies

Aegean Dive Shop, Pandhóras 31, Glyfádha, off map, on the coast to the southeast (☎89 45 409). Good-value one-day dive trips to a reef near Vouliagméni, sporadically during the week but regularly on weekends.

Alberto's, Patissíon 37 (in the arcade) *B2*; plus many others on same street heading towards Omónia. This is in effect the "bike bazaar", for repairs, parts and sales. For mountain bikes, try Gatsoúlis at Thessaloníkis 8 in Néa Filadhélfia (off map; #18 trolley bus).

Alpamayo, Panepistimíou 44, *D3*. Small hiking store which also stocks some *Korfes* back issues (see also "Books", above).

Army & Navy, Kynéttou 4, on Ayíou Filíppou square, *E2*. Good for ponchos, stoves, mess kits, boots, knives and survival gear in general.

Kazos, in the arcade between Panepistimíou and Koraï, *D3*. A bit pricey due to its central location, but handy for small items like socks, knives, water bottles, etc.

Marabout, Sólonos 74, behind the university, *C3*. Soft goods only – parkas, packs, sleeping bags, etc.

No-Name Bike Shop, Trítis Septemvríou 40/cnr Stournári, *C2*.

Pindhos, Patissíon 52, *B2*. Extensive state-of-the-art hiking/climbing gear: Lowe packs, ice axes, stoves, water containers, parkas, foam pads, etc.

Records and CDs

If you hear music you like, or want to explore Greek sounds of bygone days (or today), refer to the discographies in Contexts (p.812–821) and then try the outlets below. When shopping, beware of records warped by poor stacking in the racks. The big advantage of shopping here is that the **vinyl industry** is still alive and well, having survived the CD onslaught; you may find pressings discontinued elsewhere.

Jazz Rock, Akadhimías 45, *D3*. Specializes in just that, and also a good source of information and tickets for upcoming concerts.

Music Corner, basement of Panepistimíou 36, nr Ippokrátous, *D3*. A good range of traditional Greek music, plus rock and jazz.

Metropolis, Panepistimíou 64, *D3*. Strictly CD's; the branch at #54 sells just vinyl. Often has discounted items.

Philodisc, Gambétta 1, cnr Benáki, *C2/C3*. Good for R & B, classical, jazz, CDs, plus lots of moderately priced sounds on Greek vinyl.

Tzina, Panepistimíou 57, *D3*. Stop in here if Metropolis or Xylouris doesn't have what you're after; it has its own label of Greek folk.

Virgin Megastore, Stadhíou 7-9 (*D3*). Two floors of tapes and CDs, with video cassettes in the basement; expensive.

Xylouris, Panepistimíou 39, in the arcade, *D3*. Run by the widow of the late, great Cretan singer Nikos Xylouris, this is currently one of the best places for Greek popular, folk and (of course) Cretan music. On the expensive side, but stocks items unavailable elsewhere.

Listings

Airlines Almost all the following – Singroú and Eólou addresses apart – are within 100m or so of Sýndagma: Olympic, ticket office at Óthonos 6, on Sýndagma, *E4* (☎92 67 555, (reservations) ☎96 66 666), main office at Singroú 96, *G3* (☎92 69 111); Air Canada, Óthonos 10, *E4* (☎32 23 206); Alitalia, Bouliagménis 577, near airport (☎99 59 200); British Airways, Óthonos 10, *E4* (☎32 22 521); Canadian Airlines (Amfitreon Air Services), 3rd floor, Singrou 7, *E3* (☎ 92 12 470-80); CSA, Panepistimíou 15, *D3* (☎32 32 303); Cyprus Airways, Filellínon 10, *E3* (☎32 47 801); Delta, Óthonos 4, *E4* (☎32 35 242); Egyptair, Óthonos 10, *E4* (☎32 33 575); El Al, Óthonos 8, *E4* (☎33 11 673); Kenya Airways, Khariláou Trikoúpi 6-10, *C3* (☎36 21 176); KLM, cnr Vouliagménis & Lóndou, Glifádha, off map (☎96 48 865); Malev, Panepistimíou 15, *D3* (☎32 41 116); Qantas (represented by British Airways); Sabena, cnr Vouliagménis & Lóndou (☎96 00 217); Singapore Airlines, Xenofóndos 9, *E4* (☎32 39 111); South African Airways, Vassilísis Sofías 11, *D/E4* (☎36 16 305); Turkish Airlines, Filellínon 19, *E4* (☎32 46 024); TWA, Xenofóndos 8, *E4* (☎32 26 451); United, Syngroú 5, *F3* (☎92 42 645); Virgin Atlantic, Tziréon 8-10 (behind Athens Gate Hotel), *E3* (☎92 49 100).

Airport enquiries ☎93 69 111 for Olympic flight enquiries; ☎96 94 111 for all other carriers.

American Express Poste restante and money changing at the main branch at Ermoú 2 (1st floor), cnr Sýndagma (*E3*). Mail pick-up desk open in summer Mon–Fri 7.30am–8pm, Sat 7.30am–2pm; shorter weekday hours in winter.

Banks The National Bank of Greece at Sýndagma (*E3*), stays open for **exchange** Mon–Fri 8am–2pm & 3.30–6.30pm, Sat 9am–3pm & Sun 9am–1pm. The nearby, less crowded Yeniki Trapeza/General Bank cnr Ermoú and Sýndagma, has longer hours: Mon–Thurs 8am–6.30pm, Fri 8am–6pm, Sat 8am–2pm, closed Sun. **Foreign banks**, keeping normal hours of Mon–Thurs 8am–2pm, Fri 8am–1.30pm, include Barclays, Voukourestíou 15, off Panepistimíou, *D4* (☎36 44 311); Citibank, Óthonos 8, *E4* (☎32 38 020); Midland Bank, Sekéri 1a, Kolonáki, *D5* (☎36 47 410); and National Westminster, Koraï 5, *D3* (☎32 50 924). Royal Bank of Scotland have a branch in Pireás at Aktí Miaoúli 61 (☎42 93 210). Most of these branches have cash dispensers which should accept standard European and US banking cards. Outside of normal banking hours, you can use automatic foreign note changing machines – most are located around Sýndagma. Along Leofóros Amalías, and on Sýndagma itself, there are also a number of staffed kiosks that stay open until around 9pm.

Buses For information on buses out of Athens (and the respective terminals), see "Travel Details" at the end of this chapter.

Camera repair Most central at Pikopoulos, Lékka 26, off Ermoú, 3rd floor, *E3*, and Kriton Kremnitsios, Karayeóryi Servías 7, 5th floor, *E3*.

Car rental A number of companies are to be found along Leofóros Syngroú (*F3*), including InterRent/EuropCar, at no. 4 (*F3*), Holiday Autos (no. 8, *F3*), Thrifty (no. 24, *F3*), Eurodollar (no. 29, *F3*), Just (no. 43, *G3*), Avanti (no. 50, *G3*), Antena (no. 52, *G3*) and Autorent (no. 118; *G3*); the latter three give student discounts, while Payless is just off Syngroú at Hatzihristou 20 (*F3*).

Car repairs, tyres, and assistance VW vans are well looked after at Grigoris Steryiadhis, Melandhías 56, Goúva (between Pangráti and Néos Kósmos; off map just below *G4*). Mechanics for virtually any make are scattered around Néos Kósmos district, while spares stores congregate along and between Kalliróis and Vouliagménis. If they don't have the part, or the know-how, they'll refer you to someone who does. Tyre stores are grouped between Trítis Septemvríou 60–80 (north of Omónia, *B2*). **ELPA** – the Greek automobile association – gives free **help and information** to foreign motorists at Leof. Mesoyíon 2 (northeast of Lykavitós, off map) and at the Athens Tower in Ambelókipi. For **emergency assistance** call ☎104 (free, though you'll pay for any parts).

Dentists Free treatment at the Evangelismos Hospital, Ipsilándou 45, Kolonáki, *D5* and at the Pireás Dentistry School (*Odhondoiatrikó Skolío*), cnr Thívon/Livadhías, well north of the metro and public buses. For private treatment, check the ads in the *Athens News* or ask your embassy for addresses.

Embassies/Consulates include: Australia, Dhimitríou Soútsou 37, *B5* (☎64 47 303); Britain, Ploutárkhou 1, Kolonáki, *D5* (☎72 36 211); Bulgaria, Stratigoú Kallári 33a, Paleó Psihikó, off map (☎64 78 105, Mon–Fri 10am–noon); Canada, Ioánnou Yennadhíou 4, *D5* (☎72 54 011); Denmark, Vassilísis Sofías 11, *D5* (☎36 08 315); Egypt, 3 Vas. Sofías, *D4* (☎36 18 612); Hungary, Kálvou 16, Paleó Psykhikó, off map (☎67 25 994, Mon–Fri 9am–noon); Ireland, Vassiléos Konstandínou 7, *E5* (☎72 32 771); Israel, Marathonodhrómou 1, Paleó Psyihikó, off map (☎67 19 530); Netherlands, Vassiléos Konstandínou 5–7, *E5* (☎72 39 701); New Zealand (consulate), Xenías 24, Ambelókipim off map (☎77 10 112); Norway, Vassiléos Konstandínou 7, *E5* (☎72 46 173); Romania, Emmanuel Benáki 7, Paleó Psyihikó, off map (☎67 18 020, Mon–Fri 10am–noon); South Africa, Kifissías 60, Ambelókipi, off map (☎69 22 125); Sweden, Vassiléos Konstandínou 7, *E5* (☎72 90 421); USA, Vassilísis Sofías 91, off map (☎72 12 951).

Emergencies Dial the tourist police (☎171; 24hr) for medical or other assistance. In a **medical emergency**, don't wait for an ambulance if you can travel safely – get a taxi straight to the hospital address that the Tourist Police gives you. If your Greek is up to it, ☎166 summons an ambulance, ☎105 gets you a rota of night-duty doctors, and ☎106 ascertains the best hospital for you to head for. Otherwise, KAT, way out in Kifissiá at Níkis 2, is excellent for trauma and acute complaints if you can hold out that long – it's the designated casualty ward for Greater Athens.

Environment Greenpeace, Kallidhromíou 44, Exárkhia, *C3*. (☎38 40 774). Stop by if you want information, or are staying long-term in Greece and would like to participate in volunteer work and campaigns. WWF Greece, Filellínon 26, 4th floor, *E3* (☎32 47 586) have many excellent field programs.

Ferries Most central offices for major lines like ANEK, Strintzis, Hellenic Mediterranean, G&A and Ventouris flank Leofóros Amalías between Sýndagma and Hadrian's Gate; a prominent exception is Minoan Lines, on Vassiléos Konstandínou, next to the Olympic Stadium. Phone ☎143 for an information hotline (in Greek). Tickets are sold from the Flying Dolphins office at the quay from about an hour before departure. To be sure of a particular sailing in high season, book ahead in either Pireás or Athens. The main booking office is at Aktí Themistokléous 8 in Pireás, ☎42 8001. The Athens office is at Filellínon 3, ☎32 4600. If your schedule is tight, book your seat back to Pireás when you arrive.

Football The Athens team Panathinaïkós, owned by the tycoon Yiorgos Vardinoyannis, is Greece's wealthiest and as a rule most successful club. Catch them at the 25,000-capacity stadium on Leof. Alexándhras (*B5*). Their traditional rival, Olympiakós of Pireás plays at the Karaïskáki stadium (by the Néo Fáliro metro stop; see the Pireás map on p.127). Also worth looking out for are AEK, which has had some recent European success. Football being an obsession in Greece (there are several daily sports papers), matches are not hard to discover: just ask at a kiosk or bar.

Gay groups The Autonomous Group of Gay Women meet weekly at The Women's House (see "Women's movement", below). Akoe Amphi, the (predominantly male) Greek Gay Liberation Movement, have an office at Zalóngou 6 (Mon–Fri 6–11pm).

Greek language courses Athens Centre, Arkhimídhous 48, Pangráti, *F5* (☎70 12 268, fax 70 18 603), is considered the best for foreigners. The Hellenic American Union, Massalías 22, *D4*, is more geared to the needs of Greeks learning English, while the Ionic Centre, Lissíou 4, Pláka, *D4*, has a few summer courses on Hios island.

Hiking Trekking Hellas, Filellínon 7, 3rd floor, *E3*, arrange hiking tours throughout Greece.

Hospital clinics For minor injuries the Hellenic Red Cross, Trítis Septemvríou/Kapodhistríou, *C2*, is fairly good. The Women's House (see below) has addresses of English-speaking gynecologists. For **inoculations**, try the Vaccination Centre, Leof. Alexándhras 196/cnr Vassilísis Sofías, Ambelókipi (off map; Mon–Fri 8.30am–12.30pm), where most jabs are free; phone ☎64 60 493 for details.

Laundry Numerous dry/wet cleaners will do your laundry for you, or there are coin-ops at Dhidhótou 46, Exárkhia, *C3*, Ploutárckhou and Karneádhou, and Ioulianoú 72–78, *B2*.

Lost property The transport police have a lost property office (Grafío Khaménon Andikiménon) at Alexándras 173, 7th floor, *B5* (☎64 21 616).

Luggage storage Best arranged with your hotel; many places will keep the bulk of your luggage for free or a nominal amount while you head off to the islands. Pacific Ltd, Níkis 24 (*E3*), stores luggage for around 4000dr per item per month, 1500dr per week.

Motorbike rental Available from Motorent, whose head office is at Falírau 5, cnr Makriyánni, Veïkoú, *F3* (☎92 34 939, fax 92 34 885).

Mount Áthos permits See p.386 for details if you're planning a trip to Athos. In Athens, the Ministry of Foreign Affairs, Akadhimías 3, in the arcade, 5th floor, *E4*, is the first stop in securing a permit; office hours are Mon, Wed & Fri 11am–1pm.

Opticians Quick repairs at Paraskevopoulos in the arcade between Voukourestíou and Kriezótou, by the parcel post office, *D3*. Contact lens solutions available at Katsimandis, at Amerikís 11.

Pharmacies *(farmakía)* The Marinopoulos branches (in Patissíon and Panepistimíou streets, *C2/D3*) are particularly good and also sell homeopathic remedies, as does (supposedly) any establishment with a green cross outside. Bakakos, on Omónia square (*D2*), is the largest general pharmacy in Athens and stocks just about anything. Call ☎107 for after-hours pharmacies, or consult daily listings in *Athens News*.

Phones You can phone locally from a *períptero* (kiosk), where you pay afterwards. Phone boxes all require phone cards – an irritating investment (minimum 1500dr) if you won't be around very long. International calls are best made at the central OTE offices at Stadhíou 15 (*D3*) and Patissíon 25, Oktovríou 85 (*B2*); the latter is open 24hr.

Police Dialling ☎100 gets the flying squad; for thefts, problems with hotel overcharging, etc, contact the **Tourist Police** at Dimitrakoupoúlou 77, Koukáki, *E1* (☎171).

Post offices *(Takhydhromío)* For ordinary letters and parcels up to 2kg, the branch on Sýndagma (cnr Mitropóleos, *E3*) is open Mon–Fri 7.30am–8pm, Sat 7.30am–2pm, Sun 9am–1.30pm. To send home parcels of personal effects, use the post office in the arcade between Voukourestíou and Kriezótou, *D3* (Mon–Fri 7.30am–2pm) – or, closer to Omónia at Koumoundoúrou 29. Paper and string are supplied – you bring box and twine. "Surface/air lift" will get parcels home to North America or Europe in two weeks. For souvenirs, a branch at Níkis 37, *E3* expedites shipments and minimizes duty/declaration problems.

Poste restante The main post office for Athens is at Eólou 100, just off Omónia, *D2* (Mon–Fri 7.30am–8pm, Sat 7.30am–2pm, Sun 9am-1.30pm).

Train information, reservations and tickets The most central OSE offices are at Filellínon 17, *E3*, and Sína 6, *D3*.

Travel agencies Most budget and youth/student agencies are to be found just off Sýndagma, on and around Filellínon and Níkis streets. The cheapest ferry tickets to Italy are usually sold through USIT, Filellínon 1 (☎32 41 884), or Transalpino (Níkis 28), still trading despite the demise of its namesake. Among other agencies, Highway Express, Níkis 42; Periscope, Filellínon 22; Himalaya, Filellínon 7 and Arcturus, Apóllonos 20 are worth scanning for air travel deals. For the hardy, the widest range of north-bound buses is still available at Magic Bus, Filellínon 20. All these addresses are *E3/F3*.

Work/residence permits/visa extensions at the Aliens' Bureau *(Ipiresía Allodhapón)*, Leof. Alexándras 173, off map past *B5*; open Mon–Fri 8am–1pm, but go early or you won't get seen. Also, come armed with small notes for revenue stamps, large notes for the extension fee(s), wads of passport photos, pink personalized bank receipts, and plenty of patience.

AROUND ATHENS: ATTICA

Attica (Attikí), the region encompassing the capital, is not much explored by tourists. Only the great romantic ruin of the **Temple of Apollo** at Sounion is on the excursion circuit. The rest, if seen at all, tends to be en route to the islands – from the ports of **Pireás**, **Rafina** (a fast and cheap route to many of the Cyclades) or **Lávrio** (which serves Kéa).

The neglect is not surprising. The mountains of **Imittós**, **Pendéli** and **Párnitha**, which surround Athens on three sides, are progressively less successful in confining the urban sprawl, and the routes out of the city to the south and west are unenticing to say the least. But if you're planning on an extended stay in the capital, a day trip or two, or a brief circuit by car, can make a rewarding break, with much of Greece in microcosm to be seen within an hour or two's ride: mountainside at **Párnitha**, minor archeological sites in **Brauron** and **Rhamnous**, and the odd unspoilt beach, too.

Pireás (Piraeus)

PIREÁS has been the port of Athens since Classical times. Today it is a substantial metropolis in its own right, containing much of Greater Athens' industry, as well as the various commercial activities associated with a port: banking, import–export, freight and so on. For most visitors, though, it is Pireás's inter-island ferries that provide the reason for coming (see "The Ferries" below for details).

The port at Pireás was founded at the beginning of the fifth century BC by **Themistocles**, who realized the potential of its three natural harbours. His work was consolidated by Pericles with the building of the **"Long Walls"** to protect the corridor to Athens, and it remained active under Roman and Macedonian rulers. Subsequently, under Turkish rule, the place declined to the extent that there was just one building there, a monastery, by the end of the War of Independence. From the 1830s on, though, Pireás grew by leaps and bounds. The original influx into the port was a group of immigrants from Khíos, whose island had been devastated by the Turks; later came populations from Ídhra, Crete and the Peloponnese. By World War I, Pireás had outstripped the island of Síros as the nation's first port, its strategic position enhanced by the opening of the Suez and Corinth canals in 1862 and 1893 respectively. Like Athens, the city's great period of expansion began in 1923, with the exchange of populations with Turkey. Over 100,000 Asia Minor Greeks decided to settle in Pireás, doubling the population almost overnight – and giving a boost to a pre-existing semi-underworld culture, whose enduring legacy was *rembétika*, outcasts' music played in hashish dens along the waterside.

The city these days is almost indistinguishable from Athens, with its scruffy web of suburbs merging into those of the capital. Economically, it is at present on a mild upswing, boosted by two successive go-ahead mayors and the prominence of its late MP, former actress and Minister of Culture, Melina Mercouri. An unashamedly functional place, with its port despatching up to sixty ships a day in season – both to the islands and to a range of international destinations – there are few sights beyond the numbers and diversity of the sailors in the harbour. The ancient walls are long gone, and the junta years saw misguided demolition of many buildings of character. On the plus side, there's a nice enough **park** (three blocks back from the main harbour, intersected by Vassiléos Konstandínou); a scattering of genuine antique/junk shops, full of peasant copper and wood, plus a big Sunday morning **flea market**, near Platía Ipodhamías, at the top end of Goúnari (behind the train station); and a couple of more than respectable museums.

The Archeological and Maritime museums

The **Archeological Museum** at Khariláou Trikoúpi 31 (Tues–Sun 8.30am–3pm; 500dr) is the best time-filler in Pireás, and enthusiasts will certainly want to make a special trip out here. Upper-floor exhibits include a *kouros* (idealized male statue) dedicated to Apollo, which was dragged out of the sea in 1959. Dating from 520 BC, this is the earliest known life-size bronze, and is displayed with two other fifth-century bronzes of Artemis and Athena found in the same manner at about the same time.

On the ground floor are more submarine finds, this time second-century AD stone reliefs of battles between Greeks and Amazons, apparently made for export to Rome.

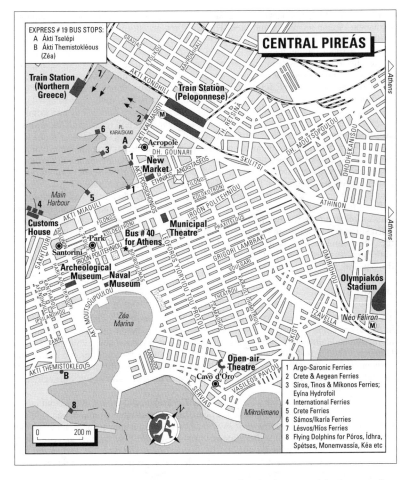

EXPRESS # 19 BUS STOPS:
A Ákti Tselépi
B Ákti Themistokléous
   (Zéa)

CENTRAL PIREÁS

Train Station
(Northern
Greece)

Train Station
(Peloponnese)

PL.
KARAISKAKI
A

Acropole

New
Market

Main
Harbour

Customs
House

Bus # 40
for Athens

Municipal
Theatre

Santorini

Archeological
Museum   Naval
         Museum

Olympiakós
Stadium

Néo Fáliron

Zéa
Marina

Open-air
Theatre

Cavo d'Oro

Mikrolimano

0   200 m

B

N

1 Argo-Saronic Ferries
2 Crete & Aegean Ferries
3 Síros, Tínos & Míkonos Ferries;
   Eyína Hydrofoil
4 International Ferries
5 Crete Ferries
6 Sámos/Ikaría Ferries
7 Lésvos/Híos Ferries
8 Flying Dolphins for Póros, Ídhra,
   Spétses, Monemvassía, Kéa etc

Athens

Athens

The sea's effect on them was far more corrosive than in the case of the bronzes, but you can still tell that some scenes are duplicated – showing that the ancients weren't above a bit of mass artistic production.

A few blocks away, on Aktí Themistokléous, adjacent to Zéa, the **Maritime Museum** (Tues–Fri 9am–2pm, Sat & Sun 9am–1pm; 400dr) is more specialized, tracing developments with models and the odd ancient piece.

The ferries

If you're staying in Athens prior to heading out to the islands, it's worth going to the tourist office at at 2 Amerikas Street to pick up a **schedule of departures** from Pireás. These can't be relied upon implicitly, but they do give a reasonable indication of what boats are leaving when and for where; note that the Argo-Saronic sailings and ships based on Sýros or Páros are omitted.

The majority of the boats – for the Argo-Saronic, Ikaría or Sámos, and the popular Cyclades – leave between 8 and 9am. There is then another burst of activity between noon and 3pm towards the Cyclades and Dodecanese, and a final battery of sailings from 4 to 10pm (sometimes later), bound for a wide variety of ports, but especially Crete, the northeast Aegean and the western Cyclades. The frequency of sailings is such that, in high season at least, you need never spend the night in Athens or Pireás.

There's no need to **buy tickets** for conventional ferries before you get here, unless you want a cabin berth or are taking a car on board (in which case, consult agents in Athens or Pireás); Flying Dolphin reservations are a good idea during July and August. In general, the best plan is to get to Pireás early, say at 7am, and check with the various **shipping agents** around the metro station and along the quayside Platía Karaïskáki. Keep in mind that many of these act only for particular lines, so for a full picture of the various boats sailing you will need to ask at three or four outlets. Prices for all domestic boat journeys are standard, but the quality of the craft and circuitousness of routes vary greatly. If you are heading for Thíra (Santórini) or Rhodes, for example, try to get a boat that stops at only three or four islands en route; for Crete settle for direct ferries only.

Boats for different destinations leave from a variety of points along the main harbour, usually following the pattern in the box opposite, though it's wise to leave time for wayward ships and look for the signs (indicating name of boat and a clockface with departure time) hung in front of the relevant boats on the waterside railings or on the stern of the boats themselves. The ticket agent should know the whereabouts of the boat on the particular day.

Practicalities

The easiest way to get to Pireás from Athens is on the **metro**. There are central stops in Athens at Platía Viktorías, Omónia and Monastiráki squares, plus Thissío for those in Veïkou, and Petrálona for those in Koukáki; the journey takes about 25 minutes from Omónia to the Pireás train station stop (the end of the line). Metro trains run from 6am, early enough to catch the first ferries, until midnight, long after the arrival of all but the most delayed boats. Tickets cost 100dr a journey, more if you start your journey north of Omónia square.

Alternatively, you could take a **bus** or a taxi. Green bus #40 (about every 20min during the day; hourly 1am–5am) will deposit you on Vassiléos Konstandínou, half a dozen blocks from the docks, but it's very slow – allow nearly an hour from Sýndagma, the most obvious boarding point. The **express buses** (see p.73) are quicker and provide a particularly useful link with the airport. **Taxis** cost about 1500dr at day tariff from the centre of Athens or the airport – worth considering, especially if you're taking one of the hydrofoils from the Zéa marina, which is a fair walk from the metro.

Accommodation

Few visitors stay in Pireás, and most of the port's **hotels** are geared to a steady clientele of seamen, resting between ships. For this reason, picking somewhere at random is not always a good idea. If you have a bit of money, consider the *Hotel Park* (☎45 24 611; ④), a couple of blocks back from the port at Kolokotróni 103, or the very pleasant and luxurious *Cavo d'Oro* (☎41 13 742; ⑤), overlooking the Mikrolímano yacht harbour. Two places close by the main harbour, and used to tourists, are the *Hotel Santorini*, Trikoúpi 6 (☎45 22 147/9; ③), and the *Acropole*, Goúnari 7 (☎41 73 313; ③): the latter has a sporadically functioning bar and sunroof.

Sleeping rough in Platía Karaïskáki, as some exhausted travellers attempt to do, is unwise. If thieves or the police don't rouse you, street-cleaners armed with hoses certainly will – at 5am.

FERRY DEPARTURE POINTS

Aegean islands (Cyclades/Dodecanese)
These leave from either Aktí Kalimasióti, the quay right in front of the metro station (#2 on the map), or from Aktí Kondhíli (#7, perpendicular to Possidhónios). The big boats going to the major Dodecanese only usually share point (#5) with some of the Cretan ferries.

Crete
Some ferries dock at Aktí Kalimasióti (#2), but most use the promontory by Aktí Miaoúli (#5), or (#7) on Aktí Kondhíli.

Sýros, Tínos, Mýkonos
The morning departures tend to go from (#3), next to the Éyina hydrofoils.

Sámos/Ikaría
Boats ending up at these islands, whether morning or evening services, use the far end of the dock beyond Platía Karaïskáki (#6).

Khíos/Lésvos
Most Khios and Mitilíni (Lésvos) boats leave from (#6), with a very few going from #7.

Argo-Saronic
Ordinary ferries leave from the junction of Aktí Possidhónios and Aktí Miaoúli, and also west along Possidhónios (#1), a ten-minute walk from the metro.

International destinations (Limassol, Haifa, Izmir, etc)
These leave further around the main harbour (#4), towards the Customs House (where you should check passports before boarding).

Hydrofoils
Except for departures direct to Éyina, which leave from Aktí Tselépi (#3), hydrofoils for Argo-Saronic and Peloponnesian destinations leave from the Zéa marina (#8), a twenty-minute uphill walk from the metro.
Tickets are on sale from the Flying Dolphins office at the quay from about an hour before departure. To be sure of a particular sailing in high season, it is wise to book ahead in Athens. Equally, if your schedule is tight, book your seat back to Pireás when you arrive.

Eating and drinking

If you're simply looking for food to take on board, or breakfast, you'll find numerous places (as well as several budget restaurants) around the market area, back from the waterside Aktí Miaoúli/Ethnikís Andistáseos, open from 6.30am.

For a real blowout, the *Vassilenas* at Etolikoú 72 (the street running inland from Aktí Kondhíli) is a fine choice. Housed in an old grocery store, its set menu provides mezédhes enough to defy all appetites; at 5000dr a head, drinks extra, it's not especially cheap, but enough Athenians consider it worth the drive that most evenings you need to book a table (☎46 12 457). There's a string of ouzerí and seafood tavernas along Aktí Themistokléous, west of the Zéa marina, most of them pretty good and reasonably priced, or try the Indian restaurant *Maharajah Navarkhou* at Notará 122.

Otherwise, a good bet for seafood is *Kefalonitis*, on the corner of Rethýmnis and Tsakálof, up by the open-air theatre. As the name implies, this place is run by a Kefallonian family, and is far superior to the tourist-traps on Mikrolímano.

Entertainment, restaurants and nightlife

Culturally, there's not a great deal going on at Pireás, though a **summer festival**, run alongside that of Athens, features events in the open-air theatre set back from the yacht harbour of Mikrolímano (or Tourkolímano, as it has been called for centuries). In winter there's always **football**: Olympiakós are the port's big team, rivals to the capital's AEK and Panathenaïkós.

Finally, a word for the port's best **rembétika venue** (see p.116), the *Ondas tis Konstandinas* at Koundouriótou 109 on the corner of Karóli Dhimitríou (☎42 20 459; closed Sun & Mon, and in summer). This is a very friendly taverna, with rembétika music each night and a special *Smyrneika* show every Tuesday. On Friday and Saturday nights there's a minimum charge of 4000dr per person.

The "Apollo Coast", Cape Sounion and Lávrio

The seventy kilometres of coast south of Athens – the tourist-board-dubbed "**Apollo Coast**" – has some good but highly developed beaches. At weekends, when Athenians flee the city, the sands fill fast, as do the innumerable bars, restaurants and discos at night. If this is what you're after, then resorts like **Glyfádha** and **Vouliagméni** are functional enough. But for most foreign visitors, the coast's lure is at the end of the road, in the form of the Temple of Poseidon at **Cape Sounion**.

Access to Sounion (Soúnio in the modern spelling) is straightforward. There are buses on the hour and half-hour from the KTEL terminal on Mavromatéon at the southwest corner of the Pedíou e Áreos Park; there's also a more central (but in summer, very full) stop ten minutes later at point "D" on Filellínon street, south of Sýndagma (corner of Xenofóndos, in front of the Middle East Airways office). There are both coastal (*paraliakó*) and inland (*mesoyiakó*) services, the latter slightly longer and more expensive. The coast route normally takes around two hours; last departures back to Athens are posted at the Sounion stop.

For Glyfádha/Voúla and Vouliagméni/Várkiza – the main resorts – take the 180 Poseidon bus from the Záppion gardens. The A2 trunk line bus for Glyfádha/Voúla also leaves from Panepistimíou.

The resorts: Glyfádha to Anávissos

Although some Greeks swim at Pireás itself, few would recommend the sea much before **GLYFÁDHA**, half an hour's drive southeast from the city centre. The major resort along the "Apollo Coast", merged almost indistinguishably with its neighbour **VOÚLA**, this is lined with seafood restaurants, ice-cream bars and discos, as well as a couple of marinas and a golf course. Its popularity, though, is hard to fathom, built as it is in the shadow of the airport. The only possible appeal is in the beaches, the best of which is the **Astir**, privately owned and with a stiff admission charge; others are gritty. Hotels are all on the expensive side, and in any case are permanently full of package tours; there is a **campsite** at Voúla (☎01/89 52 712).

VOULIAGMÉNI, which in turn has swallowed up **Kavoúri**, is a little quieter than Glyfádha, and a little ritzier. Set back from a small natural saltwater lake, it boasts a waterski school, some extremely chi-chi restaurants, and an EOT pay-beach. Again, budget accommodation is hard to come by, though there is a **campsite** – and another EOT pay-beach – just to the south at **Várkiza**.

South from Várkiza, there are further beaches en route to Sounion, though unless you've a car to pick your spot they're not really worth the effort. The resorts of **Lagoníssi** and **Anávissos** are in the Glyfádha mould, and only slightly less crowded, despite the extra distance from Athens.

Cape Sounion

Cape Sounion – Aktí Soúnio – is one of the most imposing spots in Greece, for centuries a landmark for boats sailing between Pireás and the islands, and an equally dramatic vantage point in itself to look out over the Aegean. On its tip stands the fifth-century BC **Temple of Poseidon**, built in the time of Pericles as part of a major sanctuary to the sea god.

The Temple of Poseidon

The temple (Tues–Sun 10am–sunset; 500dr) owes its fame above all to **Byron**, who visited in 1810, carved his name on the nearest pillar (an unfortunate precedent), and commemorated the event in the finale of his hymn to Greek independence, the "Isles of Greece" segment of *Don Juan*:

> *Place me on Sunium's marbled steep,*
> *Where nothing, save the waves and I,*
> *May hear our mutual murmurs sweep;*
> *There, swan like, let me sing and die:*
> *A land of slaves shall ne'er be mine –*
> *Dash down yon cup of Samian wine!*

In summer, at least, there is faint hope of solitude, unless you slip into the site before the tour groups arrive. But the temple is as evocative a ruin as any in Greece. Doric in style, it was probably built by the architect of the Thiseon in the Athens *agora*. That it is so admired and visited is in part due to its site, but also perhaps to its picturesque state of ruin – preserving, as if by design, sixteen of its thirty-four columns. On a clear day, the view from the temple takes in the islands of Kéa, Kíthnos and Sérifos to the southeast, Éyina and the Peloponnese to the west.

The rest of the site is of more academic interest. There are remains of a fortification wall around the sanctuary; a **Propylaion** (entrance hall) and **Stoa**, and cuttings for two shipsheds. To the north are the foundations of a small **Temple of Athena**.

Beaches – and staying at Sounion

Below the promontory are several **coves** – the most sheltered a five-minute walk east from the car park and site entrance. The main Sounion beach is more crowded, but has a group of tavernas at the far end – pretty reasonably priced, considering the location.

If you want to stay, there are a couple of **campsites** just around the coast: *Camping Bacchus* (the nearest; ☎0292/39 262) and *Sounion Beach Camping* (5km; ☎0292/39 358). The 1960s-style *Hotel Aegeon* (☎0292/39 262; ⑤) is right on the Sounion beach.

Lávrio

Ten kilometres north of Sounion, around the cape, is the port of **LÁVRIO**. This has daily ferry connections with Kéa and a single weekly boat to Kýthnos. It can be reached by **bus** from the Mavromatéon terminal in Athens, or from Sounion.

The port's ancient predecessor, Laurion, was famous for its silver mines – a mainstay of the classical Athenian economy – which were worked almost exclusively by slaves. The port today remains an industrial and mining town, though nowadays for less precious minerals (cadmium and manganese) and also hosts the country's principal transit camp for political refugees: mostly Kurds from Iraq and Turkey at present, with a scattering of Eastern Europeans, awaiting resettlement in North America, Australia or Europe. The island offshore, **Makrónissos**, now uninhabited, has an even more sinister past, for it was here that hundreds of ELAS members and other leftists were imprisoned in "re-education" labour camps during and after the civil war.

As you might imagine, this is not really a place to linger between buses and ferries. However, if you have time to kill, the site of **ancient Thoriko** is of some interest. It lies down a zigzag track from the village of Pláka, 5km north of Lávrio. A defensive outpost of the mining area in classical times, its most prominent ruins are of a theatre, crudely engineered into an irregular slope in the hill.

East of Athens: the Mesóyia and Brauron

The area east of Athens is one of the least visited parts of Attica. The mountain of **Imittós** (Hymettus) forms an initial barrier, with Kessarianí monastery (see p.107) on its cityside flank. Beyond extends the plateau of the **Mesóyia** (Midland), a gentle land-scape whose villages have a quiet renown for their *retsina* and for their churches, many of which date to Byzantine times. On towards the coast, there is the remote and beau-tiful site of **ancient Brauron**, and the developing resort of **Pórto Ráfti**.

The Mesóyia

The best-known attraction of the Mesóyia is at the village of **PEANÍA**, on the east slope of Imittós: the **Koutoúki cave** (daily 9.30am–4.30pm; 500dr), endowed with spectacularly illuminated stalactites and stalagmites and multicoloured curtains of rock. It is fairly easily reached by taking the Athens–Markópoulo bus, stopping at Peanía and then walking up. Close by the village – just to the east on the Spáta road – is the chapel of **Áyios Athanásios**, built with old Roman blocks and fragments.

MARKÓPOULO, the main Mesóyia village, shelters a further clutch of chapels. Within the village, in a walled garden, stand the twin chapels of **Áyia Paraskeví** and **Ayía Thékla**; ring for admission and a nun will open them up to show you the seven-teenth-century frescoes. Over to the west, on the road to Koropí, is one of the oldest churches in Attica, tenth-century **Metamórfosi** – the keys to which can be obtained from the Análipsi church in Koropí.

Heading east from Markópoulo, the road runs past the unusual double-naved **Ayía Triádha** (2500m out) and on to the coast at **PÓRTO RÁFTI**, whose bay, protected by islets, forms an almost perfect natural harbour. It's been comprehensively developed, with an EOT pay-beach and a fair number of tavernas, but remains a good place to stay if you can find a room. On the small island in the harbour is a large Roman statue of a woman whose now missing arm held the "first fruits" of crops that were sent each year to the sacred island of Delos. In the sixteenth century the statue was thought to hold scissors, and the port came to be known as the tailor's port, Pórto Ráfti.

From here, if you've your own vehicle, you can make your way over the mountain to the village of Vravróna and the site of **Ancient Brauron**.

Brauron

Brauron (site and museum Tues–Sun 8.30am–3pm; 400dr) is one of the most enjoy-able minor Greek sites. It lies just outside the modern village of Vravróna (40km from Athens), in a marshy area at the base of a low, chapel-topped hill. The marsh and sur-rounding fields are alive with birdsong, only rarely drowned out by traffic noise from the nearby busy road.

The remains are of a **Sanctuary of Artemis**, centred on a vast *stoa*. This was the chief site of the Artemis cult, legendarily founded by Iphigeneia, whose "tomb" has also been identified here. It was she who, with Orestes, stole the image of Artemis from Tauris (as commemorated in Euripides's *Iphigeneia at Tauris*) and introduced worship of the goddess to Greece. The main event of the cult was a quadrennial festival, now shrouded in mystery, in which young girls dressed as bears to enact a ritual connected with the goddess and childbirth.

The **Stoa of the Bears,** where these initiates stayed, has been substantially reconstructed, along with a stone **bridge;** both are fifth century BC and provide a graceful focus to the semi-waterlogged site. Somewhat scantier are the ruins of the temple itself, whose stepped foundations can be made out; immediately adjacent, the sacred spring still wells up, today squirming with tadpoles. Nearby, steps lead up to the chapel, which contains some damaged frescoes. At the site **museum,** a short walk from the ruins, various finds from the sanctuary are displayed.

Getting to Brauron from Athens will involve a walk if you're dependent on public transport. Bus #350 from the Záppio (*E1*) terminates at "Artémi" (Loútsa), but you can get off the bus at the site, two kilometres before the end of the line.

Rafína, Marathon and Rhamnous

The port of **RAFÍNA** has **ferries,** the **Catamaran** (in fact a sort of jet-boat) and **hydrofoils** to a wide assortment of the Cyclades, the Dodecanese, and the northeast Aegean, as well as to nearby Évvia. It is connected regularly by bus with Athens: a forty-minute trip (from Mavromatéon) through the "gap" in Mount Pendéli.

Boats aside, the appeal of the place is mainly gastronomic. Though much of the town has been spoilt by tacky seaside development, the little fishing harbour with its line of **roof-terrace seafood restaurants** remains one of the most attractive spots on the Attic coast. A lunchtime outing is an easy operation, given the frequency of the bus service. Evenings, when it's more fun, you need to arrange your own transport back, or make for the beachside **campsite** at nearby Kókkino Limanáki. The town's half-dozen **hotels** are often full, so you need to phone ahead to be sure of a room; the best value are the *Corali* (☎0294/22 477; ③) and the *Kymata* (☎0294/23 406; ③),both of which are located in the central Platía Nikifórou Plastíra.

Marathon

The site of the most famous military victory in Athenian history is not far from the village of **MARATHÓNAS,** 42km from Athens, on the same bus route as Rafína. Just over three kilometres after Néa Mákri (4 km before the village of Marathonas there is a turn to the right; the **Týmfos Marathóna** stands to the left of the road 700 yards after this turn. The ancient burial mound was raised over 192 Athenians who died in the city's famous victory over the Persians in 490 BC. Consisting only of earth piled ten metres high, it is a quietly impressive monument. Another mound, this for the eleven Plataian allies of the Athenians (including a ten-year-old boy) who died in the battle, is about 5km away, near the edge of the mountain. To reach the **Mound of the Plataians** and the **archeological museum,** return to the Rafina-Marathonas road and turn right towards the village of Marathona. Turn left and follow the small yellow signs for 2.5km to the museum (open, as is the mound precinct, Tues–Sun 8.30am–3pm; 500dr) with a sparse collection of artefacts mainly from the local Cave of Pan, a deity felt to have aided the victory.

Marathóna village itself is a dull place, with just a couple of cafés and restaurants for the passing trade. Nearby, though, to the west, and quite an impressive site, is **Límni Marathóna** – Marathon Lake – with its huge marble dam. This provided Athens's entire water supply until the 1950s and it is still used as a storage facility for water from the giant Mórnos project in central Greece.

The coast around ancient Marathon takes in some good stretches of sand, walkable from the tomb if you want to cool off. The best and most popular **beach** is to the north at **SKHINIÁS**, a long, pine-backed strand with shallow water, crowded with Athenians at weekends. There is a **campsite**, *Camping Marathon*, midway along the road from Marathónas.

Rhamnous

Further to the north, the ruins of **RHAMNOUS** (Tues–Sun 8.30am–3pm; 500dr) occupy an isolated site above the sea. Among the scattered and overgrown remains is a Doric **Temple of Nemesis**, goddess of retribution. Pausanias records that the Persians who landed nearby before their defeat incurred her wrath by carrying off a marble block – upon which they intended to commemorate their conquest of Athens. There are also the remains of a smaller temple dedicated to Themis, goddess of justice. Rhamnous can be reached just five times daily by bus from the Mavromatéon terminal; the village name to look for is Káto Soúli.

Mount Párnitha and Phyle

Scarcely an hour's bus ride north from the city centre, **Mount Párnitha** is an unexpectedly vast and – where it has escaped fire damage – virgin tract of forest, rock and ravine. If you've no time for expeditions further afield, it will give you a taste of what Greek mountains are all about, including a good selection of mountain flowers. If you're here in March or April, it merits a visit in its own right. Snow lies surprisingly late on the north side and, in its wake, carpets of crocus, alpine squills and mountain windflower spring from the mossy ground, while lower down you'll find aubretia, tulips, dwarf iris, and a whole range of orchids.

There are numerous **waymarked paths** on the mountain (look for red discs and multicoloured paint splodges on the trees). The principal and most representative ones are the approach to the Báfi refuge up the **Khoúni** ravine, and the walk to the Skípiza spring. These, along with a couple of lesser excursions, to the ancient fort at Phyle and one of the many legendary **Caves of Pan**, are detailed below.

The hike to the Báfi refuge

On Saturdays and Sundays bus A12 runs from the corner of Aharnón and Stournári (north side of Platía Váthi, *C2* on the main Athens map) twice a day (6.30am and 2.30pm) up to Párnitha. During the week take the trunk line bus A10 or B10 to the end of the line (Mesiníti) and then the local buses #724 or #737 to the suburb of Thrakomakedhónes, whose topmost houses are beginning to steal up the flanks of the mountain beside the mouth of the **Khoúni** ravine. Get off at the highest stop and keep on, bearing left, up Odhós Thrákis to where the road ends at the foot of a cliff beside two new blocks of flats. Keep straight ahead along the foot of the cliff and in a few metres you come to the start of the path, turning down left into a dry streambed, before crossing and continuing on the opposite bank.

The refuge is about two hours' walk away. The track curves slowly leftwards up the craggy, well-defined ravine, at first through thick scrub, then through more open forest of Greek fir, crossing the stream two or three times. At a junction reached after about 45 minutes, signposted "Katára–Mesanó Neró–Móla", keep straight ahead. At the next fork, some ten minutes later, keep right. After a further five minutes, at the top of a sparsely vegetated slope, you get your first glimpse of the pink-roofed refuge high on a rocky spur in front of you. Another twenty minutes brings you to the confluence of two small streams, where a sign on a tree points left to Ayía Triádha (see p.132), and a second path branches right to Móla and Koromiliá. Take the third, middle, path, up a scrubby spur. At the top a broad path goes off left to meet the ring road leading to Ayía Triádha.

From here, turn right, down into the head of a gully, where the path doubles back and climbs up to the refuge. Normally the refuge warden provides **board and lodging**, particularly on weekends, but it would be wise to check opening times and accommodation policy with the Athens EOS on Platía Kapnikaréas (weekday evenings only) in advance, as the schedule changes periodically. Water is usually available at the back of the building, except in winter.

To the Skípiza spring

For the walk to the Skípiza spring, you need to get off at the chapel of Ayía Triádha in the heart of the mountains. On the weekends there are two A12 connections a day: at 6.30am, returning at 8am; and at 2pm, returning at 4pm. If you get stuck, you can continue to the *Hotel Mount Parnes* and take the *téléférique* down if it's operating – otherwise there's a rough trail down a gully near the *Xenia Hotel*, spilling out near the Metóhi picnic grounds.

The **Skípiza spring** is an hour and a half to two hours' walk away. From the bus stop by the chapel, walk west past the *Hotel-Chalet Kiklamina*, continuing straight on to the ring road. After the first ascent and descent, you come after fifteen minutes to the Paliohóri spring on the right of the road in the middle of a left-hand bend, opposite a piece of flat ground marked with pointed-hat pipes. A beautiful and well-defined path is clearly marked by discs on trees, beginning by the spring and following the course of a small stream up through the fir woods.

From Skípiza you can continue right around the summit to **Móla** (about 90min) and from there, in another hour, back to the Báfi refuge. Alternatively, by setting your back to the Skípiza spring and taking the path that charges up the ridge almost directly behind, you can get to **Báfi** in around forty minutes. Turn left when you hit the paved road after about half an hour; follow it ten minutes more down to the ring road and turn left again. In a few paces you are in the refuge car park. To get back to Ayía Triádha by the road it's about 6km (an hour's walk).

The Cave of Pan

Another highly evocative spot for lovers of classical ghosts is the **Cave of Pan**, which Menander used as the setting for one of his plays. The best approach is by track and trail from the chapel of Ayía Triádha: a map showing local landmarks (labelled in Greek), superimposed on a topographical map, is posted just behind the church.

Phyle

Over to the west of the main Párnitha trails, another route up the mountain will take you to the ruined but still impressive fourth-century BC Athenian fort of **Phyle**, about an hour and three quarters on foot beyond the village of Filí (known locally as Khasiá). Buses to Filí leave near the Aharnón/Stournára stop on Odhós Sourméli (*C2*).

On the way up to the fort you pass the unattractively restored fourteenth-century **monastery of Klistón** in the mouth of the Goúra ravine that splits through the middle of the Párnitha range. The walking, unfortunately, is all on asphalt.

Eleusis and west to the Peloponnese

The main **highway to Kórinthos** (Corinth) is about as unattractive a road as any in Greece. For the first thirty or so kilometres you have little sense of leaving Athens, whose western suburbs merge into the industrial wastelands of first Elefsína and then Mégara. Offshore, almost closing off the bay, is **Salamína** (ancient Salamis), not a dream island in anyone's book but a nicer escape than it looks, and accessible by ferries from the mainland here at Lákki Kaloírou (and at Pérama, near Pireás).

A train or bus direct to Kórinthos or beyond, though, is perhaps the wisest option. Only the site of **ancient Eleusis** is in any way a temptation to stop, and even this is strictly for classical enthusiasts. **Drivers** should note that the Athens–Kórinthos non-toll road is one of the most dangerous in the country, switching from four-lane highway to a rutted two-laner without warning; it is best driven in daytime, or preserve your sanity and pay the toll.

Eleusis

The **Sanctuary of Demeter** at **ELEUSIS**, at the beginning of the Sacred Way to Athens, was one of the most important in the Greek world. For two millennia, the ritual ceremonies known as the Mysteries were perfomed, which had an effect on their ancient initiates the equal of any modern cult. According to Pindar, who experienced the rites in classical times and, like all others, was bound by pain of death not to reveal their content, anyone who had "seen the holy things [at Eleusis] and goes in death beneath the earth is happy, for he knows life's end and he knows the new divine beginning".

Established in Mycenaean times, perhaps as early as 1500 BC, the cult centred around the figure of Demeter (Ceres to the Romans), the goddess of corn, and the myth of her daughter Persephone's annual descent into and resurrection from the underworld, which came to symbolize the rebirth of the crops (and the gods responsible for them) in the miracle of fertility. By the fifth century BC the cult had developed into a sophisticated annual festival, attracting up to 30,000 people from all over the Greek world. Participants gathered in Athens, outside the Propylaia on the Acropolis, and, after various rituals, including mass bathing and purification in Phaleron Bay, followed the Sacred Way to the sanctuary here at Eleusis. It has been speculated by some, such as the late ethnomycologist R. Gordon Wasson, that one of the rituals entailed the ingestion of a potion containing grain-ergot fungus, the effects of which would be almost identical to those of modern psychedelic drugs.

The site

The **ruins** (Tues–Sun 8.30am–3pm; 500dr) are obscure in the extreme, dating from several different ages of rebuilding and largely reduced to foundations; any imaginings of mystic goings-on are further hampered by the spectacularly unromantic setting. The best plan is to head straight for the **museum**, which features models of the site at various stages in its history. This will at least point you in the direction of the **Telesterion**, the windowless Hall of Initiation, where the priests of Demeter would exhibit the "Holy Things" – presumably sheaves of fungus-infected grain, or vessels containing the magic potion – and speak "the Unutterable Words".

To reach the site from Athens, take **bus Ā16** from Platía Eleftherías (*E2* on the main Athens map). Ask to be dropped at the *Heröön* (Sanctuary), to the left of the main road, a short way into Elefsína. The trip can easily be combined with a visit to the monastery at Dhafní (see p.107), on the same road and bus route.

On from Elefsína

Northwest from Elefsína, the **old road to Thebes and Delphi** heads into the hills. This route is described in Chapter Three, and is highly worthwhile, with its detours to **ancient Aegosthena** and the tiny resort of **Pórto Yermenó**. At Mégara another, more minor road heads north to reach the sea at the village of Alepohóri, where it deteriorates to a track to loop around to Pórto Yermenó.

Heading directly west, on towards the Peloponnese, there are shingle beaches – more or less clear of pollution – along the old, parallel coastal road at Kinéta and Áyii

Theódhori. This highway, with the Yeránia mountains to the north and those of the Peloponnese across the water, has a small place in pre-Homeric myth, as the route where Theseus slew the bandit Sciron and threw him off the cliffs to be eaten by a giant sea turtle. Thus, Sciron met the same fate as the generations of travellers he had preyed upon.

You leave Attica at Isthmía, a village beside the **Corinth Canal** (see p.148), where most of the buses break the journey for a drink at the café by the bridge. To the north of the canal, Loutráki and Perahóra are technically part of Attica but, as they are more easily reached from Kórinthos, are covered in the Peloponnese chapter.

travel details

Trains

Trains for **Kórinthos and the Peloponnese** leave from the **Stathmós Peloponíssou**, those for **northern Greece** from **Stathmós Laríssis**. The stations adjoin each other, just west of Deliyánni (*B/C1*), on the #1 trolley bus route. To reach the Peloponnese station, use the metal overpass next to the Laríssis station.

Buses

Attica Buses for most destinations in Attica (ie within this chapter) leave from the Mavromatéon terminal (250m north of the National Archeological Museum, at the junction with Leof. Alexándhras, "B" on the Athens map, *B2*). Exceptions are specified in the text.

Destinations include: Lávrio (every 30min until 6pm, then hourly until 9pm; 1hr); Marathon Tomb (every 30min until 2pm, hourly thereafter; 1hr); Rafína (every 30min; 1hr); Sounion by the coast (hourly on the half hour; 1hr); Sounion by the inland route (hourly on the hour; 1hr 15min).

Peloponnese and western/northern Greece Most buses leave from the terminal at Kifissoú 100, a good 4km northeast of the city centre, in the industrial district of Peristéri; the easiest way to get there is on the #051 bus from the corner of Vilára and Menándhrou (near Omónia; "E" on the map, *D2*).

Destinations include: Árgos (hourly; 2hr 45min; Árta (8 daily; 6hr); Corfu (3 daily; 11hr); Igoumenítsa (3 daily; 8hr 30min); Ioánnina (8 daily; 7hr 30min); Kefalloniá (4 daily; 8hr); Kórinthos (every 30min; 1hr 30min); Lefkádha (4 daily; 6hr); Mycenae/Náfplio (hourly; 2hr 30min); Olympia (4 daily; 6hr); Pátra (every 45min; 3hr); Pýlos (2 daily; 6hr); Spárti (9

daily; 4hr 30min); Thessaloníki (10 daily; 7hr); Trípoli (12 daily; 4hr); Zákynthos (3 daily; 7hr).

Central Greece Buses for most other destinations in central Greece leave from the Liossíon 260 terminal, easiest reached by taxi. Alternatively, take either bus #024 at the Amalías entrance of the National Gardens (by Sýndagma, *E4*), almost to the end of its route (about 25min; the stop is 200m south of the terminal); or the metro from Omónia/Monastiráki to the Áyios Nikólaos station (800m southeast of the terminal; coming out, go under the rail line, turn left and look out for the buses).

Destinations include: Áyios Konstandínos (hourly at quarter past the hour; 2hr 30min); Delphi (5 daily; 3hr); Khalkídha (every 30min; 1hr); Karpeníssi (2 daily; 6hr); Kými, for Skýros ferries (6 daily; 3hr 30min); Óssios Loukás (2 daily; 4hr); Thíva/Thebes (hourly; 1hr); Tríkala (7 daily; 5hr 30min); Vólos (9 daily; 5hr).

Island ferries and hydrofoils

Information For details of ferries from **Rafína or Lávrio** call their respective port police offices (Rafína: ☎0294/22 300; Lávrio: ☎0292/25 249). For **hydrofoils** call (☎0294/ 23 500 or 23 561).

Pireás Ferries and hydrofoils to the Argo-Saronic, Monemvassía, Crete, the Cyclades, Dodecanese and northeast Aegean islands. See p.128 for details of how to get to Pireás.

Lávrio Ferries daily to Kéa; one weekly to Kýthnos. Bus from Mavromatéon (*B2*).

Rafína Ferries daily to Mármari, Kárystos and Stíra on Évvia; most days to Ándhros, Tínos, Sýros, Mýkonos, Páros and Náxos, plus less frequently to Amorgós; and two or three weekly to Khíos, Lésvos and Límnos. Hydrofoils to Évvia (Stýra, Mármari and Kárystos), Ándhros, Tínos,

Mýkonos, Páros, Náxos and beyond. Most ferries from Rafína to the Cyclades leave in the **late afternoon** – a boon if you've missed the morning Pireás boats. Bus from Mavromatéon (*B2*).

International ferries

From Pireás Destinations include: Izmir or Çeşme, Turkey (once weekly); Kuşadası, Turkey (once weekly May–Oct); Ancona, Italy (2 weekly); Limassol, Cyprus and Haifa, Israel (at least weekly, via Rhodes or Crete); Venice, Italy (3–4 monthly). Services to Alexandria, Egypt are currently suspended.

Domestic flights

Olympic Airways operate regular flights from the **west airport** to the following destinations:

Alexandhroúpoli, Astypálea, Khaniá (Crete), Khíos, Iráklion (Crete), Ioánnina, Kalamáta, Kárpathos, Kastoriá, Kavála, Kefalloniá, Kérkyra (Corfu), Kýthira, Kós, Kozáni, Léros, Límnos, Mílos, Mýkonos, Mytilíni (Lésvos), Náxos, Páros, Préveza, Ródhos (Rhodes), Sámos, Sitía (Crete), Skiáthos, Sýros, Sitía, Skýros, Thessaloníki, Thíra (Santórini) and Zákynthos.

All services are heavily reduced out of season.

CHAPTER TWO

THE PELOPONNESE

T he appeal of the Peloponnese (Pelopónnisos in Greek) is hard to overstate. This southern peninsula, technically an island since the cutting of the Corinth Canal, seems to have the best of almost everything Greek. Its ancient sites include the Homeric palaces of Agamemnon at **Mycenae** and of Nestor at **Pýlos**, the best preserved of all Greek theatres at Epidaurus, and the lush sanctuary of **Olympia**, host for a millennium to the Olympic Games. The medieval remains are scarcely less rich, with the fabulous Venetian, Frankish and Turkish castles of **Náfplio**, **Methóni** and **Kórinthos**; the strange tower-houses and frescoed churches of the **Máni**; and the extraordinarily well-preserved Byzantine shells of **Mystra** and **Monemvassía**.

Beyond this incredible profusion of cultural monuments, the Peloponnese is also a superb place to relax and wander. Its **beaches**, especially along the west coast, are among the finest and least developed in the country, and the **landscape** itself is superb – dominated by range after range of forested mountains, and cut by some of the lushest valleys and gorges to be imagined. Not for nothing did its heartland province of **Arcadia** lend its name to the concept of a classical rural idyll.

The Peloponnese is at its most enjoyable and intriguing when you venture off the beaten track: to the old hill towns of Arcadia like **Karýtena** and **Dhimitsána**; the bizarre semi-desert of the **Máni** or the castles and beaches of **Messinía** in the south; or the trip along the astonishing **rack-and-pinion railway** leading inland from **Dhiakoftó** on the north coast.

The province will amply repay any amount of time that you devote to it. The **Argolid**, the area richest in ancient history, is just a couple of hours from Athens, and if pushed you could complete a circuit of the main sights here – **Corinth**, **Mycenae** and **Epidaurus** – in a couple of days, making your base by the sea in Náfplio. Given a week, you could take in the two sites of Mystra and Olympia at a more leisurely pace. To get to grips with all this, however, plus the wonderful southern peninsulas of the Máni and Messinía, and the hill towns of Arcadia, you'll need at least a couple of weeks.

If you were planning on a combination of Peloponnese-plus-islands, the Argo-Saronic or Ionian islands are the most convenient, although you might well be better off limiting yourself to the mainland on a short trip. The **Argo-Saronic** islands (see pp.165–166) are linked by hydrofoil with the Argolid and Pireás. Of the **Ionian** islands, **Kýthira** is covered in this chapter since it's easiest reached from the southern Peloponnese ports, but **Zákynthos** (see p.234) can also be reached from the western port of Kýllíni, and Greece's second port city of **Pátra** serves as a gateway to the other islands of the Ionian group – and to southern Italy.

Travelling about the peninsula by **public transport**, you'll be dependent mostly on the **buses**, which are fast and regular on the main routes, and get to most other places at least once a day. The Peloponnese **train line**, now a century old, is in a poor state, especially on its highly scenic southern loop, with trains risking mishaps on defective sleepers if they exceed the leisurely timetable. Renting a **car** is worthwhile if you can afford it, even for just a few days – to explore the south from Kalamáta or Sparta, or Arcadia from Náfplio or Trípoli.

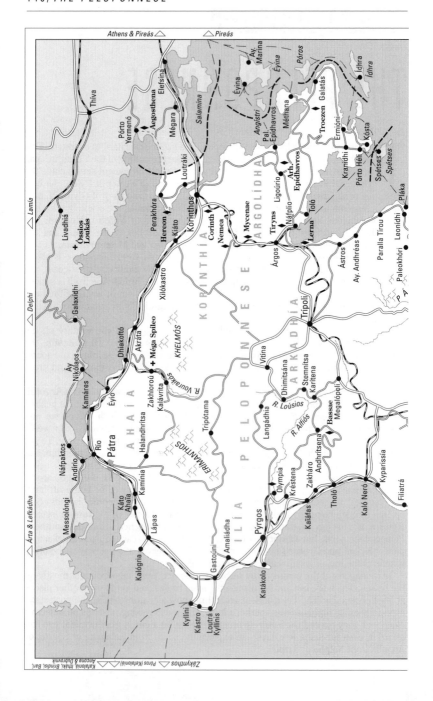

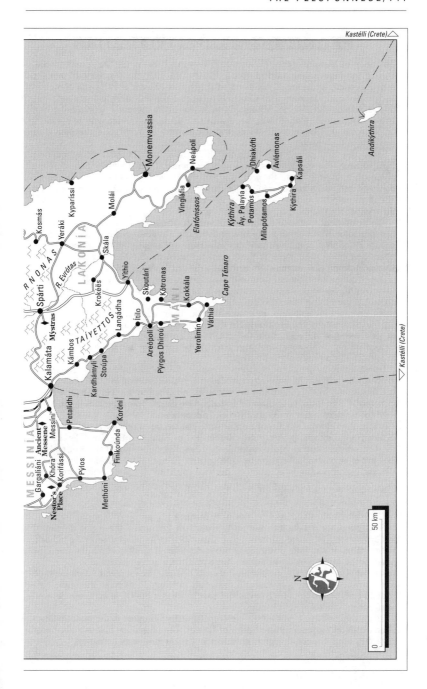

PELOPÓNISSOS – MOREÁS: SOME HISTORY

The **ancient history** of the Peloponnese is very much that of the Greek mainstream. During the **Mycenaean period** (around 2000–1100 BC), the peninsula hosted the semi-legendary kingdoms of Agamemnon at Mycenae, Nestor at Pýlos and Menelaus at Sparta. In the **Dorian** and **Classical** eras, the region's principal city-state was Sparta, which, with its allies, brought down Athens in the ruinous Peloponnesian War. Under **Roman** rule, Corinth was the capital of the southern Greek province. For more on all these periods, see the "Historical framework" on p.767, and the individual accounts in this chapter.

From the decline of the Romans, through to the Turkish conquest, the Peloponnese – or the **Moreás**, as it became known, from the resemblance of the peninsula's map-outline to the leaf of a mulberry tree (*moreás*) – pursued a more complex and individual course. A succession of occupations and conquests, with attendant outposts and castles, has left an extraordinary legacy of medieval remains throughout the region.

The Peloponnese retained a nominally Roman civilization well after the colonial rule had dissipated, with Corinth at the fore, until the city was destroyed by two major earthquakes in the sixth century. Around this time, too, came attacks from barbarian tribes of Avars and Slavs, who were to pose sporadic problems for the new rulers – the **Byzantines**, the eastern emperors of the now divided Roman Empire.

The Byzantines established their courts, castles and towns from the ninth century on; their control, however, was only partial, as large swathes of the Moreás fell under the control of the Franks and Venetians. The **Venetians** settled along the coast, founding trading ports at Monemvassía, Pýlos and Koróni, which endured, for the most part, into the fifteenth century. The **Franks**, led by the Champlitte and Villehardouin clans, arrived in 1204, bloodied and eager from the sacking of Constantinople in the piratical Fourth Crusade. They swiftly conquered large tracts of the peninsula, and divided it into feudal baronies under a prince of the Moreás.

Towards the middle of the thirteenth century, there was a remarkable **Byzantine revival**, which spread from the court at Mystra to reassert control over the peninsula. A last flicker of "Greek" rule, it was eventually extinguished by the **Turkish conquest**, between 1458 and 1460, and was to lie dormant, save for sporadic rebellions in the Máni, until the nineteenth-century **War of Greek Independence**.

In this, the Peloponnese played a major part. The banner of rebellion was raised near **Kalávryta**, in Arcadia, by Yermanos, Archbishop of Pátra, and the Greek forces' two most successful leaders – **Mavromikhalis** and **Kolokotronis** – were natives of, and carried out most of their actions in, the Peloponnese. The battle that accidentally decided the war, **Navarino Bay**, was fought off the west coast at Pýlos; and the first Greek parliament was convened here, too, at **Náfplio**. After independence, however, power passed swiftly away from the Peloponnese to Athens, where it was to stay. The peninsula's contribution to the early Greek state was a disaffected one, highlighted by the assassination of Capodistrias, the first Greek president, by Maniots.

Throughout the **nineteenth** and **early twentieth centuries**, the region developed important ports at Pátra, Kórinthos and Kalamáta, but its interior reverted to backwater status. It was little disturbed until **World War II**, during which the area saw some of the worst German atrocities; there was much brave resistance in the mountains, but also some of the most shameful collaboration. The **civil war** which followed left many of the towns polarized and physically in ruins. In its wake there was substantial **emigration** from both towns and countryside, to the US in particular, as well as to Athens and other Greek cities.

Today, the southern Peloponnese has a reputation for being one of the most traditional and politically **conservative** regions of Greece. The people are held in rather poor regard by other Greeks, though to outsiders they seem unfailingly hospitable.

CORINTH AND THE ARGOLID

The usual approach from Athens to the Peloponnese is along the highway through Elefsína and across the Corinth Canal to modern-day **Kórinthos** (Corinth); buses and trains come this way at least every hour, the former halting at the canal (see p.148). Another, more attractive approach to the peninsula is by ferry or Flying Dolphin hydrofoil, via the islands of the **Argo-Saronic** (see pp.165–167); routes run from Pireás through those islands, with brief hops over to the Argolid ports of Ermióni, Pórto Héli, Náfplio and Paleáepídhavros.

The region that you enter, to the south and southeast of Kórinthos, is known as the **Argolid** (Argolídha in modern Greek), after the city of Argos, which held sway in Classical times. The greatest concentration of ancient sites in Greece is found in this compact little peninsula, its western boundary delineated by the main road south from Kórinthos. Within an hour or so's journey of each other are Agamemnon's fortress at **Mycenae**, the great theatre of **Epidaurus**, and lesser sites at **Tiryns**, **Árgos** and **Lerna**. Inevitably these, along with the great Roman site at **Ancient Corinth**, draw the crowds, and in peak season you may want to see the sites early or late in the day to realize their magic.

When ruin-hopping palls, there are the small-town pleasures of elegant **Náfplio**, and a handful of pleasant **coastal resorts**. The best beaches in these parts, however, are to be found along the coast road south from Árgos – at the Ástros and Tirós beaches, where there are some good campsites. Technically outside the Argolid, both of these are easiest reached by bus from Árgos or by Flying Dolphin hydrofoil from Náfplio (summer only), Pórto Héli or the island of Spétses. The southern continuation of these hydrofoil routes takes you on down the coast to the Byzantine remains of Monemvassía.

Kórinthos

Like its ancient predecessor, the modern city of **KÓRINTHOS** (modern Corinth) has been levelled on several occasions by earthquakes – most recently in 1981, when a serious quake left thousands in tented homes for most of the following year. Repaired and reconstructed, with buildings of prudent but characterless concrete, the modern city has little of intrinsic interest: it is largely an industrial-agriculture centre, its economy bolstered by the drying and shipping of currants, for centuries one of Greece's few successful exports (the word currant itself derives from Corinth).

Nevertheless, you could do worse than base yourself here for a night or two, for the setting, with the sea on two sides and the mountains across the gulf, is magnificent, and there are some pleasant quarters along the shore, plus a nice provincial main square centred around a park. In addition, of course, there are the remains of ancient and medieval Corinth – **Arkhéa Kórinthos** – 7km to the southwest, as well as access to Perakhóra and a couple of other minor sites (see p.148).

The only specific sight in the modern city itself is the **Folklore Museum** (daily 8am–1pm; free), located in a tasteful modern building near the harbour. This contains the usual array of peasant costumes, old engravings and dioramas of traditional crafts.

Arrival and information

The **bus station for Athens** and most local destinations (including Arhéa Kórinthos, Isthmía, Loutráki and Neméa) is on the Ermoú side of the park, at the corner with Koliátsou. **Long-distance buses** (to Spárti, Kalamáta, Trípoli, Mycenae, Árgos and

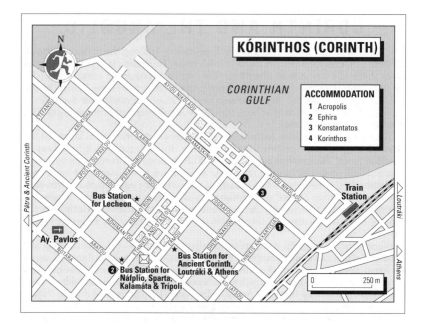

Náfplio) use a terminal on the other side of the park, at the corner of Ethnikís Andístasis and Arátou. The **train station** is a few blocks to the east.

Orientation is straightforward. The centre of Kórinthos is its **park**, bordered on the longer sides by Ermoú and Ethnikís Andístasis (formerly Konstantinou) streets. You'll find the National and Commercial **banks** along the latter, and the main **post office** on Adimantoú street, on the south side of the park. There's a **tourist police** post at Ermoú 5 (☎0741/23 282), near the Athens bus station, and a **taxi rank** on the Ethnikís Andístassis side of the park. If you want to rent your own transport, for **mopeds** and **bikes** check out Liberopoulos, at Ethnikís Andistáseos 27 (☎0741/72 937); for **cars**, try Grigoris Lagos (☎0741/22 617) at Ethnikís Andistáseos 42 or Vasilopoulis at Adímantou 30 (☎0741/28 437).

Accommodation

At most times of year, **hotels** are reasonably easy to find, with two or three on the road into town from the train station, and a couple of less expensive ones on or near the waterside. A selection is given below. Alternatively, there are a couple of **campsites** along the gulf to the west: *Korinth Beach* (☎0741/27 967; April–Oct) is 3km out at Dhiavakíta – to reach the beach, such as it is, you must cross the coastal road and the railway line. *Blue Dolphin* (☎0741/25 766; mid-May to mid-Oct) is a bit further away at Léheo, but it is on the seaward side of the tracks, and for that alone is preferable. For both sites, take the bus to Léheo (a part of Ancient Corinth) from alongside the park in modern Kórinthos.

Acropolis, Ethnikís Anexartisías 25 (☎0741/22 430). On the way into town from the train station; good value. ④.

Ephira, Ethnikís Andistáseos 52 (☎0741/22 434). One block from the park and near the long-distance bus station. A modern hotel and a good mid-priced choice. ④.

Konstantatos, Dhervenakínou 3 (☎0741/22 120). Upmarket with private bathrooms and elegant decor. ⑥.

Korinthos, Dhamaskinóu 26 (☎0741/22 631). Near the *Konstantatos*; there's little to choose between them. ④.

Eating and drinking

Kórinthos has a few **tavernas**, and rather more fast-food places along the waterfront, all modestly priced.

Anaxagoras, Áyiou Nikólaou 31. Good range of mezédhes and grilled meats.

Kanata, Dhamiskinoú 41. One of the best restaurants in the centre of town. Open all day.

Arkhontiko, (☎0741/27 968). A favourite with the locals. As this place is out near the campsites, you might want to phone first.

Ancient Corinth

Buses to Ancient Corinth, **ARKHÉA KÓRINTHOS**, leave modern Kórinthos every hour from 8am to 9pm and return on the half-hour; a taxi is also a possibility, since fares are not exorbitant at around 2500dr return, and drivers will wait. The ruins of the **ancient city**, which displaced Athens as capital of the Greek province in Roman times, occupy a rambling sequence of sites, the main enclosure of which is given a sense of scale by the majestic ruin of a Temple of Apollo. Most compelling, though, are the ruins of the medieval city, which occupy the stunning acropolis site of **Acrocorinth**, towering 565m above.

The ruins of Ancient Corinth spread over a vast area, and include sections of ancient walls (the Roman city had a fifteen-kilometre circuit), outlying stadiums, gymnasiums and necropolises. Only the central area, around the Roman forum and the Classical Temple of Apollo, is preserved in an excavated state; the rest, odd patches of semi-enclosed and often overgrown ruin, you come across unexpectedly while walking about the village and up to Acrocorinth.

The overall effect is impressive, but it only begins to suggest the majesty of this once supremely wealthy city. Ancient Corinth was a key centre of the Greek and Roman worlds, whose possession meant the control of trade between northern Greece and the Peloponnese. In addition, the twin ports of **Lechaion**, on the gulf of Corinth, and **Kenchreai**, on the Saronic Gulf, provided a trade link between the Ionian and Aegean seas – the western and eastern Mediterranean. Not surprisingly, this meant that the city's ancient (and medieval) history was one of invasions and power struggles which, in Classical times, was dominated by Corinth's rivalry with Athens – against whom it sided with Sparta in the Peloponnesian War.

SITE OPENING HOURS

Summer opening hours for the **sites** and **museums** in the Peloponnese are included with some trepidation. They are notorious for changing without notice, from one season to another, or from one week to the next due to staff shortages. Current policy has them opening as late as 9pm in August and 7pm the other summer months, and this seems set to continue.

To be sure of admission, it's best to visit between 9am and 3pm, and to be wary of Monday, when most museums and sites close for the whole day.

Despite this, Corinth suffered only one major setback, in 146 BC, when the Romans, having defeated the Greek city states of the Achaean League, razed the site to the ground. For a century the city lay in ruins before being rebuilt, on a majestic scale, by Julius Caesar in 44 BC: initially intended as a colony for veterans, it was later made the provincial capital. Once again Corinth grew rich on trade – with Rome to the west, Syria and Egypt to the east.

Roman Corinth's reputation for wealth, fuelled by its trading access to luxury goods, was soon equalled by its appetite for earthly pleasures – including sex. Corinthian women were renowned for their beauty and much sought after as *hetairai* (courtesans); a temple to Aphrodite/Venus, on the acropolis of Acrocorinth, was served by over a thousand sacred prostitutes. **St Paul** stayed in Corinth for eighteen months in 51–52 AD, though his attempts to reform the citizens' ways were met only by rioting – tribulations recorded in his two "letters to the Corinthians". The city endured until rocked by two major earthquakes, in 375 and 521, which brought down the Roman buildings, and again depopulated the site until a brief Byzantine revival in the eleventh century.

The excavations

Daily: summer 8am–7pm (Aug 8am–9pm); winter 8am–5pm; museum hours same except closed Mon; 1200dr for both.

Inevitably, given successive waves of earthquakes and destruction, the **main excavated site** is dominated by the remains of the Roman city. Entering from the north side, just behind the road where the buses pull in, you find yourself in the **Roman agora**, an enormous marketplace flanked by the substantial foundations of a huge *stoa*, once a structure of several storeys, with 33 shops on the ground floor. Opposite the *stoa* is a *bema*, a marble platform used for public announcements. At the far end are remains of a **basilica**, while the area behind the *bema* is strewn with the remnants of numerous Roman administrative buildings. Back across the *agora*, almost hidden in a swirl of broken marble and shattered architecture, there's a fascinating trace of the Greek city – a **sacred spring**, covered over by a grille at the base of a narrow flight of steps.

More substantial is the elaborate Roman **Fountain of Peirene**, which stands below the level of the *agora*, to the side of a wide excavated stretch of what was the main approach to the city, the marble-paved **Lechaion Way**. Taking the form of a colonnaded and frescoed recess, the fountain occupies the site of one of two natural springs in Corinth – the other is up on the acropolis – and its cool water was channelled into a magnificent fountain and pool in the courtyard. The fountain house was, like many of Athens' Roman public buildings, the gift of the wealthy Athenian and friend of the Emperor Hadrian, Herodes Atticus. The waters still flow through the underground cisterns and supply the modern village.

The real focus of the ancient site, though, is a rare survival from the Classical Greek era, the fifth-century BC **Temple of Apollo**, whose seven austere Doric columns stand slightly above the level of the forum and are flanked by foundations of another marketplace and baths. Over to the west is the site **museum**, housing a large collection of domestic pieces, some good Roman mosaics and a frieze depicting some of the labours of Heracles (Hercules), several of which were performed nearby – at Nemea, Stymphalia and Lerna. The city's other claim to mythic fame, incidentally, is as the home of the infant Oedipus and his step-parents, prior to his travels of discovery to Thebes.

A number of miscellaneous smaller excavations surround the main site. To the west, just across the road from the enclosing wire, there are outlines of two **theatres**: a Roman **odeion** (once again endowed by Herodes Atticus) and a larger Greek amphitheatre, adapted by the Romans for gladiatorial sea battles. To the north are the inaccessible but visible remains of an **Asclepion** (dedicated to the healing god).

Acrocorinth

Tues–Sun 8.30am–7pm; free.

Rising almost sheer above the lower town, **Acrocorinth** is sited on an amazing mass of rock, still largely encircled by two kilometres of wall. The ancient acropolis of Corinth, it became one of Greece's most powerful fortresses during the Middle Ages, besieged by successive waves of invaders, who considered it the key to the Moreás.

Despite the long, four-kilometre climb – or a taxi ride from ancient Corinth, reasonable if shared – a visit to the summit is unreservedly recommended. Looking down over the Saronic and Corinthian gulfs, you really get a sense the strategic importance of the fortress's position. Amid the sixty-acre site, you wander through a jumble of chapels, mosques, houses and battlements, erected in turn by Greeks, Romans, Byzantines, Frankish Crusaders, Venetians and Turks.

The Turkish remains are unusually substantial. Elsewhere in Greece evidence of the Ottoman occupation has been physically removed or defaced, but here, halfway up the hill, you can see a midway point in the process: the still functioning **Fountain of Hatzi Mustafa**, which has been Christianized by the addition of great carved crosses. The outer of the citadel's **triple gates**, too, is largely Turkish; the middle is a combination of Venetian and Frankish, the inner, Byzantine, incorporating fourth-century BC towers. Within the citadel, the first summit (to the right) is enclosed by a **Frankish keep** – as striking as they come – which last saw action in 1828 during the War of Independence. Keeping along the track to the left, you pass some interesting (if perilous) cisterns, remains of a Turkish bath house and crumbling Byzantine chapels.

In the southeast corner of the citadel, hidden away in the lower ground, is the **upper Peirene spring**. This is not easy to find: look out for a narrow, overgrown entrance, from which a flight of iron stairs leads down some five metres to a metal screen. Here, broad stone steps descend into the dark depths, where a fourth-century BC arch stands guard over a pool of water that has never been known to dry up. To the north of the fountain, on the second and higher summit, is the site of the **Temple of Aphrodite** mentioned above; after its days as a brothel, it saw use as a church, mosque and belvedere.

Practicalities

To explore both ancient and medieval Corinth you need a full day, or better still, to stay here overnight. A modern **village** spreads around the edge of the main ancient site and there are a scattering of **rooms** to rent in its backstreets – follow the signs or ask at the cafés. A good cheap option is the *Hotel Shadow* (☎0741/31 481; ③) which now has a small free museum in the lobby including petrified wood, minerals and local relics. More upmarket is *Marinos* rooms (☎0741/31 209; ④) with a smart new wing including a large indoor restaurant.

A rather wonderful alternative, for those with transport, or energy for the walk, would be to stay at the solitary modern building up in **Acrocorinth**: the *Acrocorinthos* café (☎0741/31 099; ②); phone ahead, as it only has a few rooms. There is a fully operational restaurant until early evening during summer months.

Around Corinth

As well as the **Corinth Canal**, which you can't help but pass en route between Kórinthos and Athens, a number of minor sites are accessible by bus (at least most of the way) from Kórinthos, both on the Peloponnese and Attic peninsulas. Just south of the canal is ancient **Isthmía**, site of the Panhellenic Isthmian Games. To the northwest are the spa of Loutráki and the classical **sanctuary of Hera** at **Perakhóra** on Cape Melangávi. If you have a car, there's a grand and rather wild route east from the cape, around the **Alkyonid Gulf** to Pórto Yermenó (see p.247). There are beaches along the way, though little settlement or development, and the final stretch of road beyond Káto Alepohóri is scarcely better than a jeep track.

Back in the Peloponnese proper, **Neméa** – as in the lion of Hercules's labour – is a brief detour southwest of Kórinthos, off the road to Árgos or Mycenae. **Sikyon** is a bit more remote, 25km up the coast towards Pátra, but again accessible by bus.

The Corinth Canal

The idea for a **Corinth Canal**, providing a short cut and safe passage between the Aegean and Ionian seas, dates back at least to Roman times, when the Emperor Nero performed initial excavations with a silver shovel and Jewish slave labour. It was only in the 1890s, however, that the technology became available to cut across the six-kilometre isthmus. Opened in July 1893, the canal, along with its near-contemporary Suez, helped establish Pireás as a major Mediterranean port and shipping centre, although

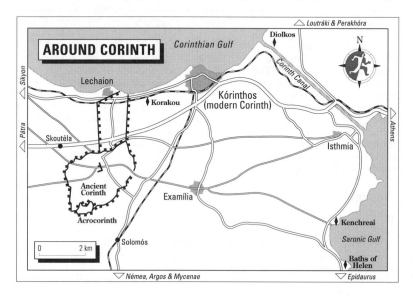

the projected toll revenues were never realized. Today supertankers have made it something of an anachronism and the canal has fallen into disrepair, but it remains a memorable sight nonetheless.

Approaching on the main Athens road, you cross the canal near its eastern end. At the **bridge** there's a line of **cafés**, where buses from Athens usually stop if they're going beyond Kórinthos. Peering over from the bridge, the canal appears a tiny strip of water until some huge freighter assumes toy-like dimensions as it passes hundreds of metres below. If you were to take one of the cruise ships from Pireás to the Ionian, you would actually sail through the canal – a trip almost worthwhile for its own sake. At the western end of the canal, by the old Kórinthos–Loutráki ferry dock, there are remains of the **diolkos**, a paved way along which a wheeled platform used to carry boats across the isthmus. In use from Roman times until the twelfth century, the boats were strapped onto the platform after being relieved temporarily of their cargo.

Ancient Isthmía

Modern Isthmía lies either side of the Saronic Gulf entrance to the canal, and is served by regular buses from Kórinthos. To the south of the modern settlement, on a hillock alongside the present-day village of Kriavríssi, is the site of ancient **ISTHMÍA**.

There is nothing very notable to see at the site, though the ancient settlement was an important one, due to its **Sanctuary of Poseidon** – of which just the foundations remain – and Panhellenic Isthmian games. The latter ranked with those of Delphi, Neméa and Olympia, though they have left scant evidence in the form of a **stadium** and **theatre**, together with a few curiosities, including starting blocks used for foot races, in the small adjacent **museum** which also houses some of the finds from Kenchreai. The opening hours of the museum are currently uncertain, but you can roam the site at will. There are decent swimming spots and some accommodation at *Loutra Elenis* and *Kehries* on the coast heading towards Paleá Epidhavros.

Loutráki

Six kilometres north of the canal is the spa resort of **LOUTRÁKI**. The epicentre of the 1981 Corinth earthquake, it may once have had its charms but today the concrete line of buildings casts a leaden air over the town. The resort is nonetheless immensely popular, with a larger concentration of hotels than anywhere else in the Peloponnese. The visitors are virtually all Greek, coming here for the "cure" at the hot springs, and to sample Loutráki mineral water – the country's leading bottled brand. A sign of the times is the new Pepsi-Cola bottling plant on the outskirts of Loutráki. There is a helpful tourist kiosk on E.Venizélou, the main road through town, just above the train station.

With your own transport, you'd be better off using the town simply as a staging post en route to the site of Ancient Perakhóra and making Lake Vouliagméni your base (see below). Otherwise, Loutráki is connected by bus and special summer trains with Athens, and by half-hourly bus with Kórinthos. If you end up staying, *Hotel Brettagne*, at Yeor Lékka 28 (☎0744/02 349; ③), makes a refreshing change from the many expensive spa-resort hotels; *Hotel Pappas* (☎0744/23 026; ⑤), to the left of the Perakhóra road, has better facilities and fine views across the gulf. The *Acropole*, P. Tsaldári II (☎0744/22 265; ⑤) is comfortable. *To Kharama* psistariá at the corner of Kanári and Ethnikís Andistáseos has good grills at decent rates.

Perakhóra

The road to **Cape Melangávi** is enjoyable in itself, running above the sea in the shadow of the Yizánia mountains, whose pine forests are slowly recovering from fire devastation in 1986. En route the road offers a loop through the modern village of

PERAKHÓRA (10km) before heading out to the cape along the shore of **Lake Vouliagméni**, a beautiful lagoon with sheltered swimming, a new hotel, the *Philoxenia* (☎0741/91 294; open all year; ④), and a small campsite, *Limni Heraiou* (☎0741/91 230; summer only). Perakhóra is connected by hourly bus with Loutráki; one daily bus makes the journey between Loutráki and Lake Vouliagméni, but runs in summer only.

Ancient Perakhóra – also known as the Heraion Melangavi – stands right on the western tip of the peninsula, commanding a marvellous, sweeping view of the coastline and mountains along both sides of the gulf. The site's position is its chief attraction, though there are the identifiable ruins of two sanctuaries, the **Hera Akraia** (*akron* is the extremity of the peninsula) and **Hera Limenia** (of the port), as well as the submerged **stoa** of the ancient port. The latter provides great snorkelling opportunities, but beware the potentially dangerous currents beyond the cove.

The initial excavation of Perakhóra, between 1930 and 1933, is described by Dilys Powell in *An Affair of the Heart*. Humfrey Payne, her husband, directed the work until his death in 1936; he was then buried at Mycenae. The site also features in myth, for it was here that Medea, having been spurned by her husband Jason at Corinth, killed their two children.

Nemea

Ancient **NEMEA**, the location for Hercules's slaying of its namesake lion (his first labour), lies 10km off the road from Kórinthos to Árgos. By public transport, take the bus to modern Neméa and ask to be dropped en route at *Arhéa Neméa*; moving on from the site, you can walk back down to the Árgos road and possibly wave down a bus on to Mycenae.

Like Olympia and Isthmía, Neméa held athletic games – supposedly inaugurated by Hercules – for the Greek world. A sanctuary rather than a town, the principal remains at the **site** (Tues–Sun 8.30am–3pm; 500dr) are of a **Temple of Nemean Zeus**, currently three slender Doric columns surrounded by other fallen and broken drums, but slowly being reassembled by a team of University of California archeologists. Nearby are a **palaestra** with **baths** and a Christian basilica, built with blocks from the temple. Outside the site, half a kilometre east, is a **stadium** whose starting line has been unearthed. There is also a **museum** (same hours; entrance included in site ticket), with excellent contextual models and displays relating to the biennial games.

The Stymphalean Lake

If you have transport, it's possible to cut across the hills from Neméa into Arcadia, via another Herculean locale, the **Stymphalean Lake** (around 35km from Neméa). In myth, this was the nesting-ground of man-eating birds who preyed upon travellers, suffocating them with their wings, and also poisoned local crops with their excrement. Hercules roused them from the water with a rattle, then shot them down – one of the more straightforward of his labours.

The lake is known in modern Greek as **Límni Stymfalías**, though it is really more marsh: an enormous depression with seasonal waters, ringed by woods and the dark peaks of Mount Kyllíni. There are no buildings for miles around, save for the ruins of the thirteenth-century Frankish Cistercian **Abbey of Zaráka** (east of the road), one of the few Gothic buildings in Greece.

If you don't have your own transport, the most promising approach to the lake is from Kiáto on the Gulf of Corinth, where there are several hotels and rooms to rent; the road, much better than that from Neméa, has the occasional bus. The nearest places to stay are the *Hotel Stymfalia* (☎0747/22 072; ②) at **Stymfália** village, just before the abbey, or the *Xenia* (☎0747/31 283; ④) 3km outside **Kastaniá**, a mountain village 20km to the west that's famed for its butterflies.

Ancient Sikyon

Six kilometres inland from Kiáto (see opposite), ancient **SIKYON** (Sikyóna) is a fairly accessible if little-known site, which deserves more than the few dozen visitors it attracts each year. Six buses a day run from Kiáto (on the bus and train routes from Kórinthos) to the village of Vasilikó, on the edge of a broad escarpment running parallel to the sea, from where it's a kilometre's walk to the site.

In ancient history, Sikyon's principal claim to fame came early in the sixth century BC, when the tyrant Kleisthenes kept a court of sufficient wealth and influence to purportedly entertain suitors for his daughter's hand for a full year. After his death the place was rarely heard from politically except as a consistent ally of the Spartans, but a mild renaissance ensued at the end of the fourth century when Demetrios Poliorketes moved Sikyon to its present location from the plain below. The town became renowned for sculptors, painters and artisans, and flourished well into Roman times; it was the birthplace of Alexander the Great's chief sculptor, Lysippus and, allegedly, of the art of sculptural relief.

The road from Vasilikó cuts through the site, which is fenced off into a number of enclosures. To the right is the **Roman baths museum** which shelters mosaics of griffins from the second to third century AD. To the left are the majority of the public buildings, with a theatre and stadium on the hillside above. As you enter the **main site** (unrestricted access), opposite the Roman baths, the foundations of a **Temple of Artemis** are visible to your left. Beyond it are traces of a **bouleuterion** (senate house) dating from the first half of the third century BC. The most important remains in this section are of the **Gymnasium of Kleinias** in the far right-hand corner, at the base of the hill; this is on two levels, the lower dating from around 300 BC, the other from Roman times.

Although only the first few rows of seats have been excavated, the outline of the **Theatre** – larger than that of Epidaurus – is impressive and obvious. Pine trees have taken root in the upper half, from where there's a marvellous view encompassing the rest of the site, the village of Vasilikó, the lemon and olive groves around Kiáto, plus gulf and mountains in the distance.

Mycenae (Mykínes)

Tucked into a fold of the hills just east of the road from Kórinthos to Árgos, Agamemnon's citadel at **MYCENAE** fits the legend better than any other place in Greece. It was uncovered in 1874 by the German archeologist Heinrich Schliemann (who also excavated the site of Troy), impelled by his single-minded belief that there was a factual basis to Homer's epics. Schliemann's finds of brilliantly crafted gold and sophisticated tomb-architecture bore out the accuracy of Homer's epithets of "well-built Mycenae, rich in gold".

Mycenaean history and legend

The Mycenae–Árgos region is one of the longest occupied in Greece, with evidence of Neolithic settlements from around 3000 BC. But it is to a period of three centuries at the end of the second millennium BC – from around 1550 to 1200 BC – that the citadel of Mycenae and its associated drama belong. This period is known as **Mycenaean**, a term which covers not just the Mycenae region but a whole civilization that flourished in southern Greece at the time.

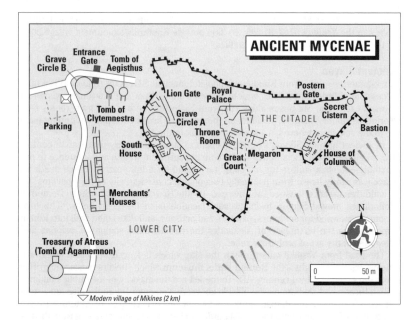

Modern village of Mikines (2 km)

According to the **legend** related in Homer's *Iliad* and *Odyssey* and Aeschylus's *Oresteia*, the city of Mycenae was founded by Perseus, the slayer of Medusa the gorgon, before it fell into the bloodied hands of the **House of Atreus**. In an act of vengeance for his brother Thyestes's seduction of his wife, Atreus murdered Thyestes's children, and fed them to their own father. Not surprisingly, this incurred the wrath of the gods. Thyestes's own daughter, Pelopia, subsequently bore him a son, Aegisthus, who promptly murdered Atreus and restored his father to the throne.

The next generation saw the gods' curse fall upon Atreus's son Agamemnon. On his return to Mycenae after commanding the Greek forces in the Trojan War – a role in which he had earlier consented to the sacrifice of his own daughter, Iphigeneia – he was killed in his bath by his wife Clytemnestra and her lover, the very same Aegisthus who had killed his father. The tragic cycle was completed by Agamemnon's son, Orestes, who took revenge by murdering his mother, Clytemnestra, and was pursued by the Furies until Athena finally lifted the curse on the house.

The **archeological remains** of Mycenae fit remarkably easily with the tale, at least if it is taken as a poetic rendering of dynastic struggles, or, as most scholars now believe it to be, a merging of stories from various periods. The buildings unearthed by Schliemann show signs of occupation from around 1950 BC, as well as two periods of intense disruption, around 1200 BC and again in 1100 BC – at which stage the town, though still prosperous, was abandoned.

No coherent explanation has been put forward for these events, since the traditional "Dorian invasions" theory (see p.770) has fallen from favour, but it seems that war among the rival kingdoms was a major factor in the Mycenaean decline. These struggles appear to have escalated as the civilization developed in the thirteenth century BC, and excavations at Troy have revealed the sacking of that city, quite possibly by forces led by a king from Mycenae, in 1240 BC. The citadel of Mycenae seems to have been replanned, and heavily fortified, during this period.

The Citadel

Daily: summer 8am–7pm (Aug 8am–9pm); winter 8am–5pm; 1500dr.

The **Citadel of Mycenae** is entered through the famous **Lion Gate**, whose huge sloping gateposts bolster walls were termed "Cyclopean" by later Greeks in bewildered explanation of their construction. Above them a graceful carved relief stands out in confident assertion: Mycenae at its height led a confederation of Argolid towns (Tiryns, Árgos, Asine, Hermione – the present-day Ermióni), dominated the Peloponnese and exerted influence throughout the Aegean. The motif of a pillar supported by two muscular lions was probably the symbol of the Mycenaean royal house, for a seal found on the site bears a similar device. Inside the walls to the right is **Grave Circle A**, the royal cemetery excavated by Schliemann and believed by him to contain the bodies of Agamemnon and his followers, murdered on their triumphant return from Troy. Opening one of the graves, he found a tightly fitting and magnificent gold mask that had somehow preserved the flesh of a Mycenaean noble; "I have gazed upon the face of Agamemnon," he exclaimed in an excited cable to the king of Greece. For a time it seemed that this provided irrefutable evidence of the truth of Homer's tale. In fact, the burials date from about three centuries before the Trojan war, though, given Homer's possible accumulation of different and earlier sagas, there's no reason why they should not have been connected with a Mycenaean king Agamemnon. They were certainly royal graves, for the finds (now in the National Archeological Museum in Athens) are among the richest archeology has yet unearthed.

Schliemann took the extensive **South House**, beyond the grave circle, to be the Palace of Agamemnon. However, a building much grander and more likely to be the **Royal Palace**, was later discovered near the summit of the acropolis. Rebuilt in the thirteenth century BC, this is an impressively elaborate and evocative building complex; although the ruins are only at ground level, the different rooms are easily discernible. Like all Mycenaean palaces, it is centred around a **Great Court**: on the south side, a staircase would have led via an anteroom to the big rectangular **Throne Room**; on the east, a double porch gave access to the **Megaron**, the grand reception hall with its traditional circular hearth. The small rooms to the north are believed to have been **royal apartments**, and in one of them the remains of a red stuccoed bath have led to its fanciful identification as the scene of Agamemnon's murder.

With the accompaniment of the sound of bells drifting down from goats scratching about the mountainside, a stroll round the ramparts is evocative. A more salutary reminder of the nature of life in Mycenaean times is the **secret cistern** at the western end of the ramparts, created in the twelfth century BC. Whether it was designed to enable the citadel's occupants to withstand siege from outsiders, rival Mycenaeans, or even an increasingly alienated peasantry, is not known. Steps lead down to a deep underground spring; it's still possible to descend the whole way, though you'll need to have a torch and be sure-footed, since there's a seventy-metre drop to the water (depth unknown) at the final turn of the twisting passageways. Nearby is the **House of Columns**, a large and stately building with the base of a stairway that once led to an upper storey.

Only the ruling Mycenaean elite could live within the citadel itself. Hence the main part of town lay outside the walls and, in fact, extensive remains of **merchants' houses** have been uncovered near to the road. Their contents included Linear B tablets recording the spices used to scent oils, along with large amounts of pottery, the quantity suggesting that the early Mycenaeans may have dabbled in the perfume trade. The discovery of the tablets has also prompted a reassessment of the sophistication of Mycenaean civilization for they show that, here at least, writing was not limited to government scribes working in the royal palaces as had previously been thought, and that around the citadel may have been a commercial city of some size and wealth.

Alongside the merchants' houses are the remains of another Grave Circle (B), dating from around 1650 BC and possibly representing an earlier, rival dynasty to the kings buried in Grave Circle A, and two **thólos** (circular chamber-type) tombs, speculatively identified by Schliemann as the **tombs of Aegisthus** and **Clytemnestra**. The former, closer to the Lion Gate, dates from around 1500 BC and has now collapsed, so is roped off; the latter dates from some two centuries later – thus corresponding with the Trojan timescale – and can still be entered.

The Treasury of Atreus

Same hours as the Citadel; admission included in Citadel entrance fee.

Four hundred metres down the road from the Citadel site is another, infinitely more startling *thólos*, known as the **Treasury of Atreus** or "Tomb of Agamemnon". This was certainly a royal burial vault at a late stage in Mycenae's history, contemporary with the "Clytemnestra Tomb", so the attribution to Agamemnon or his father is as good as any – if the king was indeed the historic leader of the Trojan expedition. In any case, it is an impressive monument to Mycenaean building skills, a beehive-like structure built without the use of mortar. Entering the tomb through a majestic fifteen-metre corridor, you come face to face with the chamber doorway, above which is a great lintel formed by two immense slabs of stone – one of which, a staggering nine metres long, is estimated to weigh 118 tonnes.

Practicalities: Mykínes

The modern village of **MYKÍNES** is 2km from the Kórinthos–Árgos road and the train station, but not all trains on the Kórinthos–Árgos–Trípoli line stop here. Buses from Athens to Árgos or Náfplio usually drop passengers at the turning rather than in the village; local buses from Nápflio serve the village itself. The walk in from the main road is along a beautiful straight road lined with eucalyptus trees, through which glimpses of the Citadel appear, flanked by the twin mountains of Zára and Ilías. The site is a further 2km uphill walk from the village.

Accommodation and eating

Unless you have your own transport, you'll probably want to stay at Mikínes, which is heavily touristy by day but quiet once the site has closed and the tour buses depart. Along the village's single street, there is quite an array of hotels – most of their names taken from characters in the House of Atreus saga – as well as a number of signs for rooms. Mycenae's two **campsites** are both centrally located, on the way into the village. There's not a great deal to choose between them, though *Camping Mykines* (☎0751/66 247; open all year) is smaller and a little closer to the site than *Camping Atreus* (☎0751/66 221; March–Oct).

All the hotels listed below have **restaurants** catering for the lunchtime tour-group trade; don't raise your expectations too high, though. Other eating places worth trying are the *Electra* (☎ 0751/76 447), the *King Menelaos* (☎0751/76 300) and the *Menelaos* (☎0751/76 311), all along the main street.

Agamemnon (☎0751/76 222). A small hotel whose modern facade belies the older comfortable rooms inside. ③.

Belle Hélène (☎0751/76 225). The village's most characterful hotel, converted from the house used by Schliemann during his excavations. Signatures in its visitors' book include Virginia Woolf, Henry Moore, Sartre and Debussy. Very friendly, with a good restaurant, this is a definite first choice. ②.

Rooms Dassis (☎0751/76 123). A pleasant, well-organized set-up, run, along with a useful travel agency, by Canadian Marion Dassis, who married into the local Dassis dynasty. ③.

Klitemnestra, up the hill (☎0751/76 451). Pleasant, modern hotel. ③.

Petite Planète (☎0751/76 240). An ugly but comfortable hotel at the top end of the village, with great views and a swimming pool. Owned by another of the Dassis dynasty, this is the closest hotel to the site. ⑤.

Youth Hostel, above the *Restaurant Iphigeneia* (☎0751/76 255). Easy-going hostel with rather cramped dorm-rooms on the roof. IYHF card required. ①.

The Argive Heraion

The little-visited **Argive Heraion** (daily 8.30am–3pm; free) is an important sanctuary from Mycenaean and Classical times and the site where Agamemnon is said to have been chosen as leader of the Greek expedition to Troy. It lies 7km south of Mycenae, off the minor road which runs east of Argos through Hónikas, and on to Náfplio. The lonely site is above the village of Hónikas; before you reach the village, look out for signs to "Ancient Ireo". There are various Mycenaean tombs near the site, but the principal remains of a temple complex, baths and a *palaestra* (wrestling/athletics gym), built over three interconnnecting terraces, all date from the fifth century BC.

The Heraion makes a pleasant diversion for anyone driving between Mycenae and Náfplio, or an enjoyable afternoon's walk from Mykínes – it takes a little over an hour on foot if you follow the old track southeast from the village, running parallel to the minor road to Ayía Triádha and Náfplio. Hónikas has the occasional bus to Árgos; Ayía Triádha, 4km on, has more frequent connections to Náfplio.

Árgos

ÁRGOS, 12km south of the Mykínes junction, is said to be the oldest inhabited town in Greece, although you wouldn't know it from first impressions. However, this turn-of-the-century trading centre has some pleasant squares and Neoclassical buildings, and a brief stop is worthwhile for the excellent museum and mainly Roman ruins. Try to time your visit to coincide with the regular **Wednesday market**, which draws locals from all the surrounding hill villages.

The modern **Archeological Museum** (Tues–Sun 8.30am–3pm; 500dr) is just off the main market square, Platía Áyios Pétrou, and makes an interesting detour after Mycenae, with a good collection of Mycenaean tomb objects and armour as well as extensive pottery finds. The region's Roman occupation is well represented here, in sculpture and mosaics, and there are also some lesser finds from Lerna on display.

Before you leave Árgos, ask to be pointed in the direction of the town's ancient remains – a few minutes' walk down the Trípoli road. The **site** (daily 8am–3pm; free) is surprisingly extensive, the **theatre**, built by Classical Greeks and adapted by the Romans, looks oddly narrow from the road, but climb up there and it feels immense. Estimated to have held 20,000 spectators – six thousand more than Epidaurus, it is matched on the Greek mainland only by the theatres at Megalopolis and Dodona. Alongside are the remains of an **odeion** and **Roman baths**.

Above the site looms the ancient **acropolis**, capped by the largely Frankish **medieval castle** of Lárissa, built on ancient foundations and later augmented by the Venetians and Turks. Massively cisterned and guttered, the sprawling ruins offer wonderful views – the reward for a long, steep haul up, either on indistinct trails beyond the theatre, or a very roundabout road.

Practicalities

You may well need to change **buses** in Árgos: its connections are considerably better than those of Náfplio. There are two KTEL kiosks, a block apart from each other and the central square; the one to the south, on Vassiléos Yioryíou tou Dheftérou, is for buses back towards Athens and various points in the Argolid; the other, at Plíthonos 24, beyond the museum, is for Trípoli, Spárti and down the coast towards Leonídhi.

For a good meal between buses, try the *Retro Restaurant* on the central square or, for a quick snack, *Miku*, 50m from the square on Papafléssa. Staying overnight shouldn't prove necessary, unless you find Náfplio full – a possibility in high season. Good, modest **hotels** on, or just off, the central square, include *Mycenae Hotel* (☎0751/68 754; ④), *Hotel Palladin* (☎0751/66 248; ③) and *Hotel Telesilla* (☎0751/68 317; ⑤).

Tiryns (Tírynthos)

In Mycenaean times **TIRYNS** stood by the sea, commanding the coastal approaches to Árgos and Mycenae. Today the Aegean has receded, leaving the fortress stranded on a low hillock in the plains, surrounded by citrus groves – alongside the Argolid's principal modern prison. It's not the most enchanting of settings, which in part explains why this accessible, substantial site is relatively empty of visitors. After the crowds at Mycenae, however, the opportunity to wander about Homer's "wall-girt Tiryns" in near-solitude is worth taking. The site lies just to the east of the Árgos–Náfplio road, and buses will drop off and pick up passengers, on request, at the café opposite.

The Citadel
Daily: summer 8am–7pm (Aug 8am–9pm); winter 8am–5pm; 400dr.

As at Mycenae, Homer's epigrams correspond remarkably well to what you can see on the ground at Tiryns. The fortress, now over 3000 years old, is undeniably impressive. The walls, formed of huge Cyclopean stones, dominate the site; the Roman guidebook writer Pausanias, happening on the site in the second century AD, found them "more amazing than the Pyramids" – a claim that seems a little exaggerated, even considering that the walls then stood twice their present height.

The entrance is on the far side of the fortress from the road, and visitors are restricted to exploring certain passages, staircases and the palace. Despite this, the sophistication and defensive function of the citadel's layout are evident as soon as you climb up the **entrance ramp**. Wide enough to allow access to chariots, the ramp is angled so as to leave the right-hand, unshielded side of any invading force exposed for the entire ascent, before forcing a sharp turn at the top – surveyed by defenders from within. The **gateways**, too, constitute a formidable barrier; the outer one would have been similar in design to Mycenae's Lion Gate, though unfortunately its lintel is missing, so there is no heraldic motif that might confirm a dynastic link between the sites.

Of the **palace** itself only the limestone foundations survive, but the fact that they occupy a level site makes them generally more legible than the ruins of hilly and boulder-strewn Mycenae and you can gain a clearer idea of its structure. The walls themselves would have been of sun-dried brick, covered in stucco and decorated with frescoes. Fragments of the latter were found on the site: one depicting a boar hunt, the other a life-sized frieze of courtly women, both now in Náfplio's museum. From the forecourt, you enter a spacious **colonnaded court** with a round sacrificial altar in the middle. A typically Mycenaean double porch leads directly ahead to the **megaron** (great hall), where the base of a throne was found – it's now in the Archeological Museum in Athens, with miscellaneous finds and frescoes from the site. The massive round clay hearth that's characteristic of these Mycenean halls – there's a perfect example at Nestor's Palace (see p.215) – is no longer to be seen at Tiryns, because some time in the sixth century BC this part of the palace became the site of a Temple to Hera, a structure whose column bases now pepper the ground. **Royal apartments** lead off on either side; the women's quarters are thought to have been to the right, while to the left is the bathroom, its floor – a huge, single flat stone – intact. The **lower acropolis**, north of the *megaron*, is currently out of bounds due to the excavation of two underground cisterns recently discovered at its far end.

A tower further off to the left of the *megaron* gives access to a **secret staircase**, as at Mycenae, which winds down to an inconspicuous **postern gate**. The site beyond the *megaron* is separated by an enormous inner wall and can only be viewed from a distance.

Náfplio

NÁFPLIO (which you may also see as Nauplia or Navplion), is a rarity amongst Greek towns. A lively, beautifully sited place, it exudes a rather grand, fading elegance, inherited from the days when it was the fledgling capital of modern Greece. The seat of government was here from 1829 to 1834 and it was in Náfplio that the first prime minister, Capodistrias, was assassinated by vengeful Maniot clansmen. It was here, too, that the Bavarian Prince Otho, put forward by the European powers to be the first King of Greece, had his initial royal residence. Today the town is becoming increasingly popular, with the result that hotel rooms and meals have crept up to Athens rates and above, but it remains by far the most attractive base for exploring the Argolid and resting up for a while by the sea.

Arrival and accommodation

Wedged between the sea and a fortress-topped headland, Náfplio is an easy town to find your way around. Arriving by **bus**, you are set down at one of two adjacent terminals just south of the interlocking squares, **Platía Tríon Navárkhon** and **Platía Kapodhistría**, on Singroú. The **train** will deposit you at the junction of Polyzoídhou and Irakléous, where a new station has been built, with two old red carriages serving as ticket office and waiting room.

Accommodation

Accommodation in Náfplio is generally overpriced for what you get, though out of season most **hotels** drop their prices significantly. There are a number of private **rooms** advertised – and sometimes touted to new arrivals; most cluster on the slope south above the main squares. A few other hotels and rooms, generally the last to fill, are located out on the road to Árgos. There is nowhere to **camp** in Náfplio itself, but southeast on the stretch of coast from Toló (11km from Náfplio) to Íria (26km away), there are a dozen or so campsites (see p.162).

Acronafplia, Vas. Konstandínou 23 (☎0752/24 481). Excellent value pension in three refurbished buildings around town. ②.

Agamemnon, Aktí Miaoúli 3 (☎0752/28 021). On the waterfront, with an upmarket restaurant and roof garden giving great views. ⑤.

Argolis, Árgos 32 (☎0752/27 721). On the left coming from Árgos, this modern, comfortable hotel can be noisy at the front. ③.

Dioscouri, junction Zygomála and Výronos (☎0752/28 550). A pleasant hotel, reached via a steep flight of steps. Rooms at the front overlook the old town and the port. ⑤.

Economou, Argonáfton 22 (☎0752/23 955). Opposite the Youth Hostel and worth the walk from the centre. Recently refurbished; all rooms with private bath. ③.

Epidauros, Kokkínou 2 (☎0752/27 541). Well-maintained building in the old town. Opposite is a pension owned by the same people, with slightly cheaper rooms. ④.

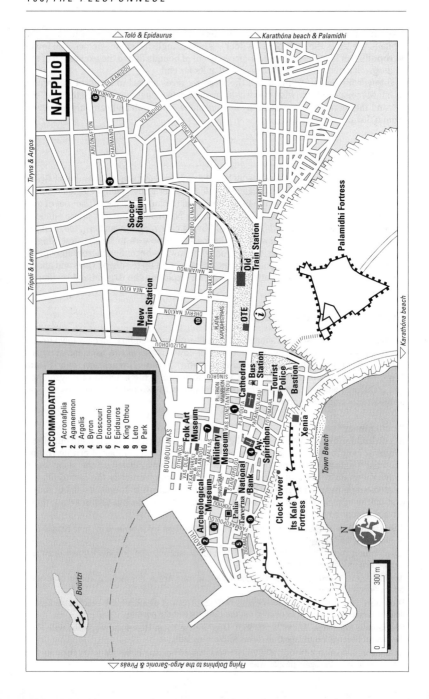

King Othon, Farmakopoúlou 2 (☎0752/27 585). Popular, well-placed hotel, close to the waterfront and Platía Sýndagma. In good weather, breakfast is served in the garden. ④.

Leto, Zygomála 28 (☎0752/28 093). Located at the base of the Íts Kalé fortress, but worth the climb, this is a more expensive sister hotel to the King Othon. ④.

Park, Dhervenakíon 1, off Platía Khapodhístrías (☎0752/27 428). Large, well-run 1960s hotel which may well have space when the smaller old-town places are full. ④.

The Town

There's ample pleasure in just wandering about Náfplio: looking around the harbourfront, walking over to the rocky town beach and, when you're feeling energetic, exploring the great twin fortresses of Palamídhi and Íts Kalé on the headland. Náfplio also offers the best restaurants and shops in the eastern Peloponnese, plus a range of useful facilities including car rental and, in summer, hydrofoils down the coast to Monemvassía and to the Argo-Saronic islands.

Palamídhi

The **Palamídhi**, Náfplio's principal fort, was one of the key military flashpoints of the War of Independence. The Greek commander Kolokotronis – of whom there's a majestically bewhiskered statue down in the Platía Kapodhistría – laid siege to the castle for over a year before finally gaining control. After independence, ironically, he was imprisoned in the fortress by the new Greek government; wary of their attempts to curtail his powers, he had kidnapped four members of the parliament.

The most direct approach to the **fortress** (daily: summer 8am–7.45pm; winter 8.30–3pm; 800dr) is by a stairway from the end of Polizídhou street, beside a Venetian bastion, though there is also a circuitous road up from the town. On foot, it's a pretty killing climb up 899 stone-hewn steps and, when you reach the summit, you're confronted with a bewilderingly vast complex. Within the outer walls are three self-contained castles, all of them built by the Venetians between 1711 and 1714, which accounts for the appearance of that city's symbol, the Lion of Saint Mark, above the various gateways. The middle fort, San Niccolo, was the one where Kolokotronis was imprisoned; it later became a notorious prison during the civil war.

The fortress takes its name, incidentally, from Náfplio's most famous and most brilliant legendary son, **Palamedes** – the inventor of dice, lighthouses and measuring scales. He was killed by the Greeks at Troy, on charges of treachery trumped up by Odysseus, who regarded himself as the cleverest of the Greeks.

Íts Kalé and Boúrtzi

The **Íts Kalé** ("Inner Castle" in Turkish), to the west of the Palamídhi, occupies the ancient acropolis, whose walls were adapted by three successive medieval restorers – hence the name. The fortifications are today far less complete than those of the Palamídhi, and the most intact section, the lower Torrione castle, has been adapted to house the *Xenia Hotel*. There's little of interest, but the hotel has meant a road has been carved out over the headland, and this brings you down to a small pay **beach**, overcrowded in season but nevertheless an enjoyable spot to cool off in the shadow of the forts. In the early evening, it is the province of just a few swimmers, though the refreshment kiosks operate only at peak hours and in season. If you walk along the path that continues from the end of the road just past the beach entrance for about ten minutes, you can pick your way down to a couple of small stone beaches below the cliffs; take provisions if you want to stay for a few hours to relax.

The town's third fort, the **Boúrtzi**, occupies the islet offshore from the harbour. Built in the fifteenth century, the castle has seen various uses in modern times: from the nineteenth-century home of the town's public executioner to a luxury hotel earlier this century. The late actress and politician, Melina Mercouri, claimed in her autobiography (*I Was Born Greek*) to have consummated her first marriage there.

Mosques and museums

In the town itself, there are a few minor sights, mainly from the town's Turkish past, and two excellent museums. **Platía Sýndagma**, the main square of the old town, is the focus of most interest. In the vicinity, three converted **Ottoman mosques** survive: one, in the southeast corner of the square, is an occasional theatre and cinema; another, just off the southwest corner, was the modern Greek state's original **Voulí** (parliament building). A third, fronting nearby Staikopoúlou, has been reconsecrated as the cathedral of **Áyios Yióryios**, having actually started life as a Venetian Catholic church. In the same area are a pair of handsome **Turkish fountains** – one abutting the south wall of the theatre-mosque, the other on Kapodhistría, opposite the church of Áyios Spíridhon. On the steps of the latter, Ioannis Capodistrias was assassinated by two members of the Mavromikhalis clan from the Máni in 1831; you can still see a scar left in the stone by one of the bullets.

The **Archeological Museum** (Tues–Sun 8.30am–3pm; 500dr) occupies a dignified Venetian mansion on the west side of Sýndagma. It has some good collections, as you'd expect in a town at the heart of the Argolid sites, including a unique and more or less complete suit of Mycenaean armour and reconstructed frescoes from Tiryns.

The fine **Folk Art Museum** on Ipsilándou, just off Solróni, which won a European "Museum of the Year" award when it opened in 1981 and features some gorgeous embroideries, costumes and traditional household items, is closed for renovation and is not expected to open until 1999.

Ayía Moní

More handicrafts are on sale at the convent of **Ayía Moní**, 4km east of Náfplio on the Epidaurus road, just south of the village of Ária. The monastic church, one of the most accomplished Byzantine buildings in the Peloponnese, dates back to the twelfth century. From the outer wall bubbles a nineteenth-century fountain, identified with the ancient spring of Kanthanos, in whose waters the goddess Hera bathed each year to restore her virginity. Modern Greeks similarly esteem the water, though perhaps with less specific miracles in mind.

Karathóna beach

The closest "proper" beach to Náfplio is at **Karathóna**, a fishing hamlet just over the headland beyond the Palamídhi fortress, which can be reached by a short spur off the drive going up to the ramparts. A more direct road around the base of the intervening cliffs was recently opened, and there's a morning bus service in season – or you can walk it in forty minutes.

The **sandy beach** stretches for a couple of kilometres, with a summer taverna at its far end. There were plans to develop it during the junta years, when the old road here was built along with the concrete foundations of a hotel, but the project was suspended in the 1970s and has yet to be revived. At present Karathóna attracts quite a few Greek day-trippers in season, along with a handful of foreigners in camper vans; there are cafés in summer, plus windsurf boards for rent.

Eating, drinking and nightlife

A good place to start restaurant menu-gazing in Náfplio is the waterside **Bouboulínas**, where the locals take their early evening volta, or **Staïkopoúlou**, off which are many enjoyable tavernas. For **breakfast**, it's hard to beat the zakharoplastío right beside the bus station; assorted bakeries and juice bars around Platía Sýndagma are also worth investigating. **Nightlife** is low key, with a few late-night bars and the occasional seasonal disco on and around Bouboulínas and Singróu. *Sirena*, on the corner of Bouboulínas and Sofróni, has Greek dancing (in summer from 9.30pm), while *Kookoo*, also on Bouboulínas features rockier sounds. A quieter drink can be had at the **cafés** on Platía Sýndagma, which stay open late, too. The real night-out haunts around town are the numerous huge discos on the beach road out towards Néos Kíos. These include *Goa* and *Liquid of Shiva*, whose exotic names indicate the increasing popularity of eastern-influenced trance music.

Karina Restaurant, Papanikólou 32. Authentic French meals served on the terrace in summer; expensive but worthwhile.

Ellas, Platía Sýndagma. One of the best on the square. Service can be slow, but the food (largely traditional dishes) is worth waiting for.

Kakanarakis, Vassilísis Ólgas 18 (☎0752/25 371). In the former Arapakos building, a lively place serving a variety of Greek dishes. Open evenings only; arrive early or book ahead.

Omorfi Poli, Vas. Olgas 16. Local specialities include *kolokotroneïko* (pork in a rich basil sauce and sweet red peppers stuffed with cheese).

Palia Taverna, towards the seafront end of Staïkopoúlou. Good traditional food at better prices than most in that street.

Paskhalis, Vas. Aléxandrou 15. Excellent friendly place on a quiet corner with unusual specialities like aubergine, bacon, peppers and cheese bake.

Savouras, Bouboulínas. Locals claim this has the freshest fish; competitive prices too.

Listings

Banks are concentrated around Platía Sýndagma and along Amalías.

Bookshops Odyssey, on Platía Sýndagma (April–Oct 8am–10pm, Nov–March 8am–2pm), has a good stock of English-language books, newspapers, cassettes, CDs and videos.

Car rental Pick from: Safeway (☎0752/22 155; including convertibles), Eyíou 2; Champ (☎0752/24 930) on Staikopoúlou, just off Platía Sýndagma; or Ikaros (☎0752/23 594).

Hydrofoils Náfplio is a stop for Flying Dolphin hydrofoils from April to September only. Services connect the town with Spétses and the other Argo-Saronic islands, plus Pireás and Monemvassía; some involve a change at Pórto Khéli. The ticket office is at Bouboulínas 2.

Moped, motorbike and bicycle rental From Nikopoulos, Bouboulínas 49; Moto Sakis, Sidhirás Merarkhías 15; Hi-Fly, 25-Martíou; or Bourtzi Tours, next door to the bus station.

Phones The OTE is on 25-Martíou.

Post office The main branch (Mon–Fri 7.30am–2pm) is on the northwest corner of Platía Kapodhistría.

Taxis There's a rank on Singroú, opposite the bus station.

Tourist office 25 Martiou 2, opposite OTE; open daily, but unpredictable hours.

Tourist police (☎0752/28 131). On the right at top of Syngróu. Helpful and open daily 7.30am–9pm.

Beaches around Náfplio: Tólo, Kastráki and beyond

Southeast from Náfplio are the fast-growing resorts of **Tólo** and **Kastráki** – popular and established enough to feature in many British holiday brochures. Inevitably, this means that they get packed at the height of the season, although they're still more tranquil than the main island resorts; you can always seek refuge at the low-key places further along the coast.

Tólo (Tolon)

TÓLO, 11km from Náfplio (hourly buses in season; last back at 8.30pm), is beginning to get rather overdeveloped, with a line of thirty or more hotels and campsites swamping its limited sands. Out of season it can still be quite a pleasant resort, but in summer it is about as un-Greek an experience as you'll find in the Peloponnese. Redeeming features include views of the islets of Platía and Romví on the horizon, and in summer a good range of watersports (windsurfing, waterskiing, paragliding).

Hotels in Tólo tend to be block-booked through the summer but you could try some of the smaller places, like the *Hotel Artemis* (☎0752/59 458; ⑤) and *Hotel Tolo* (☎0752/59 248; ⑤). If they're full or beyond your budget, it's usually possible to find **rooms** by asking around or following the signs, but be prepared for inflated prices during the summer. The three **campsites** charge similar rates: first try *Sunset* (☎0752/59 556; March–Oct); failing that, there's *Lido II* and *Tolo Beach*. The taverna closest to the *Sunset* is highly rated.

In July and August, there are **hydrofoils** to the Argo-Saronic islands of Ídhra (Hydra) and Spétses.

Kastráki and Ancient Assine

A pleasant alternative to Tólo, especially if you're looking for a campsite, is the longer beach at **KASTRÁKI**, 2km to the east; coming from Náfplio by bus, ask to be let off where the road reaches the sea – it forks right to Tólo and left (500m) to Kastráki, marked on some maps as Paralía Asínis. Here, too, development is underway, but it's a fair bit behind that of Tólo, limited to a scattering of small-scale hotels and campsites. *Camping Kastraki* (☎0752/59 386; April–late Oct) is on the beach, and has windsurfing equipment, pedaloes and canoes for hire.

If you get tired of the water, wander along the beach to the scrub-covered rock by the Náfplio road junction. This is, or was, **ancient Assine**, an important Mycenaean and Classical city destroyed by the jealous and more powerful Árgos in retribution for the Assinians having sided with the Spartans against them. There's little to see, other than a 200-metre length of ancient wall, but it's an oddly atmospheric spot.

East to Íria

Further around the coast, to the east of Kastráki, the road runs on to **DHRÉPANO**, a sizeable village with four **campsites**, and a very expensive **hotel**. The best campsite is *Triton* (☎0752/92 228; March–Nov); it's 1200m from the main square of Dhrépano – follow signs to the beach. Beyond Dhrépano, the **Vivári lagoon** has a couple of good fish tavernas on its shore. If you continue this way for another 13km, you reach a turning and poor track down to the beach and the *Poseidon* campsite (☎0752/913 41; May–mid-Oct) at **ÍRIA**.

For the coast south of here towards Pórto Khéli, Ermióni, Galatás and Méthana (each a local port for the Argo-Saronic islands) see pp.165–166.

Epidaurus (Epídhavros)

EPIDAURUS is a major Greek site, visited for its stunning **ancient theatre**, built by Polykleitos in the fourth century BC. With its extraordinary acoustics, this has become a very popular venue for the annual Athens Festival productions of **Classical drama** which are staged on Friday and Saturday nights from June through until the last weekend in August. The works are principally those of Sophocles, Euripides and Aeschylus; given the spectacular setting, they are worth arranging your plans around whether or not you understand the modern Greek in which they're performed.

The theatre, however, is just one component of what was one of the most important sanctuaries in the ancient world, dedicated to the healing god, Asclepius, and a site of pilgrimage for half a millennium, from the sixth century BC into Roman times.

The Ancient Theatre and Asclepion

Daily: summer 8am–7pm (Aug 8am–9pm); winter 8am–5pm; 2000dr. For festival performances you are admitted to the theatre after 7pm, but not to the rest of the site.

The dedication of the sanctuary at Epidaurus to **Asclepius**, the legendary son of Apollo, probably owes its origin to an early healer from northern Greece who settled in the area. There were Asclepian sanctuaries throughout Greece (Athens has ruins of one on the south slope of its Acropolis) and they were sited, rationally enough, alongside natural springs. Epidaurus, along with the island of Kós, was the most famous and inspirational of them all, and probably the richest. The sanctuary was much endowed by wealthy visitors and hosted a quadrennial festival, including drama in the ancient theatre, which followed the Isthmian games. Its heyday was in the fourth and third centuries BC; Rome, when ravaged by an epidemic in 293 BC, sent for the serpent that was kept in the sanctuary.

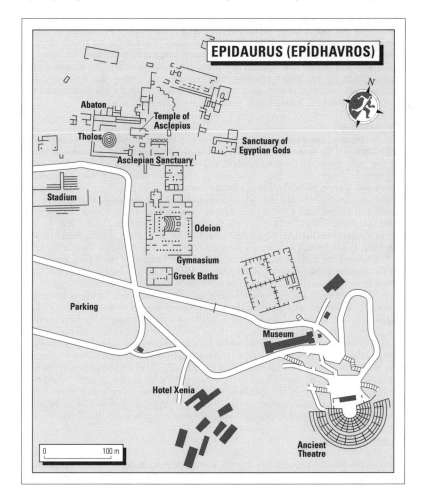

This aspect of the site, however, along with most of the associated Asclepian ruins, is incidental for most visitors; Epidaurus's **Ancient Theatre** is simply a wonderful sight. With its backdrop of rolling hills, this 14,000-seat arena merges perfectly into the landscape, so well in fact that it was rediscovered and unearthed only last century. Constructed with mathematical precision, it has an extraordinary equilibrium and, as guides on the stage are forever demonstrating, near-perfect natural acoustics – such that you can hear coins, or even matches, dropped in the circular *orchestra* from the highest of the 54 tiers of seats. Constructed in white limestone (red for the dignitaries in the front rows), the tiered seats have been repaired, but otherwise restoration has been minimal, with the beaten earth stage being retained, as in ancient times.

The museum

Close by the theatre is a small **museum** (daily: summer 8am–7pm; winter 8am–5pm; entrance fee included in site ticket price), which is best visited before you explore the sanctuary. The finds displayed here show the progression of medical skills and cures used at the Asclepion; there are tablets recording miraculous and outrageous cures – like the man cured from paralysis after being ordered to heave the biggest boulder he could find into the sea – alongside quite advanced surgical instruments.

In 86 BC, by which time Epidaurus's reputation was in decline, the Roman consul Sulla, leader of the forces invading the Peloponnese, looted the sanctuary and destroyed its buildings. Hence, most of the ruins visible today are just foundations and a visit to the museum helps identify some of the former buildings.

The sanctuary

The **Asclepian Sanctuary**, as large a site as Olympia or Delphi, holds considerable fascination, for the ruins here are all of buildings with identifiable functions: hospitals for the sick, dwellings for the priest-physicians, and hotels and amusements for the fashionable visitors to the spa. Their setting, a wooded valley thick with the scent of thyme and pine, is evidently that of a health farm.

The reasonably well-labelled **site** begins just past the museum, where there are remains of **Greek baths** and a huge **gymnasium** with scores of rooms leading off a great colonnaded court; in its centre the Romans built an **odeion**. To the left is the outline of the **stadium** used for the ancient games, while to the right, a small **Sanctuary of Egyptian Gods** reveals a strong presumed influence on the medicine used at the site.

Just beyond the stadium are the foundations of the **Temple of Asclepius** and beside it a rectangular building known as the **Abaton**. Patients would sleep here to await a visitation from the healing god, commonly believed to assume the form of a serpent. He probably appeared in a more physical manifestation than expected; harmless snakes are believed to have been kept in the building and released at night to bestow a curative lick.

The deep significance of the serpent at Epidaurus is elaborated in the next building you come to – the circular **Tholos**, one of the best-preserved buildings on the site and designed, like the theatre, by Polykleitos. Its inner foundation walls form a labyrinth which is thought to have been used as a snakepit and, according to one theory, to administer a primitive form of shock therapy to the mentally ill. The afflicted would crawl in darkness through the outer circuit of the maze, guided by a crack of light towards the middle, where they would find themselves surrounded by writhing snakes. Presumably, on occasions, it worked. Another theory is that the labyrinth was used as an initiation chamber for the priests of Asclepius, who underwent a symbolic death and rebirth in it.

Practicalities

Most people take in Epidaurus as a day trip, though there's a **hotel** at the site, the unattractive and expensive *Xenia* (☎0753/22 003; June–Sept; ⑤). There are better and more mod-

---

TICKETS AND TRANSPORT

Theatre tickets cost 4000–8000dr. As the theatre never fills, you can often buy the cheaper upper tier seats but actually sit lower down. Tickets for the plays are available at the site on the day of performance, or in advance in Athens (at the festival box office) or Náfplio (from Bourtzi Tours or Olympic Airways at Bouboulínas 2). In Athens you can buy all-inclusive tickets for performances and return bus travel. There are also special evening buses from the site to Náfplio after the show. **English translations** of the plays are available at the site and at the Odyssey bookshop in Náfplio. Normally there are six buses daily from Náfplio to the site; they are marked "Theatre", "Asklipion" or "Epidhavros" and shouldn't be confused with those to the modern villages of Néa or Paleá Epídhavros (see below).

---

estly priced hotels on the way to and in nearby **LIGOÚRIO** village, 5km northwest of the site. Possibilities here include the *Hotel Alkion* (☎0753/22 552; ③) at the turning off the main road to the village, or *Hotel Koronis* (☎0753/22 267; ②) in the village itself; both are open all year. Alternatively, it's possible to **camp** in the grass car park on days of performances, though you must wait until an hour after the play's end before setting up a tent. Beachside accommodation is available at Paleá Epídhavros, 15km to the northeast (see below).

For meals, the nearest **restaurant** to the site is the *Oasis* on the Ligoúrio road. Much better is *Taverna Leonides* (☎0752/22 115), in the village proper, a friendly spot with a garden out the back; you'd be wise to book ahead if your visit coincides with a performance at the ancient theatre. Actors eat here after shows, and photos on the wall testify to the patronage of Melina Mercouri, the Papandreous, François Mitterrand and Peter Hall.

Paleá Epídhavros

The closest beach resort to Epidaurus is **Paleá Epídhavros**, which has mushroomed since the recent improvement of the direct coast road from Kórinthos. The recent discovery of ancient remains at the village means that some road signs for the beach now indicate "Ancient Epidavros", while the main site is referred to as "Ancient Theatre of Epidavros". As far as the remains are concerned, excavations are still in progress but they are worth a quick visit. There is another smaller classical theatre on the headland past the small town beach, which is a venue for weekend musical shows in July and August, and you can find some small *thólos* tombs from the Mycenaean era up a road behind the bakery on the main street through town.

Facing the beach, there are at least a dozen **hotels**, as many purpose-built **rooms**, and four **campsites**, all very popular with festival patrons in season. If you want to book ahead, three hotels to try are the *Christina* (☎0753/41 451; ④), *Epidavria* (☎0753/41 222; ③) and *Paola Beach* (☎0753/41 397; ④); all these close over winter. The *Elena* rooms (☎0753/41 207; ④), are comfortable apartments with air-conditioning. Three of the four campsites are on the beach to the south of the village in the district known as Yialassi: they are *Verdelis* (☎0753/41 425; March–late Oct), *Bekas* (☎0753/41 714; late March–mid-Oct) and *Nicholas II* (☎0753/41 445; April–mid-Oct). A new Flying Dolphin route from Piraeus via Éyina during summer months provides alternative easy access from Athens.

The Saronic ports: Méthana to Pórto Khéli

The roads across and around the southern tip of the Argolid are sensational scenic rides, but the handful of resorts here are lacking in character and generally overdeveloped. With a car, you can pick your beaches and take a leisurely route back to Náfplio, perhaps exploring the site of **Ancient Troezen** and the **Limonódhassos** lemon groves. Otherwise, you'll probably travel this way only if heading for one of the **Argo-Saronic islands**: **Méthana** has local connections to Éyina (Aegina); **Galatás** to Póros; **Ermióni** to Ídhra (Hydra) and Spétses; **Kósta** and **Pórto Khéli** to Spétses.

Méthana and Ancient Troezen

It's a sixty-kilometre drive from Epidaurus to **MÉTHANA**, the last section along a cliff-hugging corniche road. Set on its own peninsula, Méthana is a disappointing spa-town, whose devotees are apparently attracted by foul-smelling sulphur springs. Of its half-dozen hotels, the most pleasant is the seafront *Avra* (☎0298/92 382; ④).

Close by the village of Trizína, just south and inland of the turning to the Méthana peninsula, are the ruins of ancient **TROEZEN**, the legendary birthplace of Theseus and location of his domestic dramas. The root of his problems was Aphrodite, who, having been rejected by Theseus's virgin son Hippolytus, contrived to make Phaedra – Theseus's then wife – fall in love with the boy (her stepson). She, too, was rejected and responded by accusing Hippolytus of attempted rape. Hippolytus promptly fled, and when he was killed when his horses took fright at a sea monster, Phaedra confessed her guilt and committed suicide. Originally told by Euripides (later reworked by Racine), a full account of the tragedy, together with a map of the remains, is on sale for 300dr in the modern village. For the romantic, there's always Theseus's autobiography in Mary Renault's *The King Must Die*, which starts, "The Citadel of Troizen, where the palace stands, was built by giants before anyone remembers. But the Palace was built by my great-grandfather. At sunrise . . . the columns glow fire-red and the walls are golden. It shines bright against the dark woods on the mountainside."

Such **remains** as exist of the ancient town are spread over a wide site. Most conspicuous are three ruined Byzantine chapels, constructed of ancient blocks, and a structure known as the **Tower of Theseus**, whose lower half is third century BC and top half is medieval. This stands at the lower end of a gorge, the course of an ancient **aqueduct**, which you can follow in a half an hour's walk up a bulldozer track to the **Yéfira tou Dhiavólou** (Devil's Bridge), a natural rock formation spanning a chasm; a rare black butterfly is said to be endemic to the ravine.

Galatás and Limonódhassos

GALATÁS lies only 350m across the water from the island of Póros, with which it is connected by skiffs, sailing more or less continuously in the summer months. The town has a cluster of **hotels**, of which the best value is the *Saronis* (☎0298/22 356; ④), and **rooms** for rent, plus a handy **bike rental** place, Fotis Bikes. The village is connected by a daily bus with Epidaurus and Náfplio.

On the coast road to the south, there are the beaches of **Pláka** (2km) and **Alykí** (4km); just back from the latter, a path, signposted "Restaurant Cardassi", leads into the **Limonódhassos** – a vast, irrigated lemon grove. Though one travel brochure says there are 300,000 lemon trees here, the consensus tallies about 30,000, not that it matters much as you pick your way along the various paths that meander through them, all heading upwards to an inspiringly positioned **taverna**, where a charming old man serves fresh lemonade as you sit on the terrace. Henry Miller recounts a visit here in *Colossus of Maroussi*, hyperbolizing that "in the spring young and old go mad from the fragrance of sap and blossom". There is also a good seafront taverna at Alíki beach.

Ermióni, Kósta and Pórto Khéli

Continuing clockwise around the coast from Galatás, you follow a narrow, modern road, cut from the mountainside to open up additional resorts close to Athens. Plépi (or

Hydra Beach) is a villa-urbanization, visited by boats from beachless Ídhra opposite. **ERMIÓNI** (ancient Hermione) is better: a real village, enclosed by a rocky bay and perhaps saved from development by lack of a sandy beach. It has three modest **hotels**: the *Akti* (☎0754/31 241; ③), the *Olympion* (☎0754/31 214; ①) and the *Ganossis Filoxenia* (☎0754/31 218; ③); the owner of the *Ganossis Filoxenia* also runs the *Ganossis Filoxenia* apartments (☎0754/31 218; ④) along the beach. Aris Skouris on the seafront south of the harbour, has bikes and mopeds for rent.

Further round, **KÓSTA** and **PÓRTO KHÉLI**, on either side of headland, are purpose-built resorts that have swallowed up their original hamlets and are slowly merging into each other. Both feature a rather soulless mix of package-tour hotels and facilities for yachters exploring the Argo-Saronic islands. If you want or have to stay, there is a campsite – *Camping Costa* (☎0754/51 571) at Kosta – as well as some fairly upmarket hotels like the *Hotel Lido* (☎0754/57 393; ⑤). More reasonable options near the dock in Pórto Khéli itself include *Flisvos* (☎0754/51 316; ③) and *Porto* (☎0754/51 410; ③). There are numerous restaurants and cafés as well as car and bike rental. This is the only Argolid port which has direct hydrofoil connections to Monemvassía and Kýthira.

The circuitous route back to Náfplio from Pórto Khéli runs inland, via attractive Kranídhi, scrambling its way up through the mountains. It is covered four times daily by a bus, which usually dovetails in Pórto Khéli with ferries and hydrofoils to and from Spétses and elsewhere; in low season, however, you may have to change buses in Kranídhi.

The east coast: Náfplio to Leonídhi

The **coastline** between Náfplio and Leonídhi is mountainous terrain, increasingly so as you move south towards Monemvassía where the few villages seem carved out of their dramatic backdrop. Considering its proximity to Náfplio – and Athens – the whole stretch is enjoyably low key and remarkably unexploited, remaining more popular with Greek holidaymakers than with foreign tourists.

Getting to the **beaches** – Parália Ástros, Áyios Andréas, Parália Tiroú and Pláka – is perhaps best done by car, though there are also **buses** twice daily from Árgos to Leonídhi, while **Pláka** (the port/beach of Leonídhi) is served by the Flying Dolphin **hydrofoils** en route from Spétses/Pórto Khéli to Monemvassía. However you travel, change money in advance, as there are few **banks** between Náfplio and Leonídhi.

Right at the beginning of the route, around the coast from Náfplio, the minor site of **Ancient Lérna** makes an interesting halt. If you are travelling by train from Árgos to Trípoli, you could stop off at the station of Míli, only 500m from the site; alternatively, a trip there makes a nice ride around the coast if you rent a bike in Náfplio.

Ancient Lerna

The site of ancient **LERNA** (Tues–Sun 8.30am–3pm; 500dr) lies 10km south of Árgos and 12km from Náfplio by the minor road around the coast via Néa Kíos. On the way from Argos there is an interesting detour possible to the cave-lake **monastery** at Kefalári and 4km further on to the Bronze Age **pyramid** at Ellinikó. The nearest village is Míli, at the foot of Mount Pontinus, where buses between Trípoli and Kórinthos break their journey at a group of *souvláki* stands, open virtually 24 hours. Just beyond the straggle of the village a narrow, poorly signposted lane leads to the prehistoric site, which now lies between the main road and the railway; surrounded by an orange grove and close to the sea, it makes a fine picnic spot. The warden, unused to visitors, may volunteer to show you around this important Bronze Age settlement. Excavations carried out in the 1950s unearthed ruins of an early **Neolithic house**, and a well-preserved **fortification wall**, revealing it as one of the most ancient of Greek sites, inhabited from as early as 4000 BC.

Another large house at the north end of the site is thought to have been an early palace, but was superseded, in about 2200 BC, by a much larger and more important structure known as the **House of the Tiles**. Measuring approximately 24m by 9m, this dwelling, labelled as another palace, takes its name from the numerous terracotta roof tiles found inside, where they are thought to have fallen when either lightning or enemy raiders set the building ablaze in approximately 2100 BC. The house represents the earliest known instance of the use of terracotta as a building material, and is the most impressive pre-Helladic structure to have been unearthed on the Greek mainland. A symmetrical ground plan of small rooms surrounding larger interior ones is today protected by a huge canopy, with stairs mounting to a now-vanished second storey. The substantial walls, made of sun-dried brick on stone foundations, were originally covered with plaster. Even after its destruction, this palace may have retained some ritual significance, since two Mycenaean **shaft graves** were sunk into the ruins in around 1600 BC, and the site was not completely abandoned until the end of the Mycenaean period.

As implied by the chronology, the founders and early inhabitants of Lerna were not Greeks. Certain similarities in sculpture and architecture with contemporary Anatolia suggest an Asiatic origin but this has yet to be proved conclusively. Excavated finds, however, demonstrate that the Lerneans traded across the Aegean and well up into the Balkan peninsula, cultivated all the staple crops still found in the Argolid, and raised livestock, as much for wool and hides as for food. Elegant terracotta sauce tureens and "teaspoons", which may be seen in the Árgos archeological museum (see p.155), hint at a sophisticated cuisine.

According to myth, Hercules performed the second of his labours, the slaying of the nine-headed Hydra, at Lerna. And, as if in corroboration of the legend, the nearby swamps are still swarming with eels.

Along the coast to Ástros and Paralía Tyróu

The initial section of coast from Lerna to Ástros and Áyios Andhréas is low-lying: less spectacular than the sections further south, but pleasant enough. The first village of any size is **PARALÍA ÁSTROUS**, whose houses are tiered against a headland shared by a medieval fort and the ruins of an ancient acropolis. Back from the sand and gravel beach, which extends for 6km south of the fishing harbour. There are three or four tavernas, some rooms to let and several hotels: the *Chryssi Akti* (☎0755/51 294; ④) has a decent seafront setting, the brand new *Pension Alexandros* (☎0755/51 743; ④) is also good, but the *Hotel Crystal* (☎0755/51 313; ⑤) is inland and rather overpriced. The *Thirea* campsite (☎0755/51 002; mid-March to mid-Nov) is a lively spot.

Just to the south, a trio of surprisingly neat and compact villages – Ástros, Korakavóuni and Áyios Andhréas – perch at the foothills of **Mount Párnon** as it drops to meet the lush, olive-green plain. A little beyond Áyios Andhréas (10km from Ástros), the road curls down to the coast and the first in a series of fine-pebbled swimming coves, crammed between the massive spurs of Párnon. There are seasonal **rooms** at several of the coves, plus the *Arcadia* **campsite** (☎ 0755/31 190; May–Oct) on the main road, 6km beyond Áyios Andhréas; popular with middle-aged Greeks, the site has a friendly atmosphere but is noisy, particularly at weekends. Few concessions are made to tourists along this stretch of coast, apart from the occasional makeshift taverna; out of season, you'll definitely need your own supplies.

PARALÍA TYRÓU is a fair-sized town and a reasonably popular resort, mostly with older Greeks; younger Greeks tend to go further south along the coast, to Pláka. The place feels quite sedate, with comfortable, mid-range hotels and cafés spread back from its long pebble beach. **Accommodation** options include the *Hotel Apollon* (☎0757/41

393; ③), the *Hotel Kamvyssis* (☎0757/41 424; ④), the *Hotel Galazia Thalassa* (also known as the *Blue Sea*; ☎0757/41 369; ③), and the well-equipped **campsite**, *Zaritsi* (☎0757/41 429; April–mid-Oct), on the coast north of Paralía Tiróu.

Leonídhi, Pláka and south towards Monemvassía

Gigantic red cliffs that wouldn't look out of place in deserts of the American Southwest confine **LEONÍDHI**, the terminus of the Árgos bus route. Set inland, with good agricultural land stretching down to the sea, this prosperous and traditional market town sees little need to pander to tourists. Most in any case end up down by the sea at Leonídhi's diminutive port, Pláka. If you prefer to stay here, you might find space in the town's one modest **hotel**, the *Alexaki* (also known as the *Neon*; ☎0757/22 383; ②), or the few advertised **rooms** for rent such as the new and comely *Ithaki* (☎0757/22 3394; ④) on the road out towards the coast. There are some enjoyable, small town tavernas.

Pláka to Yérakas

PLÁKA, 4km away, is a tiny place consisting of a harbour, a couple of **hotels** and **eating places**. It also has a fine pebble beach, which in recent years has become popular with Greek and European tourists, plus a sporadic influx of yachties. In summer, it would be wise to phone ahead to reserve a balconied room with sea view in the first-choice *Hotel Dionysos* (☎0757/23 455; ④), run by the family who also own the taverna opposite. There are excellent meals to be had on the beach, too, at the taverna twenty minutes' walk to the north along the bay across the river bed (dry in summer), as well as picturesquely situated little places like *Tou Psara* taverna near the harbour.

The hamlet of **POÚLITHRA**, 3km south of Pláka around the bay, marks the end of the coast road – which deteriorates to a track as it heads inland. There is a taverna, with a terrace, close by the narrow strip of beach, a **hotel**, the *Kentauros* (☎0757/51 214; ④), favoured by groups, and a large rooms place by the waterfront.

South of Leonídhi the coastline is wilder and sparsely inhabited, with just a couple of coastal settlements cut into the cliffs. To reach the two little settlements – **KYPARÍSSI** and **YÉRAKAS** – you're better off taking the Flying Dolphin **hydrofoil**, which stops at both on the way to Monemvassía. By road, it's a very roundabout route (though in better shape than it looks on the map) from Molái, on the Spárti–Monemvassía road.

Inland from Leonídhi

The route inland from Leonídhi is worth taking for its own sake, climbing over a spur of **Mount Párnon**, past the **monastery of Elónis** and the high mountain village of **Kosmás** – quite a temperature shock in the height of summer and a great place to stop and enjoy the fresh mountain air over a drink in the atmospheric square, shaded by huge plane trees. It is a decent road for cars, and brings you out at the minor Byzantine site of **Yeráki** (aka Pýrgos Yerakíou, see p.182); from there, you have a choice of roads – to Spárti and Yíthio (Githion) via Skála, and Monemvassía via Molái. Without a car, you'll have to plan very carefully: a daily **bus** runs from Leonídhi to Yeráki, and goes on to Spárti twice a week – currently on Tuesday afternoons and Saturday mornings, but check first.

Moní Elónis

Visible from Leonídhi, the **Moní Elónis** stands out as a white slash in the mountainside – though as you twist around Mount Párnon, and up a ravine, it drops away from view. The turn-off to the monastery (visitors permitted from sunrise to sunset) in fact comes 13km from Leonídhi, via an approach road which ends at a seemingly impregnable gateway; if all looks closed, pull the wire, which passes along the cliff to a large bell. Once admitted, you can wander down to a small chapel crammed with icons and lanterns and to a spring, whose icy-cold water has supposedly curative powers. Most of the monastery, originally founded in medieval times following the appearance of a miraculous and inaccessible icon, was rebuilt following the War of Independence. Today, it is maintained by four nuns, who sell a classic little history (in Greek only) of the monastery's legends and vicissitudes.

Kosmás

Continuing south, past the Elónis turning, you reach **KOSMÁS**, a handsome village set about a grand platía, with rooms and a couple of tavernas. Straddling the most important pass of Párnon, at nearly 1200m, it can be a chilly place during the spring or winter, but beautiful, too, with its streams, cherry and walnut trees, and fir forests all around. Beyond the village the road runs through an uninhabited valley, then lurches slowly down to the village and Byzantine ruins of Yeráki (see p.182).

Trípoli

Trípoli is a major crossroads of the Peloponnese, from where most travellers either head **north** through Arcadia towards Olympia, or **south** to Spárti and Mystra or Kalamáta (see below). To the **east**, a recently improved road, looping around Mount Ktenías, connects Trípoli with Árgos and Náfplio, via Lérna. To the **west**, you can reach the coast on a reasonably fast road to Kýparissía, via the evocative, scattered ruins of Ancient Megalopolis. To the **northeast**, a new fast highway links Trípoli with Kórinthos and Athens.

The Peloponnese **railway** also passes through Trípoli, continuing its meandering course from Kórinthos and Árgos to Kýparissía and Kalamáta. Those with passes might be tempted to use the train to Trípoli and then take a bus to Spárti, but it's not a good idea, as Árgos–Spárti buses are not scheduled to meet trains in Trípoli and furthermore they often pass through full; it's better to take a direct bus (seven daily from Athens to Spárti, via Árgos and Trípoli), or approach Spárti more enjoyably via the hydrofoil to Monemvassía.

The Town

The Arcadian capital doesn't live up to expectations: **TRÍPOLI** is a large, modern town, and home to one of the country's biggest army barracks. It doesn't exactly overwhelm you with its charm and has few obvious attractions, although the **Archeological Museum** (Tues–Sun 8.30am–3pm; 500dr), signposted off Vassiléos Yioryíou and housed in a Neoclassical building with a beautiful rose garden, makes a pleasant diversion. Medieval Tripolitsa was destroyed by retreating Turkish forces during the War of Independence, the Greek forces, led by Kolokotronis, having earlier massacred the town's population. Trípoli's ancient predecessors, the rival towns of Mantinea to the north and Tegea to the south, are the only local points of interest.

Getting in and out of the town can be fairly complicated. The major **bus terminal**, serving all destinations in Arcadia and the northern Peloponnese, is on Platía Kolokotróni, one of the three main squares. Services to Pátra, Messinía, Kalamáta, the outer Máni, Pýlos and Spárti leave from the "milk" shop directly opposite the train station, at the southeastern edge of town. If you need to spend a night here, there are a number of reliable **hotels** including: the *Arcadia* on Platía Koloktróni (☎071/225 551; ⑤); the *Alex*, Vassiléos Yioryíou 26 (☎071/223 465; ④); the *Anaktoric* on Ethnikís Andistáseos 48 (☎071/ 22 2545; ④); the *Menalon* on Platía Áreos (☎071/222 450; ④); and the *Artemis*, Dimitrakopoúlou 1 (☎071/225 221; ④). Cheaper **rooms** are advertised on Lambráki on the way into town from the train station. Eating establishments

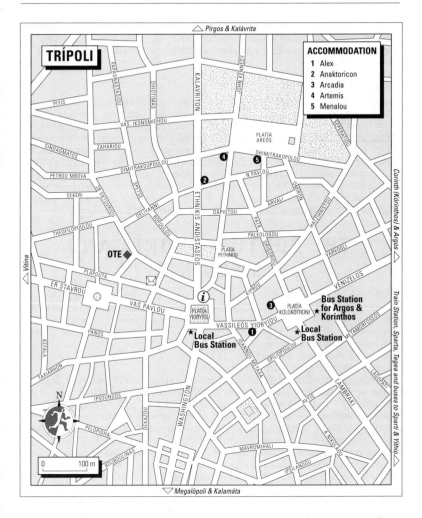

△ *Pírgos & Kalávrita*

TRÍPOLI

ACCOMMODATION
1 Alex
2 Anaktoricon
3 Arcadia
4 Artemis
5 Menalou

PAPANASTASIOU
PIYIS
DHOTIMAS
KALAVRITON
JOHN KENNEDY
SEFERINII
VAS. IKONOMIDHOU
SINDAGMATOS
ZAHARIOU
PLATÍA
AREOS
DHIMITRAKOPOLOU
PETROU MBOVA
DIMITRAKOUPOULOU
N PAVLOU
SEKERI
28 OKTOVRIOU
SPETSI
DELIYANNI
BOPOLIOU
ETHNIKIS ANDISTASEOS
DAPIOTOU
ARVALI
OMIRON
HATZIHRISTOU
THEOFILOPOULOU
PAIR
PALEOLOGOU
DELIGHORGI
Corinth (Kórinthos) & Argos ▷
OTE ◆
PLATÍA
PETRINOU
VARVOGLI
Vtina ◁
PLAPOUTA
KIPROU
VENIZELOS
ER STAVROU
(i)
VAS PAVLOU
PLATÍA
YIORYIOU
PLATÍA
KOLOKOTRONI ★
**Bus Station
for Argos &
Korinthos**
PANOS
VASSILEÓS YIORYIOU
★**Local
Bus Station**
★**Local
Bus Station**
Train Station, Sparta, Tegea and buses to Sparti & Yithio ▷
KEFALA
TAXIARHON
IOANNOU METAXA
METAMORFOSEOS
IPSOUNDOS
SPILIOPOULOU
LALIOTI
N
WASHINGTON
DEKAZOU
AVIS
LAMBRAKI
A NIKOLAOU
PELOPIDHA
BOUBOULINAS
MAVROMIHALI
IPSILANDOU

0   100 m

▽ *Megalópoli & Kalamáta*

---

are mostly of the functional variety, but for decent food in more pleasant surroundings there are two tavernas, *Neos Dionysos* and the more homely *Klimataria*, almost adjacent to one another on Kalavritón about 100m past the far end of Platía Areos.

Ancient Mantinea

Ancient **MANTINEA**, known to Homer as "pleasant Mantinea", was throughout its history a bitter rival of nearby Tegea, invariably forming an alliance with Athens when Tegea stood with Sparta, then switching allegiance to Sparta when Tegea allied with Thebes. Its site stands 15km north of Trípoli and is served by hourly buses from Platía Kolokotróni in Trípoli, between the road to Dhimitsána/Pátra and the new Kórinthos–Trípoli highway. It is unenclosed, the principal remains being a circuit of fourth-century BC **walls**, still more or less intact, though much reduced in height, and a few tiers of its theatre.

Alongside the site, however, is one of the most bizarre sights in Greece: a modern **church** constructed in an eccentric pastiche of Byzantine and Egyptian styles. Put together in the 1970s by a Greek-American architect, it is dedicated to "The Virgin, the Muses and Beethoven".

Ancient Tegea

Ancient **TEGEA**, 8km south of Trípoli, was the main city of the central Peloponnese in Classical and Roman times, and, refounded in the tenth century, was an important town again under the Byzantines. The diffuse and partially excavated site lies just outside the village of Aléa (modern Tegea), on the Spárti road. Local buses from Trípoli stop in the village beside a small **museum** (Tues–Sun 8.30am–3pm; 500dr), which is well stocked with sculptures from the site. Take the road to the left as you leave, which leads in 100m to the main remains, the **Temple of Athena Alea**, in whose sanctuary two kings of Sparta once took refuge. Keeping on the road past the site, it's a twenty-minute walk to the village of Paleá Episkopí, whose church – a huge modern pilgrim shrine – incorporates part of ancient Tegea's theatre and a number of Byzantine mosaics.

THE SOUTH: LAKONÍA AND MESSINÍA

Draw a line on a map from Kalamáta over the Taïyettos mountains, through Spárti and across to Leonídhi. Broadly, everything below this line is **Lakonía**, the ancient territories of the Spartans. It's a dramatic country of harsh mountains and, except for the lush strip of the Evrótas valley, of poor, rocky soil – terrain that has kept it isolated throughout history. **Mount Taïyettos** itself is a formidable barrier, looming ahead if you approach from Trípoli, and providing an exciting exit or entrance in the form of the Langádha Pass between Spárti and Kalamáta.

Landscapes apart, the highlights here are the extraordinarily preserved Byzantine towns of **Mystra** and **Monemvassía** – both essential visits for any tour of the Peloponnese – and the remote and arid **Máni** peninsula, with its bizarre history of feuds and unique tower houses and churches with barrel roofs. Monemvassía is a regular stop for Flying Dolphin hydrofoils (plus a weekly boat) from Pireás and the Argo-Saronic islands and would make a superb entry point to the peninsula. In summer, the Maniot port of **Yíthio** (Gythion) and tiny **Neápoli**, south of Monemvassía, are additional stops on the hydrofoil and provide the easiest links to **Kýthira**, technically an Ionian island but covered – due to its Peloponnesian access – in this section.

Moving west across the region, you enter **Messinía**, with its mellower countryside and gorgeous, little-developed coast. There are good beaches at Messinía's own duo of medieval sites – the twin fortresses of **Koróni** and **Methóni** – but if you are looking for sands to yourself in the Peloponnese, and you're unperturbed by a lack of facilities, you could do no better than explore the shore north of Pýlos. En route are the remains of **Nestor's Palace**, the foundations only, but the most important ancient site in the south and, like Mycenae, keying remarkably well with the Homeric legend.

Sparta (Spárti)

Thucydides predicted that if the city of **Sparta** were deserted, "distant ages would be very unwilling to believe its power at all equal to its fame". The city had no great temples or public buildings and throughout its period of greatness remained unfortified: Lycurgus, architect of the Spartan constitution, declared that "it is men not walls that

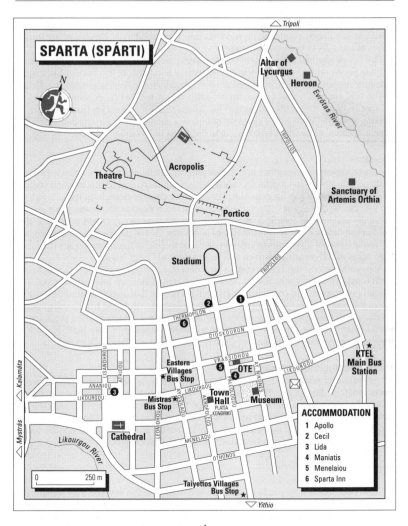

make a city". Consequently, modern **SPÁRTI**, laid out grid-style in 1834, has few ancient ruins to speak of, and is today a rather gritty market and agricultural town. Spárti's appeal is in its ordinariness – in its pedestrianized side streets, its café-lined squares, orange trees and evening *volta* – but it isn't the most rewarding of Greek towns. The reason for coming here is basically to see **Mystra**, the Byzantine town 5km to the east, that once controlled great swathes of the medieval world (see p.175).

Ancient Sparta

Descending from the mountains that ring Spárti on all side, you get a sense of how strategic was the location of the ancient city-state of **SPARTA**. The ancient "capital" occupied more or less the site of today's town, though it was in fact less a city than a grouping of villages, commanding the Laconian plain and fertile Evrótas valley from a series of low hills to the east of the river.

The Greek city was at the height of its powers from the eighth to the fourth century BC, the period when Sparta structured its society according to the laws of **Lycurgus**, defeated Athens in the Peloponnesian War, established colonies around the Greek world, and eventually lost hegemony through defeat to Thebes. A second period of prosperity came under the Romans – for whom this was an outpost in the south of Greece, with the Máni never properly subdued – though from the third century AD Sparta declined as nearby Mystra became the focus of Byzantine interest.

The sites

Traces of ancient Spartan glory are in short supply, but there are some ruins to be seen to the north of the city: follow the track behind the football stadium towards the old **Acropolis**, tallest of the Spartan hills. An immense **theatre** here, built into the side of the hill, can be quite clearly traced, even though today most of its masonry has gone – hurriedly adapted for fortification when the Spartans' power declined and, later still, used in the building of the Byzantine city of Mystra. Above the theatre, to the left, are the foundations of a **Temple to Athena**, while at the top of the acropolis sits the knee-high ruins of a **Byzantine church** and **monastery** of Osíou Níkou.

About 500m along the Trípoli road, a path descends to the remains of the **Sanctuary of Artemis Orthia**, where Spartan boys underwent endurance tests by flogging. The Roman geographer and travel writer Pausanias records that young men often expired under the lash, adding that the altar had to be splashed with blood before the goddess was satisfied. Perhaps it was the promise of such a gory spectacle that led the Romans to revive the custom: the main ruins here are of the grandstand they built. Neither of these sites is enclosed, and you can explore them along pleasant walkways.

The Archeological Museum

All movable artefacts and mosaics have been transferred to the town's small **Archeological Museum** (Tues–Sat 8.30am–3pm, Sun & holidays 8.30am–2.30pm); 500dr). Among its more interesting exhibits are a number of votive offerings found on the sanctuary site – knives set in stone that were presented as prizes to the Spartan youths and solemnly rededicated to the goddess – and a marble bust of a Spartan hoplite, found on the acropolis and said to be Leonidas, the hero of Thermopylae (see p.266).

Practicalities

If it is Mystra that brings you here, and you arrive early in the day, you may well decide to move straight on. Getting out of Spárti is straightforward. The **main bus terminal** (for Trípoli, Athens, Monemvassía, Kalamáta and the Máni) has been moved recently to the eastern edge of town at the very end of Likoúrgou. Buses for **Mystra** leave (hourly on weekdays; less frequently at lunchtime and at weekends) from the main terminal and the corner of Likoúrgou and Leonídhou; schedules are posted on the window of the café there. To reach Áyios Ioánnis, trailhead for hikes up **Mount Taïyettos**, you'll need to take a bus from the bottom of Paleológou on the south side of town.

Accommodation

There are usually enough **hotels** to go around, many of them on the main avenue of Paleológou. **Camping** is available at two sites out along the Mystra road; both can be reached via the Mystra bus, which will stop by the sites on request. The nearest, 2.5km from Spárti, is *Camping Mystra* (☎0731/22 724) which has a swimming pool and is open year-round. Two kilometres closer to Mystra is the *Castle View* (☎0731/93 303), a very clean, well-managed site.

Apollo, Thermopýlon 84, cnr Tripoléos (☎0731/22 491). A graceless but functional hotel. ④.

Cecil, Paleológou 125, cnr Thermopýlon (☎0731/24 980). Small and very friendly, now newly renovated, all rooms with bathrooms. ④.

Lida, cnr Atridou and Ananíou (☎0731/23 601). The most expensive place in town, with all mod cons, including a restaurants and parking. ⑥.

Maniatis, Paleológou 72, cnr Likoúrgou (☎0731/22 665). Modern and ugly, but with good facilities at a reasonable price. ⑤.

Menelaion, Paleológou 91 (☎0731/22 161). A modernized turn-of-the-century hotel, functional but charmless, with air-conditioning and a swimming pool. Rooms at the front are best avoided as there's an all-night taxi rank outside. ⑤.

Sparta Inn, Thermopýlon 105, cnr Gortsóglou (☎0731/25 021). Modern and better-looking than average, with a roof-garden and two swimming pools. ⑤.

Eating and drinking

There is a wide choice for meals, with most restaurants and tavernas concentrated on the main street of Paleológou – including several good psistariés towards the south end of Paleológou. The happening music bars include *Draft* featuring soft rock/dance in an imaginatively decorated garden off Likoúrgou, and the rockier *Ozone Club* which has some live acts.

Averof, Paleológou 77. A long-established and reasonably priced taverna with tasty Greek home-cooking; outdoor tables in summer.

Diethnes, Paleológou 105. Highly rated by the locals with a wide range of traditional dishes. The interior lacks atmosphere, but a delightful garden with orange and lemon trees compensates.

Dionysos, Recently moved 2km out on the road towards Mystra, this restaurant offers expensive dishes, but they're served with style – outdoors on a summer's evening.

Elysse, Paleológou 113. Run by French-Canadians, this place has a continental look and menu; good char-grilled meat dishes.

Finikas, Thermopýlon 51. Fine taverna cum psistariá.

Semiramis, Paleológou 58. Taverna, tucked away in the basement, with a traditional Greek menu; the house speciality is roast pork with aubergine.

Mystra (Mystrás)

A glorious, airy place, hugging a steep flank of Taïyettos, **Mystra** is arguably the most exciting and dramatic site that the Peloponnese can offer. Winding up the hillside is an astonishingly complete Byzantine city that once sheltered a population of some 42,000, and through which you can now wander. Winding alleys lead through monumental gates, past medieval houses and palaces and above all into a sequence of churches, several of which yield superb and radiant frescoes. The effect is of straying into a massive museum of architecture, painting and sculpture – and into a different age.

There are few facilities at the site itself, so you'll need to base yourself at either Spartí (see above) or the modern settlement of Néos Mystrás (see p.180).

Some history

Mystra was basically a Frankish creation. In 1249, Guillaume II de Villehardouin, fourth Frankish Prince of the Moreás, built a castle here – one of a trio of fortresses (the others were at Monemvassía and in the Máni) designed to garrison his domain. The Franks, however, were driven out of Mystra by the Byzantines in 1262, and this isolated triangle of land in the southeastern Peloponnese, encompassing the old Spartan territories,

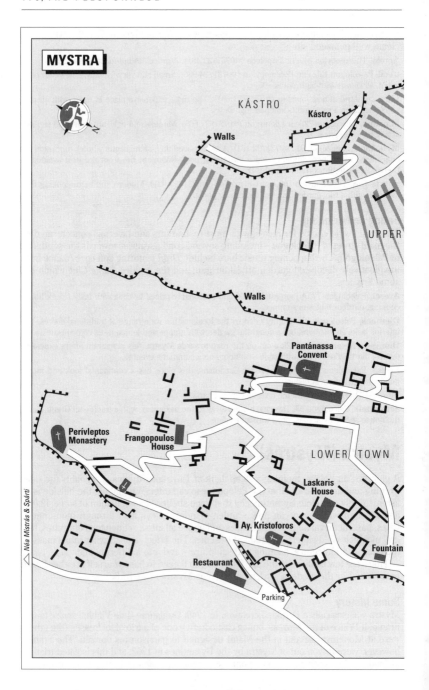

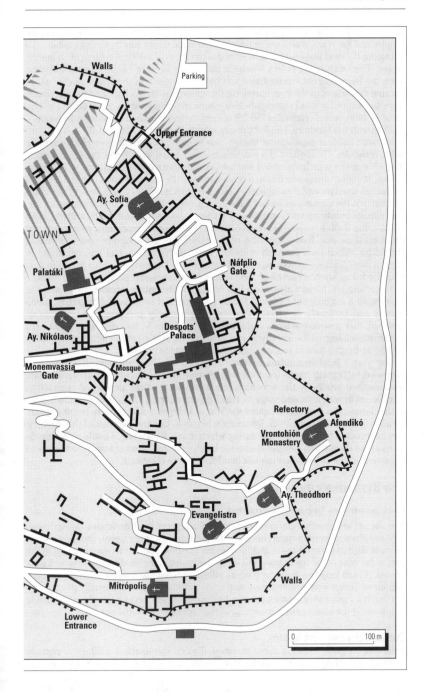

became the **Despotate of Mystra**. This was the last province of the Greek Byzantine Empire and for years, with Constantinople in terminal decay, was its virtual capital.

During the next two centuries, Mystra was the focus of a defiant rebirth of Byzantine power. The Despotate's rulers – usually the son or brother of the eastern emperor, often the heir-apparent – recaptured and controlled much of the Peloponnese, which became the largest of the ever-shrinking Byzantine provinces. They and their province were to endure for two centuries before eventual subjugation by the Turks. The end came in 1460, seven years after the fall of Constantinople, when the despot Demetrius, feuding with his brothers, handed the city over to the Sultan Mehmet II.

Mystra's political significance, though, was in any case overshadowed by its **artistic achievements**. Throughout the fourteenth and the first decades of the fifteenth centuries it was the principal cultural and intellectual centre of the Byzantine world, sponsoring, in highly uncertain times, a renaissance in the arts and attracting the finest of Byzantine scholars and theologians – among them a number of members of the imperial families, the Cantacuzenes and Paleologues. Most notable of the court scholars was the humanist philosopher **Gemisthus Plethon**, who revived and reinterpreted Plato's ideas, using them to support his own brand of revolutionary teachings, which included the assertions that land should be redistributed among labourers and that reason should be placed on a par with religion. Although his beliefs had limited impact in Mystra itself – whose monks excommunicated him – his followers, who taught in Italy after the fall of Mystra, exercised wide influence in Renaissance Florence and Rome.

More tangibly, Mystra also saw a last flourish of **Byzantine architecture**, with the building of a magnificent Despots' Palace and a perfect sequence of churches, multi-domed and brilliantly frescoed. It is these, remarkably preserved and sensitively restored, that provide the focus of this extraordinary site. In the painting, it is not hard to see something of the creativity and spirit of Plethon's court circle, as the stock Byzantine figures turn to more naturalistic forms and settings.

The town's **post-Byzantine history** follows a familiar Peloponnesian pattern. It remained in Turkish hands from the mid-fifteenth to late seventeenth centuries, then was captured briefly by the Venetians, under whom the town prospered once more. Decline set in with a second stage of Turkish control, from 1715 onwards, culminating in the destruction that accompanied the War of Independence, the site being evacuated after fires in 1770 and 1825. Restoration began in the first decades of this century, was interrupted by the civil war – during which it was, for a while, a battle site, with the ruins of the Pantánassa convent sheltering children from the lower town – and renewed in earnest in the 1950s when the last inhabitants were relocated.

The Byzantine city

Daily: summer 8am–7pm; winter 8.30am–3pm; 12,000dr.

The site of the Byzantine city comprises three main parts: the **Katokhóra** (lower town), with the city's most important churches; the **Anokhóra** (upper town), grouped around the vast shell of a royal palace; and the **Kástro** (castle). There are two entrances to the site, at the base of the lower town and up by the kástro; once inside, the site is well signposted. A road loops up from the modern village of Néos Mystrás (see p.180) past both entrances. Buses from Spárti always stop at the lower entrance, and usually go up to the top too. It's a good idea to stock up on refreshments before setting out; there's a mobile snack bar at the lower gate, but nothing at the upper one or in the site itself.

The Upper Town and Kástro

Following a course from the upper entrance, the first identifiable building you come to is the church of **Ayía Sofía**, which served as the chapel for the Despots' Palace – the enormous structure below. The chapel's finest feature is its floor, made from poly-chrome marble. Its frescoes, notably a *Pandokrator* (Christ in Majesty) and *Nativity of the Virgin*, have survived reasonably well, protected until recent years by coatings of whitewash applied by the Turks, who adapted the building as a mosque. Recognizable parts of the refectory and cells of its attached monastery also remain.

The **Kástro**, reached by a path direct from the upper gate, maintains the Frankish design of its original thirteenth-century construction, though it was repaired and mod-ified by all successive occupants. There is a walkway around most of the keep, whose views allow an intricate panorama of the town below. The castle itself was the court of Guillaume II de Villehardouin but was used primarily as a citadel in later years.

Heading down from Ayía Sofía, there is a choice of routes. The right fork winds past ruins of a Byzantine mansion, the **Palatáki** (Small Palace), and **Áyios Nikólaos**, a large seventeenth-century building decorated with crude paintings. The left fork is more interesting, passing the massively fortified **Náfplio Gate**, which was the princi-pal entrance to the upper town, and the vast, multi-storeyed, gothic-looking complex of the **Despots' Palace**.

Parts of the palace (currently closed for extensive restoration) probably date back to the Franks. Most prominent among its numerous rooms is a great vaulted audience hall, built at right angles to the line of the building, with ostentatious windows regally dominating the skyline; this was once heated by eight great chimneys and sported a painted facade. Behind it are the ruins of various official public buildings, while to the right of the lower wing, flanking one side of a square used by the Turks as a market-place, are the remains of a **mosque**.

The Lower Town

At the **Monemvassía Gate**, which links the upper and lower towns, there is a further choice of routes: right to the Pantánassa and Perívleptos monasteries or left to the Vrontohión monastery and cathedral. If time is running out, it is easier to head right first, then double back down to the Vrontohión.

When excavations were resumed in 1952, the last thirty or so families who still lived in the lower town were moved out to Néos Mystrás. Only the nuns of the **Pantánassa** ("Queen of the World") **convent** have remained; currently, there are seven in residence and they have a reception room where they sell their own handicrafts and sometimes offer a cooling *vissinadha* (cherryade) to visitors. The convent's church is perhaps the finest sur-viving in Mystra, perfectly proportioned in its blend of Byzantine and Gothic. The **frescoes** date from various centuries, with some superb fifteenth-century work, including one in the gallery (entered by an external staircase) which depicts scenes from the life of Christ. David Talbot Rice, in his classic study *Byzantine Art*, wrote of these frescoes that "Only El Greco in the west, and later Gauguin, would have used their colours in just this way". Other frescoes were painted between 1687 and 1715, when Mystra was held by the Venetians.

Further down on this side of the lower town is a balconied Byzantine mansion, the **House of Frangopoulos**, once the home of the Despotate's chief minister – who was, incidentally, the founder of the Pantánassa.

Beyond it is the diminutive **Perívleptos monastery**, whose single-domed church, partially carved out of the rock, contains Mystra's most complete cycle of frescoes, almost all of which date from the fourteenth century. They are in some ways finer than those of the Pantánassa, blending an easy humanism with the spirituality of the Byzantine icon traditions, and demonstrating the structured iconography of a Byzantine church. The position of each figure depended upon its sanctity and so here upon the dome, the image of heaven, is the *Pandokrator* (the all-powerful Christ in glory after the Ascension); on the apse is the Virgin, and the higher expanses of wall portray scenes from the life of Christ. Prophets and saints could only appear on the lower walls, decreasing in importance according to their distance from the sanctuary.

Along the path leading from Perívleptos to the lower gate are a couple of minor, much-restored churches, and, just above them, the **Laskaris House**, a mansion thought to have belonged to relatives of the emperors. Like the Frangopoulos House, it is balconied; its ground floor probably served as stables. Close by, beside the path, is an old Turkish fountain.

The **mitrópolis** or cathedral, immediately beyond the gateway, is the oldest of Mystra's churches, built between 1291–92 under the first Paleologue ruler. A marble slab set in its floor is carved with the double-headed eagle of Byzantium, commemorating the spot where Constantine XI Paleologus, the last Eastern emperor, was crowned in 1448; he was soon to perish, with his empire, in the Turkish sacking of Constantinople in 1453. Of the church's frescoes, the earliest, in the north aisle, depict the torture and burial of Áyios Dhimítrios, the saint to whom the church is dedicated. The comparative stiffness of their figures contrasts with the later works opposite. These, illustrating the miracles of Christ and the life of the Virgin, are more intimate and lighter of touch; they date from the last great years before Mystra's fall. A small **museum** (included in main admission charge), adjacent to the cathedral, contains various fragments of sculpture and pottery.

Finally, a short way uphill, is the **Vrontohión monastery**. This was the centre of cultural and intellectual life in the fifteenth-century town – the cells of the monastery can still be discerned – and was also the burial place of the despots. Of the two attached churches, the further one, **Afendikó** has been beautifully restored, revealing late frescoes similar to those of Perívleptos, with startlingly bold juxtapositions of colour.

Practicalities: Néos Mystrás

Buses run regularly through the day from Spárti to the lower Mystra site entrance, stopping en route at the modern village of **NÉOS MYSTRÁS**. This is quite attractive in its own right: a small roadside community whose half-dozen tavernas, crowded with tour buses by day, revert to a low-key life at night, except at the end of August when the town buzzes with live music and a gypsy market on the occasion of the week-long annual *paneyíri* (fête).

In general, staying in Néos Mystrás is worth the bit extra over Spárti, for the setting and early access to the site, though you will need to book ahead, or arrive early in the day, to find a place. **Accommodation** is limited to a single hotel, the *Byzantion* (☎0731/83 309; ④), which is pleasant but oversubscribed for most of the year, and a small number of private rooms – those run by Hrístos Vahaviólos (☎0731/20 047; ②) are especially recommended. There are campsites along the Mystra–Spárti road: all the details are on p.174.

The Vahaviólos family also has an excellent taverna, while the **restaurant** opposite the hotel, *To Kastro*, is also good, if a bit on the expensive side. Between the village and the site, *Taverna Marmara* is fine – and quieter in the evenings after the tour buses have gone.

West from Spartí: Mount Taïyettos and the Langádha pass

Moving on from Spárti there is a tough choice of routes: west over Mount Taïyettos, either on foot or by road through the dramatic **Langádha pass** to Kalamáta; east to the Byzantine towns of **Yeráki** and **Monemvassía**; or south, skirting the mountain's foothills, to **Yíthio** and **the Máni**. For anyone wanting to get to grips with the Greek mountains, there is **Mount Taïyettos** itself. Although the range is one of the most dramatic and hazardous in Greece, with vast grey boulders and scree along much of its length, it has one reasonably straightforward path to the highest peak, Profítis Ilías.

HIKING IN THE TAÏYETTOS RANGE

Most **hikes** beyond Anavrití need experience and proper equipment, including the relevant *Korfes* or *YIS* maps, and should definitely not be undertaken alone – a sprained ankle could be fatal up here. The area is prone to flash floods, so seek advice locally. If you are confident, however, there are various routes to the Profítis Ilías summit and beyond:

The only straightforward route is to follow the **E4 long-distance footpath**, here a forest road marked variously by yellow diamonds or red-and-white stripes, for five hours south to the **alpine refuge** at Ayía Varvára (see below).

The classic approach to the **Profítis Ilías summit** used to entail a dusty, eleven-kilometre road-walk up from the village of Paleopanayía, a short bus ride south of Spárti off the Yíthio road, to the spring and ex-trailhead at Bóliana, where there's a single ramshackle hut that serves drinks and sometimes meals in summer. You now have to proceed past Bóliana towards Anavrití on the E4 track for about thirty minutes, then bear left near a picnic ground and spring (the last reliable water on the mountain). Another half-hour above this, following E4 blazes, what's left of the old trail appears on the right, signposted "EOS Spárti Katafíyio". This short-cuts the new road except for the very last 50m to the Ayía Varvára refuge.

A more challenging option, requiring mountaineering skills and camping equipment, is to adopt the red-dotted trail veering off the E4 early on, and follow it to a point just below the 1700-metre saddle described by Patrick Leigh Fermor in *Mani*, where you must choose between dropping over the pass to the far side of the range or precarious ridge-walking to the Profítis Ilías summit (2404m). Crossing the pass would land you at the head of the **Ríndomo gorge**, where you can camp at the chapel-monastery of Panayía Kavsodhematúsa before descending the next day to either Gaïtses or Pigádhia, near the Messinian coast. Keeping to the watershed it is seven tough hours to the peak even in optimum conditions and with a light load, involving exposed rock pinnacles, sheer drops and difficult surfaces. This is not a hike to be lightly undertaken.

AYÍA VARVÁRA TO THE SUMMIT

The **Ayía Varvára refuge** (unstaffed, but open sporadically – more likely at weekends), above Bóliana, sits on a beautiful grassy knoll shaded by tremendous storm-blasted black pines. The conical peak of Profítis Ilías rises directly above; if you can get your climb to coincide with a full moon you won't regret it. There is plenty of room for camping, and the hut has a porch to provide shelter in bad weather.

The path to the **summit** starts at the rear left corner of the refuge and swings right on a long reach. Level and stony at first, it leaves the treeline and loops up a steep bank to a sloping meadow, where it is ineffectually marked by twisted, rusting signs with their lettering long obliterated. Keep heading right across the slope towards a distinct secondary peak until, once around a steep bend, the path begins to veer left in the direction of the summit. It slants steadily upward following a natural ledge until, at a very clear nick in the ridge above you, it turns right and crosses to the far side, from where you look down on the Gulf of Messinía. Turn left and you climb steeply to the summit in around 25 minutes.

There is a squat stone chapel and outbuildings on the **summit**, used during the celebrations of the Feast of the Prophet Elijah (Profítis Ilías) on July 18–20. The views, as you would expect, are breathtaking, encompassing the sea to east and west.

SUMMIT TO THE COAST

The terrain **beyond the peak** is beyond the ambitions of casual hikers. The easiest and safest way off the mountain towards the Messinian coast is to follow the E4 from Ayía Varvára to the gushing springs at Pendávli, and then over a low saddle to the summer hamlet of **Áyios Dhimítrios**. This takes just a couple of hours and you can camp in the beautiful surroundings. In the morning you're well poised, at the head of the **Výros gorge**, to handle the all-day descent to Kardhamýli through the other great Taïyettan canyon. At one point you negotiate stretches of the **Kakí Skála**, one of the oldest paths in Greece, built to link ancient Sparta and Messene.

Mount Taïyettos

Gazing up at the crags above the castle at Mystra, Mount Taïyettos (Taygettus) looks daunting and inviting in pretty equal measure. If all you want is a different perspective on the mountain, then the simplest course is to take a bus from Spárti to **ÁYIOS IOÁNNIS**, a little way to the south of Mystra and closer to the peaks. From there a spectacular *kalderími* (cobbled way) leads up from the gravel-crushing mill behind the village to **ANAVRYTÍ**, which boasts superb vistas, a single friendly hotel the *Anemodharména Ípsi* ("Wuthering Heights"; ☎0731/21 788; ②) and one very basic taverna aside from the one in the hotel. An alternative, more popular approach involves following the marked E4 overland route, partly on track, partly on trail, up from Néos Mystrás via the **monastery of Faneroméni**. Neither the E4 nor the *kalderími* take more than two hours uphill, and they can be combined as follows for a wonderful day's outing: bus to Áyios Ioánnis, taxi to rock-crushing mill (2.5km), hike up to Anavrytí, have a look around and a meal, then descend via Faneroméni to Néos Mystrás. Note that this route is best tackled from Áyios Ioánnis; the downhill start of the *kalderími* just east of Anavrytí isn't marked, and can be difficult to locate

Spárti to Kalamáta: the Langádha pass

The **Langádha pass**, the sixty-kilometre route across the Taïyettos from **Spárti to Kalamáta**, was the former alternative to the Kakí Skála and is still the only paved road across the mountain. Remote and barren, with no habitation at all for the central 25km section, it unveils a constant drama of peaks, magnificent at all times but startling at sunrise. This was, incidentally, the route that Telemachus took in *The Odyssey* on his way from Nestor's palace at Pylos to that of Menelaus at Sparta. It took him a day by chariot – good going by any standards, since today's buses take three hours.

Heading from Spárti, the last settlement is **TRÝPI**, 14km out, where there is a small **hotel**, the *Keadas* (☎0731/98 222; ③), with a restaurant, and one of the best tavernas in the Spárti area, *Bábi Vozóla*. Just beyond the village, the road climbs steeply into the mountains and enters the **gorge of Langádha**, a wild sequence of hairpins through the pines. To the north of the gorge, so it is said, the Spartans used to leave their sick or puny babies to die from exposure. Beyond the gorge, close to the summit of the pass, and 22km from Spartí, the *Canadas* hotel (☎0721/76 821; ②) is built in the style of an alpine chalet, with a restaurant that serves good *bakaliaro* (cod) and *loukániko* (sausage); both are open year-round.

The first actual village on the Kalamáta side is Artemisía, where you often have to change buses, before entering another gorge for the final zigzagging descent to Kalamáta.

East from Spárti: Yeráki

If you choose the eastern route from Spárti, then it is well worth making the effort to visit the **Byzantine antiquities** at **Yeráki**. With its **Frankish castle** and fifteen **chapels** spread over a spur of Mount Párnon, Yeráki stands a creditable third to the sites of Mystra and Monemvassía.

Medieval Yeráki

Yeráki was one of the original twelve **Frankish baronies** set up in the wake of the Fourth Crusade, and remained through the fourteenth century an important Byzantine town, straddling the road between Mystra and its port at Monemvássia. The site is spectacular, with sweeping vistas over the olive-covered Evrótas plain and across to

Taïyettos. It stands four kilometres outside the current village of Yeráki (see below), on the first outcrop of the Párnon mountains.

Although the site itself is unenclosed, all the main churches are kept locked, and to visit them you should first make enquiries at the café on the village square for one of the caretakers, one of whom will either be here, at the small office on the Kástro side of town or up at the site itself. You'll be given a tour by him, clambering around the rocks to the best-preserved **chapels**.

The most substantial remains of the medieval town are of its fortress, the **Kástro**, built in 1256 by the local Frankish baron, Jean de Nivelet, who had inherited Yeráki, with six other lordships, from his father. Its heavily fortified design is based on that of the Villehardouin fortress at Mystra, for this was one of the most vulnerable Frankish castles of the Moreás, intended to control the wild and only partially conquered territories of Taïyettos and the Máni. In the event, Jean retained his castle for less than a decade, surrendering to the Byzantines in 1262 and buying an estate near Kórinthos on the proceeds. Within the fortress are huge **cisterns** for withstanding siege, and the largest of Yeráki's churches: the thirteenth-century **mitrópolis**, also known as **Áyios Yeóryios**, which features blackened Byzantine frescoes, a Frankish iconostasis and the Villehardouin arms.

The churches on the slope below also mix Frankish and Byzantine features, and many incorporate ancient blocks from Yeráki's ancient predecessor, Geronthrai. The caretaker is usually prepared to unlock two or three, including **Áyios Dhimítrios**, **Zoödóhos Píyi**, and **Ayía Paraskeví** (at the base of the hill), each of which has restored frescoes.

Practicalities

The "modern" village of **Yeráki** has no regular accommodation, though rooms may be negotiable through the café or taverna in the square. If you're dependent on public transport, you'll need to take in Yeráki as day-trip from Spárti: **buses** run several times daily, but not along the splendid route over Mount Párnon to Leonídhi (see p.169).

Monemvassía

After Mystra you half-expect Byzantine sites to be disappointing – or at least low-key like Yeráki. **MONEMVASSÍA** is emphatically neither. Set impregnably on a great island-like irruption of rock, the medieval seaport and commercial centre of the Byzantine Peloponnese as exciting as its spiritual counterpart of Mystra, a place of grand, haunting atmosphere, whose houses and churches are all the more evocative for being populated, albeit on a largely weekend and tourist basis.

The town's name, an elision of *Moni Emvasis* or "single entrance", is a reference to its approach from the mainland, across a kilometre-long causeway and a small bridge built this century to replace a sequence of wooden bridges. Such a defensible and strategic position gave it control of the sea-lines from Italy and the West to Constantinople and the Levant. Fortified on all approaches, it was invariably the last outpost of the Peloponnese to fall to invaders, and was only ever taken through siege.

Some history

Founded by the **Byzantines** in the sixth century, Monemvassía soon became an important port. It remained in Byzantine possession for almost seven hundred years, passing only very briefly to the Franks – who took it in 1249 after a three-year siege but had to ransom it back for the captured Guillaume de Villehardouin. Subsequently, it served as the chief commercial port of the Despotate of the Moreás and was to all effects the Greek Byzantine capital. Mystra, despite the presence of the court, was never much more than a large village; Monemvassía at its peak had a population of almost 60,000.

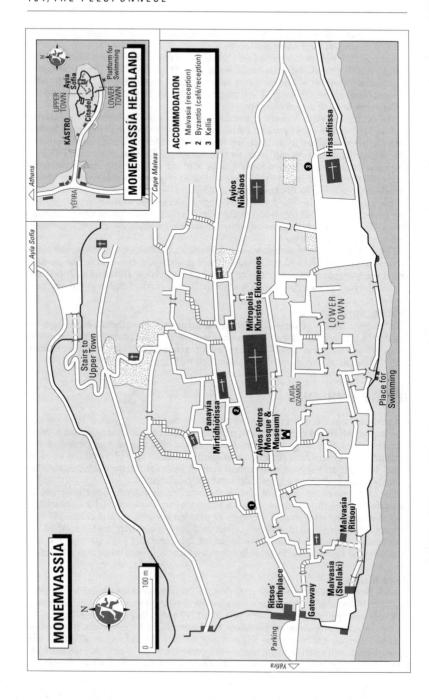

MONEMVASSÍA

N

0   100 m

△ Ayía Sofía

Stairs to Upper Town

Panayía Miridhiótissa

Áyios Pétros (Mosque & Museum)

PLATÍA DZAMÍOU

Mitrópolis Khristós Elkómenos

Áyios Nikólaos

LOWER TOWN

Place for Swimming

Hrissafítissa

Ritsos' Birthplace

Gateway

Malvasia (Stellaki)

Malvasia (Ritsou)

Parking

△ Yéfira

MONEMVASSÍA HEADLAND

N

KÁSTRO

UPPER TOWN

Ayía Sofía

Citadel

LOWER TOWN

Platform for Swimming

YÉFIRA

△ Athens

▽ Cape Maléas

ACCOMMODATION

1 Malvasia (reception)
2 Byzantio (café/reception)
3 Kellia

Like Mystra, Monemvassía had something of a golden age in the thirteenth century; during this period, it was populated by a number of noble Byzantine families, and reaped considerable wealth from estates inland, from the export of wine (the famed Malmsey, mentioned by Shakespeare) and from roving corsairs who preyed on Latin shipping heading for the East. When the rest of the Moreás fell to the Turks in 1460, Monemvassía was able to seal itself off, placing itself first under the control of the Papacy, later under the **Venetians**. Only in 1540 did the **Turks** gain control, the Venetians having abandoned their garrison after the defeat of their navy at Préveza.

Turkish occupation precipitated a steady decline, both in prestige and population, though the town experienced something of a revival during the period of Venetian control of the Peloponnese. Monemvassía was again thrust to the fore in the **War of Independence**, being the first of the major Turkish fortresses to fall, after a terrible siege and wholesale massacre of the Turkish inhabitants, in July 1821.

After the war, there was no longer the need for such strongholds, and, at the end of the nineteenth century, shipping routes changed too, with the opening of the Corinth Canal. The population plummeted and the town drifted into a village existence, its buildings for the most part allowed to fall into ruin. By the time of World War II – during which 4000 New Zealand troops were dramatically evacuated from the rock – only eighty families remained. Today there are just ten in permanent residence.

The rock: medieval Monemvassía

From the mainland village of **Yéfira** – where the causeway to **Monemvassía** (or **Kástro**, as locals call it) begins – nothing can be seen of the medieval town, which is built purely on the seaward face of the rock. Little more is revealed as you walk across the causeway, past a garage with a Mobil sign. Then suddenly the road is barred by huge castellated walls. Once through the fortified entrance gate, wide enough only for a single person or a donkey, everything looms into view: piled upon one another amid narrow stone streets and alleyways are houses with tiled roofs and walled gardens, distinctively Byzantine churches, and high above, the improbably long castle walls protecting the upper town on the summit.

The Lower Town

Standing at the **gateway** to the rock there is the same sense of luxury and excitement as at Mystra: the prospect of being able to walk each street, explore every possible turn of this extraordinary place. The **Lower Town** here once numbered forty churches and over eight hundred homes, an incredible mass of building, which explains the intricate network of alleys. A single main street – up and slightly to the left from the gateway – shelters most of the restored houses, as well as a scattering of cafés, tavernas and souvenir shops. One of the tavernas is owned by the Ritsos family, relatives of the late Yannis Ritsos, one of Greece's leading poets and a lifelong communist, who was born on the rock; a plaque on a house above the main gate commemorates his birthplace.

At the end of this street is the lower town's main square, a beautiful public space, with a cannon and a well in its centre, a kafenío along one side, and, on the other, the great, vaulted **cathedral** built by the Byzantine Emperor Andronicus II Comnenus when he made Monemvassía a see in 1293. The largest medieval church in southern Greece, it is dedicated to Christ in Chains, and is thus known as *Hristós Elkómenos*. Across the square is the domed church of **Áyios Petros**, which was transformed by the Turks into a mosque and now houses a small museum of local finds (open, but keeps unpredictable hours). Unusually for Ottoman Greece, the Christian cathedral was allowed to function during the occupation, and must have done so beside this mosque – hence the name of this square, Platía Dzamíou, the square of the mosque.

Down towards the sea is a third notable church, the **Khryssafítissa**, whose bell hangs from a bent-over old acacia tree in the courtyard. It was restored and adapted by the Venetians in their second, eighteenth-century, occupation. The **Portello** is a small gate in the sea wall, due south of Platía Tzamíou; you can **swim** safely off the rocks here.

In peaceful times, the town was supplied from the tiny harbour, **Kourkoúla**, outside the town and below the road as you approach the entrance gateway. There are two minor churches just off the main street. **Panayía Myrtidhiótissa**, to the north of the cathedral, is a small, single-aisled basilica with a single dome; inside there is a beautifully carved *iconostási* – ask around for the priest if the basilica is locked. The big grey church built alongside the main street, above the Hrissafítissa, is **Áyios Nikólaos**. it dates from the early seventeenth century, and was used for many years as a school.

The Upper Town

The climb to the **Upper Town** is highly worthwhile – not least for the solitude, since most of the day-trippers stay down below. To get the most from the vast site, it's a good idea to bring some food and drink (from Yéfira: Monemvássia has no supermarket), to enable you to explore at leisure. There are sheer drops from the rockface, and unguarded cisterns, so descend before dusk and if you have young children, keep them close by.

The fortifications, like those of the lower town, are substantially intact; indeed the **entrance gate** retains its iron slats. Within, the site is a ruin, unrestored and deserted – the last resident moved out in 1911 – though many structures are still recognizable. The only building that is relatively complete, even though its outbuildings have long since crumbled to foundations, is the beautiful thirteenth-century **Ayía Sofía**, by the gateway. Founded as a monastery by Andronikos II, along a plan similar to that of Dhafní, the chapel candles still flicker perilously in the wind.

Beyond the church extend acres of ruins: in medieval times the population here was much greater than that of the lower town. Among the remains are the stumpy bases of Byzantine houses and public buildings, and, perhaps most striking, a vast **cistern** to ensure a water supply in time of siege. Monemvassía must have been more or less self-sufficient in this respect, but its weak point was its food supply, which had to be entirely imported from the mainland. In the last siege, by Mavromihalis's Maniot army in the War of Independence, the Turks were reduced to eating rats – and, so the propagandists claimed, Greek children.

Practicalities

Monemvassía can be approached by road or sea. There are twice-weekly **ferries** from Pireás, and Kastélli on Crete, and more frequent **hydrofoils** in season, linking the town to the north with Leonídhi, Pórto Khéli, Spétses and Pireás, and to the south with Neápoli and the island of Kýthira; currently there is no hydrofoil link with Yíthio. Direct **buses** connect with Spárti three times daily and twice (in season only) with Yíthio; occasionally a change at Mólai is necessary. Out of season it's best to alight at Skála, 17km from Yíthio, and take a local bus or taxi.

The boat or hydrofoil will drop you at a mooring midway down the causeway; buses arrive in the modern village of Yéfira on the mainland. This is little more than a straggle of hotels, rooms and restaurants for the rock's tourist trade, with a pebble beach; for a **beach** day-trip, it's best to head 3–4km north along the coast.

Accommodation on the rock is expensive – in season and out – and from June to September, you'll need to book ahead. The choice is between three very attractive and upmarket **hotels**, each of which has beautifully restored and traditionally furnished rooms. The most renowned is the *Malvasia* (☎0732/61 323; ④), which occupies three separate locations between the main street and the sea; call first at the hotel reception, well signposted just inside the main gateway. The similarly characterful *Byzantio* (☎0732/61 351; ⑤) further along the main street is marginally more expensive: ask at the café of the same name. Down near the Hrissafítissa, looking out over the sea, is the *Kellia* (☎0732/61 520; ⑤), a small and rather remote place: advance booking is recommended. Several other **furnished apartments** on the rock are available for long-term rental. If you ask around at the shops and taverna on the main street, it's just possible that you might get one of these on a more temporary basis, out of season. Or you could seek the help of Malvasia Travel (see below). **Eating out** in the old village is enjoyable, as much for location as food. Of the several restaurants, the best all round place is *Matoúla*, which has a leafy garden overlooking the sea.

Yéfira

There's more accommodation in **YÉFIRA**, along with various other useful tourist services: **bank, post office, OTE** and a **travel agent**, Malvasia Travel (☎0732/61 432), which can help with rooms, sells ferry tickets and rents out **mopeds**; the Mobil garage just across the bridge towards the rock (☎0732 /61 219) handles the **hydrofoils**. There are several **hotels** near the causeway. The cheapest are the refurbished *Akroyiali* (☎0732/61 360; ③) and the *Aktaion* (☎0732/61 234; ④); the latter's enterprising owner has also recently opened the *Filoxenia* (☎0732/61 716; ④), with balconies and wonderful sea views. The *Monemvassia* (☎0732/61 381; ⑤) is also newish, with colourful decor inspired by the Aegean scenery. If these are full, there are plenty of others to choose from, plus dozens of **rooms** for rent, advertised along the waterfront. One good option is *Kontorinis House* (☎0732/61 186; ④), at the back of the village with views of the rock. The nearest **campsite** is 3km to the south, along the coast road; *Kapsis Paradise* (☎0732/61 123) is open year-round, and has water skis and mopeds for rent. Back in the village, the best **taverna** is undoubtedly the *Nikolaos*; if you have transport, you could also try the *Pipinelis* (☎0732/61 044; May–Oct), about 2km out on the road south to the campsite, but ring first to be sure it's open and to make a reservation if the weather's cool, as indoor seating is limited. Even closer to the campsite is the pleasant *Kamares* taverna with good grilled and oven food.

South to Neápoli and Elafónissos

The isolated southeasternmost "finger" of the Peloponnese below Monemvassía is a bit disappointing, with little of interest in either its villages or its landscape. However, the area around **Neápoli**, the southernmost town in mainland Greece, offers access to the islet of Elafónissos, just offshore, and to the larger Ionian islands of Kýthira and Andíkithira, midway to Crete.

Neápoli

NEÁPOLI is a mix of old buildings and modern Greek concrete behind a grey sand beach – hardly compelling, aside from its ferry and hydrofoil connections. For such an out of the way (and not especially attractive) place, it is surprisingly developed, catering mainly to Greek holidaymakers. Besides **rooms**, there are two modest hotels: the *Aivali* (☎0734/22 287; ④) and the *Arsenakos* (☎0734/22 991; ④), both small and worth booking ahead in summer. The huge new *Hotel Limira Mare* (☎0734/22 236; ⑤) is a fall-back, though an expensive one. If you are waiting for the ferry or hydrofoil, you can eat well at the *Restaurant Metaxia Manalitsi*, by the bridge on the seafront; *Captain D. Alexandrakis* (☎0734/22 940), also on the seafront, acts as an agent for ferries, hydrofoils and rooms.

Neápoli **beach** extends north to the village of Vingláfia and the recently upgraded harbour of Poúnda, which has ferry crossings every 45 minutes over the short strait to the islet of Elafónissos in high season, and several daily at other times. Currently there is only one early morning sailing from Neápoli to the islet.

Elafónissos island

Like Neápoli, **Elafónissos** is relatively busy in summer, and again is frequented mainly by Greek visitors. The island's lone village is largely modern and functional, but has plenty of rooms and some good fish tavernas. The three **pensions**, the *Asteri* (☎0734/61 271; ④), *Elafonissos* (☎0734/61 210; ③) and *Lafotel* (☎0734/61 138; ④), are worth booking.

Although scenically barren, the island has one of the best **beaches** in this part of Greece at **Káto Nísso**, a large double bay of fine white sand; it's 5km southeast of the village, from where a caique leaves every morning in summer. There's one basic sandwich-and-drinks stand at the beach, and usually a small community of people camping here. Another beach, **Símos**, to the southwest of the village is quieter but less spectacular.

Arkhángelos

Further up the coast from Neápoli, just off the more northerly route from Monemvassia, **ARKHÁNGELOS** is a pleasant little resort at the southern end of a quiet sandy and deserted bay. By a quaint twist the village's name means "archangel", yet it is the harbour of Dhemonía ("devilry"), several kilometres inland. Rooms are to be had at a good restaurant, *Limanaki* (☎0732/44 123; ④; March–Oct), or at the smarter apricot-coloured *Hotel Palazzo* (☎0732/44 111; ⑤), open all year. The *Anokato* bar is a popular hang-out for the whole peninsula, especially in winter.

Kýthira island

Isolated at the foot of the Peloponnese, the island of **Kýthira** traditionally belongs to the Ionian islands, and shares their history of Venetian, and later, British rule; under the former it was known as Cerigo. For the most part, the similarities end there. The island architecture, whitewashed and flat-roofed, looks more like that of the Cyclades, albeit with a strong **Venetian** influence. The landscape is different, too: wild scrub- and gorse-covered hills or moorland sliced by deep valleys and ravines.

Depopulation has left the land underfarmed and the abandoned fields overgrown, for, since the war, most of the islanders have left for Athens or Australia, giving Kýthira the reputation of being a classic emigrant island; it is known locally as "Australian Colony" or "Kangaroo Island", and Australia is referred to as "Big Kýthira". Many of the villages are deserted, their platías empty and the schools and kafenía closed. Kýthira was never a rich island, but, along with Monemvassía, it did once have a military and economic significance – which it likewise lost with Greek independence and the opening of the Corinth Canal. These days, tourism has brought a little prosperity (and a few luxury hotels), but most summer visitors are Greeks and especially Greek-Australians. For the few foreigners who reach Kýthira, it remains something of a refuge, with its fine and remarkably undeveloped **beaches** the principal attraction. Up until recently very little stayed open out of season outside **Potamós** but nowadays **Livádhi** and **Khóra** keep going as well.

Arrival and getting around

Arrival on the island is in the throes of dramatic change. In 1997 a huge new all-weather **harbour** was opened at Dhiakófti and it is anticipated that by 1998 all ferries and hydrofoils will be docking here instead of Ayía Pelayía or Kapsáli. The airport is

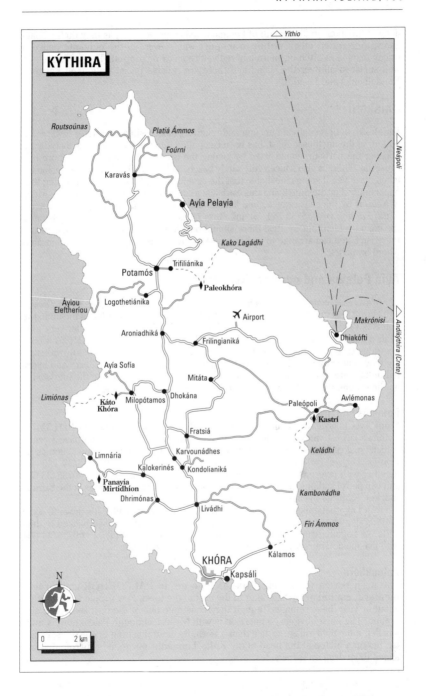

deep in the interior, 8km south of Potamós; taxis meet arrivals, as they do the boats. Sadly, there is no other **public transport** whatsoever, so the only alternative to pricey taxis is to hitch or, more advisedly, hire a **car** or **moped**. The roads are now well surfaced all over the island and there are reliable petrol stations at Potamós, Kondoliánika and Livádhi.

Dhiakófti

Dhiakófti, until recently an unsung and relatively inaccessible backwater towards the bottom of the northeast coast, has been catapulted into the forefront of activity by the opening the harbour, constructed by joining the islet of Makrónisi to the shore by a causeway. There is also a nice white sandy beach, and although no major expansion has taken place yet, it seems inevitable that the developers will not be long in seizing their opportunity. For the time being there are just a couple of tavernas, including the friendly *Notaras* by the causeway, a good kafenío and a few rooms and apartments such as *Eritili Zantioti* (☎0735/33 760; ④) and *Porto Diakofti* (☎0735/33 760; ⑤). Transport is the main problem but by 1998 there should be a branch of Panayiotis vehicle rent. If there isn't, you can arrange to be brought a car or a moped by phoning the Kapsáli or Khóra branches.

Ayía Pelayía and northern Kýthira

There's a reasonable choice of **tavernas** and **rooms** in Ayía Pelayía; the *Faros Taverna* (☎0735/33 282; ③) offers both, from its waterfront location. Best value of the upmarket hotels is *Venardos* (☎0735/34 305; ⑥), which is open all year and can offer very good deals off season. The clean and comfortable *Hotel Kytheria* (☎0735/33 321; ②) is more luxurious, as are the more recent *Filoxenia Apartments* (☎0735/33 100; ⑥), with striking blue shutters and an imaginative layout around small courtyards. Ferry and hydrofoil **tickets** are available from Conomos Travel (☎0735/33490), inside the tourist shop on the ground floor of the *Kytheria*. *To Paleo* ouzerí is recommended.

Potamós and around

From Ayía Pelayía, the main road winds up the mountainside towards **POTAMÓS**, Kýthira's largest village – a pleasant and unspoiled place which, if you have a rented vehicle, makes a good base for exploring the island. It has a few **rooms**, such as the *Pension Porfyra* (☎0735/33 329; ④), and *Alevizopoulos* rooms (☎0735/33 245; ④), together with tavernas, a bank, a post office, Olympic Airways office (☎0735/33 688) and two petrol stations. Most of the shops on the island are here, too, as is the **Sunday market**, Kýthira's liveliest regular event.

From Logothetiánika, just south of Potamós, an unpaved road leads down to Ayíou Eleftheríou, where you can **swim** from the rocks on the west coast, backed by high cliffs. At Logothetiánika itself, there is a popular taverna, *Karidhies* (☎0735/33 664) with live music Thursday–Saturday, when booking is advisable.

Paleokhóra

The main reason for visiting Potamós is to get to **PALEOKHÓRA**, the ruined **medieval capital** of Kýthira, 3km to the east of the town. Few people seem to know about or visit these remains, though they constitute one of the best Byzantine sites around. The most obvious comparison is with Mystra: although Paleokhóra is much smaller, a fortified village rather than a town, its natural setting is equally spectacular. Set on a hilltop at the head of the **Káko Langádhi gorge**, it is surrounded by a sheer 100m drop on three sides.

The site is lower than the surrounding hills and invisible from the sea and most of the island, something which served to protect it from the pirates that have plagued Paleokhóra through much of its history. The town was built in the thirteenth century by Byzantine nobles from Monemvassía, and when Mystra fell to the Turks, many of its noble families also sought refuge here. Despite its seemingly impregnable and perfectly concealed position, the site was discovered and sacked by **Barbarossa**, commander of the Turkish fleet, in 1537, and the island's 7000 inhabitants were sold into slavery.

The town was never rebuilt, and tradition maintains that it is a place of ill fortune, which perhaps explains the emptiness of the surrounding countryside, none of which is farmed today. The hills are dotted with Byzantine **chapels**, which suggests that, in its heyday, the area must have been the centre of medieval Kýthira; it is rumoured to have once had 800 inhabitants and 72 churches. Now the principal remains are of the surviving churches, some still with traces of frescoes, and the castle. The site is unenclosed and has never been seriously investigated, although excavations are now planned.

If you have your own transport, there's a rough dirt road to Paleokhóra, signposted off the main road from Potamós to Aroniadhiká. By foot, it's quicker and more interesting to take the path from the tiny village of Trifiliánika, just outside Potamós – look out for a rusting sign to the right as you enter the village. The path is overgrown in parts and not easy to follow; the ruins only become visible when you join the road above the gorge.

Karavás

KARAVÁS, 6km north of Potamós, is untypical of the island's villages – its architecture and the setting, in a deep wooded valley with a stream, are more reminiscent of the other Ionian islands. One of Kýthira's most pleasant villages, it would be a superb base, though there is (as yet) nowhere to stay. There is, however, a restaurant *Amir Ali*, with frequent live music.

Platiá Ámmos, at the end of the valley, is a sandy beach with a seasonal fish **taverna**. There is also an ouzerí and café and a few rooms at *Moudheas* restaurant (☎0735/33 960; ④). The little pebble beach at **Foúrni**, 2km south, is quieter and more attractive.

Kapsáli

KAPSÁLI, in addition to its harbour function, is the one place on Kýthira largely devoted to tourism. Most foreign visitors to Kýthira stay here, and it's a popular port of call for yachts heading from the Aegean to the Ionian islands and Italy. Set behind double pebble-sand bays, it is certainly picturesque. The larger of its two bays has a line of **tavernas**; the *Magus*, nearest the harbour, has good food at reasonable prices as does *To Venetsianiko*, half way along the front, but the best of all is *Hydragogio* at the Khorá end of the beach which serves up good veggie options. For nightlife the liveliest place is *Shaker*, playing the standard mix of Greek and foreign hits.

The best **accommodation** is in high demand and can be expensive. Top of the tree is the *Porto Delfino* (☎0735/31 940; ⑥; April–Oct); a few hundred metres above the bay are *Rigas* (☎0735/31 265; ⑥) and *Hotel Raikos* (☎0735/31 629; ⑥). The *Aphrodite Apartments* (☎0735/31 328; ⑤) have more reasonable rates, as do *Megaloudis* rooms (☎0735/31 340; ④). A fairly basic **campsite** (June–Sept) nestles in the pine trees behind the village.

There's a mobile **post office** in summer, and a couple of travel agents near the harbour: Kytheros International (☎0735/31 925) arranges travel, accommodation and vehicle rental, while Roma Travel (☎0735/31 561) deals with accommodation only. Panayiotis (☎0735/31 600) and Nikos (☎0735/31 5700) both rent **cars**, **motorbikes** and **mopeds**. As well as watersports facilities the former has a friendly reliable service; you can call off season (☎0735/31 551) and get wheels when most places are closed.

Khóra

KHÓRA (or Kýthira town), a steep 2km haul above Kapsáli, has an equally dramatic site, its Cycladic-style houses tiered about the walls of a Venetian castle. Within the **castle**, most of the buildings are ruined, but there are spectacular views of Kapsáli and, out to sea, to the islet of Avgó (Egg), legendary birthplace of Aphrodite. Below the castle are the remains of older Byzantine walls, and 21 Byzantine churches in various states of dereliction. A small **museum** (Tues–Sat 8.45am–3pm; Sun 9.30am–2.30pm) houses modest remnants of the island's numerous occupiers, in particular Minoan finds from excavations at Paleópoli.

Compared with Kapsáli, Khóra stays quiet and many places are closed out of season. A few **tavernas** open in summer, of which *Zorba* is by far the best, but the climb from Kapsáli discourages the crowds. Out of season, only one café/fast-food place stays open, near the square. **Accommodation** is slightly easier to find than in Kapsáli. The homeliest and best deal is the pension run by Yiorgos Píssis (☎0735/31 070; ②) with shared facilities including kitchen and some balcony views. Other options are the *Castello Studios* (☎0735/31 068; ④) and the old-style *Hotel Margarita* (☎0735/31 711; ⑤). At **MANITOKHÓRI**, 2km further inland, are the *Hotel Keti* (☎0735/31 318; ②) and the *Pension Kythira* (☎0735/31 563; ④). Other facilities include a couple of **banks**, an **OTE**, **post office**, and branches of Panayiotis (☎0735/31 004) and Nikos (☎0735/31 767) vehicle rental. The only real bar is *Mercato*, which stays open in the winter and also has exhibitions of local art.

The southeast coast

The beach at Kapsáli is decent but gets very crowded in July and August. For quieter, undeveloped beaches, it's better to head out to the east coast, towards Avlémonas.

Firí Ámmos and Kombonádha

Firí Ámmos, the nearest good sand beach to Kapsáli, is popular but not overcrowded, even in summer. To get there, you can follow a paved road as far as the sleepy village of Kálamos (take the northerly side road between Kapsáli and Khóra); the beach is signposted down a dirt track on the far side of the village. Firí Ámmos can also be reached from the inland village of Livádhi, on the Khóra–Arodhiánika road – as can **Kombonádha**, the next beach north. There are summer canteens at both beaches.

Paleópoli and Avlémonas

PALEÓPOLI, a hamlet of a few scattered houses, is accessible by a paved road from Aroniádhika. The area is the site of the ancient city of **Skandia**, and excavations on the headland of **Kastrí** have revealed remains of an important Minoan colony. There's little visible evidence, apart from shards of pottery in the low crumbling cliffs, but happily, tourist development in the area has been barred because of its archeological significance. Consequently, there's just one solitary **taverna**, the *Skandia* (June–Oct), on the excellent two-kilometre sand-and-pebble **beach** that stretches to either side of the headland. This place has recently been taken over by seven hippyish Anglo-Greek siblings and has great atmosphere with home cooking and frequent musical evenings.

The surrounding countryside, a broad, cultivated valley surrounded by wild hills, is equally attractive. **Paleokástro**, the mountain to the west, is the site of ancient Kýthira and a sanctuary of Aphrodite, but again, there's little to be seen today. Heading across the valley and turning right, an unpaved road leads up to a tiny, whitewashed church above the cliffs. From there, a track leads down to **Kaládhi**, a beautiful pebble beach with caves and rocks jutting out to sea.

AVLÉMONAS, 2km east of Paleópoli, is a tiny fishing port with two tavernas, of which *Sotiris* is recommended for fish, plus a few rooms including the large *Sklavos* apartments (☎0735/33 066; ⑤) and those run by Petrohilos (☎0735/33 034; ④) and his sister Mandy (☎0735/33 039; ④). There is a rather unimpressive Venetian fortress, the coast is rocky, the scenery bleak and exposed, and the village has something of an end-of-the-world feel.

North and west of Khóra

LIVÁDHI, 4km north of Khóra, has **rooms** and, on the main road, the newish *Hotel Aposperides* (☎0735/31656; ⑤) which, together with the *Toxotis* restaurant opposite, would make a good base if you had transport. Livádhi is also home to the most efficient travel agency on the island, Porfyra Travel, which is the main ANEK agent (☎0734/31 888); from here you can arrange hiking tours of the island. At Katoúni (2km out), there is an incongruous arched bridge; a legacy of the nineteenth century when all the Ionian islands were a British protectorate – it was built by a Scottish engineer. From the village, a fork heads west to Kalokerinés, and continues 3km further to the island's principal monastery, **Panayía Myrtidhíon**, set among cypress trees above the wild and windswept west coast. Beyond the monastery, a track leads down to a small anchorage at Limnária; there are few beaches along this rocky, forbidding shore. At **Káto Livádhi**, a kilometre to the east of Livádhi, there is an excellent new Byzantine museum (Mon–Sat 9am–2.30pm, Sat & Sun 9am–1.30pm; free) next to the large central church. It contains frescoes, painstakingly removed from island churches, dating from the sixth to the eighteenth centuries, a mosaic and some icons. Not far away there is also a cooperative pottery workshop (open all day except 2–4pm) and, near an old bridge built by the English, a popular taverna called *O Faros*.

Mylopótamos, Káto Khóra and the Ayía Sofía cave

North of Livádhi, the main road crosses a bleak plateau whose few settlements are near-deserted. At Dhokána it's worth making a detour off the main road for **MYLOPÓTAMOS**, a lovely traditional village and a virtual oasis, set in a wooded valley occupied by a small stream. The shady *Platanos* kafenío makes a pleasant stop for a drink. Nearby is a waterfall, hidden from view by lush vegetation – follow the sign for "Neraidha" past an abandoned restaurant. The valley below the falls is overgrown but contains the remains of the watermill that gave the village its name.

Káto Khóra, 500m down the road, was Mylopótamos's predecessor. Now derelict, it remains half-enclosed within the walls of a Venetian fortress. The fortress is small and has a rather domestic appearance: unlike the castle at Khóra, it was built as a place of refuge for the villagers in case of attack, rather than as a base for a Venetian garrison. All the houses within the walls, and many outside, are abandoned. Beyond here, a paved and precipitous road continues 5km through spectacular scenery to **Limiónas**, a rocky bay with a small beach of fine white sand.

The reason most visitors come to Milopótamos is to see the **cave of Ayía Sofía**, the largest and most impressive of a number of caverns on the island. A half-hour signposted walk from the village, the cave is open regularly from mid-June to mid-September (Tues–Thurs, Sat & Sun 11am–3pm, Wed & Fri 4–8pm; 600dr). When the cave is closed, you can probably find a guide in Milopótamos; ask at the village, giving a day's notice, if possible. The cave is worth the effort to see: the whitewashed entrance has been used as a church and has a painted iconostasis. Beyond, the cave system comprises a series of chambers which reach 250m into the mountain, although the thirty-minute guided tour (in Greek and English) only takes in the more interesting outer chambers. These include some startling formations like the "shark's teeth", but you have to ask to be shown "Aphrodite's chambers". A minute new species of disc-shaped insect has been discovered here.

Andikýthira island

The tiny island of **Andikýthira** has twice-weekly connections in summer only on the Kýthira–Kastélli run. Rocky and poor, it only received electricity in 1984. Attractions include good birdlife and flora, but it's not the place if you want company. With only fifty or so inhabitants divided between two settlements – **Potamós**, the harbour, and **Sokhória**, the village – people are rather thin on the ground. A resident doctor and a teacher serve the dwindling community (there are three children at the village school, as compared with nearly forty in the 1960s). The only official accommodation is the set of **rooms** run by the local community at Potamós, which also has the sole **taverna**. In Sohória the only provisions available are basic foodstuffs at the village shop.

Yíthio (Gythion)

YÍTHIO, Sparta's ancient port, is the gateway to the dramatic Máni peninsula, and one of the south's most attractive seaside towns in its own right. Its somewhat low-key harbour, with ferries to Pireás, Kýthira and Crete, gives onto a graceful nineteenth-century waterside of tiled-roof houses – some of them now showing their age. There's a beach within walking distance and rooms are relatively easy to find. In addition, the town has a site as exotic and alluring as any in Greece. In the bay, tethered by a long narrow mole, is the **islet of Marathónissi**, ancient Kranae, where Paris of Troy, having abducted Helen from Menelaus's palace at Sparta, dropped anchor, and where the lovers spent their first night.

The Town

Marathónissi is the town's main sight, a pleasant place to while away an hour or so in the early evening, with swimming off the rocks towards the lighthouse (beware sea urchins). Amid the island's trees and scrub stands a recently restored tower-fortress built in the 1810s by the Turkish-appointed Bey of the Máni to guard the harbour against his lawless countrymen. It now houses the **Museum of the Máni** (9.30am–5pm; 500dr), which deals with the exploration of the Máni from Ciriaco de Pizzicoli (1447) to Henri Belle (1861), with captions in Greek and English.

For an aerial view of the islet and town, climb up through Yíthio's stepped streets on to the hill behind – the town's ancient acropolis. The settlement around it, known as **Laryssion**, was quite substantial in Roman times, enjoying a wealth from the export of murex, the purple-pigmented mollusc used to dye imperial togas.

Much of the ancient site now lies submerged but there are some impressive remains of a **Roman theatre** to be seen at the northeast end of the town. Follow the road past the post office for about 300m, until you reach an army barracks, where a sign in the road says "stop" and the theatre stands just to the left. A modest 40m in diameter but with most of its stone seats intact, it illustrates perfectly how buildings in Greece take on different guises through the ages: built to one side is a Byzantine church (now ruined) which, in turn, has been pressed into service as the outer wall of the barracks.

Beaches near Yíthio

For swimming, there are a number of coves within reach of Yíthio, on both sides of which rise an intermittent sequence of cliffs. The **beach** at Mavrovoúni, by the campsites detailed below, is one of the best; a smaller one, north of the town, has a nominal admission charge. Many of the buses serving Yíthio from Spárti routinely continue to Mavrovoúni – ask on board. Alternatively, if you've transport, there are the superb beaches in Váthi Bay, further along, off the Areópoli road (see p.195).

Practicalities

Buses drop you close to the centre of town, with the main waterfront street, **Vassiléos Pávlou**, right ahead of you. There are three **banks** near the bus station. Moto Máni by the causeway, on the Areópoli road (☎0733/22 853), has mopeds for rent, and Supercycle on the main square (☎0733/24 407), rents out **motorcycles** by the day and, by negotiation, for longer periods. If you are headed for Kýthira, Pireás, Monemvassía or Crete, you can check **ferry** sailings at the Rozakis Shipping and Travel Agency (☎0733/22 207) on the waterfront; the latter will also change travellers' cheques and money. A trip of at least three days is worth considering for the Máni; the Ladopoulou and Andreikos **bookstores** are worth scouring for books on the area.

Accommodation

Finding **accommodation** shouldn't be hard, with a fair selection of hotels and rooms – most along the waterfront, signposted up the steps behind, or facing the Marathónissi islet. There are three **campsites** along Mavrovoúni beach, which begins 3km south of the town off the Areópoli road. The nearest and best of these is the *Meltémi* (☎0733/23 260; April–Oct); a couple of kilometres further on are the *Gythion Beach* (☎0733/22 522; year-round) and *Mani Beach* (☎0733/23 450; mid-April to mid-Oct).

Githion, Vassiléos Pávlou (☎0733/23 452). A fine old hotel on the waterfront; good value for money. ④.

Kondoyannis, Vassiléos Pávlou 19 (☎0733/22 518). A small, friendly pension with a family feel, up steep steps alongside – and above – the management's jewellery shop. ②.

Koutsouris, junction Larysíou and Morétti (☎0733/22 321). Excellent-value pension, friendly and comfortable, with a lovely garden, a dog and five tortoises. Turn right at the clocktower 100m inland from Platía Mavromiháli and it's on the left. ③.

Kranae, Vassiléos Pávlou 15 (☎0733/24 394). On the waterfront, next to the police station; try for a room at the front with a balcony. ④.

Milton, (☎0733/22 091). Open year-round, this hotel is out on the headland of Mavrovoúni beach. ④.

Saga, Dzanetáki (☎733/23 220). Pension run by a French family, with a popular restaurant on the ground floor. Overlooks the Marathónissi islet; recommended. ④.

Spanakas rooms, (☎0733/22 490). Homely pension on the route into town from Spárti. ③.

Eating and drinking

For **meals**, the waterside is the obvious location – though choose carefully from among the tavernas since most have inflated prices for fish and seafood. A much more genuine local taverna serving traditional casseroles, *Petakos* is to be found tucked away in the sports stadium at the northern end of town. *Kostas*, by the bus station and facing the shore, is also a no-nonsense place. Besides these, and the restaurant in the *Pension Saga* (see above), look out for the *Taverna Poulikakos*, by the taxi rank, which offers good home cooking at reasonable prices.

The Máni

The southernmost peninsula of Greece, **the Máni**, stretches from Yíthio in the east, Kardhamíli in the west and down to Cape Ténaro, mythical entrance to the underworld. Its spine, negotiated by road at just a few points, is the vast grey mass of Mount Taïyettos and its southern extension, Sangiás. It is a wild landscape, an arid Mediterranean counterpart to Cornwall, say, or the Scottish highlands, and with an idiosyncratic culture and history to match. Nowhere in Greece does a region seem so close to its medieval past – which continued largely unchanged until the end of the last century.

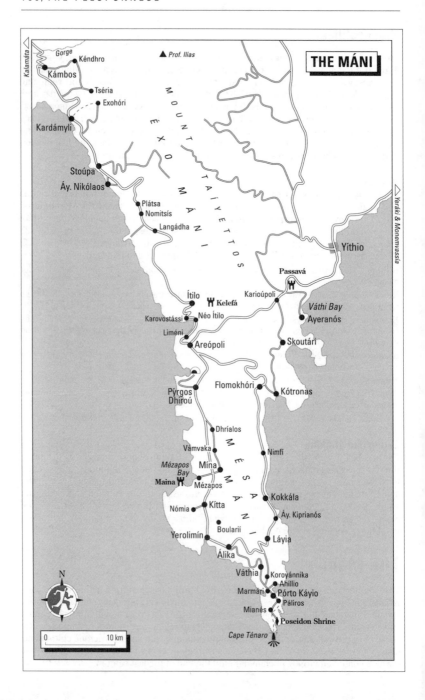

THE MÁNI

MANIOT BLOOD FEUDS

These were the result of an intricate **feudal society** that seems to have developed across the peninsula in the fourteenth century. After the arrival of refugee Byzantine families, an aristocracy known as **Nyklians** arose and the various clans gradually developed strongholds in the tightly clustered villages. The poor, rocky soil was totally inadequate for the population and over the next five centuries the **clans clashed** frequently and bloodily for land, power and prestige.

The feuds became ever more complex and gave rise to the building of strongholds: marble-roofed **tower houses** which, in the elaborate rule-system of the peninsula, could be raised only by those of Nyklian descent. From these local forts the clans – often based in the same village – conducted their vendettas according to strict rules and aims. The object was to annihilate both the tower house and the male members of the opposing clan. The favourite method of attack was to smash the prestigious tower roofs; the forts consequently rose to four and five storeys.

Feuds would customarily be signalled by the ringing of church bells and from this moment the adversaries would confine themselves to their towers, firing at each other with all available weaponry. The battles could last for years, even decades, with women (who were safe from attack) shuttling in food, ammunition and supplies. With the really **prolonged feuds**, temporary truces were declared at harvest times, then with business completed the battle would recommence. Ordinary villagers – the non-Nyklian peasantry – would, meanwhile, evacuate for the duration of the conflict. The feuds would end in one of two ways: destruction of a family in battle, or total surrender of a whole clan in a gesture of **psykhikó** (a thing of the soul), when they would file out to kiss the hands of enemy parents who had lost "guns" (the Maniot term for male children) in the feud; the victors would then dictate strict terms by which the vanquished could remain in the village.

The last full-scale feud took place as late as 1870, in the village of Kítta, and required a full detachment of the regular army to put down.

The peninsula has two distinct regions: the Éxo (Outer) Máni and the Mésa (Inner) Máni. The **Mésa Máni** – that part of the peninsula south of a line drawn east from Areópoli – is the classic Máni territory, its jagged coast relieved only by the occasional cove, and its land a mass of rocks. It has one major sight, the remarkable caves at **Pýrgos Dhyroú**, which are now very much on the tourist circuit. Beyond this point, though, tourists thin out fast. The attractions are in small part the coastal villages, like **Yerolimín** on the west coast, or **Kótronas** on the east, but the pleasure is mainly in the walking, and in exploring the **tower houses** and **churches**. A fair number of the tower houses survive, their groupings most dramatic at **Kítta**, **Váthy** and **Flomokhóri**. The churches are harder to find, often hidden away from actual villages, but worth the effort. Many were built during the tenth and twelfth centuries, when the Maniots enthusiastically embraced Christianity; almost all retain primitive-looking frescoes.

The **Éxo Máni** – the coast up from Areópoli to Kalamáta – sees the emphasis shift much more to beaches. **Stoúpa** and **Kardhamýli** are both beautiful resorts, developing now but far from spoiled. And the road itself is an experience, threading precipitously up into the foothills of Taïyettos before looping down to the sea.

Some Maniot history

The **mountains** offer the key to Maniot history. Formidable natural barriers, they provided a refuge from, and bastion of resistance to, every occupying force of the last two millennia. The Dorians never reached this far south in the wake of the Mycenaeans. Roman occupation was perfunctory and Christianity did not take root in the interior until the ninth century (some 500 years after the establishment of Byzantium). Throughout the years of Venetian and Turkish control of the

---

PRACTICALITIES IN THE MÁNI

Getting around can be time-consuming unless you have your own transport, and you may want to consider renting a **moped** or **motorbike** from Yíthio or Kalamáta, or a **car** from Kalamáta. Without a vehicle, you will need to walk or hitch to supplement the buses. In Mésa Máni, there are just two services: Areópoli–Yerolimín–Váthy (daily in summer; 3 weekly out of season); Areópoli–Kótronas–Láyia (daily).

An alternative is to make use of the handful of **taxis**, generally negotiable at Areópoli, Yerolimín and Kótronas, as well as at Yíthio. Currently, for example, a taxi from Areópoli to Váthy would cost 4500dr, and then you could return by bus.

The Mésa Máni has no regular **bank**. You can change travellers' cheques at the **post offices** (Mon–Fri 7.30am–2pm) in Yerolimín or Areópoli, but it's wise to bring as much as you think you'll need for a visit from either Yíthio or Kalamáta.

Peloponnese there were constant rebellions, climaxing in the Maniot uprising on March 17, 1821, a week before Archbishop Yermanos raised the Greek flag at Kalávryta to launch the War of Independence.

Alongside this national assertiveness was an equally intense and violent internal tribalism, seen at its most extreme in the Maniots' bizarrely elaborate tradition of **blood feuds** (see box on p.197), probably prolonged, and certainly exploited, by the **Turks**. The first Maniot uprising against them had taken place in 1571, a year after the Ottoman occupation. There were to be renewed attempts through the succeeding centuries, involving plots with Venetians, French and Russians. But the Turks, wisely, opted to control the Máni by granting a level of local autonomy, investing power in one or other clan whose leader they designated "Bey" of the region. The position provided a focus for the obsession with arms and war and worked well until the nineteenth-century appointment of **Petrobey Mavromikhalis**. With a power base at Liméni he managed to unite the clans in revolution, and his Maniot army was to prove vital in the success of the War of Independence.

Perhaps unsurprisingly, the end of the war and the formation of an **independent Greece** was not quite the end of Maniot rebellion. Mavromihalis swiftly fell out with the first president of the nation, Capodistrias and, with other members of the clan, was imprisoned by him at Náfplio – an act which led to the president's assassination at the hands of Petrobey's brothers. The monarchy fared little better until one of the king's German officers was sent to the Máni to enlist soldiers in a special Maniot militia. The idea was adopted with enthusiasm, and was the start of an enduring tradition of Maniot service in the modern Greek military.

In this century, sadly, all has been decline, with persistent **depopulation** of the villages. In places like Váthy and Kítta, which once held populations in the hundreds, the numbers are now down to single figures, predominantly the old. Socially and politically the region is notorious as the most conservative in Greece. The Maniots reputedly enjoyed an influence during the colonels' junta, when the region first acquired roads, mains electricity and running water. They voted almost unanimously for the monarchy in the 1974 plebiscite, and this is one of the very few parts of Greece where you may still see visible support for the far-right National Party.

Into the Máni: Yíthio to Areópoli

The road from Yíthio into the Máni begins amid a fertile and gentle landscape, running slightly inland of the coast and the Yíthio/Mavrovoúni beaches, through tracts of orange and olive groves. About 12km beyond Yíthio, the Máni suddenly asserts itself as the road enters a gorge below the Turkish **Castle of Passavá**.

The castle is one of a pair (with Kelefá to the west) guarding the Máni, or perhaps more accurately guarding against the Máni. From the Avin petrol station just to the west it's quite a scramble up, with no regular path, but the site is ample reward, with views out across two bays and for some miles along the defile from Areópoli. There has been a fortress on Passavá since Mycenaean times; the present version is an eighteenth-century Turkish rebuilding of a Frankish fort that the Venetians had destroyed on their flight from the Peloponnese in 1684. It was abandoned by the Turks in 1780 following the massacre of its garrison by the Maniot Grigorakis clan – their vengeance for the arrest and execution by the Turks of the clan chief.

Shortly after Passavá a turning to the left, signposted "Belle Hélène", leads down to a long sandy beach at **Váthy Bay**, which is dominated by German tourists. Before you reach the beach, there is the *Pension Tassia* (☎0733/93 433; ②), with four comfortable rooms, each with a kitchen. At the southern end of the beach is the grand *Hotel Belle Hélène* (☎0733/93 001; ⑥), which is often block-booked by German groups, and, halfway along, behind the reasonable *Gorgona* restaurant, the *Kronos* campsite (☎0733/93 320; mid-April to Oct) which is well suited to families.

The road beyond the beach deteriorates rapidly, though it is possible to continue through woods to the village of **Ayeranós**, with a couple of tower houses, and from there – if you can find your way among the numerous rough tracks – to Skoutári, below which is another good beach with some Roman remains. A better road to Skoutári leaves the main Yíthio–Areópoli road at Karyoúpoli, itself dominated by an imposing tower house.

Continuing towards Areópoli from Passavá, the landscape remains fertile until the wild, scrubby mass of Mount Kouskoúni signals the final approach to Mésa Máni. You enter another pass, with **Kelefá Castle** (see p.204) above to the north, and beyond it several southerly peaks of Mount Taïyettos. Areópoli, as you curl down from the hills, radiates a real sense of arrival.

Areópoli and around

An austere-looking town, **AREÓPOLI** sets an immediate mood for the region. It was, until the last century, secondary to Ítilo, 6km north, as the gateway to Mésa Máni, but the modern road has made it, to all intents, the region's centre. Its name, meaning the Town of Ares (the god of war), was bestowed for its efforts during the War of Independence. It was here that Mavromikhalis (commemorated by a statue in the main platía) declared the uprising.

The town's sights are archetypically Maniot in their apparent confusion of ages. The **Taxiárkhis** cathedral, for example, has primitive reliefs above its doors which look twelfth century until you notice their date of 1798. Similarly, its tower houses could readily be described as medieval, though most of them were built in the early 1800s. On its own, in a little platía, is the church of **Áyios Ioánnis**, the Mavromihalis family church; the interior has strip-cartoon frescoes.

Buses leave Areópoli from the main platía; if you are heading north, towards Kalamáta, you may need to change at Ítilo. On or just off the platía is a **bank** (Mon–Fri 9am–noon), a **post office**, **OTE** and a useful **supermarket**.

There are several **rooms** around the cathedral and two **hotels**: the *Kounis* (☎0733/51 340; ④) on the main platía, and the *Mani* (☎0733/51 269; ④) three minutes from the main platía and 50m beyond the bank. One of the towers, the *Pyrgos Kapetanakou* (☎0733/51 479; ④), has been restored by the EOT as a "traditional guesthouse"; the rooms are beautiful but expensive. Nearby is the *Pension Londas* (☎0733/51 360; ⑥), another converted tower house, and the much cheaper *Pyrgos Tsimova* (☎0733/51 301; ④), which has more of a lived-in feel – all the rooms have TV and there is a private war museum in the tower.

There are a number of **café-restaurants** around the main platía; the most popular (and the bus agent) is *Nikola's Corner*, which does good mezédhes; try the general assortment. *Barba Petros* has a sweet little courtyard off a pedestrian street towards Pýrgos Kapetanákov.

North to Liméni

Areópoli stands back a kilometre or so from the sea – an enjoyable walk. **LIMÉNI**, the town's tiny traditional port, lies 3km to the north, whose scattering of houses are dominated by the restored tower house of Petrobey Mavromihalis, which looks like nothing so much as an English country parish church. On one of the hairpin bends on the road from Areópoli to Liméni is the newly completed *Limeni Village* (☎0733/51 111; ⑤), a re-creation (in unusually good taste) of Maniot towers, high above the rocky shore and with its own swimming pool. Further round the bay, on the waterside, there are a few tavernas including *To Limeni* (☎0733/51 458; ④), which has rooms.

South to the Pýrgos Dhyroú caves

Eight kilometres south from Areópoli, at the village of **PÝRGOS DHYROÚ**, the road forks off to the underground caves – the Máni's major tourist attraction. The village itself has an isolated 21-metre-tower house, but is otherwise geared to the cave trade, with numerous tavernas and cafés, and dozens of **rooms** for rent. The closest to the caves – and the sea – are at the *Panorama* restaurant (☎0733/52 280; ④); the rooms are better than the meals, which are only marginally offset by the view. If you want to stay in the village itself, the modern *Hotel Diros* (☎0733/52 306; ④) is a fair option.

The **Pýrgos Dhyroú caves** (June–Sept 8am–5.30pm; Oct–May 8am–2.30pm; 3500dr) are 4km beyond the main village, set beside the sea and a small beach. They are very much a packaged attraction but, unless caves leave you cold, they are worth a visit, especially on weekday afternoons when the wait is shorter. Visits consist of a thirty-minute punt around the underground waterways of the **Glyfádha caves**, well-lit and crammed with stalactites, whose reflections are a remarkable sight in the two-to twenty-metre-deep water. You are then allowed a brief tour on foot of the **Alepótripa caves** – huge chambers (one of them 100m by 60m) in which excavation has unearthed evidence of prehistoric occupation. Unfortunately there is no foreign-language commentary.

You should buy a ticket as soon as you arrive at the caves: this gives you a priority number for the tours. On a mid-season weekend you can wait for an hour or more, so it's best to arrive as early as possible in the day with gear to make the most of the adjacent beach. If time is short, taxis from Areópoli will take you to the caves, then wait and take you back; prices, especially split four ways, are reasonable.

The adjoining **museum** (Tues–Sun 8.30am–3pm; 400dr) of neolithic finds from the caves is interesting, but again the few captions are in Greek only; a guide leaflet in several languages is promised.

South to Yerolimín

The narrow plain between Pýrgos Dhiroú and Yerolimín is one of the more fertile parts of Mésa Máni. This seventeen-kilometre stretch of the so-called "shadow coast" supported, until this century, an extraordinary number of villages. It retains a major concentration of **churches**, many of them Byzantine, dating from the eleventh to the fourteenth centuries. These are especially hard to find, though well detailed in Peter Greenhalgh's *Deep Into Mani*. The main feature to look for is a barrel roof. Almost all are kept locked, though a key can often be found.

Among Greenhalgh's favourites on the seaward side are the eleventh-century **church of the Taxiárkhis** at Kharoúdha (3km south of Pýrgos Dhyroú), **Trissákia church** by a reservoir near Tsópokas (5km south of Pýrgos Dhyroú) and **Ayía Varvára** at Éremos (8km south of Pýrgos Dhyroú).

Mézapos and the Castle of the Maina

An easier excursion from the main road is to the village of **MÉZAPOS**, whose deep-water harbour made it one of the chief settlements of Máni, until the road was built this century. From the main road, take the side road to Áyios Yioryios and then to Mézapos, where there are a few rooms. The best of some fine coastal walks leads to the castle at **Tigáni** ("Frying Pan") **rock**, 4km around the cliffs, past the twelfth-century **church of Vlakherna**, which has a few fresco fragments, including a memorable John the Baptist.

The fortress, by general consensus, seems to have been the **Castle of the Maina**, constructed like those of Mystra and Monemvassía by the Frankish baron, Guillaume de Villehardouin, and ceded with them by the Byzantines in 1261. Tigáni is as arid a site as any in Greece – a dry Monemvassía in effect – whose fortress seems scarcely man-made, blending as it does into the terrain. It's a jagged walk out to the castle across rocks fashioned into pans for salt-gathering; within the walls are ruins of a Byzantine church and numerous cisterns. If you ask at one of the cafés in Mézapos it's sometimes possible to negotiate a boat trip out to Tigáni, or even around the cape to Yerolimín.

The nearby village of **STAVRÍ** offers traditional **tower-house accommodation** in the converted *Tsitsiris Castle* (☎0733/56 297; ⑤), much the same price as the other tower hotels in Areópoli and Váthy, but in a more exciting setting. To the north of Stavrí, but within walking distance, is the twelfth-century **church of Episkopí**; the roof has been restored, while inside there are some fine but faded frescoes, and columns crowned by Ionic capitals, with a surprising marble arch at the entry to the *ikonostási*.

Kítta and Boulariï

Continuing along the main road, **KÍTTA**, once the largest and most powerful village in the region, boasts the crumbling remains of more than twenty tower houses. It was here in 1870 that the last feudal war took place, eventually being suppressed by a full battalion of four hundred regular soldiers. Over to the west, visible from the village, is another eruption of tower houses at Kítta's traditional rival, Nómia.

Two kilometres south of Kítta and east of the main road, **BOULARIÏ** is one of the most interesting and accessible villages in Mésa Máni. It is clearly divided into "upper" and "lower" quarters, both of which retain well-preserved tower houses and, in varying states of decay, some twenty churches. The two most impressive are tenth-century **Áyios Pandelímon** (roofless and unlocked, with several frescoes) and eleventh-century **Áyios Stratigós**, which is just over the brow of the hill at the top of the village. This second church is locked and the keys are with the priest at Eliá village, but it is usually possible to gain peaceable entry without them since the doorframe itself is barely secured by a piece of twisted wire; many seem to have squeezed in this way, as the pile of donated money inside confirms. The effort is well rewarded for the church possesses a spectacular series of frescoes from the twelfth to the eighteenth centuries.

Yerolimín and south to the Mátapan

After the journey from Areópoli, **YEROLIMÍN** (Yeroliménas) has an end-of-the-world air, and it makes a good base for exploring the southern extremities of the Máni. Despite appearances, the village was only developed in the 1870s – around a jetty and warehouses built by a local (a non-Nyklian migrant) who had made good on the island of Sýros. There are a few shops, a **post office**, a couple of **cafés** and two

hotels. Of these, the *Akroyiali* (☎0733/54 204; ④) is the more comfortable, with some air-conditioned rooms; the *Akrotenaritis* (☎0733/54 205; ③) is slightly cheaper and now has four new rooms that rival those at the *Akroyiali*. There are several **places to eat** between the two hotels, but the baked fish in lemon juice and olive oil served at the *Akroyiali* takes some beating.

At the dock, occasional boat trips are offered – when the local owners feel like it – around Cape Ténaro (see below).

Álika to Pórto Káyio

South from Yerolimín, a good road (and the bus) continues to **Álika**, where it divides. One fork leads east through the mountains to Láyia (see opposite), and the other continues to Váthy and across the Marmári isthmus to Páliros. Between Álika and Váthy there are good coves for swimming. One of the best is a place known as **Kypárissos**, reached by following a riverbed (dry in summer) about midway to Váthy. On the headland above are scattered Roman remains of ancient Kaenipolis, including (amid the walled fields) the excavated ruins of a sixth-century basilica.

VÁTHIA, a group of tower houses set uncompromisingly on a scorching mass of rocks, is one of the most dramatic villages in Mésa Máni. It features in Colonel Leake's account of his travels, one of the best sources on Greece in the early nineteenth century. He was warned to avoid going through the village as a feud had been running between two families for the previous forty years. Today it has the feel of a ghost town even though EOT has completed its restoration of a dozen tower houses to accommodate guests (☎0733/ 55 244; ⑥). These are undoubtedly atmospheric places to stay, and good value with a group of four or five, but there's only one café and the nearest restaurants are 7km away at Pórto Káyio.

From Váthia the road south to the cape starts out uphill, edging around the mountain in what appears to be quite the wrong direction. It slowly descends, however, bringing you out at the beach and hamlet of **PÓRTO KÁYIO** (7km from Váthy). There are comfortable rooms at the *Akroteri Domatia* (☎0733/52 013; ④), and two or three tavernas, the best of which is the *Hippocampos*. Above the village, a road branches west (past a rusting, bullet-ridden sign for Páliros) around the headland, capped by ruins of a Turkish **castle** contemporary with Kelefá, to sandy **beaches** at the double bay of Marmári. Rooms and great food with a cliff-top view are available here at *To Marmari* (☎0733/52 101; ④).

On to Cape Ténaro

Finding your way to **Cape Ténaro** from the bullet-ridden sign where the track bears left from the road to Marmári, follow the signs for the fish taverna, *To Akrotenaro*. After you've wound your way over the Maní's last barren peninsula and down to the taverna, where rooms should be available, the road ends in a knoll crowned with the squat **chapel of Asómati**, constructed largely of materials from an ancient Temple of Poseidon.

To the left (east) as you face the chapel is the little pebbly **bay of Asómati**, often with a fishing boat at anchor; on the shore is a small **cave**, another addition to the list of sites said to be the mythical entrance to the underworld. Patrick Leigh Fermor, in *Mani*, writes of another "Gates of Hades" cave, which he swam into on the western shore of Mátapan, just below Marmári. To the right (west) of the Asómati hill, the main path, marked by red dots, continues along the shore of another cove and through the metre-high foundations of a **Roman town** that grew up around the Poseidon shrine; there is even a mosaic in one structure. From here the old trail, which existed before the road was bulldozed, reappears as a walled path, allowing 180° views of the sea on its 25-minute course to the lighthouse on **Cape Ténaro**.

The east coast

The east coast of Mésa Máni is most easily approached from **Areópoli**, where there's a daily **bus** through Kótronas to Láyia. However, if you have transport, or you're prepared to walk and hitch, there's satisfaction in doing a full loop of the peninsula, crossing over to Láyia from Yerolimín or Pórto Káyio. The east-coast landscape is almost remorselessly barren, little more than scrub and prickly pears. This is the Mésa Máni's "sunward coast", far harsher than the "shadow coast" of the west side. There are few beaches, with most of the scattered villages hanging on the cliffs.

Láyia to Kokkála

From the fork at Álika (see opposite), it is about a ninety-minute walk by road to **LÁYIA**. Coming from Pórto Káyio it takes around three hours, though the route, at times on narrow tracks, is more dramatic, passing the virtually deserted hilltop village of **Korogoniánika**. Láyia itself is a multi-towered village that perfectly exemplifies the feudal setup of the old Máni. Four Nyklian families lived here, and their four independently sited settlements, each with its own church, survive. One of the taller towers, so the locals claim, was built overnight by the four hundred men of one clan, hoping to gain an advantage at sunrise. During the eighteenth century the village was home to the Mésa Máni doctor – a strategic base from which to attend the war-wounded across the peninsula. Today there is a single kafenío, with a few snacks and some cheap rooms (②) run by the same family who own the Marmári hotel and the nearby *Kastro* at Kokkála.

The first village beyond Láyia, over on the east coast, is **ÁYIOS KYPRIANÓS**. Inexplicably towerless, it, too, has a few rooms, though the proprietor may prove elusive in the off-season. Five kilometres on is **KOKKÁLA**, a larger village and enclosed by a rare patch of greenery. It has a harbour, a very pretty cove, a longer beach to the north and walking possibilities. Three kilometres to the northwest, up on the mountainside, is a spot known as Kiónia (columns), with the foundations of two Roman temples. The village boasts several café-restaurants, the *Pension Kokkala* (☎0733/21 107; ③) and several rooms for rent above the *Taverna Marathos* (summer only; ☎0733/21 118; ③) on the beach. Overlooking the village is the *Kastro* (☎0733/21 620; ④), expensive but value for money. Another smart new place is *Hotel Soloteri* (☎0733/21 126; ④).

Kótronas and Flomokhóri

KÓTRONAS is still a fishing village, and its pebble beach (there are sandy strips further around the bay) and causeway-islet make it a good last stop in the region. The village is frequented by a fair number of tourists (mainly Germans) each summer, and has a trio of pensions. The most pleasant is the *Kali Kardia* (☎0733/21 246; ③) on the seafront. The *Dhio Adherfia* (☎0733/21 209; ②), is marginally cheaper. The land hereabouts is relatively fertile, and **FLOMOKHÓRI**, thirty minutes' walk in the hills behind, has maintained a reasonable population as well as a last imposing group of tower houses.

The Éxo Máni: Areópoli to Kalamáta

The forty kilometres of road between Areópoli and Kalamáta is as dramatic and beautiful as any in Greece, a virtual corniche route between **Mount Taïyettos** and the **Gulf of Messinía**. The first few settlements en route are classic Maniot villages, their towers packed against the hillside. As you move north, with the road dropping to near sea level, there are three or four small resorts, which are becoming increasingly popular but are as yet relatively unspoiled. For walkers, there is a reasonably well-preserved *kalderimi* paralleling (or short-cutting) much of the paved route, and a superb **gorge hike** just north of Kardhamýli.

Ítilo and around

ÍTILO, 11km from Areópoli, is the transport hub for the region. If you are heading towards Kalamáta, either from Yíthio or Areópoli, you may need to change here. It looks tremendous from a distance, though close up it is a little depressing; its population is in decline, and many of the tower houses are collapsing into decay. In better days, Ítilo was the capital of the Máni, and from the sixteenth to the eighteenth century it was the region's most notorious base for piracy and slave trading. The Maniots traded amorally and efficiently in slaves, selling Turks to Venetians, Venetians to Turks, and, at times of feud, the women of each others' clans. Irritated by their piracy and hoping to control the important pass to the north, the Turks built the **Castle of Kelefá**. This is just a kilometre's walk from Ítilo across a gorge and its walls and bastions, built for a garrison of five hundred, are substantially intact. Also worth exploring is the monastery of **Dhekoúlou**, down towards the coast; its setting is beautiful and there are some fine eighteenth-century frescoes in the chapel.

There are a few **rooms** to rent in Ítilo, and a smart hotel just out of town, the *Xenonas Pyrgos Alevra* (☎0733/59 388; ⑤). A better option is to look for accommodation by the beach in **NÉO ÍTILO**, which is just round the bay from Ítilo's ancient seaport, Karavostássi. Néo Ítilo is a tiny hamlet, but as well as rooms for rent it boasts the luxury *Hotel Itilo* (☎0733/59 222; ⑤), which also runs the slightly cheaper *Alevras* guesthouse.

Langádha, Nomitsís and Thalamés

If you want to walk for a stretch of the onward route, you can pick up the *kalderimi* just below the main road out of Ítilo. As it continues north, the track occasionally crosses the modern road, but it is distinct at least as far as Ríglia. The most interesting of the villages along the way are **LANGÁDHA**, for its setting that bristles with towers, and **NOMITSÍS**, for its trio of frescoed Byzantine churches strung out along the main street. A couple more churches are to be found off the road just to the north; in one of these, the **Metamórfosi**, there are delightful sculpted animal capitals. Just before Nomitsís, you pass the hamlet of **THALAMÉS**, where a local enthusiast has set up a widely advertised **Museum of Maniot Folklore and History** (May–Sept daily 8am–8pm). The tag "museum" is perhaps a bit inflated for what is really a collection of junkshop items, but it's a nice stop nonetheless and sells superb local honey.

Áyios Nikólaos and Stoúpa

The beaches of Éxo Máni begin at **ÁYIOS NIKÓLAOS**, whose quiet little harbour, flanked by old stone houses, seems fated for higher things. At present it's a delightful place, with four tavernas and a scattering of **rooms** and apartments. A good choice for rooms is the *Lofos* (☎0721/77 371; ③), just above the village with a nice garden for breakfast.

Just to the north, **STOÚPA** is much more developed, and justifiably so. It has possibly the best sands along this coast with two glorious **beaches** (Stoúpa and the smaller Kalógria) separated by a headland, each sloping into the sea and superb for children. Submarine freshwater springs gush into the bay, keeping it unusually clean – if also a bit cold – while banana trees lend an exotic air. Ten minutes to the north of Kalógria beach is a delightful rocky and deserted cove. The resort was home for a while to Nikos Kazantzakis, who is said to have based his novel *Zorba the Greek* on a worker at the coal mine in nearby Pástrova.

Out of peak season, Stoúpa is certainly recommended. In July and August, you may find the crowds a bit overwhelming, and space at a premium. There are plenty of tavernas and a **bank** (Mon–Fri 9am–3pm), but the local supermarket will change money and travellers' cheques during opening hours. Accommodation includes numerous **rooms** and apartments for rent, and several **hotels**. The cheapest is the *Halikoura Bay*

(☎0721/77 303; ③), while the *Lefktron* (☎0721/77 322; ⑤) and the *Stoupa* (☎0721/77 485; ⑤) are more upmarket. A good rooms option is *Petros Nikolareas* (☎0721/77 063; ③). At Kalógria there is a smart new **campsite**, *Kalogria Camping* (☎0721/77 319) up the hill towards Stoúpa, and the good but rather expensive pension *Kalogria* (☎0721/77 479; ⑤) at the back of the beach. Halfway to Kardhamíli there is another livelier campsite, *Ta Delfina* (☎0721/54 318).

Kardhamýli

KARDHAMÝLI, 10km north of Stoúpa, is also a major resort, by Peloponnese standards at least, with ranks of self-catering apartments and pensions, block-booked by the package trade in season. But once again the **beach** is superb – a long pebble strip north of the village and fronted by acres of olive trees.

Back from the road, it's a nice walk up to "Old Kardhamýli", the medieval quarter on the hillside. Here a group of abandoned tower houses are gathered about the eighteenth-century church of **Áyios Spíridhon** with its unusual multi-storey bell tower. Further back is a pair of ancient tombs and the old acropolis, where the Maniot chieftains Kolokotronis and Mavromihalis played human chess with their troops during the War of Independence.

On the main road and platía, you'll find a branch of the Agricultural Bank (Mon, Wed & Fri), a **post office** (Mon–Fri), which will change money and travellers' cheques, and Morgan Holiday (☎0721/73 220), which is open mornings and evenings and will help you with everything from accommodation to **moped rental**. Bookable **hotels** include the *Patriarhea* (☎0721/73 366; ④), by the main road but attractive, and the imaginatively named *Kardamyli Beach* (☎0721/73 180; ⑥). Also on the way along the beach, near the campsite, is *Lela's* (☎0721/73 541; ③), a good taverna with fine sea-view **rooms** which should be booked well ahead in summer. The **campsite**, *Melitsina* (May–Sept; ☎0721/73 461), is 2km from the village and has an extremely aggressive proprietor. Among Kardhamíli's **tavernas**, try *Kiki's* as well as *Lela's*, whose eponymous owner was once housekeeper to Patrick Leigh Fermor, who lives locally. Otherwise, all along the through road there are a few low-key bars and a superb ice-cream place.

Inland to the Výros gorge

North of Kardhamýli the road leaves the coast, which rises to cliffs around a cape, before dropping back to the sea in the bay around Kalamáta. But before moving on, a day or two spent exploring Kardhamýli's immediate environs on foot is time well spent.

The giant **Výros gorge** plunges down from the very summit of Taïyettos to meet the sea just north of the resort, and tracks penetrate the gorge from various directions. From Kardhamýli, a path at the acropolis continues to the village and church of Ayía Sofía, and then proceeds on a mixture of tracks and lanes either across a plateau to the hamlet of Exohóri or down into the gorge, where two **monasteries** nestle at the base of sheer walls. An hour or so inland along the canyon, more cobbled ways lead up to either Tséria on the north bank (taverna but no accommodation) or back towards Exokhóri on the south flank. Linking any or all of these points is an easy day's hiking at most; forays further upstream require full hiking gear and detailed local maps.

Kalamáta and beyond

KALAMÁTA is by far the largest city of the southern Peloponnese, spreading for some four kilometres back from the sea, and into the hills. It's quite a metropolitan shock after the small-town life of the rest of the region. The city has a long-established export trade in olives and figs from the Messinian plain, and, until recently, it had a prospering industrial base. In 1986, however, Kalamáta was near the epicentre of a severe

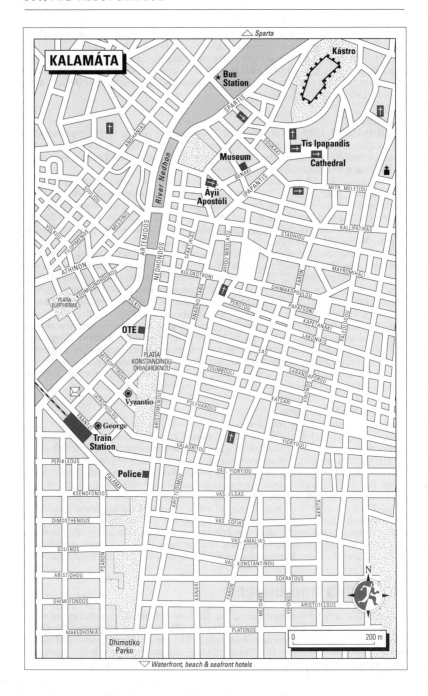

KALAMÁTA

△ Sparta

★ Bus Station

SPARTIS

Kástro

River Nedhon

Museum

Áyii Apostóli

BENAKI

IPAPANTIS

ROUKAK

✝ Tis Ipapandis

✝ Cathedral

MITR. MELETIOU

ANDHARIAS

SOULIOU

MESSINIS

VOLKOU

FLORESTENOS

ATHINON

KOUMOUNDHOUROU

PLATÍA ELEFTHERIAS

ARTEMIDOS

NEDHONDOS

KILKIS

SPARTIKAS

ANAGNOSTARA

KOLOKOTRONI

PEROTOU

AYIOU NIKOLAOU

STADHIOU

KALLIPATIRAS

DHIMAKOPOULOU

FARON

MAVROMIHALI

PAPATSONI

PALEOLOGOU

KAPETANAKI

LAKONIKIS

EAS

OTE ■

PLATÍA KONSTANDINOU DHIADHOKNOU

MITROPETROVA

TATROPOLITOU

ZOUMBOULI

SARANDAPOROU

VIRONOS

Vyzantio ◉

ARISTOMENOUS

POLYHAROUS

KATSARI

George ◉

Train Station

TRANIS

VALAORITOU

YIORYOULI

PERIKLEOUS

PALAMA

ARISTODIMOU

✝

Police ■

KSENOFONDOS

VAS. YIORYIOU

DIMOSTHENOUS

VAS. OLGAS

VAS. SOFIAS

AKRITA

SOLONOS

PSARON

VAS. AMALIAS

ARISTIDHOU

VAS. KONSTANTINOU

SOKRATOUS

DHIMOFONDOS

KANARI

FARON

MEZONOS

VIRONOS

ARISTOTELOUS

N

MAKEDHONIAS

Dhimotiko Parko

PLATONOS

0   200 m

▽ Waterfront, beach & seafront hotels

earthquake that killed twenty people and left 12,000 families homeless. But for the fact that the quake struck in the early evening, when many people were outside, the death toll would have been much higher. As it was, large numbers of buildings were levelled throughout the town. The intensity of the damage was in part due to the city's position over several subterranean streams, but mostly, it seems, the legacy of poor 1960s construction. The result was an economic depression across the whole area, from which the town is only now recovering properly.

The City

The physical effects of the earthquake are still evident in temporary housing around the suburbs of the city, and few visitors will want to linger here. However, if you are travelling for a while, it's a good place to get things done, and there are other simple pleasures such as eating at untouristy tavernas on the waterfront or around the centre, which comprises the wide avenue formed by Platía Yeoryíou and the larger Platía Konstandínos Dhiadhóknou.

With a little time to fill, a twenty-minute walk north of the centre will bring you to the most pleasing area of the city, around the **Kástro**. Built by the Franks and destroyed and adapted in turn by the Turks and Venetians, the kástro survived the quake with little damage; an **amphitheatre** at its base hosts summer concerts. A short way south of the Kástro on Benáki is the excellent **Benakiou Archeological Museum** (Tues–Sun 8am–2pm; 300dr), which houses a modest but well-labelled collection of tomb reliefs, sculptures and smaller artefacts from the surrounding areas, as well as a colourful Roman mosaic from Desylla.

Kalamáta's **beach**, a ten-minute bus ride (#1) south of the centre, is always crowded along the central section. The gritty sands are functional but the harbour itself has a welcome touch of life and activity. If you prefer to walk to the harbour from the centre, it's a thirty-minute walk down Aristoménous, and you can loiter in the park alongside and admire the old steam engines and rolling stock from the three-foot gauge Peloponnese railway.

Practicalities

If you're looking to get transport straight through, arrive early to make connections. The **bus station** is about 600m north of the centre; follow the river along Nedhóndos and look out for the **market** nearby. The most regular buses run north to Megalópoli/Trípoli and southwest to Koróni; the magnificent route over the Taÿettos to Spárti is covered twice daily, and the one to Kardhamíli and Ítilo (connection to Areópoli) four times daily.

The **train station** is 300m to the west of Platía Konstandínou Dhiadhóknou. Kalamáta is the railhead for trains chugging along the slow but enjoyable route to Kyparissía (and ultimately to Pátra, with a possible detour to Olympia) or inland to Trípoli and Árgos. There are daily **flights** to and from Athens; tickets are sold at the Olympic Airways office across from the train station. The **airport** is 6km west off the road to Messini and Pylos but Olympic run their own buses to and from the centre. **Taxis** usually meet trains; otherwise there is a taxi rank on Platía Konstandínou Dhiadhóknou and another at the junction with Navarínou. Three rival agencies offer **car rental**: Maniatis, Iatropoúlou 1 (π0721/27 694), Theodorakopoulos, Kessári 2 (π0721/20 352), and Stavrianos, Nedhóndos 89 (π0721/23 041). There are two reliable **moped rental** outlets: Bastakos, Fáron 190 (π0721/26 638), and Alpha, Výronos 156 (π0721/93 423).

Most facilities, including the **banks**, **post office** and **OTE** are in the streets around Platía Konstandínou Dhiadhóknou, though there is a second **post office** near the customs house at the seaward end of Aristoménous. In the summer, Hobby at Fáron 237 sells English-language newspapers and books.

Accommodation

In the city centre, there are very few mid-range **hotels** left. Two of the best in terms of value for money are the *George*, Frantzí 5 (☎0721/27 225; ③) and the larger *Vizantio*, Stathmoú 13 (☎0721/86 824; ③). Both belong to the same management, are very close to the train station and have TV in all rooms. In general you'll do better down by the waterfront, where there are many more hotels. Some of these are expensive, though they seem to have spent more on the reception areas than the bedrooms. Even so, they are often full by mid-afternoon and if you have not booked ahead you may have to shop around.

Choices include the *Flisvos*, Navarínou 135 (☎0721/82 177; ④), which has quiet, comfortable rooms on the waterfront next to the church of Ayía Anástasis. Nearby and next to the platía, the *Haikos*, Navarínou 115 (☎0721/88 902; ④), is a modern hotel with pleasant rooms, TV, air-conditioning and helpful staff. The cosy *Nevada*, Santaróza 9 (☎0721/82 429; ②), is carefully tended by a Greek matriarch; there are a number of house rules (in Greek and interpreted by her son). There is no breakfast, but you can eat very cheaply on the waterfront close by.

The nearest **campsites** are to be found along the stretch of beach to the east of the city. The first, about 5km from the waterfront, is the *Elite* (☎0721/80 365; April–mid-Oct). It is behind the *Hotel Elite* (☎0721/25 015; ⑤), where campers can eat, and swim in the pool. If you want to swim off the pebble beach you will have to cross the Areópoli–Kalamáta highway, or stay at the *Maria*, also known as the *Sea and Sun*, (☎0721/41 060), a popular and friendly campsite 500m down the road, which fronts onto the sea. However, unless you are stuck, you'd do better heading west towards Petalídhi (see opposite).

Eating and drinking

The best **restaurants** in the summer months are down by the **harbour**, which has been set up as a yacht marina. Moving from west to east, you have quite a selection: *Krini* at Evangelistrías 40, is a neighbourhood fish-and-wine taverna open most of the year; *Pyrofani* on Salaminos, west of the marina, has a large selection of meat and vegetarian dishes and good local wine; *Katofli* on Salamínos near the marina, has outdoor summer seating and a huge menu; *Meltemi*, near the corner of Navarínou and Fáron, is a very basic psistariá with tasty food; *Tabaki*, Navarínou 91, features a wide menu and cheerful service; almost opposite, the *Akroyiali* has a better sea view and good but pricey fish, though the service can be surly.

Only in winter does the **centre** of town get into its culinary stride. At this time, pick from *Koutivas*, 100m north of the bus station, with spicy food and bulk wine; *Kannas*, Lakonikis 18, an atmospheric place with occasional live music which featured in Sheelagh Kanelli's novel, *Earth and Water*; or *Kioupi*, Alexíki 52 (off the Areópoli road), idiosyncratically decorated and with clay-pot cooking (as the name implies).

If you're not after a full meal, Kalamáta has plenty of *mezedhopolía*, the better among them serving the traditional local snack – roast pork and potatoes. Down at the harbour, the ouzerí west of the post office does a nice fish mezédhes; and there's another good one at the bottom of Fáron, near a *souvláki* stand and video-games arcade, which does an excellent *pikilía* (grand selection of mezédhes).

Ancient Messene

The ruins of ancient **MESSENE** (Ithómi) lie 25km northwest of Kalamáta and 20km northwest of modern Messini. The ancient city was the fortified capital of the Messenians, and achieved some fame in the ancient world as a showcase of military architecture. The highlights of the widely dispersed site are the outcrops of its giant walls, towers and gates.

The ruins share the lower slopes of Mount Ithómi (800m) with the pretty village of **MAVROMÁTI**. A climb to the summit is rewarded with spectacular views of the region of Messinía and the southern Peloponnese. If you wish to stay and see the sunset from the site of the Temple of Zeus which crowns this peak, there are **rooms** at the *Zeus* (☎0724/51 025; ②), a pension in the village.

The site is a tricky place to get to, unless you're driving. Buses run only twice a day from Kalamáta (earliest departure 6am). With a car it's a fairly easy detour en route to either Kyparissía, Pýlos or Petalídhi/Koróni.

The site

Messene's fortifications were designed as the southernmost link in a defensive chain of **walled cities** (others included Megalópolis and Árgos) masterminded by the Theban leader Epaminondas to keep the Spartans at bay. Having managed to halt them at the battle of Leuctra in 371 BC, he set about building a nine-kilometre circuit of walls and restoring the Messenians to their native acropolis. The Messenians, who had resisted Spartan oppression from the eighth century BC onwards, wasted no time in re-establishing their capital; the city, so chronicles say, was built in 85 days.

The most interesting of the remains is the **Arcadia gate** at the north end of the site, through which the side road to Meligalá still runs. It consisted of an outer and inner portal separated by a circular courtyard made up of massive chunks of stone precisely cut to fit together without mortar. The outer gate, the foundations of which are fairly evident, was flanked by two square towers from where volleys of javelins and arrows would rain down on attackers. The inner gate, a similarly impregnable barrier, comprised a huge monolithic doorpost, half of which still stands. You can still trace the ruts of chariot wheels in paved stretches of ancient road within the gateway.

Further south, and signposted "Ithomi: Archeological site" on the road running northwest from Mavromáti, is a newly excavated **Sanctuary of Asclepius**. This site, which was first mistakenly marked out as the *agora*, consisted of a temple surrounded by a porticoed courtyard. The bases of some of the colonnades have been unearthed along with traces of benches. Next to it you can make out the site of a theatre or meeting place. Excavations continue in the summer with archeologists digging in the shade of semi-permanent canopies.

Other remains are to be seen up Mount Ithómi, an hour's hike along a steep path forking north from the track at the Laconia gate, which is to the southeast of the site. Along the way you pass remains of an Ionic **Temple of Artemis**. At the top, on the site of a Temple of Zeus, are the ruins of the small **Monastery of Vourkanó**, founded in the eighth century but dating in its present form from the sixteenth. Spread below are the lush and fertile valleys of Messinía.

Around the coast to Koróni

Beaches stretch for virtually the entire distance southwest from Kalamáta to Koróni, along what is steadily developing as a major resort coast. At present, however, it is more popular with Greeks than foreigners, and the resorts, tucked away in the pines, consist primarily of campsites, interspersed with the odd room for rent.

The beach at Boúka, 5km south of modern Messini, is a fine stretch of sand with views of the Máni. It is popular with the locals, especially as a place to go for Sunday lunch. The best of the beaches are around **PETALÍDHI**, 25km west around the coast from Kalamáta. The village itself is not unattractive and there are a couple of good **campsites**: *Petalidi Beach* (☎0722/31 154; April–Sept), 3km north of the village, is well established and reasonably priced; *Sun Beach* (☎0722/31 200; May–Oct), 500m south of the village, is not on the beach, which is reached by a subway under the road. There are ample tavernas and cafés around the spacious sea-facing square and very cheap rooms at the *Blue Sea Hotel* (②), 150m north of the funfair between the square and the sea. Moving on south, if you have your own transport, there are numerous restaurants, rooms and hotels along the stretch of coast to Koróni.

Koróni and Methóni

The twin **fortresses** at Koróni and Methóni were the Venetians' oldest and longest-held possessions in the Peloponnese: strategic outposts on the route to Crete and known through the Middle Ages as "the eyes of the Serene Republic". Today they shelter two of the most attractive small resorts in the south.

Thankfully, public transport around the Messinian peninsula has improved of late and as well as the customary good connections between Kalamáta and Koróni and Pýlos and Methóni, there are now several buses a day from Kalamáta through to Methóni and Finikoúnda via Pýlos. Direct connections between Methóni and Koróni are still elusive though.

Koróni

KORÓNI has one of the most picturesque sites in Greece, stacked against a fortified bluff and commanding grand views across the Messenian gulf to the Taïyettos peaks. The town is beautiful in itself, with tiled and pastel-washed houses arrayed in a maze of stair-and-ramp streets that can have changed little since the medieval Venetian occupation. Koróni's **Citadel** is one of the least militaristic-looking in Greece, crowning rather than dwarfing the town. Much of it is given over to private houses and garden plots, but the greater part is occupied by the flower-strewn nunnery of **Timíou Prodhrómou**, whose chapels, outbuildings and gardens occupy nearly every bastion.

From the southwest gate of the fortress, stairs descend to the park-like grounds of **Panayía Elestrías**, a church erected at the end of the last century to house a miraculous icon – unearthed with the assistance of the vision of one Maria Stathaki (buried close by). The whole arrangement, with fountains, shrubbery and benches for watching the sunset, is more like the Adriatic than the Aegean.

Continuing downhill, you reach the amazing **Zánga beach**, a two-kilometre stretch of sand and preternaturally clear water that sets the seal on Koróni's superiority as a place to relax, drink wine and amble about a countryside lush with vineyards, olives and banana trees. This leads into the equally attractive Mémi beach.

Practicalities

To be sure of a room in summer, it's worth trying to phone ahead. The only large hotel, the *Hotel de la Plage* (☎0725/22 401; ⑤) is way out on the road towards Mémi beach. Looking for **private rooms** on arrival, try the places to the right of the fishing port as you face the water, and don't leave it too late in the day. Several of the tavernas rent rooms on a regular basis, including the *Parthenon* (☎0725/22 146; ③) near the port and the *Pension Koroni* (☎0725/22 385; ③) above the *Symposium* restaurant on the main street. An attractive and slightly more expensive option, with a leafy setting and views of the bay and castle, is *Marinos Bungalows* (☎0725/22 522; ④) on the road north out of town. There are two **campsites**: *Memi Beach* (☎0725/22 130; May–Oct) is 2km before Koróni as you approach from Petalídhi or Methóni, and *Koroni* (☎0725/22 119; May–Sept) on the road into town; both have sandy beaches, though from *Memi Beach* you have to cross the road.

There is a reasonable selection of **restaurants** on the waterfront, and some authentic **tavernas** (barrel-wine and oven-food places) along the main shopping street. The

Parthenon has good food and efficient service, and the *Symposium* serves moussaka and fish dishes. The *Flisvos* remains a good restaurant despite its closure as a hotel.

Many people make wine or raki in their basement and the heady local tipple figures prominently in the nightlife. There are two or three tavernas on the beach and by night a solitary disco, though all of these close down by mid-September. Otherwise, there is a surprisingly fancy zakharoplastía for such a small place, plus two **banks** and a **post office** for money matters. The main venue for nightlife is the sprawling *Astra Club* out towards Mémi beach.

Finikoúnda

FINIKOÚNDA, 20km west of Koróni, is a small fishing village with a superb cove-beach. Over recent years it has gained a reputation as a backpackers' – and especially windsurfers' – resort, with half the summer intake at a pair of campsites on either side of the village, the others housed in a variety of rooms. It can be a fun, laid-back place.

To book **rooms** in advance, try the **hotels** *Finikounda* (☎0723/71 208; ④) and *Finissia* (☎0723/71 358; ④; summer only), the smart new *Korakakis Beach* (☎0723/71 221; ④) or the *Moudakis* rooms at the restaurant *To Kyma* (☎0723/71 224; ③). The local **campsites** are the *Ammos* (☎0723/71 262; May–Oct), 2km to the east of the village, and the *Loutsa* (☎0723/71 445; June–Sept), 3km to the east. Among the other restaurants, *Elena* is recommended for good traditional fare and for a drink; *Theasis* features a mixture of old and new rock music.

Methóni

In contrast to the almost domesticated citadel at Koróni, the fortress at **METHÓNI** is as imposing as they come – massively bastioned, washed on three sides by the sea, and cut off altogether from the land by a great moat. It was maintained by the Venetians in part for its military function, in part as a staging post for pilgrims en route, via Crete and Cyprus, to the Holy Land, and from the thirteenth to the nineteenth centuries it sheltered a substantial town.

Within the **fortress** (Mon–Sat 8.30am–7pm, Sun 9am–7pm; closes 3pm in winter), entered across the moat along a stone bridge, are the remains of a Venetian cathedral (the Venetians' Lion of Saint Mark emblem is ubiquitous), along with a Turkish bath, the foundations of dozens of houses and some awesome underground passages, the last unfortunately cordoned off. Walking around the walls, a sea gate midway along leads out across a causeway to the **Boúrtzi**, a small fortified island. The octagonal tower was built by the Turks in the sixteenth century to replace an earlier Venetian fortification.

Practicalities

The modern village, on the landward side of the moat, has a **bank**, **OTE** and **post office**, all easily located in the three-street-wide grid.

Methóni is geared more conspicuously to tourism than Koróni and gets very crowded in season when accommodation can be expensive and often oversubscribed. Out of season, the **hotels** are cheaper and a number stay open all year. The *Amalia* (☎0723/31 129; ⑤) is the height of luxury, with a fine view over the town, but is only open from May to October. The *Castello* (☎0723/31 300; ⑤) is a new hotel near the entrance to the fortress, with beautiful gardens, balconies and a stunning view. The *Aris* (☎0723/31 336; ④) on a small platía in the town centre is friendly and good value. The *Dionysos* (☎0723/31 317; ③) is a small, welcoming hotel in town, which is worth booking in advance; the owner's son speaks English. The recently renovated *Anna* (☎0723/31 332; ④) is also friendly and great value – all rooms have TV and there's a good restaurant. In addition, there is the usual collection of cheaper **rooms**, including some above the *Rex* (☎0723/31 239; ②; Jan–Oct). At the east end of the beach is a municipal **campsite**, the *Methoni* (☎0723/31 228; mid-May–mid-Oct). It's popular and gets crowded, but the facilities are good and the beach pleasant.

Methóni has one of the best **restaurants** you'll come upon anywhere in the Peloponnese, the *Klimataria* (☎0723/31 544; May–Oct, evenings only), which serves a mouthwatering selection of dishes (including good veggie choices) in a courtyard garden. At the *Rex*, which is open all day, you can eat in the shade of tamarisk trees. Among the dozen or so other eateries, *Dinousses* is also recommended for beach-side dining.

Pýlos and around

PÝLOS (Pýlos) is a little like a small-scale, less sophisticated Náfplio – quite a stylish town for rural Messinía, all the more so after Kalamáta. It is fronted by a pair of medieval castles and occupies a superb position on one of the finest natural harbours in Greece, the landlocked **Navarino Bay** (see box below). Given the town's romantic associations with the Battle of Navarino, and, more anciently, with Homer's "sandy Pýlos", the domain of "wise King Nestor" whose palace (see p.215) has been identified 16km to the north, a better base for exploring this part of the Peloponnese is hard to imagine – particularly if equipped with a car or moped (both for rent here). Relying on public transport, however, you'll find the long afternoon gaps in services make day trips difficult.

The Town

The main pleasures of Pýlos are exploring the hillside alleys, waterside streets and fortress. Getting your bearings is easy as it's not a large town, and buses drop you close by the central Platía Tríon Navárkhon and the port.

THE BATTLES OF NAVARINO BAY

Arriving at Pýlos your gaze is inevitably drawn to the bay, virtually landlocked by the offshore island of Sfaktiría (Sphacteria). Its name, Ormós Navarínou – **Navarino Bay** – commemorates the battle that effectively sealed Greek independence from the Turks on the night of October 20, 1827. The battle itself seems to have been accidental. The Great Powers of Britain, France and Russia, having established diplomatic relations with the Greek insurgent leaders, were attempting to force an armistice on the Turks. To this end they sent a fleet of 27 warships to Navarino, where Ibrahim Pasha had gathered his forces – 16,000 men in 89 ships. The declared intention was to coerce Ibrahim into leaving Messinía, which he had been raiding.

In the confusion of the night an Egyptian frigate, part of the Turks' supporting force, fired its cannons and full-scale battle broke out. Without intending to take up arms for the Greeks, the "allies" found themselves responding to attack and, extraordinarily, sank and destroyed 53 of the Turkish fleet without a single loss. There was considerable international embarrassment when news filtered through to the "victors" but the action had nevertheless ended effective Turkish control of Greek waters and within a year Greek independence was secured and recognized.

Navarino Bay also features in one of the most famous battles of Classical times, described in great detail by Thucydides. In 425 BC, during the Peloponnesian War, an Athenian force encamped in Paleó Kástro (the old castle of Pýlos) laid siege to a group of Spartans on the island of **Sfaktiría**, just across the straits. In a complete break with tradition, which decreed fighting to the death, the Spartans surrendered. "Nothing that happened in the war surprised the Hellenes as much as this," commented Thucydides.

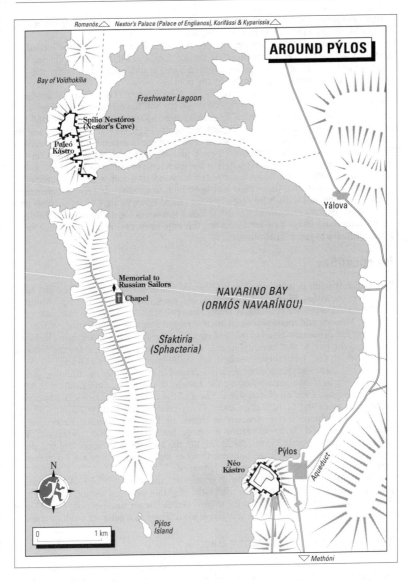

Romanós △ Nestor's Palace (Palace of Englianos), Korifássi & Kyparissía △

AROUND PÝLOS

Bay of Voïdhokília

Freshwater Lagoon

Spílio Nestóros
(Nestor's Cave)

Paleó
Kástro

Yálova

Memorial to
Russian Sailors

Chapel

*NAVARINO BAY
(ORMÓS NAVARÍNOU)*

*Sfaktiría
(Sphacteria)*

Pýlos

Néo
Kástro

Aqueduct

N

Pýlos
Island

0   1 km

△ Methóni

Shaded by a vast plane tree and scented by limes, **Platía Tríon Navárkhon** is a beautiful public platía, completely encircled by cafés and very much the heart of the town. At its centre is a **war memorial** commemorating Admirals Codrington, de Rigny and von Heyden, who commanded the British, French and Russian forces in the Battle of Navarino (see box on p.212). Nearby, just off the main waterside platía on Filellínon, a little **museum** (Tues–Sun 8.30am–3pm; 500dr) also boasts remains from the battle, along with archeological finds from the region.

Further memories of the Navarino battles can be evoked by a visit to the **island of Sfaktiría**, across the bay, where there are various tombs of Philhellenes, a chapel, and a memorial to the Russian sailors. In summer, some of the fishing boats offer trips. If you're interested, enquire at the cafés by the port.

The principal sight in town, however, is the **Néo Kástro** (Tues–Sun 8.30am–9pm; 800dr), close by the port on the south side of the bay (off the Methóni road). The "new castle" was built by the Turks in 1572, and allows a 1500-metre walk right around the arcaded battlements. For much of the last two centuries, it served as a prison and its inner courtyard was divided into a warren of narrow yards separated by high walls, a design completely at odds with most Greek prisons, which were fairly open on the inside. This peculiar feature is explained by the garrison's proximity to the Máni. So frequently was it filled with Maniots imprisoned for vendettas, and so great was the crop of internal murders, that these pens had to be built to keep the imprisoned clansmen apart. The pens and walls have recently been pulled down as part of an ongoing programme to restore and convert the castle into a **museum** for underwater archeology (same hours and ticket as Kástro). So far, the only attraction is a collection of René Puaux pictures of the 1821 revolution.

Practicalities

The National Bank is to be found on the central platía, and the **post office** just back from there on Niléos. **Mopeds, motorbikes** and **cars,** ideal for taking in both Methóni and Nestor's Palace, are available at Venus Rent (☎0723/22 312) on the road north out of town. Mopeds and motorbikes can also be rented from Sapienza Travel (☎0723/23 207) near the *Miramare* (see below), and cars from the *Miramare* itself. You can hire a **boat** from the port to visit Sfaktiría island, where you can snorkel and see the remains of the Turkish fleet lying on the sea bed; ask at the Harbourmaster's Office.

Pýlos has somewhat limited accommodation and in the summer months you should definitely try to phone ahead. Among the **hotels,** the *Arvaniti* (☎0723/23 050; ④) – beyond the post office on Niléos – is the best of the mid-priced options, but is closed between October and March. The *Galaxy*, Platía Tríon Navárkhon (☎0723/22 780; ④), is a fall-back choice if the *Arvaniti* is closed or full. The *Karalis*, Kalamatas 26 (☎0723/22 960; ⑤), is an attractive if pricey hotel with a good restaurant. The *Miramare*, Myrtidiotissis 35 (☎0723/22 751; ⑥), has a restaurant and bar and fine views by the port, but it is also closed between October and March. There are many rooms around the road on the hill out towards Kyparissía.

For **drinks,** the Platía Tríon Navárkhon cafés are the obvious choice. Among **tavernas,** try *Grigori's*, signposted from the platía. Nightlife revolves around bars such as *Sunset*, *Legitimus* and *Zoglo* around the square, and the larger summer-only discos *Gigi's* and *Zoglo Summer Matter*, both a little out of town. There is a summer outdoor cinema.

The northern rim of Navarino Bay

Pýlos's northern castle, and ancient acropolis, **Paleó Kástro**, stands on a hill almost touching the island of Sfaktiría, at the end of the bay. It has substantial walls, and identifiable courtyards and cisterns within fortifications which are a mix of Frankish and Venetian, set upon ancient foundations. It's a seven-kilometre trip from the town, for which you'll need transport. To get there, follow the main road north towards Korifássi and then take a side road southwest to the hamlet of Románnos; turn off along a track signposted (in Greek) "Navarino", and cross a bridge over a freshwater lagoon. If you find your way here, you will end up at one of the best beaches in the Peloponnese – a lovely sweep of sand curling around the **Bay of Voïdhokiliá**. A simpler alternative to the coastal route to the beach, is to go north through Yialóva, ignore the sign to Voïdhokiliá, turn left just before the second church on the left and keep straight on this unmarked dirt track.

A path from the castle descends to the **Spílio toú Nestóros** (Nestor's Cave). This is fancifully identified as the grotto in which, according to the *Odyssey*, Nestor and Neleus kept their cows, and in which Hermes hid Apollo's cattle. It is not impossible that the cave sparked Homer's imagination, for this location is reckoned by archeologists to have been the Mycenaean-era harbour of King Nestor (see below).

The Bay of Navarino encompasses a couple of additional **beaches** and hamlets. **YIALÓVA**, 4km out of Pýlos and the first resort around the bay, has tamarisk trees shading the sands, two **hotels** – the delightful *Zoe* (☎0723/22 025; ④) which is also opening the new *Voula Apartments* back towards Pýlos, and *Helonaki House* (☎0723/23 080; ③) with a variety of rooms and apartments for rent – and the *Navarino Beach* **campsite** (☎0723/22 761; April–Oct). Just north of here, the beach of **Maistrós** is a popular windsurfing strip. For eating, you can't beat the excellent home-cooking at *Oasis* by the corner of the pier, with a good view across the bay.

North to Nestor's Palace

Nestor's Palace (also known as the Palace of Englianós, after the hill on which it stands) was discovered in 1939, but left virtually undisturbed until after World War II; thus its excavation – unlike Mycenae, or most of the other major Greek sites – was conducted in accordance with modern archeological techniques. In consequence, its remains are the best preserved of all the Mycenaean royal palaces, though they shelter rather prosaically beneath a giant metal roof. The site guide by Carl Blegen and Marion Rawson is an excellent buy.

The palace is located some 16km from modern Pýlos, a half-hour drive. Using public transport, take any of the **buses** from Pýlos towards Kyparissía; these follow the main road inland past Korifássi to the site and its museum at Khóra (3km to the east).

The palace site

Flanked by deep, fertile valleys, the **palace site** (Tues–Sun 8.30am–3pm; 500dr) looks out towards Navarino Bay – a location perfectly suiting the wise, measured and peaceful king described in Homer's *Odyssey*. The scene of the epic that's set here is the visit of Telemachus, the son of Odysseus, who journeys from Ithaca to seek news of his father from King Nestor. As Telemachus arrives at the beach, accompanied by the disguised goddess Pallas Athena, he comes upon Nestor with his sons and court making a sacrifice to Poseidon. The visitors are welcomed and feasted, "sitting on downy fleeces on the sand", and although the king has no news of Odysseus he promises Telemachus a chariot so he can enquire from Menelaus at Sparta. First, however, the guests are taken back to the palace, where Telemachus is given a bath by Nestor's "youngest grown daughter, beautiful Polycaste", and emerges, anointed with oil, "with the body of an immortal".

By some harmonious twist of fate, a bathtub was unearthed on the site, and the palace ruins as a whole are potent ground for Homeric imaginings. The walls stand a metre high, enabling you to make out a very full plan. They were originally half-timbered (like Tudor houses), with upper sections of sun-baked brick held together by vertical and horizontal beams, and brilliant frescoes within. Even in their diminished state they suggest a building of considerable prestige. No less should be expected, for Nestor sent the second largest contingent to Troy – a fleet of "ninety black ships". The remains of the massive complex are in three principal groups: the **main palace** in the middle, on the left an earlier and **smaller palace**, and on the right either **guardhouses** or **workshops**.

The basic design will be familiar if you've been to Mycenae or Tiryns: an internal court, guarded by a sentry box, gives access to the main sections of the principal palace.

This contained some 45 rooms and halls. The **Megaron** (throne room), with its characteristic open hearth, lies directly ahead of the entrance, through a double porch. The finest of the frescoes was discovered here, depicting a griffin (perhaps the royal emblem) standing guard over the throne; this is now in the museum at Khóra. Arranged around are domestic quarters and **storerooms**, which yielded literally thousands of pots and cups during excavations; the rooms may have served as a distribution centre for the produce of the palace workshops. Further back, the famous **bathroom**, its terracotta tub in situ, adjoins a smaller complex of rooms, centred on another, smaller *megaron*, identified as the **queen's quarters**. Finally, on the other side of the car park there is a *thólos* (beehive) tomb, a smaller version of the famous ones at Mycenae.

Archeologically, the most important find at the site was a group of several hundred tablets inscribed in **Linear B**. These were discovered on the first day of digging, in the two small rooms to the left of the entrance courtyard. They were the first such inscriptions to be discovered on the Greek mainland and proved conclusively a link between the Mycenaean and Minoan civilizations; like those found by Sir Arthur Evans at Knossos on Crete, the language was unmistakably Greek. The tablets were baked hard in the fire which destroyed the palace around 1200 BC, perhaps as little as one generation after the fall of Troy.

The museum at Khóra

At Khóra, the **museum** (Tues–Sun 8.30am–3pm; 500dr) adds significantly to a visit to the site. If you've no transport, it might be better to take a bus here first, and then walk the 45 minutes to the site after viewing the exhibits. In spring or autumn this is a pleasure; shy golden orioles have been seen in trees alongside the road. In hot weather, or if pressed for time, you can hitch fairly easily or get a taxi.

Pride of place in the display goes to the **palace frescoes**, one of which, bearing out Homer's descriptions, shows a warrior in a boar-tusk helmet. Lesser finds include much pottery, some beautiful gold cups and other objects gathered both from the site and from various Mycenaean tombs in the region.

The coast north of Pýlos

The stretch of **coast** between Pýlos and Pýrgos is defined by its **beaches**, which are on a different scale to those elsewhere in the Peloponnese, or indeed anywhere else in Greece – fine sands, long enough (and undeveloped enough) to satisfy the most jaded Australian or Californian. Their relative anonymity is something of a mystery, though one accounted for in part by the poor communications. For those without transport this entails slow and patient progress along the main "coast" road, which for much of the way runs two or three kilometres inland, and a walk from road junction to beach.

Heading north from the Bay of Voïdhokiliá, near the turning inland to Korifássi and Nestor's Palace, you can take a beautiful recently paved road, flanked by orange and olive orchards. This keeps close to the sea for most of the way to Kyparissía, allowing access to isolated beaches and villages.

If you're travelling to Olympia by **train** from this coast, you can save the detour to Pýrgos (not really an exhilarating town – see p.232) by getting a connection at Alfiós, a tiny station at the junction of the Olympia line and as bucolic a halt as any on the network.

Marathópoli and Filiatrá

If you are looking for the rudiments of accommodation and a little more than a village café then Marathópoli and Filiatrá hold most promise. **MARATHÓPOLI** has a long beach, rockier than most along this coast and facing the little islet of Próti. It has two **hotels**: on the beach, the *Artina* (☎0723/61 400; ④) has en suite facilities and should be booked in advance; in the village, the *Rania* (☎0723/61 404; ④) is a new hotel which opens all year. The rooms all have small kitchenettes. There are some **rooms** for rent; a **campsite**, *Proti* (☎0723/61 211; May–Oct), with a swimming pool on account of the rocky beach; and two or three summer tavernas by the sea. A small taxi boat makes the short crossing to the islet of Próti, with its sandy beach and monastery, for a reasonable fixed rate.

Further on the road passes through Áyia Kiriakí, a fishing village with a sweet little harbour and a few rooms, before reaching **FILIATRÁ**, which is linked by bus with Pýlos and Kyparissía. There are two **hotels**: in the village itself, the recently renovated *Trifylia* (☎0761/34 290; ④) is more like a pension, though the rooms have en suite facilities including a small kitchenette and TV; the run-of-the-mill *Limenari* (☎0761/32 935; ④) is down by the sea.

Fournier's Castle

By a curious pattern of emigration, just as Kýthira is home to Greek-Australians, the villages along the Kyparissía coast have a concentration of returned Greek-Americans, virtually all of them having done a stint of work in New York or New Jersey. Disgraced ex-Vice President Spiro Agnew (1968–1973) was perhaps the most infamous local boy.

However, the Greek-American who has left most mark on his home domain is one Haris Fournakis, also known as **Harry Fournier**, a doctor from Chicago who came back in the 1960s and started building his fantasies. At the entrance to Filiatrá, Fournier constructed a garden-furniture version of the **Eiffel Tower** (illuminated at night by fairy lights) and a mini-replica of the globe from the 1964 New York Expo.

His most ambitious project, however, was his **Kástro Ton Paramýthión** ("Castle of the Fairytales"; 9am–2pm & 5pm–8pm; 500dr), a truly loopy folly with white concrete battlements and outcrops of towers, plus thirty- to forty-foot-high statues of Poseidon's horse (flanked by vases of flowers) and the goddess Athena. The castle is located right on the sea, near Filiatrá beach, and can be reached from Filiatrá by following the road for 6km north, through the hamlet of Agríli.

Kyparissía

KYPARISSÍA is a small, congenial market town, positioned hard against the Egáleo mountains. On the first outcrop of the range is a Byzantine-Frankish **castle**, around which is spread the **old town**. Its ochre-hued mansions stand abandoned, having suffered heavy damage in the civil war, though a couple of tavernas still function here, lovely old places and very welcoming.

Below the hill, the modern town goes about its business, with a small harbour and real shops. A few tourist boutiques and a night club or two have sprung up recently, but it's still a pleasant place to rest up, and certainly preferable to a night in Kalamáta if you're on your way to Olympia by bus or train (Kyparissía is the junction of the Kalamáta and Pýrgos lines). Within walking distance of the town are long, near-deserted sands and rocky cliff paths.

Practicalities

The centre of the modern town, a couple of blocks inland from the train station, is Platía Kalantzákou, where you'll find a **bank**, **OTE** and **post office**. Accommodation consists of a half-dozen **hotels**, divided between the modern town and the beach. The cheapest place to stay in town is the *Trifolia*, 25-Martíou (☎0761/22 066; ③), a down-to-earth and welcoming pension. Other town hotels are the *Vasilikon*, Alexopoúlou 7 (☎0761/22 655; ④), which is well kept, though without any particular charm, and the comfortable *Ionion* (☎0761/22 511; ⑤), an older hotel facing the train station. By the beach, the best value is the *Apollon* (☎0761/24 411; ⑥); there is also a **campsite**, *Kyparissía* (☎0761/23 491). There are a handful of no-nonsense **restaurants** and pizzerias in Platía Kalantzákou and in the adjacent streets; one of the best is *Nynio*, at 25 Martíon 52. For atmosphere it's better to eat down at the beach, where the taverna *Ta Porákia*, towards the campsite, is a fine choice, or up at the old town, where the liveliest place to eat is the psisteria *Arcadia*.

Beaches north from Kyparissía

Between Kyparissía and Kaïáfas, the road and rail lines continue a kilometre or so back from the coast, with the occasional **campsite** advertising its particular stretch of beach. These include the *Apollo Village* (☎0625/61 200) at Yiannitsohóri (18km along), and a better site at **Tholó** (8km further on) – the *Tholo Beach* (☎0625/61 345; March–Oct). *Neo Hori*, just past Tholó, has a few rooms to rent, as does *Yiannitsohóri*. Just south of there, unofficial camping in the pine forest behind the beach at Élia is possible. On the beach itself there's an ecological kiosk with information about the turtles that land there; behind the forest there's a good shady taverna, *O Mythos*.

All of the hamlets on this coast have superb stretches of sandy beach, edged with olive groves – their lack of development seems almost miraculous. One of the nicest of all the beaches is at **KAKOVÁTOS** (5km beyond Tholó), which combines breakers with incredibly shallow, slowly shelving waters. The area is slightly more commercialized now with the *Grigoris* taverna and the *Baywatch* café (complete with watchtower) on the beach, while the village has a number of pensions, including *Kallifidhas* (☎0625/31 167; ②) and *Timoleon* (☎0625/32 253; ③), plus a traditional *inomayirío*-style restaurant, *To Pigadhi*, in an old house.

At **ZAKHÁRO**, the largest village between Kyparissía and Pýrgos, and a train stop, there are a few shops and four **hotels**. The *Rex* (☎0625/31 221; ④) has en suite facilities and some rooms have kitchenettes; the *Nestor* (☎0625/31 206; ④) has clean if spartan rooms; the *Sugar Town* (☎0625/31 985; ②) is a new and slightly inelegant hotel by the train station; and the *Diethnes* (☎0625/31 208; ④), which also has en suite facilities, is near the church at the top end of the village. Midway to the excellent beach is the *Banana Place* (☎0625/34 400; ③), set in a banana plantation. It offers chalet-type accommodation with cooking facilities, and is open between mid-April and mid-October; booking is advisable.

Another enormous strand, backed by sand dunes and pine groves, is to be found just before the roads loop inland at **Kaïáfas**. At the beach there's just a single, rather uninspired taverna and the train station. A couple of kilometres inland, however, the village of **LOUTRÁ KAÏÁFAS** assumes the atmosphere of a spa. Strung out alongside a lagoon are a dozen or so hotels and pensions, frequented mainly by Greeks seeking hydrotherapy cures. Each morning a small shuttle-boat takes the patients from their hotels to the hot springs across the lagoon. The best deal for accommodation is probably at the friendly *Hotel Jenny* (☎0625/32 234; ③), which also has a decent restaurant. Two kilometres north of the lake, as the national road loops around a spur in the hills, you can just make out the walls of ancient Samía on the hillside.

ARCADIA AND THE NORTH

Arcadia (Arkadhía in modern Greek), the heartland province of the Peloponnese, lives up to its name. It contains some of the most beautiful landscapes in Greece: verdant and dramatic hills crowned by a string of medieval towns, and the occasional Classical antiquity. The best area of all is around **Andhrítsena**, **Stemnítsa** and **Karýtena**, where walkers are rewarded with the luxuriant (and rarely visited) **Loúsios gorge**, and archeology buffs by the remote, though permanently covered, **Temple of Bassae**. En route, if approaching from Trípoli, you may also be tempted by the ancient theatre at

Megalópoli. The one site everyone heads for is, of course, **Olympia**, whose remains, if at times obscure, are again enhanced by the scenery.

Beaches are not a highlight in this northwest corner, nor along the north coast between Pátra and Kórinthos – technically the province of Aháïa. However, if you are travelling this way, or are arriving in or leaving Greece at the (modern) port of Pátra, a detour along the rack-and-pinion **Kalávryta railway** should on no account be missed. This takes off through a gorge into the mountains at Dhiakoftó.

If heading for Delphi, or central or western Greece, car-drivers and pedestrians alike can save backtracking to Athens by using the **ferry links** across the Gulf of Kórinthos at either Río–Andírio (the most routine) or Éyio–Áyios Nikólaos.

Megalópoli

Modern **MEGALÓPOLI** (Megalopolis) is an important road and bus junction, and your first thoughts on arrival are likely to be directed towards getting out. Like Trípoli, it's a dusty, characterless place, with a military presence and two vast power stations; there's little in the way of hotels or food. The adoption of its ancient name, "Great City", was an altogether empty joke.

However, the impulse to leave should be resisted, at least for an hour or two, because just outside the city to the northwest is one of the most extensive and least touristy sites in the Peloponnese: **ancient Megalopolis**.

Practicalities

Megalópoli has good **bus connections** with Trípoli (and on to Árgos and Athens) and Kalamáta. Arrive at a reasonable hour and you should be able to make either of these connections. Moving north or west into Arcadia is slightly more problematic, with just two buses daily to Karítena/Andhrítsena (currently at noon and 7pm). However, hitching is a viable proposition along this route, as local drivers are aware of the paucity of transport, and it's also possible to negotiate a **taxi** to Karítena. Facilities such as **banks**, **post office** and **OTE** are also to be found around the central platía.

There are four or five **hotels** in Megalópoli, most of them catering to local business travellers rather than tourists. The cheapest are all in the vicinity of the central Platía Gortiníás and include the *Pan*, Papanastassíou 7 (☎0791/22 270; ③), which is rather old but acceptable, with private facilities in the more expensive rooms; the better presented *Paris*, Ayíou Nikólaou 5 (☎0791/22 410; ③); and the *Achillion*, Papaionánnou 67 (☎0791/22 311; ④), which has clean, comfortable rooms with en suite showers.

Ancient Megalopolis

Ancient Megalopolis (Tues–Sun 8.30am–3pm; free) was one of the most ambitious building projects of the Classical age, a city intended by the Theban leader Epaminondas, who oversaw construction from 371 to 368 BC, to be the finest of a chain of Arcadian settlements designed to hold back the Spartans. However, although no expense was spared on its construction, nor on its extent – nine kilometres of walls alone – the city never took root. It suffered from sporadic Spartan aggression and the citizens, transplanted from forty local villages, preferred, and returned to, their old homes. Within two centuries it had been broken up, abandoned and ruined.

As you approach the site, along a tree-lined track off the Andhrítsena road (signposted "Ancient Theatre"), the countryside is beautiful enough; a fertile valley whose steaming cooling towers seem to give it added grandeur; beyond the riverbed is just a low hill, and no sign of any ruins. Suddenly, you round the corner of the rise and its function is revealed: carved into its side is the largest **theatre** built in ancient Greece. Only the first few rows are excavated, but the earthen mounds and ridges of the rest are clearly visible as stepped tiers to the summit where, from the back rows, trees look on like immense spectators.

The theatre was built to a scale similar to those at Árgos and Dodóna, and could seat 20,000; the **Thersileion** (Assembly Hall) at its base could hold 16,000. Today you're likely to be alone at the site, save perhaps for the custodian (who has plans of the ruins). Out beyond the enclosed part of the site you can wander over a vast area, and with a little imagination make out the foundations of walls and towers, temples, gymnasiums and markets. "The Great City", wrote Kazantzakis in *Journey to the Morea*, "has become a great wasteland". But it's the richest of wastelands, gently and resolutely reclaimed by nature.

Megalópoli to Dhimitsána

North of Megalópoli the best of Arcadia lies before you: minor roads that curl through a series of lush valleys and below the province's most exquisite medieval hill towns. The obvious first stop and a possible base for exploring the region is **Karýtena**. From here you can visit the dramatic and remote site of **ancient Gortys** and explore the **Loúsios gorge**, above which, outrageously sited on 300-metre-high cliffs, is the eleventh-century **monastery of Ayíou Ioánni Prodhrómou** (commonly abbreviated just to Prodhrómou).

Moving on from Karýtena, there is a choice of roads. The "main" route loops west through **Andhrítsena** to Késtena, from where irregular buses run to Olympia. An alternative route to the northwest winds around the edge of the Ménalo mountains to the delightful towns of **Stemnítsa** and **Dhimitsána**, meeting the main Trípoli–Pýrgos road at Karkaloú. If you have time on your hands, perhaps the most attractive option is to explore the region north as far as Dhimitsána, then backtrack to Karýténa to proceed on to Olympia via Andhrítsena.

Karýtena

Set high above the Megalópoli–Andhrítsena road, **KARÝTENA** may look familiar; with its medieval bridge over the River Alfíos (Alpheus), it graces the 5000-drachma note. Like many of the Arcadian hill-towns hereabouts, its history is a mix of Frankish, Byzantine and Turkish contributions, the Venetians having passed over much of the northern interior. It was founded by the Byzantines in the seventh century and had attained a population of some 20,000 when the Franks took it in 1209. Under their century-long rule, Karýtena was the capital of a large barony under Geoffroy de Bruyères, the paragon of chivalry in the medieval ballad *The Chronicle of the Moreás*, and virtually the only well-liked Frankish overlord.

The village these days has a population of just a couple of hundred; there were at least ten times that figure until the beginning of this century. Approaching, you can stop on the modern bridge over the Alfíos and peer down at the **medieval bridge**, which is immediately adjacent. It is missing the central section, but is an intriguing structure nonetheless, with a small Byzantine chapel built into one of the central pillars.

From the main road, there's a winding three-kilometre road up to the village, in the upper part of which is a small central platía with a kafenío. Off the platía are signposted the Byzantine churches of **Zoödhóhos Piyí** (with a Romanesque belfry) and **Áyios Nikólaos** (with crumbling frescoes) to the west, down towards the river; ask at the kafenío for the keys. Also off the platía is the **Frourio**, the castle built by the Franks and with added Turkish towers. It was here that Theodoros Kolokotronis held out against Ibrahim Pasha in 1826 and turned the tide of the War of Independence; hence the view of Karýtena on the 5000-drachma note and a portrait of Kolokotronis on the reverse.

There are two places to rent **rooms**: one signposted opposite the post office, run by Stamatía Kondopoúlou (☎0791/31 262; ②); the other, a very comfortable apartment 1km beyond the platía, run by Khristos and Athanasia Papodopoulos (☎0791/31 203; ②), who, given notice, will provide fine evening meals and wine. A good new taverna, *To Konaki*, has opened in the square.

North through the Loúsios River valley

The site of **ancient Gortys** can be approached either from Karýtena or from Stemnítsa (8km northwest of the site). From Karýtena the most direct route to the valley runs up and through the town to Astílohos (11km), a village 2km southwest of the site; a taxi should cost in the region of 3000dr return. This route is no more than a jeep track, and twenty minutes from the site it becomes a trail. If you don't have a car, it is easier to follow the road north towards Stemnítsa and Dhimitsána for 6km to the hamlet of Ellinikó. From the edge of Ellinikó, a dirt track signposted "Gortys" descends west; after a rough six kilometres (ignore the right-hand fork at the five-kilometre point – this heads north to Prodhrómou before winding east towards Stemnítsa) it ends at the bank of the Loúsios River. Here is an old bridge, which you cross to reach the site of ancient Gortys. It is possible to camp overnight at Gortys, or to stay at the nearby monastery of Prodhrómou.

The town of Stemnítsa probably makes a better base for exploring the area, and walkers may want to do so by following the Stemnítsa–Prodhrómou–Gortys–Ellinikó–Stemnítsa circuit (see below).

Ancient Gortys
Ancient Gortys is one of the most stirring of all Greek sites, set beside the rushing river known in ancient times as the Gortynios. The relics are widely strewn amongst the vegetation on the west (true right) bank of the stream, but the main attraction, below contemporary ground level and not at all obvious until well to the west of the little chapel of Áyios Andhréas (by the old bridge), is the huge excavation containing the remains of a **Temple to Asclepius** (the god of healing) and an adjoining **bath**, both dating from the fourth century BC.

The most curious feature of the site is a circular **portico** enclosing round-backed seats which most certainly would have been part of the therapeutic centre. It's an extraordinary place, especially if you camp with the roar of the Loúsios to lull you to sleep. The only drawback is the climate: temperatures up here plummet at night, no matter what the season, and heavy mists, wet as a soaking rain, envelop the mountains from midnight to mid-morning.

The Loúsios gorge and monastery of Prodhrómou
The farmland surrounding ancient Gortys belongs to the monks of the nearby **Monastery of Prodhrómou**, who have carved a donkey path along the **gorge of the Loúsios** between Áyios Andhréas and the monastery. It's about forty minutes' walk upstream, with an initially gradual and later steady ascent up a well-graded, switchbacked trail. A set of park benches by a formal gate heralds arrival at the cloister, and the whole area is well stamped about by the monks' mules. If you look up through the trees above the path, the monastery, stuck on to the cliff like a swallow's nest, is plainly visible a couple of hundred metres above.

The interior of the monastery does not disappoint this promise; the local villagers accurately describe it as *politisméno* (cultured) as opposed to *ágrio* (wild). Once inside it is surprisingly small; there were never more than about fifteen tenants, and currently there are twelve monks, four of them very young and committed. Visitors are received in the *arkhondarikí* (guest lounge and adjoining quarters), and then shown the tiny frescoed katholikón, and possibly invited to evening services there. The strictest rules of dress apply, but the monks welcome visitors who wish to stay the night. The only problem, especially on weekends, is that there are only a dozen or so beds, and people from Trípoli and even Athens make pilgrimages and retreats here, arriving by the carload along a circuitous dirt track from Stemnítsa. Be prepared for this possibility, and arrive in time to get back to level ground to camp.

Prodhrómou to Stemnítsa

Beyond Prodhrómou the path continues clearly to the outlying monasteries of **Paleá** and **Néa Filosófou**. The older dates from the tenth century but, virtually ruined, is easy to miss since it blends into the cliff on which it's built. The newer (seventeenth-century) monastery has been restored, but has fine frescoes inside; there is now a permanent caretaker monk to show you around. North from here the trail becomes almost impassable, though there is a jeep track from near Néa Filosófou upstream to Dhimitsána.

At Prodhrómou you can pick up the dirt track (described above as the fork off the Ellinikó–Gortys track) and head for Stemnítsa. If you are walking it is more pleasant, and quicker, to follow instead the old *kalderími* from Prodhrómou to Stemnítsa – a climb, but not a killing one, of about ninety minutes through scrub oak with fine views over the valley. Usually one of the monks or lay workers will be free to point out the start of the path; once clear of the roadhead confusion by the modern little chapel at the edge of the canyon, there's little possibility of getting lost.

If Stemnítsa is your base rather than your destination, you can take this route in reverse by heading out of town on the paved road to Dhimitsána and (500m after the town-limits sign) bear down and left onto the obvious beginning of the upper end of the *kalderími*. The loop can be completed by following the walk all the way back to Ellinikó, where a proper trail leads north back to Stemnítsa.

Stemnítsa

Fifteen kilometres north of Karýtena, **STEMNÍTSA** (or Ipsoúnda in its official Hellenized form, or Ipsoús on many maps) was for centuries one of the premier metal-smithing centres of the Balkans. Although much depopulated, it remains a fascinating town, with a small folklore museum, a revived artisan school (and workshop near the bus stop) and a handful of quietly magnificent medieval churches.

The town is divided by ravines into three distinct quarters: the Kástro (the ancient acropolis hill), Ayía Paraskeví (east of the stream) and Áyios Ioánnis (west of it). The **Folklore Museum** (Mon & Wed–Fri 6–8pm, Sat 11am–1pm & 6–8pm, Sun 11am–1pm; closed in Feb; free) is just off the main road in the Ayía Paraskeví Ioánnis quarter, and repays the trip out in itself. The ground floor is devoted to mock-ups of the workshops of indigenous crafts such as candle-making, bell-casting, shoe-making and jewellery. The next floor up features re-creations of the salon of a well-to-do family and a humbler cottage. The top storey is taken up by the rather random collections of the Savopoulos family: plates by Avramides (a refugee from Asia Minor and ceramics master), textiles and costumes from all over Greece, weapons, copperware, and eighteenth- and nine-teenth-century icons. Across the way you can visit the **Artisan School** (Mon–Fri 8am–2pm & some Mon evenings), staffed by the remaining local silver-, gold- and coppersmiths. Next door to the school is the seventeenth-century **basilica of Tríon Ierarkhón**, the most accessible of the town's Byzantine churches; its caretaker lives in the low white house west of the main door.

To visit the other churches, all of which are frescoed and locked, requires more determined enquiries to find a key. The katholikón of the seventeenth-century **monastery of Zoödhókhos Piyí** has perhaps the finest setting, on the hillside above Ayía Paraskeví, but the tiny windows do not permit much of an interior view. The little adjoining monastery hosted the first *yerousía* (convention) of guerrilla captains in the War of Independence, giving rise to the local claim that Stemnítsa was Greece's first capital.

Near the summit of the Kástro hill are two adjacent chapels: the tenth-century **Profítis Ilías** (with a convenient window for fresco-viewing) and the twelfth-century **Panayía Vaferón** (with an unusual colonnade). The last of the town's five churches, **Áyios Pandelímon**, is located at the western edge of the town, to the left of the paved road to Dhimitsána.

Accommodation is limited to the pleasant *Hotel Trikolonion* (☎0795/81 297; ③), which has regular rooms and some luxurious suites in a fine traditional building in the centre of town; the inclusive breakfasts are substantial and, with adequate notice, you can dine here. Failing that, you can eat well in town at the simple *Iy Klinitsa* on the square or *To Kastro*. There are two **buses** a day linking Stemnítsa with Trípoli via Dhimitsána.

Dhimitsána

Like Stemnítsa, **DHIMITSÁNA** has an immediately seductive appearance, its cobbled streets and tottering houses straddling a twin hillside overlooking the Loúsios River. Views from the village are stunning: it stands at the head of the gorge, and looking downriver you can just see the cooling towers of the Megalópoli power plant and the bluff that supports Karýtena. To the east are the lower folds of the Ménalo mountains, most visible if you climb up to the local **Kástro**, whose stretch of Cyclopean walls attests to its ancient use.

In the town, a half-dozen churches with tall, squarish belfries recall the extended Frankish, and especially Norman, tenure in this part of the Moreás during the thirteenth century. Yet none should dispute the deep-dyed Greekness of Dhimitsána. It was the birthplace of Archbishop Yermanos, who first raised the flag of rebellion at Kalávryta in 1821, and of the hapless patriarch, Grigoris V, hanged in Constantinople upon the Sultan's receiving news of the insurrection mounted by his co-religionist. During the hostilities the ubiquitous Kolokotronis maintained a lair and a powder mill in the then almost inaccessible town. Before the War of Independence, the nunnery of **Emyalón** (daylight hours, except 2–5pm), 3km south towards Stemnítsa, was used by the Kolokotronis clan as a hideout.

Accommodation is limited to a couple of rooms establishments like *Kazas* (☎0795/31 084; ③) or the modern and well-appointed *Dimitsana* (☎0795/31 518; ④), 1km out on the road to Stemnítsa, which is popular with rambling groups. The *Taverna Iy Kali Thea*, just across the road from the hotel, is Dhimitsána's best and not too expensive.

Moving on to Olympia

Keep in mind that through buses from Dhimitsána are scarce, and you may well need to hitch (or take a taxi) to Karkaloú or Vitína, on the main Trípoli–Pýrgos road, where you can pick up buses more easily. Once on the road, the most enjoyable halt is **LANGÁDHIA** (18km from Dhimitsána), whose tiers of houses and bubbling sluices tumble downhill to the river far below the road. Often you can stop on a late-morning bus, eat lunch and pick up the next through service with little lost time. If you decide to stay the night, there are a couple of **hotels** on the main road: the rather ritzy *Kentrikon* (☎0795/43 221; ③) and the municipal motel *Langadia* (☎0795/43 202; ②).

You may well find that you have fewer changes and stops if you backtrack south to join the **Karýtena–Andhrítsena route** and travel on to Olympia from there. Alternatively, if you're approaching Olympia from the north, through Arcadia from Pátra, then a pleasant staging post is the twin village of **Lámbia-Dhívri**, roughly halfway between Trípoli and Pátra. There is a good psistariá, *Iy Divri* as well as the *Lámbia Pension* (☎0624/81 205; ②), both of which enjoy fine views.

Andhrítsena and the Temple of Bassae

Moving west from Karýtena towards Andhrítsena, the Alfíos River falls away to the north and the hills become mountains – Líkeo to the south and Mínthi to the west. The route, only slightly less remote than the twists of road around Dhimitsána, is a superb one for its own sake, with the added attractions of **Andhrítsena**, a traditional mountain town, and the **Temple of Apollo at Bassae** up in the flanks of Mount Líkeo.

Andhrítsena

ANDHRÍTSENA, 28km west of Karýtena, is a beautiful stop, and the traditional base from which to visit the Temple of Apollo at Bassae up in the mountains to the south. Though very much a roadside settlement today, it too was a major hill town through the years of Turkish occupation and the first century of independent Greece. It is remarkably untouched, with wooden houses spilling down to a stream, whose clear ice-cold headwaters are channelled into a fountain that's set within a plane tree in the central platía. There is a small **folk museum**, which opens on demand (200dr). Contact Vassilikí Tsigoúri (☎0626/22 197) at the *Tsigouris* restaurant on a side street near the plane tree.

Hotel accommodation is available at the *Pan* (☎0626/22 213; ②; summer only) which has clean, comfortable rooms, and is located at the west end of town by the Shell station; the fancier *Theoxenia* (☎0626/22 219; ④) is on the Karýtena side of town. For **meals**, try any of the restaurants on the main platía, and especially the one up the steps beside the old (and closed) *Vassae* hotel.

The Temple of Apollo at Bassae

Daily 8am–8pm; 500dr.

Fourteen kilometres into the mountains south from Andhrítsena, the **Temple of Apollo** at **BASSAE** (Vassés) is the most remote and arguably the most spectacular site in Greece. In addition, it is, after the Thiseion in Athens, the best-preserved Classical monument in the country, and for many years was considered to have been designed by Iktinos, architect of the Parthenon – though this theory has recently fallen from favour.

There the superlatives must cease. Romantic though the temple was in the past, for the forseeable future it is swathed in a gigantic grey marquee supported on metal girders and set in concrete with wire stays; its entablature and frieze lie dissected in neat rows on the ground to one side. No doubt the **restoration** is badly needed for its preservation – and the marquee is quite a sight in itself – but it has to be said that visitors are likely to be a bit disappointed. If you are not put off, take the Kréstena road out of town and then, almost immediately, turn off to the left and you begin the climb to the temple. The simplest approach is to share a taxi, which should charge 3500–4000dr for the round trip, waiting an hour at the site. On foot it's a pretty agonizing ascent, with little likelihood of a lift. The site is not enclosed, but has a full-time guardian who lives alongside. It's a lonely place, and must have felt even more isolated in ancient times.

The temple was erected in dedication to **Apollo Epikourios** ("the Succourer") by the Phigalians. It's known that they built it in gratitude for being spared from plague, but beyond this it is something of a puzzle. It is oddly aligned on a north–south axis and, being way up in the mountains, is only visible when you are comparatively near. There are oddities, too, in the architecture: the columns on its north side are strangely thicker than in the rest of the building, and incorporated into its *cella* was a single Corinthian column, the first known in Greece (though now vanished save for its base). Unusually again, the cult statue, probably a four-metre-high bronze, would have stood in front of this pillar.

Athens street scene

Parliamentary guard in Athens

Detail on tomb, Eleusis

MICHAEL JENNER

Athens postcards

PETER WILSON

The Acropolis at night

Panorama of Athens

The Palaestra, Olympia, Peloponnese

Byzantine church, Mystra

Shepherd in the Zagorian mountains

The Tholos, Delphi

Acrocorinth: west curtain walls,
Peloponnese

Church in Miliés village, Pílion peninsula

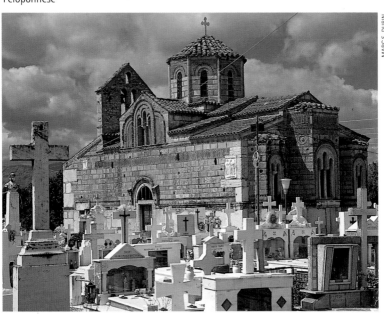

Twelfth-century church, Mérbaka, Argolid

Moving on from Bassae or Andhrítsena

Leaving the Bassae/Andhrítsena area, you've a number of choices. From Andhrítsena there are two daily **buses** back up towards Karýtena/Megalópoli and two down to Pýrgos. If you are headed for **Olympia**, take the Pýrgos bus and get off in Kréstena, from where you can hitch or take a taxi along the 12km side road up to the site. You'll certainly save time and maybe some money.

For the adventurous, a partly surfaced road winds through the mountains from Bassae down to the coast at **Tholó** (see p.218). It takes quite a while to cover the 46km and the road is pretty bumpy in places, but for the unhurried there's an opportunity to stop at Perivólia (10km) which is a surprisingly lively little place with a couple of restaurants, cafés and even a bar full of well-dressed youth. This mountain hamlet has a two-kilometre dirt road connecting it with the similarly diminutive Figalía, close by the ruins of the enormous Classical walls of **ancient Phigalia**.

Olympia (Olymbía)

The historic associations and resonance of **OLYMPIA**, which for over a millennium hosted the most important **Panhellenic games**, are rivalled only by Delphi or Mycenae. It is one of the largest and most beautiful sites in Greece, and the setting is as perfect as could be imagined: a luxuriant valley of wild olive and plane trees, spread beside twin rivers of Alfíos (Alpheus) and Kládhios, and overlooked by the pine-covered hill of Krónos. Sadly, the actual ruins of the sanctuary are jumbled and confusing, and seem to cry out for reconstruction, even on a modest scale. The great temple columns lie half-buried amid the trees and undergrowth: picturesque and shaded, perfect ground for picnics, but offering little real impression of their ancient grandeur or function. Their fame, however, prevails over circumstance, and walking through the arch from the sanctuary to the stadium it is hard not to feel in awe of the Olympian history. Despite the crowds, the tour buses, the souvenir shops and other trappings of mass tourism, it demands and deserves a lengthy visit.

The modern village of Olimbía acts as a service centre for the site, and has little in the way of distractions, save a somewhat dutiful **Museum of the Olympic Games** (Tues–Sat 8am–3.30pm, Sun & Mon 9am–4.30pm; 500dr), with commemorative postage stamps and the odd memento from the modern games, including the box that conveyed the heart of Pierre de Coubertin (reviver of the modern games) from Paris to Olympia, where it was buried.

The site

Daily: May to mid-Oct 8am–7pm (Aug till 9pm; Sept till 8pm); mid-Oct to April 8am–5pm, Sat & Sun 8.30am–3pm; 1200dr.

From its beginnings the site was a sanctuary, with a permanent population limited to the temple priests. At first the games took place within the sacred precinct, the walled, rectangular **Altis**, but as events became more sophisticated a new **stadium** was built to adjoin it. The whole sanctuary was throughout its history a treasure-trove of public and religious statuary. Victors were allowed to erect a statue in the *Altis* (in their likeness if they won three events) and numerous city-states installed treasuries. Pausanias, writing in the fourth century AD, after the Romans had already looted the sanctuary several times, fills almost a whole book of his *Guide to Greece* with descriptions.

The entrance to the site leads along the west side of the **Altis wall**, past a group of public and official buildings. On the left, beyond some Roman baths, is the **Prytaneion**, the administrators' residence where athletes were lodged and feasted at official

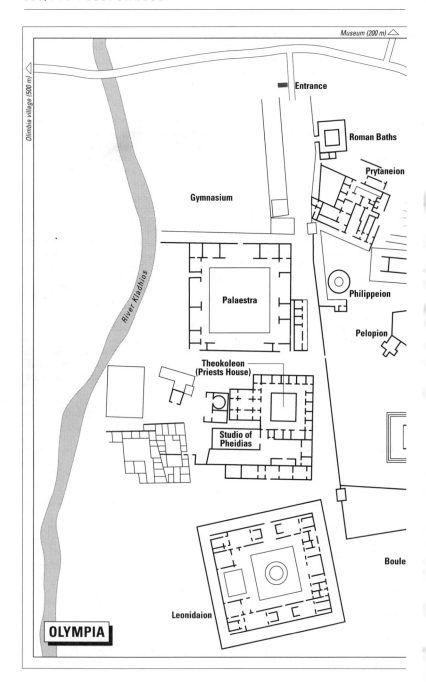

Museum (200 m) △

Olimbia village (500 m) △

Entrance

Roman Baths

Prytaneion

Gymnasium

River Kladhios

Palaestra

Philippeion

Pelopion

Theokoleon
(Priests House)

Studio of
Pheidias

Boule

Leonidaion

OLYMPIA

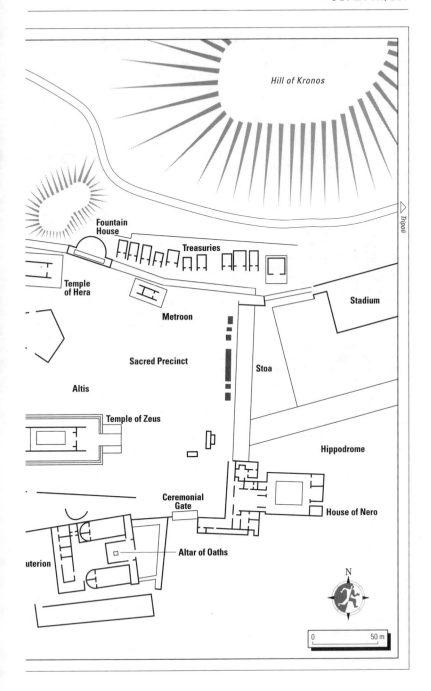

Hill of Kronos

Fountain
House

Treasuries

Temple
of Hera

Metroon

Stadium

Sacred Precinct

Stoa

Altis

Temple of Zeus

Hippodrome

Ceremonial
Gate

House of Nero

Altar of Oaths

uterion

Tripoli

N

0   50 m

THE OLYMPIC GAMES: SOME HISTORY

The origins of the games at Olympia are rooted in **legends** – the most predominant relating to the god **Pelops**, revered in the region before his eclipse by Zeus, and to **Herakles**, one of the earliest victors. Historically, the contests probably began around the eleventh century BC, growing over the next two centuries from a local festival to the quadrennial celebration attended by states from throughout the Greek world.

The impetus for this change seems to have come from the **Oracle of Delphi**, which, with the local ruler of Elis, **Iphitos**, and the Spartan ruler **Lycurgus**, helped to codify the Olympic rules in the ninth century BC. Among their most important introductions was a **sacred truce**, the *Ekeheiria*, announced by heralds prior to the celebrations and enforced for their duration. It was virtually unbroken throughout the games' history (Sparta, ironically, was fined at one point) and as host of the games, Elis, a comparatively weak state, was able to keep itself away from political disputes, growing rich meanwhile on the associated trade and kudos.

From the beginning, the main Olympic **events** were athletic. The earliest was a race over the course of the stadium – roughly 200m. Later came the introduction of two-lap (400m) and 24-lap (5000m) races, along with the most revered of the Olympiad events, the **Pentathlon**. This encompassed running, jumping, discus and javelin events, the competitors gradually reduced to a final pair for a wrestling-and-boxing combat. It was, like much of these early Olympiads, a fairly brutal contest. More brutal still was the **Pancratium**, introduced in 680 BC and one of the most prestigious events. *Pancratium* contestants fought each other, naked and unarmed, using any means except biting or gouging each others' eyes; the olive wreath had on one occasion to be awarded posthumously, the victor having died at the moment of his opponent's submission. Similarly, the **chariot races**, introduced in the same year, were extreme tests of strength and control, only one team in twenty completing the seven-kilometre course without mishap.

The great gathering of people and nations at the festival extended the games' importance and purpose well beyond the winning of olive wreaths; assembled under the tem-

expense. On the right are the ruins of a **Gymnasium** and a **Palaestra** (wrestling school), used by the competitors during their obligatory month of pre-games training.

Beyond these stood the Priests' House, the **Theokoleion**, a substantial colonnaded building in the southeast corner of which is a structure adapted as a Byzantine church. This was originally the **studio of Pheidias**, the fifth-century BC sculptor responsible for the great cult statue in Olympia's Temple of Zeus. It was identified by following a description by Pausanias, and through the discovery of tools, moulds for the statue and a cup engraved with the sculptor's name. The studio's dimensions are exactly those of the *cella* in which the statue was to be placed.

To the south of the studio lie further administrative buildings, including the **Leonidaion**, a large and doubtless luxurious hostel endowed for the most important of the festival guests. It was the first building visitors would reach along the original approach road to the site.

The Altis

Admission to the **Altis** was in the earlier centuries of the games limited to free-born Greeks – whether spectators or competitors. Throughout its history it was a male-only preserve, save for the sanctuary's priestess. An Olympian anecdote records how a woman from Rhodes disguised herself as her son's trainer to gain admission, but revealed her identity in the joy of his victory. She was spared the legislated death penalty, though subsequently all trainers had to appear naked.

porary truce, **nobles** and **ambassadors** negotiated treaties, while **merchants** chased contacts and foreign markets. **Sculptors** and **poets**, too, would seek commissions for their work. Herodotus read aloud the first books of his history at an Olympian festival to an audience that included Thucydides – who was to date events in his own work by reference to the winners of the *Pancratium*.

In the early Olympiads, the **rules of competition** were strict. Only free-born – and male – Greeks could take part, and the rewards of victory were entirely honorary: a palm, given to the victor immediately after the contest, and an olive branch, presented in a ceremony closing the games. As the games developed, however, the rules were loosened to allow participation by athletes from all parts of the Greek and Roman world, and nationalism and professionalism gradually crept in. By the fourth century BC, when the games were at their peak, the athletes were virtually all professionals, heavily sponsored by their home states and, if they won at Olympia, commanding huge appearance money at games elsewhere. Bribery became an all too common feature, despite the solemn religious oaths sworn in front of the sanctuary priests prior to the contests.

Under the **Romans**, predictably, the process was accelerated. The palms and olive branches were replaced by rich monetary prizes, and a sequence of new events was introduced. The nadir was reached in 67 AD when the Emperor Nero advanced the games by two years so that he could compete in (and win) special singing and lyre-playing events – in addition to the chariot race in which he was tactfully declared victor despite falling twice and failing to finish.

Notwithstanding all this abuse the Olympian tradition was popular enough to be maintained for another three centuries, and the games' eventual **closure** happened as a result of religious dogma rather than lack of support. In 393 AD the Emperor Theodosius, newly converted to Christianity, suspended the games as part of a general crackdown on public pagan festivities. This suspension proved final, for Theodosius's successor ordered the destruction of the temples, a process completed by barbarian invasion, earthquakes and, lastly, by the Alfios River changing its course to cover the sanctuary site. There it remained, covered by seven metres of silt and sand, until the first excavation by German archeologists in the 1870s.

The main focus of the precinct, today as in ancient times, is provided by the great Doric **Temple of Zeus**. Built between 470 and 456 BC, it was as large as the (virtually contemporary) Parthenon, a fact quietly substantiated by the vast column drums littering the ground. The temple's decoration, too, rivalled the finest in Athens; partially recovered, its sculptures of Pelops in a chariot race, of Lapiths and Centaurs, and the Labours of Herakles, are now in the museum. In the *cella* was exhibited the (lost) gold-and-ivory cult statue by Pheidias, one of the seven wonders of the ancient world. Here, too, the Olympian flame was kept alight, from the time of the games until the following spring – a tradition continued at an altar for the modern games.

The smaller **Temple of Hera**, behind, was the first built in the *Altis*; prior to its completion in the seventh century BC, the sanctuary had only open-air altars, dedicated to Zeus and a variety of other cult gods. The temple, rebuilt in the Doric style in the sixth century BC, is the most complete building on the site, with some thirty of its columns surviving in part, along with a section of the inner wall. The levels above this wall were composed only of sun-baked brick, and the lightness of this building material must have helped to preserve the sculptures – most notably the *Hermes of Praxiteles* – found amid the earthquake ruins.

Between the temples of Hera and Zeus is a grove described by Pausanias, and identified as the **Pelopeion**. In addition to a cult altar to the Olympian hero, this enclosed a small mound formed by sacrificial ashes, among which excavations unearthed many of the terracotta finds in the museum. The sanctuary's principal altar, dedicated to Zeus, probably stood just to the east.

West of the Temple of Hera, and bordering the wall of the *Altis*, are remains of the circular **Philippeion**, the first monument in the sanctuary to be built to secular glory. It was begun by Philip II after the Battle of Chaeronea gave him control over the Greek mainland, and may have been completed by Alexander the Great. To the east of the Hera temple is a small, second-century AD **fountain house**, the gift of the ubiquitous Herodes Atticus. Beyond, lining a terrace at the base of the Hill of Kronos, are the **state treasuries**. All except two of these were constructed by cities outside of Greece proper, as they functioned principally as storage chambers for sacrificial items and sporting equipment used in the games. They are built in the form of temples, as at Delphi; the oldest and grandest, at the east end, belonged to Gela in Sicily. In front of the treasuries are the foundations of a the **Metroön**, a fourth-century BC Doric temple dedicated to the mother of the gods.

The ancient ceremonial entrance to the *Altis* was on the south side, below a long **stoa** taking up almost the entire east side of the precinct. At the corner was a house built by Nero for his stay during the games. The emperor also had the entrance remodelled as a triumphal arch, fit for his anticipated victories. Through the arch, just outside the precinct, stood the **Bouleuterion** or council chamber, where before a great statue of Zeus the competitors took their oaths to observe the Olympian rules. As they approached the stadium, the gravity of this would be impressed upon them: lining the way were bronze statues paid for with the fines exacted for foul play, bearing the name of the disgraced athlete, his father and city.

The stadium

In the final analysis, it's neither foundations nor columns that make sense of Olympia, but the 200-metre track of the **Stadium** itself, entered by way of a long arched tunnel. The starting and finishing lines are still there, with the judges' thrones in the middle and seating ridges banked to either side.

Originally unstructured, the stadium developed with the games' popularity, forming a model for others throughout the Greek and Roman world. The tiers here eventually accommodated up to 20,000 spectators, with a smaller number on the southern slope overlooking the **Hippodrome** where the chariot races were held. Even so, the seats were reserved for the wealthier strata of society. The ordinary populace – along with slaves and all women spectators – watched the events from the Hill of Krónos to the north, then treeless and a natural grandstand.

The stadium was unearthed only in World War II, during a second phase of German excavations between 1941 and 1944, allegedly on the direct orders of Hitler. It's a sobering thought to see this ancient site in the context of the 1936 Berlin Olympics.

The Archeological Museum

May to mid-Oct Mon 12.30–7pm, Tues–Sun 8am–7pm (Aug till 9pm; Sept till 8pm); mid-Oct to April Mon 10.30am–5pm, Tues–Fri 8am–5pm, Sat & Sun 8.30am–3pm; 1200dr.

Olympia's site museum lies a couple of hundred metres north of the sanctuary; some of the signposts still refer to it as the "New Museum". It contains some of the finest Classical and Roman sculptures in the country, all superbly displayed.

The most famous of the individual sculptures are the **Head of Hera** and the **Hermes of Praxiteles**, both dating from the fourth century BC and discovered in the Temple of Hera. The Hermes is one of the best preserved of all Classical sculptures, and remarkable in the easy informality of its pose; it retains traces of its original paint. On a grander scale is the **Nike of Paionios**, which was originally ten metres high. Though no longer complete (and currently sequestered for restoration), it hints at how the sanctuary must once have appeared, crowded with statuary.

The best of the smaller objects are housed in Room 4. They include several fine bronze items, among them a **Persian Helmet**, captured by the Athenians at the Battle of Marathon, and (displayed alongside) the **Helmet of Miltiades**, the victorious Athenian general; both were found with votive objects dedicated in the stadium. There is also a superb terracotta group of **Zeus abducting Ganymede** and a group of finds from the workshop of **Pheidias**, including the cup with his name inscribed.

In the main hall of the museum is the centrepiece of the Olympia finds – statuary and sculpture reassembled from the **Temple of Zeus**. This includes three groups, all of which were once painted. From the *cella* is a frieze of the **Twelve Labours of Herakles**, delicately moulded and for the most part identifiably preserved. The other groups are from the east and west pediments. The east, reflecting Olympian pursuits, depicts Zeus presiding over a **chariot race** between Pelops and Oinamaos. The story has several versions. King Oinamaos, warned that he would be killed by his son-in-law, challenged each of his daughter Hippomadeia's suitors to a chariot race. After allowing them a start he would catch up and kill them from behind. The king (depicted on the left of the frieze) was eventually defeated by Pelops (on the right with Hippomadeia), after – depending on the version – assistance from Zeus (depicted at the centre), magic steeds from Poseidon or, most un-Olympian, bribing Oinamaos's charioteer to tamper with the wheels.

The west pediment, less controversially mythological, illustrates the **Battle of Lapiths and Centaurs** at the wedding of the Lapith king, Peirithous. This time, Apollo presides over the scene while Theseus helps the Lapiths defeat the drunken centaurs, depicted, with fairly brutal realism, attacking the women and boy guests. Many of the metope fragments are today in the Louvre in Paris, and some of what you see here are plaster-cast copies.

In the last rooms of the museum are a collection of objects relating to the games – including *halteres* (jumping weights), discuses, weightlifters' stones, and so on. Also displayed are a number of **funerary inscriptions**, including that of a boxer, Camelos of Alexandria, who died in the stadium after praying to Zeus for victory or death.

Practicalities: Olymbía

Modern **OLYMBÍA** is a village that has grown up simply to serve the excavations and tourist trade. It's essentially one long main avenue, **Praxitéles Kondhíli**, with a few side streets. Nevertheless, Olymbía is quite a pleasant place to stay, and is certainly preferable to Pýrgos (see p.252), with the prospect of good countryside walks along the Alfíos River and around the hill of Krónos.

Most people arrive at Olympia **via Pýrgos**, which is on the main Peloponnese rail line and has frequent bus connections with Pátra and a couple daily with Kalamáta/Kyparissía. The last of five daily **trains** from Pýrgos to Olympia leaves at 7.20pm; if you have time to kill between buses or trains, the city square, two blocks north, is pleasant. **Buses** leave sixteen times daily on weekdays (ten on weekends) between Pýrgos and Olympia, with a break between 12.30pm and 3.30pm; the last service is at 9pm. The only other direct buses to Olympia are **from Trípoli**, via Langádhia. These run twice daily in either direction. If you are approaching **from Andhrítsena**, either take the bus to Pýrgos and change, or stop at Kréstena and hitch or take a taxi the final 12km on from there.

There is a most helpful **tourist office** (May–Oct daily 9am–10pm; Nov–April Mon–Sat 11am–5pm; ☎0624/23 100), on the right of Praxiteles Kondhíli as you head towards the site. Olimbía has two **banks** and an **OTE** on the main avenue, a **post office** (just uphill) with Saturday and Sunday morning hours. **English-language books** are to be found at the back of the *Galerie d'Orphée* crafts shop on Praxitéles Kondhíli.

Accommodation

Accommodation is fairly easy to come by, with a swift turnaround of clientele and a range of hotels and private rooms whose prices are kept modest by competition. Most **rooms** are signposted on Stefanopoúlou or on the road parallel to and above Praxiteles Kondhíli, though you may well be offered one on arrival. As elsewhere, rates can drop substantially out of season, though many of the smaller and cheaper places close during the off season (never precisely defined), and it's best to check in advance. The **youth hostel** at Praxiteles Kondhíli 18 (☎0624/22 580; ①), which is open all day and has no curfew, is probably the cheapest option for lone travellers. There are three **campsites**, closest of which is *Diana* (☎0624/22 314), 1km back from the main street, with a pool and good facilities. The others are *Alphios* (☎0624/22 950; April–Sept), 1km out on the Kréstena road, and *Olympía* (☎0624/22 745; April–Oct), 2km out on the Pýrgos road.

Achilles, Stefanopoúlou 4 (☎0624/22 562). A pension on a side street behind the National Bank; large and comfortable rooms above a snack bar. ②.

Antonios (☎0624/22 348). A hotel in the woods on the Kréstena road; expensive and not particularly well furnished, but peaceful, with a swimming pool and a stunning view; open April–Oct. ⑥.

Europa (☎0624/22 650). A modern hotel on the hill overlooking the village; it's a good hotel, which also has a swimming pool. ⑤.

Heracles (☎0624/22 696). A welcoming hotel on a side street off Praxitéles Kondhíli; big breakfasts and small balconies. ④.

Hermes (☎0624/22 577). A comfortable hotel 400m out on the Pýrgos road; rooms have private facilities and there is a good restaurant. ③.

Pelops, Barélas 2 (☎0624/22 543). A hotel run by a Greek/Australian couple and strongly recommended by those who stay there; open March–Oct. ④.

Praxiteles, Spiliopoúlou (☎0624/22 592). Quiet hotel next to the police station; there's a good restaurant, and both meals and rooms are competitively priced. ③.

Eating and drinking

Many of the hotels have excellent **restaurants**, where non-residents can eat. The main avenue is lined with **tavernas**, which offer standard tourist meals at mildly inflated prices in high season, and there is a growing number of fast-food kerbside cafés. The *Kladhios* taverna, out of the village on the banks of the Kládhios River, serves good food in a pleasant setting. In **Miráka** village (1km out on the Trípoli road), the family-run *Taverna Drosiá* offers a friendly service and fresh, home-made food; the excellent "house" wine is made by the owner's father. For picnics, bread from the bakery on the road to Kréstena is very good.

The northwest coast to Pátra

Despite the proximity of Olympia and Pátra, the northwest corner of the Peloponnese is not much explored by foreign visitors. Admittedly, it's not the most glamorous of coasts, except for the glorious beach at **Kalógria**, but a stay at the old port of **Katákolo** or around **Loutrá Kyllínis/Arkoúdhi** can provide a pleasant enough diversion.

Ferry connections may add further purpose: from Kyllíni there are regular crossings to Zákynthos, and in summer to Kefalloniá, while Katákolo has (summer-only) kaïkia to Zákynthos.

Pýrgos

PÝRGOS has a grim recent history. When the Germans withdrew at the end of World War II, it remained under the control of Greek Nazi collaborators. These negotiated surrender with the Resistance, who were met by gunfire as they entered the town. Full-scale battle erupted and for five days the town burned. Today, it's a drab, 1950s-looking place, which earns few plaudits from casual visitors. If you can avoid an enforced overnight stay, do so. The hotels are overpriced, the food uninspiring and diversions nonexistent. If you have to stay the night, the cheapest hotels are the *Marily*, Deliyiánni 48 (☎0621/28 133; ④), and the *Pantheon*, Themistokleous 7 (☎0621/29 748; ④).

The main escape routes are by **train** or **bus** to Pátra, Kyparissía or Olympia; there is a daily bus to Itéa, usually in the morning and this should put you within striking distance of Delphi on the same day. Closer to hand, there are frequent buses to Katákolo by local bus #4. The bus station is at the top of the hill and the train station 400m away at the bottom, so allow a little time for interchange.

Katákolo

Thirteen kilometres west of Pýrgos, **KATÁKOLO** is somewhat more enticing: a decayed, ramshackle old port with good beaches close by. Until the last few decades, when new roads improved connections with Pátra, it controlled the trade for Ilía province. Today only a few tramp steamers rust at anchor, though the navy calls occasionally and, oddly, the port remains a stop for Italian summer-cruise ships. Consequently, the town has become aware of a potentially lucrative tourist trade, and most of the old warehouses have been converted into boutiques and trinket shops. But arriving from Pýrgos it feels an easy place to settle into, and to the south there's a pleasant twenty-minute walk out to the **lighthouse**, set on a plateau among arbutus and pine.

There are three reasonable **hotels**, best value of which the *Delfíni* (☎0621/41 795; ③), is most popular with the locals, who play cards and backgammon on green-baize tables in the snack bar on Sundays. At the top of steps leading from the road are several **room** establishments with cabins fronted by peach and apricot trees. Try to avoid staying on the main drag, which can be noisy at night, belying the town's torpid daytime appearance. For **meals**, there are a handful of excellent tavernas on the quay.

Beaches

Katákolo's beach, the **Spiátza**, stretches away for miles to the north, a popular spot with Greeks, many of whom own shuttered little cottages set just back from the sea. It is sandy, though hard-packed and is more of a spot for football or jogging, with the sea too shallow for real swimming. However, a thirty-minute walk north, past the overgrown Byzantine-Frankish **Castle of Beauvoir**, will take you to much better swimming at **Áyios Andhréas** beach: two hundred metres of sloping, outcrop-studded sand, with views over a few attendant islets and out to Zákynthos. There are summer tavernas here and a few rooms to let. An even better beach is to be found at **Skafídhia**, 3km north of Katákolo and accessible by road via Korakohóri.

The cape north of Pýrgos

North from Pýrgos, road and rail meander through a series of uneventful market towns, but there are two forks west to a sandy cape and the coast. The first is at Gastoúni and heads for the spa of **Loutrá Kyllínis** (occasional buses from Pýrgos and Pátra); the second is at Kavássilas, where a side road (buses from Pátra) heads down to **Kyllíni** proper. Take care not to confuse the two.

LOUTRÁ KYLLÍNIS has a long beach, and at its north end you'll find a crop of upmarket **hotels** catering for the resort's spa-trade, including the over-priced and under-resourced *Kyllini Spa Xenia Tourist Complex* run by the EOT. It's better to walk south where the development soon gives way to sand dunes. There are two **campsites** – the *Aginara Beach* (☎0623/96 411) and the *Ionian Beach* (☎0623/96 395), both bordered by trees and beaches of fine shingle and sand – further to the southeast and best approached from Lygía on the road from Gastoúni.

Only a few kilometres south of the EOT complex, at the point where this most westerly coast of the Peloponnese bends back east into the long bay that curves towards Pýrgos, is **ARKOÚDHI**, a far better place to stay. This compact village resort has something of an island feel to it and a fine sandy bay enclosed by a rocky promontary. As well as a campsite, there are a surprising number of hotels and rooms. On the edge of the village is the posh and good value hotel *Arcoudi* (☎0623/96 480), which has a pool. In the village centre more spacious apartments are available at *Soulis* (☎0623/96 379; ⑤) or *Elena* (☎0623/96 493; ④). For meals try the central *Spyros* psistariá, or the *Akrogiali*, which offers a sea view and a wide selection of dishes.

Cheerless little **KYLLÍNI** (which can be reached by taxi from Loutrá Kyllínis) has little more to offer than its **ferry connections**. It is the principal port for **Zákynthos** (eight departures daily in summer, five in winter) and Póros on **Kefalloniá** (five departures daily in summer, two in winter). If you're stuck overnight in Kyllíni, **places to stay** are limited: the choice is between the *Hotel Ionian* (☎0623/92 318; ④) on the main street where some rooms have private facilities, rooms (also on the main street), or sleeping on the beach. The *Taverna Anna*, beyond the harbour, serves a wide range of traditional dishes and is particularly popular with locals at Sunday lunchtimes.

Using Loutrá Kyllínis, Arkoúdhi or Kyllíni as a base, it's worth taking time to hitch or walk to the village of **KÁSTRO**, at the centre of the cape. Looming above the village is the Frankish **Castle of Khlemoútsi** (8am–8pm; free), a vast hexagonal structure built in 1220 by Guillaume de Villehardouin, the founder of Mystra. Its function was principally to control the province of Akhaïa, though it served also as a strategic fortress on the Adriatic. Haze permitting, there are sweeping views across the straits to Zákynthos, and even to Kefalloniá and Itháki, from the well-preserved and restored ramparts. Kástro has a hotel, the welcoming *Chryssi Avgi* at Loutropoleos 9 (☎0623/95 224; ④), which is open from May to mid-October. You can eat here by arrangement, or dine equally well at the nearby *Apollon* taverna.

Kalógria and Niforéïka Patróu

Midway between Kyllíni and Pátra, **KALÓGRIA** is an eight-kilometre strand of beach, bordered by a swathe of **pine forests**. A fair proportion of Pátra descends here at the weekend as it's the nearest good **beach** to the city, but it's also a respected place (the beach for its sands and the forest for its birdlife) and permanent development remains low key. It is not actually a village – the nearest bona fide town is Metókhi – but rather a cluster of tavernas and stores. At the far north end of the beach there's the *Kalogria Beach* (☎0693/31 276; ⑥), a large hotel complex with many facilities. There's not much official accommodation apart from that, but free camping is tolerated among the pines behind the beach. A novelty for wildlife aficionados are the estuaries nearby in which you may find yourself swimming alongside harmless metre-long watersnakes.

Around the northwest coast towards Pátra, 3km west of Káto Akhaïa, another busy little resort is that of **NIFORÉÏKA PATRÓN**, where accommodation options include the pricey *Hotel Acheos* complex (☎0693/25 370; ⑤), with cheaper bungalows attached, and *Aliki* camping. There is a choice of several restaurants.

Pátra

PÁTRA (Patras) is the largest town in the Peloponnese and, after Pireás, the major port of Greece; from here you can go to Italy as well as to certain Ionian islands. The city is also the hub of the Greek-mainland transport network, with connections throughout the Peloponnese and, via the ferry at Río, across the straits to Delphi or western Greece.

Unless you arrive late in the day from Italy, you shouldn't need to spend more than a few hours in the city. A conurbation of close to a quarter of a million souls, it's not the ideal holiday retreat: there are no beaches, no particular sights, and traffic noise well

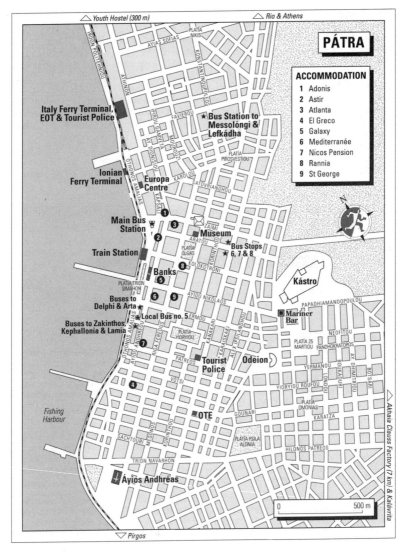

into the night and earlier than you'd want to get up. Nor has there been much effort to make the place attractive to visitors, save for a **summer festival** which sponsors events from late June to mid-September. These include classical plays and the occasional rock concert in the Roman **Odeion**, and art and photographic exhibitions that bring a bit of life to the warehouses by the harbour (details from the EOT, Tourist Police or the theatre on Platía Yioryíou). The three-week **carnival** (ending on the Sunday before Lent Monday – *Kathari Dheftera*) is one of the biggest in the country, with a grand parade through the city centre on the final day.

The Town

The best places to make for are the café-table-studded **Platía Psilá Alónia** or the **Kástro** (daily 8am–7pm; free), a mainly Byzantine citadel. This is not particularly exciting, but it is away from the city bustle, surrounded by a park and only a ten-minute walk up from the water. At the southwest end of the waterfront itself is the neo-Byzantine **church of Áyios Andhréas**, which opened in 1979 and houses relics of St Andrew, said to have been martyred on this spot. The church is a massive confection of yellow and cream walls, red-tiled domes and marmoreal excess that takes in the pillars and arches. A small **museum** on the corner of Mésonos and Arátov contains a number of exquisite objects from the county of Ahaïa dating from the Mycenean to the Roman eras.

Swimming near Pátra isn't really advisable, with the sea polluted for some kilometres to the southwest. Locals go to the **beaches** around Río (7km northeast; bus #6 from the stop on Kanakári) or to Kalógria (40km southwest, see p.234; bus from KTEL station).

The Akhaïa Clauss factory

The **Akhaïa Clauss** factory (daily tours 9am–5pm) is an out-of-town time-filler, 9km southeast of Pátra; take the #7 bus from the stop on Kanakári (see map on p.235). Tours

---

FERRY ROUTES AND COMPANIES

Innumerable ticket agents along the waterfront each sell different permutations of **ferry crossings** to Italy on one or more of the lines detailed below. It is worth spending an hour or so researching these, especially if you're taking a car, since costs, journey times and routes all differ from one company to another. Ferry company **brochures** quoting times and prices are freely available from the agents. En route to Italy, it is possible to make stopovers on Kefalloniá and, most commonly, Igoumenítsa and Corfu (Kérkyra). Domestic tickets to these Greek island stops (plus Itháki) are also available from Pátra.

ROUTES Pátra–Ancona has become the standard route. Until recently this entailed two nights on board, but high-speed ferries operated by ANEK, Minoan Lines and Superfast Ferries can now complete the crossing in 20–24hr. Other routes include Pátra–Brindisi, Pátra–Bari, Pátra–Trieste and Pátra–Venice. Minoan Lines plan to introduce a high-speed ferry (23hr) on the Pátra–Venice route in 1998.

HIGH SEASON All frequencies of ferry crossings detailed below are for the high season, the definition of which varies slightly from company to company. Broadly, for crossings from Italy to Greece, high season is between early July and mid-August; from Greece to Italy, it is between early August and early September. Check with company agents for exact dates. Out of season, all services are reduced.

FARES All companies offer a variety of fares for cabin, airline-type seats, and deck passage, with reductions according to age and student or rail-card status. High-speed ferries cost only fractionally more than the normal ones. All ferry companies offer a substantial discount (normally thirty percent) on return trips if booked together with the outward journey.

EMBARKATION TAX All international departures carry a levy of 1500dr per person and per car.

CHECKING IN If you have bought tickets in advance, or from a travel agent other than the official agent listed below, you must check in (to the appropriate agent's office, or at their booth in the departure hall) at least two hours before departure.

STOPOVERS Free if you specify them when booking, though you may have to pay re-embarkation taxes.

show you around the wine-making process, and feature some treasured, century-old barrels of Mavrodhafni – a dark dessert wine named after the woman Clauss wanted to marry. You're given a glass of white wine to sample on reaching the factory's rather Teutonic bar, an echo of its founder's nationality. Along the walls are signed letters from celebrity recipients of Mavrodhafni. A shop sells all the factory's products, if you want a bottle for yourself.

Practicalities

If you are driving in or through Pátra, you will find the traffic and one-way system no less frustrating than Athens; an EOT map showing the direction of traffic, if not vital, will at least save time and probably maintain sanity. For **tourist information**, try the **EOT** office, at the entrance to the Italy ferry terminal (Mon–Fri 7am–9pm; ☎061/62 0353); and the helpful **Tourist Police** (daily 7am–11pm; ☎061/45 1893) inside the same building.

For **money exchange**, there is an automatic machine outside the National Bank of Greece on the waterside Platía Tríou Simáhou, which also keeps special daily evening hours (6–8pm). Numerous other banks offer exchange during normal hours. For better

Companies, agents and destinations

ANEK
United Ferries, Óthonos Amalías 25 (☎061/226 053).

Ancona: Tues, Fri direct (26hr); Wed, Sat & Sun via Igoumenítsa (32hr).

Trieste: Mon & Wed via Igoumenítsa (36hr); Thurs via Igoumenítsa and Corfu (36hr).

Adriatica
Charilaos Cacouris, Óthonos Amalías 8 (☎061/421 995).

Brindisi: via Igoumenítsa and Corfu alternate days (18hr); direct on alternate days (15hr).

Hellenic Mediterranean Lines
Hellenic Mediterranean Lines, Pénde Pigadhioú and Iróön Polyteckhnióu (☎061/452 521).

Brindisi: daily via Kefalloniá, Igoumenítsa and Corfu (19hr 30min).

Marlines
Marlines, Óthonos Amalías 56 (☎061/223 444).

Ancona (36hr): Mon, Tues & Thurs via Igoumenítsa (18hr).

Minoan Lines
Minoan Lines, Athónon 2 (☎061/421 500).

Venice: via Corfu and Igoumenítsa daily (37hr).

Ancona: direct daily (22hr).

Strintzis
Tsimaras, Óthonos Amalías 14 (☎061/622 602).

Ancona: Tues & Sat via Igoumenítsa (34hr); Mon & Sun via Corfu and Igoumenítsa (34hr); otherwise direct.

Venice: Wed & Thurs via Igoumenítsa and Corfu (37hr).

Itháki via Kefalloniá (port of Sámi).

Ventouris
Express Shipping Agencies Co, Óthonos Amalías 81 (☎061/222 958).

Bari: direct alternate days (17hr 30min); via Kefalloniá alternate days (18hr).

Superfast
Superfast ferries, Óthonos Amalías 12 (☎061/622 500).

Ancona: daily except Tues (20hr).

exchange rates try the Kapa foreign exchange bureau at Othónos Amalías 5 (☎061/43 7261). The main **OTE** building (daily 7am–midnight) is on the corner of Goúnari and Kanakári and the main **post office** (Mon–Fri 7.30am–8pm) on the corner of Mesonós and Záïmi.

Departures

The **ferry agents, train station** and main **KTEL bus terminal** could hardly be easier to find, grouped on the harbour road, Óthonos Amalías. Full details of **ferry routes** are shown in the box on p.237. **Buses** go almost everywhere from Pátra. From the **main KTEL** station, there are departures to Athens, Pýrgos and other towns in the Peloponnese, as well as to Ioánnina and Thessaloníki. From the **KTEL station on Faviérou**, the Étolo-Akarnanía service will take you to Messolóngi and Agrínio, where you can change for Lefkádha. You can pick up the Athens–Zákynthos and Athens–Keffalloniá buses (for information call ☎061/27 2246) at Óthonos Amalías 58. Direct buses to Delphi (for information call ☎061/62 1200) leave twice a day from Óthonos Amalías 44.

Trains go from Pátra down the west coast of the Peloponnese, with changes at Alfiós for Olympia, and at Kaló Neró for routes inland to Kalamáta, Trípoli, Kórinthos and Athens. Trains go east along the southern shore of the Gulf of Kórinthos to Dhiakoftó, Kórinthos, Athens and Pireás. For train and bus frequencies see travel details on p.244.

Accommodation

Most of Pátra's **hotels** are on Ayíou Andhréou, one block back from Óthonos Amalías, or on Ayíou Nikólaos, which runs back from the sea, near the train station and Platía Tríon Simáhon. Don't expect too much in the way of standards or value for money; most of the places cater for a very passing trade and don't make great efforts. The best budget option is the **youth hostel** at Iróon Politehníou 68 (☎061/427 278; ①), a kilometre-plus walk northeast of the train station along the waterfront; it's clean, cheap, very popular, has no curfew and is housed in a nineteenth-century mansion within a small courtyard. Most of the older hotels nearer the waterfront have closed, or indeed collapsed. Of those still standing, choices include the following.

Adonis, cnr Kapsáli & Záïmi (☎061/224 213). On the junction with Kapsáli opposite the bus station. It's well furnished and maintained and includes a buffet-style breakfast; good value. ⑤.

Astir, Ayíou Andhréou 16 (☎061/277 502). Modern hotel with a swimming pool, sauna, roof garden and car parking, which still don't justify the price. ⑥.

Atlanta, Záïmi 10 (☎061/220 098). Central hotel, but still quiet and good value; out of season you should get a competitive price. ⑥.

El Greco, Ayíou Andhréou 145 (☎061/272 931). A good bargain hotel and top of its class; the manager is attentive and speaks English. ④.

Galaxy, Ayíou Nikoláouss 9 (☎061/275 981). A well-placed hotel, if a touch pretentious; serves a good breakfast. ⑥.

Mediterranée, Ayíou Nikólaouss 18 (☎061/279 602). Modern and adequate hotel, if undistinguished, with helpful staff. ④.

Nicos, cnr Patréos 3 & Ayíou Andhréou 121 (☎061/623 757). Clean, cheerfully run pension with character; good terrace and bar; cheaper if you share facilities; 4am curfew. ②.

Rannia, Ríga Feréou 53 (☎061/220 114). Clean, faultless and well placed, with a café and snack bar. ⑤.

Saint George Hotel, Ayíou Andhréou 73 (☎061/225 092). A good new clean and central hotel. ⑤.

Eating and drinking

Pátra's **restaurants** are fairly wretched, with countless fast-food places around Platía Tríon Simákhon, and along Ayíou Andhréou and Ayíou Nikólaou. But even here there are some reliable restaurants with character, and a mouth-watering patisserie-bakery at Kolokotróni 46. For fish, the best places are a couple of tavernas down by the fishing harbour, home to a somewhat half-hearted fleet, while for spit-roast specialities, several psistariés are grouped around Platía Omonías and Platía Pyrosvestíou. **Nightlife** in town is largely concentrated around a noisy selection of bars at the steps of Ayíou Nikoláou. Further up beside the castle you can enjoy a quiet drink at the *Mariner* bar.

If you're stuck for the night and feel the urge to escape to a quieter stretch of sea, hop on any #5 blue bus labelled "Tsoukaleíka" and alight at either **Monodhéndhri** or **Vrahneíka**, 10km south-west of the city. There is now a practically unbroken chain of tavernas stretching 2km from Monodhéndhri to Vrahneíka, of which *Thalassa* ouzerí has the best selection of food. The others vary in price, range and quality but all share the seaside and sunset view. Real gourmets will want to check out the terrific cuisine at *Mesogeios/Mouragios*, in the suburb of **Boznítika**, 6km east of Pátra. Specialities include artichoke soufflé and seafood pasta served in a conch shell; the prices are reasonable. Choices in Pátra include the following.

Apostolis, cnr Londou and Yeorgíou Roúfou. A basic but great taverna with quiet garden, twenty minutes' walk from centre.

Faros, cnr Othónos Amalías and Sakhtoúri. One of the best fish tavernas for quality and prices.

Hartofilacas, cnr Ríga Feréou/Karólou. A good-value estiatório, serving traditional food.

Krini, Pandokrátoros 57. An endearing place at the top of the old town, by the kástro. It has a limited but exemplary menu, and is a favourite with locals; it's possible to eat in the little garden at the back.

Majestic, Ayíou Nikoláou 2/4. Old-style estiatório, where you can choose from the day's hot dishes, which are tasty but expensive.

Nikolaous, Ayíou Nikoláou 50. Another old-style estiatório, serving good, traditional food.

Peking, cnr Iröón Politéhniou and Terpsithéas. A rare Chinese restaurant; rather pricey but none too bad.

Listings

American Express Handled by Albatros Travel, Óthonos Amalías 48 (☎061/220 993).

Books and newspapers Book's Corner, Ayíou Nikólaou 32, stocks useful maps and English-language newspapers. Kyklos, Riga Feréou 33, has guide books, second-hand books and a large selection of paperbacks, some in English. Lexis, Mesonos 38, stocks maps and a selection of Penguins. Romios on Kapsáli, behind the bus station, sells English-language books, and English-language papers are available from kiosks on the waterfront.

Car rental Major operators include: Avis, Kapsali 11(☎061/275 547); Budget, Othónos Amalías 14 (☎061/623 200); Delta, Óthonos Amalías 32 (☎061/272 764); Eurodollar, Albatros Travel, Óthonos Amalías 48 (☎061/220 993); Hertz, Karolóu 2 (☎061/220 990); InterRent-EuropCar, Ayíou Andhréou 6 (☎061/621 360); Just, Óthonos Amalías 37 (☎061/275 495); and Thrifty, Óthonos Amalías 14 (☎061/623 200).

Consulates Britain, Vótsi 2 (☎061/277 329); Finland, Riga Feréou 46 (☎061/277 707); Germany, Mesonós 98 (☎061/221 943); Netherlands, Philopimónos 39 (☎061/271 846); Norway, Karolóu 85c (☎061/435 090); Sweden, Óthonos Amalías 62 (☎061/271 702).

Laundry Skafi Self Service, cnr Zäimi and Korínthou (Mon–Sat 9am–9pm).

Poste restante Contact the main post office on the corner of Mesonós and Zäimi.

Travel agents These can help with information and reservations, and all line Óthonos Amalías: Albatros Travel (☎061/220 993); Marine Tours (☎061/621 166); Olympias Shipping and Travel Enterprises (☎061/275 495); Thomas Cook (☎061/226 053).

The north coast and the Kalávryta railway

From Pátra you can reach Kórinthos in two hours by **train** or **bus** along the national highway; the onward journey to Athens takes another ninety minutes. The resorts and villages lining the Gulf of Kórinthos are nothing very special, though none are too developed. At most of them you find little more than a campsite, a few rooms for rent and a couple of seasonal tavernas. At both **Río** and **Éyio**, you can cross the gulf by ferry. Beyond **Dhiakoftó**, if you're unhurried, it's worth taking the old **coast road** along the Gulf of Kórinthos; this runs below the national highway, often right by the sea.

However, to travel from Pátra to Kórinthos without taking the time to detour along the **Kalávryta railway** from Dhiakoftó would be to miss one of the best treats the Peloponnese has to offer – and certainly the finest train journey in Greece. Even if you have a car, this trip should still be part of your plans.

Río and Éyio

RÍO, connected by local bus #6 to Pátra (30min), signals the beginning of swimmable water, though most travellers stop here only to make use of the **ferry** across the gulf to Andírio. This runs every fifteen minutes through the day and early evening (hourly or half-hourly thereafter), shuttling cars (1500dr including driver) and passengers (150dr) across to the central mainland. It is a long-established crossing, testimony to which are a pair of diminutive Turkish **forts** on either side of the gulf.

If you are crossing into the Peloponnese from Andírio, you might be tempted to stop by the sea here, rather than at Pátra. There are several **hotels**, including the *Georgios* (☎061/992 627; ④) and *Rio Beach* (☎061/991 421; ④) and the ultra swish *Hotel Porto Rio* (☎061/992 102; ⑥). There are two **campsites**: the *Rio Mare* (☎061/992 263; May–Oct), just before the jetty and 120m from the beach, and the *Rion* (☎061/993 388; April–Oct) beyond the jetty but closer to the beach, which is poor. The best of the restaurants is the *Four Seasons* with bargain prices in a romantic setting opposite the railway crossing. Río also boasts some of the most tub-thumping disco bars in the Pátra area – *Mojo* is particularly popular.

Moving east, there are better beaches, and a further **campsite**, the *Tsolis* (☎0691/31 469), at **ÉYIO**. Although not a place many people would choose to stay, there are a few hotels and rooms in Éyio. It's more likely you might want to eat there though and the town has several decent psistariés, while just east of the harbour around Dhódheka Vrísses square are more eating establishments; the *Plessas* inomayirío is authentic and cheap; nearby stands an ancient plane tree from 200 AD dedicated to the historian Pausanias. Nearby a ravine cuts sharply into the hillside near the Panayía Tripití church, marking the spot where local hero Miralis escaped from the Turks in 1821 by jumping in with his horse.

The best sands are at the village of **RHODHODHÁFNI**, 2km northwest of Éyio, the *Corali Beach* (☎0691/71 546; May–Sept) and the *Acoli Beach* (☎0691/71 317; April–Oct) **campsites** are close to the beach. At Éyio, a **ferry** crosses the gulf nine times daily (7.30am–8.30pm; car and driver 3000dr, passengers 500dr) to Áyios Nikólaos, well placed for Delphi.

Dhiakoftó and beyond

It is at **DHIAKOFTÓ** that the rack-and-pinion railway heads south into the Vouraïkós gorge for Kalávryta (see opposite). If you arrive late in the day, it's worth spending the night here and making the train journey in daylight; the town can, in any case, be an attractive alternative to staying overnight in Pátra. There are four **hotels**: the pleasant, upmarket *Chris-Paul* (☎0691/41 715; ⑤); the beautiful but basic *Helmos* (☎0691/41 236; ②; closed in winter); the *Lemonies* (☎0691/41 821; ③) set in a lemon grove by the road to the beach; and the *Panorama* (☎0691/41 614; ④) by the beach itself. The *Spiros* taverna, attached to the *Lemonies*, has decent food, as does the *Kohili* on the corner of the beach road and the restaurant at the *Panorama*.

Beyond Dhiakoftó there are minor resorts at Akráta and Xilókastro. **AKRÁTA**, a small town with a beach hamlet, is a little crowded, with three hotels and three campsites set along a rather drab, exposed stretch of beach. **DHERVÉNI**, another 8km east, is more attractive, though there is no hotel or campsite; there are **rooms** for rent, and those offered by Konstandinos Stathakopoulos (☎0743/31 223; ③) are comfortable. **XILÓKASTRO**, a popular weekend escape from Kórinthos, has both good beaches and accommodation, and a pleasant setting below Mount Zíria. Cheapest of its dozen **hotels** are the *Hermes*, Ioánou 81 (☎0743/22 250; ③), and *Kyani Akti*, Tsaldhári 68 (☎0743/28 930; ④). More expensive is the *Apollon*, housed in a fine old building at Ioánou 119 (☎0743/25 240; ⑤). The long seafront boasts a number of restaurants of which *Iy Zesti Gonia* is friendly with good fish and tray food, while *Iy Palea Exedhra* has more variety.

Dhiakoftó to Kalávryta: the rack-and-pinion railway

Even if you have no interest in trains, the **rack-and-pinion railway** from Dhiakoftó to Kalávryta is a must. It's a crazy feat of engineering, rising at gradients of up to one in seven as it cuts through the course of the **Vouraïkós gorge**. En route is a toy-train fantasy of tunnels, bridges and precipitous overhangs.

The railway was built by an Italian company between 1889 and 1896 to bring minerals from the mountains to the sea. Its steam locomotives were replaced some years ago – one remains by the line at Dhiakoftó and another at Kalávryta – but the track itself retains all the charm of its period. The tunnels, for example, have delicately carved windows, and the narrow bridges zigzagging across the Vouraïkós seem engineered for sheer virtuosity.

It takes up to an hour to get from Dhiakoftó to Zahloroú (confusingly listed on timetables as Méga Spílio), and about another twenty minutes from there to Kalávryta. The best part of the trip is the stretch to **Zahloroú**, along which the gorge narrows to a few feet at points, only to open out into brilliant, open shafts of light beside the Vouraïkós, clear and fast-running even in midsummer. In peak season the ride is very popular, so you'll probably need to buy tickets some hours before your preferred departure (including the return journey).

Zakhloroú and Méga Spílio

ZAKHLOROÚ is as perfect a train stop as could be imagined: a tiny hamlet echoing with the sound of the Vouraïkós River, which splits it into two neighbourhoods. It's a lovely, peaceful place with a gorgeous old wooden hotel, the very friendly and very reasonably priced *Romantzo* (☎0692/22 758; ③), which has a fine separately owned restaurant below. The only other hotel is the adjacent *Messina* (☎0692/22 789; ②), sometimes closed during summer.

The **Monastery of Méga Spílio** (Great Cave) is a 45-minute walk from the village, up a rough donkey track along the cliff; this joins an access drive along the final stretch, which is often chock-a-block with tour buses. The monastery is reputedly the oldest in Greece, but it has burned down and been rebuilt so many times that you'd hardly guess at its antiquity. The last major fire took place in the 1930s, after a keg of gunpowder left behind from the War of Independence exploded. Dress conduct for visitors is strict: skirts for women and long sleeves and trousers for men. Only men are allowed to stay overnight, and the monks like visitors to arrive before 8pm, serving up a rough repast before closing the gates.

The view of the gorge from the monastery is for many the principal attraction. However, the cloister was once among the richest in the Greek world, owning properties throughout the Peloponnese, in Macedonia, Constantinople and Asia Minor. In consequence, its treasury, arranged as a small **museum**, is outstanding. In the church, among its icons is a curiously moving charred black image of the Virgin, one of three in Greece said to be by the hand of Saint Luke. The monastery was founded by saints Theodhoros and Simeon, after a vision by the shepherdess Euphrosyne in 362 AD led to the discovery of the icon in the large cave behind the site of the later church.

Kalávryta and around

From Méga Spílio a new road has been hacked down to **KALÁVRYTA**. The train line is more in harmony with the surroundings, but coming from Zahloroú the drama of the route is diminished as the gorge opens out. Kalávryta itself is beautifully positioned, with Mount Khelmós as a backdrop, though it has a sad atmosphere. During World War II the Germans carried out one of their most brutal reprisal massacres, killing the entire male population – 1436 men and boys – and leaving the town in flames. Rebuilt, it is both depressing and poignant. The first and last sight is a mural, opposite the station, that reads: "Kalávryta, founder member of the Union of Martyred Towns, appeals to all to fight for world peace." The left clocktower on the central church stands fixed at 2.34pm – the hour of the massacre. Out in the countryside behind the town is a shrine to those massacred, with the single word, "Peace" (*Iríni*).

The Nazis also burnt the **monastery of Ayía Lávra**, 6km out of Kalávryta. As the site where Yermanos, Archbishop of Pátra, raised the flag to signal the War of Independence, the monastery is one of the great Greek national shrines. It, too, has been rebuilt, along with a small historical museum.

Staying at Kalávryta has a sense of pilgrimage about it for Greeks, and it's crowded with school parties during the week and with families at weekends. It probably will not have the same appeal for the casual visitor, but if you miss the last train back to Zakhloroú (currently at 7.30pm, but check on the day) there are several pleasant **hotels**. Among them are the *Megas Alexandhros*, Lokhagón Vassiléos Kapóta 1 (☎0692/22 221; ④) with small rooms but value for money; the *Paradissos*, Lokhagón Vassiléos Kapóta 12 (☎0692/22 303; ④), a clean and agreeable hotel; *Polixeni*, Lokhagón Vassiléos Kapóta 13 (☎0692/23 051; ④); and the *Villa Kalavrita* (☎0692/22 712; ③) across the rail track from the station, which has comfortable, modern rooms, some with a small kitchen. There are several adequate restaurants around the square – *To Tzaki* has a nice atmosphere and good, mostly grilled food. Kalávryta is also the main base for the **Khelmós Ski Centre**, which is rapidly growing in popularity. There are a number of shops which can hire equipment, give information about the state of the slopes and maybe help with transport up to the centre.

A thirty-minute drive southeast of Kalávryta is the **Spílio Límnon** or Cave of the Lakes (summer daily 9am–6pm; winter Mon–Fri 9.30am–4.30pm, Sat & Sun 9.30am–6pm; 800dr; ☎0692/31 633). Mineral-saturated water trickling through a two-kilometre cavern system has precipitated natural dams, trapping a series of small underground lakes. Only the first 300m or so are as yet open to the public but the chambers are still well worth the trip.

The cave is on the same **bus** line from Kalávryta as the villages of Káto Loussí, Kastriá and Planitéro, and is 2km north of Kastriá. Buses also run from Kalávryta to Pátra four times daily.

Mount Khelmós

The highest peaks of the imposing Helmós range rear up a dozen or so kilometres to the southeast of Kalávryta. **Mount Khelmós** itself, at 2341m, is only 60m short of the summit of Taïyettos to the south. However, the walk from Kalávryta is not an interesting approach, the trail having vanished under a paved road and the new ski centre approached by it. To get the most from hiking on the mountain you need to climb up from the village of **Sólos**, on the west side – a five-hour-plus walk which takes you to the **Mavronéri waterfall**, source of the legendary Styx, which the souls of the dead had to cross in order to enter Hades.

The hike from Sólos

To reach the path opening at Sólos, start at **Akráta** on the Pátra–Kórinthos road. From here it's a slow but beautiful haul up a winding paved road. Buses run only three times a week, but hitching isn't too difficult in high summer.

SÓLOS is a tiny place, a cluster of stone cottages on a steep hillside just below the fir trees, and inhabited only in summer. Facing it across the valley is the larger but more scattered village of Peristéra, past which runs the easiest of the routes to Mavronéri.

Follow the **track** through Sólos, past the combined inn (all of ten beds), and *magazí* (café-store), where you can get a simple meal. Beyond the last houses the track curves around the head of a gully. On the right, going down its wooded flank, is a good path which leads to a bridge over the river at the bottom. Just beyond (15min; this and all subsequent times are from Sólos), you reach another track. There is a **chapel** on the left, and, on the wall of a house on the right, a sign saying "Pros Gounariánika" that points up a path to the left. Follow it past a **church** on a prominent knoll and on to the jeep track again, where, after 75 minutes, you turn left to the half-ruined hamlet of **Gounariánika**. From there continue steadily upwards along the west (right) flank of the valley through abandoned fields until you come to a stream-gully running down off the ridge above you on your right. On the far side of the stream the fir forest begins. It's an ideal camping place (2hr 30min; 1hr 30min going back down).

Once into the **woods**, the path is very clear. After about an hour (3hr 30min) you descend to a boulder-strewn **stream bed** with a rocky ravine to the right leading up to the foot of a huge bare crag, the east side of the Neraïdhórahi peak visible from Kalávryta. Cross the stream and continue leftwards up the opposite bank. In June there are the most incredible wild flowers, including at least half a dozen different orchids, all the way up from here.

After fifteen minutes' climb above the bank, you come out on top of a **grassy knoll** (3hr 30min), then dip back into the trees again. At the four-hour mark, you turn a corner into the mouth of the **Styx ravine**. Another five minutes' walk brings you to a **deep gully** where enormous banks of snow lie late into the spring. A few paces across a dividing rib of rock there is a second gully, where the path has been eroded and you have to cross some slippery scree.

Here you come to a wooded spur running down from the crag on the right. The trail winds up to a shoulder (4hr 20min), descends into another gully, and then winds up to a second shoulder of level rocky ground by some large blue pines (4hr 30min), known as *To Dhiasselo tou Kinigou* (the Hunter's Saddle). From there you can look into the Styx ravine. Continue down the path towards the right until it dwindles at the foot of a vast crag (4hr 45min). You can now see the **Mavronéri waterfall**, a 200-metre-long, wavering plume of water pouring off the red cliffs up ahead.

To get to it, angle across the scree bank without losing altitude – the track is obliterated soon after the saddle – until you reach the base of the falls (5hr). There's a small **cave** under the fall, where a rare columbine grows. It is possible to continue up the valley, past some turf next to a seasonal pond where people camp, but the summit area proper is a bit of a let-down after the majesty of the Styx valley. Fairly clear and easy trails lead down from the south side of the watershed to the villages of Káto Loussí or Planitéro; the appropriate *Korfes* or *YIS* maps have more details on these routes.

travel details

Trains

There are two types of train: **ordinary** and **express** (Intercity or IC), which are much faster than punctual.

There are two main Peloponnesian lines:

Athens–Kórinthos–Dhiakoftó–Pátra–Pýrgos –Kyparissía–Kalamáta 1 train daily makes the full run in each direction. Another 8 daily run between Athens and Pátra, 7 continuing to Pýrgos, 5 as far as Kyparissía. Another 1 train daily covers the route between Pátra and Kalamáta.

Approximate journey times are:

Athens–Kórinthos (1hr 30min–2hr)

Kórinthos–Dhiakoftó (1–1hr 30min)

Dhiakoftó–Pátra (45min–1hr 15min)

Pátra–Pýrgos (1hr 30min–2hr)

Pýrgos–Kyparissía (1hr–1hr 30min)

Kyparissía–Kalamáta (1hr 40min).

Athens (starts in Pireás)–Kórinthos–Mykínes (Mycenae)–Árgos–Trípoli–Kalamáta 3 trains daily cover the full route, in each direction.

Approximate journey times are:

Athens–Kórinthos (1hr 30min–2hr)

Kórinthos–Mykínes (50min)

Mykínes–Árgos (10min)

Árgos–Trípoli (1hr 30min)

Trípoli–Kalamáta (2hr 20min).

In addition, there are the following branch lines:

Pýrgos–Olympia 5 trains daily (40min).

Pýrgos–Katákolo 5 daily (25min).

Dhiakoftó–Zakhloroú–Kalávryta 6 daily (Dhiakoftó–Zakhloroú 50min; Zakhlaroú–Kalávryta 20min).

Buses

Buses detailed have similar frequency in each direction, so entries are given just once; for reference check under both starting-point and destination.

Connections with Athens: Kórinthos (hourly; 1hr); Mykínes (Mycenae)/Árgos/Tíryns/Náfplio (hourly to 8.30pm; 2hr/2hr 15min/2hr 45min/3hr);

Spárti (9 daily; 4hr 30min); Olympia (4 daily; 5hr 30min).

Areópoli to: Yerolimín (daily in season only; 1hr); Kalamáta (4 daily changing at Ítilo; 2hr 30min); Láyia (daily; 1hr).

Árgos to: Náfplio (half hourly; 30min); Mykínes (Mycenae; 6 daily; 30min); Neméa (3 daily; 1hr); Ástros/Leonídhi (3 daily; 1hr/3hr); Trípoli (9 daily; 1hr 20min); Spárti (8 daily; 3hr); Andhrítsena (daily at 10am; 3hr); Olympia (3 daily on weekdays; 4hr 30min).

Kalamáta to: Koróni (8 daily; 1hr 30min); Ítilo/Areópoli (4 daily; 1hr 30min); Pátra (2 daily; 4hr); Pýlos (9 daily; 1hr 20min); Megalópoli/Trípoli (8 daily; 1hr/1hr 45min).

Kórinthos to: Mykínes (Mycenae)/Árgos/Tíryns/ Náfplio (hourly; 30min/1hr/1hr 15min/1hr 30min); Loutráki (half-hourly; 20min); Neméa (5 daily; 45min); Trípoli (9 daily; 1hr 30min); Spárti (8 daily; 4hr); Kalamáta (7 daily; 4hr).

Megalópoli to: Andhrítsena/Pýrgos (2 daily; 3hr/4hr); Trípoli (8 daily; 40min).

Náfplio to: Epidaurus (5 daily; 45min); Tólo (half-hourly; 25min); Trípoli (4 daily;1hr15min).

Pýlos to: Methóni (6 daily; 20min); Kalamáta (9 daily; 1hr 20min); Kyparissía (6 daily, but none 3–7pm; 2hr).

Pátra to: Kalávryta (4 daily; 2hr 30min); Zákynthos (4 daily; 2hr 30min including ferry from Kyllíni); Ioánnina (3 daily; 5hr); Kalamáta (2 daily; 4hr); Vólos (daily; 6hr).

Pýrgos to: Olympia (hourly, but none 12.30–3.30pm; 45min); Andhrítsena (2 daily; 2hr); Pátra (11 daily; 2hr); Kyparissía/Kalamáta (2 daily; 1hr/2hr).

Spárti to: Mystrás (11 daily, 6 on Sun; 15min); Monemvassía (3 daily; 3hr); Kalamáta (2 daily; 2hr 30min); Yíthio (5 daily; 1hr); Neápoli (4 daily; 4hr).

Trípoli to: Megalópoli (8 daily; 40min); Spárti (2 daily; 1hr 20min); Olympia (3 daily, in stages; 5hr); Pátra (via Lámbia; 2 daily; 4hr); Pýrgos (3 daily; 3hr); Andhrítsena (2 daily; 1hr 30min); Dhimitsána (2 daily; 1hr 30min); Kalamáta (8 daily; 2hr); Pýlos (3 daily; 3hr); Kyparissía (2 daily; 2hr).

Yíthio to: Areópoli (4 daily; 50min); Láyia (daily; 1hr); Monemvassía (2 daily; 2hr 30min).

Ferries

Across the Gulf of Kórinthos Andírio–Río (every 15min, much less often between 11pm and dawn; 20min); Éyio–Áyios Nikólaos (9 daily; 35min).

Galatás to: Póros (every 15min from dawn till past midnight; 5min).

Kalamata to Kastélli (Crete) (once a week, currently Mon)

Kyllíni to: Zákynthos (daily 8 summer 5 winter; 2hr); Kefaloniá (5 summer 2 winter; 1hr).

Kýthira to: Kastélli, Crete (twice weekly in season; 4hr).

Pátra to: Igoumenítsa and Corfu (2 or 3 daily; 7–9hr/9–11hr); Kefaloniá and Itháki (daily; 4–5hr); Paxí (2 or 3 weekly; 6hr); also to Brindisi, Ancona, Bari, Trieste (Italy). See under "Pátra" for details.

Pireás–Kyparíssi–Monemvassía–Neápoli–El afónissos–Kýthira–Andýkithira–Kastélli (Crete). At least once weekly – currently Sunday – a boat departs Kastélli for Pireás via all of the ports listed, returning on the same route on Monday; the complete trip takes about 16 hours. For current schedules, phone Miras Ferries (☎01/41 27 225) or Ventouris Ferries (☎01/41 14 911).

Yíthio to: Kýthira (almost daily service; 2hr 30min); contact Haloulakos (☎0733/24 501) or Rozakis (☎0733/22 207) for current information.

Hydrofoils

For details and frequencies of services, which vary drastically with season, contact local agents or the Ceres Hydrofoils' main office in Pireás (Aktí Themistokléous 8; ☎01/412 8001).

"Flying Dolphin" hydrofoils run between the following ports:

Kyparíssi/Monemvassía/Leonídhi to Pórto Khéli, Spétses, Póros and Pireás.

Neápoli/Kýthira to Pireás.

Méthana to Éyina and Póros.

Ermióni to Ídhra (Hydra) and Spétses.

Náfplio (midsummer only) to Monemvassía, Toló, Spétses, Póros and Pireás.

Paleá Epídhavros to Éyina-Pireás.

Summer-only excursion boats

Pórto Khéli: Water-taxis to Spétses according to demand (20min).

Flights

To/from **Athens–Kalamáta** (1 daily; 50min); Kýthira (1–2 daily; 50min).

CHAPTER THREE

THESSALY AND CENTRAL GREECE

Central Greece is a region of scattered highlights – above all the site of the ancient oracle at **Delphi**, and, further to the north, the unworldly rock-monasteries of the **Metéora**. The area as a whole, dominated by the vast agricultural plain of Thessaly, is less exciting, with rather drab market and industrial towns. For scenic drama – and most of the historic sights – you have to head for the fringes.

The southern part of this region, before you enter Thessaly proper, is known as **Stereá Elládha** – literally "Greek Continent", a name that reflects its nineteenth-century past as the only independent Greek mainland territory, along with Attica and the quasi-island of the Peloponnese. It corresponds to the ancient divisions of Boeotia and Phocis, the domains respectively of Thebes and Delphi. Most visitors head straight through these territories to Delphi but, if you have time, there are rewarding if minor detours in the monastery of **Óssios Loukás** – with the finest Byzantine frescoes in the country – and **Gla**, the largest and most obscure of the Mycenaean sites. For hikers there is also the opportunity of climbing **Mount Parnassós**, the Muses' mountain.

The central plains of **Thessaly** (Thessalía), beyond, formed the bed of an ancient inland sea – rich agricultural land that was ceded reluctantly to the modern nation by the Turks in 1878. The province's attractions lie on the periphery, chained in by the mountain ranges of Ólymbos (Olympus), Píndhos (Pindus), Óssa and Pílion (Pelion). There are a number of routes to choose from. East from the major city and port of Vólos extends the slender peninsula of **Mount Pílion**, whose luxuriant woods and beaches are easily combined with island-hopping to the Sporades. To the west, **Kalambáka** gives access to the Metéora (not to be missed) and across the dramatic **Katára Pass** over the Píndhos to Epirus. To the north, the horizon is dominated by **Mount Olympus** (covered in Chapter Five), home of the gods.

ACCOMMODATION PRICE CODES

Throughout the book we've used the following **price codes** to denote the cheapest available room in high season; all are prices for a double room, except for category ①, which represents per person rates. Out of season, rates can drop by up to fifty percent, especially if you are staying for three or more nights. Single rooms, where available, cost around seventy percent of the price of a double.

① 1400–2000dr	④ 8000–12,000dr
② 4000–6000dr	⑤ 12,000–16,000dr
③ 6000–8000dr	⑥ 16,000dr and upwards

For more accommodation details, see pp.39–42.

Looming across a narrow gulf from Stereá Elládha, and joined by a bridge at Khalkídha, is the island of **Évvia** (Euboea). Though this feels like an extension of the mainland (from where there are many ferry crossings), it is nonetheless a bona fide island and we have detailed its attractions in Chapter Three.

STEREÁ ELLÁDHA: THE ROADS TO DELPHI AND BEYOND

The inevitable focus of a visit to Stereá Elládha is **Delphi**, 150km northwest of Athens. Buses cover the route from the capital several times a day, or can be picked up at **Livadhiá**, the nearest rail terminus. However, if you're in no hurry, there are rewards in slowing your progress: taking the "old road" to Thebes (Thíva), or detouring from Livadhiá, to the Byzantine monastery of **Óssios Loukás**, or to Mycenaean **Gla**.

To the northeast of the Athens–Delphi road, traffic thunders along the **National Road 1** towards Lárissa and Thessaloníki, skirting the coast for much of the way, with the long island of Évvia only a few kilometres across the gulf. Along this route there are ferries over to Évvia at **Arkítsa, Áyios Konstandínos** (where you can also pick up ferries or hydrofoils to the Sporades) and **Glýfa**.

Moving on from Delphi, two routes head north into Thessaly – west to the Metéora, east to Pílion. Another road leads southwest to the Gulf of Corinth, offering an approach to – or from – the **Peloponnese**, via the ferry at Andírio–Río. A fourth, more remote route, leads to **Karpeníssi** and through the southern foothills of the Píndhos mountains.

The Old Road to Thebes (Thíva)

The ancient road from Athens to Delphi began at the Parthenon as the **Sacred Way to Eleusis**, and from there climbed into the hills towards Thebes. It is possible to follow this route, almost unchanged since Oedipus supposedly trod it, by taking the minor road into the hills at modern Elefsína (see p.136). Leaving the polluted and industrial port, things improve fast, as the road winds up and out into a landscape of pines and grey stony hills. There are two buses daily along this road to Thíva and connections from there on to Livadhiá and Delphi.

Pórto Yermenó, Aegosthena and Eleutherai

The first thing to tempt you off the Sacred Way is a look at the best preserved stretch of ancient walls in Greece – the fourth century BC fort of **Aegosthena** – above the mouth of a valley running between Mounts Kythairon and Pateras, and overlooking the Gulf of Kórinthos. Historically it is insignificant, being merely an outpost of Spartan ally Megara, but the ruins themselves are impressive, the two end towers rising up more than 12m above the walls. The seaward ramparts have mostly vanished; up on the acropolis, a church with frescoes survives from a medieval monastery which took root here.

But there is little to keep you at **Pórto Yermenó**, a little family resort at this extreme northeast corner of the Gulf. It has just one **hotel**, the *Egosthenion* (☎0263/41 226; ④) well above the shore, several rooms squeezed behind the waterfront, and four or five fish tavernas all in a row. The beaches are gravel and sand with pine- and olive-draped hills as a backdrop, and can get very crowded in summer. But for those with transport (there is no bus service covering the 23km from the Elefsína–Thíva road) and a penchant for old walls, the twenty-five-minute drive down to the beach is worth it.

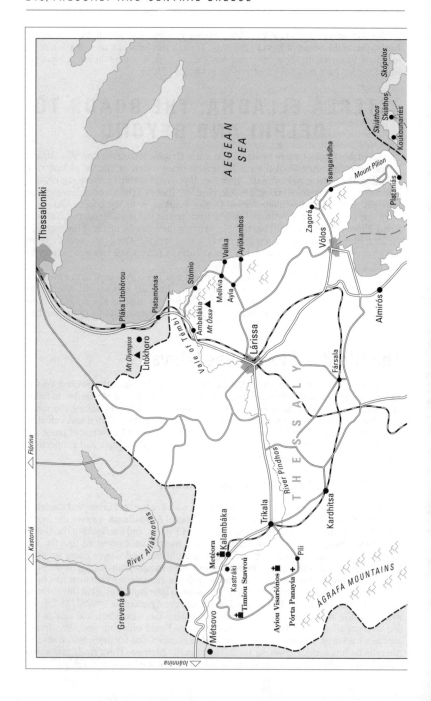

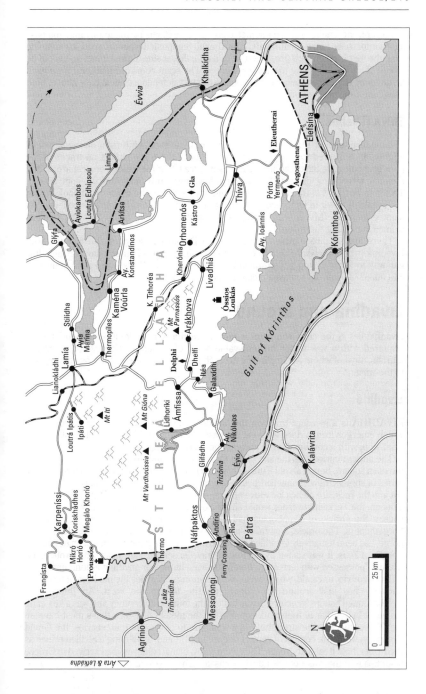

Back on the Thebes road, a kilometre north of the Pórto Yermenó turning, you pass another fortress, fourth-century BC **Eleutherai**. Signposted from the road, 400m to the east, the fort is again well preserved, with its northeast side almost intact and six of its circuit of towers surviving to varying degrees. The scant ruins of Eleutherai town itself lie down by the Aegosthena junction, while the fort defends a critical pass above; both sites have unlimited access.

Thíva (Thebes)

The modern town of **THÍVA** lies 20km north of Eleutherai, built right on the site of its mighty, ancient predecessor. For this very reason, there are almost no traces of the past: archeologists have had little success in excavating the crucial central areas, and the most interesting visit is to the excellent town **museum** (daily 9.30am–7pm; 500dr). This is to be found at the far (downhill) end of Pindhárou, the main street; look out for the Frankish tower in its forecourt. Among many fine exhibits is a unique collection of painted *larnakes* (Mycenaean sarcophagi) depicting, in bold expressionistic strokes, women lamenting their dead.

There are no direct **buses** from Thíva to Delphi but services run frequently to Livadhiá (where there are better connections) and a couple of times a day to Khalkídha, gateway to Évvia. If you get stranded between buses, the *Niobe* **hotel** at Epaminónda 63 (☎0262/27 949; ②) makes a pleasant enough stop.

Livadhiá and around

Livadhiá lies at the edge of a great **agricultural plain**, much of it reclaimed lakebed, scattered with a few minor but enjoyable sites. It's a part of Greece that sees few tourists, most of whom are in a hurry to reach the glories of the Parnassós country just to the west.

Livadhiá

LIVADHIÁ is a pleasant town on the banks of the Herkína, a river of ancient fame which emerges from a dark gorge at the base of a fortress. It's an attractive place for a brief stop, with a combination of ancient and medieval sights.

The ancient curiosity is the site of the **Oracle of Trophonios**, a ten-minute walk from the main square, beside an old Turkish bridge. Here the waters of the Herkína rise from a series of springs, now channelled beside the (signposted) *Xenia* café. Above the springs, cut into the rock, are niches for votive offerings – in one of which, on a large chamber with a bench, the Turkish governor would sit for a quiet smoke. In antiquity, all who sought to consult the Oracle of Trophonios had first to bathe in the Springs of Memory and Forgetfulness. The oracle, a circular structure which gave entrance to caves deep in the gorge, has been tentatively identified at the top of the hill, near the remains of an unfinished Temple of Zeus. It was visited by the Roman traveller-scholar Pausanias, who wrote that it left him "possessed with terror and hardly knowing himself or anything around him".

The **Froúrio**, or castle, which overlooks the springs, provides the medieval interest; its entrance lies just around the corner up the hill to the west. An impressive, well-bastioned square structure, it was built in the fourteenth century and was a key early conquest in the War of Independence. But it's the medieval history that's most interesting. The castle was the stronghold of a small group of Catalan mercenaries, the Grand Company, who took control of central Greece in 1311 and, appointing a Sicilian prince as their ruler, held it for sixty years. They were a tiny, brutal band who had arrived in Greece from Spain in the wake of the Fourth Crusade. They wrested control from the Franks, who were then established in Athens and Thebes, in a cunning deviation from traditional rules of engagement. As the Frankish nobility approached Livadhiá, the vastly outnumbered Catalans diverted the river to flood the surrounding fields. The Frankish cavalry advanced into the unexpected marsh and were cut down to a man.

Practicalities

The town today is a minor provincial capital with a trade in milling cotton from the area. Though completely off the tourist route, new landscaping along the springs is making it an even more enjoyable daytime pause before, or after, Delphi. Be warned that in season buses on towards Delphi often arrive and leave full, though two local ones start from Livadhiá around noon. Arriving by **bus**, you'll be dropped near the central square, **Platía Dhiákou**; the **train station** is a few kilometres out, but arrivals may be met by a shuttle bus (or more likely taxis) into town.

Staying overnight is highly problematic since the closure of several central hotels. If your budget doesn't run to the pricey *Livadhia* on Platía Kotsóni (☎0261/23 611; ⑥), or if you don't fancy the noisy *Philippos* (☎0261/24931; ⑤), you'd be well advised to press on towards Dhelfí. There are a few **eating** options. Several tavernas and psistariés are scattered about town, the most obvious being the trio clustered at the T-junction five minutes west of the main square.

Orkhomenos

Just 10km east of Livadhiá (10min; buses every hour) is the site of ancient **ORKHOMENOS**, inhabited from Neolithic to Classical times. As the capital of the Minyans, a native Thessalian dynasty, it was one of the wealthiest Mycenaean cities.

Near the middle of the rather drab modern village, along the road signposted Diónisos village, is the **Treasury of Minyas** (Tues–Sat 9am–3pm, Sun 10am–2pm), a stone *tholos* similar to the tomb of Atreus at Mycenae. The roof has collapsed but it is otherwise complete, and its inner chamber, hewn from the rock, has an intricately carved marble ceiling. Much closer to the road are the remains of a fourth-century BC **theatre**, and behind, on the rocky hilltop, a tiny fortified acropolis from the same period.

Across the road from the theatre is the ninth-century Byzantine **Church of the Dormition**, built entirely of blocks from the theatre and column drums from a classical temple – as is the minute Byzantine church in the main village square. The larger triple-apsed church has some fine reliefs including a sundial, with the remains of a monastery just to the south.

The Citadel of Gla

Continuing east, in a highly worthwhile diversion, it's a further twenty minutes by bus (2 buses daily, 2.30pm & 7.15pm) to the village of Kástro, right next to the National Road towards Lárissa. If you walk through the village, cross the highway and then walk south (towards Athens) for about 100m you come to an unsignposted road behind a Shell garage and tyre store. This leads after around 200m to the Mycenaean **Citadel of Gla**.

An enormous and extraordinary site, **GLA** (unrestricted entrance) stands within a three-kilometre circuit of Cyclopean walls – a far larger citadel than either Tiryns or Mycenae. Almost nothing, however, is known about the site, save that it was once an island in Lake Kopais (which was drained in the last century) and that it may have been an outpost of the Minyans. The **walls** and **city gates** still stand to five metres in places, and are almost three kilometres in length, despite having been damaged when the city fell. Inside, on the higher ground, what is thought to have been a huge Mycenaean **palace** has been revealed; it appears to include a *megaron* (throne room) and various storerooms, though archeologists are puzzled by differences from the standard Mycenaean palace form. Further down, and currently being excavated, is a vast walled area believed to have been the **marketplace**.

Almost anywhere you walk in this rarely visited site, you come across evocative traces of its former buildings. One **word of warning** about the site: there are said to be snakes among the ruins, so tread with care.

Chaironeia

Directly north of Livadhiá, on the main road to Lamía, is **Chaironeia**, once the home of the writer Plutarch, but more famous as the site of one of the most **decisive battles** of ancient Greece. Here, in 338 BC, Philip of Macedon won a resounding victory over an alliance of Athenians, Thebans and Peloponnesians put together by Demosthenes. This defeat marked the death of the old city-states, from whom control passed forever into foreign hands: first Macedonian, later Roman.

Set beside the road, at modern Herónia, is a remarkable six-metre-high **stone lion**, originally part of the funerary monument to the Thebans (or, some say, to the Macedonians) killed in the battle. Adjacent is a small museum of local finds, and there are remains of ancient **acropolis** fortifications, with a theatre at their base, above the village.

The Oedipus crossroads, Óssios Loukás and Arákhova

West from Livadhiá, the scenery becomes ever more dramatic as Mount Parnassós and its attendant peaks loom high above the road. At 24km, about halfway to Delphi, you reach the so-called **Schist** (split) or **Triodos** (triple way) **Crossroads** – also known as the **Oedipus crossroads** – junction of the ancient roads from Delphi, Daulis (today Dávlia), Thebes (Thíva) and Ambrossos (Dhístomo). The old road actually lay in the gorge, below the modern one.

Pausanias identified the crossroads as the site of Oedipus's murder of his father, King Laertes of Thebes, and his two attendants. According to the **myth**, Oedipus was returning on foot from Delphi while Laertes was speeding towards him from the opposite direction on a chariot. Neither would give way, and in the altercation that followed Oedipus killed the trio, ignorant of who they were. It was to be, as Pausanias put it mildly, "the beginning of his troubles". Continuing to Thebes, Oedipus solved the riddle of the Sphinx, which had been ravaging the area, and was given the hand of widowed Queen Jocasta in marriage – unaware that he was marrying his own mother.

Getting to Óssios Loukás: Dhístomo

If you have transport, you can turn left at the crossroads and follow the minor road to Dhístomo, and thence to the **Monastery of Óssios Loukás**. Travelling by bus, you may need to take a more roundabout route: first from Livadhiá, to Dhístomo, then another bus on from there towards Kyriakí – getting off at the fork to Óssios Loukás (leaving just a 2500m walk). Alternatively, it's possible to charter a taxi in **DHÍSTOMO**, which also has a couple of small hotels, on the town square facing the church: the *America* (☎0267/22 079; ④) and *Koutriaris* (☎0267/22 268; ③).

It is a drab place, with a tragic wartime history: the Germans shot over two hundred of the inhabitants on June 10, 1944, in reprisal for a guerrilla attack. The event is immortalized in a bleak grey and white memorial on a nearby hilltop – follow the signs to the "mausoleum".

Óssios Loukás Monastery

The **Monastery of Óssios Loukás** (daily: summer 8am–2pm & 4–7pm; winter 8am–6pm; 500dr) was a precursor of that last defiant flourish of **Byzantine art** that produced the great churches at Mystrá in the Peloponnese. It is modest in scale, but from an architectural or decorative point of view, ranks as one of the great buildings of medieval Greece. The setting, too, is exquisite – as beautiful as it is remote. Hidden by trees along the approach from Dhístomo, the monastery's shady terrace suddenly appears, and opens out on to a spectacular sweep of the Elikónas peaks and countryside.

The main structure comprises two domed churches, the larger **Katholikón** of Óssios Loukás and the attendant chapel of the **Theotókos**. They are joined by a common foundation wall but otherwise share few architectural features. Ten monks still live in the monastic buildings around the courtyard, but the monastery is essentially maintained as a museum, with a café (occasionally open) in the grounds. Skirts or long trousers – no shorts – must be worn.

The Katholikón

The **Katholikón**, built in the early eleventh century, is dedicated to a local beatified hermit, Saint Luke of Stiri (not the Evangelist). Its design formed the basis of Byzantine octagonal-style churches, and was later copied at Dhafní and at Mystra. Externally it is modest, with rough brick and stone walls surmounted by a well-proportioned dome. The inside, however, is startling. A conventional cross-in-square plan, its atmosphere switches from austere to exultant as the eye moves along walls lined in red and green marble to the gold-backed **mosaics** on the high ceiling. Light filtering through marble-encrusted windows reflects across the curved surfaces of the mosaics in the narthex and the nave and bounces onto the marble walls, bringing out the subtlety of their shades.

The original mosaics were damaged by an earthquake in 1659, and in the dome and elsewhere have been replaced by unremarkable frescoes. But other surviving examples testify to their effect. The mosaic of *The Washing of the Apostles' Feet* in the narthex is one of the finest; its theme is an especially human one, the expressions of the apostles ranging between diffidence and surprise. This dynamic and richly humanized approach is again illustrated by the *Baptism*, high up on one of the curved squinch arches that support the dome. Here the naked Jesus reaches for the cross amid a swirling mass of water, an illusion of depth created by the angle and curvature of the wall. The church's original **frescoes** are confined to the vaulted chambers at the corners of the cross plan and, though less imposing than the mosaics, employ subtle colours and shades, notably in *Christ Walking towards the Baptism*.

The Theotókos and Crypt

The church of the **Theotókos** (literally "God-Bearing", meaning the Virgin Mary) is a century older than the Katholikón. From the outside it overshadows the main church with its elaborate brick decoration culminating in a highly Eastern-influenced, marble-panelled drum. The interior seems gloomy and cramped by comparison, highlighted only by a couple of fine Corinthian capitals and an original floor mosaic, now dimmed by the passage of time.

Finally, do not miss the vivid frescoes in the **crypt** of the Katholikón, entered on the lower right-hand side of the building. It's a good idea to bring a torch, since the lighting is limited to preserve the colours of the frescoes.

Arákhova

Arriving at **ARÁKHOVA**, the last town east of Delphi (just 11km further on), you are properly in Parnassós country. The peaks stand tiered above, sullied somewhat by the wide asphalt road cut to a ski-resort – the winter-weekend haunt of BMW-driving Athenians. If you want to **ski**, it's possible to hire equipment on a daily basis at the resort and even to get an all-in day package from Athens (see p.58). The resort's main problem is high winds, which often lead to the closure of its ski lifts, so check the forecast before you set off.

Skiing aside, the town is a delight, despite being split in two by the Livadhiá–Delphi road. If you're not making for any other mountain areas, Arákhova is well worth an afternoon's pause before continuing to Delphi, and if you've got your own transport you might consider staying here as a base for visiting the site. Houses in Arákhova are predominantly traditional in style, twisting up narrow lanes into the hills and poised to the south on the edge of the olive-tree-choked Pleistós gorge. The area is renowned for its strong purply wines, honey, *flokátes* (shaggy rugs) and woollen weavings; all are much in evidence in the roadside shops, though some of the goods are nowadays imported from Albania and northern Greece. Also of note is the local **Festival of Áyios Yeóryios** (23 April, or the Tuesday after Easter if this date falls within Lent), which is centred on the church at the top of the hill, and is one of the best opportunities to catch genuine folk-dancing during almost two days of continuous partying.

For details of hiking on Parnassós from Arákhova, see p.261.

Practicalities

Five **buses** daily go to Athens and more to Delphi and Itéa, two of which go on to Náfpaktos; bus timetables are displayed in the window of the *Celena Cafeteria Bar* (see below).

In the summer most people just stop for a meal and to shop, so finding **accommodation** is easy. In winter, particularly at weekends, rooms are at a premium. At the cheaper end of the scale, there are two pleasant and modest **hotels**, side by side at the Livadhiá end of town: *Apollon Hotel* (☎0267/31 427; ③) and *Hotel Parnassos* (☎0267/31 307; ②). At the Delphi end of town, the *Pension Nostos* (☎0267/31 385; ③), *Xenia Hotel* (☎0267/31 230; ④) and the new *Apollon Inn* (☎0267/31 057; ③), an offshoot of the *Apollon Hotel*, are all worth a try.

There is also an excellent **taverna**, the *Karathanasi* (open evenings only), while the *Celena Cafeteria Bar*, also on the main street opposite the small square which doubles as a bus station, is open all day; its helpful Danish owner offers information on rooms and buses.

Delphi (Dhelfí)

With its site raised on the slopes of a high mountain terrace and dwarfed to either side by the great and ominous crags of Parnassós, it's easy to see why the ancients believed **DELPHI** to be the centre of the earth. But more than the natural setting or even the occasional earthquake and avalanche were needed to confirm a divine presence. This, according to Plutarch, was achieved through the discovery of a rock chasm that exuded strange vapours and reduced all comers to frenzied, incoherent and undoubtedly **prophetic** mutterings.

The Oracle: some history

The first **oracle** established on this spot was dedicated to **Gea** ("Mother Earth") and to **Poseidon** ("the Earth Shaker"). The serpent **Python**, son of Gea, was installed in a nearby cave, and communication made through the Pythian priestess. Python was subsequently slain by **Apollo**, whose cult had been imported from Crete (legend has it that he arrived in the form of a dolphin – hence the name *Delphoi*). The **Pythian Games** were established on an eight-year cycle to commemorate the feat, and perhaps also to placate the ancient deities.

The place was known to the **Mycenaeans**, whose votive offerings (tiny striped statues of goddesses and worshipping women) have been discovered near the site of Apollo's temple. Following the arrival of the **Dorians** in Greece at the beginning of the twelfth century BC, the sanctuary became the centre of the loose-knit association of Greek city-states known as the **Amphyctionic League**. The territory still belonged however, to the city of Krissa, which, as the oracle gained in popularity, began to extort heavy dues from the pilgrims arriving at the port of Kirrha. In the sixth century BC the League was called on to intervene, and the first of a series of **Sacred Wars** broke out. The League wrested Delphi from the Krissaeans and made it an autonomous state. From then on Delphi experienced a rapid ascent to fame and respect, becoming within a few decades one of the major sanctuaries of Greece, with its tried-and-tested oracle generally thought to be the arbiter of truth.

For over a thousand years thereafter, a steady stream of **pilgrims** worked their way up the dangerous mountain paths to seek divine direction in matters of war, worship, love or business. On arrival they would sacrifice a sheep or a goat and, depending on the omens, wait to submit questions inscribed on lead tablets. The Pythian priestess, a simple and devout village woman of fifty or more years, would chant her prophecies from a tripod positioned over the oracular chasm. Crucially, an attendant priest would then "interpret" her utterings and relay them to the enquirer in hexameter verse.

Many of the **oracular answers** were equivocal: Croesus, for example, was told that if he embarked on war against neighbouring Cyrus he would destroy a mighty empire – he did, and destroyed his own. But it's hard to imagine that the oracle would have retained its popularity and influence for so long without offering predominantly sound advice. Indeed, Strabo wrote that "of all oracles in the world, it had the reputation of being the most truthful". One explanation is that the Delphic priests were simply better informed than any other corporate body around at the time. Positioned at the centre of the Amphyctionic League, which became a kind of "United Nations" of the Greek city-states, they were in a position to amass a wealth of political, economic and social information – and from the seventh century BC on, Delphi had its own network of informants throughout the Greek world.

The **influence** of the oracle spread abroad with the age of classical colonization and its patronage grew, reaching a peak in the sixth century BC, with powerful benefactors such as Amasis, King of Egypt, and the unfortunate King Croesus of Lydia; many of the Greek city-states also dedicated treasuries at this time. Privileged position and enormous wealth, however, made Delphi vulnerable to Greek rivalries: the first Sacred Wars left it autonomous, but in the fifth century BC the oracle began to be too closely identified with individual states. Worse, it maintained a defeatist, almost treacherous attitude towards the Persian invasions – only partially mitigated when a Persian force, sent by Xerxes to raid Delphi, was crushed at the entrance to the Sanctuary by a well-timed earthquake.

It never quite regained the same level of trust – and consequently of power – after these instances of bias and corruption. However, real **decline** did not set in until the fourth century BC, with the resumption of the Sacred Wars and the emergence of Macedonian control. Following prolonged squabbling among the Greek city-states, the Sanctuary was seized by the Phocians in 356 BC, leading to Philip of Macedon's intervention to restore the Amphyctionic League to power. Seven years later, when the League again invited Philip to settle a dispute, this time provoked by the Amphissans, he responded by invading southern Greece. The independence of the city-states was brought to an end at the Battle of Chaironeia (see p.252), and Delphi's political intriguing was effectively over.

Under **Macedonian** and later **Roman** control, the oracle's role became increasingly domestic and insignificant, dispensing advice on marriages, loans, voyages and the like. The Romans thought little of its utterances and of its treasure: Sulla plundered the sanctuary in 86 BC and Nero, outraged when the oracle pronounced judgement on the murder of his mother, carted away some five hundred bronze statues. Finally, with the demise of paganism under Constantine and Theodosius in the fourth century AD, the oracle became defunct.

In modern times, the sanctuary site was rediscovered towards the end of the seventeenth century and explored, haphazardly, from the 1840s onwards. Real **excavation** of the site came only in 1892 when the French School of Archeology leased the land, in exchange for a French government agreement to buy the Greek currant crop. There was little to be seen other than the outline of a stadium and theatre, but the villagers who lived there were persuaded (with the help of an army detachment) to move to a new town 1km west, and digging commenced. Over the next decade or so most of the excavations and reconstruction visible today were completed.

The most interesting development in Delphi's recent history came through the efforts of the poet Angelos Sikelianos and his wife Eva Palmer to set up a "University of the World" in the 1920s. The project eventually failed, though it inspired an annual **Delphic Festival**, held now in June of each year, with performances of classical drama in the ancient theatre.

The Sites

Split by the road from Arákhova, the ancient site divides essentially into three parts: the **Sacred Precinct**, the **Marmaria** and the **Castalian spring**. In addition there is a worthwhile, though poorly presented, **museum**, which is currently undergoing a much needed expansion to double its size. All in all it's a large and complex ruin, best taken in two stages, with the sanctuary ideally at the beginning or end of the day, or at lunchtime, to escape the crowds.

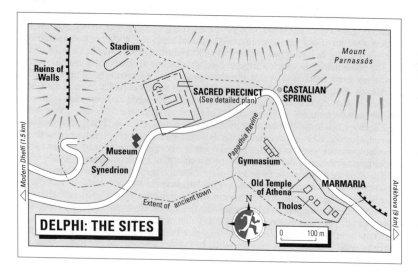

DELPHI: THE SITES

Make sure you have sturdy footwear as there's a lot of clambering up rough stone steps and paths, and take food and drink if you're planning a full day's visit; good picnicking spots are the amphitheatre with its seats and panorama of the sanctuary, or try the stadium for fewer interruptions.

The Sacred Precinct

The **Sacred Precinct** (Mon–Fri 8am–7pm, Sat & Sun 8.30am–3pm; 1200dr), or Temenos (Sanctuary) of Apollo, is entered, as in ancient times, by way of a small **Agora** enclosed by ruins of Roman porticoes and shops for the sale of votive offerings. The paved **Sacred Way** begins after a few stairs and zigzags uphill between the foundations of memorials and treasuries to the Temple of Apollo. Along each edge is a litter of statue bases where gold, bronze and painted marble figures once stood; Pliny counted more than three thousand on his visit, and that was after Nero's infamous raid.

The choice and position of these **memorials** were dictated by more than religious zeal; many were used as a deliberate show of strength or often as a direct insult against a rival Greek state. For instance, the **Offering of the Arcadians** on the right of the entrance (a line of bases that supported nine bronzes) was erected to commemorate their invasion of Laconia in 369 BC, and pointedly placed in front of the Lacedaemonians' own monument. Beside this, and following the same logic, the Spartans celebrated their victory over Athens by erecting their **Monument of the Admirals** – a large recessed structure, which once held 37 bronze statues of gods and generals – directly opposite the Athenians' **Offering of Marathon**.

Further up the path, past the Doric remains of the **Sikyonian Treasury** on the left, stretch the expansive foundations of the **Siphnian Treasury**, a grandiose Ionic temple erected in 525 BC. Siphnos had rich gold mines and intended the building to be an unrivalled show of opulence. Fragments of the caryatids that supported its west entrance, and the fine Parian marble frieze that covered all four sides, are now in the museum. Above this is the **Treasury of the Athenians**, built, like the city's "Offering", after Marathon (490 BC). It was reconstructed in 1904–6 by matching the inscriptions that completely cover its blocks. These include honorific decrees in favour of Athens, lists of Athenian ambassadors to the Pythian Festival, and a hymn to Apollo with its musical notation in Greek letters above the text.

Next to it are the foundations of the **Bouleuterion**, or council house, a reminder that Delphi needed administrators, and above is the remarkable **Polygonal Wall** whose irregular interlocking blocks have withstood, intact, all earthquakes. It, too, is covered with inscriptions, but these almost universally refer to the emancipation of slaves; Delphi was one of the few places where such freedom could be made official and public by an inscribed register. An incongruous outcrop of rock between the wall and the Treasuries marks the original **Sanctuary of Gea**. It was here, or more precisely on the recently built-up rock, that the Sibyl, an early itinerant priestess, was reputed to have uttered her prophecies.

Finally, the Sacred Way leads to the Temple Terrace and you are confronted with a large altar, erected by the island of Chíos. Of the main body of the **Temple of Apollo**, only the foundations stood when it was uncovered by the French. Six Doric columns have since been re-erected, giving a vertical line to the ruins and providing some idea of the temple's former dominance over the whole of the sanctuary. In the innermost part of the temple was the *adyton*, a dark cell at the mouth of the oracular chasm where the Pythian priestess would officiate. No sign of cave or chasm has been found, nor any vapours that might have induced a trance, but it is likely that such a chasm did exist and was simply opened and closed by successive earthquakes. On the architrave of the temple – probably on the interior – were inscribed the maxims "Know Thyself" and "Nothing in Excess".

The theatre and stadium used for the main events of the Pythian Festival are on terraces above the temple. The **theatre**, built in the fourth century BC with a capacity of

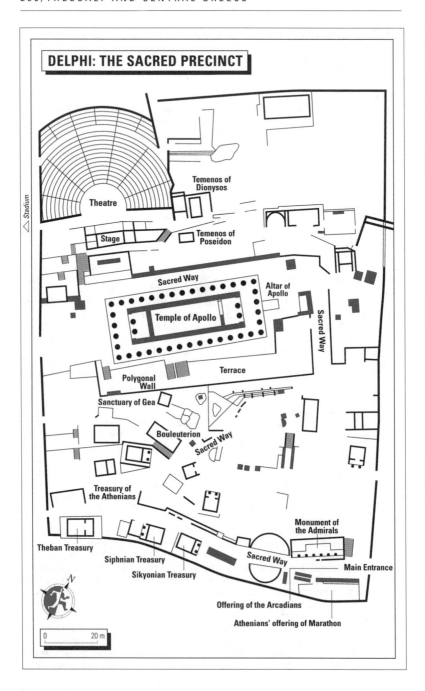

DELPHI: THE SACRED PRECINCT

△ Stadium

Theatre

Temenos of Dionysos

Stage

Temenos of Poseidon

Sacred Way

Altar of Apollo

Temple of Apollo

Sacred Way

Terrace

Polygonal Wall

Sanctuary of Gea

Bouleuterion

Sacred Way

Treasury of the Athenians

Monument of the Admirals

Theban Treasury

Main Entrance

Siphnian Treasury

Sacred Way

Sikyonian Treasury

N

Offering of the Arcadians

Athenians' offering of Marathon

0   20 m

five thousand, was closely connected with Dionysos, the god of ecstasy, the arts and wine, who reigned in Delphi over the winter months when the oracle was silent. A path leads up through cool pine groves to the **stadium**, a steep walk which discourages many of the tour groups. Its site was artificially levelled in the fifth century BC, though it was banked with stone seats (giving a capacity of seven thousand) only in Roman times – the gift, like so many other public buildings in Greece, of Herodes Atticus. For even greater solitude, climb up above to the pine trees that have engulfed the remains of the fourth-century BC walls.

The Museum

Delphi's **museum** (Mon noon–6.45pm, Tues–Fri 8am–6.45pm, Sat & Sun 8.30am–2.45pm; 1200dr) contains a rare and exquisite collection of archaic sculpture, matched only by finds on the Acropolis. It features pottery, figures and friezes from the various treasuries, which, grouped together, give a good picture of the sanctuary's riches.

The most famous exhibit, placed at the far end of the central corridor, is the **Charioteer**, one of the few surviving bronzes of the fifth century BC. It was unearthed in 1896 along with other scant remains of the "Offering of Polyzalos", which probably toppled during the earthquake of 373 BC. The charioteer's eyes, made of onyx and set slightly askew, lend it a startling realism, while the demure expression sets the scene as a lap of honour. It is thought that the odd proportions of the body were designed by the sculptor (possibly Pythagoras of Samos) with perspective in mind; they would be "corrected" when the figure was viewed, as intended, from below.

Other major pieces include two huge **Kouroi** (archaic male figures) from the sixth century BC in the second room at the top of the stairs. To the right of this room, in the "Hall of the Siphnian Treasury", are large chunks of the beautiful and meticulously carved **Syphnian frieze**; they depict Zeus and other gods looking on as the Homeric heroes fight over the body of Patroclus, and the gods battling with the giants. In the same room is an elegant Ionic sculpture of the winged **Sphynx of the Naxians**, dating from around 560 BC. Back along the main corridor is the **Athenian Treasury**, represented by fragments of the metopes, which depict the labours of Herakles, the adventures of Theseus and a battle with Amazons. Further on and to the right, the **Hall of the Monument of Daochos** is dominated by a group of three colossal dancing women, carved from Pentelic marble around an acanthus column. The figures, celebrating Dionysus, probably formed the stand for a tripod.

The Castalian spring

Following the road east of the sanctuary, towards Arákhova, you reach a sharp bend. To the left, marked by niches for votive offerings and by the remains of an archaic fountain house, the celebrated **Castalian spring** (partially fenced in; free admission) still flows from a cleft in the Phaedriades cliffs.

Visitors to Delphi (only men were allowed in the early centuries) were obliged to purify themselves in its waters, usually by washing their hair, though murderers had to take the full plunge. **Byron**, impressed by the legend that it succoured poetic inspiration, jumped in. This is no longer possible, since the spring is fenced off. Sadder still, the Phaedriades cliffs, which tower above the spring, are threatened with collapse due to the impact of traffic vibration, and so are swathed in scaffolding.

The Marmaria

Across and below the road from the spring is the **Marmaria** (Mon–Fri 8am–7pm, Sat & Sun 8.30am–3pm; free), or Sanctuary of Athena, whom the Delphians worshipped as Athena Pronoia ("Guardian of the Temple"). The name Marmaria means "marble quarry" and derives from the medieval practice of filching the ancient blocks for private use.

The most conspicuous building in the precinct, and the first visible from the road, is the **Tholos**, a fourth-century BC rotunda. Three of its dome-columns and their entablature have been set up, but while these amply demonstrate the original beauty of the building (which is *the* postcard image of Delphi), its purpose remains a mystery.

At the entrance to the sanctuary stood the **Old Temple of Athena**, destroyed by the Persians and rebuilt in the Doric order in the fourth century BC; foundations of both can be traced. Outside the precinct on the northwest side (above the Marmaria) is a **Gymnasium**, again built in the fourth century BC, but later enlarged by the Romans who added a running track on the now collapsed terrace; prominent among the ruins is a circular plunge bath which, filled with cold water, served to refresh the athletes after their exertions.

Practicalities: Modern Dhelfí

Modern Dhelfí is as inconsequential as its ancient namesake, 1500m to the east, is impressive. Entirely geared to tourism, its attraction lies in its mountain setting, proximity to the ruins, and access to Mount Parnassós (see the following section).

There is a single **bus terminal**, located at the Itéa (west) end of town. Westbound buses go to Ámfissa (whence you can pick up connections north), Itéa and (usually with a change) Náfpaktos, while eastbound services go only to Livadhiá or Athens. The main difficulty, since all coaches originate elsewhere, is that seats allocated for the Dhelfí ticket booth are limited and they sell out some hours in advance. If you're going to be stuck standing all the way to Athens, it's better to get off at Livadhiá and continue by train – there are four morning departures and five later departures. Bus timetables are available from the helpful **tourist office** (Mon–Fri 7.30am–2.30pm; ☎0265/82 900) in the spiffy new Town Hall, done up in modern Neoclassical style. Other amenities include **banks**, a **post office** and an **OTE**, all along the main street.

Accommodation

Accommodation is plentiful: like most Greek site villages, Dhelfí has a quick turn-around of visitors and, with close on twenty hotels and pensions, finding a place to stay should present few problems. There are three **campsites** in the area: the closest is *Camping Apollon* (☎0265/82 762; open all year), alongside the road to Ámfissa/Itéa and less than 1km west of Dhelfí. *Camping Delphi* (☎0265/82 475; open all year) is 3km further along the same road, just after Chrysso, and *Camping Chrissa* (☎0265/82 050; April–Oct) is another 3km on, along the same road.

Athena, Vassiléos Pávlou 55 (☎0265/82 239). Near the bus station at the Itéa (west) end of town, this rather tatty hotel has views of the gulf from back rooms. ③.

Hermes, Vassiléos Pávlou keh Frederíkis 27 (☎0265/82 318). Relatively new and quiet, with wondeful views. ⑤.

Loula Sotiríou, Apollonos 84 (☎0265/82 349). Attractive, inexpensive *dhomátia* rooms. ③.

Odysseus, Isaía 1 (☎0265/82 235). On a street below and parallel to the main street, this quiet pension has a flowered terrace and fine views. ③.

Olympic Hotel, Vassiléos Pávlou keh Frederíkis 57 (☎0265/82 793). Tasteful, pricey hotel with the same owner as the cheaper *Hermes*. Value for money though, and the price includes breakfast. ⑥.

Pan, Vassiléos Pávlou keh Frederíkis 53 (☎0265/82 294). The same owner (currently the mayor) as the *Pythia*. Adequate and comfortable with fine views of the gulf. ④.

Panorama, Óssio Louká 47 (☎0265/82 061). This peaceful hotel with lovely views is situated above most of the shops, in a residential area. Price includes breakfast. ⑤.

Pythia, Vassiléos Pávlou 68 (☎0265/82 328). Close to the site and museum. ④.

Varonos, Vassiléos Pávlou keh Frederíkis 27 (☎0265/82 345). Welcoming hotel, with private facilities in all rooms. Copious breakfasts are extra. ④

Eating and drinking

Meals are best at the incredibly cheap *Taverna Vakhos*, next to the church, and at the nearby *Lefkaria*, Dhelfí's only typical taverna, which is dearer, but no less popular; both have views down to the gulf from their terraces. Nearer to the museum and site is the *Apollonio Restaurant*, which is ideal for a quick lunch or snack. Back in town, try the *souvláki*, next to the *Hotel Pan* and, beyond it, *Gargantua*, for cheap, good meals with a view, at the westernmost end.

Mount Parnassós

For a taste of the Greek alpine scene, **Parnassós** is probably the most convenient peak in the land, though it is no longer a wilderness, having been disfigured by the ski-station above Arákhova and its accompanying paraphernalia of lifts, snack bars and access roads. The best routes for walkers are those up from Dhelfí to the **Corycian Cave** (practicable from April to November), or to the **Liákoura summit ascent** (May to September only). Those with their own transport can take advantage of metalled **roads** up the mountain from Arákhova and Graviá or the jeep track from Amfíklia; these could easily be combined with a walk.

Dhelfí to the Corycian Cave

To reach the **trailhead** for this walk – and the initial path up the mountain – take the right-hand (approaching from Athens), uphill road through Dhelfí village. At the top of the slope turn right onto a road that doubles back to the **museum-house** (9am–3pm; closed Tues; 200dr) where the poet **Angelos Sikelianos** – he of the revived ancient festival (see p.256) – once lived. There is a bust of him outside.

Continue climbing from here, on a gravel surface, and you reach the highest point of the fence enclosing the sanctuary ruins. Where it ends at a locked gate, adopt a trail on your left, initially marked by a black and yellow rectangle on a white background. From the top of the hill the trail continues, well marked by black-on-yellow metal diamonds: it's part of the E4 European long-distance trail. Initially steep, the way soon flattens out on a grassy knoll overlooking the stadium, and continues along a ridge next to a line of burned cypresses.

Soon after, you join up with an ancient cobbled trail coming from inside the fenced precinct, the **Kakí Skála**, which zigzags up the slope above you in broad reaches. The view from here is fantastic, stretching back over the Gulf of Kórinthos to the mountains of the Peloponnese. The cobbles come to an end by a large concrete inspection cover in the Dhelfí water supply, an hour above the village, at the top of the Phaedriades cliffs. Nearby stand a pair of rock pinnacles, from one of which those guilty of sacrilege in ancient times were thrown to their deaths – a custom perhaps giving rise to the name *Kakí Skála* or "Evil Stairway".

E4 markers remain visible in the valley which opens out ahead of you. You can get simultaneous views south, and northeast towards the Parnassan summits, by detouring a little to the right to a wooden hut and a barn, then to a slight rise perhaps 150m further. The principal route becomes a gravel track bearing northeast; beyond, you take the right fork near a spring and watering troughs, with some shepherds' huts scattered under the trees. The track passes a picnic ground and a chapel within the next fifteen minutes, and acquires intermittent paved surface before skirting a sheepfold and another hut on the left. Some two hours above Dhelfí, you emerge from the fir woods with a view ahead to the rounded mass of the Yerondóvrakhos peak (2367m) of the Parnassós massif.

Another fifteen minutes brings you to a spring, followed by another chapel and lean-to on the left, with a patch of grass that does for camping. Just beyond is a muddy tarn backed by a low ridge. To the left rises a much steeper ridge, on whose flank lies the ancient

Corycian cave. Scramble up the slope, meeting a dirt road about three-quarters of the way up; turn left and follow it to the end, about 10m below the conspicuous cave mouth.

This was sacred to Pan and the nymphs in ancient times, the presiding deities of Delphi during the winter months when Apollo was said to desert the oracle. Orgiastic rites were celebrated in November at the cave by women acting as the nymphs, who made the long hike up from Delphi on the Kakí Skála by torchlight. The cavern itself is chilly and forbidding, but if you look carefully with a torch you can find ancient inscriptions near the entrance; without artificial light you can't see more than a hundred metres inside. By the entrance you'll notice a rock with a man-made circular indentation – possibly an ancient altar to hold libations.

Descending to Dhelfí takes rather less than the roughly three-hour ascent. The marked E4 route, on the other hand, continues almost due north over a mixture of trails and tracks to the village of **Eptálofos**, on the Arákhova–Graviá paved road, where simple **rooms** and meals are available.

The Liákoura summit

Liákoura is Parnassós's highest and finest peak (2457m) and can be approached either from the Dhelfí side or from around the mountain to the north. The latter is the best walk, starting **from Áno Tithoréa**, but it involves taking a bus or train and then local taxi to the trailhead – plus camping out on the mountain. If you want a more casual look at Parnassós, it's probably better to walk up **from the Delphi side**. This is very enjoyable as far as the EOS (Hellenic Alpine Club) refuge – about six hours' walk – and you could either turn back here or a couple of hours lower down on the Livádhi plateau if you don't fancy a night on the mountain and the final, rather dull, four hours' slog up to Liákoura.

For the energetic, it's possible to traverse the whole massif in around fifteen hours' walking, starting from Dhelfí and descending at Áno Tithoréa, or vice versa.

Áno Tithoréa to Liákoura via the Velítsa Ravine

This last surviving wilderness route up Parnassós to Liákoura involves starting with a trip by train or bus as far as Káto Tithoréa, which is on the Livadhià–Amfíklia road and the Athens–Thessaloníki railway. You then need to get to the higher, twin village of **Áno Tithoréa**, a four-kilometre haul easiest accomplished by taxi (usually available, but bargain for the price beforehand). You should allow at least six hours for the ascent, and around four and a half hours for the descent, so it's best to arrive early in the day; come equipped for camping out on the mountain as lodging can be difficult to find.

From the platía in Áno Tithoréa, head southwest out of town until you reach some park benches overlooking the giant **Velítsa Ravine**. Adjacent is a "waterfall" (in reality a leak in an aqueduct) which crosses the path beginning here a few minutes above the benches. A hundred metres further, bear left away from what seems to be the main track and descend towards the bed of the canyon. Once you're on the far side you can see the aqueduct again, now uncovered. Follow it until you reach the isolated chapel of Áyios Ioánnis (1hr from Áno Tithoréa).

Past the chapel, a fine alpine path heads off through the firs before you. The way is obvious for the next ninety minutes, with tremendous views of the crags filing up to the Liákoura summit, on your right across the valley. You emerge on a narrow neck of land, with a brief glimpse over the Ayía Marína valley and its namesake monastery to the east (left). The path, faint for an interval, heads slightly downhill and to the right to meet the floor of the Velítsa at the Tsáres spring (3hr 30min) – it's the last reliable water supply, so best fill up.

On the far bank of the river, head up a steep, scree-laden slope through the last of the trees to some sheep pens (4hr), then climb up to another pastoral hut (4hr 30min) at the base of the defile leading down from the main summit ridge. Beyond this point the going is gentler for much of the final ascent to the northwest (top right-hand) corner of this valley. A brief scramble up a rockfall to a gap in the ridge and you are at the base of Liákoura (5hr 30min). Orange paint-splashes – primarily oriented for those descending – stake out most of the approach from the Tsáres spring.

The **final ascent** is an easy twenty-minute scramble more or less up to the ridge line. On a clear morning, especially after rain, you're supposed to be able to see Mount Olympus in the north, the Aegean to the east, the Ionian to the west and way down into the Peloponnese to the south. The best viewing is said to be in midsummer, but all too often you can see only cloud.

Down to the gulf: Delphi to Náfpaktos

The train-less, almost beach-less north shore of the **Gulf of Kórinthos** is far less frequented than the south coast. The arid landscape, with harsh mountains inland, can be initially off-putting, but there are attractive, low-key resorts in **Galaxídhi** and **Náfpaktos** – both reasonably well connected by bus, and offering connections on south to the Peloponnese, via the ferries at Áyios Nikólaos–Éyio or Andírio–Río. From both Éyio and Río, you can reach Pátra by rail or road. Alternatively, heading in the opposite direction, it is easy to reach Dhiakoftó and the Kalávryta rack-and-pinion railway (see p.241).

All buses heading southwest of Delphi towards the Gulf of Kórinthos stop first at Itéa, a gritty little town (literally, owing to the bauxite-ore dust everywhere) where you may have to change buses for the next leg of the journey. (For the continuation of the route west from Andírio to Messolóngi and Agrínio, see p.331.)

Galaxídhi

GALAXÍDHI, 17km southwest of Itéa, is a quiet port, rearing mirage-like out of an otherwise lifeless shore. The old town stands on a raised headland, crowned by the photogenic church of Áyios Nikólaos, patron saint of sailors. Two and three masted kaïkia and schooners were built alongside the old harbour to the north of the headland until the beginning of this century. Still standing is the superb waterfront of nineteenth-century shipowners' houses. These have lately become the haunt of Athenian second-homers. Despite the restorations and a bit of a marina ethos down at the "new" southern harbour, the town still remains just the right side of tweeness, with an animated market high street and a variety of watering-holes. Above the new harbour, a small **archeological and maritime museum** (Sat–Tues 9.30am–1pm, Wed–Fri 9.30am–2pm; free) contains paintings and models of ships as well as old figureheads, while a modest **folk art museum** (9.30am–1.30pm, closed Tues; 500dr) near the main square has three rooms of turn-of-the-century embroideries and fashions.

There is no real beach – something that's no doubt acted as a healthy brake on development – but if you stroll around the pine-covered headland to the north, you'll find some pebbly **coves**, with chapel-crowned islets offshore. Another good walk is to the thirteenth-century **Moní Metamórfosis**, an archetypal rural monastery looking out over the bay towards Parnassós. It's an hour on foot to the west, through terraced fields and olive and almond groves; take the track under the flyover at the western edge of the village and look out for a footpath to the right after about twenty minutes.

Practicalities

Accommodation is on the pricey side and hard to find in summer. The cheapest place, also very clean and quiet, is the *Hotel Koukonas* (☎0265/41 179; ④) inland from the end of the old harbour. A bit more expensive are the *Rooms Scorpios* (☎0265/41 198; ④), over the supermarket next to the post office, and near the bus station. More charming options are the *Hotel Galaxidi* (☎0265/41 850; ④), opposite the *Koukonas*, the *Hotel Galaxa* (☎0265/41 620; ⑤), beyond the new harbour (ask for a front room; price includes breakfast), and the delightful Italian-run *Ganimede Hotel* (☎0265/41 328; ⑤), in an old sea captain's house off the market street, with antiques, a beautiful garden and homemade jams at breakfast.

For budget **eating**, far and away the best meals are to be had at the *Albatross* taverna, inland on the road near Áyios Nikólaos, while *To Porto*, at the end of the old harbour, is wonderful for fish. Serving a wider variety of seafood in a more glamorous ambience is the *Omilos*, if you're feeling flush, while for dessert, the sweets prepared by the Arab pastrycook at *To Konaki*, on the market street, are hard to resist.

The Áyios Nikólaos–Éyio ferry

West of Galaxídhi is some of the sparsest scenery of the Greek shoreline; there are few villages with scrappy beaches, none which really warrants a stop. At **Áyios Nikólaos** however, there's a year-round **ferry** across the gulf to the Peloponnese – an alternative to the crossing at Andírio–Río, 60km further west (see opposite). Boats leave Áyios Nikólaos for Éyio for the forty-minute journey (9 times daily, 6.30am–10pm; 550 dr, 3153dr for a car; ☎0266/31 854).

If you miss the last sailing, **accommodation** possibilities include the nearby rooms grandiosely called *Hotel San Nikolas* (☎0266/31 176; ②) with a taverna, and Theodore Katharakis's rooms (☎0266/31 177; ③) by the café. On a bluff, high above the coastal road and bay, is the well-maintained campsite, the *Doric Village* (☎0266/31 195), which also has bungalows (④).

If you really want to get off the beaten track, make the detour to **Khánia** on the coast about half way between Áyios Nikólaos and Náfpaktos, and take a little boat (200dr per person) across the narrow channel to the green island of **Trizónia**, a favourite shelter/stopover with yachtsmen. The *Hotel Drymna* (☎0266/71204; ④) offers comfortable, peaceful rooms and *Lizzie's Yacht Club* (restaurant) is the best place to eat.

Náfpaktos

The one place that stands out to the west of Galaxídhi is **NÁFPAKTOS**, a lively resort sprawling along the seafront below a rambling Venetian castle. Two hours by bus from Dhelfí, and an hour by bus and ferry from Pátra, it makes a convenient stopover, though diversion of the very heavy traffic through town would enhance its charm.

The **Kástro** provides a picturesque backdrop to the town, an enjoyable stroll to the top of its fortifications. The walls run down to the sea, enclosing the old harbour and the **beach**, which are entered through one of the original gates. The castle was long a formidable part of the Venetian defences, and the **Battle of Lepanto** was fought offshore from here in 1571. Under the command of John of Austria, an allied Christian armada devastated an Ottoman fleet – the first European naval victory over the Turks since the death of the dreaded pirate-admiral Barbarossa; Cervantes, author of *Don Quixote*, lost his left arm to a cannonball in the conflict.

Practicalities

Buses run northwest to Agrínio (where you can pick up services to Ioánnina or Lefkádha), and east to Itéa and Ámfissa (for connections north into Thessaly). Local city buses go to the ferry at Andírio, or you can sometimes get a seat on a long-distance bus heading to Pátra.

Despite the dozen or so hotels and assorted rooms places, **accommodation** can be in short supply in summer. The shabby *Hotel Amaryllis* (☎0634/27 237; ③), on Platía

Liménos, is tolerable if you have a back room looking onto the castle walls; in the same price range, *Hotel Aegli* (☎0634/27 271; ③), at Ilárkhou Tzavéla 75, is central and noisy. For a more tranquil setting, there's a cluster of comfortable hotels on the beach: the *Nafpaktos* (☎0634/29 551; ⑥) is a modern place which promises an "American-style" breakfast, the *Akti* (☎0634/28 464; ④) across the street is less pretentious, while the spanking clean *Hotel Afroditi* (☎0634/2992; ④) is closer to the shore. There's a good **campsite**, *Platanitis Beach* (☎0634/31 555; mid-May–Sept), 5km west of the town towards Andírio; to get there, catch a blue city bus from the main square – the last one leaves at 10pm.

There are a number of well shaded **restaurants** along the waterfront and, around the old port, several new and lively cafés; on the outskirts of town to the west there are a few other tavernas along a stretch of beach.

The Andírio–Río Ferry

The ferry at **Andírio** runs across the Gulf of Kórinthos to Río (see p.240) every fifteen minutes from 6.45am until 10.45pm, and less frequently during the night. The trip takes just fifteen minutes, and fares are 110dr per passenger, 1300dr per car and driver. Once across, you can generally pick up a city bus immediately for Pátra, but as through bus services between the Dhelfí area and Pátra have improved in recent years, it might be worth hanging on for one. In summer, drivers should count on waiting for around thirty minutes for the ferry. There's a moderately priced restaurant and the *Hotel Andirrion* (☎0634/31 450; ④), or the *Dounis Beach* campsite (☎0634/31 565; May–Oct) on the Náfpaktos/Andírio road, 1km from the ferry.

North to Lamía

Lamía is a half-day's journey north from Dhelfí, with a connection at Ámfissa: a slow but pleasant route skirting mounts Parnassós, Gióna and (to the northwest) Íti. At the historic pass of **Thermopylae**, the road joins the **coastal highway** from Athens.

Inland via Ámfissa

The inland road west from Dhelfí climbs slowly through a sea of olive groves to **ÁMFISSA**, a small town in the foothills of Mount Gióna. Like Livadhiá, this strategic military location was a base for the Catalan Grand Company, who have left their mark on the **castle**. If you have time to kill between buses, its ruins, which include remnants of an ancient acropolis, make for a pleasant walk, if only to enjoy the shade of the pine trees and examine a few stretches of classical polygonal masonry. The **market** quarter of the town is also good for a stroll. Ámfissa was once one of the major bell-making centres in the Balkans, and copper-alloy sheep bells are still produced and sold here. The local green olives are also acclaimed.

Serious **walkers** may want to use Ámfissa as a jumping-off point for the mountains west and north towards Karpeníssi: **Gióna**, **Vardhoússia** and **Oxía**. There are routes through from Ámfissa (and from Lidhoríki, west of Ámfissa) **to Karpeníssi**. Most travellers, however, continue north on the dramatic **Lamía road**, dividing Mounts Parnassós and Gióna, or along the **rail line** from Livadhiá to Lamía. This is one of the most dramatic stretches of railway in Europe, and has a history to match: it runs through the foothills of Mount Íti and over the precipitous defile of the **Gorgopótamos River**, where in 1942 the Greek Resistance – all factions united for the first and last time, under the command of the British intelligence officer C.M.Woodhouse – blew up a railway viaduct, cutting one of the Germans' vital supply lines to their army in North Africa.

The coastal highway

The first 60km of the **Athens–Lamía** coastal highway are fast, efficient and generally dull. But as some patches beyond are being modernized slowly, drivers should proceed with caution. Generally fairly flat, it runs a little inland, skirting various pockets of artificial lake, like Límni Ilíki, north of Thíva, before reaching the coast. The most interesting stop, along with Thíva (see p.250) is the Mycenaean citadel of **Gla** (see p.251), near the village of Kástro.

There are various links with the island of **Évvia**: first at Khalkídha, where there's a causeway; then by ferry at **Arkítsa** to Loutrá Edhipsoú (every hour in season, every 2hr out of season, last at 9pm; 50min; passengers 500dr, cars 1800dr). Arkítsa itself is a rather upmarket resort, popular mainly with Greeks.

Áyios Konstandínos and Kaména Voúrla

Áyios Kostandínos is the closest port to Athens if you're heading for the islands of the Sporades. There are daily car **ferries**, usually just after midday, to Skiáthos and Skópelos, with an additional evening departure in season which sometimes continues to Alónissos. In summer there are also at least three daily Flying Dolphin **hydrofoils** (passengers only) to Skiáthos, Skópelos and Alónissos; these are about twice as fast and twice as expensive as the ferry. For ferry information contact Alkyon Travel (☎0235/31 920); for hydrofoil information call the Ceres-Flying Dolphin Office (☎0235/ 318 71), next to each other on the main square.

There should be no reason to stay in Áyios Konstandínos, but if you're stranded you can choose from eight or so **hotels** – try the very simple *Hotel Poulia* (☎0235/31 663; ③) or the more pleasant *Amfitryon* (☎0235/31702; ③) on the waterfront – and a **campsite**, *Camping Blue Bay* (☎0235/314 25). *O Pharos Taverna* by the sea serves up a variety of fresh fishy delights.

A better beach is at **Kaména Voúrla**, 9km north; this is, however, very much a resort, used mainly by Greeks attracted by the spas here and at neighbouring Loutrá Thermopylíon (see below). Seafood aficionados are well looked after at the long line of decent fish tavernas along the promenade here, and there are dozens of acceptable hotels and rooms on the main street and shady backstreets.

Thermopylae and its spa

Just before joining the inland road, the highway enters the **Pass of Thermopylae**, where Leonidas and three hundred Spartans made a last stand against Xerxes's thirty-thousand-strong Persian army in 480 BC. The pass was much more defined in ancient times, a narrow defile with Mount Kalídhromo to the south and the sea – which has silted and retreated nearly 4km – to the north.

The tale of Spartan bravery is described at length by **Herodotus**. Leonidas, King of Sparta, stood guard over the pass with a mixed force of seven thousand Greeks, confident that it was the only approach an army could take to enter Greece from Thessaly. At night, however, Xerxes sent an advance part of his forces along a mountain trail and broke through the pass to attack the Greeks from the rear. Leonidas ordered a retreat of the main army, but remained in the pass himself, with his Spartan guard, to delay the Persians' progress. He and all but two of the guard fought to their deaths.

Loutrá Thermopylíon, midway through the pass, is named for the hot springs present since antiquity. The grave mound of the fallen Spartans lies 500m away, opposite a gloriously heroic statue of Leonidas. The spa and restaurant facilities are intimidatingly built up, but there are a few cascades and drainage sluices where you can bathe undisturbed in the open air, if you can stomach the sulphurous stench.

Lamía and onward routes

LAMÍA is a busy provincial capital and an important transport junction for travellers. It sees few overnight visitors, but has a worthwhile sight in the Catalan castle, and it abounds in excellent ouzerís and kafenía.

Heading **north from Lamía** there's a choice of three routes: to Tríkala and Kalambáka, to Lárissa, or around the coast to Vólos, but none is especially memorable. Fársala and Kardhítsa, on the routes to Lárissa and Tríkala respectively, are small, very ordinary country towns. The **Vólos road**, however, leading east along the coast, has a little more to delay your progress.

Lamía

The town is arranged around three main squares: Platía Párkhou, Platía Eleftherías and Platía Laoú, all good venues for sipping a *frappé* and watching Greek life go by. **Platía Eleftherías** is the town's social hub, full of outdoor cafés and restaurants, and the scene of the evening volta. The cathedral and town hall occupy two sides of the square; every Sunday evening, the flag that flies above the square is lowered in solemn ceremony, to the wayward accompaniment of the local military band. To the west of the square a replica of an old boat, the *Kyrenia*, stands on its own tiny square, an incongruous gift to this inland town from the people of Cyprus.

Just to the south of Eleftherías is the atmospheric **Platía Laoú**, shaded by plane trees which in autumn are crowded with migratory birds. Here you'll find the town's main taxi rank and an all-night kiosk. Leading off to the right is Karaiskáki – a vegetarian's nightmare of a street, with meat roasting on spits and the smell of *patsás* (tripe-and-trotter soup) hanging in the air. For a look at **bread-making** by the oldest of methods, leave Platía Laoú on Isaía and follow it for 200m into the old part of town: the bakery is on the left, recognizable by the quarter-glazed windows and stable door. Another noteworthy bakery, supplying good *tyrópites*, is on the corner of Platía Laoú.

The third square, **Platía Párkhou** is the main shopping area, with **banks** also grouped around it. On Saturdays, the streets below Párkhou turn into a lively **market**, with everything from rheumatism cures to plastic combs on sale.

Looking down on the city is the fourteenth-century Catalan castle, which boasts superb views – and houses a new archeological **museum** (Tues–Sun 8.30am-3pm; 500dr) exhibiting a variety of finds – Neolithic, Mycenaean, Classical, Hellenistic and Roman – in a Neoclassical building dating from King Otho's time.

Other diversions in Lamía include authentic live **bouzouki music** on the Stilídha road, opposite the high school; a **theatre** on Ipsilándou, used for art exhibitions and in winter as an art-film cinema; and *The Velvet Underground*, behind the cathedral on Andhroútsou, the best of the winter-only clubs. Finally, every Sunday there is a **puppet show** in the small theatre 200m up the road past the OTE; it's designed for children, telling classic Greek stories that are understandable even with a very hazy knowledge of the language.

Practicalities

The **buses**, including a local service from the train station (6km out), arrive at terminals scattered throughout the town, though none is much further than ten minutes' walk away from Platía Párkhou. Ámfissa and Karpeníssi services use a terminal on Márkou Bótsari; those for Lárissa, Tríkala and the north, a stop on Thermopylíon;

those for Vólos, the stop at the corner of Levadhítou and Rozáki-Ángeli; while buses for Athens and Thessaloníki go from the corner of Papakiriazí and Satovriándou.

Accommodation prospects are disappointing in Lamía; there are a couple of drab hotels on Ódhos Rozáki-Ángeli: *Thermopylae* (☎0231/21 366; ④) at no. 36 and *Athina* (☎0231/20 700; ④) at no. 41. The *Samaras* (☎0231/42 701; ⑤) on pretty Platía Dhiákou south of Eleftherías is a more reputable, attractive alternative.

For **food and drink**, good ouzerís exist on Androutsóu, between platías Laoú and Eleftherías. *Aman Aman* and *Allo Skedhio* are the best, with palatable barrelled wine, closely followed by *Asterias*, one of three fine places to eat in a small courtyard below Eleftherías. *Psilidhas*, on the road out towards Vólos has a glowing reputation and is more upmarket. The trendiest cafés in Platía Eleftherías are the *Viva*, *Remezzo* and *Castro*. From a smaller square above Platía Párkhou, steps lead up to a peaceful but more pricey hilltop café-restaurant, *Ayios Loukas*, with great views from the terrace. There is also a café up on the Kástro, which closes at 9pm.

Lamía to Vólos

The first temptation on the coast road to Vólos is **Ayía Marína**, 12km east of Lamía, where the seafood tavernas – a popular weekend jaunt for Lamian families – are much better than the rather pathetic beach.

A couple of kilometres further, **STYLÍDHA** was once one of the major ports of the Aegean – it was at the opera house here that Maria Callas's grandfather outsang a visiting Italian star and started a dynasty. Today the unsightly town is chiefly concerned with olive-oil bottling and cement: not an inspiring prospect. Probably the only reason to stop is to catch the seasonal hydrofoil to the Sporades. If you get stuck, there a couple of cheap hotels like *Hotel Skyland* (☎0238/22798; ③) and two campsites. At Karavómilos and Akhládhi, 8km and 19km east of Stylídha respectively, the fish tavernas are more inviting than the beaches, though you'll need your own transport. Look out for nesting herons on the road back to Lamía.

The best beaches along this route are near **Glyfá**, 30km further north, though it is 11km off the highway and served only by one afternoon bus from Lamía. It has the mainland's northernmost ferry crossing to **Évvia**: eight times daily in July and August to Áyiokambos (last ferry at 8.15pm; 30min; 336dr, cars 2600dr), with a reduced service the rest of the year. **Rooms** are on offer in private houses and at half a dozen hotels, the cheapest of which is the *Oassis* (☎0238/61 201; ②). Akhílio, 7km north, is less attractive; it has a **campsite**.

Finally, rounding the Pagasitic Gulf towards Vólos, car-drivers might want to stop at **Néa Ankhíalos**, where five early Christian basilicas have been uncovered. Their mosaics and the small site museum are interesting, though perhaps not enough to make it worth risking a three-hour wait between buses.

West to Karpeníssi – and beyond

The road west from Lamía climbs out of the Sperkhiós valley, with glimpses on the way of mounts Íti, Gióna and Vardhoússia, 10km to the south. If you want to do some **hiking**, there are spectacular routes on Mount Íti (the classical *Oita*), easiest approached from the village of Ipáti. The **Karpeníssi valley**, too, lends itself to walking trips amid a countryside of dark fir forest and snow-fringed mountains, which the EOT promotes (with some justice) as "the Greek Switzerland". Neither area sees more than a few dozen foreign summer tourists, most of these on rafting trips arranged by Trekking Hellas (see p.124).

Ipáti and paths on Mount Íti

Mount Íti is an unusually accessible mountain. There are buses almost hourly from Lamía to Ipáti, its main trailhead; if you arrive by train, these can be picked up en route at Lamía's "local" station, Lianokládhi, 6km from the town. Be sure not to get off the bus at the sulphurous spa of Loutrá Ipátis, 5km north of Ipáti proper.

IPÁTI is a small village, clustered below a castle, with two good-value **hotels**, catering mainly for Greek families: the *Panorama* (☎0231/98 222; ②) and *Panhellinion* (☎0231/98 340; ②). There are also a couple of reasonable tavernas.

Trail-finding on Mount Íti can be an ambitious undertaking and requires detailed maps and/or a hiking guidebook. A limited trek, however, should be feasible if you've reasonable orientation skills. From the village, a path loosely marked by red splashes of paint leads in around four hours to an EOS refuge known as **Trápeza** (usually locked, but with a spring and camping space nearby). This is a steep but rewarding walk, giving a good idea of Íti's sheer rock ramparts and high lush meadows.

Karpeníssi

The main road west from Ipáti, after scaling a spur of Mount Timvristós, and passing the turnoff to a tiny **ski centre** (uncrowded and with equipment to rent), drops down to the town of **KARPENÍSSI**. Its site is spectacular – huddled at the base of the peak and head of the Karpenissiótis valley, which extends south all the way to the wall-like Mount Panetolikó – though the town itself is entirely nondescript, having been destroyed in World War II by the Germans and again during the civil war. During the latter, it was captured and held for a week by Communist guerrillas in January 1949. In the course of the fighting, an American pilot was shot down – thereby gaining, as C.M.Woodhouse observes in *Modern Greece*, "probably the unenviable distinction of being the first American serviceman to be killed in action by Communist arms".

Except on weekends in summer or skiing season, **accommodation** is easily found, if not that appealing; most of the eight hotels are noisy and expensive. The cheapest and quietest is the *Galini* (☎0237/22 914; ④), followed by *Elvetia* at Zinopoúlou 33 (☎0237/22 465; ⑤) and *Anesis* (☎0237/22 840; ⑥). The first two are within sight of the central square and its adjacent bus terminal, the last lies 660m towards Lamia. A much cheaper, more tranquil alternative is provided by a wide selection of rooms at 10,000 or less; enquire at the tourist office. All prices drop drastically during the week.

Eating options are also limited; exceptions to the bland array of fast food snack bars are the *Psistaria Poniras*, opposite the bus station, *Adherfi Triandafilli*, opposite the OTE, just southwest of the square, the *Panorama*, under the police station — rated best by the locals — and *Esi Oti Pis*, near the *nomarkhía*, at the start of the road to Agrinion.

The friendly municipal **tourist office** (☎0237/21016), opposite the bus station, is a mine of information on accommodation, eating and public transport in the whole area.

Around Karpeníssi

A pleasant four-kilometre walk from Karpeníssi is the traditional mountain village of **Koriskhádhes**, whose stone houses display the ornate wooden balconies typical of the region. It has a traditional inn and a kafenío where you can order mezédhes and gaze over the trees at Mount Helidhóna. To reach the village, follow the road south out of town (towards Proussós) and look for the turning to the right after about 1km.

If your appetite is whetted for more of this stunning countryside, a twice-daily bus trundles 15km downriver, again along the Proussós road, to **Megálo Khorió** and **Mikrí Khorió** ("Big Village" and "Little Village"). Both have **inns**, rooms and the possibility of day hikes up the respective peaks presiding over them.

Beyond these villages, the valley narrows to a gorge, and a paved road has made a visit to the monastery and village of **Proussós** (33km out of Karpeníssi) much easier, though only two buses a week do the trip. The **monastery** is large and much rebuilt after a succession of fires (started by candles), and presently inhabited by just five monks. Visitors are welcomed and are shown curiosities in the ninth-century katholikón, such as paper made from the skin of goat-kid embryo and an icon of the Panayía with its eyes gouged out. (According to the monks, the Communist rebels of the 1940s were responsible for this, though the Turks were wont to perform the same sacrilege, and credulous villagers attributed magical powers to the dust thus obtained.)

In summer the monastery will host men for a one-night stay; otherwise there are a couple of tavernas in the **village** (1km further on) and many rooms.

The road to Agrínio

The roads west from Karpeníssi climb high into the mountains of **Ágrafa**, the southernmost extension of the Píndhos. In winter critical passes are generally closed, but through the summer they're generally serviceable.

The most remote and dramatic route, with no bus service, is on **south from Proussós** (see above): 33km of rough dirt track which eventually brings you out at **Thérmo**, on the shores of Lake Trihonídha. There you are within striking distance (and a daily bus ride) of Agrínio, with its connections to Patrá and Ioánnina (see p.263 and p.331 respectively).

The direct **Karpeníssi–Agrínio** road is paved, but extremely sinuous, so it still takes the one morning bus a good three and a half hours to cover the 115km. The beauty of the first half of the journey cannot be overemphasized; it's largely empty country, with the only place of any size (having a filling station and a taverna) being the village of **Frangísta**, which straddles a valley, 41km from Karpeníssi. Beyond Frangísta, the bus lumbers past the giant **Kremastón dam** on the Tavropós, Trikeriótis and Ahelóös rivers, skirts Panetolikó, then winds down through tobacco-planted hills to Agrínio. If you wish to explore the Ágrafa wilderness to the north, leave the bus at the turnoff for Kerasohóri, 27km out of Karpeníssi.

THESSALY

The highlights of travelling through **Thessaly** are easily summarized. Over to the east, curling down from the industrial port-city of Vólos, is the **Pílion** (Pelion) mountain peninsula. The villages on its lush, orchard-covered slopes are among the most beautiful in the country – an established resort area for Greeks and numerous camper van tourists, though still surprisingly unspoiled. To the west is a sight not to be missed on any mainland exploration – are the extraordinary "monasteries in the air" of the **Metéora**.

The **central plains** are to be passed through, rather than visited. That said, **Lárissa**, the region's capital, is making itself into a pleasant city, besides providing efficient connections by bus, and rather slower ones by train, to Vólos and to Kalambáka (via Tríkala).

Heading north or west from Lárissa, you'll find yourself in one mountain range or another. The dramatic route over the Píndhos, from Kalambáka to Ioánnina, is covered in the following chapter. North from Kalambáka there are reasonable roads, though few buses, into western Macedonia, with the lakeside town of Kastoriá an obvious focus. Most travellers, however, head north from Lárissa towards Thessaloníki, a very beautiful route in the shadow of Mount Olympus (see Chapter Five).

Vólos

Arriving at the city of **VÓLOS** gives little hint of Pílion's promise. This is Greece's fastest-growing industrial centre and a major depot for long-distance truck drivers. It's hard to imagine the mythological past of this busy modern port, but it is the site of ancient Iolkos, from where Jason and the Argonauts set off on their quest for the Golden Fleece. Rebuilt after a devastating 1955 earthquake, and now edging to its natural limits against the Pílion foothills behind, Vólos is a lively city, beginning to revel in its recently acquired prosperity. It would be no hardship to spend a few hours or even a night here while waiting for a bus up the mountain or a boat to Skiáthos, Skópelos or Alónissos, for which Vólos is the **main port**.

The most attractive place to linger is along the eastern waterfront esplanade, between the landscaped **Platía Yeoryíou** and the archeological museum, which is itself a highly recommended diversion. Imaginatively laid out and clearly labelled in English, the **Archeological Museum** (daily except Mon 8.30am–3pm; 500dr) features a unique collection of painted grave *stelai* depicting, in now-faded colours, the everyday scenarios of fifth-century BC life, as well as a variety of graves complete with skeletons. It also has one of the best European collections of Neolithic pottery, tools and figurines, from the local sites of Sesklo and Dimini (both of which – respectively 15km and 3km west of Vólos – can be visited, though they are of essentially specialist interest).

Practicalities

Ferries and hydrofoils arrive and depart from the central **port**, and most other services are found within a couple of blocks. An exception is the **bus station**, off our map on Grigoríou Lambráki and ten minutes' walk southwest of the main square, **Platía Ríga Feréou**. Arrayed around the latter are the **train station** and the helpful **EOT** office (☎0421/23 500 or 37 417), which provides information on bus and ferry services as well as accommodation. Like Áyios Konstandínos, Vólos has regular ferries and in summer (for nearly double the price) the quicker Flying Dolphin hydrofoils to the Sporades. **Ferries** leave two to four times daily for Skiáthos and Skópelos, with at least one continuing to Alónissos; the last departure is generally 7pm (1pm on Sun); for information phone the port police at ☎0421/38 888 or the tourist police at ☎0421/72 421.

Hydrofoils (☎0421/39 786) run two or three times daily to Skiáthos, Skópelos and Alónissos, continuing two or three times a week to Skýros. In midsummer there are also hydrofoils to the islands from **Plataniás** at the foot of Mount Pílion (see p.280).

If you want to **rent a car** to explore Mount Pílion, try European Cars (☎0421/36 238) at Iassónos 83, one block inland and parallel to the waterfront.

Accommodation

Hotels are fairly plentiful, with a concentration of acceptable ones in the grid of streets behind the port. Budget options include the humble *Avra* at Sólonos 3 (☎0421/25370; ③), the very basic *Iolcos* at 37 Dhimitriádhos (☎0421/23416; ②), and the *Iasson* (☎0421/26075; ④), near the port at Pávlou Melá 1; further out at Tzánou 1, the slightly scruffy *Roussas* (☎0421/21732; ③) is handy for the museum and ouzerís, and has helpful staff. The *Philippos* (☎0421/37 607-8; ⑤) at Sólonos 9 is in the middle range, while the *Aigli* (☎0421/24471; ⑥) at Argonáfton 24, an Art Deco hotel on the quayside, is strictly for splurging.

Restaurants and nightlife

Vólos specializes in one of Greece's most endearing institutions – the authentic **ouzerí**, serving a huge variety of mezédhes washed down, not necessarily with ouzo

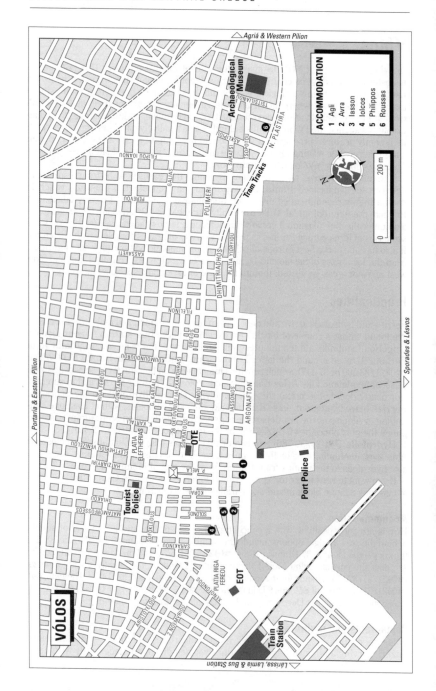

VÓLOS

△ Agriá & Western Pílion

△ Portaría & Eastern Pílion

▽ Lárissa, Lamía & Bus Station

▽ Sporades & Lésvos

ACCOMMODATION

1 Agli
2 Avra
3 Iasson
4 Iolcos
5 Philippos
6 Roussas

0   200 m

Archaeological Museum

Tram Tracks

Port Police

Tourist Police

EOT

Train Station

OTE

N. PLASTIRA
TSISTILIANOU
TSOPOTOU
D. SARATSI
ASKLIPIOU
FILIPOU IOANOU
GALIAS
PEREVOU
POLIMERI
PLATIA YIORYOU
DHIMITRIADHOS
KASSAVETI
FILELINON
OREOS
KOUMOUNDOUROU
CONSTANDA
RIGA FEREOU
KARTALI
26 OCTOVRIOU (ALEXANDHRAS)
ERMOU
ASSONOS
ARGONAFTON
SOKRATOUS
ELEFTHERIOU VENIZELOU
HATZIARYIRI
PLATIA ELEFTHERIAS
P. MELA
KORAI
SOLONOS
METAMORFOSSEOS
DHIAKOU
SOFOKLEOUS
SARAKINOU
PLATIA RIGA FEREOU
KENDOTOU
SPIRIDHI
AMSTOLIDHOU
ANALIPSEOS

but with *tsípouro*, the local and lethal spirit. Among the *ouzerís* strung out along Argonáfton on the waterfront, *O Yiorgos* is the best, followed by *Ouzeri Argonaftes* and *Naftilia*. More pricey, but excellent, **tavernas** are on Nikifórou Plastíra, near the museum: these include *Papadis, Monosandalon, Remvi* and *Akti Tselepi*, all specializing in seafood. For more conventional and cheap casserole dishes, try *Harama* at Dhimitriádhos 49.

As for **nightlife**, concerts and plays are frequently performed in the open-air theatre (tickets can be bought at Kekhaïdis music store at the corner of Iássonas and Kartáli streets, one block in from the waterfront), and there are plenty of swish cafés on the waterfront where Vólos youth hang out, dozens of discos on the outskirts of town, and a few casual spots where local musicians take the floor, some regularly, some spontaneously, as at *I Skala tou Milanou* at the corner of E Venizélou and Analípseos.

Mount Pílion (Pelion)

There is something decidedly un-Greek about the **Mount Pílion peninsula**, with its lush orchards of apple, pear and nut trees and dense forests of beech and oak. Scarcely a rock is visible along the slopes, and the sound of water comes gurgling up from crevices beside every track; summer temperatures here are a good 15°F cooler than the rest of Thessaly. Pílion is reputed to be the land of the mythical centaurs, and the site of ancient gods' revelries.

Pílion **villages** are idiosyncratic, spread out along the slopes – due to easy availability of water – and with their various quarters linked by winding cobbled paths. They formed a semi-autonomous district during the Turkish occupation, and during the eighteenth century became something of a nursery for Greek culture, fostered by an Orthodox education (imparted through semi-underground schooling) and a revival of **folk art** and **traditional architecture**. There is also a strong regional **cuisine**, with specialities such as *spedzofaí* (sausage and pepper casserole), *kounéli kokkinistó* (rabbit stew) and *gída vrastí* (goat pot-au-feu). Herbs, a wide range of fruit, home-made preserves and honey are important local products.

Many of the villages have changed little in appearance over the centuries, and offer rich rewards with their mansions, churches and sprawling platías – invariably shaded by one or more vast plane trees, sheltering the local cafés. The slate-roofed **churches** are highly distinctive, built in a low, wide style, often with a detached belltower and always ornamented with carved wood. Two communities, **Makrinítsa** and **Vizítsa**, have been designated by the EOT as protected showpieces of the region, but almost every hamlet boasts its own unique attractions.

Add to the above the delights of a dozen or so excellent **beaches**, and you have a recipe for an instant holiday idyll – or disaster, if your timing is wrong. Lying roughly midway between Athens and Thessaloníki, Pílion is a favourite with Greek vacationers, and you'd be pushing your luck more than usual to show up in August without a reservation. Prices are comparatively high for the mainland.

Getting around Pílion

The peninsula is divided into three regions, with the best concentration of traditional villages **north** of Vólos and along the **east coast**. The **west** coast is less scenically interesting, with much more development along the Pagasitic Gulf. The **south**, low-lying and sparsely populated, has just one major resort, Plataniás, and a few small inland hamlets.

Travelling between the villages can be tricky without your own transport. **Buses** to the east cover two main routes: Vólos–Khánia–Zagorá (3–5 daily) and Vólos–Tsangarádha–Áyios Ioánnis via Miliés (2 daily), with just one daily service linking

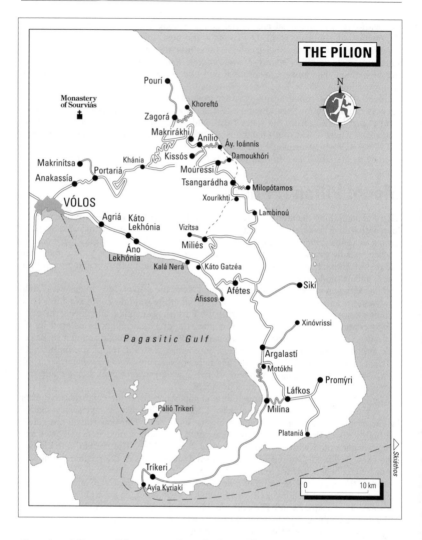

THE PÍLION

N

Pourí

Monastery of Sourviás

Khoreftó

Zagorá

Makrirákhi

Anílio

Áy. Ioánnis

Makrinítsa

Khánia

Kissós

Damoukhóri

Portariá

Moúressi

Anakassía

Tsangarádha

Milopótamos

VÓLOS

Xouríkhti

Agriá

Káto Lekhónia

Vizítsa

Lambinoú

Áno Lekhónia

Miliés

Kalá Nerá

Káto Gatzéa

Siki

Áfissos

Afétes

Xinóvrissi

Pagasitic Gulf

Argalastí

Motókhi

Promýri

Láfkos

Palió Trikeri

Milína

Plataniá

Tríkeri

Ayía Kyriakí

0   10 km

△ *Skiáthos*

Zagorá and Tsangarádha to complete the loop. The far south is equally sparsely served, with just two or three departures a day to Plataniás and Tríkeri, though the respective northern and western highlights of Makrinítsa and Vizítza both have excellent connections.

Alternatives are to **rent a car** in Vólos (especially advisable if you're pushed for time), some very uncertain hitching, or **walking**. The latter means slow progress, since roads snake around ravine contours, seeming never to get closer to villages just across the way, though a limited number of old cobbled **paths** (*kalderímia*) provide short cuts.

Leaving Pílion, you needn't necessarily return to Vólos but can take advantage of a daily summer **hydrofoil** from Plataniás to islands of the Sporades.

The north

Before crossing over to the east coast on the main Vólos–Zagorá axis, consider pausing en route: both **Portariá** and **Makrinítsa** villages have intrinsic attractions and make good first or last stops out of Vólos.

Anakassiá and Portariá

The first of the Pílion villages, **Anakassiá** is just 4km out of Vólos, and few casual visitors give it more than a passing glance. What they miss is a small but very beautiful museum (signposted) dedicated to the "naive" painter **Theóphilos** (1873–1934). A great eccentric, originally from Lésvos, Theóphilos lived for long periods in both Athens and Vólos, where he wandered around, often dressed in traditional costumes, painting frescoes for anyone prepared either to pay or feed him. In Pílion you find his work in the most unlikely places, mostly unheralded, including a number of village tavernas and kafenía. Here, the **museum** (daily 9am–3pm) occupies the **Arkhondikó Kóndos**, an eighteenth-century mansion whose first floor he entirely frescoed with scenes from the Greek War of Independence – one of his favourite themes.

PORTARIÁ, 10km east, has a more mountainous feel with a startling soundtrack of running streams. Of late, regrettably, the areas closest to the busy road have become tacky and commercialized, but the back streets are still quiet and charming. The chief glory, as so often in Pílion, is the main square, shaded by tremendous plane trees, one planted in 1220. If you decide to stay, you can pick from almost a dozen pensions, traditional inns and **hotels**, cheapest among which are the *Filoxenia* (☎0428/99 160; ④) and *Pelias* (☎0428/99 290; ④), or rooms at *Viky's* (☎0428/99 520; ②) just outside Portariá on the road to Makrinítsa, next to a mini-waterfall.

Makrinítsa

From Portariá many buses detour northwest to **MAKRINÍTSA**, 17km from Vólos, where stone houses are picturesquely scattered on the mountainside. If your time in Pílion is limited, this is perhaps the best single target. Founded in 1204 by refugees from the first sacking of Constantinople, it boasts six outstanding churches and a monastery, and a group of **traditional mansions** – three of which have been restored as lodges by the EOT. Up against stiff competition, Makrinítsa, with its splendid views, ranks as one of Greece's prettiest villages. Inevitably, there are souvenir shops and plenty of day-trippers, but these are easy to escape, and exploration can be rewarding.

There's a two hundred-metre altitude difference between the upper and lower quarters of Makrinítsa, so to get a full sense of the village takes a full day's rambling. Most impressive of the churches are **Áyios Ioánnis**, next to the fountain on the shady main platía, and the beautiful eighteenth-century **Monastery of Panayía Makrinítissa**, right under the clock tower. Many of the sanctuaries and frescoes here are only a few centuries old, but the marble relief work on some of the apses (the curvature behind the altar) is the best of its type in Greece. A few metres on from the Áyios Ioánnis square there are **Theóphilos frescoes** (see above) in a café. If you are looking for a more challenging walk in Pílion, the village is also the starting point for a long **trail** over to the deserted Monastery of Sourviás. A thirty-minute walk from the car park (at the end of the road next to the entrance to the village) leads to Áyios Yerásimos.

Accommodation in Makrinítsa is not cheap. The EOT lodges are very pleasant but pricey; the best ones are *Arkhondiko Mousli*, east of the main square (☎0428/99 228; ⑤), and *Pension Xiradaki* west of the square (☎0428/99 250; ⑤). Cheaper private operations also located near the square – some in traditional mansions – are the newish *Pilioritiko Spiti* (☎0428/99 432; ⑤), the atmospheric *Arkhondiko Diomidi* (☎0428/99 430; ④) and the cosy *Arkhontiko Routsou* (☎0428/99 090; ④). There are four eateries in the platía.

Khánia

Travelling on over the mountain, beyond Portariá, the road hairpins up to the **Khánia pass**, and the village of the same name, a stark cluster of modern houses and a smattering of hotels. To the south a road leads in 4km to a small, winter **ski resort** (open Jan–March). Once over the Khánia pass, the view suddenly opens to take in the whole east coast, as you spiral down to a fork: the left turning leads to Zagorá, the right towards Tsangarádha.

The east coast

Pílion's best (and most popular) beaches and lushest scenery are to be found on the Aegean-facing **east coast**. The transport hub for the region and major producer and packer of fruit is **Zagorá**, the apple capital of Greece.

Zagorá and Pourí

The largest Pílion village, **ZAGORÁ**, has a life more independent of tourism than its neighbours, and is a lot more interesting than first impressions of its concrete main street suggest. In addition to this modern section of the village, there are four well-preserved and architecturally more varied areas, based around the squares of **Ayía Paraskeví, Ayía Kyriakí, Áyios Yeóryios**, and **Ayía Sotíra**, strung out over five kilometres. Coming from Vólos, turn left at the first filling station to find Ayía Paraskeví (Perakhóra) up the hillside; Ayía Kyriakí is in the centre of the village. Bearing left past the road down to Khoreftó will bring you to the majestic Áyios Yiórgios, which languishes in the shadow of a lovely plane tree and the beautiful eighteenth-century church, while Ayía Sotíra lies beyond it above the road to Pourí. Close to the second bend of the road to Khoreftó beach, is the **Riga Fereou** school, now a gallery/folk museum, open in July and August. Four hundred metres from the school, down the dirt road next to it, is *Villa Horizonte* (☎0426/23 342), a cultural centre which organizes concerts, seminars, exhibitions and trekking holidays, and is a possibility for accommodation.

Accommodation in Zagorá is more reasonably priced than elsewhere in the region. There are several places, such as *Marika Vlahou* (☎0426/22 153; ②) and *Yiannis Halkias* (☎0426/22 159; ③), near the turn for Horeftó, and one impeccably restored mansion, the *Hotel Arkhontiko Konstantinidi* (☎0426/23 391; ⑥) with a beautiful garden and home-made jams for breakfast. All four squares host grill-tavernas: *O Takis* in Ayía Kiriakí is reasonable, *Kyriazis* in Ayía Sotíra is good, but the best food in Zagorá is at *O Petros*, just up from Áyios Yiórgios, where Faní will cook you Pílion specialities. There are also plenty of card phones, a **post office** and bank agent – the main official services between here and Tsangarádha, though the nearby coastal resorts provide similar amenities.

The road from Zagorá to **Pourí**, one of the northernmost communities on Pílion, is a spectacular approach to a regally situated and quietly appealing village. Khiótis Theoharis rents rooms here in his new pension 250m beyond the square, but finding a meal is still a problem in Pouri, though he will provide a light breakfast. There are two dazzling, deserted beaches below the village, to give you an idea of what Khoreftó and Áyios Ioánnis looked like twenty years ago.

Khoreftó

A great coastal base is eight twisting kilometres down the mountain at **KHOREFTÓ** (5 buses daily in summer, 2 in winter). There is a choice of beaches here: an excellent one in front of the former fishing village, and another smaller bay (used by nude bathers) around the headland at the north end, where the road stops. Determined explorers can follow a coastal path for twenty minutes more to the coves of **Análipsi** – the southerly one a little paradise with a spring, popular with freelance campers, the further road-accessible and rockier.

Khoreftó supports half a dozen **hotels** and lots of rooms for rent. The best-value and best-located hotels are the *Hayiati* (☎0426/22 405; ④) and *Erato* (☎0426/22 445; ④), both at the quiet, southern end of the coast road. Other attractive possibilities are *Flamingo Studio Hotel* (☎0426/22 579; ⑤), on a dirt road very near the beach, and Kosta Kapaniari's simple but spotless little apartments (☎0426/63 779; ④), among the trees. Be warned that if you want to come in high season (July 20–August 25), you need to make a reservation. The village also has a **campsite** (☎0426/22 180), with decent amenities at the extreme south end of the main beach.

Eating in Khoreftó is sadly disappointing. The *Milo tis Eridhos*, run by the Apple Growers Cooperative, has the best food in the village. Two or three bars provide evening distraction.

Áyios Ioánnis and around

Bearing east at the junction below Khánia, the road winds down from Mount Pílion past Makrirákhi and Anílio (meaning "without sun"), both spoilt by concrete development, towards **KISSÓS**. This is a much more traditional slice of Pílion – and an enjoyable stop. Set just off the main road, it is virtually buried in foliage, with sleepy residential quarters ascending in terraces and, in eighteenth-century Ayía Marína, one of the finest churches on the peninsula. **Rooms** and **meals** are available at the *Ksenonas Kissos* (☎0426/31 214; ③), among the best value spots in Pílion; the friendly family there serve homemade delicacies such as *ktipití*, a piquant cheese dip, and their own yoghurt, nuts and honey. Half-overgrown tracks meander from the village up towards the ski-lift ridge.

Heading for the coast, it's six kilometres of twisting paved road down to **ÁYIOS IOÁNNIS**, eastern Pílion's major resort. Despite the many hotels and private rooms, finding a bed here is as problematic as anywhere on the peninsula in summer; a small **tourist office** can advise on where there are vacancies or, if necessary on times of buses out. Budget **accommodation** doesn't really exist, so the best options are the very basic but clean *Evripidis* (☎0426/31 338; ④), *Armonia* (☎0426/31 242; ④), with a decent taverna, and at the south end of the village, the kitschly furnished *Zephyros* (☎0426/31 335; ④), quieter and set near woods behind a pleasant patio. As for **eating**, the locals recommend *Akroyiali*, *Akti* and *To Kyma*, in addition to *Armonia*. For a splurge meal, try the elegant *Ostria* taverna inland, which features traditional Pílion dishes.

The **beach** at Áyios Ioánnis is popular and commercialized, with windsurfing boards and waterskis for rent. For a quieter time, walk either ten minutes north to **Pláka** beach, with its mostly young, Greek clientele, or fifteen minutes south (past the **campsite**) to **Papaneró** beach, the best bronzing spot in the vicinity, fronted by a few rooms for rent and two good tavernas. South from Papaneró, a new paved road leads to **Damoúkhari**, a hamlet set amid olive trees and fringing a secluded fishing harbour.

The construction of another road down from Moúressi has put an end to its seclusion, and villas and hotels are springing up fast amongst the olive trees. However, there is a large pebble beach, two pleasant tavernas and the overgrown ruins of a Venetian castle. If you'd like to stay, try *To Kastro* (☎0426/49 475; ④).

From Damoúhari, it's possible to walk to **Tsangarádha** (see below) in a little over an hour. At the mouth of the ravine leading down to the larger bay, a spectacular *kalderími* or stairway begins its ascent, allowing glimpses of up to six villages simultaneously, and even the Sporades on a clear day, from points along the way. The path emerges in the Ayía Paraskeví quarter of Tsangarádha.

Tsangarádha and Moúressi

TSANGARÁDHA, the largest northeastern village after Zagorá, is divided into four distinct quarters, spread out along several kilometres of road. Each of these is scattered around a namesake church and platía, the finest of which is **Ayía Paraskeví**, shaded by reputedly the largest plane tree in Greece – a thousand years old and with an eighteen-metre trunk.

Most **accommodation** in this area is on the noisy main road. Exceptions include the modern, friendly *Villa ton Rodhon* (☎0426/49 340; ④), on the cobbled path to Damoúhari, and the *Konaki Hotel* (☎0426/49 281; ④), just before Ayía Paraskeví square but set back from the road. There are also some rooms for rent in the southern parish of **Taxiárhes** (linked by a *kalderími* with Ayía Paraskeví), and an acceptable **taverna**, *To Kalivi*. Below the massive tree in Ayía Paraskeví is a kafenío, while *Aleka's Taverna* above it serves decent food.

In general, better cooking is to be had at **MOÚRESSI**, a few kilometres northwest on the road. At either *Iy Dhrosia* or *To Tavernaki* here, you can get specialities like *fasólies hándres* (delicately flavoured pinto beans) and assorted offal-on-a-spit. The rooms in *Arkhontiko Olga* (☎0426/49 651; ⑤), on the square, are furnished in traditional style.

Mylopótamos and the coast to Lambinoú

From Tsangarádha a hairpin road (with a daily bus) snakes seven kilometres down to **MYLOPÓTAMOS**, a collection of attractive pebble coves, two of which are separated by a naturally tunnelled rock wall. Above them, there are a couple of excellent tavernas. They attract an international summer crowd, who are catered for by a series of rooms for rent on the approach road; the nearest is the rundown *Diakoumis* (☎0423/49 203; ④), with spectacular views from precarious wooden terraces. The *Christos-Marina* bungalows (☎0423/49 400; ⑤) a few hundred metres higher have cosy Pílion-style rooms with balconies and a pool.

If you want to swim in more solitude, try **Fakístra beach**, a cliff-girt, white-gravel bay, just to the north; the new road from Tsangarádha may soon bring the crowds, though. If they do, the beautiful empty beach of **Limiónas** is only a thirty-minute walk to the south. Other beaches on the south side of Milopótamos include **Lambinoú** and **Kalamáki**, both well signposted, along with their inland villages. They have a more open feel, since the dramatic terrain begins to subside here.

En route from Tsangarádha to Lambinoú, the village of Xoríkhti is the eastern trailhead for an enjoyable three-hour **trail to Miliés**. The path, which wends its way through a mix of open hillside and shady dell, is marked all along its length. Before the road around the hill via Lambinoú and Kalamáki was built in 1938, this was the principal thoroughfare between the railhead at Miliés and the Tsangarádha area.

Miliés, Vizítsa and the western coast

Lying in the "rain shadow" of the mountain, the western Pílion villages and coast have a drier, more Mediterranean climate, with olives and arbutus shrubs. The beaches, at least until you get past Kalá Nerá, are a bit overdeveloped, and in any case lack the character of those on the east side. Inland it is a different story, with pleasant foothill villages and, for a change, a decent bus service. **Miliés** and **Vizítsa** both make good bases for exploring local traditions and taking short walks in the Pílion interior.

Miliés

Like Tsangarádha, **MILIÉS** is a sizeable village that was an important centre of culture during the eighteenth century. It retains a number of imposing mansions and an interesting church, the **Taxiárkhis**, whose narthex (usually kept open) is decorated with brilliant frescoes. There is also a small **folk museum** (Tues–Sun 10am–2pm; free), which displays local artefacts and sponsors a crafts festival in early July. Another attraction is the old *trenáki* – miniature railway – line between Vólos and Miliés. The line, in service until 1972, was laid out early this century by an Italian company. In 1997 a summer steam locomotive service was reintroduced on weekends as a tourist attraction. Covering a lovely 16km route, the train leaves Áno Lehónia on the coast at 11am, arrives at Miliés ninety minutes later, and departs again at 4pm. Both train stations have been charmingly restored. Tickets cost 1000dr each way and go on sale at 9–9.30am with priority given to groups. Following the tracks down to Áno Lehónia also makes for a non-taxing two- to three-hour walk.

Accommodation is a choice between a couple of traditional mansions and *O Paleos Stathmos* (☎0423/86 425; ⑤), a cosy inn and restaurant converted from the old train station below the town. Other food choices are a couple of café-restaurants on the village square; a simple grill, *Panorama*; and *To Aloni*, a fancy place on the Vizítsa road. But the most distinctive food in town comes from a superb **bakery** down on the road by the bus stop, which cranks out every kind of Pílion bread, pie, turnover and cake imaginable.

Vizítsa
VIZÍTSA, 3km further up the mountain and full of babbling brooks, is preserved as a "traditional settlement" by the EOT. It has a more open and less lived-in appearance than Makrinítsa, and it draws surprisingly large crowds of day-trippers in summer. The best way to enjoy the place is to stay at one of the EOT or privately run **guesthouses**, converted from the finest of the mansions – try *Vafiadis* (☎0423/86 765; ⑥) and *Karayianopoulos* (☎0423/86 717; ⑤). To get the feel of staying in an *arkhondiko* without the expense, try the small hotel/café *Thetis* (☎0423/86 111; ④). There are two tavernas on the platía.

Agriá, Káto Gatzéa and inland
Most of the coast between Vólos and Koropí (below Miliés) is unenticing. At **AGRIÁ**, for example, a cement plant casts its shadow over rashes of hotels and neon-garish tavernas, while spilling a horrid brown sludge into the Pagasitic Gulf. Heading southeast, things improve temporarily around **Káto Gatzéa**, with olive groves lining the road, which now runs well inland; of the two **campsites** here, *Hellas* has the edge over the *Marina*.

A better inland route, if you have your own transport, is through the larger settlements of **DHRAKIÁ** and **ÁYIOS LAVRÉNDIS**. Dhrakiá boasts the Triandafíllou mansion and an August 23 festival; Áyios Lavréndis is more homogeneous and has the *Pension Kentavros* (☎0421/96 224; ④), if you want to stay in a typical, quieter Pílion village.

The south
Once **south** of the loop road around the mountain, Pílion becomes drier, emptier and less dramatic, its villages lacking the historic interest and character of their northern counterparts. There are, though, some interesting pockets, and considerably less tourism.

The area can be reached a little tortuously by bus, but much more easily by sea. In summer, **hydrofoils** from Vólos call at least daily at the port of **Ayía Kyriakí** (Tríkeri), and pause first at the little island of **Paleó Tríkeri**.

Argalastí and around
To get a better idea of the low-lying olive-grove countryside of western Pílion, press on south from Kalá Nerá to the junction of **ARGALASTÍ**, the "county town", with its obligatory square, and two good tavernas, *To Sokkaki* near the square, and *Klimataria*, on the outskirts at the start of the road to Milína. From here you can get several daily buses to **Áfissos**, a crowded, swish resort. **Khórto** (7km) and **Milína** (10km) are nicer though, small coastal villages with seasonal **campsites**, a few hotels, rooms for rent and tavernas lining the waterfront. Just south of Milína, there's a picturesque bay

where fishing boats moor, and the good *Favios* restaurant, which serves barrelled retsina. Much more beautiful and wilder are the beaches at **Páltsi**, on the west coast.

For walkers, an excellent **mule track** leads from Milína to Láfkos, an interesting inland village where many of Pílion's herbs are grown, while the coast at Líri and Katiyiórgis is still unspoilt. An alternative to hiking in this part of Pílion would be to go on a one-to-ten-day trek on **horseback** organized by *Kentavros Farm* (☎0423/ 54 131 or 439), near Argalastí.

Plataniás

Argalastí or Kalá Nerá are also the pick-up points for Vólos-based buses passing three times daily on their way to **PLATANIÁS**, a small resort near the end of the Pílion peninsula. The beach is excellent, though the resort is often a bit crowded with Greek holidaymakers: walk to the second beach, **Mikró**, for more seclusion. From the quayside, hydrofoils ply the short distance over to the Sporades islands, and also back to Vólos (see "Travel Details" on p.292).

Among the half-dozen **hotels**, the cheapest are *Kyma* (☎0423/71 269; ③) and *Platania* (☎0423/71 266; ③). Most of the waterside **restaurants** serve tasty seafood, but none really stands out.

Tríkeri peninsula

Stranded at the far end of Pílion, the semi-peninsula of **Tríkeri** still feels very remote. It was used after the 1946–49 civil war as a place of exile for political prisoners (along with the island of Paleó Tríkeri), and until a few years ago there was no real road connecting it with the rest of Pílion. It now boasts the best road in Pílion, connecting it with Milína in less than thirty minutes. There are a few daily buses from Vólos, but the area can also be reached by hydrofoil from Vólos or the Sporades (daily from April to October, going up to twice daily between June and September).

The port of **AYÍA KYRIAKÍ** is still strictly a working fishing village, something of a rarity in modern Greece. There are a few simple **rooms** to rent, but otherwise minimal concessions to tourism, perhaps because there's no good beach. However, orange fishing boats, paths adorned with bougainvillea and excellent seafood combine to make it a captivating, unspoilt little port. In the local boatyard, large kaïkia, and occasionally yachts, are built in much the same way they have been for the last hundred years.

From Ayía Kyriakí, it's a 25-minute walk up to the village of **Tríkeri**, by an old *kalderími* that starts behind the port police building – by road it's twice the distance. This is a pleasant hilltop village with a scattering of mansions and a useful post office and money exchange; the most common mode of transport for villagers is horse or donkey, though the new road will undoubtedly bring changes. The tree-shaded platía has a kafenío and an excellent traditional ouzerí; there's also a taverna, with some **rooms** above, by the road down to the harbour.

Paleó Tríkeri

Paleó Tríkeri (or Nisí Tríkeri – Tríkeri island) has a village, two hotels, a couple of tavernas and sand – which perhaps makes it the smallest Greek island with everything you really need. Little more than a kilometre end to end, it consists of a few olive-covered hills and a fringe of small, rocky beaches; it is friendly and uncrowded, and has its own charm.

The port and village, **Aïyánni**, is tiny, with a single shop and a good taverna by the harbour. Around the island from here, there are just donkey tracks. Following the track up from the village, for around ten minutes, you reach the nineteenth-century **Evangelistrías monastery** (daily 8am–3pm & 6–8pm), the scene of a work-holiday camp for European teenagers, at the centre of the island. Past here, you reach a large bay and the island **hotel** – the *Filoxenia* (✆0423/55 209; ③), with a restaurant over-looking the beach. The *Galatia* also offers a few **rooms** (✆0423/91 031; ③), and there's generally no problem camping under the olive trees nearby.

The island is connected with Ayía Kyriakí by Flying Dolphin **hydrofoil**: these run daily in July and August (twice a week at other times of year), and take just ten minutes. Standard **ferries** to the Sporades only stop here once a week (Saturday), returning to Vólos on Sunday evening. For specific times, ask hotel proprietors or call the port police in Vólos (✆0421/38 888).

Lárissa

LÁRISSA stands at the heart of the Thessalian plain: a large market centre approached across a prosperous but dull landscape of wheat and corn fields. It is for the most part modern and unremarkable, but retains a few old streets that hint at its recent past as a Turkish provincial capital. The highest point of the town — the ancient acropolis — is dominated by the remains of a medieval fortress, which is closed to the public. Down below, the centre is being made into a series of landscaped squares, connected by pedestrian streets lined with upmarket boutiques. Life focuses on **Platía Makaríou**, also called Post Office Square (Takhidhromíou), which boasts several fountains, flowerbeds and statues, and rows of trendy cafés shaded by smart white umbrellas. Save at least an hour for the newly renovated **archeological museum**, 31 Avgoustou 2 (Tues–Sun 8.30am–3pm; free), with its fascinating collection of Neolithic finds. The modern Greek paintings in the Lárissa **pinakothiki** (Tues–Sun 11am–2.30pm & 6.30–10pm; 100dr), Roosevelt 59 are considered second only to those in the National Gallery in Athens. Otherwise, the **Alcazar** park, beside the Piniós, Thessaly's major river, remains a pleasant place to wile away a few hours. As a major **road and rail junction**, the town has efficient connections with most places you'd want to reach: Vólos to the east; Tríkala and Kalambáka to the west; Lamía to the south; the Vale of Témbi (see below), Mount Olympus and Thessaloníki along the national highway to the northeast.

You probably won't choose to stay in Lárissa, but if you need to, there are numerous **hotels**. The cheapest are a trio of places in the square by the train station: the *Diethnes* (✆041/234 210; ②), the last resort *Neon* (✆041/236 268; ①) and the renovated *Pantheon* (✆041/236 726; ③). More savoury options include the *Metropol* at Roosevelt 14 (✆041/227 843; ⑤) and the *Atlantic* at Panagoúli 1 (✆041/287 711; ④). *Ellas*, at Roosevelt 28, serves inexpensive **meals** and is always packed with locals, while *Filoxenia*, a few doors up on the square itself, is also good value if slightly fancier.

North towards Mount Olympus: the Vale of Témbi and the coast

Travelling north from Lárissa, the National Highway heads towards Thessaloníki, a highly scenic route through the **Vale of Témbi**, between Mounts Olympus and Óssa, before emerging on the coast. Accounts of the valley and the best of the **beaches** east of Mount Óssa follow; for details on Mount Olympus, see p.360.

Ambelákia

If you have time, or a vehicle, a worthwhile first stop in the Témbi region is **AMBELÁKIA**, a small town in the foothills of Mount Óssa. In the eighteenth century, this community supported the world's first **industrial cooperative**, producing, dyeing and exporting textiles, and maintaining its own branch offices as far afield as London. With the cooperative came a rare and enlightened prosperity. At a time when most of Greece lay stagnant under Turkish rule, Ambelákia was largely autonomous; it held democratic assemblies, offered free education and medical care, and even subsidized weekly performances of ancient drama. The brave experiment lasted over a century, eventually succumbing to the triple ravages of war, economics and the industrial revolution. In 1811 Ali Pasha raided the town and a decade later any chance of recovery was lost with the collapse of the Viennese bank in which the town's wealth was deposited.

Until World War II, however, over six hundred mansions survived in the town. Today there are just 36, most in poor condition. You can still get some idea of the former prosperity by visiting the **Mansion of George Schwarz**. The home of the cooperative's last president, this *arkhondikó* (Tues–Sun 9.30am–3.30pm; 500dr) is built in grand, old-Constantinople style. The exterior has been admirably restored, but the charming Anatolian/rococo interior is in dire need of conservation. Schwarz, incidentally, was a Greek, despite the German-sounding name, which was merely the Austrian bank's translation of his real surname, Mavros (Black).

The town is connected by bus with Lárissa (3 daily); or you can walk up a cobbled way in about an hour from the Témbi train station. There is a single **inn**, the *Ennea Mousses* (☎0495/93 405; ④), and a couple of tavernas.

The Vale of Témbi

Two kilometres beyond the Ambelákia turn-off, you enter the **Vale of Témbi**, a valley cut over the eons by the Piniós, which runs for nearly ten kilometres, between the steep cliffs of the Olympus (Ólymbos) and Óssa ranges. In antiquity it was sacred to Apollo and constituted one of the few possible approaches into Greece – being the path taken by both Xerxes and Alexander the Great – and it remained an important passage during the Middle Ages. Walkers might consider a hike along the valley, which can also be traversed by canoe on the Piniós. However, both National Road 1 and the railway forge through Témbi, impinging somewhat on its beauties. One of the most popular stops is the **Spring of Venus**. Halfway through the vale (on the right, coming from Lárissa) are the ruins of the **Kástro tis Oreás** (Castle of the Beautiful Maiden), one of four Frankish guardposts here, while marking the northern end of the pass is a second **medieval fortress** at Platamónas, also built by the Crusaders.

Platamónas marks the beginning of **Macedonia** and heralds a rather grim succession of resorts fronting the narrow, pebbly beaches of the Thermaíkos gulf. The coast south of the castles is a better bet (see below). Inland, the mountain spectacle continues, with **Mount Olympus** (Óros Ólymbos) casting ever-longer shadows; the trailhead for climbing it is Litóhoro, 7km to the north (see p.360).

Stómio and the Óssa Coast

A side road, close by the Kástro tis Oreás, takes you the 13km to **STÓMIO**, an unexceptional seaside village at the mouth of the river Piniós. The dense beech trees of Óssa march down almost to the shore, masking some of Stómio's more recent construction. The marshes around the river make the beach a fine spot for **birdwatchers**, and swimmers can bathe in clear waters, while gazing at Mount Olympus.

Outside July and August – when Stómio draws big crowds from the hinterland – you shouldn't have any trouble finding **accommodation**, though the rooms available on the waterfront are apt to be noisy. *Anatoli* (☎0495/91 350; ②) offers the bare essentials, while *Vlasis*, higher and quieter, has two-room places (☎0495/91 301; ④). Camping would be a better option but the free municipal **campsite** north of the river is a bit squalid, offering cold-water sinks and toilets only, though there are showers on the beach. Along the seafront, a clutch of fish tavernas and bars are the focus of Stómio's low-key nightlife.

Down the coast towards Pílion, Koutsupiés and Kókkino Neró have smaller beaches and are also rather scruffy resorts for Lárissans and Tríkalans. **Ayiókambos** and **Velíka**, east and southeast of the attractive Óssa hill villages of **Ayía** and **Melívia**, have long sandy beaches. All four villages are served by bus from Lárissa; for **accommodation** try the *Golden Beach* (☎0494/51 222; ⑤) at Ayiókambos which has a pool and tennis courts, or the modest eight-room *Melivia Beach* (☎0494/51 128; ③) on the shore at Velíka. There are also plenty of campsites in the area. The road is paved all along the coast.

West from Lárissa: Tríkala and Pýli

West from Lárissa, the road trails the river Pindhós to **Tríkala**, a quiet provincial town with a scattering of Byzantine monuments nearby. For most travellers, it's simply a staging post en route to Kalambáka and the Metéora; five buses daily connect it with Lárissa and there are connections north and west also. The railway loops around between Vólos, Lárissa, Tríkala and Kalambáka, via the uninteresting market town of Kardhítsa.

Tríkala

TRÍKALA is quite a lively metropolis after the agricultural towns of central Thessaly, spread along the banks of the Lethéos, a tributary of the Piniós, and backed by the mountains of the Koziakas range. It was the main town of the nineteenth-century Turkish province and retains quite a few houses from that era, around the clock tower at the north end of town. Downriver from the bus station, a minaret-less yet very stately Turkish mosque, the **Koursoum Tzami**, survives, too, a graceful accompaniment to the town's numerous stone churches.

The town's **fortress**, a Turkish adaptation of a Byzantine structure, is closed to the public, but around it are attractive gardens, a pleasantly shaded café and the meagre remains of a **Sanctuary of Asclepius** – according to some accounts, the cult of the healing god originated here (see p.164). The liveliest part of town, encompassing what's left of the old **bazaar**, is in the streets around the central Platía Iróön Politekhníou on the riverside.

Practicalities

The **post office** and **OTE** are situated off Platía Iróön Politekhníou. The **bus station** is on the west bank of the river, 300m southeast of the square; the **train station** is found at the southwestern edge of town, at the end of Odhós Asklipíou. Accommodation should pose few problems, with two bare, inexpensive **hotels** across the river from the main square in the lively area around Platía Ríga Feréou: the rock-bottom, hundred-year-old *Panhellinion*, Vassilísis Olgas 2 (☎0431/27 644; ②), and the slightly more comfortable *Palladion*, Víronos 4 (☎0431/28 091; ③). Other mid-range alternatives include two renovated hotels, the *Lithaeon*, Óthonos 18, above the bus station (☎0431/20 690; ④), and the slightly cushier *Hotel Dina*, on the corner of Asklipíou and Karanasíou, near the square (☎0431/74 777; ④).

Aside from the ouzerí places in the old bazaar, **restaurants** are scattered throughout the town. A good, cheap lunch can be had at *O Elatos*, at the junction of Asklipíou and Víronos in the pedestrian zone behind the hotels, while *Taverna O Babis*, next to *Hotel Dina*, is highly thought of by the locals. Other possibilities are *Dimitri's* ouzerí on Gousíon street, *Pliatsikas* on Adhám and *Khanis*, across the train line on the road to

Pýli. Like Lárissa, Tríkala has been gentrified in the last few years and boasts its share of chic cafés. There's no shortage of cafés and bars as well as some good zakharoplastía along Asklipíou, but prices tend to be higher here. If you have time to spare, take a look at the traditional Thessalian cheese shop *Galaktos Batayanni*, on parallel Adhám 10 – identifiable by the range of goatbells hanging inside.

Pýli

It takes some effort of will to delay immediate progress to Kalambáka and the Metéora. Byzantine aficionados, however, may be tempted by a detour to **PÝLI**, 20km southwest of Tríkala, for the thirteenth-century church of **Pórta Panayía**, one of the unsung beauties of Thessaly, in a superb setting at the beginning of a gorge. Nearby, there is an outstanding cycle of frescoes at the monastery of **Ayíou Visaríonos Dousíkou** (men only admitted), which would be a major tourist attraction were it not overshadowed by its spectacular neighbour, Metéora.

Regular **buses** run to Pýli from Tríkala. Near Pórta Panayía and beside a fountain-fed oasis there are two **tavernas** – a far nicer lunch stop than Tríkala; in the village there is a single **hotel**, the *Babanara* (☎0431/22 325; ④). More tavernas are located on the Pýli side of the river, and the whole area is a very popular Sunday outing spot with the locals; the scenery beyond up to the ski resort at Eláti is alpine.

The Pórta Panayía

The **Pórta Panayía** (daily: summer 8am–noon & 4–8pm; winter 9am–1pm & 3–5pm; 100dr) is a ten-minute walk uphill from the bus-stop in Pýli village. Cross the Portaikós River on the footbridge, then bear left on the far bank until you see its dome in a clump of trees below the rough road; a slightly longer route is via the roadbridge. The caretaker lives in a white house below the nearby tavernas.

Much of the church was completed in 1283 by one Ioannis Doukas, a prince of the Despotate of Epirus. Its architecture is somewhat bizarre, in that the current narthex is probably a fourteenth-century Serbian remodelling of the original dome and transept. The original nave on its west side collapsed in an earthquake, and its replacement to the east gives the whole a "backwards" orientation. In the Doukas section, perpendicular barrel vaults over a narrow transept and more generous nave lend anti-seismic properties, with further support from six columns. The highlights of the interior are a pair of **mosaic icons** depicting Joseph, Mary and the Child, and a marble iconostasis, whose modern icons are placed unusually (for Orthodox iconography) with Christ on the left of the Virgin. The **frescoes** have fared less well and many of the figures are blackened by fire and barely discernible. The most interesting image is next to the tiny font, over Ioannis Doukas's tomb, where a lunette shows the Archangel Michael leading a realistically portrayed Doukas by the hand to the enthroned Virgin with Child.

A kilometre upstream, best reached along the Pýli bank of the river, a graceful **medieval bridge** spans the Portaïkós at the point where it exits a narrow mountain gorge. A couple of cafés and snack bars take advantage of the setting, and you can cross the bridge to follow paths some distance along the gorge on the opposite side; the tranquil beauty is best appreciated on a weekday.

Ayíou Visaríonos Dousíkou

The monastery of **Ayíou Visaríonos Dousíkou** – known locally as Aï Vissáris – has a stunning setting, 500m up a flank of Mount Kóziakas, looking out over most of Thessaly. The small community of monks is keen to maintain its isolation, excluding women from visits, and admitting men only with suspicion. In theory, visits are allowed from 8am to noon and 3.30pm to 7.30pm, with preference given to Orthodox visitors and/or Greek speakers. To reach the monastery, cross the road bridge over the Portaïkós as for Pórta Panayía, but turn right instead, then left almost instantly onto a signed dirt track which leads up for 4km.

The monastery was founded in 1530 by Visarionos (Bessarion), a native of Pýli, and contains a perfect **cycle of frescoes** by Tzortzis – one of the major painters on Mount Athos – executed between 1550 and 1558 and recently restored to brilliance. These, and the cloister as a whole, miraculously escaped damage in 1940, when two Italian bombs fell in the court but failed to explode.

Originally, the monastery perched on a cliff as steep as any at Metéora, but in 1962 the abyss was largely filled in with kitchen gardens, and a new road and gate opened. This rendered ornamental the pulleys and ladder on the east wall, which, like much of the place, had survived intact since its foundation. In its heyday, nearly three hundred monks lived at the monastery; currently there are around ten.

The Monasteries of Metéora

The **Monasteries of Metéora** are one of the great sights of mainland Greece. These extraordinary buildings, perched on seemingly inaccessible pinnacles of rock, occupy a valley just to the north of **Kalambáka**; the name *metéora* means literally "rocks in the air". Arriving at the town, your eye is drawn in an unremitting vertical ascent to the first weird grey cylinders. Overhead to the right you can make out the closest of the monasteries, Ayíou Stefánou, firmly entrenched on a massive pedestal; beyond stretch a chaotic confusion of spikes, cones and cliffs – beaten into bizarre and otherworldly shapes by the action of the prehistoric sea that covered the plain of Thessaly around thirty million years ago.

Some history

The Meteorite monasteries are as enigmatic as they are spectacular. Legend has it that **St Athanasios**, who founded Megálou Meteórou (the Great Meteoron) – the earliest of the buildings – flew up to the rocks on the back of an eagle. A more prosaic suggestion is that the villagers of Stáyi, the medieval precursor of Kalambáka, may have become adept at climbing, and helped the original monks up. The difficulties of access and building are hard to overstate; a German guide published for rock climbers grades almost all the Metéora routes as "advanced", even with modern high-tech climbing gear.

The earliest religious communities here appeared in the late tenth century, when groups of **hermits** made their homes in the caves that score many of the rocks. In 1336 they were joined by two monks from Mount Athos, **Gregorios**, Abbot of Magoula, and his companion, **Athanasios**. Gregorios returned shortly to Athos but he left Athanasios behind, ordering him to establish a monastery. This Athanasios did, whether supernaturally aided or not, imposing a particularly austere and ascetic rule. He was quickly joined by many brothers, including, in 1371, **John Paleologos**, who refused the throne of Serbia to become the monk Ioasaph.

The royal presence was an important aid to the **endowment** of the monasteries, which followed swiftly on all the accessible, and many of the inaccessible rocks. They reached their zenith during the Ottoman reign of Süleyman the Magnificent (1520–66), by which time 24 of the rocks had been surmounted by monasteries and hermitages. The major establishments accumulated great wealth, flourishing on revenues of estates granted them in distant Wallachia and Moldavia, as well as in Thessaly itself. They retained these estates, more or less intact, through to the eighteenth century, at which time monasticism here, as elsewhere in Greece, was in decline.

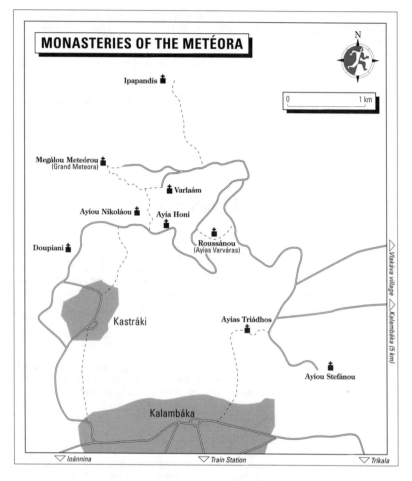

MONASTERIES OF THE METÉORA

N

0   1 km

Ipapandís

Megálou Meteórou
(Grand Meteora)

Varlaám

Ayíou Nikoláou

Ayía Honí

Doupiani

Roussánou
(Ayías Varváras)

Kastráki

Ayías Triádhos

Vlakáva village ▷ / Kalambáka (5 km) ▷

Ayíou Stefánou

Kalambáka

▽ Ioánnina   ▽ Train Station   ▽ Tríkala

During the intervening centuries, numerous disputes arose over power and precedence among the monasteries. However, the principal factors in the Metéora's fall from glory were physical and economic. Many of the buildings, especially the smaller hermitages, were just not built to withstand centuries of use and, perhaps neglected or unoccupied, gradually disintegrated. The grander monasteries suffered **depopulation**, conspicuously so in the nineteenth century as a modern Greek state was established to the south – with Thessaly itself excluded – and monasticism lost its link with Greek nationalism and resistance to Turkish rule.

In the present century the crisis accelerated after the monastic lands and revenues, already much reduced from their heyday, were taken over by the state for the use of Greek refugees from Asia Minor, after the Greco-Turkish war of 1919–22. By the 1950s, there were just five active monasteries, struggling along with little more than a dozen monks between them – an epoch that's superbly chronicled in Patrick Leigh Fermor's *Roumeli*. Ironically, before their expropriation for **tourism** over the last three decades, the monasteries had begun to revive a little, attracting a number of young and intellectual brothers. Today, put firmly on the map by appearances in such films as James Bond's *For Your Eyes Only*, the four most accessible monasteries and convents are today essentially museum-piece monuments. Only two, **Ayías Triádhos** (the Holy Trinity) and **Ayíou Stefánou**, continue to function with a primarily monastic purpose.

Practicalities: Kalambáka and Kastráki

Visiting the Metéora demands a full day, which means staying at least one night in **Kalambáka** or at the village of **Kastráki**, 2km to the north. If at all possible, opt for Kastráki; it wins hands down on atmosphere and situation, set as it is right in the shadow of the rocks. It also has two of the best local campsites.

Kalambáka

KALAMBÁKA has no particular allure, save for its position near the rocks. The town was burned by the Germans in the last war and very few pre-war buildings remain, save for the old cathedral. This, the **Mitrópolis** (daily late afternoons; 200dr) stands a couple of streets above its modern successor, at the top end of the town. It was founded in the seventh century on the site of a temple to Apollo and incorporates various classical drums and fragments in its erratically designed walls. Inside are fourteenth-century Byzantine frescoes and, most unusually in a Greek church, a great double marble pulpit in the central aisle.

Arriving by **bus or train**, in season, you are likely to be offered a **room** by waiting householders. Unfortunately, not all of them are reputable, so it's best to hunt for accommodation independently, to avoid being cheated. This should not be difficult, as there are numerous signs on the road into town from the bus station and plenty of rather undistinguished **hotels**, most of which have a tendency to noise, with minimal views and character and above-average rates, reflecting the tourist status of the Metéora. Least expensive, and fairly quiet, is the *Astoria*, Kondhíli 93 (☎0432/22 213; ②) in sight of the train station; mid-budget options include the *Famissi* (☎0432/24 117; ④) on the main road through town and the *Edelweiss* (☎0432/23 966; ④) on the first square. Both have good views if you get a back room.

Kastráki

KASTRÁKI is twenty minutes' walk out of Kalambáka; there's a short cut if you follow a footpath out of the northwest corner of the town. In season there are occasional buses.

Along the way to the village you pass the first of two **campsites** here, *Camping Vrakhos* (☎0432/22 293, fax 23 134), which offers **rock-climbing** and **hang-gliding** lessons in English: sign up on the premises. The other, *Camping Boufidhis/The Cave* (☎0432/24 802), is a bit more cramped, but incomparably set on the far side of the village with the monasteries of Ayíou Nikoláou and Roussánou rearing above. Both have swimming pools, as do the other more distant sites out on the Tríkala and Ioánnina roads.

The village has hundreds of **rooms** for rent (all around 7,000dr), and several affordable and agreeable small hotels. The *Hotel Meteora* (☎0432/22 367; ③), up a side street to the right as you leave Kalambáka for Kastráki, sits at the foot of the extraordinary rocks. *Doupiani House* (☎0432/75 326; ③), acclaimed as "the balcony of Metéora", and *Hotel Kastraki* (☎0432/75 336; ⑤), also fantastically situated and a more pricey but a very comfortable choice, are both on the left side of the road through Kastráki towards the monasteries. There are also an almost infinite number of **places to eat**. Arrayed around the central church and platía, are four reasonable tavernas, of which *Gardhenia* is probably the best. Other good meals can be had at *Philoxenia* (1km past Vrakhos on the main road), *Stelios* (near the square) and *Koka Roka*, this last in upper Kalambáka.

Visiting the monasteries

There are six Metéora monasteries, each open to visits at slightly different hours and days (see below). To see them all in a day, start early to take in Ayíou Nikoláou, Varlaám and Megálou Meteórou before 1pm, leaving the afternoon for Roussánou, Ayías Triádhos and Ayíou Stefánou.

The road route from **Kastráki to Ayíou Stefánou** is just under 10km. Walking, you can veer off the tarmac occasionally onto a few short-cut paths; at Ayíou Stefánou the "circuit" stops (the road signposted Kalambáka just before Ayías Triádhos is a highly indirect 5km). In season there are a couple of daily buses from Kalambáka up the road as far as Megálou Meteórou/Varlaám; even taken just part of the way they will give you the necessary head start to make a hiking day manageable. Hitching is also pretty straightforward.

Before setting out it is worth buying **food and drink** to last the day; there are only a couple of drinks/fruit stands on the circuit, by Varlaám and Megálou Meteórou. And finally, don't forget to carry money with you: each monastery levies an admission charge – currently 300–400dr depending on the monastery, with students half price except at Ayías Triádhos.

For visits to all the monasteries, **dress code** is strict. For women this means wearing a skirt – not trousers; for men, long trousers. Both sexes must cover their shoulders. Skirts are often lent to female visitors, but it's best not to count on this.

Doupianí and Ayíou Nikoláou Anapavsás

North from Kastráki the road loops around between huge outcrops of rock, passing below the chapel-hermitage of **Doupianí**, the first communal church of the early monastic settlements. This stretch takes around twenty minutes to walk from the centre of Kastráki. A further ten minutes and you reach a stepped path to the left, which winds around and up a low rock, on which is sited **Ayíou Nikoláou Anapavsás** (daily summer 9am–6pm; winter 9am–1pm & 3–5pm). A small, recently restored monastery, this has some superb sixteenth-century frescoes in its katholikón (main chapel) by the Cretan painter Theophanes. Oddly, the katholikón faces almost due north rather than east because of the rock's shape. As well as the Theophanes paintings there are later, naive images that show Adam naming the animals, including a basilisk – the legendary lizard-like beast that could kill by a breath or glance. Ayíou Nikoláou is also accessible, more directly, by dirt track and path, directly from the platía of Kastráki in fifteen minutes.

Next to Ayíou Nikoláou, on a needle-thin shaft, sits **Ayía Moní**, ruined by an earthquake in 1858.

Roussánou

Bearing off to the right, fifteen minutes or so further on from Ayíou Nikoláou, a well-signed and cobbled path ascends to the tiny and compact convent of **Roussánou** (daily: summer 9am–6pm; winter 9am–1pm & 3.30–6pm), also known as Ayías Varváras; from another descending trail off a higher loop of road, the final approach is across a dizzying bridge from an adjacent rock. Roussánou has perhaps the most extraordinary site of all the monasteries, its walls built right on a knife edge. Inside, the narthex of its main chapel, or katholikón, has particularly gruesome seventeenth-century frescoes of martyrdom and judgement, the only respite from sundry beheadings, spearings and mutilations being the lions licking Daniel's feet in his imprisonment, near the window.

A short way beyond Roussánou the road divides, the left fork heading towards Varlaám and the Megálou Meteórou. Both monasteries are also more directly accessible on foot via a partly cobbled and shaded path leading off the road, 250m past Ayíou Nikoláou; twenty minutes up this path bear right at a T-junction to reach Varlaám in ten minutes, or left for Megálou Meteórou within twenty steeper minutes.

Varlaám (Barlaam)

Varlaám (daily except Fri, 9am–1pm & 3.20–6pm) is one of the earliest established monasteries, standing on the site of a hermitage established by St Varlaam – a key figure in Meteorite history – shortly after Athanasios's arrival. The present building was founded by two brothers from Ioánnina in 1517 and is one of the most beautiful in the valley.

The monastery's katholikón, dedicated to Ayíon Pándon (All Saints), is small but glorious, supported by painted beams and with walls and pillars totally covered by frescoes. A dominant theme, well suited to the Metéora, are the desert ascetics, and there are many scenes of martyrdom. The highly vivid *Last Judgement* (1548), has a gaping Leviathan swallowing the damned, and, dominating the hierarchy of paintings, a great *Pandokrátor* (Christ in Majesty) in the inner of two domes (1566). In the refectory is a small museum of icons, inlaid furniture and textiles; elsewhere the monks' original water barrel is displayed.

Varlaám also retains intact its old **Ascent Tower**, with a precipitous reception platform and dubious windlass mechanism. Until the 1920s the only way of reaching most of the Meteorite monasteries was by being hauled up in a net drawn by rope and windlass, or by the equally perilous retractable ladders. Patrick Leigh Fermor, who stayed at Varlaám in the 1950s, reported a macabre anecdote about a former abbot: asked how often the rope was changed, he replied, "when it breaks."

Steps were eventually cut to all of the monasteries on the orders of the Bishop of Tríkala, doubtless unnerved by the vulnerability of his authority on visits. Today the ropes are used only for carrying up supplies and building materials.

Megálou Meteórou (Great Meteora)

The **Megálou Meteórou** (daily except Tues, 9am–1pm & 3.20–6pm) is the grandest and highest of the monasteries, built on the "Broad Rock" some 600m above sea level. It had extensive privileges and held sway over the area for several centuries: in an eighteenth-century engraving (displayed in the museum) it is depicted literally towering above the others. How Athanasios got onto this rock is a wonder.

The monastery's **katholikón**, dedicated to the *Metamórfosis* (Transfiguration), is the most magnificent in Metéora, a beautiful cross-in-square church, its columns and beams supporting a lofty dome with another *Pandokrátor*. It was rebuilt in the sixteenth century, with the original chapel, constructed by Athanasios and Ioasaph, forming just the *ierón*, the sanctuary behind the intricately carved *témblon*, or altar screen. Frescoes, however, are much later than those of the preceding monasteries and not as significant artistically; those in the narthex concentrate almost exclusively on grisly martyrdoms. The other monastery rooms comprise a vast, arcaded cluster of buildings. The *kellari* or storage cellar holds an exhibit of rural impedimenta, including a stuffed wolf; in the domed and vaulted refectory is a **museum**, featuring a number of exquisite carved-wood crosses, rare icons and an incense-burner made from a conch shell, as well as a wooden calendar of saints. You can also visit the ancient domed and smoke-blackened kitchen.

Ipapandí, Ayías Triádhos and Ayíou Stefánou

If you are visiting the valley in midsummer, you may by this point be impressed by the buildings but depressed by the crowds, which detract from much of the wild, spiritual romance of the valley. The remaining monasteries on the "east loop" are less visited, and for a real escape, you can take a path leading north from just past the Varlaám/Great Meteora fork which will bring you out, in around half an hour's walk, at the abandoned fourteenth-century monastery of **Ipapandí**. The church, huddled inside a small cave, was being restored in 1997, so it may not stay remote for long.

Following the main road, it's about thirty minutes' walk from the Varlaám/Great Meteora fork to **Ayías Triádhos** (closed in 1997 for repairs), whose final approach consists of 130 steps carved into a tunnel in the rock. You emerge into a light and airy cloister, recently renovated. There's a small folk museum of weavings and kitchen/farm implements, but in general less to be seen than elsewhere – many of the frescoes in the katholikón are black with soot and damp, a project to clean and restore them having stalled at an early stage. Most tour buses, mercifully, do not stop here, and the life of the place remains essentially monastic – even if there are only three brothers to maintain it.

Ayíou Stefánou (Tues–Sun 9am–1pm and 3.20–6pm), the last and easternmost of the monasteries, is twenty minutes' walk beyond here, appearing suddenly at a bend in the road. Again it is active, occupied this time by nuns, but the buildings are a little disappointing, having been bombed during the war. Still, the katholikón has been painted in the last few years with attractive frescoes, the garden has been given much loving care, and the place conveys a spirituality somewhat lacking in most of the other monasteries. One small chapel, undamaged, contains lovely frescoes, and the small museum is a jewel. Needless to say, the view is amazing – like every turn and twist of this valley – and many visitors leave the convent refreshed by the absence of commerciality.

The path back to Kalambáka from here is disused and dangerous.

On from Kalambáka

West from Kalambáka runs one of the most dramatic roads in Greece, negotiating the **Katára Pass** across the Píndhos mountains to Métsovo and Ioánnina. This route, taking you into northern Epirus, is covered at the beginning of the next chapter.

North from Kalambáka a road leads through Grevená into Macedonia, and then forks: north to Kastoriá, or east to Siátista, Kozáni, Véria and Thessaloníki (see Chapter Five). The **Grevená road**, despite its uncertain appearance on most maps, is quite reasonable: its only drawback is that there are just two daily buses to dull Grevená itself, and not a lot of other transport. Finally, there's a possible side trip into the mountains west of Metéora to visit one of Greece's most peculiar churches.

The church of Timíou Stavroú

If you have your own transport, the flamboyant medieval **church of Timíou Stavroú**, 42km northwest from Kalambáka, between the villages of Kranía (Kranéa on some maps) and Dholianá, is well worth a visit. The church itself, eighteenth century but seeming far older, is a masterpiece of whimsy, matched in concept only by two specimens in Romania and Russia. It sports no less than twelve turret-like cupolas, higher than they are wide: three are over the nave, one over each of the three apses, and six over the ends of the triple transept. The church is in perfect repair, despite some ill-advised restoration and bulldozing, and a terrace below with a fountain makes an ideal picnic spot.

To reach the church, head 10km north of Kalambáka and instead of taking the Métsovo/Ioánnina-bound highway, bear left into a narrower road with multiple signposts for high villages. Climb steadily over a pass on the shoulder of Mount Tringía and then drop sharply into the densely forested valley of the River Aspropótamos, one of the loveliest in the Píndhos. From the *Aspropotamos* taverna, continue 1500m further south to a tiny bridge and a signposted track on the left which leads after 500m to the church, at a height of 1150m. There's a bus from Tríkala to Kranía most days in the summer; a small hotel, the *Aspropotomos* (☎0432/87 277; ②) is open from May to November.

travel details

Trains

Athens–Thíva–Livadhiá–Lianokládhi (Lamía)–Lárissa

14 trains daily, in each direction: some expresses (marked IC on schedules) don't stop at Thíva or Livadhiá. The intercity express takes only 4 hours and costs 10,000dr, one way, to Lárissa.

Approximate journey times:
Athens–Thíva (1hr 15min)
Thíva–Livadhiá (30min)
Livadhiá–Lianokládhi (1hr–2hr)
Lianokládhi–Lárissa (1hr 30min–2hr 30min).

Lárissa–Kateríni–Thessaloníki

12 daily in each direction.
Approximate journey times:
Lárissa–Kateríni (1hr 10min)
Kateríni–Thessaloníki (1hr 10min).

Vólos–Lárissa–Platamónas–Litókhoro –Kateríni–Thessaloníki

3 daily in each direction; all involve a change of trains in Lárissa.
Approximate journey times:
Vólos–Lárissa (1hr 10min)
Lárissa–Platamónas (45min)
Platamónas–Litókhoro (25min)
Litókhoro–Kateríni (15–30min)
Kateríni–Thessaloníki (1hr 30min).
Lárissa–Vólos 15 daily in each direction (1hr 10min).

Vólos–Fársala–Kardhítsa–Tríkala–Kalambáka

5 daily in each direction.
Approximate journey times:
Vólos–Farsála (1hr 30min)
Farsála–Kardhítsa (1 hr)
Kardhítsa–Tríkala (30min)
Tríkala–Kalambáka (20min).

Buses

Buses detailed have similar frequency in each direction, so entries are given just once; for reference check under both starting-point and destination.

Connections with Athens Thíva/Livadhiá (hourly; 1hr 30min/2hr 10min); Dhelfí (4–6 daily; 3hr); Lamía (hourly; 3hr 15min); Karpeníssi (2 daily; 6hr); Vólos (9 daily; 4hr 30min); Lárissa (6 daily; 5hr); Tríkala (7 daily; 5hr 30min).

Ámfissa to: Lamía (3–4 daily; 2hr 30min).

Andírio to: Messolóngi/Agrínio (12 daily; 1hr 30min).

Dhelfí to: Itéa (5 to 16 daily; 30min); Ámfissa (4 daily; 40min); Náfpaktos (4 daily – not direct; 2hr); Patzas (1–2 daily; 3hr).

Elefsína to: Thíva (Thebes) (2 daily; 1hr 30min).

Itéa to: Galaxídhi/Náfpaktos (4 daily; 30min/1hr 30min).

Kalambáka to: Métsovo/Ioánnina (3 daily; 1hr 30min/3hr 30min); Grevená (2 daily; 1hr 30min); Vólos (4 daily; 2hr 30 min).

Karpeníssi to: Agrínio (1 or 2 daily; 3hr 30min).

Lamía to: Karpeníssi (4 daily; 2hr); Vólos (2 daily; 3hr); Lárissa (4 daily; 3hr 30min); Tríkala, via Kardhítsa (4 daily; 3hr); Thessaloníki (2 daily; 4hr 30min).

Lárissa to: Stómio (3 daily; 1hr 25min); Litóhoro junction (almost hourly; 1hr 45min); Tríkala (every half-hour; 1hr); Kalambáka (hourly; 2hr).

Livadhiá to: Arákhova/Delphi (6 daily; 40min/1hr); Dhístomo, for Óssios Loukás (10 daily; 45min); Óssios Loukás, direct (daily at 1pm; 1hr).

Náfpaktos: City bus to Andírio for most connections.

Thíva to: Livadhiá (hourly; 1hr); Khalkídha (2 daily; 1hr 20min).

Tríkala to: Kalambáka (hourly; 30min); Kalambáka–Métsovo–Ioánnina (3 daily; 30min/2hr/4hr); Kalambáka–Grevená (2 daily; 30min/2hr).

Vólos to: Lárissa (hourly; 1hr 15min); Tríkala (4 daily; 2hr 30min); Thessaloníki (5 daily; 3hr 20min); Portariá/Makrinítsa (10 daily; 40min/50min); Zagorá (4 daily; 2hr); Tsangarádha/Áyios Ioánnis (2 daily; 2hr/2hr 30min); Miliés/Vizítsa (6 daily; 1hr/1hr 10min); Plataniás (3 daily; 2hr); Tríkeri (2 daily; 2hr).

Ferries

Áyios Konstandínos to: Skiáthos (daily; 2hr 30min); Skópelos (daily; 3hr 30min) and Alónissos (daily; 4hr 40min); ☎0235/31 920 for information.

Vólos to: Skiáthos (2–4 daily; 2hr 30min–3hr) and Skópelos (2–4 daily; 4–5hr), at least one continuing to Alónissos (5–6hr); at least one weekly to Tríkeri and Tríkeri island; call ☎0421/31 059 for information. Also twice weekly to Thessaloníki.

To Évvia Arkítsa-Loutrá Edhípsou (hourly, every 2hr in winter, last at 11pm/8pm; 50min); Glyfá-Ayiókambos (8 daily, 4 in winter; last at 8.15pm/5pm; 30min).

Across the Gulf of Kórinthos Andírio–Río (every 15min, much less often after midnight; 20min journey); Áyios Nikólaos–Éyio (3 times daily, 5 in summer; 35–40min journey).

Hydrofoils

Flying Dolphins run from the following ports (call ☎01/32 44 600 for information on any route).

Áyios Konstandínos At least 3 daily in season to Skiáthos, Skópelos and Alónissos, some stopping at Tríkeri, Paleó Tríkeri and Plataniás in southern Pílion.

Plataniás At least 1 daily in season to Skiáthos, Skópelos and Alónissos, except Thurs.

Stylídha 1 weekly in season to Skiáthos, Skópelos and Alónissos, Oreí, Skýros and Kými.

Tríkeri and Paleó Tríkeri At least 2 daily in season to Skiáthos, Skópelos and Alónissos.

Vólos 2–4 daily in season to Skiáthos, Skópelos and Alónissos, with 2 weekly continuing to Skýros; last reliable departure to Skiáthos 7pm; at least one daily stops at Plataniás, Tríkeri and Paleó Tríkeri.

For details of services, which vary drastically with the seasons, your best bet is to contact local agents (in Áyios Konstandínos ☎0235/31 614; in Vólos ☎0241/39 786; in Plataniás ☎0423/71 231; in Tríkeri ☎0423/91 556) or call ☎01/32 44 600 for information on any route.

CHAPTER FOUR

EPIRUS AND THE WEST

Epirus (Ípiros in modern Greek) has the strongest regional identity in mainland Greece. It owes this character to its mountains: the rugged peaks and passes, forested ravines and turbulent rivers of the **Píndhos** (Pindus) **range**. They have protected and isolated Epirus from outside interference, securing it a large measure of autonomy even under Turkish rule.

Because of this isolation, the region's role in Greek affairs was peripheral in ancient times. There are just two archeological sites of importance, both of them oracles chosen for their isolation. At **Dodona**, the sanctuary includes a spectacular classical theatre; at **Ephyra**, the Necromanteion (Oracle of the Dead) was touted by the ancients as the gateway to Hades.

In more recent times, **Lord Byron** has been the region's greatest publicist. Byron visited in 1809 when the tyrannical ruler Ali Pasha was at the height of his power, and the poet's tales of brigandage and braggadocio sent a frisson of horror down Romantic western spines. Byron went on to distinguish himself in the southern province of **Étolo-Akarnanía** by supplying and training troops for the Greek War of Independence, and of course dying at **Messolóngi**.

Despite eventual Greek victory in the War of Independence, the Turks remained in Epirus, and were not finally ousted until February 1913. A disputed frontier territory throughout the nineteenth century, the region never recovered its medieval prosperity. When the Italians invaded in 1940, followed by the Germans in 1941, its mountains became first the stronghold of the Resistance, then a battleground for rival political factions, and finally, after 1946, the chief bastion of the Communist Democratic Army in the **civil war**. The events of this period (see the box on p.295) are among the saddest of modern Greek history, and continue to reverberate today.

However, the **mountains** are still the place to head for in Epirus. The people are friendly and hospitable, and certain aspects of their traditional way of life survive. Vlach and Sarakatsan shepherds (see Contexts, p.784) still bring their flocks to the high mountain pastures in summer. Bears leave footprints on riverbanks and raid beehives, risking an (illegal) bullet, while wolves keep a hungry eye out for stray ewes and goats.

The best single area to visit is around **Mounts Gamíla** and **Smólikas**, with the **Aóös** and **Víkos gorges** to walk through and the splendid **villages of Zagóri** to stay

---

ACCOMMODATION PRICE CODES

Throughout the book we've used the following **price codes** to denote the cheapest available room in high season; all are prices for a double room, except for category ①, which represents per person rates. Out of season, rates can drop by up to fifty percent, especially if you are staying for three or more nights. Single rooms, where available, cost around seventy percent of the price of a double.

① 1400–2000dr	④ 8000–12,000dr
② 4000–6000dr	⑤ 12,000–16,000dr
③ 6000–8000dr	⑥ 16,000dr and upwards

For more accommodation details, see pp.39–42.

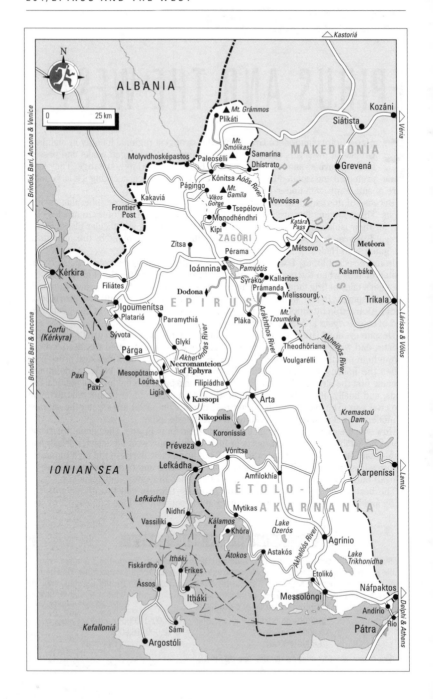

in. The Píndhos is a popular area for hiking, and you really have to explore on foot to get a full flavour of the place. Some of the road routes offer less strenuous travelling highlights – above all the Kalambáka–Ioánnina highway as it negotiates the **Katára pass**. En route is **Métsovo**, perhaps the easiest location for a taste of mountain life, though increasingly commercialized. **Ioánnina**, Ali Pasha's capital, is a town of some character, with its island and lake, and is the main transport hub for trips into Zagóri. Other than **Árta**, prettily set and with some fine Byzantine churches, there are few other urban attractions.

The **coasts** of both Epirus and Étolo-Akarnanía, are in general disappointing. **Igoumenítsa** is a useful ferry terminal for Corfu and Italy, but otherwise will win few admirers. **Párga**, the major Epirot resort, has been developed beyond its capacity, though **Préveza** has retained some character and is now a major gateway for charter-package patrons. Between these two towns is a string of functional beaches and, just inland, a scenic highlight – the gorge of the **Akheróndas River**. South of Préveza, you

---

WORLD WAR II AND THE CIVIL WAR IN EPIRUS

In **November 1940**, the **Italians** invaded Epirus, pushing down from Albania as far as Kalpáki, just south of Kónitsa. United as a nation for the first time in decades, the Greeks repulsed the attack and humiliated Mussolini. However, the euphoria was short-lived as the following April the Germans attacked and rapidly overran Greece.

When parcelling out key portions of the country to their allies for administration, the Germans initially assigned Epirus to the Italians, who trod lightly in the province where they had just been so soundly beaten. After Mussolini's capitulation, the Germans assumed direct responsibility for Epirus, and conditions worsened. Together with the mountains of central Greece to the south, the Epirot Píndhos was the main staging point for various **guerrilla bands**, foremost among them the Communist-dominated **ELAS**. Resistance harassment and ambush of the occupying forces incurred harsh reprisals, including the burning in early 1944 of virtually every Vlach village along the Aóös River.

The wartime flight to the cities from the mountains dates more or less from these atrocities, and the vicissitudes of the subsequent **civil war** (1946–49) dashed any lingering hope of a reasonable existence in the mountains. Victims of reprisals by either the Communists or the Royalist/Nationalist central government, villagers fled to safety in the cities, and many never returned. Wherever you go in the back country you'll hear people talk of these times. Some blame the Communists, some blame the Nationalists and all blame the British: "They set us at each other's throats," many will say, and with much justice.

Since 1975, many men (and a few women) who fought in ELAS, either as volunteers or conscripts, have returned to their villages – some of them after thirty years of **exile** in the USSR and other Eastern Bloc countries. Many of them had been carried off as children to Albania, and made to work in labour camps before being distributed to various East European states. The political Right claims that this **pedhomázema** – the roundup of children – was a cynical and merciless ploy to train up an army of dedicated revolutionaries for the future, while the Left retorts that it was a prudent evacuation of non-combatants from a war zone.

One thing, however, is certain. The Right won, with the backing of the British and, more especially, the Americans, and they used that victory to maintain an undemocratic and vengeful regime for the best part of the following quarter century. Many Epirot villagers, regardless of political conviction, believe that the poverty and backwardness in which their communities have remained was a deliberate punishment for being part of Communist-held territory during the civil war. For decades they were constantly harassed by the police, who controlled the issue of all sorts of licences and permits needed to find work, travel, put children in better schools, run a business and so forth. Only since the early 1980s have things really changed, and the past is finally treated as another age.

enter a low, marshy landscape of lakes and land-locked gulfs hemmed in by bare hills, of interest mainly to birdwatchers. For better beach escapes in this part of the world go to the Ionian Islands; Lefkádha (see p.740) is even connected to the mainland by a movable bridge.

THE PÍNDHOS MOUNTAINS

Even if you have no plans to go hiking, the **Píndhos range** deserves a few days' detour. The remoteness and traditional architecture, the air, the peaks – all constitute a very different Greece from the popular tourist image, and the range is still relatively unspoiled.

If you are coming from central Greece, the best of the main routes is **Kalambáka–Métsovo–Ioánnina**, which divides the **north Píndhos** from the **south Píndhos**. If you are arriving by ferry at Igoumenítsa, getting up to **Ioánnina** enables you to reverse this itinerary, which is quite the most attractive route into the mainland. **Walkers** will want to make directly for **Zagóri**, north of Ioánnina.

A number of **hiking routes** are detailed in the text; others can be found in the specialist guides (see "Books", p.822). Most of the routes are arduous rather than dangerous. But nonetheless this is high-mountain country, with unpredictable microclimates, and it's inadvisable to set off on the longer, more ambitious itineraries unless you are a fairly experienced walker.

Kalambáka to Ioánnina

West of Kalambáka (see p.287), the 1694-metre **Katára pass** cuts across the central range of the Píndhos to link Thessaly and Epirus. This route, the only motor road across these mountains that is kept open in winter (except during blizzards), is one of the most spectacular in the country and worth taking for the journey alone. It is the shortest east–west crossing in Greece, though distances here are deceptive. The road zigzags through folds in the enormous peaks, which rise to more than 2300m around Métsovo, and from November to April the snowline must be crossed. But all this will soon be in the past, as an enormous tunnel, scheduled to open by 1999, is being bored through the ridge.

Just two **buses** daily cover the entire route, running between Tríkala and Ioánnina, with stops at Kalambáka and Métsovo. If you're **driving**, allow half a day for the journey from Kalambáka to Ioánnina (114km), and in winter check on conditions before setting out. Anyone planning on **hitching** from Kalambáka should take a lift only if it's going through to Ioánnina or Métsovo, as there's little but mountain forest in between.

Métsovo

MÉTSOVO lies just west of the Katára pass, off the Kalambáka–Ioánnina highway. It is a small, often rainy **alpine town** built on two sides of a ravine and guarded by a forbidding range of peaks to the south and east. This startling site is matched by a **traditional architecture** and way of life. Immediately below the highway are tiers of eighteenth- and nineteenth-century stone houses with wooden balconies. They spill down the slope past the main platía, where a dwindling number of old men loiter, especially after Sunday mass, magnificent in full traditional dress: flat black caps and pom-pommed shoes. The women, enveloped in rich blue weave and with kerchiefs over their braided hair, have a more subdued appearance.

If you arrive outside of the two high seasons, stay overnight and take the time to walk in the valley below, the place can seem magical. During the summer, however, your experience may not be so positive. Métsovo has become a favourite target for bus tours, and its beauty veers perilously close to the artificially quaint. Souvenir shops selling "traditional" handicrafts (often from Albania) proliferate, while the stone roofs of the mansions have been replaced by ugly pantiles (it's claimed the slates cracked too readily under the weight of the yearly snowfall).

Nonetheless, it would be a shame to pass through Métsovo too speedily, for its history and status as the Vlach "capital" (see p.313) are unique. Positioned on the only commercially and militarily viable route across the Píndhos, it won a measure of independence, both political and economic, in the earliest days of Turkish rule. These privileges were greatly extended in 1659 by a grateful **Turkish vizier** who, restored to the sultan's favour, wanted to say a proper thank you to the Metsovite shepherd who had protected him during his disgrace. Métsovo's continued prosperity, and the preservation of some of its traditions, are largely due to Baron Tosítsas, banker scion of a Metsovite family living in Switzerland, who left his colossal fortune to an endowment that benefits industries and crafts in and around the town.

The town and around

The Métsovo **museum** occupies the eighteenth-century **Arkhondikó Tosítsa** (daily except Thurs 8.30am–1pm & 4–6pm; mandatory tours every 30min; 500dr), the old Tosítsa mansion just off the main thoroughfare. This has been restored to its full glory, and with its panelled rooms, rugs and fine collection of Epirot crafts and costumes, gives a real sense of the town's wealth and grandeur in that era. The **Ídhryma Tosítsa** (Tosítsa Foundation) building down in the platía serves as an outlet for contemporary handicrafts, stocking some of the more tasteful and finely woven cloth, rugs and blankets to be found in Greece – no relation to the schlock in the souvenir stalls. The goods are expensive, but not outrageously so, considering their quality.

The other major Métsovo attraction is the relatively remote monastery of **Áyios Nikólaos**, signposted from the main platía but in fact twenty minutes' walk below town, just off the *kalderími* to Anílio, the village across the ravine. The katholikón was built in the fourteenth century to a bizarre plan. It is topped by a simple barrel vault, and what might once have been the narthex became over time a *yinaikonítis* or women's gallery, something seen rarely elsewhere in Greece, except Kastoriá. The highly unusual eighteenth-century **frescoes**, recently cleaned and illuminated, mostly depict scenes of the life of Christ and assorted martyrdoms. Since there is no dome, the Four Evangelists are painted on four partly recessed columns rather than on pendentives, as is the norm. The barrel vault features three medallions – the Virgin and Child, an Archangel and a *Pandokrátor* (Christ in Majesty) – forming an unusual series of iconographies. A warden couple live on the premises and receive visitors until 7.30pm. You'll be shown the monks' former cells, with insulating walls of mud and straw, and the abbot's more sumptuous quarters; a donation or purchase of postcards is expected.

The village of **Anílio** (Sunless) is a further half-hour down, then up, and you'll have to make the gruelling trek back the same way. Like Métsovo, the population is Vlach-speaking, but life is more genuinely traditional here. There are no pretensions to tourist appeal, and the buildings are executed in dull cement. You can, however, get an excellent, reasonably priced lunch at the platía before starting back. The municipality of Métsovo is currently preparing a booklet/map detailing forty other trail walks around the town, ranging in length from an hour to a day.

Practicalities

The **bus stop** is in the town centre; the **post office** is on the main street, as are three **banks** with cash dispensers. Métsovo has a wide range of **accommodation** with thirteen hotels plus rooms and apartments for rent. Outside of the ski season, late August, or the town's festival (July 26), you should have little trouble in getting a bed. **Hotels** include the welcoming *Bitounis* (☎0656/41 217, fax 41 545; ⑤) at the top of the main street, and the *Acropolis* (☎0656/41 672; ③), rather inconveniently located at the very top of town. The friendly *Athens/Athenai* (☎0656/41 332; ③), just off the main platía, with clean rooms and en-suite showers, was one of the first hotels in Epirus (1925); it has a slightly fancier annexe called the *Filoxenia* (☎0656/41 021; ④). The *Kassaros* (☎0656/41 346; ⑤) a few steps south is comfortable, compact and quiet, though like the *Bitounis* it occasionally fills with tours; some rooms have views over to Anílio. The *Tolis* (☎0656/42 300, fax 42298; ⑤), peacefully sited just above the main square has the biggest, plushest rooms in town.

Eating in Métsovo is overwhelmingly meat-oriented. Three of the simpler grills are *Kryfi Folia* on the main platía, *To Koutouki tou Nikola* and *To Arkhondiko* directly below and behind the post office; all function principally in the evening. The main vegetarian and lunchtime option, with the fullest menu, is the restaurant attached to the *Athens*, which does good, reasonably priced casserole food accompanied by decent house wine. Wine buffs may want to try the fabled *katoyí*, a moderately expensive limited bottling from tiny vineyards down on the Árakhthos River. These and other local specialities such as *trakhanádhes* (sweet- and sour-dough grain-soup base) and *khilópites* (like tagliatelli, long or chopped into cubes), can be obtained from shops like Iy Piyí, downhill from the Bitounis.

Nightlife takes the form of a few conspicuously noisy pubs, cafés and discos uphill from the post office on the main street.

Villages of the Eastern Zagóri

For wilder, remoter scenery, and a truer, grittier picture of contemporary mountain life, follow the paved road up into the Píndhos from the Baldhoúma junction on the Métsovo–Ioánnina highway. This precipitous route snakes its way north along the valley of the Várdhas River, through a lush landscape of broad-leafed trees and scrub. At **GREVENÍTI**, the first of a series of predominantly Vlach villages, a black pine forest takes over and continues virtually all the way to Albania; you can stay here at the *Tourist Pavillion* (☎0656/31 212; ③).

The neighbouring villages of **Flambourári** and **Elatokhóri** have basic *xenónes* (inns) and places to eat, plus bus services from Ioánnina three days weekly. The villages are badly depopulated, having failed to recover from wartime destruction inflicted by Germans in pursuit of Resistance fighters, but what remains is very attractive: stone-roofed churches, vine-shaded terraces and courtyards full of flowers and stacked with logs for winter. Best of all is the beautiful village of **Makrinó** and its fine monastery, an hour's glorious walk across the ravine from Elatokhóri (or a more circuitous twenty-minute drive).

The main road continues, winding northeast to **VOVOÚSSA**, which lies right on the Aóös River, its milky green waters spanned here by a high-arched eighteenth-century bridge. On either side, wooded ridges rise steeply to the skyline. The village has a couple of psistariés and a single (poorly stocked) shop, open more or less year-round. The large riverside **hotel**, the *Perivoli* (no phone; ③), is worth a look for its rambling, slightly spooky layout; there are a few rooms available in peak season. If you prefer to **camp**, turn left off the road onto the old path just past the Vovoússa road sign, and walk for about fifteen minutes downstream to where a stretch of riverbank meadow makes an idyllic site. Fresh bear paw-prints are often seen in the riverside mud here, but the locals swear they are timid creatures who avoid contact with humans.

There is a sporadic **bus services** to Vovoússa from Ioánnina at 1.15pm on Monday and Friday, returning to Ioánnina the next morning at 6am; on Sundays they leave from Ioánnina at 7.45am, returning at 2pm. Alternatively, you could hike along the "E6", a marked long-distance route down the Aóös River valley to Dhístrato on Mount Smólikas, where there's an inn and early morning bus service (Tues, Thurs, Sat am & Sun pm) to Kónitsa (see p.313). The trek keeps to the east bank of the Aóös and takes a full day to accomplish.

Ioánnina and around

Descending from Métsovo, you approach **IOÁNNINA** through more spectacular folds of the Píndhos, emerging high above the great lake of **Pamvótis** (Pamvotídha). The old town stands on a rocky promontory jutting out into the water, its fortifications punctuated by towers and minarets. From this base, Ali Pasha wrested from Ottoman authority a fiefdom that encompassed much of western Greece – an act of contemptuous rebellion that portended wider defiance in the Greeks' own War of Independence.

Disappointingly, most of the city is modern and undistinguished – a testimony not so much to Ali Pasha, although he did raze much in the siege of 1820, as to developers in the 1950s and 1960s. However, there are several old stone **mosques** which evoke the Turkish era, and the fortifications of Ali Pasha's citadel, the Froúrio, survive more or less intact.

ALI PASHA

Ali Pasha, a highly ambivalent "heroic rebel", is the major figure in Ioanninan and Epirot history. The so-called "Lion of Ioánnina", on balance a highly talented sociopath, pursued a policy that was consistent only in its ambition and self-interest. His attacks on the Ottoman imperial government were matched by acts of appalling and vindictive **savagery** against his Greek subjects. Despite all this, he is still held in some regard by locals, the rationale being "a son of a bitch, but at least *our* son of a bitch"; a platía in the citadel is even named for him.

He was born in 1741 in Tepelene, Albania and rose to power under Turkish patronage, being made pasha of Tríkala in 1788 in reward for his efforts in the sultan's war against Austria. But his ambitions were of a grander order and that same year he **seized Ioánnina**, an important town since the thirteenth century, with a population of 30,000 – probably the largest in Greece at the time. Paying sporadic tribute to the sultan, he operated from this power-base for the next 33 years, allying in turn, and as the moment suited him, with the British, French and Ottomans.

In 1809, when his dependence upon the sultan was nominal, Ali was visited by the young **Lord Byron**, whom he overwhelmed with hospitality and attention. (The tyrant's sexual tastes were famously omnivorous, and it is recorded that he was particularly taken with the poet's "small ears", a purported mark of good breeding.) Byron, impressed for his part with the renegade's daring and stature, and the lively **revival of Greek culture** in Ioánnina (which, he wrote, was "superior in wealth, refinement and learning" to any town in Greece), commemorated the meeting in *Childe Harold*. The portrait that he drew, however, is an ambiguous one, aware that beneath the Pasha's splendid court and deceptively mild countenance there were "deeds that lurk" and "stain him with disgrace".

In a letter to his mother Byron was more explicit, concluding that "His highness is a remorseless tyrant, guilty of the most horrible cruelties, very brave, so good a general that they call him the Mahometan Buonaparte . . . but as barbarous as he is successful, roasting rebels, etc, etc". Of the rebels, the most illustrious was Katsandonis the Klepht, who racked by smallpox, was captured by Ali in a cave in the Ágrafa mountains. He imprisoned the unfortunate wretch in a waterlogged lakeside dungeon, and finally executed him in public by breaking his bones with a sledgehammer.

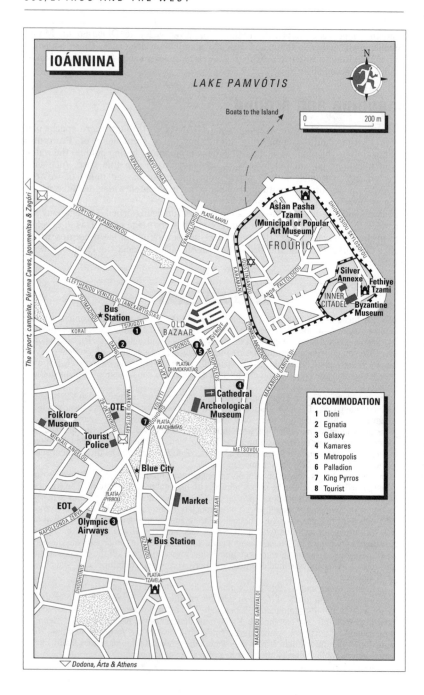

IOÁNNINA

N

LAKE PAMVÓTIS

Boats to the Island

0   200 m

The airport, campsite, Pérama Caves, Igoumenitsa & Zagóri

PAPAGOU

PAMVOTIHAS

YEORYIOU PAPANDREOU

EVANGELIDHOU

PLATÍA MAVILI

ELEFTHERIOU VENIZELOU

TANEKARTISSIAS

KARAMANI

Aslan Pasha
Tzami
(Municipal or Popular
Art Museum)

FROÚRIO

IOUSTINIANOU

ANDR. PALEOLOGOU

DHIONYSSIOU SKYLOSOGOU

Silver
Annexe

Fethiye
Tzami

INNER
CITADEL

Byzantine
Museum

ETHNIS ANDSTAS

Bus
Station

KOTMANOUDI

TSIRIGOTI

KORAÏ

1

OLD
BAZAAR

KARAMANI

AVEROF

2

MANGI

VYRONOS

8

5

6

IVY.LAPI

PLATÍA
DHIMOKRATÍAS

MITROPOLEOS

MARKOU BOTSARI

KOLLETTI

4

☩ **Cathedral**

**Archeological
Museum**

MAKARIOU GARIVALDI

OTE

TS.DROSOU

DHOUROUTI

7

PLATÍA
AKADHIMIAS

ACCOMMODATION

**Folklore
Museum**

MIKHAIL ANGELOU

**Tourist
Police**

★ **Blue City**

PLATÍA
PYRROU

METSOVOU

H. KATSARI

1   Dioni
2   Egnatia
3   Galaxy
4   Kamares
5   Metropolis
6   Palladion
7   King Pyrros
8   Tourist

EOT

NAPOLEONDA ZERVA

**Olympic
Airways**

3

Market

★ **Bus Station**

BIZANIOU

DHIODHOROU

PLATÍA
TZAVELA

MAKARIOU GARIVALDI

▽ *Dodona, Árta & Athens*

Ioánnina is also the jump-off point for visits to the **caves of Pérama**, some of Greece's largest, on the west shore of the lake, and the longer excursion to the mysterious and remote Oracle of Zeus at **Dodona**, as well as to Epirus' most rewarding corner, **Zagóri** (see p.306)

Arrival, orientation and information

Ioánnina **airport** is on the road out to the Pérama caves; it's connected to the town by city bus #7 (the most frequent); #1 and #13 also pass by. All such blue-and-white buses leave Ioánnina from a stop below the central **Platía Pýrrou**.

The main bus station is at **Zozimádhou 4**, north of Platía Pýrrou; this serves most points north and west, including Métsovo, Kalambáka, Igoumenítsa, Kónitsa and the Zagóri villages. A smaller terminal at **Bizaníou 19** connects Árta, Préveza, Dodona and all villages in the south or east parts of Epirus. It is advisable, especially on summer weekends, to buy tickets for both coast and mountains the day before. For more efficient explorations of the poorly served Zagória area, consider **car rental** from Avis at Dhodhónis 96 (☎0651/46 333), Budget at Dhodhónis 109 (☎0651/43 901) or European at Koundourióti 2 (☎0651/70 086, mobile ☎093/302770).

The axis of the town centre is the confusing, oddly angled jumble of streets between Platía Pýrrou and the **Froúrio**, Ali Pasha's citadel. Near the latter is the old bazaar area – still in part an artisans' marketplace. Within sight of Platía Pýrrou are most essential services: most of the **banks** (all with cash dispensers), the **OTE** and the central **post office** (Mon–Fri 7.30am–8pm), the latter both on 28-Oktovríou. There's a second post office closer to the lake on Yeoryíou Papandhréou. **Information** on current bus timetables and departure points can be obtained at the friendly **EOT** (July–Aug Mon–Fri 7.30am–2.30pm & 5.30–8.30pm, Sat 9am–1pm; Sept–June Mon–Fri 7.30am–2.30pm); when the office is shut, refer to the **tourist police** on 28-Oktovríou.

Accommodation

Most Ioánnina **hotels** are noisy and expensive for what's on offer, though at slow times they may cut prices by a category. The pay-and-display parking scheme in town is pretty comprehensive, so hotels with garages are indicated. If you arrive early enough in the day, and value tranquillity above luxury, it's worth heading straight out to Nissí island (see p.333), where the **inn** offers the cheapest, most attractive accommodation available. You'll also find dozens of **rooms** in Pérama village as you walk to the caves. *Camping Limnopoula*, 2km out of town on the Pérama road (city bus #2 or a 20min walk from Platía Mavíli), is a pleasant, mosquito-free **campsite**, though more geared towards camper vans than tents.

Dioni, Tsirigóti 10 (☎0651/27 864). The most pleasant of several hotels on this street leading away from the Zozimádhon bus station; has a car park. ⑤.

Egnatia, Danglí 2, cnr Aravandínou (☎0651/25 667). Another decent hotel near Zozimádhou bus station, though favoured by trekking groups and often block-booked. ④.

Galaxy, Platía Pýrrou, south cnr (☎0651/25 056, fax 30 724). Comfortable, quiet and pleasant, with spectacular mountain views from the balconies. Central, but fairly expensive. ⑤.

Kamares, Zalakósta 74 (☎0651/79 348). Rooms in a restored mansion in a quiet neighbourhood near the citadel. ⑤.

King Pyrros, Gounári 3, just off Platía Akadhimías (☎0651/27 652, fax 29 980). Comfortable, fair-sized rooms with en-suite facilities; best if you can get a room facing the pedestrianized side-street Goúnari, though front-facing rooms are double-glazed. ④.

Metropolis, Krystálli 2, cnr Avéroff (☎0651/26 207). Pretty basic and noisy, but a clean enough budget hotel. ②.

Sotiris Dellas (☎0651/81 494). A good if simple pension on Nissí with eight non-en-suite rooms; you'll find the owners at the house right next to the school, or adjacent the inn at their *Snak-Bar Seraï*. ②.

Tourist, Kolétti 18, cnr Krystálli (☎0651/26 443). Around the corner from the *Metropolis*, but quieter and more comfortable; the rooms all have baths. ⑤.

The Town

The **Froúrio** is an obvious point to direct your explorations. In its heyday the walls dropped abruptly to the lake, and were moated on their (southwest) landward side. The moat has been filled in, and a quay-esplanade now extends below the lakeside ramparts, but there is still the feel of a citadel; inside lies a quiet residential zone with narrow alleys and its own shops.

Signs inside direct you to the **Municipal (Popular Art) Museum** (summer Mon–Fri 8am–8pm, Sat–Sun 9am–3pm; winter daily 9am–3pm; 700dr), an elegantly arranged collection of Epirot costumes, guns and jewellery. More poignant is a section devoted to synagogue rugs and tapestries recently donated by the dwindling, fifty-strong Jewish community; the so-called Muslim wing features a mother-of-pearl suite, including the pipe of Esat Pasha, last Ottoman governor here. The museum is housed in the well-preserved **Aslan Pasha Tzami**, allowing a rare glimpse of the interior of a Greek mosque; it retains decoration on its dome and has recesses in the vestibule for worshippers' shoes. Tradition has it that in the adjacent quarters, Ali's rape and subsequent murder in 1801 of Kyra Phrosyne, the mistress of his eldest son took place. Her "provocation" had been to refuse the 62-year-old tyrant's sexual advances; together with seventeen of her companions, she was bound, weighted and thrown alive into Lake Pamvótis. The incident gave rise to several folk songs, and her ghost is still said to hover over the water on moonlit nights.

To the east of the Aslan Pasha Tzami is the **inner citadel** or acropolis of the fortress (daily 7am–10pm; free). This was used for some years by the Greek military, and most of its buildings – including Ali's palace where Byron was entertained – have unfortunately been adapted or restored to a point where they can no longer be recognized as eighteenth-century structures. Ali Pasha's tomb is purported to be close by the old **Fethiye Tzami** (Victory Mosque), though no identifiable trace of it remains. The tyrant's former palace has been pressed into service as the **Byzantine Museum** (Tues–Sat 8.30am–3pm; 500dr): six rooms containing masonry from assorted Epirot basilicas, troves of coins, medieval pottery and post-Byzantine icons. The only genuinely Byzantine painting is a fresco fragment of *The Betrayal*, from a damaged church in Voulgarélli. A few paces away, in the purported treasury of Ali Pasha's seraglio, is a marginally better auxiliary exhibit devoted to Ioánnina's long-running silver industry.

Apart from the Froúrio, the town's most enjoyable quarter is that of the old **bazaar**, a roughly semicircular area focused on the citadel's main gate. This retains a cluster of Ottoman-era buildings (including some imposing houses with ornate window grilles), as well as a scattering of copper and tinsmiths, and the silversmiths that were for centuries a mainstay of the town's economy.

Just off the central Platía Dhimokratías, set beside a small park behind the National Bank, is the well-lit and well-labelled **archeological museum** (Mon 12.30–6pm, Tues–Fri 8am–6pm, Sat & Sun 8.30am–3pm; 500dr). It's certainly a must if you're planning a visit to the theatre and oracle of Dodona, for on display here – along with some exceptionally well-crafted bronze seals – is a fascinating collection of lead tablets inscribed with questions to the oracle. There are ornate relief-carved Roman sarcophagi from Paramythiá and Igoumenítsa and, among numerous bronze statuettes, two Hellenistic children, one throwing a ball and one holding a dove. The ancient collection is rounded off by burial finds and pottery from Ambracia (Árta), Acheron (the Necromanteion of Ephyra) and Vítsa; the incongruous modern-art collection at the rear is of minimal interest.

Nissí island

The island of **NISSÍ** on Lake Pamvótis is connected by motor-launches (summer every 30min, otherwise hourly, 8am–11pm; 200dr) from the quay northwest of the Froúrio on Platía Mavíli. The beautiful island village, founded in the sixteenth century by refugees from the Máni in the Peloponnese, is flanked by five **monasteries**, providing a perfect focus for an afternoon's visit. By day the main lane leading up from the boat dock is crammed with stalls selling jewellery and kitsch souvenirs. Quiet descends with the sun, except at the pair of restaurants on the waterfront and another cluster by Pandelímonos; outside cars are not allowed, and the islanders have just a few vehicles which they haul across on a chain-barge to the mainland. Sadly, **Lake Pamvótis** itself is not only polluted, but also slowly shrinking. The springs which fed it suddenly dried up in the early 1980s, and the lake stopped draining towards the Adriatic. Contaminated runoff from Ioánnina and surrounding farmland began to accumulate, a problem exacerbated by four dry years between 1989 and 1992. The inhabitants of the island struggle to continue **fishing**: locals generally refuse to eat anything out of the lake, so the islanders are forced to sell their catch at a pittance for shipment to Thessaloníki, where it retails for ten times the price.

The **Monastery of Pandelímonos**, just to the east of the village, is perhaps the most dramatic of Ioánnina's Ali Pasha sites, though it is in fact a complete reconstruction, as the original building was smashed some years ago by a falling tree. In January 1822 Ali was assassinated here, his hiding place having been revealed to the Turks, who had finally lost patience with the wayward ruler. Trapped in his rooms on the upper storey, he was shot from the floor below, then decapitated; his head was sent to the Sultan as a trophy. The fateful bullet holes in the floorboards form the centrepiece of a small **museum** (summer daily; 100dr) to the tyrant, along with wonderful period prints and knick-knacks like Ali's splendid hubble-bubble. Right behind Pandelímonos is **Ioánnou Prodhrómou** (the keys are kept at Pandelímonos), whose interior is of scant interest; the exterior, with its three-windowed gables and brickwork, is the thing.

Three other monasteries – **Ayíou Nikoláou Filanthropinón**, **Stratigopoúlou Dilíou**, and **Eleoússas** (closed for restoration) – lie south of the village. They are quite clearly signposted and stand within a few hundred yards of one another along a lovely tree-lined lane which loops around the island; the first two are maintained by resident families, who allow brief visits except during siesta hours (knock for admission if the door is shut). Both monasteries are attractively situated, with pleasant courtyards: visits essentially consist of being shown the katholiká with their late and post-Byzantine **frescoes**.

The finest frescoes are those of Filanthropinón, a simple barrel-vaulted structure with two side-chapels or *pareklísia*. A complete cycle of the life of Christ in the inner nave dates from just after the monastery's foundation in 1292; there are images on boats in the Sea of Galilee, as befits a lake-island church. Lower down, throughout the building, are the saints, including (just east of the door to the south *pareklísion*) the apocryphal Khristóforos (Christopher). Higher up, in the outer nave and north *pareklísion*, graphic martyrdoms predominate: sundry beheadings, draggings, impalings and boilings. At the east end of the north chapel, Adam names the beasts in the Garden of Eden, while the ceiling of the narthex holds a fine Transfiguration. In the south chapel, just west of the door, ancient Greek sages (Solon, Aristotle, Plutarch) make a rare appearance, indicating that this may have been a school for Hellenic culture during the Turkish period.

Eating, nightlife and entertainment

For **eating**, the **island** is the most atmospheric location, its tavernas featuring fresh-water specialities like eel (*khéli*), crayfish (*karavídhes*) and frogs' legs, as well as the rarer *kýprino*. The lakefront *Seraï* is a friendly, inexpensive local hangout. If you'd rather not sample anything fished from the murky waters of the lake, the farmed trout (*péstrofa*) is cheaper and possibly safer. In winter the tavernas provide lunch only.

In **town**, more standard fare can be found around the bazaar near the Froúrio gate; try the basic, oven-food *Ivi* restaurant, or, for grills, the excellent and inexpensive *To Kourmanio*, exactly opposite the gate. Worth the traipse away from the old town is *Taverna Mezedhopolio Kipos*, at Karaïskáki 20, overlooking landscaped Platía Zalóngou: it's nothing extraordinary menu-wise, but well executed. Note that Ioánnina is also the original home of the *bougátsa* (custard-tart), fresh at breakfast time with sweet or savoury fillings from *Select* at Platía Dhimokratías 3. To eat by the lake, go to one of the half-dozen psistariés and ouzerís along Odhós Pamvotidhas. By far the best of these is the furthest one, *Mezedhadhiko Syn 2*, with an imaginative and lengthy menu, reason-able prices and a local clientele. About 100m beyond this is *Kyknos*, a taverna aimed at the student crowd, which has live music and only really gets going after 11pm.

Nightlife oscillates between the calmer **cafés** on and around Platía Pýrrou and the **bars** and (generally mediocre) tavernas on Platía Mavíli, heart of the Mólos or lake-front. The bars, especially *Yperokeanios* and *Gallery*, are more fun, and the gas-lantern carnival atmosphere outside is enlivened by sellers of *halvás* (sweetmeat) and roast corn. There are more theme bars and kafenía on the approaches to the castle, along Karamanlí, Avéroff and at the far end of Ethnikís Andistásis, at the southern corner of the citadel.

Back up on Platía Pýrrou, there are also three **cinemas**, which – thanks to the uni-versity students – usually host quite a decent programme of first-run films. In mid-July to mid-August, the Politistikó Kalokéri (Cultural Summer) **festival** features music and theatre performances, plus the odd cultural exhibition. Most of the events take place in a hillside theatre, known as the **Fróntzos** or **EHM theatre**, just outside the town (there is also a pleasant summer restaurant here, with fine views down to the town and lake). Tickets are available from the EOT office or the Folklore Museum (Mon 5.30–8pm & Wed 10am–1pm) at Mikhaïl Angélou 42. Some years there are a few performances of classical drama and contemporary music at the ancient **theatre of Dodona** (see opposite).

North to the Pérama caves

Five kilometres north of Ioánnina, the village of **PÉRAMA** boasts what are reputed to be Greece's largest system of **caves** (daily: summer 8am–8pm; winter 8am–sunset; 1000dr), which extend and echo for kilometres beneath a low hill. They were discov-ered during the last war by a guerrilla in hiding from the Germans. The half-hour tours of the complex are a little perfunctory (consisting in the main of a student reeling off the names of various suggestively shaped formations), but not enough to spoil the experience, though the same can't be said for the ugly concrete path which threads through the caverns.

To reach the caves, take a #8 blue city bus (buy your ticket in advance from a kiosk) from the terminal below Platía Pýrrou to Pérama village; the caves are a ten-minute walk inland from the bus stop, past tacky souvenir shops. If you are driving, you can make a circuit of the expedition. The road splits shortly after Pérama, one fork leading up towards Métsovo with superb views down over Ioánnina and the lake, the other run-ning around the lake, with a shoreline café midway.

South to Dodona: the Oracle of Zeus

At **DODONA**, 22km southwest of Ioánnina, in a wildly mountainous and once-isolated region, lie the ruins of the **Oracle of Zeus**, dominated by a vast and elegant theatre. The oracle is a very ancient site indeed; "Wintry Dodona" is mentioned in Homer, and the worship here of Zeus and of the **sacred oak tree** seems to have been connected with the first Hellenic tribes who arrived in Epirus around 1900 BC.

The origins of the site – the oldest in Greece – are shadowy. Herodotus tells an enigmatic story about the arrival of a *peleiae* or dove from Egyptian Thebes which settled in an oak tree and ordered a place of divination to be made. The word *peleiae* in fact meant both dove and old woman, so it's possible that the legend he heard refers to an original priestess – perhaps captured from the Middle East and having some knowledge of divination. The **oak tree**, stamped on the ancient coins of the area, was central to the cult. Herodotus recorded that the oracle spoke through the rustling of the oak's leaves in sounds amplified by copper vessels suspended from its branches. These would then be interpreted by frenzied priestesses and strange priests who slept on the ground and never washed their feet.

The site

Entering the **site** (summer Mon–Fri 8am–7pm, Sat & Sun 8am–3pm; winter 8am–5pm, Sat & Sun 8am–3pm; 500dr) past a few seat-tiers of a third-century BC **Stadium**, you are immediately confronted by the massive western retaining wall of the **Theatre**. Built during the time of Pyrrhus (297–272 BC), this was one of the largest on the Greek mainland, rivalled only by those at Árgos and Megalopolis. Later, the Romans made adaptations necessary for their blood sports, adding a protective wall over the lower seating and also a drainage channel, cut in a horseshoe shape around the orchestra. The site was meticulously restored in the late nineteenth century.

The theatre is used occasionally, to marvellous effect, for weekend ancient drama and music performances during Ioánnina's summer cultural festival (see p.304). This is one of the most glorious settings in Greece, facing out across a green, silent valley to the slopes of Mount Tómaros. At the top of the *cavea*, or seating curve, a grand entrance gate leads into the **Acropolis**, an overgrown and largely unexcavated area. The foundations of its walls, mostly Hellenistic, are a remarkable 4–5m wide.

Beside the theatre, and tiered uncharacteristically against the same slope, are the foundations of a *bouleuterion*, beyond which lie the complex ruins of the **Sanctuary of Zeus**, site of the oracle itself. There was no temple as such until the end of the fifth century BC; until then, worship had centred upon the sacred oak, which stood alone within a circle of votive tripods and cauldrons. Building began modestly with a small stone temple-precinct, and in the time of Pyrrhus the precinct was enclosed with Ionic colonnades. In 219 BC the sacred house was sacked by the Aetolians and a larger temple was built with a monumental *propylaion*. This survived until the fourth century AD, when the oak tree was hacked down by Christian reformists. It is remains of the later precinct that can be seen today. They are distinguishable by an oak planted at the centre by a reverent archeologist.

Many **oracular inscriptions** were found scattered around the site when it was excavated in 1952. Now displayed in Ioánnina's archeological museum, they give a good idea of the personal realm of the oracle's influence in the years after it had been eclipsed by Delphi. More interestingly, they also offer a glimpse of the fears and inadequacies that motivated the pilgrims of the age to journey here, asking such domestic questions as: "Am I her children's father?" and, memorably, "Has Pleistos stolen the wool from my mattress?".

Ruins of an early Christian **Basilica**, constructed on a Sanctuary of Herakles, are also prominent nearby – distinguished by rounded column stumps.

Practicalities

Relatively few people make the detour to Dodona, so the site and **DHODHÓNI** – the little village to the west of it – are completely unspoiled. **Transport** is accordingly sparse, with only two buses direct from Ioánnina (Mon–Wed, Fri & Sat 6.30am & 4pm, Sun 4pm only). Alternatively, buses for the village of Zotikó (Mon–Fri, 1pm) pass within 2km of the site; the bus conductor will point out the kafenío where you should alight for the final, downhill walk. The return bus calls at the site car park at about 5pm. Hitching to the site from the junction 7km south of Ioánnina should be feasible in summer, or a round trip by taxi from Ioánnina with an hour at the site can be negotiated for a reasonable amount – say 5000dr per carload. You could always stay the night here: there are some lovely spots to **camp**, a friendly if basic **taverna** in the village which has rooms (6000dr), and a small, less welcoming **hotel/taverna** at the site, the *Andromachi* (☎0651/82 296; ③), which fills only at festival time.

Zagóri

Few parts of Greece are more surprising, or more beguiling, than **ZAGORÍ**. A wild, infertile region, it lies to the north of Ioánnina, bounded by the roads to Kónitsa and Métsovo on the west and south and the Aóös River valley to the northeast. The drama of its landscape is unquestionable: miles of forest, barren limestone wastes, rugged mountains furrowed by foaming rivers and subterranean streams. But there is hardly an arable inch anywhere, and scarcely a job for the few remaining inhabitants. The last place, in fact, that one would expect to find some of the most imposing architecture in Greece.

Yet the **Zagorokhória**, as the 46 villages of Zagóri are called, are full of grand stone *arkhondiká* (mansions), enclosed by semi-fortified walls and with deep-eaved gateways opening onto immaculately cobbled streets. Though they look older, the *arkhondiká* are mostly late eighteenth or early nineteenth century. Many have fallen into disrepair or been insensitively restored, but the government now ensures (in several listed villages, anyway) that repairs are carried out in the proper materials, rather than cheap brick and sheet metal; new structures are required to have local stone cladding. The living quarters are upstairs, arranged on an **Ottoman** model. Instead of furniture, low platforms line the rooms on either side of an often elaborately hooded fireplace; strewn with rugs and cushions, they serve as couches for sitting during the day and sleeping at night. The wall facing the fire is usually lined with panelled and sometimes painted storage cupboards called *misándres*. In the grander houses the intricately fretted wooden ceilings are often painted as well. Additionally, most houses have a *bímsa* (secret bunker) for hiding the family gold and perhaps a wife and child or two when Albanian or other Muslim marauders threatened; even if the house was torched, the survivors could dig out their wealth and start again.

As for the countryside, much the best way of savouring its joys is on foot, **hiking** on the dozens of paths connecting the outlying villages, through forest and sheepfold, over passes and hogbacks. The most popular outing – now very much part of the holiday trekking-company circuit – is along the awesome **Víkos gorge**. It's not to be missed, though for more of a feel of the back country, you may want to continue northwest, over towards **Mount Gamíla** and the remoter Vlach villages at the base of **Mount Smólikas** (see p.315).

Kostas Vasiliou at Robinson Travel, Ogdhóïs Merarkhías 10, Ioánnina (☎0651/29 402, fax 25 071), near the campsite by a BP filling station, provides organized outings; if you don't contact him in advance you risk waiting a few days between departures.

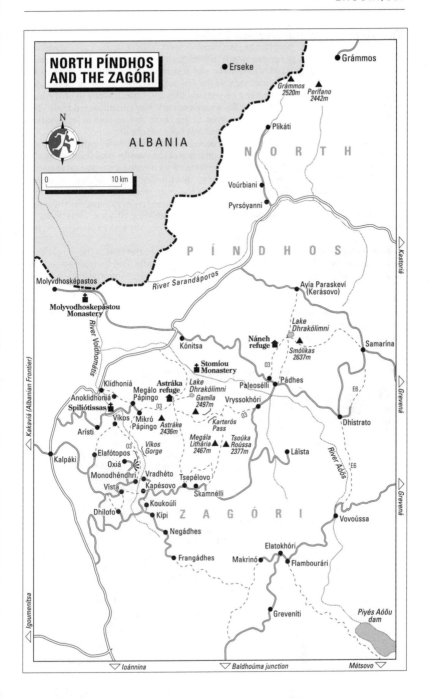

NORTH PÍNDHOS AND THE ZAGÓRI

N

ALBANIA

0   10 km

Erseke

Grámmos

Grámmos 2520m
Perifano 2442m

Plikáti

NORTH

Voúrbiani

Pyrsóyanni

PÍNDHOS

Molyvdhosképastos

River Sarandáporos

Ayía Paraskeví (Kerásovo)

Kastoriá

Molyvodhoskepástou Monastery

River Voïdhomátis

Kónitsa

Náneh refuge

Lake Dhrakólimni

Smólikas 2637m

Samarína

Stomíou Monastery

D3

Pádhes

Grevená

Kakaviá (Albanian Frontier)

Klidhoniá

Astráka refuge
Megálo Pápingo

Lake Dhrakólimni

Paleosélli

E6

Anoklidhoniá
Spiliótissas

D3

Gamila 2497m

Vryssokhóri

Mikró Pápingo

Víkos

Astráka 2436m

Karterós Pass

D3

Dhístrato

Arísti

Víkos Gorge

Megála Lithária 2467m

Tsoúka Roússa 2377m

Láïsta

Kalpáki

Elafótopos

D3

River Aóös

E6

Grevená

Oxiá
Monodhéndhri

Vradhéto

Tsepélovo

Vista

Kapésovo

Skamnélli

Dhílofo

Koukoúli

Kípi

ZAGÓRI

Vovoússa

Negádhes

Frangádhes

Makrinó

Elatokhóri

Flambourári

Greveníti

Piyés Aóöu dam

Igoumenítsa

Ioánnina

Baldhoúma junction

Métsovo

The Víkos gorge and western Zagóri

The walls of the **Víkos gorge** are nearly 1000m high in places, cutting right through the limestone tablelands of Mount Gamíla, and separating the villages of the western and central Zagóri. It is quite the equal of the famous Samarian gorge in Crete and a **hike** through or around it, depending on your abilities and time, is likely to be the highlight of a visit to the Zagóri. Since 1975 a national park has encompassed both Víkos and the equally gorgeous Aóös River canyon to the north and, to date at least, various plans for ski centres, téléfériques and dams have been fought off.

Tourist development, however, has proceeded apace since the early 1980s, and today almost every hamlet within spitting distance of the canyon (and indeed any sizeable village elsewhere in Zagóri) has some form of accommodation and tavernas. Be warned, though, that you won't get a room at short notice in July or August, when a tent is an essential fallback. During the rest of the year, weekends and three-day holidays are also unwise times to show up without advance reservations. Furthermore, you may have to settle for staying in some of the outlying villages, away from the immediate environs of the gorge – though this will be slightly less expensive and may have a more genuine community feel.

Monondhéndhri is the most popular starting point for a traverse of the gorge, but is by no means the only one; explorations in the area generally lend themselves to linear or loop trips of some days' length, rather than basing yourself somewhere for a week.

Monodhéndhri

Near the south end of the gorge, perched right on the rim, is the handsome village of **MONODHÉNDHRI**. It is one of the best preserved of the western Zagóri communities, all of which escaped the wartime devastation suffered by their eastern cousins. The wide,

---

HIKING WARNINGS

Despite the gorge's popularity, and recent improvements in trail maintenance, mapping and waymarking, it is worth emphasizing that the traverse is not a Sunday stroll, and that there is still plenty of scope for getting lost or worse. During April or early May, snowmelt often makes the Monodhéndhri end **impassable**, and in a rainstorm the sides of the gorge can become an oozing mass of mud, tree-trunks and scree.

At the best of times it's not really a hike to be attempted with low-cut trainers and PVC water bottles, as so many do. It is also strongly recommended that walkers go in parties of four or more, since isolated hikers are more vulnerable to attack by desperate, possibly armed Albanians living rough in the bushes. A stout stick for warding off snakes and belligerent livestock, and purchase when traversing scree-slopes, wouldn't go amiss either. Finally, owing partly to the decrease in grazing and the gradual re-forestation of the area, the local **bear population** is on the increase; sightings are becoming commonplace, especially around Kípi and Pápingo, though the bears are shy and (except for females with cubs) flee humans who stumble on them.

The Ioánnina EOT hand out photocopies of the *Korfes* magazine's topographical map of the Víkos gorge area, but this is old and full of dangerous errors. If you are going beyond the gorge, the collection of **maps** which the EOS reps in Megálo and Mikró Pápingo keep on hand are more authoritative and should at least be glanced at. Recently, the EU-funded "Life" program has signposted and waymarked a large number of "Z"-prefixed trails in western and central Zagóri, but elapsed times given are often unreliable, and the accompanying booklet is only published in Greek. Additionally, signposts seem to be vandalized by hunters almost as quickly as they're put up, so you really do need a map, a **specialist guide** and some trekking nous if you plan to venture off the most trodden routes.

rather tasteless modern *kalderími* leading off from the far end of the lower platía leads to the uninhabited monastery of **Áyia Paraskeví**, teetering on the very brink of the gorge. If you have a good head for heights, continue on around the adjacent cliff face and the path eventually comes to a dead end near **Megáli Spiliá**, a well-hidden cave where the villagers used to barricade themselves in times of danger. In all, count on just under an hour for visiting these sites. For an even more spectacular view of the gorge, follow signs towards **Oxiá** (7km by car, slightly shorter by path), where a short kalderími leads out from road's end onto a natural balcony where all of Víkos is spread vertiginously at your feet.

On weekdays there are two daily **buses** here from Ioánnina, at 6am and 4.15pm. The handful of inns by the upper platía where the bus calls – such as *Arkhondiko Zarkadas* (☎0653/71 305; ④) and *Monodhendhri* (☎0653/71 300; ⑤) – are pricey. The only marginally cheaper outfit is an unnamed "rooms" close to the lower platía, where those with their own transport should leave vehicles. For **meals**, the best option is *To Petrino Dhasos* near the upper platía which features local recipes such as *alevrópitta*. There is no shop however, so come supplied for your trek.

At nearby **VÍTSA**, 2km below, additional en-suite accommodation is available at *Arkhondiko Dhanou* (☎0653/71 271; ④) in the upper quarter, and at *Selini* (☎0653/71 350; ④) in the lower of the two ridgeline neighbourhoods, with its own access drive well marked. To some tastes Vítsa is a less claustrophobic, more attractive village than Monodhéndhri, with a few **tavernas**, a fine platía and alternative access to the gorge. This is via the signposted Skála Vítsas, a half-hour's gentle descent, partly on engineered stair-path, to the handsome single-arched Mitsíou bridge; from there it's possible to continue upstream to Kípi village (see p.312) or veer downstream along the heart of the gorge.

If you've no luck with vacancies in Vítsa, **ÁNO PEDHINÁ**, 4km west, offers three hotels or rooms, including the long-standing *Spiti tou Oresti* (☎0653/71 202; ⑤) and some tavernas; it's served by the same bus as for Vítsa and Monodhéndhri.

Monodhéndhri to Pápingo: through the gorge

The most-used **path down to the gorge** begins beside the arcaded church of Áyios Athanásios in Monodhéndhri's lower platía. Having first passed the village's municipal amphitheatre, the path is paved for most of the way down to the riverbed, whose stony course you can quite easily parallel for the first hour or so of the walk. The walk along the gorge is not difficult to follow, since the entire route is waymarked, in parts a bit faintly, by red-paint dots and white-on-red stencilled metal diamonds with the legend "O3". This refers to a long-distance path, which begins south of Kípi and at the time of writing can be followed across Mount Gamíla all the way to Mount Smólikas. In fact all you need to do is keep straight, occasionally crossing from one side to the other of the riverbed or climbing for a while through the wooded banks.

About two-and-a-half hours out of Monodhéndhri you draw even with the mouth of the **Mégas Lákkos ravine**, the only major breach in the eastern wall of the gorge; a spring here has recently been improved with piping to make it more reliable later in the year. Another forty minutes' walk brings you past the small, white shrine of **Ayía Triádha** with a recessed well opposite. A further hour yet (around 4hr 30min from Monodhéndhri), the gorge begins to open out and the sheer walls recede.

As the gorge widens you are faced with a choice. Continuing straight, on the best-defined path, takes you close to a beautifully set eighteenth-century chapel of the Panayía, past which the route becomes a well-paved *kalderími*, climbing up and left to the hamlet of **VÍKOS** (Vitsikó). This route has been kept in good repair by the locals and takes half an hour to walk. The hamlet has a single small **inn** (☎0653/41 176; ④), run by Kostas Karpouzis.

Most walkers, however, prefer to follow the marked O3 route to the two **Pápingo** villages, crossing the gorge bed at the **Voïdhomátis springs**, some five hours from Monodhéndhri. It's about two hours' walk to Mikró Pápingo, slightly less to Megálo, with the divide in the trail nearly ninety minutes above the riverbed crossing.

The Pápingo villages
MEGÁLO PÁPINGO is, as its name suggests, the larger of these paired villages. It is patronized by wealthy trendy Greeks, making it a poor choice of base in peak season, though it is still delightful at other times, when most **accommodation** proprietors will knock a few thousand drachmes off room rates. Behind the central café is the recently refurbished eighteen-bed *Pension Koulis* (☎0653/41 138 or 41 115; ④) with en-suite rooms, run by the Khristodhoulos family, who are also the local EOS representatives. As such, they can advise on space in the Astráka hut and walks towards Mount Gamíla (see below). On the south side of the village, a second inn, *Xenonas Kalliopi* (☎0653/41 081; ④), offers good home-style meals at the only year-round reliable taverna, and there are a number of rooms for rent on the way. If money is no object, *Ta Spitia tou Saxoni*, an immaculate, eighteen-bed pension on the lane leading to the Klidhoniá path (☎0653/41 615 or 41 890; ⑥) is the place to part with it. In high season more tavernas operate, including one across from *Pension Koulis*.

MIKRÓ PÁPINGO, around half the size of its neighbour, crouches below an outcrop of grey limestone rocks known as the *Pýrgi* (Towers). The village has one main **inn**, *O Dhias* (☎0653/41 257/41 357; ④), whose proprietor is sympathetic to trekkers; he can arrange shuttles back to cars left in Monodhéndhri, and often gives discounts to those with backpacks. Slightly less pricey are various rented **rooms** around the inn, and self-catering studios. If you are still stuck for accommodation, there are almost always vacancies in **ARÍSTI**, 13km across the Voïdhomátis River; the best of a handful here is the *Zissis* (☎0653/41 147; ④), a family-run outfit with a good restaurant.

From Pápingo to Ioánnina, the return **bus** trip can be a rather haphazard affair. Scheduled departures from Ioánnina (Mon, Wed & Fri 5am & 2.30pm) turn around for the return trip immediately upon arrival at Megálo Pápingo, an hour or so later; in midsummer there's also a service on Sunday, leaving Ioánnina at 9.30am and getting back to town in the late afternoon. If you miss the bus, the best course is to walk to the village of Klidhoniá on the Kónitsa–Ioánnina highway, which has regular buses. It's around a two-and-a-half-hour walk west from Megálo Pápingo, via the nearly abandoned hamlet of Áno Klidhoniá, on a better-than-average marked path, and certainly quicker than the dreary nineteen-kilometre haul to the highway along the paved road which passes through Arísti.

The lower Voïdhomátis River valley
Roughly halfway between the Kónitsa–Ioánnina highway and Megálo Pápingo, the paved side road descends to cross the Voïdhomátis as it flows out of the Víkos gorge. The immediate environs of the bridge is a popular picnic area in summer (no camping allowed), but river-bank trails allow you to hike to more peaceful, tree-shaded spots upstream before the gorge blocks further progress. **Kayaking** and **rafting** are the only ways to visit these narrows; swimming in the Voïdhomátis is a privilege enjoyed only by the (not to be fished) trout: anyone ignoring the ban would be in danger of perishing in the icy waters. Downstream lies the restored, cliff-clinging monastery of **Spiliótissas**; a track (closed to cars) leads to it through a plane grove, west of the road, about 400m before the bridge. It must be said, though, that the best views of the monastery are from the road as it begins ascending to Pápingo.

Hikes across the Gamíla range

For walkers keen on fairly arduous hiking, there are a number of routes on from the Pápingo villages, up and across the **Gamíla** range into the central Zagóri. These are linked by the O3 long-distance trail.

Mikró Pápingo to the Astráka refuge

All onward hikes east into Gamíla begin with the steep but straightforward ascent to the **refuge** on **Astráka** col. Though the refuge is clearly visible from Megálo Pápingo, the trail essentially starts at Mikró Pápingo. The two villages are linked by a three-kilometre asphalt road, which takes 45 minutes to walk; it's better to take the marked path off the road, via a historic bridge, which reduces the journey time to half an hour.

At the top of Mikró Pápingo, the well-signed, regularly maintained O3 trail resumes. Ten minutes out, you pass the chapel of Áyios Pandelímon, then head through forest to the Antálki spring (about 40min from Mikró Pápingo). From here the forest thins as you climb towards the Tráfos spring (1hr 40min from Mikró). Twenty minutes beyond Tráfos, a signposted trail branches right towards the **Astráka summit** (2436m), which is a three-hour round-trip from this point. If you ignore this trail, and keep straight with the O3 markers, in around half an hour you will reach the **EOS refuge**, perched on the saddle joining Astráka with Mount Lápatos (2hr 45min from Mikró Pápingo).

The hut is open and permanently staffed from mid-May to mid-October, but space is at a premium and bunks are the refuge standard 2500dr (twenty percent discount for affiliated European alpine club members), and meals are also relatively expensive. If you want to squeeze in amongst the Greek and foreign trekking/climbing groups, phone the *Pension Kouli* at Megálo Pápingo; they're in radio contact with the hut, who can confirm space.

East of Astráka

Northeast of the refuge, on the far side of the boggy Lákka Tsoumáni valley below, the gleaming **lake of Dhrakólimni** is tucked away on the very edge of the Gamíla range. This is about an hour from the refuge, along a well marked path.

East of the refuge, the O3 route takes you on a strenuous nine-hour hike to the village of Vryssokhóri via the **Karterós pass**. Despite the waymarking, the casual

---

PACKHORSE BRIDGES

A perennial pleasure as you stumble down boulder-strewn ravine beds that are bone-dry an hour after a thunderstorm is coming upon one of the many fine **packhorse bridges** that abound in Zagóri. These arched bridges, and the old cobbled paths serving them, were the only link with the outside world for these remote parts until motor roads were opened up in the 1950s. They were erected mainly in the nineteenth century by gangs of **itinerant craftsmen**, and were financed by local worthies.

Like the semi-nomadic Vlach and Sarakatsan shepherds of Epirus, these wandering construction gangs or *bouloúkia* were away from home between the feasts of Áyios Yeóryios (St George's Day) in April and Áyios Dhimítrios in October. As in other mountainous regions of Europe – the Alps, for example – they came from isolated and poor communities, Pyrsóyianni and Voúrbiani in particular in the Kónitsa area, and Ágnanda, Prámanda and Khouliarádhes southeast of Ioánnina. Closely guarding the secrets of their trade with their own invented argot, they travelled the length and breadth of Greece and the Balkans, right up to World War II.

While you're in the Zagóri region, a good side trip, easiest done from Vítsa, Kípi or Tsepélovo, would be to take a look at the half-dozen fantastic bridges in the vicinity. One is below Vítsa, one right beside the main road, one between Kípi and Koukoúli, and the remainder to either side of Kípi: one spectacular triple span downstream, three more upstream from the village. These bridges span the upper reaches of the Víkos gorge and its tributaries, and constitute the most representative and accessible examples of the vanished craft of packhorse-bridge building.

walker may find this an intimidating hike; it's best attempted only if you're an experienced trekker and equipped with the appropriate maps. At first, the trail heads for **Mount Gamíla** (2497m), itself a good two-and-a-half-hour climb from the refuge, but then veers off south from the final summit approach to negotiate the pass between the Karterós and Gamíla peaks, with a nasty scree slide on the far side. Near the usually empty sheepfold of Kátsanos, this route eventually joins an easier, unmarked trail coming over from the village of Skamnélli in the south, before the final descent to Vryssokhóri (see below for details).

South to central Zagóri

A more obvious, less demanding onward trek from Astráka col is the five-hour route, on an often faint trail, south across the Gamíla uplands, via the Mirioúli sheepfold and the head of the Mégas Lákkos gorge, to the villages of central Zagóri. Besides water at Mirioúli, there is only one other tiny spring en route, and for the most part the scenery is forbidding, but **TSEPÉLOVO**, the main destination, is among the finest of Zagorokhória. New pensions and hotels seem to open here all the time, making it the biggest tourist centre in Zagóri after the Pápingo villages. An English-speaker runs a store on the platía, and also has the well-renovated *Hotel Gouris* (☎0653/81 214/81 288; ③). There is a good-value pension, the *Fanis* (☎0653/81 271; ③), higher in the village, as well as other tavernas on the platía and out on the road by the school. A recent entry on the scene is *To Palio Arkhondiko* (☎0653/81 216; ④), which provides rooms in a restored mansion. Two **buses** daily (Mon–Fri) connect the village with Ioánnina; they leave Ioánnina at 7am (6am in summer) and at 3.15pm, ending their run in Skamnélli (see below) and then returning via Tsepélovo an hour or so later.

The adjacent village of **SKAMNÉLLI**, 3.5km along, isn't the most prepossessing place, but it's a useful base as the start of a marked hiking route to Stomíou monastery in the Aóös valley, via the Goúra plateau and Karterós. The *Hotel Pindhos* down by the road (☎0653/81 280; ④) is somewhat institutional, but has the biggest restaurant for miles around; *Paradhisos* rooms, at the very top of the village (☎0653/81 378; ④) is more traditionally built.

Descending 12km by road from Tsepélovo towards Ioánnina brings you to the celebrated cluster of **old bridges** (see the box on p.311) around Kípi, plus the amazing coiled-spring *kalderími* linking Kepésovo and Vradhéto. The bridges span the very upper reaches of the Víkos gorge, which can be reached nearly as easily from here as it can from Monodhéndhri or Vítsa.

The highest of the three villages closest to the bridges, **KAPÉSOVO** is an attractive place offering yet another possible access to the Víkos gorge. The gigantic former schoolhouse, dating from 1861, is now home to an informal ethnographic collection, including wolf-traps, and also hosts special events. An en-suite **inn** here (☎0653/51 347; ④) is more than adequate, and the café-taverna on the platía does evening meals. The existing trail to Víkos, though a bit weedy, is well marked through oak forest; a more exciting corniche path, the so-called "Katafídhi", is being rehabilitated to descend to the gorge via the Mezária ravine.

KÍPI, 2km up a side turning 6km below Kapésovo, is another handsome village with **accommodation** at *Stou Artemi* (☎0653/51 262; ③) and *Evangelia Dherva* (☎0653/51 280; ③), plus an excellent **taverna** down by the road, *Stou Mikhali*. The O3 passes nearby, as do a number of "Z" trails. The twice-daily **bus** (Mon–Fri), the same one serving Tsepélovo and Skamnélli, leaves for Ioánnina at 7am and 5pm.

North towards the Aóös valley

Beyond Skamnélli, forest extends north to the **Aóös valley**. Fourteen kilometres or so out of the village, the road branches north towards Vryssokhóri, and east towards

LÁISTA, which has a fine, though damaged church, and an incongruously large **hotel**, the *Robolo* (☎0653/81 457; ④). These two villages are served by bus from Ioánnina only on Tuesday and Thursday, at 8.45am.

Rather than follow this relatively dull road to Vryssokhóri, you can get there in seven hours from Skamnélli by walking over a pass between the peaks of **Megála Lithária** (2467m) and **Tsoúka Roússa** (2377m). This is a rather easier hike than that through the Karterós pass previously described, and is covered by many of the organized trekking groups. An added bonus is the unrivalled display of mountain wildflowers in the **Goúra valley**, directly below Tsoúka Roússa.

After the approach, **VRYSSOKHÓRI** is a little anticlimactic, being almost swallowed by the dense woods at the base of Tsoúka Roússa peak. Tiny and ramshackle (this was one of the settlements burned by the Germans in the war), the village has one small **inn** run by Stamatia Tsoumani (☎0653/81 497; ③), but no proper taverna or even a store. If necessary, you can camp at the edge of town by one of two springs on either side of the O3 coming down from Karterós.

Moving on to north Píndhos

The O3 trail used to continue across the Aóös from Vryssokhóri to **Paleosélli** in the north Píndhos but the path was bulldozed in 1989, extending the road up from Skamnélli. If you are purist about cross-country hiking, you will have to follow a slightly longer, pretty, but as yet unmarked trail from Vryssokhóri via Áyios Minás chapel down to the Aóös. Ford the river (at low water only), and bushwhack a bit on the other side up to Paleosélli. You'll need to allow about three-and-a-half hours for this stretch, which allows direct access to the villages of Paleosélli and Pádhes on the southern slopes of Mount Smólikas (see p.315). Alternatively, the O3 resumes after a fashion on the far side of the bridge over the Aóös, cutting across the curves of the new road en route to Pádhes.

The north Píndhos

The region **north of the Aóös River** is far less visited than Zagóri. Its landscape is just as scenic but its villages are very poor relatives – virtually all those within sight of the river were burned in the war, accounting for their present haphazard appearance. The villagers claim that before this disaster their houses exceeded in splendour those of Zagóri, since they had ample timber to span huge widths and to provide carved interiors. The region is dominated by mounts **Smólikas** and **Grámmos**, two of the highest peaks in Greece. The former can be approached on foot from **Mount Gamíla** (see p.310) or by vehicle from **Kónitsa**, the largest settlement in these parts, just off the Ioánnina–Kastoriá highway.

Kónitsa and around

KÓNITSA is a sleepy little town whose most memorable features are a famous bridge and a view. The **bridge**, over the Aóös, is a giant; it was built around 1870 but looks far older. The **view** comes from the town's amphitheatre-like setting on the slopes of Mount Trapezítsa, above a broad flood plain where the Aóös and Voïdhomátis rivers mingle with the Sarandáporos before flowing through Albania to the sea.

The town was besieged by the Communist Democratic Army over the New Year in 1948, in their last, unsuccessful bid to establish a provisional capital. Much was destroyed in the fighting, though parts of the old bazaar and a tiny Turkish neighbourhood near the river survive. However, in July 1996 a severe earthquake damaged numerous structures in the lower quarters; many families and businesses will be housed temporarily for the near future.

The **bus terminal** (seven buses daily to Ioánnina and connections to most villages in this section) is on the central platía; the **OTE**, the **bank** and the **post office** are just to the south. Kónitsa has recently acquired some importance as a kayakers' and walkers' centre; *Paddlers* (☎0655/23 777) organizes river trips. Accordingly, *dhomátia* have sprung up on the serpentine approach road from the main highway and the bridge. Longest established, and one of the best, is *To Dhendro* (☎0655/23 982, fax 22 055; ④), whose English-speaking proprietor, one of the characters of Epirus, is a mine of local information; cooking at the attached restaurant is good too. The *Kouyias* (☎0655/23 830; ④), up on the main street between the **post office** and the **OTE**, and the *Aoos* (☎0655/22 079; ④), down on the bypass road next to the Shell station, are the only other functioning hotels in town and less inspiring choices. For rooms, the best choice from the standpoint of calm is *Yerakofolia* (☎0655/22 168; ③), 300m along the road to Pádhes. Apart from the food at *To Dhendro*, *O Makedhonas*, next to a bakery on the central platía, is a good, inexpensive taverna offering oven meals.

The Aóös gorge

Kónitsa can serve as a base for a fine afternoon's walking. Beginning at the old bridge over the Aóös, two interweaving paths on the south bank lead within ninety minutes to the eighteenth-century **monastery of Stomíou**, perched on a bluff overlooking the narrowest part of the Aóös gorge. The katholikón here is of minimal interest, and the premises have been rather brutally restored, but the setting is sublime. There are two springs to drink from, and many visitors camp in the surroundings, after bathing in the river below.

Beyond Stomíou the slopes are shaggy with vegetation constituting one of the last pristine habitats for lynx, roe deer and birds of prey. A minimally waymarked path climbs from the monastery gate up to the **Astráka area** (see p.311). This is a five-hour uphill walk, rather less in reverse, and a very useful trekkers' link between the Gamíla and the Smólikas regions, provided you have a good map. It is less arduous than the Astráka–Vryssokhóri route and allows all sorts of loops through both Gamíla and the north Píndhos.

Molyvdhosképastos: village and monastery

The tiny hillside village of **MOLYVDHOSKÉPASTOS** hugs the Albanian border 23km west of Kónista. The place was once a haunt of the seventh-century emperor, Constantine IV Pogonatos, though only a few of his monuments survive intact. One of these is the tiny chapel of **Ayía Triádha**, on a crag below; another is the present parish church of **Áyii Apóstoli**, right on the frontier. If you can get in, the church has fine frescoes, and the view from its terrace – into Albania, over the Aóös valley, and east to Smólikas and Gamíla – is among the finest in Epirus. Unfortunately, photography is forbidden locally and you may need to present ID at a military checkpoint back at the Aóös bridge.

A weekday **bus** comes out to Molyvdhosképastos at 2.45pm from Kónitsa, but it doesn't return until the next morning, in which case the only **place to stay** is at the posh *Hotel Bourazani* (☎0655/61 283, fax 61 321; ⑤), set in its own deer park by the river bridge 10km before Molyvdhosképastos. On June 29, the village itself comes to life for the **festival** of its patron saints, Peter and Paul, with music and feasting until dawn.

Five kilometres below the village is the **Monastery of Molyvdhoskepástou**, the most important of the emperor's surviving monuments. Recently repopulated and attractively restored by its half-dozen monks, the monastery enjoys a bucolic setting on the bank of the Aóös. The curiously long and narrow church, with a precariously high Serbian-type dome, is thirteenth century. The nave ceiling is supported by arches and vaults; the airier exonarthex was a later addition. The frescoes throughout are in a poor state. This is a working monastery, so don't visit between 3pm and 5pm; the monks are quite fanatical, and will urge you to visit a confessional chapel to account for your sins.

East of Kónitsa: Mount Smólikas

Mount Smólikas (2637m) is the second highest peak in Greece. It dominates a beautiful and very extensive range, covering a hundred square kilometres of mountain territory, all of it above 1700m, and including a lovely mountain lake, **Dhrakólimni** (not to be confused with its namesake on Mount Gamíla). The region is also one of the last heartlands of traditional shepherd life, which is best observed in summer at the Vlach village of **Samarína**.

Kónitsa–Dhístrato **buses** (Mon & Wed 1.45pm, Fri 2.30pm, Sun 11.30am) roll through the mountains, stopping en route at **Paleosélli** and **Pádhes**, the two best trailheads on the mountain's southern flank. Paleosélli has two simple stores and a single **inn-taverna**, run by Sotiris Rouvalis (☎0655/71 216). Evening meals can be arranged here and at the inn-taverna in Pádhes.

Hiking from Paleosélli

There is a fine trail from Paleosélli up to **Dhrakólimni** (a little over 4hr), and from there you can make an ascent of **Mount Smólikas** (another 90min). There is also a marked path to the lake from Pádhes, though a new road cuts across it at several points.

The Paleosélli–Dhrakólimni route has been waymarked as part of the O3 plus a **refuge** established midway, at a spring and sheepfold known as Náneh, an idyllic little spot 1600m up with camping space, an external water supply and a toilet. Keys for this shelter are available from the Paleosélli inn. Beyond the refuge, the trail becomes less distinct, but waymarks lead you up onto a ridge aiming for the summit of Mount Smólikas, though the path markings disappear at the treeline. Just over two hours' walk from the refuge you should emerge into the little depression containing the **lake**. You can camp here, but level space is at a premium and you'll need a tent to protect against the cold and damp.

Moving along the ridge above the lake, you can reach the **summit** of Smólikas in about an hour and a quarter, tackling a rather steep, pathless slope with grass and stone underfoot. It is not unusual to see chamoix near the top. The easiest way down from Smólikas is a scenic and well-trodden two-and-a-half-hour path to the village of **AYIÁ PARASKEVÍ** (also known as Kerásovo). The path leads off at a sheepfold in the vale between the lake and the summit. There are a couple of basic **tavernas** in the village, including one open all year on the ground floor of the central *Smolikas* hotel (☎0655/41 215; ③); if it's full, camping near the village is tolerated. Four days weekly (currently Mon, Tues, Thurs & Fri, at 7 or 8am), there's **bus** service to Kónitsa, with the return the same day at 2.30pm.

Hiking from Dhrakólimni to Samarína

If you have a good head for heights, and you're not carrying a heavy pack, the best hiking route from **Dhrakólimni to Samarína** involves tracing the ridge east from the summit, the start of a seven-hour walking day. After a full hour of cross-country progress, you'll reach a small, bleak pass in the watershed, where you link up with a real path coming up from the village of Pádhes, marked by faint yellow paint splodges on the rocks. Once through this gap, you descend into the rather lunar, northwest-facing cirque which eventually drains down to the hamlet of Ayía Paraskeví.

Next you traverse the base of one of Smólikas's **secondary peaks** as a prelude to creeping up a scree-laden rock "stair". From here, waymarks change from yellow to red, and a line of **cairns** guides you across a broad, flat-topped ridge. The path soon levels out on another neck of land. To the left yawns a dry gully (to be avoided) and way off to the right (south) can be glimpsed the other of Smólikas's lakes, as large as Dhrakólimni but difficult to reach. Try not to stray in either direction in poor visibility, as there are steep drops to either side.

Beyond, you encounter the leading edge of the black pine forest, at the foot of a peak, which is capped by a wooden altimeter. The trail threads between this knoll and another, at the foot of which lies Samarína. Twenty minutes or so beyond this pass, a spring oozes from serpentine strata, some six hours from Smólikas summit. There follows a sharper descent through thick forest, with a second spring gurgling into a log-trough set in a beautiful mountain clearing, to which there is a direct road. Below this, the woods end abruptly and you'll emerge on a bare slope directly above Samarína.

Samarína

At 1450m, **SAMARÍNA** is claimed to be the highest village in Greece. It's only inhabited in the summer when it fills up with Vlachs from the plains of Thessaly, and their sheep – some 50,000 of them. The village was burned during both World War II and the civil war, and not surprisingly looks a bit of a mess. Even so, it's a thriving and friendly place and very proud of its Vlach traditions. The high point of the year is the **Feast of the Assumption** on August 15, when there is much music and merrymaking and the place is swamped by nostalgic Vlachs from Athens and all over the country. The interior of the main church, the **Panayía**, is superb, with frescoes and painted ceilings and an intricately carved *témblon*, where the mustachioed angels, soldiers and biblical figures are dressed in *fustanélles* (the Greek kilt). Though it looks a lot older, like many other churches in the region it dates from around 1800. Its special hallmark is a black pine, at least a century old, growing out of the roof of the apse. The keys are with the priest, who lives opposite the main gate.

The improbably large stone building that confronts you at the top of the village is a **hotel** (open only mid-summer); there's is another basic **inn** on the platía, above one of the numerous psistariés, but both of these may well be full. There may be a better chance of a vacancy at the fairly basic *Hotel Kyparissi* (no phone; ③) out on the east edge of the village, though no one will mind if you camp beyond the village itself.

Leaving Samarína, you have two choices. There is a bus to **Grevená** on the Kalambáka–Kastoriá road from June to September, but not every day, though a lift is not too hard to get if you ask around. If you are committed to staying in Epirus, follow the "E6" trail via the monastery of Ayía Paraskeví and Goúrna ridge to Dhístrato, where you might coincide with an early-morning bus back to **Kónitsa** (see p.313), or keep going to Vovoússa on the east bank of the Aóös, with its less frequent buses to Ioánnina.

North of Kónitsa: Mount Grámmos

It was on **Mount Grámmos** that the Democratic Communist Army made its last stand in the civil war. Its eventual retreat into Albania followed a bitter campaign which saw tens of thousands of deaths and the world's first use of napalm (supplied by the United States). The upper slopes of the mountain remain totally bare, and as you walk the high ridges you still see rusting cartridges and trenches from the fighting. If you want to visit the range, and peer down into the wilds of Albania, the most useful base is the village of Plikáti. The simplest way here is from Kónitsa by **bus** (Mon, Wed & Fri; 2pm). Coming from the Smólikas area, you're best off walking out to **Ayía Paraskeví**, where there are daily morning **buses** to Kónitsa (see p.315).

Plikáti and a hike up Mount Grámmos

There's a singularly end-of-the-world feel to **PLIKÁTI** – it's the closest Greek village to the Albanian frontier, and trailhead for Greece's remotest, least frequented mountain, Grámmos. Some eighteen paved kilometres off the main highway, it's a traditional looking place, with stone houses, a tiny permanent population, a couple of exceedingly basic

inns (one run by Angeliki Theologou) and a taverna/general store. Brace yourself to be stared at, as relatively few foreigners make it up here.

Mount Grámmos (2520m) is the fourth highest Greek peak, and in making the ascent you should plan on a round trip of eight hours from Plikáti. The easiest strategy is to angle northeast up the gentler slopes leading to Perífano (2442m), the second highest point in the range, rather than tackling head-on the badly eroded and steep incline immediately below the main peak. The trail in the indicated direction is clear for the first two hours out of the village, crossing the river and switchbacking up through bushes and then beech trees before it peters out at a sheepfold. Just above this are the last water sources on this side of the ridge: various trickles feeding a pond. Bearing west along a plain trail, you can thread along the crest for roughly an hour to the **summit**, its cairn covered in a babel of initials and multilingual graffiti. Below, to the west, a cultivated Albanian valley stretches to the barns of Erseke, 5km distant.

In the opposite direction from the summit, you can follow the watershed to the lower **Aréna massif**, which is garnished with a trio of small lakes and clumps of beech trees. The summer-only village of Grámmos is visible from the summit ridge, and though a clear trail leads to the place, there is no onward transport.

The south Píndhos

Most hikers arriving at Ioánnina have their sights firmly set to the north, especially on the Víkos gorge and the Zagóri villages. If you're feeling adventurous, however, and are not too particular about where you sleep or what you eat, the **remote villages** of the south Píndhos provide an interesting alternative. They perch on the beetling flanks of **Mounts Tzoumérka** and **Kakardhítsa**, two overlapping ridges of bare mountains linked by a high plateau, plainly visible from Ioánnina. There are few special sights, but you'll get a solid, undiluted experience of Epirot life.

On weekdays **buses** leave from Ioánnina's southern station at 5.45am and 3.15pm for Ágnanda and Prámanda, with an additional Saturday service at 3.15pm and on Sundays at 2.30pm. Many of the villages can also be approached from Árta. Buses run a couple of times daily in either direction along the secondary road between Árta and Ioánnina, stopping at **Pláka**, which has an eighteenth-century bridge over the Arakhthós and stunning scenery. Here you can flag down one of the twice-daily Árta-based buses continuing along the side road east as far as Melissourgí.

Áganda to Melissourgí

The first village of any size is 12km above Pláka at **ÁGNANDA**, which was heavily damaged in the last war and is not particularly attractive; it has only one **inn** (☎0685/31 332; ③). It's better to continue on to **PRÁMANDA**, which is no more distinguished architecturally than Ágnanda, but enjoys a wonderful setting. Strewn across several ridges, the village is dominated by Mount Kakardhítsa and commands fine views of the Kallaritikós valley. Nearby there is a huge **cave**, inhabited in Neolithic times, to which any villager will give you directions if you ask for the *Spiliá*. The enormous church of **Ayía Paraskeví** almost uniquely escaped wartime devastation, and as an example of nineteenth-century kitsch it is hard to beat. The village has a **post office**, a rather primitive *ksenónas* (inn), plus a handful of **tavernas** and psistariés, though there is a more comfortable **hotel**, the *Tzoumerka* (☎0659/61 590; ④) in the tiny hamlet of **TSÓPELAS**, 2km out on the road to Melissourgí.

MELISSOURGÍ, 5km to the southeast of Prámanda, is more rewarding. The village escaped destruction during the war, but most buildings – including the historic church

– have lost their slate roofs in favour of ugly pantiles. There is a **taverna** and one large **inn** (☎0659/61 357; ③), though in midsummer, it's likely to be booked by holidaying relatives from the cities. There are two daily weekday **buses** to Árta from Melissourgí, at 6am and 5pm.

Hikes from Melissourgí

Melissourgí is a good base for rambles on the **Kostelláta plateau**, which separates Mount Kakardhítsa (2429m) from the more pyramidal Mount Tzoumérka (2399m). Heading south, you can cross these high pastures in a day and a half. The initial stretch of path from Melissourgí is very faintly waymarked with red-paint arrows, and there are intermittent *stánes* (summer sheepfolds) if you need water or directions. You can descend to the villages of **Theodhóriana** or **Voulgarélli (Dhrossopiyí)**, at the edge of the Akhelóös river basin; both have daily early-morning **buses** to Árta, as well as modest **inns** and **tavernas**. In the latter village is the not-so-modest *Arkhondiko Villa Sofía* (☎0685/22 713; ⑥); it's inaccessible by car and overpriced; you might want to try two more modest (③) places lower down the hill.

Prámanda to Syráko

Some days the **bus** from Ioánnina continues to **Matsoúki**, the last village on the provincial route, beautifully set near the head of a partly forested valley, and offering easy access to Mount Kakardhítsa, as well as a few rooms for rent. On days when the bus doesn't serve Matsoúki, it runs instead as far as the hamlet of **Kipína**. A famous namesake **monastery**, founded in 1381 but uninhabited today, hangs like a martin's nest from the cliff face half an hour's walk beyond the hamlet.

Kallarítes

Beyond this point, you can follow the road upstream for around thirty minutes through a tunnel and past a road bridge to join the remnant of a wonderful *kalderími* climbing up to the village of **KALLARÍTES**, which is perched superbly above the upper reaches of the Kallaritikós river. This half-deserted village, one of the southernmost Vlach settlements in the Píndhos, was a veritable eldorado up until the end of the last century. Fame and fortune were based on its specialization in **gold and silversmithing**, and even today the craftsmen of Ioánnina are mostly of Kallaritiot descent – as is Vulgari, one of the world's most celebrated contemporary jewellers. Though the village is all but deserted except during summer holidays, the grand houses are kept in excellent repair. The flagstoned platía has remained unchanged for a century, with its old-fashioned stores and *stele* commemorating local emigré Kallaritiots who helped finance the Greek revolution. There are two **café-grills** on the platía, but the municipal **inn** has not operated for some years, so you should plan on camping.

Khroússias gorge and Syráko

Just beyond Kallarítes, the awesome **Khroússias gorge** separates the village from its neighbour Syráko, visible high up on the west bank but a good hour's walk away. The trail is spectacular, including a near-vertical "ladder" hewn out of the rockface. Down on the bridge over the river you can peer upstream at a pair of abandoned watermills. The canyon walls are steep and the sun shines down here for only a few hours a day even in summer.

SYRÁKO, hugging a steep sloped ravine, is even more strikingly set than Kallarítes, with well-preserved *arkhondiká*, the archways and churches are more reminiscent of those in the Zagóri. Not to be upstaged by Kallarítes, the village has also erected a number of monuments to various national figures (including the poet Krystallis) who hailed from here. There is a **taverna** (summer only) and a kafenío, but no formal inn; though you can beg a mattress on the floor in the school during the summer.

There is an alternative route back to Ioánnina from Syráko, **via Petrovoúni**, though it is covered by just one **bus** a week (Fri, also Sun in summer), leaving from Ioánnina at 3pm and returning from Syráko at 5.30pm.

THE COAST AND THE SOUTH

The **Epirot coast** is nothing special, with **Igoumenítsa** a purely functional ferry port and **Párga**, the most attractive resort, is overdeveloped and best left for out-of-season visiting. Head a little inland, however, and things start looking up. Close by Párga, the **Necromanteion of Ephyra** (the legendary gate of Hades) is an intriguing detour; the **gorge of the Akhérondas** offers fine hiking, and the imposing Roman ruins of **Nikopolis** break the journey to Préveza. Best of all is **Árta**, an interesting little provincial town surrounded by Byzantine churches, approached either around the Amvrakikós gulf, or more impressively along the plane-shaded Loúros river gorge from Ioánnina.

Moving south into **Étolo-Akarnanía**, the landscape becomes increasingly desolate with little to delay your progress to the island of Lefkádha (see p.740) or to Andírio, for the ferry to the Peloponnese. Committed isolates might hole up on **Kálamos** islet, south of Vónitsa. Byron's heart is buried at **Messolóngi**, though it's otherwise an unglamorous town.

Igoumenítsa and around

IGOUMENÍTSA is Greece's third passenger port, after Pireás and Pátra, with almost hourly ferries to Corfu and several daily to Italy. In 1992, summer catamarans were introduced to Páxi, Corfu and Brindisi. Though these did not operate in subsequent years, they may re-appear, as have services to Croatia and Montenegro. As land travel through ex-Yugoslavia remains a dodgy option, sea traffic between Greece and Italy has increased significantly.

A lively waterfront apart, the town is pretty unappealing; it was levelled during the last war and rebuilt in a sprawling, functional style. If you can, try to get a ferry out on the day you arrive; virtually every day in season there will be morning (7–10am) and evening (9.30–11am) sailings to Italy. To get a cabin berth, or take a vehicle on afternoon or evening sailings (see box on p.320), it's best to make reservations in advance. If you find yourself stuck for the day, you are better off taking one of the limited **excursions** from Igoumenítsa than hanging around town.

Practicalities

International liners dock in the central part of the **quay**, conveniently close to the town and the **EOT office** (Mon–Fri 7am–2pm; ☎0665/22 227), which is on the dock, next to the Customs House. Local **ferries** from Corfu use the "new port" just to the south. The **bus station** is five minutes away at Kýprou 47. Drivers should beware of Igoumenítsa's **fee parking** scheme (8am–8pm): you buy tickets at kiosks, not at pay-and-display machines.

IGOUMENÍTSA FERRY COMPANIES

All frequencies of ferry crossings detailed below are for the **high season**, the definition of which varies slightly from company to company. Broadly, for crossings from Italy to Greece, high season is between early July and mid-August; from Greece to Italy it is between early August and early September. Out of season, all services are reduced.

Most travel and **ticket agencies** for international ferries are found along Ethnikís Andistásis, which lines the waterfront. Tickets for domestic services are purchased at another office on the domestic ferry quay, south of the main dock. All companies offer a variety of **fares** for cabin, "airline" seats and deck passage, as well as reductions according to student or rail-card status, as well as hefty discounts on return tickets. High-season fares to Bari, for example, range from 11,000dr for the cheapest deck seats to 30,000dr for fully-equipped two-berth cabins with baths. Cars are carried on all ferries; as a guideline count on 20,000dr for a small car to Bari. Brindisi tends to be marginally less, Ancona rather more.

All international departures carry an **embarkation tax** of 1500dr per person and per car; this figure is now usually included in quoted prices. If you have bought tickets in advance you must **check in** at least two hours before departure (at the appropriate *official* agent as listed below, or at their booth in the port). Unlike sailings from Pátra, ferries from Igoumenítsa to Italy are not allowed to sell tickets with a **stopover** on Corfu. You can, however, take the regular Corfu ferry over and then pick up most ferry routes on from there.

International ferry companies, destinations and agents

ANEK Ancona (21hr 30min), direct Thurs, Sun & Mon 10.30am; Trieste (24–26hr), direct Tues, Thurs, Fri & Sun variable 7–9am. Revis Brothers, Ethnikís Andistásis 34 (☎0665/22 104).

Adria Brindisi (9hr), daily summer only at 11pm. Thalassa Travel, Ethnikís Andistásis 16 (☎0665/22001).

Agoudimos Brindisi (9hr 30min), daily at 11am (July–early Aug), or 11pm (early Aug to early Sept). Roussanoglou Shipping, Ethnikís Andistásis 46 (☎0665/23 630).

Adriatica Brindisi (11hr) via Corfu, daily 7am. Ethnikís Andistásis 58 (☎0665/22 952).

Fragline Brindisi (10hr) via Corfu, 6–7 days weekly 7am; occasional direct sailings 10am (9hr) or via Corfu at 10.30pm. Revis Brothers, Ethnikís Andístassis 34 (☎0665/22 158).

Hellenic Mediterranean Lines Brindisi (10hr) via Corfu, daily 7am, 8.45am, 9.45am or even 9.30pm depending on month. Hellenic Mediterranean Lines, Ethnikís Andistásis 30 (☎0665/22 180).

Jadrolinija Bari (11hr 30min) and Dubrovnik (19hr), Mon only at 7.30pm. Katsios Brothers, Ethnikís Andistásis 54 (☎0665/22 877).

Marlines Ancona (23–26hr), direct Tues & Wed 8am, Fri 10am & 8pm; Bari (12hr), daily at 9pm. Marlines, Ethnikís Andistásis 42 (☎0665/23 301).

Minoan Brindisi via Corfu (10hr 30min), daily 11.30pm. Minoan Lines, Ethnikís Andistásis 58a (☎0665/22 952).

Strintzis Ancona (23hr), Tues, Thurs, Sun Mon at 10am; Venice (29hr), Thurs & Fri at 5am, check-in at Poyakis Travel, Ethnikís Andistásis 62 (☎066524 252); Brindisi (8hr 30min) via Corfu, daily at 8am & 11.30pm, separate check-in at Ferry Travel, Kostí Palamá 1 (☎0665/27 358).

Ventouris Bari (12hr–13h), via Corfu high season only, direct otherwise; daily 9pm; Brindisi (9hr), 3 weekly, daily Aug–early Sept at midnight, noon Fri–Sun. Milano Travel, Ayíon Apostólon 11b (☎0665/24 237).

Domestic ferries

Corfu Hourly ferries in season from 5.30am to 10pm (90min).

Kefalloniá, Itháki Sporadic ferry services operate in July and August.

Paxí Ferry operates daily in the high season, and five times a week otherwise.

The town is not large but hotels are plentiful if rather lugubrious; most are to be found either along, or just back from, the waterfront. The nearest hotel to the port is the non-en-suite *Acropolis* (☎0665/22 342; ②) on Ethnikís Andístasi right in front of the OTE. Inland, at the southeast corner of the main platía stands the more comfortable *Egnatia*, at Eleftherías 1 (☎0665/23 648; ③); ask for a room facing the pine grove. The *Stavrodhromi* (☎0665/22 343; ③) on Soulíou 14, the street leading diagonally uphill from the square, is a good budget choice, with a pleasant atmosphere and a restaurant that makes its own wine. The closest **campsite** is at Kalami Beach (☎0665/71 211), just before Platariá, a nine-kilometre bus ride away.

The **restaurants** and **cafés** here are generally pretty uninspiring; for lunch, try *Martinis Sotiriou* inland at Grigoríou Lambráki 32, while after dark several fish tavernas and ouzerís at the very north end of the front, near the Dhrépano turning, come to life. **Banks** with cash dispensers are scattered along the south end of the front; at the north end, just inland on Evangelistrías, the **OTE** and short-hours **post office** share a building.

Around Igoumenítsa

The best escapes are probably to the **beach**. The closest strand lies 5km west at **Dhrépano**, a crescent-shaped sand spit (the name means "sickle") shaded by myrtle and closing off a lagoon. Local city buses serve it, and there are a few simple snack bars along its two-kilometre length. Heading south, other beaches flank the campsites at Kalámi (9km) and Platariá (12km), but Sývota (23km) is by far the most attractive option.

Sývota

The sleepy coastal resort of **SÝVOTA**, surrounded by olive groves, looks out to Corfu and Paxí. Greeks holiday here, so summer apartments predominate, but foreign package companies have begun to discover the place of late. The north bay and small port has the most development, with the village centre – such as it is – lying a kilometre inland, and smaller, sandier bays to the south on the road to Pérdhika. In order of occurrence, there's small, shady **Závia**, **Mikrí Ámmos**, bigger, sunnier **Méga Ámmos** and **Méga Tráfos**, as well as the island of **Mávro Óros**, joined to the mainland by a sandspit. A potential problem here are the distances to be covered: the beaches are spread out along over three kilometres, there's no transport hire, and the **bus** service is rudimentary (4 buses Mon–Fri, 2 buses Sat).

For **accommodation**, there's the tree-shrouded *Hellas* (☎0665/93 227; ③) in the village centre, and the *Acropolis* (☎0665/93 263; ③), 400m further on near the side drive to Závia. Among the better places is *Mega Ammos*, well set behind the eponymous beach (☎0665/93 447; ⑤). The beaches all have grills or simple snack bars, but for something more substantial the harbour is the place, where amongst a half-dozen **tavernas** *O Faros* is reasonable, tasty and non-greasy. Here you can also catch the seasonal **ferry** to Paxí, less reliable and pricier (4500dr one-way) than Parga's; contact Sivota Travel (☎0665/93 264) for current details.

Inland, few destinations reward the effort expended to get to them, despite earnest promotion in EOT brochures. There is a regular bus to the "traditional village" of **Filiátes**, 19km to the northwest, but it's a drab place, with not even a taverna to redeem it. The old hill town of **Paramythiá**, 38km to the southeast (2 buses daily), is another disappointment. A castle and Byzantine church are scarcely in evidence, and despite touting as a centre for copper-working, just two mediocre metal shops remain in a tiny bazaar – nothing comparable to what you'd see more easily and conveniently in Ioánnina.

For an inland excursion, your time would be much better spent at the remarkable **Necromanteion of Ephyra** or the **Akheróndas gorge** (see p.323).

Párga and around

PÁRGA is a charming and popular coastal town, approximately 50km south of Igoumenítsa on the Epirot shoreline. Its crescent of tiered houses, set below a Norman-Venetian **kástro**, and its superb **beaches**, with a string of rocky islets offshore, constitute as enticing a resort as any in western Greece. However, since the late 1980s the outskirts have been swamped by concrete apartment buildings, and package tourism has even engulfed the next village, Anthoússa, 3km west, where numerous tavernas and accommodation places nestle under a tiny, hatbox castle. In season, it's hard to recommend more than a brief stopover in Párga (if you can find a room) before taking the local **ferry to Paxí**. The harbour is currently being enlarged, presumably to accommodate cruise liners, which will spell doom for the notion of calm here in any month.

Párga's fate is all the sadder given its idiosyncratic **history**. From the fourteenth to eighteenth centuries Párga was a lone Venetian toehold in Epirus, complementing the Serene Republic's offshore possessions in the Ionian islands; the Lion of Saint Mark – symbol of Venice – is still present on the kástro keep. Later, the Napoleonic army took the town for a brief period, leaving additional fortifications on the largest **islet**, a 200-metre swim from the harbour beach. At the start of the nineteenth century, the town enjoyed a stint of **independence**, being self-sufficient through the export of olives, still a mainstay of the region's agriculture. After that, the British acquired Párga and subsequently sold it to Ali Pasha. The townspeople, knowing his reputation, decamped to the Ionian islands, the area being resettled by Muslims who remained until the exchange of populations in 1923, when they were replaced by Orthodox Greeks from the area around Constantinople.

The town and its beaches

The town is dominated by the bluff-top **kástro** (open all day; free), a haven from Párga's bustle. A long stair-street leads up to the ruined ramparts, which offer excellent views of the town, its waterfront and a mountainous backdrop. Párga's fine **beaches** line three consecutive bays, and often get very crowded in midsummer. The small bay of **Kryonéri** lies opposite the church-studded islet. Immediately beyond the kástro lies **Váltos beach** (on foot easiest reached by the long ramp from the kástro gate; water-taxis in season), more than a kilometre in length as it sprawls around to the hamlet of the same name. **Líkhnos**, 3km in the opposite (southeast) direction, is a similarly huge beach; a shaded path through the olive groves shortcuts the winding road in.

Practicalities

Buses link Párga with Igoumenítsa and Préveza four or five times daily, less on Sunday; the stop is just north of the junction of Alexándhrou Bánga and Spýrou Livadhá across from a small café that doubles as a ticket office. The **OTE** and **post office** are both just a few paces away, in opposite directions along Bánga, the start of the main market street. Half-a-dozen local travel agencies, concentrated on the waterfront, cater mostly to package tourists but they also rent motorbikes and cars, sell tickets for the daily (in season) morning passenger **ferry** to Paxí, and run **boat tours** up the Akheróndas River to the Necromanteion of Ephyra, allowing good views of the delta birdlife en route.

From late June to early September package tourists monopolize most of the hotels; only during May and October will you more or less have the run of the place. Just three **hotels** remain which are not block-booked by companies: the *Ayios Nektarios* (☎0684/31 324, fax 32 150; ③) on the edge of town at the corner of Livadhá and the road in, which has a small self-catering kitchen and fair-sized rooms; nearby in an orchard, the mostly German-patronized *Galini* (☎0684/31 581, fax 32 221; ④) has enormous rooms; and the *Paradise* on Spýrou Livadhá opposite the school (☎0684/31 229, fax 31 266; ④), which is noisy and worthwhile only if you get a rear room. The plusher *Acropol* (☎0684/31 239; ⑤) next to the central Platía Vasilá, a two-minute walk from the harbour, is mostly booked by tour groups in season.

Rooms are plentiful, if a little pricey: someone will probably approach you on arrival at the bus station or ferry quay. Otherwise, the best strategy is to take the stairs up to the castle entrance, where the lane leading perpendicularly away is one solid line of rooms, many with unbeatable views over Váltos beach. Representative of these are three non-en-suite rooms with a kitchen on the roof, run by the friendly Haravyi Dalipi (☎0684/31 604; ③).

There are **campsites** just behind Kryonéri beach at *Parga Camping* (☎0684/31 161) and *Elaia Camping* (☎0684/31 130), among olive groves 600m inland to the north. Váltos beach also has a newer, unobtrusive site (☎0684/31 287) at the far end by the new yacht harbour, and the enormous *Enjoy Lihnos Camping* (☎0684/31 171) straddles the road access to Líkhnos beach.

For **meals**, there are two dozen tavernas around the town, though many offer a tourist-orientated menu; honourable exceptions include *To Kandouni*, at the rear of the market on Platía Ayíou Dhimitríou. On the west waterfront of Kamíni, *Psarotaverna Zorbas* (aka *Triadha's* after the proprietress) is a good venue for fish, while on the east quay, *To Kyma* is the best of roughly half-a-dozen here, with reasonably priced, non-greasy if standard food. Up on the ridge lane leading off the castle gate, none of the half-dozen establishments really stand out, though *Three Plane Trees* seems reasonable and well placed. Lastly, the creperie on Platía Ayíou Dhimitríou can be recommended for breakfast and desserts. Most Párga tavernas offer local wine from the barrel; the red is generally excellent. For more extended drinking, **nightlife** centres around a half-dozen noisy bars on the main quay.

Southeast to the Necromanteion of Ephyra

The **Necromanteion of Ephyra** (or Sanctuary of Persephone and Hades) stands just above the village of Messopótamo, 22km southeast of Párga. Compared with Greece's other sites it has few visitors, and this, coupled with its obscure location, makes it a worthwhile and slightly unusual excursion. The sanctuary is sited on a low, rocky hill, above what in ancient times was the mouth of the Akheron (Akhérondas in modern Greek), the mythical **Styx**, river of the underworld. According to mythology, this was the spot where Charon rowed the dead across the Styx to Hades, and from Mycenaean to Roman times it maintained an elaborate oracle of the dead. Ephyra never achieved the stature of Delphi or Dodona, but its fame was sufficient for Homer, writing in the ninth century BC (it is assumed), to use it as the setting for Odysseus's visit to Hades. This he does explicitly, with Circe advising Odysseus:

You will come to a wild coast and to Persephone's grove, where the hill poplars grow and the willows that so quickly lose their seeds. Beach your boat there by Ocean's swirling stream and march on into Hades' Kingdom of Decay. There the River of Flaming Fire and the River of Lamentation, which is a branch of the Waters of the Styx, unite around a pinnacle of rock to pour their thundering streams into Acheron. This is the spot, my lord, that I bid you seek out . . . then the souls of the dead and departed will come up in their multitudes.

The sanctuary

Trees still mark the sanctuary's site (daily 8am–3pm, possibly later in peak season; 500dr; site booklet 1500dr), though today they are primarily cypresses, emblems of the dead throughout the Mediterranean. The lake, which once enclosed the island-oracle, has receded to the vague line of the Akhérondas skirting the plain: from the sanctuary you can pick out its course from a fringe of Homer's willows. As for the sanctuary itself, its **ruins**, flanked by an early **Christian basilica**, offer a fascinating exposé of the confidence tricks pulled by its priestly initiates.

According to contemporary accounts, **pilgrims** arriving on the oracle-island were accommodated for a night in windowless rooms. Impressed by the atmosphere, and by their mission to consult with the souls of the dead, they would then be relieved of their votive offerings, while awaiting their consultation with the dead. When their turn came, they would be sent groping along labyrinthine corridors into the heart of the sanctuary, where, further disoriented by hallucinogenic vapours, they would be lowered into the antechamber of "Hades" itself to witness whatever spiritual visitation the priests might have devised.

The remains of the sanctuary – walls of Cyclopean masonry standing up to headheight – allowed excavators to identify the function of each room, and there is a rudimentary plan at the entrance. At the very top, visible from a considerable distance, sits a **medieval chapel** retaining eighteenth-century fresco fragments; just below, *pithária* or giant storage urns have been left in situ. At the centre of the site is a long room with high walls, flanked by chambers used for votive offerings. And from here metal steps lead to the damp, vaulted underground chamber where the necromantic audiences took place. Originally this descent was by means of a precarious windlass mechanism – which was found on the site.

Practicalities

The Necromanteion is most easily reached by boat **tour** (or rented motorbike) from Párga. Puny mopeds will not cope well with the grades and speeds of the improved main highway between the two points; you'll need at least an 80cc bike. Buses from Párga stop at Kastrí (2km before Kanaláki), 5km from the site, and since the improvement and re-routing of the coast road should call at Messopótamos as well – ask before alighting. **Buses** from Párga and Préveza also pass through **KANALÁKI**, where mopeds (a more feasible mode of transport from here) can be rented in summer. There are two basic **hotels** in Kanaláki, the *Ephyra* (☎0684/22 128; ③) and *Akheron* (☎0684/22 241; ③) beside each other near the main platía, plus a few psistariés. In theory, the village could make a useful base for leisurely exploration of both the Necromanteion and the Soúli area (see below), but it's an ugly, dusty place bearing all the hallmarks of massive wartime destruction.

East into Souliot country

The highland region east of Párga was the traditional heartland of the **Souliots**, an independent-spirited tribe of Orthodox Christians and great mountain-warriors. During the last decades of the eighteenth century and the first decade of the nineteenth, the Souliots conducted a perennial rebellion against Ali Pasha and the Albanians from their village strongholds above the **Akhérondas gorge** and the mountains to the south. Although it is hard today to think of the placid Akhérondas near the Necromanteion of Ephyra as the way to hell, only a few kilometres to the east its waters cut deep into rock strata and swirl in unnavigable eddies as the river saws a course through the gorge. While not in quite the same league as the Víkos, it is certainly a respectable wilderness, and if you're looking for an adventure inland from Párga you won't find better (except on weekends, when it's very crowded with local visitors).

Hikes up the gorge start at **GLYKÍ**, a twelve-kilometre bus ride from Kanaláki on a side road between Préveza and Paramythiá (one daily bus from the former). The river here, still relatively calm, is flanked on one bank by a mediocre *exókhiko kéndro* (see opposite for a better alternative) and on the other by a sign reading "Skála Tzavélainas", pointing up a paved road. Following this, you can bear left after 700m towards the sign-posted *Piyes Akheronda* **taverna** (1300m in total from the main road), much better and cheaper than its rival, with shaded seating and good wading for kids.

Continue another 100m on the road and bear left towards a modern chapel, 1km from the bridge; this side track deteriorates and ends 1700m from Glykí at a tunnel. The *skála* (a well-constructed path) begins just to its left; ignore, after 100m, a trail plunging down towards the river, since it's dangerously washed out within minutes. Below, the canyon walls squeeze together, and upstream a carpet of greenery covers a wilderness, rolling up to the castle of Kiáfa.

The main trail, waymarked sporadically with blue arrows and yellow rectangles, descends to the Akhérondas and crosses a bridge after twenty minutes' hiking. It then immediately takes a much older bridge over a tributary, the outflow of the Tsangariótiko River, known locally as the **Piyés Soulíou** (Souliot Springs). Beyond here the marked route climbs up through the oaks out of the Akhérondas valley. After paralleling the Tsangariótiko, the trail turns up yet another side ravine to reach the tiny, poor hamlet of **SAMONÍDHA** – around two hours' walk from Glykí, ninety minutes from the tunnel – where there's a well behind the community office; the nearest kafenío/taverna is in the village of **SOÚLI**, 3km to the north.

From Samonídha a bulldozed track leads up within another half-hour to **Kiáfa castle**, one of several the local Souliots erected in their many and protracted wars with the Turks.

South to Préveza

Approaches to Préveza (see below) from the Necromanteion and Aherónda area feature a few more minor sites and resorts before edging out onto the landlocked **Amvrakikós (Ambracian) Gulf**, where in 31 BC Octavian defeated Antony and Cleopatra at the Battle of Actium. Suitably enough, the most substantial of the ruins is Octavian's "Victory City" of **Nikopolis**, just south of the point where the Igoumenítsa–Préveza and the Árta–Préveza highways meet.

Two local **buses** cover the coastal route to Préveza from **Ammoudhiá**, a surprisingly unspoilt little beach resort 5km due west of the Necromanteion at the mouth of the Akhérondas. Germans and Italians equipped with camper vans occupy the eucalyptus grove separating the rather scrappy village from the 700-metre sandy beach. Compared with other nearby beaches, however, it's not the most scenic: plenty of litter washes up, and the river can make for cold swimming.

Better places to break your journey, if you take this route with your own vehicle, are at **Liyiá**, unmarked on many maps, and **Loútsa**, immediately to the north (same exit from the main highway). At the former there are **rooms** to rent, an impromptu campsite, several tavernas and an enormous, boulder-strewn beach, all overlooked by a crumbling castle in the distance; Loútsa's beach is longer and sandier, with a similar range of amenities. The long-distance buses to and from Párga or Igoumenítsa don't pass this way, but head inland at Messopótamo, before joining the coastal road near Nikopolis.

Inland: Zalóngo and ancient Kassopi

Some 28km on the inland route from Messopótamo, you pass a turning east to the village of **KAMARÍNA** (3km along), overlooked by the monastery and monument of Zalóngo and the ruins of ancient Kassopi. These are a steep, shadeless six-kilometre climb from the main highway, though a **bus** from Préveza goes direct to the site each morning at 6am and 2pm. An early start does have its reward as both places are glorious vantage points from which to watch the sunrise. Otherwise a taxi or your own transport is a good idea; there's also an approach (unsignposted) through the village of Kriyopiyí, also 3km off the main road, somewhat quicker if you're coming from Glykí.

The **Monastery of Zalóngo** is a staple of Greek schoolbook history, immortalized by the defiant **mass suicide** of a group of Souliot women. In 1806, Albanian troops cornered a large band of Souliots in the monastery. As this refuge was overrun, about sixty Souliot women and children fled to the top of the cliff above and, to the amazement of the approaching Muslim troops, the mothers danced one by one, with their children in their arms, over the edge of the precipice. This act is commemorated by a truly hideous modern sculpture, approached by several hundred steps. Along with the monastery just below (closed 2–4pm & Thurs), the monument attracts regular Greek coach tours.

Slightly to the west of the monastery, on a natural balcony just below the summit of a similar bluff, are the remains of **Ancient Kassopi**, a minor Thesprotian city-state today approached via a long path through a pine grove. Theoretically the site is open daily 8am to 3pm and is free; in practice the warden tries to sell you a ticket, and leaves the gate open after-hours. The ruins date mainly from the fourth century BC, with extensive rebuilding after the city was sacked by the Romans; the place was definitively abandoned in 31 BC when its citizens were commanded to inhabit Nikopolis (see below). An excellent site plan affixed to the warden's hut helps to locate highlights, the most impressive of which is a *katagoyeion* or hostelry for representatives of the Kassopian federation. Principally, though, Kassopi is memorable for its superb location – some 600m above sea level, with the Ionian Sea coast and Lefkádha below.

Nikopolis

The "Victory City" of **NIKOPOLIS** was founded by Octavian on the site where his army had camped prior to the Battle of Actium. An arrogant and ill-considered gesture, it made little geographical sense. The settlement was on unfirm ground, water had to be transported by aqueduct from the distant springs of the Loúros, and a population had to be forcibly imported from towns as far afield as Náfpaktos. However, such delusionary posturing was perhaps understandable. At **Actium**, Octavian had first blockaded and then largely annihilated the combined fleets of Antony and Cleopatra, gathered there for the invasion of Italy. The rewards were sweet, subsequently transforming Octavian from military commander to emperor of Rome, with the adopted title Augustus.

The history of Nikopolis is undistinguished, with much of its original population drifting back to their homes. As the Roman Empire declined, the city suffered sacking by Vandals and Goths. Later, in the sixth century AD, it was restored by Justininan and flourished for a while as a Byzantine city, but within four centuries it had sunk again into the earth, devastated by the combined effect of earthquakes and Bulgar raids.

The site and museum

The far-flung and overgrown ruins begin 7km north of Préveza, on either side of the main road. Travelling by **bus**, you could just ask to be set down here, though it's a long walk back to town. It would be better to hire a taxi in Préveza for a couple of hours, or visit with a rental car, as the site is really too scattered to tour on foot.

The site, access to which is unrestricted, looks impressive from the road. A great **theatre** stands to the east and as you approach the site museum, past remnants of the **baths**, there is a formidable stretch of sixth-century Byzantine **fortified walls**. Walking around, however, the promise of this enormous site is unfulfilled; few other remains reward close inspection. The ruins are also a home to snakes, butterflies, the odd tortoise and, in spring, numerous wild flowers.

From the scant foundations of the sixth-century **basilica of Bishop Alkyon**, it's a two-kilometre walk to the main **theatre**, whose arches stand amidst dangerously crumbling masonry. To the left of this you can just make out the sunken outline of the **stadium**, below the modern village of Smirtoúna. Octavian's own tent was pitched upon the hill above the village, and a massive **podium** remains from the commemorative monument that he erected. On a terrace alongside, recent excavations have revealed the remains of "beaks" (ramming protuberances) of some of the captured warships, which Octavian dedicated to the gods.

The dull **museum** (Tues–Sun 8.30am–3pm; 400dr) consists of two rooms containing an uninspiring collection of Roman sarcophagi and coins. Its caretaker's main function used to be the wardenship of the Roman and Byzantine mosaics unearthed amidst the foundations of the sixth-century **basilica of Doumetios** nearby, but these have recently been recovered by a protective layer of sand and polythene. If available, the caretaker will escort you to the Roman **Odeion**, for which he has the keys. This dates from the original construction of the city and has been well restored for use in a summer music festival (see "Préveza" below).

Préveza

Modern **PRÉVEZA**, at the tip of the Amvrakikós Gulf, is a relatively insignificant successor to Nikopolis, but is not without charm. Numerous **cafés** and **tavernas** line the waterfront, facing Actium (modern Áktio) where the forces of Antony and Cleopatra were defeated. With the advent of charter traffic to nearby Áktio airport in recent years, this provincial capital has had a facelift of sorts, and more character remains in the pedestrianized old quarter than at Párga. Préveza merits a brief stopover, not only for Nikopolis, but also for its lively evenings and particularly the deliciously fresh fish on offer at the *psarotavérnes*. In the summer months, the town also has useful **hydrofoils** to Páxi, Itháki, Kefalloniá and Zákynthos, though services are rather sporadic.

Charter flights arriving at the **airport** generally have transport laid on to Lefkádha or Párga; otherwise there are taxis. The **bus station** in Préveza is on Leofóros Irínis, a kilometre north of the ferry dock. **Ferries** across the gulf ply across to Áktio jetty, where you can pick up buses (four or five daily) to Vónitsa and Lefkádha (times are displayed on the quayside ticket office).

Sharing a building on the quay are a **post office** and **tourist office**. The **OTE** is in a pedestrian lane, near the *Minos* hotel.

Accommodation

The three in-town **hotels** are not especially inviting. Most obvious, and most expensive, is the noisy *Preveza City* on Odhós Irínis (☎0682/27 365; ⑤); much better is the *Dioni* on Platía Papayeoryíou, a quiet pedestrian zone more or less behind (☎0682/27 381, fax 27 384; ④). The *Minos*, just south on 21-Oktovríou (☎0682/28 424; ⑤) is bargainable but the management is off-putting. Failing these, there are a few rooms on the shore road on the far side of the peninsula; follow this road south out of town about 2km, which curls around the medieval fortifications at the peninsula tip. The nearest **campsites** are *Camping Indian Village* (☎0682/27 185 and *Camping Kalamitsi* (☎0682/22 368), around 4km north of the town on the broad highway which skims along a few hundred metres back from the coast. Any bus running towards Kanáli (15km out, and not to be confused with Kanaláki) will pass the summer-only sites of *Monolithi* (☎0682/51 755) and *Kanali* (☎0682/22 741), on either side of the road at Monolíthi beach, a fine stretch of sand beginning 11km from Préveza.

Eating, drinking and nightlife

There are at least a dozen **tavernas** scattered around the centre of Préveza, some on the waterfront boulevard Venizélou, but more inland in the market lanes. Good inland choices include *Psatha*, Dhardhanellíou 2 (west of the main shopping thoroughfare), for standard oven fare, and the long-running *Amvrosios*, specializing in grilled sardines and barrel wine at budget prices, virtually under the Venetian clock tower. On the water, *G. Peponis* at Venizélou 8a and *Nikopoli* at no. 11 are the standbys. *Patsas* fans might try *Treis Adherfes* at Tsaldári 51, just up from the bus station.

At **night**, the alleys in the bazaar, especially around the fish-market building and the clock tower, come alive with bars, ouzerís and cafés, crammed with locals and people from the nearby resorts. As for culture, July and August see a range of musical and theatrical events as part of the **Nikopolia festival**, held at Nikopolis. On Platía Androútsou by the port is the only **shadow puppet** (*karagiózis*) theatre left in the country.

Árta and around

Fifty kilometres northeast of Préveza lies **ÁRTA**, finely situated in a loop of the broad Árakhthos River as it meanders towards the **Amvrakikós Gulf**, 20km to the south. It is one of the more pleasant Greek towns: a quiet place, very much the provincial capital, with an old centre that retains much of its Ottoman-bazaar aspect, and some celebrated medieval monuments. From the west, you enter town past the restored packhorse **bridge**, subject of song and poetry throughout the mainland. Legend maintains that the bridge builder, continually thwarted by the current washing his foundations away, took the advice of a bird and sealed up his wife in the central pier; the bridge finally held but the woman's voice haunted the place thereafter.

The Town

In ancient times Árta was known as Ambracia, and had a brief period of fame as the capital of Pyrrhus, king of Epirus; it was the base for the king's hard-won campaigns in Italy – the original Pyrrhic victories ("Another such victory and I am lost"). The foundations of a **Temple of Apollo** and an **Odeion** lie on either side of Odhós Pýrrou, but otherwise there are very few remnants of this period. At the northeast end of the street is the **Froúrio**, the ancient acropolis and the citadel in every subsequent era; regrettably, it is now locked, seemingly indefinitely.

More substantial monuments date from Árta's second burst of glory, following the 1204 fall of Constantinople, when the town became aggrandized as the **Despotate of Epirus**, an autonomous Byzantine state. The despotate, which stretched from Corfu to Thessaloníki, was governed by the Angelos dynasty (the imperial family expelled from Constantinople) and survived until 1449, when the garrison surrendered to the Turks.

The most striking and certainly the most bizarre of the Byzantine monuments is the **Panayía Parigorítissa** (Tues–Sun 8.30am–3pm; 500dr), a grandiose, five-domed cube that rears above Platía Skoufá, at the southwest end of that street. The interior is almost Gothic in appearance, the main dome being supported by an extraordinary cantilevered-pilaster system that looks unwieldy and unsafe. Up top, this insecurity is accentuated by a looming *Pandokrátor* (Christ in Majesty) mosaic in excellent condition, overshadowing the sixteenth- and seventeenth-century frescoes in the sanctuary and nave. The church, flanked by two side chapels, was built in 1283–96 by Despot Nikiforos I as part of a monastic complex; of this, sixteen cells and the refectory remain east and south of the church, along with the excavated foundations of an early shrine, and there are plans to restore them as an archeological museum.

Two smaller Byzantine churches from the same period also survive in the town. Both have a more conventional structure but are enlivened by highly elaborate brick and tile decorations on the outside walls. They're usually locked but this is no tragedy

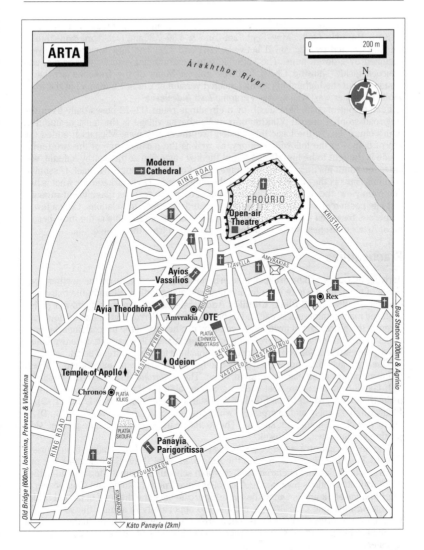

since the exteriors are the main interest. **Ayía Theódhora**, containing the fine marble tomb of the wife of the Epirot ruler Michael II, stands in its own courtyard halfway down Pýrrou. A little further north, opposite the produce market, is thirteenth-century **Áyios Vassílios**, a gem ornamented with glazed polychrome tiles and bas-reliefs.

Nearby monasteries and churches

Amid the orange groves surrounding Árta, a number of **monasteries** and **churches** were built during the despotate, many of them by members of the imperial Angelos dynasty; all are well signposted.

Within easy walking distance (2km along Odhós Komméno) stands the monastery of **Káto Panayía** (daily: May–Sept 7am–1pm & 4.30–7.30pm; Oct–April 8am–1pm & 3–6pm), erected by Michael II between 1231 and 1271 and now a working convent occupied by a dozen nuns. The katholikón has extravagant exterior decoration, and frescoes inside showing Christ in three guises. Many of the **frescoes** are badly smudged, but the highlight is an undamaged version of Christ Emmanuel in the front vault. The outer west wall sports a graphic *Last Judgement*.

Further out of Árta, 6km north by a circuitous route (11–12 buses daily from the ring-road stop), **Panayía Vlakhernón** in Vlakhérna village is the most beautiful of Árta's churches. To the basic three-aisled twelfth-century plan, Michael II added the trio of domes in the following century, as well as the narthex; one of the two tombs inside is thought to be his. Having found the key custodian at the nearby kafenío, you enter the south narthex door under a fine **relief** of the Archangel Michael. Dissimilar columns support the added cupolas, but the church is more remarkable for what is hidden from view: the warden will lift a section of carpet to reveal a magnificent **mosaic**, just one portion of a vast marble floor punctuated with such tesselations. Only a few of numerous **frescoes** thought to be under plaster are exposed. This is the most beautiful of Árta's churches, worth contemplating at length from the kafenío.

Practicalities

Arriving by **bus**, you'll be dropped at a terminus on the riverbank, on the northern outskirts of town, from where it's a ten-minute walk along **Odhós Skoufá**, the main thoroughfare, to the central **Platía Ethnikís Andístásis**. Skoufá, which is the town's pedestrianized main commercial street, and its parallel streets, Pýrrou and Konstandínou, wind through the oldest part of town. If you come by car, beware of the fee-parking scheme in effect during business hours: a red strip on the sign means free parking up to two hours, but a green strip means you must seek out a machine for a windscreen ticket.

There are just three **hotels**, normally enough for the trickle of tourists and business visitors, though none constitute great value. The *Amvrakia*, Priovólou 13 (☎0681/28 311; fax 78 544; ④), is the best choice, a comfortable hotel with a good position on a pedestrian lane, just off Platía Ethnikís Andístasis. The *Chronos* (☎0681/22 211; ⑤) on Platía Kílkis is noisy and overpriced, while the *Rex*, Skoufá 9 (☎0681/27 563; ①), is cheap and clean enough but spartan. The *Xenia* up in the castle, despite profuse signposting around town, has closed.

The town's **restaurants** are excellent value, catering for locals rather than tourists. Best by far is the *Skaraveos*, next to the *Amvrakia* hotel (Mon–Sat lunch only); it provides ample choice for vegetarians and is worth scheduling a lunch stop around. Other, more ordinary options include the *Averoff*, at the corner of Skoufá and Grimbóvou, or the *Ellinikon* at Skoufá 5. Out at the old bridge, café-bars at either end of the old bridge – *Protomastoras* and *Club Mylos* – provide the opportunity to admire the structure at leisure over a coffee or stiffer drink, but there's no food available here. In the evenings, people tend to perform their volta around Platía Ethnikís Andístasis, or congregate in its cafés.

The Amvrakikós Gulf

Árta is the undisputed highlight of the **Amvrakikós Gulf**. Further around, and in fact all the way south to the open sea, there is little to prompt a stop. Locals from Árta head at weekends for seafood meals at the fishing villages of **MENÍDHI** (21km) or the somewhat more rewarding **KORONÍSSIA** (25km), approached along a wave-lashed causeway flanked by a scrappy beach that's popular with windsurfers. Today the village here boasts a few fish tavernas, some rooms, and a tenth-century Byzantine church.

AMFILOKHÍA is promisingly situated at the head of the gulf, but in reality is a very dull, small town. The chance for a swim would also seem from the map to be a redeeming feature, but the water here is stagnant. If you're marooned here, best emergency fallback **hotel** is probably the *Oscar* (π0642/22 155; ③) at the west end of the quay. **VÓNITSA**, 35km west of Amfilokhía, is a more convenient and pleasant choice for a stopover. Again it's not an exciting place, and frustratingly distant from real sea, but it's a definite improvement on Amfilokhía, with its lively waterside, tree-lined squares and substantial **Byzantine castle** above. Among five **hotels**, the best is the comfortable *Bel Mare* (π0643/22 394; ③) on the castle end of the *paralia*; the *Leto* just inland on Platía Anaktoríou has castle views but is considerably more basic (π0643/22 246; ①). As at Préveza across the gulf, sardines figure prominently on the menus of a half-dozen waterfront **tavernas**. Infrequent local **buses** cover the 14km to **ÁKTIO**, the terminal for ferries from Préveza, passing Áktio airport.

The coast south to Messolóngi

Heading south for Messolóngi and the gulf of Kórinthos, there's not much more of interest, at least on the direct **inland route**. From Amfilokhía, you pass a few swampy patches of lake pumped to irrigate the local tobacco. Midway down the Amfilokhía–Messolóngi road, **AGRÍNIO** is little more than a transport link for this area, with buses to Árta/Ioánnina, Karpeníssi and south to Andírio, where there are local buses to Náfpaktos, as well as the ferry across the Gulf of Kórinthos to the Peloponnese.

Mýtikas, Astakós and Etolikó

The **coast south from Vónitsa** is bleakly impressive, its quiet stretch of road skirting the shoreline with nothing but an arid wilderness inland. However, if you have transport there are great opportunities for finding tiny deserted beaches. There is just one sleepy but pleasant settlement, **MÝTIKAS**, whose rows of old-fashioned houses strung along a pebbly shore look out onto the island of Kálamos (see p.332). As yet development is minimal, consisting of three **hotels** – the best of these being the *Kymata* (π0646/81 258; ④) – and rooms or studios, representative ones being those of Alekos Lekatsas (π0646/81 097; ②), with cooking facilities and a sea view. Of several **tavernas** pitched mostly at locals, *Ouzeri stou Thoma* is the most elaborate, but is still very reasonable. Two kilometres of uncommercialized beach lead east from the village, getting better as you proceed, all with a backdrop of sheer mountains.

South from here, the coast road loops around to **ASTAKÓS**, whose name means "lobster". Patrick Leigh Fermor, in *Roumeli*, fantasizes about arriving at this gastronomic-sounding place and ordering its namesake for supper; it turned out to be a crashing non-event, and you still won't get lobster at any of the half-dozen tavernas which line the quay here. Like Amfilokhía, the location of the village is its most attractive attribute, and many of the older buildings have been preserved.

Arriving by land, the bus station is at one end of the quay, while the single hotel, *Stratos* (π0646/41 911, fax 41 227; ④) sprawls at the other end, overlooking the tiny, gravelly town beach. Buses from Athens dovetail fairly well with the **ferries** across to Itháki and Kefalloniá, which leave twice daily much of the year (1pm & 9pm in summer, 10am & 6pm in the off-season).

Beyond here the scenery becomes greener as the road winds 26km over oak-covered hills to **ETOLIKÓ**, built on an island in the eponymous, rather sumpy lagoon and reached by two causeways. The town is visibly less prosperous than Messolóngi (see p.332), with a prominent gypsy presence, but it could make a good emergency halt with a perfectly acceptable en-suite **hotel** on the west-facing quay: the *Alexandra* (π0632/23019; ③). Next door is the town's fanciest **restaurant**, *To Stafnokari*, specializing in local seafood, and there's the usual complement of bars and kafenía in the centre, plus a bank and post office. Occasional buses ply to Messolóngi, just 10km southeast, past the salt factories that are today the area's mainstay.

Kálamos

Kálamos, the largest island in a mini-archipelago west of Astakós, is essentially a partly-wooded mountain rising abruptly from the sea. In summer there are usually a few yachts moored in the small harbour below the main village, Khóra, but otherwise the island, with a permanent population of about three hundred, sees few visitors, and is ill-equipped to host them. The only regular connection is a daily kaïki from Mýtikas, which leaves the mainland at noon and returns from the island at 7.30am the next day. At the time of writing there is no reliable accommodation available in Khóra; come with **camping** gear if you intend to stay the night, though even this is difficult, given the lack of flat ground.

KHÓRA, spread out among gardens and olive groves on the south coast, largely survived the 1953 earthquake which devastated so many of the Ionian islands, though there's been no lack of insensitive building since. There are two basic tavernas and a "supermarket" by the harbour, plus a bakery and sweetshop higher up, next to a **post office** where you can change money. The gravelly village **beach**, is fifteen minutes southwest; the much better beach of **Meríthia** lies twenty minutes northeast of the port, via a rough scramble along the shore. Your reward will be 500m of sand and fine gravel which can accommodate all the tourists Kálamos is ever likely to get, and is one of the better places to camp, though there's no shade or fresh water.

KÁSTRO, an old fortified settlement at the north tip of the island facing Mýtikas, is linked to the port by a seven-kilometre asphalt road; the ninety-minute walk is drudgery despite pine-shade and views, so try and thumb a lift from the sparse traffic. The small, five-bastioned castle here may possibly be Byzantine, and as well as being pirate-safe, it surveyed the straits between here and Mýtikas. Its walls are surrounded by a dozen or so houses, mostly roofless and abandoned, and the overgrown bailey is now used by villagers to keep their hens and sheep. A spring just above the road provides water, and the damp church of Áyios Nikólaos huddles beside the fortifications. Down towards Kástro's harbour, a few more houses are still inhabited, though there's no shop or café. Small, exquisite beaches dot the coast between Khóra and Kástro, though they can only be seen and reached by sea.

Messolóngi

MESSOLÓNGI (Missolongi) is for most visitors irrevocably bound to the name of **Lord Byron**, who died in the town while organizing the local Greek forces during the War of Independence (see box on p.333). The town has an obvious interest in this literary past but, as in Byron's time, it's a fairly shabby and desperately unromantic place, wet through autumn and spring, and now comprised mostly of drab, modern buildings. To be fair, the town has been spruced up of late, especially around the centre, though if you come here on a pilgrimage, it's best to plan on moving ahead within the day.

The Town

You enter the town from the northeast by the **Gate of the Exodus**, whose name recalls an attempt by nine thousand men, women and children to break out during the Turks' year-long siege in 1826. In one wild dash they managed to get free of the town, leaving a group of defenders to destroy it in their wake. But they were betrayed, and in the supposed safety of nearby Mount Zýgos were ambushed and massacred by a large Albanian mercenary force.

Just inside this gate, on the right, partly bounded by the remains of the fortifications, is the **Kípos Iróön**, or **Garden of Heroes** (summer 9am–8pm; winter 9am–5pm; signposted in English as "Heroes' Tombs") where a tumulus covers the bodies of the town's unnamed defenders. Beside the tomb of the Greek Souliot commander, Markos Botsaris, is a **statue of Byron**, erected in 1881, under which the poet's heart is buried. The rest of Byron's remains were taken back to his family home, Newstead Abbey, despite his dying request: "Here let my bones moulder; lay me in the first corner without pomp or nonsense." Perhaps he knew this would be disregarded. There is certainly a touch of pomp in the carving of Byron's coat of arms with a royal crown above; there had been speculation that Byron would be offered the crown of an independent Greece. Among the palm trees and rusty cannons there are also monuments – busts, obelisks, cenotaphs – to American, German and French Philhellenes.

Elsewhere in the town, traces of Byron are sparse. The **house** in which he lived and died was destroyed during World War II and its site is marked by a clumsy memorial garden. It's on Odhós Levídhou, reached from the central platía by walking down to the end of Khariláou Trikoúpi and turning left. Back in the central Platía Bótsari, the town hall houses a small **museum** devoted to the revolution (Mon–Fri 9am–1.30pm & 4–7pm, Sat & Sun 9am–1pm & 4–7pm; free), with some emotive paintings of the independence struggle on the upper floor (including a reproduction of Delacroix's *Gate of*

O LORDHOS VYRONOS: BYRON IN MESSOLÓNGI

Byron arrived at Messolóngi, a squalid and inhospitable place surrounded by marshland, in January 1824. The town, with its small port allowing access to the Ionian islands, was the western centre of **resistance** against the Turks. The poet, who had contributed much of his personal fortune to the war effort, as well as much publicity, was enthusiastically greeted with a 21-gun salute.

On landing, he was made **commander-in-chief** of the five thousand soldiers gathered at the garrison, a role that was as much political as military. The Greek forces, led by Klephtic brigand-generals, were divided among themselves and each faction separately and persistently petitioned him for money. He had already wasted months on the island of Kefaloniá, trying to assess their claims and quarrels before finalizing his own military plan – to march full force on Náfpaktos and from there take control of the Gulf of Corinth – but in Messolóngi he was again forced to delay.

Occasionally Byron despaired: "Here we sit in this realm of mud and discord", he wrote in his journal. But while other Philhellenes were returning home, disillusioned by the squabbles and larceny of the Greeks, or appalled by the conditions in this damp, stagnant town, he stayed, **campaigning** eloquently and profitably for the cause. Outside his house, he drilled soldiers; in the lagoon he rowed and shot, and caught a fever. On April 19, 1824, Byron died, pronouncing a few days earlier, "My wealth, my abilities, I devoted to the cause of Greece – well, here is my life to her!" It was, bathetically, the most important contribution he could have made to the struggle.

The news of the **poet's death** reverberated across northern Europe, swelled to heroic proportions by his admirers. Arguably it changed the course of the war in Greece. When Messolóngi fell again to the Ottomans, in 1826, there was outcry in the European press, and the French and English forces were finally galvanized into action, sending a joint naval force for protection. It was this force that accidentally engaged an Egyptian fleet at Navarino Bay (see p.212), casting a fatal blow against the Ottoman navy.

Byron, ever since independence, has been a **Greek national hero**. Almost every town in the country has a street – Výronos – named after him; a few men still answer to the first name Vyron; there was once an eponymous brand of cigarettes (perhaps the ultimate Greek tribute); and, perhaps more important, the respect Byron inspired was for many years generalized to his fellow countrymen – before being dissipated in this century by British interference in the civil war and bungling in Cyprus.

the Sortie), reproductions of period lithographs and a rather desperate collection of Byronia on the ground floor, padded out with a brass souvenir plaque of Newstead Abbey. Pride of place, by the entrance, goes to an original edition of Solomos's poem "Hymn to Liberty", now the national anthem. Despite the evident thinness of the exhibits, a new "Lord Byron Museum" is planned for the west of town, to be filled with who knows what.

Perhaps more interesting and enjoyable than any of this is a walk across the **lagoon**, past the **forts** of Vassiládhi and Kleissoúra, which were vital defences against the Turkish navy. The lagoon, with its salt-pans and fish farms, attracts coastal birds. Migrant waders pass through and, in spring, avocets and black-winged stilts nest here. A causeway extends for about 5km and reaches the open sea at **TOURLÍDHA**, a hamlet of prefab summer cottages on stilts, and a taverna, the *Alikes*, haunted by coach tours. Its rival, *To Iliovasilema*, only functions at high season.

Practicalities

Long-distance **buses** arrive at the KTEL on Mavrokordháto 5, next to the central Platía Bótsari, and the local blue-and-white buses park just a few paces away. You can **rent bicycles** from the *Theoxenia* hotel should you wish to explore the lagoon. The **OTE** and the **post office** are virtually adjacent just a block east of the square.

Hotels in Messolóngi are a bit cheerless, expensive and often block-booked by tour groups. Etolikó (see p.331), 10km to the west, is a cheaper, less crowded alternative for the night. If you need or want to stay in the town, a good option is the *Avra* (☎0631/22 284; ③), Khariláou Trikoúpi 5; it's adjacent to the central platía and close to the best of Messolóngi's eating and drinking venues. More upmarket and impersonal choices include the massive *Liberty* (☎0631/28 089; ④), Iróön Polytekhníou 41, one block from the Heroes' Garden, or the *Theoxenia* (☎0631/22 493; ④), a small complex amidst landscaping just south of town on the lagoon shore.

Of late, the prevailing Greek craze for innovative ouzerís and *barákia* has swept through Messolóngi, resulting in a vastly improved **eating** and **drinking** scene, and making it eminently worthwhile for a lunch stop. The town is especially famous for its eels, hunted with tridents in the lagoon. The main concentration of places is along Athanasíou Razikotsíka, one block south of Khariláou Trikoúpi: try *O Nikos* at no. 7, *Fagadhiko* and *Poseidhon* at no. 4, and *Marokia* at no. 8. In the narrow alleys linking these two broader streets are more bars, kafenía and ouzerís, for example the *Rodhon*, which has an impressive range of imported beers.

6hr); Kónitsa (7 daily; 1hr 30min); Métsovo (4 Mon–Sat, 2 Sun; 1hr 30min); Monodhéndhri (2 daily Mon–Fri 6am/4.15pm; 45min); Pápingo (Mon, Wed & Fri 5am/2.30pm; 1hr); Paramythiá/Párga (1 daily; 2hr/3hr); Pátra via Agrínio (5 daily; 4hr 30min); Prámanda (2 daily Mon–Fri 5am/3.15pm; 2hr); Préveza (10 daily, 8 Sun; 2hr 30min); Syráko (2 weekly Fri & Sun; 2hr 30min); Thessaloníki (5 daily; 8hr); Tríkala, via Métsovo and Kalambáka (2 daily; 1hr 30min/3hr); Tsepélovo (2 daily Mon–Fri 6am & 3.15pm; 1hr); Vovoússa (Mon & Fri 1.15pm, Sun 7.45am; 1hr 30min).

Messolóngi to: Astakós (2 daily; 1hr 15min); Athens (8 daily; 4hr); Ioánnina (6 daily, 2hr 30min); Pátra (8 daily, 1hr 30min).

Préveza to: Glykí (1 daily; 1hr); Lefkádha (4 daily, 45min); Párga (4 Mon–Sat, 3 Sun; 1hr 30min).

Vónitsa to: Áktio (3 daily; 30 min); Lefkádha (5 daily; 30min).

Ferries

Astakós to: Itháki and Kefalloniá (2 daily most of the year).

Igoumenítsa to: Corfu (hourly, last at 10pm; 1–2hr). Also to Ancona, Bari, Trieste, Venice and Brindisi (Italy), and Dubrovnik (Croatia) via Bari. See "Igoumenítsa and around" for details.

Párga to: Paxí (daily 9.30am May–Sept; 2hr).

Préveza to: Áktio (every 20min 9am–9pm, every half hour 6am–9am and 9pm–midnight, every hour midnight–6am; 10min).

Sývota to: Paxí (1–2 weekly, in season; 2hr).

Hydrofoils and catamarans (summer only)

Routes and services change annually, and some years don't operate at all. Check at the Igoumenítsa Port Authority (☎0665/22 240) for details of future services.

Igoumenítsa Services to Corfu, Páxi and other Ionian islands, plus Brindisi (Italy).

Préveza Infrequent services to Páxi, Itháki and Kefalloniá in season.

Flights

Ioánnina to: Athens (2 daily; 1hr10min); Thessaloníki (5–7 weekly; 45min).

Préveza to: Athens (4–5 weekly; 1hr).

Also occasional international charters between Préveza (Áktion) and Britain.

CHAPTER FIVE

THE NORTH: MACEDONIA AND THRACE

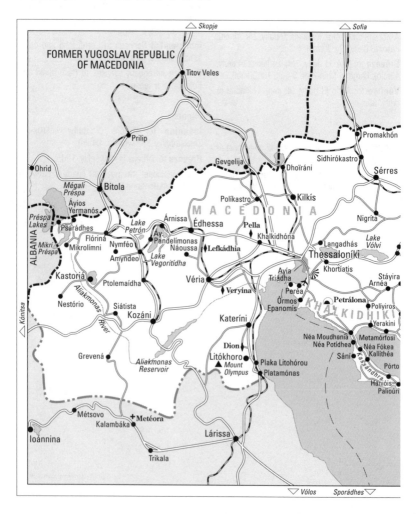

△ Skopje   △ Sofia

FORMER YUGOSLAV REPUBLIC
OF MACEDONIA

Titov Veles

Prilip

Promakhón

Ohrid

Mégali Préspa

Bitola

Gevgelija   Dhoïráni   Sidhirókastro   Sérres

Áyios Yermanós

Préspa Lakes

PolÍkastro   Kilkís

MACEDONIA

Psarádhes   Flórina   Árnissa   Édhessa   Pella   Khalkidhóna   Nigríta

ALBANIA

Lake Petrón   Ay. Pandelímonas   *Lefkádhia*   Langadhás   *Lake Vólvi*

Mikri Préspa   Mikrolímni   Nymféo   Náoussa   Thessaloníki

Amýndeo   *Lake Vegoritídha*   Ayía Triádha   Khortíatis   Stáyira Arnéa

Kastoriá   Véria   Perea   **Petrálona**   Políyiros

Aliakmonas River   Ptolemaïda   *Veryína*   Órmos Epanomís   KHALKIDHIKÍ   Yerakíni

Nestório   Siátista   Kozáni   Néa Moudhaniá   Metamórfosi

Kóitsa   Kateríni   Néa Potídhea   Néa Fókea   Kallithéa

Grevená   *Aliakmonas Reservoir*   **Dion**   Litókhoro   Sání   Pórto

Plaka Litohórou   Haniótis

▲ Mount Olympus   Platamónas   Palioúri

Métsovo   + **Metéora**

Kalambáka   Lárissa

Ioánnina

Trikala

▽ Vólos   Sporádhes ▽

The two northern regions of **Macedonia** and **Thrace** have been part of the Greek state for just less than three generations. Macedonia (Makedhonía) was surrendered by the Turks after the Balkan Wars in 1913; Greek sovereignty over Thrace (Thráki) was confirmed only in 1923. As such, they stand slightly apart from the rest of the nation – an impression reinforced for visitors by scenery and climate that are essentially Balkan. Macedonia is characterized by an abundance of lakes to the west, and in the east by heavily cultivated flood plains and the deltas of rivers with sources in former Yugoslavia or Bulgaria. The climate can be harsh, with steamy summers and bitterly cold winters, especially up in the Rhodópi mountains that form a natural frontier with Bulgaria.

These factors, along with a dearth of good beaches and thus direct charters from abroad, may explain why the north is so little known to outsiders, even those who have

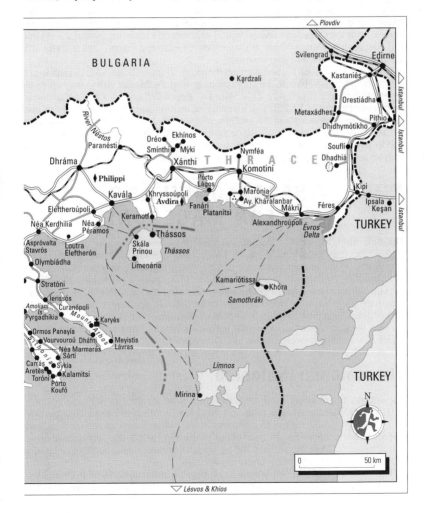

travelled widely throughout the rest of the mainland and the islands. The only areas to draw more than a scattering of visitors, even at the height of the summer, are Khalkidhíkí and Mount Olympus. **Khalkidhíkí**, the three-pronged peninsula province trailing below Thessaloníki, offers a beach-playground for that city – and for growing numbers of foreigners – in the rapidly expanding resort areas of Kassándhra and Sithonía. Stunning views are provided by the slopes of **Mount Olympus**, the mythical abode of the gods and a mecca for walkers in the south of the region. As for the rest, few travellers look beyond the dull trunk routes to Turkey and Bulgaria, along which only **Xánthi** merits more than a meal stop.

With a more prolonged acquaintance, the north may well grow on you. Part of its appeal lies in its vigorous life, independent of tourism, most evident in the sybaritic Macedonian capital of **Thessaloníki** (Salonica) and the north's second port-city, **Kavála**. Other attractions lie, as in Epirus, in the rugged western provinces, around the **Préspa national park** and the lakeside city of **Kastoriá**. Monuments are on the whole modest, with the exception of King Philip II of Macedon's tomb, discovered at **Veryína** and now open to visitors. There are lesser Macedonian and Roman sites at **Pella** and at **Philippi**, St Paul's first stop in Greece.

If you are male, over 21, and interested enough in monasticism – or Byzantine art and architecture – to pursue the applications procedure, **Mount Áthos** may prove to be a highlight of a Greek stay. This **"Monks' Republic"** occupies the mountainous easternmost prong of Khalkidhíkí, maintaining control over twenty monasteries and numerous dependencies and hermitages. Women (and most female animals) have been excluded from the peninsula since a decree of 1060, although it is possible for any-one to view the monasteries from the sea by taking a boat tour from the resorts of Ierissós and Ouranoúpoli in the "secular" part of Áthos.

THESSALONÍKI AND WESTERN MACEDONIA

Thessaloníki is the focus of Macedonian travel. If you are heading for the west of the region, the train ride from there to **Flórina** via **Édhessa**, edging around Lake Vegorítidha, is one of the most scenic in the country. **Kastoriá**, with its remote towns and Byzantine monuments, is also highly worthwhile, though reachable only by bus. Beyond Flórina, the secluded **Préspa lakes**, straddling the frontiers of three countries, constitute one of the finest wildlife refuges in the Balkans. The biggest attraction in this part of Macedonia, however, has to be **Mount Olympus** (Óros Ólymbos). The fabled home of the gods soars high above the town of Litókhoro, easily approached from the highway or rail line between Lárissa and Thessaloníki.

Thessaloníki (Salonica)

The second city of Greece and administrative centre for the two northern regions, **THESSALONÍKI** (or Salonica, as the city was known in Western Europe until this cen-tury) has a very different feel from Athens: more Balkan-European and modern, less Middle Eastern. Situated at the head of the Thermaïkos gulf, it also seems more open; you're never far from the sea, and the air actually circulates, though this is a bit of a mixed blessing since the bay is pretty much a sump.

The "modern" quality of Thessaloníki is due largely to a disastrous **1917 fire** which lev-elled most of the old plaster houses along a labyrinth of Ottoman lanes, including the entire

Jewish quarter with its 32 synagogues (see below), rendering nearly half the population homeless. The city was rebuilt over the next eight years on a grid plan prepared under the supervision of French architect and archeologist Ernest Hébrard, with long central avenues running parallel to the seafront. The part of the plan forbidding high buildings was disregarded, but Thessaloníki is still a more livable city than Athens, with a more cosmopolitan, wealthy aspect, stimulated by its major university and international trade fair. But the new opulence has its downside: the city is beginning to act as a magnet for all the misery of the upper Balkans, with unemployed Slavic and Albanian refugees gathered on park lawns and beggars and buskers making the rounds of the outdoor tavernas.

Even before this influx, Athenians loved to disparage the city as "Bulgaria", but they would be more accurate to call it "Anatolia", for the 1923 influx of refugees from that region is still reflected in Turkish surnames and in the spicy Anatolian food found nowhere else in Greece. Prior to then, the city had the largest European **Jewish** community of the age: 80,000, or nearly half of the inhabitants, for whom "Salonica" was the "Mother of Israel", before the first waves of emigration to Palestine began after World War I. Numbers had dropped to less than 60,000 at the onset of World War II, when all but a tiny fraction were deported from Platía Eleftherías to the concentration camps, in one of the worst atrocities committed in the Balkans. It was this operation in which former Austrian president Kurt Waldheim has been implicated. The vast Jewish cemeteries east of the city centre were desecrated, and later covered over by the new university and trade fair grounds in 1948.

You can catch glimpses of "Old Salonica" today in the walled **Kástra** quarter, on the hillside beyond the modern grid of streets. Even amidst the post-1917 flatlands below, there are pockets of Ottoman and Greek Art Deco buildings which miraculously survived the fire. For most visitors, however, it is Thessaloníki's excellent **Archeological Museum**, with its spectacular exhibits from the tombs of Philip II and others of his dynasty, that stands out. Additionally, there is a wealth of **churches** dating from Roman times to the fifteenth century, while a smaller number of **Islamic monuments** – virtually all of them from the fifteenth century – attest to Thessaloníki's status as the first Ottoman Balkan city, when Athens was still a village.

The downside of the city, for visitors as well as residents, is a complex of **problems** all too reminiscent of Athens. Industrial and residential waste is discarded, untreated, into the gulf, and traffic on the main avenues is often at a standstill. Ambitious 1980s plans for a metro line and a widening of the waterfront boulevard have never been acted upon. Additionally, the punishing 1991–1995 blockade of the FYROM ironically brought activity at Thessaloníki's busy port – the natural gateway to the landlocked republic – to a near-halt. Under these circumstances, the city's designation as **European Cultural Capital for 1997** has been a huge boost. The year's most tangible legacy – thanks to EU funds – has been extensive signposting and sprucing up of long-neglected medieval buildings. At the same time came an equally overdue recognition of the nearly-vanished Jewish community, in the form of a new museum and a memorial to the 1943 deportations.

Arrival, orientation and information

Arriving in Thessaloníki is fairly straightforward. The **train station** on the west side of town is just a short walk from the central grid of streets and the harbour. The scattered provincial KTELs were supposed to be gradually gathered after 1992 into one giant **bus terminal** at the bottom of 26-Oktovríou, in the Sfayiá district, but resistance to the move has been overwhelming, and you'll still arrive at a variety of points, especially

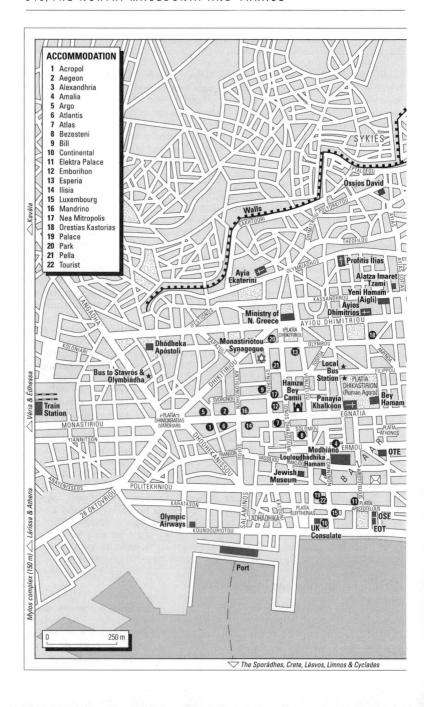

ACCOMMODATION

1 Acropol
2 Aegeon
3 Alexandhria
4 Amalia
5 Argo
6 Atlantis
7 Atlas
8 Bezesteni
9 Bill
10 Continental
11 Elektra Palace
12 Emborihon
13 Esperia
14 Ilisia
15 Luxembourg
16 Mandrino
17 Nea Mitropolis
18 Orestias Kastorias
19 Palace
20 Park
21 Pella
22 Tourist

SYKIES

Óssios David

Walls

Ayia Ekateríni

Profitis Ilias

Alatza Imaret Tzami

Yeni Hamam (Aigli)

Ministry of N. Greece

Ayios Dhimitrios

Dhódheka Apóstoli

Monastiriótou Synagogue

Bus to Stavrós & Olymbiádha

Local Bus Station

PLATIA DHIKASTIRION (Roman Agora)

Bey Hamam

Train Station

Hamza Bey Camii

Panayia Khalkéon

Modhiáno

Louloudhádhika Hamam

OTE

Jewish Museum

Olympic Airways

UK Consulate

OSE

EOT

Port

0   250 m

▽ *The Sporádhes, Crete, Lésvos, Límnos & Cyclades*

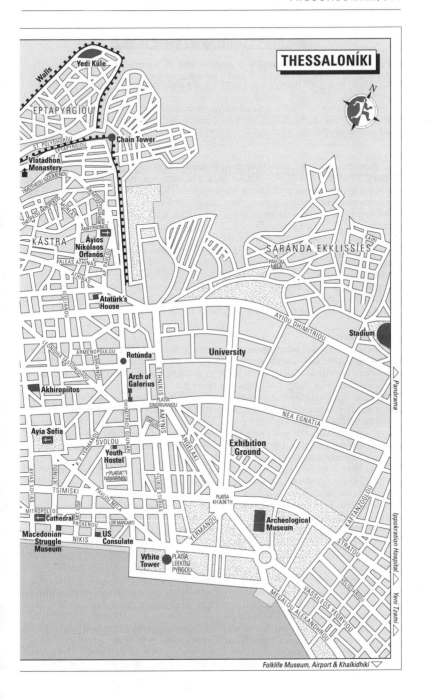

THESSALONÍKI

Walls
Yedi Küle
EPTAPYRGIOU
ST. POLYDHOROU
EPTAPYRGIOU
Chain Tower
TIMOTHEOU IGOUMENOU
Vlatádhon
Monastery
THEROU AGIOROPES
MURLES
AMFITRIONOS
KÁSTRA
Áyios
Nikólaos
Orfanós
PALEAS ATHINAS
AP. PAVLOU
IOULIANOU
ATHINAS
Atatürk's
House
AYIOU DHIMITRIOU
Stadium
LEONIDHA IASSONIDHOU
ARMENOPOULOU
ARRIANOU
Rotúnda
University
Akhiropíitos
DHIMITRIOU GUNARI
Arch of
Galerius
ETHNIKIS
PLATÍA
SINDRIVANIOU
NEA EGNATIA
OMILOU
Ayía Sofía
AMYNIS
P. P. YERMANOU
SVOLOU
Youth
Hostel
ANGELAKI
FILIKIS ETERIAS
Exhibition
Ground
AYIAS SOFIAS
DINIKI
PLATÍA
NAVARINOU
PAVLOU MELA
TSIMISKI
PLATÍA
KH.A.N.TH
MITROPOLEOS
Cathedral
PROXENOU
LORI MARGARITI
YERMANOU
Archeological
Museum
Macedonian
Struggle
Museum
NIKIS
US
Consulate
White
Tower
PLATÍA
LEFKOU
PYRGOU
MEGALOU ALEXANDHROU
VASSILEOS YEORYIOU
YELOSSABOU
KAFTANZOGLOU
STRATOU
SARÁNDA EKKLISSIES
PL.
PAVLOU
MELA
KAIRI

N

Panórama
Ippokration Hospital
Yeni Tzami

Folklife Museum, Airport & Khalkidhikí

THESSALONÍKI'S FESTIVALS

The city's festival season begins in September with the **International Trade Fair**, the major event of the year. This is followed almost immediately by a **Festival of Greek Song**, and finally, for the last week of October, by the **Dhimitría** celebrations for the city's patron saint; these coincide with the parades and parties held for Ókhi Day (see p.56) on October 28. The **Film Festival** runs from September to November. The period of the Trade Fair, particularly, is not a good time to visit. Hotels are full, and proprietors will add twenty-percent surcharges.

---

near the train station; the most useful are detailed in "Listings", p.350. Coming from the **airport**, city bus #78 (130dr) shuttles back and forth hourly between 7am and midnight; the most convenient city stops are the train station and Platía Aristotélous. A taxi into town won't set you back more than 1800dr. All **ferries** and **hydrofoils** call at the passenger port, within walking distance of the train station at the western end of the seafront. For all ferry agencies, see p.355; Aegean routes and frequencies are detailed in the "Travel Details" at the end of the chapter.

Once within the grid, **orientation** is relatively straightforward on the major avenues: Ayíou Dhimitríou, Egnatía, Tsimiskí and Mitropóleos. All run parallel to the quay, but confusingly change their names repeatedly as they head east into the city's post-medieval annexe. The divide between the older and newer parts of town is marked by the exhibition grounds and the start of the seaside park strip, known locally as Zoo Park and dominated by the **Lefkós Pýrgos** or White Tower, the city's symbol.

City transport

There are two types of **local buses**: the orange articulated "caterpillar" models which operate within the city, and the deep red or blue buses which travel further afield. The fare within the city is 75dr; it costs 100dr to the suburbs and 115dr out to nearby villages. In most cases, there's an automatic ticket machine on the bus – which is apt not to take 100-drachma coins or the old 20-drachma ones – but there are still some city buses where you pay the conductor at the rear entrance. Useful lines include #10 and #11, which both ply the length of Egnatía. From Platía Eleftherías (just behind the sea front), buses initially run east along Mitropóleos; line #5 takes you to the archeological and folklore museums, and #22/23 heads north through Kástra to the highest quarter, known as Eptapyrgíou, the most pleasant part of town.

If you bring your own **car**, it's best to use the attended fee car park that occupies all of Platía Eleftherías where day rates are available and you pay on exit. Otherwise, finding a kerbside space is a fairly hopeless task, even in the suburbs; you must go to a *períptero* to buy blue-and-red strip cards which you validate yourself for an hour at a time (200dr per hour) – buy as many as you need in advance for display in the windscreen (fees payable Mon–Fri 8am–8pm, Sat 8am to 3pm). If you intend to drive around the city, arm yourself with a map showing the one-way system (one is provided by the EOT).

Information

The main **EOT** office is at Platía Aristotélous 8 (Mon–Fri 8am–8pm, Sat 8.30am–2pm; ☎271 888); they also have a booth at the airport. When these are closed, try the **tourist police** post (Mon, Wed, Sat & Sun 8am–2pm, plus 5–9pm other days; ☎254 871) at Dhodhekaníssou.

Free handout **maps** at the tourist office are often out of stock; the bound A-to-Z-type atlas published by Malliaris, *Polyodhigos tis Thessalonikis*, is heavy, expensive and not very useful. A better **book**, with a large-scale folding map, is *Monuments of Thessaloníki* by Apostolos Papayiannopoulos (1500dr), available at Áyios Dhimítrios church.

For **listings**, try the English-language *What's On*, available from the British expatriates' shop at Ioánnou Mikhaíl 16, off Dhimitríou Goúnari; if you can read Greek you might pick up the bi-weekly free broadsheet *Politismika*, available at some record stores and art galleries.

Accommodation

Outside of the festival season, reasonably priced **hotel** rooms are fairly easy to find, if not always very attractively situated. You will, however, find accommodation relatively expensive – fifteen percent more than Athens or the Peloponnese for equivalent facilities. Modest to comfortable hotels tend to cluster in two areas: around the beginning of Egnatía – although many of the establishments here are plagued by street noise – or in the more agreeable zone between Eleftherías and Aristotélous squares. There are also some good bets between Egnatía and Ayíou Dhimitríou, also a relatively quiet area.

The closest **campsites** are at the small resorts of Ayía Triádha and Órmos Epanomís, 24km and 33km away respectively; see p.358 for more information. Both are EOT sites and Órmos Epanomís is the better, as is the beach there. Take bus #72 from Platía Dhikastiríon for Ayía Triádha and bus #69 for Órmos Epanomís.

Lower Egnatía

Acropol, Egnatía 10, cnr Tandalídhou (☎536 170). Quiet and clean, this is a good cheap option with toilet and shower down the corridor. No breakfast. ③.

Aegeon, Egnatía 19 (☎522 921, fax 522 923). Functional, comfortable and central. Breakfast is extra. ④.

Alexandria, Egnatía 18 (☎536 185). Opposite the *Aegeon*, a less dear en-suite hotel. ④.

Argo, Egnatía 11 (☎519 770). An old place with basic but acceptable rooms, some of which have private facilities. ②.

Atlantis Egnatía 14 (☎540 131). Another budget hotel, with better rooms facing a side street. ③.

Atlas, Egnatía 40 (☎537 046). Choose a room with private facilities, or for 2000dr less, you can share. Rooms at the front are noisy. Furthest from the train station of the places in this list. ④.

Averof, Sófou 24, south of Egnatía (☎538 840, fax 543 194). A good, friendly cheapie, not too noisy and used to foreigners' needs. En-suite conversions of the well-furnished rooms are scheduled for 1998. ③.

Emborikon, Syngroú 14, cnr Egnatía (☎514 431). Good value, despite the shared bathrooms, and with helpful staff. ③.

Ilisia, Egnatía 24 (☎528 492). One of the better deals in town, this has good en-suite facilities and a courteous, cheerful welcome. ④.

Mandrino, Antigonídhou 2, cnr Egnatía (☎526 321). Rather sterile 1970s building, but well-maintained and comfortable. ⑤.

ACCOMMODATION PRICE CODES

Throughout the book we've used the following **price codes** to denote the cheapest available room in high season; all are prices for a double room, except for category ①, which represents per person rates. Out of season, rates can drop by up to fifty percent, especially if you are staying for three or more nights. Single rooms, where available, cost around seventy percent of the price of a double.

① 1400–2000dr	④ 8000–12,000dr
② 4000–6000dr	⑤ 12,000–16,000dr
③ 6000–8000dr	⑥ 16,000dr and upwards

For more accommodation details, see pp.39–42.

A NOTE ON MACEDONIA

The name **Macedonia** is a geographical term of long standing, applied to an area that has always been populated by a variety of races and cultures. It is today divided unequally between Greece, Bulgaria, the Former Yugoslav Republic of Macedonia (FYROM) and Albania, with Greece retaining by far the greatest extent.

The original **Kingdom of Macedonia**, which gained pre-eminence under Philip II and Alexander the Great, was governed by Greek kings and inhabited by a predominantly Greek population. Its early borders spread south to Mount Olympus, west to present-day Kastoriá, east to Kavála, and north into parts of what was Yugoslavia. It lasted, however, for little more than two centuries. In subsequent years the region fell under the successive control of Romans, Slavs, Byzantines, Saracens and Bulgars, before eventual subjugation, with southern Greece, under Ottoman Turkish rule.

In the late nineteenth century, when the disintegration of the **Ottoman Empire** began to raise the issue of future national territories, the name Macedonia denoted simply the geographical region. Its heterogeneous population included Greeks, Slavs and Bulgarians – the latter referring to themselves and their language as "Macedonian" – as well as large numbers of Jews, Serbs, Vlachs, Albanians and Turks. No one ethnic group predominated overall, and Greek Orthodox were often in a distinct minority, particularly in Thessaloníki. The first nationalist struggles for the territory began in the 1870s, when small armies of Greek *andartes*, Serbian *chetniks* and Bulgarian *comitadjis* took root in the mountain areas, coming together against the Ottomans in the first Balkan War.

Following Turkish defeat, things swiftly became more complex. The **Bulgarians** laid sole claim to Macedonia in the second Balkan War, but were defeated, and a 1912 Greco-Serbian agreement divided the bulk of Macedonian territory between the two states along approximate linguistic/ethnic lines. During World War I however, the Bulgarians occupied much of Macedonia and Thrace, until their capitulation in 1917. After the Versailles peace conference, a small part of Slavophone Macedonia remained in Bulgaria, and there were population exchanges of Greek-speakers living in Bulgaria, and Bulgarians in Greece. This was followed, in 1923, by the arrival and settlement of hundreds of thousands of Greek refugees from Asia Minor, who – settling throughout Greek Macedonia – effectively swamped any remaining Slavophone population.

During World War II the Bulgarians again occupied all of eastern Macedonia and Thrace (beyond the River Strýmon), as allies of Nazi Germany. Their defeat by the Allies led to withdrawal and seems to have vanquished ambitions. Recent Bulgarian leaders, both Communist and post-Communist, have renounced all territorial claims and "minority rights" for "Greek-Bulgarians". The position of Yugoslavia, though, which under Tito established the **Socialist Republic of Macedonia** in its share of the historical territory, was more ambiguous. During the decades of its unity Yugoslav propaganda attempted to suggest Slav affinities with the ancient Macedonian kingdom, and, by extension, with the present Greek population.

Between Eleftherías and Aristotélous

Amalia, Ermoú 33 (☎268 321, fax 233 356). A decent, if slightly overpriced hotel, quiet enough at night, and well placed near the market. ⑤.

Continental, Komninón 5 (☎277 553). Central, characterful and quiet, with rooms with and without bath; there have however been some complaints about falling cleanliness standards. ④.

Electra Palace, Platía Aristotélous 5/a (☎232 221, fax 235 947). The most expensive hotel in town after the *Macedonia Palace*, and in the most prestigious position, but it can get noise from events in the square. ⑥.

Luxembourg, Komninón 6 (☎278 449). Another Neoclassical pile that's clean enough, but gloomy and ripe for an overhaul – a fallback choice. ④.

When the Yugoslav federation fell apart violently in mid-1991, the issue resurfaced at the top of Greece's political agenda, after the population of Yugoslav Macedonia voted overwhelmingly for an **independent nation of Macedonia**. Greek reaction was vitriolic, all the more so when the fledgling nation adopted the star of Veryína (the symbol of the ancient Macedonian dynasty) on their flag and coinage. Had the new state opted for a different name and emblem, the Greeks, doubtless, would have had no quarrel: an impoverished nation of two million, after all, posed little strategic threat. But their adoption of the Macedonian name and symbol was too much: Greeks claimed a cultural and historical copyright over both, and felt their "expropriation" as an act of aggression. The Right even called for invasion.

The Mitsotakis government, ensnared in this nightmare, managed to resist military action, but spared no effort to thwart the Yugoslav-Macedonian aspirations, spurred along by huge popular demonstrations in Thessaloníki and Athens. Ministers were sent on interminable rounds of EU capitals, imploring their allies not to recognize any state assuming the name of "Macedonia", and, their position increasingly ignored by the international community, the Greeks instigated an **economic boycott** of the fledgling state, only lifted in late 1995.

These moves severely destabilized the new country but did nothing to halt its recognition by the UN and EU – albeit under a convoluted (and presumably interim) title, **The Former Yugoslav Republic of Macedonia** (FYROM). Greeks have had to accept this de facto situation, but they still refuse to use the name, referring to the territory as Ta Skópia, after the capital, and its people as **Skopianá**. References in the press tend to use the phrase the "rump Skopje republic"; indeed it is prohibited to refer in print to Yugoslav "Macedonia" except in inverted commas. Official posters throughout Greece proclaim that "Macedonia was, is and always will be Greek and only Greek", for "three thousand years" no less, and further exhort the public to "read history".

This war of words is probably louder than any likely deeds but it is bad news for the beleaguered, landlocked republic, and for those approximately 40,000 Slavophones remaining in Greek Macedonia and Thrace, whose existence Greece refuses to admit. Activists leafleting for recognition of this minority – who were long accused of plotting to dismember the country during the Civil War – have been arrested; moreover, a respected professor, **Anastasia Karakasidou**, received death threats while resident in Thessaloníki during 1993 for presenting research establishing that many villagers in the North still identify themselves primarily as Slavs. In February 1996, Karakasidou's manuscript detailing these findings, *Fields of Wheat, Hills of Blood*, was declined for publication by Cambridge University Press, despite the ringing endorsement of its editorial review board; the reasons given were concern for the safety of CUP personnel (and for CUP's sales of English-language teaching materials) in Greece. Karakasidou eventually had her work published by the University of Chicago, but the incident highlighted the narrow limits of public discussion on this issue, both in Greece and in the Greek diaspora.

Palace, Tsimiskí 12 (☎270 855). Very clean, enormous en-suite rooms in this updated interwar hotel. ⑤.

Tourist, Mitropóleos 21 (☎276 335, fax 226 865). A rambling, Belle Epoque palace with parquet-floored lounges. The newly refurbished rooms are almost all en suite; there are very few singles. Popular and trendy, it must be booked in advance. ⑤.

Between Egnatía and Ayíou Dhimitríou

Bill, Syngroú 29, cnr Amvrossíou (☎537 666). In a quiet, tree-lined side street, this is a real find; the friendly management is inclined to bargain at slow times, and quotes reasonable single rates. ④.

Esperia, Olýmbou 58 (☎269 321, fax 269 457). A refurbished place; views north to the hills. ⑥.

Nea Mitropolis, Syngroú 22 (☎525 540, fax 539 910). Clean, well maintained, and not too noisy, despite its proximity to Egnatía. ⑥.

Orestias Kastorias, Agnóstou Stratiótou 14, cnr Olýmbou (☎276 517, fax 276 572). With most rooms of this 1930s building recently converted to en suite, this is a prime, friendly choice and easily the quietest hotel in the city; reservations suggested. ④.

Park, Íonos Dhragoúmi 81 (☎524 121, fax 524 193). Modern, sterile but spotless double-glazed rooms with limited sea view. Unbelievable bargains to be had in off-season. ⑤.

Pella, Íonos Dhragoúmi 63 (☎524 221, fax 524 223). A tall, narrow, modern hotel on a moderately quiet street; popular with wealthy tourists and frugal businessmen. ⑥.

Youth hostel

Youth Hostel, Svólou 44 (☎225 946). The official *IYHF* hostel; take bus #10 from the train station and ask for the Kamára stop. The office is closed from 11am to 7pm and there's an 11pm curfew, though it's not rigorously applied. However there have been complaints about poor management of the hostel, and lack of cleanliness. ①.

Central Thessaloníki

Although scholarly opinion now holds that the main Via Egnatia skirted the ancient city walls, there is no doubt that the modern **Odhós Egnatía** follows the course of an important Roman street or processional way. At some point during your time in town you are likely to ride or walk down the road, catching glimpses of various monuments that line it.

Near the eastern corner of Platía Dhikastiríon stands the disused fifteenth-century **Bey Hamam** or Turkish **bath**, its doorway surmounted by elaborate stalactite ornamentation. Other nearby **Ottoman monuments** include the **Bezesténi** or covered valuables market at the corner of Venizélou and Egnatía, just west of Bey Hamam, renovated in 1997 and now home to plush shops. Directly opposite the Bezesténi, on the north side of Egnatía, squats another prominent mosque, the fifteenth-century purpose-built **Hamza Bey Camii** (most mosques in Ottoman Thessaloníki were converted churches); today, home to modest shops, it bears the sign "Alcazar" from its days as a cinema of that name.

On the southwest corner of the platía, the eleventh-century **Panayía Khalkéon** church is a classic though rather unimaginative example of the cross-in-square form (see the box on Roman and Byzantine Salonica on p.348). Until restoration is complete you can't go in, but you should be able to make out the founder's dedicatory inscription over one door. As the name indicates, it served during the Ottoman occupation as the copperworkers' guild mosque; the only remnant of this is the handful of kitsch-copper-souvenir shops just across the street. For real antiques – old lamps, bedsteads and wooden furniture – you're best off heading to the city's **flea market**, two blocks up on diagonal Tossítsa.

Across from Panayía Khalkéon lies the **main bazaar** area, bounded roughly by Egnatía on the northwest, Dhragoúmi on the southwest, Ayías Sofías on the northeast, and Tsimiskí to the southeast. Much the most interesting section is a quiet grid of lanes just northeast between Ayías Sofías and Aristotélous, selling live animals, cheap furniture and crafts.

The **Modhiáno**, the central meat, fish and produce market, is named after the wealthy **Jewish** family which long owned it. Although now in decline, with many stalls vacant, it still makes an atmospheric and authentic destination for a meal (see p.352). It is said that until the last war, Ladino (Judeo-Spanish) was the principal language of commerce here and in the nearby harbour, where all work ceased for the Jewish Sabbath. Thessaloníki's only surviving pre-1943 **synagogue** is the Monastiriótat at Syngroú 35, with an imposing facade. A **Museum of the Jewish Presence** (tentative hours Mon–Fri 9am–1pm) is due to open in 1998 at Ayíou Miná 13, southwest of the Modhiáno.

Remains of Salonica's formative years in the eastern Roman empire are thin on the ground; those that survive are concentrated to either side of Egnatía. Ruins of the **Roman agora** were unearthed in the 1970s in the vast Platía Dhikastiríon, behind Panayía Khalkéon; the excavation has yielded little in the way of structures, though work is still in progress. Rather more prominent is an **odeion** in the north corner of the square.

Tucked just out of sight north of the boulevard, the church of **Panayía Akhiropíïtos** (now under scaffolding) is the oldest in the city, featuring arcades, monolithic columns and often highly elaborate capitals – a popular development under Theodosius. Only the mosaics beneath the arches survive, depicting birds, fruits and flowers in a rich Alexandrian style. Further along on the same side of Egnatía, the **Rotunda**, later converted rather strangely to the church of **Áyios Yeóryios**, is the most striking single Roman monument – designed, but never used, as an imperial mausoleum (possibly for Galerius) and consecrated for Christian use in the late fourth century by the addition of a sanctuary, a narthex and rich mosaics. Later it became one of the city's major mosques, from which the minaret remains. Unfortunately, the church's interior has been closed since the 1978 earthquake, and the minaret caged in scaffolding. It is opened for infrequent special events; if you are lucky enough to get inside, the superb mosaics of peacocks, elaborate temples and martyred saints are definitely worth a look.

The Rotunda originally formed part of a larger complex linking the **Arch of Galerius** with a palace and hippodrome. Now also swathed in scaffolding to prevent its collapse from pollution damage, the arch is the surviving span of a dome-surmounted arcade leading to a group of Roman palaces. Built to commemorate the emperor's victories over the Persians in 297 AD, its piers contain reliefs of the battle scenes interspersed with symbolic poses of Galerius himself. The scant remains of **Galerius's palace** can be viewed, below the modern street level, along pedestrianized Dhimitríou Goúnari and its extension, Platía Navarínou.

Ayía Sofia

Between Egnatía and Navarínou, and not to be confused with the city's undistinguished modern cathedral on Mitropóleos, the eighth-century church of **Ayía Sofía** was consciously modelled on its illustrious namesake in Constantinople. Its dome, ten metres in diameter, bears a splendid mosaic of the *Ascension*, for which you'll need opera glasses. Christ, borne up to the heavens by two angels, sits resplendent on a rainbow throne; below a wry inscription reads "Ye men of Galilee, why stand ye gazing up into heaven?" The dome was restored late in the 1980s; the rest of the interior decoration was plastered over after the 1917 fire. Another fine mosaic of the *Virgin Enthroned* in the apse is currently hidden by the *ikonostásis* and scaffolding; it apparently replaced a cross dating from the Iconoclast period, of which traces are visible.

The White Tower

The **White Tower (Lefkós Pýrgos)**, a short walk southeast of Ayía Sofía on the seafront, formed the southeast corner of the city's Byzantine and Turkish defences before most of the walls were demolished late in the nineteenth century. Prior to this, it was the "Bloody Tower", a place of imprisonment and (in 1826) execution of the Janissaries, until the Greeks whitewashed both the building and its image after World War I, removing at the same time a polygonal outer enclosure built by the Ottomans in 1875. Today, stripped of white pigment, it looks a little stagy in its isolation, but is a graceful symbol nonetheless; for years appeared it as the background logo on the evening TV news. The tower was restored in 1985 for Salonica's 2300th birthday celebrations and now houses a small but well-presented **museum** of Byzantine secular and sacred art – icons, jewellery, pottery, metalwork, coins – plus several displays on the history of Thessaloníki (summer Mon 12.30–7pm, Tues–Fri 8am–7pm, Sat & Sun

---

■ ROMAN AND BYZANTINE SALONICA AND ITS CHURCHES

Macedonia became a **Roman province** in 146 BC, and Salonica, with its strategic position for both land and sea access, was the natural and immediate choice of capital. Its fortunes and significance were boosted by the building of the Via Egnatia, the great road linking Rome (via Brindisi) with Byzantium and the East, along whose course Amphipolis, Philippi and Kavála were also to develop.

Christianity had slow beginnings in the city. St Paul visited twice, being driven out on the first occasion after provoking the Jewish community. On his second visit in 56 AD, he stayed long enough to found a church, later writing the two Epistles to the Thessalonians, his congregation. It was another three centuries, however, before the new religion took full root. Galerius, who acceded as eastern emperor upon Byzantium's break with Rome, provided the city with virtually all its surviving late Roman monuments – and its patron saint, Dhimitrios, whom he martyred. The first resident Christian emperor was **Theodosius** (375–395), who after his conversion issued the Edict of Salonica here, officially ending paganism.

Under Justinian's rule (527–565) Salonica became the second city of Byzantium after Constantinople, which it remained – under constant pressure from Goths and Slavs – until its sacking by Saracens in 904. The storming and sacking continued under the Normans of Sicily (1185) and with the Fourth Crusade (1204), when the city became for a time capital of the Latin Kingdom of Salonica. It was, however, restored to the Byzantine Empire of Nicea in 1246, reaching a cultural **Golden Age** amid the theological conflict and political rebellion of the next two centuries, until Turkish conquest and occupation in 1430.

The most prevalent of Roman public buildings had been the **basilica**: a large wooden-roofed hall, with aisles split by rows of columns. It was ideally suited for conversion to Christian congregational worship, a process achieved simply by placing a canopied altar at what became the apse, and dividing it from the main body of the church (the nave) by a screen (a forerunner to the *témblon*). The baptistry, a small distinct building, was then added to one side. The upper reaches of wall were adorned with mosaics illustrating Christ's transfiguration and man's redemption, while at eye level stood a blank lining of marble. (Frescoes, a far more economical medium, did not become fashionable until

---

8.30am–3pm; winter Mon 10.30am–5pm, Tues–Fri 8am–5pm, Sat & Sun 8.30am–3pm; 800dr). You can climb to the top for the views and for the very pleasant **café**.

The archeological museum

Whatever else you do in Thessaloníki, find time for the superb **archeological museum** (summer Mon 12.30–7pm, Tues–Fri 8am–7pm, Sat & Sun 8.30am–3pm; winter Mon 10.30am–5pm, Tues–Fri 8am–5pm, Sat & Sun 8.30am–3pm; 1500dr), on the oddly named Platía KH.A.N.TH (YMCA), just a few minutes' walk from the White Tower. The central gallery, opposite as you enter, is devoted to rich grave finds from ancient Sindos, a few kilometres north of the modern city, while the left-wing is devoted to Hellenistic and Roman art, in particular some exquisite blown-glass birds, found in the tumuli (*toúmbes*) that stud the plain around Thessaloníki.

But these are all just appetizers for – or anticlimaxes after – the **Veryína exhibition** in the south hall, which displays almost all of the finds from the **Royal Tombs** of Philip II of Macedon (father of Alexander the Great) and others at the ancient Macedonian capital of Aigai (modern Veryína, see p.365). They include startling amounts of gold and silver (masks, crowns, wreaths, necklaces, earrings and bracelets) of extraordinarily imaginative craftsmanship, as well as ivory and bronze pieces. Examples include a silver wine strainer with goose-head handles, a perforated bronze lampshade, and the enormous bronze *kratir* from the small site of Dhervéni, with a richly ornate rendition of the god Dionysos' life. But certainly the most celebrated artefact is the *larnax* or casket, containing the ashes of

much later – during the thirteenth and fourteenth centuries – when their scope for expression and movement was realized.)

By the sixth century architects had succumbed to eastern influence and set about improving their basilicas with the addition of a **dome**. For inspiration they turned to Ayía Sofía in Constantinople, the most striking of all Justinian's churches. Aesthetic effect, however, was not the only accomplishment, for the structure lent itself perfectly to the prevailing representational art. The mosaics and frescoes adorning its surfaces became physically interrelated or counterposed, creating a powerful spiritual aid. The eye would be lifted at once to meet the gaze of the *Pandokrátor* (Christ in Majesty) illuminated by the windows of the drum. Between these windows the prophets and apostles would be depicted, and as the lower levels were scanned the liturgy would unfold amid a hierarchy of saints.

The most successful shape to emerge during later experiments with the dome was the **Greek cross-in-square** – four equal arms that efficiently absorb the weight of the dome, passing it from high barrel vaults to lower vaulted chambers fitted inside its angles. Architecturally it was a perfect solution; a square ground plan was produced inside the church with an aesthetically pleasing cruciform shape evident in the superstructure. Best of all, it was entirely self-supporting.

By the mid-tenth century it had become the conventional form. Architects, no longer interested in new designs, exploited the old, which proved remarkably flexible; subsidiary drums were introduced above corners of the square, proportions were stretched ever taller, and the outer walls became refashioned with elaborate brick and stone patterning.

Almost all of Thessaloníki's Byzantine churches can be found in city centre. Under the Turks most of the buildings were converted for use as **mosques**, a process that obscured many of their original features and destroyed (by whitewashing) the majority of their frescoes and mosaics. Further damage came with the 1917 fire and more recently with the earthquake of 1978. Restoration seems a glacially slow process, guaranteeing that many of the sanctuaries are locked, or shrouded in scaffolding, or both, at any given moment. But these disappointments acknowledged, the churches of Thessaloníki remain an impressive and illuminating group.

a Macedonian king and a **gold oak-leaf wreath**, its cover embossed with an eight-pointed star, a device harnessed now irrevocably to the Greek-nationalist juggernaut. A more modest companion *larnax*, perhaps for a queen or other royal female, bears a twelve-pointed star on the lid, and contains a diadem in a floral design, studded with golden bees.

Through these finds, the history of the Macedonian dynasty and empire is traced: at first impression a surprisingly political act, but the discoveries at Veryína have been used by Greece to emphasize the fundamental "Greekness" of the modern provinces of Makhedonía and Thráki. The ancient sites are a significant part of the debate; during the Bulgarian occupation of the North during World War II, for example, there was a deliberate policy of vandalism towards "Greek Macedonian" and "Greek Thracian" remains. Archeology in northern Greece has always been a nationalist as well as an academic issue, and the museum itself is a brilliantly executed "educational" endeavour.

Folklife (Ethnological) Museum of Macedonia

The **folklife museum** at Vassilísis Ólgas 68 (temporarily closed for works) is the best of its kind in Greece, with well-written commentaries (in English and Greek) accompanying displays on housing, costumes, day-to-day work and crafts. The exhibits, on weaving and spinning especially, are beautiful. And there is a strong emphasis on context: on the role of women in the community, the clash between tradition and progress, and the yearly cycle of agricultural and religious festivals. Even the traditional costumes are presented in a manner that goes beyond the mere picturesque.

The collection is housed in the elegant turn-of-the-century mansion of the **Modhiáno** family, they of the meat market, and one of several Jewish-built villas hereabouts. The museum is just a twenty-minute walk (or short bus ride) from the archeological museum; catch the #5 bus as it runs east along Mitropóleos.

Yeni Cami

The orientalized Art Nouveau **Yeni Cami** is the enduring civic contribution of the Dönme, or more properly Ma'min, an offshoot sect of Judaism descended from followers of the seventeenth-century "False Messiah" Sabbatai Zvi; outwardly they embraced Islam after his forced conversion, but secretly they continued certain aspects of Jewish worship, and married only among themselves. Dating from 1904, this was the last mosque built in the city, in the same area as a number of sumptuous villas belonging to the Dönme industrialists. Designed by an Italian architect, the Yeni Cami is an engaging folly, often open for special exhibitions; in fact it long served as Thessaloníki's archeological museum after 1923. The interior, if you gain admission, is nothing other than an Iberian synagogue in disguise, its decor likely to overshadow any displays. This mosque is easy to find, well-signposted about a kilometre northwest up Vassilísis Olgás from the Folklife Museum, then 100m up a side street.

Museum of Macedonian Struggle

If the archeological museum helps you understand better the present-day importance to Greeks of the Royal Tombs at Veryína, the **Museum of Macedonian Struggle** (summer Tues–Fri 9am–2pm, Wed & Sat 5–7pm, Sun 11am–2pm; winter same hours except Wed & Sat 6–8pm; free), Proxénou Koromilá 23, helps to explain their ongoing concern about Bulgarian or FYROM claims to "Greek" Macedonia. The museum illustrates the struggle to create greater Greece, from the 1870s onwards, by means of photographs, posters, pamphlets and dioramas. It's (understandably) all in Greek, but you can borrow an English-language commentary and appreciate the significance of the building in which the museum is housed – it is the former Greek consulate, from which the struggle was masterminded. To find the museum, walk down Ayías Sofías towards the waterfront: it's on your left, on the corner with Koromilá.

Kástra and Eptapyrgíou

Above Odhós Kassándhrou, hillside **Kástra** is the main surviving quarter of Ottoman Thessaloníki. Although they are gradually becoming swamped by new apartment buildings, the streets here remain ramshackle and atmospheric, a labyrinth of timber-framed houses and winding steps. Since the 1980s the stigma of the district's "Turkishness" has been overcome as the older houses are bought up and restored, and it is justifiably one of the city's favourite nightime destinations.

Áyios Dhimítrios and other churches

At the very foot of the slope is a massive yet simple church, **Áyios Dhimítrios** (Mon 12.30–7pm, Tues, Thurs & Sat 8am–8pm, Fri 8am–11pm, Sun 10.30am–8pm; free), conceived in the fifth century though heavily restored since. The *de facto* cathedral of the city, with pride of place in Thessalonian hearts, it was almost entirely rebuilt after the 1917 fire, which destroyed all but the apse and colonnades. The church is dedicated to the city's patron saint and stands on the site of his martyrdom, and even if you know beforehand that it is the largest church in Greece, its immense interior comes as a surprise.

Amid so much space and white plaster, six small surviving **mosaics**, mostly on the columns flanking the altar, are a focal point; of these, four date back to the church's second building after the fire of 620. The mosaic of *Áyios Dhimítrios Flanked by the*

Church's Two Founders, on the south pier beside the steps to the crypt, was described by Osbert Lancaster as "the greatest remaining masterpiece of pictorial art of the pre-Iconoclastic era in Greece"; this, and the adjacent mosaics of *Áyios Sérgios* and *Áyios Dhimítrios with a Deacon* contrast well with their contemporary on the north column, a warm and humane mosaic of the saint with two young children. The fifth-century mosaics are a *Deisis* on the north pier, and, high on the west wall of the inner south aisle, a child being presented or dedicated to the saint.

The **crypt**, unearthed after the great fire, contains the *martyrion* of the saint – probably an adaptation of the Roman baths in which he was imprisoned – and a whole exhibit of beautifully carved column-capitals.

Around Áyios Dhimítrios are several more churches, utterly different in feel. West along Ayíou Dhimitríou is the somewhat remote church of **Dhódheka Apóstoli**, built with three more centuries of experience and the bold Renaissance influence of Mystra (see p.175). Its five domes rise in perfect symmetry above walls of fine brickwork, though its interior no longer does it justice. To the west, **Ayía Ekateríni**, contemporary with Dhódheka Apóstoli, has fine brickwork, exploiting all the natural colours of the stones. **Profítis Ilías**, between Ayía Ekateríni and Áyios Dhimítrios, is in the same vein as Dhódheka Apóstoli, though less imposing, with negligible surviving interior decoration.

Áyios Nikólaos Orfanós

Áyios Nikólaos Orfanós (Tues–Sun 8.45am–2.45pm; entrance from Odhós Irodhótou, warden at no. 17) is a diminutive fourteenth-century basilica to the north of Áyios Dhimítrios, whose well-preserved frescoes are the most accessible and expressive in the city. In the south aisle, St Jerome is seen with anthropomorphic lions, while Christ's miracles adorn the row above. The *naos* is devoted to episodes from the Passion, in particular the rare image of *Christ Mounting the Cross*, and *Pilate Seated in Judgement* at a wooden desk, looking just like a Byzantine scribe of the era. Above the Virgin Platytera in the apse conch looms the equally unusual *Áyion Mandílion*, an image of Christ's head superimposed on a legendary veil sent to an ancient king of Anatolian Edessa. Around the apse is a wonderful *Niptir* (Christ Washing the Disciples' Feet), in which it is thought the painter inserted an image of himself at the top right above the conch, riding a horse and wearing a white turban. Frescoes of the north aisle, illustrating the Akathistos Hymn glorifying the Virgin, are less intact, but do feature a wonderful *Dream of Joseph* on one column capital.

The ramparts and Eptapyrgíou

Sections of the fourteenth-century **Byzantine ramparts**, constructed with brick and rubble on top of old Roman foundations, crop up all around the northern part of town. The best-preserved portion begins at a large circular keep known as the "Chain Tower" (after its encircling ornamental moulding) in the northeast angle. It then rambles north around the district of **Eptapyrgíou** ("Seven Towers"), enclosing the old acropolis at the top end. For centuries it served as the city's prison – described as a sort of Greek Devil's Island in a number of plaintive old songs entitled "Yediküle" (Turkish for "Seven Towers") – until abandoned as too inhumane in 1989. It is now being restored as a museum commemorating its inmates, who included many political prisoners. On its south side, the wall is followed by Odhós Eptapyrgíou and edged by a small strip of park – a good place to sit and scan Thessaloníki. Nearby, various tavernas come alive in the late afternoon and evening (see p.353).

Although strictly speaking the following two monuments lie within Kástra, they are easier to find walking downhill from the Eptapyrgíou area. **Óssios Davíd** (daily 8–11.30am, often open later), a tiny fifth-century church on Odhós Timothéou, no longer exemplifies any architectural trend, since the Ottomans demolished much of the building when converting it to a mosque. However, it has arguably the finest mosaic in the city, depicting a clean-shaven Christ Emmanuel appearing in a vision, to the amazement of the prophets Ezekiel and Habakkuk. Nearby, the **monastery of Vlatádhon** is noteworthy for its peaceful, tree-shaded courtyard, a perfect place to complete a tour; you may be able to gain entrance to the much-restored katholikón, which has fourteenth-century frescoes inside.

Atatürk's house

If you approach or leave Kástra on its east side, it's worth casting an eye at the Turkish consulate at the bottom of Apostólou Pávlou. In the pink building beside it at no. 17, **Kemal Atatürk**, first president and creator of the modern state of Turkey, was born. The consulate maintains the house as a small museum, with its original fixtures. To visit you must apply for admission at the main building, with your passport (Mon–Fri 9am–1pm & 2–6pm). Security is tight, and with good reason – Atatürk has been held largely responsible for the traumatic exchange of Greek and Turkish populations in 1923. In 1981 a Turkish celebration of the centenary of his birth had to be called off after a Greek stunt pilot threatened a kamikaze-dive at the house.

Eating

In recent years there has been an explosion of interesting places to **eat** and **drink** in Thessaloníki, paralleling the increasing prosperity of the city. Most of the listings below, categorized both by district and price per person, are within walking distance of Platía Aristotélous, and for those that aren't we've given the appropriate transport connections. Most of the city's ouzerís will provide some sort of sweet on the house, often semolina *halvás*. Thessalonians take their summer holidays a bit earlier than Athenians, so the description "closed in midsummer" tends to mean mid-July to mid-August.

Thessaloníki offers a number of good places for **breakfast** and **snacks**. *Cookies* at Egnatía 144 is a terrific cookies-by-weight shop with imaginative varieties – there's another branch at Venizélou 10. *Corner* at Ethnikís Amýnis 6, near the White Tower, is a California-bistro-meets-London-pub with draught beer and indoor and outside seating; the wood-fired oven produces the best pizzas in the city. *Corner*'s close (and for many, superior) rival is *Family*, Mitropóleos 67, on the northeast corner of Ayías Sofías: food is cheaper if you aren't seated. There are pastries, crepes, sandwiches and good coffee or juice for breakfast, and pizzas and pasta are served after noon. Other good options for crepes and pastries are *Forum*, Aristotélous 27, in an arcaded sit-down environment, *Vavel* at Komninón 18, and *Venezia* on Dhimitríou Goúnari at the corner of Egnatía, which is most distinctive for its 24-hour service.

Downtown: between the sea and Odhós Ayíou Dhimitríou

UNDER 3500DR

Ta Adhelfia tis Pixarias, Platía Navarínou 7. Best of several similar places on this archeological-site/square, with delicacies such as *tzigerosárma* (lamb liver in cabbage) and *mýdhia saganáki* – though haphazard service and smallish portions. Often packed, so go early.

Iy Gonia tou Merakli, Avyerinoú, alley off Platía Áthonos. Inexpensive sea food and bulk wine make this the best of several ouzerís in these lanes between this plaza and Aristotélous, which by day preserve their old commercial character.

Iridha, Olýmbou 83. An inexpensive taverna under the hotel *Orestias Kastorias*, which has recently expanded its former grills-only menu. The speciality *soutzoukákias* bear little relation to the usual Greek version, being more like Turkish *inegól köfte*. Outside seating; open all year.

Koumbarakia, Egnatía 140. Tucked behind the little Chapel of the Transfiguration, the outdoor tables of this durable ouzerí groan with Macedonian-style grills, seafood and salads including *túrsi* (pickled vegetables). Closed Sunday and midsummer.

Loutros, Komninón 15. Partly housed in the former Yehuda (Jews') or Loulouládhika (Flower-Mart) baths, with summer seating spilling onto the adjacent pavement next to the modern flower market. Good fried seafood and excellent retsina, compensating somewhat for the rough-and-ready surroundings (currently under restoration). Closed in summer.

O Myrovolos tis Smyrnis, arcade in the Modhiáno, off Komninón 32. Friendly, crowded ouzerí, also known as *Tou Thanassi*, and reckoned the best (and marginally most expensive) of several clustered here. Typical fare includes cheese-stuffed squid and grilled baby fish. Attracts a crowd of local characters, who consume pitchers of *tsípouro* in the company of gypsy buskers. Open all year, air conditioned in summer; despite ample seating, reservations recommended (☎ 274 170).

Nea Ilyssia, Sófou 17. Opposite the *Averof Hotel*, this popular travellers' restaurant is open long hours (8.30am–2am) and serves highly regarded *mayireftá*.

Pazar Hamam, Komninón 15a. A newer restaurant alongside the *Loutros*, with a wider menu than its neighbour, but also more expensive and less frequented.

Platía Athonos, Dhragoúmi, alley off Platía Athonos. Another good choice in this popular area, and one that's open for lunch.

Stenaki, End of Kapetán Patríki, an alley opposite cinema *Esperos* on Svólou. A pricey but popular ouzerí with outdoor seating in the cul-de-sac. Open during summer; live music some nights.

OVER 3500DR

Aproöpto, Zefxídhos 6, pedestrian lane between Iktínou and Pávlou Melá. A somewhat snooty ouzerí with outdoor seating and rather Westernized fare (stuffed mushrooms, blue-cheese sauces). Open all year round, but closed Sun.

Aristotelous, Aristotélous 8. In a courtyard off Odhós Aristotélous, just above the platía, this upmarket ouzerí with its fine arcaded interior can get crowded. Open noon–5pm and 8pm–2am, except Sunday and during August.

Soutzoukakia, alias Rongotis, Venizélou 8, cnr Kalapotháki. Varied menu, but famous for its namesake *soutzoukákia*; consumed daily by a business clientele. Closed midsummer & Wed.

Tottis, Platía Aristotélous 2–3. Café, gelateria and (pricey) adjacent restaurant, that's as much a meeting place as a dining spot.

Tsaroukhas, Olýmbou 78, near Platía Dhikastiríon. Reputedly the best, and certainly the most famous, of the city's *patsatzídhika* – kitchens devoted to tripe-and-trotter soup. Serves lots of other *mayireftá*, and Anatolian puddings such as *kazándibi* (try it, you'll like it). Closed midsummer; otherwise open all hours, and thus prices bumped up for the convenience (and full staffing).

Kástra and Eptapyrgíou

Most of the places listed below cling to either side of the walls encircling Eptapyrgíou district; bus #22 or #23 from Platía Eleftherías spares you the climb.

UNDER 3500DR

Iy Kamara, Steryíou Polidhórou 15. Inside the main Portára gate of the Kástra. Smallish portions of good Anatolian/Cypriot food, served alongside the park strip inside the walls.

Khiotis, Graviás 2. Just inside the second (eastern) castle gate, near the Chain Tower. Mussels, kebabs and *kokorétsi* served on the terrace under the ramparts, or inside in colder weather. This is probably the best of several similar establishments arranged here cheek-by-jowl. Dinner only in summer, lunch and dinner rest of the year.

To Makedhoniko, Sykiés district. From the main Portára gate, head west, keeping to the walls as much as possible, until you reach the taverna at the west end of the walls, near a third minor gate. Very limited menu of *tís óras*, dips, salad and retsina, but also very cheap and popular with the trendy set. Bus #23 goes right through the adjacent medieval gateway.

Vangos, Kaïri 15, above Platía Pávlou Melá in the hillside area of Saránda Ekklissíes. Tiny hole-in-the-wall joint, popular with students, tucked away in an alley; ask in the square for directions (bus #15 runs to the platía). Closed mid-July–mid-Aug.

To Yedi, Paparéska 13, at the very top of Kástra, opposite the Yediküle citadel. Very full ouzerí-type menu and ample seating under trees opposite the old prison gate.

The eastern suburbs

The establishments below cater primarily to well-heeled residents, so food is consequently more elegant – and routinely more than 3500dr per person.

Archipelagos, Kanári 1, Néa Kríni. A fancy seafood place and one of the best in the area. Take bus #5 or a taxi. Open daily 1pm–midnight.

Batis, Platía Eleftherías 22, Néa Kríni. Sea view with your grilled octopus; other fish dishes as well. Bus #5.

Krikelas, Ethnikís Andistásis 32, in Byzándio district, on the way to the airport. A bit touristy, but the chef here is one of the best in Greece, drawing on half a century of experience. Closed in summer.

Ta Pringiponissia, Krítis 60, east of 25-Martíou, 600m beyond the ethnological museum. Delicious Constantinople-Greek food served in a pleasant three-level designer building; you select from trays of hot and cold mezédhes. Open all year; closed Sun.

Drinking, nightlife and entertainment

Ladhádhika, the tough old warehouse, red-light and commercial district behind the harbour, has been gentrified to become the trendiest district for **nightlife**, its pedestrianized streets lined with a succession of techno-*barákia*, complete with bouncers and sunglass-clad patrons. Establishments here have a high turnover rate, so citing them is fairly pointless. The area has more or less eclipsed a small concentration of bars on Proxénou Korimilá and Lóri Margaríta – two narrow alleys, continuations of each other, a block inland from Níkis. During the warmer months, the action shifts to various glitzy, larger establishments lining the coast road out to Kalamariá, and to the nightly volta (promenade) that takes place between the Arch of Galerius and the seafront along pedestrianized Dhimitríou Goúnari, which bulges out halfway down to include Platía Navarínou. Certain theatres and concert halls near the White Tower tend to be the venues for more formal winter events, though again there has been a recent renaissance of refurbished industrial venues near Ladhádhika and beyond.

Bars, cafés and clubs

Alambra, Níkis 19. The "in" waterfront hangout, with pricey coffees and alcohol at indoor or pavement seating. Purports to be a reincarnation of a pre-fire kafenío at roughly this location.

Chic, Lóri Margaríti 5. Women-only piano bar; shut in summer.

Kourdhisto Gourouni, Ayías Sofías 31. Ten different foreign brews on tap, more than sixty bottled varieties at this stylish bar with indoor and outdoor seating; expensive food menu as well.

Mandragoras, Mitropóleos 98. A large and elegant upstairs wine-and-mezédhes bar, run by a man who twice won the state lottery. Closed in summer.

Yeni Hamam, cnr Ayíou Nikoláou and Kassándhrou, behind Áyios Dhimítrios church. Predating the 1997 wave of renovations, this classy bar-ouzerí with Anatolian decor occupies the dependency of the nearby Alatza Imaret Camii. A double-domed main chamber of the baths hosts events, with bar seating outside in summer, when the garden becomes the *Aigli* outdoor cinema.

Zythos, Platía Katoúni 5. The first bar established in Ladhádhika, still one of the best and the only one active at lunch-time, when food is served along with two dozen varieties of foreign beer.

Events

Winter **dance, concert** and **theatre** events tend to take place in the recently redone *Kratikó Théatro* (State Theatre) and the *Vassilikó Théatro* (Royal Theatre), within sight of each other behind the White Tower. In summer things move to either the *Théatro Kípou* (Garden Theatre), near the archeological museum, or well up the hill into the *Théatro Dhássous* (Forest Theatre), in the pines beyond the upper town.

For more cutting-edge events (monthly programmes from *Blowup Records*, Aristotélous 8), *Mylos* at Andhréou Yeoryíou 56 is a multi-functional cultural centre housed in an old flour mill 2km southeast of the centre. Here you'll find a couple of bars, a live jazz café, a popular *tsipourádhiko* (open for lunch), a summer cinema, concert halls and exhibition galleries of various sizes, plus a theatre. It has spawned various smaller imitators near and far in Greece, including *Idhroyeios* at 26-Oktobríou 33, a venue for ethnic and jazz acts run by *Be Bop Records* (Sept–June; outdoor cinema in summer), and *Iskandar Polykhoros* at Psathá 2, on the corner of Karatásou, a world-music club/art gallery in Ladhádhika which has a summertime roof café.

Cinema

Indoor cinemas tend to cluster between the White Tower and the Galerius arch. Those known to concentrate on first-run material rather than porno or kung fu flicks include: *Alexandhros*, Ethnikís Amýnis 1; *Aristotelion*, Ethnikís Amýnis 2; *Esperos*, Svólou 22; *Makedhonikon*, Filikís Eterías 44; and *Navarinon*, on the namesake plaza (shut summer). **Summer cinemas** have all but vanished from downtown Thessaloníki, owing to spiralling property values; the only ones left are the *Alex*, at Olýmbou 106, recently joined by the nearby *Aigli* (see *Yeni Haman*, opposite); *Natali*, at the start of Megalou Alexandhrou by the *Macedonia Palace* hotel, is a bit further out. *What's On* does weekly **listings** and the Greek papers daily ones, or stroll by and read the playbills.

Listings

Airlines Air Greece, Íonos Dhragoúmi 4, 7th floor (☎244 250); British Airways, Íonos Dhragoúmi 4 (☎242 005); Olympic, Koundourióti 3 (☎260 122). Most other airlines are represented by general sales agents or bucket shops (see below).

Airport At Mikrá, 16km out and served by bus #78; ☎411 977 for flight information.

Books and papers Molho, Tsimiskí 10, is far and away the best shop in the city, with an excellent stock of English-language books, magazines and newspapers. Promithevs, at Ermoú 75, is also good for books. For English-language newspapers, visit the International Press kiosk on the corner of Angeláki and Svólou.

Bus terminals The large terminal on 26-Oktovríou only provides a few Athens services; most KTELs are still scattered all over town, and locations should be checked with EOT. Currently, the most useful ones include: Alexandhroúpoli, Koloniári 31; Édhessa/Véria, 26-Oktovríou 10; Flórina, Anayenníseos 42; Ioánnina, Khrístou Pípsou 19; Kastoriá, Anayenníseos 6; Kavála, Langadhá 59; Khalkidhikí, Karakássi 68, in the east of town (#10 bus to Bótsari stop); Komotiní, cnr Olympíou Yeorgáki and Irínis; Litókhoro, Sapfoús 10; Pélla, Anayenníseos 22; Tríkala, Monastiríou 65; Vólos, Anayenníseos 22; Xánthi, Ayíou Nestóros 22.

Camping gear Petridhis, Vassilíou Iraklíou 43; or World Jamboree, at Íonos Dhelíou 6, off Ethnikís Amýnis.

Car rental Many are clustered near the fairgrounds and archeological museum on Angeláki; the leading agencies have kiosks at the airport, too. Specific outfits include: Ansa/Holiday Autos, Laskarátou 19 (☎419 109); Avis, Níkis 3 (☎227 126); Budget, Angeláki 15 (☎229 519); Europcar/Inter Rent, Papandhréou 5 (☎826 333); European, Angeláki 15 (☎281 603); Eurorent, Angeláki 3 (☎286 327); Hertz, Venizelou 5 (☎224 906); Salonika, Tsimiski 114 (☎277 015); Thrifty, Angeláki 15 (☎241 241).

Consulates Important for getting letters of introduction for Mount Áthos (see "Ministry of Macedonia and Thrace", p.356), and onward travel in the Balkans. Bulgaria, Mánou 12 (☎829 210); Canada, Tsimiskí 17 (☎256 350); Denmark, Komminón 26 (☎284 065); Netherlands, Komninón 26(☎227 477); Romania, Níkis 13, 4th floor (☎225 481); UK/Commonwealth, honorary consul is at Venizélou 8, 8th floor, by appointment only (☎278 006; Mon–Fri 8am–1pm); USA, Níkis 59 (☎242 905; Tues & Thurs 9am–noon).

Cultural institutes British Council, Ethnikís Amýnis 9; free library and reading room, plus various events in the winter months. USIS Library, Mitropóleos 34, 1st floor (closed summer).

Exchange For changing notes, use the 24hr-automatic exchange machine at the Ktimatiki Trapezia on Platía Aristotélous. Thessaloníki has plenty of cash dispensers.

Ferry ticket agents The agent for the DANE ferry to Sámos and the Dodecanese is Mikron Travel, Komninón 2/Níkis 9 (☎242 121). Minoan Line sailings to the Sporádhes, Cyclades and

Crete, as well as hydrofoils to the Sporádhes, are both handled by Kriti Travel, Íonos Dhragoúmi 1, cnr Koundouriótou (☎534 376). For routes and frequencies, see "Travel details" at the end of this chapter.

Football Thessaloníki's main team is PAOK, whose stadium is in the east of the city – off our map, though visible in square A5 of the EOT "Thessaloniki/Khalkidhiki" handout.

Hospitals For minor trauma, use the Yenniko Kendriko at Ethnikiís Amýnis 41; otherwise, head for the Ippokration at Konstandinopóleos 49, in the eastern part of town.

Laundries There are several coin-ops where you can leave your clothes to be washed, and collect them later, including Bianca, Antoniádhou 3, near the Arch of Galerius (open all day), and Freskadha, Filíppou 105, beside the Rotunda.

Ministry of Macedonia and Thrace This is on Platía Dhikitiríou (officially renamed Kypríon Agonistón), and you'll have to visit to obtain a Mount Áthos permit. Go first to your consulate for a letter of recommendation (free to US citizens, 5700dr to UK and Commonwealth citizens; take your passport). At the ministry, make your way to Room 218 (Mon–Fri 11am–1.45pm).

OTE Ermoú 40, at junction with Karólou Díehl. Open daily 24hr, but only card phones available.

Post office Main branch (for poste restante and after-hours exchange) is at Tsimiskí 45 (Mon–Fri 7.30am–8pm, Sat 7.30am–2.15pm, Sun 9am–1.30pm). There are other branch post offices around the city: two useful ones are at Tsimiskí 5 and Ethnikís Amýnis 9a.

Records The best of Thessaloníki's various record stores for Greek music are (in rough order of preference) Studio 52, Dhimitríou Goúnari 46, basement, with lots of out-of-print vinyl and cassettes plus well-sorted CDs; Be Bop, Paleón Patrón Yermanoú 19, with a wide range of music (not just jazz) and its own innovative label (Ano Kato) and club venue (see p.355); and Lyra, Tsimiskí 64, selling much more than its eponymous label.

Train tickets All services depart from the giant station down on Monastiríou, the southwestern continuation of Egnatía, well served by buses. If you want to buy tickets or make reservations in advance, the OSE office at Aristotélous 18 (Tues–Fri 8am–9pm, Mon & Sat 8am–3pm) is far more central, helpful and supplied with timetables than the station ticket-windows.

Travel agents Flights out of Thessaloníki are not cheap; air ticket shops cluster around Platía Eleftherías, especially on Kalapotháki, Komninón and Mitropóleos. More specifically, Kinissi Tours, Tsimiskí 17 (☎237 000) and Oceanic World, Níkis 21 (☎265 400), are general sales agents for several major airlines. Students and youth travellers should try Etos at Ippodhromíou 15 (☎263 814), or Sunflight at Tsimiskí 114. For cheap buses to Turkey, try Bus and Atlantic Tours, Aristotélous 10, 4th floor (☎238 378). Specialist hiking and other expeditions throughout Greece are offered by Trekking Hellas, Aristotélous 11 (☎242 190).

Wine Northern Greece boasts some fine vineyards, and accordingly Thessaloníki has some fine wine stores affordably selling bottles superior to your average taverna plonk; Iy Tsaritsani, Avyerinoú 9, off Platía Áthonos, and Aneroto, Dhimitríou Goúnari 42, are two good retailers.

Out from the city

The main weekend escape from Thessaloníki is to the three-pronged **Khalkidhikí peninsula**, but to get to its better beaches requires more than a day trip. If you just want a respite from the city, or a walk in the hills, consider instead Thessaloníki's own local villages and suburbs. Further out, drivers en route to Néa Moudhaniá can take in the extraordinary **cave** near Petrálona – though half-day trips with a local tour operator make this a possibility for those without their own transport, too.

Panórama and Khortiátis

On the hillside overlooking the city 11km to the east, **PANÓRAMA**, the closest escape from the city, is exactly what its name suggests: a high, hillside viewpoint looking down over Thessaloníki and the gulf. The original village was razed to the ground by the Germans in retaliation for partisan sabotage during World War II – there's a monument to those burned alive in the action – and Panórama has been rebuilt with smart villas, coffee shops and a large, modern shopping mall. Of more appeal are a number of cafés, tavernas and zakharoplastía. The best-known of these is *Elenidhi-To Ariston*, which serves up the premier local speciality, *trígona* (custard-filled triangular confections), wonderful *dondurma* (Turkish-style ice-cream) and *salépi* (a beverage made from the ground-up root of *Orchis mascula*). The village can be reached by #57 or #58 bus from Platía Dhikastiríon, or by taxi (around 1000dr).

Still more of a retreat is **KHORTIÁTIS**, 11km further on (or 16km direct from Thessaloníki), set in an area known as Khília Dhéndhra (Thousand Trees), which since ancient times has supplied Thessaloníki with water – you can still see a ruined aqueduct to one side of the road. Khortiátis is accessible on the #61 bus, which meets passengers alighting the #57 or #58 at the crossroads where those buses head up to Panoráma. Again, it offers sweeping views over the city, good walking among the pines and some popular places to eat; the *Tsakis* taverna has a well-deserved reputation, so in summer you should book (☎349 874) to avoid disappointment.

ANASTENARIÁ: THE FIRE WALKERS OF LANGADHÁS

On May 21, the feast day of Saints Constantine and Helena, villagers at **LANGADHÁS**, 20km north of Thessaloníki, used to (and may still) perform a ritual barefoot dance across a bed of **burning coals**. The festival rites are of unknown and strongly disputed origin. It has been suggested that they are remnants of a **Dionysiac cult**, though devotees assert a purely Christian tradition which seems to relate to a fire, around 1250, in the Thracian village of Kósti. **Holy icons** were heard groaning from the flames and were rescued by villagers, who emerged miraculously unburned from the blazing church. The icons, passed down by their families, are believed to ensure protection. Equally important is piety and purity of heart: it is said that no one with any harboured grudges or unconfessed sins can pass through the coals unscathed. The Greek church authorities, however, refuse to sanction any service on the day of the ritual; it has even been accused of planting glass among the coals to try and discredit this "devil's gift".

Whatever the origin, the rite was until recently still performed each year – lately as something of a tourist attraction, with an admission charge and repeat performances over the next two days. It was nevertheless strange and impressive, beginning around 7pm with the lighting of a cone of hardwood logs. A couple of hours later their embers were raked into a circle and, just before complete darkness, a traditional Macedonian *daoúli* **drummer** and two **lýra players** preceded about sixteen women and men into the arena. These *anastenarídhes* (literally "groaners"), in partial trance, then shuffled across the coals for about a quarter of an hour.

Recently the cult members were subjected to various **scientific tests**. The only established clues were that the dancers' brain waves indicated some altered state – when brain activity returned to normal they instinctively left the embers – and that their rhythmical steps maintained minimum skin contact with the fires. There was no suggestion of fraud, however. In 1981 an Englishman jumped into the arena, was badly burnt, and had to be rescued by the police from irate devotees and dancers. In 1991, however, the rites failed to take place, owing to continued pressure from the Church and the *anastenarídhes'* own ire at being viewed merely as freak-show attractions. The ceremony's future seems uncertain, with the likelihood of it taking place, if at all, in private at an undisclosed location.

If the *anastenariá* do take place in public, arrive early at Langadhás – by 5.30pm at the latest – in order to get a good seat. Be prepared, too, for the circus-like commercialism, though this in itself can be quite fun. Other *anastenarídhes* used to "perform" at **Melíki**, near Véria, and at the villages of **Ayía Eléni** and **Áyios Pétros** near Sérres. Crowds, though, were reputed to be large and fire-walkers fewer. If you're in Greece, anywhere, and moderately interested, you can catch the show (if it happens) on the ET TV news at 9pm. Their cameramen are at Langadhás, too.

Beaches

To swim near Thessaloníki you need to get well clear of the gulf, where the pollution is all too visible – and odorous. This means heading southwest towards Kateríni and the **beaches** below Mount Olympus (along the fast National Road), or southeast towards Khalkidhikí.

If all you want is a meal by the sea, then you can take local buses around the gulf. Buses #72 or #69 run to **PERÉA**, 20km from Thessaloníki, a small resort with good seafront tavernas but a rather unpleasant beach; try the inexpensive evening grill, *O Fotis*; you could even stay at the friendly *Hotel Lena* (☎0392/22 755; ④). Bus #72 continues to **AYÍA TRIÁDHA**, where there is an EOT **campsite**, the *Akti Thermaikou* (☎0392/51 360; open all year), rooms to rent and three comfortable **hotels**, all with swimming pools: cheapest is the *Xenia Helos* (☎0392/25 551; ⑤), but better value for money is the *Galaxias* (☎0392/22 291; ⑥), 1km before Ayía Triádha.

Bus #69 sweeps north, via Epanomís, to the better strand of **ÓRMOS EPANOMÍS**, 33km from Thessaloníki, although some people prefer to travel on to Néa Kalikrátia before taking to the water. There is a second EOT **campsite** at Órmos Epanomís (☎0392/41 378; April–Oct), more attractive and with more shade than the one at Ayía Triádha.

Petrálona

Fifty kilometres southeast of Thessaloníki is the **cave of Kókkines Pétres** (Red Stones), discovered in 1959 by villagers from nearby **PETRÁLONA** looking for water. Besides an impressive display of stalagmites and stalactites, the fossilized remains of prehistoric animals were found, and, most dramatic of all, a Neanderthal skull.

The cave, kitted out with dioramas of prehistoric activities and well worth a visit, makes an interesting diversion on the way to or from the Kassándhra peninsula; you'll find the village of Petrálona itself roughly 4km north of Eleokhória, on the old road running from Thessaloníki to Néa Moudhaniá at the neck of the peninsula. It's open every day (summer 9am–7pm; winter 9am–5pm; 700dr) and there's a small café on site, though the museum there is closed indefinitely. Doucas Tours in Thessaloníki (Venizélou 8, under the UK consulate) operates a half-day trip there.

Pella

PELLA was the capital of Macedonia throughout its greatest period, and the first real capital of Greece after Philip II forcibly unified the country around 338 BC. It was founded some sixty years earlier by King Archelaus, who transferred the royal Macedonian court here from Aigai (see p.365), and from its beginnings it was a major centre of culture. The **royal palace** was decorated by Zeuxis and was said to be the greatest artistic showplace since the time of Classical Athens. Euripides wrote and produced his last plays at the court, and here Aristotle tutored Alexander the Great – born, like his father Philip II, in the city.

The site today, split by the road to Édhessa, is an easy and rewarding day trip from Thessaloníki. Its main treasures are a series of pebble **mosaics**: some in the museum, a couple in situ. For an understanding of the context, it is best to visit after looking around the archeological museum at Thessaloníki.

The site

Tues–Sun 8.30am–3pm; 500dr.

Today the **ruins** of Pella stand in the middle of a broad plain, 40km from Thessaloníki and the sea, but when Archelaus founded the city it lay at the head of a broad lake connected to the Thermaïkós gulf by a navigable river. By the second century BC the river had begun to silt up and the city fell into decline. It was destroyed by the Romans in 146 BC and never rebuilt.

Pella was located by chance finds in 1957, and preliminary excavations have revealed a vast site covering over 485 hectares. As yet, only a few blocks of the city have been fully excavated, but they have proved exciting. To the right of the road is a grand official building, probably a government office; it is divided into three large open courts, each enclosed by a *peristyle*, or portico (the columns of the central court have been re-erected), and bordered by wide streets with a sophisticated drainage system.

The three main rooms of the first court have patterned geometric floors, in the centre of which were found superb, intricate **pebble mosaics** depicting scenes of a lion hunt, a griffin attacking a deer, and Dionysus riding a panther. These are now in the **museum** across the road (same hours as site; separate 500dr admission). But in the third court three mosaics have been left in situ; one, a stag hunt, is complete, and astounding in its dynamism and use of perspective. Others represent the rape of Helen and a fight between a Greek and an Amazon.

It is the inherently graceful and fluid quality of these compositions that sets them apart from later Roman and Byzantine mosaics, and that more than justifies a visit. The uncut pebbles, carefully chosen for their soft shades, blend so naturally that the shapes and movements of the subjects seem gradated rather than fixed, especially in the action of the hunting scenes and the sloping movement of the leopard with Dionysus. Strips of lead or clay are used to outline special features; the eyes, all now missing, were probably semiprecious stones.

The **acropolis** at Pella is a low hill to the west of the modern village. Excavation is in progress on a sizeable building, probably a palace, but at present it's illuminating mainly for the idea it gives you of the size and scope of the site.

Getting there

Pella is easiest reached from Thessaloníki. Just take any of the Édhessa **buses**, which run more or less half-hourly through the day and stop by the Pella museum. If you arrive late and want to stay, the nearest **hotel** is at Khalkidhóna, 8km east on the road back to Thessaloniki: the *Fillipos* (☎0391/22 125; ③).

Continuing to Aigai/Veryína by public transport, you'll need to get a bus, or walk, back down the Thessaloníki road to the junction at Khalkidhóna. From here you can pick up the Thessaloníki–Véria buses.

Dion

Ancient **DION**, in the foothills of Mount Olympus, was the Macedonians' sacred city. At this site – a harbour before the river mouth silted up – the kingdom maintained its principal sanctuaries: to Zeus (from which the name *Dion*, or *Dios*, is derived) above all, but also to Demeter, Artemis, Asclepius and, later, to foreign gods such as the Egyptians Isis and Serapis. Philip II and Alexander both came to sacrifice to Zeus here before their expeditions. Inscriptions found at the sanctuaries referring to boundary disputes, treaties and other affairs of state suggest that the political and social importance of the city's festivals exceeded a purely Macedonian domain.

Most exciting for visitors, however, are the finds of mosaics, temples and baths that have been excavated since 1990 – work that remains in progress whenever funds allow. These are not quite on a par with the Veryína tombs, but still rank among the major discoveries of Macedonian history and culture. If you are heading for Mount Olympus, they are certainly worth a half-day detour. At the village of **DHIÓN** (formerly Malathiriá), 7km inland from Litókhoro beach or reached by #14 bus from Kateríni, take a side road 400m east from the *Hotel Dion*, past the remains of a theatre. The main **site** lies ahead (summer Mon 12.30–7pm, Tues–Fri 8am–7pm, Sat & Sun 8.30am–3pm; winter Mon 10.30am–5pm, Tues–Fri 8am–5pm, Sat & Sun 8.30am–3pm; 800dr). The integrity of the site and the wealth of its finds is due to the nature of the city's demise. At some point in the fifth century AD, a series of earthquakes prompted an evacuation of Dion, which was then swallowed up by a mudslide from the mountain. The place is still quite waterlogged, and constant pumping against the local aquifer is necessary. The main visible excavations are of the vast **public baths** complex and, outside the city walls, the **sanctuaries** of Demeter and Aphrodite-Isis. In the latter a small temple has been unearthed, along with its cult statue – a copy of which remains in situ. The finest mosaics so far discovered lie in a former banquet room; they depict the god Dionysus on a chariot, but their protective canopy renders them scarcely visible. Two Christian **basilicas** attest to the town's later years as a Byzantine bishopric in the fourth and fifth centuries AD. An observation platform allows you to view the layout of the site more clearly.

Back in the village, a large but badly labelled **museum** (summer same hours as site, winter Mon–Fri 12.30–5pm; 800dr) houses most of the finds. The sculpture, perfectly preserved by the mud, is impressive, and accompanied by various tombstones and altars. In the basement sprawls a fine **mosaic of Medusa**, off-limits but adequately viewed down through the stairwell. Upstairs, along with extensive displays of pottery and coinage, is a collection of everyday items, including surgical and dental tools (removed temporarily in 1997) perhaps connected with the sanctuary of Asclepius, the healing god. Pride of place, however, goes to the remains of a first-century BC **pipe organ**, discovered in 1992 and exhibited on the upper storey.

Note that the village and site cannot be approached directly from Mount Olympus, since an army firing range bars the way. If you want to **stay overnight**, the *Hotel Dion* stands at the crossroads by the bus stop (☎0351/53 682; 7500dr), 100m below the museum; on the pedestrian street linking the two are a few tavernas firmly pitched at the tourist trade. The nearest campsites are on the beach at Varikó, 11km away: *Stani* (☎0352/61 277) and *Niteas* (☎0352/61 290), both open all year round.

Mount Olympus (Óros Ólymbos)

The highest, most magical and most dramatic of all Greek mountains, **Mount Olympus** – Ólymbos in Greek – rears up 3000 metres from the shores of the Thermaïkos gulf. Dense forests cover its lower slopes, and its **wild flowers** are without parallel, even by Greek standards. To make the most of it, you need to allow two to three days' hiking.

Equipped with decent boots and warm clothing, no special expertise is necessary to get to the top in summer (mid-June to October), though it's a long hard pull requiring a good deal of stamina; winter climbs, of course, are another matter. At any time of year Olympus is a mountain to be treated with respect: its weather is notoriously fickle and it regularly claims lives.

Litókhoro and Olympus practicalities

The best base for a walk up the mountain is the village of **LITÓKHORO** on the eastern side. Unexciting in itself, in good weather it affords intoxicating dawn-of-climb views into the heart of the range. Reaching Litókhoro is fairly easy; there's a train station 9km distant on the coast, from where there are more or less hourly buses (or taxis late at night). You can get the same bus direct from Thessaloníki or the market town of Kateríni.

The Litókhoro youth hostel has closed down, so for similar facilities try the *dhomátia* (②) available through the management of the *Ouzerí Olympos* on the main square, or the exceedingly plain non-en-suite *Park* at Ayíos Nikoláou 23 (☎0352/81 252; ②), near the bottom of town. The *Myrto* on Ayíos Nikoláou, just downhill from the main square (π0352/81 398, fax 82 298; ④) is open all year, and is considered the best **hotel** in the village. The newish, spotless *Enipeís* (π0352/81 328; ④) is on the main square above the post office; the first floor rear rooms have the best views in town. Immediately opposite stands the *Aphrodite* (π0352/81 415, fax 22 123; ④), with only averagely clean rooms, few of which have any view. As for **eating**, there are fast-food places and simple grills in the square and down Ayíos Nikoláou, but along the uphill side streets, there are more attractive possibilities, such as the *Ouzeri Manos* on 28-Oktovríou, or the *Dhamaskinia*, on Vassiléos Konstandínos. For sustenance while walking, you'll need to buy food in Litókhoro, though water can wait until you're at the vicinity of either of two trailheads (see below).

Accommodation **on Olympus** itself is better organized than on any other mountain in Greece. There are two staffed **refuges**: the EOS-run *Spílios Agapitós* at 2100m (May 15–Oct 15; π0352/81 800, reservations recommended in summer), commonly known as Refuge "A", and the SEO-managed *Yiósos Apostolídhis* hut at 2700m (open July–Sept, though its glassed-in porch is always available for climbers in need). There is no longer a set phone number for this refuge, since the wardenship is in a state of flux; contact the SEO information booth in Litókhoro at π0352/82 300. Both currently charge around 2500dr for a bunk (you can camp at Refuge "A" for 700dr, using their bathroom), with lights out and outer door locked at 10pm. Meals at either shelter are relatively expensive, and mandatory since no cooking is allowed inside; bring more money than you think you'll need, as bad weather can ground you for a day or two longer than planned. Both the Ethniki/National and Emboriki/Commercial **banks** in Litókhoro have cash dispensers.

This guide contains all the information you need to head up the mountain, since sources of **information** in Litókhoro are patchy. EOS maintains an office 200m west of the *Hotel Myrto*, but they have no set hours off-season, and their free leaflet is quite useless; you should buy a proper **map** in advance, co-produced by *Korfes* magazine and EOS Akharnés, either from mountaineering shops in Athens or from Stanfords in London.

The mountain

To reach alpine Olympus, you have a choice of road or foot routes. With your own vehicle, you can **drive** deep into the mountain along a fairly decent road, the first 6km of which is now paved. There is a control/education post where (in high season anyway) your nationality is recorded and you're given some literature advising you of the park rules; so far there's no admission charge, though this will probably change in the future. Conservationists are agitating for a total ban on private vehicles within the park, and all and all it is much better to **walk** in from Litókhoro, as far as the monastery of Ayíou Dhionysíou, and beyond to the two trailheads following.

As for the final **ascent routes**, there are two main paths: one beginning at **Priónia**, just under 18km up the mountain at the road's end, where a primitive, summer-only taverna operates by the spring; the other at a spot called Dhiakládhosi or Gortsiá (14km up), marked by a signboard displaying a map of the range. The Priónia path is more frequented and more convenient, the Dhiakládhosi trail longer but more beautiful. A 1800-metre driveway, appearing on the main road about halfway between the two trailheads, leads down to Ayíou Dhionysíou.

The Mavrólongos canyon and Ayíou Dhionysíou monastery

Some years ago the Greek overland-trail committee rehabilitated old paths in the superlatively beautiful Mavrólongos (Enipévs) river canyon to make a fine section of the **E4 overland trail**, thus sparing hikers the drudgery of walking up the road or the expense of a taxi. Black-on-yellow diamond markers begin near Litókhoro's central platía; follow road signs for Mýli and bear down and right at the cemetery. Once out of town, they lead you along a roller-coaster course by the river for three and a half hours to Ayíou Dhionysíou. It's a delightful route, but you'll need basic hiking skills as there are some scrambles over steep terrain, and a few water crossings.

The **monastery** itself was burned by the Germans in 1943 for allegedly harbouring guerrillas, and the surviving monks, rather than rebuilding, relocated to new premises near Litókhoro. After years of dereliction and vandalism, Ayíou Dhionysíou is undergoing restoration as of writing. Drinking-water taps by the gate are much used by people camping along the riverbanks below the perimeter wall (tolerated despite this being national park territory).

From Ayíou Dhionysíou it's about an hour more along the riverside E4 to Priónia, or slightly less up the driveway and then east to the Dhiakládhosi trailhead.

The ascent from Priónia

The E4 carries on just uphill from the taverna by an EOS signpost giving the time to the refuge as two hours thirty minutes (allow 3hr). You cross a stream (last water before the *Spílios Agapitós* refuge, purification advisable) and start to climb steeply up through beech and black pine woods. This path, the continuation of the E4, is well trodden and marked, so there is no danger of getting lost. As you gain height there are superb views across the Mavrólongos ravine to your left and to the peaks towering above you.

The *Spílios Agapitós* **refuge** perches on the edge of an abrupt spur, surrounded by huge storm-beaten trees. You need to let the warden know in good time if you want a meal and a bed. It's best to stay overnight here, as you should make an early start for the three-hour ascent to Mýtikas, the highest peak at 2917m. The peaks frequently cloud up towards midday and you lose the view, to say nothing of the danger of catching one of Zeus's thunderbolts, for this was the mythical seat of the gods. Besides, nights at the refuge are fantastic: a log fire blazes, you watch the sun set on the peaks, and there are billions of stars.

The summit area

The E4 path continues behind the refuge (the last water source on the mountain), climbing to the left up a steep spur among the last of the trees. Having ignored an initial right fork towards the unstaffed *Khristos Kakalos* hut (Refuge "C"), within an hour you reach a signposted **fork** above the tree line. Straight on takes you across the range to Kokkinopylós village with the E4 waymarks, or with a slight deviation right to Mýtikas, via the ridge known as Kakí Skála (1hr 30min). An immediate right turn leads to the Yiósos Apostolídhis hut in one hour along the so-called Zonária trail, with the option after forty minutes of taking the very steep Loúki couloir left up to Mýtikas; if you do this, be wary of rockfalls.

For the safer **Kakí Skála route**, continue up the right flank of the stony featureless valley in front of you, with the Áyios Andónios peak up to your left. An hour's dull climb brings you to the summit ridge between the peaks of Skolió on the left and Skála on the right. You know you're there when one more step would tip you over a 500-metre sheer drop into the Kazánia chasm; take great care. The Kakí Skála (Evil Stairway) begins in a narrow cleft on the right just short of the ridge; paint splashes mark the way. The route keeps just below the ridge, so you are protected from the drop into Kazánia. Even so, those who don't like heights are likely to feel very uncomfortable here.

You start with a slightly descending rightward traverse to a narrow nick in the ridge revealing the drop to Kazánia – easily negotiated. Continue traversing right, skirting the base of the Skála peak, then climb leftwards up a steepish gully made a little awkward by loose rock on sloping footholds. Bear right at the top over steep but reassuringly solid rock, and across a narrow neck. Step left around an awkward corner and there in front of you, scarcely 100 metres away, is **Mýtikas summit**, an airy, boulder-strewn platform with a trigonometric point, tin Greek flag and visitors' book. In reasonable conditions it's about forty minutes to the summit from the start of Káki Skála; three hours from the refuge; five and a half hours from Priónia. A stone's throw to the north of Mýtikas is the **Stefáni peak**, also known as the Throne of Zeus.

Descending from Mýtikas, you can either go back the way you came, with the option of turning left at the signpost (see above) for the Apostolídhis hut (2hr 30min from Mýtikas by this route), or you can step out, apparently into space, in the direction of Stefáni and turn immediately down to the right into the mouth of the Loúki couloir. It takes about forty minutes of downward scrambling to reach the main path where you turn left for the hut, skirting the impressive northeast face of Stefáni (1hr), or go right, back to the familiar signpost and down the E4 to Spílios Agapitós (2hr altogether).

The ascent from Dhiakládhosi (Gortsiá)

Starting from the small parking area beyond the information placard, it's critically important to take the narrow path going up and left, not the forest track heading down and right. An hour along, you reach the meadow of **Bárba**, and two hours out you'll arrive at a messy junction with a modern water tank and various placards – take left forks en route when given the choice. The signs point hard left to the spring at **Strángo**; right for the direct path to Petróstrounga; and straight on the old, more scenic way to **Petróstrounga**, passed some two and a half hours along.

Beyond this summer pastoral colony, there's a signpost right, then the trail wanders up to the base of **Skoúrta** knoll (4hr 15min), above the tree line. After crossing the Lemós (Neck) ridge dividing the Papá Réma and Mavrólongos ravines, with spectacular views into both, five and a quarter hours should see you up on the Oropédhio Musón (Plateau of the Muses), five and a half hours to the Apostolídhis refuge, visible for the last fifteen minutes. But you should count on seven hours, including rests, for this route; going down takes about four and a half hours, a highly recommended descent if you've come up from Priónia.

It takes about an hour, losing altitude, to traverse the onward Zonária path linking Apostolídhis and the E4, skimming the base of the peaks – about the same time as coming the other way as described above.

The southern ridge route

To experience complete solitude on Olympus, continue past Áyios Andónios, the peak just south of Skála and the E4 trail, and begin to ridge-walk the line of peaks that bounds the Mavrólongos to the south. Much of this trek past Metamórfosi, Kalóyeros, and Págos summits is cross-country, but with the recommended map, route-finding is easy on a clear day. It's six and a half walking hours from the Apostolídhis hut to the dilapidated but serviceable unstaffed shelter at **Livadháki**, with unreliable cistern water only – you'll need to carry at least a couple litres in with you. From Livadháki a good trail descends via the ridges of Pelekoudhiá and Tsouknídha, coming out three and a quarter hours on at the meadow of **Déli**, where you're just above a forest road which leads 7km down to Litókhoro.

Alternatively, a faint trail at Déli dips down into a ravine and up onto **Gólna** knoll, intersecting another sporadically marked path up from Litókhoro that leads over into the Mavrólongos watershed to join up with the E4. Just above the junction woodcutters have messed up the path, but persevere, and you'll suddenly drop down on to the E4 about halfway along its course, some ninety minutes out of Déli. This last section makes a beautiful, if challenging walk. For full details, a specialist hiking guide (see " Books", p.830).

Véria and Veryína

The broad agricultural plain extending west from Thessaloníki eventually collides with an abrupt, wooded escarpment, at the panoramic edge of which several towns have grown up. The largest of these, **Véria**, has few particular sites or monuments, but it is one of the more interesting northern Greek communities and lies within twenty minutes' drive of the excavations of ancient Aigai at **Veryína**.

Véria

Visitors to **VÉRIA** arriving by bus (the train station 3km east of the centre is hopelessly inconvenient) will hike south along Odhós Venizélou from the main **KTEL** to the point where the street splits. Odhós Elías, a short but fashionable throughfare, leads south to the **Belvedere**, the escarpment park, where Odhós Anixéos snakes north along the cliff edge to re-intersect Venizélou. En route Anixéos passes the **archeological museum** (Tues–Sun 8.30am–3pm; 500dr) which has no finds from Veryína (see opposite), but contains mostly Roman oddments from the area. Partly pedestrianized **Mitropóleos** heads west from the triple junction towards the central Platía Konstandínou Ráktivan – universally called **Platía Oroloyíou**, after a long-vanished clock-tower – passing on the way **OTE** at no. 45, the **post office** at no. 35, various banks with cash dispensers, and the new cathedral. On Platía Oroloyíou is a separate, small KTEL for Kozáni services.

The old **cathedral**, opposite a gnarled plane tree from which the conquering Turks hanged the town's archbishop in 1430, is just off Odhós Vassiléos Konstandínou (better known as Odhós Kendrikís), which links Venizélou and Platía Ráktivan. Near the tree, what remains of the old **bazaar** straddles Kendrikís; downhill and to the northwest tumbles the riverside Ottoman quarter of **Barboúta** or Barboúti, easiest reached via pedestrianized Odhós Sófou. Largely **Jewish** before the 1943 deportations decimated the 850-strong community, it is today mostly abandoned and crumbling, though there are signs of restoration and, near the footbridge crossing the Tripótamos stream, there's a pricey café-restaurant. The disused, locked synagogue here can also be reached by a pedestrian lane from behind the yellow courthouse up on Platía Oroloyíou. Survivals of the **Muslim** presence in Véria are more numerous and more conspicuous: a wonderful *hamam* complex on Loutroú, west of Mitropóleos; a small mosque on Kendrikís; and a larger one on Márkou Bótsari, just south of Platía Oroloyíou.

Christianity has a venerably long history here: St Paul preached in Véria (Acts 17: 1–13 of the New Testament) on two occasions, and a gaudy alcove shrine at the base of Mavromikháli marks the supposed spot of his sermons. But the town is more famous for sixty or so small medieval **churches**, mostly sixteenth to eighteenth century. In order to avoid offending Muslim sensibilities, they were once disguised as barns or warehouses, with little dormer windows rather than domes to admit light, but today, well-labelled and often surrounded by cleared spaces, they are not hard to find. The only church regularly open is **Khristós** (Tues–Sun 8.30am–3pm) near the lower end of Mitropóleos, which has restored fourteenth-century frescoes.

Practicalities

There are plenty of **hotels** in Véria, but most offer a disincentive to stay the night, being overpriced, noisy or both. The best of the cheaper ones, an exception to the above rule, is *Polytimi* (☎0331/22 866, fax 20 014; ④) at Megálou Alexándhrou 35 (☎0331/64 902; ④). Next up is the adequate and clean *Veroi* at Kendrikís 4, just off Platía Oroloyíou. More **upmarket** choices include the *Villa Elia*, Elías 16 (☎0331/26 800, fax 21 880; ⑤), subject to street noise, and the *Macedonia* (☎ and fax 0331/66 902; ⑤), Kondoyeorgáki 50, far enough past the bars (see opposite) for nocturnal peace is the town's best.

There are a number of good **restaurants** in Véria; indeed, the town is worth a detour for a meal stop. An excellent lunch choice is *Sarafopoulos* at Kendrikís 26, with cheap *mayireftá*; more elaborate are a pair of ouzerís, *To Steki tou Goulari* and *Nikos*, opposite each other on pedestrianized Patriárkhou Ioakeím, 100m downhill from Mitropóleos. For supper, an enduring favourite is *Kostalar* (shut Mon) at Afrodhítis 2/d in the Papákia district, reached by following Mavromikháli uphill from the St Paul shrine, to a plane-tree-shaded square; this place has been going since 1939, offering clay-pot oven dishes and grills. By day, by far the most pleasant place for a coffee is the tourist pavilion at the edge of the Belvedere, with its shady terrace overlooking the plain. In the same area, *Kamelot* on Anixéos is a quiet bar with a shady courtyard and upstairs rooms for playing *távli*. For **nightlife**, a pedestrianized area west of Mitropóleos, crammed full with noisy *barákia* installed in restored Ottoman houses, comes into its own. Most of these clubs are on Kondoyeorgáki, starting from the Khristós church, and adjoining Éllis; *Enodhia* on Éllis usually has the best music.

Veryína: ancient Aigai

Excavations at **VERYÍNA**, 13km southeast of Véria, have revolutionized Macedonian archeology since the 1970s. A series of chamber tombs, unearthed here by Professor Manolis Andronikos (1919–1992), are now unequivocally accepted as those of Philip II and other members of the Macedonian royal family. This means that the site itself must be that of **Aigai**, the original Macedonian royal capital before the shift to Pella, and later its necropolis. Finds from the site and tombs, the richest Greek trove since the discovery of Mycenae, are exhibited at Thessaloníki's archeological museum. The main tombs can now be seen in situ; visitors walk down a narrow stone passage into an air-conditioned bunker which allows them to view the ornamental facades and the empty chambers beyond. Overhead, the earth of the tumulus has been replaced.

Until recently, the modern village of Veryína had limited facilities, but with the advent of tourism two reasonable **tavernas** have opened in the village centre, as have two **pensions** on the edge, conveniently near the stop for the frequent buses from Véria. The best of these is the friendly, en-suite *Oikos* (☎0331/92 366; ④), whose management may provide meals on request.

The sites

Tues–Sun 8.30am–3pm; 1200dr.

Ancient Aigai is documented as the sanctuary and **burial place** of the Macedonian kings. It was here that Philip II was assassinated and buried – and tradition maintained that the dynasty would be destroyed if any king were buried elsewhere, as indeed happened after the death of Alexander the Great in Asia. Until Andronikos's finds in November 1977 – the culmination of years working on the site – Aigai had long been assumed to be lost beneath modern Édhessa, a theory now completely discarded.

What Andronikos discovered, under a tumulus just outside Veryína, were two large and indisputably Macedonian **chamber tombs**. The first had been looted in antiquity but retained a mural of the rape of Persephone by Pluto, the only complete example of an ancient Greek painting yet found. The second, a grander vaulted tomb with a Doric facade adorned by a superb painted frieze of a lion hunt, was – incredibly – intact, having been deliberately disguised with rubble from later tomb pillagings. Among the treasures to emerge were a marble sarcophagus containing a gold casket of bones with the exploding-star symbol of the royal line on its lid, and, still more significantly, five small ivory heads, among them representations of both Philip II and Alexander. It was this clue, as well as the fact that the skull bore marks of a disfiguring facial wound Philip was known to have sustained, that led to the identification of the tomb as his.

It is these **Royal Tombs** (known as Tomb 1: Persephone and Tomb 2: Phillip II), together with two more adjacent tombs (Tomb 3: Prince's and Tomb 4: unnamed), which can now be seen underground. From outside, all that's visible is a low hillock with some skylights and long ramps leading down, but inside the facades and doorways of the tombs are well illuminated behind glass.

The so-called **Macedonian Tomb**, actually three adjacent tombs, can also be visited after a fashion (same times as above; same admission ticket). They are about 500m uphill and south of the village and, like the Royal Tombs, lie well below the modern ground level, protected by a vast tin roof. When he's around, the guard will let you into the dig, though not into the tombs themselves. Excavated by the French in 1861, the most prominent one has the form of a temple, with an Ionic facade of half-columns breached by two marble doors. Inside, you can just make out an imposing marble throne with sphinxes carved on the sides, armrests and footstool. The neighbouring pair of tombs, still under excavation, are said to be similar in design.

On a slope southeast of the village, across a ravine and 800m by road beyond a vast new car-park, the ruins of the **Palace of Palatitsa** (same times as above; same ticket) occupy a low hill. This complex was probably built during the third century BC as a summer residence for the last great Macedonian king, Antigonus Gonatus. It is now little more than foundations, but amidst the confusing litter of column drums and capitals you can make out a triple *propylaion* (entrance gate) opening onto a central courtyard. This is framed by broad porticoes and colonnades which, on the south side, preserve a well-executed if rather unexciting mosaic. Despite its lack of substance it is an attractive site, dominated by a grand old oak tree looking out across the plains, scattered with Iron-Age (tenth- to seventh-century BC) tumuli. The only substantial items dug up to date are the first two tiers of the **theatre** just below, where Philip II was assassinated, some say at the wedding of his daughter.

Édhessa, Lefkádhia and Náoussa

With your own vehicle, the other two escarpment towns can be easily and enjoyably toured in a day or less, with an unspoilt archeological site – Lefkádhia – in between. Travelling by public transport (especially by train), stopping off is time-consuming and probably more trouble than it's worth, in which case Édhessa, astride the main route between Thessaloníki and the far west of Macedonia, is the place you're most likely to stop.

Édhessa

ÉDHESSA, like Véria, makes a pleasant brief stopover, its modest fame attributed to the waters that flow through the town. Coming down from the mountains to the north, they flow swiftly through the middle of town in several courses and then, just to the east, cascade down a dramatic ravine, luxuriant with vegetation, to the plain below. From the train station, walk straight for 400m until you see the main branch of the walled-in river, paralleled by Tsimiskí street. Turn left and you will come to the **waterfalls**, focus of a park with a couple of cafés. For the **Byzantine bridge** turn right from here and follow the river for about 600m. Paths also lead down the ravine, providing access to caves below the waterfalls.

The town itself is a little ordinary, but the various streamside parks and wide pedestrian pavements are a rare pleasure in a country where the car is king, and the train and bus stations are both well placed for breaking a journey. The main **KTEL** is on the corner of Filíppou and Pávlou Melá (you follow Filíppou north into the centre); there's a second, smaller terminal for Flórina/Kastória services only, nearby at the corner of Egnatía and Pávlou Melá. The **post office** is on Dhimokratías, while three **banks** – Ethniki (National), Emboriki (Commercial) and Alpha Pisteos (Credit) – have cash dispensers.

For **accommodation**, the best of the town's hotels, is *Katarraktes* (☎0381/22 300, fax 27 237; ④), perched, as the name suggests, near the waterfalls. Slightly shabby but adequate and friendly is the *Pella* (☎0381/23 541; ③), Egnatia 26, or try the more comfortable, air-conditioned *Alfa* (☎0381/22 221; ④), next door at no. 28. Quieter but less friendly is the air-conditioned *Elena* (☎0381/23 218, fax 23 951; ④) on Platía Timenídhon, whose management (unlike the others) refuses to bargain at slack times. All three hotels are a five-minute walk from the two KTEL terminals. **Restaurants** aren't numerous, but there's enough choice for a short stay; very close to the two more modest hotels are *To Rolói* at Ayíos Dhimitríou 5, for *mayireftá*, and *O Pavlos* beyond the clock tower and OTE at Péllis 8, for grills and mezédhes. **Café** and **bar** life happens on the pedestrian zones flanking the rivulets, especially on Angelí Gátsou. The *Ilektra*, opposite the Pella and Alfa hotels, is one of the few places offering a sit-down **breakfast**, of both coffee and pastries.

Lefkádhia

Thirty kilometres south of Édhessa on the road to Véria, Lefkádhia has not been positively identified with any Macedonian city, but it is thought to have been Mieza, where Aristotle taught. The modern village of **LEFKÁDHIA** lies just west of the main road, but you should turn off east at a sign reading "To the Macedonian Tombs". There are four tombs in all – only one has a guard, who keeps the keys to the other three.

The staffed one, the so-called **Great Tomb** or **Tomb of Judgement** (closed for restoration), east of the main road just past the train tracks, is the largest Macedonian temple-tomb yet discovered. Despite extensive cement protection, it has been so badly damaged by creeping damp from the very high local water table that extensive consolidation works are under way, probably involving complete dismantling and reconstruction. It dates from the third century BC, and was probably built for a general, depicted on the left, in one of the barely surviving frescoes, being led by Hermes (the Conductor of Souls). Other faded frescoes on the right represent the Judges of Hades – hence the tomb's alias. A once-elaborate double-storeyed facade, half Doric and half Ionic, has almost completely crumbled away; on the entablature frieze you can barely make out a battle between Persians and Macedonians.

The **Anthimíon Tomb**, 150m further along the same country road, is more impressive, with its four Ionic facade columns, two marble interior sarcophagi with inscribed lids, and well-preserved frescoes. The typanum bears portraits of a couple, presumably the tomb occupants, though the man's face has been rubbed out. Ornamental designs and three giant *akrokerámata* complete the pediment decoration. Between the double set of portals, the ceiling frescoes are perhaps stylized representations of octopi.

The other two local tombs are of essentially specialist interest. The one signposted "Kinch's Macedonian Tomb", after the Dane who discovered it, is on the east side of the main road, on the way back towards the village. That of **Lyson-Kallikles** is signed west of the main road, before the turning to the village, at the end of a 1km dirt track through peach orchards; to visit you have lower yourself through a usually locked grating in the ceiling, the original entrance having been long since buried.

Náoussa

Four kilometres south of the tombs is a turning west, off the main road, to **NÁOUSSA**, a small country town whose vintners, the **Boutari** company, produce some of Greece's best wines, and whose mills turn out vast numbers of brightly coloured acrylic blankets for the nation's hotels. Along with Véria, the town is also at the heart of the country's main peach-growing region – excuse enough for a stop in July – and hosts one of Macedonia's most elaborate pre-Lenten carnivals. That said, Náoussa is generally the least distinguished of the three escarpment towns – a pleasant enough place to live but not necessarily to holiday at. In winter, however, Náoussa is very busy with Greeks enjoying the two superb ski centres overhead on Mount Vermion.

If you do drop in, the big attraction is the parkland of **Áyios Nikólaos**, 4km beyond town (itself 6km west of the main road), an oasis of giant plane trees nourished by the streams that bubble from the earth here. Most of the space is filled by a funfair and go-kart track, attractions swarmed over by school-groups during the week, all and sundry at weekends. The riverbanks are additionally lined with several more or less identically priced tavernas featuring farm-raised trout (the *Nisaki* is the most pleasantly set). Just upstream, the *Hotel Vermion* (☎0332/29 311; ⑤) is open year-round and has a fine restaurant. The torrents eventually cut through the town below, lending it some definition and a green vegetation belt, but it's a decidedly a miniature version of Édhessa. South of the large belfried church, which you pass as you wind up from the main road, there's a small park strip, lined with the bulk of Náoussa's restaurants and bars. The **bus** leaves from the KTEL at the lower end of town; the **train station** is a good 7km distant.

West from Édhessa: Flórina and the lakes

West of Édhessa lies **Límni Vegoritídha**, the first of a series of lakes that punctuate the landscape towards Kastoriá and up to and across the border with the Former Yugoslav Republic of Macedonia (FYROM). The rail line between Édhessa and Flórina traces the lake's west shore – a fine journey which could be broken at either of the two village train stops, Árnissa and Áyios Pandelímonas.

ÁRNISSA has perhaps the better setting, opposite an islet and amidst apple orchards; for a swim, head for the water, then walk right for fifteen minutes until you find a break in the shoreline reedbeds. The one-street village itself is a little drab, though it does have the convenience of the attractive hotel *Megali Hellas* (☎0381/31 232; ③). The village comes alive on Tuesdays when the weekly market attracts families from miles around, using their tractors as taxis. To the north of the village rises **Mount Kaïmaktsalán**, scene of one of one of the bloodiest battles of World War I, which raged intermittently from 1916 to 1918 until a Serbian-Greek force managed to break through the German-Bulgarian lines. The 2524-metre summit marks the Greek-"Yugoslav" frontier and bears a small memorial chapel to the fallen. If you can get a lift to the end of the road at Kalývia, it's a beautiful walk beyond, though much of the area has been developed as the Vórras ski resort.

The more attractive of the lakeside villages, however, is **ÁYIOS PANDELÍMONAS**, with its red-roofed houses crowned by a ruined windmill, and a small beach where you can swim in the slightly algae-ridden waters. The lakeside *Epikheirisi* **restaurant** has no rooms available, but keeps watch over the basic **campsite** alongside. Rail and road then pass through Amýndeo (no accommodation, and a dire place to get stuck) before turning north towards Flórina. Some 1500m west of Amýndeo, a short diversion to the right brings you to the smaller lake of **Petrón** and the hillside ruins of the Hellenistic Petres on the west shore, recently excavated and the subject of an interesting display on the first floor of the museum at Flórina (see below).

Flórina

FLÓRINA, surrounded by hills densely wooded in beech, is the last town before the FYROM border 13km to the north and as such, is quite a lively market centre. Cars can cross the border but at present there are no through trains. There is little of intrinsic interest in the town itself, other than the **archeological museum** 150m from the train station (Tues–Fri 8.30am–3pm; 500dr), and the main reason for a visit is to see the Préspa lakes, 40km west (see below).

The local economy has been hard hit by the collapse of Yugoslavia, mainly because Macedonians no longer come here to shop, and Germans and Austrians no longer pass through on their way to the Peloponnese beaches, factors only slightly offset by visits in Mercedes from wealthy Albanian *mafiosi* from Körçe (there's a border crossing 51km distant at Krystallopiyí). This hasn't had a salutary effect on **hotel** prices, which remain high; the cheapest is the *Ellinis* near the train station at Pávlou Melá 31 (☎0385/22 671, fax 22 815; ④). Further up pedestrianized Pávlou Melá, across the central square and onto the continuation Megálou Alexándhrou, stands the more comfortable and quieter *Lingos* (☎0385/28 322, fax 29 643; ⑤) at Tagmatárkhou Naoúm 1. The *Antigoni* (☎0385/23 180; ④), at Ariánou 1, diagonally opposite the KTEL, is a noisy third choice. Three proper **restaurants**, as opposed to the numerous cafés and bars on Pávlou Melá, are found on 25-Martíou, running west from the central platía towards the river bisecting the town; there's another, the *Restaurant Olympos*, nearby at Megálou Alexándhrou 22.

Given the expense of hotels here, and the dearth of local attractions, it's well worth planning to arrive early in the day, as moving on is likely to be your main priority. There's no longer any direct bus from **Flórina to Kastoriá**, and it's easy to see why, as there's little in between other than dense forest and a few crumbling villages, half-deserted since the Civil War. The road is paved, however, climbing sharply and snaking out of Flórina to the 1600-metre Pisodhéri saddle, site of one of the larger villages and the Vígla ski lift. Since its resurfacing, the road is kept snow-ploughed in winter; it follows the headwaters of the Aliákmonas River, the longest in Greece, most of the way to Kastoriá. There are, however, two daily buses (6.45am & 2.30pm) to **Áyios Yermanós** in the **Préspa** basin.

The Préspa lakes

Rising out of the Aliákmonas valley on the paved side road towards **Préspa**, you have little hint of what's ahead until suddenly you top a pass, and a shimmering expanse of water riven by islets and ridges appears. It's not postcard-pretty, but the basin has an eerie, back-of-beyond quality that grows on you with further acquaintance – and a turbulent recent history that belies its current role as one of the Balkans' most important wildlife sanctuaries.

During the Byzantine era, Préspa became a prominent place of exile for troublesome noblemen, which accounts for the surprising number of **ecclesiastical monuments** in this backwater. In the tenth century it briefly hosted the court of the Bulgarian Tsar Samuel before his defeat by Byzantine Emperor Basil II. Under the Ottomans the area again lapsed into obscurity, only to regain the dubious benefits of strategic importance in just about every European war of this century, culminating in vicious local battles during the 1947–49 Greek civil war. In 1988 a forest fire on the eastern ridge treated observers to a dangerous fireworks display, as dozens of unexploded artillery shells were touched off by the heat. After World War II Préspa lay desolate and largely depopulated, as the locals fled abroad to Eastern Europe, North America and Australia, in response to a punitive government policy of forced assimilation against Macedonian-speakers – as all the lake-dwellers are. It is only since the late 1970s that the villages, still relatively primitive and neglected, have begun to refill during the summer, when beans and hay are grown as close to the two lakes as the national park authorities allow. A common sight everywhere are lake-reeds, cut and stacked for use as bean-poles.

Mikrí Préspa, the southerly lake, is mostly shallow and reedy, with a narrow fjord curling west and just penetrating Albania. The borders of Greece, Albania and FYROM meet in the middle of deeper **Megáli Préspa**, making the area doomed to play some role in whatever Balkan uproars lie in the future. During the past few years a steady stream of Albanian refugees have used the basin as an exit corridor into Greece. Though they used to be routinely caught and returned to Albania by the army, their presence as illegal agricultural workers is now tolerated, as farms in the area are perennially short-handed. Considering that for years you needed an official permit to visit Préspa, and given the uncertain future, the Greek military presence is surprisingly unobtrusive and sovereignty lightly exercised.

The core of the **national park**, established in 1971, barely encompasses Mikrí Préspa and its shores, but the peripheral zone extends well into the surrounding mountains, affording protection of sorts to a variety of animals. You'll almost certainly see foxes crossing the road, though the wolves and bears up on the ridges are considerably shyer. The lakes have a dozen resident fish species, including *tsiróni*, a sort of freshwater sardine, and *grivádhi*, a kind of carp. But it is **bird life** for which the Préspa basin, particularly the smaller lake, is most famous. There are few birds of prey, but you should see a fair number of egrets, cormorants, crested grebes and pelicans, which nest in the spring, with the chicks out and about by summer. They feed partly on the large numbers of snakes, which include vipers, whip snakes and harmless water snakes which you may encounter while swimming. Observation towers are available at Vromolímni and near Áyios Akhíllios, but dawn spent anywhere at the edge of the reedbeds with a pair of binoculars will be immensely rewarding (though bear in mind that you're not allowed to boat or wade into the reeds). There are **park information centres** in the villages of Áyios Yermanós and Psarádhes (see below).

While you may arrive from Flórina by bus, you really can't hope to tour the area without some means of **transport** – either a mountain bike or a car. Similarly, in view of the area's past under-development, don't expect much in the way of **facilities**: food is adequate and inexpensive, but exceedingly simple. The same might be said of accommodation, though it has improved recently. Préspa is an increasingly popular target for holidaying Greeks and (for some reason) Dutch, and you'd be wise to reserve accommodation in mid-summer, especially at weekends.

The way in: Mikrolímni

MIKROLÍMNI, 5km up a side road off the main route into the valley, is the first conceivable stop. The small shop and fish taverna, on the shore square, has three **rooms** to let (☎0385/61 221; ②). In the evening, you can look towards sunsets over reedbeds and the snake-infested Vidhronísi (Vitrinítsi) islet, though swimming isn't good here, or anywhere else on Mikrí Préspa for that matter. At the far end of the hamlet is a sporadically used biological observation station, literally the last house in Greece, and beyond that the lake narrows between sheer hillsides on its way to Albania. A prominent trail, much used by fleeing Albanians, leads there, paralleling the long inlet, but it would be unwise to walk its full length.

Regain the main road, which reaches a T-junction 16km from the main Flórina–Kastoriá highway, on the spit which separates the larger and smaller lakes. It's probable that at one time there was just one lake here, but now there's a four-metre elevation difference. Bearing right at the junction leads within 4km to Áyios Yermanós; the left option splits again at the west end of the spit, bearing south towards the islet of Áyios Akhíllios or northwest toward the hamlet of Psarádhes (see opposite).

Áyios Yermanós

ÁYIOS YERMANÓS is a large village of tile-roofed houses, overlooking a patch of Megáli Préspa in the distance. It's worth making the trip up just to see two tiny late Byzantine churches, whose frescoes, dating from the time when the place belonged to the bishopric of Ohrid, display a marked Macedonian influence. The lower church, **Áyios Athanásios**, has been recently renovated but if it's open (a rare event) you can glimpse a dog-faced *Saint Christopher* among a line of saints opposite the door.

The main thing to see, however, is the tiny, eleventh-century parish church of **Áyios Yermanós** up on the square, hidden behind a new monster awkwardly tacked onto it in 1882. The Byzantine structure (currently closed for repairs) has its own entrance, and the frescoes, skilfully retouched in 1743, can be lit: the switch is hidden in the narthex. There are more hagiographies and martyrdoms than space allows to list here, but there's a complete catalogue of them (in Greek) by the door. Among the best are the *Pandokrátor* in the dome; a *Nativity* and *Baptism* right of the dome; a *Crucifixion* and *Resurrection* to the left; plus the saints *Peter and Paul*, *Kosmas and Damian*, *Triphon and Pandelimon* by the door. Less conventional scenes include the *Entry into Jerusalem* and *Simon Helping Christ with the Cross*, opposite the door, and the *Apocalypse*, with the *Succouring of Mary the Beatified by Zozimas*, in the narthex. Mary was an Alexandrine courtesan who, repenting of her ways, retired to the desert for forty years. She was found, a withered crone on the point of death, by Zozimas, abbot of a desert monastery, and is traditionally shown being spoon-fed like an infant.

The village has the excellent Préspa **information centre** (daily: mid–June to mid–Sept 9.30am–1.30pm & 5–7.30pm; mid-Sept to mid–June 10am–2pm), focusing on the wildlife of the national park; given sufficient warning the centre can arrange guides for trips into the park. It also sells locally farmed organic products. In addition to a **post office** – the only one in the Préspa basin – the village has two places to **stay**: Makis Arabatzis' *Les Pelicans* (☎0385/51 442; ③), across from Áyios Athanásios and with a bit of lake view from its terrace, or two much nicer renovated old houses at the very top of the village, run by the local Women's Cooperative and heated by wood stoves in winter. Reservations (☎0385/51 320 or 51 355; ③) are strongly advised, especially in August when a folk-dance seminar takes place here. The only **taverna** in Áyios Yermanós is *Lefteris*, up by the women's inn, though there is another in Lemós, the village 1km below.

Across the spit: Koúla and Psarádhes

At the far end of the causeway dividing the two lakes, 4km from the T-junction, is **Koúla beach**, and a cluster of what passes for tourist development hereabouts: a patch of reed-free sand from where you can swim in Megáli Préspa, a free but basic camping area, now bereft of its water tap, and an army post. Tents and vans sprout by the "sailing club", actually a seemingly defunct taverna of sorts; *Iy Koula*, up by the army guardpost, is the only other (not very good, and overpriced) alternative. Just below it, you can see where Mikrí Préspa drains into Mégali Préspa.

If you don't intend to camp, it's best to bear right just above the army post, reaching after 6km the rickety village of **PSARÁDHES**, whose lanes make for an hour's stroll. Unfortunately the wonderful old houses lining them are increasingly derelict, with nothing being done either to preserve them, or to check the spread of unsightly modern construction. A good example of that, across the rather stagnant inlet here, is the bunkerstyle *Hotel Psaradhes* (☎0385/46 015; ③), an ugly necessity given the number of summer and weekend visitors here. Best of the few **rooms** in the village itself – and very sparsely furnished at that – are those above the *Taverna Syndrofia* (☎0385/46 107; ③), which is a good spot to sample lake fish and the proprietor Lazaros' wine. Of the other three **tavernas**, *Paradhosi* seems the best of the bunch, and the most reliably open.

Although there are white-rock swimming beaches below the hotel, the best outing from Psarádhes is a **boat excursion** to (and past) various medieval shrines and *askitíria* (hermitages) tucked into the shore leading around the promontory to Albania. The going rate per boat (ask, for example, at *Syndrofia*) is 5000–6000dr, so you'll want to assemble a party of four. Even if you have no particular interest in churches, the ride alone is well worth it, as cormorants, gulls and pelicans skim the waters of

Megáli Préspa which reflect the mountains of Albania. Your guide will point out a fifteenth-century icon of the Virgin painted onto the rock opposite the village, and (on the far side of the peninsula) the thirteenth-century hermitage of Metamórfosis, whose icons have either been stolen or taken to the safety of the Flórina museum. Usually, your only landfall is the spectacular fifteenth-century rock-church of **Panayía Eleoúsas**, concealed at the top of a deep chasm some 500m before the frontier. From the top of the long stairway up, you have a fantastic framed view of the lake and Albania; the deceptively simple vaulted chapel contains a plethora of expressive frescoes. They depict episodes from the life of Christ: to the right of the door, Mary Magdalene washes Christ's feet, with the *Transfiguration* just above, while opposite are a moving *Lamentation*, the *Myrrofori* at the sepulchre and an unusual *Resurrection* showing only Adam.

Áyios Akhíllios

The leftward option at the end of the causeway takes you, after 1500m, to the jetty for the islet of **Áyios Akhíllios**, with an impoverished hamlet of the same name. Five families still live there, whose members keep watch for visitors, with a boat (1500dr for one or two people, 2000dr for more) usually appearing as if by magic within moments of your arrival Once on the island, you can climb its cross-spiked summit for unrivalled views of Mikrí Préspa, or take the ten-minute walk to the ruined Byzantine basilica of **Áyios Akhíllios**. This used to have a mosaic depicting an egret, which features in all the available tourist literature, but it was stolen or crumbled away during the early 1990s. There is also a ruined sixteenth-century monastery of Panayía Porfýras near the south end of the islet, but boatmen tend not to stop here unless specifically asked.

Kastoriá and around

Set on a peninsula extending deep into a slate-coloured lake, **KASTORIÁ** is one of the most interesting and attractive towns of mainland Greece. It is a relatively wealthy place and has been so for centuries as the centre of the Greek (and Balkan) fur trade. Although the local beavers (*kastóri* in Greek) were trapped to extinction by the nineteenth century, Kastoriá still supports a considerable industry of furriers who make up coats, gloves and other items from fur scraps imported from Canada and Scandinavia. Animal rights supporters will find the place heavy going, as the industry is well-nigh ubiquitous: you'll see scraps drying on racks, and mega-stores line all the approach highways, pitched at Russian *mafiosi* buying mink coats for their womenfolk, judging from the profuse Cyrillic signposting.

For most visitors, however, the main appeal lies in traces of the town's former prosperity: half a dozen splendid *arkhondiká* – **mansions** of the old fur families – dating from the seventeenth to nineteenth centuries, plus some fifty Byzantine and medieval **churches**, though only a handful are visitable and of compelling interest. The main reminder of the Muslim settlement is the minaretless Kursun Tzami, marooned in a ridgetop car park; there's also a patch of originally Byzantine fortification wall down on the neck of the peninsula.

Kastoriá suffered heavy damage during both World War II and the Civil War which followed it. Platía Van Fleet, by the lakeside at the neck of the promontory, commemorates the US general who supervised the Greek Nationalist Army's operations against the Communist Democratic Army in the final campaigns of 1948–49. However, most of the destruction of Kastoriá's architectural heritage is not due so much to munitions as to 1950s neglect and 1960s development. It is miraculous that so many isolated specimens of humble Balkan vernacular and Neoclassical townhouses survive, mostly higher up on the peninsula where the steep slopes have frustrated cement mixers.

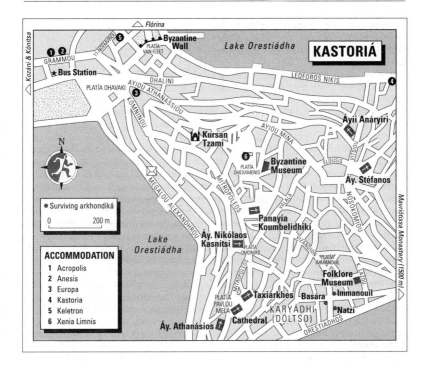

Town museums

For a sense of what Kastoriá must once have been in its heyday, the best area of town is the former lakeside quarter of **Karýdhis** (also called Dóltso), around Platía Immanouíl. Nearby at Kapetán Lázou 10, the seventeenth-century Aïvazís family mansion has been turned into a **Folklore Museum** (daily 10am–noon & 3–6pm; 200dr). The house was inhabited until 1972 and its furnishings and ceilings are in excellent repair. The caretaker, on request, will show you some of the other surviving *arkhondiká*. The most notable – the nearby **Bassáras**, **Natzís**, and **Immanouíl**, close together on Vyzandíon – are marked on the map; the last two have recently undergone restoration.

The **Byzantine Museum** up on Platía Dhexamenís, opposite the *Xenia Limnis* hotel (Tues–Sun 8.30am–3pm; 500dr) wisely goes for quality over quantity in a well-lit collection spanning the twelfth to sixteenth centuries. Highlights include an unusually expressive thirteenth-century St Nicholas and a later icon depicting the life of St George. There are also a few double-sided icons, including a rare *Deposition*, intended for use in religious processions.

Byzantine churches

Kastoriá's noteworthy Byzantine **churches** can only be visited by application to the key-keeper at the Byzantine museum; while friendly and knowledgeable, he speaks only Greek. Shown on the map, they are small structures which almost certainly began life as private chapels founded by wealthy donors from amongst the mansion owners. **Áyii Anáryiri** dates from the eleventh century, with three layers of frescoes spanning the following two hundred years. It is currently shut for further works, and only one of the frescoes, *Áyios Yióryios and Áyios Dhimítrios*, has so far been cleared of grime. Nearby **Áyios Stéfanos**, also closed at present, is of the tenth century and has been little changed over the years. Its frescoes are insignificant, but it does have an unusual women's gallery or *yinaikonítis*.

The excellent frescoes of twelfth-century **Áyios Nikólaos Kasnítsi** were returned to their former glory during the late 1980s. The unusual epithet stems from the surname of the donor, who is shown with his wife on the narthex wall presenting a model of the church to Christ. Lower down are ranks of female saints, to console the women congregated in the narthex, which long served as a women's gallery. High up on the west wall of the nave, the *Dormition* and the *Transfiguration* are in good condition, the former inexplicably backwards (the Virgin's head is usually to the left). **Taxiárkhes tís Mitropóleos**, the oldest (ninth-century) church, was built on the foundations of an earlier pagan temple, of which recycled columns and capitals are visible. Its more visible frescoes, such as that of the *Virgin Platytera and Adoring Archangels* in the conch of the apse, and a conventional *Dormition* on the west wall, are fourteenth century. In the north aisle is the tomb of Greek Macedonian nationalist Pavlos Melas, assassinated by Bulgarians at a nearby village in 1906, and commemorated by street-names across northern Greece; his widow, who survived to the age of 101 (she died in 1974), is interred with him. Lastly, the **Panayía Koumbelidhikí**, so named because of its unusual dome (*kübe* in Turkish), is currently undergoing much-needed repairs, but retains one startling and well-illuminated fresco: a portrayal – unique in Greece – of God the Father, in a ceiling mural of the *Holy Trinity*. The building was done in stages, with the apse completed in the tenth century and the narthex in the fifteenth. The dome was meticulously restored after being destroyed by Italian bombing in 1940.

If tracking down buildings seems too frustrating a pursuit, perhaps the most pleasant thing to do in Kastoriá is to follow the narrow paved track which runs all around the **lake shore** to the east of town; vehicles must circulate anticlockwise. Although the lake itself is visibly polluted, wildlife still abounds – frogs, tortoises and water snakes especially. Near the southeastern tip of the peninsula, 2500m from the cluster of mansions or 3500m from the *Hotel Kastoria*, stands the **Mavriótissa monastery**, flanked by peacocks and a fair-value restaurant that's popular with Greek tours. Two churches are all that remains of the monastery: a smaller fourteenth-century chapel, with fine frescoes of scenes from the life of Christ, abutting the larger, wood-roofed eleventh-century katholikón on whose outer wall looms a well-preserved *Tree of Jesse*, showing the genealogy of the Saviour.

Practicalities

Arriving at the **bus station**, you'll find yourself at the western edge of the peninsula. Coming by **car**, look out for the fee-parking scheme; we've indicated which hotels have car parks. Most of Kastoriá's **hotels**, especially those within easy walking distance of the bus station, are noisy and overpriced; they are also likely to be full pretty much year-round with people on fur-buying sprees, so try to phone ahead for reservations. Uninspiring choices closest to the bus station on Grámmou include the *Anessis* (☎0467/33 908; ③) at no. 10 and *Acropolis* (☎0467/83 737; ③)at no. 16, the latter having rooms with and without private facilities. The next notch up is occupied by the *Keletron* (☎0467/22 676; ③), 11-Noemvríou 52, with entrance on a side street and some rooms overlooking leafy Platía Van Fleet; the *Europa* (☎0467/23 826; fax 25 154; ⑤), Ayíou Athanasíou 12 is more comfortable but plagued by traffic noise. The fairly quiet *Kastoria* (☎0467/29 453; ④), Nikís 122, faces the lake at the far end of the northern waterfront, and offers fine views from its balconied front rooms, as well as free parking; room decor is tired though, and the hot water is unreliable. If you have the extra cash and/or a car, you're best off at the *Xenia Limnis/Xenia du Lac* (☎0467/22 565; fax 26 391; ⑤), peacefully set near the top of town by the museum, with private parking and comfortable wood-floored rooms.

The best venue for **restaurants** is Platía Omonías, where the *Omonoia* and the *Mantziaris* are both excellent for *mayireftá* and more or less identically priced, with tables on the square. Lakeside dining is pretty much restricted to either the restaurant at Mavriótissas (see opposite) or *Ta Balkania* at Orestíon 37 (the northwest quay), which has good grills. **Nightlife**, such as it is, takes place at a half-dozen *barákia* between *Ta Balkania* and Platía Van Fleet.

Around Kastoriá

If you have you own transport, you might make a trip 14km southwest to **OMOR-FÓKLISSIÁ**, an eerie village of mud-brick houses inherited post-1923 from Muslim peasants. It has a fourteenth-century Byzantine church with a lofty cupola, attached belfry and, inside, a huge, primitive carved-relief wooden **icon of Saint George** thought to date from the eleventh century.

SIÁTISTA, draped along a single ridge in a forbiddingly bare landscape 70km south of Kastoriá, is also a worthy destination. Located just above the point where the road splits for Kozáni or Kastoriá, it was an important fur centre, and boasts a handful of eighteenth-century mansions or *arkhondiká*, which you can visit. The eighteenth-century house of **Hatzimikhaïl Kanatsoúli** at Mitropóleos 1, near the police station, is still lived in but you can ring to be shown around. The first two floors are occupied; upstairs, a corner room has naive murals of mythological scenes (including Kronos's castration of Ouranos). The dilapidated **Nerantzópoulos mansion** (Mon–Sat 8.30am–3pm, Sun 9.30am–2.30pm) is on the upper square, by the *Ethniki Trapeza*. The warden here has the keys for several other houses, of which the largest and most elaborate is the **Manoúsi mansion**, dating from 1763, in a vale below the Kanatsoúli along with various other surviving *arkhondiká*. Ceiling medallions often sport a carved cluster of fruit or a melon with a slice missing where you'd expect a chandelier hook; there are more three-dimensional floral and fruit carvings up at the tops of the walls, which are adorned with stylized murals of pastoral and fictitious urban scenes. The church of **Áyia Paraskeví**, on the lowest platía, has soot-blackened seventeenth-century frescoes inside; until the scheduled cleaning happens, you're better off glancing at the exterior ones.

Almost everything you need in Siátista – **banks, OTE, post office** – are found along the single, long main street, including the impressive *Archontiko* **hotel** (☎0465/21 298, fax 22 835; ④), which has a reasonable restaurant and café on the ground floor; it often fills with Greek tours, so if you've your heart set on staying here, check for space in advance. Other options for **eating** out are limited; the *Psistaria Ouzerí O Platanos*, just below Áyia Paraskeví, has acceptable food but a rather boozy male environment – the hotel is more genteel. The easiest bus connections are with Kozáni, 28km distant.

The mountain village of **NYMFÉO**, 60km east of Kastoriá, the last 9km via an incredibly steep hairpin side road, is much publicized but functions as a "hill station" for Thessaloníki yuppies, and facilities are priced accordingly. The gruff villagers seem positively put out at the prospect of having to accommodate foreigners. The only reasonably priced lodging is the ugly, modern and non-en-suite **hotel** *Iy Neveska* (the old Slavic name for the place; ③); anything else is 12,000dr and up. Run with a degree of professionalism – and the sole source of decent, if pricey, **food** – is an inn at the outskirts, *Ta Linouryia* (☎0386/31 133), whose few beds are arranged in expensive octuples or quads. All in all, a shame, given that Nymféo straddles the E4 long-distance trail, and that horse-riding and winter sports are easily to hand.

KHALKIDHIKÍ AND EASTERN MACEDONIA

Khalkidhikí, easily reached by bus from Thessaloníki, is the clear highlight of eastern Macedonia. Its first two peninsulas, **Kassándhra** and **Sithonía,** shelter the north's main concentration of beaches; the third, **Áthos,** has the country's finest, though most secretive, monasteries. Moving east, there are a few more good beaches en route to **Kavála,** but little of interest inland, where a scattering of small market towns serve a population that – as in neighbouring Thrace – produces the main Greek tobacco crop.

Kassándhra, Sithonía and secular Áthos

The peninsula of **Khalkidhikí** begins at a perforated edge of shallow lakes east of Thessaloníki and extends into three prongs of land – Kassándhra, Sithonía, and Áthos – trailing like tentacles into the Aegean sea.

Mount Áthos, the easternmost peninsula, is in all ways separate, a "Holy Mountain" whose monastic population, semi-autonomous within the Greek state, excludes all women – even as visitors. For men who wish to experience Athonite life, a visit involves suitably Byzantine procedures which are detailed, with the monastic sights, in the section that follows. The most that women can do is to glimpse the buildings from offshore cruise kaïkia sailing from the two small resorts on the periphery of the peninsula – Ierissós and Ouranoúpoli – the "secular" part of Áthos covered in this section.

Kassándhra and **Sithonía,** by contrast, host some of the fastest-growing holiday resorts in Greece. Up until the late 1980s these were popular mainly with Greeks, but they're now in the process of a staggering development, with most European package-tour companies maintaining a presence. On Kassándhra especially, almost any reasonable beach is accompanied by a crop of villas or a hotel development, while huge billboards advertise campsite complexes miles in advance. Still larger signs at the entrance to each peninsula of Khalkidhikí reminds you that camping outside the authorized grounds is strictly prohibited, although you may have no other choice if you turn up in peak season without a reservation. One consolation is that most beaches here are equipped with free freshwater showers. The beaches themselves are of white granitic sand; less appealingly, stingless jellyfish drift about nearly everywhere.

Both Kassándhra and Sithonía are connected to Thessaloníki by a network of fast new roads which extend around their coastlines; buses run frequently to all the larger resorts. In spite of this, neither peninsula is that easy to travel around if you are dependent on **public transport.** You really have to pick a place and stay there, perhaps renting a **moped** for local excursions.

Kassándhra

Kassándhra, the nearest prong to Thessaloníki, is also by far the most developed. Unless you're very pushed for time and want a couple of days' escape from Thessaloníki, it's best to keep going to Sithonía, or, better still, the top end of Áthos. Apart from resorts, there is very little to Kassándhra, since its population took part in the independence uprising of 1821, and was defeated and massacred. As a result, there were only a few small fishing hamlets here until after 1923, when the peninsula was resettled by refugees from around the Sea of Marmara.

On the peninsula's west coast, the first resort, **NÉA MOUDHANIÁ**, is really a size-able town, complete with several cash dispensers and a post office, as well as being a minor hydrofoil port. Hydrofoils sail from here to Skiáthos, Skópelos and Alónissos, as well as Áyios Ioánnis on the Pílion peninsula (twice weekly from July to early Sept. There's a **campsite** on the sandy beach – the *Ouzouni Beach* (May–Sept; ☎0373/42 100) – and at least two hotels, of which the *Philippos*, inland opposite the school, is preferable to the *Thalia* (☎0373/23 106; ④). The best waterfront eating is at *Taverna Ouzeri Maistrali*, at the far left end of the quay as you face the sea.

The second resort, **NÉA POTÍDHEA**, at the neck of the peninsula, is a tiny place, overlooked by a medieval watchtower. It has a laid back feel, which attracts Greek families and a fairly young crowd. The new *Golden Beach* **apartments** (☎0373/41 657; ④) are friendly, while on the promenade are a number of good **tavernas** – look for the *Philippos* or the *Marina*.

Just before Néa Fókea, a turning to the right takes you to the western shore of the peninsula, where **SÁNI** has the *Blue Dream* campsite (☎0374/31 435; May–Sept); it's operated by the village and is more relaxed than most. The nearby *Sani Beach Phocea Club* (hotel, campsite and club) is more frenetic – and expensive (☎0374/31 221; ⑥). Continuing 10km south from Néa Fókea, the next east coast resort is **KALLITHÉA**, a large and busy place and a slightly better option if you want a straightforward holiday spot. There are a large number of **rooms** to let – not just package hotels – and you can rent bikes and mopeds on the main street, or windsurfers on the beach.

KHANIÓTIS, 17km further south, is an old-fashioned resort with a good long beach and numerous hotels and tavernas. If you want to stay, you'll have to arrive early in the day and shop around – the *Ermis/Hermes* (☎0374/51 245; ④) lacks charm but is good value.

Sithonía

Things improve considerably as you move east across the Khalkidhikí and away from the front line of tourism; the landscape also becomes increasingly green and hilly, cul-minating in the isolated and spectacular scenery of the Holy Mountain, looming across the gulf lapping Sithonía's east coast. As for the peninsula itself, **Sithonía** is more rugged but greener than Kassándhra, though once again there are few true villages, and those that do exist mostly date from the 1920s resettlement era. Pine forests cover many of the slopes, particularly in the south, giving way to olive groves on the coast. Small sandy inlets with relatively discreet pockets of campsites and tavernas make a welcome change from sprawling mega-resorts.

Metamórfosi

Suitably enough, **METAMÓRFOSI** ("Transfiguration"), at the western base of Sithonía, signals the transformation. Its beach is only adequate but there's good swim-ming to be had, and the village, while relentlessly modern, has an easy-going air. In addition to the friendly *Hotel Golden Beach* (☎0375/22 063; ③), with its cool courtyard and café on the village square, there are two **campsites**. The best site is *Mylos*, 3km east, on the beach side of the road; *Sithon* is 5km west (☎0375/22 414; May–Sept). In high season, both campsites and village can be a little crowded, but there are a fair number of **tavernas** clustered in and around the square.

Moving on to Sithonía proper, it's best to follow the loop road clockwise around the east coast, so that the peak of Áthos is always before you. **Bus services** are sparse, however: there are up to five buses daily around the west coast to Sárti, and up to three a day direct to Vourvouroú, but there's no KTEL connection between these two end-points. A complete circuit is only really possible with your own transport.

Órmos Panayía to Vourvouroú

ÓRMOS PANAYÍA, first of the east coast resorts, is nowadays well developed; ranks of villas dwarf the picturesque hamlet and tiny harbour, and the nearest decent beaches are 4km north en route to Pyrgadhíkia, below the inland village of **ÁYIOS NIKÓLAOS**. The only conceivable reason to stop at Órmos is to catch the excursion boats that sail around Áthos from here, but these are expensive and often reserved for tourists bused in from the big Khalkidhikí resorts.

VOURVOUROÚ, 8km down the coast, is not a typical resort, since it's essentially a vacation-villa project for Thessaloníki professors, established in the late 1950s on land expropriated from Vatopedhíou monastery on Áthos. There is a fair amount of **accommodation**; as well as a number of rooms, there's the seafront *Dhiaporos* hotel (☎0375/91 313; ⑥; half-board obligatory) with its cool rooftop restaurant, the plain but en-suite *Vourvourou* (☎0375/91 261; ③), and the new, rather sterile *Rema* just inland (☎0375/91 142, fax 91 071; ⑤) which has attractive off-season specials. The strange feel of the place is accentuated by those plot owners who haven't bothered to build villas (so far very scattered) and merely tent down, making it hard to tell which are the real campsites. Islets round the bay create a fine setting, but the beach, while sandy, is extremely narrow: Vourvouroú is really more of a yachters' haven. **Tavernas** are relatively inexpensive because they're banking on a return clientele (which includes lots of Germans); the *Itamos*, inland from the road, is the best; the *Gorgona/Pullman*, while the nicest positioned, gets coach tours as the alias implies. There are two campsites: *Dionysos* (☎0375/91 214; April–Oct), which is simple but adequate and partly faces the beach, and *Glaros* (no phone; mostly caravans), which faces Karýdhi beach at the eastern end of things.

Some of Sithonía's best **beaches** line the thirty kilometres of road between Vourvouroú and Sárti: five signposted sandy coves, each with a **campsite** and little else. The names of the bays reflect the fact that most of the land here belonged to various Athonite monasteries until confiscated by the Greek government to resettle Anatolian refugees.

Sárti

Concrete-grid **SÁRTI** itself, rising to a ridge on the north, is set slightly back from its broad, two-kilometre-long beach, with only the scale of the bay protecting it from being utterly overrun in summer by Germans (plus growing numbers of Hungarians and Czechs). There are hundreds of **rooms** (though often not enough to go around), the choicest being in the southerly part of town. At the end of the beach is another cluster of development, including the *Sarti Beach* (☎0375/94 250; ④) and the shady *Camping Sarti Beach* (☎0375/94 629; May–Sept), the campsite laid out between the road and the hotel grounds. *Iy Neraida* and *O Stavros* are two of the less expensive **tavernas** lining the landscaped shore esplanade. The perennial (if pricey) favourite amongst Greeks, *Ta Vrakhakia* (no sign), stands at the far north end of the beach, overlooking the "little rocks" of the name, and dishing up rich *mayireftá*. Inland you'll find a short-hours **bank** and a rather tattily commercialized square ringed by fast-food joints – plus the big local agency, Taousanis Tours, which does **car rental**.

Paralía Sykiás and Kalamítsi

PARALÍA SYKIÁS, 8km further along, has a beach somewhat inferior to Sárti's and thus less developed so far. What there is, however, is not very appealing: just a few tavernas well back from the sea along 2km of coastal highway, with much of the intervening space fenced off for some appalling-looking incipient development. At the north end of the beach is a **campsite**, *Melissi* (☎0375/41 631) sheltering in some trees. The best strategy here is to follow the side road at the south end of the beach towards the more scenic coves at Linaráki, where *Pende Vímata stin Ammo* is the most famous of three **tavernas** here, or beyond to Pigadháki. The "town" for these parts, with a **post office** and shops, is SYKIÁ, 2km inland, a surprisingly large place hemmed in by rocky hills and thus invisible to pirates. Far better is KALAMÍTSI, another 8km south of Paralía Sykiás, consisting of a beautiful double bay sheltered by islets, with relatively little commercialization to date. At the north bay of Pórto, there's a basic **campsite** (✆0375/41 346) containing the North Aegean scuba centre (✆0375/41 148), though staff are none too friendly and all literature and pricing is in German. More worthwhile, perhaps, is the **taverna** *O Yiorgakis* next door, with varied, reasonably priced food, and good **rooms** behind (✆0375/41 338; ③). The sandy south bay is rather monopolized by the fancier *Camping Kalamitsi* (✆0375/41 411; May–Sept).

Pórto Koufó, Toróni, Tristeníka

Sithonía's forest cover diminishes after Sárti, and as you round the tip of the peninsula it vanishes completely, with bare hills spilling into the sea to create a handful of deep bays. PÓRTO KOUFÓ, just northwest of the cape, is the most dramatic of these, almost completely cut off from the open sea by high cliffs. The name Koufó ("deaf" in Greek) is said to come from one's inability to hear the sea within the confines of this inlet, which served as an Axis submarine shelter during World War II. There's a decent beach near where the road drops down from the east, as well as a small, rather stark **hotel** and a few **rooms**. The north end of the inlet, a kilometre from the beach area, is a yacht-and-fishing harbour with a string of five somewhat expensive seafood **tavernas**; *O Pefkos* is the least expensive though not very inspired, alternative here.

TORÓNI, 3km north, is an exposed, two-kilometre-long crescent of sand with wooded hills behind. It's probably your best bet as a base if you just want to flop on a beach for a few days; for more stimulation there is a minimal **archeological site** (currently off-limits) on the southern cape, sporting the remains of an ancient fortress and early Christian basilica. The half-dozen or so combination **taverna-studio rooms** scattered the length of the beach are all pre- or suffixed *"Haus"*, for example *Haus Sakis* (✆0375/51 261; ②), with comfortable rooms upstairs and good food plus German beer on tap at street level.

Just 2km north is the turning for TRISTENÍKA (ARETÉS), now much as Toróni must have been in the 1980s: another outstanding two-kilometre beach, reached by a sand-and-dirt track past the first hopeful taverna and rooms outfit, with a tiny hamlet 1km in from the main road. At the south end of the sand, served by its own access drive, is *Camping Isa* (✆0375/51 235; May–Sept).

Pórto Carrás to Parthenónas

Beyond Tristeníka, you edge back into high-tech resort territory, epitomized by Greece's largest planned holiday complex, PÓRTO CARRÁS. Established by the Carras wine and shipping dynasty, it features an in-house shopping centre, golf course and vineyards, while from the ten-kilometre private beach in front, you can indulge in every imaginable watersport. Since the death of founder John Carras, the complex has been sold off and split into three luxury hotels: *Meliton*, *Village Inn* and *Casino Magic-Sithonia Beach*.

The nearest proper town to all this, with **banks** and a **post office**, is NÉOS MAR-MARÁS, a once-attractive fishing port with a small beach. Nowadays, it's popular with Greeks who stay at family hotels like the *Platanos* (✆0375/71 234; ④). Failing that, the last **campsite** in Sithonía is 3km to the north – *Castello* (✆0375/71 095; May–Sept) – the beach is sandy and there's tennis, volleyball and a restaurant.

If you're curious as to what Sithonía looked like before all this happened, a road leads 5km from Néos Marmarás to PARTHENÓNAS, the lone "traditional" village on

Sithonía, crouched at the base of 808m Mount Ítamos. The place was abandoned in the 1960s in favour of the shore, and never provided with mains electricity; its dilapidated but appealing houses are now slowly being sold off to wealthy Greeks and Germans. *Paul's Taverna* is a lively venue here, with Greek dancing sessions.

East to secular Áthos

From Órmos Panayía a partly paved road winds around the coast to Ierissós at the head of the Áthos peninsula. No buses cover this stretch however, and if you're dependent on public transport you'll have to backtrack as far as Yerakiní and then inland to Khalkidhikí's capital **POLÍYIROS**, a drab market town with an unexciting archeological museum. Here, or from Áyios Pródhromos 20km to the north, you can pick up buses heading for Áthos via **ARNÉA**, which has some fine old quarters and a reputation for (somewhat touristy) carpets and other colourful handwoven goods. It could be worth a brief stopover, as the local authorities have restored several old houses as high-quality accommodation, for example the *Arkhondiko Miteiou* (④), above a carpet showroom. Alternative **accommodation** is at **PALEOKHÓRI**, 5km further east, towards Stáyira, where the *Park Hotel Tasos* (☎0372/41 722; ④) on the outskirts, is a delightful place with well-furnished rooms and a country-style restaurant.

After Stáyira, the road continues on to Ierissós, and the only place you'd think to stop is **PYRGADHÍKIA**, a ravine-set fishing village now taken over by German holiday-makers during July, but otherwise peaceful. The lone hotel *Elena* is not well placed, but you still might lunch here at one of four waterfront tavernas; there's little beach to speak of.

Ierissós and Néa Ródha
IERISSÓS, with a good, long beach and a vast, promontory-flanked gulf, is the most Greek-patronized of the "secular Athos" resorts, although the sizeable town itself, built well back from the shore and with room to expand, is a sterile concrete grid dating from after a devastating 1932 earthquake. The only hint of pre-tourist life is the vast caique-building dry dock to the south.

There are numerous **rooms**, an inexpensive **hotel** – the quiet *Marcos* (☎0377/22 518; ③) overlooking its own garden at the south end of town – and two basic **camp-sites**: one at the north edge of town, the other, *Delfini* (☎0377/22 208), on the way to Néa Ródha. The beach is surprisingly uncluttered – if rather dull – with just a handful of shore **tavernas** and **bars** behind the landscaped promenade. Rounding off the list of amenities, there's a **post office**, two **banks** and a summer **cinema** by the campsite. Ierissós is also the main port for the northeast shore of Áthos; mid-summer sailings take place daily in the morning, with only three sailings weekly during the rest of the year, as the weather – which can turn very stormy on this side – allows. The road beyond Ierissós passes through the resort of **NÉA RÓDHA**, with a small beach and no more claim to architectural distinction than its neighbour, but worth knowing about as an alternative point for picking up the morning boat from Ierissós. Just beyond here your route veers inland to follow a boggy depression that's the remaining stretch of **Xerxes's canal**, cut by the Persian invader in 480 BC to spare his fleet the shipwreck at the tip of Áthos that had befallen the previous expedition eleven years before.

Ammoulianí
You emerge on the southwest facing coast at **Tripití**, not a settlement but merely the western exit of Xerxes' canal and now also the ferry jetty for the small island of **AMMOULIANÍ** (up to 7 daily crossings in summer, cars carried). This is Macedonia's only inhabited Aegean island apart from Thássos, and after decades of eking out an

existence as a refugee fishing community from the Sea of Marmara, has in recent years had to adjust to a new role as a popular target for Thessalonian weekenders and German-speaking holidaymakers from Ouranópoli (see below). Like anywhere else in Khalkidhikí, it's impossibly oversubscribed in July and August, but in spring or autumn this scrub-and-olive covered islet can make an idyllic hideaway.

The only town, where the ferries dock, is another unprepossessing grid of concrete slung over a ridge; it is, however, chock-a-block with **rooms**, many self-catering, and two **hotels** plainly visible on the left as you sail in. The better of these is the *Sunrise* (☎0377/51 273, fax 51 174; ④), with its own swimming jetty, reliable hot water and buffet breakfast included. Of the village's half-dozen **tavernas**, *Alekos* (on the front), *Iy Klimataria* (on the road out) and *Yannis* (facing the rear Limanáki port) get high marks for hygiene and good value. There are a few shops for self-caterers, but no bank or post office. As for **nightlife**, there are two bars (one, *Barka*, does breakfasts) and two discos a few hundred metres out of town on the main island road.

This leads southwest, after two paved kilometres, to **Alykés**, the islet's most famous beach, with a namesake saltmarsh inland, a taverna and separate café behind the sand, and a rather parched campsite. Ammouliani's best beaches however, lie in the far southeast, facing the straits with the Áthos peninsula. To reach them, bear left off the pavement 1500m out of town where the *Agionissi* luxury resort is signposted, onto a smooth, sand-dirt track. Some 2km along this, you pass the tiny chapel and cistern of **Áyios Yeóryios** overlooking the excellent eponymous beach. Just beyond stands the popular lunchtime-only *Sarandis*, but it's pricier than the simple fare warrants, and you might prefer to continue to the far end of the beach and the *Gripos Ouzeri*, which is better value. This also offers a half-dozen upstairs rooms (☎0377/51 049; ②), with copper antiques, beam ceilings, terracotta floor tiles and large balconies. The affable owner keeps pheasants and other exotic fowl, whose squawkings vie with those of the gulls nesting on the rock-islets of the Dhrénia archipelago just offshore. You can continue a final 500m to even more idyllically set **Megáli Ámmos** beach, where there's a café with seats in the sand, a seasonal taverna, and a pleasant, olive-shaded campsite. Other, less accessible beaches beckon in the northwest of the island, served in season by excursion boats from the town; a popular map-postcard on sale will give necessary hints if you'd like to reach them on foot or (better) rented bicycle.

Ouranópoli

Fifteen kilometres beyond Ierissós, **OURANÓPOLI** is the last community before the restricted monastic domains, with a centre that's downright tatty, showing the effects of too much Greek-weekender and German-package tourism. Local beaches, stretching intermittently for several kilometres to the north, are sandy enough but narrow and cramped – certainly not the best Khalkidhikí has to offer. If you're compelled to stay the night while waiting for passage to Áthos, the best temporary escape would be either to take a cruise, or to rent a **motor boat**, to the mini-archipelago of **Dhrénia** just opposite, with almost tropical sandy bays and tavernas on the larger islets.

The only other conceivable diversion in Ouranópoli is the Byzantine **Phosphóri tower** by the bus stop, visible from some distance. Sydney Loch – author of *Athos: the Holy Mountain*, published posthumously in 1957 and still an excellent guide to the monasteries – lived here for nearly thirty years. Loch and his wife Joyce, who died in the tower in 1982, were a Scots-Australian missionary couple who devoted most of their lives to the refugees of Khalkidhikí. The cottage industry of carpet-weaving, which they taught the local villagers, is increasingly less in evidence.

Three **ferries** – the Áyios Nikolaos, the Poseidon and the Axion Esti – take turns calling along the southwest shore of Áthos, and are probably the main reason to come here. Throughout the year there's just one daily departure, at around 9.45am; tickets should be purchased before boarding from the Athoniki agency, near the medieval tower. One of these, or perhaps another craft, also offer half-day **cruises** in season (10.30am; 3000dr) which skim along the Athonite coast, keeping females 500m off-shore, as required by the monastic authorities.

If you need to stay, there are a fair number of **rooms** and **hotels**, most en-suite. Less expensive places include the *Athos* (☎0377/71 368; ③) on the main thoroughfare, and the seafront *Akrogiali* (☎0377/71 201, fax 71 395;③) around the corner. The latter shares management with the *Makedonia* (☎0377/71 085, fax 71 395; ③), slightly uphill and inland, a pleasantly quiet spot with a small British package presence. About 300m out of town towards the monastic border, the *Avra* (☎0377/71 189, fax 71 095; ④) isn't wildly friendly but the seaview rooms are clean and spacious. If money is no object, the closest high-grade hotel to town that isn't utterly dominated by packages is the *Xenia* (☎0377/71 412, fax 71 362; ⑥) on the beach, which does have substantial off-peak discounts. A **campsite**, better appointed than those in Ierissós, is 2km north of the village, amidst a crop of luxury hotel complexes that have sprung up where there's more space to spread out. The half-dozen most obvious waterfront **tavernas** all have identical rip-off menus, though you're unlikely to care much about value for money after several lean days on Áthos. On the south waterfront, respectively just before and after the town limits sign, are two marginally more appealing alternatives: *Mantho*, a traditional-format *estiatório* with plenty of *mayireftá*, and the fancier *Athos*, next to the hotel *Avra*, with a huge menu featuring grilled vegetables, soups and (unusually) sweets. Ouranópoli has a **post office** and an **OTE** booth, but no bank.

Mount Áthos: the monks' republic

The population of the **Mount Áthos** peninsula has been exclusively male since the *ávaton* edict, banning females permanent or transient, was promulgated by the Byzantine emperor Constantine Monomachos in 1060. Known in Greek as the **Áyion Óros** (Holy Mountain), it is an administratively autonomous province of the country – a "monks' republic" – on whose slopes are gathered twenty monasteries, plus a number of smaller dependencies and hermitages.

Most of the **monasteries** were founded in the tenth and eleventh centuries. Today, all survive in a state of comparative decline but they remain unsurpassed in Greece in their general and architectural interest, and for the art treasures they contain. If you are male, over 21 years old, and have a genuine interest in monasticism or Greek Orthodoxy, or simply in Byzantine and medieval architecture, a visit is strongly recommended. It takes a couple of hours to arrange, either in Thessaloníki or Athens (see p.386 for details), but the rewards more than justify your efforts. In addition to the religious and architectural aspects of Áthos, it should be added that the peninsula, despite some horrific fires and heavy logging in recent years, is still one of the most beautiful parts of Greece. With only the occasional service vehicle, two buses and sporadic coastal boats, a visit necessarily involves walking between settlements – preferably on paths through dense woods, up the main peak, or above what is perhaps the Mediterranean's last undeveloped coastline. For many visitors, this – as much as the experience of monasticism – is the highlight of time spent on the Holy Mountain.

The Theocratic Republic: some history

By a Greek legislative decree of 1926, Áthos has the status of **Theocratic Republic**. It is governed from the small town and capital of Karyés by the *Ayía Epistasía* (Holy Superintendency), a council of twenty representatives elected for one-year terms by each of the monasteries. At the same time Áthos remains a part of Greece: all foreign monks must adopt Greek citizenship, and the Greek civil government is represented by an appointed governor and a small police force.

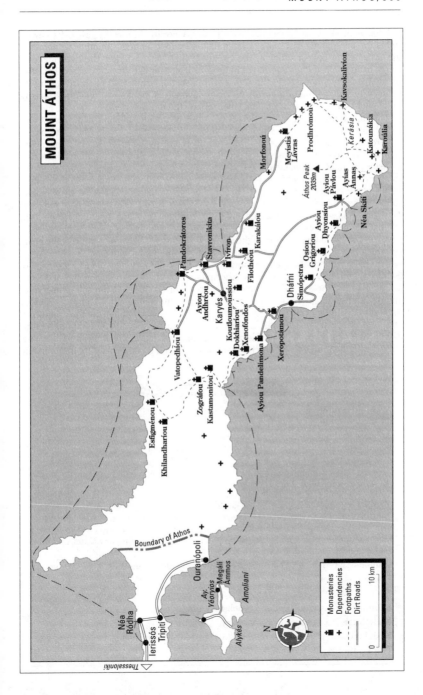

Each monastery has a distinct place in the **Athonite hierarchy**: Meyístis Lávras holds the prestigious first place, Kastamonítou ranks twentieth. All other settlements are attached to one or other of the twenty "ruling" monasteries; the dependencies range from a *skíti* (either a group of houses, or a cloister-like structure scarcely distinguishable from a monastery) through a *kellí* (a sort of farmhouse) to an *isikhastírio* (a solitary hermitage, often a cave). As many laymen as monks live on Áthos, mostly employed as agricultural or manual labourers by the monasteries.

The **development of monasticism** on Áthos is a matter of some controversy, and foundation legends abound. The most popular asserts that the Virgin Mary was blown ashore here on her way to Cyprus, and while overcome by the great beauty of the mountain, a mysterious voice consecrated the place in her name. Another tradition relates that Constantine the Great founded the first monastery in the fourth century, but this is certainly far too early. The earliest historical reference to Athonite monks is to their attendance at a council of the Empress Theodora in 843; probably there were some monks here by the end of the seventh century. Áthos was particularly appropriate for early Christian monasticism, its deserted and isolated slopes providing a natural refuge from the outside world – especially from the Arab conquests in the east, and the iconoclastic phase of the Byzantine Empire (eighth to ninth centuries). Moreover its awesome beauty, which had so impressed the Virgin, facilitated communion with God.

The most famous of the **early monks** were Peter the Athonite and St Euthimios of Salonica, both of whom lived in cave-hermitages on the slopes during the mid-ninth century. In 885 an edict of Emperor Basil I recognized Áthos as the sole preserve of monks, and gradually hermits came together to form communities known as *cenobia* (literally "common living"). The year 963 is the traditional date for the **foundation** of the first monastery, Meyístis Lávras, by Athanasios the Athonite; the Emperor Nikiforos Fokas provided considerable financial assistance. Over the next two centuries, with the protection of other Byzantine emperors, foundations were frequent, the

---

ATHONITE TERMS

Arkhondáris Guestmaster of a monastery or *skíti*, responsible for all visitors; similarly, *arkhondaríki*, the guest quarters themselves.

Arsanás Harbour annexe of each monastery or *skíti*, where the kaïkia anchor; they can be a considerable distance from the institution in question.

Cenobitic/Idiorrythmic Historically, this is (increasingly, was) the major distinction between religious foundations on the mountain. At cenobitic establishments the monks eat all meals together, hold all property in common and have rigidly scheduled days. Those remaining foundations that are idiorrhythmic are more individualistic: the monks eat in their own quarters and study or worship when and as they wish. Since the mid-1980s, all of the remaining idiorrhythmic monasteries reverted to cenobitic status, with Pandokrátoros the last hold-out until 1992. Currently monks wishing to follow a more independent path must take up residence in an idiorrhythmic *skíti* (most of them are) or a *kellí*.

Dhíkeos The "righteous one" – head of an idiorrhythmic foundation.

Dhókimos A novice monk.

Fiáli The covered font for holy water in some monastery courtyards; often very ornate.

Igoúmenos Abbot, the head of a cenobitic house.

Katholikón Main church of a monastery.

Kyriakón Central chapel of a *skíti*, where the residents worship together once weekly.

Trapezaría Refectory, or dining room.

monasteries reaching forty in number (reputedly with a thousand monks in each), alongside many smaller communities.

Troubles for Áthos began at the end of the eleventh century. The monasteries suffered sporadically from **pirate raids** and from the settlement of three hundred Vlach shepherd families on the mountain. After a reputedly scandalous time between the monks and the shepherdesses, the Vlachs were ejected and a new imperial *chryssobul* (edict) was issued, confirming that no female mammal, human or animal, be allowed to set foot on Áthos. This edict, called the *ávaton*, remains in force today, exempting hens to lay eggs and cats to control rodents.

During the twelfth century, the monasteries gained an international – or at least, a **pan-Orthodox** – aspect, as Romanian, Russian and Serbian monks flocked to the mountain in retreat from the turbulence of the age. Áthos itself was subjected to Frankish raids during the Latin occupation of Constantinople (1204–61) and, even after this, faced great pressure from the Unionists of Latin Salonica to unite with western Catholics; in the courtyard of Zográfou there is still a monument to the monks who were martyred at this time while attempting to preserve the independence of Orthodox Christianity. In the early fourteenth century the monasteries suffered two disastrous years of pillage by Catalan mercenaries but they recovered, primarily through Serbian benefactors, to enjoy a period of great prosperity in the fifteenth and sixteenth centuries.

After the fall of the Byzantine Empire to the Ottomans, the fathers wisely declined to resist, maintaining good relations with the early sultans, one of whom paid a state visit. The later Middle Ages brought **economic problems**, with heavy taxes and confiscations, and as a defence many of the monasteries dissolved their common holdings and reverted to an **idiorrhythmic system**, a self-regulating form of monasticism where monks live and worship in a loosely bound community but work and eat individually. However, Athos remained the spiritual centre of Orthodoxy, and during the seventeenth and eighteenth centuries even built and maintained its own schools.

The mountain's real decline came after the **War of Independence**, in which many of the monks fought alongside the Greek *klephts*. In Macedonia the insurrectionists were easily subdued, the region remaining under Ottoman control, and the monks paid the price. A permanent Turkish garrison was established on the mountain and monastery populations fell sharply as, in the wake of independence for southern Greece, monasticism became less of a focus for Greek Orthodox Christianity.

At the end of the last century and the beginning of this one **foreign Orthodox monks**, particularly Russian ones, tried to step in and fill the vacuum. But the Athonite fathers have always resisted any move that might dilute the Greek character of the Holy Mount, even – until recently – at the expense of its material prosperity. During the early 1960s, numbers were at their lowest ever, barely a thousand, compared with 20,000 in Áthos's heyday. Today, however, the monastic population has climbed to about 1700, its average age has dropped significantly, and the number of well-educated monks increased markedly.

This revival is due partly to the increasing appeal of the contemplative life in a blatantly materialistic age, but more importantly to a wave of rather militant sectarian sentiment, which has swept both the Holy Mountain and world Orthodoxy at large. Active recruitment and **evangelizing** has produced a large crop of novices from every continent, particularly visible in such monasteries as Simópetra, Filothéou and Vatopedhíou. Some less picturesque manifestations of worldliness have appeared at the monasteries: "pilgrims" tote mobile phones (card phones are available for the rest of us), many of the monasteries have fax machines, and much of the mountain resembles a building site, with massive restoration or new building underway, often with little regard for traditional architecture. Some of the monks (and not a few foreigners) feel that this modernization has got out of hand, and there is already something of a backlash, one effect of which will hopefully be to preserve what remains of Athos' trail system from the road-builders.

Critics assert that the zealots have transformed religious life on Áthos with little tact, compelling many supposedly lax idiorrhythmic houses to become cenobitic as the price of their revitalization. In an echo of the conflicts earlier this century, there has also allegedly been interference with the efforts of the non-Greek foundations to recruit brothers and receive pilgrims from the home country, and in general a confusion of the aims of Orthodoxy and Hellenism. There have been consistent complaints that Orthodox pilgrims from Slavic countries are routinely subject to petty harassment from the Greek authorities, and that clerics and novices from Serbia, Russia, Bulgaria and so on must be approved for entry by the Ecumenical Patriarchate in Istanbul, unlike Greek priests.

If these tensions appear unseemly in a commonwealth devoted to spiritual perfection, it's worth remembering that doctrinal strife has always been part of Athonite history; that most of the monks still are Greek; and that donning the habit doesn't quell their inborn love of politicking. Also, in a perverse way, the ongoing controversies demonstrate a renewed vitality, inasmuch as Mount Áthos, and who controls it, are seen once again as having some global importance.

Permits and entry

Until a few decades ago foreigners could visit Áthos quite easily, but during the early 1970s the number of tourists grew so great that the monasteries could no longer cope. Since then a **permit system** has been instituted, and only Greeks – and to a lesser extent foreign Greek Orthodox, who automatically rank as religious pilgrims – are exempt from it. There have, incidentally, been recent mutterings in the foreign press that Áthos, as a sub-province of Greece (which is within the EU), must cease controlling its own borders, even to the extent of admitting women, but the mountain and its foreign sympathizers promise to fight any such changes, and the permit system is likely to remain in place for some years yet.

The first step in acquiring a permit to visit and stay on Áthos is to obtain a **letter of recommendation** from your embassy or consulate in Athens or Thessaloníki; see those respective cities' "Listings" for addresses. The letter should be purely a formality; the US consulate issues it free, UK ones make a charge (currently £15) – before charging you they suggest you contact the relevant Greek ministries first to see if space is available. If you're non-Orthodox, it's best to have yourself described in the text as a university-level scholar or graduate in art, religion or architecture – or as a "man of letters", which description covers just about any published (or hopeful) writer.

Take the consular letter either to the **Ministry of Foreign Affairs in Athens** (Akadhimías 3, 5th floor; Mon, Wed & Fri 11am–1pm) or to the **Ministry of Macedonia and Thrace in Thessaloníki** (Platía Dhikitiríou, Room 222; Mon–Fri 11am–1.45pm). In exchange for the letter you will be issued a permit valid for four days' residence on Áthos, which must be used "within a reasonable amount of time" and which will have a date specified for the beginning of the visit. This may not be the date of your choice in high summer, when it's all but mandatory to apply for permission at least two months in advance. The Athens ministry described above is allotted four slots for foreigners of all nationalities on each day of the year, while the Thessaloníki ministry has ten at its disposal, for a total of fourteen new arrivals on Áthos per day. Therefore if your day, or week, of choice is full up in Athens, there is some chance that there may be space in Thessaloníki, though this can't be relied on.

To get to Áthos, take a Khalkidhikí KTEL bus from its terminal at Karakássi 68 to Ouranópoli or Ierissós (see "East to secular Áthos", p.380). From Ouranópoli just one **boat** daily throughout the year sails at 9.45am as far as **Dháfni**, the main port on the southwestern coast of Áthos, where there's a connecting service onward to the *skíti* of Ayías Ánnas. If you're setting out on the day your permit starts, you'll have to take the earliest (6am) KTEL departure to connect with the boat. At Ierissós, the boat leaves at

8.30am (1 daily July–12 Sept; Mon, Thurs, Sat otherwise), earlier in the morning than the first bus will pass through, entailing an overnight stop here – and a chance to see if bad weather will force a cancellation. This service along the northeast shore always goes as far as the monastery of **Ivíron**, usually up to Meyístis Lávras, and turns around more or less immediately. Ouranópoli–Dháfni takes about ninety minutes; Ierissós–Ivíron more than two hours.

In Ouranoúpolis, you must call at the **Grafío Proskyníton** (Pilgrims' Bureau, daily 8.10am–2pm), behind the Jet Oil filling station. Here you will exchange your ministry permit for a document called the **dhiamonitírion** (7000dr), which entitles you to stay at any of the main monasteries. Armed with this, you may get off the boat at the *arsanás* (harbour annexe) of any of the southwest coastal monasteries; despite what you may read elsewhere, it is no longer necessary to waste valuable time obtaining the *dhiamonitírion* in Karyés. Starting from Ierissós or Néa Rodha, passengers will be granted this permit from a police post at the *arsanás* of Khilandharíou, the first monastery on the northeast coast; they are then free to disembark or continue with the boat to a dock of another monastery of their choice.

Several of the monasteries, and groups of five or more turning up anywhere on Áthos, require **advance reservations** by phone or fax throughout the year. Monasteries where you have to book are identified in the text, and phone numbers given for all of them. Also, until at least 1999, Ivíron and Ayíou Pandelímona monasteries are unable to offer hospitality owing to renovation works in their guest quarters.

Many visitors wish to arrange for an **extension** of the basic four-day period. This can theoretically be done at the *Ayía Epistasía* (Holy Superintendancy) in Karyés, though you had better have a good reason, for example an invitation from a specific monastery; up to another week may be granted, and your chances are much better out of season. In the past – though this is no guarantee of future practice – nobody was terribly bothered if you stayed five days or even a week, except in summer when monastic accommodation gets quite crowded. It used to be rare that guestmasters asked to see your *dhiamonitírion*, much less scrutinize it carefully, and the four-day limit was originally enforced to discourage gawkers and others with frivolous motives for visiting. If you strike the monks as behaving presumptuously or inappropriately, no amount of time remaining on your permit will persuade them to host you. As signs on walls repeatedly remind you, "Hospitality is not obligatory".

The way of life

With *dhiamonitírion* in hand, you will be admitted to stay and eat in the main monasteries – and certain *skítes* – free of charge. If you offer money it will be refused, though Orthodox pilgrims are encouraged to buy candles, incense, icon reproductions and the like at those *skítes* which specialize in their production, or at monastery tourist shops supplied by them. **Accommodation** is usually in dormitories, and fairly spartan, but you're always given sheets and blankets; you don't need to lug a sleeping bag around. Áthos grows much of its own **food**, and the monastic diet is based on tomatoes, beans, cheese and pasta, with occasional treats like *khalvás* and fruit added. The heartiest meal of the week is after Sunday morning service and often consists of fish served with wine. Normally only two meals a day are served, the first at mid-morning, the latter about an hour and a half to two hours before sunset. You will need to be partly self-sufficient in provisions, both for the times when you fail to coincide with meals and for the long walks between monasteries. (If you arrive after the evening meal you will generally be served leftovers set aside for latecomers.) There are a few shops in Karyés, but for better selection and to save valuable time you should stock up before coming to Áthos.

If you're planning to **walk** between monasteries, you should get hold of one of two **maps**: the first simply entitled "Athos", produced in Austria at a scale of 1:50,000 by Reinhold Zwerger and Klaus Schöpfleuthner (Wohlmutstr 8, A 1020 Wien), and unreliably available in Ouranópoli; the other a simple sketch map of all the roads and trails on the mountain, by Theodhoros Tsiropoulos of Thessaloníki (☎031/430 196). The *Korfes* magazine map is now obsolete and contains potentially dangerous errors, but it's still more useful than any of the touristy maps sold in Ouranópoli. Even with these maps, you'll need to be pointed to the start of trails at each monastery, and confirm walking times and path conditions. New roads are constantly being built, and trails accordingly abandoned; they become overgrown within two years if not used.

If need be, you can supplement walking with the regular **kaïki services** that ply between the main establishments on each coast. The return time out of Ayías Ánnas to Dháfni is about 8am in summer, with onward connections towards the "border" just after noon. On the other side, the single craft leaves Meyístis Lávras at about 2pm, bound for Ierissós. On alternate days in summer there is also a useful kaïki linking Meyístis Lávras and Ayías Ánnas, stopping at the *skíti* of Kavsokalivíon on its way around the south tip of the peninsula. There is also a pair of fairly decrepit **buses** which ply between Dháfni and Ivíron via Karyés, scheduled (in theory) to coincide with the arrival times of the larger ferries.

However you move around, you must reach your destination **before dark**, since all monasteries and many *skítes* lock their front gates at sunset – leaving you outside with the wild boars and (it is claimed) a handful of wolves. Upon arrival you should ask for the *arkhondáris* (guestmaster), who will proffer the traditional welcome of a *tsípouro* (distilled spirits) and *loukoúmi* (Turkish delight) before showing you to your bed. These days guestmasters tend to speak at least some English, a reflection of the increasing numbers of Cypriot, Australian or educated Greek novices on Áthos.

You will find the monastic **daily schedule** somewhat disorienting, and adapted according to the seasonal time of sunrise and sunset. On the northeast side of the peninsula 12 o'clock is reckoned from the hour of sunrise, whereas on the opposite side clocktowers may show both hands up at sunset. Yet Vatopedhíou keeps "worldly" time, as do most monks' wristwatches. However the Julian calendar, thirteen days behind the outside world, is universally observed, and will be the date appearing on your *dhiamonitírion*. More and more monasteries are getting electric power – and all now have phones, sometimes faxes as well – but this has affected the round of life very little; both you and the monks will go to bed early, shortly after sunset. Sometimes in the small hours your hosts will awake for solitary meditation and study, followed by *órthros* or matins. Around sunrise there is another quiet period, just before the *akolouthía* or main liturgy. Next comes the morning meal, anywhere from 9.30am to 11.30am depending on the time of year. The afternoon is devoted to manual labour until the *esperinós* or vespers, actually almost three hours before sunset in summer (much less in winter). This is followed immediately by the evening meal and the short *apódhipno* or compline service.

A few words about **attitudes** and **behaviour** towards your hosts (and vice versa) are in order, as many misunderstandings arise from mutual perceptions of disrespect, real or imagined. For your part, you should be fully clad at all times, even when going from dormitory to bathroom; this in effect means no shorts, no hats inside monasteries, and sleeves that come down to the middle of the biceps. If you swim, do so where nobody can see you, and don't do it naked. Smoking in most foundations is forbidden, though a few allow you to indulge out on the balconies. It would be criminal to do so on the trail, given the chronic fire danger; you might just want to give it up as a penance for the duration of your stay. Singing, whistling and raised voices are taboo; so is standing with your hands behind your back or crossing your legs when seated, both considered overbearing stances. If you want to photograph monks you should always ask permission, though photography is forbidden altogether in several monasteries, and video cameras are completely banned from the mountain. It's best not to go poking your nose into corners of the buildings where you're not specifically invited, even if they seem open to the public.

Monasteries, and their tenants, tend to vary a good deal in their handling of visitors, and their reputations, deserved or otherwise, tend to precede them as a favourite subject of trail gossip among foreigners. You will find that as a non-Orthodox you may be politely ignored, or worse, with signs at some institutions specifically forbidding you from attending services or sharing meals with the monks. Other monasteries are by contrast very engaging, putting themselves at the disposal of visitors of whatever creed. It is not uncommon to be treated with extreme bigotry and disarming gentility at the same place within the space of ten minutes, making it very difficult to draw conclusions about Áthos. If you are non-Christian as well as non-Orthodox, and seem to understand enough Greek to get the message, you'll probably be told at some point during your visit that you'll burn in Hell unless you convert to the True Faith forthwith. While this may seem offensive, considering your probable motivation for being here, it pays to remember that the monks are expecting religious pilgrims, not tourists, and that their role is to be committed, not tolerant. On average, expect those monks with some level of education or a smattering of foreign languages to be benignly interested in you; a very soft-sell in the form of a reading library of pamphlets and books will be left at your disposal. Incidentally, idiorrhythmic *skítes* (see below) and *kelliá* are not bound by the monastic rule of hospitality, and you really need to know someone at one of these places to be asked to stay the night.

The monasteries

Obviously you can't hope to visit all twenty monasteries during a short stay, though if you're able to extend the basic four-day period for a few days you can fairly easily see the peninsula's most prominent foundations. The dirt road linking the southwestern port of Dháfni with the northeastern coastal monastery of Ivíron by way of Karyés, the capital, not only cuts the peninsula roughly in two but also separates the monasteries into equal southeastern and northwestern groups; the division is not so arbitrary as it seems, since the remaining path system seems to reflect it and the feel of the two halves is very different.

The southeastern group

IVÍRON
The vast **IVÍRON** monastery (☎0377/23 248; no overnighting at present) is not a bad introduction to Áthos, and is well poised for walks or rides in various directions. Although founded late in the tenth century by Iberian (Georgian) monks, the last Georgian died in the 1950s and today it is a cenobitic house of 35 Greek monks, some of whom moved here from nearby Stavronikíta. The focus of pilgrimage is the miraculous **icon** of the Portaítissa, the Virgin Guarding the Gate, housed in a special chapel to the left of the entrance. It is believed that if this protecting image ever leaves Áthos, then great misfortune will befall the monks. The **katholikón** is among the largest on the mountain, with an elaborate mosaic floor dating from 1030. The frescoes are recent and of limited interest, but not so various pagan touches such as the Persian-influenced gold crown around the chandelier, and two Hellenistic columns from a temple of Poseidon with rams-head capitals which once stood here. There's also a silver-leaf lemon tree crafted in Moscow; because of the Georgian connection, Russians were lavish donors to this monastery. There is also an immensely rich library and treasury, but you are unlikely to be able to see these.

KARYÉS AND MINOR MONASTERIES
Though you no longer have to call in here except for extensions of the *dhiamontírion*, a look around **KARYÉS** is rewarding: the main church of the Protáton, dating from 965, contains exceptional fourteenth-century **frescoes** of the Macedonian school.

Karyés also has a simple inn, and a few **restaurants** where you may be able to get heartier fare than is typical in the monasteries. At the northern edge of "town" sprawls the enormous cloister-like *skíti* of **Ayíou Andhréou**, a Russian dependency of the great Vatopedhíou monastery, erected hurriedly last century and today virtually deserted.

A signposted trail leads up within an hour to **KOUTLOUMOUSÍOU** (☎0377/23 226), at the very edge of Karyés. Much the most interesting thing about it is its name, which appears to be that of a Selçuk chieftain converted to Christianity.

From Ivíron a path stumbles uphill, tangling with roads, to reach **FILOTHÉOU** (☎0377/23 256, fax 23 674), which was at the forefront of the monastic revival in the early 1980s and hence is one of the more vital monasteries. It is not, however, one of the more impressive foundations from an architectural or artistic point of view – though the lawn surfacing the entire courtyard is an interesting touch – and it's one of those houses where the non-Orthodox are forbidden from attending church or eating with the monks.

The same is true at **KARAKÁLOU**, 45 minutes' walk (mostly on paths) below Filothéou, also accessible via a short trail up from its *arsanás*. The lofty keep is typical of the fortress-monasteries built close enough to the shore to be victimized by pirates; note that there's limited space in the guest wing, so advance booking is required (☎0377/23 225).

Between here and Meyístis Lávras the trail system has been destroyed or overgrown, replaced by a road (no bus) that makes for dreary tramping, so it's advisable to continue southeast on the boat, or by arranging a lift with a service vehicle.

MEYÍSTIS LÁVRAS AND THE ATHONITE WILDERNESS

MEYÍSTIS LÁVRAS (☎0377/23 758) is the oldest and foremost of the ruling monasteries, and physically the most imposing establishment on Áthos, with no fewer than fifteen chapels within its walls. Uniquely among the twenty, it has never suffered from fire. The treasury and library are both predictably rich, the latter containing over two thousand precious manuscripts, though the ordinary traveller is unlikely to view them; as is usual, several monks (out of the 25 here) have complementary keys which must be operated together to gain entrance. What you will see at mealtimes are the superior **frescoes** in the **trapezaría**, executed by Theophanes the Cretan in 1535. Hagiographies and grisly martyrdoms line the apse, while there's a *Tree of Jesse* in the south transept, the *Death of Athanasios* (the founder) opposite, and an *Apocalypse* to the left of the main entry. In the western apse is a *Last Supper*, not surprisingly a popular theme in refectories. Just outside the door stands a huge **fiáli**, largest on the mountain, with pagan columns supporting the canopy. The **katholikón**, near the rear of the large but cluttered courtyard, contains more frescoes by Theophanes.

Beyond Meyístis Lávras lies some of the most beautiful and deserted country on the peninsula, though now sullied by a track recently bulldozed over the hour's worth of path south to one of Meyístis Lávras's many dependencies, **Skíti Prodhrómou**, whose Romanian inmates seem to have departed, to be replaced by Greeks. Nonetheless, it is a fairly hospitable house, little visited, and only ten minutes away by marked path there's the **hermitage cave** of St Athanasios, watched over by five skulls.

Most first-time visitors will, however, proceed without delay on what ends up being a five-hour traverse across the tip of Áthos, through incomparably rugged territory – including an intimidating landslide of boulders and tree-trunks in a gully about an hour or so out of Prodhrómou. You might consider dropping down off the main trail to see the *skíti* of **Ayías Triádhas (Kavsokalivíon)**, its *kyriákon* surrounded by many cottages, but the commonest strategy involves heading straight for **Skíti Ayías Ánnas**, whose buildings tumble down to a perennial-summer patch of coast where lemons grow. This is the usual "base camp" for the climb of **Áthos peak** itself (2030m) – best left for the next morning.

With a (pre-)dawn start, you gain the necessary mercy of a little shade and can expect to be up top just over four walking hours from Ayías Ánnas, with the combination refuge-church of **Panayía** passed a little over an hour before reaching the summit. Some hikers plan an overnight stop at this shelter, to watch the sunrise from the peak, but for this you must be self-sufficient in **food** – as you might want to be at the *skíti*, which being idiorrhythmic does not set a particularly sumptuous table, even allowing for monastic austerities. There's no spring **water** en route – you drink from cisterns at Panayía or at **Metamórfosi**, the tiny chapel atop the peak.

Returning from the peak before noon, you'll still have time to reach one of the monasteries north of Ayías Ánnas; the path continues to be delightful, and affords a sudden, breathtaking view of **AYÍOU PÁVLOU** (☎0377/23 250) as you round a bend. Except for the ugly scar of the new access road off to the left, which continues down to its *arsanás*, little can have changed in the perspective since Edward Lear painted it in the 1850s. The monastery, just over an hour from Ayías Ánnas, is irregularly shaped owing to the constraints of the inland site at the base of Áthos peak, and is currently home to 36 monks, many of them from the island of Kefalloniá.

THE "HANGING" MONASTERIES

From Ayíou Pávlou it's another hour to **DHIONYSÍOU** (☎0377/23 687, fax 23 686), a fortified structure perched spectacularly on a coastal cliff, and among the most richly endowed monasteries. It has overcome a grim reputation and is now both one of the better houses to stay at, with neat and airy *arkhondaríki* that come as a relief after so many claustrophobic facilities. Sadly, it is difficult to make out the sixteenth-century **frescoes** by the Cretan Tzortzis in the hopelessly dim katholikón, likewise an icon attributed to the Evangelist Luke; however, those of Theophanes on the inside and out of the **trapezaría** are another story. The interior features *The Entry of the Saints into Paradise* and *The Ladder to Heaven*; the exterior wall bears a version of the *Apocalypse*, complete with what looks strangely like a nuclear mushroom cloud. Unusually, you may be offered a tour of the **library** with its illuminated gospels on silk-fortified paper, a wooden carved miniature of the Passion week, and ivory crucifixes. You've little chance, however, of seeing Dhionysíou's great treasure, the three-metre-long **chrysobull** of the Trapezuntine emperor Alexios III Komnenos. Extensive modernization has been carried out here, with mixed results: clean electric power is supplied by a water turbine up-canyon, but the old half-timbered facade has been replaced with a rather brutal concrete-stucco one.

The onward path to **OSSÍOU GRIGORÍOU** (☎0377/23 218, fax 23 671) is a bit neglected but still usable, depositing you at the front door within an hour and a quarter of leaving Dhionysíou; every building here dates from after a devastating 1761 fire. Of all the monasteries and *skítes* it has the most intimate relation with the sea. Some of the old guest rooms overlook the water – a new hostel is being built – and the monks are exceptionally hospitable.

The southwest coastal trail system ends just over an hour later at **SÍMONOS PÉTRA** (abbreviated **Simópetra**; reservations required ☎0377/23 254, fax 23 707) or "The Rock of Simon", after the foundation legend asserting that the hermit Simon was directed to build a monastery here by a mysterious light hovering over the sheer pinnacle. Though entirely rebuilt in the wake of a fire a century ago, Simópetra is perhaps the most visually striking monastery on Áthos. With its multiple storeys, ringed by wooden balconies overhanging sheer 300-metre drops, it resembles nothing so much as a Tibetan lamasery. As at Dhionysíou, of which it seems an exaggerated rendition, the courtyard is quite narrow. Thanks to the fire there are no material treasures worth mentioning, though the monastery rivals Filothéou in vigour, with sixty monks from a dozen countries around the world. Unfortunately, because of the spectacle it presents, and its feasibility as an easy first stop out of Dháfni, Simópetra is always crowded with foreigners and might be better admired from a distance.

Further walking is inadvisable and it's best to arrange a lift northwest up the peninsula, or catch the morning boat in the same direction.

The northwestern group

DHÁFNI PORT AND THE RUSSIAN MONASTERY

Though you may not ever pass through Karyés, at some point you're likely to make the acquaintance of **DHÁFNI**, if only to change boats, since the service on this coast is not continuous. There's a **post office**, some rather tacky souvenir shops, and a **customs post** – much more vigilant when you leave than upon entry; all passengers' baggage is inspected to check traffic in smuggled-out treasures. A number of eagle-brooch-capped Athonite police skulk about as well, ever ready to pounce on real or imagined violations of the Athonite dress and behaviour codes. There's a **taverna** where you can get a beer and bean soup, but no shops adequate for stocking up with food and drink.

The kaïki usually has an hour's stop here before heading back towards Ayías Ánnas, during which time the captain can often be persuaded (for a reasonable fee) to take groups as far as the Russian monastery of **AYÍOU PANDELÍMONA** (alias Roussikó; no overnight stays; ☎0377/23 252), a dull forty-minute walk from the port, allowing a look at the premises before the scheduled departure to Ouranópoli appears. Most of the monks are Russian, a predominance reflected in onion-shaped **domes** and the softer faces of the frescoes. The majority of the buildings were erected at speed just after the mid-1800s, as part of Tsarist Russia's campaign for eminence on the mountain, and have a utilitarian, barrack-like quality. The sole unique features are the green lead roofs and the enormous **bell** over the refectory, the second largest in the world, which always prompts speculation as to how it got there. Otherwise, the small population fairly rattles around the echoing halls, the effect of desolation increased by ranks of outer dormitories gutted by a fire in 1968. If you're an architecture buff, Roussikó can probably be omitted without a twinge of conscience; students of turn-of-the-century kitsch will be delighted, however, with mass-produced saints' calendars, gaudy reliquaries, and a torrent of gold (or at least gilt) fixtures in the seldom-used katholikón. If you are permitted to attend service in the top-storey chapel north of the belfry, do so for the sake of the Slavonic chanting, though it must be said that the residents don't exactly put themselves out for non-Slavs. However, since the collapse of the Soviet Union, Ayíou Pandelímona anticipates a material and spiritual renaissance of sorts, and the current works are doubtless intended to accommodate the flood of Russian Orthodox pilgrims who will not be long in coming.

Actually closer to Dháfni is the square compound of **XEROPOTÁMOU** (reservations required; ☎0377/23 251), with most of its construction and church frescoes dating from the eighteenth century, except for two wings that were fire-damaged in 1952.

GREEK COASTAL MONASTERIES

From the vicinity of Dháfni or Roussikó, most pilgrims continue along the coast, reaching **XENOFÓNDOS** (reservations required; ☎0377/23 249) along trail and tractor tracks an hour after quitting the Russian monastery. Approached from this direction, Xenofóndos's busy sawmill gives it a vaguely industrial air. The enormous, sloping, irregularly shaped court, expanded upward last century, is unique in possessing two katholiká. The small, older one – with exterior frescoes of the Cretan school – was outgrown and replaced during the 1830s by the huge upper one, currently shut for repairs. Among its many icons are two fine **mosaics** of saints Yeóryios (George) and Dhimítrios. The guest quarters occupy a modern wing overlooking the sea at the extreme south end of the perimeter.

A half-hour' walk separates Xenofóndos from **DHOKHIARÍOU** (☎0377/23 245), one of the more picturesque monasteries on this coast but not conspicuously friendly to the non-Orthodox. Early 1990s renovations left untouched the primitive but clean *arkhondaríki*, which see few foreigners. An exceptionally lofty, large **katholikón** nearly fills the court, though its Cretan-school frescoes, possibly by Tzortzis, were clumsily retouched in 1855. Much better are the late seventeenth-century frescoes in the long, narrow **refectory**, with its sea views some of the nicest on Áthos. Even Orthodox pilgrims have trouble getting to see the wonder-working icon of *Gorgoipikóöu* ("She Who is Quick to Hear"), housed in a chapel between church and *trapezaría*.

THE FAR NORTHERN MONASTERIES

The direct trail inland and up to Konstamonítou has been reclaimed by the forest, so to get there you have to go in a roundabout fashion 45 minutes along the coast to its *arsanás*, and then as much time again sharply up on tracks and then cobbled path. **KONSTAMONÍTOU** (☎0377/23 228), hidden up in a thickly wooded valley, seems as humble, bare and poor as you'd expect from the last-ranking monastery; the katholikón nearly fills the court where the grass is literally growing up through the cracks. Non-Orthodox and believers are segregated, not that many foreigners make it this far; as a consolation a carillon "concert" of some musicality announces vespers.

From here you can continue on foot for ninety minutes to **ZOGRÁFOU** (☎0377/23 247), the furthest inland of the monasteries, today populated by a handful of Bulgarian monks. More than at most large, understaffed houses, you gain an appreciation of the enormous workload that falls on so few shoulders; a walk down the empty, rambling corridors past the seventeenth- and eighteenth-century cells, now unmaintained, is a sobering experience. "Zográfou" means "of the Painter", in reference to a tenth-century legend: the Slavs who founded the monastery couldn't decide on a patron saint, so they put a wooden panel by the altar, and after lengthy prayer a painting of Áyios Yeóryios – henceforth the institution's protector – appeared.

Near Zográfou the trail splits, presenting you with three choices. In two and a half hours along the leftmost option, you arrive at the large, irregularly shaped monastery of **KHILANDHARÍOU** (☎0377/23 797), which was in the past patronized by the thirteenth-century Serbian kings and has to this day remained a Serbian house and a hotbed of Serbian nationalism. Lately it has sheltered Bosnian Serbs accused of war crimes, a dubious revival of the Holy Mountain's historic role as a no-questions-asked place of asylum. The **katholikón** dates in its present form from the fourteenth century, but its frescoes, similar in style to those in the Protáton at Karyés, have been retouched. As you'd expect for a beacon of medieval Serbian culture, the library and treasury are well endowed.

The central, down-valley route out of Zográfou leads in three hours to **ESFIGMÉNOU** (☎0377/23 796), built directly on the water and reputedly the strictest foundation on the mountain – an early 1990s banner hung out of the top-storey window reading "Orthodoxy or Death" would seem to confirm this and does not encourage a casual visit. In any case the path veers down the coast for three hours to **VATOPEDHÍOU**, a similar distance away if you are setting out directly from Zográfou. Exceeding Meyístis Lávras in size, it also vies with it in importance and wealth, and makes a good beginning or farewell to Áthos, though reservations are required (☎0377/23 219). The cobbled, slanting court with its freestanding belfry (which can be climbed) seems more like a town plaza, ringed by stairways and stacks of cells for more than three hundred inhabitants. The **katholikón**, one of the oldest on the mountain, has the usual array of frescoes painted over for better or worse, but more uniquely two **mosaics** of the *Annunciation* and the *Deisis* flanking the door of the inner narthex. The population of about forty monks, mostly young and two-thirds Cypriot (as is the abbot), includes a brotherhood of nine Australians who have had to change residence four times (a common drama for non-Greek monks on the peninsula) and hope that this is their last home.

With the proper maps it is just possible to short-cut the dusty track above Vatopedhíou en route to **PANDOKRÁTOROS** (☎0377/23 253), two and a half hours away, the last half of the journey on scenic coastal paths. Other than the setting on a hill overlooking its own picturesque fishing harbour, and the courtyard with its eight Valencia orange trees, there is little of note. But most of the 35 monks are welcoming, perhaps the more so since the community succumbed to pressure from its peers and converted to the cenobitic mode. The guest wing overlooks the sea and there is a (cold) shower – a boon after days of sweaty trekking. In a valley above looms the *skíti* of **Profítis Ilías**, a relic of the Russian expansion drive and today home to just nine monks from several different countries.

Continuing on the coastal trail, it's under an hour door-to-door to tiny **STAVRONIKÍTA**, the best example of the Athonite coastal fortress-monastery and distinctly vertical in orientation. Long one of the poorest houses, it has recently been completely redone, and, surrounded by aqueduct-fed kitchen gardens, is pin-neat. Several Australians, including the abbot, number among the fifteen monks who are ill-equipped to cope with the relatively large numbers of guests. The modernized guest quarters, despite showers, are meagre, and reservations are required (☎0377/23 255). There's little chance of a seaside room, though by virtue of its rock-top position Stavronikíta has some of the best views of Áthos peak on the peninsula. The narrow **katholikón** occupies virtually all of the gloomy courtyard, and the **refectory**, normally opposite, had to be shifted upstairs to the south wing – it's a spartan room with a single window onto the water, and fresco fragments by Theophanes of the *Death of Áyios Nikólaos* (the patron) and the *Last Supper*. From here an hour's walk separates you from Ivíron.

The coast to Kavála

Heading towards Kavála from Sithonía or Áthos by public transport is surprisingly tricky, since buses from either peninsula run only back to Thessaloníki. However, the gap between the Thessaloníki–Khalkidhikí and Thessaloníki–Kavála services is only 16km wide at one point, with a couple of places you wouldn't mind getting stuck at along the way, so if you don't have your own transport, you could always walk.

To begin, you should get off the Ouranópoli–Thessaloníki bus at the small coastal village of **STRATÓNI**. The bay here is dominated by the local mine workings, and there is little incentive to stay, though there are several tavernas on the grey-black beach and even one hotel, the *Angelika* (☎0376/22 075; ②). From Stratóni, the scenic road glides over the forested ridge north 15km to the beach resort of Olymbiádha which has regular buses (4 daily Mon–Fri, 3 on Sat, 2 on Sun) to the Thessaloníki–Kavála highway.

OLYMBIÁDHA itself is still very low-key, with **rooms**, a pair of streamside campsites, *Olympias* and *Corali* (☎0376/51 304) 1km north and 500km inland, and a pair of co-managed hotels: the quieter, garden-set *Liotopi* at the south edge of town, and the central *Germany* with a ground floor taverna (both ☎0376/51 362, fax 51 255; ⑥). There are three other **tavernas** on the southern bay, the cheapest and most characterful being the *Kapetan Manolis/Platanos* by the concrete jetty. All along this shore the local speciality is **mussels** (*mídhia*), farmed in floating nursery beds and typically served in a spicy cheese sauce, or sold raw at roadside stalls.

The small town **beaches** are fine, but there are far better ones – such as Próti Ammoudhiá – 2km back towards Stratóni, behind the promontory that is home to ancient **Stageira**, birthplace of Aristotle. This covers two hilltops joined by a saddle, and is under continuous summer excavation; you're free to have a wander around, though there's not much on view yet other than the massive western wall and towers on the landward side, a few paved streets and foundations and – at the lowest point – a stoa. It is perhaps unique in Greece for having been a city built of granite rather than marble or limestone.

STAVRÓS, 12km north of Olymbiádha – the interval again dotted with semi-accessible coves – is a much bigger, busier place than Olymbiádha, with a beautiful seafront of plane trees, and up to ten daily orange buses to Thessaloníki. The cheapest of five inexpensive **hotels** is the *Avra Strymonikou* (☎0397/61 278; ②), though the *Athos* is better placed, and you'd be most likely to end up in **rooms**.

From here you're just 4km from the main E90 highway, where just east of the junction the first coastal place of any size – **ASPRÓVALTA** – will come as a jolt after the relative calm of Khalkidhikí. Minimally attractive, it's essentially a summer suburb of Sérres and Thessaloníki, from where there's a frequent urban bus service.

Ten kilometres east of Aspróvalta, the road to Kavála crosses the River Strymónas, beyond which long-distance buses tend to veer inland to hug the base of Mount Pangéo. With your own transport it's worth following the coast road to Kavála. If you keep to the old road, rather than the flyover, you'll cross the river by a long bridge, before which – approaching from Thessaloníki – you'll see on your left the colossal marble **Lion of Amphipolis**. This was reconstructed in 1937 from fragments found when excavating the ancient city of Amphipolis nearby, and is thought to date from the end of the fourth century BC.

Twenty-eight kilometres beyond Amphipolis, **LOUTRÁ ELEFTHERÓN**, just 2km inland of the coast road to Kavála, is an old-fashioned spa set in a riverside oasis, though the thermal springs themselves are a bit difficult to bathe in, and the old Turkish domed bath has been closed down, leaving only the rather clinical indoor plunge-pools (open in the morning and evening).

Approaching Néa Péramos, a narrow frontage road seaward from the main highway threads past very impromptu **campsites** among vineyards and fine, duned **beaches**, the best in eastern Macedonia. **NÉA PÉRAMOS** itself, 14km before Kavála, sports an unheralded **castle** at one corner of its sandy, sheltered bay, and isn't a bad place to spend a couple of hours. *Camping Anatoli* (May–Sept; ☎0594/21 027) at the west end of things can be recommended if you want to spend the night; it has its own salt-water swimming pool. The only other **campsites** between here and Kavála are the *Estella*, 5km east, or the expensive EOT site, *Batis*, 10km along and already hedged by Kavála's sprawl.

Kavála

KAVÁLA, backing on to the lower slopes of Mount Symbólon, is the second largest city of Macedonia and the principal port for northern Greece. Coming in through the suburbs, there seems little to recommend a stay. But the centre is fairly pleasant and characterful, grouped about the nineteenth-century harbour area and its old tobacco warehouses. A citadel looks down from a rocky promontory to the east, and an elegant Turkish aqueduct leaps over modern buildings into the old quarter on the bluff.

The town was known in ancient times as Neapolis, and as such served for two centuries or more as a terminus of the Via Egnatía and the first European port of call for merchants and travellers from the Middle East. It was here that St Paul landed on his way to Philippi (see p.398), on his initial mission to Europe. In later years, the port and citadel took on considerable military significance, being occupied in turn by Byzantines, Normans, Franks, Venetians, Turks and (during both world wars) Bulgarians.

The Town

Although the remnants of Kavála's Turkish past are mostly neglected, the **Panayía**
quarter above the port preserves a scattering of eighteenth- and nineteenth-century
buildings, and considerable atmosphere. It is by far the most attractive part of town to
explore, with twisting lanes running up towards the citadel.

The most conspicuous and interesting building is the **Imaret**, overlooking the harbour
on Poulidhoú. An elongated, multi-domed structure with Arabic inscriptions over many
doorways, it was originally a combination of soup kitchen and hostel housing three hundred *softas*, or theological students. After many decades of dereliction it was partially
refurbished during the early 1990s, appropriately enough, as a restaurant-bar (see p.398).
Claimed to be the largest Islamic building in Europe, the Imaret was endowed by
Mehmet Ali, Pasha of Egypt and founder of the dynasty which ended with King Farouk.
The house where Mehmet Ali was born to an Albanian family in 1769, near the corner of
Pavlídhou and Méhmet Alí, is maintained as a monument. It provides an opportunity, rare
in Greece, to look over a prestigious Islamic house, with its wood-panelled reception
rooms, ground-floor stables and first-floor harem (Tues–Sun 10am–2pm; free but tip the
guide). Nearby rears an equestrian statue of the great man – a useful landmark.

You can also visit the Byzantine **citadel** (daily 10am–7pm; free) to explore the ramparts, towers, dungeon and cistern; in season it hosts a few festival performances, mainly drama and some music, in its main court. From here, down towards the middle of
town, north of Panayía's narrow maze of streets, the **aqueduct**, built on a Roman model
in the reign of Süleyman the Magnificent (1520–66), spans the traffic in Platía Nikotsára.

Finally, on the other side of the harbour from the old town, there are two museums of moderate interest. The **Archeological Museum** (Tues–Sun 8.30am–6pm; 500dr) on Erythroú Stavroú contains a fine dolphin-and-lily mosaic upstairs in the Abdira room, plus painted sarcophagi in the adjacent section devoted to Thasian colonies. By far the most intriguing object here, though, is a bronze statuette-lamp in the form of a kneeling, bound barbarian prisoner. Downstairs in the ground-floor rear left gallery are a reconstructed Macedonian funeral chamber, many terracotta figurines still decorated in their original paint and gold ornaments from tombs at Amphipolis. Just inland, wedged between former tobacco warehouses at Filíppou 4, is the **Folk and Modern Art Museum** (Mon–Fri 8am–2pm, Sat 9am–1pm; free). Along with various collections of traditional costumes and household utensils, this has some interesting rooms devoted to the Thássos-born sculptor Polygnotos Vayis.

Practicalities

The main **bus station** is on the corner of Mitropolítou and Filikís Eterías, near the main anchorage; buses for Alexandhroúpoli stop some blocks away on Erythroú Stavroú, in front of the *Hotel Oceanis*. **Taxis** are coloured deep orange. In the main square, Platía Eleftherías, you'll find an **EOT** office, which can provide details (and sell tickets) for the summer drama festivals at Philippi. Right next door is a long-hours money **exchange** booth, Midas, and the Ionian Bank has erected an automatic note-changer on the fishing wharf. Kaválaˊs **airport**, used by package holiday-makers en route to Thássos, lies between the town and Keramotí, 29km southeast (see p.398).

Accommodation

Abundant, good-value **hotel** rooms are not the order of the day in KaVála, though proprietors can often be bargained down a category or two in the off season. Especially if you're arriving on an afternoon charter in summer, you might well prefer to transfer from the airport to Keramotí for a ferry to Thássos with its wide choice of accommodation (see p. 688), reserving Kavála for a day trip.

The cheapest acceptable outfits are the *Panorama* at Venizélou 26/c (☎051/224 205, fax 224 685; ③) or the *Akropolis* (☎051/223 543, fax 830 752; ③) at Eleftheríou Venizélou 29, west of Platía Eleftherías, with English-speaking management and large, eccentric rooms. Of two nearly adjacent hotels out on Erythroú Stavroú opposite the archeological museum, the *Esperia* (☎051/229 621, fax 220 621; ④) at no. 44 is to be preferred – for its air-conditioning, quieter double-glazed rooms – to the *Nefeli* (☎051/227 441, fax 227 440; ⑤) at no. 50. The only private **rooms** in the centre are those of Yiorgos Alvanos at Anthemíou 35 (☎051/228 412; ②), in an old house at the heart of the old Panayía quarter – worth trying for if you arrive early in the day. An alternative place to stay, frequented by many Greek tourists, is the beach-suburb of Kalamítsa, to the west of town. The closest **campsite** is *Irini* (☎051/229 785; open all year), on the shore 3km east of the port; city bus #2 goes there.

Eating and drinking

Eating out in Kavála is a more cheerful prospect than staying the night; ignore the tourist traps along the waterfront and walk instead up into the Panayía district, where rows of tavernas with outdoor seating on Poulídhou tempt you with good and reasonably priced grills and seafood. Starting opposite the lower end of the Imaret, you'll see as you proceed uphill: *O Thomas, O Kanadhos, Antonia*, and *To Koutoukaki*, with *O Kanadhos* being the most attended at lunchtime. Beyond the single open entrance to the Imaret lies one more eatery, *To Tavernaki tis Panayias*, but if you've made it this far, you may as well plump for the Imaret itself, certainly the most atmospheric premises in the province. The courtyard floor is a café-bar, while somewhat pricey meals are served on the upper gallery overlooking whitewashed arcades and the harbour.

Ferry services

Car ferries sail from Kavála to **Thássos** almost hourly in season; virtually all run to the port of Skála Prínou (75min). Out of season, when services drop to just a handful of boats daily, you may be better off taking the bus or driving to Keramotí, 46km southwest, and then using the car ferry from there to Thássos. **KERAMOTÍ** itself provides an alternative, though unexciting, stopover. It's a small, rather drab village, with a functional beach, a few rooms and a half-dozen hotels which you shouldn't have to patronize, as the last ferry leaves for Thássos at about 10pm.

Other ferry services from Kavála are less predictable. From late July until late August, there are generally five weekly departures to **Samothráki** (Mon, Tues, Wed, Fri & Sat; 4hr), and the same number to **Límnos** (Tues, Wed, Thurs, Fri, Sat & Sun), dwindling to two and three sailings respectively during the off-season. Two or three of these continue to various islands, among them Áyios Efstrátios, Lésvos, Khíos and Rafína/Pireás. Details for Límnos and beyond are available from Nikos Miliadhes, tucked away behind Platía Karaolí Dhimitríou (☎051/226 147 or 223 421), while the Samothráki services can be checked at the nearby agency Arsinoi-Saos (☎051/835 671).

Philippi

As you might expect, **PHILIPPI** was named after Philip II of Macedon, who wrested the town from the Thracians in 356 BC. However, it owed its later importance and prosperity to the Roman building of the Via Egnatia, which ran from the Adriatic to Byzantium. With Kavála/Neápolis as its port, Philippi was essentially the easternmost town of Roman-occupied Europe.

Here also, as at Actium, the fate of the Roman Empire was decided on Greek soil, at the **Battle of Philippi** in 42 BC. After assassinating Julius Caesar, Brutus and Cassius had fled east of the Adriatic and, against their better judgement, were forced into confrontation on the Philippi plains with the pursuing armies of Antony and Octavian. The "honourable conspirators", who could have successfully exhausted the enemy by avoiding action, were decimated by Octavian in two successive battles, and, as defeat became imminent, first Cassius, then Brutus killed himself – the latter running on his comrade's sword with the purported Shakespearean sentiment, "Caesar now be still, I killed thee not with half so good a will".

St Paul landed at Kavála and visited Philippi in 49 AD and so began his mission in Europe. Despite being cast into prison here he retained a special affection for the Philippians, his first converts, and the congregation that he established was one of the earliest to flourish in Greece. It furnished the principal remains of the site: several impressive, although ruined, basilican churches.

Philippi is easily reached from Kavála, just 14km distant; buses (which continue to Dhráma) leave every half hour, and drop you by the road that now splits the site.

The Site

Tues–Sun 8.30am–3pm; 500dr.

The most conspicuous of the churches is the **Direkler** (Turkish for "columns" or "piers"), to the south of the modern road which here follows the line of the Via Egnatia. Also known as Basilica B, this was an unsuccessful attempt by its sixth-century architect to improve the basilica design by adding a dome. In this instance the entire east wall collapsed under the weight, leaving only the narthex convertible for worship. The central arch of its west wall and a few pillars of reused antique drums stand amid remains of the Roman **forum**. A line of second-century porticoes spreads outwards in front of the church, and on their east side are the foundations of a colonnaded octagonal church which was approached from the Via Egnatia by a great gate. Behind the Direkler, and perversely the most interesting and best-preserved building of the site, is a huge monumental **public latrine** with nearly fifty of its original marble seats still intact.

Across the road on the northern side, stone steps climb up to a terrace passing on the right a Roman crypt, reputed to have been the **prison of St Paul** and appropriately frescoed. The terrace flattens out onto a huge paved atrium that extends to the foundations of another extremely large basilica. Continuing in the same direction around the base of a hill you emerge above a **theatre** cut into its side. Though dating from the original town it was heavily remodelled as an amphitheatre by the Romans – the bas-reliefs of Nemesis, Mars and Victory (on the left of the stage) all belong to this period. It is used for the annual drama festival, held every weekend from mid-July to early August. The **museum** (Tues–Sun 8.30am–3pm; separate 500dr admission), above the road at the far end of the site, is rather dreary.

The best general impression of the site – which is very extensive despite a lack of obviously notable buildings – and of the battlefield behind it can be gained from the **acropolis**, a steep climb along a path from the museum. Its own remains are predominantly medieval.

THRACE (THRÁKI)

Separated from Macedonia to the west by the Néstos River and from (Turkish) Eastern Thrace by the Évros river delta, **Western Thrace** is the Greek state's most recent addition. Under effective Greek control from 1920, the Treaty of Lausanne (1923) confirmed Greek sovereignty over the area, and also sanctioned the exchange of 390,000 Muslims, principally from Macedonia and Epirus, for more than a million ethnic Greeks from Eastern Thrace and Asia Minor. But the Muslims of Western Thrace, in reciprocity for a continued Greek presence in and around Constantinople, were exempt from the exchanges and continue to live in the region.

Thrace was originally inhabited by a people with their own non-Hellenic language and religion. From the seventh century BC onwards it was colonized by Greeks, and after Alexander the area took on a strategic significance as the land route between Greece and Byzantium. It was later controlled by the Roman and Byzantine empires, and after 1361 by the Ottoman Turks.

Nowadays, out of a total population of 360,000, there are around 120,000 Muslims, made up (approximately) of 60,000 **Turkish-speakers**, 40,000 **Pomaks** and 20,000 **Gypsies**. These figures are disputed by Turkish Muslims who put their numbers alone at something between 100,000 and 120,000. The Greek government lumps all three groups together as "a Muslim minority" principally of Turkish descent, and provides Turkish-language education for all of them (despite the fact that the Pomaks speak a language very similar to Bulgarian). Greek authorities also point to the 336 functioning mosques, the Turkish-language newspapers and a Turkish-language radio station in Komotiní as evidence of their goodwill. However, since 1968 only graduates from a special academy in Thessaloníki have been allowed to teach in the Turkish-language schools here, thus isolating Thracian Turks from mainstream Turkish culture, and on various occasions the Greek authorities have interfered with Muslim religious appointments. In 1985, when the Mufti of Komotiní died, he was replaced by a government appointee. When he resigned, another Mufti was appointed by the authorities. In August 1991, the Greeks appointed a new Muslim leader in Xánthi, again without consulting the Muslim community.

There is no doubt in the minds of local Turks and Pomaks that in secular matters, too, they are the victims of **discrimination**. Muslim villages, they say, receive less help from the state than Greek villages: some are without electricity and many lack proper roads. Muslim schools are underfunded, Muslims are unable to join the police force, and it is extremely difficult for them to buy property or get bank loans – although most ethnic Turks do also acknowledge that they are still materially better off than their counterparts in Turkey.

There have been occasional explosions of inter-communal violence and matters have only worsened since the re-incorporation, in neighbouring Bulgaria, of the Turkish minority into the commercial and political life of that country, with the Greeks becoming increasingly aware of the potential for unrest. In July 1991 the Greek government put forward a plan to demilitarize the whole of Thrace, including the Bulgarian and Turkish sectors. The plan received a positive reply from the Bulgarian government, but ominously Turkey reserved its position, and Greece remains fearful of Turkish agitation in Western Thrace that might lead to a Cyprus-type military operation where Turkish forces "come to the assistance" of an oppressed minority. The Turkish consulate at Komotiní has long been considered a conduit for fifth-column activities, with incumbent consuls regularly expelled by Greece for "activities incompatible with diplomatic status". These activities constitute not espionage, but alleged attempts to foment local disturbances. Occasionally the Greek secret service has been accused of playing rougher, as in the case of the outspoken former MP for Thrace, Ahmet Sadiq, who was killed in an allegedly "manufactured" road accident in July 1995.

As an outsider you will probably not notice the intercommunal tensions, but you will not be able to avoid the many military installations in the province; moreover some Muslim areas near the Bulgarian border north of Komotiní and Xánthi are subject to police and army restrictions. However, there are mixed villages where Muslims and Greeks appear to coexist quite amicably, and Thracians, both Muslim and Orthodox, have a deserved reputation for hospitality.

Compared with the rest of the mainland, there is little tangible to see, and most travellers take a bus straight through to **Alexandhroúpoli**, for the ferry to Samothráki, or head straight on to **Istanbul**. But Thrace's many rulers left some mark on the area, and there are a few well-preserved monuments, most significant the remains of the coastal cities of Avdira, south of Xánthi, and Maroneia, southeast of Komotiní – Greek colonies in the seventh century BC that were abandoned in Byzantine times when the inhabitants moved inland to escape pirate raids. Otherwise, the landscape itself holds most appeal, with the train line forging a circuitous but scenic route below the foothills of the Rodhópi mountains that's at its best in the **Néstos valley** between Paranésti and Xánthi. If you make time to explore the backstreets of the towns, or venture up the myriad tracks to tiny, isolated villages in the Rhodópi mountains, you'll find an atmosphere quite unlike any other part of Greece.

Xánthi and around

Coming from Kavála, after the turning to the airport and shortly after the side road to Keramotí you cross the Néstos River, which with the **Rhodópi mountains** forms the border of Greek Thrace. The Greek/Turkish, Christian/Muslim demographics are almost immediately apparent in the villages: the Turkish settlements, long established, with their tiled, whitewashed houses and pencil-thin minarets; the Greek ones, often adjacent, built in drab modern style for the refugees of the 1920s.

Ancient Kassope, Epirus

Metéora, Northern Greece

Dhokhiaríou monastery, Mount Athos

Ayíou Pávlou seen from its bay

Ayíos Akhíllios basilica, Mikrí Préspa

Goats on a cliff, Northern Greece

Triple-arched bridge near Kípi

Mansion with bougainvillea, Ídhra

Port of Ídhra

River base in Víkos gorge, Zagória

Harbour in Éyina

Bay in Párga

Xánthi

XÁNTHI (Iskeçe to the Turks), the first town of any size, is perhaps the most interesting point to break a journey. There is a busy market area, good food, and, up the hill
to the north of the main café-lined square, a very attractive old quarter. The town is also
home to the University of Thrace, which lends a lively air to the place, particularly in
the area between the bazaar and the campus, where bars, cinemas and bistros are busy
in term time. Try if you can to visit on Saturday, the day of Xánthi's **street market** – a
huge affair, attended equally by Greeks, Pomaks and Turks, held in a large open space
near the fire station on the eastern side of the town.

The narrow, cobbled streets of the **old town** are home to a number of very fine mansions, most of them dating from the mid-nineteenth century when Xánthi's tobacco
merchants made their fortunes. One of them has been turned into a **Folk Museum**
(Mon, Wed, Fri, Sat 1am–1pm & 7–9.30pm; Tues, Thurs & Sun 11am–1pm; 300dr), at
Antiká 7, at the bottom of the slope up into the right-bank quarter of the old town. A
Siamese-twin dwelling originally built for two tobacco magnate brothers, it has been
lovingly restored with painted wooden panels, decorated plaster and floral designs on
the walls and ceilings, as well as displays of Thracian clothes and jewellery, a postcard
collection and cakes of pressed tobacco.

Further up, the roads become increasingly narrow and steep, and the Turkish presence (about fifteen percent of the total urban population) is more noticeable: most of
the women have their heads covered and the more religious ones wear full-length
cloaks. Churches and mosques hide behind whitewashed houses with tiled roofs, and
orange-brown tobacco leaves are strung along drying frames. Numerous houses, no
matter how modest, sport a dish for tuning into Turkish satellite television.

To the north, overlooking the town from on high, is the **Panayía Convent**, while
beyond stands the **Áyios Nikólaos Monastery**, from which there are fine views north
into the forested Rhodópi mountains. To reach them by car from the river bridge, follow road signs for "*Monastíria*"; on foot, walk fifteen minutes up through the left-bank
neighbourhood of Samakóv.

Practicalities

Arriving, you'll be either at the **train station**, 2km south of the centre, just off the
Kavála road (cheap taxis to hand), or at the very central main **KTEL**, just off Platía
Eleftherías, at the northeast corner of the central market hall; there's a separate terminal for Kavála services opposite the south end of the market, on Sarándon Ekklissíon.
28-Oktovríou is the main south–north thoroughfare, passing just east of Platía
Eleftherías and terminating at the central platía with its prominent clock tower. Xánthi's
pay-and-display **parking** scheme (Mon–Fri 8.30am–9pm) is pretty comprehensive. The
OTE, the **post office** and Olympic Airways all lie within sight of the central platía, on
its uphill side. **Taxis** are avocado green, with white tops.

Hotel choices are limited and generally expensive; the central *Xenia*, despite its continued appearance in various tourism literature, has shut down. Cheapest, a bit
unsavoury, though quietly positioned on a pedestrian zone, is the non-en-suite *Lux* at
Yeoryíou Stavroú 18 (☎0541/22 341; ②). The next niche up is occupied by the
Dimokritos on 28-Oktovríou 41 (☎0541/25 111; ④) near the KTEL, whose well-worn but
en-suite rooms (rear ones quiet) are a bit better than the gloomy lobby and halls
promise. More or less around the corner at Mikhaïl Karaolí 40, the *Orfeas* (☎0541/20
121, fax 20 998; ⑤) is newer and worth the extra money. At the *Xanthippio* (☎0541/77
061, fax 77 076; ⑤), 28-Oktovríou 212, you're at the top of the range.

Restaurant options are somewhat better. The best is *Nisaki*, with an incomparable
setting on the banks of the Podhonífi River dividing the town. To find it, follow Odhós
Pindhárou upstream from behind the abandoned *Xenia* hotel, to where the street ends

at the base of the old town. Just off the main square on pedestrianized Yeoryíou Stavroú are two adjacent ouzerís, with *To Dhromaki* having the edge over *Ta Fanarakia*. At the upper end of cobbled Paleológou, essentially the entrance to the old town, are three places – *Arhondissa*, *Kyvotos* and *Kharadhra* (reached from a side street) – all with similar menus and prices. Odhós Vassilísis Sofías, leading down off Paleológou from the little park to the river, is the focus of Xánthi's **nightlife**. Doyen of the various bars here is the enormous *Kyverneio*, opposite the university's engineering faculty, although the alternative set head for *Katafíyio* bar near the square. A good cinema – the Olympia – is at the bottom of the old town behind the municipal library.

North of Xánthi

Much of the countryside north of Xánthi, towards the Bulgarian border, is a military "controlled area", dotted with signs denoting the fact. Greeks will tell you that access to areas like this is restricted because of the sensitivity of the frontier with Bulgaria; ethnic Turks and Pomaks claim the army uses the border as an excuse to keep tabs on them. It is possible to enter the controlled areas, but you need a pass from the police and army in Mýki.

If you do venture up into the mountains here, the reward is some magnificent scenery and fine traditional architecture, the road twisting up through forests and tobacco terraces into the highest and wildest part of the Rhodópi range. There are a number of Muslim villages: **SMÍNTHI**, a large and dispersed Pomak settlement with a mosque and tall minaret, and, further on and much more isolated, **MÝKI**, with long, single-storey stone houses and a large mosque. The road north of here, towards Ekhínos, leads into a restricted area, and you will need a pass to get through. If you do have a pass, continue to **EKHÍNOS**, a fine-looking town that is the main market for the surrounding Pomak community – Bogomil-Christian Slavs forcibly converted to Islam in the sixteenth century. They still speak a corrupt dialect of Bulgarian with generous mixtures of Greek and Turkish.

Otherwise, the furthest you can get to without a pass is **ORÉO**, north of Smínthi, another Pomak village set on a steep hillside with cloud-covered peaks behind and terraces falling away to the riverbed – a dramatic setting in the extreme. It has a mosque and Turkish-language school, but it is grindingly poor: the ground floors of the houses are used for corralling animals or storing farm produce, and it has no bar or taverna, at least not for visitors. If you show up here, don't expect much of a welcome.

South of Xánthi: along the coast

Travelling south from Xánthi – across a coastal plain, bright with cotton, tobacco and cereals, stretching to the sea – is less problematic. Heading towards Ávdira, you might stop briefly in **YENISSÉA** (Yeniçe), an unspectacular farming village with a mixed Greek-Turkish population, and – behind its nondescript centre – one of the oldest mosques in Thrace, more than four hundred years old. Now derelict, it's a low whitewashed building, with a tiled roof: a wooden portico running round its four sides is dangerously rotten and its minaret has been truncated. Across the road, behind a service station, is a second mosque, door locked and windows boarded, though its minaret still stands.

Ávdira and along the coast

A few kilometres further on, regular buses go to the village of **ÁVDIRA**, and, in summer, to the beach of the same name, 7km beyond and passing through the ancient site of **Avdira** (daily 9am–3pm; free). The walls of the ancient acropolis are visible on a low headland above the sea, and there are traces of Roman baths, a theatre and an ancient acropolis. However, the best finds have been taken off to museums in Kavála and Komotiní, the remains are unspectacular, and the setting not particularly attractive. If you have time only for one site, you're better off going to Marónia (see below).

For the most part, the coast between Ávdira and Marónia is flat and dull. At the southern end of brackish Lake Vistonídha is **PORTO LÁGOS**, a semi-derelict harbour partly redeemed by the nearby monastery of **Áyios Nikólaos** (shut daily 1–5pm) built on two islets in the lagoon – though the structure itself is modern and dull. The surrounding marshland is an important site for birdlife, and is more accessible than the Évros delta; a few observation towers have been provided along the reedy shoreline.

Nearby, 7km southeast and 32km from Xánthi, the small resort of **FANÁRI** has a long, sandy beach (good for Thrace, average for Greece) with two co-managed **hotels**: the all-white, modern *Fanari Hotel* (☎0535/31 300, fax 31 388; ④), set well back from the beach at the eastern edge of the village, and the smaller, potentially noisier *Pension Theodora* (☎0535/31 242, same fax; ③) out on the village promontory by the fishing port. The *Fanari* has a restaurant and there are a number of other fish **tavernas**. There's also an EOT campsite, the *Fanari* (☎0535/31 270; May–Oct), 500m east of the *Fanari Hotel*, just before the public beach. Fanári village is popular with Komotiniots in the evenings and at weekends, and its beach gets busy in the high summer, but there are less crowded spots southeast along the coast.

Marónia and further east
Further along the coast, **ancient Maroneia** has little more to see than Ávdira, but the site is altogether more attractive. Most of it is still unexcavated, and the visible remains are scattered among the olive trees and undergrowth at the foot of Mount Ísmaros, now anachronistically crowned with the large, white "golf balls" of a radar station. The founder of the city is reckoned to be Maron, the son of the god of wine, Dionysus (Ísmaros is known locally as the Mountain of Dionysus) and the city became one of the most powerful in all of ancient Thrace. The site, which can be explored at will, is badly signposted, but you should be able to track down traces of a theatre, a sanctuary of Dionysus, and various buildings including a house with a well-preserved mosaic floor. The land walls of the city are preserved to a height of two metres, together with a Roman tower above the harbour. Over time, the sea has done its own excavation, eroding the crumbling cliffs to reveal shards of pottery and ancient walls. There can be fewer more magical places to watch the sun set over the Thracian Sea.

The pleasant, modern village of **MARÓNIA**, 4km inland with six daily buses from Komotiní, has a few surviving old Thracian mansions with jutting balconies, and some **rooms** (☎0533/41 158; ③) offered through a women's cooperative, though eating options around the shady square aren't brilliant. The women's cooperative will supply daily meals during July and August, but only at weekends otherwise.

Marónia's harbour of **Áyios Kharálambos**, below the edge of the archeological site and 4km south of modern Marónia, was "improved" recently in anticipation of a tourism boom that never happened: it's frankly a miserable place, baking in the heat of the surrounding cliffs, with no usable beach, and two overpriced tavernas. By contrast **Platanítis**, 4km west of Marónia by another paved but unsigned road, has a small but adequate gravel-and-sand beach – essentially a gap in the red cliffs – and a good, reasonably priced fish taverna, *O Yerasimos*.

Towards Alexandhroúpoli, there are passable beaches at **MESIMVRÍA** and **MÁKRI**, though with few facilities except for Mákri's *Hotel Kleio/Cleo* (☎0551/71 411; ③), which has a good restaurant.

Komotiní

KOMOTINÍ, 48km east of Xánthi along a road skirting the Rodhópi foothills, is an unattractive town with ranks of apartment buildings and gridded suburbs to the south and west, and dusty, noisy streets clogged with traffic. It is more markedly Turkish than Xánthi with its fourteen functioning mosques, and social mixing between the different ethnic groups – roughly at parity population-wise – is less common, although Orthodox and Muslim continue to live in the same neighbourhoods.

During the thirteenth century, the city gained importance and wealth due to its position on the Via Egnatia. When the Ottomans took the city in 1361, they changed its name to Gümülçine, which is what it was called during the long centuries of their rule. In 1912, at the outbreak of the First Balkan War, Komotiní fell to the Bulgarians; it was liberated by Greek forces in the following year, only to be taken once more by the Bulgarians during World War I. It was finally and definitively joined to Greece on May 14, 1920.

The old **bazaar**, to the north of the central Platía Irínis and the through boulevard Orféos, is very pleasant, caught between mosques and a fine Ottoman-era clocktower. Shady cafés and tiny shops sell everything from carpets to iron buckets, and it's especially busy on Tuesdays when the villagers from the surrounding area come into town to sell their wares. Behind this old quarter, you can see the modern **Cathedral** and the remains of Komotiní's **Byzantine walls**, in one corner of which once stood a fine synagogue, destroyed recently after its dome collapsed.

Traditionally a city with both Greek and Turkish inhabitants, Greek influence began to dominate in the waning years of the Ottoman Empire, with rich Greeks funding schools and colleges in the city to develop Greek culture and ideals. Some of these educational foundations still survive: one, the **Hellenic Civic School of Nestor Tsanakali**, a Neoclassical structure on Dhimokritoú, is now the official residence of the Dean of the University of Thrace; another, at Áyios Yeóryios 13, on the other side of the park, has become Komotiní's **Folk Museum** (Tue–Sat 10am–1pm; free), displaying examples of Thracian embroidery, traditional Thracian dress, silverware, copperware and a collection of religious seals. The **archeological museum** at Simeonídhi 4 (daily 9am–5pm; free), just to the right of the main road from Xánthi and well signposted, is also worth a visit, giving a lucid overview of Thracian history by means of plans and finds from local sites, from its beginnings up to the Byzantine era. On display are a number of statues, busts, bas reliefs, jewellery and artefacts from the archeological sites around Komotiní.

Practicalities

If you need to stay, be aware that the **hotel** situation is even less promising than Xánthi's. If you can afford it, you'd be best off at the *Anatolia* (☎0531/36 242; fax 23 170; ⑥), Ankhiálou 53; the overpriced *Astoria* (☎0531/35 054, fax 22 707; ⑥) is housed in a restored mansion at Platiá Irínis. Rock-bottom is the spartan *Hellas* (☎0531/22 055; ②) at Dhimokrítou 31 at a noisy intersection in the west of town.The more central, air-conditioned *Olympos* at Orféos 37 (☎0531/37 690; ④) is a much better choice, though it tends to fill with business types. The best **eating** is in the narrowest lanes of the bazaar just north of Orféos, where the *Yiaxis* and *Apolavsis* ouzerís put out tables under arbours; there's also a good psistariá opposite the clocktower– behind the main mosque – run by Mumin Mehmet Muhsin.

Alexandhroúpoli

A modern city, designed by Russian military architects during the Russian-Turkish war of 1878, **ALEXANDHROÚPOLI** – Dedeağaç to the Turks and Bulgars – does not, on first acquaintance, have much to recommend it: a border town and military garrison,

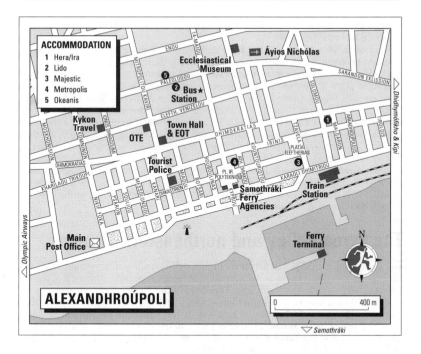

ACCOMMODATION
1 Hera/Ira
2 Lido
3 Majestic
4 Metropolis
5 Okeanis

ALEXANDHROÚPOLI

0 ——— 400 m

▽ *Samothráki*

with overland travellers and Greek holidaymakers in transit competing for limited space in the few hotels and the campsite.

The town became Greek in 1920, when it was renamed Alexandhroúpoli following a visit from the Greek King Alexander. There are no obvious sights and the heavy military presence can be oppressive – especially for single women. The Turkish quarter, literally on the wrong side of the tracks, may or may not whet the appetite for the unadulterated article across the border. Otherwise it's the seafront that best characterises the town. Dominated by a huge **lighthouse** built in 1880 (and adopted as the town's symbol), the area comes alive at dusk when the locals begin their evening volta. Traffic is diverted and the cafés spill out onto the road and around the lighthouse; makeshift stalls along the pavements sell salted seeds, pirate cassettes and grilled sweetcorn. There is also a little funfair on waste ground between the lighthouse and the harbour. On summer evenings, there are concerts and shows in the makeshift amphitheatre in the municipal gardens beyond the western end of the seafront.

Practicalities

Arriving by **train**, you'll be deposited conveniently next to the port; the **KTEL** is at Venizélou 36, several blocks inland.

For the island of **Samothráki** (see p.682), there is at least one daily **ferry** year-round and, in July and August, two a day – often three on Fridays, Saturdays and Sundays. Tickets can be bought from either the Vatsis agency at Kyprou 5 (☎0551/26 721) or the Arsinoi/Saos agent across the way (☎0551/22 215). Drivers should be aware that this is an expensive monopoly sailing: 10,000dr for a small car on the one-way, two-hour journey. **Hydrofoil** departures to Samothráki and occasionally beyond, are handled by Arsinoi or Caravettis Shipping (☎0551/37 074). The once-weekly G&A

ferry to Rhodes and several intervening islands is represented by Kykon Tours at Venizélou 68 (☎0551/32 398).

The **hotels** nearest the port and train station cater for those just passing through, whether by ferry to and from Samothráki or by train into Turkey or back to Thessaloníki. Choices get more comfortable, and quieter, as you move inland. The best value place is the *Lido* at Paleológou 15 (☎0551/28 808; ②), a bargain with its large en-suite rooms. Close to the train station is the *Majestic*, Platía Eleftherias 7 (☎0551/26 444; ②), a friendly, old-fashioned cheapie; the overpriced *Metropolis*, Athanasíou Dhiákou 11 (☎0551/26 443; ④) is nearby. More luxury means either the air-conditioned *Okeanis* at Paleológou 20 (☎0551/28 830, fax 34 118; ④), or the *Ira/Hera* at Dhimokratías 179 (☎0551/23 941, fax 34 222; ⑤), worthwhile if you get a quieter side room.

Restaurants are relatively limited in number, *Psarotaverna Anesti* at Athanasíou Dhiákou 5 being the best option, especially for supper. Just inland from the ticket agencies on Platía Iróon Polytekhníou, are two overpriced establishments; of the two, *Iy Klimataria* is more wholesome than *Iy Neraïda*.

The Évros Valley and northeastern Thrace

The **Évros Valley**, extending northeast of Alexandhroúpoli, is a prosperous but dull agricultural area. Most towns are in general ugly, modern concrete affairs full of bored soldiers; others, such as **Souflí** and **Dhidhymótikho**, retain some character and medieval monuments, and the main route through the valley is well served by public transport. The highlight here by a long way is the **Dhadhiá Forest** and wildlife reserve, also reachable by bus; if you have your own transport, you can head east from Alexandhroúpoli to the **Évros delta**, one of Europe's most important wetland areas for birds – and one of Greece's most sensitive military areas.

The Évros Delta

To the southeast, the **Évros Delta** is home to more than 250 different species of birds, including sea eagles. The easiest way to get there (if you have a car) is to leave Alexandhroúpoli on the main road (E90/E85) towards Turkey and Bulgaria. After passing the airport on the right after 7km, continue to **Loutrá Traianópolis**, 13km away, the site of an ancient Roman spa and its modern continuation. There are three modest hotels (all ②–③) in the vicinity, any of which would make a good base for exploring the delta, best approached by turning right off the main road and taking the dirt track that runs alongside the *Hotel Isidora*. The delta is crisscrossed with tracks along the dykes used by farmers taking advantage of the plentiful water supply for growing sweet corn and cotton. The south is the most inspiring part, well away from the army installations to the north; as you go further into the wetlands, the landscape becomes utterly desolate, with decrepit clusters of fishing huts among the sandbars and inlets. At the mouth of the delta is a huge saltwater lake called **Límni Dhrakónda**. Obviously what you see depends on the time of year, but even if birdlife is a bit thin on the ground, the atmosphere of the place is worth experiencing.

Féres

Northeast into the valley proper, 28km from Alexandhroúpoli, the otherwise unremarkable town of **FÉRES**, draped over several hills and ravines, has the imposing twelfth-century Byzantine church of **Panayía Kosmosótira** (usually open). Though rather vaguely signposted, it's recognizable from afar by its broad, lead-sheathed dome and commanding hilltop position. Founded by a member of the Comnene dynasty, it was originally part of a fortified monastery, of which only two ruined towers on the south remain. The church's exterior seems a bit unpromising, and the frescoes inside have been obliterated except for some saints at the transept ends. Mostly what impresses are the huge capitals of the paired pier-columns, and the lofty airiness of the twelve-windowed cupola, surrounded by four subsidiary domes, a design rare in Greece outside of Thessaloníki.

If you have to change buses en route to the border post at Kípi, as sometimes happens, and have some time to wait, the church is well worth seeking out; it's just a few paces east of the main commercial street. With your own car, it's an easy five-minute detour from the main highway. There's a hotel in Féres, the *Anthi* (☎0555/24 201; ④) on the way into town as you approach from the south.

The Dhadhiá Forest

Continuing north, the next attraction is the **Dhadhiá Forest Reserve**, reached by a road off to the left 1km after Likófi (Likófos). After a seven-kilometre drive through the rolling, forested hills, you reach the reserve **information centre** (daily 9am–8pm; ☎0554/32 290), at the heart of 35,200 hectares of protected oak and pine forest covering volcanic ridges. The diversity of landscape and vegetation and the proximity of important migration routes make for extremely diverse flora and fauna, but raptors are the star attraction, and main impetus for this WWF project. All cars – except for a special tour van which makes sorties several times daily (500dr) – are banned from core areas, and foot access is restricted to two marked trails: a two-hour route up to the reserve's highest point, 520-metre **Gíbrena** with its ruined Byzantine castle, and another ninety-minute loop route to an observation hide overlooking **Mavrórema** canyon. The region is claimed to be the last European home of the **black vulture** outside of Spain; they, and griffin vultures, make up the bulk of sightings from this post. You'll need a bird manual, as identification keys at the hide are in Greek only.

If you're a keen birder you'll want to stay the night, as the best raptor viewing is before 9am or after 6pm in summer (they can be seen all day Oct–March). Next to the visitors' centre stands a very clean **ecotourism hostel** (☎0554/32 263; ③), where the en-suite rooms have been given bird names instead of numbers (keys from the café across the car-park, until 11pm). The café supplies breakfast, but for other **meals** you'll retire to **DHADHIÁ** village, 1km back on the route in, which can offer the inexpensive *Psistaria tou Yirogou* near the Mobil station, plus a surprisingly active nightlife at a handful of **bars**.

Souflí and Dhidhymótikho

The nearest town to Dhadhiá, 7km north of the side turning, is **SOUFLÍ**, renowned for a now all-but-vanished silk industry. This is commemorated in a well signposted **museum** (Mon–Fri 8am–3.30pm, Sat & Sun 9am–2pm), a few hundred metres uphill and west of the main through road. It's lodged in a fine old ochre-tinted mansion, one of a number of surviving vernacular houses which lend Souflí some distinction. If you want to stay, there's just one **hotel**, the overpriced and noisy Orfeas (☎0554/22 922; ⑤), at no. 172 off the main highway. **Eating** and **drinking** options aren't great either, comprising mainly pizzerias, *souvladzídhika* and *barákia* for the lads in the armed forces.

DHIDHYMÓTIKHO, 30km further northeast by the border, is the only other stop along the trunk route of any interest. The old part of town is still partially enclosed by the remains of double Byzantine fortifications (hence the name, which means "double wall"), and some old houses and churches survive, but the area has a feeling of decay despite continuing efforts at restoration. Like Komotiní, the town once had a fine **synagogue** for its thousand-strong Jewish community, but this was sold and demolished in 1985, after having been ransacked during World War II at the instigation of the Nazis – who had spread the (false) rumour that treasure was secreted in its walls. Below the fortified hill, on the central platía, stands the most important surviving monument, a fourteenth-century **mosque**, the oldest and second largest in Greece. Its overall design, a great square box with a pyramidal roof, harks back to Seljuk and other pre-Ottoman prototypes in central Anatolia, and you'll see nothing else like it between here and Divriği or Erzurum in Turkey. Unfortunately, the interior is closed indefinitely for restoration, though you can still admire the ornate north portal.

Staying presents a problem, as neither of the town's **hotels** is wonderful. The less expensive and more central is the none too welcoming *Anesis* (☎0553/24 850; ④), 250m northwest of the mosque on Vassiléos Alexándhrou. The other choice is the *Plotini* (☎0553/23 400; ⑤) a rather gaudy building, inconveniently set 1km south of town across the river, on the west side of the road. For **eating**, one of the best restaurants in northern Greece is *To Koutoukaki* on the main road through town. Try also the *Zythestiatorio Kypselaki* (lunch only), in the central market hall just above the mosque.

Metaxádhes and Orestiádha

Further north still, smaller roads take you through isolated communities and beautiful countryside. **METAXÁDHES** is one of the most handsome villages in the area, sited on a steep hill, its large houses built traditionally of stone and wood with tiled roofs and lush gardens. Fought over by Bulgars and Turks, Metaxádhes used to support a Turkish community but now its population is exclusively Greek, although older residents still speak some Turkish. Beyond Metaxádhes, you descend north into the vast, fertile **Árdhas River plain** that dominates the northeastern tip of Greek Thrace. Rich farmland – the main crops are sunflowers, sweet corn and (increasingly) sugar beet – supports a large number of modern villages, many of them populated by settlers from Asia Minor.

Hemmed in on three sides by Bulgaria and Turkey, it has been a Greek priority to establish a Greek population in this extremely sensitive corner of Thrace; lately the process has continued, with Greeks repatriated from the ex-Soviet Union. Apart from its agricultural importance, the area has great strategic significance. Barracks are liberally scatted through the hinterland and along the eastern border with Turkey; there are numerous surveillance posts, all flying Greek flags, and looking over to the minarets of Turkey across the Évros river valley.

The main centre in this northeastern corner is **ORESTIÁDHA**, a busy market town with restaurants, bars and lots of cake shops in its main square. It also has at least one bank, something worth bearing in mind when returning from Bulgaria or Turkey, though you'll get a poor rate exchanging the currencies of those countries. You could spend an expensive night here before or after crossing the border; **hotels** include the new *Alexandros* (☎0552/27 000, fax 29 632; ⑤), the older *Elektra* (☎0552/23 540, fax 23 133; ⑤) at Pandazínou 50, with the *Iridanos* **restaurant** alongside, and the now very old *Vienni/Vienna* (☎0552/22 578; ④). One hundred metres up the road from the side of the *Vienni* is a very pleasant local taverna.

On to Turkey or Bulgaria

Crossing into Turkey from Alexandhroúpoli, you are presented with a bewildering choice of routes; currently there's only one daily rail link to Bulgaria.

British passport holders now need a **Turkish visa**, which costs £10 at the border; Americans also require a visa, costing $20. Border guards can be very exigent about linking currencies to nationalities – Brits for example, can only pay with sterling, not any other hard currency – and will often only accept other denominations with ruinous surcharges, so come prepared. **Bulgarian visas** are required for all nationals and are expensive; prices fluctuate, but count on paying $70 (have US currency ready) for a transit pass at the border, somewhat less if you obtain it at a consulate beforehand.

By bus to Turkey

The simplest way to travel from northern Greece to Turkey, if you can get a ticket, is to go by **bus** direct to Istanbul. There are several departures daily, one run by OSE (tickets from the train station), the others by private companies (ask at travel agents). The problem is that most of the buses start in Thessaloníki, and by this stage most are full. In addition to buses to Istanbul, there are private buses three or four times a week to Edirne, just across the border; ask for details at travel agents in Xánthi, Komotiní or Alexandhroúpoli.

An alternative is to take a local bus to the border at **KÝPI** (6 daily). You are not allowed to cross the frontier here on foot, but it is generally no problem to get a driver to shuttle you the 500m across to the Turkish post, and perhaps even to give you a lift beyond. The nearest town is Ipsala (5km further on), but if possible get as far as Keşan (30km), from where buses to Istanbul are much more frequent.

By train to Turkey

Travelling by **train** to Istanbul should be simpler than getting the bus. However, the only through connection leaves Alexandhroúpoli at 6am, crossing the border at Píthio by 8am and taking (in theory) nine more hours (including a long halt at the frontier) to reach Istanbul. In recent years this has been downgraded from express status to a slow local, so don't be surprised if the train – which originates in Thessaloníki – shows up late.

You might prefer to take a more frequent local train through Píthio and on to **KASTANIÉS**, opposite Turkish Edirne. The most useful departure from Alexandhroúpoli is currently at 6am; later ones arrive after the border post (daily 9am–1pm) has closed. There's no accommodation in Kastaniés, but unlike Kýpi you are allowed to walk across the border (under army escort). Once on the Turkish side there's bus service to the first Turkish village, 2km beyond the frontier; it's 7km in total from the border to Edirne (Adhrianoúpoli to the Greeks) – an attractive and historic city with some important Ottoman monuments and frequent buses making the three-hour trip to Istanbul. For more information, see the *Rough Guide to Turkey*.

Into Bulgaria

To Bulgaria from Alexandhroúpoli there is just one connecting **train** daily, leaving at 6am and reaching Greek Orménio just under three hours later, where you may have to change trains for the fifteen-minute journey to Svilengrad inside Bulgaria. This turns around less than an hour later for a service back to Alexandhroúpoli. From Svilengrad (which has just one expensive hotel), it is best to plan on moving on the same day towards Plovdiv.

travel details

Note: Onward services in the states of the former Yugoslavia are currently sharply reduced, and with the exception of trains into the FYROM from Thessaloníki it is impossible to obtain reliable information on schedules; most of these routes are, in any case, inadvisable for independent travellers.

Trains

Alexandhroúpoli–Istanbul (Turkey) Semi-direct (change cars at Píthio or Uzunköprö) day train (6am), arriving Istanbul around 5pm, after an hour or longer wait at the border.

Alexandhroúpoli–Dhidhymótihko–Orestiádha–Kastaniés (for Edirne) 6 daily, but only 2 departures (5.22am and 6.01am) reach frontier post while open; 2hr 45min for whole journey.

Alexandhroúpoli–Svilengrad (Bulgaria) 1 daily (6.01am); 3hr.

Thessaloníki–Sofia, via Promakhón (1 daily; 8hr 30min).

Thessaloníki–Gevgeli (FYROM) 3 daily; 1hr 30min–2hr.

Thessaloníki–Kateríni/Lárissa/Athens 4 express, 5 slower trains daily in each direction (6–7hr 30min for entire journey).

Thessaloníki–Lárissa/Vólos 3 daily in each direction, changing at Lárissa (4hr total).

Thessaloníki–Véria/Édhessa/Amýndeo/Flórina 7 daily in each direction, changing as necessary at Amýndeo; connections between Amýndeo and Kozáni 7 times daily; 1 daily only up to Édhessa.

Thessaloníki–Sérres–Dhráma–Xánthi–Komotiní–Alexandhroúpoli 3 daily expresses, well spaced, plus 3 slower trains (Thessaloníki–Xánthi 4hr–5hr; Xánthi-Alexandhroúpoli 1hr 30min–2hr).

N.B. OSE also has **long-distance buses** from Thessaloníki to Istanbul, Sofia, Milan, Paris, London, Vienna and towns in Germany.

Buses

Alexandhroúpoli to: Dhadhiá (2 daily; 1hr 20min); Dhidhymótikho (17 daily Mon–Fri, 14 daily Sat–Sun; 2hr); Istanbul (daily OSE and other private buses; 8hr); Kípi (5 daily; 45min); Komotiní (14 daily; 1hr).

Édhessa to: Flórina (4 daily; 2hr); Kastoriá (4 daily; 2hr 30min, change at Amýndeo); Véria (6 Mon–Sat, 2 Sun; 50min).

Flórina to: Préspa basin, 2 daily (1 hr).

Kastoriá to: Flórina (4 daily indirect services via Amýndeo; 3hr including layover).

Kateríni to: Dhíon (12 daily, 20min); to Litókhoro, for Mount Olympus (18 Mon–Sat, 12 Sun; 30min).

Kavála to: Keramotí (12 daily; 1hr); Philippi (half-hourly 6am–8.30pm; 20min); Xánthi/Komotiní (half-hourly 6am–9pm; 1hr–2hr); Alexandhroúpoli (5 daily; 3hr).

Komotiní to: Fanári (7 daily Mon–Fri, 6 Sat, 5 Sun)

Kozáni to: Grevená (8 daily; 1hr); Siátista (4 daily; 30min).

Thessaloníki to: Alexandhroúpoli (5 daily; 6hr); Arnéa-Ierissós/Ouranópoli (5–7 daily; 2hr–3hr 30min); Athens (16 daily; 7hr); Flórina (6 daily; 3hr 30min); Istanbul (daily OSE, others privately operated; 14hr); Kalambáka (7 daily; 4hr 30min); Ioánnina (5 daily; 7hr); Kastoriá (5 daily; 4hr); Litókhoro, for Mount Olympus (14 daily; 1hr 30min); Kavála (hourly 6am–10pm; 3hr); Pella/Édhessa (hourly; 1hr–1hr 15min); Sárti, via Políyiros (3 daily; 4hr 30min); Sofia (2 weekly; 7hr 30min); Véria (half-hourly; 1hr 15min); Vólos (4 daily; 4hr); Vourvouroú, via Políyiros (3 daily; 3hr).

Véria to: Édhessa, via Náoussa (6 daily; 1hr 15min); Kozáni (8 daily; 1hr).

Xánthi to: Ekhínos (6 daily; 45min); Kavála (half-hourly, 6am–9pm; 1hr); Komotiní (17–18 daily, via coast or inland; 50min); Thessaloníki (6–7 daily; 4hr).

Ferries

Alexandhroúpoli to: Límnos, Lésvos, Khíos, Sámos, Kós or Kálymnos, Rhodes (1 weekly); Samothráki (1–2 daily in season, 4 weekly out of season).

Kavála to: Thássos (Skála Prínou; 4–15 daily, average 8, depending on season); to Samothráki (2–5 weekly in season); to Límnos and Áyios Efstrátios (2–4 weekly); to Lésvos and Khíos (2–3 weekly).

Keramotí to: Thássos (Liménas) (10 daily, year-round).

Thessaloníki to: Límnos, Lésvos and Khíos (1–2 weekly) Sámos, Kós, Rhodes (1 weekly); Iráklion (Crete) via Vólos, Skiáthos, Tínos, Sýros, Náxos, Páros and Thíra (2–3 weekly March–Oct); to Skýros, Skópelos, Alónissos (3 weekly in summer).

Hydrofoils

Alexandhroúpoli to: Samothráki (1–2 daily); Thássos (Liménas; 3 weekly); Límnos (1 weekly, mid-June–early Sept).

Kavála to: Thássos (Liménas; 8–15 daily); Thássos (west coast resorts; 2–4 daily).

Thessaloníki to: Skiáthos, Skópelos and Alónissos (5 weekly June to early July, daily early July to early September).

Flights

Alexandhroúpoli to: Athens (1–3 daily; 1hr).

Kastoriá to: Athens (3–6 weekly; 1hr 15min).

Kozáni to: Athens (3–6 weekly; 1hr 10min).

Thessaloníki to: Athens (6–7 daily year-round; 50min); Corfu (2 weekly; 1hr); Ioánnina (5–7 weekly; 50min); Iráklion, Crete (2–3 weekly; 2hr); Khaniá, Crete (2 weekly; 2hr); Khíos (2weekly; 1hr 50min); Lésvos (6–8 weekly; 1–2hr); Límnos (4–7 weekly; 50min); Sámos (2 weekly; 1hr 40min).

PART THREE

THE

ISLANDS

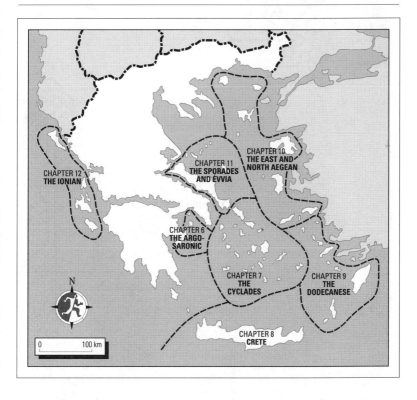

CHAPTER 12
THE IONIAN

CHAPTER 11
THE SPORADES
AND ÉVVIA

CHAPTER 10
THE EAST AND
NORTH AEGEAN

CHAPTER 6
THE ARGO-
SARONIC

CHAPTER 7
THE
CYCLADES

CHAPTER 9
THE
DODECANESE

CHAPTER 8
CRETE

N

0   100 km

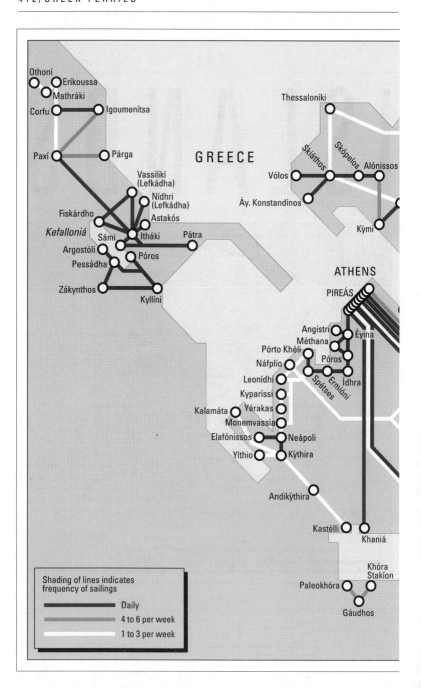

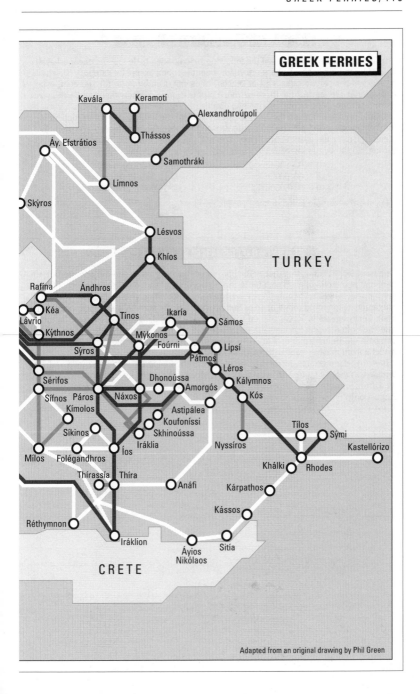

GREEK FERRIES

Kavála
Keramotí
Alexandhroúpoli
Áy. Efstrátios
Thássos
Samothráki
Límnos
Skýros
Lésvos
Khíos
TURKEY
Rafína
Ándhros
Kéa
Tínos
Ikaría
Sámos
Lávrio
Kýthnos
Mýkonos
Foúrni
Lipsí
Sýros
Pátmos
Sérifos
Dhonoússa
Léros
Kálymnos
Sífnos
Páros
Náxos
Amorgós
Kós
Kímolos
Astipálea
Koufoníssi
Tílos
Síkinos
Skhinoússa
Sými
Mílos
Folégandhros
Íos
Iráklia
Nyssíros
Kastellórizo
Thírassía
Thíra
Khálki
Rhodes
Réthymnon
Anáfi
Kárpathos
Iráklion
Áyios
Nikólaos
Sitía
Kássos
CRETE

Adapted from an original drawing by Phil Green

ACCOMMODATION PRICE CODES

Throughout the book we've used the following **price codes** to denote the cheapest available room in high season; all are prices for a double room, except for category ①, which represents per person rates. Out of season, rates can drop by up to fifty percent, especially if you are staying for three or more nights. Single rooms, where available, cost around seventy percent of the price of a double.

Rented private rooms on the islands usually fall into the ② or ③ categories, depending on their location and facilities, and the season; a few in the ④ category are more like plush self-catering apartments. They are not generally available from late October through to the beginning of April, when only hotels tend to remain open.

① 1400–2000dr   ④ 8000–12,000dr

② 4000–6000dr   ⑤ 12,000–16,000dr

③ 6000–8000dr ·   ⑥ 16,000dr and upwards

For more accommodation details, see pp.39–42.

FERRY ROUTES AND SCHEDULES

Details of ferry routes, together with approximate journey times and frequencies, are to be found at the end of each chapter in the "travel details" section. Please note that these are for general guidance only. Ferry schedules change with alarming regularity and the only information to be relied upon is that provided by the port police in each island harbour. Ferry agents in Pireás and on the islands are helpful, of course, but keep in mind that they often represent just one ferry line and won't neccessarily inform you of the competition. Be aware, too, that ferry services to the smaller islands tend to be pretty skeletal from mid-September through to May.

In many island groups, ferries are supplemented by Flying Dolphin hydrofoils – which tend to be twice as quick and twice the price. Most of the major hydrfoil routes are operated from May to early September, with lesser ones sometimes running to July and August only.

CHAPTER SIX

THE ARGO-SARONIC

T he rocky, volcanic chain of **Argo-Saronic** islands, most of them barely an olive's throw from the Argolid, differ to a surprising extent not just from the mainland but from one another. Less surprising is their massive popularity, with Éyina (Aegina) especially becoming something of an Athenian suburb at weekends.

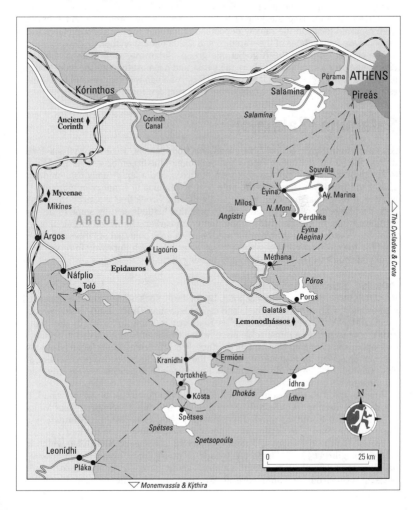

Ídhra (Hydra), Póros and Spétses are not far behind in summer, though their visitors tend to be predominantly cruise- and package-tourists. More than any other group, these islands are at their best out of season, when populations fall dramatically and the port towns return to quiet, provincial-backwater life.

Éyina, important in antiquity and more or less continually inhabited since then, is the most fertile of the group, famous for its pistachio nuts, as well as for one of the finest ancient temples in Greece. Its main problem – the crowds – can be escaped by avoiding weekends, or taking the time to explore its satellite isles, **Angístri** and **Moní**.

The three southerly islands, **Spétses**, **Ídhra** and **Póros**, are pine-cloaked and relatively infertile. They were not really settled until medieval times, when refugees from the mainland – principally Albanian Christians – established themselves here. In response to the barrenness of their new home the islanders adopted piracy as a livelihood, and the seamanship and huge fleets thus acquired were placed at the disposal of the Greek nation during the War of Independence. Today foreigners and Athenians have replaced locals in the rapidly depopulating harbour towns, and windsurfers and sailboats are faint echoes of the warships and kaïkia once at anchor.

The closest island of the Argo-Saronic group, **Salamína**, is virtually a suburb of Pireás, just over a kilometre offshore to its east, and it almost touches the industrial city of Mégara to the west as well. It is frequented by Athenian weekenders and is also used as a base for commuting to the capital, but sees very few foreign visitors.

Salamína (Salamis)

Salamína is the quickest possible island hop from Athens. Take the Kyfissia–Pireás train to the end of the line in Pireás and then one of the green buses marked Pérama to the shipyard port of Pérama, just west of Pireás, and a ferry (daily 5am–midnight; 120dr) will whisk you across to the little port of Paloukía in a matter of minutes. The ferry crosses the narrow strait where, in 480BC, the Greek fleet trounced the Persian fleet, despite being outnumbered three to one; this battle is said by some to be more significant than the battle of Marathon, ten years earlier. On arrival in Paloukía, you won't be rewarded by desirable or isolated beaches – the pollution of Pireás and Athens is a little too close for comfort although the water has much improved in recent years – but you soon escape the capital's *néfos* and city pace.

Paloukía, Salamína and Selínia

PALOUKÍA is really just a transit point. By the ferry dock is a taverna and opposite is a bus station, with services to the island capital Salamína Town (3km), and beyond.

SALAMÍNA TOWN (also known as Kouloúri) is home to 18,000 of the island's 23,000 population. It's a ramshackle place, with a couple of banks, a fish market and an over-optimistic (and long-closed) tourist office. Pretty much uniquely for an island town – and emphasizing the absence of tourists – there is no bike or moped rental outlet, and also no hotel (not that you'd want to stay). Fortunately, bus services are excellent, linking most points on the island.

Buses marked **Faneroméni** run to the port at the northwest tip of the island, the **Voudoro peninsula**, where there are ferries across to Lákki Kalomírou, near Mégara on the Athens–Kórinthos road. En route it passes close by the **Monastery of Faneroméni** (6km from Salamína), rather majestically sited above the gulf.

Around 6km to the south of Paloukía is a third island port, **SELÍNIA**, which has connections direct to the Pireás ferry dock (winter 9.30am, summer five crossings daily between 8am–2.30pm; 330dr; 30min). This is the main summer resort, with a pleasant waterfront, a bank, several tavernas and two inexpensive hotels, the

Akroyali (☎01/46 73 263; ②) and *Votsalakia* (☎01/46 71 334; ③). Selínia can be reached direct by bus from Paloukía.

Eándio and the south
South from Salamína Town, the road edges the coast towards Eándio (6km; regular buses). There are a few tavernas along the way, but the sea vistas are not inspiring. **EÁNDIO**, however, is quite a pleasant village, with a little pebble beach and the island's best **hotel**, the *Gabriel* (☎01/46 62 275; ④), owned by poet and journalist Giorgos Tzimas, who can be prevailed upon to recite a poem or two. The hotel overlooks the bay, whose waters are returning to health.

Two roads continue from Eándio. The one to the southeast runs to the unassuming village resorts of Peráni and Paralía (both around 4km from Eándio). The more interesting route is southeast to Kanákia (8km from Eándio; no buses), over the island's pine-covered mountain, and passing (at around 5km) a monastery – dedicated, like almost all Salamína churches, to Áyios Nikólaos. At the monastery you could turn off the road (left) along a track to the harbour and small-scale resort of Peristéria (5km). This is a much more attractive settlement than the littered beach and scruffy huts of Kanákia itself.

Éyina (Aegina)

Given its current population of a little over 10,000, it seems incredible that **Éyina** (Aegina) was a major power in Classical times – and a rival to Athens. It carried on trade to the limits of the known world, maintained a sophisticated silver coinage system (the first in Greece) and had prominent athletes and craftsmen. However, during the fifth century BC the islanders made the political mistake of siding with their fellow Dorians,

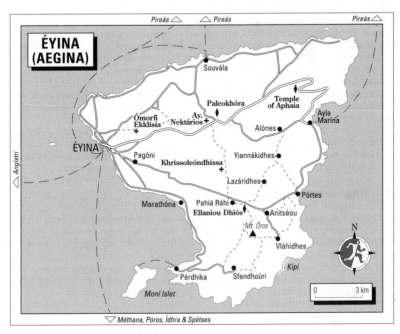

the Spartans, which Athens seized on as an excuse to act on a long-standing jealousy; her fleets defeated those of the islanders in two separate sea battles and, after the second, the population was expelled and replaced by more tractable colonists.

Subsequent history was less distinguished, with the familiar central Greece pattern of occupation – by Romans, Franks, Venetians, Catalans and Turks – before the War of Independence brought a brief period as seat of government for the fledgling Greek nation. These days, the island is most famous for its **pistachio orchards**, whose thirsty trees lower the water table several feet annually; hence the notices warning you of the perennial water crisis.

Athenians regard Éyina as a beach annexe for their city, being the closest place to the capital most of them would swim at, though for tourists it has a monument as fine as any in the Aegean in its beautiful fifth-century BC **Temple of Aphaia**. This is located on the east coast, close to the port of **Ayía Marína**, and if it is your primary goal, you'd do best to take one of the ferries or hydrofoils which run directly to that port in season. If you plan to stay, then make sure your boat will dock at **Éyina Town**, the island capital. Ferries and hydrofoils also stop at **Souvála**, a Greek weekend retreat between the two ports devoid of interest to outsiders. Hydrofoils, incidentally, are far more frequent, run from the same quay in Pireás as the conventional boats, and cost hardly any more for this particular destination.

Éyina Town

A solitary column of a Temple of Apollo beckons as your ferry or hydrofoil steams around the point into the harbour at **ÉYINA TOWN**. The island's capital, it makes an attractive base, with some grand old buildings from the time (1826–28) when it served as the first capital of Greece after the War of Independence. And for somewhere so close to Athens, it isn't especially overrun by foreign tourists, nor are accommodation prices unduly inflated except on weekends.

The **harbour** is workaday rather than picturesque, but is nonetheless appealing: fishermen talk and tend their nets, and kaïkia loaded with produce from the mainland bob at anchor. North of the port, behind the small town beach, the rather weather-beaten Apollo temple column stands on a low hill that was the ancient acropolis and is known, logically enough, as **Kolóna** (Column). Around the temple are rather obscure **ruins** (daily 8.30am–3pm; 500dr), only worth it for the sweeping view from Moní islet on the south to the mainland shore on the northwest. There is a small museum in the grounds. On the north flank of Kolóna hill there's an attractive bay with a small, sandy **beach** – the best spot for swimming in the immediate vicinity of the town.

The town's other sights, such as they are, are the frescoed thirteenth-century church of **Ómorfi Ekklisía**, fifteen minutes' walk east of the port, and a house in the suburb of Livádhi, just to the north, where a plaque recalls the residence of **Nikos Kazantzakis**, when he was writing his most celebrated book, *Zorba the Greek*.

Arrival and accommodation

The **bus station** is also on the recently refurbished Platía Ethneyersías, with an excellent service to most villages on the island, while the largest moped and cycle rental place – Sklavenas Rent-a-Car (☎0297/22 892), which also rents open-sided cars at slightly above normal island rates – is just beyond the pink corner building immediately to the north. There are a few mountain bikes available, but Éyina is large and hilly enough to make motorized cycles worthwhile for anything other than a pedal to the beaches between Éyina Town and Pérdhika. Three **banks** line the waterfront; the **post office** is on Platía Ethneyersías; while the **OTE** lies well inland beyond the cathedral. There's a **tourist police** post in the same building as the regular police, immediately behind the post office but reached from Leonárdhou Ladhá. Aegina Island Holidays

(☎0297/26 430) on the waterfront, offers excursions to the Epidavros theatre festival and handles tickets for the Sea Falcon Hydrofoils.

Good inexpensive **accommodation** can be found in the rooms rented by Andonis Marmarinos at Leonárdhou Ladhá 30 (☎0297/22 954; ④); they're spotless, fairly but though not en suite. For more comfort try the *Hotel Marmarinos* nearby at no. 24, run by a branch of the same family (☎0297/23 510; ④). Across the street, *Hotel Artemis* (☎0297/25 195; ④) is appealingly set in a pistachio orchard. The slightly fancier but no more expensive *Areti* (☎0297/23 593; ④) and *Avra* (☎0297/22 303; ④) hotels are on the seafront between Platía Ethneyersías and Kolóna, where ocean views compensate for the traffic noise. Next to the *Avra* is the inexpensive and friendly *Plaza Hotel* (☎0297/25 600; ③).

Eating and entertainment

Perhaps the best **food** in town is to be had at the newly opened *En Agini* restaurant in a courtyard in Spiro Rodi street just below the huge St Nikolas church. The food is of high quality, and the prices reasonable. Directly behind the fish market is a particularly good and inexpensive seafood **taverna**, the *Psarotaverna Agora*, with outdoor seating on the cobbles in summer. Similar in concept, though not quite as good value, is *Ta Vrekhamena*, a little hole-in-the-wall on Leonárdhou Ladhá just seaward from the police station, offering a very limited menu of bulk wine, ouzo and grilled octopus. Next to the *Hotel Areti*, the small *Lekkas* is excellent for no-nonsense meat grills by the waterside. At the other end of the block next to the Plaza Hotel is *Floisvos*, offering food grilled over charcoal on tables by the sea. At the south end of the quay, by the Alpha Trapeza Pisteos (Credit Bank), *Maridhaki* is a less carnivorous traditional place, dishing up the usual Greek oven standards. For a mild blowout, try Petros's *Ippokambos* on the road alongside the football ground on the corner with the old prison; it's superb for mezédhes.

In terms of **nightlife**, Éyina Town boasts two summer **cinemas**, the Olympia near the football grounds before the *Miranda* hotel and the new Akroyiali at the end of Eyina harbour on the Pérdhika road, which shows quality foreign films; the winter cinema, the Titina, is by the park with the medieval tower-house, a block below OTE. On the corner of Aiándos and Piléos, the *Belle Epoque* bar is worth a visit for its ornate turn-of-the-century architecture. Nightclubs and discos are mostly to be found across the island in Ayía Marína but the *Eltiana* nightclub is just behind the Ávra beach.

The Temple of Aphaia

The Doric **Temple of Aphaia** (Mon–Fri 8.30am–7pm, Sat & Sun 8.30am–3pm; 800dr) lies 12km east of Éyina Town, among pines that are tapped to flavour the local retsina, and beside a less aesthetic radio mast. It is one of the most complete and visually complex ancient buildings in Greece, with superimposed arrays of columns and lintels evocative of an Escher drawing. Built early in the fifth century BC, or possibly at the end of the sixth century, it predates the Parthenon by around sixty years. The dedication is unusual: Aphaia was a Cretan nymph who had fled from the lust of King Minos, and seems to have been worshipped almost exclusively on Éyina. As recently as two centuries ago the temple's pediments were intact and virtually perfect, depicting two battles at Troy. However, like the Elgin marbles they were "bought" from the Turks – this time by Ludwig of Bavaria, which explains their current residence in the Munich Glyptothek museum.

There are buses to the temple from Éyina Town, or you could walk from Ayía Marína along the path that takes up where Kolokotróni leaves off, but the best approach is by rented motorbike, which allows you to stop at the monastery of Áyios Nektários, and the island's former capital of Paleokhóra.

Áyios Nektários and Paleokhóra

Áyios Nektários, a whitewashed modern convent situated around halfway to the Temple of Aphaia, was named in honour of the Greek Orthodox Church's most recent saint, who died in 1920 and was canonized in 1962. A huge church belonging to the convent was recently completed on the main road below. Opposite the convent car park a partly paved road leads up into the hills towards the seventeenth-century convent of Khryssoleóndissa – primarily worth seeing for its views.

Paleokhóra, a kilometre or so further east, was built in the ninth century as protection against piracy, but it failed singularly in this capacity during Barbarossa's 1537 raid. Abandoned in 1827 following Greek independence, Paleokhóra is now utterly deserted, but possesses the romantic appeal of a ghost village. You can drive right up to the site: take the turning left after passing the new large church and keep going about 400m. Some twenty of Paleokhóra's reputed 365 churches and monasteries – one for every saint's day – remain in recognizable state, and can be visited, but only those of Episkopí (locked), Áyios Yeóryios and Metamórfosis (on the lower of the two trails) retain frescoes of any merit or in any state of preservation. Little remains of the town itself; when the islanders left, they simply abandoned their houses and moved to Éyina Town.

The East: Ayía Marína and Pórtes

The island's major package resort of **AYÍA MARÍNA**, 15km from Éyina Town, lies on the east coast of the island, south of the Aphaia Temple ridge. The concentrated tackiness of its jam-packed high street is something rarely seen this side of Corfu: signs for Guinness, burger bars and salaciously named ice creams and cocktails. The beach is packed and overlooked by constantly sprouting, half-built hotels, and the water is not good. It's really only worth coming here for connections to Pireás. There are some five ferries a day in season, with departures in the morning and late in the afternoon, and now the Sea Falcon Line hydrofoils (☎0297/26 430) link both Ayía Marína and Souvála with Pireás.

Beyond the resort, the paved road continues south 8km to **PÓRTES**, a pokey, low-key shore hamlet, dramatically set with a cliff on the north and wooded valleys behind. Among the uneasy mix of new summer villas-in-progress (no short-term accommodation) and old basalt cottages are scattered two or three tiny fish **tavernas** and snack bars, with a functional beach between the two fishing anchorages. Soon the road deteriorates to a steep, rough dirt track climbing to the village of Anitséou, just below a major saddle on the flank of Mount Óros. A small taverna, *The Hunter's Inn* (☎0297/40 210), tucked away above the village, serves home cooked food and locally baked bread at weekends, and is run by English-speaking Greeks returned from abroad. The road surface improves slightly as it forges west towards the scenic village of **Pakhiá Rákhi**, almost entirely rebuilt in traditional style by foreign owners. From here, a sharp descent leads to the main west-coast road at Marathóna (for which see opposite), or a longer, paved and tree-lined route back to Éyina Town.

Mount Óros

Just south of the saddle between Pahiá Ráhi and Anitséou, mentioned above, are the massive foundations of the shrine of **Ellaníou Dhiós**, with the monastery of Taxiárkes squatting amid the massive masonry. The 532m summit of **Mount Óros**, an hour's walk from the highest point of the road, is capped by the modern Chapel of the Ascension, and has views across the entire island and over much of the Argo-Saronic Gulf.

A few other **paths** cross the largely roadless, volcanic flanks of Óros from Vlakhídhes. Amazingly in this bulldozer-mad country, one to **Sfendhoúri** hamlet still survives, initially marked by white paint dots. Sfendhoúri itself has a road link with Pérdhika (see opposite). Gerald Thompson's *A Walking Guide to Aegina*, available locally, describes in detail a series of walks across the range of mountains and wooded valleys between Mount Oros and the Aphaias temple and down to the port of Souvala, all avoiding main roads.

The West: Marathóna, Pérdhika and Moní islet

The road due south of Éyina Town running along the west coast of the island is served by regular buses (8–10 daily). **MARATHÓNA**, 5km from Éyina, constitutes the only sandy-beach resort on the west coast and is tolerable enough, with its clutch of rooms and tavernas along the shore.

PÉRDHIKA, 9km along and the end of the line, is more scenically set on its little bay and certainly has the best range of non-packaged accommodation on the island, besides the main town. There are **rooms**, and the *Hotel Hippocampus* (☎0297/61 363; ③). On the pedestrianized esplanade overlooking the water are a dozen **tavernas**; the best is *Argyris To Proreo*, which boasts log-cabin-like decor. At the head of the bay by the bus stop is the *Votsitsanos* taverna and bar running the length of the small beach and shaded by eucalyptus trees.

The only other diversion at Pérdhika is a trip to **Moní islet** just offshore (300dr one way; 10min; several departures daily). There was once an EOT-run campsite on Móni, but this is now abandoned and derelict. There are no facilities on the islet and most of it is fenced off as a nature conservation area. It's really only worth the trip for a swim in wonderfully clear water, as Pérdhika bay itself is of dubious cleanliness and has very small beaches.

Angístri

Angístri, a half-hour by boat from Éyina, is small enough to be overlooked by most island-hoppers, though it's now in many foreign holiday brochures. The island fosters an uneasy coexistence between Athenian and German old-timers, who bought property here years ago, and British newcomers on package trips. Beaches, however,

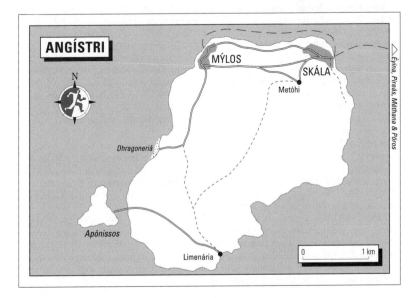

remain better and less crowded than on Éyina, and out of season the pine-covered island succumbs to a leisurely village pace, with many islanders still making a living from fishing and farming. Headscarves worn by the old women indicate the islanders' Albanian ancestry, and until recently they still spoke *Arvanítika* – a dialect of medieval Albanian with Greek accretions – amongst themselves.

The Angístri dock in Éyina Town, separate from the main harbour, is directly opposite the *Ethniki Trapeza* (National Bank). **Boats** from Éyina and Pireás call at both the main villages, Skála and Mílos. **From Pireás**, a direct ferry runs at least twice daily in season, once a day out of season: the journey takes two hours. From Éyina (departures from the fish market harbour), there are boats four or five times a day in season, twice a day out of season.

Skála and Mýlos

The essentially modern resort of **SKÁLA** is dominated by dreary modern apartment buildings and hotels with little to distinguish or commend them; they tend to face either inland or the windswept north side of the peninsula over which Skála is rapidly spreading. The popular town beach, the island's only sandy one, nestles against the protected south shore of this headland, below an enormous church that is the local landmark. Between the beach and the ferry dock are two **hotels** with a bit more going for them position-wise: the *Akti* (☎0297/91 232; ④) and the *Anayennisis* (☎0297/91 332; ④); on summer weekends you would be well advised to reserve ahead at one of these. The tavernas here are pretty nondescript. Both **mopeds** and **mountain bikes** are available for rent at slightly inflated rates (even compared with Éyina); Limenária, the end of the trans-island road, is only 8km distant, so in cooler weather you can comfortably cross Angístri on foot or by bike. A road to the left of the harbour leads within fifteen minutes to the *Angistri Club*, with a disco-bar on the rocks above the sea. From there, it's another ten minutes' walk to a secluded **pebble beach** backed by crumbling cliffs and pine-covered hills; along with Dhragoneriá (see below), this is the best the island has to offer, and is clothing-optional.

Metókhi, the hillside hamlet just above Skála, was once the main village, and in recent years has been completely bought up and restored by foreigners and Athenians; there are no facilities.

Utterly overbuilt Skála threatens in the near future to merge with **MÝLOS**, just 1500m west along the north coast. Once you penetrate a husk of new construction, you find an attractive village centre built in the traditional Argo-Saronic style. Although there's no decent beach nearby, it makes a preferable base to Skála, with plenty of rented **rooms** and some **hotels**. The *Milos Hotel* (☎0297/91 241; ④) is a good, well-positioned choice, and Maroussa Tours, on the ground floor of the hotel, is very helpful. *Ta Tria Adherfia*, in the centre of the village, is the island's best taverna.

The rest of the island

A regular bus service, designed to dovetail with the ferry schedule, connects Skála and Mýlos with Limenária on the far side of the island – or you could hike from Metókhi along a winding track through the pine forest, with views across to Éyina and the Peloponnese. The paved west-coast road takes you past the turning for **Dhragoneriá**, an appealing pebble beach with a dramatic backdrop.

LIMENÁRIA is a small farming community, still largely unaffected by tourism. There are two tavernas, a few rooms and a sign pointing to a misleadingly named "beach", which is really just a spot, often monopolized by male naturists, where you can swim off the rocks. A half-hour walk northwest of here, through olive and pine trees, and past a shallow lake, will bring you to a causeway linking Angístri with the tiny islet of **Dhoroússa**, where there's a seasonal taverna.

Póros

Separated from the mainland by a 350-metre strait, **Póros** ("the ford") only just counts as an island. But qualify it does and, far more than the other Argo-Saronic Gulf islands, it is package tour territory, while its proximity to Pireás also means a weekend invasion by Athenians. Unspoiled it isn't, and the beaches are few and poor, especially compared with neighbouring Ídhra and Spétses. The island town has a bit of character though, and the topography is interesting. Póros is in fact two islands, **Sferiá** (which shelters Póros Town) and the more extensive **Kalávria**, separated from each other by a shallow engineered canal.

In addition to its regular ferry and hydrofoil connections with Pireás and the other Argo-Saronics, Póros has frequent boats shuttling across from the mainland port of **Galatás** in the Peloponnese: there's a car ferry every twenty minutes. This allows for some interesting excursions – locally to the lemon groves of Limonódhassos (see p.166), Ancient Troezen (see p.166) near Trizíni, and the nearby Devil's Bridge (see p.166). Further afield, day-trips to Náfplio (see p.157) or to performances of ancient drama at the great theatre of Epidaurus (see p.162) are possible by car, or by taking an excursion, available through travel agents in Póros Town (see below).

Póros Town

Ferries from the Argo-Saronics or from Galatás drop you at **PÓROS**, the only town on the island, which rises steeply on all sides of the tiny volcanic peninsula of Sferiá. The harbour and town are picturesque, and the cafés and the waterfront lively. There are no special sights, save for a little **archeological museum** (Mon–Sat 9am–3pm; free) with a display on the mainland site of Troezen.

Near the boat dock is Hellenic Sun Travel, which has a large number of rooms available (☎0298 25 901/3; ③–⑥). Just back from the waterfront are three other **travel agents**:

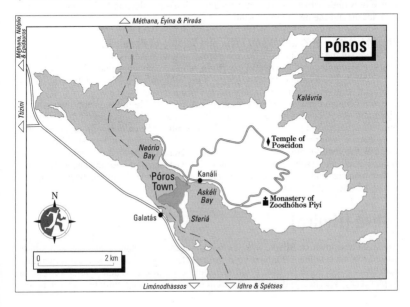

Marinos Tours (☎0298/23 423), sole agents for the Flying Dolphin hydrofoils, Family Tours (☎0298/23 743) and Saronic Gulf Travel (☎0298/24 555). All these agencies **exchange money**, sell island **maps**, arrange **accommodation** in rented rooms, and handle **tours** off the island. If you want to look around on your own, the quieter and preferable places are in the streets back – and up – from the clocktower, although prices are generally on the high side. Here you'll find two reasonable hotels; *Dimitra* (☎0298/22 697; ④) and *Latsi* (☎0298/22 392; ④). Most of the other hotels are across the canal on Kalávria. Camping is not encouraged anywhere on the island and there is no official campsite.

Down on the quayside, good-value **restaurants** include *Grill Oasis* and *Mouragio*, at the far end away from the ferry dock. The *Amvrosia*, up behind the small post office square, serves good fresh fish, and the *Kypos* restaurant beyond it on the left is well worth a visit. Up in town nearer the clocktower, the *Dimitris* taverna is run by a butcher and, unsurprisingly, has good meat. The *Akroyiali*, on the right hand side of the road some 300m down the shore to the left after the Naval Cadet's Training School, is a good family fish taverna with a fine view back over the town.

Additional facilities around the waterfront include a couple of **moped** and **bicycle** rental outlets (you can take either across on boats to the mainland), a **bank**, **post office**, and the helpful **tourist police** (☎0298/22 462; mid-May–Sept).

Kalávria

Most of Póros's **hotels** are to be found on Kalávria, the main body of the island, just across the canal beyond the Naval Cadets' Training School. They stretch for two kilometres or so on either side of the bridge, with some of those to the west ideally situated to catch the dawn chorus – the Navy's marching band. If you'd rather sleep on, head beyond the first bay where the fishing boats tie up. Here, on **Neório Bay** 2km from the bridge, is the pleasant *Hotel Pavlou* (☎0298/22 734; ⑤).

Alternatively, turn right around **Askéli Bay**, where there is a group of posh hotels and villas facing good clear water, if not much in the way of beaches. The best island beach is **Kanáli**, which usually charges admission – a reflection both of Póros's commercialism and the premium on sand.

The Monastery of Zoödhókhou Piyís and Temple of Poseidon

At the end of the four-kilometre stretch of road around Askéli is the simple eighteenth-century **Monastery of Zoödhókhou Piyís**, whose monks have fled the tourists and been replaced by a caretaker to collect the admission charges. It's a pretty spot, with a couple of summer tavernas under the nearby plane trees.

From here you can either walk up across to the far side of the island through the pines and olives, or bike along the road. Either route will lead you to the few columns and ruins that make up the sixth-century BC **Temple of Poseidon** – though keep your eyes open or you may miss them; look for a small white sign on a green fence to the right of the road coming from the monastery. Here Demosthenes, fleeing from the Macedonians after taking part in the last-ditch resistance of the Athenians, took poison rather than surrender to the posse sent after him. A road leads on and back down in a circular route to the "grand canal".

Ídhra (Hydra)

The port and town of **Ídhra**, with its tiers of substantial stone mansions and white-walled, red-tiled houses climbing up from a perfect horseshoe harbour, is a beautiful spectacle. Unfortunately, thousands of others think so, too, and from Easter until September it's packed to the gills. The front becomes one long outdoor café, the hotels are full and the discos flourish. Once a fashionable artists' colony, established in the 1960s as people restored the grand old houses, it has experienced a predictable meta-morphosis into one of the more popular (and expensive) resorts in Greece. But this acknowledged, a visit is still to be recommended, especially if you can get here some time other than peak season.

Ídhra Town

The waterfront of **ÍDHRA TOWN** is lined with mansions, most of them built during the eighteenth century, on the accumulated wealth of a remarkable merchant fleet of 160 ships which traded as far afield as America and, during the Napoleonic Wars, broke the British blockade to sell grain to France. Fortunes were made and the island also enjoyed a special relationship with the Turkish Porte, governing itself, paying no tax, but providing sailors for the Sultan's navy. These conditions naturally attracted Greek immigrants from the less-privileged mainland, and by the 1820s the town's population stood at nearly 20,000 – an incredible figure when you reflect that today it is under 3000. During the War of Independence, Hydriot merchants provided many of the ships for the Greek forces and inevitably many of the commanders.

The **mansions** of these merchant families, designed by architects from Venice and Genoa, are still the great monuments of the town. If you are interested in seeking them out, a town map is available locally – or ask the tourist police (see p.426) for help in locating them. On the western waterfront, and the hill behind, are the **Voulgaris** mansion, with its interesting interior, and the **Tombazis** mansion, used as a holiday hostel for arts students. Higher up, the **Koundouriotis** mansion was once the proud home of George Koundouriotis, a wealthy shipowner who fought in the War of Independence and whose great grandson, Pavlos Koundouriotis, was president of Greece in the 1920s. On the eastern waterfront are the **Kriezis** mansion, the **Tsamados** mansion, now the national merchant navy college which you can visit between lectures, and the **Spiliopoulous** mansion.

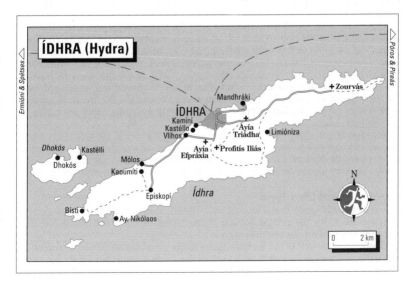

ÍDHRA FESTIVALS

On the second or third weekend in June, Ídhra Town celebrates the **Miaoulia**, in honour of Admiral Andreas Miaoulis whose **fire boats**, packed with explosives, were set adrift upwind of the Turkish fleet during the War of Independence. The highlight of the celebrations is the burning of a boat at sea as a tribute to the sailors who risked their lives in this dangerous enterprise.

On an altogether more peaceful note, the **International Puppet Theatre Festival** takes place here at the end of July, and appeals to children of all ages.

Ídhra is also reputedly hallowed by no less than 365 churches – a total claimed by many a Greek island, but here with some justice. The most important is the cathedral of **Panayía Mitropóleos**, built around a courtyard down by the port, and with a distinctive clocktower.

Practicalities

The town is small and compact, but away from the waterfront the streets and alleyways are steep and finding your way around can be difficult. There are several **banks** along the waterfront, and the **tourist police** (☎0298/52 205; daily mid-May–mid-Oct, 9am–10pm) are on Votsi, opposite the **OTE**.

There are a number of **pensions** and **hotels** along, or just behind, the waterfront in Ídhra town, often charging up to a third more than usual island rates. Some of the restaurants along the waterfront act as agents for the outlying pensions and hotels, which could save you time and footwork; better still, phone ahead and book. *Hotel Amarylis* at Tombazi 15 (☎0298/53 611; ④) is a small hotel with comfortable rooms and private facilities, or there are a couple of beautifully converted old mansions, *Pension Angelika*, Miaouli 42 (☎0298/52 202; ⑤) and *Hotel Hydra*, at Voulgari 8 (☎0298/52 102; ⑤). On the waterfront, but entered from Miaouli, is the slightly run-down but very welcoming *Hotel Sofia* (☎0298/52 313; ③). Of the new pensions, try *Antonio's*, Harami (☎0298/53 227; ④).

There's no shortage of **restaurants** around the waterfront, of which the *Veranda Restaurant* (below the *Hotel Hydra*) has stunning views of the sunset, but for good tavernas you would do well to head a little inland. *The Garden* taverna, known for good meat, is on the road heading up from the hydrofoil dock, with the equally good *Kseri Elia* down the narrow street outside *The Garden*'s wall. Above the *Amarylis Hotel* is the small *Barba Dimas* taverna, which has wonderful mezédhes, snails and fish. Farther up on the same road, *To Kryfo Limani* is a pleasant taverna in a small garden. A bit farther yet you will find good home cooking at the *Yeitoniko*, which has tables on its small verandah.

For **nightlife**, the long-established *Kavos* above the harbour is the best disco, while *Heaven* has impressive views from its hillside site. *Amalour*, straight up from the hydrofoil dock and *Hydronetta* at the edge of town towards Kamíni are lively and play foreign music. The very popular *Sirocco*, also on the waterfront in Ídhra town, plays Greek music.

Beaches around Ídhra Town

The island's only sandy beach is at **MANDHRÁKI**, 2km east of Ídhra Town along a concrete track; it's the private domain of the *Miramare Hotel* (☎0298/52 300; ⑥), although the windsurfing centre is open to all.

On the opposite side of the harbour, to the southeast, a coastal path leads around to **KAMÍNI**, about a twenty-minute walk. Just as you reach Kamíni on the right is a small pension, *Antonia* (☎0298/52 481; ④) On the left, across the street, Eléni Petrolékka has a rival pension (☎0298/52 701; ④), with just two studio flats. Also on the left is the *Kondylenia* restaurant, with fresh fish and a wonderful view of the sunset. About ninety yards up the dry streambed to the left is *Christina's*, a fine traditional Greek fish taverna. Continuing along the water on the unsurfaced mule track you'll come to **Kastéllo**, another small, rocky beach with the ruins of a tiny fort.

Thirty minutes' walk beyond Kamíni (or a boat ride from the port) will bring you to **VLYKHÓS**, a small hamlet with two tavernas, **rooms** and a historic nineteenth-century bridge. The first taverna is *Maria's*, a bit inland and well shaded for lunch. The second is *Marina's*, set on the rocks over the water. Both of these restaurants can call a water taxi to whisk you back to town. **Camping** is tolerated here (though nowhere else closer to town) and the swimming in the lee of an offshore islet is good. Further out is the island of **Dhokós**, only seasonally inhabited by goatherds and people tending their olives.

The interior and south coast

There are no motor vehicles of any kind on Ídhra, except for two lorries to pick up the rubbish, and no surfaced roads away from the port: the island is mountainous and its interior accessible only by foot or donkey. The net result of this is that most tourists don't venture beyond the town, so with a little walking you can find yourself in a quite different kind of island. The pines devastated by forest fires in 1985 are now recovering.

Following the streets of the town upwards and inland you reach a path which winds up the mountain, in about an hour's walk, to the **Monastery of Profítis Ilías** and the **Convent of Ayía Efpraxía**. Both are beautifully situated; the nuns at the convent (the lower of the two) offer hand-woven fabrics for sale. Further on, to the left if you face away from the town, is the **Monastery of Ayía Triádha**, occupied by a few monks (no women admitted). From here a path continues east for two more hours to the cloister of **Zourvás** in the extreme east of the island.

The donkey path continues west of Vlíkhos to **Episkopí**, a high plateau planted with olives and vineyards and dotted by perhaps a dozen summer homes (no facilities). An inconspicuous turning roughly half an hour below leads to **Mólos Bay**, sea-urchin infested and reportedly recently purchased by foreigners who don't welcome visitors, and to the more pleasant farming hamlet of **Kaoumíti**. From Episkopí itself faint tracks lead to the western extreme of the island, on either side of which the bays of **Bísti** and **Áyios Nikólaos** offer solitude and good swimming. Bísti has a pebble beach with good rocks for swimming off at one side. Ayios Nikólaos has a small sand beach. Any point on the coast can be reached by the water taxis, which will drop you off and then pick you up again at any time you arrange.

The best cove of the many on the south coast is **Limióniza** (beyond Ayía Triádha), with a pebble beach and pine trees.

Spétses (Spetsai)

Spétses was the island where John Fowles once lived and which he used, thinly disguised as Phraxos, as the setting for *The Magus*. It is today very popular with well-to-do Athenians and with foreigners, and seems to have risen above the bad reputation an unhealthy proportion of cheap package tours and "lager louts" blighted it with in the 1980s. The architecture of Spétses Town is characterful and distinguished, if less dramatic than that of Ídhra. And, despite a bout of forest-fire devastation in 1990, the landscape described by Fowles is still to be seen: "away from its inhabited corner [it is] truly haunted . . . its pine forests uncanny". Remarkably, at Spétses's best beach, Áyii Anáryiri, development has been limited to a scattering of holiday villas.

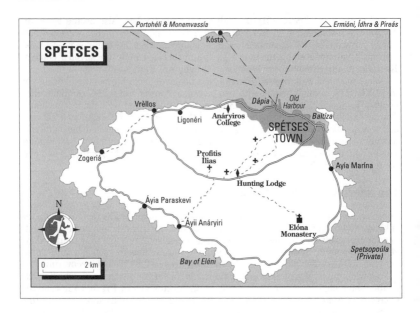

△ Portohéli & Monemvassía   △ Ermióni, Ídhra & Pireás

SPÉTSES

Kósta

Vrèllos   Dápia   Old Harbour

Ligonéri   Anáryiros   SPÉTSES   Baltíza
            College   TOWN

Profitis Ilias

Zogeriá   Ayía Marína

Hunting Lodge

N

Áyia Paraskeví

Áyii Anáryiri   Elóna Monastery

Spetsopoúla (Private)

0   2 km   Bay of Eléni

Spétses Town

SPÉTSES TOWN is the island's port – and its only settlement. It shares with Ídhra the same history of late eighteenth-century mercantile adventure and prosperity, and the same leading role in the War of Independence, which made its foremost citizens the aristocrats of the newly independent Greek state. Pebble-mosaic courtyards and streets sprawl between 200-year-old mansions, whose architecture is quite distinct from the Peloponnesian styles across the straits. Though homeowners may bring private cars onto the island, their movement inside the town limits is prohibited. A few taxis supplement the horse-drawn buggies, whose bells ring cheerfully night and day along the long waterfront, though animal welfare activists are justifiably worried by the condition of some of the horses by summer's end. Otherwise, motorbikes are the preferred mode of transport.

The sights are principally the majestic old houses and gardens, the grandest of which is the magnificent Mexis family mansion, built in 1795 and now used as the **local museum** (Tues–Sun 8.30am–2.30pm; 400dr), housing a display of relics from the War of Independence that includes the bones of the Spetsiot admiral-heroine Lascarina Bouboulina. Bouboulina's home, to the rear of the cannon-studded main harbour known on the island as the Dápia, has been made into a **museum** (daily 10am–7pm; 1000dr) by her descendants and is well worth visiting. Guided tours (30 min) are given in English several times a day.

Just outside the town, Fowles aficionados will notice **Anáryiros College**, a curious Greek re-creation of an English public school where the author was employed and set part of his tale; it is now vacant, save for the occasional conference or kids' holiday programme. Like the massive Edwardian **Hotel Possidonion**, another *Magus* setting, on the waterside, it was endowed by Sotirios Anáryiros, the island's great nineteenth-century benefactor. An enormously rich self-made man, he was also responsible for planting the pine forest that now covers the island. His former house, behind the *Hotel Roumani*, is a monument to bad taste, decked out like a Pharaoh's tomb.

Perhaps more interesting than chasing *Magus* settings though, is a walk east from the Dápia. En route, you pass the smaller "old harbour", still a well protected mooring, and the church of **Áyios Nikólaos** with its graceful belfry and some giant pebble mosaics. At the end of the road you reach the **Baltíza** inlet where, among the sardine packed yachts, half a dozen boatyards continue to build kaïkia in the traditional manner; it was one of these that recreated the *Argo* for Tim Severin's re-enactment of the "Jason Voyage".

Practicalities

A good way to get around the island is by bike and, despite the hills, you can reach most points or make a circuit without too much exertion. Several reliable **bike** and **moped** rental outlets are scattered through town.

All kinds of **accommodation** are available in Spétses Town, though the *Possidonion*, where kings and presidents have slept, no longer operates as a hotel. Be warned that prices are inflated in high season, but the town is smaller and less steep than Ídhra, so hunting around for a good deal is not such hard work. If you don't fancy pounding the streets yourself, try Alasia Travel (☎0298/74 098) or Melédon Tourist and Travel Agency (☎0298/74 497), both by the Dápia. Two simple but comfortable places are *Faros* (☎0298/72 613; ④) and *Stelios* (☎0298/72 971; ③). Good, though less central options are *Studios Orlof* near Ayía Marína beach and *Makis/Costas Studios* in Kounoupítsa, west of the Dápia. Few places stay open all year – exceptions include the central *Pension Alexandris* (☎0298/72 211; ④) and the *Klimis Hotel* (☎0298/74 497; ④), a quiet and pleasant place.

In Spétses Town, **food** and **drink** tend to be a bit on the pricey side. Among the best options are *Roussos*, 300m east of the Dápia just beyond Klimis; the Bakery Restaurant, about 100m up from the Dápia; and *Lazaros's Taverna*, another 300m beyond it. For fish, go to the long established *Patralis* on the water at Kounoupítsa beyond the Spetses Hotel; *Siora's* in the Old Harbour is also good but expensive and crowded. The ouzerí *Byzantino*, also on the Old Harbour, is popular, too.

By day, *Stambolisos To Kafenio*, beyond the Flying Dolphin office at the Dápia, remains steadfastly traditional. By night, clubbers head for *Figaro* in the Old Harbour, and the places at the other end of town around Kounoupítsa. Few of these places shut until the fishermen are setting out.

Spétses has a couple of good **craft shops**: *Pityousa* and *O Palios Eleonas* (behind the *Hotel Soleil*) offer some attractive original work.

Around the island

For **swimming** you need to get clear of the town. Beaches within walking distance are at **Ayía Marína** (twenty minutes east, with the very pleasant *Paradise* restaurant), at various spots beyond the **old harbour**, and several other spots half an hour away in either direction. The tempting islet of **Spetsopoúla**, just offshore from Ayía Marína, is unfortunately off-limits: it's the private property of the heirs of shipping magnate Stavros Niarchos.

For heading further afield, you'll need to hire a **bike** or **moped**, or use the **kaïkia** rides from the Dápia, which run to beaches around the island in summer. A very expensive alternative are **waterboat taxis**, though they can take up to ten people. **Walkers** might want to go over the top of the island to Áyii Anáryiri; forest fire has ravaged most of the pines between Ayía Marína and Áyii Anáryiri, though happily they are growing back. The route out of town starts from behind *Lazaros's Taverna*.

West from Spétses Town

Heading west from the Dápia around the coast, the road is paved or in good condition almost all around the island. The forest stretches from the central hills right down to the shore and it makes for a beautiful coastline with little coves and rocky promontories, all shaded by trees. *Panas* taverna at Ligoneri provides wonderful respite from the bustle of town. You can swim below and then have lunch or dinner under the pines.

Vréllos is one of the first places you come to, at the mouth of a wooded valley known locally as "Paradise", which would be a fairly apt description, except that, like so many of the beaches, it becomes polluted every year by tourists' rubbish. However, the entire shore is dotted with coves and in a few places there are small tavernas – there's a good one at **Zogeriá**, for instance, where the scenery and rocks more than make up for the inadequate little beach.

Working your way anti-clockwise around the coast towards Áyii Anáryiri you reach **Áyia Paraskeví** with its small church and beach – one of the most beautiful coves on Spétses and an alternate stop on some of the kaïki runs. There's a basic beach café here in summer. On the hill above is the house John Fowles used as the setting for *The Magus*, the **Villa Yasemiá**. It was once owned by the late Alkis Botassis, who claimed to be the model for the *Magus* character – though Fowles denies "appropriating" anything more than his "outward appearance" and the "superb site" of his house.

Áyii Anáryiri

Áyii Anáryiri, on the south side of the island, is the best, if also the most popular, beach: a beautiful, long, sheltered bay of fine sand. Gorgeous first thing in the morning, it fills up later in the day, with bathers, windsurfers and, at one corner, speedboat-driving waterski instructors. On the right-hand side of the bay, looking out to sea, there's a sea cave, which you can swim to and explore. There's a good taverna on the beach and, just behind, *Tasso's*, run by one of the island's great eccentrics.

travel details

Ferries

From the central harbour at **Pireás** at least 4 boats daily run to Ayía Marína (1hr) and 11 to Éyina (1hr 30min); 1–2 daily to Skála and Mílos (2hr); 4 daily to Póros (3hr 30min); 1–2 daily to Ídhra (4hr 30min) and Spétses (5hr 30min). About 4 connections daily between Éyina and Póros; 4–5 daily between Éyina and Angístri; from Angístri about 4 weekly to Paleá Epídhavros, far less frequently to Póros and Méthana.

Most of the ferries stop on the mainland at Méthana (between Éyina and Póros) and Ermióni (between Ídhra and Spétses); it is possible to board them here from the Peloponnese. Some continue from Spétses to Pórto Khéli. There are also constant boats between Póros and Galatás (10min) from dawn until late at night, and boat-taxis between Spétses and Pórto Khéli.

NB There are more ferries at weekends and fewer out of season (although the service remains good); for Éyina and Póros they leave Pireás most fre-

quently between 7.30am and 9am, and 2pm and 4pm. Do not buy a return ticket as it saves no money and limits you to one specific boat. The general information number for the Argo-Saronic ferries is ☎01/41 75 382.

Flying Dolphin hydrofoils

Approximately hourly services from the central harbour at Pireás to **Éyina** only 6am–8pm in season, 7am–5pm out of season (40min).

All hydrofoils going beyond Éyina leave from the **Zea Marina**: 4–15 times daily to Póros (1hr), Ídhra (1hr 40min), and Spétses (2–2hr 30min). All these times depend upon the stops en route, and frequencies vary with the season.

Éyina is connected with the other three islands twice a day; Póros, Ídhra and Spétses with each other 3–5 times daily. Some hydrofoils also stop at Méthana and Ermióni and all of those to Spétses continue to Porto Khéli (15min more). This is a junction of the hydrofoil route – there is usually one a day onwards to Toló and Náfplio (and vice versa; 30 and 45min) in season and another (almost year-round) to Monemvassía (2hr). The Monemvassía hydrofoil continues 2–4 times a week to the island of Kýthira.

NB Services are heavily reduced out of season, though all the routes between Pórto Khéli and Pireás still run. Hydrofoils are usually twice as fast and twice as expensive as ordinary boats, though to Éyina the price is little different. You can now buy round trip tickets to destinations in the Argo-Saronic Gulf. In season, it's not unusual for departures to be fully booked for a day or so at a time.

Details and tickets available from the Ceres Pireás ticket office at Ákti Themistokléous 8 (☎01/42 80 001, number perennially engaged). The Ceres Athens office at Filellínon 3 (☎01/32 44 600) is more convenient if you are in Athens. Tickets can also be bought at the departure quays on Aktí Tselépi in Pireás and at Zéa.

CHAPTER SEVEN

THE CYCLADES

N amed after the circle they form around the sacred island of Delos, the **Cyclades** (Kykládhes) is the most satisfying Greek archipelago for island-hopping. On no other group do you get quite such a strong feeling of each island as a microcosm, each with its own distinct traditions, customs and path of modern development. Most of these self-contained realms are compact enough to walk around in a few days, giving you a sense of completeness and identity impossible on, say, Crete or most of the Ionian islands.

The islands do share some features however, the majority of them (Ándhros, Náxos, Sérifos and Kéa excepted) being arid and rocky; most also share the "Cycladic" style of brilliant-white, cubist architecture. The extent and impact of tourism, though, is markedly haphazard, so that although some English is spoken on most islands, a slight detour from the beaten track – from Íos to Síkinos, for example – can have you groping for your Greek phrasebook.

But whatever the level of tourist development, there are only two islands where it has come completely to dominate their character: **Íos**, the original hippie-island and still a paradise for hard-drinking backpackers, and **Mýkonos**, by far the most popular of the group, with its teeming old town, selection of nude beaches and sophisticated clubs and gay bars. After these two, **Páros**, **Sífnos**, **Náxos**, and **Thíra** (Santoríni) are currently the most popular, with their beaches and main towns drastically overcrowded at the height of the season. To avoid the hordes altogether – except in August, when nearly everywhere is overrun and escape is impossible – the most promising islands are **Síkinos**, **Kímolos** or **Anáfi**, or the minor islets around Náxos. For a different view of the Cyclades, visit **Tínos** and its imposing pilgrimage church, a major spiritual centre of Greek Orthodoxy, or **Sýros** with its elegant townscape, and (like Tínos), large Catholic minority. Due to their closeness to Athens, adjacent **Kýthnos** and **Kéa** are predictably popular – and relatively expensive – weekend havens for Greeks. The one

---

ACCOMMODATION PRICE CODES

Throughout the book we've used the following **price codes** to denote the cheapest available room in high season; all are prices for a double room, except for category ①, which represents per person rates. Out of season, rates can drop by up to fifty percent, especially if you are staying for three or more nights. Single rooms, where available, cost around seventy percent of the price of a double.

Rented private rooms on the islands usually fall into the ② or ③ categories, depending on their location and facilities, and the season; a few in the ④ category are more like plush self-catering apartments. They are not generally available from late October through to the beginning of April, when only hotels tend to remain open.

① 1400–2000dr	④ 8000–12,000dr
② 4000–6000dr	⑤ 12,000–16,000dr
③ 6000–8000dr	⑥ 16,000dr and upwards

For more accommodation details, see pp.39–42.

major ancient site is **Delos** (Dhílos), certainly worth making time for; the commercial and religious centre of the Classical Greek world, it's visited most easily on a day trip, by kaïki or jet boat from Mýkonos.

When it comes to **moving on**, many of the islands – in particular Mílos, Páros, Náxos and Thíra – are handily connected with Crete (easier in season), while from Tínos, Mýkonos, Sýros, Páros, Náxos, Thíra or Amorgós you can reach many of the Dodecanese by direct boat. Similarly, you can regularly get from Mýkonos, Náxos, Síros and Páros to Ikaría and Sámos (in the eastern Aegean – see pp.646 and 634).

One consideration for the timing of your visit is that the Cyclades often get frustratingly **stormy**, particularly in early spring or late autumn, and it's also the group worst affected by the *meltémi*, which blows sand and tables about with ease throughout much of July and August. Delayed or cancelled ferries are not uncommon, so if you're heading back to Athens to catch a flight leave yourself a day or two's leeway.

Kéa (Tziá)

Kéa is the closest of the Cyclades to the mainland, and is extremely popular in summer, and at weekends year-round, with Athenians. Their impact is mostly confined to certain small coastal resorts, leaving most of the interior quiet, although there is a preponderance of expensive apartments and villas, and not as many good tavernas as you might expect because so many visitors self-cater. Midweek, or outside peak season, Kéa is a more enticing destination, with its rocky, forbidding perimeter and inland oak and almond groves.

As ancient Keos, the island and its strategic well-placed harbour supported four cities – a pre-eminence that continued until the nineteenth century when Sýros became the main Greek port. Today tourists account for the sea traffic – regular ferry connections with Lávrio on the mainland (only a ninety-minute bus ride from Athens), plus useful hydrofoils and ferries to and from Zéa, Kýthnos and Rafína.

The northwest coast: Korissía to Otziás

The small northern ferry and hydrofoil port of **KORISSÍA** has fallen victim to uneven expansion and has little beauty to lose; if you don't like its looks upon disembarking, try to get a bus to Písses (16km), Otziás (6km) or Ioulidha (6km). Buses usually meet the boats; from July until August there's a regular fixed schedule around the island, but at other times they can be very elusive. There are just four **taxis** on Kéa, and two motorbike rental outfits, which are more expensive than on most islands, though Nikos Laliótis (☎0288/21 485), 200m along the road to Khóra, has much better prices than the harbour shop.

There's a list of rooms in the seafront tourist information office, and the kindly agents for the Flying Dolphin hydrofoils (To Stegadhi gift shop) sell maps and guides, and can phone around in search of **accommodation**. The best choices are *Nikitas* pension (☎0288/21 193; ④), open all year and very friendly, *Pension Korissia* (☎0288/21 484; ④), well inland along the stream bed, *Iy Tzia Mas* (☎0288/21 305; ④), right behind the best end of the otherwise uninspiring port beach, and the somewhat noisy *Karthea* (☎0288/21 204; ④), which does, however, boast single rooms and year-round operation – and a cameo appearance in recent Greek history. When the junta fell in July 1974, the colonels were initially imprisoned for some weeks in the then-new hotel, while the recently restored civilian government pondered what to do with them; Kéa was then so remote and unvisited that the erstwhile tyrants were safely out of reach of a vengeful populace. For **eating**, *Iy Akri* is the best of a small bunch, while *O Kostas* near the jetty

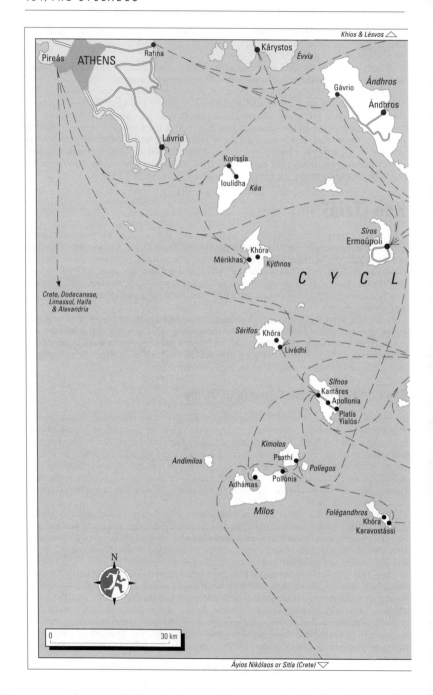

Khíos & Lésvos △

Pireás

ATHENS

Rafina

Kárystos

Évvia

Gávrio

Ándhros

Ándhros

Lávrio

Korissía

Ioulídha

Kéa

Síros
Ermoúpoli

Khóra

Mérikhas

Kýthnos

C Y C L

Crete, Dodecanese,
Limassol, Haifa
& Alexandria

Sérifos Khóra

Livádhi

Sífnos
Kamáres
Apollonía
Platís
Yialós

Kímolos

Andímilos

Psathí

Políegos

Adhámas

Pollónia

Mílos

Folégandhros
Khóra
Karavostássi

N

0 30 km

Áyios Nikólaos or Sitía (Crete) ▽

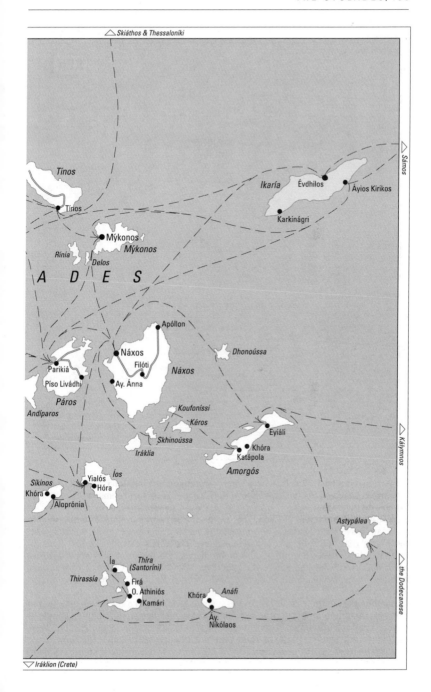

△ Skiáthos & Thessaloníki

△ Sámos

Tínos

Tínos

Ikaría   Évdhilos   Áyios Kirikos

Karkinágri

Mýkonos

Rínia   Mýkonos

Delos

A   D   E   S

Apóllon

Dhonoússa

Náxos

Parikiá   Filóti   Náxos

Píso Livádhi   Ay. Ánna

Koufoníssi

Páros   Kéros   Eyiáli

Andíparos   Skhinoússa   Khóra

Iráklia   Katápola   △ Kálymnos

Amorgós

Síkinos   Yialós   Íos

Khóra   Hóra

Aloprónia   Astypálea

Ía   Thíra
(Santoríni)

Thirassía   Firá   ▷ the Dodecanese

O. Athiniós   Khóra   Anáfi

Kamári   Ay.
Nikólaos

▽ Iráklion (Crete)

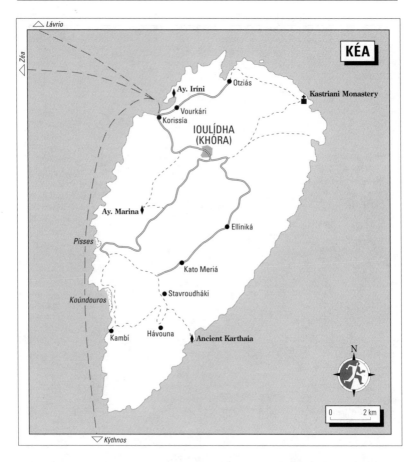

is functional but fairly decent. There's good swimming at **Yialiskári**, a small, eucalyptus-fringed beach on the headland above Korissía; the *Yialiskari* rooms (☎0288/21 197; ⑤) enjoy a good view.

VOURKÁRI, a couple of kilometres to the north, is more compact and arguably more attractive than Korissía, serving as the favourite hangout of the yachting set; there's no real beach or accommodation here. Three fairly expensive and indistinguishable **tavernas**, serve up good seafood dishes, and there's a very good ouzerí – *Strofi tou Mimi* – located where the road cuts inland towards Otziás. The few **bars** include *Vinylio*, popular with an older crowd, and the slightly more happening *Kouros* and *Prodhikos*.

Another 4km to the east, **OTZIÁS** has a small beach that's a bit better than that at Korissía, though more exposed to prevailing winds; facilities are limited to a couple of tavernas and a fair number of apartments for rent. Kéa's only functioning monastery, the eighteenth-century **Panayía Kastriani**, is an hour's walk along a dirt road from Otziás. The hostel at the monastery (☎0288/21 348; ②) is the cheapest accommodation deal on the island, albeit rather basic and isolated. Although more remarkable for its fine setting on a high bluff than for any intrinsic interest, from here you can take the pleasant walk on to the island capital, Ioulídha, in another two hours.

Ioulídha

IOULÍDHA, ancient Ioulis, was the birthplace of the renowned early fifth-century BC poets Simonides and Bacchylides. With its numerous red-tiled roofs, Neoclassical buildings and winding flagstoned paths, it is by no means a typical Cycladic village, but, beautifully situated in an amphitheatric fold in the hills, is architecturally the most interesting settlement on the island. Accordingly it has "arrived" in recent years, with numerous trendy bars and bistros much patronized on weekends. The **Archeological Museum** (Tues–Sun 8.30am–3pm; free) displays finds from the four ancient city-states of Kéa, although the best items were long ago spirited away to Athens. The lower reaches of the town stretch across a spur to the **Kástro**, a tumbledown Venetian fortress incorporating stones from an ancient temple of Apollo. Fifteen minutes' walk northeast, on the path toward Panayía Kastrianí, you pass the **Lion of Kea**, a sixth-century BC sculpture carved out of the living rock. Six metres long and two metres high, the imposing beast has crudely powerful haunches and a bizarre facial expression. There are steps right down to the lion, but the effect is most striking from a distance.

There are two **hotels** in Ioulídha, quieter than anything down in Korissía, and both much in demand: the somewhat pokey *Filoxenia* (☎0288/22 057; ③) is perched above a shoe shop and has no en-suite plumbing and saggy beds; the more comfortable *Ioulis* (☎0288/22 177; ④) up in the kástro has superb views from its terrace and west-facing rooms.

You're spoiled for choice in the matter of **eating** and **drinking**, with quality generally higher here than near Korissía. *Iy Piatsa*, just as you enter the lower town from the car park, has a variety of tasty dishes, while *To Kalofagadhon* up on the platía enjoys great views and is the best place for a full-blown meat feast. Further up there is good standard fare on the terrace of *To Steki tis Tzias*. The aptly named *Panorama* serves up pastries and coffee and is a good place to watch the sun set, while after-dark action seems to oscillate between such bars as *Kamini*, *Leon* and, best of all, *Mylos*. A newly opened kéndro, *Ta Pedhia Pezi* (which means "the guys are playing"), a few kilometres out off the road towards Písses is terrific for a full-on bouzoúki night. An **OTE**, **post office** and **bank agent** round up the list of amenities.

The south

About 8km southwest of Ioulídha, reached via a mix of tracks and paths, or by mostly paved road, the crumbling Hellenistic watchtower of **Ayía Marína** sprouts dramatically from the grounds of a small nineteenth-century monastery. Beyond, the paved main road twists around the dramatically scenic head of the lovely agricultural valley at **PÍSSES**, emerging at a large and little-developed beach. There are three tavernas behind, plus a pleasant **campsite**, *Camping Kea*, which has good turfy ground and also runs the studios (☎0288/31 302; ④) further inland. The pension above the taverna (☎0288/31 301; ③) is the best deal around. Of the tavernas, the best is *To Akroyiali*, with a good range and excellent rosé wine.

Beyond Písses, the asphalt – and the bus service – peters out along the 5km south to **KOÚNDOUROS**, a sheltered, convoluted bay popular with yachters; there's a taverna behind the largest of several sandy coves, none cleaner or bigger than the beach at Písses. The luxury *Kea Beach* hotel (☎0288/31 230; ⑥) sits out on its own promontory with tennis courts and pool, and there is a hamlet of dummy windmills; built as holiday homes, they are "authentic" right down to their masts, thatching and stone cladding. At the south end of the bay, *Manos* taverna and rooms (☎0288/31 214; ③) is by far the best value, with TV in all rooms. If you want to base yourself on this side of the island it's worth noting that the hydrofoil stops at the *Kea Beach* hotel. A further 2km south at **Kambí**, there's a nice little beach and a good taverna, *To Kambi*.

Besides the very scant ruins of ancient Poiessa near Písses, the only remains of any real significance from Kéa's past are fragments of the temple of Apollo at **ancient Karthaia**, tucked away on the southeastern edge of the island above Póles Bay, with an excellent deserted twin beach that's easiest reached by boat. Otherwise, it's a good three hour round-trip walk from the hamlet of Stavroudháki, some way off the lower road linking Koúndouros, Khávouna and Káto Meriá. Travelling by motorbike, the upper road, which more directly plies between Písses and Káto Meriá, is worth following as an alternative return along the island's summit to Ioulídha; it's paved between Ioulídha and Káto Meriá, and the entire way affords fine views, over the thousands of magnificent oaks which constitute Kéa's most distinctive feature.

Kýthnos (Thermiá)

Though perhaps the dullest and certainly the most barren of the Cyclades, a short stay on **Kýthnos** is a good antidote to the exploitation likely to be encountered elsewhere. Few foreigners bother to visit – the island is quieter than Kéa, even in midsummer – while the inhabitants (except in more commercialized Mérikhas) are overtly friendly. All these factors compensate for the paucity of specific diversions: it's a place where Athenians come to buy land for villas, go spear-fishing, and sprawl on generally mediocre beaches without having to jostle for space. You could use it as a first or, better, last island stop; there are weekly ferry connections with Kéa, more frequent services to and from Sérifos, Sífnos and Mílos, as well as seasonal hydrofoils to Kéa, Zéa and Rafína.

Mérikhas and around

In good weather boats dock on the west coast at **MÉRIKHAS**, a rather functional ferry and fishing port with most of the island's facilities. This fact almost obliges you to stay here, and makes Mérikhas something of a tourist ghetto, but it's redeemed by proximity to the island's best beaches. The closest beach of any repute is **Episkopí**, a 500m stretch of averagely clean grey sand with a single taverna, thirty minutes' walk north of the town; you can shorten this considerably by sticking to coast-hugging trails and tracks below the road. Far better are the adjacent beaches of **Apókroussi**, which has a canteen, and **Kolóna**, the latter essentially a sandspit joining the islet of Áyios Loukás to Kýthnos. They lie about an hour's walk northwest of Episkopí, and are easiest reached by boat-trip from the harbour. Camping is generally tolerated, even on Martinákia beach, the nearest to Mérikhas, which has an eponymous taverna.

Accommodation proprietors often meet the ferries, and a relative abundance of rooms makes for good bargaining opportunities. Few places have sea views, one exception being the *Kythnos Hotel* (☎0281/32 092; ③) near the ferry dock. Behind the seafront, *Pension Yiasemi* (☎0281/32 248; ④) is a decent choice; studios there and elsewhere can be good value too. The best **restaurants** are *To Kandouni*, furthest from the ferry, a tasty grill with tables right by the water and specialities like *sfougato*, and *Yialos*, about halfway along the seafront, which has a good section of salads and dips. Among purveyors of a modest nightlife, by far the friendliest and liveliest place is *To Vyzantio*, just back from the water, whose animated owner plays varied rock music. *Remezzo*

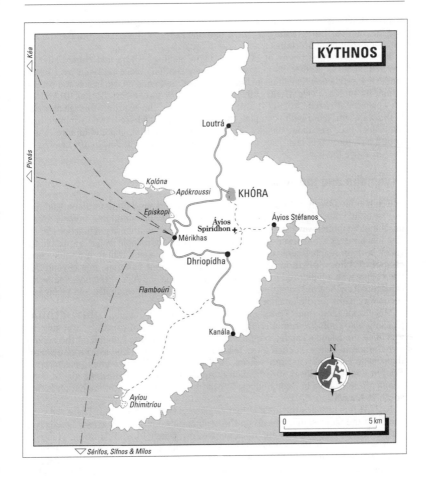

behind the beach has a fine location and plays good music, and eclectic Greek folk music can be heard at the modern *New Corner*, 100m along the road to Dhriopídha.

The **bus service**, principally to Loutrá, Khóra, Dhryopídha and Kanála, is reasonably reliable, in season at least; the only motorbike rental is through the main Milos Express ticket agency and is noticeably more expensive than on many islands. The Cava Kythnos shop doubles as the official **National Bank** outlet (exchange all day), and is the agent for hydrofoil tickets and the boat to Kéa.

Khóra and Loutrá

KHÓRA is 6km northeast of Mérikhas, set in the middle of the island. Tilting south off an east–west ridge, and laid out to an approximate grid plan, it's an awkward blend of Kéa-style gabled roofs, Cycladic churches with dunce-cap cupolas, and concrete monsters. Khóra supports the main **OTE** branch, and a **post office** (open only until noon); at present the closest accommodation is at Loutrá (see p.440). You can **eat** at the taverna run by Maria Tzoyiou near the small square, or at the *To Steki* grill, and there's a single outdoor **bar**, *Apokalypsi*. You'll find another good taverna, *Paradisos*, on the approach road from Mérikhas.

The much-vaunted resort of **LOUTRÁ** (3km north of Khóra and named after its thermal baths) is scruffy, its nineteenth-century spa long since replaced by a sterile modern construction. Facilities include a few good **tavernas** on the beach and several **pensions** such as *Porto Klaras* (☎0281/31 276; ④), *Delfini* (☎0281/31 430; ③) and the very pleasant *Meltemi* (☎0281/31 271; ④), all on or near the seafront. You can also stay in the state-run *Xenia* baths complex (☎0281/31 217; ④), where a twenty-minute bath plus check-up costs about 1000dr. The small bay of Ayía Iríni, just a kilometre east of Loutrá, is a more pleasant place to swim and boasts the decent *Trehandiri* taverna on the hill above the bay.

Dryopídha and the south

You're handily placed in Khóra to tackle the most interesting thing to do on Kýthnos: the beautiful **walk** south to Dhryopídha. It takes about ninety minutes, initially following the old cobbled way that leaves Khóra heading due south; critical junctions in the first few minutes are marked by red paint dots. The only reliable water is a well in the valley bottom, reached after thirty minutes, just before a side trail to the triple-naved **chapel of Áyios Sprídhon** which has recycled Byzantine columns. Just beyond this, you collide with a bulldozed track between Dhryopídha and Áyios Stéfanos, but purists can avoid it by bearing west towards some ruined ridgetop windmills, and picking up secondary paths for the final forty minutes of the hike.

More appealing than Khóra by virtue of spanning a ravine, **DHRYOPÍDHA**'s pleasing tiled roofs are reminiscent of Spain or Tuscany. A surprisingly large place, it was once the island's capital, built around a famous cave, the Katafíki, at the head of a well watered valley. Tucked away behind the cathedral is a tiny **folklore museum** that opens erratically in high season. Beside the cathedral is a cheap psistariá, *Ly Pelagra* and a good local ouzerí called *O Apithanos* ("the unbelievable guy"). Some people do let rooms in their houses, but the nearest official accommodation is 6km south at Kanála.

KANÁLA is perhaps the most attractive place to stay on the island. There are some rooms in the older settlement up on the promontory and a fine taverna, *Louloudhas*, with a huge terrace overlooking the larger western beach, **Megáli Ámmos**, which has itself been sympathetically developed with a taverna and rooms. Two good adjacent pensions on the beach are *Margarita* (☎0281/32 265; ④) and *Anna* (☎0281/32 035; ④).

From Kanála, a succession of small coves extends up the east coast as far as **ÁYIOS STÉFANOS**, a small coastal hamlet with two high season tavernas opposite a chapel-crowned islet linked by a causeway to the body of the island. Southwest of Dhryopídha, reached by a turning off the road to Kanála, **Flamboúri** is the most presentable beach on the west coast. The double bay of **Ayíou Dhimitríou** at the extreme southern tip of the island is reached over a rough road, and is not really worth the effort, although there are now two restaurants and rooms to rent in high season.

Sérifos

Sérifos has long languished outside the mainstream of history and modern tourism. Little has happened here since the legendary Perseus returned with the Gorgon's head, in time to save his mother Danaë from being ravished by the local king Polydectes. Many would-be visitors are deterred by the apparently barren, hilly interior which, with the stark, rocky coastline, makes Sérifos appear uninhabited until your

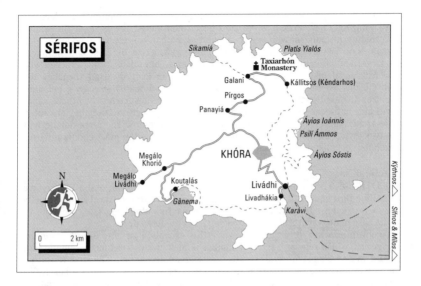

ferry turns into Livádhi bay. The island is recommended for serious **walkers**, who can head for several small villages and isolated coves in the little-explored interior. Modern Serifots love seclusion, and here, more than anywhere else in the Cyclades, you will find farmsteads miles from anywhere, with only a donkey path to their door. Everyone here seems to keep livestock, and to produce their own wines, and many also cultivate the wild **narcissus** for the export market.

Few islanders speak much English, and many have a deserved reputation of being slow to warm to outsiders; one suspects that the locals still don't quite know what to make of the hordes of northern Europeans who descend on the place for the brief but intense July and August season. American yachties drop anchor here in some numbers as well, to take on fresh water which, despite appearances, Sérifos has in abundance.

Livádhi and the main beaches

Most visitors stay in the port, **LIVÁDHI**, set in a wide greenery-fringed bay and handy for most of the island's beaches. The usually calm bay here is a magnet for island-hopping yachts, whose crews chug to and fro in dinghies all day and night. It's not the most attractive place on Sérifos – and to stay here exclusively would be to miss some fine walks – but Livádhi and the neighbouring cove of Livadhákia are certainly the easiest places to find rooms and any other amenities you might need, all of which are very scarce elsewhere.

Unfortunately, the long **beach** at Livádhi is nothing to write home about: the sand is hard-packed and muddy, and the water weedy and prone to intermittent jellyfish flotillas – only the far northeastern end is at all usable. Walk uphill along the street from the *Mylos* bakery, or over the southerly headland from the cemetery, to reach the neighbouring, far superior **Livadhákia**. This golden-sand beach, shaded by tamarisk trees, offers snorkelling and other watersports, one rather average taverna and some furtive nudism. If you prefer more seclusion, five minutes' stroll across the headland to the south brings you to the smaller **Karávi** beach, which is cleaner and almost totally naturist, but has no shade or facilities.

A slightly longer 45-minute walk north of the port along a bumpy track leads to **Psilí Ámmos**, a sheltered, white-sand beach considered the best on the island. Accordingly, it's popular, with two rival tavernas, both of which tend to be full in high season. Naturists are pointed – via a ten-minute walk across the headland – towards the larger and often deserted **Áyios Ioánnis** beach, but this is rather exposed with no facilities at all, and only the far south end is inviting. Both beaches are theoretically visited by kaïkia from Livádhi, as are two nearby sea-caves, but don't count on it. Additionally, and plainly visible from arriving ferries, two more sandy coves hide at the far southeastern flank of the island opposite an islet; they are accessible on foot only, by a variation of the track to Psilí Ámmos. The more northerly of the two, Áyios Sóstis, has a well with fresh water and is the most commonly used beach for secluded freelance camping.

Practicalities

The **OTE** office is at the foot of the quay in Livádhi, and you can rent a **bike** or **car** from Blue Bird next to the single filling station, or from Krinas Travel above the jetty, and there are three **boat-ticket agents**. The public **bus stop** and posted schedule are at the base of the yacht and fishing boat jetty, not the ferry dock.

Accommodation proprietors – with the exception of the *Coralli Camping Bungalows*, which regularly sends a minibus – don't always meet ferries, and in high season you'll have to step lively off the boat to get a decent bed. The most rewarding hunting grounds are on the headland above the ferry dock, or Livadhákia beach (see below); anything without a sea view will be a notch cheaper. Up on the headland, the *Pension Cristi* (☎0281/51 775; ④) has an excellent, quiet position overlooking the bay; the nearby *Areti* (☎0281/51 479; ④) is a little snootier for the same price. Alternatively, down in the flatlands, the relatively inexpensive seafront *Kyklades Hotel* (☎0281/51 553; ④) has the important virtues of year-round operation and kindly management, though the bay-view rooms get some traffic noise. The new *Hotel Anna* (☎0281/51 666; ④) by the yacht harbour is another fall-back, while the cheapest rooms in Livádhi are next to each other at the far end of the bay: *Margarita* (☎0281/51 321; ③) and *Adonios Peloponnisos* (☎0281/51 113; ③).

Livadhákia, ten to fifteen minutes' walk south, offers more nocturnal peace, choice and quality, though it has a more touristy feel and the mosquitoes are positively ferocious – bring insecticide coils or make sure your room is furnished with electric vapour pads. One of the oldest and largest complexes of rooms and apartments, close to the beach and with verdant views, is run by Vaso Stamataki (☎0281/51 346; ④). Newer and higher-standard choices include the *Helios Pension* (☎0281/51 066; ③), just above the road as you arrive at Livadhákia and, further along, the *Medusa* (☎0281/51 127; ④). Cheaper are the rooms in adjacent buildings just after *Helios*, run by two sisters, Yioryia (☎0281/51 336; ③) and Mina (☎0281/51 545; ③) – the latter place has sea views. Further along is *Dhorkas* (☎0281/51 422; ④) and right by the beach above a restaurant, is *O Alexandros* (☎0281/51 119; ④). Near the built up area, beside one of only two public access tracks to the beach and behind the best patch of sand, *Coralli Camping Bungalows* (☎0281/51 500; ⑤) has a restaurant, bar, shop and landscaped camping area, but no prizes for a warm welcome.

A makeshift road runs the length of the Livádhi seafront, crammed with restaurants, shops, and all the services you might need. At the strategic southerly crossroads, the *Mylos* bakery has exceptionally good cheese pies and wholegrain bread; a butcher and a handful of fruit shops and **supermarkets** are scattered along the beach, while there's a **pharmacy** at the foot of the quay.

You'll pay through the nose for **eating** in the obvious places near the quay in Livádhia (although *Mokkas* fish taverna is friendly and good value); walk up the beach, and meals get less expensive and more authentically Greek. The two best traditional tavernas are the busy *Stamatis*, and the welcoming restaurant under the *Hotel Cyclades*. At the extreme far northeast end of the beach, *Sklavenis* (aka *Margarita's*) has loyal adherents to its down-home feel and courtyard seating, but many find the food overly deep-fried and too pricey. Closer to the yacht harbour, *Meltemi* is a good – if slightly expensive – ouzerí, something out of the ordinary for the island. For crepes and ice cream, try *Meli*, in the commercial centre by the port police.

Nightlife is surprisingly lively, though few establishments stay in business more than two consecutive seasons. The main cluster is about a third of the way along the seafront and includes the westernized *Vitamin C, Karnayio* and *Agria Menta*, as well as the skiládhiko-style bouzoúki joint *AlterEgo*, and a smaller bar with a pool table named *Aiolos*.

Buses connect Livádhi with Khóra, 2km away, some ten times daily, but only manage one or two daily trips to Megálo Livádhia, Galaní, and Kállitsos. You may well want to walk, if you're travelling light; it's a pleasant if steep forty minutes up a cobbled way to Khóra, with the *kalderími* leading off from a bend in the road about 300m out of Livádhia. By the beginning of October, you'll have no choice, since the bus – like nearly everything else – ceases operation for the winter.

Khóra

Quiet and atmospheric **KHÓRA**, teetering precariously above the harbour, is one of the most spectacular villages of the Cyclades. The best sights are to be found on the town's borders: tiny churches cling to the cliff edge, and there are breathtaking views across the valleys below. At odd intervals along its alleyways you'll find part of the old castle making up the wall of a house, or a marble statue leaning incongruously in one corner. A pleasant diversion is the hour-long **walk** down to **Psilí Ámmos**: start from beside Khóra's cemetery and aim for the lower of two visible pigeon towers, and then keep close to the phone wires, which will guide you towards the continuation of the double-walled path descending to a bend in the road just above the beach.

Among two or three **tavernas**, the nicest place is *Iy Piatsa*, a tiny establishment near the church on the upper square serving local dishes such as wild fennel fritters; *Stavros* just east of the bus-stop platía, is consistent and can arrange beds too. The island's **post office** is found in the lowest quarter, and a few more expensive **rooms** for rent lie about 200m north of town, on the street above the track to the cemetery.

The north

North of Khóra, the island's high water table sometimes breaks the surface to run in delightful rivulets swarming with turtles and frogs, though in recent years many of the open streams seem to have dried up. Reeds, orchards, and even the occasional palm tree still take advantage of the unexpected moisture, even if it's no longer visible. This is especially true at **KÁLLITSOS** (Kéndarhos), reached by a ninety-minute path from Khóra, marked by fading red paint splodges along a donkey track above the cemetery. Once at Kállitsos (no facilities), a paved road leads west within 3km to the fifteenth- to seventeenth-century **monastery of Taxiarkhón**, designed for sixty monks but presently home only to one of the island's two parish priests, one of a dying breed of farmer-fisherman monks, If he's about, the priest will show you treasures in the monastic church, such as an ivory-inlaid bishop's throne, silver lamps from Egypt (to where many Serifots emigrated), and the finely carved *témblon*.

As you loop back towards Khóra from Kállitsos on the asphalt, the fine villages of Galaní and Panayía (named after its tenth-century church) make convenient stops. In **GALANÍ** you can get simple **meals** at the central store, which also sells excellent, tawny-pink, sherry-like wine; its small-scale production in the west of the island is highly uneconomic, so you'll find it at few other places on Sérifos. Below the village, trails lead to the remote and often windswept beach of **Sikaminiá**, with no facilities and no camping allowed; a better bet for a local swim is the more sheltered cove of **Platýs Yialós** at the extreme northern tip of the island, reached by a partly-paved track (negotiable by moped) that branches off just east of Taxiarkhón. The beach now has a taverna and a number of rooms and seems set for further development. The church at **Panayía** is usually locked, but comes alive on its feast day of Ksilopanayía (August 16). Traditionally the first couple to dance around the adjacent olive tree would be the first to marry that year, but this led to unseemly brawls – so the priest always goes first these days.

The southwest

A little way south of Panayía, you reach a junction in the road. Turn left to return to Khóra, or continue straight towards **Megálo Khorió** – the site of ancient Sérifos, but with little else to recommend it. **Megálo Livádhi**, further on, is a remote and quiet beach resort 8km west of Khóra, with two tavernas and some rooms. Iron and copper ore were once exported from here, but cheaper African deposits sent the mines into decline and today most of the idle machinery rusts away, though some gravel-crushing still goes on. There is a monument at the north end of the beach to four workers killed during a protest against unfair conditions in 1916. An alternate turning just below Megálo Khorió leads to the small mining and fishing port of **Koutalás**, a pretty if shade-less sweep of bay with a church-tipped rock, and a tiny beach – it has become rather a ghost settlement and the workers' restaurants have all closed down. The winding track from here back to Livádhi is easy to drive or walk along, passing the more attractive **Gánema** beach, which has a taverna of the same name.

Sífnos

Sífnos is a more immediately appealing island than its northern neighbours: prettier, more cultivated and with some fine architecture. This means that it's also much more popular, and extremely crowded in July or August, when rooms are very difficult to find. Take any offered as you land, come armed with a reservation, or, best of all, time your visit for June or early in September, though bear in mind that most of the trendier bars and the souvenir shops will be shut for the winter by the middle of the latter month. In keeping with the island's somewhat upmarket clientele, freelance camping is forbidden (and the two designated sites are substandard), while nudism is tolerated only in isolated coves. The locals tend, if anything, to be even more dour and introverted than on Sérifos.

On the other hand, Sífnos' modest size – no bigger than Kýthnos or Sérifos — makes it eminently explorable. The **bus service** is excellent, most of the roads quite decent and there's a network of paths that are fairly easy to follow. Sífnos has a strong tradition of pottery and was long esteemed for its distinctive cuisine, although most tourist-orientated cooking is average at best. However, the island's shops and greengrocers are well stocked in season.

Ferry connections have improved in recent years, keeping pace with the island's increasing popularity. The main lines head south, via Kýmolos to Mílos, with occasional extensions to Thíra, Crete and select Dodecanese, or north, via Sérifos and Kýthnos to Pireás. The only links with the central Cyclades are provided by the weekly visits of the Páros Express, currently on Sunday, which gets you to Páros or Sýros rather late at night; there are occasional connections on the Ilios Lines hydrofoil in the summer months.

Kamáres

KAMÁRES, the island's port, is tucked away at the foot of high, bare cliffs in the west which enclose a beach. A busy, fairly downmarket resort with concrete blocks of villas edging up to the base of the cliffs, Kamáres' seafront crammed with bars, travel agencies, ice-cream shops and fast-food places. You can store luggage at the semi-official **tourist office**, Aegean Thesaurus, while hunting for a room (proprietors tend not to meet boats) – they also change money and can advise on bed availability throughout the island.

Accommodation is relatively expensive, though bargaining can be productive outside peak season. Try the rooms above the Katzoulakis Tourist Agency near the quay, as well as the reasonable *Hotel Stavros* (☎0284/31 641; ④), just beyond the church; the good but expensive *Voulis Hotel* (☎0284/32 122; ⑤) lies across the bay. The **campsite** around the bay is rather lacking in shade but has adequate facilities; it is attached to the good value *Korakis* rooms (☎0284/32 366; ④).

The best **restaurants** are the *Meropi*, ideal for a pre-ferry lunch or a more leisurely meal, the *Boulis* with its collection of huge retsina barrels, the *Kamares* ouzomezed-hopolio and the *Kapetan Andreas* fish taverna. Kamáres also boasts a fair proportion of the island's **nightlife**: try the *Collage Bar* for a sunset cocktail, and move on to the *Mobilize Dancing Club* or the *Cafe Folie*. The best place to hire a moped is at *Diónysos*, next to *Mobilize Dancing Club*, which is run by the amiable mechanic's son.

Apollonía and Artemónas

A steep twenty-minute bus ride (hourly service until late at night) takes you up to **APOLLONÍA**, the centre of the Khóra, an amalgam of three hilltop villages which have merged over the years into one continuous community. With white buildings, flower-draped balconies, belfries and pretty squares, it is eminently scenic, though not self-consciously so. On the platía itself, the **Folk Museum** (open on request; 2000dr) is well worth a visit. Most of the exhibits celebrate a certain Kyría Tseleméndi, who wrote a famous local recipe book (fragments of which are kept here), and there's also an interesting collection of textiles, laces, artwork, costumes and weaponry.

Radiating out from the platía is a network of stepped marble footways and the main pedestrian street, flagstoned Odhós Styliánou Prókou, which is lined with shops, churches and restaurants. The garish, cakebox cathedral of **Áyios Spíridhon** is nearby, while the eighteenth-century church of **Panayía Ouranoforía** stands in the highest quarter of town, incorporating fragments of a seventh-century BC temple of Apollo and a relief of St George over the door. **Áyios Athanásios**, next to Platía Kleánthi Triandafílou, has frescoes and a wooden *témblon*. Some 3km southeast, a short distance from the village of Exámbela, you'll find the active monastery of **Vrýssis** which dates from 1612 and is home to a good collection of religious artefacts and manuscripts.

ARTEMÓNAS, fifteen minutes south of Apollonía on foot, is worth a morning's exploration for its churches and elegant Venetian and Neoclassical houses alone. **Panayía Gourniá** (key next door) has vivid frescoes, the clustered-dome church of **Kokhí** was built over an ancient temple of Artemis (also the basis of the village's name), and seventeenth-century **Áyios Yeóryios** contains fine icons. Artemónas is also the point of departure for **Kherónissos**, an isolated hamlet with two tavernas and a few potteries behind a deeply indented, rather bleak bay at the northwestern tip of the island. There's a motorable dirt track there – and occasional boat trips from Kamáres, though these are only worth the effort on calm days.

Practicalities

The **bank**, **post office**, **OTE** and **tourist police** are all grouped around Apollonía's central platía. Most of the village's **rooms** establishments are along the road towards Fáros, and thus a bit noisy; the *Margarita* (✆0284/31 701; ④) is comfortable and fairly representative. If you want quieter premises with a better view, be prepared to pay more: your best bet is to look on the square for the main branch of the excellent travel agency, Aegean Thesaurus (✆0284/31 151, fax 31 145), which can book you into more expensive rooms (③–④). They also sell a worthwhile package consisting of an accurate topographical map, bus/boat schedules and a short text on Sífnos for a few hundred drachmas. Near the central platía, there's the late-arrival fall-back *Sofia* (✆0284/31 238; ③), though most people find somewhere else the next day, as it's a rather cheerless 1970s construction; the *Galini*, 400m south, up in Katavatí (✆0284/31 011; ③), is preferable.

In Khóra there are still a bare handful of quality **tavernas**, the doyen of which is the *Liotrivi* up in Artemónas, which has moved from the old oil-press suggested by its name to extended new premises on the village square. Next to the post office in Apollonía, *Iy Orea Sifnos* has standard fare and a flower-decked garden; *To Apostoli to Koutouki* in the backstreets is also reasonable.

Nightlife in Apollonía tends to be dominated by the thirty-something crowd which, having dined early by Greek-island standards, lingers over its oúzo until late. The central *Argo* music bar features the currently fashionable mix of rock early on and Greek pop later; the *Kivotos* club out of town features live skíládhíko, while gentler rembétika can be heard at Aloni.

The east coast

Most of Sífnos' coastal settlements are along the less precipitous eastern shore, within a modest distance of Khóra and its surrounding cultivated plateau. These all have good bus services, and a certain amount of food and accommodation, Kástro being far more appealing than the touristy resorts of Platís Yialós and Fáros.

Kástro

An alternative east-coast base which seems the last place on Sífnos to fill up in season, **KÁSTRO** can be reached on foot from Apollonía in 35 minutes, all but the last ten on a clear path beginning at the *Hotel Anthoussa* and threading its way via Káto Petáli hamlet. Built on a rocky outcrop with an almost sheer drop to the sea on three sides, the ancient capital of the island retains much of its medieval character. Parts of its boundary walls survive, along with a full complement of sinuous, narrow streets graced by balconied, two-storey houses and some fine sixteenth- and seventeenth-century churches with ornamental floors. Venetian coats-of-arms and ancient wall-fragments can still be seen on some of the older dwellings; there are remains of the ancient acropolis (including a ram's head sarcophagus by one of the medieval gates), as well as a small **archeological museum** (Tues–Sat 9am–3pm, Sun 11am–2pm; free) installed in a former Catholic church in the higher part of the village.

Among the several rooms establishments, the newly modernized *Aris* apartments (☎0284/31 161; ④) have something for most budgets and are open all year. The *Star* and *Zorbas* are the obvious tavernas to try out, while the *Sierra Maestra* café-bar, run by an old hippy, is suitably laid back and has a fantastic view. On the edge of town, the *Castello* disco-bar is a livelier hang-out. There's nothing approximating a beach in Kástro; for a swim you have to walk to the nearby rocky coves of **Serália** (to the southeast, and with more rooms) and **Paláti**. You can also hike – from the windmills on the approach road near Káto Petáli – to either the sixteenth-century monastery of **Khryssostómou**, or along a track opposite to the cliff face that overlooks the church of the **Eptá Martíres** (Seven Martyrs); nudists sun themselves and snorkel on and around the flat rocks below.

Platýs Yialós

From Apollonía there are almost hourly buses to the resort of **PLATÝS YIALÓS**, some 12km distant, near the southern tip of the island. Despite claims to be the longest beach in the Cyclades, the sand can get very crowded at the end near the watersport facilities rental. Diversions include a pottery workshop, but many are put off by the ugly *Platys Yialos* hotel at the southern end of the beach, and the strong winds which plague it. **Rooms** are expensive, although the comfortable *Pension Angelaki* (☎0284/71 28; ④), near the bus stop, is more reasonably priced. The *Hotel Eurosini* (☎0284/71 353; ⑤) is comfortable, and breakfast is included in the price. The local **campsite** is rather uninspiring: a stiff hike inland, shadeless, and on sloping, stony ground. Among several fairly pricey **tavernas** are the straightforward *To Steki* and *Bus Stop*.

A more rewarding walk uphill from Platýs Yialós brings you to the convent of **Panayía to Vounoú** (though it's easy to get lost on the way without the locally sold map); the caretaker should let you in, if she's about.

Fáros and around

Less crowded beaches are to be found just to the northeast of Platýs Yialós (though unfortunately not directly accessible along the coast). **FÁROS**, again with regular bus links to Apollonía, makes an excellent fall-back base if you don't strike it lucky elsewhere. A small and friendly resort, it has some of the cheapest **accommodation** on the island, and a few early-evening **tavernas**, the best of which is *To Kyma*. The closest beaches are not up to much: the town strand itself is muddy, shadeless and crowded, and the one to the northeast past the headland not much better. Head off in the opposite direction, however, through the older part of the village, and things improve at **Glyfó**, a longer, wider beach favoured by naturists and snorkellers.

Continuing from Glyfó, a fifteen-minute cliffside path leads to the beach of **Apokoftó**, with the good *Lembessis* taverna, and, up an access road, the *Pension Flora* (☎0284/71 278; ③) which has superb views. The shore itself tends to collect seaweed, however, and a rock reef must be negotiated to get into the water. Flanking Apokoftó to the south, marooned on a sea-washed spit and featuring on every EOT poster of the island, is the disestablished, seventeenth-century **Khryssopiyís monastery**, whose cells are rented out in summer (☎0284/31 255; ②) – other rooms are available if the cells are full in high season. According to legend, the cleft in the rock appeared when two village girls, fleeing to the spit to escape the attentions of menacing pirates, prayed to the Virgin to defend their virtue.

The interior and Vathý

Apollonía is a good base from which to start your explorations of remoter Sífnos. You can rent **bikes** at Moto Apollo, beside the BP station on the road to Fáros, but the island is best explored on foot.

Taking the path out from Katavatí (the district south of Apollonía) you'll pass, after a few minutes, the beautiful empty **monastery of Firáyia** and – fifteen minutes along the ugly new road – the path climbing up to **Áyios Andhréas**, where you'll be rewarded with tremendous views over the islands of Sýros, Páros, Íos, Folégandhros and Síkinos. Just below the church is an enormous Bronze-Age archeological site.

Even better is the all-trail walk to Vathý, around three hours from Katavatí and reached by bearing right at a signed junction in Katavatí. Part-way along you can detour on a conspicuous side trail to the **monastery of Profítis Ilías**, on the very summit of the island, with a vaulted refectory and extensive views.

Vathý

A fishing village on the shore of a stunning funnel-shaped bay, **VATHÝ** is the most attractive and remote base on the island and, remarkably, the new road doesn't seem to be leading to extra development. There are still just a few rooms places, the best deals probably being at *Manolis* taverna (②), or those attached to the tiny **monastery of the Archangel Gabriel**. Unusually, camping rough is positively encouraged by the locals, a reflection of their friendly attitude towards outsiders. For **food**, *Manolis* does excellent grills and has a fascinating gyrating clay oven in the courtyard, *Iy Okeanidha* has good mezédhes such as chickpea balls and cheesy aubergine patties, while *To Tsikali* behind the monastery is cheaper but less varied.

Now that there are regular buses (8 daily in high season, 2 daily at other times) the kaïkia no longer run from Kamáres. It is possible to walk to Platýs Yiálos in ninety minutes, but the path is not well marked. At the far end of the bay a traditional pottery still functions.

Mílos

Mílos has always derived prosperity from its strange geology. Minoan settlers were attracted by obsidian, and other products of its volcanic soil made the island – along with Náxos – the most important of the Cyclades in the ancient world. Today the quarrying of barite, perlite and porcelain brings in a steady revenue, but has left deep and unsightly scars on the landscape. The rocks, however, can be beautiful in situ: on the left as your ferry enters Mílos Bay, two outcrops known as the Arkoúdhes (Bears) square off like sumo wrestlers. Off the north coast, accessible only by excursion boat,

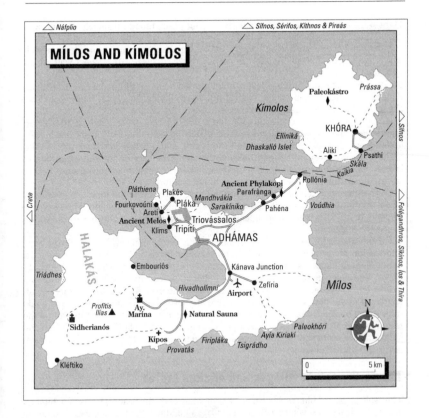

the Glaroníssia (Seagull Isles) are shaped like massed organ pipes, and there are more weird formations on the southwest coast at Kléftiko. Inland, too, you frequently come across strange, volcanic outcrops, and thermal springs burst forth.

The landscape has been violated, but as with most weathered volcanic terrain, Mílos is incredibly fertile; away from the summits of **Profítis Ilías** in the southwest and lower hills in the east, a gently undulating countryside is intensively cultivated to produce grain, hay and orchards. The island's domestic architecture, with its lava-built, two-up-and-two-down houses, is reminiscent of Níssyros, while parts of the coast, with their sculpted cliffs and inlets, remind some visitors of Cyprus.

Yet the drab whole is less than the sum of the often interesting parts; Mílos is not and never will become another Santoríni, despite a similar geological history, and is probably the better for it. The locals are reconciled to a very short tourist season lasting from late June to early September, and make most of their money during late July and August, when prices are rather high.

Adhámas

The main port of **ADHÁMAS**, known as Adhámandas to locals, was founded by Cretan refugees fleeing a failed rebellion in 1841. Despite sitting on one of the Mediterranean's best natural harbours (created by a volcanic cataclysm similar to, but earlier than,

Thira's), Adhámas is not a spectacularly inviting place, though it's lively enough and has all the requisite facilities.

Most hotel **accommodation** manages to be simultaneously noisy, viewless and relatively expensive. Exceptions are the *Delfini* (☎0287/22 001; ⑤), a short way inland from the first beach north of the harbour, and the *Semiramis* (☎0287/ 22 117; ⑤) left of the road to Pláka, which has a lovely quiet garden setting and good deals off-season. Rooms are concentrated on the conical hill above the harbour, and range from real cheapies with shared facilities like those of *Anna Gozadhinou* (☎0287/ 22 364; ②), to smart studios with TV and all mod cons, like those of Mallís (☎0287/22 612; ⑤). During high season the highly organized **tourist office** opposite the ferry dock has a daily updated list of available rooms around the island, and a handy brochure with all the numbers at any given time. There is no proper campsite here or anywhere else on the island, but freelance camping goes undisturbed at the small **Frangomnímata** beach, ten minutes' walk northwest by the French war memorial.

Of the three adjacent **tavernas** along the seafront towards the long tamarisk-lined beach south of town, *Navagio* is the best value, while close to the jetty *Flisvos* is reasonable. Just off the main street inland, *Ta Pitsounakia* is a good cheap psistariá with a pleasant courtyard.

On the quayside, several travel agencies such as the efficient Vichos Tours have information about coastal boat trips, sell maps of the island, and rent out mopeds. Otherwise, Adhámas is the hub of the island's **bus services**, which run hourly to Pláka, nine times daily in high season to Pollónia, seven times daily to Paleokhóri via Zefíria, and to Provatás. Some visitors arrive by plane from Athens: the **airport** is 5km southeast of the port, close to Zefíria. There are several banks, a post office and a taxi rank with a posted list of fixed rates. An unmissable day out is the **boat tour** round the island on one of three boats; weather permitting, these leave at 9am and make several stops at inaccessible swimming spots like the magnificent Kléftiko, as well as taking in late lunch on Kímolos.

The northwestern villages and ancient Melos

The real appeal of Mílos resides in an area that has been the island's focus of habitation since Classical times, where a cluster of villages huddle in the lee of a crag 4km northwest of the harbour.

PLÁKA (MÍLOS) is the largest of these communities and is the official capital of the island, a status borne out by the presence of the hospital, **OTE, post office**, a part-time **bank** and three **motorbike rental** outfits along the approach road. Unfortunately, Pláka's **rooms** are housed in three or four modern blocks overlooking this busy boulevard, and prompt few thoughts of staying. But a number of ouzería have opened up in recent years, making it a real **eating** paradise: highly recommended are *Arkhondoula*, *Dhiporto* and *To Kastro* up in the centre of the village, as well as *Plakiani Gonia* on the approach road.

The attractive village of **TRYPITÍ** (meaning "perforated" in Greek), which takes its name from the cliffside tombs of the ancient Melian dead nearby, covers a long ridge a kilometre south of Pláka. Despite semi-desolation (many houses are for sale), it probably makes the best base if you're after a village environment, with its three modest **rooms** establishments, two of which are just down the steep street from the tiny platía below the main church. Here also the modest *Kafenio Iy Hara* does simple **meals**, and has a fantastic view of the vale of Klíma (see opposite); more elaborate and expensive fare is available at the *Methismeni Politia* ouzerí, at the top of the road to the catacombs. From Trypití, it's possible to walk more or less directly down to Adhámas via Skinópi on the old *kalderími*, which begins on the saddle linking Trypití with the hamlet of Klimatovoúni.

TRIOVÁSSALOS and its twin PÉRAN TRIOVÁSSALOS are more workaday, less polished than Pláka or Trypití. There are "rooms to rent" signs out here as well, but they'll inevitably be noisier. Péran also offers the idiosyncratic taverna *O Khamos* (which means "chaos"), and a naive pebble mosaic in the courtyard of Áyios Yeóryios church – created in 1880, the mosaic features assorted animal and plant motifs.

Local sites – and the coast

Pláka boasts **two museums** of moderate interest. Behind the lower car park, at the top of the approach boulevard through the newer district, the **archeological museum** (Tues–Sun 8.30am–3pm; 500dr) contains numerous obsidian implements, plus a whole wing of finds from ancient Phylakopi (see p.453) whose highlights include a votive lamp in the form of a bull and a rather Minoan-looking terracotta goddess. Labelling is scant, but isn't really needed for a plaster cast of the most famous statue in the world, the *Venus de Milo*, the original of which was found on the island in 1820 and appropriated by the French; her arms were knocked off in the melée surrounding her abduction. Up in a mansion of the old quarter, the **Folklore Museum** (Tues–Sat 10am–2pm & 6–9pm, Sun 10am–2pm; 400dr) offers room re-creations but is otherwise a Greek-labelled jumble of impedimenta pertaining to milling, brewing, cheese-making, baking and weaving, rounded off by old engravings, photos and mineral samples.

A stairway beginning near the police station leads up to the old Venetian **Kástro**, its slopes clad in stone and cement to channel precious rainwater into cisterns. Near the top looms the enormous chapel of **Panayía Thalassítra**, where the ancient Melians made their last stand against the Athenians before being massacred in 416 BC. Today it offers one of the best views in the Aegean, particularly at sunset in clear conditions.

From the archeological museum, signs point you towards the **early Christian catacombs** (Tues–Sun 8am–8pm; free), 1km south of Pláka and just 400m from Trypití village; steps lead down from the road to the inconspicuous entrance. Although some 5000 bodies were buried in tomb-lined corridors which stretch some 200m into the soft volcanic rock, only the first 50m are illuminated and accessible by boardwalk. They're worth a look if you're in the area, but the adjacent ruins of **ancient Melos**, extending down from Pláka almost to the sea, justify the detour. There are huge Dorian walls, the usual column fragments lying around and, best of all, a well preserved Roman **amphitheatre** (unrestricted access) some 200m west of the catacombs by track, then trail. Only seven rows of seats remain intact, but these evocatively look out over Klíma to the bay. Between the catacombs and the theatre is the signposted spot where the *Venus de Milo* was found; promptly delivered to the French consul for "safekeeping" from the Turks, this was the last the Greeks saw of the statue until a copy was belatedly forwarded from the Louvre in Paris.

At the very bottom of the vale, **KLÍMA** is the most photogenic of several fishing hamlets on the island, with its picturesque boathouses tucked underneath the principal living areas. There's no beach to speak of, and only one place to stay – the impeccably sited *Panorama* (☎0287/21 623; ⑤), whose restaurant currently seems to be resting on its laurels.

Pláthiena, 45 minutes' walk northwest of Pláka, is the closest proper beach, and thus is vastly popular in summer. There are no facilities, but the beach is fairly well protected and partly shaded by tamarisks. Head initially west from near the police station on the marked footpath towards **ARETÍ** and **FOURKOVOÚNI**, two more cliff-dug, boathouse-hamlets very much in the Klíma mould. Although the direct route to Pláthiena is signposted, it's no longer to go via Fourkovoúni; both hamlets are reached by side turnings off the main route, which becomes a jeep track as you approach Fourkovoúni. By moped, access to Pláthiena is only from Plakés, the northernmost and smallest of the five northwestern villages.

The south

The main road to the south of the island splits at **Kánava junction**, an unrelievedly dreary place at first glance owing to the large power plant here. But opposite this, indicated by a rusty sign pointing seaward, is the first of Mílos' **hot springs**, which bubble up in the shallows and are much enjoyed by the locals.

Taking the left or easterly fork leads to **ZEFÍRIA**, hidden among olive groves below the bare hills; it was briefly the medieval capital until an eighteenth-century epidemic drove out the population. Much of the old town is still deserted, though some life has returned, and there's a magnificent seventeenth-century church.

South of here it's a further 8km down a winding road to the coarse-sand beach of **Paleokhóri**. Actually a triple strand totalling about 800m in length and unarguably the island's best, clothing is optional at the westerly cove, where steam vents heat both the shallow water and the rock overhangs onshore. There are a number of places to stay, such as the inland *Broutsos Studios* (☎01/34 78 425; ⑤), and the *Artemis* restaurant (☎0287/31 221; ④) nearer the beach, but the best value are Panayiota Vikelli's rooms (☎0287/31 228; ④). Apart from the *Artemis*, there are a couple of other tavernas including the new *Pelagos*, which has a large raised patio.

The westerly road from Kánava junction leads past the airport gate to **Khivadholímni**, considered to be the best beach on Mílos bay itself. Not that this is saying much: Khivadholímni is north-facing and thus garbage-prone, with shallow sumpy water offshore although there is a taverna, a disco bar and a sizeable community of campers during the summer. It's better to veer south to **Provatás**, a short but tidy beach, closed off by colourful cliffs on the east. Being so easy to get at, it hasn't escaped some development: there are two-room establishments plus, closer to the shore, a new luxury complex. The best value for food and accommodation is the *Maistrali* (☎0287/31 206; ③).

Some 2km west of Provatás, you'll see a highway sign for **Kípos** just before the asphalt fizzles out. Below and to the left of the road, a small **medieval chapel** dedicated to the Kímisis (Assumption) sits atop foundations far older – as evidenced by the early Christian reliefs stacked along the west wall and a carved, cruciform baptismal font in the *ieron* behind the altar screen. At one time a spring gushed from the low tunnel-cave beside the font – sufficiently miraculous in itself on arid Mílos. Several kilometres before Provatás, a road forks east through a dusty white quarry to the trendy and popular beach of **Firipláka**, beautifully set but sadly dominated in high summer by a noisy canteen pumping out techno. Further east, **Tsigrádho** beach is accessible by boat, or by the novel means of a rope hanging down a crevice in the cliff face.

For the most part **Khálakas**, the southwestern peninsula centred on the wilderness of 748-metre Profítis Ilías, is uninhabited and little built upon, with the exception of the **monastery of Sidherianós**. The roads are memorable, if a little tiring, and several spots are worth making the effort to see. **Emboriós** on the east side of the peninsula has a fine little beach and a great local taverna with a few cheap rooms (☎0287/21 389; ④). On the mostly rugged west coast, **Triádhes** is one of the finest and least spoilt beaches in the Cyclades, but you'll have to bring your own provisions. **Kléftiko** in the southwest corner is only reachable by boat, but repays the effort to get there with its stunning rock formations, semi-submerged rock tunnels, and colourful coral.

The north coast

From either Adhámas or the Pláka area, good roads run roughly parallel to the **north coast** which, despite being windswept and largely uninhabited, is not devoid of interest. **Mandhrákia**, reached from Péran Triovássalos, is another boathouse settlement, and **Sarakíniko**, to the east, is a sculpted inlet with a sandy sea bed and a summer beach café. About 8km from Adhámas, the little hamlet of **Pákhena**, not shown on many maps, has a cluster of rooms and a small beach – the best value rooms are *Terry's* (☎0287/22 640; ④). About a kilometre beyond this, the remains of three superimposed Neolithic settlements crown a small knoll at **Filakopí** (ancient Phylakopi); the site was important archeologically, but hasn't been maintained and is difficult to interpret. Just before the site is another one of Milos' coastal wonders: the deep-sea inlet of **Papafránga**, set in a ravine and accessible through a gap in the cliffs.

Pollónia

POLLÓNIA, 12km northeast of Adhámas, must be the windiest spot on the island, hence the name of its longest-lived and best **bar**, *Okto Bofor* (meaning "Force 8 gales"), near the church. The second resort on Mílos after Adhámas, it is, not surprisingly, immensely popular with windsurfers. Pollónia is essentially a small harbour protected by a storm-lashed spit of land on the northeast, where self-catering units are multiplying rapidly, fringed by a long but narrow, tamarisk-fringed beach to the rear, and closed off on the south by a smaller promontory on which the tiny original settlement huddles. Besides the town beach, the only other convenient, half-decent beach is at **Voúdhia**, 3km east, where you will find more of the island's hot springs, although it is effectively spoiled by its proximity to huge mining works, which lend it the desolate air of a *Mad Max* scene.

On the quay are a row of four **tavernas**, the best of these being *Kapetan Nikolaos* (aka *Koula's*; open year-round) and *Araxovoli* with an unusual menu. Inland and south of here you'll find another concentration of **accommodation**, more simple rooms and fewer apartments, most with the slight drawback of occasional noise and dust from quarry trucks. Among the newest and highest-quality units here are the *Kapetan Tasos Studios* (☎0287/41 287; ③), with good views of the straits between Mílos and Kímolos. Up behind the quay, *Corina* (☎0287/41 209; ④) is a more reasonable option, as is *Flora* (☎0287/41 249; ④) on the road towards the spit, which also rents out bikes. Pollónia has no bank or post office, but there is a helpful **travel agency**, Blue Waters (☎0287/41 442), which can change money, rent cars, book accommodation and sell ANEK ferry tickets (services to Sitía on Crete). A **motorbike rental** place behind the beach, and a well-stocked **supermarket**, completes the list of amenities. There is a huge map fixed on a metal frame near the bus stop, which shows all the facilities and gives telephone numbers.

Getting to Kímolos (see below) may be the main reason you're here. Either the Tria Adhelfia or one other kaïki makes the trip daily year-round at 6.45am and 2pm, returning from Kímolos an hour later; during high season, there are five crossings a day.

Kímolos

Of the three islets off the coast of Mílos, Andímilos is home to a rare species of chamois, Políegos has more ordinary goats, but only **Kímolos** has any human habitation. Volcanic like Mílos, with the same little lava-built rural cottages, it profits from its geology and used to export chalk (*kimolía* in Greek) until the supply was exhausted. Still a source of fuller's earth, the fine dust of this clay is a familiar sight on the island, where mining still outstrips fishing and farming as an occupation. Rugged and barren in the interior, there is some fertile land on the southeast coast where low-lying wells provide water, and this is where the population of about eight hundred is concentrated.

Kímolos is sleepy indeed from September to June, and even in August sees hardly any visitors. This is probably just as well, since there are fewer than a hundred beds on the whole island, and little in the way of other amenities.

Psathí and Khóra

Whether you arrive by ferry, or by kaïki from Pollónia, you'll dock at the hamlet of **PSATHÍ**, pretty much a non-event except for the excellent *To Kyma* **taverna** midway along the beach. The laissez-faire attitude towards tourism is demonstrated by the fact that there are no rooms here, but equally, nobody minds if you sleep on the small beach. **Ferry tickets** are sold only outside the expensive café at the end of the jetty, an hour or so before the anticipated arrival of the boat; the Pollónia kaïki comes and goes unremarked from the base of the jetty five times a day in summer. There is no bus on the island, but at the time of writing a licence had been obtained for a taxi, and only a driver was required.

Around the bay there are a few old windmills and the dazzlingly white **KHÓRA** perched on the ridge above them. Unsung – and neglected, although there are plans to reconstruct it and build government rooms – is the magnificent, two-gated **kástro**, a fortified core of roughly the same design as those at Andíparos and Síkinos; the perimeter houses are intact but its heart is a jumble of ruins. Just outside the kástro on the north stands the conspicuously unwhitewashed, late-sixteenth-century church of **Khryssóstomos**, the oldest and most beautiful on the island. It takes fifteen minutes to walk up to the surprisingly large town, passing the recommended *Villa Maria* (☎0287/51392; ④) about five minutes along the way and nearer to Psathí; you'll also find accommodation, managed by Margaro Petraki (☎0287/51 314; ②), tucked away in the rather unglamourous maze of backstreets. The aptly named *Panorama*, near the east gate of the kástro, is the most elaborate and consistently open **taverna**, and there are a couple of basic psistariés. Self-catering is an easy proposition – and may be a necessity before June or after August – with a well-stocked supermarket, produce stalls and a butcher. Finally, there's a friendly **OTE** office behind Khryssóstomos church, a boat agency and a **post office** which does exchange. By 1998 the small archeological **museum** (Tues–Sun 8am–2pm), currently on the road into Khóra, should have moved to more spacious premises near the church; its collection comprises pottery from the Geometric to the Roman period.

Around the island

During summer at least, the hamlet of **ALYKÍ** on the south coast is a better bet for staying than Psathí and Khóra; it only takes about thirty minutes to walk there on the paved road that forks left just before the *Villa Maria*. Alikí is named after the salt pan which sprawls between a rather mediocre beach with no shade or shelter, and has a pair of **rooms** – *Sardis* (☎0287/51 458; ④) and *Passamihalis* (☎0287/51 340; ③) – and simple **tavernas**. You can stroll west one cove to **Bonátsa** for better sand and shallow water, though you won't escape the winds. Passing another cove you come to the even more attractive beach of Kalamítsi, with better shade and the good little taverna and rooms of Ventourís (☎093/611685; ③). To the east, between Alikí and Psathí, the smaller, more secluded beach of **Sténda** is better for camping.

The 700m coarse-sand beach of **Elliniká** is 45 minutes' walk west of Alikí: starting on the road, bear left – just before two chapels on a slope – onto a narrower track which runs through the fields at the bottom of the valley. Divided by a low bluff, the beach is bracketed by two capes and looks out over Dhaskalió islet, and tends to catch heavy weather in the afternoon; there are no facilities here.

Another road leads northeast from Khóra to a beach and radioactive springs at **Prássa**, 7km away. The route takes in impressive views across the straits to Políegos and there are several shady peaceful coves where you could camp out. Innumerable goat tracks invite exploration of the rest of the island; in the far northwest, on Kímolos' summit, are the ruins of an imposing Venetian fortress known as **Paleókastro**. The local community has plans to open an official campsite at Klíma Bay 2km northeast of Khóra, once it has relocated the rubbish dump that currently befouls the place.

Ándhros

Ándhros, the second largest and northernmost of the Cyclades, has a number of fine features to offer the visitor, although you have to search them out. Thinly populated but prosperous, its fertile, well-watered valleys have attracted scores of Athenian holiday villas whose red-tiled roofs and white walls stand out among the greenery. Some of the more recent of these have robbed many of the villages of life and atmosphere, turning them into scattered settlements with no nucleus, and have created a weekender mentality manifest in noisy Friday and Sunday evening traffic jams at the ferry dock. The island neither needs, nor welcomes, independent travellers, and it can be almost impos-

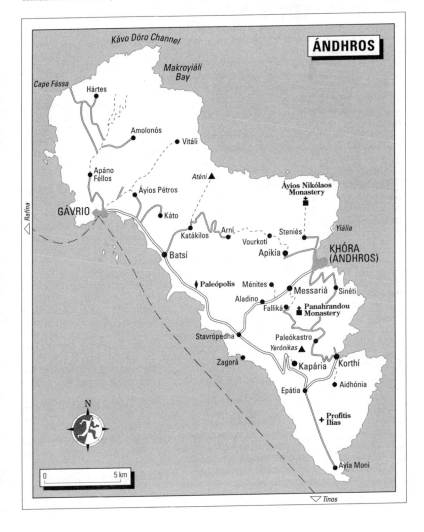

sible to get a bed in between the block-bookings during high season. On the positive side, the permanent population is distinctly hospitable; traditionally working on ships, they are only too happy to practise their English on you. Together with some of the more idiosyncratic reminders of the Venetian period, such as the *peristereónes* (pigeon towers) and the *frákhtes* (dry-stone walls, here raised to the status of an art form), it is this friendliness that lends Ándhros its charm.

Ferries connect the island with Rafína on the mainland, only an hour from Athens on the bus, and you can loop back onto the central Cycladic routes via Mýkonos or Sýros. The bus service is poor, and you'd be well advised to consider renting a bike to tour the sights – otherwise you'll face a lot of walking.

Northern and western Ándhros

All ferries and catamarans arrive at the main port, **GÁVRIO**, a nondescript place whose dirty, windswept beach is usually deserted. The sea in the enclosed harbour is so murky that even the wildfowl aren't interested. A converted dovecote houses a sporadically functioning **tourist office**, and the ferry **ticket agent** only opens half an hour before boats arrive. There's also a part-time **bank**, and a **post office** on the waterfront.

The cheapest **accommodation** is in the clean and reasonable *Galaxy* (☎0282/71 228; ④) or the *Bati* rooms behind the beach (☎0282/71 010; ④); *Camping Andros*, 2km down the road, has decent facilities, including a swimming pool and a good café. **Restaurants** worth trying include the good if basic estiatório *Tria Asteria*, the *Vengera* taverna with its nice leafy courtyard 100m inland, and the smart new *Trehandiri* ouzerí opposite the catamaran dock. **Nightlife** revolves around the *Idhroussa* and *Tropical* bars, or at livelier outdoor places on Áyios Pétros beach several kilometres south, where the *Marabou* taverna frequently features live guitar music.

The road north begins behind the *Hotel Gavrion Beach*. Around 3km northwest are two beaches named **Fellós**: one with holiday villas and a taverna, the other hidden beyond the headland and popular with freelance campers. Beyond Ápano Fellós, the countryside is empty except for a few hamlets inhabited by the descendants of medieval Albanians who settled here and in southern Évvia several hundred years ago.

Most traffic heads 8km south down the coast, past the excellent *Yiannouli* taverna, to **BATSÍ**, the island's main package resort, with large hotels and bars around its fine natural harbour. The beautiful though crowded beach curves round the port, and the sea is cold, calm and clean (except near the taxi park). **Hotels** range from the cheap but seedy *Avra* (☎0282/41 216; ②), through the comfortable *Chryssi Akti* (☎0282/41 236; ⑤) with TV and air conditioning, to the very upmarket *Aneroussa Beach Hotel* (☎0282/41 045; ⑥), south of town past the Stivári area towards Áyia Marína Beach. There are plenty of rooms, and good food can be had at *O Stamatis*, an old place with a nice atmosphere, or at *Ta Kavouria*, which specializes in fish – both are near the harbour. Further out at **Stivári**, a pleasant café/taverna, *Stivari Gardens*, is run by an English woman. For **nightlife** there are five bars, mostly featuring the standard foreign/Greek musical mix, although *Diva* plays some psychedelic sounds. Finally, there are two banks where you can change money.

From Batsí you're within easy walking distance of some beautiful inland villages. At **KÁTO KATÁKILOS**, one hour inland, three **tavernas** host "Greek nights" organized in Bátsi; a rough track leads to **ATÉNI**, a hamlet in a lush, remote valley, as yet unvisited by the dreaded donkey safaris. **ANO KATÁKILOS** has a couple of undervisited tavernas with fine views across the village. A right-hand turning out of Katákilos heads up the mountain to **ARNÍ**, whose lone taverna is often shrouded in mist. Another rewarding trip is to a well-preserved, 20-metre-high **Classical tower** at Áyios Pétros, 5km from Gávrio or 9km coming from Batsí.

South of Batsí along the main road are Káto and Áno Apróvato. **Káto** has rooms, a café and a path to a quiet beach, while nearby is the largely unexplored archeological site of **Paleópolis**.

Khóra and around

A minimal bus service links the west coast with **KHÓRA** or **ÁNDHROS** town, 35km from Gávrio. With its setting on a rocky spur cutting across a huge bay, the capital is the most attractive place on the island. Paved in marble and schist from the still-active local quarries, the buildings around the bus station are grand nineteenth-century affairs, and the squares with their ornate wall fountains and gateways are equally elegant. The hill quarters are modern, while the small port acts as a yacht supply station, and below are the sands of Parapórti – a fine beach, if a little exposed to the *meltémi* winds in summer.

The few **hotels** in town are on the expensive side, and tend to be busy with holidaying Greeks: try the *Aigli* (☎0282/22 303; ④), opposite the big church on the main walkway. Most rooms are clustered behind the long **Nimboúrio** beach north of town, and range from good cheap old-style family guesthouses like those of Firiou (☎0282/22 921; ③) or Pandazi (☎0282/22 777; ③), to modern apartments such as *Alkioni Inn* (☎0282/24 522; ⑥), as well as the seasonal **campsite**. For **eating**, most cafés are up in Khóra, although the restaurant right by the bus station is good, and there's a decent psistariá on the main drag. The nicest taverna is *O Nonas*, tucked away at the town end of the beach behind the ugly *Xenia* hotel. Up in Khóra there's the *Rock Café* for a **drink**, but the epicentre of nightlife is the two-storey *Vecera*, a thumping disco halfway along the beach. There's an **OTE**, post office and bank around town, a couple of travel agents and three moped rentals, two behind the beach, and one on the road to Gavrío.

From the square right at the end of town you pass through an archway and down to windswept **Platía Ríva**, with its statue of the unknown sailor scanning the sea. Beyond lies the thirteenth-century Venetian **Kástro**, precariously joined to the mainland by a narrow-arched bridge, which was damaged by German munitions in World War II. The **Modern Art Museum** (Wed–Sun 10am–2pm, also 6–8pm in summer; 1000dr) has a sculpture garden and a permanent collection that includes works by Picasso and Braque, as well as temporary exhibits. Don't be discouraged by the stark modern architecture of the **Archeological Museum** (Tues–Sun 8.30am–3pm; 500dr); it turns out to be well laid out and labelled with instructive models. The prize items on view are the fourth-century "Hermes of Ándhros", reclaimed from a prominent position in the Athens archeological museum, and the "Matron of Herculaneum".

Hiking inland and west from Ándhros, the obvious destination is **MÉNITES**, a hill village just up a green valley choked with trees and straddled by stone walls. The church of the **Panayía** may have been the location of a Temple of Dionysus, where water was turned into wine; water still flows continuously from the local rocks. Nearby is the medieval village of **MESSARIÁ**, with the deserted twelfth-century Byzantine church of *Taxiárkhis* below and the pleasantly shady *Platanos* taverna. The finest monastery on the island, **Panakhrándou**, is only an hour's (steep) walk away, via the village of Falliká; reputedly tenth-century, it's still defended by massive walls but occupied these days by just three monks. It clings to an iron-stained cliff southwest of Khóra, to which you can return directly with a healthy two- to three-hour walk down the creek valley, guided by red dots. There is a wonderful taverna, *Pertesis*, at Strapouriés, which boasts a view all the way down to the coast and excellent food.

Hidden by the ridge directly north of Khóra, the prosperous nineteenth-century village of **STENIÉS** was built by the vanguard of today's shipping magnates, and today you can splash out at the good fish tavernas here. Just below, at Yiália, there's a small pebble beach with a café and watersports facilities. Beyond Steniés is **APIKÍA**, a tidy little village which bottles Sariza-brand mineral water for a living; there are a few **tavernas** and a very limited number of **rooms**, as well as the new luxury hotel *Dighi Sarisa* (☎0282/23 799 or 23 899; ⑥), just below the spring itself. The road is now asphalted up to Vourkotí and even past this point is quite negotiable via Arní to the west coast. There are some stunning views all along this road but bike riders need to take care when the *meltémi* is blowing – it can get dangerously windy.

Southern Ándhros

On your way south, you might stop at **Zagorá**, a fortified Geometric town – unique in having never been built over – that was excavated in the early 1970s. Located on a desolate, flat-topped promontory with cliffs falling away on three sides, it's worth a visit for the view alone. With your own transport, the sheltered cove of Sinéti is also worth a detour.

The village of **KORTHÍ**, the end of the line, is a friendly though nondescript village set on a large sandy bay, cut off from the rest of the island by a high ridge and so relatively unspoiled – and pleasant enough to merit spending the night at *Pension Rainbow* (☎0282/61 344; ③) or at the austere-looking *Hotel Korthion* (☎0282/61218; ④). There are also several good seafood **restaurants**. You could also take in the nearby convent of **Zoödhókhou Piyís** (open to visitors before noon), with illuminated manuscripts and a disused weaving factory.

To the north is **PALEÓKASTRO**, a tumbledown village with a ruined Venetian castle – and a legend about an old woman who betrayed the stronghold to the Turks, then jumped off the walls in remorse, landing on a rock now known as "Old Lady's Leap". In the opposite direction out of Korthí are **AÏDHÓNIA** and **KAPÁRIA**, dotted with pigeon towers (*peristereónes*) left by the Venetians.

Tínos

Tínos still feels one of the most Greek of the larger islands. A few foreigners have discovered its beaches and unspoiled villages, but most visitors are Greek, here to see the church of **Panayía Evangelístria**, a grandiose shrine erected on the spot where a miraculous icon with healing powers was found in 1822. A Tiniote nun, now canonized as Ayia Pelayía, was directed in a vision to unearth the relic just as the War of Independence was getting underway a timely coincidence which served to underscore the links between the Orthodox Church and Greek nationalism. Today, there are two major annual pilgrimages, on March 25 and August 15, when, at 11am, the icon bearing the Virgin's image is carried in state down to the harbour over the heads of the faithful.

The Ottoman tenure here was the most fleeting in the Aegean. **Exóbourgo**, the craggy mount dominating southern Tínos and surrounded by most of the island's sixty-odd villages, is studded with the ruins of a Venetian citadel which defied the Turks until 1715, long after the rest of Greece had fallen. An enduring legacy of the long Venetian rule is a persistent Catholic minority, which accounts for almost a third of the population, and a sectarian rivalry said to be responsible for the numerous graceful belfries scattered throughout the island – Orthodox and Catholic parishes vying to build the tallest. The sky is pierced, too, by distinctive and ornate dovecots, even more in evidence here than on Ándhros. Aside from all this, the inland village architecture is striking and there's a flourishing folk-art tradition which finds expression in the abundant local marble. The islanders have remained open and hospitable to the relatively few foreigners and the steady stream of Greek visitors who touch down here, and any mercenary inclinations seem to be satisfied by booming sales in religious paraphernalia to the faithful.

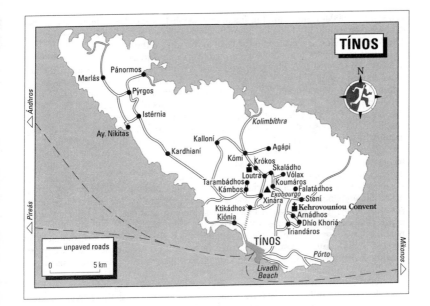

Tínos Town and the southern beaches

At **TÍNOS** town, trafficking in devotional articles certainly dominates the streets leading up from the busy waterfront to the Neoclassical **church** (daily 8am–8pm) which towers above. Approached via a massive marble staircase, the famous **icon** inside is all but buried under a dazzling mass of gold and silver *tammata* (votive offerings); below is the crypt (where the icon was discovered) and a mausoleum for the sailors drowned when the Greek warship *Elli*, at anchor off Tínos during a pilgrimage, was torpedoed by an Italian submarine on August 15, 1940. Museums around the courtyard display more objects donated by the faithful (who inundate the island for the two big yearly festivals), as well as icons, paintings and work by local marble sculptors

The shrine aside – and all the attendant stalls, shops and bustle – the port is none too exciting, with just scattered inland patches of nineteenth-century buildings. You might make time for the **Archeological Museum** (Tues–Sun 8.30am–3pm; 500dr) on the way up to the church, whose collection includes a fascinating sundial from the local Roman Sanctuary of Poseidon and Amphitrite (see p.460).

Practicalities

Ferries dock at any of three different **jetties**; this can depend on weather conditions. There are at least three boats a day from Pireás and four from Rafína, with connections to Ándhros, Mýkonos, Páros and Sýros. When you're leaving, ask your ticket agent which jetty to head for. **Buses** leave from a small parking area in front of a cubbyhole-office on the quay, to Pánormos, Kalloní, Stení, Pórto and Kiónia (timetables available here; no buses after 7.30pm). A **moped** is perhaps a more reliable means of exploring – Vidalis, Zanáki Alavánou 16, is a good rental agency.

Windmills Travel (☎0283/ 23 398), on the front towards the new jetty, can help with information as well as hotel and **tour bookings**; they even have a book exchange. In season an excursion boat does day trips taking in Delos (see p.467) and Mýkonos

(Tues–Sun; 4000dr round trip); this makes it possible to see Delos without the expense of staying overnight in Mýkonos, but only allows you two and a half hours at the site. The **tourist police** are located on the road to the west of the new jetty.

To have any chance of securing a reasonably priced **room** around the pilgrimage day of March 25 (August 15 is hopeless), you must arrive several days in advance. At other times there's plenty of choice, though you'll still be competing with out-of-season pilgrims, Athenian tourists and the sick and the disabled seeking a miracle cure. Of the hotels, the *Eleana* (☎0283/22 561; ④), east of the quay about 400m inland at the edge of the bazaar, is a good budget option. The conspicuous waterfront *Yannis Rooms* (☎0283/22 515; ④) is just in front of the reasonable *Thalia* (☎0283/22811; ④), all the way around the bay from the old jetty. Slightly pricier options include the *Avra* (☎0283/22 242; ④), a Neoclassical relic on the waterfront, and the *Favie Souzane* just inland (☎0283/22 693 or 22 176; ④). *Hotel Tinion* (☎0283/22 261; ⑤) is a stylish 1920s hotel near the post office. The *Vyzantio*, Zanáki Alavánou 26 (☎0283/22 454; ④), on the road out towards Pórto and the villages, is not especially memorable but it and the *Meltemi* (☎0283/22 881; ⑤) at Filipóti 7, near Megalokháris (☎0283/22 881; ④), are the only places open out of season. Finally, there is a smart hotel with swimming pool near the beginning of the beach road east of the promontory – *Aeolos Bay Hotel* (☎0283/23 410; ⑥). Otherwise, beat the crowds by staying at *Tinos Camping* which also has a few nice rooms to let (☎0283/22 344; ②); follow the signs from the port, it's a ten-minute walk. A farmers' **market** for locally produced fruit and vegetables takes place every morning in the Palládha area (towards the new jetty between the bars and the waterfront).

As usual, most seafront **restaurants** are rather overpriced and indifferent, with the exception of a friendly psitopolio right opposite the bus terminal, the *Zefyros* estiatório next to the post office, and the upmarket *Xinari* restaurant and pizzaria on Evangelístrias. A cluster of places around the bazaar just to the left of Megalokháris as you face the church include *Palea Pallada* and *Peristereonas*, both of them reasonable. Tucked away in a small alley near the seafront off Evangelistrías, *Pigada* does a fine clay-pot moussaka, as well as some more unusual dishes, while *O Kipos*, further inland on the way to the church, has a pleasant garden setting. Wash down your meal with the island's very good barrelled retsina, which is available just about everywhere.

There are quite a few **bars**, mostly in a huddle near the new quay. *Fevgatos* has a pleasant atmosphere, and *Kala Kathoumena* is pretty lively with a mixture of international hits and Greek music.

Nearby beaches

Kiónia, 3km northwest (hourly buses), is the site of the **Sanctuary of Poseidon and Amphitrite** which was discovered in 1902; the excavations yielded principally columns (*kionia* in Greek), but also a temple, baths, a fountain, and hostels for the ancient pilgrims. The **beach** is functional enough, but it's better to walk past the large *Tinos Beach Hotel*, the last stop for the bus, and follow an unpaved road to a series of sandy coves beyond.

The beach beyond the headland east of town starts off rocky but improves if you walk 500 metres further along. Further east, **Pórto** (six buses daily) boasts two good beaches to either side of **Áyios Sóstis** headland, with a couple of good tavernas as well as rooms at the reasonably priced restaurant belonging to Akti Aegeou (☎0283/24 248; ⑤) on the first beach of Áyios Pandelímon. *Porto Tango* (☎0283/24 411; ⑥) is a good upmarket hotel here.

Northern Tínos

A good beginning to a foray into the interior is to take the stone stairway – the continuation of Odhós Ayíou Nikoláou – that passes behind and to the left of Evangelístria. This climbs for ninety minutes through appealing countryside to **KTIKÁDHOS**, a fine village with a good sea-view taverna, *Iy Dhrosia*. You can either flag down a bus on the main road or stay with the trail until Xinára (see "Around Exóbourgo" below).

Heading northwest from the junction flanked by Ktikádhos, Tripótamos and Xinára, there's little to stop for – except the fine dovecotes around Tarambádhos – until you reach **KARDHIANÍ**, one of the most strikingly set and beautiful villages on the island, with its views across to Sýros from amid a dense oasis. Nestled in the small sandy bay below is a fine little restaurant by the name of *Anemos*, which serves octopus stew and other dishes at good prices. Kardhianí has been discovered by wealthy Athenians and expatriates, and now offers the exotic *To Perivoli* taverna. **ISTÉRNIA**, just a little beyond, is not nearly so appealing but it does have a pension at the top of the village and a few cafés, perched above the turning for **Órmos Isterníon**, a comparatively small but overdeveloped beach.

Five daily buses along this route finish up at **PÝRGOS**, a few kilometres further north and smack in the middle of the island's marble-quarrying district. A beautiful village, its local artisans are renowned throughout Greece for their skill in producing marble ornamentation; ornate fanlights and bas-relief plaques crafted here adorn houses throughout Tínos. With an attractive shady platía, Pýrgos is popular in summer, but you should be able to find a **room** easily enough, and you have a choice of two **tavernas**, *Vinia* being the more elegant by far.

The marble products were once exported from **PÁNORMOS** (Órmos) harbour, 4km northeast, with its tiny but commercialized beach; there's little reason to linger, but if you get stuck there are rooms and some tavernas.

Around Exóbourgo

The ring of villages around **Exóbourgo** mountain is the other focus of interest on Tínos. The fortified pinnacle itself (570m), with ancient foundations as well as the ruins of three Venetian churches and a fountain, is reached by steep steps from **XINÁRA** (near the island's major road junction), the seat of the island's Roman Catholic bishop. Most villages in north central Tínos have mixed populations, but Xinára and its immediate neighbours are purely Catholic; the inland villages also tend to have a more sheltered position, with better farmland nearby – the Venetians' way of rewarding converts and their descendants. Yet **TRIPÓTAMOS**, just south of Xinára, is a completely Orthodox village with possibly the finest architecture in this region – and has accordingly been pounced on by foreigners keen to restore its historic properties.

At **LOUTRÁ**, the next community north of Xinára, there's an Ursuline convent and a good **Folk Art Museum** (summer only 10.30am–3.30pm; 300dr) in the old Jesuit Monastery here; to visit, leave the bus at the turning for Skaládho. From Krókos has a couple of scenically situated restaurants, it's a forty-minute walk to **VÓLAKAS** (Volax), one of the most remote villages on the island, a windswept oasis surrounded by bony rocks. Here, half a dozen elderly Catholic basketweavers fashion some of the best examples of that craft in Greece. There is a small **Folklore Museum** (free); you have to ask for it to be opened up.

At Kómi, 5km beyond Krókos, you can take a detour for **KOLYMBÍTHRA**, a magnificent double beach: one part wild, huge and windswept, the other sheltered and with a taverna and rooms, but no camping. The bus to Kalloní goes on to Kolimbíthra twice a day in season; out of season you'll have to get off at Kómi and walk 4km.

From either Skaládho or Vólakas you go on to Koúmaros, where another long stairway leads up to Exóbourgo, or skirt the pinnacle towards Stení and Falatádhos which appear as white speckles against the fertile Livádha valley. From Stení you can catch the bus back to the harbour (seven daily). On the way down, try and stop off at one of the beautiful settlements just below the important twelfth-century **convent of Kekhrovouníou**, where Ayía Pelayía had her vision. Particularly worth visiting are

DHÝO KHORIÁ with a fine main square where cave-fountains burble, and TRIANDÁROS which has a two good, reasonable **eating** places – *Iy Lefka* and *Eleni's* taverna, a tiny place at the back of the village. If you have your own transport, there are quite wide and fairly negotiable tracks down to some lovely secluded bays on the east of the island from the area of Steni. One such is **Santa Margarita**; given the lack of tourist development here, it's a good idea to take something to drink.

This is hardly an exhaustive list of Tiniot villages; armed with a map and good walking shoes for tackling the many old trails that still exist, you could spend days within sight of Exóbourgo and never pass through the same hamlets twice. Take warm clothing out of season, especially if you're on a moped, since the forbidding mountains behind Vólakas and the Livadhéri plain keep things noticeably cool.

Mýkonos

Originally visited only as a stop on the way to ancient Delos, **Mýkonos** has become easily the most popular (and the most expensive) of the Cyclades. Boosted by direct air links with Britain and domestic flights from Athens, an incredible 800,000 tourists pass through in a good year, producing some spectacular overcrowding in high summer on Mýkonos' 75 square kilometres. But if you don't mind the crowds, or – and this is a much more attractive proposition – you come out of season, the prosperous capital is still one of the most beautiful of all island towns, its immaculately whitewashed houses concealing hundreds of little churches, shrines and chapels.

The sophisticated nightlife is pretty hectic, amply stimulated by Mýkonos' former reputation as *the* gay resort of the Mediterranean – a title lost in recent years to places like Ibiza and Sitges in Spain; whatever, the locals take this comparatively exotic clientele in their stride. Unspoiled it isn't, but the island does offer excellent (if crowded) beaches, picturesque windmills and a rolling arid interior. An unheralded Mýkonian quirk is the legality of scuba diving, a rarity in Greece, and dive centres have sprung up on virtually every beach.

Mýkonos Town

Don't let the crowds put you off exploring **MÝKONOS TOWN**, the archetypal post-card image of the Cyclades. Its sugar-cube buildings are stacked around a cluster of seafront fishermen's dwellings, with every nook and cranny scrubbed and shown off. Most people head out to the beaches during the day, so early morning or late afternoon are the best times to wander the maze of narrow streets. The labyrinthine design was intended to confuse the pirates who plagued Mýkonos in the eighteenth and early nineteenth centuries, and it still has the desired effect.

You don't need any maps or hints to explore the convoluted streets and alleys of town; getting lost is half the fun. There are, however, a few places worth seeking out: coming from the ferry quay you'll pass the **Archeological Museum** (Tues–Sat 9am–3pm, Sun 9.30am–2.30pm; 400dr) on your way into town, which displays some good Delos pottery; the town also boasts a **Marine Museum** displaying various nautical artefacts including a lighthouse re-erected in the back garden (Tues–Sun 8.30am–3pm; 200dr). Alternatively, behind the two banks there's the **Library**, with Hellenistic coins and late medieval seals, or, at the base of the Delos jetty, the **Folklore Museum** (Mon–Sat 5.30–8.30pm, Sun 6.30–8.30pm; free), housed in an eighteenth-century mansion and cramming in a larger-than-usual collection of bric-a-brac, including a vast four-poster bed. The museum shares the same promontory as the old Venetian kástro, the entrance to which is marked by Mýkonos' oldest and best-known church, **Paraportianí**, which is a fascinating asymmetrical hodge-podge of four chapels amalgamated into one.

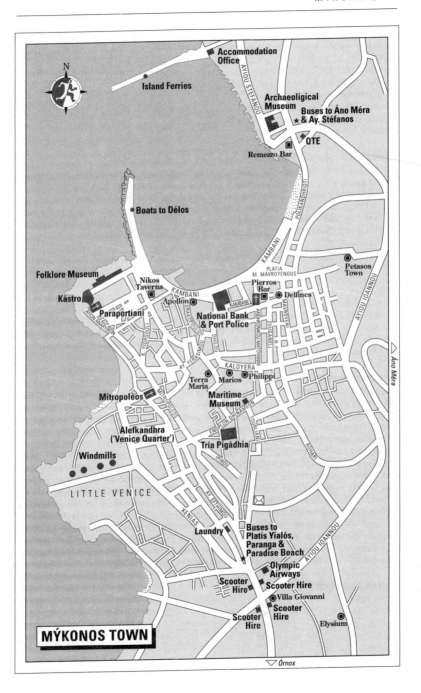

N

Accommodation Office

Island Ferries

Archaeoligical Museum

Buses to Áno Méra & Ay. Stéfanos

OTE

Remezzo Bar

Boats to Délos

POLIKANDHRIOTI

KAMBANI

PLATIA M. MAVROYENOUS

Petasos Town

Folklore Museum

Nikos Taverna

Pierros Bar

Delfines

AYIOU IOANNOU

Kástro

Apollon

KAMBANI

Paraportiani

KAMBANI

MAVROYENI

National Bank & Port Police

ANDRONIKOU MATOYANNI

ENOPLON DINAMEON

AY. YERASIMOU

DILIOU

DHRAKOPOULOU

AY. ANARYIRON

KALOYERA

Terra Maria

Marios

Philippi

Maritime Museum

Mitropoléos

MITROPOLEOS

ENOPLON DINAMEON

TOURLIANI

ROMAH

Áno Méra

Alefkandhra ('Venice Quarter')

Tría Pigádhia

Windmills

IPIROU

L I T T L E   V E N I C E

AV. EFTHIMIOU

XENIAS

Laundry

Buses to Platis Yialós, Paranga & Paradise Beach

Olympic Airways

AYIOU IOANNOU

Scooter Hire

Scooter Hire

Villa Giovanni

Scooter Hire

Scooter Hire

Elysium

MÝKONOS TOWN

Órnos

The shore leads to the area known as "Little Venice" because of its high, arcaded Venetian houses built right up to the water's edge. Its real name is **Alefkándhra**, a trendy district packed with art galleries, chic bars and discos. Back off the seafront, behind Platía Alefkándhra, are Mýkonos' two **cathedrals**: Roman Catholic and Greek Orthodox. Beyond, the famous **windmills** look over the area, a little shabby but ripe for photo opportunities. Instead of retracing your steps along the water's edge, follow Énoplon Dhinaméon (left off Mitropóleos) to **Tría Pigádhia** fountain. The name means "Three Wells", and legend has it that should a maiden drink from all three she is bound to find a husband.

Arrival and information

There is some accommodation information at the **airport**, but unless you know where you're going it's easier to take a taxi for the 3km into town, and sort things out at the jetty. The vast majority of visitors arrive by boat at the new northern **jetty**, where a veritable horde of room-owners pounce on the newly arrived. The scene is actually quite intimidating and so, if you can avoid the grasping talons, it is far better to go a hundred metres further where a row of offices deal with official hotels, rented rooms and camping information.

The harbour curves around past the dull, central Polikandhrióti beach; south of which is the **bus station** for Toúrlos, Áyios Stéfanos and Áno Méra. The **post office**, Olympic Airways office and **tourist police** are all in the Lákka area near the Platís Yialós bus station. A second **bus terminus**, for beaches to the south, is right at the other end of the town, beyond the windmills. Buses to all the most popular beaches and resorts run frequently, and till the early hours. **Taxis** go from Platía Mavroyénous on the seafront, and their rates are fixed and quite reasonable; try Mýkonos Radio Taxi (☎0289/22 400). It is also here that the largest cluster of **motorbike rental** agencies is to be found: prices vary little.

Accommodation

Accommodation **prices** in Mýkonos rocket in the high season to a greater degree than almost anywhere else in Greece. If you're after **rooms**, it's worth asking at *O Megas* grocery store on Andhroníkou Matoyiánni – they tend to know what's available. One **hotel** that comes recommended is *Villa Giovanni* (☎0289/22 485; ⑥), on Ayíou Ioánnou, the busy main road above the bus station. **In town**, try *Delfines* on Mavroyenous (☎0289/22 292; ⑥), *Apollon* on Kambani (☎0289/22 223; ⑤), *Maria* at Kaloyéra 18 (☎0289/24 212; ⑥), or the *Philippi* at Kaloyéra 25 (☎0289/22 294; ④–⑤). There are plenty of very expensive splurge hotels like *Elysium* (☎0289/23 952; ⑥) on Skholíou Kalón Tehnon which has a gym, sauna and jacuzzi as well as pool, and *Petasos* (☎0289/22608; ⑥) above Polikandhrióti. As a last resort, the *Apollo 2001* disco may rent out roof space. Otherwise, there are two **campsites**: *Mykonos Camping* (☎0289/24 578; 2,300dr) above Paranga beach is smaller and has a more pleasant setting than nearby *Paradise Camping* (☎0289/22 852) – but both are packed in season, and dance music from the 24-hour bars on Paradise Beach makes sleep difficult. The campsite restaurants are best avoided. Hourly bus services to Paranga and Paradise Beach continue into the early hours but can get very overcrowded.

Eating and nightlife

Even **light meals** and **snacks** are expensive in Mýkonos, but there are several bakeries – the best is *Andhrea's*, just off Platía Mavroyénous – and plenty of supermarkets and takeaways in the backstreets, including *Spilia* on Énoplon Dhinaméon, which does decent burgers. For **late-night** snacks, try *Margarita's* on Flórou Zouganéli, or after 3am head for the port, where the Yacht Club is open until sunrise.

The area around Kaloyéra is a promising place to head for a full **meal**. The *Edem Garden* at the top of Kaloyéra, is a popular gay restaurant with an adventurous menu, and *El Greco* at Tría Pigádhia is expensive but romantic. Alefkándhra can offer *La Cathedral*, by the two cathedrals on the platía, the pricey but well-sited *Pelican*, behind the cathedrals, the *Oasis Garden Restaurant* nearby on Mitropóleos, in a quiet garden with reasonable food, and *Spiro's* for good fish on the seafront. *Kostas*, also behind the two cathedrals, has competitive prices, a good selection including barrelled wine (not easily found on Mýkonos) and friendly service. Less than fifty metres further along Mitropóleos, the small *Yiavroutas Estiatorio* is probably the least expensive and most authentically Greek place on the island, again with good barrelled wine. There's something for most tastes in the Lákka (bus station) area: a variety of salads at *Orpheas*, French cuisine at *Andromeda*, and Italian at *Dolce Vita*. Just behind the Town Hall is *Nikos' Taverna* – crowded, reasonable and recommended – and 1km north you can dine by a floodlit pool overlooking the cruise ships at the luxury *Hotel Cavo Tagoo*.

Nightlife in town is every bit as good as it's cracked up to be – and every bit as pricey. *Remezzo* (near the OTE) is one of the oldest bars, now a bit over the hill but a nice place to watch the sunset before the onslaught of the hilarious Greek dancing lessons. *Skandinavian Bar-Disco* is a cheap and cheerful party spot, as is the nearby *Irish Bar*, and there are more drinking haunts over in the Alefkándhra area. For classical music, try *Kastro's* for an early evening cocktail, moving on later to the fairly swanky *Montparnasse*. *Bolero's* and *Piano Bar* both have live music, while *Le Cinema* is a newish club worth trying. The **gay** striptease and drag-show scene has shifted to the *Factory* by the windmills; *Manto* and adjacent bars are also popular.

The beaches

The closest **beaches** to town are those to the north, at **Toúrlos** (only 2km away but horrid) and **Áyios Stéfanos** (4km, much better), both developed resorts and connected by a very regular bus service to Mýkonos. There are tavernas and rooms to let (as well as package hotels) at Áyios Stéfanos, away from the beach; *Nikos* taverna at the far end of the bay has a pleasant setting and good prices.

Other nearby destinations include southwest peninsula resorts, with undistinguished beaches tucked into pretty bays. The nearest to town, 1km away, is **Megáli Ammos**, a good beach backed by flat rocks and pricey rooms, but nearby Kórfos bay is disgusting, thanks to the town dump and machine noise. Buses serve **Órnos** – home to the Lucky Divers Scuba Club (☎0289/23 220) – and an average beach, and **Áyios Ioánnis**, a dramatic bay with a tiny, stony beach and a chapel.

The south coast is the busiest part of the island. Kaḯkia ply from town to all of its beaches, which are among the straightest on the island, and still regarded to some extent as family strands by the Greeks. You might begin with **Platýs Yialós**, 4km south of town, though you won't be alone: one of the longest-established resorts on the island, it's not remotely Greek any more, the sand is monopolized by hotels, and you won't get a room to save your life between June and September. **Psaroú**, next door, is very pretty – 150m of white sand backed by foliage and calamus reeds, crowded with sunbathers. Facilities here include a diving club (☎0289/23 579), waterskiing and windsurfer rental, but again you'll need to reserve well in advance to secure a room between mid-June and mid-September.

A dusty footpath beyond Platís Yialós crosses the fields and caves of the headland across the clifftops past *Mykonos Camping*, and drops down to **Paradise Beach**, a crescent of golden sand that is packed in season. Behind are the shops, self-service restaurants and noisy 24-hour beach bars of *Paradise Camping*. The next bay east contains

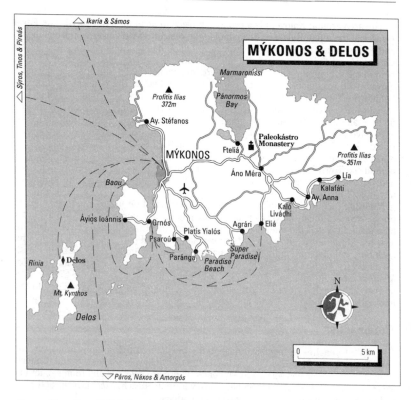

Super Paradise (officially "Plindhrí") beach, accessible by footpath or by kaïki. Once renowned as an exclusively gay, nudist beach, it's now pretty mixed, and a has a good, friendly atmosphere and a couple of tavernas.

Probably the **best beach** on Mýkonos, though, is **Elía**, the last port of call for the kaïkia. A broad, sandy stretch with a verdant backdrop, it's the longest beach on the island, though split in two by a rocky area. Almost exclusively nudist, it boasts an excellent restaurant, *Matheos*. If the crowds have followed you this far, one last escape route is to follow the bare rock footpath over the spur (look for the white house) at the end of Elía beach. This cuts upwards for grand views east and west and then winds down to **Kaló Livádhi** (seasonal bus service), a stunning beach adjoining an agricultural valley scattered with little farmhouses; even here there's a restaurant (a good one at that) at the far end of the beach. **Lía**, further on, is smaller but delightful, with bamboo windbreaks and clear water, plus another taverna.

The rest of the island

If time is limited, any of the beaches above will be just fine. There are others, though, away from Mýkonos Town, as well as a few other destinations worth making the effort for.

East of Elía, roughly 12km by road from the town, **Ayía Ánna** boasts a shingle beach and taverna, with the cliffs above granting some fine vistas; the place achieved its moment of fame as a location for the film *Shirley Valentine*. **Tarsaná**, on the other side of the isthmus, has a long, coarse sand beach, with watersports, a taverna and smart bungalows on offer. **Kalafáti**, almost adjacent, is more of a tourist community, its white-sand beach supporting a few hotels, restaurants and a disco. There's a local bus service from here to Áno Méra (see below), or you can jump on an excursion boat to **Tragoníssi**, the islet just offshore, for spectacular coastal scenery, seals and wild birds. The rest of the east coast is difficult – often impossible – to reach: there are some small beaches, really only worth the effort if you crave solitude, and the region is dominated by the peak of Profítis Ilías, sadly spoiled by a huge radar dome and military establishment. The **north coast** suffers persistent battering from the *meltémi*, plus tar and litter pollution, and for the most part is bare, brown and exposed. **Pánormos Bay** is the exception to this – a lovely, relatively sheltered beach, and one of the least crowded on the island, with a couple of decent tavernas.

From Pánormos, it's an easy walk to the only other settlement of any size on the island, **ÁNO MÉRA**, where you should be able to find a **room**. The village strives to maintain a traditional way of life: in the main square there's a proper kafenío and fresh vegetables are sold, ouzo and a local cheese are produced, and there's just one hotel. The taverna *Tou Apostoli to Koutouki* is popular with locals. The red-roofed church near the square is the sixteenth-century **monastery of Panayía Tourlianí**, where a collection of Cretan icons and the unusual eighteenth-century marble baptismal font are worth seeing. It's not far, either, to the late twelfth-century **Paleokástro monastery** (also known as Dárga), just north of the village, in a magnificent green setting on an otherwise barren slope. To the northwest are more of the same dry and wind-buffeted landscapes, though they do provide some enjoyable, rocky walking with expansive views across to neighbouring islands – stroll down to Áyios Stéfanos for buses back to the harbour.

Delos (Dhílos)

The remains of **ancient Delos**, Pindar's "unmoved marvel of the wide world", though skeletal and swarming now with lizards and tourists, give some idea of the past grandeur of this sacred isle a few sea-miles west of Mýkonos. The ancient town lies on the west coast on flat, sometimes marshy ground which rises in the south to **Mount Kínthos**. From the summit – an easy walk – there's a magnificent view across the Cyclades: the name of the archipelago means "those [islands] around [Delos]".

The first excursion boats to Delos leave Mýkonos daily at 8.30am (1600dr round trip), except Mondays when the site is closed. You have to return on the same boat but in season each does the trip several times and you can choose what time you leave. The last return is usually about 3pm, and you'll need to arrive early if you want to make a thorough tour of the site. In season a daily kaïki makes return trips from the beaches (2500dr) with pick-up points at Paránga, Platís Yialós and Ornos, but only allows you three hours on the island. It's a good idea to bring your own food and drink as the tourist pavilion's snack bar is a rip-off.

Some history

Delos' ancient fame was due to the fact that Leto gave birth to the divine twins Artemis and Apollo on the island, although its fine harbour and central position did nothing to hamper development. When the Ionians colonized the island around 1000 BC it was already a cult centre, and by the seventh century BC it had become the commercial and religious centre of the **Amphictionic League**. Unfortunately Delos also attracted the attention of Athens, which sought dominion over this prestigious

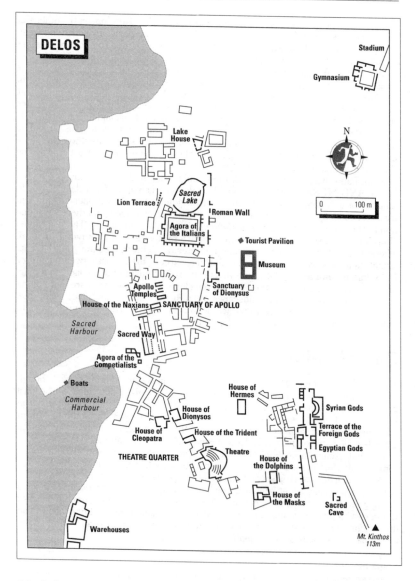

island; the wealth of the Delian Confederacy, founded after the Persian Wars to protect the Aegean cities, was harnessed to Athenian ends, and for a while they controlled the Sanctuary of Apollo. Athenian attempts to "purify" the island began with a
decree that no one could die or give birth on Delos – the sick and the pregnant were
taken to the islet of Rheneia – and culminated in the simple expedient of banishing
the native population.

Delos reached its peak in the third and second centuries BC, after being declared a free port by its Roman overlords. In the end, though, its undefended wealth brought ruin: first Mithridates (88 BC), then Athenodorus (69 BC), plundered the treasures and the island never recovered. By the third century AD, Athens could not even sell it, and for centuries, every passing seafarer stopped to collect a few prizes.

The site

Tues–Sun 8.30am–3pm; 1200dr.

As you land, the Sacred Harbour is on your left, the Commercial Harbour on your right; and straight ahead is the **Agora of the Competialists**. Competialists were Roman merchants or freed slaves who worshipped the Lares Competales, the guardian spirits of crossroads; offerings to Hermes would once have been placed in the middle of the *agora*, their position now marked by a round and a square base. The **Sacred Way** leads north from the far left corner; it used to be lined with statues and the grandiose monuments of rival kings. Along it you reach three marble steps which lead into the **Sanctuary of Apollo**: much was lavished on the god, but the forest of offerings has been plundered over the years. On your left is the Stoa of the Naxians, while against the north wall of the House of the Naxians, to the right, a huge statue of Apollo stood in ancient times. In 417 BC the Athenian general Nicias led a procession of priests across a bridge of boats from Rheneia to dedicate a bronze palm tree; when it was later blown over in a gale it took the statue with it. Three **Temples of Apollo** stand in a row to the right along the Sacred Way: the Delian Temple, that of the Athenians, and the Porinos Naos, the earliest of them, dating from the sixth century BC. To the east towards the museum you pass the **Sanctuary of Dionysus**, with its marble phalluses on tall pillars.

The best finds from the site are in Athens, but the **museum** still justifies a visit. To the north is a wall that marks the site of the **Sacred Lake** where Leto gave birth, clinging to a palm tree. Guarding it are the superb **lions**, their lean bodies masterfully executed by Naxians in the seventh century BC; of the original nine, three have disappeared and one adorns the Arsenale at Venice. On the other side of the lake is the City Wall, built in 69 BC – too late to protect the treasures.

Set out in the other direction from the Agora of the Competialists and you enter the residential area, known as the **Theatre Quarter**. Many of the walls and roads remain, but there is none of the domestic detail that brings such sites to life. Some colour is added by the mosaics: one in the **House of the Trident**, and better ones in the **House of the Masks**, most notably a vigorous portrayal of Dionysus riding on a panther's back. The **Theatre** itself seated 5500 spectators, and, though much ravaged, offers some fine views. Behind the theatre, a path leads past the **Sanctuaries of the Foreign Gods** and up **Mount Kínthos** for more panoramic sightseeing.

Sýros

Don't be put off by first impressions of **Sýros**. From the ferry it looks grimly industrial, but away from the Neórion shipyard things improve quickly. Very much a working island with no real history of tourism, it is probably the most Greek of the Cyclades; there are few holiday trappings and what there is exists for the benefit of the locals. You probably won't find, as Herman Melville did when he visited in 1856, shops full of ". . . fez-caps, swords, tobacco, shawls, pistols, and orient finery . . .", but you're still likely to appreciate Sýros as a refreshing change from the beautiful people. Of course, outsiders do come to the island; in fact there's a thriving permanent foreign community, and the beaches are hardly undeveloped, but everywhere there's the underlying assumption that you're a guest of an inherently private people.

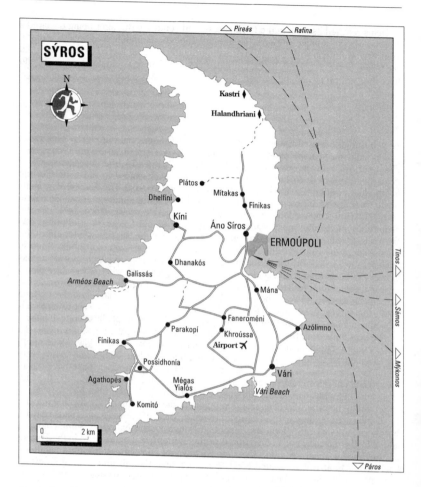

Ermoúpoli

The main town and port of **ERMOÚPOLI** was founded during the War of Independence by refugees from Psará and Khíos, becoming Greece's chief port in the nineteenth century. Although Pireás outran it long ago, Ermoúpoli is still the largest town in the Cyclades, and the archipelago's capital. Medieval Sýros was largely a Catholic island, but an influx of Orthodox refugees during the War of Independence created two distinct communities; almost equal in numbers, the two groups today still live in their respective quarters, occupying two hills that rise up from the sea.

Ermoúpoli itself, the **lower town**, is worth at least a night's stay, with grandiose buildings a relic of its days as a major port. Between the harbour and **Áyios Nikólaos**, the fine Orthodox church to the north, you can stroll through its faded splendour. The **Apollon Theatre** is a copy of La Scala in Milan and once presented a regular Italian opera season; today local theatre and music groups put it to good use. The long, central **Platía Miaoúli** is named after an admiral of the revolution whose statue stands there, and in the evenings the population parades in front of its arcaded kafenía, while the children ride the mechanical animals. Up the stairs to the left of the Town Hall is the small **Archeological Museum** (Tues–Sun 8.30am–3pm; free) with three rooms of finds from Sýros, Páros and Amorgós. To the left of the clock tower more stairs climb up to **Vrondádho**, the hill that hosts the Orthodox quarter. The wonderful church of the **Anástasi** stands atop the hill, with its domed roof and great views over Tínos and Mýkonos – if it's locked, ask for the key at the priest's house.

On the taller hill to the left is the intricate medieval quarter of **Áno Sýros**, with a clutch of Catholic churches below the cathedral of St George. There are fine views of the town below, and, close by, the **Cappuchin monastery of St Jean**, founded in 1535 to do duty as a poorhouse. It takes about 45 minutes of tough walking up Omírou to reach this quarter, passing the Orthodox and Catholic cemeteries on the way – the former full of grand shipowners' mausoleums, the latter with more modest monuments and French and Italian inscriptions (you can halve the walking time by taking a short cut on to the stair-street named Andhréa Kárga, part of the way along). Once up here it's worth visiting the local art and church exhibitions at the Vamvakeri **museum** (daily 10.30am–1pm & 7–10pm; 500dr), and the Byzantine museum attached to the monastery.

Arrival, facilities and accommodation

The **quayside** is still busy, though nowadays it deals with more tourist than industrial shipping; Sýros is a major crossover point on the ferry-boat routes. Also down here is the **bus station**, along with the **tourist police** and several **bike rental** places. Between them shops sell the *loukoumia* (Turkish delight) and *halvadhopita* (sweetmeat pie) for which the island is famed. **Odhós Khíou**, the market street, is especially lively on Saturday when people come in from the surrounding countryside to sell fresh produce.

Keeping step with a growing level of tourism, **rooms** have improved in quality and number in recent years; many are in garishly decorated, if crumbling, Neoclassical mansions. Good choices include *Kastro* rooms, Kalomenopóulou 12 (☎0281/88 064; ③), *Dream* on the seafront near the bus station (☎0281/84 356; ④), and the central rooms on Platía Miaoúli (☎0281/88 509; ④) and at *Paradise*, Omírou 3 (☎0281/83 204; ⑤). A notch up in price and quality is the well-sited *Hotel Hermes* (☎0281/83 011; ⑥) on Platía Kanári, overlooking the port or, for a slice of good-value opulence, try the *Xenon Ipatias* (☎0281/83 575; ⑤), beyond Áyios Nikólaos. At peak times the Team Work agency (on the waterfront) may be able to help with accommodation. For plusher places around town and hotels and rooms of all categories around the island there is a kiosk belonging to the Rooms and Apartments Association of Syros (☎0281/87 360) along the waterfront – turn right after disembarking.

Eating, drinking and nightlife

The most authentic and reasonably priced of the harbour **tavernas** is *Medusa*, at Ándhrou 3, a block in from the water; places actually on the quay, such as *1935*, tend to be more touristy and expensive. There are one or two exceptions, including the very reasonable *Caro D'Oro* which serves up casseroles and barrelled wine, and the popular *Psaropoula* ouzerí. Highly recommended for an Italian treat is *Il Giardino*, set in a beautifully restored villa opposite the *Apollon*. On Platía Miaoúli, the *Manousos* taverna is a good traditional place. Way up in Vrondádho, at Anastáseos 17, on the corner of Kalavrítou, the cooking at *Tembelis* makes up for the limited seating and grouchy service; *Folia*, at Athanasíou Dhiakoú 6, is more expensive but serves such exotica as rabbit and

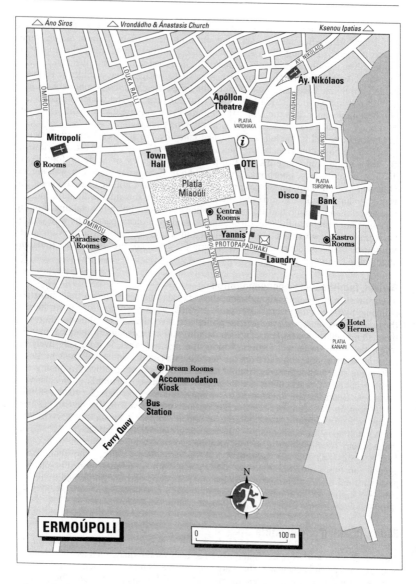

Áy. Níkólaos

Apóllon
Theatre

PLATIA
VARDHAKA

Mitropolí

Town
Hall

OTE

Rooms

Platía
Míaoúli

Disco   Bank

PLATIA
TSIROPINA

Central
Rooms

Paradise
Rooms

Yannis'

PROTOPAPADHAKI

Kastro
Rooms

Laundry

Hotel
Hermes

PLATIA
KANARI

Dream Rooms

Accommodation
Kiosk

Bus
Station

Ferry Quay

N

ERMOÚPOLI

0   100 m

pigeon. In Ano Sýros, the *Thea* taverna, signposted in Greek from the car park, is fine and affords the views its name would suggest; the *Iy Piatsa* ouzerí is also worth a try.

Incidentally, Sýros still honours its contribution to the development of **rembétika** (see "Music" on p.816); bouzoúki-great Markos Vamvakaris hailed from here and a platía in Áno Sýros has been named after him. **Taverna-clubs** such as *Lillis* (up in Áno Sýros) and *Rahanos*, with music on weekends, now take their place beside a batch of more conventional disco-clubs down near the Apollon Theatre. There are several other (often expensive) bouzoúki bars scattered around the island, mostly strung along routes to beach resorts. The seafront has a rash of lively **bars** – *Tramps* has a relaxed atmosphere and the most eclectic music. There's another cluster around the Platía Miaoúli: *Clearchos* piano bar is rather smooth, *Agora* has imaginative decor and a musical mix, while *Piramatiko* is best for up-to-date indie sounds. The big venue for nightowls is *Rodo*, a huge disco in a converted warehouse out past the Neórión shipyard opposite the turning to Vári. Finally, the newly opened *Aegean Casino* on the seafront features live music at the restaurant, and is open till 6am for those who have money to burn (and are sufficiently well-dressed).

Around the island

The main loop road (to Gallissás, Fínikas, Mégas Yialós, Vári and back), and the road west to Kíni, are good: **buses** ply the routes hourly in season, and run until late. Elsewhere, expect potholes – especially to the **north** where the land is barren and high, with few villages. The main route north from Áno Sýros has improved and is quite easily negotiable by bike; en route, the village of **Mýtikas** has a decent taverna just off the road. A few kilometres further on the road forks, with the left turn leading, after another left, to the small settlement of **Siroúga** where there's an interesting cave to explore, or straight on to **Kámbos**, from where a path leads down to Lía Beach; the right fork eventually descends to the north-east coast after passing an excellent kafenío, *Sgouros*, with views across to Tínos.

The well-trodden route **south** offers more tangible and accessible rewards. Closest to the capital, fifteen minutes away by bus, is the coastal settlement of **KÍNI**. There are two separate beaches, the *Sunset Hotel* (☎0281/71 211; ③–④), with the excellent *Zalounis* taverna just below and, just away from the seafront, the *Hotel Elpida* (☎0281/71 224; ③). **GALISSÁS**, a few kilometres south, but reached by different buses, has developed along different lines. Fundamentally an agricultural village, it's been taken over in recent years by backpackers attracted by the island's only **campsites** (both have good facilities and send minibuses to all boats, but *Camping Yianna* has the advantage over *Two Hearts* of being closer to the sea) and a very pretty beach, more protected than Kíni's. This new-found popularity has created a surplus of unaesthetic **rooms**, which at least makes bargaining possible, and five bona fide hotels, of which the cheapest is *Petros* (☎0281/42 067; ③), though the *Benois* (☎0281/42 833; ⑤) is decent value, with buffet breakfast included. Amongst the many eating choices, *Diskovolos* and *Cavos*, overlooking the bay, are worth a try. Galissás' identity crisis is exemplified by the proximity of bemused, grazing dairy cattle, a heavy-metal music pub, and upmarket handicrafts shops. Still, the people are welcoming, and if you feel the urge to escape, you can rent a moped, or walk ten minutes past the headland to the nudist beach of **Arméos**, where there's fresh spring water and unofficial camping. Note that buses out are erratically routed; to be sure of making your connection you must wait at the high-road stop, not down by the beach. **Dhelfini** just to the north is also a fine beach, though it's slowly falling prey to the developers under the translated name of Dolphin Bay.

A pleasant one-hour walk or a ten-minute bus ride south from Galissás brings you to the more mainstream resort of **FÍNIKAS**, purported to have been settled originally by the Phoenicians (although an alternative derivation could be from *fínikas*, meaning "palm tree" in Greek). The beach is narrow and gritty, right next to the road but protected to some extent by a row of tamarisk trees; the pick of the hotels is the *Cyclades* (☎0281/42 255; ⑤), which also has an acceptable restaurant, though the *Amaryllis* rooms (☎0281/42 894; ③) are much cheaper. The *Panorama* restaurant on the seafront is recommended.

Fínikas is separated by a tiny headland from its neighbour **POSSIDHONÍA** (or Delagrazzia), a nicer spot with some idiosyncratically ornate mansions and a bright blue church right on the edge of the village. It's worth walking ten minutes further south, past the naval yacht club and its patrol boat to **Agathopés**, with a sandy beach and a little islet just offshore. Komitó, at the end of the unpaved track leading south from Agathopés, is nothing more than a stony beach fronting an olive grove. **Accommodation** around Possidhonía ranges from the luxurious and extremely expensive *Hotel Eleana* (☎0281/42 601; ⑥), reckoned by some to be the best in the Cyclades, to the cheerful *Elpida Pension* (☎0281/42 577; ③), while *Meltemi* is the best seafood taverna.

The road swings east to **MÉGAS YIALÓS**, a small resort below a hillside festooned with brightly painted houses. The long, narrow beach is lined with shady trees and there are pedal boats for hire. Of the **room** set-ups, *Mike and Bill's* (☎0281/43 531; ④) is a reasonable deal, and the pricier *Alexandra Hotel* (☎0281/42 540; ⑤) on the bay enjoys lovely views. **VÁRI** is more – though not much more – of a town, with its own small fishing fleet. Beach-goers are in a goldfish bowl, as it were, with tavernas and **rooms** looming right overhead, but it is the most sheltered of the island's bays, something to remember when the *meltémi* is up. The *Kamelo* hotel (☎0281/61 217; ⑤) provides the best value, and has TV in all the rooms. The adjacent cove of **AKHLÁDHI** is far more pleasant and boasts two small good-value hotels, including the *Emily* (☎0281/61400; ④) on the seafront, and has one taverna.

Páros and Andíparos

Gently and undramatically furled around the single peak of Profítis Ilías, **Páros** has a little of everything one expects from a Greek island – old villages, monasteries, fishing harbours, a labyrinthine capital – and some of the best nightlife and beaches in the Aegean. Parikía, the Khóra, is the major hub of inter-island ferry services, so that if you wait long enough you can get to just about any island in the Aegean. However, the island is almost as heavily touristy and expensive as Mýkonos: in peak season, it's touch-and-go when it comes to finding rooms and beach space. At such times, the attractive inland settlements or the satellite island of **Andíparos** handle the overflow. Incidentally, the August 15 festival here is one of the best such observances in Greece, with a parade of flare-lit fishing boats and fireworks delighting as many Greeks as foreigners, but it's a real feat to secure accommodation around this time.

Parikía and around

PARIKÍA sets the tone architecturally for the rest of Páros, with its ranks of typically Cycladic white houses punctuated by the occasional Venetian-style building and church domes. But all is awash in a constant stream of ferry passengers, and the town is relentlessly commercial. The busy waterfront is jam-packed with bars, restaurants, hotels and ticket agencies, while the maze of houses in the older quarter behind, designed to baffle both wind and pirates, has surrendered to an onslaught of chi-chi boutiques.

Just beyond the central clutter though, the town has one of the most architecturally interesting churches in the Aegean – the **Ekatondapiliani**, or "The One-Hundred-Gated". What's visible today was designed and supervised by Isidore of Miletus in the sixth century, but construction was actually carried out by his pupil Ignatius. It was so beautiful on completion that the master, consumed with jealousy, is said to have grappled with his apprentice on the rooftop, flinging them both to their deaths. They are portrayed kneeling at the column bases across the courtyard, the old master tugging at his beard in repentance and his rueful pupil clutching a broken head. The church was substantially altered after a severe earthquake in the eighth century, but its essen-

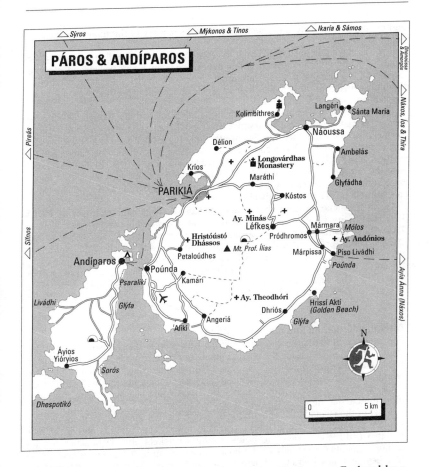

PÁROS & ANDÍPAROS

△ Sýros   △ Mýkonos & Tínos   △ Ikaría & Sámos

◁ Pireás
◁ Sífnos

Kolimbíthres
Langéri
Sánta María
Náoussa
Délion
Ambelás
Longovárdhas Monastery
Kríos
Maráthi
Glyfádha
PARIKIÁ
Kóstos
Ay. Minás
Léfkes
Mármara   Mólos
Hristóústó Dhássos
Pródhromos
Ay. Andónios
Petaloúdhes
Mt. Prof. Ílias
Márpissa   Piso Livádhi
Andíparos
Poúna
Poúnda
Psaralikí
Kamári
Livádhi
Glýfa
Ay. Theodhóri
Dhriós
Hrissí Aktí (Golden Beach)
Angeriá
Glýfa
Alikí
Áyios Yióryios
Sorós
Dhespotikó

Dhonoússa & Amorgós ▷
Náxos, Íos & Thíra ▷
Ayía Ánna (Náxos) ▷

N

0   5 km

tially Byzantine aspect remains, its shape an imperfect Greek cross. Enclosed by a great wall to protect its icons from pirates, it is in fact three interlocking churches; the oldest, the chapel of Áyios Nikólaos to the left of the apse, is an adaptation of a pagan building dating from the early fourth century BC. To the right of the courtyard, the **Byzantine Museum** (daily 9am–1pm & 5.30–9.30pm; 500dr, free on Tues) displays a collection of icons. Behind Ekatondapilianí, the **Archeological Museum** (Tues–Sun 8.30am–2.30pm; 500dr) has a fair collection of antique bits and pieces, its prize exhibits being a fifth-century winged Nike and a piece of the *Parian Chronicle*, a social and cultural history of Greece up to 264 BC engraved in marble.

These two sights apart, the real attraction of Parikía is simply to wander the town itself. Arcaded lanes lead past Venetian-influenced villas, traditional island dwellings and the three ornate wall fountains donated by the Mavroyénnis family in the eighteenth century. The town culminates in a seaward Venetian **Kástro**, whose surviving east wall incorporates a fifth century round tower and is constructed using masonry pillaged from a temple of Athena. Part of the base of the temple is still visible next to the beautiful, arcaded church of Áyios Konstandínos, and Áyia Eléni crowns the highest point, from where the fortified hill drops sharply to the quay in a series of hanging gardens.

If you're staying in town, you'll want to get out into the surroundings at some stage, if only to the beach. The most rewarding **excursion** is the hour's walk along an unsurfaced road starting just past the museum up to **Áyii Anáryiri** monastery. Perched on the bluff above town, this makes a great picnic spot, with cypress groves, a gushing fountain and some splendid views.

There are **beaches** immediately north and south of the harbour, though none are particularly attractive when compared with Páros' best. In fact, you might prefer to avoid the northern stretch altogether: heading **south** along the asphalt road is a better bet. The first unsurfaced side track you come to leads to a small, sheltered beach; fifteen minutes further on is **PARASPÓROS**, with a reasonable **campsite** (☎0284/21 100) and beach near the remains of an ancient *asklepeion*. Continuing for 45 minutes (or a short hop by bus) brings you to arguably the best of the bunch, **AYÍA IRÍNI**, with good sand and a taverna next to a farm and shady olive grove.

Off in the same direction, but a much longer two-hour haul each way, is **PETA-LOÚDHES**, the so-called "Valley of the Butterflies", a walled-in oasis where millions of Jersey tiger moths perch on the foliage during early summer (June–Sept 9am–8pm; 200dr). The trip pays more dividends when combined with a visit to the eighteenth-century nunnery of **Khristoú stó Dhássos**, at the crest of a ridge twenty minutes to the north. Only women are allowed in the sanctuary, although men can get as far as the courtyard. The succession of narrow drives and donkey paths linking both places begins just south of Parikía, by the *Xenon Ery*. Petaloúdhes can be reached from Parikía by bus (in summer), by moped, or on an overpriced excursion by mule.

Arrival, information and accommodation

Ferries **dock** in Parikía by the windmill; the **bus stop** is 100m or so to the left. Bus routes extend to Náoussa in the north, Poúnda (for Andíparos) in the west, Alikí in the south, and Dhríos on the island's east coast (with another very useful service between Dhríos and Náoussa). Buses to Náoussa carry on running hourly through the night, while other services stop around midnight. The **airport** is around 12km from town, close to Alikí – from where ten daily buses run to Parikía.

Most of the island is flat enough for bicycle rides, but mopeds are more common and are available for rent at several places in town. Polos Tours is one of the more together and friendly **travel agencies**, issuing air tickets when Olympic is shut, and acting as agents for virtually all the boats. Luggage can be left at Santorineos Travel, 50m beyond Polos Tours (heading south along the front). Olympic Airways itself is at the far end of Odhós Probóne, while the **tourist police** occupy a building at the back of the seafront square.

As for **accommodation**, Parikía is a pleasant and central base, but absolutely mobbed in summer. You'll be met off the ferry by locals offering rooms, even at the most unlikely hours; avoid persistent offers of rooms or hotels to the north as they'll invariably be a long walk away from town. One of the best deals is to be had is at the *Pension Festos* on the back streets inland, managed by young Brits (☎0284/21 635; ④); it has beds in shared rooms making it a good choice for single travellers. Popular **hotels** include *Dina* (☎0284/21 325; ④) near Platía Veléntza, *Kontes* (☎0284/21 096; ⑤) near the harbour windmill and *Hotel Oasis* (☎0284/21 227; ③–④) on Prombóna, very close to the harbour. *Hotel Kypreou* (☎0284/21 383; ④) is a small family-run hotel on Prombóna, which, like *Oasis* and *Kontes*, stays open through the winter. A good upmarket choice is *Hotel Doukissa* (☎0284/22 442; ⑥) near the Archeological Museum, while *Irini Triadafilou* (☎0284/23 022; ③) has a few basic rooms within the kástro, some with good sea views.

Eating, drinking and nightlife

Many Parikía **tavernas** are run by outsiders operating under municipal concession, so year-to-year variation in proprietors and quality is marked. However, the following seem to be long-established and/or good-value outfits. Rock-bottom is the *Koutouki Thanasis*, which serves oven food for locals and bold tourists and lurks in a back street to the left of the (expensive) *Hibiscus*. Also in the picturesque backstreets are *Kyriakos Place* on Lohágou Grivári, which has seats out under a fine tree, and the *Garden of Dionysos* nearby. In the exotic department, *May Tey* serves average Chinese food at moderate markup, while Italian dishes can be found at *La Barca Rossa* on the seafront or *Bella Italia* across a waterfront square.

There is a welter of places of varying quality and prices along the **seafront** towards the bar enclave. Of these, *Asteras Grill House* is very good with some decent specials as well as the usual grilled meats. Down a backstreet just to the north of the harbour, *Nisiotissa* has a highly entertaining chef-proprietor and is rarely crowded; *Delfini*, on the first paved drive along the road to Poúnda, is long-established and famous for its Sunday barbecue with live music. There are a couple of specialist eating places: *The Happy Green Cow*, a friendly café with vegetarian and vegan food behind the National Bank, and *Wired Café*, a new Internet café on the market street running behind the kástro (2000dr per hour).

Parikía has a wealth of **pubs, bars** and low-key **discos**, not as pretentious as those on Mýkonos or as raucous as the scene on Íos, but certainly everything in between. The most popular cocktail bars extend along the seafront, all tucked into a series of open squares and offering competing but staggered (no pun intended) "Happy Hours", so that you can drink cheaply for much of the evening. *Kafenio O Flisvos*, about three-quarters of the way south along the front, is the last remaining traditional outfit among the rash of pizzerias, snack-bars, juice and ice-cream joints. A rowdy crowd favours the conspicuous *Saloon D'Or*, while the *Pirate Bar* features jazz and blues. *Evinos* and *Pebbles* are more genteel, the latter pricey but with good sunset views and the occasional live gig. The "theme" pubs are a bit rough and ready for some: most outrageous is the *Dubliner Complex*, comprising four bars, a snack section, disco and seating area.

Finally, a thriving cultural centre, *Arhilokhos* (near Ekatondapilianí) caters mostly to locals, with occasional **film** screenings – there are also two open-air cinemas, *Neo Rex* and *Paros*, where foreign films are shown in season.

Náoussa and around

The second port of Páros, **NÁOUSSA** was once an unspoiled, sparkling labyrinth of winding, narrow alleys and simple Cycladic houses. Alas, a rash of new concrete hotels and attendant trappings have all but swamped its character, though down at the small harbour, fishermen still tenderize octopuses by thrashing them against the walls. The local festivals – an annual Fish and Wine Festival on July 2, and an August 23 shindig celebrating an old naval victory over the Turks – are also still celebrated with enthusiasm; the latter tends to be brought forward to coincide with the August 15 festival of the Panayía. Most people are here for the local beaches (see p.478) and the relaxed nightlife; there's really only one sight, a **museum** (daily 9am–1.30pm & 7–9pm; free) in the monastery of Áyios Athanásios, with an interesting collection of Byzantine and post-Byzantine icons from the churches and monasteries around Náoussa.

Despite encroaching development, the town is noted for its nearby beaches and is a good place to head for as soon as you reach Páros. **Rooms** are marginally cheaper here than in Parikía; track them down with the help of the **tourist office** which is just over the bridge, west from the harbour. The *Sea House* (☎0284/52 198; ④) on the rocks above Pipéri beach was the first place in Náoussa to let rooms and has one of the best locations, and the *Manis Inn* (☎0284/51 744; ⑥) is an upmarket hotel with pool behind Pipéri beach; out of season you should haggle for reduced prices at the *Madaki* (☎0284/51 475; ④) and the *Stella* (☎0284/52 198; ④). There are two **campsites** in the vicinity: the relaxed and friendly *Naoussa* campsite (☎0284/51565), out of town towards Kolimbíthres (see below), and the newer *Surfing Beach* (☎0284/51 013) at Sánta Maria, northeast of Náoussa; both run courtesy mini-buses to and from Parikía.

Most of the harbour **tavernas** are surprisingly good, specializing in fresh fish and seafood; *O Barbarossas* ouzerí is the best of these. There are more places to eat along the main road leading inland from just beside the little bridge over the canal. *Zorbas*, with good barrelled unresinated wine, and the *Glaros* next door are both open 24 hours. **Bars** cluster around the old harbour: *Linardo* is the big dance spot, *Agosta* plays rock, *Camaron* and the *Pirate* bar play only Greek music, and *Pico Pico* also plays Greek music, with an emphasis on *nisiotiká*.

Local beaches

Pipéri **beach** is couple of minutes' walk west of Náoussa's harbour; there are other good-to-excellent beaches within walking distance, and a summer kaïki service to connect them. To the west, an hour's tramp brings you to **Kolymbíthres** (Basins), where there are three tavernas and the wind- and sea-sculpted rock formations from which the place draws its name. A few minutes beyond, **Monastíri** beach, below the abandoned Pródhromos monastery, is similarly attractive, and partly nudist. If you go up the hill after Monastíri onto the rocky promontory, the island gradually shelves into the sea via a series of flattish rock ledges, making a fine secluded spot for diving and snorkelling, as long as the sea is calm. Go northeast and the sands are better still, the barren headland spangled with good surfing beaches – **Langéri** is backed by dunes; the best surfing is at **Sánta María**, a trendy beach connected with Náoussa by road which also has a pleasant taverna named *Aristofanes*; and **Platiá Ámmos** perches on the northeastern tip of the island.

The northeast coast and inland

AMBELÁS hamlet marks the start of a longer trek down the **east coast**. Ambelás itself has a good beach, a small taverna, and some rooms and hotels, of which the *Hotel Christiana* (☎0284/51 573; ④) is excellent value, with great fresh fish, local wine in the restaurant and extremely friendly proprietors. From here a rough track leads south, passing several undeveloped stretches on the way: after about an hour you reach **Mólos** beach, impressive and not particularly crowded. **MÁRMARA**, twenty minutes further on, has rooms to let and makes an attractive place to stay, though the marble that the village is built from and named after has largely been whitewashed over.

If Mármara doesn't appeal, then serene **MÁRPISSA**, just to the south, might – a maze of winding alleys and ageing archways overhung by floral balconies, all clinging precariously to the hillside. There are rooms here too, and you can while away a spare hour climbing up the conical Kéfalos hill, on whose fortified summit the last Venetian lords of Páros were overpowered by the Ottomans in 1537. Today the monastery of **Áyios Andónios** occupies the site, but the grounds are locked; to enjoy the views over eastern Páros and the straits of Náxos fully, pick up the key from the priest in Máripissa before setting out. On the shore nearby, **PÍSO LIVÁDHI** was once a quiet fishing village, but has been ruined by rampant construction in the name of package tourism. The main reason to visit is to catch a (seasonal) kaïki to Ayía Ánna on Náxos; if you need to **stay** overnight here, *Hotel Andromache* (☎0284/41 387 or 42 565; ④) is a good place behind the beach. The *Captain Kafkis Camping* (☎0284/41 392) – a small quiet site – is out of town on the road up to Márpissa.

Inland

The road runs west from Píso Livádhi back to the capital. A medieval flagstoned path once linked both sides of the island, and parts of it survive in the east between Mármara and the villages around Léfkes. **PRÓDHROMOS**, encountered first, is an old fortified farming settlement with defensive walls girding its nearby monastery, while **LÉFKES** itself, an hour up the track, is perhaps the most beautiful and unspoiled settlement on Páros. The town flourished from the seventeenth century on, its population swollen by refugees fleeing from coastal piracy; indeed it was the island's Khóra during most of the Ottoman period. Léfkes' marbled alleyways and amphitheatrical setting are unparalleled and, despite the few rooms, a disco and a taverna on the outskirts, and the presence of two oversized hotels – the *Hotel Pantheon* (☎0284/41 646; ④), a large 1970s hotel at the top of the village and *Lefkes Village* (☎0284/41 827 or 42 398; ⑥), a very upmarket place just outside – the area around the main square has steadfastly resisted change; the central kafenío and bakery observe their siestas religiously.

Thirty minutes further on, through olive groves, is **KÓSTOS**, a simple village and a good place for lunch in a taverna. Any traces of path disappear at **MARÁTHI**, on the site of the ancient marble quarries which once supplied much of Europe. Considered second only to Carrara marble, the last slabs were mined here by the French in the nineteenth century for Napoleon's tomb. From Maráthi, it's easy enough to pick up the bus on to Parikía, but if you want to continue hiking, strike south for the monastery of **Áyios Minás**, twenty minutes away. Various Classical and Byzantine masonry fragments are worked into the walls of this sixteenth-century foundation, and the friendly couple who act as custodians can put you on the right path up to the convent of **Thapsaná**. From here, other paths lead either back to Parikía (two hours altogether from Áyios Minás), or on up to the island's summit for the last word in views over the Cyclades.

The south of the island

There's little to stop for south of Parikía until **POÚNDA**, 6km away, and then only to catch the ferry to Andíparos (see p.480). What used to be a sleepy hamlet is now a concrete jungle, and neighbouring **ALIKÍ** appears to be permanently under construction. The **airport** is close by, making for lots of unwelcome noise; the sole redeeming feature is an excellent beachside restaurant, by the large tamarisk tree. The end of the southern bus route is at Angeriá, about 3km inland of which is the **convent of Áyii Theodhóri**. Its nuns specialize in weaving locally commissioned articles and are further distinguished as *paleomeroloyites*, or old-calendarites, meaning that they follow the medieval Orthodox (Julian) calendar, rather than the Gregorian one.

Working your way around the **south coast**, there are two routes east to Dhríos. Either retrace your steps to Angeriá and follow the (slightly inland) coastal jeep track, which skirts a succession of isolated coves and small beaches; or keep on across the foothills from Áyii Theodhóri – a shorter walk. Aside from an abundant water supply (including a duck pond) and surrounding orchards, **DHRÝOS** village is mostly modern and characterless, lacking even a well-defined platía. Follow the lane signed "Dhríos Beach", however, and things improve a bit.

Between here and Píso Livádhi to the north are several sandy coves – Khryssí Aktí (Golden Beach), Tzirdhákia, Mezádha, Poúnda and Logarás – prone to pummelling by the *meltémi*, yet all favoured to varying degrees by campers, and windsurfers making a virtue out of necessity. **KHRYSSÍ AKTÍ** is now thoroughly overrun with tavernas, room complexes and the whole range of watersports; there are also tavernas at Logarás, but other facilities are concentrated in Dhríos, which is still the focal point of this part of the island.

Andíparos

Andíparos was once quiet and unspoiled, but now the secret is definitely out. The waterfront is lined with new hotels and apartments, and in high season it can be full of the same young, international crowd you were hoping to leave behind on Páros. It has, however, has kept its friendly small island atmosphere and still has a lot going for it, including good sandy beaches and an impressive cave, and the rooms and hotels are less expensive than on Páros.

Most of the population of 800 live in the large low-lying northern **village**, across the narrow straits from Páros, the new development on the outskirts concealing an attractive traditional settlement around the kástro. A long, flagstoned pedestrian street forms its backbone, leading from the jetty to the Cycladic houses around the outer wall of the kástro, which was built by Leonardo Loredano in the 1440s as a fortified settlement safe from pirate raids: the Loredano coat of arms can still be seen on a house in the courtyard. The only way into the courtyard is through a pointed archway from the platía, where several cafés are shaded by a giant eucalyptus. Inside, more whitewashed houses surround two churches and a cistern built into the surviving base of the central tower.

Andíparos' **beaches** begin right outside town: Psaralíki just to the south with golden sand and tamarisks for shade is much better than Sifnéïko (aka "Sunset") on the opposite side of the island. Villa development is starting to follow the newly paved road down the east coast, but has yet to get out of hand. Glýfa, 4km down, is another good beach and, further south, Sóros has rooms and tavernas. On the west coast there are some fine small sandy coves at Áyios Yeóryios, the end of the road, and a long stretch of sand at Livádhia. Kaïki make daily trips round the island and, less frequently, to the uninhabited islet of Dhespotikó, opposite Áyios Yeóryios.

The great **cave** (summer daily 10.45am–3.45pm; 500dr) in the south of the island is the chief attraction for day-trippers. In these eerie chambers the Marquis de Nointel, Louis XIV's ambassador to Constantinople, celebrated Christmas Mass in 1673 while a retinue of 500, including painters, pirates, Jesuits and Turks, looked on; at the exact moment of midnight explosives were detonated to emphasize the enormity of the event. Although electric light and cement steps have diminished its mystery and grandeur, the cave remains impressive. Tour buses run from the port every half hour in season (1200dr return), giving you an hour to explore; out of season, bus services and opening hours are reduced and in winter you'll have to fetch the key for the cave from the village.

Practicalities

To get here, you have a choice of **boats** from Parikía (hourly; 40min), arriving at the jetty opposite the main street, or the car ferry from Poúnda (half-hourly; 10min), arriving 150m to the south. In season there's no need to use the car ferry unless you take a moped over or miss the last boat back to Parikía; the car ferry keeps running until midnight. The service to Parikía is reduced out of season and runs only once a day in winter.

There are plenty of **hotels** along the waterfront, including *Anargyros* (☎0284/61 204; ④), which has good rooms and air-conditioned apartments. More upmarket places to the north of the jetty include *Mantalena* (☎0284/61 206; ⑥) and *Artemis* (☎0284/61 460; ⑤), while inland there are some cheaper rooms as well as the *Hotel Galini* (☎0284/61 420; ⑤) to the left of the main street and next to a disco. The popular **campsite** (☎0284/61 221) is a ten-minute walk northeast along a track, next to its own nudist beach; the water here is shallow enough for campers to wade across to the neighbouring islet of Dhipló. For peace and quiet with a degree of comfort try *Studios Delfini* (☎093/275 911; ⑤) with its own taverna at Áyios Yeóryios.

The best of the waterfront **tavernas** is *Anargyros*, below the hotel of the same name. *Klimataria*, 100m inland to the left off the main street, has tables in a pleasant, shady garden, and *To Kastro* is one of the better restaurants outside the kástro. There are plenty of **bars** in the same area but the locals usually stick to the excellent *To Kendro* zakharoplastía in the eucalyptus-filled platía. For quiet music and views of the mountains try *Cafe Yam*, an outdoor café-bar near the Klimataria. A short-schedule **bank**, an **OTE** booth with morning and evening opening hours, a **post office**, a cinema and several **travel agents** round up the list of amenities.

Náxos

Náxos is the largest and most fertile of the Cyclades, and with its green and mountainous highland scenery seems immediately distinct from many of its neighbours. The difference is accentuated by the **unique architecture** of many of the interior villages: the Venetian Duchy of the Aegean, which ruled from the thirteenth to the sixteenth century, left towers and fortified mansions scattered throughout the island, while medieval Cretan refugees bestowed a singular character upon Náxos' eastern settlements.

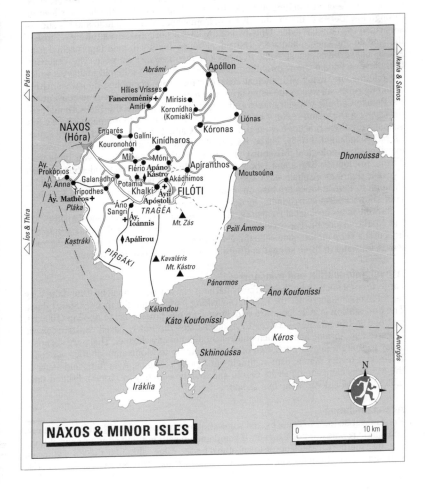

Today Náxos could easily support itself without tourism by relying on its production of potatoes, olives, grapes and lemons, but has thrown its lot in with mass tourism, so that parts of the island are now almost as busy and commercialized as Páros in season. But the island certainly has plenty to see if you know where to look: the highest mountains in the Cyclades, intriguing central valleys, a spectacular north coast, and marvellously sandy beaches in the southwest.

Náxos Town

A long causeway, built to protect the harbour to the north, connects **NÁXOS TOWN** (or Khóra) with the islet of Palátia – the place where, according to legend, Theseus abandoned Ariadne on his way home from Crete. The huge stone portal of a **Temple of Apollo** still stands there, built on the orders of the tyrant Lygdamis in the sixth century BC, but never completed. Most of the town's life goes on down by the crowded port esplanade or just behind it; back streets and alleys behind the harbour lead up through low arches to the fortified **Kástro**, from where Marco Sanudo and his successors ruled over the Cyclades. Only two of the kástro's original seven towers – those of the Sanudo and Glezos families – remain, although the north gate (approached from Apóllonos) survives as a splendid example of a medieval fort entrance. The Venetians' Catholic descendants, now dwindling in numbers, still live in the old mansions which encircle the site, many with ancient coats-of-arms above crumbling doorways. Other brooding relics survive in the same area: a seventeenth-century Ursuline convent and the Roman Catholic Cathedral, restored in questionable taste in the 1950s, though still displaying a thirteenth-century crest inside. Nearby is one of Ottoman Greece's first schools, the French School; opened in 1627 for Catholic and Orthodox students alike, its pupils included, briefly, Nikos Kazantzakis. The school building now houses an excellent **Archeological Museum** (Tues–Sun 8.30am–3pm; 500dr) with finds from Náxos, Koufoníssi, Keros and Dhonoússa, including an important collection of Early Cycladic figurines. Archaic and Classical sculpture, and pottery dating from Neolithic through to Roman times are also on display. On the roof terrace a Hellenistic mosaic floor shows a nereid surrounded by deer and peacocks.

As well as archeological treasures, Náxos has some very good sandal-makers: try the Markos store on Papavassilíou. The island is also renowned for its wines and liqueurs; a shop on the quay sells the *Prombonas* white and vintage red, plus *kitron*, a lemon firewater in three strengths (there's also a banana-flavoured variant).

Arrival, information and transport

Large **ferries** dock along the northerly harbour causeway; all small boats and the very useful Skopelitis ferry use the jetty in the fishing harbour, not the main car-ferry dock. The **bus station** is at its landward end: buses run five times a day to Apóllon (1000dr), and one of the morning services to Apóllon takes the newly paved coastal road via Engares and Ábrami, and is much quicker though not any cheaper. There are six buses a day to Apiranthos via Filoti, two of these going on to Moutsoúna on the east coast. Buses run (every 30min; 8am–midnight) to Áyios Prokopios, Ayía Ánna and as far as the Maragas campsite on Pláka beach, and four times a day to Pirgáki. Printed timetables are available from the bus station.

Accommodation

Rooms can be hard to come by and somewhat overpriced in the old quarter of Khóra, and single rooms are non-existent. If you come up with nothing after an hour of hunting, the southern extension of town offers better value, although there's significant night-time noise from the clubs and discos. *Litsa's Rooms* (☎0285/24 272; ⑤) comprise good new rooms and studios just to the south of the kástro, or try *Iliada Studios* (☎0285/23 303 or 24 277; ⑤) on the cliffs beyond Grotta Beach, with good views over the town and out to sea. *Panos Studios* (☎0285/26 078 or 22 087; ⑤) are reasonable, and are located near Áyios Yioryios beach.

Hotel choices include the *Panorama* on Afitrítis (☎0285/24 404; ④), the nearby *Anixis* (☎0285/22 112; ④), or, as a last resort, the *Dionyssos* (☎0285/22 331; ②) near the kástro, which also has dorm beds for 1500dr. Around the back of the kástro, is the friendly *Kastell* (☎0285/23 082; ④), and other options include: *Hotel Pantheon* (☎0285/24 335; ④), with a few rooms in a traditionally furnished house on Apollonos, going up to the kástro, *Hotel Anna* (☎0285/22 475; ④), a good family run hotel in the Grotta area north of the kástro which stays open through the winter; and *Hotel Galaxy* (☎0285/22 422; ⑥), an upmarket beach hotel with a pool, behind Áyios Yioryios beach.

Eating, drinking and nightlife

One of the best quayside breakfast bars is the *Bikini* creperie. Further along to the south are a string of relatively expensive but simple oven-food **tavernas** – *Iy Kali Kardhia* is typical, serving acceptable casserole dishes washed down with barrelled wine. Much better for the money are *Papagalos* in the new southern district, almost all the way to Áyios Yeóryios bay, and the good but pricey fish taverna *Karnayio* on the front. A hidden gem is *To Roupel*, a good old kafenío in the backstreets between the front and the kástro. *Cafe En Plo* and *Musique Café* are two reasonable places in the middle of the quay, both popular with locals; *Cafe Picasso*, near Papagalos, serves Mexican food, and is only open in the evenings. The *Elli Cafe Bar Restaurant* behind Grotta Beach is a little more expensive but serves really imaginative food, and *Portokali Club* on the headland to the south of town is a club, café and restaurant with good views over Áyios Yeóryios bay.

Much of the evening action goes on at the south end of the waterfront, and slightly inland in the new quarter. **Nightlife** tends more towards drinking places, though there is the lively *Ocean Club*, subsisting on pop-chart fodder, *Ole Club* towards the middle of the quay for dance music, and *Lakrindi Jazz Bar*, a tiny place on Apóllonos. There's also an open-air cinema, the Ciné Astra, on the road to the airport at the southern end of town. It's a fair walk out but the Ayía Anna bus stops here.

The southwestern beaches

The **beaches** around Náxos Town are worth sampling. For some unusual swimming just to the **north** of the port, beyond the causeway, **Grotta** is easiest to reach. Besides the caves for which the place is named, the remains of submerged Cycladic buildings are visible, including some stones said to be the entrance to a tunnel leading to the unfinished Temple of Apollo. The finest spots, though, are all **south** of town, the entire southwestern coastline boasting a series of excellent **beaches** accessible by regular bus. **ÁYIOS YEÓRYIOS**, a long sandy bay fringed by the southern extension of the hotel "colony", is within walking distance. There's a line of cafés and tavernas at the northern end of the beach, and a windsurfing school, plus the first of four **campsites**, whose touts you will no doubt have become acquainted with at the ferry jetty. This first campsite (*Camping Naxos* ☎0285/23 500) isn't recommended; *Maragas* and *Plaka* (see p.484) have far more attractive locations on Pláka beach. A word of warning for campers: although this entire coast is relatively sheltered from the *meltémi*, the plains behind are boggy and you should bring along mosquito repellent.

Buses take you to **ÁYIOS PROKÓPIOS** beach, with reasonably priced hotels, rooms and basic tavernas, plus the relaxed *Apollon* campsite nearby. Or follow the busy road a little further to **AYÍA ÁNNA** (habitually referred to as "Ayi'Ánna"), a small resort where there are plenty of **rooms** and tavernas. *Bar Bagianni* on the road from

Áyia Ánna to Áyios Prokópios is a colourful and popular bar which serves vegetarian food, the sea-view *Hotel Ayia Anna* (☎0285/23 870; ④) and adjacent *Gorgona* taverna are highly recommended. Away from the built-up area, the beach here is nudist, and the busy *Maragas* **campsite** (☎0285/24 552) thrives; it also has double rooms (②).

Beyond the headland stretch the five kilometres of **PLÁKA** beach, a vegetation-fringed expanse of white sand becoming built up with tavernas and rooms. Pláka **campsite** (☎0285/42 700), 700 metres down the beach is a good new site: small and quiet and away from the busier built up end of the beach. The *Hotel Orkos Village* (☎0285/75 321; ⑤) comprises apartments in an attractive location, on a hillside above the coast between Pláka beach and Mikrí Vígla.

For real isolation, go to the other side of Mikrí Vígla headland, along a narrow footpath across the cliff edge, to **KASTRÁKI** beach; towards the middle of the beach *Areti* (☎0285/75 292; ④) has apartments and a restaurant. A few people camp around the taverna on the small headland a little further down. In summer this stretch, all the way from Mikrí Vígla down to Pirgáki, attracts camper vans and windsurfers from all over Europe. On the Aliko promontory to the south of Kastráki there is a small nudist beach.

From Kastráki, it's couple of hours' walk up to the castle of **Apalírou** which held out for two months against the besieging Marco Sanudo. The fortifications are relatively intact and the views magnificent. **PYRGÁKI** beach has a couple of tavernas and a few rooms; four kilometres further on is **Ayiássos** beach.

The rest of the **southern coast** – indeed, virtually the whole of the southeast of the island – is remote and mountain-studded; you'd have to be a dedicated and well-equipped camper/hiker to get much out of the region.

Central Náxos and the Tragéa

Although buses for Apóllon (in the north) link up the central Naxian villages, the core of the island – between Náxos town and Apíranthos – is best explored by moped or on foot. Much of the region is well off the beaten track, and can be a rewarding excursion if you've had your fill of beaches; Christian Ucke's *Walking Tours on Naxos*, available from bookshops in Náxos town, is a useful guide for hikers.

Out of Khóra, you quickly arrive at the neighbouring villages of **GLINÁDHO** and **GALANÁDHO**, forking respectively right and left. Both are scruffy market centres: Glinádho is built on a rocky outcrop above the Livádhi plain, while Galánadho displays the first of Náxos' fortified mansions and an unusual "double church". A combined Orthodox chapel and Catholic sanctuary separated by a double arch, the church reflects the tolerance both of the Venetians during their rule and of the locals to established Catholics afterwards. Continue beyond Glinádho to **TRÍPODHES** (ancient Biblos), 9km from Náxos Town. Noted by Homer for its wines, this old-fashioned agricultural village has nothing much to do except enjoy a coffee at the shaded kafenío. The start of a long but rewarding walk is a rough road (past the parish church) which leads down the colourful Pláka valley, past an old watchtower and the Byzantine church of Áyios Mathéos (mosaic pavement), and ends at the glorious Pláka beach (see above).

To the east, the twin villages of **SANGRÍ**, on a vast plateau at the head of a long valley can be reached by continuing to follow the left-hand fork past Galanádho, a route which allows a look at the domed eighth-century church of **Áyios Mámas** (on the left), once the Byzantine cathedral of the island but neglected during the Venetian period and now a sorry sight. Either way, **Káto Sangrí** boasts the remains of a Venetian castle, while **Áno Sangrí** is a comely little place, all cobbled streets and fragrant courtyards. Thirty minutes' stroll away, on a path leading south out of the village, are the partially reconstructed remains of a Classical temple of Demeter.

The Tragéa

From Sangrí the road twists northeast into the **Tragéa** region, scattered with olive trees and occupying a vast highland valley. It's a good jumping-off point for all sorts of exploratory rambling, and **KHALKÍ** is a fine introduction to what is to come. Set high up, 16km from the port, it's a noble and silent town with some lovely churches. The **Panayía Protóthronis** church, with its eleventh- to thirteenth-century frescoes, and the romantic **Grazia (Frangopoulos) Pýrgos**, are open to visitors, but only in the morning. Tourists wanting to stay here are still something of a rarity, although you can usually get a room in someone's house by asking at the store. The olive and citrus plantations surrounding Halkí are criss-crossed by paths and tracks, the groves dotted with numerous Byzantine chapels and the ruins of fortified *pírgi* or Venetian mansions. Between Khalkí and Akadhimí, but closer to the latter, sits the peculiar twelfth-century "piggyback" church of **Áyii Apóstoli**, with a tiny chapel (where the ennobled donors worshipped in private) perched above the narthex; there are brilliant thirteenth-century frescoes as well.

The road from Khalkí heads north to **MONÍ**. Just before the village, you pass the sixth-century monastery of **Panayía Dhrossianí**, a group of stark grey stone buildings with some excellent frescoes; the monks allow visits at any time, though you may have to contend with coach tours from Náxos Town. Moní itself enjoys an outstanding view of the Tragéa and surrounding mountains, and has three tavernas, and some rooms. A dirt road leads on to Kinídharos with the old marble quarry above the village; a few kilometres beyond a signpost points you down a rough track to the left, to **FLÉRIO** (commonly called Melanés). The most interesting of the ancient marble quarries on Náxos, this is home to two famous **koúri**, dating from the sixth century BC, that were left recumbent and unfinished because of flaws in the material. Even so, they're finely detailed figures, over five metres in length: one of the statues lies in a private, irrigated orchard; the other is up a hillside some distance above, and you will need to seek local guidance to find it.

From Flério you could retrace your steps to the road and head back to the Khóra via Míli and the ruined Venetian castle at Kouronohóri, both pretty hamlets connected by footpaths. If you're feeling more adventurous, ask to be directed south to the footpath which leads over the hill to the Potamiá villages. The first of these, **ÁNO POTAMIÁ**, has a fine taverna and a rocky track back towards the Tragéa. Once past the valley the landscape becomes craggy and barren, the forbidding Venetian fortress of **Apáno Kástro** perched on a peak just south of the path. This is believed to have been Sanudo's summer home, but the fortified site goes back further if the Mycenean tombs found nearby are any indication. From the fort, paths lead back to Khalkí in around an hour. Alternatively you can continue further southwest down the Potamiá valley towards Khóra, passing first the ruined **Cocco Pýrgos** – said to be haunted by one Constantine Cocco, the victim of a seventeenth-century clan feud – on the way to **MÉSO POTA-MIÁ**, joined by some isolated dwellings with its twin village **KÁTO POTAMIÁ**, nestling almost invisibly among the greenery flanking the creek.

At the far end of the gorgeous Tragéa valley, **FILÓTI**, the largest village in the region, lies on the slopes of Mount Zas (or Zeus) which, at 1000m, is the highest point in the Cyclades. To get an idea of the old village, climb the steps up the hill from the platía, near to which the *Babulas Grill-Restaurant* (☎0285/31 426; ②) has rooms. A turning at the southern end of the village is signposted to the Pýrgos Himárou, a remote 20m Hellenistic watchtower, and Kalándou beach on the south coast; beyond the turning the road is unpaved. There are no villages in this part of the island so bring supplies if you're planning to camp. From the village, it's a round-trip walk of two to three hours to the summit of Zas, a climb which rewards you with an astounding panorama of virtually the whole of Náxos and its Cycladic neighbours. From the main Filóti–Apóllon road, take the side road towards Dhánakos until you reach a small chapel on the right, just beside the start of the waymarked final approach trail.

APÍRANTHOS, a hilly, winding 10km beyond, shows the most Cretan influence of all the interior villages. There are four small **museums** and two Venetian fortified mansions, while the square contains a miniature church with a three-tiered belltower. Ask to be pointed to the start of the spectacular path up over the ridge behind; this ends either in Moní or Kalóxilos, depending on whether you fork right or left respectively at the top. Cafés and tavernas on the main street look out over a terraced valley below. Rooms are available but are not advertised – ask in the cafés or in the embroidery shop. Apíranthos is good quiet place to stay for a few days, and being high in the mountains is noticeably cooler and greener than the coast.

Apíranthos has a beach annexe of sorts at **Moutsoúna**, 12km east. Emery mined near Apíranthos used to be transported here, by means of an aerial funicular, and then shipped out of the port. The industry collapsed and the sandy cove beyond the dock now features a growing colony of holiday villas. An unpaved road heads south along the coast to a remote sandy beach at Psilí Ámmos – ideal for self-sufficient campers, but you must take enough water. From here a track carries on to Panórmos beach in the southeastern corner of the island.

Northern Náxos

The route through the mountains from Apíranthos to Apóllon is very scenic, and the roads are in good condition all the way. Jagged ranges and hairpin bends confront you before reaching Kóronos, the halfway point, where a road off to the right threads through a wooded valley to **Liónas**, a tiny and very Greek port with a pebble beach. You'd do better to continue, though, past Skadhó to the remote, emery-miners' village of **KOMIAKÍ** which is a pleasing, vine-covered settlement – the highest village in the island and the original home of *kitron* liqueur.

Back on the main road, a series of slightly less hairy bends lead down a long valley to **APÓLLON** (Apóllonas), a small resort with two beaches: a tiny and crowded stretch of sand backed by cafés and restaurants, and a longer and quieter stretch of shingle, popular mainly with Greek families. If you are staying, try the friendly *Hotel Eolos* (☎0285/67 088; ③) overlooking the larger beach, or the *Hotel Adonis* (☎0285/67 060; ④) opposite. The only major attraction is a **koúros**, approached by a path from the main road just above the village. Lying in situ at a former marble quarry, this largest of Náxos's abandoned stone figures is just over ten metres long, but, compared with those at Flério, disappointingly lacking in detail. Here since 600 BC, it serves as a singular reminder of the Naxians' traditional skill; the famous Delian lions (see p.469) are also made of Apollonian marble. Not surprisingly, bus tours descend upon the village during the day, and Apóllon is now quite a popular little resort. The local festival, celebrated on August 29, is one of Náxos's best.

From Náxos town there is now a daily bus service direct to Apóllon (taking about an hour). It's easy to make a round trip by bus of the north coast and inland villages in either direction. The coastal road is spectacularly beautiful, going high above the sea for most of the way – it's more like parts of Crete or the mainland than other islands. Ten kilometres past the northern cape sprouts the beautiful **Ayía** *pirgos*, or tower, another foundation (in 1717) of the Cocco family. There's a tiny hamlet nearby, and, 7km further along, a track leads off to **Ábrami** beach, an idyllic spot with a family-run taverna and **rooms** to let, *Pension and Restaurant Efthimios* (☎0285/63 244; ③). Just beyond the hamlet of Khília Vrýssi is the abandoned **monastery of Faneroménis**, built in 1606. Nearby, there's another deserted beach, **Amíti**, and then the track leads inland, up the Engarés valley, to Engarés and Galíni, only 6km from Khóra. On the final stretch back to the port you pass a unique eighteenth-century Turkish fountain-house and the fortified monastery of **Ayíou Ioánnou Khryssostómou**, where a couple of aged nuns are still in residence. A footpath from the monastery and the road below lead straight back to town.

Koufoníssi, Skhinoússa, Iráklia and Dhonoússa

In the patch of the Aegean between Náxos and Amorgós there is a chain of six small islands neglected by tourists and by the majority of Greeks, few of whom have heard of them. **Kéros** – ancient Karos – is an important archeological site but has no permanent population, and **Káto Koufoníssi** is inhabited only by goatherds. However, the other four islands – **Áno Koufoníssi**, **Skhinoússa**, **Iráklia** and **Dhonoússa** – are all inhabited, served by ferry, and can be visited. Now just beginning to be discovered by Greeks and foreigners alike, the islets' increasing popularity has hastened the development of better facilities, but they're still a welcome break from the mass tourism of the rest of the Cyclades, especially during high season. If you want real peace and quiet – what the Greeks call *isykhia* – get there soon.

A few times weekly in summer a Pireás-based **ferry** – usually the *Apollon Express* or the tardy *Ergina* – calls at each of the islands, linking them with Náxos and Amorgós and (usually) Páros, Sýros, Sérifos and Sífnos. A kaïki, the *Skopelitis*, is a reliable daily fixture, leaving Náxos in mid-afternoon for relatively civilized arrival times at all the islets. Ilio Lines' hydrofoil calls on demand at all the islands (except Dhonoússa) on its twice-weekly foray to Amorgós; you must let the steward, if you're on the hydrofoil, or agent, if you're on the island, know if you want to be picked up or put down.

Koufoníssi and Kéros

Ano Koufoníssi is the most populous island of the group; there is a reasonable living to be made from fishing and, with some of the best beaches in the Cyclades, it is attracting increasing numbers of Greek and foreign holidaymakers. Small enough to walk round in a morning, the island can feel overcrowded in July and August.

The old single-street village of **KHÓRA**, on a low hill behind the harbour, is being engulfed by new room and hotel development, but still has a friendly, small-island atmosphere. A map by the jetty shows where to find all the island's **rooms**: *To Limani* (☎0285/71 851 or 71 450; ④) is a café with new rooms near the harbour; the popular restaurant and pension *Iy Melissa* (☎0285/71 454; ④) is on the main street; the new and upmarket *Hotel Aigaion* (☎0285/74 050 or 74 051; ⑤) is by the village beach; *To Akroyiali* (☎0285/71 685; ④) is on the front just beyond the beach; Yiorgia Kouveou has rooms at *Hondros Kavos* (☎0285/71 707; ④), to the east of the village; and the *Petros Club* (☎0285/71 728; ⑤) is in a quiet position inland, with excellent views.

Koufoníssi is noted for its fish **tavernas**; the *Karnayio* ouzerí on the bay to the west of the harbour is cheaper than most and has a fine array of seafood. The nearby *To Steki Tis Marias* is a good breakfast place and café with views over the narrow channel to Káto Koufoníssi. The most popular nightspot is *Soroccos*, an expensive café/bar on the front, while good alternatives include *Ta Kalamia*, with a quieter choice of music, and *Scholeio*, a creperie and bar. The OTE office and ticket agency are on the main street, and money can be changed at the post office (limited hours).

All the good beaches are in the southeast of the island, starting at **Fínikas**, a ten-minute walk from the village, where there are rooms, a self-service restaurant and a **campsite** (☎0285/71 683) with rather poor facilities. Fínikas is the first of a series of small bays and coves of gently shelving golden sand, some with low cliffs hollowed out into sea-caves. Further east, a path round a rocky headland leads to **Porí**, a much longer and wilder beach, backed by dunes and set in a deep bay. It can be reached more easily from the village by following a track heading inland through the low scrub-covered hills.

KÁTO KOUFONÍSSI, the uninhabited island to the southwest, has a seasonal taverna and some more secluded beaches; a kaïkia shuttles people across until late in the

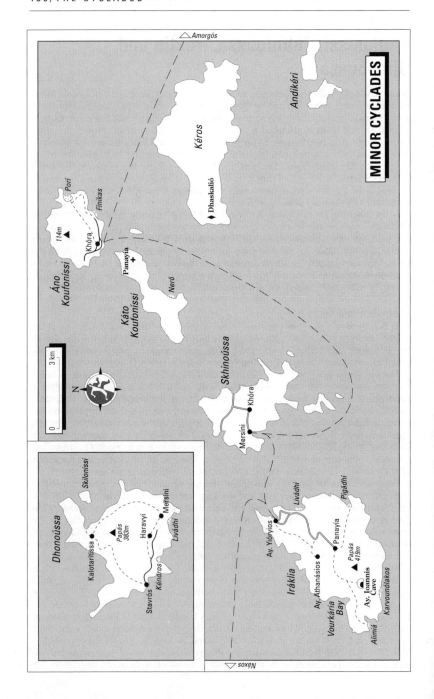

MINOR CYCLADES

evening. A festival is held here on August 15, at the church of the Panayía. The island of **Kéros** is harder to reach, but if there is a willing group of people keen to visit the ancient site, a boat and boatmen can be hired for around 15,000dr for the day.

Skhinoússa

A little to the west, the island of **Skhinoússa** is just beginning to awaken to its tourist potential, largely due to the energetic efforts being made in that direction by one Yiorgos Grispos.

Boats dock at the small port of Mirsíni, which has one pension (☎0285/71 157; ④) and a couple of cafés; a road leads up to **KHÓRA**, the walk taking just over ten minutes. As you enter the village, the well-stocked shop of the Grispos family is one of the first buildings on the left and the aforementioned Yiorgos is a mine of information. Indeed, he is personally responsible for the island's map and postcards, as well as being the boat/hydrofoil agent, having the OTE phone and selling the Greek and foreign press.

Accommodation is mostly in fairly simple rooms, such as *Pension Meltemi* (☎0285/71 195; ⑤), *Anesis* (☎0285/71180; ③), *Drossos* and *Nomikos* (no phone; both ④). The main concentration of **restaurants**, cafés and bars is along the main thoroughfare, including a lively ouzerí and, further along on the left, the pleasant *Schoinoussa* restaurant – another Grispos family venture.

There are no less than sixteen beaches dotted around the island and accessible by a lacework of trails. Freelance campers congregate on **Tsigoúri beach**, a little over five minutes from Khóra; the only other beach with any refreshments is **Almiros**, which has a simple canteen.

Iráklia

The westernmost of the minor Cyclades, **Iráklia** (pronounced Irakliá by locals) is a real gem, with an atmosphere reminiscent of the Greece of fifteen years ago, despite increasing visitor numbers.

Ferries and hydrofoils call at **ÁYIOS YEÓRYIOS**, a small but sprawling settlement behind a sandy tamarisk-backed beach. Irini Koveou (☎0285/71 448; ③) has a café-restaurant and rooms opposite the harbour, and more rooms and places to eat can be found along the old road to Livádhi beach. *Anna's Place* (☎0285/71 145; ④) provides the most upmarket accommodation, as well as a tourist shop with maps showing the route to a fine **cave** (see p.490) on the far side of the island. Theofanis Gavalas (☎0285/71 565; ②), Dhimítrios Stefanídhis (☎0285/71 484; ③), Alexandra Tournaki (☎0285/71 482; ③) and Angelos Koveos (☎0285/71 486; ④) all have rooms nearby. *O Pefkos* is a pleasant **taverna**, with tables shaded by a large pine tree, while the café/shop *Melissa* acts as the main ticket agency for ferries.

Livádhi, the best beach on the island, is a 15-minute walk past a taverna, whose friendly and animated proprietor usually meets ferries at the dock. The beach really is lovely, both deep and wide, with plenty of large bushes, a few trees for shade, and a crystal-clear sea. The village of Livádhi, deserted since 1940, stands on the hillside above, its houses ruined and overgrown; among the remains are Hellenistic walls incorporated into a later building, and fortifications from the time of Marco Sanudo. Marietta Markoyianni (☎0285/71 252; ②) has the only rooms on the beach; *Zografos Rooms* (☎0285/71 946; ④), above the road to Panayía, has fine views but is rather remote.

PANAYÍA or **KHÓRA**, an unspoiled one-street village at the foot of Mount Papas, is another hour's walk inland along the newly paved road. It has a bakery, two café/shops and the excellent and cheap *O Kritikos* ouzerí, but no rooms. A track to the east heads down to Pigádhi, a rocky beach with sea urchins, at the head of a narrow inlet. To the west a track from the near deserted hamlet of **Áyios Athanásios** leads back to the port.

The **cave of Áyios Ioánnis** lies behind the mountain, at the head of a valley leading to Vourkaria bay. From Panayía, follow a signposted track west before zigzagging
up to a saddle well to the north of the summit, with views over Skhinoússa,
Koufoníssi, Kéros, Náxos and Amorgós; the path drops down to the south around the
back of the mountain. A painted red arrow on the left indicates the turning to the
cave, just over an hour from Panayía. A church bell hangs from a cypress tree above
the whitewashed entrance, and inside there's a shrine, and the cave opens up into a
large chamber with stalactites and stalagmites. It can be explored to a depth of 120m
and is thought to be part of a much larger cave system, yet to be opened up; a festival is held here every year on August 18.

The main trail continues beyond the cave to a small sandy beach at **Alimía** but this
can be reached more easily with the beach boat from Áyios Yeóryios. In season the boat
sails daily to either Skhinoússa, Alimiá or the nearby pebble beach of Karvounólakos.

Dhonoússa

Dhonoússa is a little out on a limb compared with the others, and ferries and hydrofoils call less frequently. Island life centres on the pleasant port settlement of
STAVRÓS, spread out behind the harbour and the village beach.

Rooms, most without signs, tend to be booked up by Greek holidaymakers in
August; try Mikhalis Prasinos (☎0285/51 578; ③) with rooms along a lane behind the
church, Dhimitris Prasinos ☎(☎0285/51 579; ③) with rooms open year-round near the
Iliovasilema restaurant or Nikos Prasinos (☎0285/51 551; ④) who has good new studios above the rocks west of the harbour. *Ta Kymata* is the most popular of the four tavernas but *Meltemi* and *Iliovasilema* are also good. Nikitas Roussos (☎0285/51 648) has
a **ticket agency** above the harbour and can change money and book rooms.

The hills around Stavrós are low and barren and scarred by bulldozed tracks, but a
little walking is repaid with dramatic scenery and a couple of fine beaches. Freelance
campers and nudists head for **Kéndros**, a long and attractive stretch of sand fifteen
minutes to the east, although shade is limited and there are no facilities. A road is being
built on the hillside above, replacing the donkey track to the farming hamlets of
Kharavyí and Mersíni; these have more hens and goats in the streets than people, and
there are no cafés, shops or rooms. **Mersíni** is an hour's walk from Stavrós and has a
welcome spring beneath a plane tree, the island's only running water. A nearby path
leads down to Livádhi, an idyllic white sand beach with tamarisks for shade. In July and
August there's a daily beach boat from the port.

KALOTARÍTISSA in the north can still only be reached on foot or by boat – a track
heading inland from Stavrós climbs a valley west of Papás, the island's highest point,
before dropping down rapidly to the tiny village with a simple **taverna** and one room to
rent (☎0285/51 562; ②). There are two small pebble beaches and a path that continues
above the coast to Mersíni. It takes four to five hours to walk round the island.

Amorgós

Amorgós, with its dramatic mountain scenery and laid-back atmosphere, is attracting
visitors in increasing numbers; most ferries and hydrofoils call at both Katápola in the
southwest and Eyiáli in the northeast. The island can get extremely crowded in mid-
summer, the numbers swollen by French paying their respects to the film location of
Luc Besson's *The Big Blue*, although few actually venture out to the wreck of the
Olympia, at the island's west end, which figured so prominently in the movie. In general it's a low-key, escapist clientele, happy to have found a relatively large, interesting
and uncommercialized island with excellent walking.

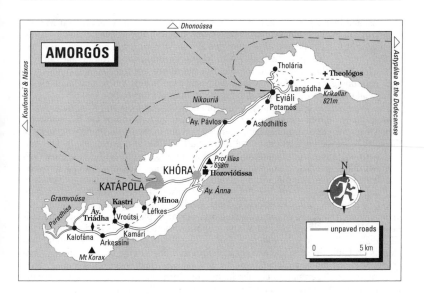

The southwest

KATÁPOLA, set at the head of a deep bay, is actually three separate hamlets: Katápola proper on the south flank, Rakhídhi on the ridge at the head of the gulf, and Xilokeratídhi along the north shore. There is a beach in front of Rahídhi, but the beach to the west of Katápola is better, though not up to the standards of Eyiáli. In season there is also a regular kaïki to nearby beaches at **Maltézi** and **Plákes** (400dr return) and a daily kaïki to the islet of **Gramboúsa** off the western end of Amorgós (2000dr return).

There are plenty of small **hotels** and **pensions** and, except in high summer when rooms are almost impossible to find, proprietors tend to meet those boats arriving around sunset – though not necessarily those that show up in the small hours. A good new place next to the beach at the western end of Katápola is *Eleni Rooms* (☎0285/71 543 or 71 628; ④). *Dhimitri's Place* in Rahídhi (③) is a compound of interconnecting buildings in an orchard, where rooms with bath and use of kitchen vary in price, depending on the season and the number of people. On the same road, *Angeliki Rooms* (☎0285/71 280; ③) is well-run, friendly and good value, as Angeliki doesn't put up her prices for August; the fancy *Hotel Minoa* (☎0285/71 480; ⑤) on the waterfront is considerably noisier. *Panayiotis Rooms* (☎0285/71 890; ④) in Xilokeratídhi is good value.

In Katápola proper, *Mourayio* is the most popular **taverna** in town; alternatively try the *Akrogiali* taverna. What **nightlife** there is focuses on a handful of cafés and pubs. A bar called *Le Grand Bleu* in Xilokeratídhi regularly shows *The Big Blue* on video but there are other less expensive and pretentious places to drink, *Ippokampos*, a café and bar on the front at Rakhídhi being a good choice.

Prekas is the one-stop **boat ticket agency**, and a new **OTE** stays open until 11pm. **Moped rental** is available at Corner Rentabike (☎0285/71 867), though the local bus service is more than adequate and walking trails delightful. The **campsite** (☎0285/71 802) is well signed between Rahídhi and Xilokeratídhi; in the latter district are three **tavernas**, of which the middle one – *Vitzentzos* – is by far the best.

Steps, and then a jeep track, lead out of Katápola to the remains of **ancient Minoa**, which are apt to disappoint up close: some Cyclopean wall four or five courses high, the foundations of an Apollo temple, a crumbled Roman structure and bushels of unsorted pottery shards. It's only the site, with views encompassing Khóra and ancient Arkessíni, that's the least bit memorable. Beyond Minoa the track soon dwindles to a trail, continuing within a few hours to Arkessíni (see below) via several hamlets – a wonderful **excursion** with the possibility of catching the bus back.

The **bus** shuttles almost hourly until 11pm between Katápola and Khóra, the island capital; several times daily the service continues to Ayía Ánna via Hozoviotíssas monastery, and once a day (9.45am) there's a run out to the "Káto Meriá", made up of the hamlets of Kamári, Arkessíni and Kolofána. **KHÓRA**, also accessible by an hour-long path beginning from behind the Rakhídhi campsite, is one of the best preserved khóras in the Cyclades, with a scattering of tourist shops, cafés, tavernas and rooms. Dominated by a rock plug wrapped with a chapel or two, the thirteenth-century Venetian fortifications look down on countless other bulbous churches – including Greece's smallest, **Áyios Fanoúrios**, which holds just three worshippers – and a line of decapitated windmills beyond. Of the half-dozen or so **places to stay**, the fanciest is *Pension Hora* (☎0285/71 110; ④), whose minibus sometimes meets ferries, outside the village above the road from Katápola. *Liotrivi* restaurant, down the steps from the bus stop, is probably the best place to **eat** in town. In addition to the pair of traditional tavernas, *Kastanis* and *Klimataria*, there are several noisy bistro-café-pubs, with *To Steki* in the upper plaza perennially popular in the late afternoon. On the same square are the island's main **post office** and a **bank**; further up the hill is the main OTE office, with somewhat limited opening hours.

From the top of Khóra, next to the helipad, a wide cobbled *kalderími* drops down to two major attractions, effectively short-cutting the road and taking little longer than the bus to reach them. Bearing left at an inconspicuous fork after ten minutes, you'll come to the spectacular **monastery of Khozoviótissas** (daily 8am–1pm & 5–7pm; donation), which appears suddenly as you round a bend, its vast wall gleaming white at the base of a towering orange cliff. Only four monks occupy the fifty rooms now, but they are quite welcoming, considering the number of visitors who file through; you can see the eleventh-century icon around which the monastery was founded, along with a stack of other treasures. The foundation legend is typical for such institutions in outlandish places: during the Iconoclastic period a precious icon of the Virgin was committed to the sea by beleaguered monks at Khózova, somewhere in the Middle East, and it washed up safely at the base of the palisade here. The view from the katholikón's terrace, though, overshadows all for most visitors, and to round off the experience, visitors are ushered into a comfy reception room and treated to a sugary lump of *loukoúmi*, a fiery shot of *kitró* and a cool glass of water.

The right-hand trail leads down, within forty minutes, to the pebble **beaches** at **Ayía Ánna**. Skip the first batch of tiny coves in favour of the path to the westernmost bay, where naturists cavort, almost in scandalous sight of the monastery far above. As yet there are no tavernas here, nor a spring, so bring food and water for the day.

For alternatives to Ayía Ánna, take the morning bus out toward modern Arkessíni, alighting at Kamári hamlet (where there's a single taverna) for the twenty-minute path down to the adjacent beaches of **Notiná**, **Moúros** and **Poulopódhi**. Like most of Amorgós' south-facing beaches, they're clean, with calm water, and here, too, a fresh-water spring dribbles most of the year. The road is paved as far as Kolofana, where there is one place with rooms. From here unpaved roads lead to the western tip of the island, and remote beaches at Káto Kámbos and at Paradhísa, facing the islet of Gramuoussa.

Archeology buffs will want to head north from Kamári to Vroútsi, start of the overgrown hour-long route to **ancient Arkessini**, a collection of tombs, six-metre-high walls and houses out on the cape of Kastrí. The main path from Minoa also passes through Vroútsi, ending next to the well-preserved Hellenistic fort known locally as the "Pýrgos", just outside modern **ARKESSÍNI**. The village boasts a single taverna with rooms, and, more importantly, an afternoon bus back to Khóra and Katápola.

The northeast

The energetically inclined can walk the four to five hours from Khóra to Eyiáli. On the Khóra side you can start by continuing on the faint trail just beyond Khozoviótissas, but the islanders themselves, in the days before the road existed, preferred the more scenic and sheltered valley route through Terláki and Rikhtí. The two alternatives, and the modern jeep road, more or less meet an hour out of Khóra. Along most of the way, you're treated to amazing views of **Nikouriá islet**, nearly joined to the main island, and in former times a leper colony. The only habitations en route are the summer hamlet of **Asfodilídhi**, with well water but little else for the traveller, and **Potamós**, a double village you encounter on the stroll down towards Eyiáli bay.

EYIÁLI (Órmos), smaller than Katápola, is a delightful beachside place stuck in a 1970s time-warp. **Accommodation** includes *Hotel Pelagos* (☎0285/73 206; ④), a largish new hotel a short walk up from the harbour (near Akrogiali), *Nikitas* (☎0285/73 237; ④) and *Akrogiali* (☎0285/73 249; ④), both above the harbour, and *Lakki* (☎0285/73 244; ②), which has a fine setting along the beach but a rather fierce management style. Overlooking the bay on the road up to Tholária is a luxury hotel with a swimming pool, the *Aegialis* (☎0285/73 107 or 73 393; ⑥). Behind the *Lakki* there is a very friendly official **campsite**, *Amorgos Camping* (☎0285/ 73 500). For **eating out**, try *To Limani* (aka *Katerina's*) on the single inland lane, packed until midnight by virtue of its excellent food and barrel wine. Other good options are the *Amorgialos* kafenío, right by the harbour which serves up octopus, and *Delear*, a smart beach bar with live music some evenings, and rather pricey drinks. A few seasonal music **bars**, such as *Selini*, attempt to compete with *Katerina's*.

The main Eyiáli **beach** is more than serviceable, getting less weedy and reefy as you stroll further north, the sand interrupted by the remains of a Roman building jutting into the sea. A trail here leads over various headlands to an array of clothing-optional bays: the first sandy, the second mixed sand and gravel, the last shingle. There are no facilities anywhere so bring along what you need.

Eyiáli has its own **bus service** up to each of the two villages visible above and east, with eight departures daily up and down (a timetable is posted by the harbour bus stop in town), but it would be a shame to miss out on the beautiful **loop walk** linking them with the port. A path starting at the far end of the beach heads inland and crosses the road before climbing steeply to **THOLÁRIA**, named after vaulted Roman tombs found around Vígla, the site of ancient Eyiáli. Vigla is on a hill opposite the village but there is little to see beyond the bases of statues and traces of city walls incorporated into later terracing. Another path winds down behind the hill to a tiny pebble beach at Míkrí Vlihádha far below. A handful of **taverna-cafés**, including a handsome wooden-floored establishment near the church, are more contemporary concerns, and there are now several places to stay, including some fairly fancy **rooms** (reserve through *Pension Lakki* in Eyiáli), the large and upmarket *Vigla* (☎0285/73 288; ⑤), and the *Thalassino Oneiro* (☎0285/73 345; ④), which has a fine restaurant and an extremely friendly owner. **LANGÁDHA** is another hour's walk along a path starting below Tholaria; to the left of the trail is the chapel of Astratios with an altar supported by the capital of a Corinthian column. Past here there are views down to the inlet of Megáli Vlihádha and, on a clear day, across to Ikaria to the north. The path descends through the village of Stroumbos, abandoned apart from three or four houses restored as holiday homes, and into a small gorge before climbing the steps up to Langádha. The place is home to a sizeable colony of expatriates – something reflected in the German-Greek cooking at *Nikos'* **taverna** at the lower end of the village, which also has some **rooms** (☎0285/73 310; ④), as does *Yiannis'* taverna.

Beyond Langádha, another rocky path leads around the base of the island's highest peak, the 821-metre-high **Kríkellos**, passing on the way the fascinating church of **Theológos**, with lower walls and ground plan dating to the fifth century. Somewhat easier to reach, by a slight detour off the main Tholária–Langádha trail, are the church and festival grounds of **Panayía Panokhorianí** – not so architecturally distinguished but a fine spot nonetheless.

Íos

No other island is quite like **Íos**, nor attracts the same vast crowds of young people, although attempts are being made to move the island's tourism upmarket; the island now enforces Greece's early closing laws (3am except Fri & Sat) and bars no longer stay open all night. The only real villages – **Yialós**, **Khóra** and **Mylopótamos** – are in one small corner of the island, and until recently development elsewhere was restricted by poor roads. As a result there are still some very quiet beaches with a few rooms to rent. Yialós has one of the best and safest natural harbours in the Cyclades and there is talk of building a new yacht marina.

Most visitors stay along the arc delineated by the port – at Yialós, where you'll arrive (there's no airport), in Khóra above it, or at the beach at Mylopótamos; it's a small area, and you soon get to know your way around. **Buses** constantly shuttle between Koumbára, Yialós, Khóra and Mylopótamos, with a daily service running roughly from 8am to midnight; you should never have to wait more than fifteen minutes, but at least

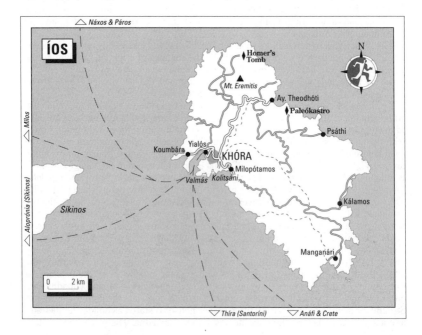

once try the short walk up (or down) the stepped path between Yialós and Khóra. Various travel offices run their own buses to the beaches at Manganári and Ayia Theodhóti; they sell return tickets only, and are a bit expensive. To rent your own transport, try Jacob's Car and Bike Rental (☎0286/91 047) in Yialós, and Vangelis Bike Rental (☎0286/91 919) in Khóra.

Despite its past popularity, **sleeping on the beach** on Íos is really worth avoiding these days. Crime and police raids are becoming more frequent as the island strains under the sheer impact of increasing youth tourism, and the police have been known to turn very nasty. They prefer you to sleep in the official campsites and, given the problem of theft, you should probably take their advice.

Yialós and Khóra

From **YIALÓS** quayside, **buses** turn around just to the left, while Yialós **beach** – surprisingly peaceful and uncrowded – is another five minutes' walk in the same direction. You might be tempted to grab a room in Yiálos as you arrive: owners meet the ferries, hustling the town's **accommodation**, and there are also a couple of kiosks by the jetty that will book rooms for you. At the far end of the beach is a plush option: *Ios Beach Bungalows* (☎0286/91 267; ⑤); *Galini Rooms* (☎0286/91 115; ④) down a lane behind the beach is a good quiet choice, if a little out of the way. There are more rooms on the stepped path from Yialós to Khóra although they can be noisy at night: the *Hotel-Bar Helios* (☎0286/91 500; ③) has a few simple, older rooms, the *Princess Sissy Hotel* (☎0286/91 244; ④) further up the steps towards Khóra is also reasonable, and *Ios Camping* (☎0286/91 329) has new management and has been improved recently, with a new swimming pool and café. Yialós has all the other essentials – accommodation kiosks, a reasonable supermarket (to the right of the bus stop), and a few **tavernas**. The *Octopus Tree*, a small kafenío by the fishing boats, serves cheap fresh seafood caught by the owner, while on the front heading towards the beach the *Waves Restaurant* does good Indian food. A twenty-minute stroll over the headland at **KOUMBÁRA**, there's a smaller and less crowded beach, with a taverna and a rocky islet to explore. The *Polydoros* taverna in Koumbára is one of the better places to eat on Íos, and is worth the bus ride.

KHÓRA (aka Íos Town) is a twenty-minute walk up behind the port, though you've got a better chance of getting something reasonable by haggling if you intend to stay for several days. The old white village is overwhelmed by the crowds of tourists in season, but with any number of arcaded streets and whitewashed chapels, it does have a certain charm.

Khóra divides naturally into two parts. The old town climbing the hillside to the left as you arrive is separated by an open space from newer development to the right. There are plenty of basic **rooms** in the old part (although the bars can make sleep difficult): *The Hotel Filippou* (☎0286/91 290; ④) is above the National Bank and next to the cathedral; *Yánnis Stratís* (☎0286/91 494; ②) has a few very simple rooms next door; and *Markos Pension* (☎0286/91 059; ④; ask for the ten percent discount for Rough Guide readers) with a poolside bar is one of the best choices in the new part. *Iliovassilema Rooms* (☎0286/91 997; ④) just out of town down a path past the Íos Club, is quiet and has fine views over the port, and the *Four Seasons Pension* (☎0286/91 308; winter 0286/92 081; ④) up a turning by Vangelis Bike Rental is also well away from the noise of the bars and clubs. The snack bar downstairs serves – bizarrely – a full Scottish breakfast.

What Khóra is still really about, though, is **nightlife**. Every evening the streets throb to music from ranks of competing discos and clubs – mostly free, or with a nominal entrance charge, though drinks tend to be expensive. Most of the smaller **bars** and pubs are tucked into the thronging narrow streets of the old village on the hill, offering

> A note of warning: bars on Íos are more expensive than they used to be, but still cheap compared with other islands. One way to keep prices down is to replace spirits with homemade alcohol, and Greeks call the resulting drinks **bombas** for obvious reasons. Beware of free drinks and cheap cocktails; a crackdown has been attempted but bombas are still around.

something for everyone – unless you just want a quiet drink. A welcome exception to the techno-pop dancing fodder can be found at the *Taboo* bar, run by two friendly brothers and featuring underground rock, eclectic decor and a clientele to match; *Pegasus* and the *Kahlua Bar* are also recommended. The larger **dancing clubs**, including the *Anjuna Club* which plays techno and trance music, and the *Disco Scorpion* are to be found on the main road to Mylopótamos. Finally the *Ios Club*, perched right up on the hill, plays quieter music, has reasonable food and is a good place to watch the sunset.

Eating is a secondary consideration but there are plenty of cheap and cheerful psistariés and take-away joints: sound choices include *Iy Folia*, near the top of the village, and the *Lord Byron* mezedhopoleio in an alley near the cathedral – it's open year round and tries hard to recreate a traditional atmosphere, with old rembétika music and some good and unusual Greek food.

Around the island

The most popular stop on the island's bus routes is **MYLOPÓTAMOS** (universally abbreviated to Mylópotas), the site of a magnificent beach and a mini-resort. There are two **campsites**: *Far Out* (☎0286/91 468), towards the far end of the beach, is more popular but can get very noisy and crowded, and *Stars* (☎0286/91302), by the road up to Khóra, is showing its age but is a bit quieter with more shade. At the far end of the bay *The Purple Pig* (☎0286/91 301; ④), a new Australian-run **backpackers' hotel** with beds in shared rooms (3500dr) and a café and bar, is a good alternative to the campsites and one of the best choices on Íos for single travellers. Across the road *Gorgona* (☎0286/91 307; ④) and *Dracos* (☎0286/91 281 or 91 010; ④) have reasonable rooms. *Dracos* also has a good taverna on its own little quay, serving freshly caught fish. The *Far Out Hotel* (☎0286/91 446 or 91 702; ⑤) on the road down from Khóra and the pricey *Ios Palace Hotel* (☎0286/91 269; ⑥) above the near end of the beach are the best upmarket choices. The *Harmony Restaurant* on the rocks beyond the *Ios Palace* is one of the better places to eat, serving pizzas and Mexican food. The restaurants and self-service cafés behind the beach are uninspiring, and only the *Faros Café* rates a mention for staying open through the night to cater for the crowds returning from Khóra in the early hours. Mylopótamos itself has surprisingly little in the way of nightlife.

From Yialós, daily boats depart at around 10am (returning in the late afternoon) to **MANGANÁRI** on the south coast, where there's a beach and a swanky hotel; you can also get there by moped. There's an expensive speedboat (4000dr return) from Yialós to Manganári, but most people go by bus (1500dr return). These are private buses run by travel agencies, leaving Yialós about 11am, calling at Khóra and Mylopótamos and returning later in the afternoon. Predominantly nudist, Manganári is the beach to come to for serious tans, although there's more to see, and a better atmosphere at **AYÍA THEODHÓTI** up on the east coast. There's a new paved road across the island to Ayía Theodhóti – the daily excursion bus costs 1000dr return. A couple of kilometres south of Ayía Theodhóti is a ruined Venetian castle which encompasses the ruins of a marble-finished town and a Byzantine church. In the unlikely event that the beach – a good one and mainly nudist – is too crowded, try the one at **PSÁTHI**, 14km to the southeast. Frequented by wealthy Athenians, this small resort has a couple of pricey tavernas, making it better for a day-trip than an extended stay. The road is very poor and not really safe for mopeds, although there are plans to improve it. Another island beach is at **KÁLAMOS**; get off the Manganári bus at the turning for Kálamos, which leaves you with a 4km walk.

Homer's "tomb" is the only cultural diversion on the island. The story goes that, while on a voyage from Sámos to Athens, Homer's ship was forced to put in at Íos, where the poet subsequently died. The tomb can be reached by moped along a safe new unpaved road (turning left from the paved road to Ayía Theódhoti 4.5km from Khóra). The town itself has long since slipped down the side of the cliff, but the rocky ruins of the entrance to a tomb remain, as well as some graves – one of which is claimed to be Homer's, but which in reality probably dates only to the Byzantine era.

Síkinos

Síkinos has so small a population that the mule-ride or walk up from the port to the village was only replaced by a bus late in the 1980s and, until the new jetty was completed at roughly the same time, it was the last major Greek island where ferry passengers were still taken ashore in launches. With no dramatic characteristics, nor any nightlife to speak of, few foreigners make the short trip over here from neighbouring Íos and Folégandhros or from sporadically connected Páros, Náxos, or Thíra. There is no bank on the island, but there is a **post office** up in Kástro-Khóra, near the **OTE**, and you can sometimes change cash at the store in Aloprónia.

Aloprónia and Kástro-Khóra

Such tourist facilities as exist are concentrated in the little harbour of **ALOPRÓNIA**, with its long sandy beach and the recent additions of an extended breakwater and jetty. More and more formal **accommodation** is being built here, but it's still possible to

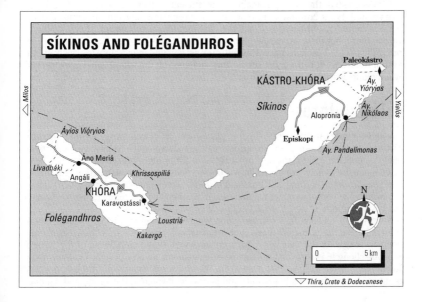

SÍKINOS AND FOLÉGANDHROS

camp or just sleep out under the tamarisks behind the beach. For rooms, try *Flora* (☎0286/51 214; ④), *Loukas* (☎0286/51 076; ③) or the friendly *Sigalas* (☎0286/51 233; ④) above the jetty; alternatively, the comfortable and traditional *Hotel Kamares* (☎0286/51 234; ④) is more affordable than the conspicuous *Porto Sikinos* luxury complex (☎0286/51 247; ⑥). *To Meltemi* **taverna** on the quay is the locals' hangout, while the fancier *Ostria* is affiliated with the *Hotel Kamares* and the *Loukas* has standard fare. The *Vrachos Rock Cafe* above the quay is where the kids hang out, while *Vengera* music bar on the opposite side of the bay is a smoother joint.

The double village of **KÁSTRO-KHÓRA** is served by the single island bus, which shuttles regularly from early morning till quite late in the evening between the harbour and here, though the route should soon be extended to Episkopí with the completion of the new road. On the ride up, the scenery turns out to be less desolate than initial impressions suggest. Draped across a ridge overlooking the sea, Kástro-Khóra makes for a charming day trip, and the lovely oil-press **museum** (July to mid-Sept 6.30–8.30pm; free), run privately by a Greek-American is definitely not to be missed. A partly ruined monastery, **Zoödhókhou Piyís** ("Spring of Life", a frequent name in the Cyclades), crowns the rock above; the architectural highlight of the place, though, is the central quadrangle of **Kástro**, a series of ornate eighteenth-century houses arrayed defensively around a chapel-square, their backs to the exterior of the village. The quality of rooms has improved, and both Markos Zagoreos (☎0286/51 263; ③) and Haroula (☎0286/51 212; ③) have competitive prices – the former has great views. A good selection of food is available, along with fine local wine, at both *Klimataria* and *Kastro*.

Around the island

West of Kástro-Khóra, an hour-plus walk (or mule ride) takes you through a landscape lush with olive trees to **Episkopí**, where elements of an ancient temple-tomb have been ingeniously incorporated into a seventh-century church – the structure is known formally as the **Iróön**. Ninety minutes from Kástro-Khóra, in the opposite direction, lies **Paleokástro**, the patchy remains of an ancient fortress. The beaches of **Áyios Yióryis** and **Áyios Nikólaos** are reachable by a regular kaïki from Aloprónia; the former is a better option because it has the daytime *Almira* restaurant. It is possible to walk to them, but there is no real path at the later stages. A more feasible journey by foot is the pebble beach at **Áyios Pandelímonas**: just under an hour's trail walk southwest of Aloprónia, it is the most scenic and sheltered on the island, and is also served by a kaïki in season.

Folégandhros

The cliffs of **Folégandhros** rise sheer in places over 300m from the sea – until the early 1980s as effective a deterrent to tourists as they always were to pirates. Used as an island of political exile right up until 1974, life in the high, barren interior has been eased since the junta years by the arrival of electricity and the construction of a lengthwise road from the harbour to Khóra and beyond. Development has been given further impetus by the recent exponential increase in tourism and the mild commercialization this has brought.

A veritable explosion in accommodation for most budgets, and slight improvement in ferry arrival times, means there is no longer much need for – or local tolerance of – sleeping rough on the beaches. The increased wealth and trendiness of the heterogeneous clientele is reflected in fancy jewellery shops, an arty postcard gallery and a newly constructed helipad. Yet away from the showcase Khóra and the beaches, the countryside remains mostly pristine, and is largely devoted to the spring and summer cultivation of barley, the mainstay of many of the Cyclades before the advent of tourism. Donkeys and donkey-paths are also still very much in evidence, since the terrain on much of the island is too steep for vehicle roads.

Karavostássi and around

KARAVOSTÁSSI, the rather unprepossessing port whose name simply means "ferry stop", serves as a last-resort base; it has several **hotels** but little atmosphere. Best value, if you do decide to stay is *Hotel Ailos* (☎0286/41 205; ④), while the *Poseidon* (☎0286/41 272; ⑤) throws in breakfast at its decent restaurant *To Kati Allo*, which means "Something Else". The *Vardia Bay* (☎0286/41 277; ⑥) above the harbour is extremely pricey, but has the excellent *Iy Kali Kardhia* below it, while the *Smyrna* ouzerí in a converted boathouse is nice for a drink. There are many buses a day in summer to Khóra, and three of those go on to Ano Meriá. Jimmy's motorbike rental (☎0286/41 448) has better prices than the one in Khóra.

The closest **beach** is the smallish, but attractive enough, sand-and-pebble **Vardhiá**, signposted just north over the headland. Some twenty minutes' walk south lies **Loustriá**, a rather average beach with tamarisk trees and the island's official **campsite** which is good and friendly, although the hot water supply can be erratic.

Easily the most scenic beach on Folégandhros, with an offshore islet and a 300m stretch of pea-gravel, is at **Katergó**, on the southeastern tip of the island. Most people visit on a boat excursion from Karavostássi or Angáli, but you can also get there on foot from the hamlet of Livádhi, a short walk inland from Loustriá. Be warned, though, that it's a rather arduous trek, with some nasty trail-less slithering in the final moments.

Khóra

The island's real character and appeal are to be found in the spectacular **KHÓRA**, perched on a cliff-top plateau some 45 minutes' walk from the dock; an hourly high-season **bus** service (6 daily spring/autumn) runs from morning until late at night. Locals and foreigners – hundreds of them in high season – mingle at the cafés and tavernas under the almond, flowering judas and pepper trees of the two main platías, passing the time unmolested by traffic, which is banned from the village centre. Toward the cliff-edge, and entered through two arcades, the defensive core of the medieval **kástro** is marked by ranks of two-storey houses, whose repetitive, almost identical stairways and slightly recessed doors are very appealing.

From the square where the bus stops, a zigzag path with views down to both coastlines climbs to the crag-top, wedding-cake church of **Kímisis Theotókou**, nocturnally illuminated to grand effect. Beyond and below it hides the **Khryssospiliá**, a large cave with stalactites, accessible only to proficient climbers; the necessary steps and railings have crumbled away into the sea, although a minor, lower grotto can still be visited.

Practicalities

Khóra's **accommodation** seems slightly weighted to favour hotels over rooms, with concentrations around the bus plaza at the east entrance to the village and at the western edge. Recommended rooms places include the purpose-built complex run by Irini Dekavalla (☎0286/41 235; ③), east of the bus stop. The nearby *Hotel Polikandia* (☎0286/41 322; ⑤) has an engaging proprietress and far lower rates than appearances suggest, especially off season. The most luxurious facilities are at the cliff-edge *Anemomilos Apartments* (☎0286/41 309; ⑥), immaculately appointed and with stunning views. The only hotel within the Khóra – the *Castro* (☎0286/41 230; ⑤) is a bit overpriced, despite recent renovation and undeniable atmosphere, with three rather dramatic rooms looking directly out on an alarming drop to the sea. At the western edge of Khóra near the police station, densely packed rooms outfits tend to block each other's views; the least claustrophobic is the long-established *Odysseas* (☎0286/41 276; ③), which also manages some attractive apartments near the *Anemomilos*. By the roadside on the way to Áno Meriá, the *Fani-Vevis* (☎0286/41 237; ④), in a Neoclassical mansion overlooking the sea, seems to function only in high season.

Khóra's dozen or so **restaurants** are surprisingly varied. The *Folegandhros* ouzerí in water-cistern plaza, is fun, if a bit eccentrically run. Breakfast can be enjoyed on the adjacent Platía Kondaríni at *Iy Melissa*, which does good fruit and yoghurt, omelettes and juices. *Iy Piatsa* has a nightly changing menu of well-executed Greek dishes, while their neighbour and local hangout *O Kritikos* is notable only for its grills. *Iy Pounda* near the bus stop is the most traditional place and has a small garden, while *Apanemo* at the far end of town has good food and a quieter setting, despite its proximity to the main bar area. Self-catering is an attractive option, with two well-stocked fruit shops and two supermarkets. Khóra is inevitably beginning to sprawl unattractively at the edges, but this at least means that the burgeoning **nightlife** – two dancing bars and a quantity of musical pubs and ouzerís – can be exiled to the north, away from most accommodation. *Methexis* plays mostly old rock, while *Greco* has more up-to-date sounds, and *Patitiri* features live rembétika. A combination **OTE/post office** (no bank) completes the list of amenities, though the single **ferry agent** also does money exchange as does the Italian-run Sottavento agency, which offers a wide range of services.

The rest of the island

Northwest of Khóra a narrow, cement road threads its way towards **ÁNO MERIÁ**, the other village of the island; after 4km you pass its first houses, clustered around the three churches of Áyios Pandelímonas, Áyios Yióryios and Áyios Andhréas. Four tavernas operate in high season only: *O Mimis* is about halfway along, and *Iy Sinandisi* is at the turning for Áyios Yeóryios beach, while *Barba Kostas* and *Iliovasilema*, at the far end of the sprawling village, complete the list. Several rooms are also available; particularly recommended are *Stella's* (☎0286/41 329; ②)

Up to six times a day in high season a **bus** trundles out here to drop people off at the footpaths down to the various sheltered beaches on the northwest shore of the island. Busiest of these is **Angáli** (aka Vathý), with five rather basic room outfits (no phones; all ②) and three equally simple summer-only tavernas, reached by a fifteen-minute walk along a dirt road from the bus stop.

Nudists are urged to take the paths which lead twenty minutes east or west to **Firá** or **Áyios Nikólaos** beaches respectively; the latter in particular, with its many tamarisks, coarse sand and view back over the island, is Katergó's only serious rival in the best-beach sweepstakes. At Áyios Nikólaos, a lone taverna operates up by the namesake chapel; Firá has no facilities at all. From the *Iliovasilema* taverna, a motorable track continues north to a point from where a 500m path takes you down to the pleasant little bay of Ambéli, which also has facilities.

Thíra (Santoríni)

As the ferry manoeuvres into the great caldera of **Thíra**, the land seems to rise up and clamp around it. Gaunt, sheer cliffs loom hundreds of feet above, nothing grows or grazes to soften the view, and the only colours are the reddish-brown, black and grey pumice striations layering the cliff face. The landscape tells of a history so dramatic and turbulent that legend hangs as fact upon it.

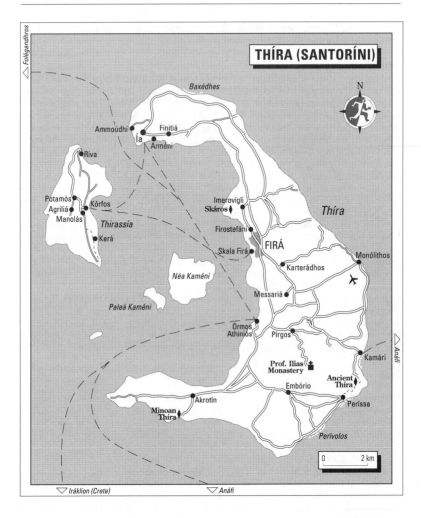

From as early as 3000 BC the island developed as a sophisticated outpost of Minoan civilization, until around 1550 BC when catastrophe struck: the volcano-island erupted, its heart sank below the sea, and earthquakes reverberated across the Aegean. Thíra was destroyed and the great Minoan civilizations on Crete were dealt a severe blow. At this point the island's history became linked with legends of Atlantis, the "Happy Isles Submerged by Sea". Plato insisted that the legend was true, and Solon dated the cataclysm to 9000 years before his time – if you're willing to accept a mistake and knock off the final zero, a highly plausible date.

These apocalyptic events, though, scarcely concern modern tourists, who are here mostly to stretch out on the island's dark-sand beaches and absorb the peculiar, infernal atmosphere: as recently as a century ago, Thíra was still reckoned to be infested with vampires. Though not nearly so predatory as the undead, current visitors have in fact succeeded in pretty much killing off any genuine island life, creating in its place a rather expensive and stagey playground.

Arrival and departure

Ferries dock at the somewhat grim port of **Órmos Athiniós**; **Skála Firás** and **Ía** in the north are reserved for local ferries, excursion kaïkia and cruise ships. **Buses**, astonishingly crammed, connect Athiniós with the island capital Firá, and, less frequently, with the main beaches at Kamári and Périssa – disembark quickly and take whatever's going, if you want to avoid a long walk. You're also likely to be accosted at Athiniós by people offering rooms all over the island; it may be a good idea to pay attention to them, given the scramble for beds in Firá especially. If you alight at Skála Firás, you have the traditional route above you – 580 mule-shit-splattered steps to Firá itself. It's not that difficult to walk, but the intrepid can also go up by mule or by cable car (summer only 6.40am–10pm, every 20min; 800dr). The **airport** is located towards the other side of the island, near Monólithos; there is a regular shuttle bus service to the Firá bus station, which runs until 10pm.

When it comes to **leaving** – especially for summer/evening ferry departures – it's best to buy your ticket in advance. Note, too, that although the bus service stops around midnight, a shared taxi isn't outrageously expensive. Incidentally, **ferry information** from any source is notoriously unreliable on Thíra, so departure details should be quadruple-checked. If you do get stranded in Athiniós waiting for a ferry connection, there's no place to stay, and the tavernas are pretty awful. With time on your hands, it's well worth zigzagging the 3500m up to the closest village, **MEGALOKHÓRI**. Between Megalokhóri and Pýrgos village, quite near the junction of the main and Athiniós road, is *Hotel Zorbas* (☎0286/31 433; ⑥), with very personable Greek and American management. At the centre of Megalokhóri, the *Yeromanolis* is a surprisingly reasonable and tasty grill which offers the increasingly rare homemade Santoríni wine.

Firá

Half-rebuilt after a devastating earthquake in 1956, **FIRÁ** (also known as Thíra or Khóra) still lurches dementedly at the cliff's edge. With a stunningly attractive setting, it appears on postcards and tourist brochures and, naturally, you pay the price for its position. Busy with day-trippers in summer at least, initial impressions of Firá are of gross commercialism, and it is perhaps best avoided in season.

However, Firá's cliff-top position does justify a visit, and you should also make time for the **Archeological Museum** (Tues–Sun 8.30am–3pm; 800dr), near the cable car to the north of town, whose collection includes a curious set of erotic Dionysiac figures. The interesting **Museum Megaro Ghyzi** (Mon–Sat 10.30am–1.30pm & 5–8pm, Sun 10.30am–4.30pm; 350dr) is in an old mansion owned by the Catholic diocese of Santoríni and restored as a cultural centre. It has a good collection of old prints and maps as well as photographs of the town before and after the 1956 earthquake.

Practicalities

Caldera-side hotels and studios in **Firá** itself are expensive but there are plenty of rooms without caldera views at the back of town. Otherwise there are three **youth hostels** in the northern part of town, cheap, often full, but not too bad if you have your own bedding and sleep on the roof; the *Kamares* hostel (☎0286/24 472) on Erythroú Stavroú is the official hostel and the cheapest, but the other two hostels are better and also have reasonably priced double rooms. The *International Youth Hostel* (☎0286/22 387; ①) is across the alleyway from *Kamares* in a large old house: both are close to the bars and clubs and can be a bit noisy at night. *Kontohori Hostel* (☎0286/22 722 or 22

577; ①) is in a quiet location on the edge of town, down a turning off 25 Martiou, the road to Firostefáni and Ía.

FIROSTEFÁNI, between Firá and Imerovígli, is the best bet for reasonably priced rooms with views over the caldera. Rooms in Firostefáni of varying prices and standards include *Apartments Gaby* (☎0286/22 057; ④), *Stathis Rooms* (☎0286/22 835; ④), *Hotel Mylos* (☎0286/23 884; ④) and *Ioannis Roussos* (☎0286/22 511 or 22 862; ③). *Villa Haroula* (☎0286/24 226; ⑤) is a good new hotel on the road down to *Santorini Camping* (☎0286/22 944) at the back of town, which stays open with heating through the winter. You might try **KARTERÁDHOS**, a small village about twenty minutes' walk south of Firá, where there are rooms and the pleasant *Hotel Albatross* (☎0286/23 435, fax 23 431; ⑤), or Messariá, another 2km further, with some more expensive hotels.

Firá's **restaurants** are primarily aimed at the tourist market, but there are a few worth trying: the *Flame of the Volcano* is the last of the caldera-side restaurants heading north past the cable car station (towards Firostefáni) and is better and more reasonably priced than most, although you are still paying extra for the view. *Nikolas* on Erythroú Stavroú is an old-established and defiantly traditional taverna but it can be hard to get a table. Otherwise try *Koutouki* and *Bella Thira*, next to each other on 25 Martiou. As for **nightlife**, the places listed below are all on Erythroú Stavroú (walking south from the Kamares Youth Hostel), along with various other clubs and bars. *Enigma*, a soul disco, occupies a converted house and garden, the *Casablanca Club*, below *Kyra Thira* which is good jazz bar, is popular for dance music.

Theoskepasti Tours (☎0286/22 256 or 22 176) on 25-Martiou, next to the OTE, is helpful and is the only tourist agency in Firá with reliable information about ferries to Thirassía. **Buses** leave Firá from the just south of Platía Theotokopoúlou to Périssa, Perívolos, Kamári, Monólithos, Akrotíri, Athiniós and the airport. **Taxis** (☎0286/22 555) go from near the bus station. If you want to see the whole island in a couple of days a rented **moped** is useful; Moto Chris at the top of the road that leads down to *Santorini Camping* is particularly recommended.

The north

Once outside Firá, the rest of Santoríni comes as a nice surprise, although development is beginning to encroach. The volcanic soil is highly fertile, with every available space terraced and cultivated: wheat, tomatoes (most made into paste), pistachios and grapes are the main crops, all still harvested and planted by hand. The island's *visándo* and *nikhtéri* wines are a little sweet for many tastes but are among the finest produced in the Cyclades.

A satisfying – if demanding – approach to Ía, 12km from Firá in the northwest of the island, is to walk the stretch from **IMEROVÍGLI**, 3km out of Firá, using a spectacular footpath along the lip of the caldera; the walk takes around two hours. Imerovígli has a taverna and one moderate hotel, the *Katerina* (☎0286/22 708; ④) and if you carry on to Ía you'll pass Toúrlos, an old Venetian citadel on Cape Skáros, on the way. *Chromata* (☎0286/23 278; ⑥) at Imerovígli are smart and extremely expensive caldera-side villas that require booking well in advance.

ÍA was once a major fishing port of the Aegean, but it has declined in the wake of economic depression, wars, earthquakes and depleted fish stocks. Partly destroyed in the 1956 earthquake, the town has been sympathetically reconstructed, its pristine white houses clinging to the cliff face. Apart from the caldera and the village itself there are a couple of things to see, including a **Naval Museum** (9am–1pm & 5–8pm, closed Tues) and the very modest remains of a Venetian castle. With a **post office**, part-time **bank** and **bike-rental** office, Ía is a good, and quieter alternative to Firá. Much of the town's **accommodation** is in its restored old houses; expensive choices include the troglodytic *Hotel Lauda* (☎0286/71 157; ④), the *Hotel Anemones* (☎0286/71 342; ④), and the *Hotel Fregata* (☎0286/71 221; ④). The *Chelidonia Villas* (☎286/71 287; ⑤) are attractive restored cliff-side houses.

Quite near the bus terminal, also reachable by the main road that continues round to the back end of the village, is an excellent new hostel – the *Oia Youth Hostel* (☎0286/71 465; ①), with a terrace and shady courtyard, a good bar, clean dormitories and breakfast included. Recommended **restaurants** include *Petros* (for fish) and *Cafe Flora*, a friendly new place with reasonable prices; generally, the further you go along the central ridge towards the new end of Ía, the better value the restaurants. **Nightlife** revolves around sunset-gazing, for which people are bussed in from all over the island, creating traffic chaos; when this pales, there's *Strofi* rock-music bar.

Below the town, 200-odd steps switchback hundreds of metres down to two small harbours: **Ammoúdhi**, for the fishermen, and **Arméni**, where the excursion boats dock. Off the cement platform at Ammoúdhi you can swim past floating pumice and snorkel among shoals of giant fish, but beware the currents around the church-islet of Áyios Nikólaos. At Arméni, a single taverna specializes in grilled-octopus lunches. **FINIKIÁ**, 1km east of Ía, is a very quiet and traditional little village with a good restaurant – the expensive but varied *Finikias*. *Lotza Rooms* (☎0286/ 71 051; ③) are located in an old house in the middle of the village, while *Villa Agnadi* (☎0286/71 647; ⑥) comprises good apartments above the village, near the main road. Just north of Ía is **Baxédhes** beach, a quiet alternative to Kamári and Périssa (see below), with a few tavernas including the *Paradhisos*, which has good food and reasonable prices.

The east and south

Beaches on Santoríni, to the east and south, are bizarre – long black stretches of volcanic sand which get blisteringly hot in the afternoon sun. They're no secret, and in the summer the crowds can be a bit overpowering. Closest to Firá, **MONÓLITHOS** has a couple of tavernas but is nothing special. Further south, **KAMÁRI** has surrendered lock, stock and barrel to the package-tour operators and there's not a piece of sand that isn't fronted by concrete villas.

Nonetheless it's quieter and cleaner than most, with some beachfront **accommodation** including *Hotel Nikolina* (☎0286/31 702; ③), with basic but cheap rooms towards the southern end of the beach, as well as the *White House* (☎0286/31 441; ④), *Poseidon Hotel* (☎0286/31 698; ④) and the recommended *Sea Side Rooms* (☎0286/33 403; ③) further along the beach. *Kamari Camping* (☎0286/31 453) is a small and quiet municipal-run site with limited facilities, a fifteen-minute walk on the road out of Kamári.

Psistaria O Kritikos, a taverna-grill frequented by locals rather than tourists, is one of the best places to **eat** on the island. It's a long way out of Kamári on the road up to Messariá, and too far to walk, but the bus stops outside. There are plenty of cafés and restaurants behind the beach, though many are expensive or uninspired. *Saliveros*, in front of the *Hotel Nikolina*, has taverna food at reasonable prices, and *Almira*, next to *Sea Side Rooms*, is a smarter restaurant and only a little more expensive. Kamári is a family resort with little in the way of clubs and nightlife, but there is a good open-air **cinema** near the campsite, and in summer buses run until 1am so there's no problem getting back to Firá after seeing a film.

Things are scruffier at **PÉRISSA**, around the cape. Despite (or perhaps because of) its attractive situation and abundance of cheap rooms, it's noisy and crowded with backpackers. *Camping Perissa Beach* (☎0286/81 343) is right behind the beach and has plenty of shade but is also next to a couple of noisy late-night bars. There are two youth hostels on the road into Périssa: *Anna* (☎0286/82 182; ②) is fairly basic but better than the unofficial hostel across the road. There are plenty of cheap rooms in the same area and some upmarket hotels behind the beach including the smart and expensive *Hotel*

Veggara (☎0286/82 060; ⑤). The beach itself extends almost 7km to the west, sheltered by the occasional tamarisk tree.

Kamári and Périssa are separated by the Mésa Vounó headland, on which stood **ancient Thíra** (Tues–Sun 9am–3pm), the post-eruption settlement dating from the ninth century BC. Excursion buses go up from Kamári (2000dr), staying two hours at the site (ask at Kamári Tours behind the beach) but you can walk the **cobbled path** starting from the square by the Argo General Store. The path zigzags up to a white-washed church by a **cave**, containing one of Thira's few freshwater springs, before crossing over to meet the road and ending at a saddle between Mésa Vounó and Profítis Ilías, where a refreshments van sells expensive drinks. From here, the path to the site passes a chapel dating back to the fourth century AD before skirting round to the Temenos of Artemidoros with bas-relief carvings of a dolphin, eagle and lion representing Poseidon, Zeus and Apollo. From here the path follows the sacred way of the ancient city through the remains of the agora and past the theatre. Most of the ruins (dating mainly from Hellenistic and Roman times) are difficult to place, but the site is impressively large and the views are awesome. The site can also be reached by a path from Périssa, and either way it's an hour's walk.

Inland along the same mountain spine is the monastery of **Profítis Ilías**, now sharing its refuge with Greek radio and TV pylons and the antennae of a NATO station. With just one monk remaining to look after the church, the place only really comes to life for the annual Profítis Ilías festival, when the whole island troops up here to celebrate. The views are still rewarding, though, and from near the entrance to the monastery an old footpath heads across the ridge in about an hour to ancient Thíra. The easiest ascent is the thirty-minute walk from the village of Pýrgos.

PÝRGOS itself is one of the oldest settlements on the island, a jumble of old houses and alleys that still bear the scars of the 1956 earthquake. It climbs to another Venetian fortress crowned by several churches and you can clamber around the battlements for sweeping views over the entire island and its Aegean neighbours. By way of contrast **MESSARIÁ**, a thirty-minute stroll north, has a skyline consisting solely of massive church domes that lord it over the houses huddled in a ravine.

Akrotíri

Evidence of the Minoan colony that once thrived here has been uncovered at the other ancient site of **Akrotíri** (Tues–Sat 8.30am–3pm; 1200dr), at the southwestern tip of the island. Tunnels through the volcanic ash uncovered structures, two and three storeys high, first damaged by earthquake then buried by eruption; Professor Marinatos, the excavator and now an island hero, was killed by a collapsing wall and is also buried on the site. Only a small part of what was the largest Minoan city outside of Crete has been excavated thus far. Lavish frescoes adorned the walls, and Cretan pottery was found stored in a chamber; most of the frescoes are currently exhibited in Athens.

Akrotíri itself can be reached by bus from Firá or Périssa; the excellent *Glaros* taverna on the way to Kókkini Ámmos beach has excellent food and barrelled wine. Kókkini Ámmos is about 500m from the site and is quite spectacular with high reddish brown cliffs above sand the same colour (the name means "red sand"). There's a drinks stall in a cave hollowed into the base of the cliff. It's a better beach than the one below the site, but gets crowded in season.

The Kaméni islets and Thirassía

From either Firá or Ía, boat excursions and local ferries run to the charred volcanic islets of **Paleá Kaméni** and **Néa Kaméni**, and on to the relatively unspoiled islet of Thirassía, which was once part of Santoríni until shorn off by an eruption in the third century BC. At Paleá Kaméni you can swim from the boat to hot springs with sulphurous mud, and Néa Kaméni, with its mud-clouded hot springs features a demanding hike to a volcanically active crater.

The real attraction though, is **Thirassía**, the quietest island in the Cyclades. The views are as dramatic as any on Santoríni, and tourism has little effect on island life. The downside is that there is no sandy beach, no nightlife and nowhere to change money.

Most tour boats head for **Kórfos**, a stretch of shingle backed by fishermen's houses and high cliffs. It has a few tavernas, including *Tonio* which stays open when the day trippers have gone, but no rooms. From Kórfos a stepped path climbs up to **MANOLÁS**, nearly 200m above. Donkeys are still used for transport and stables can be seen in both villages. Manolás straggles along the edge of the caldera, an untidy but attractive small island village that gives an idea of what Santoríni was like before tourism arrived there. It has a bakery, a couple of shops and some indifferent tavernas that open only for the midday rush: the **restaurant** at the *Hotel Cavo Mare* (☎0286/29 176; ⑤) wins out by giving diners the use of the swimming pool. Dhimítrios Nomikós has **rooms** (☎0286/29 102; ②) overlooking the village from the south.

The best **excursion** from Manolás is to follow the unmade road heading south; about halfway along you pass the church of Profítis Ilías on a hilltop to the left. From here an old and overgrown trail descends through the deserted caldera-side village of **Kerá**, before running parallel with the road to the **Monastery of Kímisis** above the southern tip of the island. Minoan remains were excavated in a pumice quarry to the west of here in 1867, several years before the first discoveries at Akrotíri, but there is nothing to be seen today.

Ferries run to Thirassía four times a week in season and three times a week through the winter. There is no problem taking a car or rental bike over, but fill up with petrol first. Day trips take in Néa Kaméni and Paleá Kaméni but are expensive (5000dr) and only stay two or three hours on Thirassía. In Firá, Theoskepastí Tours (☎0286/22 256 or 22 176), next to the OTE office on 25-Martíou, is the only reliable source of ferry information, and its day trips allow you to take a vehicle over to Thirassía at no extra charge.

Anáfi

A ninety-minute boat ride to the east of Thíra, **Anáfi** is the last stop for ferries and hydrofoils, and something of a travellers' dead end, with only one weekly ferry on to the Dodecanese. Not that this is likely to bother most of the visitors, who intentionally come here for weeks in mid-summer, and take over the island's beaches with a vengeance.

At most other times the place seems idyllic, and indeed may prove too sleepy for some: there are no bona fide hotels, mopeds, discos or organized excursions, and donkeys are still the main method of transport in the interior. Anáfi, though initially enchanting, is a harsh place, its mixed granite/limestone core overlaid by volcanic rock spewed out by Thíra's eruptions. Apart from the few olive trees and vines grown in the valleys, the only plants that seem to thrive are prickly pears.

The harbour and Khóra

The tiny harbour hamlet of **ÁYIOS NIKÓLAOS** has a single taverna, *To Akroyiali*, with a few rooms (☎0286/61 218; ②), while *Dave's Cafe*, with straw umbrellas above the beach, is a colourful English-run drinking spot. Jeyzed Travel (☎0286/61 253, fax 61 352) can provide information as well as issuing ferry tickets, changing money and booking rooms. In August there are enough Greek visitors to fill all the rooms on the island and it's a good idea to book ahead. Most places to stay are in Khóra. In season a bus runs from the harbour every two hours or so from 9am to 11pm.

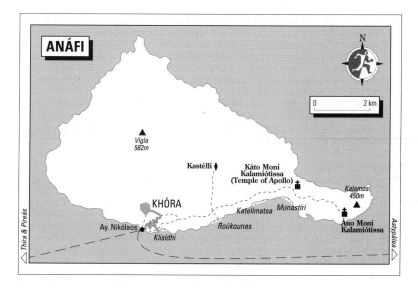

KHÓRA itself, adorning a conical hill overhead, is a stiff, 25-minute climb up the obvious old mule path which shortcuts the modern road. Exposed and blustery when the *meltémi* is blowing, Khóra can initially seem a rather forbidding ghost town. This impression is slowly dispelled as you discover the hospitable islanders taking their coffee in sheltered, south-facing terraces, or under the anti-earthquake barrel vaulting that features in domestic architecture here.

The modern, purpose-built **rooms** run by Kalliopi Halari (☎0286/61 271; ②) and Voula Loudharou (☎0286/61 279; ③), and those run by Margarita Kollidha (☎0286/61 292; ③) at the extreme east edge of the village, are about the most comfortable – and boast stunning views south the islets of Ftená, Pakhiá and Makriá, and the distinctive monolith at the southeastern corner of Anáfi. Somewhat simpler are the rooms of the Gavalas family (②), looking down over the village from the top of the mule path. Evening **diners** seem to divide their custom between the simple, welcoming *To Steki*, with reasonable food and barrel wine served on its terrace, and the more upmarket *Alexandhra's* on the central walkway with a bar upstairs. Otherwise there are shops, a bakery, a **post office** and an OTE station.

East along the coast: beaches and monasteries

The glory of Anáfi is a string of south-facing beaches starting under the cliffs at Áyios Nikólaos. Freelance campers head for **KLISÍDHI**, a short walk to the east of the harbour, where 200m of tan, gently shelving sand is pounded by gentle surf, and splendidly malopropic signs announce that "Nubbism is not allowed". Above the calamus-and-tamarisk oasis backing the beach there are two cafés and a taverna, including the *Kafestiatorion tis Margaritas* with popular rooms (☎0286/61 237; ③). The *Villa Apollon* on the hillside above has the island's most upmarket accommodation (☎0286/61 348; ④). Klisídhi can be reached by a new road but it's quicker to take the cliff-top path starting behind the power station at the harbour. East of here the beaches can only be reached by foot or boat.

From a point on the paved road just east of Khóra, the **main path** skirting the south flank of the island is signposted: "Kastélli – Paleá Khóra – Roúkouna – Monastíri". The primary branch of this trail roller-coasters in and out of several agricultural valleys that provide most of Anáfi's produce and fresh water. Just under an hour along, beside a well, you veer down a side trail to **Roúkounas**, easily the island's best beach, with some 500m of broad sand rising to tamarisk-stabilized dunes, which provide welcome shade. A single taverna, *To Papa*, operates up by the main trail in season; the suggestively craggy hill of **Kastélli**, an hour's scramble above the taverna, is the site both of ancient Anaphi and a ruined Venetian castle.

Beyond Roúkounas, it's another half hour on foot to the first of the exquisite half-dozen **Katelímatsa** coves, of all shapes and sizes, and 45 minutes to **Monastíri** beach – all without facilities, so come prepared. Nudism is banned on Monastíri, because of its proximity to the monasteries.

The monasteries

Between Katelímatsa and Kálamos, the main route keeps inland, past a rare spring, to arrive at the **monastery of Zoödhókhou Piyís**, some two hours out of Khóra. A ruined temple of Apollo is incorporated into the monastery buildings to the side of the main gate; according to legend, Apollo caused Anáfi to rise from the waves, pulling off a dramatic rescue of the storm-lashed Argonauts. The courtyard, with a welcome cistern, is the venue for the island's major festival, celebrated eleven days after Easter. A family of cheesemakers lives next door and can point you up the start of the spectacular onward path to **Kalamiótissa**, a little monastery perched atop the abrupt pinnacle at the extreme southeast of the island. It takes another hour to reach, but is eminently worthwhile for the stunning scenery and views over the entire south coast. Kalamiótissa comes alive only during its 7–8 September festival; at other times, you could haul a sleeping bag up here to witness the amazing sunsets and sunrises, with your vantage point often floating in a sea of cloud. There is no water up here, so bring enough with you. It's a full day's outing from Khóra to Kalamiótissa and back; you might wish to take advantage, in at least one direction, of the excursion **kaïki** that runs from Áyios Nikólaos to Monastíri (6 times daily in high season). There is also a slightly larger mail-and-supplies boat (currently Mon & Thurs 11am) which takes passengers to and from Thíra (Athiniós), supplementing the main-line ferries to Pireás.

travel details

Ferries

Most of the Cyclades are served by mainline ferries from **Pireás**, but there are also boats which depart from **Lávrio** (for Kéa and, less often, Kýthnos) and **Rafína**, which has become increasingly important of late, as work proceeds on the new international airport at nearby Spáta. At the moment there are regular services from Rafína to Ándhros, Tínos, Mýkonos, Sýros, Páros, Náxos and Amorgós, with less frequent sailings to the North and East Aegean. All three ports are easily reached by bus from Athens.

The frequency of sailings given below is intended to give an idea of services from April to October, when most visitors tour the islands. During the winter expect departures to be at or below the minimum level listed, with some routes cancelled entirely. Conversely, routes tend to be more comprehensive in spring and autumn, when the government obliges shipping companies to make extra stops to compensate for numbers of boats still in dry dock.

By 1998 the long-awaited computerized booking system should be operational, and all agents will be required to issue computerized tickets. This move is designed to conform to EU regulations and prevent the overcrowding of ferries so common in the past. It means that in high season, certain popular routes may be booked up days in advance, so if you're visiting a few islands it is important to check availability on arrival in Greece, and book your outward and final pre-flight tickets well ahead. There is not usually so much problem with space between islands, as there is to and from Pireás.

Amorgós 5–6 ferries weekly to Náxos and Páros, some of these continuing to Rafína rather than Pireás; 4–5 to Sýros; 3–4 weekly to Tínos; 4 to Mýkonos; 2–3 weekly to Ándhros, Koufoníssi, Skhinoússa, Iráklia and Dhonoússa; 1–3 weekly to Astypálea; 1 weekly to Kálymnos and Kós.

Anáfi 3 weekly to Pireás (12hr 30min) via Thíra (1hr 30min), Íos, Náxos, Páros; 1 weekly to Sýros, Astypálea, Síkinos and Folégandhros; 2 weekly mail boats to Thíra (2hr).

Ándhros At least 3 daily to Rafína (2hr), Tínos (2hr), and Mýkonos; 4 weekly to Sýros; 1 weekly to Amorgós and the minor islets behind Náxos.

Dhonoússa 3–4 weekly to Amorgós; 1–3 weekly to Náxos; 1–2 weekly to Koufoníssi, Skhinoússa, Iráklia, Páros, Sýros, Pireás; 1 weekly to Mýkonos, Tínos, Astypálea, Pátmos, Lipsí, Léros, Kós, Níssyros, Tílos, Sými and Rhodes.

Íos At least 2 daily to Pireás (10hr), Páros (5hr), Náxos (3hr) and Thíra (2hr); 5–6 weekly to Síkinos and Folégandhros; 4 weekly to Crete; 1–3 weekly to Mílos, Kímolos, Sérifos, Sífnos and Kýthnos; 1 weekly to Tínos, Skiáthos and Thessaloníki; 2–3 weekly to Kárpathos and Kássos; 2 weekly to Rhodes.

Kéa 1–3 daily to Lávrio (1hr 30min); 2 weekly to Kýthnos.

Kímolos 2 daily kaïkia to Mílos (Pollónia) year-round, 5 in summer; 2–5 weekly to Mílos (Adhámas), Sífnos, Sérifos, Kýthnos, and Pireás (7hr); 1 weekly to Folégandhros, Síkinos and Thíra.

Kýthnos 4–12 weekly to Pireás (3hr 15min); 4–10 weekly to Sérifos, Sífnos, and Mílos; 2–4 weekly to Kímolos, Folégandhros, Síkinos, Íos and Lávrio.

Koufoníssi, Skhinoússa, Iráklia 2–3 weekly Náxos, 2 weekly to Mýkonos; 1–2 weekly to Páros, Sýros and Tínos; 1 weekly to Dhonoússa, Amorgós, Astypálea, Ándhros, Rafína and Pireás.

Mýkonos At least 2 daily to Pireás (5hr), Rafína (3hr 30min), Tínos (1hr), Ándhros (3hr 30min) and Sýros (2hr); 3–4 weekly to Amorgós; 3 weekly to Crete (Iráklion), Skiáthos and Thessaloníki; 2–3 weekly to Dhonoússa; 1–2 weekly to Koufoníssi, Skhinoússa and Iráklia; 1 weekly to Kýthnos, Kéa, Pátmos, Lipsí, Léros, Kós, Níssyros, Tílos, Sými and Rhodes; daily (except Monday) excursion boats to Delos.

Mílos At least daily to Pireás (8hr); 5–10 weekly to Sífnos (2hr), Sérifos and Kýthnos; 2–5 daily kaïkia or 4–6 weekly ferries to Kímolos; 2–3 weekly to Folégandhros, Síkinos, Íos and Thíra; 1–3 weekly to Crete (Iráklion or Sitía); 1 weekly to Náxos, Amorgós, Náfplio (Peloponnese), Kássos, Kárpathos, Khálki, Sými and Rhodes (Ródhos).

Náxos At least 3 daily to Pireás (8hr), Páros (1hr), Íos and Thíra; at least 1 daily to Sýros; 5–7 to Amorgós; 6 weekly to Crete (Iráklion); 5–7 weekly to Amorgós; 5–6 to weekly Tínos; 5 weekly to Síkinos and Folégandhros; 3–4 weekly to Ándhros and Rafína; 3–4 weekly to Anáfi; 3 to Rhodes; 2–6 weekly to Ikaría and Sámos; 2–3 weekly to Astypálea, Kássos, Kárpathos, Pátmos, Léros Kálimnos, Kós, Skiáthos, Thessaloníki, Iráklia, Skhinoússa, Koufoníssi and Dhonoússa; 1 to Foúrni, Kýthnos, Kéa and Khálki.

Páros At least 3 daily to Pireás (7hr), Andíparos, Náxos, Íos, Thíra; at least 1 daily to Sýros and Tínos; daily to Iráklion (Crete); 3–6 weekly to Ikaría and Sámos; 5 weekly to Síkinos, Folégandhros and Amorgós; 4–5 weekly to Rafína; 3–5 weekly to Skiáthos and Thessaloníki; 3 weekly to Rhodes, Kárpathos; 2–3 weekly to Anáfi; 2 weekly to Sífnos, Sérifos, Foúrni, Pátmos, Léros, Kálymnos, Kós, Astypálea and Kássos; 1–3 weekly to Koufoníssi, Skhinoússa, Iráklia; 1 weekly to Vólos, Kéa, Kýthnos, Mílos, Kímolos and Khálki; at least hourly from Parikía to Andíparos in summer, dropping to 3 weekly in winter. There is also a car ferry from Poúnda to Andíparos at least hourly throughout the year.

Sérifos and Sífnos 5–12 weekly to Pireás (4hr 30min) and each other; 5–10 weekly to Mílos; 2–5 weekly to Kímolos; 2–3 weekly to Folégandhros, Sýkinos, Íos, and Thíra (Santoríni); once weekly to Sýros; once weekly to eastern Crete and select Dodecanese; daily (June–Aug) from Sífnos to Páros.

Síkinos and Folégandhros 2–6 weekly between each other, and to Pireás (10hr), Kýthnos, Sérifos, Sífnos and Mílos; 1–3 weekly to Íos, Thíra, Sýros, Páros, Náxos and Kímolos.

Sýros At least 2 daily to Pireás (4hr), Tínos (1hr), Mýkonos (2hr), Náxos, and Páros; 4 weekly to Rafína (3hr 30min), 2 weekly to Amorgós and the islets behind Náxos; 2 weekly to Íos, Síkinos, Folégandhros and Thíra; 2 weekly to Ikaría, Sámos and Astypálea; 1–2 weekly to Pátmos, Léros, Kálimnos, Kós, Níssyros, Tílos and Rhodes.

Thíra At least 3 daily to Pireás (10–12hr), Páros, Íos and Náxos; daily to Iráklion, Crete (5hr); 5–7 weekly to Síkinos and Folégandhros; 4 weekly to Anáfi, Sífnos and Mýkonos; 3–5 weekly to Sýros, Tínos, Skiáthos and Thessaloníki; 3–4 weekly to Mílos and Kímilos; 3 weekly to Kárpathos; 2–3 weekly to Sérifos; 2 weekly to Kássos; 2 weekly to Rhodes; 1 weekly to Astypálea, Khálki, Kýthnos and Vólos; 3–4 weekly to Thirassía (plus lots of expensive daily excursion boats in season); 2 weekly mail boats to Anáfi.

Tínos At least 2 daily to Pireás (5hr), Rafína (4hr), Ándhros, Sýros and Mýkonos; 5–6 weekly to Páros and Náxos; 4–5 weekly to Thíra and Iráklion (Crete); 3–5 weekly Skiáthos and Thessaloníki; 3–4 weekly to Amorgós; 1 weekly to Íos, Koufoníssi, Skhinoússa, Iráklia, Kéa, Kýthnos, Vólos, Pátmos, Lipsí, Léros, Kós, Níssyros, Tílos, Sými and Rhodes; also excursion boats calling at Delos and Mýkonos, 1 daily except Monday.

Other services

To simplify the lists above, certain strategic **hydrofoil** and **small-boat services** have been omitted. Of these, the *Skopelitis* plies daily in season between Mýkonos and Amorgós, spending each night at the latter and threading through all of the minor isles between it and Náxos, as well as Náxos and Páros (Píso Livádhi), in the course of a week. Note that, as well as being overcrowded and unreliable, this boat has no café or restaurant on board, so take provisions for what can be quite lengthy journeys. The Páros Express is actually a small car ferry based on Sýros (despite its name), which does a very useful weekly circle route linking that island with Páros, Náxos, Íos, Thíra, Síkinos, Folégandhros,

Sífnos, Sérifos and Kýthnos. The Seajet catamaran – a small-capacity (and expensive) jet-boat (☎0294/22 888 for details), operates almost daily during summer out of Rafína and connects Sýros, Tínos, Mýkonos, Páros and Náxos. Ceres "Flying Dolphins" hydrofoils operate between Zéa (Pireás), Kéa and Kýthnos – twice daily Friday to Monday in high season, once daily mid-week. A new company, Speed Lines hydrofoils, is competing with Ilio Lines in the central and eastern Cyclades.

Flights

There are **airports** on **Páros**, **Mýkonos**, **Thíra**, **Sýros**, **Mílos** and **Náxos**. In season, or during storms when ferries are idle, you have little chance of getting a seat on less than three days' notice. The Athens–Mílos route is probably the best value for money; the other destinations seem deliberately overpriced, in a usually unsuccessful attempt to keep passenger volume manageable. Expect off-season (Oct–April) frequencies to drop by at least eighty percent.

Athens–Páros (4–5 daily; 45min)

Athens–Mýkonos (4–7 daily; 50min)

Athens–Thíra (4–8 daily; 1hr)

Athens–Sýros (2–3 daily; 35min)

Athens–Mílos (2 daily; 45min)

Athens–Náxos (2 daily; 45min)

Mýkonos–Thíra (2–3 weekly; 40min)

Mýkonos–Iráklion (Crete) (1 weekly; 1hr 10min)

Mýkonos–Rhodes (1 weekly; 1hr 10min)

Thíra–Iráklion (Crete) (1–2 weekly; 40min)

Thíra–Rhodes (3 weekly; 1hr).

CHAPTER EIGHT

CRETE

Crete (Kríti) is a great deal more than just another Greek island. In many places, especially in the cities or along the developed north coast, it doesn't feel like an island at all, but rather a substantial land in its own right – a mountainous, wealthy and surprisingly cosmopolitan one. But when you lose yourself among the mountains, or on the less-known coastal reaches of the south, it has everything you could want of a Greek island and more: great beaches, remote hinterlands and hospitable people.

In **history**, Crete is distinguished above all as the home of Europe's earliest civilization. It was only at the beginning of this century that the legends of King Minos and of a Cretan society that ruled the Greek world in prehistory were confirmed by excavations at **Knossós** and **Festós**. Yet the **Minoans** had a remarkably advanced society, the centre of a maritime trading empire as early as 2000 BC. The artworks produced on Crete at this time are unsurpassed anywhere in the ancient world, and it seems clear, that life on Crete in those days was good. This apparently peaceful culture survived at least three major natural disasters. Each time the palaces were destroyed, and each time they were rebuilt on a grander scale. Only after the last destruction, probably the result of an eruption of Thíra (Santoríni) and subsequent tidal waves and earthquakes, do significant numbers of weapons begin to appear in the ruins. This, together with the appearance of the Greek language, has been interpreted to mean that Mycenaean Greeks had taken control of the island. Nevertheless, for nearly 500 years, by far the longest period of peace the island has seen, Crete was home to a culture well ahead of its time.

The Minoans of Crete came probably originally from Anatolia; at their height they maintained strong links with Egypt and with the people of Asia Minor, and this position as meeting point and strategic fulcrum between east and west has played a major role in Crete's subsequent history. Control of the island passed from Greeks to Romans to Saracens, through the Byzantine Empire to Venice, and finally to Turkey for more than two centuries. During World War II, the island was **occupied** by the Germans and attained the dubious distinction of being the first place to be successfully invaded by paratroops.

ACCOMMODATION PRICE CODES

Throughout the book we've used the following **price codes** to denote the cheapest available room in high season; all are prices for a double room, except for category ①, which represents per person rates. Out of season, rates can drop by up to fifty percent, especially if you are staying for three or more nights. Single rooms, where available, cost around seventy percent of the price of a double.

Rented private rooms on the islands usually fall into the ② or ③ categories, depending on their location and facilities, and the season; a few in the ④ category are more like plush self-catering apartments. They are not generally available from late October through to the beginning of April, when only hotels tend to remain open.

① 1400–2000dr	④ 8000–12,000dr
② 4000–6000dr	⑤ 12000–16,000dr
③ 6000–8000dr	⑥ 16,000dr and upwards

For more accommodation details, see pp.39–42.

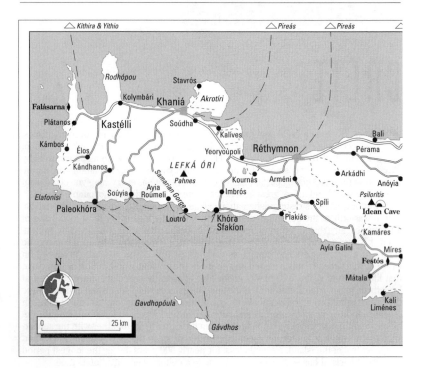

Today, with a flourishing **agricultural economy**, Crete is one of the few islands which could probably support itself without tourists. Nevertheless, **tourism** is heavily promoted. The northeast coast in particular is overdeveloped, and though there are parts of the south and west coasts that have not been spoiled, they are getting harder to find. By contrast, the high mountains of the interior are still barely touched, and one of the best things to do on Crete is to **rent a vehicle** and explore the remoter villages.

Where to go
Every part of Crete has its loyal devotees and it's hard to pick out highlights, but generally if you want to get away from it all you should head west, towards **Khaniá** and the smaller, less well connected places along the south and west coasts. It is in this part of the island that the White Mountains rise, while below them yawns the famous **Samarian Gorge**. The far east, around **Sitía**, is also relatively unscathed.

Whatever you do, your first main priority will probably be to leave **Iráklion** (Heraklion) as quickly as possible, having paid the obligatory, and rewarding, visit to the **archeological museum** and nearby **Knossós**. The other great Minoan sites cluster around the middle of the island: **Festós** and **Ayía Triádha** in the south (with Roman **Górtys** to provide contrast), and **Mália** on the north coast. Almost wherever you go, though, you'll find a reminder of the island's history, whether it's the town of **Gourniá** near the cosmopolitan resort of **Áyios Nikólaos**, the exquisitely sited palace of **Zákros** in the far east, or the lesser sites scattered around the west. Unexpected highlights include Crete's Venetian forts at **Réthymnon** and **Frangokástello**; its hundreds of fres-

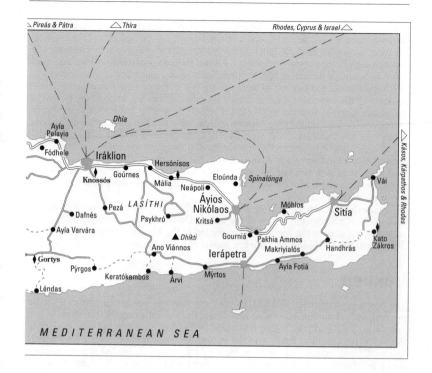

coed Byzantine churches, most famously at **Kritsá**; and, at Réthymnon and Khaniá, the cluttered old Venetian and Turkish quarters.

Climate

Crete has by far the longest summers in Greece, and you can get a decent tan here right into October and swim at least from May until November. Several annual harvests also make it a promising location for finding **casual work**. The cucumber green houses and pickling factories around Ierápetra have proved to be winter lifelines for many long-term Greek travellers. The one seasonal blight is the *meltémi*, which blows harder here and more continuously than anywhere else in Greece – the best of several reasons for avoiding an **August** visit.

IRÁKLION, KNOSSÓS AND CENTRAL CRETE

Many visitors to Crete arrive in the island's capital, **Iráklion** (Heraklion), but it's not a beautiful city, nor one where you'll want to stay much longer than it takes to visit the **archeological museum** and nearby **Knossós**. Iráklion itself, though it has its good points – superb fortifications, a fine market, atmospheric old alleys, and some interesting lesser museums – is for the most part an experience in survival: it's modern, raucous, traffic-laden and overcrowded.

The area immediately around the city is less touristy than you might expect, mainly because there are few decent beaches of any size on this central part of the coast. To the west, mountains drop straight into the sea virtually all the way to Réthymnon, with just two significant coastal settlements – **Ayía Pelayía**, a sizeable resort, and **Balí**, which is gradually becoming one. Eastwards, the main resorts are at least 40km away, at **Khersónissos** and beyond, although there is a string of rather unattractive developments all the way there. Inland, there's agricultural country, some of the richest on the island, Crete's best vineyards, and a series of wealthy but rather dull villages. Directly behind the capital rises **Mount Ioúktas** with its characteristic profile of Zeus; to the west the Psilorítis massif spreads around the peak of **Mount Ídha** (Psilorítis), the island's highest mountain. On the south coast there are few roads and little development of any kind, except at **Ayía Galíni** in the southwest, a nominal fishing village long since swamped with tourists, and **Mátala**, which has thrown out the hippies that made it famous and is now crowded with package-trippers. **Léndas** has to some extent occupied Mátala's old niche.

Despite the lack of resorts, there seem constantly to be thousands of people trekking back and forth across the centre of the island. This is largely because of the superb archeological sites in the south: **Festós**, second of the Minoan palaces, with its attendant villa at **Ayía Triádha**, and **Górtys**, capital of Roman Crete.

Iráklion

The best way to approach **IRÁKLION** is by sea: that way you see the city as it should be seen, with Mount Ioúktas rising behind and the Psilorítis range to the west. As you get closer, it's the city walls that first stand out, still dominating and fully encircling the oldest part of town; finally you sail in past the great **fort** defending the harbour entrance. Unfortunately, big ships no longer dock in the old port but at great modern concrete wharves alongside, which neatly sums up Iráklion itself. Many of the old parts have been restored from the bottom up, but they're of no relevance to the dust and noise that characterizes much of the city today. In recent times, however, Iráklion's administrators have been giving belated attention to dealing with some of the image problems, and large tracts of the centre are currently undergoing landscaping and refurbishment schemes designed to present a less daunting prospect to the visitor.

Orientation, arrival and information

Virtually everything you're likely to want to see in Iráklion lies within the walled city, and even here the majority of the interest falls into a relatively small sector, the northeastern corner. The most vital thoroughfare, **25-Avgoústou**, links the harbour with the commercial city centre. At the bottom it is lined with shipping and travel agencies and rental outlets, but as you climb these give way to banks, restaurants and stores. **Platía Venizélou** (or Fountain Square), off to the right, is crowded with cafés and restaurants; behind Venizélou is **El Greco Park**, with the OTE office and more bars, while on the opposite side of 25-Avgoústou are some of the more interesting of Iráklion's older buildings. Further up 25-Avgoústou, **Kalokerinoú** leads down to Khaniá Gate and westwards out of the city; straight ahead, **Odhós 1821** is a major shopping street, and adjacent 1866 is given over to the animated **market**. To the left,

The telephone code for Iráklion is ☎081

Dhikeosínis, heads for **Platía Eleftherías**, paralleled by the touristy pedestrian alley, Dhedhálou, the direct link between the two squares. The newly revamped Eleftherías is very much the traditional centre of the city, both for traffic, which swirls around it constantly, and for life in general; it is ringed by more expensive tourist cafés and restaurants and comes alive in the evening with crowds of strolling locals.

Points of arrival

Iráklion **airport** is right on the coast, 4km east of the city. The #1 bus leaves for Platía Eleftherías every few minutes from the car park in front of the terminal; buy your ticket (150dr) at the booth before boarding. There are also plenty of taxis outside (which you'll be forced to use when the buses stop at 10.30pm), and prices to major destinations are posted – it's about 1000dr to the centre of town.

There are three main **bus stations** and a small terminus. Services along the coastal highway to or from the **east** (Mália, Áyios Nikólaos, Sitía and so on) use the terminal just off the main road between the ferry dock and the Venetian harbour; the #2 local bus to Knossós runs from the city bus stop, adjacent to the east bus station. Main road services **west** (Réthymnon and Khaniá) leave from a terminal right next to the east bus station on the other side of the road. Buses for the **southwest** (Festós, Mátala or Ayía Galíni) and along the inland roads west (Tílissos, Anóyia) operate out of a terminal just outside Khaniá Gate, a very long walk from the centre along Kalokerinoú (or jump on any bus heading down this street). The **southeast** (basically Ierápetra and points en route) is served by a small terminus just outside the walls in Platía Kýprou at the end of Odhós Evans on Trikoúpi.

From the wharves where the **ferries** dock, the city rises directly ahead in steep tiers. If you're heading for the centre, for the archeological museum or the tourist office, cut straight up the stepped alleys behind the bus station onto Dhoúkos Bofór and to Platía Eleftherías; this will take about fifteen minutes. For accommodation though, and to get a better idea of the layout of Iráklion's main attractions, it's simplest to follow the main roads by a rather more roundabout route. Head west along the coast, past the major east-bound bus station and on by the Venetian harbour before cutting up towards the centre on 25-Avgoústou.

Information

Iráklion's **tourist office** (Mon–Fri 8am–2.30pm; ☎228 203, fax 226 020) is just below Platía Eleftherías, opposite the archeological museum at Zanthoudhídhou 1. The **tourist police** – more helpful than most – are on Dhikeosínis, halfway between Platía Eleftherías and the market.

Accommodation

Finding a **room** can be difficult in season. The best place to look for inexpensive rooms is in the area around Platía Venizélou, along Khandhákos and towards the harbour to the west of 25-Avgoústou. Other concentrations of affordable places are around El Greco park and in the streets above the Venetian harbour. Better hotels mostly lie closer to Platía Eleftherías, to the south of Platía Venizélou and near the east- and west-bound bus stations. The dusty park between the main bus station and the harbour is often crowded with the sleeping bags of those who failed to find, or couldn't afford, a room; if you're really hard up, crashing here is a possibility, but a pleasant environment it is not.

The **youth hostel** at Výronos 5 (☎286 281; ①), which has operated since 1963, is family run and very friendly and helpful, with plenty of space and up to fifty beds on the roof if you fancy sleeping out under the stars. In addition to dormitories, family and double rooms are also available; there are hot showers, breakfast (400dr) and

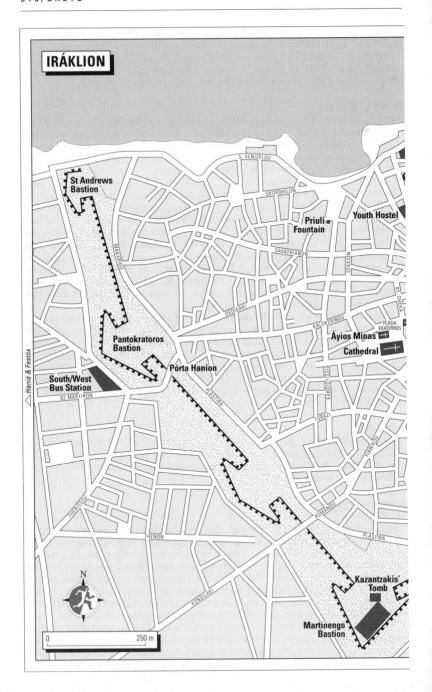

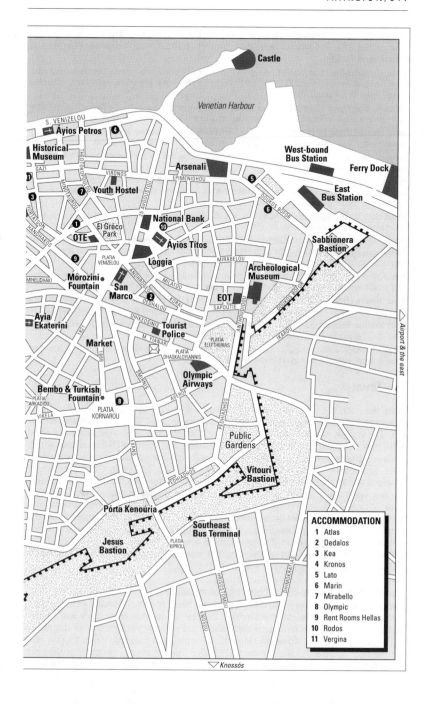

Castle

Venetian Harbour

S VENIZELOU
Áyios Petros **4**
Historical
Museum
GAZI
VIRONOS
West-bound
Bus Station
Ferry Dock
Arsenali
EPIMENIDHOU
5
East
Bus Station
Youth Hostel
DOUKOS BOTOR
6
National Bank
10
El Gréco
Park
OTE
Áyios Títos
Sabbionera
Bastion
9
PLATIA
VENIZELOU
Loggia
MIRABELOU
Môrozini
Fountain
San
Marco
2
DHIKEOSINIS
MILATOU
Archeological
Museum
EOT
SAPOUTIE
Ayia
Ekaterini
Tourist
Police
M. YIANARI
PLATIA
ELEFTHERIAS
Market
PLATIA
DHASKALOYIANNIS
Olympic
Airways
Bembo & Turkish
Fountain
8
PLATIA
ARKADIOU
VIKELA
PLATIA
KORNAROU
EVANS
Public
Gardens
PEDHIADHOS
Vitouri
Bastion
Pórta Kenoúria
Southeast
Bus Terminal
PLATIA
KIPROU
Jesus
Bastion
KNOSSOU
HRISOSTOMOU
DHIMOKRATIAS

▽ Airport & the east

MINOTAVROU
THEOTOKOPOULOU
25 AVGOUSTOU
ANDHROGEO
KORAI
ANTHOUDIDOU
DOUKOS BOFOR
IKAROU
PEDHIADHOS
AVEROF
SMIRNIS
1866
1821
MIHELIDHAKI
IDOMENEOS
HANDHAKOS
GIAMBOUDHAKIS
DHEDHALOU

ACCOMMODATION

1 Atlas
2 Dedalos
3 Kea
4 Kronos
5 Lato
6 Marin
7 Mirabello
8 Olympic
9 Rent Rooms Hellas
10 Rodos
11 Vergina

▽ Knossós

TV. There are no **campsites** near to Iráklion. The nearest sites are both found to the east of the city – *Creta Camping* at Goúves (16km), and *Caravan Camping* at Hersonisos (28km).

Atlas, Kandanoléon 11 (☎288 989). A rather run-down old pension in a convenient but noisy alley between Platía Venizélou and El Greco park. There's a pleasant roof garden, and freshly squeezed orange juice for breakfast. ②.

Dedalos, Dhedhálou 15 (☎244 812, fax 224 391). Very centrally placed on the pedestrianized alley between Venizélou and Eleftherías. Decent balcony rooms with private bath. ③.

Lato, Epomenídhou 15 (☎228 103, fax 240 350). Stylish and luxurious hotel where the air-conditioned rooms have mini-bar, TV and sea-view balcony. Good value for the price. ⑥.

Kronos, Agaráthou 2, west of 25-Avgoústou (☎282 240, fax 285 853). Pleasant, modern hotel with sea view and baths in all rooms. ③.

Marin, Doukos Bofór 10, (☎288 582). Comfortable and good-value rooms with baths, overlooking the Venetian harbour; get a balcony room at the front for a great view. Very convenient for the bus stations and the archeological museum. ④.

Mirabello, Theotokopoúlou 20 (☎285 052, fax 225 852). Good-value, family-run place in a quiet street close to El Greco park. ③.

Olympic, Platía Kornárou (☎288 861, fax 222 512). Overlooking the busy platía and the famous Bembo and Turkish fountains. One of the many hotels built in the 1960s, but one of the few that has been refurbished. ⑤.

Rea, Kalimeráki 1 (☎223 638). A friendly, comfortable and clean hotel in quiet street. Some rooms with washbasin, others with own shower. One of the best of the cheaper hotels. ②.

Rent Rooms Hellas, Khándakos 24 (☎280 858, fax 284 442). Hostel-type place with simple doubles, and dormitory rooms favoured by younger travellers. Also has a roof garden and snack bar. ①.

Rent Rooms Vergina, Khortátson 32 (☎242 739). Basic but pleasant rooms (with washbasins) in quiet street around a courtyard with an enormous banana tree. ②.

Pension Rodos, Platía Áyios Títos (☎228 519). Homely no frills double and triple rooms place, on a picturesque square with a great breakfast bar next door. ②.

The Town

From the port, the town rises overhead, and you can cut up the stepped alleys for a direct approach to **Platía Eleftherías** (Liberty Square) and the **archeological museum**. The easiest way to the middle of things, though, is to head west along the coast road, past the main bus stations and the *arsenáli*, and then up 25-Avgoústou, which leads into **Platía Venizélou**. This is crowded with Iráklion's youth, patronizing outdoor cafés (marginally cheaper than those on Eleftherías), and with travellers who've arranged to meet in "Fountain Square". The recently restored **fountain** itself is not particularly spectacular at first glance, but on closer inspection is really a very beautiful work; it was built by Venetian governor Francesco Morosini in the seventeenth century, incorporating four lions which were some 300 years old even then. From the platía you can strike up Dhedhálou, a pedestrianized street full of tourist shops and restaurants, or continue on 25-Avgoústou to a major traffic junction. To the right, Kalokerinoú leads west out of the city, the **market** lies straight ahead, and Platía Eleftherías is a short walk to the left up Dhikeosínis.

Platía Eleftherías and the archeological museum

Platía Eleftherías is very much the traditional heart of the city: traffic swirls around it constantly, and in the evening strolling hordes jam its expensive cafés and restaurants. Most of Iráklion's more expensive shops are in the streets leading off the platía.

The **Archeological Museum** (Mon 12.30–6pm, Tues–Sun 8am–6pm; 1500dr, Sun free) is nearby, directly opposite the EOT office. Almost every important prehistoric and Minoan find on Crete is included in this fabulous, if bewilderingly large, collection. The museum tends to be crowded, especially when a guided tour stampedes through, but it's worth taking time over. You can't hope to see everything, nor can we attempt to describe it all (several good museum guides are sold here; the best probably being the glossy one by J.A. Sakellarakis) but highlights include the **town mosaics** in Room 2 (galleries are arranged basically in chronological order), the famous **inscribed disc** from Festós in Room 3 (itself the subject of several books), most of Room 4, especially the magnificent bull's head **rhyton** (drinking vessel), the **jewellery** in Room 6 (and everywhere) and the engraved **black vases** in Room 7. Save some of your time and energy for upstairs, where the **Hall of the Frescoes**, with intricately reconstructed fragments of the wall paintings from Knossós and other sites, is especially wonderful.

Walls and fortifications

The massive **Venetian walls**, in places up to fifteen metres thick, are the most obvious evidence of Iráklion's later history. Though their fabric is incredibly well preserved, access is virtually nonexistent. It is possible, just, to walk along them from St Anthony's bastion over the sea in the west, as far as the tomb of Nikos Kazantzakis, Cretan author of *Zorba the Greek*, whose epitaph reads: "I believe in nothing, I hope for nothing, I am free." At weekends, Iraklians gather here to pay their respects and enjoy a free view of the soccer matches played by the island's first-division team, OFI Crete, in the stadium below. If the walls seem altogether too much effort, the **port fortifications** are very much easier to see. Stroll out along the jetty (crowded with courting couples after dark) and you can get inside the sixteenth-century **castle** (Mon–Sat 8am–6pm, Sun 10am–3pm; 400dr) at the harbour entrance, emblazoned with the Venetian Lion of St Mark. Standing atop this, you can begin to understand how Iráklion (or Candia as it was known until the seventeenth century) withstood a 22-year siege before finally falling to the Ottomans. On the landward side of the port, the Venetian **arsenali** can also be seen, their arches rather lost amid the concrete road system all around.

Churches, icons and the Historical Museum

From the harbour, 25-Avgoústou will take you up past most of the rest of what's interesting. The **church of Áyios Títos**, on the left as you approach Platía Venizélou, borders a pleasant little platía. It looks magnificent principally because, like most of the churches here, it was adapted by the Turks as a mosque and only reconsecrated in 1925; consequently it has been renovated on numerous occasions. On the top side of this platía, abutting 25-Avgoústou, is the Venetian **City Hall** with its famous loggia, again almost entirely rebuilt. Just above this, facing Platía Venizélou, is the **church of San Marco**, its steps usually crowded with the overflow of people milling around in the platía. Neither of these last two buildings has found a permanent role in its refurbished state, but both are generally open to house some kind of exhibition or craft show.

Slightly away from the obvious city-centre circuit, but still within the bounds of the walls, there are a couple of lesser museums worth seeing if you have the time. First of these is the excellent collection of **icons** in the **church of Ayía Ekateríni** (Mon–Sat 10am–1pm, Tues, Thurs & Fri also 4–6pm; 500dr), an ancient building just below the undistinguished cathedral, off Kalokerinoú. The finest here are six large scenes by Mikhalis Damaskinos (a near-contemporary of El Greco) who fused Byzantine and Renaissance influences. Supposedly both Damaskinos and El Greco studied at Ayía Ekateríni in the sixteenth century, when it functioned as a sort of monastic art school.

The **Historical Museum** (Mon–Sat 9am–2pm; 500dr) is some way from here, down near the waterfront opposite the stark *Xenia* hotel. Its display of folk costumes and jumble of local memorabilia includes the reconstructed studies of both Nikos Kazantzakis and Emanuel Tsouderos (Cretan statesman and Greek prime minister). There's enough variety to satisfy just about anyone, including the only El Greco painting on Crete, *View of Mount Sinai and the Monastery of St Catherine*.

The beaches

Iráklion's **beaches** are some way out, whether east or west of town. In either direction they're easily accessible by public bus: #6 west from the stop outside the *Astoria* hotel in Platía Eleftherías; #7 east from the stop opposite this, under the trees in the centre of the platía.

Almyrós (or Amoudhári) to the west has been subjected to a degree of development, taking in a campsite, several medium-size hotels and one giant one (the *Zeus Beach*, in the shadow of the power station at the far end), which makes the beach hard to get to without walking through or past something built up.

Amnissós, to the east, is the better choice, with several tavernas and the added amusement of planes swooping in immediately overhead to land. This is where most locals go on their afternoons off; the furthest of the beaches is the best, although new hotels are encroaching here, too. Little remains here to indicate the once-flourishing port of Knossós aside from a rather dull, fenced-in dig. If you're seriously into antiquities, however, you'll find a more rewarding site in the small villa, known as **Nírou Kháni** (Tues–Sun 8.30am–3pm) at **Kháni Kokkíni**, the first of the full-blown resort developments east of Iráklion.

Eating

Big city as it is, Iráklion disappoints when it comes to eating. The cafés and tavernas of platías **Venizélou** and **Eleftherías** are essential places to sit and watch the world pass, but their food is expensive and mediocre. One striking exception is *Bougátsa Kirkor*, by the Morosini fountain in Venizélou, where you can sample authentic *bougátsa*; alternatively, try a plate of *loukoumádhes*, available from a number of cafés at the top of Dhikeosínis. The cafés and tavernas on **Dhedhálou**, the pedestrian alley linking the two main platías, are very run of the mill, persistent waiters enticing you in with faded photographs of what appears to be food.

A more atmospheric option is to head for the little alley, **Fotíou Theodhosáki**, which runs through from the market to Odhós Evans. It is entirely lined with the tables of rival taverna owners, certainly authentic and catering for market traders and their customers as well as tourists. Compared with some, they often look a little grimy, but they are by no means cheap, which can come as a surprise. Nearby, at the corner of Evans and Yiánari, is the long-established *Ionia* taverna, which is the sort of place to come to if you are in need of a substantial, no-nonsense feed, with a good range of Greek dishes.

A relaxed lunchtime venue in the **centre** of town is *Geroplantos* with tables on the leafy Platía Áyios Titos beside the church of the same name. Across from here is a stunning new bar *Pagopoleion* (Ice Factory), good for breakfast and snacks. It's the creation of photographic artist Chrissy Martiros, who has preserved a strident inscription on one wall, left by the Nazi occupiers who used local labour to run what was then Iráklion's only ice factory. Still near the centre, just off Eleftherías at **Platía Dhaskaloyiánnis** (where the post office is), are some inexpensive and unexceptional tavernas; the platía is however a pleasant and relaxing venue, if not for a meal then to sit at one of its cafés. Nearer Venizélou, try exploring some of the back streets to the east, off Dhedhálou and behind the loggia. The *Taverna Giovanni*, on the alley Korai parallel to Dhedhálou, is one of the better tavernas in Iráklion: a friendly lively place with a varied menu that uses fresh, good quality ingredients but with reasonable prices;

it also caters for vegetarians. Should you have a craving for non-Greek food, there is **Italian** at the pricey *Loukoulos* and **Chinese** at the *New China Restaurant*, both with leafy courtyards and both in the same street as the *Taverna Giovanni*. **Mexican** tacos and beers are on offer at *El Azteca*, Psaromilíngon 32, west of Khándhakos – a lively bar with similar establishments nearby.

The **waterfront** is dotted with fish tavernas with little to recommend them. Instead, walk across the road to *Ippokambus*, which specializes in mezédhes at moderate prices. It is deservedly popular with locals and is often crowded late into the evening: you may have to wait in line or turn up earlier than the Greeks eat. Even if you see no space it is worth asking as the owner may suddenly disappear inside the taverna and emerge with yet another table to carry further down the pavement.

For **snacks** and **takeaways**, there's a whole group of *souvláki* stalls clustering around 25-Avgoústou at the entrance to El Greco park, which is handy if you need somewhere to sit and eat. For cheese or spinach pies and other pastries, sweet or savoury, there are no shortage of zakharoplastía, such as the *Samaria* next to the Harley Davidson shop across from the park, and a couple of places at the park's southwest corner. If you want to buy your own food, the **market** on Odhós 1866 is the place to go; it's an attraction in itself, which you should see even if you don't plan to buy anything.

Drinking, nightlife and entertainment

Iráklion is a bit of a damp squib as far as **nightlife** goes, certainly when compared with many other towns on the island. If you're determined, however, there are a few city-centre possibilities, and plenty of options if all you want to do is sit and **drink**. In addition, there are a number of **cinemas** scattered about: check the posters on the boards by the tourist police office.

Bars

Bars tend to fan out into the streets around Khándhakos; among a number of new-style places, *Jasmin* is tucked in an alley mid-way down Khándhakos, and serves a variety of teas (including the Cretan *dhíktamo*) with easy jazz and rock as background music. At the beginning of Khándhakos is *Tasso's*, a popular hang-out for young hostellers, lively at night and with good breakfasts to help you recover in the morning; *Odysseia* Khándhakos 63); *El Azteca* (Psaromilíngon 32, west of Khándhakos), a Mexican bar serving tacos; *Utopia*, also on Khándhakos; and the nearby *Bonsai*.

The most animated place is a platía behind Dhedhálou (up from the *Giovanni*), where there are several trendy bars (including *Flash* and *Notos*) with outdoor tables, which are popular with students in term time. Enjoy a game of backgammon here during the day or early evening; later it can get extremely lively with many distractions. In and around **Platía Venizélou**, there are many bars, again some are very fashionable, with *De Facto* being one of the most popular. This is one of the new breed of kafenío emerging in Iráklion, attracting younger people: the drinks are **cocktails** rather than *raki*, the music is Western or modern Greek and there are prices to match. Another is the *Idaean Andron*, on Perdhikári around the corner from the *Selena* hotel, which has a good atmosphere, and there are more along Kandanoléon, off El Greco park.

Iráklion looks a great deal better than you'd expect from above, and there are fancier **rooftop places** above most of the restaurants in Platía Eleftherías, the *Cafe-Bar Dore* for example. This serves food as well, and while it's not exactly the sort of place to wear cut-offs and T-shirt, it's no more expensive than the restaurants on the platía below. Many hotels around the city have rooftop bars which welcome non-residents; those just above the bus stations and harbour, such as the *Alaira*, have particularly stunning views.

Clubs and discos

For **discos** proper, there is a large selection, even if they are all playing "techno" at the moment, interspersed with Greek music (not the Greek music you get for tourists). *Trapeza* is the most popular, down towards the harbour at the bottom of Doukos Bofor, below the archeological museum. *Makao* also has a following and is on the opposite side of the street to *Trapeza*, or try *Genesis* next door. Another cluster of nightclubs can be found on Ikárou, about a twenty-minute walk away. Retrace your steps towards the archeological museum, but before emerging onto Platía Eleftherías turn left downhill and follow the main road, Ikárou. Here you'll find the *Minoica*, the *Korus Club* and the *Athina*, all playing similar music and popular with young Iraklions.

Listings

Airlines Olympic, Platía Eleftherías (☎229 191), is the only airline with a permanent office in Iráklion. Charter airlines flying in to Iráklion mostly use local travel agents as their representatives.

Airport For airport information call ☎245 644. Bus #1 runs from Platía Eleftherías to the airport every few minutes.

Banks The main branches are on 25-Avgoústou, many of which have 24hr cash machines (not always working); there's also a VISA machine at Ergo Bank on Dhikeosínis.

Car and bike rental 25-Avgoústou is lined with rental companies, but you'll find cheaper rates on the backstreets; it's always worth asking for discounts. Good places to start include: Blue Sea, Kosma Zotou 7, near the bottom of 25-Avgoústou (☎241 097) for bikes; Eurocreta, Sapotie 2 (☎226 700) near the archeological museum for cars; Ritz in the *Hotel Rea*, Kalimeráki 1 (☎223 638) for cars; and Sun Rise, 25-Avgoústou 46 (☎221 609), for cars and bikes.

Ferry tickets Available from Minoan Lines (25-Avgoústou 78; ☎229 646), Kavi Club near the tourist office (☎221 166), or any of the travel agents listed below.

Hospital Most central is the hospital on Apollónion, southwest of Platía Kornárou, between Albér and Moussoúrou.

Laundry Washsalon, Khándhakos 18 (daily 9am–7pm).

Left luggage Offices in the east-bound and southwest bus stations (daily 6am–8pm; 200dr per bag per day), as well as commercial agencies at 25-Avgoústou (daily 7am–11pm; 450dr per bag per day) and Khándhakos 18 (open 24hrs; large locker 400dr per day). You can also leave bags at the youth hostel (even if you don't stay there) for 200–300dr per bag per day. If you want to leave your bag while you go off on a bike for a day or two, the rental company should be prepared to store it.

Newspapers and books For English-language newspapers and novels, as well as local guides and maps, Dhedhálou is the best bet. Planet International Bookstore behind Platía Venizélou at the corner of Khándhakos and Kydhonías, has a huge stock of English-language titles.

Pharmacies Plentiful on the main shopping streets – at least one is open 24hr on a rota basis: the others will have a sign on the door indicating which it is.

Post office Main office in Platía Dhaskaloyiánnis, off Eleftherías (Mon–Fri 7.30am–8pm). There's also a temporary office (a van) at the entrance to El Greco Park (daily 7.30am–7pm), handy for changing money.

Taxis Major taxi ranks in Platía Eleftherías and El Greco Park, or call ☎210 102 or 210 168. Prices displayed on boards at ranks.

Telephones The OTE head office is on the west side of El Greco Park; it's an efficient 24hr service, though expect long waits.

Travel agencies Budget operators and student specialists include the extremely helpful Blavakis Travel, Platía Kallérgon 8, just off 25-Avgoústou by the entrance to El Greco Park (☎282 541) and Prince Travel, 25-Avgoústou 30 (☎282 706). For excursions around the island, villa rentals and so on, the bigger operators are probably easier: Irman Travel, Dhedhálou 26 (☎242 527) or Creta Travel Bureau, 20–22 Epimenídhou (☎243 811). The latter is also the local American Express agent.

Knossós

KNOSSÓS, the largest of the **Minoan palaces**, reached its cultural peak more than 3000 years ago, though a town of some importance persisted here well into the Roman era. It lies on a low, largely man-made hill some 5km southeast of Iráklion; the surrounding hillsides are rich in lesser remains spanning 25 centuries, starting at the beginning of the second millennium BC.

Barely a hundred years ago the palace existed only in mythology. Knossós was the court of the legendary King Minos, whose wife Pasiphae bore the Minotaur, half-bull, half-man. Here the labyrinth was constructed by Daedalus to contain the monster, and youths were brought from Athens as human sacrifice until Theseus arrived to slay the beast, and with Ariadne's help, escape its lair. The discovery of the palace, and the interplay of these legends with fact, is among the most amazing tales of modern archeology. Heinrich Schliemann, the excavator of Troy, suspected that a major Minoan palace lay under the various tumuli here, but was denied the necessary permission to dig by the local Ottoman authorities at the end of the last century. It was left for Sir Arthur Evans, whose name is indelibly associated with Knossós, to excavate the site, from 1900 onwards.

The #2 local **bus** sets off every ten minutes from the Iráklion's city bus stop (adjacent to the east bus station), runs up 25-Avgoústou (with a stop by Platía Venizélou) and

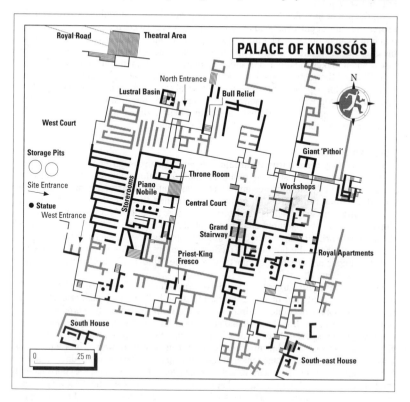

out of town on Odhós 1821 and Evans. At Knossós, outside the fenced site, is the *caravanserai* where ancient wayfarers would rest and water their animals. Head out onto the road and you'll find no lack of watering holes for modern travellers either – a string of rather pricey tavernas and tacky souvenir stands. There are several **rooms** for rent here, and if you're really into Minoan culture, there's a lot to be said for staying out this way to get an early start. Be warned that it's expensive and unashamedly commercial.

The Site

Daily: April–Sept 8am–6pm; Oct–March 8.30am–3pm; 1500dr.

As soon as you enter the **Palace of Knossós** through the West Court, the ancient ceremonial entrance, it is clear how the legends of the labyrinth grew up around it. Even with a detailed plan, it's almost impossible to find your way around the site with any success. The best advice is not to try; wander around for long enough and you'll eventually stumble upon everything. If you're worried about missing the highlights, you can always tag along with one of the constant guided tours for a while, catching the patter and then backtracking to absorb the detail when the crowd has moved on. You won't get the place to yourself, whenever you come, but exploring on your own does give you the opportunity to appreciate individual parts of the palace in the brief lulls between groups.

Knossós was liberally "restored" by Evans, and these restorations have been the source of furious controversy among archeologists ever since. It has become clear that much of Evans's upper level – the so-called *piano nobile* – is pure conjecture. Even so, his guess as to what the palace might have looked like is certainly as good as anyone else's, and it makes the other sites infinitely more meaningful if you have seen Knossós first. Without the restorations, it would be almost impossible to imagine the grandeur of the multi-storey palace or to see the ceremonial stairways, strange, top-heavy pillars and gaily painted walls that distinguish the site. For some idea of the size and complexity of the palace in its original state, take a look at the cutaway drawings (wholly imaginary but probably not too far off) on sale outside.

Royal Apartments

The superb **Royal Apartments** around the central staircase are not guesswork, and they are plainly the finest of the rooms at Knossós. Unfortunately, extensive renovations are currently taking place and these mean that the apartments are likely to be closed for some time, although glimpses can be had through the wooden railings. The **Grand Stairway** itself is a masterpiece of design: not only a fitting approach to these sumptuously appointed chambers, but also an integral part of the whole plan, its large well bringing light into the lower storeys. Light wells such as these, usually with a courtyard at the bottom, are a constant feature of Knossós and a reminder of just how important creature comforts were to the Minoans, and of how skilled they were at providing them.

For evidence of this luxurious lifestyle you need look no further than the **Queen's Suite**, off the grand **Hall of the Colonnades** at the bottom of the staircase. Here, the main living room is decorated with the celebrated **dolphin fresco** (a reproduction; the original is now in the Iráklion archeological museum) and with running friezes of flowers and abstract spirals. On two sides, it opens out onto courtyards that let in light and air; the smaller one would probably have been planted with flowers. The room would have been scattered with cushions and hung with plush curtains, while doors and further curtains between the pillars would have allowed for privacy, and for cool shade in the heat of the day. This, at least, is what they'd have you believe, and it's a very plausible scenario. Remember, though, that all this is speculation and some of it is pure hype;

the dolphin fresco, for example, was found in the courtyard, not the room itself, and would have been viewed from inside as a sort of *trompe l'oeil*, like looking through a glass-bottomed boat. Whatever the truth, this is an impressive example of Minoan architecture, the more so when you follow the dark passage around to the queen's **bathroom**. Here is a clay tub, protected behind a low wall (and again probably screened by curtains when in use), and the famous "flushing" toilet (a hole in the ground with drains to take the waste away – one flushed it by throwing a bucket of water down).

The much-pored over **drainage system** was a series of interconnecting terracotta pipes running underneath most of the palace. Guides to the site never fail to point these out as evidence of the advanced state of Minoan civilization, and they are indeed quite an achievement, in particular the system of baffles and overflows to slow down the runoff and avoid any danger of flooding. Just how much running water there would have been, however, is another matter; the water supply was, and is, at the bottom of the hill, and even the combined efforts of rainwater catchment and hauling water up to the palace can hardly have been sufficient to supply the needs of more than a small elite.

Going up the Grand Stairway to the floor above the queen's domain, you come to a set of rooms generally regarded as the **King's Quarters**. These are chambers in a considerably sterner vein; the staircase opens into a grandiose reception chamber known as the **Hall of the Royal Guard**, its walls decorated in repeated shield patterns. Immediately off here is the **Hall of the Double Axes**, believed to be have been the ruler's personal chamber, a double room that would allow for privacy in one portion while audiences were held in the more public section. Its name comes from the double-axe symbol carved into every block of masonry.

The Throne Room and the rest of the palace

Continuing to the top of the Grand Stairway, you emerge onto the broad **Central Court**. Open now, this would once have been enclosed by the walls of the buildings all around. On the far side, in the northwestern corner of the courtyard, is the entrance to another of Knossós's most atmospheric survivals, the **Throne Room**. Here, a worn stone throne sits against the wall of a surprisingly small chamber; along the walls around it are ranged stone benches, and behind there's a reconstructed fresco of two griffins. In all probability this was the seat of a priestess rather than a ruler (there's nothing like it in any other Minoan palace), but it may just have been an innovation wrought by the Mycenaeans, since it seems that this room dates only from the final period of Knossós's occupation. The Throne Room is now closed off with a wooden gate, but you can lean over this for a good view, and in the antechamber there's a wooden copy of the throne on which everyone perches to have their picture taken.

The rest you'll see as you wander, contemplating the legends of the place which blur with reality. Try not to miss the giant *pithoi* in the northeast quadrant of the site, an area known as the palace workshops; the storage chambers which you see from behind the Throne Room and the reproduction frescoes in the reconstructed room above it; the fresco of the Priest-King looking down on the south side of the central court, and the relief of a charging bull on its north side. This last would have greeted you if you entered the palace through its north door; you can see evidence here of some kind of gatehouse and a lustral bath, a sunken area perhaps used for ceremonial bathing and purification. Just outside this gate is the **theatral area**, an open space a little like a stepped amphitheatre, which may have been used for ritual performances or dances. From here the **Royal Road**, claimed as the oldest road in Europe, sets out. At one time, this probably ran right across the island; nowadays it ends after about a hundred yards in a brick wall beneath the modern road. Circling back around the outside of the palace, you get more idea of its scale by looking up at it; on the south side are a couple of small reconstructed Minoan houses which are worth exploring.

Beyond Knossós

If you have transport, the drive beyond Knossós can be an attractive and enjoyable one, taking minor roads through much greener country, with vineyards draped across low hills and flourishing agricultural communities. If you want specific things to seek out, head first for **MYRTIÁ**, an attractive village with the small **Kazantzakis Museum** (Mon, Wed & Sat 9am–1pm & 4pm–8pm, Tues & Fri 9am–1pm; 500dr) in a house where the writer's parents once lived. **ARKHÁNES**, at the foot of Mount Ioúktas, is a much larger place that was also quite heavily populated in Minoan times. None of the three archeological sites here is open to the public, but one of them, **Anemospília**, has caused huge controversy since its excavation in the 1980s: many traditional views of the Minoans, particularly that of Minoan life as peaceful and idyllic, have had to be rethought in the light of the discovery of an apparent human sacrifice. An excellent new museum (daily 8.30am–2.30pm, closed Tues; free) displays finds from this and other excavations. From Arhánes you can also drive to the top of Mount Ioúktas to enjoy the panoramic views. At **VATHÝPETRO**, south of the mountain, is a **Minoan villa** (Mon–Sat 8.30am–2pm; free), which once controlled the rich farmland south of Arkhánes. Inside a remarkable collection of farming implements was found, and a wine press. Substantial amounts of the farm buildings remain, and it's still surrounded by a vineyard three thousand five hundred years later – making it probably the oldest in Europe.

Southwest from Iráklion: sites and beaches

If you take a **tour** from Iráklion (or one of the resorts), you'll probably visit the **Górtys**, **Festós** and **Ayía Triádha** sites in a day, with a lunchtime swim at **Mátala** thrown in. Doing it by public transport, you'll be forced into a rather more leisurely pace, but there's still no reason why you shouldn't get to all three and reach Mátala within the day; if necessary, it's easy enough to hitch the final stretch. **Bus services** to the Festós site are excellent, with some nine a day to and from Iráklion (fewer run on Sunday), five of which continue to or come from Mátala; there are also services direct to Ayía Galíni. If you're arriving in the afternoon, plan to visit Ayía Triádha first, as it closes early.

The route to Áyii Dhéka

The road from Iráklion towards Festós is a pretty good one by the standards of Cretan mountain roads, albeit rather dull. The country you're heading towards is the richest agricultural land on the island, and right from the start the villages en route are large and business-like. In the largest of them, Ayía Varvára, there's a great rock outcrop known as the **Omphalos** (Navel) of Crete, supposedly the very centre of the island.

Past here, you descend rapidly to the fertile fields of the Messará plain, where the road joins the main route across the south near the village of **ÁYII DHÉKA**. For religious Cretans Áyii Dhéka is something of a place of pilgrimage; its name, "The Ten Saints", refers to ten early Christians martyred here under the Romans. In a crypt below the modern church you can see the martyrs' tombs. It's an attractive village to wander around, with several places to eat and even some **rooms** along the main road.

Górtys

Daily 8.30am–3pm; 800dr.

Within easy walking distance of Áyii Dhéka, either through the fields or along the main road, sprawls the site of **Górtys**, ruined capital of the Roman province that included not only Crete but also much of North Africa. Cutting across the fields will give you some idea of the scale of this city, at its zenith in approximately the third century AD; an enormous variety of other remains, including an impressive **theatre**, are strewn across your route. Even in Áyii Dhéka you'll see Roman pillars and statues lying around in people's yards or propping up their walls.

There had been a settlement here from the earliest times, but the extant ruins date almost entirely from the Roman era. Only now is the site being systematically excavated, by the Italian School. At the main entrance to the fenced site, alongside the road, are the ruins of the still impressive **basilica of Áyios Títos**; the eponymous saint converted the island to Christianity and was its first bishop. Beyond this is the **Odeion** which houses the most important discovery on the site, the **Law Code**. These great inscribed blocks of stone were incorporated by the Romans from a much earlier stage of the city's development; they're written in an obscure early Greek-Cretan dialect, and in a style known as *boustrophedon* (ox-ploughed), with the lines reading alternately in opposite directions like the furrows of a ploughed field. At ten metres by three metres, this is reputedly the largest Greek inscription ever found. The laws set forth reflect a strictly hierarchical society: five witnesses were needed to convict a free man of a crime, only one for a slave; raping a free man or woman carried a fine of a hundred staters, violating a serf only five. A small **museum** in a loggia (also within the fenced area) holds a number of large and finely worked sculptures found at Górtys, more evidence of the city's importance.

Míres

Some 20km west of Górtys, **MÍRES** is an important market and focal point of transport for the Messará plain: if you're switching buses to get from the beaches on the south coast to the archeological sites or the west, this is where you'll do it. There are good facilities including a **bank**, a few **restaurants** and plenty of **rooms**, though there's no particular reason to stay unless you are waiting for a bus or looking for work (it's one of the better places for agricultural jobs). Heading straight for Festós, there's usually no need to stop.

Festós

Daily 8am–6pm; 1200dr.

The **Palace of Festós** was excavated by the Italian, Federico Halbherr (also responsible for the early work at Górtys), at almost exactly the same time as Evans was working at Knossós. The style of the excavations, however, could hardly have been more different. Here, to the approval of most traditional archeologists, reconstruction was kept to an absolute minimum – it's all bare foundations, and walls which rise at most a metre above ground level. This means that despite a magnificent setting overlooking the plain of Messará, the palace at Festós is not as immediately arresting as those at Knossós or Mália. Much of the site is fenced off and, except in the huge central court, it's almost impossible to get any sense of the place as it was; the plan is almost as complex as at Knossós, with none of the reconstruction to bolster the imagination.

It's interesting to speculate why the palace was built halfway up a hill rather than on the plain below – certainly not for defence, for this is in no way a good defensive position. Psychological superiority over the peasants or reasons of health are both possible, but it seems quite likely that it was simply the magnificent view that finally swayed the decision. The site looks over Psilorítis to the north and the huge plain, with the Lasíthi mountains beyond it, to the east. Towards the top of Psilorítis you should be able to make out a small black smudge: the entrance to the Kamáres cave (see p.537).

On the ground closer at hand, you can hardly fail to notice the strong similarities between Festós and the other palaces: the same huge rows of storage jars, the great courtyard with

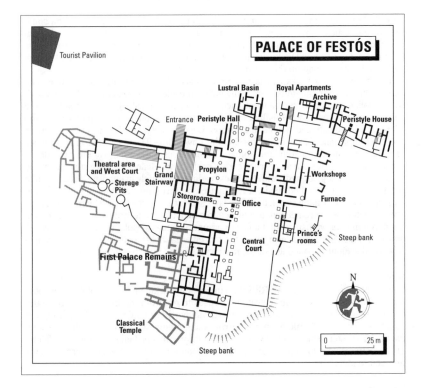

PALACE OF FESTÓS

Tourist Pavilion

Lustral Basin   Royal Apartments
Archive
Entrance   Peristyle Hall
Peristyle House
Theatral area
and West Court   Grand   Propylon
Storage   Stairway   Workshops
Pits
Storerooms   Office   Furnace
First Palace Remains   Prince's
rooms   Steep bank
Central
Court
Classical
Temple
Steep bank
N
0   25 m

its monumental stairway, and the theatral area. Unique to Festós, however, is the third court-yard, in the middle of which are the remains of a **furnace** used for metalworking. Indeed, this eastern corner of the palace seems to have been home to a number of craftsmen, including potters and carpenters. Oddly enough, Festós was much less ornately decorated than Knossós; there is no evidence, for example, of any of the dramatic Minoan wall paintings.

The **Tourist Pavilion** at Festós serves drinks and food and also has a few beds, though these are very rarely available (thanks to advance bookings) and expensive when they are. The nearby village of **ÁYIOS IOÁNNIS**, along the road towards Mátala, has a few more **rooms**, including some at *Taverna Ayios Ioannis* (☎0892/42 006) which is also a good place to eat.

Ayía Triádha

Daily 8.30am–3pm; 500dr.

Some of the finest artworks in the museum at Iráklion came from **Ayía Triádha**, about a 45-minute walk (or a short drive) from Festós. No one is quite sure what this site is, but the most common theory has it as some kind of royal summer villa. It's smaller than the palaces, but if anything even more lavishly appointed and beautifully situated. In any event, it's an attractive place to visit, far less crowded than Festós, with a wealth of interesting little details. Look out in particular for the row of **stores** in front of what was apparently a marketplace, and for the remains of the **paved road** that once led down to the Gulf of Messará. The sea itself looks invitingly close, separated from the base of the hill only by Timbáki airfield (mainly used for motor racing these days), but if you try to drive down there, it's almost impossible to find your way around the unmarked dust tracks. There's a fourteenth-century **church** at the site, worth visiting in its own right for the remains of ancient frescoes.

Mátala

MÁTALA has by far the best-known **beach** in Iráklion province, widely promoted and included in tours mainly because of the famous **caves** cut into the cliffs above its beautiful sands. These are believed to be ancient tombs first used by Romans or early Christians, but more recently inhabited by a sizeable hippie community. You'll still meet people who will assure you that this is *the* travellers' beach on Crete. Not any more it isn't. Today, the town is full of package tourists and tries hard to present a respectable image; the cliffs are now cleared and locked up every evening.

A few people still manage to evade the security, or sleep on the beach or in the adjacent campsite, but on the whole the place has changed entirely. The last ten years have seen the arrival of crowds and the development of hotels, discos and restaurants to service them; early afternoon, when the tour buses pull in for their swimming stop, sees the beach packed to overflowing. If you're prepared to accept Mátala for what it is – a resort of some size – you'll find the place more than bearable. The town beach is beautiful, and if the crowds get excessive, you can climb over the rocks in about twenty minutes (past more caves, many of which are inhabited through the summer) to another excellent stretch of sand, known locally as "Red Beach". In the evening, when the trippers have gone, there are waterside bars and restaurants looking out over invariably spectacular sunsets.

The chief problems concern prices and crowds: rooms are both expensive and oversubscribed, food is good but not cheap. If you want **accommodation**, try looking up the little street to the left as you enter town, just after the *Zafiria* hotel (☎0892/45 112; ④), where there are several rooms for rent, such as *Matala View* (☎0892/45 114; ②), and *Pension Nikos* (☎0892/42 375; ②). If these are full, then everywhere closer in is likely to be, too, so head back out on the main road, or try the **campsite**, *Camping of Matala* (☎0892/45 720), next to the beach above the car park; *Kommos Camping* (☎0892/45 596), is a nicer site, but a few kilometres out of Mátala and reached by heading back towards Pítsidia and turning left along a signed track. There are places to **eat and drink** all over the main part of town. Also impossible to miss are most other facilities, including stores, currency exchange, car and bike rental, travel agents, post office, and an OTE office in a temporary building in the car park behind the beach.

Around Mátala: Pitsídhia and Kalamáki

One way to enjoy a bit more peace is to stay at **PITSÍDHIA**, about 5km inland. This is already a well-used option, so it's not quite as cheap as you might expect, but there are plenty of rooms, lively places to eat and even music bars. If you decide to stay here, the beach at **KALAMÁKI** is an alternative to Mátala. Both beaches are approximately the same distance to walk, though there is a much better chance of a bus or a lift to Mátala. Kalamáki itself is beginning to develop somewhat, with a number of rooms and a couple of tavernas, but so far it's a messy and unattractive little place. The beach stretches for miles, surprisingly wild and windswept, lashed by sometimes dangerously rough surf. At the southern end (more easily reached by a path off the Pitsídhia–Mátala road) lies **Kómmos**, once a Minoan port serving Festós and now the site of a major archeological excavation. It's not yet open to the public, but you can peer into the fenced-off area to see what's been revealed so far, which is pretty impressive: dwellings, streets, hefty stonework and even the ship sheds where repairs on the Minoan fleet were carried out.

Iráklion's south coast

South of the Messará plain are two more beach resorts, Kalí Liménes and Léndas, with numerous other little beaches along the coast in between, but nothing spectacular. **Public transport** is very limited indeed; you'll almost always have to travel via Míres (see p.527). If you have your own transport, the roads in these parts are all passable, but most are very slow going; the Kófinas Hills, which divide the plain from the coast, are surprisingly precipitous.

Kalí Liménes

While Mátala itself was an important port under the Romans, the chief harbour for Górtys lay on the other side of Cape Líthinon at **KALÍ LIMÉNES**. Nowadays, this is once again a major port – for oil tankers. This has rather spoiled its chances of becoming a major resort, and there's no paved road or proper facilities. Some people like Kalí Liménes: the constant procession of tankers gives you something to look at, there are a number of places offering **rooms** – the best is the *Karavovrousi Beach* (☎0892/42 197; ②), a kilometre or so east of the village – the coastline is broken up by spectacular cliffs and, as long as there hasn't been a recent oil spill, the beaches are reasonably clean and totally empty. But (fortunately) not too many share this enthusiasm.

Léndas

LÉNDAS, further east along the coast, is far more popular, with a couple of buses daily from Iráklion and a partly justified reputation for being peaceful (sullied by considerable summer crowds). Many people who arrive think they've come to the wrong place, as at first sight the village looks filthy, the beach is small, rocky and dirty, and the rooms are frequently all booked. A number of visitors leave without ever correcting that initial impression, but the attraction of Léndas is not the village at all but on the other (west) side of the headland. Here, there's an enormous, excellent sandy beach, part of it usually taken over by nudists, and a number of taverna/bars overlooking it from the roadside. The beach is a couple of kilometres from Léndas, along a rough track; if you're walking, you can save time by cutting across the headland. A considerably more attractive prospect than staying in Léndas itself is **camping** on the beach to the west of the village, or with luck getting a **room** at one of the few beach tavernas – try *Tsarakis* (☎0892/95 378; ②) for sea-view rooms. After you've discovered the beach, even Léndas begins to look more welcoming, and at least it has most of the facilities you'll need, including a shop which will change money and numerous places to eat.

Once you've come to terms with the place, you can also explore some less good but quite deserted beaches eastwards, and the scrappy remains of **ancient Lebena** on a hilltop overlooking them. There was an important *Asclepieion* (temple of the god Asclepios) here around some now-diverted warm springs, but only the odd broken column and fragments of mosaic survive in a fenced-off area on the village's northern edge.

East of Iráklion: the package-tour coast

East of Iráklion, the startling pace of **tourist development** in Crete is all too plain to see. The merest hint of a beach is an excuse to build at least one hotel, and these are outnumbered by the concrete shells of resorts-to-be. It's hard to find a room in this monument to the package-tour industry, and expensive if you do.

Goúrnes and Goúves

As a general rule, the further you go, the better things get: when the road detours all too briefly inland, the real Crete of olive groves and stark mountains asserts itself. You certainly won't see much of it at **GOÚRNES**, where there used to be a US Air Force base, or at nearby Kato Goúves, where there's a **campsite**, *Camping Creta* (☎0897/41 400), which will be quiet unless and until the Greek Air Force move in next door as planned. From here, however, you can head inland to the old village of **GOÚVES**, a refreshing contrast, and just beyond to the **Skotinó Cave**, one of the largest and most spectacular on the island (about an hour's walk from the coast).

Not far beyond Goúrnes is the turning for the direct route up to the Lasíthi plateau, and shortly after that you roll into the first of the big resorts, Hersónisos (or, more correctly, Límin Hersonísou; Hersónisos is the village in the hills just behind, also overrun by tourists).

Khersónisos (Límin Khersonísou)

KHERSÓNISOS was once the port that served the Minoan city of Knossós, and was more recently just a small fishing village; today it's the most popular of Crete's package resorts. If what you want is plenty of bars, tavernas, restaurants and Eurodisco nightlife then come here. The resort has numerous small patches of sand beach between rocky outcrops, but a shortage of places to stay in peak season.

Along the modern seafront, a solid line of restaurants and bars is broken only by the occasional souvenir shop: in their midst you'll find a small pyramidal Roman **fountain** with broken mosaics of fishing scenes, the only real relic of the ancient town of Chersonesos. Around the headland above the harbour and in odd places along the seafront, you can see remains of Roman harbour installations, mostly submerged.

Beach and clubs excepted, the distractions of Khersónisos comprise **Lychnostatis** (daily 9.30am–2pm; 1000dr), an open-air "museum" of traditional Crete, on the coast on the eastern edge of the town; a small **aquarium** just off the main road at the west end of town, opposite the *Hard Rock Cafe* (daily 10am–9pm; 800dr); the watersports paradise *Star Water Park* (admission free, charges for individual sports) at the eastern end of the resort; and, a few kilometres inland, the slides, cascades and whirlpools of the newly opened and immense *Aqua Splash Water Park* (daily 10am–7pm; 3700dr, discounted rates after 2.30pm).

A short distance inland are the three **hill villages** of Koutoulafári, Piskopianó and "old" Khersónisos, which all have a good selection of tavernas, and are worth searching out for accommodation.

Practicalities

Khersónisos is well provided with all the back-up **services** you need to make a holiday go smoothly. Banks, bike and car rental, post office and OTE are all on or just off the main drag, as are the taxi ranks. **Buses** in either direction leave every thirty minutes.

Finding somewhere to stay can be difficult in July and August. Much of the **accommodation** here is allocated to package-tour operators and what remains is not that cheap. To check for availability of accommodation generally, the quickest and best option is to enquire at one of the many travel agencies along the main street, or ask at the helpful **tourist office** – officially housed on Giaboudháki, just off the main street towards the harbour, but at the time of writing temporarily evicted to a small kiosk beside the newsstands in front of the church at the western end of the main street. Reasonably priced central options include the *Nancy* on Ayía Paraskevís (☎0897/22 212; ④), and *Virginia* on

Mákhis Krítis (☎0897/22 466; ②), but be prepared for a fair amount of noise. There are two good **campsites**, one at the eastern end of town, *Caravan Camping* (☎0897/22 025 or 24 718) which also has several reed-roofed bungalows, and *Hersonissos Camping* (☎0897/22 902 or 23 792), just to the west of town. The youth hostel was recently closed, and there are no current plans for a replacement.

Despite the vast number of **eating places**, there are few in Khersónisos worth recommending, and the tavernas down on the harbour front should be avoided. One of the few Greek tavernas that stands out is *Kavouri* along Arkhéou Theátrou, but it is fairly expensive, so it's better to head out of town on the Piskopianó road where, near the junction to Koutoulafári, the friendly *Fengari* taverna serves good Greek food at a reasonable price. Sitting at your table overlooking the street below you can marvel at the steady trek of clubbers heading down the hill to the bars and nightclubs of Khersónisos. The hill villages have the greatest selection of tavernas, particularly Koutoulafári, where you can have a relaxed evening amongst the narrow streets and small platías.

Khersónisos is renowned for its **nightlife**, and there's no shortage of it. Most of the better bars and clubs are along the main road. Especially popular are *La Luna*, with up-to-date music, and the *Hard Rock Café*, which has live music. *Aria*, a large glass-fronted disco, is the biggest on Crete. Other popular haunts include *Legend*, and the beach bar-disco pub *Pirates*, both at the eastern end of town, and, towards the harbour, *Camelot*, *Blackout* and *New York*. If you fancy a quiet drink then you have come to the wrong resort, but you could try *Kahluai Beach Cocktail Bar* or *Haris Ouzo* and *Raki Place* (beneath the *Hotel Virginia*). There is an open-air **cinema** at the *Creta Maris* hotel.

Stalídha

STALÍDHA is a Cinderella town, sandwiched in between its two louder, brasher and some would say uglier sisters, Mália and Khersónisos , but is neither quiet or undeveloped. This rapidly expanding beach resort, with more than sixty tavernas and bars and a few discos, can offer the best of both worlds with a friendlier and more relaxed setting, a better beach (and usual array of water sports) and very easy access to its two livelier neighbours. The town essentially consists of a single, relatively traffic-free street which rings the seafront for more than two miles, before the apartment blocks briefly become fewer and further, until the mass development of Mália begins.

Finding a place to stay can be difficult as **accommodation** is almost entirely in studio and apartment blocks which are booked by package companies in high season. Out of season, however, you may well be able to negotiate a very reasonable price for a studio apartment complete with swimming pool; ask in the central travel agencies first, as they will know what is available, and expect to pay at least 8000dr for two. Finding somewhere to **eat** is less difficult as there are plenty of rather ordinary tavernas, the best and most authentic being *Maria's* and the *Hellas Taverna*, both at the western end of the resort.

Stalídha is completely overshadowed by its neighbours when it comes to **nightlife**, though you can dance at *Bells* disco, on the main coast road, or at *Rhythm*, on the beach; the *Sea Wolf Cocktail Bar* and *Akti Bar* are near each other along the beach.

Mália

Much of **MÁLIA** is taken up by the package industry, so in peak season finding a place to stay is not always easy. You're best off, especially if you want any sleep, trying one of the numerous **rooms** and **pensions** (③) signposted in the old town, such as the *Esperia* (☎0897/31 086; ②). Tracking back from here, along the main Iráklion road, there are a number of reasonably priced **pensions** on the left including the *Argo* (☎0897/31 636; ④), though these can be noisy. If you really want to be in the centre of things, try *Kostas* (☎0897/31 485; ④), a family-run pension incongruously located behind the mini golf at the end of the beach road. Otherwise, on arrival visit one of the travel companies along the main road – for example, Foreign Office (☎0897/31 217) – to enquire about accommodation availability. To the east of town, the new **youth hostel** (☎0897/31 555; ①) is extremely pleasant, but should be booked in advance in high season.

Eating in Mália is unlikely to be a problem as **restaurants** jostle for your custom at every step, especially along the beach road. None of these are particularly good, but that's the price of mass production. The best places are around Platía Ayíou Dhimitríou, a pleasant square beside the church in the centre of the old town. Try a meal at *Kalesma, Yiannis, Kalimera* or *Petros*, after an aperitif at the *Ouzeri Kapilla*, where they serve excellent local wine from the wood. There are a number of other welcoming tavernas and very pleasant bars, including the *Stone House* and *Temple*, lining, or just off, the platía.

The beach road comes into its own at night, when the profusion of **bars**, **discos** and **clubs** erupt into a pulsating cacophony. *Zoo* is a relatively new club, and once past midnight, one of the internal walls parts to reveal an even larger dance area. The club's newest attraction, its body piercing studio (the only one in Crete), opens at 2am. *Zig Zag, Takis* and *Highway* are the other really popular clubs in Mália. *Desire*, along the beach road, concentrates on rock and has good-quality live music some nights. Unfortunately, a good night's clubbing and dancing is frequently spoiled by groups of drunken youths pouring out of the bars. The situation has got so bad that tour operators have threatened to pull out of the resort if action isn't taken to deal with the hooligans.

The Palace of Mália

Daily 8.30am–3pm; 800dr, Sun free.

Much less imposing than either Knossós or Festós, the **Palace of Mália**, 2km east of Mália town, in some ways surpasses both. For a start, it's a great deal emptier and you can wander among the remains in relative peace. While no reconstruction has been attempted, the palace was never reoccupied after its second destruction, so the ground plan is virtually intact. It's a great deal easier to comprehend than Knossós and, if you've seen the reconstructions there, it's easy to envisage this seaside palace in its days of glory. There's a real feeling of an ancient civilization with a taste for the good life, basking on the rich agricultural plain between the Lasíthi mountains and the sea.

From this site came the famous **gold pendant** of two bees (which can be seen in the Iráklion museum or on any postcard stand), allegedly part of a horde that was plundered and whose other treasures can now be found in the British Museum in London. The beautiful leopard-head axe, also in the museum at Iráklion, was another of the treasures found here. At the site, look out for the strange indented stone in the central court, which probably held ritual offerings, for the remains of ceremonial stairways, and for the giant *pithoi* which stand like sentinels around the palace. To the south and west, digs are still going on as a large town comes slowly to light, and these will soon be viewable via an overhead walkway, under construction at the time of writing.

Any passing **bus** should stop at the site, or you could even rent a **bike** for a couple of hours as it's a pleasant, flat ride from Mália town. Leaving the archeological zone and turning right, you can follow the road down to a lovely stretch of clean and relatively peaceful beach, backed by fields, scrubland and a single makeshift taverna,

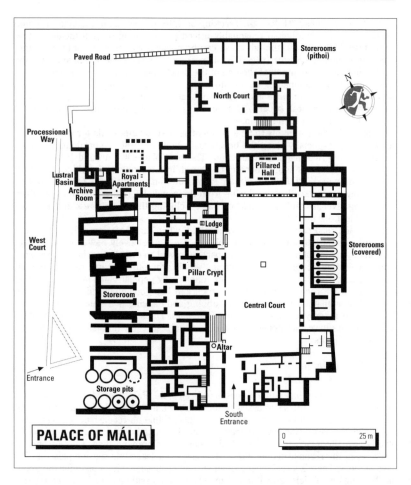

Paved Road

Storerooms (pithoi)

North Court

N

Processional Way

Lustral Basin

Royal Apartments

Archive Room

Pillared Hall

Lodge

West Court

Storerooms (covered)

Pillar Crypt

Storeroom

Central Court

Altar

Entrance

Storage pits

South Entrance

PALACE OF MÁLIA

0   25 m

which serves excellent fresh fish. From here you can walk back along the shore to Mália or take a bus (every thirty minutes in either direction) from the stop on the main road.

Sísi and Mílatos

Head **east** from the Palace of Mália, and it's not long before the road leaves the coast, climbing across the hills towards Áyios Nikólaos. If you want to escape the frenetic pace of all that has gone before, try continuing to **SÍSI** or **MÍLATOS**. These little shore villages are bypassed by the main road as it cuts inland, and are still very much in the early stages of the tourist industry, though both have several tavernas. Sísi, the more developed of the two, also has its first disco bar (*Minoa*), a large new holiday complex (*Kalimera Krita*) a couple of kilometres to the east, and even a post office – a sure sign of resort status. Accommodation in both is mainly in studios and apartments; it's best to ask in the travel agencies for details of availability. In Sísi there's also a small pension, *Elena* (②) just behind the harbour, and a **campsite** (☎0841/71 247), whilst in Mílatos, rooms can be found in the old village, 2km inland. The village beaches aren't great, but the resorts make for a refreshing change of pace, and there are some fine, deep aprons of sand in the rocky coves beyond the resort centres.

West of Iráklion: around Psilorítis

Most people heading west from Iráklion, speed straight out on the new **coastal highway**, nonstop to Réthymnon. If you're in a hurry this is not such a bad plan; the road is fast and spectacular, hacked into the sides of mountains which for the most part drop straight to the sea, though there are no more than a couple of places where you might consider stopping. By contrast, the old roads inland are agonizingly slow, but they do pass through a whole string of **attractive villages** beneath the heights of the Psilorítis range. From here you can set out to explore the **mountains** and even walk across them to emerge in villages with views of the south coast.

The coastal route towards Réthymnon

Leaving the city, the **new highway** runs behind a stretch of highly developed coast, where the hotels compete for shore space with a cement works and power station. As soon as you reach the mountains, though, all this is left behind and there's only the clash of rock and sea to contemplate. As you start to climb, look out for **Paleókastro**, beside a bridge which carries the road over a small cove; the castle is so weathered as to be almost invisible against the brownish face of the cliff.

Ayía Pelayía and Fódhele

Some 3km below the highway, as it rounds the first point, lies the resort of **AYÍA PELAYÍA**. It looks extremely attractive from above but, once there, you're likely to find the narrow, taverna-lined beach packed to full capacity; this is not somewhere to roll up without a reserved room, although the Pagosimo travel agency (☎081/811 402) can usually come up with something, even at the last minute. Out of season you might find a real bargain at an apartment and, despite the high season crowds, the resort maintains a dignity long since lost in Mália and Hersonisos, and even a certain exclusivity; a couple of Crete's most luxurious hotels, including the enormous *Paradise Creta* (☎0834/51 570, fax 51 151; ⑨) nestle on the headland just beyond the main town beach.

Not far beyond Ayía Pelayía, there's a turning inland to the village of **FÓDHELE**, allegedly El Greco's birthplace. A plaque from the University of Toledo acknowledges the claim and, true or not, the community has built a small tourist industry on that basis. There are a number of craft shops and some pleasant tavernas where you can sit outside along the river. A peaceful 1km walk (or drive) takes you to the spuriously titled "El Greco's house" and the picturesque Byzantine **church of the Panagia** (Mon–Fri 9.30am–5pm; free). None of this amounts to very much but it is a pleasant, relatively unspoiled village if you simply want to sit in peace for a while. A couple of **buses** a day run here from Iráklion, and there's the odd tour; if you arrive on a direct bus, the walk back down to the highway (about 3km), where you can flag down a passing service, is not too strenuous.

Balí and Pánormos

BALÍ, on the coast approximately halfway between Iráklion and Réthymnon, also used to be tranquil and undeveloped, and by the standards of the north coast it still is in many ways. The village is built around a couple of small coves, some 2km from the highway (a hot walk from the bus), and is similar to Ayía Pelayía except that the beaches are not quite as good and there are no big hotels, just an ever-growing proliferation of studios, apartment buildings, rooms for rent, and a number of "modest hotels" (brochure-speak). You'll have plenty of company here; the last and best beach, known as "Paradise", no longer really deserves the name; it's a beautiful place to splash about, surrounded by mountains rising straight from the sea, but there's rarely a spare inch on the sand.

Continuing along the coast, the last stop before you emerge on the flat stretch leading to Réthymnon is at **PÁNORMOS**. This makes a good stopover if you're in search of somewhere more peaceful and authentic. The small sandy beach can get crowded when boats bring day trippers from Réthymnon, but most of the time the attractive village remains relatively unspoiled, and succeeds in clinging to its Greek identity. There are several decent tavernas and rooms places, one large hotel and the very comfortable *Pension Lucy* (☎0834/51 212; ③).

Inland towards Mount Psilorítis

Of the **inland routes**, the old main road (via Márathos and Dhamásta) is not the most interesting. This, too, was something of a bypass in its day and there are few places of any size or appeal, though it's a very scenic drive. If you want to dawdle, you're better off on the road which cuts up to **Tílissos** and then goes via **Anóyia**. It's a pleasant ride through fertile valleys filled with olive groves and vineyards, a district (the Malevísi) renowned from Venetian times for the strong, sweet Malmsey wine.

Týlissos and Anóyia

TÝLISSOS has a significant archeological site (daily 9am–3pm; 500dr) where three Minoan houses were excavated; unfortunately, its reputation is based more on what was found here (many pieces in the Iráklion museum) and on its significance for archeologists than on anything which remains to be seen. Still, it's worth a look, if you're passing, for a glimpse of Minoan life away from the big palaces, and for the tranquillity of the pine-shaded remains.

ANÓYIA is a much more tempting place to stay, especially if the summer heat is becoming oppressive. Spilling prettily down a hillside close below the highest peaks of the mountains, it looks traditional, but closer inspection shows that most of the buildings are actually concrete; the village was destroyed during World War II and the local men rounded up and shot – one of the German reprisals for the abduction of General Kreipe. The town has a reputation as a **handicrafts** centre (especially for woven and woollen goods), skills acquired both through bitter necessity after most of the men had been killed, and in a conscious attempt to revive the town. At any rate it worked, for the place is thriving today – thanks, it seems, to a buoyant agricultural sector and the number of elderly widows keen to subject any visitor to their terrifyingly aggressive sales techniques.

Quite a few people pass through Anóyia during the day, but not many of them stay, even though there are some good pensions and rented rooms in the upper half of the town, including the *Kriti* (☎0834/31 048; ②), *Avis* (☎0834/31 360, fax 31 058; ②) and *Ariste* (☎0834/31 459; ③) which has en-suite rooms. The town has a very different, more traditional ambience at night, and the only problem is likely to be finding somewhere to **eat**: although there are plenty of snack bars and so-called tavernas, most have extremely basic menus, more or less limited to barbecued lamb which is the local speciality.

Mount Psilorítis and its caves

Heading for the mountains, a rough track leads 13km from Anóyia to the **Nídha plateau** at the base of Mount Psilorítis. Here there's a taverna that used to let rooms but seems now to have closed to the public altogether, though it's still used by groups of climbers. A short path leads from the taverna to the celebrated **Idhéon Ándhron** (Idean Cave), a rival of that on Mount Dhíkti (see p.538) for the title of Zeus's birthplace, and certainly associated from the earliest of times with the cult of Zeus. There's a major archeological dig going on inside, which means the whole cave is fenced off, with a miniature railway running into it to carry all the rubble out. In short, you can see nothing.

The taverna also marks the start of the way to the top of **Mount Psilorítis** (2456m), Crete's highest mountain, a climb that for experienced, properly shod hikers is not at all arduous. The route is well marked with the usual red dots, and it should be a six- to seven-hour return journey to the chapel at the summit, although in spring, thick snow may slow you down.

If you're prepared to camp on the plateau (it's very cold, but there's plenty of available water) or can prevail on the taverna to let you in, you could continue on foot next day down to the southern slopes of the range. It's a beautiful hike, at least while the road they're attempting to blast through is out of sight, and also relatively easy, four hours or so down a fairly clear path to **VORÍZIA**. If you're still interested in caves, there's a more rewarding one above the nearby village of **KAMÁRES**, a climb of some three hours on a good path. Both Vorízia and Kamáres have a few **rooms** and some tavernas, at least one daily **bus** down to Míres, and alternate (more difficult) routes to the peak of Psilorítis if you want to approach from this direction.

EASTERN CRETE

Eastern Crete is dominated by **Áyios Nikólaos**, and while it is a highly developed resort, by no means all of the east is like this. Far fewer people venture beyond the road south to **Ierápetra** and into the eastern isthmus, where only **Sitía** and the famous beach at **Vái** ever see anything approaching a crowd. Inland, too, there's interest, especially on the extraordinary **Lasíthi** plateau, which is worth a night's stay if only to observe its abidingly rural life.

Inland to the Lasíthi plateau

Leaving the palace at Mália, the highway cuts inland towards **NEÁPOLI**, soon beginning a spectacular climb into the mountains. Set in a high valley, Neápoli is a market town little touched by tourism. There is one hotel, some rooms, a modern church and a couple of museums. Beyond the town, it's about twenty minutes before the bus suddenly emerges high above the Gulf of Mirabéllo and Áyios Nikólaos, the island's biggest resort. If you're stopping, Neápoli also marks the second point of access to the **Lasíthi Plateau**.

Scores of bus tours drive up here daily to view the "thousands of white-cloth-sailed windmills" which irrigate the high plain, and most groups will be disappointed. There are very few working windmills left, and these operate only for limited periods (mainly in June). This is not to say the trip is not justified, as it would be for the drive alone, and there are many other compensations. The plain is a fine example of rural Crete at work, every inch devoted to the cultivation of potatoes, apples, pears, figs, olives and a host of other crops; stay in one of the villages for a night or two and you'll see real life return as the tourists leave. There are plenty of easy rambles around the villages as well, through orchards and past the rusting remains of derelict windmills. You'll find rooms in the main town of **TZERMIÁDHO**, and at Áyios Konstandínos, Áyios Yeóryios – where you'll find a **folk museum**, and the friendly *Hotel Dias* (☎0844/31 207; ②) – and Psykhró.

Psykhró and the Dhiktean cave

PSYKHRÓ is much the most visited, as it's the base for visiting Lasíthi's other chief attraction, the birthplace of Zeus, the **Dhiktean Cave** (daily 8am–6.45pm, reduced hours off season; 800dr; watch out for slippery stones inside). In legend, Zeus's father, the Titan Kronos, was warned that he would be overthrown by a son and accordingly ate all his offspring; however, when Rhea gave birth to Zeus in the cave, she fed Kronos a stone and left the child concealed, protected by the Kouretes, who beat their shields outside to disguise his cries. The rest, as they say, is history (or at least myth). There's an obvious path running up to the cave from Psykhró and, whatever you're told, you don't have to have a guide if you don't want one, though you will need some form of illumination. On the other hand, it is hard to resist the guides, who do make the visit much more interesting, and they're not expensive if you can get a small group together (2000dr for up to ten people). It takes a Cretan imagination to pick out Rhea and the baby Zeus from the lesser stalactites and stalagmites.

Buses run around the plateau to Psykhró direct from Iráklion and from Áyios Nikólaos via Neápoli. Both roads offer spectacular views, coiling through a succession of passes guarded by lines of ruined windmills.

Áyios Nikólaos and around

ÁYIOS NIKÓLAOS ("Ag Nik" to the majority of its British visitors) is set around a supposedly bottomless **salt lake**, now connected to the sea to form an inner harbour. It is supremely picturesque and has some style and confidence, which it exploits to the full. The lake and port are surrounded by restaurants and bars, which charge above the odds, and whilst still very popular, some tourists are distinctly surprised to find themselves in a place with no decent beach at all.

There are swimming opportunities further north however, where the pleasant low-key resort of **Eloúnda** is the gateway to the mysterious islet of **Spinalónga**, and some great back country to the north – perfect to explore on a scooter. Inland from Áyios Nikólaos, **Kritsá**, with its famous church and textile sellers is a tour-bus mecca, but just a couple of kilometres away, the imposing ruins of **ancient Lató** are usually deserted.

Áyios Nikólaos practicalities

The greatest concentration of **stores** and **travel agents** are on the hill between the bridge and Platía Venizélou. The main **ferry agent** is LANE (☎0841/26 465 or 23 090) opposite the OTE (daily 7am–10pm in high season), on the corner of 25-Martíou and K Sfakianáki. The **post office** (Mon–Fri 7.30am–8pm, Sat 7.30am–2pm) is halfway up Koundoúrou. The **tourist office** (daily 8.30am–9.30pm; ☎0841/22 357, fax 82 534), situated between the lake and the port, is one of the best on the island for information about accommodation. To hire a scooter or mountain bike try Mike Manolis, 25-Maritíou (☎0841/24 940), near the OTE office. Good car deals are available at Club Cars, 28-Oktobríou 24, near the post office.

Accommodation

The town is no longer packed solid with tourists, so it is much easier to find a place to stay, though in the peak season you won't have so much choice. One thing in your favour is that there are literally thousands of **rooms**, scattered all around town. The tourist office normally has a couple of boards with cards and brochures about hotels and rooms, including their prices. If the prices seem very reasonable it is because they

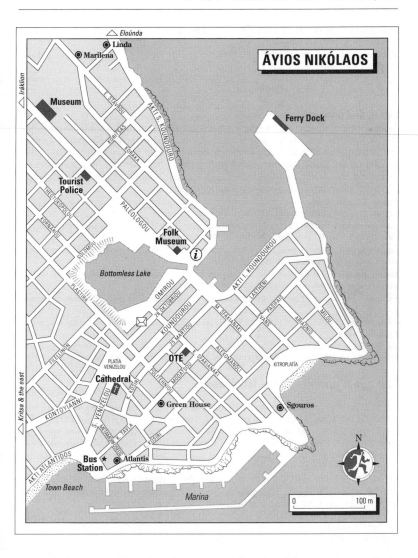

are for the low season. There is no longer a youth hostel, and the nearest **campsite** is *Gournia Moon*, 17km away (see p.541).

Atlantis, (☎0841/28 964) Nothing special but handy for the bus station; there's a snack bar below for breakfast. ②.

Green House, Modhátsou 15 (☎0841/22 025). Probably the best cheap place to stay in town; clean with shared facilities. ①.

Katerina, Stratigoú Kóraka 30 (☎0841/22 766). A pension close to the *Marilena* and another good choice in the same price bracket. ②.

Lida, Salamínos 3a (☎0841/22 130, fax 26 433). All the rooms in this friendly hotel have a shower, balcony and a partial seaview. ③.

Marilena, Érithrou Stavroú 14 (☎0841/22 681, fax 22 681). One of the cheaper pensions, this is excellent value. ③.

Sgouros, Kotroplatía (☎0841/28 931, fax 25 568). Modern hotel overlooking one of the town's beaches, and close to plenty of tavernas. ④.

Eating and drinking

At least when it comes to eating there's no chance of missing out, even if the prices are fancier than the restaurants. There are tourist-oriented **tavernas** all around the lake and harbour and little to choose between them, apart from the different perspectives you get on the passing fashion show. Have a **drink** here perhaps, or a mid-morning coffee and choose somewhere else to eat. The places around the Kiroplatía are generally fairer value, but again you are paying for the location.

Aouas, Paleológou 40. This taverna serves good, traditional Cretan food in and under a plant-covered trellised courtyard, and is reasonably cheap.

Café Migomis, Nikoláov Plastíra 22. Pleasant café high above the bottomless lake with a stunning view. Perfect place for breakfast, afternoon or evening drinks.

La Strada, just below the west side of Platía Venizélou. Authentic and good value pizza and pasta, should you fancy a change of cuisine.

Itanos, Kýprou 1, off the east side of Platía Venizélou. Popular with locals, this taverna serves Cretan food and wine, and has a terrace across the road opposite.

Pelagos, on Kóraka, just back off the lake behind the tourist office. A stylish fish taverna, serving good pricey food.

Ofou To Lo, Kitroplatía. Best of the moderately priced places on the seafront here: the food is consistently good.

To Ellinikon, just off the west side of Platía Venizélou. Great little traditional taverna run by the ebullient Yanna, who cooks up tasty country dishes accompanied by local wine and raki.

The coast north of Áyios Nikólaos

North of Áyios Nikólaos, the swankier hotels are strung out along the coast road, with upmarket restaurants, discos and cocktail bars scattered between them. **ELOÚNDA**, a resort on a more acceptable scale, is about 8km out along this road. Buses run regularly, but if you feel like renting a moped it's a spectacular ride, with impeccable views over a gulf dotted with islands and moored supertankers. Ask at the bookshop on the central square facing the sea, about the attractive seaview *Delfinia Apartments* (☎0841/41 641, fax 41 515; ③), or try the friendly *Pension Oasis* (☎0841/41 076, fax 41 218; ②) just off the square. Alternatively, one of the many travel agents around the main square, such as Olous Travel, can help with finding a room or apartment.

Just before the village a track (signposted) leads across a causeway to the "sunken city" of **Oloús**. There are restored windmills, a short length of canal, Venetian salt pans and a well preserved dolphin mosaic, but of the sunken city itself no trace beyond a couple of walls in about two feet of water. At any rate swimming is good, though there are sea urchins to watch out for.

From Eloúnda, kaïkia run to the fortress-rock of **Spinalónga**. As a bastion of the Venetian defence, this tiny islet withstood the Turkish invaders for 45 years after the mainland had fallen; in more recent decades, it served as a leper colony. As you watch the boat which brought you disappear to pick up another group, an unnervingly real sense of the desolation of those years descends. **PLÁKA**, back on the mainland, used to be the colony's supply point; now it is a haven from the crowds, with a small pebble beach and a couple of ramshackle tavernas. There are boat trips daily from Áyios Nikólaos to Oloús, Eloúnda and Spinalónga, usually visiting at least one other island along the way.

Inland to Kritsá and Lató

The other excursion everyone from Áyios Nikólaos takes is to **KRITSÁ**, a "traditional" village about 10km inland. Buses run at least every hour from the bus station, and despite the commercialization it's still a good trip: the local **crafts** (weaving, ceramics and embroidery basically, though they sell almost everything here) are fair value, and it's also a welcome break from living in the fast lane at "Ag Nik". In fact, if you're looking for somewhere to stay around here, Kritsá has a number of advantages: chiefly availability of **rooms**, better prices, and something at least approaching a genuinely Greek atmosphere; try *Argyro* (☎0841/51 174; ②) on your way to the village. There are a number of decent places to eat, too, or just to have a coffee and a cake under one of the plane trees.

On the approach road, some 2km before Kritsá, is the lovely Byzantine **church of Panayía Kyrá** (Mon–Sat 9am–3pm, Sun 9am–2pm; 800dr), inside which is preserved perhaps the most complete set of Byzantine frescoes in Crete. The fourteenth- and fifteenth-century works have been much retouched, but they're still worth the visit. Excellent (and expensive) reproductions are sold from a shop alongside. Just beyond the church, a surfaced road leads off towards the archeological site of **Lató** (Tues–Sun 8.30am–3pm; free), a Doric city with a grand hilltop setting. The city itself is extensive, but neglected, presumably because visitors and archeologists on Crete are concerned only with the Minoan era. Ruins aside, you could come here just for the views: west over Áyios Nikólaos and beyond to the bay and Oloús (which was Lató's port), and inland to the Lasíthi mountains.

The eastern isthmus

The main road south and then east from Áyios Nikólaos is not a wildly exciting one, essentially a drive through barren hills sprinkled with villas and above the occasional sandy cove. Five kilometres beyond a cluster of development at Kaló Khório, a track is signed on the right for the **Moní Faneroméni**. The track is a rough one and climbs dizzily skywards for 6km, giving spectacular views over the Gulf of Mirabélo along the way. The view from the monastery itself must be the among the finest in Crete. To get into the rather bleak looking monastery buildings, knock loudly. You will be shown up to the chapel, built into a cave sanctuary, and the frescoes are quite brilliant.

Gourniá, Pakhiá Ámmos and Mókhlos

Back on the coast road, it's another 2km to the site of **Gourniá** (Tues–Sun 8.30am–3pm; 500dr), slumped in the saddle between two low peaks. The most completely preserved **Minoan town**, its narrow alleys and stairways intersect a throng of one-roomed houses centred on a main square, and the house of the local ruler. Although less impressive than the great palaces, the site is strong on revelations about the lives of the ordinary people ruled from Knossós. Its desolation today (you are likely to be alone save for a dozing guard) only serves to heighten the contrast with what must have been a cramped and raucous community 3500 years ago.

It is tempting to cross the road here and take one of the paths through the wild thyme to the sea for a swim. Don't bother – the bay and others along this part of the coastline act as a magnet for every piece of floating detritus dumped off Crete's north coast. There is a larger beach, and rooms to rent, in the next bay along at **PAKHIÁ ÁMMOS**, about twenty minutes' walk, where there is also an excellent fish taverna, *Aiolus*; or in the other direction, there's the campsite of *Gournia Moon*, with its own small cove and a swimming pool.

This is the narrowest part of the island, and from here a fast new road cuts across the isthmus to Ierápetra in the south. In the north though, the route on towards Sitía is one of the most exhilarating in Crete. Carved into cliffs and mountain sides, the road teeters above the coast before plunging inland at Kavoúsi. Of the beaches you see below, only **MÓKHLOS** is at all accessible, some 5km below the main road. This sleepy village has a few rooms, a hotel or two and a number of tavernas; if you find yourself staying the night, try the rooms at *Limenaria* (☎0841/94 206; ②). Nearer Sitía the familiar olive groves are interspersed with vineyards, and in late summer the grapes, spread to dry in the fields and on rooftops, make an extraordinary sight in the varying stages of their slow change from green to gold to brown.

Sitía

SITÍA is the port and main town of the relatively unexploited eastern edge of Crete. It's a pleasant if unremarkable place, offering a plethora of waterside restaurants, a long sandy beach and a lazy lifestyle little affected even by the thousands of visitors in peak season. There's an almost Latin feel to the town, reflected in (or perhaps caused by) the number of French and Italian tourists, and it's one of those places you may end up staying longer than you intended. For entertainment, there's the **beach**, providing good swimming and windsurfing, and in town a mildly entertaining **folklore museum** (Tues–Sun 9.30am–2.30pm; Wed & Thurs also 6pm–8pm; 500dr), a Venetian fort and Roman fish tanks to explore, and an interesting **archeological museum** (Tues–Sun 8.30am–3pm; 500dr). Look out, too, for the town's resident pelican, Níkos, who has his own living quarters on the harbour quay.

Practicalities

There are plenty of cheap pensions and **rooms**, especially in the streets around the **OTE**, a good **youth hostel** (☎0843/22 693; ①) on the main road as it enters town, and rarely any problem about sleeping on the beach (though it is worth going a little way out of town to avoid any danger of being rousted by the police). For rooms, try *Pension Venus*, Kondhiláki 60 (☎0843/24 307; ②), *Hotel Arhontiko*, Kondhiláki 16 (☎0843/28 172; ②), and *Hotel Nora*, Rouseláki 31 (☎0843/23 017; ②) near the ferry port; if you have problems finding somewhere to stay, the **tourist police** at Anthéon 5 near the bus station (8.30am–7pm; ☎0843/23 590) may be able to help.

For **food**, the waterside places are rather expensive; the best value choices near here are the *Itanos Cafe* for mezédhes and *Creta House* serving traditional island dishes, both at the start of the beach road (Konstadínou Karamanlí). Authentic Belgian crepes are to be had at *Creperie Mike*, Elvenizélou 162, to the east of Zorbas. **Nightlife** centres on a few bars and discos near the ferry dock and out along the beach. The town's monster disco, *Planitarion*, attracts crowds from all over the east. It's a kilometre beyond the ferry port (see map), and is best reached by taxi. The one major excitement of the year is the August **Sultana Festival** – a celebration of the big local export, with traditional dancing and all the locally produced wine you can consume included in the entrance to the fairground.

Onward to Vái beach and Palékastro

Leaving Sitía along the beach, the Vái road climbs above a rocky, unexceptional coastline before reaching a fork to the **Monastery of Toploú** (daily 9am–1pm & 2pm–6pm; 700dr). The monastery's forbidding exterior reflects a history of resistance to invaders, but doesn't prepare you for the gorgeous flower-decked cloister within. The blue-robed monks keep out of the way as far as possible, but their cells and refectory are left discreetly on view. In the church is one of the masterpieces of Cretan art, the eighteenth-century icon *Lord Thou Art Great*. Outside you can buy enormously expensive reproductions.

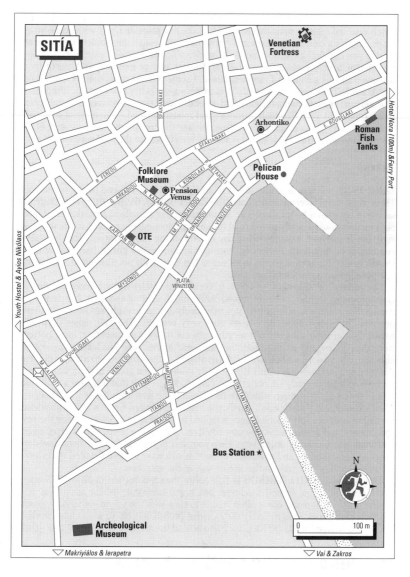

SITÍA

Venetian
Fortress

Arhontiko

Roman
Fish
Tanks

Folklore
Museum

Pelican
House

Pension
Venus

OTE

PLATÍA
VENIZELOU

Bus Station ★

N

Archeological
Museum

0   100 m

SFAKIANAKI

SFAKIANAKI

E. ROUSELAKI

R. FEREOU

I. KONDILAKI

METAXAKI

G. ARKADIOU

N. KAZANTZAKI

I.M. FOUNDALIDOU

EL. VENIZELOU

V. KORNAROU

KAPITAN SIFI

MYSONOS

G. VOURLIDAKI

EL. VENIZELOU

4 SEPTEMBRIOU

DIMOKRITOU

ITANOU

PRAISOU

KONSTANTINOU KARAMANLI

N. KAPOLI

△ Youth Hostel & Ávios Nikólaos

▷ Hotel Nora (100m) &Ferry Port

▽ Makriyiálos & Ierapetra

▽ Vai & Zakros

Vái beach itself features alongside Knossós or the Lasíthi plateau on almost every Cretan travel agent's list of excursions. Not surprisingly, it is now covered in sunbeds and umbrellas, though it is still a superb beach. Above all, it is famous for its palm trees, and the sudden appearance of the grove is indeed an exotic shock; lying on the fine sand in the early morning, the illusion is of a Caribbean island. As everywhere, notices warn that "Camping is forbidden by law", and for once the authorities seem to mean it

– most campers climb over the headlands to the south or north. If you do sleep out, watch your belongings since this seems to be the one place on Crete with crime on any scale. There's a café and an expensive taverna at the beach, plus toilets and showers. By day you can find a bit more solitude by climbing the rocks or swimming to one of the smaller beaches which surround Vái. **Ítanos**, twenty minutes' walk north by an obvious trail, has a couple of tiny beaches and some modest ruins of the Classical era.

PALÉKASTRO, some 9km south, is in many ways a better place to stay. Although its beaches can't begin to compare, you'll find several modest places with rooms –notably *Hotel Hellas* (☎0843/61 240; ②) which provides good rooms and food – a number of reasonable restaurants, and plenty of space to camp out without the crowds; the sea is a couple of kilometres down a dirt track. Palékastro is also the crossroads for the road south to Zákros.

Zákros

ZÁKROS town is a little under 20km from Palékastro, at the end of the paved road. There are several tavernas and a hotel, the *Zakros* (☎0843/61 284; ③), in the village that seems to have seen better days. The Minoan palace is actually at Káto (lower) Zákros, 8km further down a newly paved road to the sea. Most buses run only to the upper village, but in summer, a couple every day do run all the way to the site. Part way along you can, if on foot, take a short cut through an impressive **gorge** (the "Valley of the Dead", named for ancient tombs in its sides) but it's usually not difficult to hitch if your bus does leave you in the village.

The **palace of Zákros** (Tues–Sun 8.30am–7pm; 500dr) was an important find for archeologists; it had been occupied only once, and abandoned hurriedly and completely. Later, it was forgotten almost entirely and as a result was never plundered or even discovered by archeologists until very recently. The first major excavation began only in 1960; all sorts of everyday objects (tools, raw materials, food, pottery) were thus discovered intact among the ruins, and a great deal was learned from being able to apply modern techniques (and knowledge of the Minoans) to a major dig from the very beginning. None of this is especially evident when you're at the palace, except perhaps in a particularly simple ground plan, so it's as well that it is also a rewarding visit in terms of the setting. Although the site is some way from the sea, in places it is often marshy and waterlogged: partly the result of eastern Crete's slow subsidence, partly the fault of a spring which once supplied fresh water to a cistern beside the royal apartments, and whose outflow is now silted up. Among the remains of narrow streets and small houses higher up, you can keep your feet dry and get an excellent view down over the central court and royal apartments. If you want a more detailed overview of the remains, buy the guide to the site on sale at the entrance.

The village of **KÁTO ZÁKROS** is little more than a collection of tavernas, some of which rent out rooms around a peaceful beach and minuscule fishing anchorage. It's a wonderfully restful place, but is often unable to cope with the volume of visitors seeking rooms in high season. You could try the *Poseidon* (☎0843/93 316; ③) which has fine views, and *Rooms George* (☎0843/93 316; ③), 200m behind the archeological site, is also good.

Ierápetra and the southeast coast

From Sitía, the route south is a cross-country roller-coaster ride until it hits the south coast at **MAKRYIALÓS**. This little fishing village has one of the best beaches at this end of Crete, with fine sand which shelves so gently you feel you could walk the 340km to Africa. Unfortunately, in the last few years it has been heavily developed, so while still a very pleasant place to stop for a swim or a bite, it's not somewhere you're likely to find a cheap room.

From here to Ierápetra there's little reason to stop; the few beaches are rocky and the coastal plain submerged under ranks of polythene-covered greenhouses. Beside the road leading into Ierápetra, are long but exposed stretches of sand, including the appropriately named "Long Beach", where you'll find a campsite, *Camping Koutsounari* (☎0842/61 213), which has plenty of shade.

Ierápetra

IERÁPETRA itself is a bustling modern supply centre for the region's farmers. It also attracts an amazing number of package tourists and not a few backpackers looking for work, especially out of season. The tavernas along the tree-lined front are scenic enough and the EU blue-flagged beach stretches a couple miles east. But as a town, most people find it pretty uninspiring. Although there has been a port here since Roman times, only the **Venetian fort** guarding the harbour and a crumbling minaret remain as reminders of better days. What little else has been salvaged is in the one-room **museum** (Tues–Sat 8.30am–3pm; 400dr) near the post office.

If you want to stay, head up Kazantzakís from the chaotic bus station, and you'll find **rooms** at the *Four Seasons* (☎0842/24 390; ③), or in the nearby *Cretan Villa*, Lakerda 16 (☎0842/26 522; ③), a beautiful 180-year-old house. More central, and also good value, is the *Hotel Ersi*, Platía Eleftherías 20 (☎0842/23 208; ②). You'll find places to **eat** and **drink** all along the waterfront (the better places being towards the Venetian fort); there is a clutch of bars and fast-food places along the central Kyrba, behind the promenade.

West from Ierápetra

Heading west from Ierápetra, the first stretch of coast is grey and dusty, the road jammed with trucks and lined with drab ribbon development. There are a number of small resorts along the beach, though little in the way of public transport. If travelling under your own steam, there is a scenic detour worth taking at Gra Ligiá: the road, on the right for Anatolí climbs to Máles, a village clinging to the lower slopes of the **Dhíkti range**. Here would be a good starting point if you want to take a walk through some stunning mountain terrain. Otherwise, the dirt road back down towards the coast (sign-posted Mýthi) has spectacular views over the Libyan Sea, and eventually follows the Mýrtos river valley down to Mýrtos itself.

Mýrtos and Árvi

MÝRTOS is the first resort that might actually tempt you to stop, and it's certainly the most accessible, just off the main road with numerous daily **buses** to Ierápetra and a couple direct to Iráklion. Although developed to a degree, it nonetheless remains tranquil and inexpensive, with lots of young travellers (many of whom sleep on the beach, to the irritation of locals). If you want a **room**, try *Rooms Angelos* (☎0842/51 106; ②), or *Nikos House* (☎0842/51 116; ②), though there are plenty of others. Just off the road from Ierápetra are a couple of excavated **Minoan villas** you might want to explore: Néa Mýrtos and Pýrgos.

After Mýrtos the main road turns inland towards Áno Viánnos, then continues across the island towards Iráklion; several places on the coast are reached by a series of rough sidetracks. That hasn't prevented one of them, **ÁRVI**, from becoming a larger resort than Mýrtos. The beach hardly justifies it, but it's an interesting little excursion (with at least one bus a day) if only to see the bananas and pineapples grown here and to experience the microclimate – noticeably warmer than neighbouring zones, especially in spring or autumn – that encourages them. For rooms you could try the central *Pension Gorguna* (☎0895/71 211; ②).

Beyond Árvi

Two more villages, **KERATÓKAMBOS** and **TSOÚTSOUROS**, look tempting on the map. Keratókambos has a rather stony beach and only basic rooms – the *Morning Star* taverna (☎0895/51 209; ②) is a good bet and the food is tasty too – but it's popular with Cretan day-trippers and great if you want to escape from the tourist grind for a spell. Tsoútsouros is developed and not really worth the tortuous thirteen-kilometre dirt road in.

If you hope to continue across the **south** of the island, be warned that there are no buses, despite completion of the road towards Mýres after years of work. It's an enjoyable, rural drive, but progress can be slow; there's very little traffic if you're trying to hitch.

RÉTHYMNON AND AROUND

The relatively low, narrow section of Crete which separates the Psilorítis range from the White Mountains in the west seems at first a nondescript, even dull part of the island. Certainly in scenic terms it has few of the excitements that the west can offer; there are no major archeological sites and many of the villages seem modern and ugly. On the other hand, **Réthymnon** itself is an attractive and lively city, with some excellent beaches nearby. And on the south coast, in particular around **Plakiás**, there are beaches as fine as any Crete can offer, and as you drive towards them the scenery and villages improve by the minute.

Réthymnon

In the past ten years or so, **RÉTHYMNON** has seen a greater influx of tourists than perhaps anywhere else on Crete, with the development of a whole series of large hotels extending almost 10km along the beach to the east. For once, though, the middle of town has been spared, so that at its heart Réthymnon remains one of the most beautiful of Crete's major cities (only Khaniá is a serious rival), with an enduringly provincial air. A wide sandy beach and palm-lined promenade border a labyrinthine tangle of Venetian and Turkish houses lining streets where ancient minarets lend an exotic air to the skyline. Dominating everything from the west, is the superbly preserved outline of the **fortress** built by the Venetians after a series of pirate raids had devastated the town.

The Town

With a **beach** right in the heart of town, it's tempting not to stir at all from the sands, but Réthymnon repays at least some gentle exploration. For a start, you could try checking out the further reaches of the beach itself. The waters, protected by the breakwaters in front of town have their disadvantages – notably crowds and dubious hygiene – but less sheltered sands stretch for miles to the east, crowded at first but progressively less so if you're prepared to walk a bit.

Away from the beach, you don't have far to go for the most atmospheric part of town, immediately behind the **inner harbour**. Almost anywhere here, you'll find unexpected old buildings, wall fountains, overhanging wooden balconies, heavy, carved doors and rickety shops, many still with local craftsmen sitting out front, gossiping as they ply their trades. Look out especially for the **Venetian loggia**, which houses a shop selling high quality and expensive reproductions of classical art; the **Rimóndi fountain**, another of the more elegant Venetian survivals; and the **Nerandzes mosque**, the best preserved in Réthymnon but currently closed for renovation. Simply by walking past these three,

RÉTHYMNON

△ Khaniá

★ Bus Station

SINTAGMATOS

△ Spili

Fortress

MAVILI

Public Garden

NIKIFOROU FOKA

Historical Museum

Porta Guora

Nerándzes Mosque

Rimondi Fountain

ETHNIKIS ANDISTASIS

PLATÍA MARTIRON

Minaret

Youth Hostel

Loggia

PLATÍA PLASTIRA

OTE

Inner Harbour

DHIMOKRATIAS

V. KALERGI

Ferry Dock

Veli Pasha Mosque

Kara Pasha Mosque

EOT

PLATÍA AGNOSTOU

△ Iráklion

ACCOMMODATION

1 Anna
2 Atelier
3 Barbara Dokimaki
4 Byzantine
5 Ideal
6 Leo
7 Olga's
8 Réthimnon House
9 Rooms George
10 Sea Front
11 Zania

0   250 m

you'll have seen many of the liveliest parts of Réthymnon. Ethnikís Andistásis, the street leading straight up from the fountain, is also the town's **market** area.

The old city ends at the Porta Guora at the top of Andistásis, the only surviving remnant of the city walls. Almost opposite are the quiet and shady **Public Gardens**. These are always a soothing place to stroll, and in the latter half of July, the **Réthymnon Wine Festival** is staged here. Though touristy, it's a thoroughly enjoyable event, with spectacular local dancing as the evening progresses and the barrels empty. The entrance fee includes all the wine you can drink, though you'll need to bring your own cup or buy one of the souvenir glasses and carafes on sale outside the gardens.

The museums and fortress

A little further up the street from the Nerandzes mosque at M Vernardou 28, a beautifully restored seventeenth-century Venetian mansion is the new home of the small but tremendously enjoyable **Historical and Folk Art Museum** (daily 9am–1pm, Mon & Tues also 6–8pm; 400dr). Gathered within four, cool, airy rooms are musical instruments, old photos, basketry, farm implements, an explanation of traditional breadmaking techniques, smiths' tools, traditional costumes and jewellery, lace, weaving and embroidery, pottery, knives and old wooden chests. It makes for a fascinating insight into a fast disappearing rural (and urban) lifestyle, which had often survived virtually unchanged from Venetian times to the 1960s, and is well worth a look.

Heading in the other direction from the fountain you'll come to the fortress and **archeological museum** (Tues–Sun 8.30am–3pm; 500dr), which occupies a building almost directly opposite the entrance to the fortress. This was built by the Turks as an extra defence, and later served as a prison, but it's now entirely modern inside: cool, spacious and airy. Unfortunately, the collection is not particularly exciting, and really only worth seeing if you're going to miss the bigger museums elsewhere on the island.

The massive **Venetian Fortress** (Tues–Sun 8am–8pm; reduced hours out of season; 6000dr) is a must, however. Said to be the largest Venetian castle ever built, this was a response, in the last quarter of the sixteenth century, to a series of **pirate raids** (by Barbarossa among others) that had devastated the town. Inside now is a vast open space dotted with the remains of all sorts of barracks, arsenals, officers' houses, earthworks and deep shafts, and at the centre a large domed building that was once a church and later a **mosque**. It was designed to be large enough for the entire population to take shelter within the walls, and you can see that it probably was. Although much is ruined, it remains thoroughly atmospheric, and you can look out from the walls over the town and harbour, or in the other direction along the coast to the west. It's also worth walking around the outside of the fortress, preferably at sunset, to get an impression of its fearsome defences, plus great views along the coast and a pleasant resting point around the far side at the *Sunset* taverna.

Practicalities

The **bus station** in Réthymnon is by the sea to the west of town just off Periferiakós, the road which skirts the waterfront around the fortress. The **tourist office** (Mon–Fri 8am–5.30pm, Sat 9am–2pm; ☎0831/24 143) is across on the other side of the historical centre, backing onto the main town beach, close to the mobile post office (summer only) and a couple of conveniently sited cash dispensers (Visa and Mastercard). If you arrive by **ferry**, you'll be more conveniently placed, over at the western edge of the harbour.

Accommodation

There's a great number of places to stay in Réthymnon, and only at the height of the season are you likely to have difficulty finding somewhere, though you may get weary looking. The greatest concentration of **rooms** is in the tangled streets west of the inner harbour, between the Rimóndi fountain and the museums; there are also quite a few places on and around Arkadhíou and Platía Frakidháki. The cheapest beds in town are in the **youth hostel**, Tombázi 41 (☎0831/22 848; ①), where you can also sleep on the roof. It's large, clean, very friendly and popular, and there's food, showers, clothes-washing facilities and even a library, with books in various languages.

There are a couple of **campsites** 4km east of town; take the bus for the hotels (marked *Scaleta/El Greco*) from the long-distance bus station to get there. *Camping Elizabeth* (☎0831/28 694) is a pleasant, large site on the beach, with all facilities. Only a few hundred metres further east along the beach is *Camping Arkadia* (☎0831/28 825), a bigger and slightly less friendly site.

Anna, Katekháki (☎0831/25 586). Comfortable pension in a quiet position on the street that runs straight down from the entrance to the fortress to Melissinou. ④.

Atelier, Khimáras 32 (☎0831/24 440). Pleasant rooms close to *Rooms George*, run by a talented potter, who has her studio in the basement and sells her wares in a shop on the other side of the building. ③.

Barbara Dokimaki, Plastíra 14 (☎0831/22 319). Strange warren of a rooms place, with one entrance at the above address, just off the seafront behind the *Ideon*, and another on Dambergi; ask for the newly refurbished top-floor rooms, which have balconies. ③.

Byzantine, Vospórou 26 (☎0831/55 609). Excellent-value rooms in a renovated Byzantine palace. The tranquil patio bar is open to all, and breakfast is included in price. ④.

Ideon, Platía Plastíra 10 (☎0831/28 667, fax 28 670). Hotel with a brilliant position just north of the ferry dock; little chance of space in season, though. ⑥.

Leo, Vafé 2 (☎0831/26 197). Good hotel with lots of wood and a traditional feel; the price includes breakfast, and there's a good bar. ④.

Olga's Pension, Soulíou 57 (☎0831/53 206, fax 29 851). The star attraction at this very friendly pension on one of Rethimnon's most touristy streets is the resplendent flower-filled roof garden. ②.

Réthymnon Haus, V. Kornárou 1 (☎0831/23 923). Very pleasant rooms of a high standard in an old building just off Arkadhíou. Bar downstairs. ②.

Rooms George, Makedhonías 32 (☎0831/50 967). Decent rooms (some with fridge), near the archeological museum. ③.

Sea-Front Rent Rooms, Arkadhíou 159 (☎0831/51 981, fax 51 062). Rooms with sea views and balconies in an attractively refurbished mansion with ceiling fans and lots of wood. ③.

Zania, Pávlou Vlástou 3 (☎0831/28 169). Pension right on the corner of Arkadhíou by the old youth hostel building; a well-adapted old house, but only a few rooms. ③.

Eating and drinking

Immediately behind the town beach are arrayed the most touristy **restaurants**. One that maintains its integrity (and reasonable prices) is the *Samaria* taverna, almost opposite the tourist office. Around the inner **harbour**, there's a second, rather more group of expensive tavernas, specializing in fish, though as often as not the intimate atmosphere in these places is spoiled by the stench from the harbour itself: *O Zefyros* and *Seven Brothers* are two of the less outrageously pricey.

The cluster of kafenía and tavernas by the **Rimóndi fountain** and the newer places spreading into the surrounding streets generally offer considerably better value, and a couple of old-fashioned kafenía serve magnificent yoghurt and honey. Places to try include *Kyria Maria* at Moskhovítou 20, tucked down an alley behind the fountain (after the meal, everyone gets a couple of delicious *tiropitákia* with honey on the house); *Agrimi*, a reliable standard on Platía Petikháki; and the *Zanfoti* kafenío overlooking the fountain which is relatively expensive, but a great place to people-watch over a coffee; and, for a slightly cheaper option *O Psaras* (the Fisherman), a simple, friendly taverna by the church on the corner of Nikiforou Foka and Koronaíou. A good lunchtime stop close to the archeological museum is *O Pontios*, Melissinoú 34, a simple place with tables outside and an enthusiastic female proprietor. Healthy, home-baked lunches can also be had at *Stella's Kitchen*, a simple café linked to Olga's Pension at Soulíou 55, where meals can be enjoyed up on the leafy roof garden. A noisier evening alternative is *Taverna O Gounos*, Koronéou 6 in the old town; the family who run it perform live *lyra* every night, and when things get really lively the dancing starts.

If you want takeaway food, there are numerous **souvláki** stalls, including a couple on Arkadhíou and Paleológou and another at Petikháki 52, or you can buy your own ingredients at the **market** stalls set up daily on Ethnikís Andistásis below the Porta Guora. There are small general stores scattered everywhere, particularly on Paleológou and Arkadhíou; east along the beach road you'll even find a couple of mini supermarkets. The **bakery** *I Gaspari* on Mesolongíou, just behind the Rimóndi fountain, sells the usual cheese pies, cakes and the like, and it also bakes excellent brown, black and rye bread. There's a good zakharoplastío, *N.A. Skartsilakos*, on Paleológou, just north of the fountain, and several more small cafés which are good for breakfast or a quick coffee.

Nightlife

Nightlife is concentrated in the same general areas as the tavernas. At the west end of Venizélou, in the streets behind the inner harbour, the overflow from a small cluster of noisy music bars – *Templum*, *252*, *Dimmam* and *Venetianikoa* – begins to spill out onto the pavement as party-goers gather for the nightly opening of the *Fortezza Disco* in the inner harbour, which is the gliziest in town. Heading up Salamínos, a string of more subdued cocktail bars – *Memphis*, *Santan* and *Palmira* – cater for those in search of a quieter drink. The larger discos are mostly out to the east, among the big hotels, but *Venizelou* right by the inner harbour, is a touristy Cretan music and dancing place, with live performances every evening from 9.30pm.

Around Réthymnon

While some of Crete's most drastic resort development spreads ever eastwards out of Réthymnon, to the west a sandy coastline, not yet greatly exploited, runs all the way to the borders of Khaniá. But of all the short trips that can be made out of Réthymnon, the best known and still the most worthwhile is to the **Monastery of Arkádhi**.

Southeast to Arkádhi

The **Monastery of Arkádhi** (daily 8am–8pm; 300dr), some 25km southeast of the city and immaculately situated in the foothills of the Psilorítis range, is also something of a national Cretan shrine. During the 1866 rebellion against the Turks, the monastery became a rebel strongpoint in which, as the Turks gained the upper hand, hundreds of Cretan guerrillas and their families took refuge. Surrounded and, after two days of fighting, on the point of defeat, the defenders ignited a powder magazine just as the Turks entered. Hundreds (some sources claim thousands) were killed, Cretan and Turk alike, and the tragedy did much to promote international sympathy for the cause of Cretan independence. Nowadays, you can peer into the roofless vault where the explosion occurred and wander about the rest of the well-restored grounds. The sixteenth-century Rococo church survived, and is one of the finest Venetian structures left on Crete; other buildings house a small museum devoted to the exploits of the defenders of the (Orthodox) faith. The monastery is easy to visit by public bus or on a tour.

West to Yeoryoúpoli and beyond

Leaving Réthymnon to the west, the main road climbs for a while above a rocky coastline before descending (after some 5km) to the sea, where it runs alongside sandy **beaches** for perhaps another 7km. An occasional hotel offers accommodation, but on the whole there's nothing but a line of straggly bushes between the road and the windswept sands.

If you have your own vehicle, there are plenty of places you can stop at here for a swim, and rarely anyone else around – but beware of some very strong currents.

If you want to stay for any time, probably the best base is **YEORYOÚPOLI** at the far end, where the beach is cleaner, wider and further from the road. There's been a distinct acceleration in the pace of development at Yeoryoúpoli over the last few years and it's now very much a resort, packed with rooms to rent, small hotels, apartment buildings, tavernas and travel agencies; there's even a small land train to transport visitors along the sea front and on short excursions. But everything remains on a small scale, and the undeniably attractive setting is untarnished, making it a very pleasant place to pass a few days, as long as you don't expect to find many vestiges of traditional Crete. Most of the better rooms, including *Rent Rooms Stelios* (☎0825/61 308; ②), *Irene* (☎0825/61 278; ②) and *Cretan Cactus* (☎0825/61 027; ②), are away from the main platía along the road down towards the beach. More central possibilities include *Rooms Voula* (☎0825/61 359; ②) above a gift shop to the east of the platía, and the *Paradise Taverna* (☎0825/61 313; ③) off the southeast corner of the platía, which has rooms and is a good place to eat.

Within walking distance inland – though it can also be visited on the tourist train from Yeoryoúpoli – is **Kournás**, Crete's only lake, set deep in a bowl of hills and almost constantly changing colour. There are a few tavernas with rooms to rent along the shore here, or you could try for a bed in the nearby village of Moúri. A few kilometres uphill in Kournás village, the *Kali Kardia* taverna is a great place to sample the local lamb and sausages.

Beyond Yeoryoúpoli, the main road heads inland, away from a cluster of coastal villages beyond Vámos. It thus misses the Dhrápano peninsula, with some spectacular views over the sapphire Bay of Soudha, several quiet beaches and the setting for the film of *Zorba the Greek*. **Kókkino Khorió**, the movie location, and nearby **Pláka** are indeed postcard-picturesque (more so from a distance), but **Kefalás**, inland, outdoes both of them. On the exposed north coast there are good beaches at **Almyrídha** and **Kalýves**, and off the road between them. Both are fast developing into resorts in their own right; accommodation is mostly in apartments and rooms are scarce, although there are a few mid-range and more upmarket hotels, and a decent pension, *Katrina* (☎0825/38 775; ③), a short walk uphill from the centre of Almyrídha. With a string of good fish tavernas along the beach and a pleasantly refreshing sea breeze, Almyrídha makes an enjoyable lunch stop.

South from Réthymnon

There are a couple of alternative routes south from Réthymnon, but the main one heads straight out from the centre of town, an initially featureless road due south across the middle of the island towards **Ayía Galíni**. About 23km out, a turning cuts off to the right for **Plakiás** and **Mýrthios**, following the course of the spectacular Kourtaliótiko ravine.

Plakiás and the south coast

PLAKIÁS has undergone a major boom and is no longer the pristine village all too many people arriving here expect. That said, it's still quite low key, and there's a satisfactory beach and a string of good tavernas around the dock. There are hundreds of **rooms**, but at the height of summer you'll need to arrive early if you hope to find one; the last to fill are generally those on the road leading inland, away from the waterside. For rooms try *Christos's Taverna* (☎0832/31 871; ②) on the seafront, or the excellent balcony rooms at *Ipokambos* (☎0832/31 525; ②) slightly inland on the road to the **youth hostel** (☎0832/31 306; ①), which is 500m inland and signed from the seafront. The beach is long and nobody is likely to mind if you sleep out on the southern section – but Dhamnóni (see below) is far better if that's your plan.

Once you've found a room there's not a lot else to discover here. You'll find every facility strung out around the waterfront, including a temporary post office, bike rental, money exchange, supermarket and even a laundry. Places to eat are plentiful too. The attractive **tavernas** on the waterfront in the centre are a little expensive; you'll eat cheaper further inland – seek out *Medusa* taverna – or around the corner at one of the tavernas facing west where *Sunset* taverna is the first in line.

Mýrthios

For a stay of more than a day or two, **MÝRTHIOS**, in the hills behind Plakiás, also deserves consideration. It's no longer a great deal cheaper, but at least you'll find locals still outnumbering the tourists and something of a travellers' scene based around another popular **youth hostel** (☎0832/31 202; ①), with a friendly taverna and several rooms for rent. The Plakiás bus will usually loop back through Mýrthios, but check; otherwise, it's less than five minutes' walk from the junction. It takes twenty minutes to walk down to the beach at Plakiás, a little longer to Dhamnóni, and if you're prepared to walk for an hour or more, there are some entirely isolated coves to the west – ask for directions at the hostel.

Dhamnóni

Some of the most tempting **beaches** in central Crete hide just to the east of Plakiás, though unfortunately they're now a very poorly kept secret. These three splashes of yellow sand, divided by rocky promontories, are within easy walking distance and together go by the name **Dhamnóni**. At the first, Dhamnóni proper, there's a taverna with showers and a wonderfully long strip of sand, but there's also a lot of new development including a number of nearby rooms for rent and a huge new Swiss timeshare complex, which has colonized half of the main beach. At the far end, you'll generally find a few people who've dispensed with their clothes, while the little cove which shelters the middle of the three beaches (barely accessible except on foot) is entirely nudist. Beyond this, **Ammoúdhi** beach has another taverna (with good rooms for rent) and a slightly more family atmosphere.

Préveli and "Palm Beach"

Next in line comes **PRÉVELI**, some 6km southeast of Lefkóyia. It takes its name from a **monastery** (daily 8am–7pm; 500dr) high above the sea which, like every other in Crete, has a proud history of resistance, in this case accentuated by its role in the last war as a shelter for marooned Allied soldiers awaiting evacuation off the south coast. There are fine views and a monument commemorating the rescue operations, but little else to see. The evacuations took place from "**Palm Beach**", a sandy cove with a small date-palm grove and solitary drink stand where a stream feeds a little oasis. The beach usually attracts a summer camping community and is now also the target of day-trip boats from Plakiás. Sadly, these two groups between them have left this lovely place filthy, and despite a belated clean-up campaign it seems barely worth the effort. The climb down from the monastery is steep, rocky and surprisingly arduous: it's a great deal easier to come here by boat.

Spíli and Ayía Galíni

Back on the main road south, **SPÍLI** lies about 30km from Réthymnon. A popular coffee break for tours passing this way, Spíli warrants time if you can spare it. Sheltered under a cliff are narrow alleys of ancient houses, all leading up from a platía with a famous 24-spouted fountain. If you have your own transport, it's a worthwhile place to stay, peacefully rural at night but with several good **rooms** for rent. Try the *Green Hotel* (☎0832/22 225; ②) or the pleasant *Rooms Herakles* (☎0832/22 411; ②) just behind.

The ultimate destination of most people on this road is **AYÍA GALÍNI**. If heading here was your plan, maybe you should think again since this picturesque "fishing village" is so busy that you can't see it for the tour buses, hotel billboards and British package tourists. It also has a beach much too small for the crowds that congregate here. Even so, there are some saving graces – mainly some excellent restaurants and bars, plenty of rooms and a friendly atmosphere that survives and even thrives on all the visitors. Out of season, it can be quite enjoyable, and from November to April the mild climate makes it an ideal spot to spend the winter. A lot of long-term travellers do just that, so it's a good place to find work packing tomatoes or polishing cucumbers. If you want somewhere to stay, start looking at the top end of town, around the main road: the good-value *Hotel Minos* (☎0832/91 292; ②) with superb views is a good place to start, but there are dozens of possibilities, and usually something to be found even at the height of summer.

The coastal plain east of Ayía Galíni, hidden under acres of polythene greenhouses and burgeoning concrete sprawl, must be among the ugliest regions in Crete, and **Timbáki** the dreariest town. Since this is the way to Festós and back to Iráklion, however, you may have no choice but to grin and bear it.

The Amári Valley

An alternative route south from Réthymnon, and a far less travelled one, is the road which turns off on the eastern fringe of town to run via the **Amári Valley**. Very few buses go this way, but if you're driving it's well worth the extra time. There's little specifically to see or do (though hidden away are a number of frescoed Byzantine churches), but it's an impressive drive under the flanks of the mountains and a reminder of how, in places, rural Crete continues to exist regardless of visitors. The countryside here is delightfully green even in summer, with rich groves of olive and assorted fruit trees, and if you **stay** (there are rooms in Thrónos and Yerákari), you'll find the nights are cool and quiet. It may seem odd that many of the villages along the way are modern; they were systematically destroyed by the Germans in reprisal for the 1944 kidnapping of General Kreipe.

KHANIÁ AND THE WEST

The substantial attractions of Crete's westernmost quarter are all the more enhanced by its relative lack of visitors, and despite the now-rapid spread of tourist development, the west is likely to remain one of the emptier parts of the island. This is partly because there are no big sandy beaches to accommodate resort hotels, and partly because it's so far from the great archeological sites. But for mountains and empty (if often pebbly) beaches, it's unrivalled.

Khaniá itself is one of the best reasons to come here, perhaps the only Cretan city which could be described as enjoyable in itself. The immediately adjacent coast is relatively developed and not overly exciting; if you want beaches head for the south coast. **Paleokhóra** is the only place which could really be described as a resort, and even this is on a thoroughly human scale; others are emptier still. **Ayía Rouméli** and **Loutró** can be reached only on foot or by boat; **Khóra Sfakíon** sees hordes passing through but few who stay; **Frangokástello**, nearby, has a beautiful castle and the first stirrings of development. Behind these lie the **Lefká Óri** (White Mountains) and, above all, the famed walk through the **Gorge of Samariá**.

Khaniá

KHANIÁ, as any of its residents will tell you, is spiritually the capital of Crete, even if the nominal title passed (in 1971) to Iráklion. For many, it is also by far the island's most attractive city, especially if you can catch it in spring, when the Lefká Óri's snow-capped peaks seem to hover above the roofs. Although it is for the most part a modern city, you might never know it as a tourist. Surrounding the small outer harbour is a wonderful jumble of half-derelict **Venetian streets** that survived the wartime bombardments, and it is here that life for the visitor is concentrated. Restoration and gentrification, consequences of the tourist boom, have made inroads of late, but it remains an atmospheric place.

> The telephone code for Khaniá is ☎0821

Arrival, information and orientation

Large as it is, Khaniá is easy to handle once you've reached the centre; you may get lost wandering among the narrow alleys of the old city but that's a relatively small area, and you're never far from the sea or from some other obvious landmark. The **bus station** is on Kidhonías, within easy walking distance from the action – turn right out of the station, then left down the side of Platía 1866 and you'll emerge at a major road junction opposite the top of Hálidhon, the main street of the old quarter leading straight down to the Venetian harbour. Arriving by **ferry**, you'll anchor about 10km from Khaniá at the port of Soúdha: there are frequent buses which will drop you by the **market** on the fringes of the old town, or you can take a taxi (around 1500dr). From the **airport** (15km east of town on the Akrotíri peninsula) taxis (around 2500dr) will almost certainly be your only option, though it's worth a quick check to see if any sort of bus is meeting your flight. The **tourist office** is in the new town, just off Platía 1866 at Kriári 40 (Mon–Fri 7.30am–2.30pm).

Accommodation

There must be thousands of **rooms** to rent in Khaniá and, unusually, quite a few comfortable **hotels**. Though you may face a long search for a bed at the height of the season, eventually everyone does seem to find something.

There are two **campsites** within striking distance, the nearer being *Camping Khania* (☎31 138), some 4km west of Khaniá behind the beach, served by local bus (see p.559). The site is lovely, if rather basic – just a short walk from some of the better beaches. *Camping Ayía Marína* (☎68 596) lies about 8km west of Khaniá, on an excellent beach at the far end of Ayía Marína village. This is beyond the range of Khaniá city buses, so to get here by public transport you have to go from the main bus station. Check before turning up, because the site is earmarked for redevelopment.

Harbour area

Perhaps the most desirable rooms of all are those overlooking the **harbour**, which are sometimes available at reasonable rates: be warned that this is often because they're very noisy at night. Most are approached not direct from the harbourside itself but from Zambelíou, the alley behind, or from other streets leading off the harbour further around (where you may get more peace). The nicest of the more expensive places are here, too, usually set back a little so that they're quieter, but often with views from the upper storeys.

Amphora, Theotokopóulou 20 (☎ & fax 93 224). Large, traditional hotel, and beautifully renovated; worth the expense if you get a view, but probably not for the cheaper rooms with no view. ⑥.

Artemis, Kondhiláki 13 (☎92 802). One of many in this touristy street running inland from Zambelíu. ③.

Lucia, Akti Koundouriótou (☎90 302). Harbour-front hotel with balcony rooms; less expensive than you might expect for one of the best views in town. ③.

Meltemi, Angélou 2 (☎ 92 802). First of a little row of pensions in a great situation on the far side of the harbour; perhaps noisier than its neighbours, but ace views and a good café downstairs. ③.

Pension Lena, Theotokopoula 60 (☎ and fax 72 265). Charming rooms in an old wooden Turkish house restored by friendly German proprietor. Pleasant breakfast café below. ③.

Rooms Eleonora, Theotokúpoula 13 (☎50 011). One of several in the backstreets around the top of Angélou. ③.

Rooms George, Zambelíou 30 (☎88 715). Old building with steep stairs and eccentric antique furniture; rooms vary in price according to position and size. ②.

Rooms Stella, Angélou 10 (☎73 756). Creaky, eccentric old house above a ceramics shop, close to the *Lucia*, with plain, clean rooms. ③.

Theresa, Angélou 8 (☎40 118). Beautiful old house in a great position, with stunning views from roof terrace and some of the rooms; classy decor, too. A more expensive pension than its neighbours but deservedly so; unlikely to have room in season unless you book. ④.

The old town: east of Khálidhon

In the eastern half of the old town rooms are far more scattered, and in the height of the season your chances are much better over here. **Kastélli**, immediately east of the harbour, has some lovely places with views from the height. Take one of the alleys leading left off Kaneváro if you want to try these, but don't be too hopeful since they are popular and often booked up.

Fidias, Sarpáki 8 (☎52 494). Signposted from the cathedral, this favourite backpackers' meeting place is rather bizarrely run, but is an extremely friendly pension and has the real advantage of offering single rooms or fixing shares. ③.

Kastelli, Kanevárou 39 (☎ and fax 45 314). Not in the prettiest location, but a comfortable, modern, reasonably priced pension and very quiet at the back. The owner is exceptionally helpful and also has a few apartments and a beautiful house (for up to five people) to rent. ③.

Kydonia, Isódhion 15 (☎57 179). Between the cathedral platía and Platía Sindrívani, in the first street parallel to Khálidhon. Rather dark, but good value for so central a position. ③.

Lito, Episkópou Dhorothéou 15 (☎53 150). Pension very near the cathedral, in a street with several other options. ③.

Marina Ventikou, Sarpáki 40 (☎57 601). Small, personally run rooms place in a quiet corner of the old town. ③.

Monastiri, Ayíou Márkou 18, off Kanevárou (☎54 776). Pleasant rooms, some with a sea view in the restored ruins of a Venetian monastery. ③.

Nikos, Dhaskaloyiánnis 58 (☎54 783). One of a few down here near the inner harbour; relatively modern rooms all with shower. ②.

The City

Khaniá has been occupied almost continuously since Neolithic times, so it comes as a surprise that a city of such antiquity should offer little specifically to see or do. It is, however, a place which is fascinating simply to wander around, stumbling upon surviving fragments of city wall, the remains **ancient Kydonia** which is being excavated, and odd segments of Venetian or Turkish masonry.

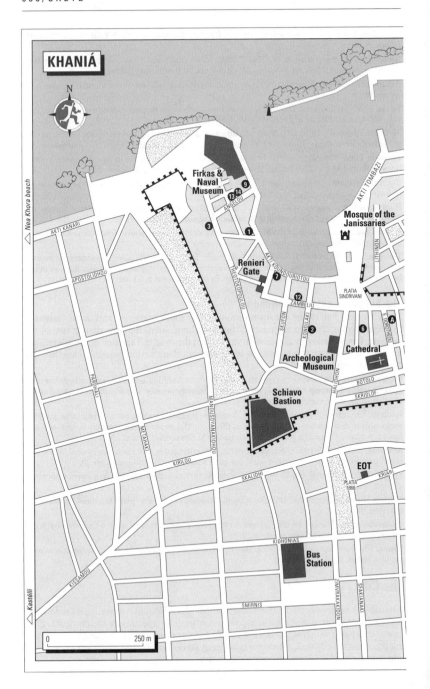

KHANIÁ

N

Nea Khora beach △

Kastélli △

Firkas &
Naval
Museum

Mosque of the
Janissaries

Renieri
Gate

Archeological
Museum

Cathedral

Schiavo
Bastion

EOT

Bus
Station

AKTI KANARI

APOSTOLIDHOU

PARDHALI

METAHAKI

KIRILOU

SKALIDHI

KISSAMOU

SMIRNIS

MANOUSOYANAKIDHOU

THEOTOKOPOULOU

SKUFON

KONDILAKI

HALIDHON

ANGELOU

AKTI KOUNDOURIOTOU

ZAMBELIU

BOTOLO

SKRIDLOF

KIDHONIAS

ZIMVRAKAKIDON

SFAKIANAKI

KRIARI

PLATIA
1866

PLATIA
SINDRIVANI

E.ORFANOUDHOU

LITHINON

AKTI TOMBAZI

3

1

7

13 14

9

12

2

6

A

0   250 m

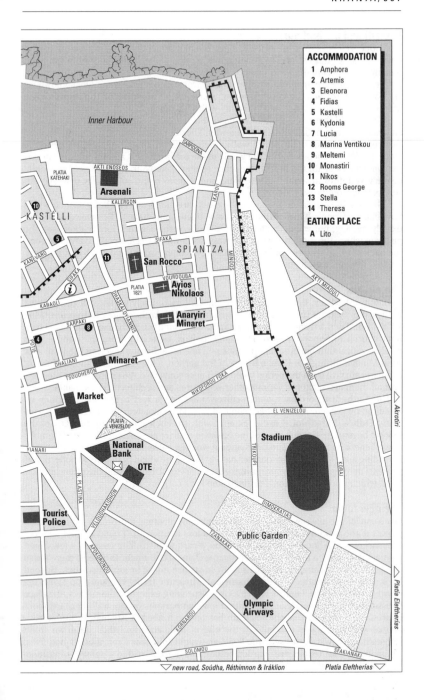

ACCOMMODATION

1 Amphora
2 Artemis
3 Eleonora
4 Fidias
5 Kastelli
6 Kydonia
7 Lucia
8 Marina Ventikou
9 Meltemi
10 Monastiri
11 Nikos
12 Rooms George
13 Stella
14 Theresa

EATING PLACE

A Lito

Inner Harbour

PLATIA KATEHAKI

AKTI ENOSEOS

Arsenali

KALERGON

SARPIDONA

IKAROU

KASTÉLLI

KANEVARO

SIFAKA

SIFAKA

SPIANTZA

MINOOS

San Rocco

VOURDOUBA

PLATIA 1821

Ayios Nikolaos

KARAOLI

DHASKALOYIANNIS

SARPAKI

Anaryiri Minaret

AKTI MIAOULI

POTIE

DHALIANI

TSOUDHERON

Minaret

NIKOFOROU FOKA

KIPROU

Market

PLATIA S. VENIZELOU

EL VENIZELOU

YIANARI

National Bank

OTE

TRIKOUPI

Stadium

KORAI

N. PLASTIRA

VELOUDHAKIDHON

DIMOKRATIAS

▷ Akrotíri

Tourist Police

TZANAKAKI

Public Garden

APOKORONOU

Olympic Airways

KORNAROU

SOLOMOU

SFAKIANAKI

▷ Platía Eleftherías

Kastélli and the harbour

The **port** area is as ever the place to start, the oldest and the most interesting part of town. It's at its busiest and most attractive at night, when the lights from bars and restaurants reflect in the water and crowds of visitors and locals turn out to promenade. By day, things are quieter. Straight ahead from Platía Sindriváni (also known as Harbour Square) lies the curious domed shape of the **Mosque of the Janissaries**, until 1991 the tourist office, but currently without a function.

The little hill that rises behind the mosque is **Kastélli**, site of the earliest habitation and core of the Venetian and Turkish towns. There's not a great deal left, but it's here that you'll find traces of the oldest **walls** (there were two rings, one defending Kastélli alone, a later set encompassing the whole of the medieval city) and the sites of various excavations. Beneath the hill, on the inner (eastern) harbour, the arches of sixteenth-century **Venetian arsenals** survive alongside remains of the outer walls; both are currently undergoing restoration.

Following the esplanade around in the other direction leads to a hefty bastion which now houses Crete's **Naval Museum** (daily 10am–4pm; 400dr). The collection is not exactly riveting, but wander in anyway for a look at the seaward fortifications and the platform where the modern Greek flag was first flown on Crete (in 1913). Walk around the back of these restored bulwarks to a street heading inland and you'll find the best-preserved stretch of the outer walls.

The old city

Behind the harbour, lie the less picturesque but more lively sections of the old city. First, a short way up Hálidhon on the right, is Khaniá's **Archeological Museum** (Mon 12.30–7pm, Tues–Fri 8am–7pm, Sat & Sun 8.30am–3pm; 500dr) housed in the Venetian-built church of San Francesco. Damaged as it is, especially from the outside, this remains a beautiful building and it contains a fine little display, covering the local area from Minoan through to Roman times. In the garden, a huge fountain and the base of a minaret survive from the period when the Turks converted the church into a mosque; around them are scattered various other sculptures and architectural remnants.

The **Cathedral**, ordinary and relatively modern, is just a few steps further up Hálidhon on the left. Around it are some of the more animated shopping areas, particularly **Odhós Skrídhlof** (Leather Street), with streets leading up to the back of the market beyond. In the direction of the Spiántza quarter are ancient alleys with tumble-down Venetian stonework and overhanging wooden balconies; though gentrification is spreading apace, much of the quarter has yet to feel the effect of the city's modern popularity. There are a couple more **minarets** too, one on Dhaliáni, and the other in Platía 1821, which is a fine traditional platía to stop for a coffee.

The new town

Once out of the narrow confines of the maritime district, the broad, traffic-choked streets of the **modern city** have a great deal less to offer. Up Tzanakáki, not far from the market, you'll find the **Public Gardens**, a park with strolling couples, a few caged animals (including a few *kri-kri* or Cretan ibex) and a café under the trees; there's also an open-air auditorium which occasionally hosts live music or local festivities. Beyond here, you could continue to the **Historical Museum** (Mon–Fri 9am–1pm), but the effort would be wasted unless you're a Greek-speaking expert on the subject; the place is essentially a very dusty archive with a few photographs on the wall. Perhaps more interesting is the fact that the museum lies on the fringes of Khaniá's desirable residential districts. If you continue to the end of Sfakianáki and then go down Iróön Polytekhníou towards the sea, you'll get an insight into how Crete's other half lives. There are several (expensive) garden restaurants down here and a number of fashionable café-bars where you can sit outside.

The beaches

Khaniá's beaches all lie to the west of the city. For the packed **city beach**, this means no more than a ten-minute walk following the shoreline from the naval museum, but for good sand you're better off taking the local bus out along the coast road. This leaves from the east side of Platía 1866 and runs along the coast road as far as **Kalamáki beach**. Kalamáki and the previous stop, **Oasis beach**, are again pretty crowded but they're a considerable improvement over the beach in Khaniá itself. In between, you'll find emptier stretches if you're prepared to walk: about an hour in all (on sandy beach virtually all the way) from Khaniá to Kalamáki, and then perhaps ten minutes from the road to the beach if you get off the bus at the signs to *Aptera Beach* or *Camping Khania*. Further afield there are even finer beaches at **Ayía Marína** to the west, or **Stavrós** (see p.561) out on the Akrotíri peninsula (reached by KTEL buses from the main station).

Eating

You're never far from something to **eat** in Khaniá: in a circle around the harbour is one restaurant, taverna or café after another. All have their own character, but there seems little variation in price or what's on offer. Away from the water, there are plenty of slightly cheaper possibilities on Kondhiláki, Kanevárou and most of the streets off Khálidhon. For snacks or lighter meals, the cafés around the harbour on the whole serve cocktails and fresh juices at exorbitant prices, though breakfast (especially "English") can be good value. For more traditional places, try around the market and along Dhaskaloyiánnis (*Singanaki* here is a good traditional bakery serving *tyrópitta* and the like, with a cake shop next door). Fast food is also increasingly widespread, with numerous *souvláki* places on Karaolí; at the end of the outer harbour, near the naval museum; and around the corner of Plastíra and Yianári, across from the **market** (see "Listings", p.561, for details of the market and supermarkets).

Anaplous, Sífaka 37. A couple of blocks west of Platía 1821, this is a popular new open-air restaurant inside a stylishly "restored" ruin of a Turkish mansion bombed in the war. Serves both mezédhes and full meals.

Boúyatsa, Sífaka 4. Tiny place serving little except the traditional creamy *bougátsa*: eat in or take away.

Dino's, inner harbour by bottom of Sarpidhóna. One of the best choices for a pricey seafood meal with a harbour view; *Apostolis*, almost next door, is also good.

Karnáyio, Platía Katekháki 8. Set back from the inner harbour near the port police. Not right on the water, but one of the best harbour restaurants nonetheless.

Lito, Episkópou Dhorothéou 15. Café/taverna with live music (usually Greek-style guitar), one of several in this street.

Meltemi, Angélou 2. Slow, relaxed place for breakfast, and where locals (especially expats) sit whiling the day away or playing *tavli*.

Neorion, Sarpidhóna. Café to sit and be seen in the evening; some tables overlook the harbour. Try an expensive but sublime lemon *graníta*.

Rudi's Bierhaus, Sífaka 24. Austrian Rudi Riegler's bar stocks more than a hundred of Europe's finest beers to accompany mezédhes.

Tamam, Zambelíou just before Renieri Gate. Young, fashionable place with adventurous Greek menu including much vegetarian food. Unfortunately only a few cramped tables outside, and inside it's very hot. Slow service.

Tasty Souvlaki, Khálidhon 80. Always packed despite being cramped and none-too-clean, which is a testimonial to the quality and value of the *souvláki*. Better to take away.

Taverna Ela, top of Kondhiláki. Live Greek music to enliven your meal in yet another roofless taverna townhouse.

Tholos, Agíon Dhéka 36. Slightly north of the cathedral, *Tholos* is another "restaurant in a ruin", this time Venetian/Turkish, with a wide selection of Cretan specialities.

To Dhiporto, Betólo 31, one block north of Skridhlóf. Long-established, very basic taverna amid all the leather shops. Multilingual menu offers such delights as "Pigs' Balls", or, more delicately, *Testicules de Porc.*

Vasilis, Platía Sindriváni. Perhaps the least changed of the harbourside cafés. Reasonably priced breakfasts.

Bars and nightlife

Khaniá's **nightlife** has more than enough venues to satisfy the most insomniac night-owls. Most of the clubs and disco bars are gathered in the area around the inner harbour, whilst there are plenty of terrace bars along both harbour fronts with more scattered throughout the old quarter.

The smartest and newest places are on and around **Sarpidhóna**, in the far corner of the inner harbour: bars like *Fraise* on Sarpidóna; and late night disco-bars such as *Berlin Rock Café*, on Radimánthous, just around the corner at the top of Sarpidóna. Heading from here around towards the outer harbour, you'll pass others including the *Four Seasons*, a very popular bar by the port police, and then reach a couple of the older places including *Remember* and *Scorpio* behind the Plaza. *Fagotto*, Angélou 16, is a pleasant, laid-back jazz bar, often with live performers. **Discos** proper include *Ariadni*, on the inner harbour (opens 11.30pm, but busy later), and *Millenium*, a big, bright place on Tsoudherón behind the market, which doesn't really get going until 2am. Tucked down a passage near the Schiavo Bastion (Skalídhi and Khálidhon), *Anayennisi Club* is a new place that becomes frenetic after midnight.

A couple of places that offer more traditional entertainment are the *Café Kriti*, Kalergón 22, at the corner of Andhroyíou, basically an old-fashioned kafenío where there's **Greek music** and **dancing** virtually every night, and the *Firkas* (the bastion by the naval museum), with Greek dancing at 9pm every Tuesday – pricey but authentic entertainment. It's also worth checking for events at the open-air auditorium in the public gardens, and for performances in restaurants outside the city, which are the ones the locals will go to. Look for posters, especially in front of the market and in the little platía across the road from there.

For **films**, you should also check the hoardings in front of the market. There are open-air screenings at *Attikon*, on Venizélou out towards Akrotíri, about 1km from the centre, and occasionally in the public gardens.

Listings

Airlines Olympic, Tzanakáki 88 (Mon–Fri 9am–4pm; ☎57 701). There's a bus from here connecting with their flights. For airport information call ☎63 245.

Banks The main branch of the National Bank is directly opposite the market. Convenient smaller banks for exchange are next to the bus station, at the bottom of Kaneváro just off Platía Sindrivani, or at the top of Khálidhon. There are also a couple of exchange places on Khálidhon, open long hours, and a post-office van parked through the summer in the cathedral platía.

Bike and car rental Possibilities everywhere, especially on Khálidhon, though these are rarely the best value. For bikes and cars try Duke of Crete, Sífaka 3 (☎21 651), Skalídhi 16 (☎57 821) and branches in Ayía Marína and Plataniás (discount for cash); for cars try Tellus Rent a Car, Kaneváro 9, east of Platía Sindriváni (☎50 400, fax 91 716).

Boat trips Various boat trips are offered by travel agents around town, mostly round Soúdha Bay or out to beaches on the Rodhópou peninsula. Domenico's on Kanevárou offers some of the best of these.

Ferry tickets The agent for Minoan is Nanadakis Travel, Khálidhon 8 (☎23 939); the agent for ANEK is on Venizélou, right opposite the market (☎23 636).

Laundry There are three, at Kanevárou 38 (9am–10pm), Episkópou Dorothéou 7 and Áyii Dhéka 18; all do service washes.

Left luggage The bus station has a left luggage office.

Market and supermarkets If you want to buy food or get stuff together for a picnic, the market is the place to head for. There are vast quantities of fresh fruit and vegetables as well as meat and fish, bakers, dairy stalls and general stores for cooked meats, tins and other standard provisions. There are also several small stores down by the harbour platía which sell cold drinks and a certain amount of food, but these are expensive (though they do open late). A couple of large supermarkets can be found on the main roads running out of town, for instance Inka on the way to Akrotíri.

Post office The main post office is on Tzanakáki (Mon–Fri 7am–8pm, Sat 8am–2pm for exchange). In summer, there's a handy Portakabin branch set up in the cathedral platía.

Taxis The main taxi ranks are in the cathedral platía and, especially, Platía 1866. For radio taxis try ☎29 405 or ☎58 700.

Telephones OTE headquarters (daily 6am–midnight) is on Tzanakáki just past the post office. It's generally packed during the day, but often empty late at night.

Tourist police Kareskáki 44 (☎94 477). Town and harbour police are on the inner harbour.

Travel agencies For cheap tickets home try Bassias Travel, Skridhlóf 46 (☎44 295), very helpful for regular tickets too. They also deal in standard excursions. Other travel agents for tours and day trips are everywhere.

Around Khaniá: the Akrotíri and Rodhopoú peninsulas

Just north of Khaniá, the **Akrotíri peninsula** loops around to protect the Bay of Soúdha and a NATO military base and missile-testing area. In an ironic twist, the peninsula's northwestern coastline is fast developing into a luxury suburb; the beach of Kalathás, near Khorafákia, long popular with jaded Khaniotes, is surrounded by villas and apartments. **STAVRÓS**, further out, has not yet suffered this fate, and its **beach** is absolutely superb if you like the calm, shallow water of an almost completely enclosed lagoon. It's not very large, so it does get crowded, but rarely overpoweringly so. There's a makeshift taverna/souvláki stand on the beach, and a couple of tavernas across the road, but for accommodation you need to search slightly south of here, in the area around **Blue Beach**, where there are plenty of apartment buildings.

Inland are the **monasteries** of **Ayía Triádha** (daily 9am–2pm & 5–7pm; 300dr) and **Gouvernétou** (daily 9am–12.30pm & 4.30–7pm). The former is much more accessible and has a beautiful seventeenth-century church inside its pink-and-ochre cloister, though ongoing renovations have recently caused many of the monks to relocate and on occasions make the normally peaceful enclosure more like a building site. Beyond Gouvernétou, which is in a far better state of preservation and where traditional monastic life can still be observed, you can clamber down a craggy path to the abandoned ruins of the monastery of Katholikó and the remains of its narrow (swimmable) harbour.

West to Rodhopoú

The coast to the west of Khaniá was the scene of most of the fighting during the German invasion in 1941. As you leave town, an aggressive diving eagle commemorates the German parachutists, and at Máleme there's a big German cemetery; the Allied cemetery is in the other direction, on the coast just outside Soúdha. There are also beaches and considerable tourist development along much of this shore. At **Ayía Marína** there's a fine sandy beach, and an island offshore said to be a sea monster petrified by Zeus before it could swallow Crete. Seen from the west, its "mouth" still gapes open.

Between **Plataniás** and **Kolymbári** an almost unbroken strand unfurls, by no means all sandy, but deserted for long stretches between villages. The road here runs through mixed groves of calamus reed (Crete's bamboo) and oranges; the windbreaks fashioned from the reeds protect the ripening oranges from the *meltémi*. At Kolymbári, the road to Kastélli cuts across the base of another mountainous peninsula, **Rodhopoú**. Just off the main road here is a monastery, **Goniá** (daily 9am–2pm & 5–7pm; respectable dress), with a view most luxury hotels would envy. Every monk in Crete can tell tales of his proud ancestry of resistance to invaders, but here the Turkish cannon balls are still lodged in the walls to prove it, a relic of which the good fathers are far more proud than of any of the icons.

South to the Samarian Gorge

From Khaniá the **Gorge of Samariá** (May to mid-Oct; 1200dr for entry to the national park) can be visited as a day trip or as part of a longer excursion to the south. At over 16km, it's Europe's longest gorge and is startlingly beautiful. **Buses** leave Khaniá for the top at 6.15am, 7.30am, 8.30am and 1.30pm, and you'll normally be sold a return ticket (valid from Khóra Sfakíon at any time). It's well worth catching the early bus to avoid the full heat of the day while walking through the gorge, though be warned that you will not be alone – there are often as many as five coachloads setting off before dawn for the nail-biting climb into the White Mountains. There are also direct early-morning buses from Iráklion and Réthymnon, and bus tours from virtually everywhere on the island. Despite all the crowds, the walk is hard work, especially in spring when the stream is a roaring torrent. Early and late in the season, there is a danger of **flash floods**, which are not to be taken lightly: in 1993, a number of walkers perished when they were washed out to sea. If in doubt, phone the Khaniá Forest Service (☎0821/67 140) for information.

Omalós

One way to avoid the early start would be to stay at **OMALÓS**, in the middle of the mountain plain from which the gorge descends. There are some ordinary **rooms** for rent and a couple of surprisingly fancy **hotels**; try the *Neos Omalos* (☎0821/67 269; ③). But since the village is some way from the start of the track, and the buses arrive as the sun rises, it's almost impossible to get a head start on the crowds. Some people sleep out at the top (where there's a bar-restaurant and kiosks serving drinks and sandwiches), but a night under the stars here can be a bitterly cold experience. The one significant advantage to staying up here would be if you wanted to undertake some other climbs in the White Mountains, in which case there's a **mountain hut** (☎0821/24 647; ①) about ninety minutes' walk from Omalós or from the top of the gorge.

The gorge

The **Gorge** itself begins at the *Xilóskala*, or "wooden staircase", a stepped path plunging steeply down from the southern lip of the Omalós plain. Here, at the head of the track, opposite the sheer rock face of Mount Gíngilos, the crowds pouring out of the buses disperse rapidly as keen walkers march purposefully down while others dally over breakfast, contemplating the sunrise for hours. You descend at first through almost alpine scenery: pine forest, wild flowers and very un-Cretan greenery – a verdant shock in the spring, when the stream is at its liveliest (and can at times be positively dangerous). Small churches and viewpoints dot the route, and about halfway down you pass the abandoned village of **Samariá**, now home to a wardens' station, with picnic facilities and filthy toilets. Further down, the path levels out and the gorge walls

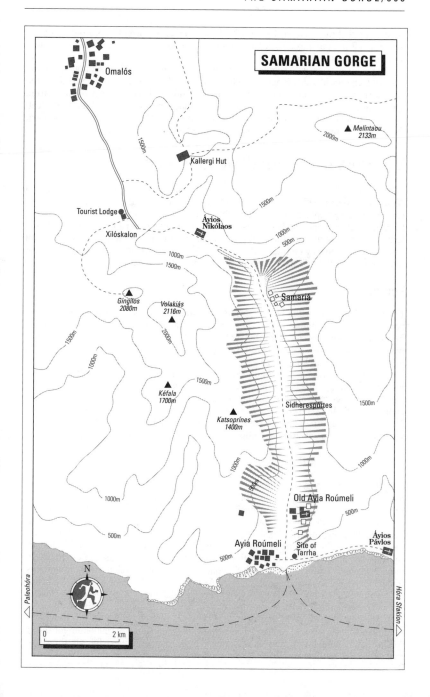

SAMARIAN GORGE

Omalós

Melíntaou 2133m

2000m

1500m

Kallergi Hut

1500m

Tourist Lodge

Áyios Nikólaos

1000m

500m

Xilóskalon

1000m

1500m

Samariá

Gíngilos 2080m

Volakiás 2116m

2000m

1500m

1000m

Kéfala 1700m

1500m

Sidherespórtes

1500m

Katsoprínes 1400m

1000m

1000m

500m

Old Ayía Roúmeli

1000m

500m

500m

Áyios Pávlos

Ayía Roúmeli

Site of Tarrha

N

Paleohóra

Hóra Sfakíon

0   2 km

close in until at the narrowest point (the *Sidherespórtes* or "Iron Gates") one can practically touch both tortured rock faces at once, and, looking up, see them rising sheer for almost a thousand feet.

At an average pace, with regular stops, the walk down takes five or six hours, and the upward trek considerably longer. It's strenuous (you'll know all about it next day), the path is rough, and solid shoes vital. On the way down, there is plenty of water from springs and streams (except some years in September and October), but nothing to eat. The park that surrounds the gorge is the only mainland refuge of the Cretan wild ibex, the *kri-kri*, but don't expect to see one; there are usually far too many people around.

Villages of the southwest coast

When you finally emerge from the gorge, it's not long before you reach the village of **AYÍA ROUMÉLI**, which is all but abandoned until you reach the beach, a mirage of iced drinks and a cluster of tavernas with **rooms** for rent. If you want to get back to Khaniá, buy your boat tickets now, especially if you want an afternoon on the beach; the last boat (connecting with the final 6.30pm bus from Khóra Sfakíon) tends to sell out first. If you plan to stay on the south coast, you should get going as soon as possible for the best chance of finding a room somewhere nicer than Ayía Rouméli.

Loutró

For tranquillity, it's hard to beat **LOUTRÓ**, two-thirds of the way to Khóra Sfakíon, and accessible only by boat or on foot. The chief disadvantage of Loutró is its lack of a real beach; most people swim from the rocks around its small bay. If you're prepared to walk, however, there are **deserted beaches** along the coast to the east. Indeed, if you're really into walking there's a **coastal trail** through Loutró which covers the entire distance between Ayía Rouméli and Khóra Sfakíon, or you could take the daunting zigzag path up the cliff behind to the mountain village of Anópoli. Loutró itself has a number of **tavernas** and **rooms**, though not always enough of the latter. Call the *Blue House* (☎0825/91 127) if you want to book ahead; this is also the best place to eat. There is also space to **camp** out on the cape by a ruined fort, but due to a long history of problems, you should be aware that campers are not very popular in the village.

Khóra Sfakíon and beyond

KHÓRA SFAKÍON is the more usual terminus for walkers traversing the gorge, with a regular boat service along the coast to and from Ayía Rouméli. Consequently, it's quite an expensive and not an especially welcoming place; there are plenty of rooms and some excellent tavernas, but for a real beach you should jump straight on the evening bus going toward Plakiás. Plenty of opportunities for a dip present themselves en route, one of the most memorable at **Frangokástello**, a crumbling Venetian attempt to bring law and order to a district that went on to defy both Turks and Germans. Its square, crenellated fort, isolated a few kilometres below a chiselled wall of mountains, looks like it's been spirited out of the High Atlas or Tibet. The place is said to be haunted by ghosts of Greek rebels massacred here in 1829; every May, these *dhrossoulítes* (dewy ones) march at dawn across the coastal plain and disappear into the sea near the fort. The rest of the time Frangokástello is peaceful enough, with a superb beach and a number of tavernas and rooms, but is somewhat stagnant if you're looking for things to do. Slightly further east, and less influenced by tourism or modern life, are the attractive villages of **Skalotí** and **Rodhákino**, each with basic lodging and food.

Soúyia

In quite the other direction from Ayía Rouméli, less regular boats also head to **SOÚYIA** and on to Paleokhóra. Soúyia, until World War II merely the anchorage for Koustoyérako inland, is low key with a long, grey pebble beach and mostly modern buildings (except for a church with a sixth-century Byzantine mosaic as the foundation). Since the completion of the new road to Khaniá, the village has started to expand; even so, except in the very middle of summer, it continues to make a good fallback for finding a room or a place to camp, eating cheaply and enjoying the beach when the rest of the island is seething with tourists.

Kastélli and the western tip

Apart from being Crete's most westerly town, and the end of the main road, **KASTÉLLI** (Kíssamos, or Kastélli Kissámou as it's variously known) has little obvious attraction. It's a busy town with a rocky beach visited mainly by people using the boat that runs twice weekly to the island of Kýthira and the Peloponnese. The very ordinariness of Kastélli, however, can be attractive: life goes on pretty much regardless of outsiders, but there's every facility you might need. The **ferry agent's office** in Kastélli is right on the main platía (Xirouxákis; ☎0822/22 655), and nothing else is far away apart from the dock, a two-kilometre walk (or inexpensive taxi ride) from town.

Falásarna to Elafoníssi

To the west of Kastélli lies some of Crete's loneliest, and, for many visitors, finest coastline. The first place of note is ancient **Falásarna**, city ruins which mean little to the nonspecialist, but they do overlook some of the best beaches on Crete, wide and sandy with clean water. There's a handful of tavernas and an increasing number of rooms for rent; otherwise, you have to sleep out, as many people do. This can mean that the main beaches are dirty, but they remain beautiful, and there are plenty of others within walking distance. The nearest real town is **Plátanos**, 5km up the recently paved road, along which there are a couple of daily buses.

Further south, the western coastline is still less discovered and the road is surfaced only as far as Kámbos; there's little in the way of official accommodation. **Sfinári** has several houses which rent rooms, and a quiet pebble beach a little way below the village. **Kámbos** is similar, but even less visited, its beach a considerable walk down a hill. Beyond them both is the **monastery of Khrissoskalítissa**, increasingly visited by

---

A ROUND TRIP

If you have transport, a circular drive from Kastélli, taking the coast road in one direction and the inland route through Élos and Topólia, makes for a stunningly scenic circuit. Near the ocean, villages cling to the high mountain sides, apparently halted by some miracle in the midst of calamitous seaward slides. Around them, olives ripen on the terraced slopes, the sea glittering far below. Inland, especially at **ÉLOS**, the main crop is the chestnut, whose huge old trees shade the village streets.

In **TOPÓLIA**, the chapel of Ayía Sofía is sheltered inside a cave which has been used as a shrine since Neolithic times. Cutting south from Élos, a paved road continues through the high mountains towards Paleokhóra. On a motorbike, with a sense of adventure and plenty of fuel, it's great: the bus doesn't come this way, villagers still stare at the sight of a tourist, and a host of small, seasonal streams cascade beside or under the asphalt.

tours from Khaniá and Paleokhóra now the road has been sealed, but well worth the effort for its isolation and nearby beaches; the bus gets as far as Váthy, from where the monastery is another two hours' walk away.

Five kilometres beyond Khryssoskalítissa, the road bumps down to the coast opposite the tiny uninhabited islet of **Elafonísi**. You can easily wade out to the islet with its sandy beaches and rock pools, and the shallow lagoon is warm and crystal-clear. It looks magnificent, but daily boat trips from Paleokhóra and coach tours from elsewhere on the island ensure that, in the middle of the day at least, it's far from deserted. Even bigger changes are now on the horizon here as Greek and German companies have bought up large tracts of land to create a monster tourist complex, although these plans are currently stalled, with developers in dispute with the government about how things should proceed. If you want to stay, and really appreciate the place, there are a couple of seasonal tavernas, but bring some supplies unless you want to be wholly dependent on them.

Kándhanos and Paleokhóra

Getting down to Paleokhóra by the main road, now paved the whole way, is a lot easier, and several daily buses from Khaniá make the trip. But although this route also has to wind through the western outriders of the White Mountains, it lacks the excitement of the routes to either side. **Kándhanos**, at the 58-kilometre mark, has been entirely rebuilt since it was destroyed by the Germans for its fierce resistance to their occupation. The original sign erected when the deed was done is preserved on the war memorial: "Here stood Kándanos, destroyed in retribution for the murder of 25 German soldiers".

When the beach at **PALEOKHÓRA** finally appears below it is a welcome sight. The little town is built across the base of a peninsula, its harbour on one side, the sand on the other. Above, on the outcrop, Venetian ramparts stand sentinel. These days Paleokhóra has become heavily developed, but it's still thoroughly enjoyable, with a main street filling with tables as diners spill out of the restaurants, and with a pleasantly chaotic social life. A good place to **eat** with some good imaginative vegetarian specials is *The Third Eye*, just out of the centre towards the sandy beach. There are scores of places to stay (though not always many vacancies) and there's also a fair-sized **campsite**; in extremis, the beach is one of the best to sleep out on, with showers, trees and acres of sand. Nearby discos and a rock'n'roll bar, or the soundtrack from the open-air cinema, combine to lull you to sleep. When you tire of Paleokhóra and the excellent windsurfing in the bay, there are excursions up the hill to Prodhrómi, for example, or along a five-hour coastal path to Soúyia.

You'll find a helpful **tourist office** (daily 9.30am–1pm & 5.30–9pm) in the town hall on Venizélos in the centre of town; they have full accommodation lists and a map (though you'll hardly need this). The **OTE**, **banks** and **travel agents** are all nearby; the **post office** is on the road behind the sandy beach. **Boats** run from here to Elafonísi, the island of Gávdhos, and along the coast to Soúyia and Ayía Rouméli.

Gávdhos

The island of **Gávdhos**, some fifty kilometres of rough sea south of Paleokhóra, is the most southerly landmass in Europe. Gávdhos is small (about 10km by 7km) and barren, but it has one major attraction: the enduring **isolation** which its inaccessible position has helped preserve. There are now a few package tours (travel agents in Paleokhóra can arrange a room if you want one), and there's a semi-permanent community of campers through the summer, but if all you want is a beach to yourself and a taverna to grill your fish, this remains the place for you.

travel details

Flights

Khaniá Several flights a day to Athens; one weekly to Thessaloníki.

Iráklion Many daily flights to Athens; 4 weekly to Rhodes; 2 weekly to Mýkonos; and 3 weekly to Thessaloníki.

Ferries

Áyios Nikólaos and Sitía 1–3 ferries a week to Kássos, Kárpathos, Khálki, Rhodes and the Dodecanese; 1–2 weekly to Thíra, Folégandhros, Mílos, Sífnos and Pireás.

Khaniá 1 or 2 ferries daily to Pireás (12hr).

Khóra Sfakíon 5 ferries daily to Loutró/Ayía Rouméli; 3 weekly to Gávdhos in season.

Iráklion 2 ferries daily to Pireás (12hr); 3 ferries weekly to Thessaloníki; at least one daily ferry to Thíra (4hr), also fast boats and hydrofoils (2hr 30min); daily ferries to Páros in season; most days to Mýkonos and Íos; at least twice weekly to Náxos, Tínos, Skýros, Skíathos, Kárpathos and Rhodes. Ferries to Ancona (Italy) twice weekly and Çeşme (Turkey) weekly; also weekly to Limassol (Cyprus) and Haifa (Israel).

Kastélli (Kíssamos) 1–3 ferries weekly to Kýthira, Yíthio (8hr), Monemvassía and Pireás.

Paleokhóra 3 boats a week in season to Gávdhos. Also daily sailings to Elafonísi and Soúyia.

Réthymnon 3 ferries a week to Pireás (12hr); weekly service and seasonal day trips to Thíra.

Buses

Áyios Nikólaos–Sitía (6 daily 6.30am–6pm; 2hr).

Khaniá–Réthymnon–Iráklion (30 daily 5.30am– 9.30pm; 3hr total).

Khaniá–Khóra Sfakíon (3 daily 8.30am–2pm; 2hr).

Khaniá–Paleokhóra (5 daily 8.30am–5pm; 2hr).

Iráklion–Áyios Nikólaos (38 daily 6.30am– 7.30pm; 1hr 30min).

Iráklion–Ierápetra (7 daily 7.30am–6.30pm; 2hr 30min).

Iráklion–Ayía Galíni (38 daily 6.30am–7pm; 2hr 15min).

Iráklion–Festós (9 daily 7.30am–5.30pm; 1hr 30min).

Kastélli–Khaniá (15 daily 5am–7.30pm; 1hr 30min).

Réthymnon–Spíli–Ayía Galíni (6 daily 6.30am– 5pm; 45min–1hr 30min).

CHAPTER NINE

THE DODECANESE

T he furthest Greek island group from the mainland, the **Dodecanese** (Dhodhekánisos) lie close to the Turkish coast – some, like Kós and Kastellórizo, almost within hailing distance of the shore. Because of this position, and their remoteness from Athens, the islands have had a turbulent history: they were the scene of ferocious battles between German and British forces in 1943–44, and were only finally included in the modern Greek state in 1948 after centuries of occupation by Crusaders, Ottomans and Italians. Even now the threat (real or imagined) of invasion from Turkey is very much in evidence. When you ask about the heavy military presence, many locals talk in terms of "when the Turks come", rarely "if".

Whatever the rigours of the various occupations, their legacy includes a wonderful blend of architectural styles and of Eastern and Western cultures. Medieval Rhodes is the most famous, but almost every island has some Classical remains, a Crusaders' castle, a clutch of traditional villages, and abundant grandiose public buildings. For these last the Italians, who occupied the islands from 1912 to 1943, are mainly responsible. In their determination to beautify the islands and turn them into a showplace for fascism they undertook public works, excavations and reconstruction on a massive scale; if historical accuracy was often sacrificed in the interests of style, only an expert is likely to complain. A more sinister aspect of the Italian administration was the attempted forcible Latinization of the populace: spoken Greek and Orthodox observance were banned in public from 1923 to 1943. The most tangible reminder of this policy is the (dwindling) number of older people who can still converse – and write – more fluently in Italian than in Greek.

Aside from this bilingualism, the Dodecanese themselves display a marked topographic and economic schizophrenia. The dry limestone outcrops of **Kastellórizo**, **Sými**, **Khálki**, **Kássos** and **Kálymnos** have always been forced to rely on the sea for their livelihoods, and the wealth generated by the maritime culture – especially in the nineteenth century – fostered the growth of attractive port towns. The sprawling, rel-

---

ACCOMMODATION PRICE CODES

,Throughout the book we've used the following **price codes** to denote the cheapest available room in high season; all are prices for a double room, except for category ①, which represents per person rates. Out of season, rates can drop by up to fifty percent, especially if you are staying for three or more nights. Single rooms, where available, cost around seventy percent of the price of a double.

Rented private rooms on the islands usually fall into the ② or ③ categories, depending on their location and facilities, and the season; a few in the ④ category are more like plush self-catering apartments. They are not generally available from late October through to the beginning of April, when only hotels tend to remain open.

① 1400–2000dr	④ 8000–12,000dr
② 4000–6000dr	⑤ 12,000–16,000dr
③ 6000–8000dr	⑥ 16,000dr and upwards

For more accommodation details, see pp.39–42.

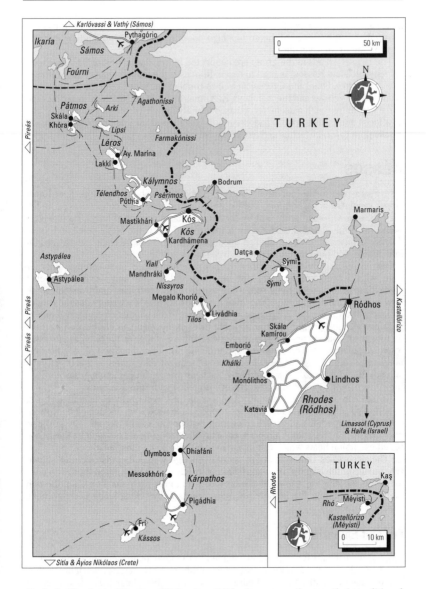

atively fertile giants, **Rhodes** (Ródhos) and **Kós**, have recently seen their traditional agricultural economies almost totally displaced by a tourist industry drawn by good beaches and nightlife, as well as the Aegean's most exciting historical monuments. **Kárpathos** lies somewhere in between, with a (formerly) forested north grafted on to a rocky limestone south; **Tílos**, despite its lack of trees, has ample water, though the green volcano-island of **Níssyros** does not. **Léros** shelters softer contours and more amenable terrain than its map outline would suggest, while **Pátmos** and **Astypálea** at the fringes of the archipelago boast architecture and landscapes more appropriate to the Cyclades.

The largest islands in the group are connected by regular ferries, and none (except for Astypálea and Kássos) is hard to reach. Rhodes is the main transport hub, with services to Turkey, Israel and Cyprus, as well as connections with Crete, the northeastern islands, the Cyclades and the mainland. Kálymnos and Kós are jointly an important secondary terminus, with a useful ferry based on Kálymnos, hydrofoil services using Kós as a focus and transfer point, and excursion boats based on Kós providing a valuable supplement to larger ferries arriving at uncivil hours.

Kássos

Like Psará islet in the northeast Aegean, **Kássos** contributed its large fleet to the Greek revolutionary war effort, and likewise suffered appalling consequences. In late May 1824, an Ottoman army sent by Ibrahim Pasha, Governor of Egypt, besieged the island; on June 7, aided perhaps by a traitor's tip as to the weak point in Kássos' defences, the invaders descended on the populated north-coastal plain, slaughtered the inhabitants, and put houses, farms and trees to the torch.

Barren and depopulated since then, numerous sheer gorges slash through lunar terrain, with fenced smallholdings of olives providing the only permanent relief. Springtime grain crops briefly soften the usually empty terraces, and livestock somehow survives on a thin furze of thornbush. Kássos attracts few visitors despite regular air links with Rhodes and Kárpathos. What remains of the population is grouped together in five villages facing Kárpathos, leaving most of the island accessible only to those on foot or on boat excursions. There's little sign here of the wealth brought into other islands by diaspora Greeks or tourists; crumbling houses and disused hillside terraces poignantly recall better days. Evidence of subsequent emigration to the US is widespread: American logo-T-shirts and baseball caps are de rigueur summer fashion, and the conversation of vacationing expatriates is spiked with Americanisms.

Kássos can be tricky to reach; Frý's anchorage just west of Boúka fishing port is so poor that passing ferries won't stop if any appreciable wind is up. In such cases, you disembark at Kárpathos and fly the remaining distance in a light aircraft. The air ticket plus a taxi fare to Kárpathos airport is comparable to the amount charged by Kárpathos-based excursion boats which can manoeuvre into Boúka in most weathers.

The airport lies 1km west of Frý, an easy enough walk, otherwise a cheap (400dr) ride on one of the island's three taxis. Except in July and August, when there's an unreliable bus service and a few rental motorbikes and boat excursions on offer, the only method of exploring the island's remoter corners is by hiking along fairly arduous, shadeless tracks.

Frý and Emboriós

Most of the capital **FRÝ**'s appeal is confined to the immediate environs of the wedge-shaped fishing port of **Boúka**, protected from the sea by two crab-claws of breakwater and overlooked by the town cathedral of Áyios Spirídhon. Inland, Frý is engagingly unpretentious, even down-at-heel; no attempt has been made to prettify what is essentially a dusty little town poised halfway between demolition and reconstruction. **Accommodation** is found at the seafront hotels *Anagenissis* (☎0245/41 323, fax 41 036; ②) and, just behind, the less expensive *Anessis* (☎0245/41 201, fax 41 730; ②). The manager of the *Anagenessis* also has a few pricier apartments (④), and runs the all-in-one travel agency just below. Both hotels tend to be noisy owing to morning bustle on the waterfront – and the phenomenal number of small but lively **bars** in town, one right under the *Anessis*. During high season a few **rooms** operate; these tend to be in the suburb of Emboriós, fifteen minute's walk east, and also more expensive.

Perched overlooking the Boúka, *Iy Oraia Bouka* is easily the best of Frý's **tavernas**, and is reasonably priced. *To Meltemi* ouzerí, on the way to Emboriós, is an honourable runner-up. Shops in Frý, including two fruit stalls, are fairly well stocked for self-catering.

Frý's town **beach**, if you can call it that, is at **Ammouá** (Ammoudhiá), a thirty-minute walk beyond the airstrip along the coastal track. This sandy cove, just before the landmark chapel of Áyios Konstandínos, is often caked with seaweed and tar, but persevere five minutes more and you'll find much cleaner pea-gravel coves. Otherwise, it's worth shelling out for high-season boat excursions to far better beaches on a pair of islets visible to the northwest, **Armathiá** and **Makrá**. There are no amenities (nor shade) on either islet.

The interior

Kássos' inland villages cluster in the agricultural plain just inland from Frý, and are linked to each other by road; all, except the dull grid of Arvanitokhóri, are worth a passing visit, accomplishable by foot in a single day.

Larger in extent and more rural than Frý, **AYÍA MARÍNA**, 1500m inland and uphill, is most attractive seen from the south; one of its two belfried churches is the focus of the island's liveliest festival, on July 17. Just beyond the hamlet of Kathístres, a further 500m southwest, the cave of **Ellinokamára** is named for the Hellenistic wall partially blocking the entrance; from there a path continues another ninety minutes in the same direction to the larger, more natural cave of **Seláï**, with impressive stalactites. On the opposite side of the plain, **PANAYÍA** is famous for its now-neglected mansions – many of Kássos' wealthiest ship captains hailed from here – and the oldest surviving church on the island, the eighteenth-century **Panayía tou Yeóryi**. From **PÓLIO**, 2km above Panayía and site of the island's badly deteriorated medieval castle, a track leads southeast within ninety minutes to **Áyios Mámas**, one of two important rural monasteries.

Between Ayía Marína and Arvanitokhóri, a dirt track heads southwest from the paved road linking the two villages; having skirted the narrows of a fearsome gorge, you are unlikely to see another living thing aside from goats or an occasional wheeling hawk. After about an hour the Mediterranean appears to the south, a dull expanse ruffled only by the occasional ship bound for Cyprus and the Middle East. When you finally reach a fork, adopt the upper, right-hand turning, following derelict phone lines and (initially) some cement paving towards the rural monastery of **Áyios Yeóryios Khadhión**, 11km (3hr on foot) from Frý, and only frequented during its the late-April festival time, and during mid-summer by the resident caretaker. There are a few open guest cells and cistern water here if you need to fill up canteens; the only other water en route is a well at the route's high point.

From the monastery it's another 3km – bikes can make it most of the way – to **Khélathros**, a lonely cove at the mouth of one of the larger, more forbidding Kassiote canyons. The sand-and-gravel beach itself is small and mediocre, but the water is pristine and – except for the occasional fishing boat – you'll probably be alone. The lower, left-hand option at the fork is the direct track to Khélathros, but this is only 2km shorter, and following severe storm damage, impassable to any vehicle and all but the most energetic hikers.

Kárpathos

A long, narrow island between Rhodes and Crete, wild **Kárpathos** has always been something of an underpopulated backwater, although it is the third largest of the Dodecanese. A mountainous spine, habitually cloud-capped, rises to over 1200 metres, and divides the more populous, lower-lying south from an exceptionally rugged north. Despite a magnificent windswept coastline of cliffs and promontories interrupted by little beaches, Kárpathos has succumbed surprisingly little to tourism. This has much to do with the appalling road system – rutted where paved, unspeakable otherwise – the paucity of interesting villages, and the often high cost of food, which offsets reasonable room prices.

Kárpathos hasn't the most alluring of interiors: the central and northern uplands were badly scorched by forest fires in the 1980s, and agriculture plays a slighter role than on any other Greek island of comparable size. Frankly, the Karpathians are too well off to bother much with farming – massive emigration to America and the resulting remittance economy has transformed Kárpathos into one of the wealthiest Greek islands. Most visitors come here for a glimpse of the traditional village life that prevails in the isolated north of the island, and for the numerous superb, secluded beaches. Although the airport can take direct international flights, only a few charters use it, and visitors are concentrated in a couple of resorts in the south.

Kárpathos' four Mycenean and Classical cities figure little in ancient chronicles. Alone of the major Dodecanese, the island was held by the Genoese and Venetians after the Byzantine collapse and so has no castle of the crusading Knights of Saint John, nor any surviving medieval fortresses of consequence. The Ottomans couldn't be bothered to settle or even garrison it; instead they left a single judge or *kadi* at the main town, making the Greek population responsible for his safety during the many pirate attacks.

Pigádhia (Kárpathos Town)

PIGÁDHIA, the capital, often known simply as Kárpathos, nestles at the south end of scenic Vróndi Bay, whose sickle of sand extends 3km northwest. The town itself, curling around the jetty and quay where ferries and excursion boats dock, is as drab as its setting is beautiful, an ever-increasing number of concrete blocks creating an air of a vast building site; by comparison the Italian-era port police building seems an heirloom. Although there's nothing special to see, Pigádhia does offer just about every facility you might need.

Practicalities

There's an **OTE** at the top end of Ethnikís Andistásis; Olympic Airways is on Apodhímon Karpathíon ("Street of the Overseas Karpathians"), at the corner of Mitropolítou; while the **post office** is on 28-Oktovríou, the main inland street running parallel to Apodhímon Kapathíon.

If you want to explore the island there are regular **buses** to Pilés, via Apéri, Voládha and Óthos, as well as to Ammopí, and a less regular service to Arkássa and Finíki. Set-rate, unmetered **taxis** aren't too expensive to get to these and other points (such as the airport) on the paved road system, but charge a fortune to go anywhere further afield. Outfits near the post office like Holiday (☎0245/22 813) or Circle (☎0245/22 690) rent **cars** at vastly inflated rates, while Hermes (☎0245/22 090) does **bike rental**. Be warned that the only fuel on the island is to be found just to the north and south of town, and the tanks on the small bikes are barely big enough to complete a circuit of the south, let alone head up north – which is, in any case, expressly forbidden by most outfits. For seagoing jaunts, **windsurfers** and **canoes** are rented from various stalls on Vróndi beach.

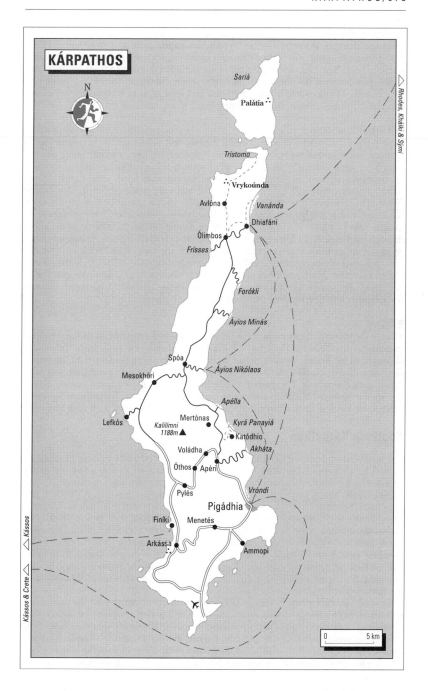

KÁRPATHOS

N

Sariá

Palátia

Trístomo

Vrykoúnda

Avlóna ●   *Vanánda*

Ólimbos ●   Dhiafáni ●

Frísses

Forókli

Áyios Minás

Spóa ●

Mesokhóri ●   *Áyios Nikólaos*

Apélla

Lefkós ●   Mertónas ●   *Kyrá Panayiá*

Kalilímni
1188m ▲   ● Katódhio

Voládha ●   *Akháta*

Óthos ● ● Apéri

Pylés ●   *Vróndi*

Pigádhia

Finíki ●   Menetés ●

Arkássa ●   ● Ammopí

✈

0   5 km

△ *Rhodes, Khálki & Sými*

△ *Kássos*

Kássos & Crete △

The north is most usually reached by **boat**. Olympos Travel (☎0245/22 993), on the front near the jetty, offers good deals on all-in **day-tours** (from around 4500dr to Ólymbos), though the rival boat (Chrisovalandou Lines; pay on board) is more attractive and stable in heavy sea. Less well-publicized is the fact that you can use these boats to travel **one-way** between the north and the south, paying about one-third of the going rate for day trips. Olympos and other agents can also offer trips to Kássos and to isolated east coast beaches without facilities (bring lunch if not included).

ACCOMMODATION

Most ferries are met by people offering **rooms**, and unless you've arranged one in advance, you might as well take up an offer – standards seem generally good, and the town is so small that no location is too inconvenient. If you prefer to hunt for yourself, possibilities near the jetty, signposted past the (not recommended) *Hotel Coral*, include *Anna's Rooms* (☎0245/22 313; ②), good value and very well positioned. The nearby *Vittoroulis Furnished Apartments* (☎0245/22 639; ④) are available only on a weekly basis, but worth it if you're staying that long. Other, simpler rooms establishments include *Sofia's* (☎0245/22 154; ②), the rambling *Konaki* (☎0245/22 908; ②) on the upper through-road west of the town hall, or *Filoxenia* (☎0245/22 623; ②) on Anastasíou, a cul-de-sac on the east side of town. Inland hotels include the basic *Avra* (☎0245/22 388; ②), open year-round, and the more comfortable *Karpathos* (☎0245/22 347; ③) at the far end of Dhimokratías. More luxurious places lie north towards, and behind, **Vróndi** beach and tend to be occupied by package groups as far as the ruined fifth-century basilica of **Ayía Fotiní**, with development gradually spreading beyond here.

EATING

Most of the waterfront **tavernas** are indistinguishable and expensive, with some notable exceptions: the *Olympia* psistariá will appeal to meat-lovers, while fish aficionados should head for *Iy Kali Kardhia*, at the north end of the shore boulevard on the way to the beach. Places inland tend to work out cheaper: try *Mike's*, up a pedestrian way from Apodhímon Karpathíon. Live **music** can be heard nightly at the *Halkia* kafenío, one of the few surviving old buildings next to the church on Apodhímon Karpathíon. At Vróndi there's just a single, decent taverna at the south end, *To Limanaki*, open only for lunch.

Southern Kárpathos

The southern extremity of Kárpathos towards the airport is extraordinarily desolate, its natural barrenness exacerbated by recent fires. There are a couple of empty, sandy beaches on the southeast coast, but they're not at all attractive and are exposed to prevailing winds. You're better off going no further in this direction than **AMMOPÍ**, just 7km from Pigádhia. This, together with the recent development at Vróndi and Arkássa (see below), is the closest thing on Kárpathos to a purpose-built beach resort: two sandy, tree-fringed coves serviced by a couple of tavernas and a few rooms places or small hotels – recommendable among these is the *Votsalakia* (☎0245/22 204; ③). Heading west from Pigádhia rather than south, the road climbs steeply 9km up to **MENETÉS**, an appealing ridgetop village with handsome old houses, a tiny folklore museum and a spectacularly sited church. There's a good taverna here, *Manolis*, and a memorial with views back to the east.

Beyond Menetés, you descend to **ARKÁSSA**, tucked into a ravine on the west coast, with excellent views to Kássos en route. Arkássa has been heavily developed, with hotels and restaurants dotted along the largely rocky coastline to either side; most facilities are aimed squarely at the package market, but you could try *Pension Filoxenia* (☎0245/61 341; ②) or the well-regarded *Taverna Petaloudha*, both in the village itself.

A few hundred metres south of where the ravine meets the sea, a signposted cement side road leads to the whitewashed chapel of Ayía Sofía, marooned amidst various remains of Classical and Byzantine Arkessia. These consist of several mosaic floors with geometric patterns, including one running diagonally under the floor of a half-buried chapel, emerging from the walls on either side. The Paleókastro headland beyond was the site of Mycenean Arkessia.

The tiny fishing port of **FINÍKI**, just a couple of kilometres north, offers a minuscule beach, occasional excursions to Kássos, three or four **tavernas** with seafood menus, and several **rooms** establishments lining the road to the jetty, including *Fay's Paradise* (☎0245/61 308; ③). The asphalt on the west-coast road currently runs out well short of the attractive resort of **LEFKÓS** (Paraliá Lefkoú). Although this is a delightful place for flopping on the beach, only three weekly buses call, and Lefkós marks the furthest point you can reach from Pighádhia on a small motorbike and return safely before running out of fuel. Your efforts will be rewarded by the striking landscape of cliffs, hills, islets and sandspits surrounding a triple bay. The *Sunlight Restaurant* has an enviable tamarisk-shaded position on the southern cove, and several **rooms** places dot the promontory overlooking the two more northerly, and progressively wilder, bays.

Back on the main road, you climb northeast through one of the few sections of pine forest not scarred by fire, to **MESOKHÓRI**. The village tumbles down towards the sea around narrow, stepped alleys; the access road ends at the top of town, where a snack bar constitutes the only tourist facility. Alternatively, you can carry on to Spóa, overlooking the east coast.

Central Kárpathos

The centre of Kárpathos supports a quartet of villages blessed with superb hillside settings and ample running water. In these settlements nearly everyone has "done time" in North America, then returned home with their nest eggs: New Jersey, New York and Canadian car plates tell you exactly where repatriated islanders struck it rich. West-facing **PYLÉS** is the most attractive, while **ÓTHOS**, noted for its red wine and a private ethnographic museum is the highest and chilliest, just below 1214-metre Mount Kalilímni and a huge wind turbine. On the east side of the ridge you find **VOLÁDHA** with its tiny Venetian citadel. From **APÉRI**, the largest, lowest and wealthiest settlement, you can drive 7km along a very rough road to the dramatic pebble beach of **Akháta**, with a spring but no other facilities.

Beyond Apéri, the road up the **east coast** is extremely rough in places, passing above beaches most easily accessible by boat trips from Pigádhia. **Kyrá Panayiá** is the first encountered, reached via a rutted side road through Katódhio hamlet; there's a surprising number of villas, rooms and tavernas in the ravine behind the 150m of fine gravel and sheltered, turquoise water. **Apélla** is the best of the beaches you can – just about – reach by road, but has no amenities other than a spring. The end of this route is **SPÓA**, high above the shore on the island's spine, with a snack bar at the edge of the village; there's also a good traditional kafenío a short way down. **Áyios Nikólaos**, 5km below, is a beach and port with tavernas and a large, if overgrown, early Christian town to explore.

Northern Kárpathos

Although connected by dirt road with Spóa, much the easiest way to get to northern Kárpathos is by boat – inter-island ferries call at Dhiafáni once a week, or there are smaller tour boats from Pigádhia daily. These take a couple of hours, and are met at Dhiafáni by buses for the eight-kilometre transfer up to Ólymbos, the traditional village that is the main attraction of this part of the island.

Ólymbos and around

Originally founded as a pirate-safe refuge in Byzantine times, windswept **ÓLYMBOS** straddles a long ridge below slopes studded by mostly ruined windmills. Two restored ones, beyond the main church, grind wheat and barley during late summer, and the basement of one houses a small ethnographic museum (odd hours; free). Indeed the village has long attracted foreign and Greek ethnologists, who treat it as a living museum of peasant dress, crafts, dialect and music long since gone elsewhere in Greece. It's still a very picturesque place, yet traditions are vanishing by the year; nowadays it's only the older women and those working in the several tourist shops who wear the striking and magnificently colourful traditional dress.

After a while you'll notice the prominent role that the women play in daily life: tending gardens, carrying goods on their shoulders, or herding goats. Nearly all Ólymbos men emigrate or work outside the village, sending money home and returning only on holidays. The long-isolated villagers also speak a unique dialect, said to maintain traces of its Doric and Phrygian origins – thus "Ólymbos" is pronounced "Élymbos" locally. Traditional music is still heard regularly and draws crowds of visitors at festival times, in particular Easter and August 15, when you've little hope of finding a bed.

At other times, the daytime commercialization of Ólymbos makes a good reason to **stay** overnight in one of an increasing number of **rooms** places. The *Ólymbos* (✆0245/51 252; ②), near the village entrance, is a good bare-bones option, while *Hotel Aphrodite* (✆0245/51 307; ③) offers both en-suite facilities and a southerly ocean view. There are also plenty of places to **eat** – *Parthenonas*, on the square by the church, is excellent; try their *makaroúnes*, a local dish of homemade pasta with onions and cheese.

From the village, the west coast and tiny port and beach at **Frísses** are a dizzy drop below, or there are various signposted **hikes** up into the mountains. It's also possible to walk between Ólymbos and Spóa or Messokhóri in the south, a six-to-seven hour trek made less scenic by the aftermath of fires. Perhaps the most attractive option, and certainly the easiest, is to walk back down to Dhiafáni, beginning just below the two working windmills. The route is well marked, eventually dropping to a ravine amidst extensive forest. The hike takes around ninety minutes downhill – too long to accomplish in the standard three or four hours allowed on day trips if you want to explore Ólymbos as well. By staying overnight in the village, you could also tackle the trail north to the Byzantine ruins at **Vrykoúnda**, via the seasonally inhabited hamlet of Avlóna.

Dhiafáni

Although its popularity is growing – especially since the completion of a new dock – rooms in **DHIAFÁNI** are still inexpensive, and the pace of life slow outside of August. There are plenty of places at which to stay and eat, shops that will change money and even a small travel agency. The obvious non-en-suite hotels opposite the quay are noisy; try instead the garrulously friendly *Pansion Delfini* (✆0245/51 391; ②) or *Pansion Glaros* (✆0245/51 259; ②; high season only), up on the southern hillside. On the front, the favourite taverna is *Anatoli*, easily recognizable by the folk reliefs that sprout from its roof.

There are boat trips to various nearby **beaches** – as well as to Byzantine ruins on the uninhabited islet of **Sariá** or through the narrow strait to Trístomo anchorage and the ruins of Vrykoúnda (see above) – or there are several coves within walking distance. Closest is **Vanánda**, a stony beach with an eccentric campsite-snack bar in the oasis behind. To get there, follow the pleasant signposted path north through the pines, but don't believe the signs that say ten minutes – it's over thirty minutes away, shortcutting the more recent road.

Rhodes (Ródhos)

It's no accident that **Rhodes** is among the most-visited Greek islands. Not only is its east coast lined with numerous sandy beaches, but the capital's nucleus is a beautiful and remarkably preserved medieval city, the legacy of the crusading Knights of Saint John who used the island as their main base from 1309 until 1522. Unfortunately this showpiece is jammed to capacity with up to 100,000 tourists a day, nine months of the year. Of transient visitors, Germans, Brits, Swedes, Italians and Danes predominate in

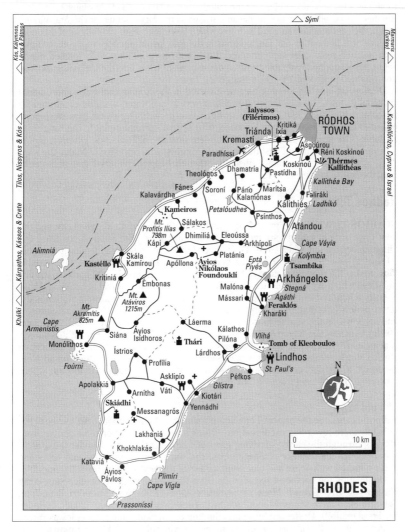

that order; accordingly fish fingers, smörgåsbord and pizza jostle alongside moussaká on menus at tourist tavernas.

Blessed with an equable climate and strategic position, Rhodes was important from earliest times despite a lack of many good harbours. The best natural port spawned the ancient town of Lindos which, together with the other city states, Kameiros and Ialyssos, united in 408 BC to found the new capital of Rhodes at the northern tip of the island. At various moments the cities allied themselves with Alexander, the Persians, Athenians or Spartans as prevailing conditions suited them, generally escaping retribution for backing the wrong side by a combination of seafaring audacity, sycophancy and burgeoning wealth as a trade centre. Following the failed siege of Demetrios Polyorkites in 305 BC, Rhodes prospered even more, displacing Athens as the major venue for rhetoric and the arts in the east Mediterranean. The town, which lies underneath virtually all of the modern city, was laid out by one Hippodamus in the grid layout much in vogue at the time, with planned residential and commercial quarters. Its perimeter walls totalled nearly 15km, enclosing nearly double the area of the present town, and the Hellenistic population was said to exceed 100,000, a staggering figure for late antiquity.

Decline set in when Rhodes became involved in the Roman civil wars, and Cassius sacked the town; by late imperial times, it was a backwater, a status confirmed by numerous Barbarian raids during the Byzantine period. The Byzantines were compelled to cede the island to the Genoese, who in turn surrendered it to the Knights of St John. The second great siege of Rhodes, during 1522–23, saw Ottoman sultan Süleyman the Magnificent oust the stubborn knights, who retreated to Malta; the town once again lapsed into relative obscurity, though heavily colonized and garrisoned, until the Italian seizure of 1912.

Ródhos Town

RÓDHOS TOWN divides into two unequal parts: the compact old walled city, and the new town which sprawls around it in three directions. The latter dates from the Ottoman occupation, when Greek Orthodox – forbidden to dwell in the old city – founded several suburb villages or *marásia* in the environs. In the walled town, the tourist is king, and in the modern district of Neokhóri west of Mandhráki yacht harbour, the few buildings which aren't hotels are souvenir shops, car rental or travel agencies and bars – easily a hundred in every category. Around this to the north and west stretches the **town beach** (standing room only for latecomers), complete with deckchairs, parasols and showers. At the northernmost point of the island an **Aquarium** (daily 9am–9pm; 600dr), officially the "Hydrobiological Institute", offers some diversion with its subterranean maze of seawater tanks. Upstairs is a less enthralling collection of half-rotten stuffed sharks, seals and even a whale. Some 200m southeast stands the **Murad Reis mosque**, a Muslim cemetery, and just west of this the **Villa Cleobolus**, where Lawrence Durrell lived from 1945 to 1947.

The old town

Simply to catalogue the principal monuments and attractions cannot do full justice to the infinitely more rewarding **medieval city**. There's ample gratification to be derived from slipping through the eleven surviving gates and strolling the streets, under flying archways built for earthquake resistance, past the warm-toned sandstone and limestone walls splashed with ochre and blue paint, and over the *khokhláki* (pebble) pavement.

Dominating the northeast sector of the city's fourteenth-century fortifications, is the **Palace of the Grand Masters** (summer Mon 12.30–7pm, Tues–Fri 8am–7pm, Sat–Sun 8am–3pm; winter Mon 12.30–3pm, Tues–Sun 8.30am–3pm; 1200dr, includes medieval exhibit). Destroyed by an ammunition depot explosion in 1856, it was reconstructed by the Italians as a summer home for Mussolini and Victor Emmanuel III

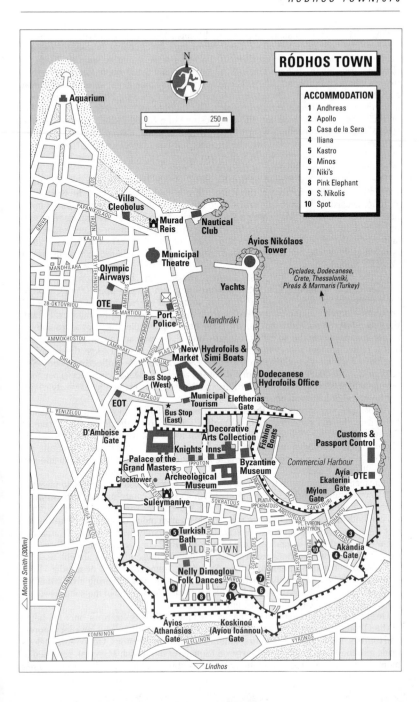

RÓDHOS TOWN

ACCOMMODATION
1 Andhreas
2 Apollo
3 Casa de la Sera
4 Iliana
5 Kastro
6 Minos
7 Niki's
8 Pink Elephant
9 S. Nikolis
10 Spot

Aquarium

Villa Cleobolus

Murad Reis

Nautical Club

Áyios Nikólaos Tower

Olympic Airways

Municipal Theatre

OTE

Port Police

Cyclades, Dodecanese, Crete, Thessaloníki, Pireás & Marmaris (Turkey)

Yachts

Mandhráki

New Market

Hydrofoils & Sími Boats

Bus Stop (West)

Municipal Tourism

Eleftherías Gate

Dodecanese Hydrofoils Office

EOT

Bus Stop (East)

D'Amboise Gate

Decorative Arts Collection

Knights' Inns

Customs & Passport Control

Palace of the Grand Masters

Byzantine Museum

Commercial Harbour

Clocktower

Archeological Museum

Áyia Ekaterini Gate

OTE

Mýlon Gate

Suleymaniye

Turkish Bath

OLD TOWN

Akándia Gate

Nelly Dimoglou Folk Dances

Áyios Athanásios Gate

Koskinoú (Ayíou Ioánnou) Gate

Fishing Boats

△ Monte Smith (300m)

▽ Líndhos

0   250 m

N

("King of Italy and Albania, Emperor of Ethiopia"), neither of whom ever visited Rhodes. The exterior, based on medieval engravings and accounts, is passably authentic, but inside matters are on an altogether grander scale: a marble staircase leads up to rooms paved with Hellenistic mosaics from Kós, and the movable furnishings rival many a northern European palace. The ground floor is home to the splendid **Medieval Exhibit** (Tues–Sat 8am–2.30pm; same ticket), whose collection highlights the importance of Christian Rhodes as a trade centre. The Knights are represented with a display on their sugar-refining industry and a gravestone of a Grand Master; precious manuscripts and books precede a wing of post-Byzantine icons, moved here permanently from Panayía Kástrou (see below). On Tuesday and Saturday afternoons, there's a supplementary tour of the **city walls** (one hour, 2.45pm; 1200dr), beginning from a gate next to the palace and finishing at the Koskinoú gate.

The heavily restored **Street of the Knights** (Odhós Ippotón) leads due east from the Platía Kleovoúlou in front of the Palace; the "Inns" lining it housed the Knights of St John, according to linguistic and ethnic affiliation, until the Ottoman Turks compelled them to leave for Malta after a six-month siege in which the defenders were outnumbered thirty to one. Today the Inns house various government offices and cultural institutions vaguely appropriate to their past, but the whole effect of the renovation is predictably sterile and stagy (indeed, nearby streets were used in the filming of *Pascali's Island*).

At the bottom of the hill, the Knights' Hospital has been refurbished as the **Archeological Museum** (Tues–Sat 8.30am–6pm, Sun 8.30am–3pm; 600dr), though the arches and echoing halls of the building somewhat overshadow the badly labelled contents – largely painted pottery dating from the sixth and seventh centuries. Behind the second-storey sculpture garden, the Hellenistic statue gallery is more accessible: in a rear corner stands the so-called "Marine Venus", beloved of Lawrence Durrell, but lent a rather sinister aspect by her sea-dissolved face – in contrast to the friendlier *Aphrodite Bathing*. Virtually next door is the **Decorative Arts Collection** (Tues–Sun 8.30am–3pm; 4600dr), gleaned from old houses across the Dodecanese; the most compelling artefacts are carved cupboard doors and chest lids painted in naïve style with mythological or historical episodes.

Across the way stands the **Byzantine Museum** (Tues–Sun 8.30am–3pm; 600dr), housed in the old cathedral of the Knights, who adapted the Byzantine shrine of Panayía Kástrou for their own needs. Medieval icons and frescoes lifted from crumbling chapels on Rhodes and Khálki, as well as photos of art still in situ, constitute the exhibits; it's worth a visit since most of the Byzantine churches in the old town and outlying villages are locked.

If instead you head south from the Palace of the Grand Masters, it's hard to miss the most conspicuous Turkish monument in Rhodes, the candy-striped **Süleymaniye mosque**. Rebuilt in the nineteenth century on foundations three hundred years older, it's currently under scaffolding like most local Ottoman monuments. The old town is in fact well sown with mosques and *mescids* (the Islamic equivalent of a chapel), many of them converted from Byzantine shrines after the 1522 conquest, when the Christians were expelled from the medieval precinct. A couple of these mosques are still used by the sizeable **Turkish-speaking minority** here, some of them descended from Muslims who fled Crete between 1898 and 1913. Their most enduring civic contribution is the imposing **hamam** or Turkish bath on Platía Ariónos up in the southwest corner of the medieval city (Wed & Sat pm; 500dr).

Heading downhill from the Süleymaniye mosque, **Odhós Sokrátous**, once the heart of the Ottoman bazaar, is now the "Via Turista", packed with fur and jewellery stores, and tourists. Beyond the tiled central fountain in Platía Ippokrátous, Odhós Aristotélous leads into the Platía tón Evréon Martyrón (Square of the Jewish Martyrs), renamed in memory of the large local community that was almost totally annihilated in summer

1944. You can sometimes visit the ornate **synagogue** on Odhós Simíou just to the south, maintained essentially as a memorial to the 2000 Jews of Rhodes and Kós sent from here to the death camps; plaques in French – the language of educated Ottoman Jews across the east Aegean – commemorate the dead.

About a kilometre west of the old town, overlooking the west-coast road, the sparse remains of **Hellenistic Rhodes** – a restored theatre and stadium, plus a few columns of an Apollo temple – perch atop Monte Smith, the hill of Áyios Stéfanos renamed after a British admiral who used it as a watchpoint during the Napoleonic wars. The wooded site is popular with joggers and strollers, but for summer shade and greenery the best spot is probably the **Rodini park**, nearly 2km south of town on the road to Líndhos. On August evenings a wine tasting festival (8pm–midnight) is held here by the municipal authorities.

Practicalities

All international and inter-island **ferries** dock at the middle of Rhodes' three ports, the commercial harbour; the only exceptions are local **boats** to and from Sými, and the **hydrofoils**, which use the yacht harbour of Mandhráki. Its entrance was supposedly once straddled by the Colossus, an ancient statue of Apollo built to celebrate the end of the 305 BC siege; today two columns surmounted by bronze deer are less overpowering replacements.

The **airport** is 13km southwest of town, near the village of Paradhíssi; public urban buses bound for Paradhíssi, Kalavárdha, Theológos or Sálakos pass the gate on the main road fairly frequently between 6.30am and 9pm. A taxi fare into town is 2000–2500dr. Orange-and-white KTEL **buses** for both the west and east coasts of Rhodes leave from two almost adjacent terminals on Papágou and Avérof, just outside the Italian-built New Market (a tourist trap). Between the lower eastern station and the **taxi** rank at Platía Rimínis there's a helpful **tourist office** (May–Oct daily 9am–9pm), while some way up Papágou on the corner of Makaríou is the **EOT office** (Mon–Fri 8am–2pm); both dispense bus and ferry schedules.

ACCOMMODATION

Inexpensive pensions abound in the old town, contained almost entirely in the quad bounded by Omírou to the south, Sokrátous to the north, Perikléous to the east and Ippodhámou to the west. In addition, there are a few more possibilities in the former Jewish quarter, east of Perikléous. At crowded seasons, or late at night, it's prudent to accept the offers of proprietors meeting the ferries and change base next day if necessary.

Andreas, Omírou 28d (☎0241/34 156, fax 74 285). Perennially popular, this hotel is the most imaginative of the local old-house restorations. All rooms have sinks. There is a terrace bar with a view, and French and English is spoken. ④.

Apollo, Omírou 28c (☎0241/35 064). Basic but clean and friendly rooms place; the self-catering kitchen makes it good for longer stays. ③.

Casa de la Sera, Thisséos 38 (☎0241/75 154). A Jewish-quarter renovation, with wonderful floor tiles in the en-suite rooms, and a breakfast bar. ④.

Kastro, Platía Ariónos (☎0241/20 446). The proprietor is a famous eccentric artist renowned for his royalist leanings, but the hotel is fine for budget rooms; garden rooms are quieter than those overlooking nearby restaurants. ③.

Iliana, Gavála 1 (☎0241/30 251). This former Jewish mansion exudes a Victorian boarding-house atmosphere, but is clean and quiet enough with private facilities. ③.

Minos, Omírou 5 (☎0241/31 813). Modern and hence a bit sterile, but with great views, this neat pension is managed by an English-speaking family. ③.

Niki's, Sofokléous 39 (☎0241/25 115). Rooms can be on the small side, but ground-floor units are en suite, and upper-storey ones have fine views. ③.

Pink Elephant, Irodhótou 42 (☎0241/22 469). A recent entry on the scene, managed by *Cleo's Restaurant*, with Scots reception; a variety of rooms, en suite and not. ③.

S. Nikolis, Ippodhámou 61 (☎0241/34 561, fax 32 034). A variety of establishments in the west of the old town. Hotel rates ⑥ include a huge breakfast, and there's the option of self-catering apartments (⑤) or a simple pension (③). Booking essential for hotel and apartments, but accepted only with credit-card number.

Spot, Perikléous 21 (☎0241/34 737). Not the most inspired renovation, but this hotel is spotless, and you won't find en-suite rooms elsewhere for this price, except at *Niki's*. ③.

EATING AND DRINKING

Eating well for a reasonable price in and around Ródhos Town is a challenge, but not an insurmountable one. As a general rule, the further back from Sokrátous you go, the better value you'll find.

Aigaion, Eskhílou 47, cnr Aristofánous. Run by a welcoming Kalymniot family, this ouzerí features brown bread and curiosities such as *foúski* (soft-shell oyster).

Alatopipero/Salt and Pepper, Mihkaïl Petrídhi 76 (☎0241/65 494), southwest edge of new town, northwest of Rodíni Park. Upmarket ouzerí serving such vegetarian oddities as stuffed cyclamen leaves and *khortópittes* (wild green pies) plus more conventional delicacies, accompanied by limited bottlings from Greece's microwineries. It'll cost 3000dr if you stick to mezédhes, 4500 if you do a main course. Supper only, closed Mon.

Cleo's, Ayíou Fanouríou 17 (☎0241/28 415). Rather overpriced but tasty nouvelle Italian, strong on appetizers and pasta dishes. Count on 4500dr a head; reservations recommended. Closed Sun.

Le Bistrot, Omírou 22–24. Open for lunch and supper daily except Sunday, this is a genuine French-run bistro with excellent if pricey food. Always full, with a loyal expatriate clientele.

O Meraklis, Aristotélous 32. This *pátsas* (tripe-and-trotter soup) kitchen is only open 3–7am for a motley clientele of post-club lads, Turkish stallholders, night-club singers and travellers just stumbled off an overnight ferry. Great free entertainment, and the soup's good, too.

Metaxi Mas, Claude Pepper, Ámmos district. An excellent, tiny ouzerí overlooking Zéfyros beach, with unusual vegetarian and seafood dishes.

Mikis, alley behind Sokrátous 17. Very inexpensive hole-in-the-wall place, serving only fish, salads and wine.

Nireas, Platía Sofkléous 22 (☎0241/21 703). A good, family-run Greek ouzerí; reservations advised in the evenings.

Palia Istoria, Mitropóleos 108 (☎0241/32 421), cnr Dhendhrínou, in south extension of new town, Álmoss district. Reckoned to be the best ouzerí on Rhodes, but very expensive for such dishes as celery hearts in egg-lemon sauce and scallops with artichokes. Supper only; reservations essential.

Yiannis, Apéllou 41, below *Hotel Sydney*. Fair portions of *mayireftá*, dished out by a family long resident in New York.

NIGHTLIFE

The old town formerly had a well-deserved reputation for being tomb-silent at night, though this has changed as establishments have cropped up catering to those bored with the estimated two hundred bars and clubs in Neokhóri, where theme nights and various other gimmicks predominate. Dance clubs and bars are mostly along the streets and alleys bounded by Alexándhrou Dhiákou, Orfanídhou (aka "Skandi Street", after the latter-day Vikings), Fanouráki and Nikifórou Mandhilará.

Sedate by comparison, Ministry-of-Culture-approved folk dances (April–Oct Mon–Fri 9.20pm; 2500dr) are presented by the Nelly Dimoglou Company, performed in the landscaped "Old Town Theatre" off Andhroníkou, near Platía Ariónos. More of a techno extravaganza is the **Sound and Light** show, spotlighting sections of the city walls, playing in a garden just off Platía Rimínis. There's English-language narration nightly except Sunday, its screening time varying from 8.15pm to 10.15pm (2000dr).

Thanks to a large contingent from the local university, there are several cool-season (indoor) **cinemas** in the new town showing first-run fare. Choose from among the Rodon Municipal Theatre, next to the Town Hall in Neokhóri; the Metropol, southeast of the old town opposite the stadium; the nearby Pallas on Dhimokratías; and the Titania on Kolokotróni, off Kanadhá, open most of the year.

Araliki, Aristofánous 45, Old Town. The bohemian set hangs out at this old-style kafenío on the ground floor of a medieval house; simple *mezédhes* provided by Italian proprietress Miriam accompany drinks, which even include Nissirot *soumádha*. Open all year.

Arkhaia Agora, Omírou 70, Old Town. Very elegant, upscale bar with good taped music, food service and a garden at the rear, shared with the affiliated *Sotiris Nikolis* hotel.

Blue Lagoon Pool Bar, 25-Martíou 2, Neokhóri. One of the better theme bars, in this case a "desert island" with palm trees, waterfalls, a shipwrecked galleon – and taped music.

Café Chantant, Aristotélous 22, Old Town. Respected as a long-established music café (Greek popular and *rembétika*), but steel yourself for the drink prices and often ear-shattering noise.

Christos' Garden, Dhilberáki 59, Neokhóri. This combination art-gallery/bar/café, run by Christos Voulgaris, occupies a carefully restored old house and courtyard with pebble-mosaic floors throughout. Incongruously classy for the area.

Hard Rock Café, Orfanídhou 29, Neokhóri. Yes there's one here too, whether a genuine affiliate or a trademark ripoff is hard to say. "Hard rock, soft lights, driving music" promised.

Mango Bar, Platía Dhoriéos 3, Old Town. Piped music and a variety of drinks at this durable bar on an otherwise quiet plaza; also a good source of breakfast after 8am, served under a plane tree.

Nyn kai Aei, cul-de-sac off Sofokléous 4t, Old Town. An elegant, live-music bar in a vaulted, thirteenth-century building, attracting a thirty-something clientele; the name means "now and forever" in ancient Greek.

Popeye's, Sofokléous 38, Old Town. Serves cheap beer and house wine to a collegiate crowd; favourite haunt of yacht hostesses between assignments.

Presley's, Íonos Dhragoúmi 27, Neokhóri. A small and thus often crowded bar, featuring a wide range of 50s and 60s music (the cocktails are named after Elvis's hits).

Roloï, Orféos 1, Old Town. The baroque clocktower erected by Ahmet Fetih Pasha in 1857 is now the focus of possibly the most exclusive café/bar in the old town. Admission charge to climb the tower, and steeply priced drinks, but you are paying for the terrific view.

Shooters, Apolloníou Rodhíou 61, Neokhóri. The haunt of divers, as it's run by the Waterhoppers scuba outfitters; live acoustic music Tuesday and Thursday.

Sticky Fingers, Anthoúla Zérvou 6, Neokhóri. Long-lived music bar with reasonable drinks; *the* place for rock, often live, nightly from 10pm onwards.

Listings

Airlines British Airways, Platía Kýprou 1 (☎0241/27 756); KLM, Ammokhóstou 3 (☎0241/21 010); Air Greece, c/o Triton Holidays Plastíra 9 (☎0241/21 690); Olympic, Iérou Lókhou 9 (☎0241/24 571). Scheduled flights are exorbitant; there's a very faint chance of picking up an unclaimed return charter seat to northern Europe – ask at the various group tour offices.

Car rental Prices at non-international chains are fairly standard at £33/US$50 per day, but can be bargained down to about £27/US$43 a day, all-inclusive, out of peak season. More flexible local outfits, all in the new town, include Alexander, Afstralías 58 (☎0241/27 547); Alamo, Mandihlará 64 (☎0241/38 400); Just, Orfanídhou 45 (☎0241/31 811); Kosmos, Papaloúka 31 (☎0241/74 374); MBC, 25-Martíou 29 (☎0241/28 617); Orion, Yeoryíou Leóndos 36 (☎0241/22 137); and Payless, Íonos Dhragoúmi 29 (☎0241/26 586).

Exchange Most bank branches are near Platía Lýprou in Neokhóri, keeping weekday evening and Saturday morning hours; at other times use the cash dispensers of the Commercial Bank, Credit Bank, Ionian Bank (with a useful branch in the old town), or National Bank.

Ferries Tourist office handouts list the bewildering array of representatives for the numerous boat and hydrofoil companies which operate here; authoritative schedule information is available at the *limenarkhío*, on Mandhráki esplanade near the post office.

Laundries Express Service, Dhilberáki 97, cnr Orfanídhou and Neokhóri; Lavomatic, 28-Oktovríou 32, Neokhóri; Hobby, Plátonos 32, old town.

Motorbike rental Mopeds will make little impact on Rhodes; sturdier Yamaha 125s, suitable for two people, go for as little as 3500dr a day. There are plenty of outlets in Neokhóri, especially around Odhós Dhiákou.

Phones At the corner of Amerikís and 25-Martíou in the new town, and at the foot of the jetty in the commercial harbour; the latter also has several booths dedicated to ATT Direct and MCI service to North America.

Post office Main branch with outgoing mail, poste restante and exchange windows on Mandhráki harbour, open Mon–Fri 7.30am–8pm; less reliable mobile office on Órfeos in the old town, open shorter hours.

Travel agencies Recommended in the old town is Castellania, Evripídhou 1–3, corner Platía Ippokrátous; GEM Travel at Papaloúka 31 (☎0241/76 206) is good for cheap flights back to the UK, in particular unclaimed return seats or one-way tickets. Visa at Grigóri Lambráki 54 (☎0241/33 282) and Contours at Ammokhóstou 9 (☎0241/36 001) are also worth contacting.

The east coast

Heading down the coast from the capital you have to go some way before you escape the crowds from local beach hotels, their numbers swelled by visitors using the regular buses from town or on boat tours out of Mandhráki. You might look in at the decayed, abandoned spa of **Thérmes Kallithéas**, dating from the Italian period. Located 3km south of Kallithéa resort proper, down an unsigned road through pines, the spa is set in a palm grove and is illuminated at night to create a hugely enjoyable spectacle of mock-orientalia. The former fishing village of **FALIRÁKI**, which draws a youngish package clientele, is all too much in the mode of a Spanish *costa* resort, while the scenery just inland – arid, scrubby sand-hills at the best of times – has been made that much more dreary by fire damage that stretches way beyond Líndhos.

The enormous mass of **Tsambíka**, 26km south of town, is the first place at which most will seriously consider stopping. Actually the very eroded flank of a much larger extinct volcano, the hill has a monastery at the summit offering unrivalled views along some 50km of coastline. From the main highway, a steep, 1500-metre cement drive leads to a small car park and a snack bar, from which steps lead to the summit. The monastery here is unremarkable except for its September 8 festival: childless women climb up – sometimes on their knees – to be relieved of their barrenness, and any children born afterwards are dedicated to the Virgin with the names Tsambikos or Tsambika, which are particular to the Dodecanese. From the top you can survey **Kolýmbia** just to the north, a beach stretching south from a tiny cove ringed with volcanic rocks, backed by a dozen, low-rise hotels. Shallow **Tsambíka bay** on the south side of the headland warms up early in the spring, and the excellent beach, though protected by the forest service from development other than a taverna and a few cantina caravans, teems with people all summer.

The next beach south, gravelly **Stégna**, can only be reached by a steep road east from **ARKHÁNGELOS**, a large village just inland overlooked by a crumbling castle and home to a dwindling leather crafts industry. Though you can disappear into the warren of alleys between the main road and the citadel, the place is now firmly caught up in package tourism, with a full complement of banks, tavernas, mini-marts and jewellery stores.

A more peaceful overnight base on this stretch of coast would be **KHARÁKI**, a pleasant if undistinguished two-street fishing port with mostly self-catering accommodation (generally ③) overlooked by the stubby ruins of **Feraklós castle**, the last stronghold of the Knights to fall to the Turks. You can swim off the town beach if you don't mind an audience from the handful of waterfront cafés and tavernas, but most people head west out of town, then north 800m to the secluded **Agáthi beach**. Best tavernas at Kharáki are *Tommy's*, run by a professional fisherman, and *Efterpi* 200m south at so-called Massári beach.

Líndhos

LÍNDHOS, the island's number-two tourist attraction, erupts from barren surround-ings 12km south of Kharáki. Like Ródhos Town itself, its charm is heavily undermined by commercialism and crowds – up to half a million visitors in a typical year. At midday dozens of coaches park nose-to-tail on the narrow access road, with even more on the drive down to the beach. Back in the village itself, those few vernacular houses not snapped up by package operators have, since the 1960s, been bought up and refur-bished by wealthy British and Italians. The old *agorá* or serpentine high street presents a mass of fairly indistinguishable bars, creperies, mediocre restaurants and travel agents. Although high-rise hotels have been prohibited inside the municipal bound-aries, the result is a relentlessly commercialized theme park, hot and airless in August, but quite ghostly in winter.

Nonetheless, if you arrive before or after peak season, when the pebble-paved streets between the immaculately whitewashed houses are relatively empty of both people and droppings from the donkeys shuttling up to the acropolis (see below), you can still appreciate the beautiful, atmospheric setting of Líndhos. The most imposing fifteenth-to-eighteenth-century **captains' residences** are built around *khokhláki* courtyards, their monumental doorways often fringed by intricate stonework, with the number of braids or cables supposedly corresponding to the number of ships owned. Several are open to the public, most notably the **Papkonstandis Mansion**, the most elaborate and now home to an unofficial museum; entrance to the "open" mansions is free but some pressure will probably be exerted on you to buy something, especially the lace and embroidery for which the place is noted.

On the bluff above the town, the ancient acropolis with its scaffolding-swaddled Doric **Temple of Athena** is found inside the Knights' **castle** (summer Mon–Fri 8.30am–6.40pm, Sat–Sun 8.30am–2.40pm; rest of year Tues–Sun 8.30am–3pm; 1200dr) – a surprisingly felicitous blend of two cultures. Though the ancient city of Lindos and its original temple date from at least 1100 BC, the present structure was begun by the tyrant Kleovoulos in the sixth century BC and replaced by the present structure after a fourth-century fire.

Líndhos' north beach, once the main ancient harbour, is overcrowded and polluted; if you do base yourself here, cleaner, quieter **beaches** are to be found one cove beyond at Pállas beach (with a nudist annexe around the headland), or 5km north at **Vlikhá** bay. South of the acropolis huddles the small, perfectly sheltered **St Paul's harbour**, where the apostle is said to have landed in 58 AD on a mission to evangelize the island.

PRACTICALITIES

There are almost no places to **stay** that are not booked semi-permanently by overseas tour companies. The oft-cited exceptions of *Pension Electra* (☎0244/31 226; ④) and *Pension Katholiki*, next door to each other on the way to the north beaches, are both of a relatively low standard and vastly overpriced. It could be more productive to throw yourself on the mercy of *Pallas Travel* (☎0244/31 494, fax 31 595) for any stray vacan-cies. Another useful contact is the Independent Association of Lindian Property Owners (☎0244/31 221, fax 31 571).

Local **restaurants** tend to be bland, although *Agostino's* by the southerly car park, possesses the important virtues of bulk Émbonas wine and real country sausages (not imported hot dogs). The apotheosis of **nightlife** is the *Epos Club*, a disco with a capac-ity of a thousand, a swimming pool and rooftop bar; the bar *Jody's Flat* can also be rec-ommended for its video-cinema matinees. A unique combination laundry/lending library behind Pallas Travel, open during normal shop hours, is run by an American expat; she both sells and lends second-hand books. Local **car rental** rates tend to be cheaper than in Ródhos Town, though the cars less roadworthy. There are two proper **banks**, working normal hours and giving normal exchange rates.

The west coast

Rhodes' west coast is the windward flank of the island, so it's damper, more fertile and more forested; most beaches, however, are exposed and decidedly rocky. None of this has deterred development, and as in the east the first few kilometres of the busy shore road down from the capital have been surrendered entirely to tourism. From the aquarium down to the airport the asphalt is fringed by an uninterrupted line of Miami-beach-style hotels, though such places as Triánda, Kremastí and Paradhíssi are still nominally villages. This was the first part of the island to be favoured by the package operators, and tends to be frequented by a decidedly middle-aged, sedate clientele.

There's not much inducement to stop, till you reach the important archeological site of **KAMEIROS**, which with Líndhos and Ialyssos was one of the three Dorian powers that united in the fifth century BC to found the powerful city-state of Rhodes. Soon eclipsed by the new capital, Kameiros was abandoned and only rediscovered in the last century. As a result it is a particularly well-preserved Doric townscape, doubly worth visiting for its beautiful hillside site (Tues–Sun 8.30am–3pm; 800dr). While none of the individual remains are spectacular, you can make out the foundations of a few small temples, the restored pillars of a Hellenistic house, and the *stoa* of the *agora*, complete with a water catchment basin. Because of the gentle slope of the site, there were no fortifications, nor was there an acropolis. On the beach below Kameiros there are several tavernas, ideal while waiting for one of the two daily buses back to town (if you're willing to walk 4km back to Kalavárda you'll have a better choice of service).

There are more restaurants clustered at **SKÁLA KAMÍROU** 15km south, a tiny anchorage which somewhat inexplicably is the target of coach tours. Less heralded is the daily pair of competing kaïkia which leave for the island of **Khálki** at 2.30pm, weather permitting, returning early the next morning; on Wednesdays and Sundays there are day trips departing at 9am and returning at 4pm.

A couple of kilometres south of Skála, the "Kastello", signposted as **Kástro Kritinías**, is from afar the most impressive of the Knights' rural strongholds, and the access road is too rough for tour buses to pass. Close up it proves to be no more than a shell, but a glorious shell, with fine views west to assorted islets and Khálki. You make a "donation" to the formidable little old lady at the car park in exchange for fizzy drinks, seasonal fruit or flowers.

Beyond Kritinía itself, a quiet hillside village with a few rooms and tavernas, the main road winds south through the forests of Mount Akramítis to **SIÁNA**, the most attractive mountain settlement on the island, famous for its aromatic pine-sage honey and *soúma*, a grape-residue distillation identical to Italian *grappa*. Bus tours also stop at the church on the square, with heavily restored eighteenth-century frescoes. The tiered, flat-roofed farmhouses of **MONÓLITHOS**, 4km southwest at the end of the public bus line, are scant justification for the long trip out here, and food at the two **tavernas** is indifferent owing to the tour-group trade, but the view over the bay is striking and you could use the village as a base by staying in rooms or at the pricier *Hotel Thomas* (☎0246/22 741 or 61 291; ③), self-catering and open most of the year. Diversions in the area include yet another **Knights' castle** 2km west of town, photogenically perched on its own pinnacle (the "monolith" of the name) and enclosing a couple of chapels, and the fine gravel beach of **Foúrni**, five bumpy, curvy kilometres below the castle, its 800-metre extent unsullied except for a seasonal drinks stand. Beyond the headland, to the left as you face the water, are some caves that were hollowed out by early Christians fleeing persecution.

The interior

Inland Rhodes is hilly, and still mostly wooded, despite the depredations of arsonists. You'll need a vehicle to see its highlights, especially as the main enjoyment is in getting away from it all; no single site justifies the tremendous expense of a taxi or the inconvenience of trying to make the best of the sparse bus schedules.

Ialyssos and the Valley of the Butterflies

Starting from the west coast, turn inland at the central junction in Tríanda for the five-kilometre uphill ride to the scanty acropolis of ancient **Ialyssos** (Tues–Fri 8.30am–6pm, Sat–Mon 8.30am–3pm; 800dr) on flat-topped Filérimos hill; from its Byzantine castle Süleyman the Magnificent directed the 1522 siege of Rhodes. Filérimos means "lover of solitude", after the tenth-century settlement here by Byzantine hermits. The existing **Filérimos monastery**, restored successively by Italians and British, is the most substantial structure here. As a concession to the Rhodian faithful, the church alone is usually open to pilgrims after the stated hours. Directly in front of the church sprawl the foundations of third-century **temples to Zeus and Athena**, built atop a far older Phoenician shrine. Below this, further towards the car park, lies the partly subterranean church of **Áyios Yeóryios**, a simple, barrel-vaulted structure with fourteenth- and fifteenth-century frescoes, not as vivid or well-preserved as those at Thári or Asklipío. A bit southeast of the parking area, a hillside **Doric fountain** with a columned facade was only revealed by subsidence in 1926. Southwest of the monastery and archeological zone, a "Way of the Cross", with the fourteen stations marked out in copper plaques during the Italian era, leads to an enormous concrete crucifix, a recent replacement of an Italian-era one; you're allowed to climb out onto the cross-arms for a supplement to the already amazing view. Illuminated at night, the crucifix is clearly visible from the island of Sými and – perhaps more pertinently – infidel Turkey across the way.

The only highly publicized tourist "attraction" in the island's interior, **Petaloúdhes** or the **"Butterfly Valley"** (April–Sept daily 9am–5pm; 300dr) reached by a seven-kilometre paved side road bearing inland from the west coast road between Paradhíssi and Theológos, is actually a rest stop for Jersey tiger moths (*Panaxia quadripunctaria*). Only in summer do these creatures congregate here, attracted for unknown reasons by the abundant *Liquidambar orientalis* trees. In season, the moths roost in droves on the tree trunks; they cannot eat during this final phase of their life cycle, must rest to conserve energy, and die of starvation soon after mating. When sitting in the trees, the moths are a well-camouflaged black and yellow, but flash cherry-red overwings in flight.

Eptá Piyés to Profítis Ilías

Heading inland from Kolýmbia junction on the main highway, it's a four-kilometre walk or drive to **Eptá Piyés**, a superb oasis with a tiny dam created by the Italians for irrigation. A shaded streamside **taverna**, immensely popular at weekend with islanders and visitors alike, serves no-nonsense, hearty fare. A trail, or a rather claustrophobic Italian aqueduct-tunnel, both lead from the vicinity of the springs to the reservoir.

Continuing inland, you reach **ELEOÚSSA** after another 9km, in the shade of the dense forest at the east end of Profítis Ilías ridge. Two other undisturbed villages, Platánia and Apóllona, nestle on the south slopes of the mountain overlooking the start of the burned area, but most people keep straight on 3km further from Eleoússa to the late Byzantine church of **Áyios Nikólaos Foundoúkli** (St Nicholas of the Hazelnuts). The partly shaded site has a fine view north over cultivated valleys, and locals descend in force for picnics on weekends; the frescoes inside, dating from the thirteenth to the fifteenth centuries, could do with a good cleaning but various scenes from the life of Christ are recognizable.

Negotiating an unsignposted but fairly obvious welter of dirt tracks gets you finally to **Profítis Ilías**, where the Italian-vintage chalet-hotel *Elafos/Elafína* (shut down) hides in deep woods just north of the 798-metre marker, Rhodes' third-highest point. There's good, gentle strolling around the summit and the namesake monastery, and a nearby snack bar is generally open in season.

Atáviros villages

All tracks and roads west across Profítis Ilías converge upon the main road from Kalavárda bound for **ÉMBONAS**, a large and architecturally nondescript village backed up against the north slope of 1215-metre **Mount Atáviros**. Émbonas, with its two pensions and meat-oriented tavernas, is more geared to handling tourists than you might expect, since it's the venue for summer "folk-dance tours" from Ródhos Town. The village also lies at the heart of the island's most important wine-producing districts, and CAÏR – the Italian-founded vintners' cooperative – produce a range of acceptable mid-range varieties. However, products of the smaller, family-run Emery winery (☎0246/41 208; Mon–Fri 9am–3pm for tasting tours) at the village outskirts are even more esteemed. To see what Émbonas would be like without tourists, carry on clockwise around the peak past the Artámiti monastery, to less-celebrated **ÁYIOS ISÍDHOROS**, with as many vines and tavernas (try *Snag* (sic) *Bar Atavíros*), a more open feel, and the **trailhead** for the five-hour return ascent of Atáviros. This path, beginning at the northeast edge of the village, is the safest and easiest way up the mountain, which has extensive foundations of a Zeus temple on top.

Thári Monastery

The road from Áyios Isídhoros to Siána is paved; not so the appalling one that curves for 12km east to Láerma, but it's worth enduring if you've any interest in Byzantine monuments. The **Monastery of Thári**, lost in pine forests five kilometres south, is the oldest religious foundation on the island, re-established as a living community of half a dozen monks in 1990 by a charismatic abbot from Pátmos. The striking kathólikon (open all day) consists of a long nave and short transept surmounted by barrel vaulting. Despite two recent cleanings, the damp of centuries has smudged the frescoes, dating from 1300 to 1450, but they are still exquisite: the most distinct, in the transept, depict the Evangelist Mark and the Archangel Gabriel, while the nave boasts various acts of Christ, including such rarely illustrated scenes as the *Storm on the Sea of Galilee*, *Meeting Mary Magdalene* and *Healing the Cripple*.

The far south

South of a line connecting Monólithos and Lárdhos, you could easily begin to think you had strayed onto another island. Gone are the five-star hotels and roads to match, and with them most of the crowds. Gone too are most tourist facilities and public transport. Only three weekly buses serve the depopulated villages here, approaching along the east coast; tavernas grace the more popular stretches of sand, and there are a few places to stay outside the package enclaves of Lárdhos and Péfkos.

A new auxiliary airport is planned for the area, however, so this state of affairs won't persist indefinitely. Already massive construction is beginning behind the sandier patches south of **LÁRDHOS**, solidly on the tourist circuit despite an inland position between Láerma and the peninsula culminating in Líndhos. The beach 2km south is gravelly and the water can be dirty, so it's best to continue 3km to Glístra cove, a small but delightful crescent which sets the tone for the coast from here on. Four kilometres east, **PÉFKOS** (Péfki on some maps) is a low-key package resort on the beach road to Líndhos; the sea is cleaner than at Lárdhos, and the beaches are small and well hidden.

Asklipío

Nine kilometres beyond Lárdhos, a paved side road heads 4km inland to **ASKLIPÍO**, a sleepy village guarded by a crumbling castle and graced by the Byzantine church of **Kímisis Theotókou**. To gain admission, call at the priest's house behind the apse, or if that doesn't work, haul on the belfry rope. The building dates from 1060, with a ground plan nearly identical to that of Thári, except that two subsidiary apses were added during the eighteenth century, supposedly to conceal a secret school in a subterranean crypt. The frescoes within are in far better condition than Thári's owing to the drier local climate; the priest claims that the final work at Thári and the earliest here were executed by the same hand, a master from Khíos.

The format and subject matter of the frescoes is rare in Greece: didactic "cartoon strips" which extend completely around the church in some cases, and extensive Old Testament stories in addition to the more usual lives of Christ and the Virgin. There's a complete sequence from Genesis, from the Creation to the Expulsion from Eden; note the comically menacing octopus among the fishes in the panel of the Fifth Day. A seldom-encountered *Revelation of John the Divine* takes up most of the east transept, and pebble mosaic flooring decorates both the interior and the vast courtyard.

To the southern tip

Back on the coast road, the beachfront hamlet of **KIOTÁRI** gets few visitors, partly because it's omitted from most maps, and also because the Orthodox Church, major landowner hereabouts, isn't selling to developers. The gravel beach has a line of tavernas behind and a few self-catering units.

There are far more ample facilities at **YENÁDHI**, including **car rental**, a **post office**, some rooms and a few **tavernas** behind the seemingly endless sand-and-gravel beach. South of Yennádhi, just 2km inland, **LAKHANIÁ** village with its eponymous **hotel** (☎0244/43 089; ③) and smattering of private rooms makes another possible base. On the main platía at the lower, eastern end of the village, the *Platanos* taverna has seating between the church and two wonderful fountains, one with an Ottoman inscription.

You can go directly from Lakhaniá to Khokhlakás, which straddles the paved side road south to **Plimíri**, an exceptionally well-protected sandy bay backed by dunes; so far the only facility is a good-value rustic **taverna**. Beyond Plimíri the road curves inland to **KATAVIÁ**, over 100km from the capital, marooned amidst grain fields. There are several tavernas at the junction that doubles as the platía, a few rooms to rent, and a filling station; the village, like so many in the south, is three-quarters deserted, the owners of the closed-up houses off working in Australia or North America.

From Kataviá a wide dirt track leads on to **Prassoníssi**, Rhodes' southernmost extremity. From May to October you can stroll across the wide sands to visit, but winter storms swamp this tenuous link and render Prassoníssi a true island. Even in summer the prevailing northwesterly winds drive swimmers to the lee side of the spit, leaving the exposed shore to the world-class windsurfers who come here to train. In season the scrubby junipers rustle with tents and caravans; water comes from two **tavernas** flanking the access road. The outfit next to the old windmill is more characterful, but beware of their fish grills – tasty but among the most expensive in Greece.

The far southwest

From Lakhaniá it's also possible to head 9km northwest along a narrow paved road to the picturesque hilltop village of **MESSANAGRÓS**. This already existed in some form by the fifth century AD, if foundations of a ruined basilica at the village outskirts are anything to go by. A smaller, but equally venerable thirteenth-century chapel squats amidst mosaic-floor patches of the larger, earlier church, with a *khokhláki* floor and stone barrel arches (key from the nearby kafenío).

The onward road to Skiádhi monastery, 6km distant, is shown incorrectly on most maps. Take the Katavá-bound road initially, then bear right onto an unsigned dirt track after about 2km; the last 4km are quite badly surfaced. Known formally as Panayía Skiadhení, **Skiádhi monastery** – despite its undistinguished modern buildings – was founded in the thirteenth century to house a miraculous icon of the Virgin; in the fifteenth century a heretic stabbed the painting, and blood flowed from the wound in the Mother of God's cheek. The offending hand was, needless to say, instantly paralysed; the fissure, and intriguing brown stains around it, are still visible. The immediate surroundings of the monastery are rather dreary since a fire in 1992, but the views west are stunning. Khténia islet is said to be a petrified pirate ship, so rendered by the Virgin in answer to prayers from desperate locals. Except on September 7/8, the festival of the icon, you can stay the night on arrangement with the caretaker priest Ioannis Kermaïtzis and his wife (☎0244/46 006; donation).

West of Kataviá, the island loop road – now completely paved – emerges onto the deserted, sandy southwest coast; Skiádhi can easily be reached from this side too, the road up from here better signposted than from Messanagrós. If freelance camping and nudism are your thing, this is the place to indulge, though you'll need to be completely self-sufficient. Only strong swimmers should venture far offshore here.

The nearest inland village is nondescript, agricultural **APOLAKIÁ**, 7km north of the Skiádhi turning and equipped with a couple of pensions and shops. Northwest the road leads to Monólithos, due south back to Kataviá, and the northeasterly road cuts quickly back to Yennádhi via Váti.

Khálki

Khálki, a tiny (20 square kilometres), waterless, limestone speck west of Rhodes, is a fully fledged member of the Dodecanese, though all but three hundred of the former population of three thousand have decamped (mostly to Rhodes or to Florida) in the wake of a devastating sponge blight early in this century. Despite a renaissance through tourism in recent years, the island is tranquil compared with its big neighbour, with a slightly weird, hushed atmosphere. The big event of the day is the arrival of the regular afternoon kaïkia from Skála Kámiros on Rhodes.

Emborió

EMBORIÓ's houses are pretty much block-booked from April to October by the tour companies and occupied by a rather staid, upper-middle-class clientele; independent travellers will be lucky to find anything at all, even early or late in the season. Non-package **accommodation**, all requiring advance reservations, includes the delightful, en-suite *Captain's House* (☎0241/45 201; ④), where the English manager can point you in likely directions if she's full; *Pension Cleanthe* (☎0241/45 334) near the school; the hillside studios of *Pension Argyrenia* (☎0241/45 205; ④) below the municipal cistern; and *Hotel Manos* (☎0241/45 295; ③), in a converted sponge factory. Of the half-dozen **tavernas** along the field-stoned, pedestrianized waterfront, *O Khouvardas*, *Arapakis* and *Omonia* are good for reasonable standard fare, while *Mavri Thalassa* is worth the extra expense for its good mezédhes and crab salad. **Bars** and **cafés** cluster at mid-quay: *Areti* for cake and coffee, *Kostas* dispensing foreign beer on tap, and *To Steki* with a central bar and music. There's a **post office** (the best place to change money), three stores, two bakeries, and two **travel agencies** which sell boat tickets.

The rest of the island

Three kilometres west lies the old pirate-safe village of **KHORIÓ**, abandoned in the 1950s but still crowned by the Knights' castle. Except during the major August 14–15 festival, the church here is kept securely locked to protect its frescoes. Across the valley, the little monastery of **Stavrós** is the venue for the other big island bash on September 14. There's little else to see or do inland, though you can spend three hours **walking** across the island on the recently opened road, the extension of the cement "Tarpon Springs Boulevard" donated by the expatriate community in Florida. At the end of the road you'll come to the monastery of **Ayíou Ioánnou Prodhrómou**; the caretaking family there can put you up in a cell (except around August 29, the other big festival date), but you'll need to bring supplies. The terrain en route is monotonous, but compensated by views over half the Dodecanese and Turkey. Occasionally the island's lone, twenty-seater **bus** runs excursions out here, with an hour to look around.

Longish but narrow **Póndamos**, fifteen minutes' walk west of Emborió, is the only sandy beach on Khálki. The sole facility is the somewhat pricey *Nick's Pondamos Taverna*, serving lunch only. Small and pebbly **Yialí**, west of and considerably below Khorió via a jeep track, lies an hour's hike away from Póndamos. A thirty-minute walk north of Emborió lies **Kánia**, with a rocky foreshore and a rather industrial ambience from both power lines and the island's only petrol pump, adjacent.

Since these three coves are no great shakes, it's worth signing on at Emborió quay for **boat excursions** to more remote beaches. More or less at the centre of Khálki's southern shore, directly below Khorió's castle, **Trakhía** consists of two coves to either side of an isthmus. North-coast beaches figuring as excursion-boat destinations include the pretty **Arétta**, **Áyios Yeóryios** just beyond, and the remote double bay of **Dhýo Yialí**.

Alimniá (Alimiá) islet

The most interesting boat excursion is to **Alimniá (Alimiá) islet**, roughly halfway between Khálki and Rhodes, a favourite swimming and barbecuing venue for both islanders and tour clients. Despite a reliable spring, the deserted village here, overlooked by a few palm trees and yet another Knights' castle, was never re-inhabited after World War II. It is claimed the locals were deported after they admitted to assisting British commandos sent to sabotage the Italian submarines who used the deep harbour here. The commandos themselves were captured here by the Nazis, bundled off to Rhodes and summarily executed as spies rather than regular prisoners of war; Kurt Waldheim allegedly countersigned their death sentences. If you go snorkelling, you can glimpse outlines of the submarine pens to one side of the deep bay. Most of the houses are now boarded up; some bear sombre lines of bullet-holes, while inside others you can glimpse crude paintings of ships and submarines sketched by bored soldiers. Today just one is inhabited on a seasonal basis, when Alimniá is used by shepherds grazing livestock.

Kastellórizo (Meyísti)

Kastellórizo's official name, Méyisti (biggest), seems more an act of defiance than a statement of fact. While the largest of a tiny group of islands, it is actually the smallest of the Dodecanese, over seventy nautical miles from its nearest Greek neighbour (Rhodes) but barely more than a nautical mile off the Turkish coast at the narrowest straits. At night its lights are quite outnumbered by those of the Turkish town of Kaş, across the bay, with whom Kastellórizo generally has excellent relations.

Less than a century ago there were 14,000 people here, supported by a fleet of schooners that transported goods, mostly timber, from the Greek towns of Kalamaki (now Kalkan) and Andifelos (Kaş) on the Anatolian mainland opposite. But the advent of steam power, the withdrawal of privileges after the 1908 "Young Turk" revolution and the Italian seizure of the Dodecanese in 1912 sent the island into decline. A French occupation of 1914–21 prompted destructive shelling from the Ottoman-held mainland, a harbinger of worse to come (see below). Shipowners failed to modernize their fleets, preferring to sell ships to the British for the Dardanelles campaign, and the new frontier between the island and republican Turkey, combined with the expulsion of all Anatolian Greeks in 1923, deprived any remaining vessels of their trade. During the 1930s the island enjoyed a brief renaissance when it became a major stopover point for French and Italian seaplanes, but events at the close of World War II put an end to any hopes of the island's continued viability.

When Italy capitulated to the Allies in the autumn of 1943, a few hundred Commonwealth commandos occupied Kastellórizo, leaving in response to German dive-bombing late in the spring of 1944. In early July, a harbour fuel dump caught fire and an adjacent arsenal exploded, taking with it more than half of the two thousand houses on Kastellórizo. Even before these events most of the population had left for Rhodes, Athens, Australia (especially Perth) and North America. Today there are fewer than 200 people living permanently on Kastellórizo, largely maintained by remittances from over 30,000 emigrants and by subsidies from the Greek government, which fears that the island will revert to Turkey should their numbers diminish any further.

Notwithstanding its apparently terminal plight, Kastellórizo may have a future of sorts. Expatriated "Kassies" have recently begun renovating their crumbling ancestral homes as a retirement or holiday home. Each summer, the population is swelled by returnees of Kassie ancestry, some of whom celebrate traditional weddings in the **Áyios Konstandínos** cathedral at Khoráfia, which incorporates ancient columns from Patara in Asia Minor.

Perhaps the biggest recent boost for Kastellórizo was its role as location for the 1991 film *Mediterraneo*, which has resulted in a tidal wave of Italian visitors. You will either love it and stay a week, or crave escape after a day; detractors dismiss Kastellórizo as a human zoo maintained by the government for the edification of nationalists, while partisans celebrate an atmospheric, barely commercialized outpost of Hellenism.

Kastellórizo Town

The current population is concentrated in the northern town of **KASTELLÓRIZO** – the finest harbour, so it is claimed, between Beirut and Pireás – and its little "suburb" of **Mandhráki**, just over the fire-blasted hill with its half-ruined castle of the Knights. Its keep now houses the local **museum** (Tues–Sun 7.30am–2.30pm; free), with displays including plates from a Byzantine shipwreck, frescoes rescued from decaying churches, and a reconstruction of an ancient basilica underneath a contemporary, gaudy church at Khoráfia. Just below and beyond the museum, in the cliff-face opposite Psorádhia islet, is Greece's only **Lycian house-tomb**; it's unmarked, but you can find it easily enough by following the shoreline walkway, then climbing some steps opposite the first wooden lamp standard.

Most of the town's surviving mansions are ranged along the waterfront, their tiled roofs, wooden balconies and long, narrow windows having obvious counterparts in the originally Greek-built houses of Kalkan and Kaş just across the water. One street behind the port, however, many properties are derelict – abandonment having succeeded where World War I shelling, a 1926 earthquake and the 1944 explosions failed – sepia-toned posters and postcards on sale show the town in its prime.

Practicalities

Pensions in the old houses tend to be fairly basic, with long climbs up and down stairs to a single bathroom. If you're not met off the boat, the best budget option is the restored mansion-pension of the Mavrothalassitis family (☎0241/49 202; ②), one of the very few with en-suite baths. Otherwise, try *Paradhisos* (☎0241/49 074; ②) at the west end of the seafront, *Barbara* (☎0241/49 295; ②), at the opposite end of things, or the more modern *Kristallo* (☎0241/41 209; ②). More luxury is available at the *Hotel Meyisti* (☎0241/49 272, fax 49 221; ⑤), on the opposite side of the bay from the ferry jetty.

Apart from fish, and whatever can be smuggled over from Kaş, Kastellórizo has to bring foodstuffs and often drinking water from Rhodes; prices for **eating** out are consequently higher than usual, bumped up further by the island's recent celebrity status. Apart from *Mikro Parisi/Little Paris* on the waterfront, the better restaurants are to be found inland. Especially recommended are *Iy Orea Meyisti*, run by the Mavrothalassitis family (they of the pension), and the *O Meyisteas* ouzerí, behind the disused municipal market building, which specializes in goat chops. The simple *Ta Platania*, opposite Áyios Konstandínos in Khoráfia district, is good for *mayireftá* and homemade desserts.

The **post office** is behind *Hotel Meyisti*; there's no OTE or bank. Most ferry companies are represented by one of several grocery stores, while the only travel agency, DiZi Travel, has a monopoly on **flights** back to Rhodes (you cannot book a return flight in Ródhos Town) and will also change money.

It is usually possible to arrange a ride over **to Turkey** on the supply boat Varvara, run by the *Taverna Apolavsi*; you'll have to pay a "special visa fee" to customs, and an additional 5000dr per person for the boat.

The rest of the island

Kastellórizo's austere hinterland is predominantly bare rock, flecked with stunted vegetation; incredibly, two generations ago much of the countryside was carefully tended, producing wine of some quality. A rudimentary road system links points between Mandhráki and the airport, but there aren't many specific places to go and no scooters for rent. Karstic cliffs drop sheer to the sea, offering no anchorage for boats except at the main town.

The shoreline and Rhó
Swimming is complicated by a total absence of beaches and an abundance of sea urchins and razor-sharp limestone reefs; the safest entry near town lies beyond the graveyard at Mandhráki, or at the tiny inlet of **Áyios Stéfanos**, a forty-minute walk north of town along the obvious trail beginning behind the post office. Once clear of the shore, you're rewarded by clear waters with a rich variety of marine life. Over on the southeast coast, accessible only by a 45-minute boat ride from town, the grotto of **Perastá** deserves a look for its stalactites and strange blue light effects; the low entrance, negotiable only by inflatable raft, gives little hint of the enormous chamber within. Two-hour raft trips (2000dr per person) visit only the cave, or for 5000dr on a larger kaïki, you can take it in as part of a five-hour tour that includes Rhó islet.

Should you make the trip out to **Rhó**, the tomb of *Iy Kyrá tis Rhó* (**The Lady of Rhó**), aka Dhespina Akhladhiotis (1893–1982) – who resolutely hoisted the Greek flag each day on that islet in defiance of the Turks on the mainland – is the first thing you see when you dock at the sandy, northwestern harbour. From here a path heads southeast for 25 minutes to the islet's southerly port, past the side trail up to the intact Hellenistic fortress on the very summit. The islet has no facilities – just one caretaker, several dogs and hundreds of goats – so bring your own food and water.

Rural monasteries and ruins
Heat permitting, you can hike up the obvious, zigzag stair-path, then south through desolate, recently fire-charred vineyards for forty minutes, to the rural **monastery of Áyios Yeóryios toú Vounioú**. The sixteenth- to eighteenth-century church boasts fine rib vaulting and a carved *témblon*, but its highlight is a **crypt**, with the frescoed, **sub-**

terranean chapel of Áyios Kharálambos off to one side; access is via a steep, narrow passage descending from the church floor – bring a torch. The only way to gain access is to go early in the morning with the key-keeper, who lives behind *Little Paris* taverna. Alternatively, a fifteen-minute, walk west of the port leads to the peaceful monastery of **Ayías Triádhas**, perched on the saddle marked by the OTE tower.

The onward path arrives after 25 minutes at the ancient citadel of **Paleókastro**, where you'll find masonry from Classical to medieval times, a warren of vaulted chambers, tunnels, cisterns plus another, ruined monastery with a *khokhláki* courtyard. From any of the heights above town there are tremendous views north over sixty kilometres of Anatolian coast.

Sými

Sými's most pressing problem, lack of water, is in many ways also its saving grace. As with so many dry rocky Dodecanese, if the rain cisterns don't fill during the winter, water must be imported at great expense from Rhodes. As a result the island can't hope to support more than a handful of large hotels; instead hundreds of people are shipped in daily during the season from Rhodes, relieved of their money and sent back. This arrangement suits both the islanders and those visitors lucky enough to stay longer, or even to own houses here.

Sými Town

The island's capital – and only proper town – consists of **Yialós**, the port, and **Khorió**, on the hillside above, collectively known as **SÝMI**. Incredibly, less than a hundred years ago the town was richer and more populous (30,000) than Rhodes, its wealth generated by shipbuilding and sponge-diving, skills nurtured since pre-Classical times. Under the Ottomans, Sými, like most of the smaller Dodecanese, enjoyed considerable autonomy in exchange for a yearly tribute in sponges to the sultan; but the Italian-imposed frontier, the 1919–22 war, the advent of synthetic sponges, and the gradual replacement of the crews by Kalymniotes spelled doom for the local economy. Vestiges of past nautical glories remain at still-active boatyards at Pédhi and Kharáni, but today the souvenir-shop sponges come mostly from overseas, and many of the magnificent nineteenth-century mansions stand roofless and deserted, their windows gaping blankly across the excellent natural harbour.

The 2500 remaining Symiotes are scattered fairly evenly throughout the mixture of Neoclassical and more typical island dwellings; despite the surplus of properties many outsiders have preferred to build anew, rather than restore derelict shells accessible only by donkey or on foot. As on Kastellórizo, a wartime ammunition blast – this time set off by the retreating Germans – levelled hundreds of houses up in Khorió. Shortly afterwards, the official surrender of the Dodecanese to the Allies was signed here on May 8, 1945: a plaque marks the spot at the present-day *Restaurant Les Katerinettes*, and each year on that date there's a fine festival with music and dance.

At the lively **port**, an architecturally protected area since the early 1970s, spice-and-sponge stalls are thronged with Rhodes-based day-trippers. But one street back from the water the more peaceful pace of village life takes over. Two massive stair-paths, the Kalí Stráta and Katarráktes, effectively deter many of the day-trippers and appear most dramatic if climbed towards sunset; massive ruins along the lower reaches of the Kalí Stráta are lonely and sinister after dark.

A series of blue arrows through Khorió leads to the excellent local **museum** (Tues–Sun 10am–2pm; 500dr). Housed in a fine old mansion at the back of the village,

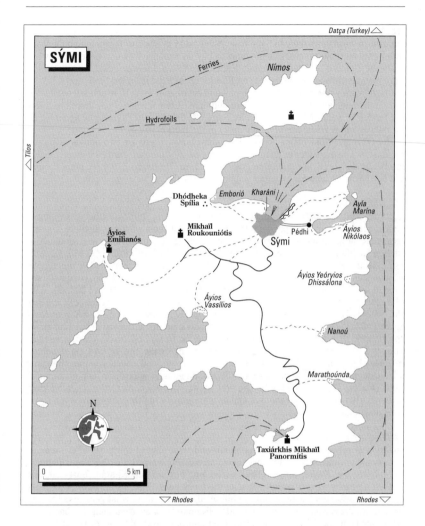

the collection concentrates on Byzantine and medieval Sými, with exhibits on frescoes in isolated, locked churches and a gallery of medieval icons. On the way back to central Khorió, the nineteenth-century pharmacy, with its apothecary jars and wooden drawers labelled for exotic herbal remedies, is worth a look.

At the very pinnacle of things, a **castle of the Knights** occupies the site of Sými's ancient acropolis, and you can glimpse a stretch of Cyclopean wall on one side. A dozen churches grace Khorió; that of the Ascension, inside the fortifications, is a replacement of the one blown to bits when the Germans torched the munitions cached there. One of the bells in the new belfry is the nose-cone of a thousand-pound bomb, hung as a memorial.

Practicalities

Excursion boats run daily to Sými from Mandhráki in Ródhos Town, but you'll come under considerable pressure at the quay to buy an expensive return ticket – not what you want if you're off island-hopping. Either insist on a one-way ticket, or buy tickets more cheaply through travel agents on Rhodes or take the islanders' own unpublicized and significantly cheaper boats, the Symi I and catamaran Symi II, which sail to Rhodes in the morning, returning between 2pm and 6pm. A few times a week there are main-line ferries as well. ANES, the outlet for Symi I/II tickets, and Psyhas, the agent for all big inter-island **ferries**, are one alley apart in the market place.

The **OTE** and **post office** are open standard hours; there are two **banks** with cash dispensers. During summer an unmarked green-and-white van shuttles between Yialós and Pédhi via Khorió at regular intervals until 11pm. There are also three taxis, though this is a perfect island for boat and walking excursions.

ACCOMMODATION

Accommodation for independent travellers is limited. Studios, rather than simple rooms, predominate, and package operators control most of these; if there are any vacancies, proprietors meet arriving boats. Among the best value are rooms with kitchen facilities let by the English-speaking Katerina Tsakiris (☎0241/71 813; ③), with a grandstand view over the harbour; reservations usually essential. Rather more basic are two standbys down by the market area, the *Glafkos* (☎0241/71 358; rooms ②, studios ③) on the square, and the fairly cramped, last-resort *Egli* (☎0241/71 392; ②). With a bit more to spend, there are rooms, studios and houses managed by the *Jean & Tonic* bar (☎0241/71 819; ③), or the *Hotel Khorio* (☎0241/71 800; ④) and the adjacent *Hotel Fiona* (☎0241/72 088; ④) are good, traditional-style outfits at the top of the Kalí Stráta up in Khorió. If money's no object, the *Alyki* (☎ & fax 0241/71 665; ⑤), a few paces right from the clocktower, is also a famous monument, while the *Dorian* right behind (☎0241/71 181, fax 72 292; ⑤) is comfortable enough, and cheaper within the same price category. Failing all of these, the best strategy is to appeal for help from Sunny Land (☎0241/71 320, fax 71 413), the first agency you encounter after disembarking: their weekly rates for villas, houses and apartments are highly competitive even if you don't stay a full seven days.

EATING AND DRINKING

You're best off avoiding entirely the north and west side of the port, where menus, prices and attitudes tend to have been terminally warped by the day-trip trade. Exceptions are *Tholos*, an excellent ouzerí out beyond the Kharáni boatyard, and *Mythos*, a nearby, pricier ouzerí opposite the ferry dock. Matters improve perceptibly as you press further inland or up the hill. At the very rear of what remains of Sými's bazaar, *O Meraklis* has polite service and well-cooked dishes; *Neraidha*, well back from the water near the OTE, has delicious food and is reasonably priced. Up in Khorió, *Georgios* is a decades-old institution, serving large portions of Greek *nouvelle cuisine* in a pebble-mosaic courtyard – excellent value, but open for dinner only.

With a large ex-pat community, a few **bars** are run by foreigners: in Khorió, *Jean & Tonic* caters to a mixed clientele; down at Yialós, *Vapori* is the oldest bar on the island, welcoming customers with desserts, breakfast and free newspapers.

Around the island

Sými has no big sandy beaches, but there are plenty of pebbly stretches at the heads of the deep narrow bays which indent the coastline. **PÉDHI**, a 45-minute walk from Yialós, retains some of its former identity as a fishing hamlet, with enough water in the plain behind – the island's largest – to support a few vegetable gardens. The beach is average-to-poor, though, and the giant *Pedhi Beach* hotel (packages only) has considerably bumped up prices at the three local tavernas, of which the most reasonable and authentic is *Iy Kamares*. Many will opt for another thirty minutes of walking via a rough but obvious path along the south shore of the almost landlocked bay to **Áyios Nikólaos**. The only all-sand beach on Sými, this offers sheltered swimming, tamarisks for shade and a mediocre taverna. Alternatively, a marked path on the north side of the inlet leads within an hour to **Ayía Marína**, where there's another, better taverna and a monastery-capped islet which you can easily swim to.

Around Yialós, you'll find tiny **Nós** "beach" ten minutes past the boat yards at Kharáni, but there's sun here only until lunchtime and it's packed with daytrippers. You can continue along the coastal track here past tiny gravel coves and rock slabs where nudists disport themselves, or cut inland from the Yialós platía past the abandoned desalination plant, to the appealing **Emborió** bay, with a taverna at one end and an artificially sand-strewn beach at the other. Inland from this are Byzantine mosaic fragments under a protective shelter, and, nearby, a catacomb complex known locally as **Dhódheka Spília**.

Plenty of other, more secluded coves are accessible by energetic walkers with sturdy footwear, or those prepared to pay a modest sum for the taxi-boats (daily in season 10am–1pm, returning 4–5pm; return fares only). These are the best way to reach the southern bays of **Marathoúnda** and **Nanoú**, and the only method of getting to the spectacular, fjord of **Áyios Yeóryios Dhissálona**. Dhissálona lies in shade after 1pm, and Marathoúnda lacks a taverna, making Nanoú the most popular destination for day trips. The 200-metre beach there consists of gravel, sand and pebbles, with a scenic backdrop and a reasonable taverna behind.

On foot, you can cross the island – which has retained patches of its natural juniper forest – in two hours to **Áyios Vassílios**, the most scenic of the gulfs, or in a little more time to **Áyios Emilianós** at the island's extreme west end, where you can stay the night (bring supplies) in a cloister. On the way to the latter you might look in at the monastery of **Mikhaïl Roukouniótis**, Sými's oldest, with lurid eighteenth-century frescoes and a peculiar ground plan: the current kathólikon is actually superimposed on an earlier, lower structure abandoned to the damp. The less intrepid can explore on guided walks to several beaches led by Hugo Tyler (☎0241/71 670), which are generally met by a boat for the ride home.

The Archangel is also honoured at the huge monastery of **Taxiárkhis Mikhaïl Panormítis**, Sými's biggest rural attraction and generally the first port of call for the excursion boats from Rhodes. These allow only a quick thirty-minute tour; if you want more time, you'll have to come on a "jeep safari" from Yialós, or arrange to stay the night (for a donation), in the *xenónas* set aside for pilgrims. There are numbers of these in summer, as Mikhaïl has been adopted as the patron of sailors in the Dodecanese.

Like many of Sými's monasteries, it was thoroughly pillaged during the last war, so don't expect too much of the building or its treasures. An appealing pebble-mosaic court surrounds the central kathólikon, tended by the single remaining monk, lit by an improbable number of oil lamps and graced by a fine *témblon*, though the frescoes are recent and mediocre. The small museum (nominal fee) contains a strange mix of precious antiques, junk (stuffed crocodiles and koalas), votive offerings, models of ships, and a chair piled with messages-in-bottles brought here by Aegean currents – the idea being that if the bottle or toy boat arrived, the sender got their wish. There's a tiny beach, a shop/kafenío and a taverna; near the taverna stands a memorial commemorating three Greeks, including the monastery's abbot, executed in February 1944 by the Germans for aiding British commandos.

Tílos

The small, blissfully quiet island of **Tílos** has a population of only 350 (shrinking to 80 in winter), and is one of the least frequented of the Dodecanese, although it can be visited on a day trip by hydrofoil once or twice a week. Why anyone should want to come for just a few hours is unclear: while it's a great place to rest on the beach or go walking, there is nothing very striking at first glance. After a few days, however, you may have stumbled on several of the seven small castles of the Knights of St John which stud the crags, or gained access to several inconspicuous medieval chapels, some with frescoes or with *khokhláki* (pebble-mosaic) court-yards, clinging to hillsides.

Tílos shares the characteristics of its closest neighbours: limestone mountains resembling those on Khálki, plus volcanic lowlands, pumice beds and red-lava sand as on Níssyros. Though rugged and scrubby on the heights, the island has ample water – mostly pumped up from the agricultural plains – and groves of oak and terebinth near the cultivated areas. The volcano on neighbouring Níssyros has contributed pumice beds and red-lava-sand beaches to the landscape as well. From many points on the island you've fine views across to Sými, Turkey and Níssyros. Tílos's main cement-paved road runs 7km from Livádhia, also the port village, to Megálo Khorió, the capi-tal and only other significant habitation. When boats arrive, a fleet of three **buses** – including a large one for high season – links the two. At other times at least one bus adheres to a schedule of sorts; there's also a single **taxi**, or you can rent a **motorbike** from two outlets in Livádhia, or charter one of the minibuses.

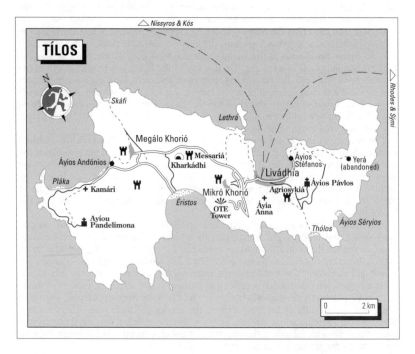

Livádhia

Of the two settlements, **LIVÁDHIA** remains better equipped to deal with tourists, and is closer to good walking opportunities. If there are vacancies, **room** and **hotel** owners meet the
ferries, but in peak season it's well worth phoning ahead. Budget options include *Paradise*
(aka *Stamatia's*; ☎0241/44 334; ②) on the waterfront, or the recently refurbished and good-
value *Hotel Livadhia* (☎0241/44 266; ②) inland, which also runs *Studios Sofia* (③) just
behind. Nearby, on the east side of the tiny platía here, stands the *Pension Periyali* (☎0241/44
398; ②), while 400m east down the beach, then inland, is *Kastello* (☎0241/44 292; ②). At the
top end of things is the *Irini*, 200m from mid-beach (☎0241/44 293, fax 44 238; ④).

Of the seafront **tavernas**, *Sofia's* is a convivial meeting place for ex-pats, in particular Laskarina clients, but you'll probably get a better, more authentically Greek meal
at *Irina* or *Stelios*, at the far east end of the beach. The best place for fish grills is *Blue
Sky*, an unmissable place perched above the ferry dock. For **breakfast** or pre-dinner
drinks, *Omonia* – under the trees strung with fairy lights, near the post office – is
enduringly popular, though lately rivalled by the *Vayos* breakfast bar and creperie, next
to the *Periyali*. Organized **nightlife** in or near Livádhia is limited to two bars: *La Luna*
at the ferry pier (scheduled to move shortly out next to *Stelios*) and a durable music
pub in Mikró Khorió (see below).

The **post office** is the only place to change money; the two **card-phones** are usual-
ly out of order, in which case you'll have to patronize the metered one at Stefanakis
Travel, one of two agencies at the jetty dividing the **ferry-ticket** trade between them.
There's also a **bakery** and three **supermarkets**.

Around the island

From Livádhia you can trail-walk an hour north to the pebble bay of **Lethrá**, or for slightly longer south to the sandy cove of **Tholoú**. The track to the latter begins by the cemetery and the chapel of **Áyios Pandelímon** with its Byzantine *khokhláki* court, then curls
around under the seemingly impregnable castle of **Agriosykiá**; from the saddle overlooking the descent to Tholoú, a route marked with cairns leads northwest to the citadel
in twenty minutes. It's less than an hour's walk west by trail, cutting across the road
curves, up to the ghost village of **Mikró Khorió**, whose 1200 inhabitants left for Livádhia
during the 1950s. The only intact structures are the church (locked except for the August
15 festival) and an old house which has been restored as a long-hours **music pub**.

Megálo Khorió and Éristos

The rest of Tílos's inhabitants live in or near **MEGÁLO KHORIÓ**, with an enviable
perspective over the vast agricultural *kámbos* stretching down to Éristos (see p.600),
and are overlooked in turn by the vast Knights' castle which encloses a sixteenth-century chapel. The castle was built on the site of ancient Tílos – from which recycled
masonry is evident – and is reached by a stiff, thirty-minute climb that begins on the
lane behind the Ikonomou **supermarket** before threading its way through a vast jumble of cisterns, house foundations and derelict chapels, the remains of the much large
medieval Megálo Khorió. Two more flanking fortresses stare out across the plain: the
easterly one of **Messariá** helpfully marks the location of the **Kharkádhi** cave where
Pleiocene midget-elephant bones were discovered in 1971. A 500-metre track goes
there from the road, ending just beyond the spring-fed cypress below the cave-mouth,
which was hidden for centuries until a World War II artillery barrage exposed it. The
bones themselves have been transferred to a small **museum** in Megálo Khorió, which
opens only on application to the town hall.

Your choices for **accommodation** in the village are the *Pension Sevasti* (☎0241/44 237; ②), the central *Miliou Apartments* (☎0241/44 204; ③), or *Studios Ta Elefandakia* (☎0241/44 213; ③) by the car park. Among a handful of **tavernas**, the *Kali Kardhia*, next to the *Pension Sevasti*, is under energetic young management and has the best view – in addition to good food. Megálo Khorió now also has a few **nightspots**, one of them at the start of the track north for remote **Skáfi** beach (sandy but often windy).

South of and below Megálo Khorió, a sign directs you along the six-kilometre paved side road to the long, pink-sand **Éristos** beach, the island's best, where nudism will goes unremarked. About halfway down the road on the right amongst the orchards is *Taverna-Rooms Tropikana* (☎0241/44 242; ②), nothing special in either category but the only reliable year-round eating place near the beach; at peak season a simple snack bar may operate behind the sand.

The far northwest

The main road beyond Megálo Khorió hits the coast again at **Áyios Andónios**, with a single **hotel/taverna**, the *Australia* (☎0241/44 296; ③), and an exposed, average beach. At low tide you can find more lava-trapped skeletons strung out in a row – human this time, presumably tide-washed victims of a Nissirian eruption in 600 BC, and discovered by the same archeologists who found the miniature pachyderms.

There's better swimming at isolated **Pláka** beach, 2km west of Áyios Andónios, where people camp rough despite a total lack of facilities. The road finally ends 8km west of Megálo Khório at the fortified monastery of **Ayíou Pandelímonas**, founded in the fifteenth century for the sake of its miraculous spring. Now the place is usually deserted except from July 25 to 27, when it hosts the island's major festival. A tower-gate and oasis setting more than two hundred forbidding metres above the west coast seem its most memorable features, though the eminently photogenic inner courtyard boasts yet another *khokhláki* floor, and the church a fine tessellated marble floor. On the interior walls, an early eighteenth-century fresco, recently restored, shows the founder-builder holding a model of the monastery, while behind the ornate altar screen hides another fresco of the Holy Trinity.

To guarantee access, you need to visit with the regular Sunday-morning minibus tour from Megálo Khorió (fare 1000dr; 1hr to look around), or contact Pandelis Yiannourakis, the key-keeper, in Megálo Khorió. To vary the return, you can walk back on a signposted path; it's shown correctly on the FOTA-sponsored map, and ends at the minor monastery of Kamári near Áyios Andónios.

Níssyros

Volcanic **Níssyros** is noticeably greener than its southern neighbours Tílos, Khálki, and Sými, and has proved attractive and wealthy enough to retain more of its population, staying lively even in winter. While remittances from abroad (particularly Astoria, New York) are necessarily important, much of the island's income is derived from quarrying gypsum and pumice.

The main island's peculiar geology is potentially a source of other benefits: DEI, the Greek power company, spent much of the years between 1988 and 1992 sinking exploratory **geothermal wells** and attempting to convince the islanders of the benefits of cheap electricity.

In 1993, a local referendum went massively against the project, and DEI, together with its Italian contractor, took the hint and packed up. The desalination plant, reliant on expensive power from the fuel-oil generator, scarcely provides enough fresh water to spur a massive growth in package tourism. The relatively few tourists who stay the night, as opposed to the daytrippers from Kós, still find peaceful villages with a minimum of concrete eyesores, and a friendly tight-knit population. Níssyros also offers

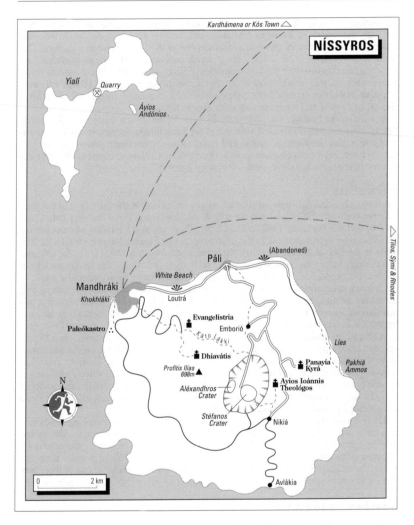

good walking opportunities, and wherever you stroll you'll hear the contented grunting of pigs as they gorge themselves on acorns from the many oak trees. Autumn is a wonderful time, especially when the landscape has perked up after the first rains, and the late-January almond-blossoming is one of the island's glories.

Mandhráki

MANDHRÁKI is the deceptively large port and island capital, where the wooden balconies and windows of its tightly packed white houses provide splashes of bright colour. Except for the drearier fringes near the ferry dock, the bulk of the place looks cheerful, arrayed around the community orchard or *kámbos* and overlooked by two ancient fortresses.

Into a corner of the first of these, the fourteenth-century Knights' castle, is wedged the little monastery of **Panayía Spilianí**, built on this spot in accordance with the instructions of the Virgin, given in a vision to one of the first Christian islanders. The monastery's prestige grew in the form of a rich collection of Byzantine icons; raiding Saracens failed to discover the vast quantities of silver secreted here. On the way up to the monastery, you might stop in at the house restored for the **Historical and Popular Museum** (erratic hours; free admission), two small rooms full of archival photos, heirlooms and other ethnographic memorabilia.

As a defensive bastion, the 2600-year-old Doric **Paleókastro** (unrestricted access), twenty minutes' well-signposted walk out of the Langadháki district, is infinitely more impressive than the Knights' castle, and ranks as one of the more underrated ancient sites in Greece. You can clamber up onto the massive, Cyclopean-block walls by means of a broad staircase beside the still-intact main gateway.

Practicalities

You'll see a handful of **hotels** on your left as you disembark at the port; best of the mid-range options are the helpful and friendly *Hotel/Restaurant Three Brothers* (☎0242/31 344; ③) and the *Romantzo* (☎0242/31 340; ③). There are also a number of more atmospheric, quieter establishments in the town proper. The *Pension Nissyros* (☎0241/31 052; ③) is at the foot of the castle, or try the small *Hotel Ipapandi* (☎0241/31 485; ③) near Mandhráki's luxury accommodation, the *Hotel Porfyris* (☎0242/31 376; ④), set back from the sea, but overlooking the *kámbos*, with gardens and a large, deep swimming pool.

Culinary **specialities** include pickled caper greens, *pittiá* (chickpea croquettes), and *soumádha*, an almond-syrup drink nowadays only made by one family and served at two tavernas (*Romantzo* and *Karava*). Shoreline **tavernas** include *Kleanthis*, a popular local hangout at lunchtime, and adjacent *Mike's* which offers such treats as yoghurt with candied grapes. Just inland from these, *Taverna Nissiros* – the oldest in town – is inexpensive and always packed after dark. However the best eating is inland: on the nocturnally lively Platía Ilikioméni, shaded by ficus trees, the excellent *Taverna Irini* has arguably the best food and most generous portions on the island, while *Panorama*, a bit east towards the Porfyris, has more idiosyncratic dishes such as snails and suckling pig. The focus of **nightlife** is again not the shore but various bars and cafés near Platía Ilikioméni, the most durable being *Cactus Bar*.

There's a short-hours **OTE** near the same platía. One of the two **travel agencies** acts as a bank rep, and a post office in the Italian-built "palace" at the harbour. Also by the jetty is a small **bus station**, with (theoretically) early morning and early afternoon departures into the interior and more frequent jaunts as far as Páli. In practice these are subject to cancellation, so you might consider renting a **motorbike** at one of three outlets on the main street.

Beaches – and Páli

Beaches on Níssyros are in even shorter supply than water, so much so that the tour agency here can successfully market excursions to a sandy cove on **Áyios Andónios** islet, just next to the mining apparatus on Yialí. Closer at hand, the black-rock beach of **Khokhláki**, behind the Knights' castle, is impossible if the wind is up, and the town beach of **Miramáre** at the east edge of the harbour would be a last resort in any weather. It's better to head east along the main road, passing the refurbished spa of **Loutrá** (hot mineral-water soaks June–Oct; 550dr per day) and the smallish **"White Beach"** (properly Yialiskári), 2km along and dwarfed by an ugly eponymous hotel (☎0242/31 498, fax 31 389; ④), generally booked by tour groups.

A kilometre or so further, the fishing village of **PÁLI** makes a more attractive base. Here you'll find the *Hotel Ellenis* (☎0242/31 453; ③), two **rooms** places (fanciest at the west end of the quay) and a good taverna, *Afroditi*, featuring white Cretan wine and homemade desserts. Another dark-sand beach extends east of Páli to an apparently abandoned new spa, but to reach Níssyros' best beaches, continue in that direction for an hour on foot (or twenty minutes by moped along the road), past an initially discouraging seaweed- and cowpat-littered shoreline, to the delightful cove of **Líes**, where the track ends. Walking a further ten or fifteen minutes along a trail over the headland brings you to the idyllic, 300-metre expanse of **Pakhiá Ámmos**.

The interior

It is the central, dormant **volcano** which gives Níssyros its special character and fosters the growth of the abundant vegetation – and no stay would be complete without a visit. When excursion boats arrive from Kós, the Polyvotis Tours coach and usually one of the public buses are pressed into service to take customers into the interior. Tours tend to set off at about 10.30am and 2.30pm, so time yourself accordingly for relative solitude, and ideally make the trip on foot or by moped.

The road up from Páli winds first past the virtually abandoned village of **EMBORIÓ**, where pigs and cows far outnumber people, though the place is slowly being bought up and restored by Athenians and foreigners. New owners are often surprised to discover natural saunas, heated by volcano steam, in the basements of the crumbling houses; at the outskirts of the village there's a public **steam bath** in a grotto, whose entrance is outlined in white paint. If you're descending to Páli from here, an old cobbled way offers an attractive short cut of the four-kilometre road.

NIKIÁ, the large village on the east side of the volcano's caldera, is more of a going concern, and its spectacular situation 14km from Mandhráki offers views out to Tílos as well as across the volcanic crater. Of the three **kafenía** here, the one on the engaging, round platía is rarely open, while the one in the middle of town usually has food. There are also a few **rooms**, but these tend to be substandard and overpriced. By the bus turnaround area, signs point to the 45-minute **trail** descending to the crater floor; a few minutes downhill, you can detour briefly to the eyrie-like **Monastery of Áyios Ioánnis Theológos**. The picnic benches and utility buildings come to life at the annual festival, the evening of September 25. To **drive** directly to the volcanic area you have to take the unsignposted road which veers off just past Emborió.

However you approach the **volcano**, a sulphurous stench drifts out to meet you as fields and scrub gradually give way to lifeless, caked powder. The sunken **main crater** of Stéfanos is extraordinary, a moonscape of grey, brown and sickly yellow; there is another, less visited double crater (dubbed Aléxandhros) to the west, equally dramatic, with a clear trail leading up to it from the access road. The perimeters of both are pocked with tiny blowholes from which jets of steam puff constantly and around which little pincushions of pure sulphur crystals form. The whole floor of the larger crater seems to hiss, and standing in the middle you can hear something akin to a huge cauldron bubbling away below you. According to legend this is the groaning of Polyvotis, a titan crushed here by Poseidon under a huge rock torn from Kós. When there are tourists around, a small, overpriced café functions in the centre of the wasteland.

Since the destruction of the old trail between the volcano and Mandhráki, pleasant options for walking back to town are limited. If you want to try, backtrack along the main crater access road for about 1km to find the start of a clear but unmarked path which passes the volcanic gulch of **Káto Lákki** and the monastery of **Evangelistrías** on its two-hour course back to the port. You can lengthen the trip by detouring from Evangelistrías south to Profítis Elías, the island's summit – a two-hour detour roundtrip, the route well marked with cairns and white paint.

Kós

After Rhodes, **Kós** is the second largest and most popular island in the Dodecanese, and there are superficial similarities between the two. Here also the harbour is guarded by an imposing castle of the Knights of St John; the streets are lined with grandiose Italian public buildings, and minarets and palm trees punctuate extensive Hellenistic and Roman remains.

Though sandy and fertile, the hinterland of Kós lacks the wild beauty of Rhodes' interior, and it must also be said that the main town has little charm aside from its antiquities. Rhodes-scale tourist development imposed on an essentially sleepy, small-scale island economy, and a population of only 22,000, has resulted most obviously in even higher food and accommodation prices than on Rhodes. Except for the main town and perhaps Mastikhári resort, this is not an island that attracts many independent travellers, and from early July to early September you'll be lucky to find any sort of room at all without reservations far in advance, or a pre-booked package. All this acknowledged, Kós is still definitely worth a few days' time while island-hopping; its handful of mountain villages are appealing, the tourist infrastructure excellent (even extending to such amenities as cycle paths) and swimming opportunities are limitless – virtually the entire coast is fringed by beaches of various sizes, colours and consistencies.

Kós Town

The town of **KÓS**, home to most of the island's population, spreads in all directions from the harbour; apart from the Knights' castle, the first thing you see on arrival, its most compelling attraction lies in the wealth of Hellenistic and Roman remains, many of which were only revealed by an earthquake in 1933, and excavated afterwards by the Italians. It was they also who planned and laid out the "garden suburb" that extends east of the central grid. Elsewhere, vast areas of open space alternate with a hotchpotch of Ottoman monuments and later mock-medieval or Art-Deco buildings.

The **castle** (Tues–Sun 8.30am–3pm; 800dr) is reached via a causeway over its former moat, now filled in and planted with palms (hence the avenue's Greek name, Finíkon). The existing double citadel, built in stages between 1450 and 1514, replaced an original fourteenth-century fort deemed not capable of withstanding advances in medieval artillery. A fair proportion of ancient Koan masonry has been recycled into the walls, where the escutcheons of several Grand Masters of the Knights of St John can also be seen.

Immediately opposite the castle entrance stands the riven trunk of Hippocrates' plane tree, its branches now propped up by scaffolding instead of the ancient columns of yore; at seven hundred years, it's not really old enough to have seen the great healer, though it has a fair claim to being one of the oldest trees in Europe. Adjacent are a hexagonal Ottoman fountain and the eighteenth-century mosque of Hassan Pasha, also known as the Loggia Mosque after the portico on one side; its ground floor – like that of the **Defterdar mosque** on Platía Eleftherías – is taken up by rows of shops.

Opposite the latter stands the Italian-built **Archeological Museum** (Tues–Sun 8.30am–3pm; 800dr), with a predictable Latin bias in the choice of exhibits. Four rooms of statuary are arrayed around an atrium with a mosaic of Hippocrates welcoming Asklepios to Kós; the most famous item, purportedly a statue of Hippocrates, is indeed Hellenistic, but most of the other highly regarded works (such as Hermes seated with a lamb) are Roman.

The largest single section of ancient Kós is the **agora**, a sunken, free-access zone containing a confusing jumble of ruins, owing to repeated earthquakes between the second and sixth centuries AD. More comprehensible are the so-called western excavations, lent definition by two intersecting marble-paved streets and the restored

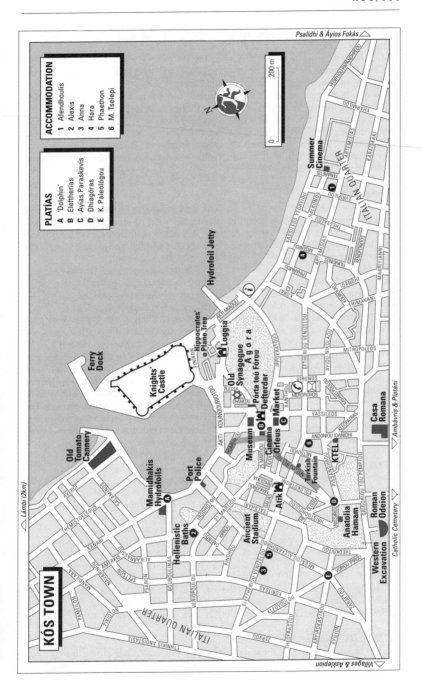

KÓS TOWN

◁ *Lámbi (2km)*

△ *Psalídhi & Áyios Fokás*

ITALIAN QUARTER

ACCOMMODATION
1 Afendhoulis
2 Alexis
3 Anna
4 Hara
5 Phaethon
6 M. Tselepi

PLATÍAS
A 'Dolphin'
B Eleftherías
C Ayías Paraskevís
D Dhiagóras
E K. Paleológou

Summer Cinema

Hydrofoil Jetty

Ferry Dock

Knights' Castle

Hippocrates' Plane Tree

Loggía

Old Synagogue

Agora

Pórta toú Fórou

Defterdar

Market

Old Tomato Cannery

Mamidhakis Hydrofoils

Port Police

Hellenistic Baths

Museum

Cinema

Orfeus

Turkish Fountain

Atik

Ancient Stadium

Anatolia Hamam

Roman Odeion

Western Excavation

Casa Romana

KTEL

◁ *Ambávris & Platáni*

◁ *Catholic Cemetery*

◁ *Villages & Asklepíon*

ITALIAN QUARTER

colonnade of the covered running track. In the same area lie several floor mosaics, such as the famous one of Europa, though these tend to be hidden under protective gravel or off-limits. To the south, across Grigoríou toú Pémptou, are a Roman-era odeion and the **Casa Romana** (Tues–Sun 8.30am–3pm; 500dr), a third-century house built around three atria with suriviving patches of mosaic floors.

Kós also boasts a thoroughly commercialized **old town**, lining the pedestrianized street running from behind the market on Eleftherías as far as Platía Dhiagóras and the isolated minaret overlooking the western archeological zone. One of the few areas of town to survive the 1933 earthquake, today it's crammed with expensive tourist boutiques, cafés and snack bars. About the only genuinely old thing remaining here is a capped **Turkish fountain** with an calligraphic inscription, found where the walkway cobbles cross Odhós Venizélou.

Practicalities

Large **ferries** anchor just outside the harbour at a special jetty by one corner of the castle; **excursion boats** to neighbouring islands sail right in and dock all along Aktí Koundouriótou. **Hydrofoils** tie up south of the castle at their own berth, on Aktí Miaoúli. Virtually all ferry and excursion boat agents sit within 50m of each other at the intersection of pedestrianized Vassiléos Pávlou and the waterfront.

The **airport** is 26km west of Kós Town in the centre of the island; an Olympic Airways shuttle bus meets Olympic flights, but if you arrive on any other flight you'll have to either take a taxi or head towards the giant roundabout outside the airport gate and find a KTEL bus – they run from here to Mastikhári, Kardhámena and Kéfalos as well as Kós Town. The **KTEL terminal** in town is a series of stops around a triangular park 400m back from the water; the municipality also runs a **local bus** service through the beach suburbs and up to the Asclepion, with a ticket and information office at Aktí Koundouriótoun 7.

The municipal **tourist office** at Vassiléos Yeoryíou 3 (July–Aug daily 7am–9pm; winter Mon–Fri 8am–3pm; spring/autumn Mon–Fri 7.30am–8pm & Sat 8am–3pm), keep stocks of local maps, bus timetables and ferry schedules (the latter not to be trusted implicitly). The Trapeza Pisteos/Credit Bank on the waterfront has an automatic notechanger as well as a cash dispenser; several other banks also have cash dispensers. The **post office** is at Venizélou 14, while the **OTE** at Výronos on the corner of Xánthou is open until 11pm daily. **Laundries** include Happy Wash laundry at Mitropóleos 14 and Laundromat Centre at Alikarnassoú 124.

ACCOMMODATION

If you're just in transit, you're virtually obliged to **stay** in Kós Town, and even if you plan a few days on the island, it still makes a sensible base, as it is the public transport hub and has the greatest concentration of transport hire and nightlife. Good budget choices in the centre include the deservedly popular *Pension Alexis* (☎0242/28 798; ③), Irodhótou 9 at the corner of Omírou, across from the Roman *agora*; the same welcoming family has the *Hotel Afendoulis* (☎0242/25 321; ④), about 600m south at Evripílou 1. If they're full, try the well-maintained *Hotel Phaethon* at Venizélou 75 (☎0242/28 901; ④), the simpler, adjacent *Pension Anna* at no. 77 (☎024/223 030; ③), or the popular *Hara* at Khálkonos 6 (☎0242/22 500; ③). For longer stays, the rooms let by Moustafa Tselepi (☎0242/28 896; ④) at Venizélou 29, on the corner of Metsóvou, are good, and some have cooking facilities. The well-appointed **campsite** is 2500m out towards Cape Psalídhi, and can be reached by the city bus service, but is open only during the summer.

EATING, DRINKING AND NIGHTLIFE

It's easy to **eat** well, and even cheaply as long as you search inland, north of the harbour. You can pretty much write off most of the waterfront tavernas, though the

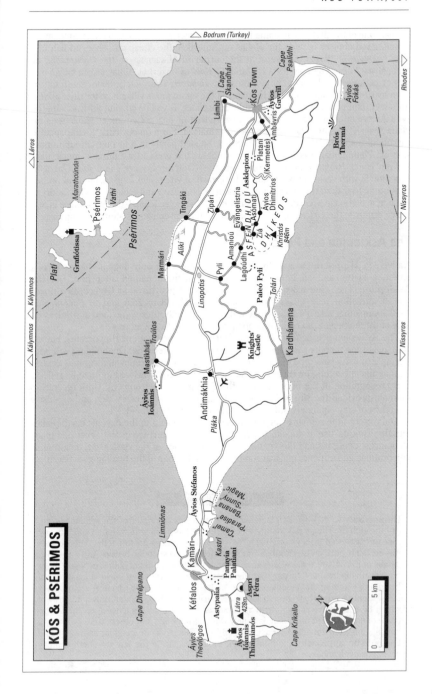

KÓS & PSÉRIMOS

Limnos, one of the first as you come from the ferry jetty, still lays on a reasonable table. Inland, good choices include the Hellas on Amerikís, the cheap and cheerful fish taverna *Nikolaos O Psaras* on Avérof at the corner of Alikarnassoú, the *Olympiadha* at Kleopátras 2 near Olympic Airways, and *To Kokhili* ouzerí at Alikarnassoú 64 on the corner of Amerikís. Equal to any of these is *Ambavris* (May–Oct), 800m south out of town by the road from near Casa Romana, in the eponymous village; go for their *pikilía* (medley), and expect to wait for a table in summer. If you're craving an English – or even American – **breakfast**, two cafés serve that or just coffee under giant trees on Platía Ayías Paraskevís, behind the produce market. For a quiet **drink** in atmospheric surroundings, there's the *Anatolia Hamam*, housed partly in a former Ottoman mansion off Platía Dhiagóras (eating there is not such a good idea); durable music bars include *Blues Brothers*, on the front near the "Dolphin Square", and *Jazz Opera* at Arseníou 5, with varied music for an older crowd. If you prefer loud techno and house, look no further than the "Pub Lanes", officially Nafklírou and Dhiákou; every address is a bar, just choose according to the crowd and the noise level. Otherwise there is one active **cinema**, the Orfeas, with summer and winter premises as shown on the map.

The Asklepion and Platáni

Native son **Hippocrates** is justly celebrated on Kós; not only does he have a tree, a street, a statue and an international medical institute named after him, but the **Asklepion** (Tues–Sun 8.30am–3pm; 800dr), one of just three in Greece, is a major tourist attraction (city buses run to site via Platáni 8am–2pm and to Platáni only 4–10.30pm; otherwise it's a 45-minute walk). Incidentally, there is no food or drink available at the Asklepion, so come equipped, or pause in Platáni en route.

The Asklepion was actually founded shortly after the death of Hippocrates, but it's safe to assume that the methods used and taught here were his. The building was both a temple to Asklepios (god of medicine, son of Apollo) and a renowned curative centre; its magnificent setting on three artificial hillside terraces overlooking Anatolia reflects early recognition of the importance of the therapeutic environment. Until recently, a fountain provided the site with a constant supply of clean, fresh water, and extensive stretches of clay piping are still visible, embedded in the ground.

Today very little remains standing above ground, owing to the chronic earthquakes and the Knights' use of the site as a quarry. The lower terrace in fact never had many structures, being instead the venue for the observance of the *Asklepieia*, quadrennial celebrations and athletic/musical competitions in honour of the healing god. Sacrifices

---

HIPPOCRATES

Hippocrates (c. 460–370 BC) is generally regarded as the father of scientific medicine, and through the Hippocratic oath – which probably has nothing to with him and is in any case much altered from its original form – he still influences doctors today. Hippocrates was certainly born on Kós, probably at Astypalia near present-day Kéfalos, but otherwise details of his life are few and disputed; what seems beyond doubt is that he was a great physician who travelled throughout the Classical Greek world but spent at least part of his career teaching and practising at the Asklepion on his native island. A vast number of **medical writings** have been traditionally attributed to Hippocrates, only a minority of which he could have actually written; *Airs, Waters and Places*, a treatise on the importance of environment on health, is widely thought to be his, but others were probably a compilation from a medical library kept on Kós. This stress on good air and water, and the **holistic approach** of ancient Greek medicine, can in the late twentieth century seem positively modern.

to Asklepios were conducted at an **altar**, the oldest structure on the site, whose foundations can still be seen near the middle of the second terrace. Just to its west, the Corinthian columns of a second-century AD **Roman temple** were partially re-erected by the nationalistic Italians. A monumental **staircase** mounts from the altar to the second-century BC Doric temple of Asklepios on the topmost terrace, the last and grandest of a succession of the deity's shrines at this site.

About halfway to the Asklepion, the village of **PLATÁNI** (also Kermetés, from the Turkish name *Germe*) is, along with the Kós Town, the remaining place of residence for the island's dwindling community of ethnic Turks. Until 1964 there were nearly three thousand of them, but successive Cyprus crises and the worsening of relations between Greece and Turkey prompted mass emigration to Anatolia, and a drop in the Muslim population to currently under a thousand. Near or at main crossroads junction, with a working Ottoman fountain, are several tavernas and kafenía, the better of them run by Turks: *Arap* (summer only) and *Gin's Palace* (all year), each offering Anatolian-style mezédhes and kebabs are better than most places in Kós Town.

Just outside Pláni on the road back to the port, the island's **Jewish cemetery** lies in a dark conifer grove, 300m beyond the Muslim graveyard. Dates on the headstones stop after 1940, after which none of the local Jews were allowed the luxury of a natural death prior to their deportation in summer 1944. Their former synagogue, a wonderfully orientalized Art-Deco specimen at Alexándhrou Dhiákou 4, has recently been refurbished as a municipal hall.

Eastern Kós

If you're looking for anything resembling a deserted **beach** near the capital, you'll need to make use of the city bus line connecting the various resorts to either side of town, or else rent a vehicle; pedal bikes can take advantage of the cycle paths extending as far east as Cape Psalídhi. Closest is **Lámbi**, 3km north towards Cape Skandhári with its military watchpoint, the last vestige of a vast army camp which has deferred to the demands of tourism.

The far end of the city bus line beginning at Lámbi is Áyios Fokás, 8km southeast, with the unusual and remote **Brós Thermá** 5km further on, easiest reached by rented vehicle. Here **hot springs** pour out of a sluice into a shoreline pool protected by boulders, heating the seawater to an enjoyable temperature. Winter storms typically disperse the boulder wall, rebuilt every spring, so that the pool changes from year to year. There's a small taverna above the parking area but no other facilities.

Tingáki and Marmári

The two neighbouring beach resorts of Tingáki and Marmári are separated from each other by the salt marsh of **Alykí**, which retains water until June after a wet winter. Between January and April Alykí is host to hundreds of migratory birds, and most of the year you'll find tame terrapins to feed near the outlet to the warm, shallow sea. There's almost always a breeze along this coast, which means plenty of windsurfers for hire at either resort. The profiles of Kálymnos, Psérimos and Turkey's Bodrum peninsula all make for spectacular scenery. If you're aiming for either of these resorts from town, especially on a bike of any sort, it's safest and most pleasant to go by the obvious **minor road** which takes off from the southwest corner of town; the entire way to Tingáki is paved, and involves the same distance as using the main trunk road and marked turnoff. Similarly, a grid of paved rural lanes links the inland portions of Tingáki and Marmári.

TINGÁKI, a busy beachside resort with half-a-dozen medium-sized hotels, lies 12km west of the harbour. Oddly, there's very little accommodation near the beach; most of this is scattered inland through fields and cow pastures. One of the better choices is

Hotel Ilios (☎0242/29 411; ③), a well designed bungalow complex; closer to the seafront turnaround square, the *Meni Beach* (☎0242/29 217; ④) is perhaps more convenient if less peaceful. The best taverna here is *Ambelis* (supper only), way off at the east end of the developed area, south of the minor road noted above. The beach itself is white-sand, long and narrow – it improves, and veers further out of earshot from the frontage road, as you head southwest.

MARMÁRI, 15km from town, has a smaller built-up area than Tingáki, and the beach itself is broader, especially to the west where it forms little dunes. Most hotels here are monopolized by tour groups, but further inland, on the west side of the access road down from the island trunk road, *Exokhiki Psistaria Apostolis* is a real find for **eating**, offering fresh fish and meat-grills, an amazing wine list, engaging decor, and reasonable prices. You can also **horse-ride** locally at the Marmari Riding Centre (☎0242/41 783), on the east side of the usual access road.

The Asfendhioú villages

Inland, the main interest of eastern Kós resides in the villages of **Mount Dhíkeos**, a handful of settlements collectively referred to as **Asfendhioú**, on the slopes of the island's only natural forest. Together they give a good idea of what Kós looked like before tourism and ready-mix concrete, and all are now severely depopulated by the mad rush to the coast. They are accessible via the curvy side-road from Zipári, a badly marked but paved minor road to Lagoúdhi, or by the shorter access road for Pylí.

The first Asfendhioú village you reach up the Zipári road is Evangelístria, where a major crossroads by the parish church and the *Asfendhiou* taverna leads to Lagoúdhi and Amanioú (west), Asómati (east) and Ziá (uphill). **ZIÁ**'s spectacular sunsets make it the target of evening tour buses, though the village has barely ten families still resident. Best of the **tavernas** here is the *Olympiada*, at the start of the pedestrian walkway up to the church; runner up, by the same church, is *Iliovasilema/Sunset*, with an unbeatable, car-free situation. Ziá is also the trailhead for the ascent of 846-metre Dhíkeos peak, a two-and-a-half-hour round-trip, initially on track but mostly by path. The route is fairly obvious, and the views from the pillbox-like summit chapel of Metamórfosis are ample reward for the effort.

Heading east from Ziá or Evangelístria, roads converge at **ASÓMATI**, home to about thirty villagers and numbers of outsiders restoring abandoned houses; the evening view from the church of Arkhángelos with its pebble mosaic rivals that of Zía, though there are no facilities as yet. **ÁYIOS DHIMÍTRIOS**, 2km beyond on a steadily worsening track, is marked by its old name of Khaïkhoúdhes on some maps, and is today completely abandoned except for a shepherd living next to the attractive church; you can continue from here on 3.5km of more rough road to the junction with the paved road linking Plimáni with the municipal rubbish tip.

Pylí

PYLÍ can be reached via the paved road through Lagoúdhi and Amanioú, or from the Linopótis pond on the main island trunk road. In the upper of its two neighbourhoods, 100m west of the pedestrianized square and church, the simple *Piyi* taverna serves inexpensive fare in a superb setting beside the giant cistern-fountain (*piyi*), decorated with carved lion-head spouts. Pylí's other attraction is the so-called **Kharmýlio** (Tomb of Kharmylos), vaguely signposted near the top of the village. This consists of a subterranean, niched vault, probably a Hellenistic family tomb; immediately above, traces of an ancient temple have been incorporated into the medieval chapel of Stavrós.

Paleó (medieval) **Pylí**, roughly 3km southeast of its modern descendant, was the Byzantine capital of Kós. Head there via Amanioú, keeping straight at the junction where painted lettering on a house corner points left to Ziá and Lagoúdhi. In any case, the castle should be obvious on its rock, straight ahead; the deteriorating road ends next to a spring, opposite which a stair-path leads within fifteen minutes to the roof of the fort. En route you pass the remains of the abandoned town tumbling southward down the slope, as well as three chapels often locked to protected fresco fragments within.

Western Kós

Near the arid, desolate centre of the island, well sown with military installations, a pair of giant roundabouts by the airport funnels traffic northwest towards the Mastikhári, northeast back towards town, southwest towards Kéfalos, and southeast to Kardhámena.

Mastikhári and Andimákhia

The least developed, least "packaged" and least expensive of the northern shore resorts, **MASTIKHÁRI** has a shortish, broad beach extending west, and a less attractive one at **Troúllos**, 1.5km east. At the end of the west beach, inside a partly fenced enclosure, lie remains of the fifth-century basilica of **Áyios Ioánnis**, one of several on the island. If you want to stay, quieter digs near the west beach include the well run *Studios Irini* (☎0242/51 269; ②) or the nearby *Filio* (☎0242/51 518; ③). *O Makis*, one street inland from the quay, is the place to eat. Mastikhári is also the port for the least expensive small **ferries** to Kálymnos; there are three well spaced departures in each direction most of the year, timed more or less to coincide with Olympic Airways flight schedules.

The workaday village of **ANDIMÁKHIA**, 5km southeast of Mastikhári, straggles over several ridges; the only concession to tourism is a much-photographed windmill on the main street, preserved as a working museum with its unfurled sails. For a token fee you can climb up to the mast loft and observe its workings. East of Andimákhia, reached via a marked, three-kilometre side road, an enormous, triangular **Knights' castle** overlooks the straits to Níssyros. Once through the imposing north gateway (unrestricted access), you can follow the well-preserved west parapet, and visit two interior chapels: one with patches of fresco, the other with fine rib vaulting.

Kardhámena

KARDHÁMENA, on the southeast coast 31km from Kós Town, is the island's largest package resort after the capital itself, with visitors (mostly Brits) outnumbering locals by twenty to one in peak season. Runaway local development has banished whatever redeeming qualities the place may once have had; the logos of Carling Black Label or Foster's, and bar names like the *Bubble and Squeak Bistro*, pretty much set the tone of the place. A hefty sand beach stretches to either side of the town, hemmed in to the east with ill-concealed military bunkers and a road as far as Tolári, home to the massive *Norida Beach* all-inclusive complex.

Kardhámena is most worth knowing about as a place to catch a **boat to Níssyros**. There are supposedly two daily sailings in season: the morning tourist excursion kaïki at approximately 9.30am, and another, less expensive one – the Chyrssoula – at 2.30pm, but in practice the afternoon departure is only reliable on Mondays and Thursdays, at some time between 1.30pm and 6.30pm, depending on when the Nissyrians have finished their shopping.

Outside high season, there are generally a few **rooms** not taken by tour companies, and prices are not outrageous. For more comfort, the *Hotel Rio* (☎0242/91 627, fax 91 895; ③) gets good reviews, and like most accommodation here is underpriced for its class. **Tavernas** are predictably poor, though the longest-lived and most reasonable one is *Andreas*, right on the harbour; inland, a **bakery** (signed with red arrows) does homemade ice cream, yoghurt and sticky cakes.

South coast beaches

The thinly populated portion of Kós southwest of the airport and Andimákhia boasts the most scenic and secluded beaches on the island, plus a number of minor ancient sites. Though given fanciful names and shown as separate extents on tourist maps, and the south-facing **beaches** form essentially one long stretch at the base of a cliff. **Magic**, officially Poléni, is the longest, broadest and wildest. **Sunny**, easily walkable from Magic, has sunbeds and a taverna. **Banana** (Langádha) is the cleanest and most picturesque, with junipers tumbling off its dunes. **Paradise**, often dubbed Bubble Beach (because of volcanic gas vents in the tidal zone) is small and oversubscribed.

Uninterrupted beach resumes at **Áyios Stéfanos**, overshadowed by a huge Club Med complex, and extends 5km west to Kamári (see below). A badly marked public access road leads down to the beach just west of a small peninsula, crowned with the exquisite remains of two triple-aisled, sixth-century basilicas. Though the best preserved on the island, several columns have been toppled since the 1980s, and wonderful bird mosaics languish under a permanent layer of "protective" gravel. The basilicas overlook tiny but striking Kastrí islet with its little chapel; in theory it's an easy swim (sometimes wading) across from the westerly beach, with some of the best snorkelling on Kós around the rock formations, but you must run the gauntlet of boats from the local water-ski school.

The far west

Essentially the shore annexe of Kéfalos (see below), **KAMÁRI** is a growing package resort pitched a few notches above Kardhámena; it's a major water-sports centre, and an alternative departure point for Níssyros, up to five days weekly in season. Independent hotels or pensions that can be recommended include *Sydney* (☎0242/71 286; ④) and the adjacent *Maria* (☎0242/71 308; ③), on the seafront west of the main road up to **KÉFALOS**, 43km from Kós Town. Squatting on a bluff looking down the length of the island, this is the end of the line for buses: dull but worth knowing about for its post office and as a staging point for expeditions into the rugged peninsula terminating dramatically at Cape Kríkello.

Main highlights of a half-day tour here are a Byzantine church incorporating an ancient temple, 1km south of the village; the late Classical amphitheatre (May–Oct), with two rows of seats remaining, of **ancient Astypalia**, 500m further at the side-path signposted "Palatia"; and the cave of **Asprí Pétra** (inhabited in the Neolithic period), marked rather vaguely off the paved ridge road. A rough dirt track west from after Astypalia leads to an often windy beach, taverna and small chapel at **Áyios Theológos**, 7km from Kéfalos; keeping to the main paved road until the end of the line brings you to the appealing (but mostly locked) monastery of **Áyios Ioánnis Thymianós**, also 7km from the village.

About 1.5km north of Kéfalos on the road tracing the island's summit ridge, an obvious dirt track veers north again for 3.5km to **Limniónas**, the only north-facing beach and fishing anchorage on this part of Kós. Of the two fish tavernas, *Limionas* – nearer the jetty – is preferable. Two compact sandy beaches sit either side of the peninsula.

Psérimos

PSÉRIMOS could be an idyllic little island if it weren't so close to Kós and Kálymnos, a factor which results in day-trippers by the boatload every day of the season. Numerous excursion boats compete to dock at the undersized harbour, and not surprisingly the islanders are apt to respond in a surly fashion to visitors. There are a couple of other, less attractive beaches to hide away on during the day: Vathý (sand), a thirty-minute walk east, or Marathoúnda (pebble), a forty-five-minute walk north.

Nowhere on Psérimos, including the monastery of Grafiótissa (its festival is on August 15), is much more than an hour's walk away.

Even during the season there won't be too many other overnighters, since there's a limited number of **rooms** available. Pick of the several small pensions are *Pension Tripolitis* (☎0243/23 196; ③) over the *Saroukos* taverna, and rooms managed by the postmistress, Katerina Xyloura (☎0243/23 497; ③) above her taverna on the eastern side of the harbour. There's just one small **store**, and most of the island's supplies are brought in daily from Kálymnos. **Eating out** however, won't break the bank, and there's often fresh fish in the handful of **tavernas**.

Virtually all boats based at Kós harbour operate triangle tours, which involve departure between 9.30am and 10am, followed by a stop for swimming on either Platí islet or adjacent Psérimos, lunch in Póthia, the port of Kálymnos, and another swimming stop at whichever islet wasn't visited in the morning. If you want to spend the entire day on Psérimos, you must ride one-way on a boat taking it as the first stop, and then cadge a lift back on another boat having Psérimos as its afternoon call, around 4pm. You should pay no more than forty percent of the full excursion price (currently about 5000dr) for each leg of the journey, and it would probably be a good idea to pack basic overnight gear in case the afternoon boat refuses to take you back to Kós.

The islanders themselves don't bother with the excursion boats, but use their own small craft, the Grammatiki, to visit Kálymnos for shopping on Monday, Wednesday and Friday (returning early afternoon); if you've been staying a few days, you might ask for a ride on this, or on your host's own boat.

Astypálea

Geographically, historically and architecturally, **Astypálea** would be more at home among the Cyclades – on a clear day you can see Anáfi or Amorgós in the west far more easily than any of the other Dodecanese (except the western tip of Kós), and it looks and feels more like these than its neighbours to the east. Astypálea is not the most beautiful of islands. The heights, which offer modest walking opportunities, are bleak and covered in thornbush. Yet the herb *alisfakiá*, brewed as a tea, flourishes too, and somehow hundreds of sheep survive – as opposed to snakes, which are (uniquely in the Aegean) entirely absent. Lush citrus groves and vegetable patches in the valleys signal a relatively ample water supply, hoarded in a reservoir. The few beaches along the generally featureless coastline are often stony or strewn with seaweed.

In antiquity the island's most famous citizen was **Kleomedes**, a boxer disqualified from an early Olympic Games for causing the death of his opponent. He came home so enraged that he demolished the local school, killing all its pupils. Things have calmed down a bit in the intervening 2500 years, and today Astypálea is renowned mainly for its honey and fish. However, the abundant local catch has only been shipped to Athens since the late 1980s, a reflection of the traditionally poor ferry links in every direction. These have improved recently with the introduction of new services to Piréas and Kós, but you still risk being marooned here for an extra day or three; indeed Laskarina Holidays deleted the island from their list in 1995, frustrated by chronically unreliable connections to the nearest airport.

Despite the relative isolation, plenty of people find their way to Astypálea during the short, intense summer, when the 1200 permanent inhabitants are all but overrun by upwards of seven thousand guests a day, and the noise and commotion at the densely built port is incredible. Most arrivals are Athenians, supplemented by large numbers of Italians and foreign owners of holiday homes in the understandably popular Khóra. At such times you won't find a bed without reserving well in advance, and camping rough is expressly frowned upon.

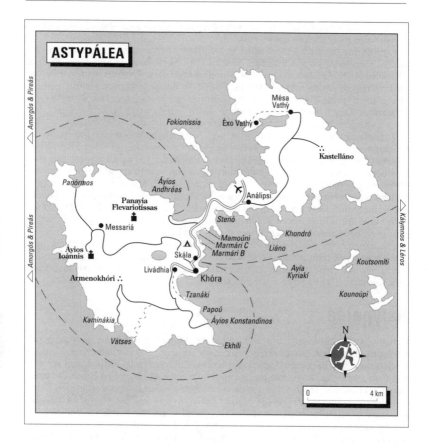

Skála and Khóra

The main harbour of **SKÁLA** or Péra Yialós dates from the Italian era (Astipálea was the first island the Italians occupied in the Dodecanese) and most of the settlement between the quay and the line of nine windmills is even more recent. As you climb up beyond the port towards **KHÓRA** though, the neighbourhoods get progressively older and more attractive, their steep streets enlivened by the *poúndia* or colourful wooden balconies of the whitewashed houses. The whole culminates in the thirteenth-century **kástro**, one of the finest in the Aegean, erected by the Venetian Quirini clan and subsequently modified by the Ottomans. Until well into this century over three hundred people lived inside the kástro, but depopulation, World War II damage and a 1956 earthquake have combined to leave only a desolate shell today. The fine rib vaulting over the entrance supports the church of Evangelístria Kastrianí, one of two intact here, the other being Áyios Yeóryios (both usually locked).

Skála, and to a lesser extent Khóra, have **accommodation** ranging from spartan rooms to new luxury studios; proprietors meet ferries if there are vacancies. Owing to high-season noise – particularly the sound of ferries dropping anchor at 3am – you might prefer the remoter, restored self-catering units up in Khóra. Obvious, inexpensive **hotels** down in the port include the *Astynea* (☎0243/61 209; ④) and the elderly *Paradisos* (☎0243/61 224; ③), both en suite. *Vangelis* (☎0243/61 281; ③) and *Karlos* (☎0246/61 330; ③) are well appointed studio units on the east shore of the bay, the former above a good restaurant. A high-season **campsite** operates about 4km along the road to Análipsi, though it's water-logged in winter and thus mosquito-plagued in summer.

At peak season, something like 45 **tavernas** set up shop across the island, few of which are memorable. Among the more reliable year-round options, *To Akroyiali* behind Skála's tiny beach has good food offsetting haphazard service; its nearby inland rival, *Australia*, has less tasty food but friendly management. *Iy Monaxia* (aka *Viki's*), one block inland from the ferry jetty by the old power plant, has excellent home-style cooking. For carnivorous meals, *Psitopolio* Galini behind the *Hotel Astynea* is fine, while *Dhimitris*, just above the downhill road from Khóra does fish dishes.

Most **nightlife** happens up in more atmospheric Khóra, where two traditional kafenía on the main square are joined in season by music bars such as *Kastro* and *La Luna*. The **post office** and most shops are here, though **OTE** and the island's only **bank** (Emboriki), complete with cash dispenser, are down at Skála quay.

A single **bus** runs along the paved road between Khóra, Skala, Livádhia and Análipsi in July and August, and less frequently out of season – posted timetables are unreliable. There are only two official **taxis**, far too few to cope with passenger numbers in season; several places rent out **scooters**, the most reliable being Lakis and Manolis, with branches at Khóra and Skála. The island **map** sold locally is grossly inaccurate, even by flexible Greek standards.

Around the island

A thirty-minute walk (or a short, frequent bus journey) from the capital lies **LIVÁDHIA**, a fertile green valley with a popular, good beach but a rather motley collection of restaurants behind. You can **rent a room** or bungalow in the beach hamlet – for example from the Kondaratos family (☎0243/61 269; ②), or for more comfort, at *Studios Electra* (☎0243/61 270; ③), with castle views. Among the **tavernas**, *Thomas* and *Kalamia* are decent enough.

If the busy beach here doesn't suit, continue southwest fifteen minutes on a footpath to three small single coves at **Tzanáki**, packed out with naturists in mid-summer. The third bay beyond, easier reached by motorbike, is **Áyios Konstandínos**, a partly shaded, sand-and-gravel cove with a good seasonal taverna. Around the headland, the lonely beaches of **Vátses** and **Kaminákia** are more usually visited by excursion boat from Skála.

A favourite outing in the west of the island is the two-hour walk or 45-minute motor-bike trip from Khórato the oasis of **Áyios Ioánnis**, 10km distant. Proceed northwest along the dirt track beginning from the fifth or sixth windmill, veering left away from the side track to Panayía Flevariotíssas monastery. Beyond this point the main track, briefly dampened by a spring-seep, curls north towards farming cottages at Messariá before reaching a junction with gates across each option. Take the left-hand one, and soon the walled orchards of the uninhabited farm-monastery of Áyios Ioánnis come into view. From the balcony of the church, a steep, faint path leads down to the base of a ten-metre waterfall with bathing pools.

Northeast of the harbour, are three coves, known as **Marmári A, B** and **C**. The first is home to the power plant, the next hosts the campsite (see above), while the third, reasonably attractive, also marks the start of the path east to the coves of **Mamoúni** ("bug" or "critter" in Greek). Beyond Marmari C, the middle beach at **Stenó** ("narrow", after the isthmus here) with clean sand and a seasonal taverna, is the best.

ANÁLIPSI, widely known as Maltezána after medieval Maltese pirates, is about a ten-kilometre bus-trip or taxi-ride from town. Although it's the second-largest settlement on Astipálea, there's little for outsiders save a narrow, sea-urchin-speckled beach (there are better ones east of the main bay) and a nice view south to some islets. Despite this, blocks of **rooms** are sprouting like mushrooms, spurred by the proximity of the airport, 700m away. At the edge of the surrounding olive groves are the well-preserved remains of **Roman baths**, with floor mosaics representing zodiacal signs and the seasons. Facilities are limited to a pair of small **tavernas** (*Obelix* is the better one) and a high-season disco, one of just two on the island.

The motorable road ends at Mésa Vathý, from where an appalling track continues to **ÉXO VATHÝ**, a sleepy fishing village with a single reasonable taverna and a superb small-craft harbour. Following several accidents, this is no longer the **backup ferry port** in winter, when Skála is buffeted by the prevailing southerlies; foot passengers (but no vehicles) are transferred ashore to the unlit quay at **Ávios Andhréas**, just west of Marmári C.

Kálymnos

Most of the population of **Kálymnos** lives in or around the large port of Póthia, a wealthy but not conventionally beautiful town famed for its sponge divers. Unfortunately almost all the Mediterranean's sponges, with the exception of a few deep-water beds off Italy, have been devastated by disease, and only three or four of the fleet of thirty-odd boats can now be usefully occupied. In response to this disaster, the island has recently established a tourist industry – so far confined to one string of beach resorts – and has also customized its sponge boats for deep-sea fishing. Warehouses behind the harbour still process and sell sponges all year round, though most of these are imported from Asia and America. There are also still numbers of elderly gentlemen about who rely on two sticks or zimmer frames, stark evidence of the havoc wrought in their youth by nitrogen embolism (the "bends"), long before divers understood its crippling effects. The departure of the remaining sponge fleet, usually just after Easter, is preceded by a festive week known as *Iprogrós*, with food, drink and music; the fleet's return, approximately six months later, has historically also been the occasion for more uproarious, male-orientated celebration in the port's bars.

Kálymnos essentially consists of two cultivated and inhabited valleys sandwiched between three limestone ridges, harsh in the full glare of noon but magically tinted towards dusk. The climate, especially in winter, is alleged to be drier and healthier than that of neighbouring Kós or Léros, since the quick-draining limestone strata, riddled with many caves, doesn't retain as much moisture. The rock does, however, admit seawater, which has invaded Póthia's wells; drinking water must be brought in by tanker truck from Vathý. In the cultivated valley bottoms, mosquitoes can be a problem; chemical or electrical remedies are sold locally.

Since Kálymnos is the home port of the very useful local namesake ferry (see p.630), and moreover where the long-distance ferry lines from the Cyclades and Astypálea join up with the main Dodecanesian routes, many travellers arrive unintentionally, and are initially most concerned with how to move on quickly. Yet Kálymnos has sufficient attractions to justify a stay of several days while island-hopping – or even longer, as the package industry at the western beaches suggests.

Póthia

PÓTHIA, without being particularly picturesque, is colourful and authentically Greek, its houses arrayed in tiers up the sides of a natural rock amphitheatre. Your first, and likely overwhelming impression will be of the phenomenal amount of noise engendered by motorbike traffic and the cranked-up sound systems of the dozen waterfront cafés. This is not entirely surprising, since with about 11,000 inhabitants, Póthia ranks as the third largest city in the Dodecanese after the main towns of Rhodes and Kós.

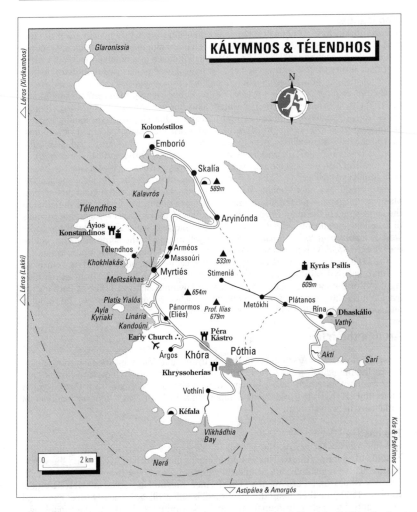

Perhaps the most rewarding way to acquaint yourself with Póthia is by wandering the backstreets, where elegant Neoclassical houses are surrounded by surprisingly large gardens, and craftsmen ply their trade in a genuine workaday bazaar. During the Italian occupation, local houses were painted blue and white to irritate the colonial overlords, and though the custom is beginning to die out, the Greek national colours are still evident, interspersed amongst pink and ochre buildings – even some of the churches, such as the eighteenth-century **Khristós**, are painted blue.

The local **museum** (Tues–Sun 10am–2pm; 500dr; guided tours only), is lodged in a grand former residence of the Vouvallis family, local sponge magnates. A rather eclectic collection, including a kitsch-furnished Belle Epoque parlour and small troves from the island's several caves, it's not exactly required viewing.

Practicalities

Accommodation is rarely a problem, since pension proprietors usually meet the ferries. The town's best, and quietest **hotel**, though often monopolized by package groups, is the *Villa Themelina* (☎0243/22 682; ④), partly housed in a nineteenth-century mansion near the museum, with gardens and a pool. Three places in Amoudhára district (west of the harbour) are worth contacting: the en-suite *Pension Greek House* (☎0243/29 559; ②; open most of year) with volubly friendly management and kitsch decor; the more subdued but non-en-suite *Rooms Katerina Smalliou* (☎0243/22 186; ②; April–Oct), 100m above, with good views; and above this, slightly to the south, the well-signposted *Hotel Panorama* (☎0243/23 138; ④; April–Oct), with balconied view rooms. More sea views are available, near the east edge of town on the Vathý road, at *Pension Gourlas* (☎0243/29 087; ②) and the adjacent *Pension Panorama* (☎0243/29 249; ②).

For **eating out**, the best strategy is to follow the waterfront northeast past the Italian-built municipal "palace" to a line of fish **tavernas** and **ouzerís**. The local speciality is octopus croquettes, more tender than you'd expect. Get these, and a good mix of meat plates and vegetable mezédhes, at *Minore tis Avyis*, one of the first establishments. At the far east end of the quay, *Barba Petros* (aka *Adherfi Martha*), serves sizeable portions of excellent, reasonably priced seafood. Sticky-cake fans will want to take three paces west to *Zakharoplastiki O Mikhalaras*, while still further in the same direction, before the church, *Apothiki* is an old warehouse refurbished as a bar and live music venue.

The **OTE** and the **post office** are virtually opposite each other inland on Venizélou; all **boat** and **hydrofoil** agents, as well as an **EOT** post, line the waterfront as you bear right out of the pier-area gate, and there's an Olympic Airways office at Patriárkhou Maxímou 17, 200m inland from the quay. Finally, waterfront branches of the National and Ionian **banks** both have cash dispensers.

Around the island

Buses run as far as Aryinóndas in the northwest and Vathý in the east, from a stop beside the municipal "palace", with schedules helpfully posted. Departures are not terribly frequent, in which case you may want to use shared **taxis** from Platía Kýprou (more than KTEL rates, less costly than a normal taxi), or rent a **scooter** from one of outlets on the waterfront.

The castles

Heading northwest across the island, the first place you reach is a castle of the Knights of St John, **Kástro Khryssokherías**, in the suburb of Mýli. From the white-washed battlements there are wonderful views southeast over town to Kós, and north towards Khóra and Péra Kástro. The former Kalymnian capital of **KHÓRA** (aka Khorió), 1500m further along the main road, is still a village of nearly three thousand inhabitants. Steep steps lead up from its easterly summit to the Byzantine citadel-town of **Péra Kástro**, appropriated by the Knights of St John and inhabited until late in the eighteenth century. Once inside the imposing gate, all is rubble now, except several well maintained, whitewashed chapels, some unlocked to permit a glimpse of late medieval fresco fragments.

West coast resorts

From the ridgetop pass at Khorió the road dips into a tree-shaded valley leading to the consecutive **beach resorts** of Kandoúni, Myrtiés and Massoúri. **KANDOÚNI**, some 200m of brown, hard-packed sand favoured by the locals, is the shore annexe of the rich agricultural valley-village of **Pánormos** (aka Eliés). At the north end of the same bay, **Linária**, has better sand and is set apart from Kandoúni proper by a rock outcrop. The next beach north, **Platýs Yialós**, though a bit shorter than Kandoúni, is arguably the best on the island: cleaner than its southern neighbours, more secluded, and placed scenically opposite Ayía Kyriakí islet. A lone taverna at the base of the cliff behind the sand will do for lunch; those after even more privacy can hunt out tiny coves in the direction of Linária, reachable only on foot.

The main road, descending in zigzags, finally meets the sea again 8km from Póthia at **MYRTIÉS**, which together with **MASSOÚRI** 1km to the north sees most of Kálymnos's tourism: lots of neon-lit music bars, souvenir shops and the like. The beach at Myrtiés is narrow, pebbly and cramped by development, though it does improve as you approach Massoúri. The closest really good beach to Myrtiés lies 500m south, at **Melitsakhás** cove. Possibly this coast's most appealing feature is its position opposite the evocatively shaped islet of Télendhos (see below), which frames some of the most dramatic sunsets in Greece. It's also possible to go from Myrtiés directly to Léros aboard the daily mid-morning kaïki. *Atlantis Hotel*, on the landward side of the road in Myrtiés, represents fair value (☎0243/47 497; ③), while the smallish *Pension Hermes* (☎0243/47 693; ③) overlooks the sea. A bit more remote, but enjoying the best views of all, is *Niki's Pension* (☎0243/47 201; ③), up the hill between Myrtiés and Massoúri. For **eating out**, *To Iliovasilema* at Myrtiés is a fine carnivorous option despite its tacky decor; homely, standard-Greek *Barba Yiannis* at Massoúri is amongst the last tavernas to shut in autumn.

Some 5km beyond Massoúri, **ARYINÓNDA** has a pebble beach backed by a single taverna and some rooms; try *Akroyiali* (☎0243/47 521; ③). The end of the bus line, **EMBORIÓ**, 19km from the port, offers more **tavernas** and **accommodation** – *Harry's Taverna Paradise*, with attached garden apartments (☎0243/47 434, ④) and *Themis* (☎0243/47 277; ③) much further inland. If the irregular bus service fails you, there is sometimes a shuttle boat back to Myrtiés.

Télendhos

The trip across the strait to the striking, volcanic-plug islet of **TÉLENDHOS** is arguably the best reason to come to Myrtiés; little boats shuttle to and fro constantly throughout the day and into the night. According to local legend, Télendhos is a petrified princess, gazing out to sea after her errant lover; her rocky profile is most evident at dusk. The hardly less pedestrian geological explanation has the islet sundered from Kálymnos by a cataclysmic earthquake in 554 AD; traces of a submerged town are said to lie at the bottom of the straits.

Télendhos is car-free and blissfully tranquil. For diversion and sustenance you'll find the ruined thirteenth-century **monastery of Áyios Vasílios**, a castle at remote Áyios Konstandínos, a tiny beach, several tavernas and inexpensive pensions, all in or near the single village. If you want to book ahead (mandatory in summer), try *Pension Uncle George* (☎0243/47 502; ②), atop an excellent taverna; *Pension Rita* (☎0243/47 914; ②) next door, above its welcoming café; *Dhimitris Harinos* (☎0243/47 916; ②), at the north end of the waterfront; or *Foukena Galanomati* (☎0243/47 401; ②), with another taverna, off by itself beyond the ruined monastery. The recent *Hotel Port Potha* (☎0243/47 321, fax 48 108; ③) is comparatively luxurious. A well signed, ten-minute path leads over the ridge to **Khokhlakás** pebble beach, small but very scenic, with sunbeds for hire. Heart and soul of **nightlife**, at the very north end of things, is the Greek-Australian-run *On the Rocks Cafe*, in the grounds of Áyios Kharálambos chapel, which also incorporates a Byzantine baths complex.

Vathý

Heading east from Póthia, an initially unpromising, ten-kilometre ride ends dramatically at **VATHÝ** a long, fertile valley, carpeted with orange and tangerine groves, whose colour provides a startling contrast to the lifeless greys elsewhere on

Kálymnos. At the simple fjord port of **RÍNA**, little distinguishes the adjacent **tavernas** *Panormitis* and *Popy's*, both pricier than you'd expect owing to patronage from the numerous yachts which call here. Nevertheless, Rína doesn't make a bad base, especially for a walking holiday; you could **stay** at the *Hotel Galini* (☎0243/31 241; ③), overlooking the boatyard, or the *Pension Manolis* (☎0243/31 300; ②), on the slope to the south, with cooking facilities and a helpful proprietor. If necessary, the tavernas can also muster a few simple rooms.

The steep-sided inlet has no beach to speak of; the closest, about 3km back towards Póthia, is **Aktí**, a functional pebble beach with sunbeds and a single snack bar, reached by a steep cement driveway. Boat excursions sometimes visit the stalactite cave of **Dhaskálio**, inhabited in Neolithic times, out towards the fjord mouth on its north flank. For **walkers** the lush valley behind, criss-crossed with rough tractor-tracks and narrower lanes, may prove an irresistible lure, but be warned that it will take you the better part of three hours, most of it shadeless once you're out of the orchards, to reach either Póthia or Aryinóndas via the old paths. You'll need to carry food and water with you, and be wary of maps showing the Aryinónda-bound trail going via Stiménia – it doesn't.

The southwest

Some 6km southwest of Póthia, the small bay of **Vlyhádhia** is reached via a narrow ravine draining from the nondescript village of Vothíni. The sand-and-pebble beach here isn't really worth a special trip, unless you're headed for the local **scuba** operation, since Vlyhádhia is one of the limited number of legal diving areas in Greece.

Póthia-based kaïkia also make well publicized excursions to the cave of **Kéfala** just to the west, the most impressive of half-a-dozen caverns around the island. You have to walk thirty minutes from where the boats dock, but the vividly coloured formations repay the effort; the cave was inhabited before recorded history, and later served as a sanctuary of Zeus (who is fancifully identified with a particularly imposing stalagmite in the biggest of six chambers).

Léros

Léros is so indented with deep, sheltered anchorages that during World War II it harboured, in turn, the entire Italian, German, and British Mediterranean fleets. Unfortunately, many of these magnificent fjords and bays seem to absorb rather than reflect light, and the island's relative fertility can seem scraggy and unkempt when compared with the crisp lines of its more barren neighbours. These characteristics, plus the island's lack of spectacularly good beaches, meant that until the late 1980s just a few thousand foreigners (mostly Italians who grew up on the island), and not many more Greeks, came to visit each August. Such a pattern is now history, with German, Dutch and British package operators forming the vanguard of those "discovering" Léros and the company of islanders unjaded by mass tourism. But foreign tourism has stalled of late, with matters unlikely to change until and unless the tiny airport is expanded to accommodate jets.

Not that the island needs, nor particularly encourages, mass tourism; various prisons and sanatoriums have dominated the Lerian economy since the 1950s, directly or indirectly employing about a third of the population. Under the junta the island hosted an infamous detention centre at Parthéni, and today the **mental hospital** on Léros is still the repository for many of Greece's more intractable psychiatric cases; another asylum is home to hundreds of mentally handicapped children. The island's domestic image problem is compounded by its name, the butt of jokes by mainlanders who pounce on its similarity to the word *léra*, connoting rascality and unsavouriness.

In 1989 a major scandal emerged concerning the administration of the various asylums, with EU maintenance and development funds found to have been embezzled by administrators and staff, and the inmates kept in degrading and inhumane conditions. Since then, an influx of EU inspectors, foreign psychiatrists and extra funding have resulted in drastic improvements in patient treatment, including the establishment of halfway houses across the island.

More obvious is the legacy of the **Battle of Léros** of November 12–16, 1943, when overwhelming German forces displaced a British division which had landed on the island following the Italian capitulation. Bomb nose cones and shell casings turn up as gaily painted garden ornaments in the courtyards of churches and tavernas, or are pressed into service as gateposts. Each year for three days following September 26, memorial services and a naval festival commemorate the sinking of the Greek battleships *Queen Olga* and *Intrepid* during the German attack.

Unusually for a small island, Léros has abundant ground water, channelled into cisterns at several points. These, plus low-lying ground staked with the avenues of eucalyptus trees planted by the Italians, makes for an active mosquito contingent, so come prepared. The island is compact enough to walk around, but there is a bus service and several cycle-rental outfits, with enough hills to give mountain-bikers a good work-out.

Lakkí and Xirókambos

All large **ferries** arrive at the main port of **LAKKÍ**, once the headquarters of a bustling Italian naval base. Boulevards far too wide for today's paltry amount of traffic are lined with some marvellous Art-Deco edifices, including the cinema (closed since 1985), the primary school and the defunct *Leros Palace Hotel*.

Buses don't meet the ferries – instead there are taxis that charge set fares to standard destinations. Few people stay at any of the three moribund hotels in Lakkí, preferring to head straight for the resorts of Pandéli, Álinda or Vromólithos (see below). There's just one bona-fide **taverna**, *To Petrino*, next to the **post office** inland, and both of the island's cash dispensers are here, attached to the National and Commercial banks. Gribelos is the island's sole G&A ferry agent. The nearest approximation of a **beach** is at Kouloúki, 500m west, where there's a seasonal taverna and some pines for shade, though it's too close to the ferry jetty for most tastes. You can carry on to the pavement's end at Merikiá which is a slight improvement and also has a taverna.

XIRÓKAMBOS, nearly 5km from Lakkí in the extreme south of the island, is the point of arrival for kaïkia from Myrtiés on Kálymnos. Billed as a resort, it's essentially a fishing port – the beach here is poor to mediocre, improving as you head west. **Accommodation** is available at *Villa Maria* (☎0247/22 827; ③) on the beach or, a bit inland, at the well-maintained *Yianoukas Rooms* (☎0247/23 148; ②); the island's **campsite** is in an olive grove at the village of Lepídha, 750m back up the road to Lakkí. **Meals** can be had at *Taverna Tzitzifies*, just by the jujube trees at the east end of things, where the road hits the shore.

Pandéli and Vromólithos

Just less than 3km north of Lakkí, Pandéli and Vromólithos together form the fastest-growing resort on the island – and are certainly two of the more attractive and scenic places to stay.

PANDÉLI is still very much a working port, the cement jetty primarily for local fishermen rather than the yachts which call here. A negligible beach is compensated for by a relative abundance of non-package **accommodation**, such as *Pension Kavos* (☎0247/23 247; ③), with a pleasant breakfast terrace, or *Pension Happiness* (☎0247/23 498; ③), where the road down from Plátanos meets the sea. Up on the ridge dividing Pandéli from Vromólithos, the *Pension Fanari* (☎0247/23 152; ④) is a good choice for its calm setting below the road and views across to the castle, while the peace at the *Hotel Rodon* (☎0247/23 524; ③) is disturbed only by wafts of music from the *Beach Bar*, perched on a rock terrace below, facing Vromólithos. The other long-lived bar is the civilized *Savana*, at the opposite end of Pandéli, but the soul of the place is its waterfront **tavernas**, which come alive after dark. These get less expensive and less pretentious as you head east, culminating in *Maria's*, a local institution, decked out in coloured lights and whimsically painted gourds – but the grilled octopus is reliable. *Zorba's* is about the best of the other three pricier tavernas, usually offering fresh fish.

VROMÓLITHOS boasts the best easily accessible beach on the island, car-free and hemmed in by hills studded with massive oaks. The **beach** is gravel and coarse sand, and the water's fine, but as so often on Léros you have to cross a nasty, sharp reef at most points before reaching a dropoff to deeper water. Two tavernas behind the beach trade more on their location than their cuisine, but the standard of **accommodation** here is higher than at Pandéli, with the result that much of it tends to be monopolized by package companies; try *Studios Paradise* (☎0247/23 247; ④) or *Pension Margarita* (☎0247/22 889; ④), both slightly inland.

Plátanos and Ayía Marína

The Neoclassical and vernacular houses of **PLÁTANOS**, the island capital 1km west of Pandéli, are draped gracefully along a saddle between two hills, one of them crowned by the inevitable Knights' castle. Locally known as the **Kástro**, this is reached either by a paved but rutted road peeling off the Pandéli road, or via a more scenic stair-path from the central square; the battlements, and the views from them, are dramatic, especially near sunrise or sunset. The medieval church of Panayía tou Kástrou, inside the gate, houses a small museum (daily 8.30am–12.30pm, also Wed, Sat & Sun 4–8pm; token admission), though its carved *témblon* and naive oratory are more remarkable than the sparse exhibits, which incongruously include a chunk of the Berlin Wall.

Except for *Hotel Eleftheria* (☎0247/23 550; ③), elevated and quiet enough to be desirable, Plátanos is not really a place to stay or eat, although it has plenty of **shops** and **services**. Olympic Airways (☎0247/24 144) is south of the junction to Pandéli, while the **post office** and short-hours **OTE** are down the road towards Ayía Marína. **Buses** ply four to six times daily between Parthéni in the north and Xirókambos in the south.

Plátanos merges seamlessly with **AYÍA MARÍNA**, 1km north on the shore of a fine bay. If you're travelling to Léros on an excursion boat or hydrofoil, this will be your port of entry. Although there's no accommodation here, it's arguably the best place to **eat** on the island. On route to the quay, the *Ayia Marina* taverna is the oldest and best established place for mayireftá, open year-round with stylish indoor seating. Just west of the police station, on the water, *Mezedhopolio Kapaniri* is a good, reasonable ouzerí, at its best after dark, featuring plenty of fried vegetable first courses. Just inland opposite the *Agrotiki Trapeza* in a little alley, the *Kapetan Mikhalis* ouzerí claims to be open all day and proffers a range of inexpensive local specialities, including various fish marinated in salt (*pastós*). A semblance of **nightlife** is provided by various bars, such as *Garbo's* near Kapaniri, and *Kharami* on the quay. Among a cluster of tourist shops 300m up the road back towards Plátanos, the pottery studio of expatriate Richard Smith merits a mention for his engaging raku ware.

Álinda and the north

ALÍNDA, 3km northwest of Ayía Marína, ranks as the longest-established resort on Léros, with development just across the road from a long, narrow strip of beach. It's also the first area for accommodation to open in spring, and the last to shut in autumn. Many of the dozen **hotels** and **pensions** here are block-booked by tour companies, but you may have better luck at *Hotel Gianna* (☎247/23 153; ④) or *Studios Diamantis* (☎247/23 213; ③) just inland, both overlooking the war cemetery (see below), or at *Rooms Papafotis* (☎0247/22 247; ③) at the north end of the strip. At Krithóni, 1.5km south, there's also the en-suite *Hotel Konstantinos*, overlooking the sea (☎0247/22 337; ④). **Restaurant** options aren't brilliant, except for *To Steki* next to the war cemetery, open year round with good grills and mezédhes plates attracting a local clientele.

An **Allied War Graves Cemetery**, mostly containing casualties of the November 1943 battle, occupies a walled enclosure at the south end of the beach; immaculately maintained, it serves as a moving counterpoint to the holiday hubbub outside. The other principal sight at Álinda is the privately run **Historical and Ethnographic Museum** (summer daily 9am–noon & 6–9pm), housed in the castle-like Bellini mansion; along with the usual rural artefacts, you'll find extensive exhibits on the printing trade including rare documents and clippings.

Alternative beaches near Álinda include **Panayiés**, a series of gravel coves (one naturist) at the far northeast of the bay, and **Goúrna**, the turning for which lies 1km or so off the trans-island road. The latter, Léros's longest sandy beach, is hard-packed and gently shelving; it's also wind-buffeted, bereft of any nearby facilities, and fringed at the back with an impromptu car park and construction rubble. A separate road beyond the Goúrna turning leads to **Kokálli**, no great improvement beach-wise, but flanked to one side by the scenic islet of **Áyios Isídhoros** which is tethered to the mainland by a causeway, its eponymous chapel perched on top.

Seven kilometres from Álinda along the main route north is the marked side track for the **Temple of Artemis**, on a slight rise just west of the airport. In ancient times, Léros was sacred to the goddess, and the temple here was supposedly inhabited by guinea fowl – the grief-stricken sisters of Meleager, metamorphosed thus by Artemis following their brother's death. All that remains now are some jumbled, knee-high walls, but the view is superb. The onward road skims the shores of sumpy, reed-fringed Parthéni Bay, with its dreary army base, until the paved road ends 11km along at **Blefoútis**, a rather more inspiring sight with its huge, virtually landlocked bay. The beach has tamarisks to shelter under and a decent taverna, *Iy Thea Artemi*, for lunch.

Pátmos

Arguably the most beautiful, certainly the best known of the smaller islands in the Dodecanese, **Pátmos** has a distinctive, immediately palpable atmosphere. It was in a cave here that St John the Divine (in Greek, *O Theologos*), received the New Testament's Revelations and unwittingly shaped the island's destiny. The monastery which commemorates him, founded here in 1088 by the Blessed Khristodhoulos (1021–1093), dominates Pátmos both physically – its fortified bulk towering high above everything else – and, to a considerable extent, politically. While the monks inside no longer run the island as they did for more than six centuries, their influence has nevertheless stopped Pátmos going the way of Rhodes or Kós.

Despite vast numbers of visitors, and the island's firm presence on the cruise, hydrofoil and yacht circuits, tourism has not been allowed to completely take Pátmos over. Although there are a number of clubs and even one disco around Skála, drunken rowdiness is virtually unknown, and this is one island where you do risk arrest for nude bathing. Package clients have only recently begun to outnumber independent visitors, and are pretty much confined to Gríkou and a few newish megahotels on the west side of Skála. There are still more daytrippers than overnighters, and Pátmos seems an altogether different place once the last cruiser has gone at sunset. Away from Skála, development is appealingly subdued if not deliberately retarded, thanks to the absence of an airport.

Skála and around

SKÁLA seems initially to contradict any solemn, otherworldly image of Pátmos, the waterside lined with ritzy-looking cafés. During peak season, the quay and commercial district heave by day with hydrofoil and cruise-ship passengers souvenir-hunting or being shepherded onto coaches for the ride up to the monastery; after dark there's still a considerable traffic in well-dressed cliques of visitors. In winter, the town seems moribund as most shops and restaurants close, their owners and staff back in Rhodes or Athens.

Melöi Beach is 1500m to the north (see p.628), and one of the most convenient and popular coves on the island; Khóra, a bus or taxi-ride up the mountain, is a more attractive base but has few rooms. Yet given time – especially in spring or autumn – Skála reveals some more enticing corners in the residential fringes to the east and west, where vernacular mansions hem in pedestrian lanes creeping up the hillsides. The

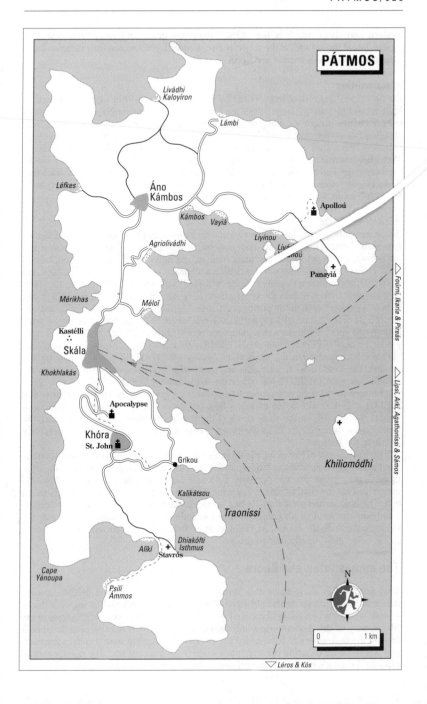

modern town dates only from the 1820s, when the Aegean had largely been cleared of pirates, but at the summit of the westerly rise, **Kastélli**, you can see the extensive foundations of the island's ancient acropolis.

Practicalities

Almost everything else of interest can be found within, or within sight of, the Italian-built municipal "palace": large ferries anchor opposite, the port police occupy the front, the **post office** the corner, along with an Ethniki **cash dispenser** (Emboriki has a free-standing one on the quay), and the fairly helpful municipal **tourist information** office (Mon–Sat 9am–1pm & 5–8pm) takes up the back, with timetables posted outside. **Motorbike rental** outfits are common, with lowish rates owing to the modest size of the island; the two main ferry and hydrofoil **agents** are Apollon and Astoria. Two particularly good **souvenir shops**, with jewellery, pottery, puppets, driftwood art, batik fabric and so on, are Selene, on the front, and Ekfrasis inland.

ACCOMMODATION

Accommodation touts meet all ferries and hydrofoils, and their offerings tend to be a long walk distant and/or inland – not necessarily a bad thing, as any location near the waterfront, which doubles as the main road, will be noisy. If you hunt yourself, calmer hotel choices include – opposite the fishing anchorage – the *Delfini* (☎0247/32 060, fax 32 061; ④) and adjacent *Captain's House* (☎0247/31 793, fax 32 277; ⑤); some 150m further towards Gríkou stands the comfortable *Blue Bay* (☎0247/31 165, fax 32 303; ④). Best of a cluster north of the power plant, near Mérikhas cove, are the *Hotel Australis* (☎0247/31 576; ③), run by an Australian-Greek family, with full breakfast for the price and myriad small kindnesses that guarantee repeat clientele. If they're full they'll refer you to the nearby *Villa Knossos* (☎0247/32 189; ③), run by the son-in-law, whose rooms all have attractive terraces, or *Pension Sydney* (☎0247/31 139; ③), owned by the brother. Out near rocky Khokhlakás bay, good-value options include the comfortable, hillside *Summer* (☎0247/31 769; ④) or the more modest *Sunset* (☎0247/31 411; ③). If you're keen to stay nearer a proper beach, there's a good but overpriced **campsite** at **MELÓÏ**, together with some **rooms** – best are those run by Loula Koumendhourou (☎0247/32 281; ③), on the slope south of the bay. There are a couple of tavernas, the best of these being *Melloi* (alias *Stefanos*): excellent, reasonably priced and open early or late in the season.

There are plenty of places for **meals** in Skála: a prime contender is *O Grigoris*, on the front at the junction with the road up to Khóra; runners-up might be *O Vrakhos*, a traditional, barrel-wine taverna opposite the yacht anchorage, or the good *Khiliomodhi* ouzerí, just off the road to Khóra, featuring seafood such as limpets and various salted fish. The biggest and most durable **bar** is the panelled and barn-like *Café Arion* on the waterside, the local youth hangout; others include *Konsolato*, a dancing bar near the fishing port, or *Byblos* inland. At Melóï, next to *Stefanos*', is an outdoor **cinema-bar**: a movie ticket gets you discounted drinks.

The monasteries and Khóra

Your first stop is likely to be the Monastery of St John, sheltered behind massive defences in the hilltop capital of Khóra. There is a regular KTEL bus up, or a thirty-minute walk by a beautiful old cobbled path. Just over halfway, you might pause at the **Monastery of the Apocalypse** (daily 8am–2pm & Mon, Wed & Fri 4–6pm; free) built around the cave where St John heard the voice of God issuing from a cleft in the rock, and where he sat dictating his words to a disciple. In the cave wall, the nightly resting place of the saint's head is fenced off and outlined in beaten silver.

This is merely a foretaste of the **Monastery of St John** (daily 8am–2pm & Mon, Tues, Thurs & Sun 4–6pm). In 1088, the soldier-cleric Ioannis "The Blessed" Khristodhoulos was granted title to Pátmos by Byzantine Emperor Alexios Komnenos; within three years he and his followers had completed the essentials of the existing monastery, the threats of piracy and the Selçuk Turks dictating a heavily fortified style. A warren of interconnecting courtyards, chapels, stairways, arcades, galleries and roof terraces, it offers a rare glimpse of a Patmian interior; hidden in the walls are fragments of an ancient Artemis temple which stood here before being destroyed by Khristodhoulos. Off to one side, the **treasury** (same hours; 500dr) merits a leisurely visit for its magnificent array of religious treasure, mostly medieval icons of the Cretan school, but pride of place goes to the eleventh-century parchment chrysobull (edict) of Emperor Alexios Komnenos, granting the island to Khristodhoulos.

Khóra

The promise of security afforded by St John's stout walls spurred the growth of **KHÓRA** immediately outside the fortifications. It remains architecturally homogeneous, with cobbled lanes sheltering dozens of shipowners' mansions from the island's seventeenth- to eighteenth-century heyday. High, windowless walls and imposing wooden doors betray nothing of the opulence within: painted ceilings, pebble-mosaic terraces, flagstoned kitchens, and carved furniture. Away from the principal thoroughfares are lanes that rarely see traffic, and by night, when the monastery ramparts are floodlit to startling effect, it's hard to think of a more beautiful Dodecanesian village. Neither should you miss the **view** from Platía Lódza (named after the remnant of an adjacent Venetian *loggia*), particularly at dawn or dusk. Landmasses to the north, going clockwise, include Ikaría, Thýmena, Foúrni, Sámos with the brooding mass of Mount Kérkis, Arkí, and the double-humped Samsun Dağ (ancient Mount Mykale) in Turkey.

You can **eat** well at *Vangelis* on the inner square, which has a wonderful old jukebox in addition to a varied, reasonable menu. There are, however, very few places to **stay**; foreigners here are mostly long-term occupants, who have bought up and restored almost a third of the crumbling mansions since the 1960s. Getting a short-term room can be a pretty thankless task, even in spring or autumn; the best strategy is to contact *Vangelis* taverna early in the day, or phone ahead for reservations to Yeoryia Triandafyllou (☎0247/31 963; ④) or Marouso Kouva (☎0247/31 026; ④).

The rest of the island

Pátmos, as a locally published guide once memorably proclaimed, "is immense for those who know how to wander in space and time". Lesser mortals may find it easier to get around on foot, or by bus. There's still scope for **walking** despite a dwindling network of paths; otherwise a single **bus** offers surprisingly reliable service between Skála, Khóra, Kámbos and Gríkou – the main stop, with a posted timetable, is right in front of the main ferry dock.

After its extraordinary atmosphere and magnificent scenery, **beaches** are Patmos's principal attraction. From Khóra, a paved road (partly shortcut by the path) winds east to the sandiest part of rather overdeveloped and cheerless **GRÍKOU**, the main venue for Patmian package tourism. The beach itself, far from the island's best, forms a narrow strip of hard-packed sand giving way to large pebbles towards the south. En route you pass the hillside *Flisvos* taverna, oldest and most reliable here, with a few simple rooms (☎0247/31 380; ③). From either Gríkou or Khóra, you can ride a moped over dirt roads as far as Stavrós over the Dhiakoftí isthmus, beyond which a thirty-minute walk southwest leads to **Psilí Ámmos** beach. This is the only pure-sand cove on the island with shade lent by tamarisks, and there's a good lunchtime **taverna**. There's also a summer kaḯki service here from Skála, departing by 10am and returning at 3.30pm.

More good beaches are to be found in the north of the island, tucked into the startling eastern shoreline; most are accessible from side roads off the main route north from Skála. **Melóï** is handy and quite appealing, with tamarisks behind the slender belt of sand, and good snorkelling offshore. The first beach beyond Méloï, **Agriolivádhi**, has a patch of sand at its broad centre, kayak rental and a high-season taverna. The next beach, **Kámbos**, is popular with Greeks, and the most developed remote resort on the island, with seasonal watersports facilities and tavernas, though its appeal is diminished by the road just inland and a rock shelf in the shallows. East of Kámbos are several less frequented coves, including pebble **Vayiá** and sand-and-gravel **Livádhi Yeranoú**, the latter with more tamarisks, a seasonal drinks cantina and an islet to swim out to. From Kámbos you can also journey north to the bay of **Lámbi**, best for swimming when the prevailing wind is from the south, and renowned for an abundance of multicoloured volcanic stones. Of the two adjacent **tavernas**, the first encountered, *Lambi*, is better for food, while the second, *To Dhelfíni tis Lambis*, rents simple **rooms** (☎0247/34 074; ②). Weather permitting, this is also the most northerly port of call for the daily excursion kaïkia that ply the east coast in season.

Lipsí

Of the various islets to the north and east of Pátmos, **LIPSÍ** is the largest, most interesting and most populated, and the one that is beginning to get a significant summer tourist trade.

During quieter months, however, Lipsí still makes an idyllic halt, its sleepy pace making plausible a purported link between the island's name and that of **Calypso**, the nymph who held Odysseus in thrall. Deep wells water many small farms, but there is only one spring in the west, and pastoral appearances are deceptive – four times the relatively impoverished full-time population of 450 is overseas (many in Tasmania, for some reason). Most of those who stayed cluster around the fine harbour, as does most of the food and lodging.

A prime **accommodation** choice in all senses is the welcoming *Apartments Galini* (☎0247/41 212, fax 41 012; ③), the first building you see above the ferry jetty; the proprietor is a fishermen and takes kaïki tours on request. Other good options include *Rena's Rooms* (☎0247/41 363; ③), overlooking Liendoú, the *Flisvos Pension* at the east end of the port (☎0247/41 261; ②) and *Studios Barbarosa* (☎0247/41 312; ④), just up the stairway into the town centre. Top of the heap is the new *Aphrodite Hotel* (☎0247/41 000; ④), a studio-bungalow complex designed to accommodate package clients, though they're not adverse to walk-ins at slow times.

The half-dozen **tavernas** are comparable in quality, though they specialize: *Barbarosa*, on the slope near *Rena's Rooms*, does good vegetable-based *mayireftá*; *Fish Restaurant* on the quay only opens when the owner has caught something, and *To Dhelfíni*, next to the police station, falls somewhere in between. On the waterfront to either side of the *Kalypso* (the grill is recommended but the hotel isn't), idiosyncratic kafenía and ouzerís with minimal decor offer mezédhes outdoors: an atmospheric pre-supper ritual. On or near the square up by the cathedral, you'll find the **post office** and **OTE** (but no bank), and a hilariously indiscriminate **Ecclesiastical Museum** featuring such "relics" as oil from the sanctuary on Mount Tabor and water from the Jordan River.

The island's **beaches** are rather scattered: closest to town is **Liendoú**, immediately west, but the most attractive is **Katsadhiá**, a collection of small, sandy coves south of the port, with a good, simple taverna, *Andonis* (May–Sept only), just inland from a music bar, *Dilaila*, which dominates the main cove here and runs an informal campsite (free but you must buy a meal daily). **Khokhlakoúra**, on the east coast, by contrast consists of rather grubby shingle with no facilities. An hour's walk along the paved road leading west from town brings you to **Platýs Yialós**, a small, sheltered, sandy bay with a single taverna (June–Sept). In high season enterprising individuals run pick-up trucks, with bench seats, along a route between town and all three of the above bays; a schedule of sorts is posted on a kafenío window. **Monodhéndhri**, on the northeast coast, is accessible on foot or by **moped** only; there are now a few rental outlets for the latter.

A bare handful of surviving paths and narrow tracks provide opportunities for **walks** through the undulating countryside, dotted with blue-domed churches. One of the better treks heads west from Liendoú to the bay of **Kímisi** (3hr round trip), where an octogenarian religious hermit dwells in a tiny monastery above the shore, next to the single island spring. An ugly track has been bulldozed in from the north to disturb his solitude – it's only suitable for jeeps, not bikes.

Arkí, Maráthi and Agathónissi

About two-thirds the size of Lipsí, **Arkí** is considerably more primitive, lacking drinking water, mains electricity (there are solar panels), a ferry dock, or any discernible village centre. Just 39 permanent inhabitants cling to life here, most engaged in fishing, though complete depopulation is conceivable within the next decade. It's an elective, once-weekly stop on the *Nissos Kalymnos* and Miniotis Lines routes: if you want to disembark here, you must warn the captain well in advance, so he can radio for the shuttle service from the island. Of the two taverna rooms (☎0247/32 371 and ☎0247/32 230; both ②), the remoter one doubles as a music pub, courtesy of the owner's enormous collection of jazz tapes. There's no proper beach on Arkí; the nearest one is just offshore on the islet of **Maráthi**, where another pair of tavernas cater to the daytrippers who come several times a week from Pátmos or Lipsí – links with Arkí are unreliable. Both tavernas let some fairly comfortable **rooms**, (no phones; ②), making Maráthi perhaps a better option than Arkí for acting out Robinson Crusoe fantasies.

The small, sheer-sided, waterless islet of **Agathóníssi (Gaïdharo)** is too remote – much closer to Turkey than Pátmos, in fact – to be included in day excursions, so that only intrepid backpackers include it in their itineraries. Even though hydrofoil connections dovetail well with appearances of the *Nissos Kalymnos*, you should count on staying three days, especially if the wind's up. Despite the lack of springs (cisterns are ubiquitous), the island is greener and more fertile than apparent from the sea; scrub on the heights overlooks two arable plains in the west. Just 140 people live here, down from several hundred before the last war, but those who've opted to stay seem determined to make a go of raising goats or fishing, and there are virtually no abandoned or neglected dwellings. Most of the population lives in the hamlet of **MEGÁLO KHORIÓ**, just visible on the ridge above the harbour of **Áyios Yeóryios**, and level with tiny **Mikró Khorió**. Except for two café restaurants (*Dhekatria Adherfia* is best for lunch) and the *Katsoulieri Pension* (☎0247/24 385; ②) in Megálo Khorió, all amenities are in the port. Here the choice is between rooms operated by Theoloyia Yiameou (☎0247/23 692; ②), Maria Kamitsi (☎0247/23 690; ②) and those inland at *George's Pension* (☎0247/24 385; ②). **Eating** options in Áyios Yeóryios are limited to *Seagull/Glaros*, at mid-quay, and *George's* at the base of the jetty.

As on Lipsí, **walking** consists of following the cement or dirt road network, or striking out cross-country over rough terrain. If you don't swim at the port, which has the only beach, you can walk twenty minutes southwest along a track to shingle-gravel **Spiliás**, or an hour-plus to **Thóli** in the far southeast of the island. Here there's a passable beach, one of a few small fish farms around the coastline, and (just inland) an arcaded Byzantine structure, probably a combination granary and trading post. Along with snorkelling over the tiny reef here, it's by far the most interesting sight on Agathóníssi.

travel details

To simplify the lists below, the *Nissos Kalymnos* has been left out. This small car ferry is the most regular lifeline of the smaller islands (aside from Kárpathos and Kássos) – it visits them all twice a week between March and December. Its schedule is currently as follows: Monday and Friday 7am, leaves Kálymnos for Kós, Níssyros, Tílos, Sými, Rhodes; out to Kastellórizo late afternoon, turns around at midnight. Tuesday and Saturday 9am, departs Rhodes for Sými, Tílos, Níssyros, Kós, Kálymnos, with an evening return trip to Astypálea; Wednesday and Sunday departs Kálymnos 7am for Léros, Lipsí, Pátmos, Arkí (Wed only), Agathónissi, Pythagório (Sámos), returning from Sámos at 2.30pm bound for Kálymnos via the same islands; Thursday morning 7am from Kálymnos to Astypálea and back, some years with a return trip to Kós done in the afternoon. This ship can be poorly publicized on islands other than its home port; if you encounter difficulties, you should phone the central agency on Kálymnos (☎0243/29 612).

Ferries

Be aware that the following frequencies are only valid for the period mid-June to mid-September; in spring or autumn some of the more esoteric links, such as Astypálea to Tílos or Sými to Lipsí, will not be operating.

Agathoníssi 1 weekly to Arkí, Lipsí, Pátmos, Sámos.

Astypálea 2–3 weekly to Amórgos, Náxos, Páros, Sýros, Pireás; 1–2 weekly to Kós, Kálymnos, Léros, Rhodes, Níssyros, Tílos.

Kálymnos Similar ferry service to Kós, plus 1 weekly to Astypálea, Amorgós (both ports), Náxos, Páros, Sýros, and no departure to Thessaloníki. Morning kaïki, afternoon speedboat to Kós Town; 3 daily kaïkia to Mastikhári. Daily kaïki (1pm) from Myrtiés to Xirókambos on Léros.

Kárpathos (Pigádhia) and Kássos 2 weekly with each other and Rhodes Town; 1 weekly to Khálki, Crete (Áyios Nikólaos and/or Sitía), Mýlos, Santoríni, Íos, Páros, and Pireás. NB Dhiafáni is served by only one weekly mainline ferry to Rhodes, Khálki, Kássos, Crete, and select western Cyclades.

Kastellórizo (Méyisti) 1–2 weekly to Rhodes; 1–2 weekly to Pireás indirectly, via select Dodecanese and Cyclades.

Khálki 1–2 weekly to Rhodes Town, Kárpathos (both ports), Kássos, Crete and select Cyclades, all subject to cancellation in bad weather. Once-daily kaïki (5.30am) to Rhodes (Skála Kámiros).

Kós 7–10 weekly to Rhodes and Pireás; 6 weekly to Kálymnos, Léros and Pátmos; 1 weekly to Tílos and Níssyros; 1 weekly to Sámos and Thessaloníki; 1 weekly to Astipálea, Sými, Lipsí, Náxos, Páros, Sýros. Excursion boats 3 daily year-round from Mastikhári to Kálymnos; 1–2 daily from Kós Town to Kálymnos; 1 daily (9.30am) to Psérimos; 1 daily from Kardhámena to Níssyros; 4–6 weekly from Kós Town and Kéfalos to Níssyros.

Léros daily to Pireás, Pátmos, Kálymnos, Kós and Rhodes; 1 weekly to Lipsí, Náxos, Páros, Sýros; seasonal daily excursion boats from Ayía Marína to Lipsí and Pátmos (2pm), and from Xirókambos to Myrtiés on Kálimnos (7.30am).

Lipsí 1–2 weekly to Sýros, Páros, Náxos, Pireás, Pátmos, Sými, Tílos, Níssyros, Kós, Kálymnos, Léros.

Níssyros and Tílos Same as for Sými, plus additional 1 weekly between each other, Rhodes, Kós, Kálymnos, Léros, Lipsí, Pátmos and Pireás. Excursion boats between Níssyros and Kós as follows: to Kardhámena daily at 3.30pm; to Kéfalos 4 weekly at 4pm; and the islanders' cheaper "shopping special", 4 weekly at 7.30–8am; 4–6 weekly to Kós town (seasonal and expensive).

Pátmos Similar ferry service to Léros, with the addition of 1 weekly to Foúrni, Arkí, Lipsí, Ikaría, Sámos; seasonal tourist boats to Sámos (Pythagório), Lipsí, and Maráthi on a daily basis; less often to Arkí.

Rhodes 10–12 weekly to Kós and Pireás; 7–10 weekly to Kálymnos; daily to Léros and Pátmos; 2 weekly to Crete (Sitía or Iráklion); 1–2 weekly to Sými, Lipsí, Tílos, Níssyros, Astypálea, Kárpathos, Kássos, Khálki; 1 weekly to Santoríni, Náxos, Páros, Sýros, Sámos, Thessaloníki. Excursion boats twice daily to Sými.

Sými 1 weekly to Rhodes, Tílos, Níssyros, Kós, Kálymnos, Léros, Lipsí, Pátmos, Náxos, Páros and Pireás. Excursion boats twice daily to Rhodes.

Hydrofoils

Two hydrofoil companies, Samos Hydrofoils and Nearkhos Mamidhakis (aka Dodecanese Hydrofoils) serve the Dodecanese between late

May and mid-October, operating out of Rhodes, Kós, Kálymnos and Sámos. Typically, the single craft of Sámos Hydrofoils leaves that island at 7am, reaching Kós along a varying itinerary by 11am or noon, returning via the same islands at 1 or 2pm. Dodecanese Hydrofoils have three craft, and schedules are accordingly more complicated; in peak season, one leaves Rhodes at 8am for Kós, returning in the evening; another leaves Kálymnos or Kós at 7 or 8am for Sámos (Pythagório) via select islands, returning at 2.30pm; while the third craft tends to serve a changing cast among the small Dodecanese between Kálymnos and Rhodes, including (occasionally) Astypálea. For current routes and schedules, phone ☎0241/24 000 or 0242/25 920 for Nearkhos Mamidhakis, ☎0273/27 337 for Sámos Hydrofoils.

Flights

Kárpathos 2–3 daily to Rhodes; 2–4 weekly to Kássos; 2–4 weekly to Athens; 1 weekly to Crete (Sitía).

Kássos 2–4 weekly to Kárpathos; 4–7 weekly to Rhodes; 1 weekly to Crete (Sitía).

Kastellórizo (Meyísti) 1 daily to Rhodes.

Kós 2–3 daily to Athens; 2–3 weekly to Rhodes.

Léros 1 daily to Athens.

Rhodes 4–5 daily to Athens; 4 weekly to Iráklion; 3–4 weekly to Santoríni; 2 weekly to Thessaloníki.

International ferries

Kós 3–14 weekly to Bodrum, Turkey (45min). Greek boat leaves 9am, returns 4pm; £19/$30 return Greek tax inclusive, £18/$28 one-way; no cheap day return, no Turkish tax. Turkish boat, departing 4.30pm, is dearer at £33/$52 return, £22/$35 one way, but provides the only service in winter.

Rhodes Daily to Marmaris, Turkey (1–2hr) by Greek hydrofoil or more expensive Turkish car ferry; 2–3 weekly to Limassol, Cyprus (18hr) and Haifa, Israel (39hr).

CHAPTER TEN

THE EAST AND NORTH AEGEAN

T he seven substantial islands and four minor islets scattered off the north Aegean coast of Asia Minor and northeast Greece form a rather arbitrary archipelago. Although there is a passing similarity in architecture and landscape, virtually the only common denominator is the strong individual character of each island. Despite their proximity to modern Turkey, members of the group bear few signs of an Ottoman heritage, especially when compared with Rhodes and Kós. There's the occasional mosque, often shorn of its minaret, but by and large the enduring Greekness of these islands is testimony to the 4000-year Hellenic presence in Asia Minor, which ended only in 1923. This heritage is regularly referred to by the Greek government in its propaganda war with Turkey over the sovereignty of these far-flung outposts. Tensions here are, if anything, worse than in the Dodecanese, aggravated by potential undersea oil deposits in the straits between the islands and the Anatolian mainland. The Turks have also persistently demanded that Límnos, astride the sea lanes to and from the Dardenelles, be demilitarized, but so far Greece has shown no signs of agreeing.

The heavy military presence can be disconcerting, especially for lone woman travellers, and large tracts of land are off-limits as military reserves. But as in the Dodecanese, local tour operators do a thriving business shuttling passengers for inflated tariffs (thanks to punitively high docking fees at both ends) between the easternmost islands and the Turkish coast with its amazing archeological sites and busy resorts. Most of these islands' main ports and towns are not quaint, picturesque spots, but rather urbanized bureaucratic, military and commercial centres. In most cases you should suppress an initial impulse to take the next boat out, and press on into the interiors.

ACCOMMODATION PRICE CODES

Throughout the book we've used the following **price codes** to denote the cheapest available room in high season; all are prices for a double room, except for category ①, which represents per person rates. Out of season, rates can drop by up to fifty percent, especially if you are staying for three or more nights. Single rooms, where available, cost around seventy percent of the price of a double.

Rented private rooms on the islands usually fall into the ② or ③ categories, depending on their location and facilities, and the season; a few in the ④ category are more like plush self-catering apartments. They are not generally available from late October through to the beginning of April, when only hotels tend to remain open.

① 1400–2000dr	④ 8000–12,000dr
② 4000–6000dr	⑤ 12,000–16,000dr
③ 6000–8000dr	⑥ 16,000dr and upwards

For more accommodation details, see pp.39–42.

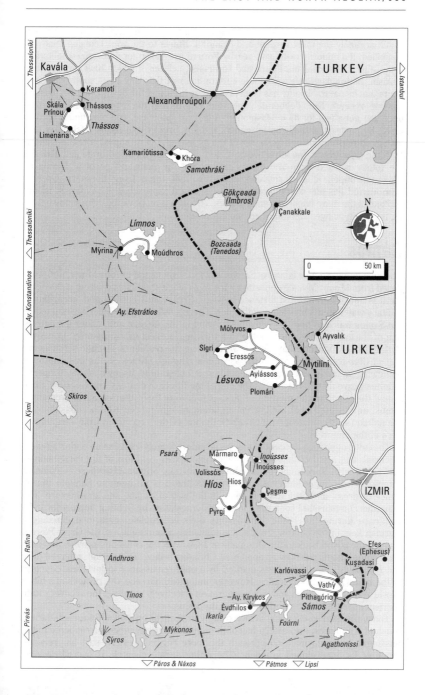

Sámos is the most visited island of the group, but if you can leave the crowds behind, is still arguably the most verdant and beautiful. Ikaría to the west remains relatively unspoiled, if a minority taste, and nearby Foúrni is a haven for determined solitaries, as are the Khíos satellites Psará and Inoússes, neither of which have any package tourism. Khíos itself offers far more cultural interest than any of its southern neighbours, but its natural beauty has been ravaged by fires, and the development of tourism has until recently been deliberately retarded. Lésvos may not impress initially, though once you get a feel for its old-fashioned, Anatolian ambience, you may find it hard to leave. By contrast virtually no foreigners and few Greeks visit Áyios Efstrátios, and with good reason. Límnos to the north is a bit livelier, but its appeal is confined mostly to the area around the attractive port town. To the north, Samothráki and Thássos are totally isolated from the others, except via the mainland ports of Kavála or Alexandhroúpoli, and it remains easier to visit them from northern Greece. Samothráki has one of the most dramatic seaward approaches of any Greek island, and one of the more important ancient sites. Thássos is more varied, with sandy beaches, mountain villages and minor archeological sites.

Sámos

The lush and seductive island of Sámos was formerly joined to Asia Minor, until sundered from Mount Mycale opposite by Ice Age cataclysms. The resulting 2500-metre strait is now the narrowest distance between Greece and Turkey, and, accordingly, military watchpoints bristle on both sides. There's little tangible evidence of it today, but Sámos was also once the wealthiest island in the Aegean and, under the patronage of the tyrant Polycrates, home to a thriving intellectual community: Epicurus, Pythagoras, Aristarchus and Aesop were among the residents. Decline set in as the star of Classical Athens was in the ascendant, though Sámos' status was improved somewhat in early Byzantine times when it constituted its own *theme* (imperial administrative district). Towards the end of the fifteenth century, the Genoese abandoned the island to the mercies of pirates; following their attacks, Sámos remained almost uninhabited until 1562, when an Ottoman admiral received permission from the sultan to repopulate it with Greek Orthodox settlers recruited from various corners of the empire.

The heterogeneous descent of today's islanders largely explains an enduring identity crisis and a rather thin topsoil of indigenous culture. Most of the village names are either clan surnames, or adjectives indicating origins elsewhere – constant reminders of refugee descent. Consequently there is no genuine Samiote music, dance or dress, and little that's original in the way of cuisine and architecture. The Samiotes compensated somewhat for their deracination by fighting fiercely for independence during the 1820s, but, despite their accomplishments in decimating a Turkish fleet in the narrow strait and annihilating a landing army, the Great Powers handed the island back to the Ottomans in 1830, with the consoling proviso that it be semi-autonomous, ruled by an appointed Christian prince. This period, referred to as the *Iyimonía* (Hegemony), was marked by a mild renaissance in fortunes, courtesy of the hemp and tobacco trades. However, union with Greece, the ravages of a bitter World War II occupation and mass emigration effectively reversed the recovery until tourism appeared on the horizon during the 1980s.

Today the Samian economy is increasingly dependent on package **tourism**, far too much of it in places; the eastern half of the island has pretty much surrendered to the onslaught of holidaymakers, although the more rugged western part has retained much of its undeveloped grandeur. The rather sedate clientele is overwhelmingly

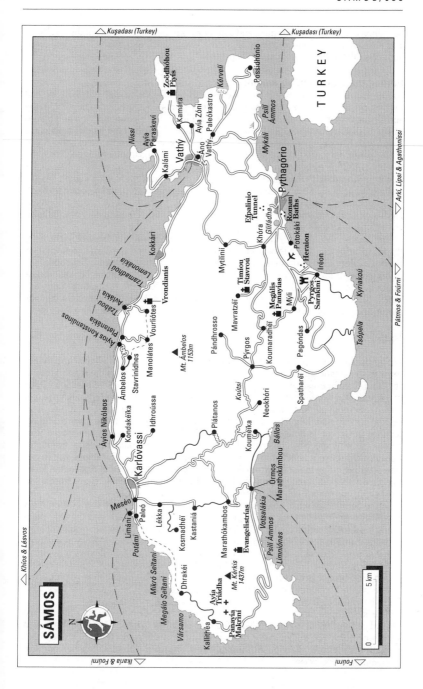

SÁMOS

Scandinavian, Dutch and German, and a far cry from the singles scene of the Cyclades. The absence of an official campsite on such a large island, and phalanxes of self-catering villas, hint at the sort of custom expected.

Getting there and getting around

Sámos has an **airport**, which lies 14km southwest of Vathý and just 3km west of Pythagório, as well as no fewer than three **ferry ports** – Karlóvassi in the west, Vathý and Pythagório in the east. All ferries between Pireás, the Cyclades, Ikaría and Sámos call at both Karlóvassi and Vathý, as do the smaller Miniotis Line ferries linking the island with Khíos, Foúrni, Ikaría and Pátmos. Vathý also receives the weekly G&A sailing between northern Greece and the Dodecanese, via most intervening islands, the weekly DANE ferry between Thessaloníki and Rhodes, plus hydrofoils and small ferries from Kuşadasi. Pythagório siphons off a bit of the Turkey shipping in high season, and additionally sees two regular weekly ferry connections from as far south as Kós in the Dodecanese. Both ports have hydrofoil services: Vathý is the home base of Samos Hydrofoils, Pythagório the northerly touch-point for Dodecanese/Mamidhakis Hydrofoils, both lines extending down to Kós.

The **bus terminals** in Pythagório and Vathý lie within walking distance of the ferry dock; at Karlóvassi, a bus is occasionally on hand to take you the 3km into town from the port. There is no airport bus service; **taxi** fares to various points are controlled, and in high season taxis (☎0273/28 404) to the airport or docks must be booked several hours in advance. The KTEL service itself is excellent along the Pythagório–Vathý and Vathý–Karlóvassi via Kokkári routes, but poor otherwise; with numerous car and motorbike rental outlets, it's easy to find a good deal outside August.

Vathý

Lining the steep northeast shore of a deep bay, **VATHÝ** is a busy provincial town which grew from a minor anchorage after 1830, when it replaced Khóra as the island's capital. It's of minimal interest for the most part – although the pedestrianized bazaar and tiers of Neoclassical houses have some attraction – and the only real highlight is the excellent **Archeological Museum** (Tues–Sun 9am–2.30pm; 800dr), set behind the small central park beside the restored Neoclassical town hall. One of the best provincial collections in Greece is housed in both the old Paskallion building and a modern wing across the way, specially constructed to house the star exhibit: a majestic, five-metre-tall *kouros*, discovered out at the Heraion sanctuary (see p.641). The *kouros*, the largest free-standing effigy to survive from ancient Greece, was dedicated to Apollo, but found together with a devotional mirror to Mut (the Egyptian equivalent of Hera) from a Nile workshop, one of only two discovered in Greece to date.

In the compelling small-objects collection of the Paskallion, more votive offerings of Egyptian design prove trade and pilgrimage links between Sámos and the Nile valley going back to the eighth century BC. The Mesopotamian and Anatolian origins of other artwork confirm the exotic trend, most tellingly in a case full of ivory miniatures: Perseus and Medusa in relief, a kneeling, perfectly formed mini-*kouros*, a pouncing lion, and a drinking horn with a bull's head. The most famous local artefacts are the dozen or so bronze **griffin-heads**, for which Sámos was the major centre of production in the seventh century BC; mounted on the edge of bronze cauldrons, they were believed to ward off evil spirits.

The single best target for a short stroll inland is **ÁNO VATHÝ**, an officially preserved community of tottering, tile-roofed houses, a few of which date from the seventeenth century. The village's late medieval churches are neglected, but still worth a look: the tiny chapel of **Áyios Athanásios** near the main cathedral boasts a fine *témblon* and naive frescoes.

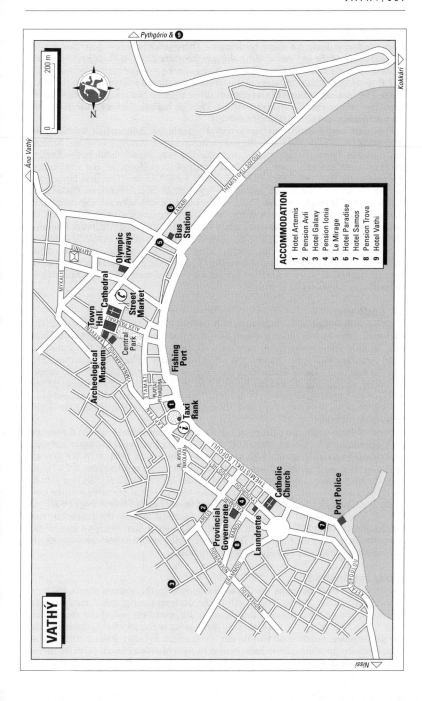

VATHÝ

Pythgório & ⑨

Kokkári ▽

△ Áno Vathý

Nissí ▽

0 — 200 m

N

ACCOMMODATION

1 Hotel Artemis
2 Pension Avli
3 Hotel Galaxy
4 Pension Ionia
5 Le Mirage
6 Hotel Paradise
7 Hotel Samos
8 Pension Trova
9 Hotel Vathi

Bus Station

Olympic Airways

Street Market

Cathedral

Town Hall

Archeological Museum

Central Park

Fishing Port

Taxi Rank

Provincial Governorate

Laundrette

Catholic Church

Port Police

Practicalities

From the **ferry dock** the shore boulevard – Themistoklí Sofoúli – describes a 1300-metre arc around the bay. About 400m along is the traffic circle of Platía Pythagóra, distinguished by its lion statue; some 800m along there's a major turning inland to the **KTEL** terminal, a chaos of buses at a perennially cluttered intersection by the ticket office. The municipal **tourist information** office is on 25-Martíou (summer Mon–Fri 9am–3pm; winter variable hours), worth a stop for leaflets, comprehensive bus and ferry schedules and accommodation listings.

The most useful waterfront **ferry/travel agents** for independent travellers are Tzoutzakis (☎0273/27 337) under the old Catholic church, handling G&A and Miniotis boats; Samos Tours (Horiatopoulos), opposite the jetty, have helpful, native-English-speaking staff and sell most other boat tickets except Agapitos and Dodecanese Hydrofoils; By Ship (☎0273/27 337) sell tickets for DANE and Nomikos ferries; and Samina Tours at Themistoklí Sofoúli 67 (☎0273/28 841), represent Dodecanese Hydrofoils and Olympic Airways. Vathý is chock-a-block with **bike** and **car rental** franchises, which keeps rates reasonable. For bikes try Louie's (☎0273/24 438), on Kefalopoúlou just before the hospital, while for cars the preferred outlets are Budget at Themistoklí Sofoúli 31 (☎0273/28 856), Eurodollar/Aramis at no. 5 (☎0273/22 682) or Autoplan, a division of Samina Tours. Other amenities include the **post office** (Mon–Fri only) on Smýrnis, inland from the Olympic offices, the **OTE** across the way from the cathedral, three waterfront **banks** with cash dispensers, and a **laundry** on pedestrianized Lykoúrgou Logothéti.

ACCOMMODATION

Most **accommodation** for independent travellers clusters in the hillside district of Katsoúni, more or less directly above the ferry dock; except in August, you'll have little trouble finding affordable vacancies. Budget choices include the waterfront *Hotel Artemis* (☎0273/27 792; ③) just off "Lion Square"; *Pension Ionia* (☎0273/28 782; ②) inland at Manoli Kalomíri 5; the *Pension Trova* (☎0273/27 759; ②) around the corner at Kalomíri 26; and the *Pension Avli* (☎0273/22 939; ②), a wonderful period piece up a nearby stair-street at Aréos 2. This is the former convent school of the French nuns, so the rooms, arrayed around a courtyard(*avlí* in Greek) are appropriately institutional.

None of these outfits are palaces by any means; for more luxury start at the surprisingly affordable *Hotel Galaxy* (☎0273/22 665; ③) at Angéou 1 near the top of Katsoúni, set in garden surroundings and with a small pool. *Samos Hotel* (☎0273/28 377; ④) right by the ferry dock, frequently drops its rates in winter, and is open all year, if a bit noisy. Only the front rooms of the *Hotel Paradise* at Kanári 21 (☎0273/23 911; ④) look at lined-up KTEL coaches – side and rear rooms have views of local orchards and the pool. Some 50m north right across from the KTEL at Ioánni Lekáti 11, *Le Mirage* (☎0273/23 868; ③) is grimly placed but quiet enough at night and benefits from a roof terrace. Finally, the *Vathi* (☎0273/28 124, fax 24 045; ③), quite a hike south up into hillside Neapolis district near the cemetery, is an excellent choice with its balconied rooms with bay view, small pool and friendly family management.

Eating and drinking

The only waterfront **tavernas** worth a second glance are the *Stefanos* ouzerí, just north of the Lion Square; *Stelios*, 150m north of the dock on the right, fine for a pre-ferry lunch; and the pricier *Apanemia* ouzerí, at the far southwest end of the shore boulevard. Up in Áno Vathý, the most obvious place to eat is the popular *Agrambeli*, where low prices reflect rather small portion sizes; you might do better 100m further into the village, where the atmospheric kafenío next to Ayía Matróna church provides mezédhes. Vathý nightlife revolves around its **bars**, the longest lived of these being *Escape*, on a sea-view terrace at Kefalopoúlou 9 (north of the jetty). *Eternity*, on the ground floor of the closed-down Catholic church (sic), is the newest entry. *Metropolis*, in the orchards behind the *Hotel Paradise*, is Vathý's bona fide **disco**.

Around Vathý

The immediate environs of Vathý offer some modest beaches and small hamlets, ideal targets for day trips. Two kilometres east of (and above) Vathý spreads the vast inland plateau of Vlamarí, devoted to vineyards and supporting the hamlets of **AYÍA ZÓNI** and **KAMÁRA**, each with simple tavernas. From Kamára you can climb up a partly cobbled path to the cliff-top **monastery of Zoödhókhou Piyís**, for views across the end of the island to Turkey.

Heading north out of Vathý, the narrow road ends after 7km at the pebble bay and fishing port of **AYÍA PARASKEVÍ** (or Nissí), with good swimming. Of two tavernas here, *Nissi* is by far the best, with grilled meats and seafoods, a well-selected *dhískos* (tray) of proffered mezédhes and cheerful terrace service offsetting the slightly bumped-up prices.

As you head southeast from Vathý along the main island loop road, the triple chapel at **Treis Ekklisíes** marks an important junction, with another fork 100m along the left-hand turning. Bearing left twice takes you through the hilltop village of **Paleókastro**, 3km beyond which is another junction. Forking left yet again, after another 3km you reach the quiet, striking bay of **Kérveli**, with a small beach, a pair of tavernas (*Iy Kharavyi* is better) by the water and another characterful favourite, *Iy Kryfi Folia*, about 500m uphill along the access road. It's not worth continuing along the right fork to the road's end at **Possidhónio**, whose single taverna is mediocre and beach negligible. Turning right at the junction before Paleókastro leads to the beaches of Mykáli and Psilí Ámmos, the only spots in this section with a bus service. **Mykáli**, a kilometre of windswept sand and gravel, has recently been encumbered with three package-only hotels; the sole place to try on spec here is *Villa Barbara* (☎0273/25 192; ④), apartments behind the Sirenes Beach hotel. **Psilí Ámmos**, further east around the headland, is a crowded, sandy cove, whose best and longest-established taverna is on the right as you arrive. If you swim to the islet beware of strong currents which sweep through the narrow straits.

Pythagório and around

Most traffic south of Vathý heads for **PYTHAGÓRIO**, the island's premier resort, renamed in 1955 to honour native son Pythagoras, ancient mathematician, philosopher and mystic. Until then it was known as Tigáni (Frying Pan) – in mid-summer you'll learn why. The sixth-century BC tyrant Polycrates had his capital here, and excavations of the site have forced modern Pythagório to expand northeast and uphill. The village core of cobbled lanes and thick-walled mansions abuts a small **harbour**, fitting almost perfectly into the confines of Polycrates' ancient port, but today devoted almost entirely to pleasure craft and overpriced cocktail bars.

Sámos's **castle**, the nineteenth-century *pýrgos* of local chieftain Lykourgos Logothetis, overlooks both the town and the shoreline. Logothetis, together with "Kapetan Stamatis" and Admiral Kanaris, chalked up decisive victories over the Turks in the summer of 1824. The final battle was won on Transfiguration Day (6 August), and accordingly the church beside the tower bears a huge sign in Greek announcing that "Christ Saved Sámos 6 August 1824". More ancient antiquities include the fairly dull **Roman baths** 400m west of town (Tues–Sun 8.30am–3pm; free) and a minuscule **archeological collection** in the town hall (Tues–Thur & Sun 9am–2pm, Fri–Sat 10am–2pm; free). Considerably more interesting is the **Efpalinio tunnel** (Tues–Sun 9am–2.30pm; 500dr), a 1040-metre aqueduct bored through the mountain just north of

Pythagório at the behest of Polycrates. To get there, take the signposted path from the shore boulevard at the west end of town, which meets the vehicle access road towards the end of a twenty-minute walk.

You can also climb to the five remaining chunks of the Polycratian **perimeter wall** enclosing his hilltop citadel. There's a choice of routes: one leading up from the Glyfádha lagoon west of Pythagório past an **ancient watchtower** now isolated from any other fortifications, and the other – which is easier – leading from the monastery of **Panayía Spilianí**. Though most of this has been insensitively restored and touristified, beyond the courtyard lies a grotto, at one end of which is a subterranean shrine to the Virgin (open daylight hours; free). This was the presumed residence of the ancient oracular priestess Fyto, and a pirate-safe hideout in medieval times.

Practicalities

If there are any **accommodation** vacancies – and it's best not to assume this in mid-season – proprietors meet incoming ferries. The **tourist information booth** (☎0273/61 389), on the main thoroughfare Lykoúrgou Logothéti, can help in finding rooms, and also dispenses town plans and transport schedules. Quietly located at the seaward end of Odhós Pythagóra, south of Lykoúrgou Logothéti, the modest *Tsambika* (☎0273/61 642; ③) and *Sydney* (③) pensions are worth considering; 50m inland from the north side of the harbour past the customs house, *Lambis Rooms* on Odhós Íras (☎0273/61 396; ③) also comes recommended. Another peaceful area is the hillside north of Platía Irínis, where *Pension Despina* (☎0273/61 472; ③) sits just north of the square, while *Hotel Galini* is one of the better small outfits (☎0273/61 167; winter ☎01/98 42 248; ④). Further uphill, on the road to Vathý, the rear units of *Studios Anthea* (☎0273/62 086; ④) are fairly noise-free and allow you to self-cater.

Eating out can be frustrating in Pythagório, with value for money often a completely alien concept. Away from the water, the *Platania* taverna, under two eucalyptus trees opposite the town hall, is a good choice for a relatively simple meal; for waterside dining, you're best off at the extreme east end of the quay, where the *Remataki* ouzerí features plenty of vegetarian dishes such as *angináres ala políta* (artichokes cooked with carrots, potatoes, vinegar and oil). Night-owls gather at either *Disco Labito* in town, or *Edem* (aka *San Lorenzo*) 1km out on the Vathý road.

If none of this appeals, the outbound **bus stop** lies just west of the intersection of Lykoúrgou Logothéti and the road to Vathý. Two **banks** (both with cash dispensers) and the **post office** are also on Lykoúrgou Logothéti; there is currently no OTE. The flattish country to the west is ideal for cycling, a popular activity, and if you want to rent a **moped**, there are several outfits on the main street.

Around Pythagório

The main local beach stretches for several kilometres west of the Logothetis "castle", punctuated about halfway along by the end of the airport runway, and the cluster of nondescript hotels known as **POTOKÁKI**. Just before the turnoff to the heart of the beach sprawls the ultra-luxurious *Doryssa Bay* complex, which includes a meticulously concocted fake village, guaranteed to confound archeologists of future eras. No two of the units, joined by named lanes, are alike, and there's even a platía with an expensive café. If you actually intend to stay in the area, however, the *Fito Bungalows Hotel* (☎0273/61 582; ⑤) is more affordable. If you don't mind the hotel crowds and low-flying jets, the sand-and-pebble **beach** here is well groomed and the water clean; you'll have to head out to the end of the road for more seclusion.

The Potokáki access road is a dead end, with the main island loop road pressing on past the turnoff for the airport and Iréon hamlet. Under layers of alluvial mud, plus today's runway, lies the processional Sacred Way joining the ancient city with the **Heraion**, the massive shrine of the Mother Goddess (Tues–Sun 8.30am–3pm; 800dr). Much touted in tourist literature, this assumes humbler dimensions – one surviving column and assorted foundations – upon approach. Yet once inside the precinct you sense the former grandeur of the temple, never completed owing to Polycrates' untimely death at the hands of the Persians. The site chosen, near the mouth of the still-active Imvrassós stream, was Hera's legendary birthplace and site of her trysts with Zeus; in the far corner of the fenced-in zone you glimpse a large, exposed patch of the paved Sacred Way.

The modern resort of **IRÉON** nearby is a nondescript grid of dusty streets behind a coarse-shingle beach, attracting a slightly younger and more active clientele than Pythagório. Here you'll find more non-package rooms and two small hotels: *Venetia* (☎0273/61 195; ③) and *Heraion* (☎0273/61 180; ③), both within sight of the water. The oldest and most authentic **taverna** is the *Ireon*, at the far west end by the fishing harbour.

Southern Sámos

Since the circum-island bus only passes through or near the places below once or twice daily, you really need your own vehicle to explore them. Some 4km west of Khóra, an inconspicuous turning leads uphill to the still-active monastery of **Timíou Stavroú**, whose annual September 14 festival is more an excuse for a tatty bazaar in the courtyards than for any music or feasting. Another 1km on, another detour bears off to **MAVRATZÉÏ**, one of two Samian "pottery villages"; this one specializes in the *Koúpa tou Pythagóra* or "Pythagorean cup", supposedly designed by the sage to leak over the user's lap if he over-indulged. More practical wares can be found in **KOUMARADHÉÏ**, back on the main road, another 2km along.

From here you can descend a paved road through burned forest to the sixteenth-century monastery of **Megális Panayías** (in theory daily mornings & 4.30–6.30pm, ring keeper on ☎61 449 to check), containing the finest frescoes on the island. This route continues to **MÝLI**, submerged in lemon groves and also accessible from Iréon. Four kilometres above Mýli sprawls **PAGÓNDAS**, a large hillside community with a splendid main square and an unusual communal fountain house on the south hillside. From here, a scenic paved road curls 9km around the hill to **SPATHARÉÏ** – its surroundings devastated by fire in 1993 – but set on a natural balcony offering the best sea views this side of the island. From Spatharéï, the road loops back 6km to **PÝRGOS**, lost in pine forests at the head of a ravine, and the centre of Samian honey production.

The rugged and beautiful coast south of the Pagóndas–Pýrgos route is largely inaccessible, glimpsed by most visitors for the first and last time from the descending road bringing them to Sámos. **Tsópela**, a highly scenic sand-and-gravel cove at a gorge mouth, is the only beach here with marked track access and a good seasonal taverna; you'll need a sturdy motorcycle (not a scooter) or jeep to get down there. The western reaches of this shoreline, which suffered comprehensive fire damage in 1994, are approached via the small village of **KOUMÉÏKA**, with a massive inscribed marble fountain and a pair of kafenía on its square. Below extends the long, pebble bay at **Bállos**, with sand, a cave and naturists at the far east end. Bállos itself is merely a sleepy collection of summer houses, several **rooms** to rent and a few **tavernas**, the best of which is the *Cypriot*, tucked away inland. Returning to Kouméïka, the dubious-looking side road just before the village marked "Velanidhiá" is in fact usable by any vehicle, and a very useful short cut if you're travelling towards the beaches beyond Órmos Marathokámbou (see p.644).

Kokkári and around

Leaving Vathý on the north coastal section of the island loop road, there's little to stop for until you reach **KOKKÁRI**, the third major Samian tourist centre after Pythagório and the capital. Sadly, while lower Vathý and Pythagório had little beauty to sacrifice, much has been irrevocably lost here. The town's profile, covering two knolls behind twin headlands, remains unaltered, and several families still doggedly untangle their fishnets on the quay, but in general its identity has been altered beyond recognition, with constant inland expansion over vineyards and the abandoned fields of baby onions that gave the place its name. With exposed, rocky beaches buffeted by near-constant winds, developers have made a virtue of necessity by developing the place as a highly successful windsurfing resort.

Practicalities

As in Vathý and Pythagório, a fair proportion of Kokkári's **accommodation** is block-booked by tour companies; one establishment not completely devoted to such trade is the pleasant *Hotel Olympia Beach* (☎0273/92 353; ④), on the western beach road, co-managed with the *Olympia Village* apartments (☎0273/92 420; ⑤). Another amenable pension is that of Ioannis Perris (☎0273/92 040; ③), also on the west beach. Otherwise Yiorgos Mikhelios has a wide range of rooms and apartments to rent (☎0273/92 456; ③), including the *Pension Green Hill*. If you get stuck, seek assistance from the seasonal **EOT post** (☎0273/92 217), housed in a portacabin near the main church.

Most **tavernas** line the north waterfront, and charge above the norm, though they're steadily losing ground to breakfast or cocktail bars. At the eastern end of things, *Ta Adhelfia* is as close as you'll get to a simple, unpretentious psistariá, while on the less commercialized western beach, *To Koutouki* does standard taverna fare without too many airs and graces. Inland, *Farmer's* – on the village through-road, a few steps east of the summer **cinema** – is highly regarded for its locally grown food, and in autumn may offer *moustalevriá* (grape-must dessert). The *Cabana Disco-Club* is the hot new entry on the nightlife scene.

Other amenities include a short-hours **bank** on the through road, a **post office** in a portacabin on a seaward lane, and a **laundry** next to that.

West of Kokkári: the coast

The closest sheltered beaches are thirty to forty minutes' walk away to the west, all with permanently anchored umbrellas. The first, **Lemonákia**, is a bit too close to the road, with an obtrusive café; 1km beyond, the graceful crescent of **Tzamadhoú** figures in virtually every EOT poster of the island. With path-only access, it's a bit less spoiled, and each end of the saucer-shaped pebble beach is by tacit consent a nudist zone. There's one more pebble bay west of Avlákia called **Tzábou**, but it's not worth a special detour when the prevailing northwest wind is up.

The next spot of any interest along the coast road is **Platanákia**, essentially a handful of tavernas and rooms for rent at a bridge by the turn off for Manolátes (see p.643); best in each category are *Taverna Apolafsi* and *Rooms Kalypso* (☎0273/94 124; ③), both on the shore side of the road. Platanákia is actually the eastern suburb of **ÁYIOS KON-STANDÍNOS**, whose surf-pounded esplanade has been "improved". However, there are no usable beaches within walking distance, so the collection of warm-toned stone buildings constitutes a peaceful alternative to Kokkári. In addition to modest **hotels** such as the *Four Seasons* (③) or the *Atlantis* (☎0273/94 329; ③) just above the highway, there's a new generation of more modern rooms below the road, such as *Maria's* (☎0273/94 460). For food, look no further than the excellent *To Kyma* at the east end of the quay.

Once past "Áyios", as bus conductors habitually bellow it out, the mountains hem the road in against the sea, and the terrain doesn't relent until **Kondakéïka**, whose diminutive shore annexe of **Áyios Nikólaos** is an excellent venue for fish meals, particularly at *Iy Psaradhes*, its terrace lapped by the waves. There's also a reasonable beach here ten minutes walk east past the last studio units.

Hill villages

Inland between Kokkári and Kondakéïka, an idyllic landscape of pine, cypress and orchards is overawed by dramatic mountains, so far little burned. Despite destructive nibblings by bulldozers, some of the trail system linking the various **hill villages** is still intact, and walkers can return to the main highway to catch a bus home. Failing that, most of the communities can provide a bed at short notice.

The monastery of **Vrondianís** (Vrónda), directly above Kokkári, is a popular destination, although since the army now uses it as a barracks, the place only really comes alive during its annual festival (7–8 September). **VOURLIÓTES**, 2km west of the monastery, has beaked chimneys and brightly painted shutters sprouting from its typical tile-roofed houses. On the photogenic central square, the oldest and arguably best of several tavernas is *The Blue Chairs*, serving two local specialities: *revithokeftédhes* (chickpea patties), and the homemade *moskháto* dessert wine.

MANOLÁTES, further uphill and an hour-plus walk away via a deep river canyon, also has several simple tavernas (the best of these being *Loukas* at the top of the village), and is the most popular trailhead for the five-hour round-trip up **Mount Ámbelos** (Karvoúnis), the island's second highest summit. From Manolátes you can no longer easily continue on foot to Stavrinídhes, the next village, but should plunge straight down, partly on a cobbled path, through the shady valley known as **Aïdhónia** (Nightingales), to Platanákia.

Karlóvassi

KARLÓVASSI, 35km west of Vathý and the second town of Sámos, is decidedly sleepier and more old-fashioned than the capital, despite having roughly the same population. Though lacking in distinction, it's popular as a base from which to explore western Sámos's excellent beaches and walking. The name, despite a vehement denial of Ottoman legacy elsewhere on Sámos, appears to be a corruption of the Turkish for "snowy plain" – the plain in question being the conspicuous saddle of Mount Kérkis overhead. The town divides into four straggly neighbourhoods: Néo, well inland, whose untidy growth was spurred by the influx of post-1923 refugees; Meséo, across the usually dry river bed, tilting appealingly off a knoll towards the shore; and postcard-worthy Paleó (or Áno), above Limáni, the small harbour district.

Most tourists stay at or near **LIMÁNI**, which has a handful of rooms and several expensive hotels. The **rooms**, all in the inland pedestrian lane behind the through road, are quieter – try those of Vangelis Feloukatzis (☎0273/33 293; ③) or Yiorgos Moskhoyiannis (☎0273/32 812; ③). The port itself is an appealing place with a working boatyard at the west end and all the **ferry-ticket agencies** grouped at the middle; often a shuttle bus service operates from Néo Karlóvassi, timed to boat arrivals and departures. Tavernas and bars are abundant, but none are worth singling out.

Immediately overhead is the partly hidden hamlet of **PALEÓ**, its hundred or so houses draped on either side of a leafy ravine. The only facilities are the sporadically functioning café *To Mikro Parisi*, and a seasonal taverna on the path down towards **MESÉO**. The latter is a conceivable alternative base to Limáni, with **rooms** along the 500m between the playground and the sea, and the *Aspasia* (☎0273/32 363; ④) well-sited 100m west of the wood-fired bakery. Following the street linking the central square to the waterfront, you pass one of the improbably huge, turn-of-the-century churches, topped with twin belfries and a blue-and-white dome, which dot the coastal plain here. Just at the intersection with the shore road you'll find the friendly, good-value *To Kyma* ouzerí (April–Oct), the best place in town to watch the sunset over a selection of mezédhes.

NÉO has little to recommend it besides a wilderness of derelict stone-built warehouses and mansions down near the river mouth, reminders of the long-vanished leather industry which flourished here during the first half of this century. However, if you're staying at Limáni, you'll almost certainly visit one of the three **banks** (cash dispensers), the **post office**, the **OTE** or the **bus stop** on the main lower square.

Western Sámos

Visitors tolerate dull Karlóvassi for the sake of western Sámos' excellent **beaches**. Closest of these is **Potámi**, forty minutes' walk away via the coast road from Limáni or an hour by a more scenic, high trail from Paleó. This broad arc of sand and pebbles gets crowded at summer weekends, when virtually the entire population of Karlóvassi descends on the place. Near the end of the trail from Paleó stands *To Iliovasilema*, a friendly fish taverna; there are also a very few **rooms** signposted locally, and you can camp along the lower reaches of the river which gives the beach its name.

A streamside path leads twenty minutes inland, past the eleventh-century church of **Metamórfosis** – the oldest on Sámos – to an apparent dead end. Beyond here you must swim and wade 100m in heart-stoppingly cold water through a sequence of fern-tufted rock pools before reaching a low but vigorous waterfall; bring shoes with good tread and perhaps even rope if you want to explore above the first cascade. You probably won't be alone until you dive in, since the canyon is well known to locals and tour agencies. Just above the Metamórfosis church, a clear if precipitous path leads up to a small, contemporaneous **Byzantine fortress**. There's little to see inside other than a subterranean cistern and badly crumbled lower curtain wall, but the views out to sea and up the canyon are terrific, while in October the place is carpeted with pink autumn crocuses.

The coast beyond Potámi ranks among the most beautiful and unspoiled on Sámos; since the early 1980s it has served as a protected refuge for the rare monk seal. The dirt track at the west end of Potámi bay ends after twenty minutes on foot, from which you backtrack a little to find the side trail running parallel to the water. After twenty minutes along this you'll arrive at **Mikró Seïtáni**, a small pebble cove guarded by sculpted rock walls. A full hour's walk from the trailhead, through partly fire-damaged olive terraces, brings you to **Megálo Seïtáni**, the island's finest beach, at the mouth of the intimidating Kakopérato gorge. You'll have to bring food and water, though not necessarily a swimsuit – there's no dress code at either of the Seïtáni bays.

Southwestern beach resorts

Heading south out of Karlóvassi on the island loop road, the first place you'd be tempted to stop off is **MARATHÓKAMBOS**, a pretty, amphitheatrical village overlooking the eponymous gulf; there's a taverna or two, but no short-term accommodation. Its port, **ÓRMOS MARATHOKÁMBOU**, 18km from Karlóvassi, has recently emerged as a tourist resort, though some character still peeks through in its backstreets. The port has been improved, with kaïkia offering day trips to Foúrni and the nearby islet of Samiopoúla, while the pedestrianized quay has become the focus of attention, home to several indistinguishable tavernas.

The beach immediately east from Órmos is hardly the best; for better ones continue 2km west to **VOTSALÁKIA** (officially signposted as "Kámbos"), Sámos' fastest-growing resort, straggling a further 2km behind the island's longest (if not its most beautiful) beach. But for most Votsalákia is still a vast improvement on the Pythagório area, and the mass of 1437-metre Mount Kérkis overhead rarely fails to impress (see below). As for **accommodation**, Emmanuil Dhespotakis (☎0273/31 258; ③) has premises towards the quieter, more scenic western end of things. Also in this vicinity is *Akroyialia*, the most traditional **taverna**, with courtyard seating and fish and meat grills. Other facilities include branches of nearly all the main Vathý travel agencies, offering **vehicle rental** (necessary, as only two daily buses call here) and money exchange.

If Votsalákia doesn't suit, you can continue 3km past to the 600-metre beach of **Psilí Ámmos**, more aesthetic and not to be confused with its namesake beach in the southeast corner of Sámos. The sea shelves very gently here, and cliffs shelter clusters of naturists at the east end. Surprisingly there is still little development: one fair-sized apartment complex in the pines at mid-beach, and two tavernas back up on the road as you approach, both of these fine for a simple lunch. Access to **Limniónas**, a smaller cove 2km further west, snakes past a villa complex rather grandiosely dubbed "Samos Yacht Club". Yachts do occasionally call at the protected bay, which offers decent swimming away from a rock shelf at mid-strand, especially at the east end where there's a simple **taverna**; inland are a very few accommodation facilities.

Mount Kérkis and around

Gazing up from a supine seaside position, you may be inspired to climb **Mount Kérkis**. The classic route begins at the west end of the Votsalákia strip, along the bumpy jeep track leading inland towards Evangelistrías convent. After thirty minutes on the track system, through fire-damaged olive groves and past charcoal pits (a major local industry), the path begins, more or less following power lines up to the convent. A friendly nun may proffer an oúzo in welcome and point you up the paint-marked trail, continuing even more steeply up to the peak. The views are tremendous, though the climb itself is humdrum once you're out of the trees. About an hour before the top there's a chapel with an attached cottage for sheltering in emergencies. All told, it's a seven-hour outing from Votsalákia and back, not counting rest stops.

Less ambitious walkers might want to circle the flanks of the mountain, first by vehicle and then by foot. The road beyond Limniónas to Kallithéa and Dhrakéï, truly backof-beyond villages with views across to Ikaría, is paved as far as Kallithéa, making it possible to venture out here on an ordinary motorbike. The bus service is better during the school year, when a vehicle leaves Karlóvassi (12.30pm, Mon–Fri) bound for these remote spots; during summer it only operates two days a week (currently Mon & Fri).

From **DHRAKÉÏ**, the end of the line with just a pair of very simple kafenía to its credit, a ninety-minute trail descends through partly burned forest to Megálo Seïtáni, from where it's easy enough to continue on to Karlóvassi within another two-and-a-half hours. People attempting to reverse this itinerary often discover to their cost that the bus (if any) returns from Dhrakéï early in the day, at 2.30pm, compelling them to stay at one of two rather expensive **rooms** establishments (summer only) in **KALLITHÉA**, and dine there at either the simple psistariá on the square or a newer, more varied taverna on the western edge of the village. From Kallithéa, a newer track (from beside the cemetery) and an older trail both lead up within 45 minutes to a spring, rural chapel and plane tree on the west flank of Kérkis, with path-only continuation for another thirty minutes to a pair of cave-churches. **Panayía Makriní** stands detached at the mouth of a high, wide but shallow grotto, whose balcony affords terrific views of Sámos' west tip. By contrast **Ayía Triádha**, a ten-minute scramble overhead, has most of its structure made up of cave wall; just adjacent, another long, narrow, volcanic cavern can be explored with a torch some hundred metres into the mountain.

After these subterranean exertions, the closest spot for a swim is **Vársamo** (Válsamo) cove, 4km below Kallithéa and reached via a well-signposted dirt road. The beach here consists of multicoloured volcanic pebbles, with two caves to shelter in and a single taverna just inland.

Ikaría

Ikaría, a narrow, windswept landmass between Sámos and Mýkonos, is little visited and invariably underestimated; the name supposedly derives from the legendary Icarus, who fell into the sea just offshore after the wax bindings on his wings melted. For years the only substantial tourism was generated by a few **hot springs** on the south coast, some reputed to cure rheumatism and arthritis, some to make women fertile, though others are so highly radioactive that they've been closed for some time.

Ikaría, along with Thessaly on the mainland, western Sámos and Lésvos, has traditionally been one of the Greek Left's strongholds. This tendency dates from the long decades of right-wing domination in Greece, when (as in past ages) the island was used as a place of **exile** for political dissidents. Apparently the strategy backfired, with the transportees outnumbering and even proselytizing their hosts; at the same time, many Ikarians emigrated to North America, and ironically their regular capitalist remittances help keep the island going. It can be a bizarre experience to be treated to a monologue on the evils of US imperialism, delivered by a retiree in perfect Alabaman English.

These are not the only Ikarian quirks, and for many the place is an acquired taste. Except for forested portions in the west, it's not a strikingly beautiful island, with most of the terrain consisting of scrub-covered schist used as building material. The mostly desolate south coast is fringed by steep cliffs, while the north face is less sheer but nonetheless furrowed by deep canyons creating hairpin bends which are extreme even by Greek standards. Neither are there many picturesque villages, since the rural schist-roofed houses are generally scattered so as to be next to their famous apricot orchards, vineyards and fields.

The Ikarians have resisted most attempts to develop their island for conventional tourism: no charter flights land here, since the northeastern airport can't accommodate jets. Long periods of seemingly punitive neglect by Athens have made the locals profoundly self-sufficient and idiosyncratic, and tolerant of the same characteristics in others.

Áyios Kírykos

About two-thirds of ferries call at the south-coast port and capital of **ÁYIOS KÍRYKOS**, about 1km southeast of the island's main thermal resort. Because of the spa trade, beds are at a premium in town; arriving in the evening from Sámos, accept any reasonable offers of rooms at the jetty, or – if in a group – proposals of a taxi ride to the north coast, which shouldn't be more than 7500dr per vehicle to the end of the line. A cream-and-green **bus** sets out across the island from the main square (daily, in theory 10am & 1.30pm on Mon, Wed & Fri to Armenistís; Mon–Fri noon to Évdhilos only).

The baths (daily 8am–1pm) in **Thérma** are rather old-fashioned, with preference given to those under medical care. A better bet for a less formal soak are the more natural, shoreline hot springs at **Thérma Lefkádhos**, 3km southwest of Áyios Kírykos, below a cluster of villas. Here the seaside spa is derelict, leaving the water to boil up right in the shallows, mixing with the sea between giant volcanic boulders to a pleasant temperature.

Practicalities

Hydrofoils and the kaïki for Foúrni use the small east jetty; large ferries dock at the main west pier. There are several **hotels**, such as the *Isabella* (☎0275/22 839; ④), or the friendly, basic but spotless *Akti* (☎0275/22 694; ②), on a knoll east of the hydrofoil and kaïki quay, with views of Foúrni from the garden. Otherwise, **pensions** and **rooms** are not especially cheap: directly behind the base of the ferry jetty and a little to the west

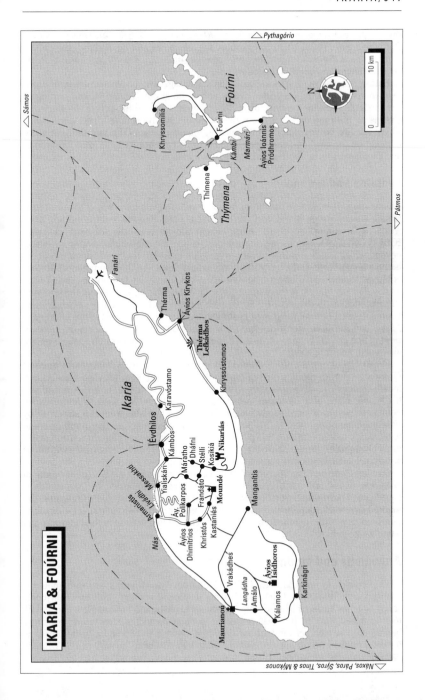

IKARÍA & FOÚRNI

△ *Pythagório*

△ *Sámos*

▽ *Pátmos*

Foúrni

Khryssomiliá

Foúrni

Thimena

Thimena

Kámbi

Marmári

Áyios Ioánnis
Pródhromos

Thýmena

N

0   10 km

Fanári

Ikaría

Thérma

Áyios Kírykos

**Thérma
Lefkádhos**

Karavóstamo

Khryssóstomos

Évdhilos

Kámbos

Messakrti

Mbrátho

Dháfni

Livádhi

Yialiskári

Stélli

Koskiá

Nikariás

Áy.
Políkarpos

Frandáto

Moundé

Armenistís

Nás

Áyios
Dhimítrios

Khristós

Kastaniés

Manganítis

Vrakádhes

**Áyios
Isídhoros**

Maurianoú

Langádha

Amálo

Kálamos

Karkinágri

there's the well-appointed *Pension Maria-Elena* (☎0275/22 543; ③), with sea views. Both the *Studios* (☎0275/22 276; ④) above the *Snack Bar Dedalos* and the prominently marked, clean *dhomátia* run by Ioannis Proestos (☎0275/23 496; ③), get noise from the several kafenía and snack bars below.

Eating out, you've even less choice than in lodging. Give the obvious quayside eateries a miss in favour of the grilled dishes served up at the *Tzivaeri* ouzerí, just inland from Ioannis Proestos's rooms, or *Iy Klimataria* just around the corner for *mayireftá*. Glitz is all the rage on the front, with *Casino* the last remaining traditional kafenío. There are two **banks** with cash dispensers, a limited-hours **OTE** and the post office adjacent on the road out, and three ferry/hydrofoil **agents**. You can **rent** motorbikes and cars here, too, but both are cheaper in Armenistís.

Évdhilos and around

The twisting, 41-kilometre road from Áyios Kírykos to Évdhilos is one of the most hairraising on any Greek island, and the long ridge extending the length of Ikaría often wears a streamer of cloud, even when the rest of the Aegean is clear. **KARAVÓSTAMO**, with its tiny, scruffy port, is the first substantial north coast place, beyond which a series of three beaches leads up to **ÉVDHILOS**. Although this is the island's second town and a ferry stop three to four times weekly in summer, it's far less equipped to deal with visitors than Áyios Kírykos. There are two **hotels**, the *Evdoxia* on the slope southwest of the harbour (☎0275/31 502, fax 31 571; ④) and the low-lying *Atheras* (☎0275/31 434, fax 31 926; ④) with a small pool – plus a few rather average **rooms**. Among several waterfront **restaurants**, the nameless kafestiatorio between *O Flisvos* and the *Blue Nice* travel agency is the most reliable and reasonable option. A **post office** and **OTE** up towards the *Evdoxia*, and a good town **beach** to the east, are also worth knowing about.

KÁMBOS, 2km west, offers a small hilltop museum with finds from nearby **ancient Oinoe**; the twelfth-century church of Ayía Iríni lies just below, with the remains of a fourth-century Byzantine basilica serving as the entry courtyard. Lower down still are the sparse ruins of a Byzantine palace (just above the road) used to house exiled nobles, as well as a large sandy beach. **Rooms** are available from the store run by Vassilis Dhionysos (☎0275/31 300; ③), which also acts as the unofficial and enthusiastic tourist office for this part of Ikaría, keeping the keys for church and museum. For **nightlife**, *Petrino* above the east end of the beach has a diet of traditional music at variance with the techno currently the rage in Greece.

Starting from the large church in Évdhilos, you can also visit the Byzantine **castle of Nikariás** (Koskiná), just over 15km south. The road signposted for Manganítis is paved until Kosikiá, just over 9km away; thereafter you've 2km of steep dirt road to the marked side track, along which you can get a bike or jeep to within a short walk of the tenth-century castle, perched on a distinctive conical hill, with an arched gateway and a fine vaulted chapel.

Armenistís and around

Most people carry on to **ARMENISTÍS**, 57km from Áyios Kírykos, and with good reason: this little resort lies below Ikaría's finest wooded scenery, with two enormous, sandy beaches battered by near-constant surf – **Livádhi** and **Messakhtí** – five and fifteen minutes' walk to the east respectively. Campers in the river-mouth greenery behind each stretch set the tone for the place, though an official campsite functions behind Livádhi in peak season, and the islanders' tolerance doesn't extend to nude bathing, as signs advise you.

A dwindling number of older buildings, plus fishing boats hauled up in a sandy cove, lend Armenistís the air of a Cornish fishing village; it's a tiny place, reminiscent of similar youth-oriented spots in southern Crete, though gentrification has definitely set in. Several "music bars" operate seasonally behind the nearer beach – these often with live Greek sessions – and at the quay's north end, but for most visitors **nightlife** is mostly about extended sessions in the tavernas and cafés overlooking the anchorage. Along the shore lane, the adjacent *Paskhalia* and *Delfini* **tavernas** are the best, the former offering full breakfasts as well as good-value, en-suite **rooms** (☎0275/71 302; winter 01/24 71 411; ③). On the hill to the south the *Armena Inn* (☎0275/71 320; ③) is of a similar standard, plus there are several other "rooms" along the road west to Nás. For more luxury, there are two adjacent hotels about 700m east of the main junction here, both with pools and hosting the local package custom: the *Cavos Bay* (☎0275/71 381, fax 71 380; ④) and the *Daidalos* (☎0275/71 390, fax 71 393; ④). Better than either, just above Messakhtí, is the *Messakhti Village* complex (☎0275/71 331, fax 713 30; ④), with a large pool (necessary here, as the deep water off the beach is often unsafe due to undertow) and fine common areas and private terraces making up for the rather plain rooms. Just east of here is the fishing settlement of **YIALISKÁRI**, which has a handful of tavernas and half-a-dozen "rooms" looking out to a picturesque church on the jetty.

Among four travel agencies/car rental/money exchange outfits in Armenistís, Marabou is about the most helpful, offering mountain bikes as well as walking tours of western Ikaría; Glaros has reasonably maintained scooters. The sole drawback to staying in Armenistís is getting away, since both taxis and buses are elusive. Theoretically, **buses** head for Áyios Kírykos daily at 2 or 3pm, usually with a change or layover in Évdhilos, and out of school term only at 7am most days, but all these departures are unreliable even by Ikarian standards and should be double-checked. If you've a ferry to catch, it's far easier on the nerves to pre-book a taxi.

Rákhes

Armenistís is actually the shore annexe of four inland hamlets – Áyios Dhimítrios, Áyios Polýkarpos, Kastaniés and Khristós – collectively known as **RÁKHES**. Despite the modern, mostly paved access roads through the pines (trails shortcut them), the settlements retain a certain Shangri-La quality, with the older residents speaking a positively Homeric dialect. On an island not short of foibles, Khristós is particularly strange inasmuch as the locals sleep much of the day, but shop and eat from early afternoon to the small hours; in fact most of the villages west of Évdhilos adhere to this schedule, defying central-government efforts to bring them in line with the rest of Greece.

Near the small main square, paved in schist and studded with gateways fashioned from the same rock, there's a **post office** and a **hotel/restaurant** (☎0275/71 269; ③), but for lunch you'll have to scrounge something at one of two unmarked tavernas or the more prominent kafenía. The slightly spaced-out demeanour of those serving may be attributable to over-indulgence in the excellent home-brewed **wine** which everyone west of Évdhilos makes. The local festival is August 6, though better ones take place further southwest in the woods at Langádha valley (August 14–15) or at Áyios Isídhoros monastery (May 14).

Nás

By tacit consent, Greek or foreign hippies, naturists and dope-fiends have been allowed to shift 3km west of Armenistís to **Nás**, a tree-clogged river canyon ending in a small but sheltered sand-and-pebble beach. This little bay is almost completely enclosed by weirdly sculpted rock formations, and it's very unwise to swim outside the cove's natural limits. The crumbling foundations of the fifth-century temple of **Artemis**

Tavropoleio (Patroness of Bulls) overlook the permanent deep pool at the mouth of the river. If you continue inland along this past colonies of campers, you'll find secluded rock pools for freshwater dips. Back at the top of the stairs leading down to the beach from the road are several tavernas (the oldest and best is *O Nas*), most offering **rooms** – *Pension Artemis* (☎0275/71 255; ②) can be booked in advance.

Satellite islands: Thímena and Foúrni

The straits between Sámos and Ikaría are speckled with islets, though the only ones permanently inhabited are Thímena and Foúrni. More westerly **Thímena** has one tiny hillside settlement, at which a regular kaïki calls on its way between Ikaría and Foúrni, but there are no tourist facilities, and casual visits are explicitly discouraged. Foúrni is home to a huge fishing fleet and one of the more thriving boatyards in the Aegean. Thanks to these, and the improvement of the jetty to receive car ferries, Foúrni's population is stable, unlike so many small Greek islands. The islets were once the lair of Maltese pirates, and indeed many of the islanders have a distinctly North African appearance.

The above-cited **kaïki** leaves Ikaría at about 1pm (Mon, Wed & Fri), stays overnight at Foúrni and returns the next morning. Another twice-weekly kaïki from Karlóvassi, and the larger car ferries which appear every few days, are likewise not tourist excursion boats but exist for the benefit of the islanders. The only practical way to visit Foúrni on a day trip is by using one of the summer morning hydrofoils out of Sámos (Vathý or Pythagório).

Foúrni

Apart from the remote hamlet of Khryssomiliá in the north, where the island's main road goes, most of Foúrni's inhabitants are concentrated in the **port** and Kámbi hamlet just to the south. The harbour community is larger than it seems from the sea, with a generally friendly ambience. Among several **rooms** establishments, the most desirable are those run by Manolis and Patra Markakis (☎0275/51 268; ③), immediately to your left as you disembark. If they're full you can head inland to the modern blocks of *Evtykhia Amoryianou* (☎0275/51 364; ③) or *Maouni* (☎0275/51 367; ③).

Of three waterfront **tavernas**, the local favourite is *Rementzo*, better known as *Nikos'*; if you're lucky the local *astakós* or Aegean lobster, actually an oversized saltwater crayfish, may be on the menu. The central "high street", fieldstoned and mulberry-shaded, ends well inland at a little platía with traditional kafenía under each of two plane trees; between them stands a Hellenistic sarcophagus found in a nearby field, and overhead is a conical hill, site of the ancient acropolis. There's a **post office** (but no bank) where you can change money, plus several well-stocked shops.

A fifteen-minute walk south from the school, skirting the cemetery and then slipping over the windmill ridge, brings you to **KÁMBI**, a scattered community overlooking a pair of sandy, tamarisk-shaded coves which you'll share with chickens and hauled-up fishing boats. There are two cafés, the lower one with seven **rooms** that are admittedly spartan but have arguably the best views on the island. A path continues to the next bay south, which like Kámbi cove, is a preferred anchorage for wandering yachts.

Heading north from the harbour via steps, then a trail, you'll find more **beaches**: **Psilí Ámmos** in front of a derelict fish-processing plant, with shade at one end, plus two more secluded ones at **Kálamos**, reached by continuing along the path. At the extreme north of the island, idyllic **KHRYSSOMILIÁ** is still best approached by boat, despite the improved road. The village, split into a shore district and a hill settlement at the top of a canyon, has a decent beach flanked by better but less accessible ones. Near the dock are very rough-and-ready combination kafenía/tavernas; simple **rooms** can be arranged on the spot.

Khíos

"Craggy Khíos", as **Homer** aptly described his probable birthplace, has a turbulent history and (unlike neighbouring Sámos) a strong identity. It has always been relatively prosperous, in medieval times through the export of mastic resin – a trade controlled by Genoese overlords between 1346 and 1566 – and later under the **Ottomans**, who dubbed the place Sakız Adası (Resin Isle). Since 1912, several shipping dynasties have emerged here continuing the pattern of wealth. Participation in

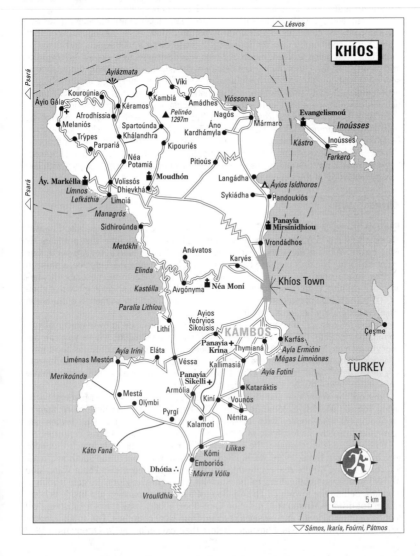

the maritime way of life is widespread, with many people serving as radio operators or officers in the merchant navy.

The more powerful shipowning families and the military authorities did not encourage tourism until the late 1980s, but with the worldwide shipping crisis, and the saturation of other, more obviously "marketable" islands, resistance has dwindled. Increasing numbers of foreigners are discovering Khíos beyond its rather daunting port capital: fascinating villages, important **Byzantine monuments** and a respectable complement of beaches. While unlikely ever to be dominated by tourism, the local scene has a distinctly modern flavour – courtesy of numerous returned Greek-Americans and Greek-Canadians – and English is widely spoken.

Unfortunately, the island has suffered more than its fair share of catastrophes during the past two centuries. The Turks perpetrated their most infamous, if not their worst, anti-revolutionary atrocity here in 1822, massacring 30,000 Khiots and enslaving or exiling even more. In 1881, much of Khíos was destroyed by a violent **earthquake**, and throughout the 1980s the natural beauty of the island was markedly diminished by several devastating forest fires, compounding the effect of generations of tree-felling by boat-builders. Nearly two-thirds of the majestic pines are now gone, with substantial patches of woods persisting only in the far northeast and the centre of Khíos.

In 1988 the first charters from northern Europe were instituted, an event that signalled equally momentous changes for the island. There are now perhaps 5,000 guest beds on Khíos, the vast majority of them in the capital or the nearby beach resort of Karfás. Further expansion, however, is hampered by the lack of direct charters between most countries and Khíos, and the refusal of property owners to part with land for the extension of the airport runway.

Khíos Town

KHÍOS, the harbour and main town, will come as a shock after modest island capitals elsewhere; it's a bustling, concreted commercial centre, with little that predates the 1881 quake. Yet in many ways it is the most satisfactory of North Aegean ports; time spent exploring is amply rewarded with a large and fascinating marketplace, a museum or two, some good, authentic tavernas and, on the waterfront, possibly the best attended evening volta (promenade) in Greece. Although it's a sprawling town of about 30,000, most things of interest to visitors lie within a hundred or so metres of the water, which is fringed by Leofóros Egéou.

South and east of the main platía, officially Plastíra but known universally as Vounakíou, extends the marvellously lively tradesmen's **bazaar**, where you can find everything from live monkeys to cast-iron woodstoves. The bakers of Khíos boast more varieties of bread than any other in Greece – including corn, wholewheat, multigrain, so-called "dark" and "village". Like nearby Lésvos and Sámos, the island makes respectable oúzo – the best commercial brand is Tetteris.

Opposite the Vounakíou taxi rank, the grandiosely titled "Byzantine Museum", occupying the old **Mecidiye Mosque** (Mon–Fri 9am–2pm; free), is little more than an archeological warehouse, with marble fragments such as Turkish, Jewish and Armenian gravestones testifying to the island's varied population in past centuries.

Until the 1881 earthquake, the Genoese **Kástro** was completely intact; thereafter developers razed the seaward walls, filled in much of the moat to the south and made a fortune selling off the real estate thus created around present-day Platía Vounakíou. Today the most satisfying entry to the citadel is via Porta Maggiora, the gate leading to a square behind the town hall. The top floor of a medieval mansion just inside is home to the **Justiniani Museum** (Tues–Sun 9am–3pm; 500dr), which has a satisfying collection of unusual icons and mosaics rescued from local churches. The small dungeon adjacent briefly held 75 Khiot hostages before their execution by the Ottomans in 1822.

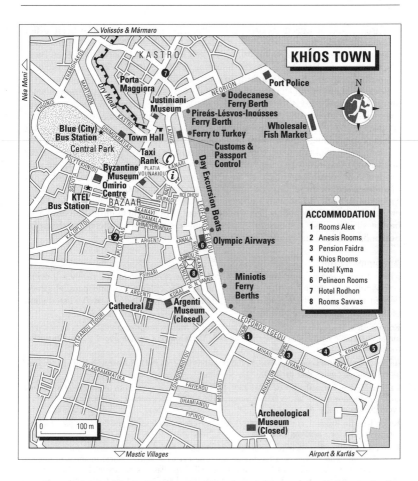

KHÍOS TOWN

△ Volissós & Mármaro

Néa Moní ◁

KASTRO

Porta Maggiora

Justiniani Museum

Blue (City) Bus Station ★

Central Park

Town Hall

Byzantine Museum

Omirio Centre

KTEL Bus Station

BAZAAR

Port Police

Dodecanese Ferry Berth

Pireás-Lésvos-Inoússes Ferry Berth

Ferry to Turkey

Customs & Passport Control

Wholesale Fish Market

Taxi Rank

PLATIA VOUNAKIOU

Day Excursion Boats

Olympic Airways

Miniotis Ferry Berths

Cathedral

Argenti Museum (closed)

LEOFOROS EGEOU

ACCOMMODATION

1 Rooms Alex
2 Anesis Rooms
3 Pension Faidra
4 Khios Rooms
5 Hotel Kyma
6 Pelineon Rooms
7 Hotel Rodhon
8 Rooms Savvas

Archeological Museum (Closed)

0   100 m

▽ Mastic Villages   Airport & Karfás ▽

The old residential quarter inside what remains of the castle walls, formerly the Muslim and Jewish neighbourhoods, is well worth a wander; among the wood-and-plaster houses you'll find assorted Ottoman monuments in various states of decay, including a cemetery, a small mosque, several inscribed fountains and a former dervish convent converted into a church after 1923.

Arrival, information and services

The **airport** lies 4km south along the coast at Kondári; any of the blue urban buses labelled "Kondári Karfás" departing from the station on the north side of the park pass the airport gate. **Ferry** agents cluster to either side of the customs building, towards the north end of the waterfront Egéou and its continuation Neoríon: NEL is a few paces south of customs (☎0271/23 971) and Miniotis Lines, at Neoríon 21–23 (☎0271/24 670), operates a regular morning service to Çeşme and small ferries to many neighbouring islands, and as well as representing G&A boats. The Turkish evening ferry to Çeşme, as well as the most regular boat to Inoússes (see p.661), are currently handled by Faros Travel at Egéou 26 (☎0271/27 240). The helpful municipal **tourist office** (May–Sept Mon–Fri 7am–2.30pm & 6–9.30pm, Sat 10am–1.30pm, Sun 10am–noon; Oct–April Mon–Fri 7am–2.30pm; ☎0271/44 389) is at Kanári 18, near the Ionian Bank. The conspicuous "Hadzelenis Tourist Information Office" (☎0271/26 743) on the quay is a private concern, geared primarily to accommodation.

Because of its central location on the island's east shore, and the preponderance of tourist facilities, Khíos is the obvious base for exploration, especially if you're without a vehicle. The green-and-cream **KTEL buses** leave from a parking area on the opposite side of the park, behind the Omirio Cultural Centre. While services to the south of Khíos are adequate, those to the centre and northwest of the island are almost nonexistent. For explorations there it's well worth renting a powerful **motorbike** or a car, or sharing a **taxi** – they're bright red here, not grey as in most of Greece. Three independent **car rental** agencies sit in a row along Evyenías Khandhrí, behind the *Chandris Hotel*; of these, George Sotirakis/European Rent a Car (☎0271/29 754) and MG (☎0271/23 377), also with a branch at Karfás, can be recommended. The **OTE** is directly opposite the tourist office, while the **post office** is on Omírou, and numerous **banks** all have cash dispensers. A final Khiot idiosyncrasy is afternoon **shopping hours** limited to Monday and Thursday in summer.

Accommodation

Khíos Town has a relative abundance of affordable accommodation, rarely – if ever – completely full. Most line the water or the perpendicular alleys and parallel streets behind, and almost all are plagued by traffic noise to some degree – we've listed some of the more peaceful establishments.

Rooms Alex, Mikhaíl Livanoú 29 (☎0271/26 054). The friendly proprietor often meets ferries arriving at unsociable hours; otherwise ring the bell. There's a roof garden above the well-furnished rooms. ③.

Anesis, cnr Vasilikári and Aplotariás, in the bazaar (☎0271/44 801). Rooms with bath, fridges and air-conditioning; quiet after dark. ④.

Faidra, Mikhaíl Livanoú 13 (☎0271/41 130). Well-appointed pension, in an old mansion with stone arches in the downstairs winter bar; in summer the bar operates outside, so ask for a rear room to avoid nocturnal noise. ④.

Khios Rooms, Kokáli 1, cnr Egéou (☎0271/27 295). Clean, antique, second-floor rooms, which are relatively quiet for a seafront locale. ②.

Kyma, east end of Evyenías Khandhrí (☎0271/44 500). A Neoclassical mansion with a modern extension, splendid service and big breakfasts. The old wing saw a critical moment in modern Greek history in September 1922, when Colonel Nikolaos Plastiras commandeered it as his HQ after the Greek defeat in Asia Minor, and announced the deposition of King Constantine I. ⑤.

Pelineon Rooms, Omírou 9, cnr Egéou (☎0271/28 030). Many rooms have a sea view (though not the singles). ③.

Rodhon, Zakharíou 17 (☎0271/24 335). The owners can be crotchety, and the more basic rooms are a bit steeply priced, but it's just about the only place inside the kástro, and is very quiet. ③.

Rooms Savvas, Roïdhou 15 (☎0271/24 892). Fairly quiet pension tucked onto a tiny plaza just inland from the water; the rear rooms unfortunately overlook the public toilets. ④.

Eating

Eating out in Khíos Town can be more pleasurable than the fast-food joints and *barákia* on the waterfront would suggest; it is also usually a fair bit cheaper than on the neighbouring islands of Sámos and Lésvos.

Agrifoglio, Stávrou Livanoú 2 (start of road to Karfás). *The* place for an Italian blowout.

Ouzeri Aïvali, Egéou 80. Newest and (marginally) best of a handful of such outfits on the front.

Ta Dhyo Adherfia, Mikhaïl Livanoú 38. Standard taverna where students and soldiers go for a cheap feed.

Dhodhoni, Egéou 102. Local outlet of Greece's best (and priciest) ice-cream chain; also pastries.

Estia, cnr Roïdhou and Venizélou, near *Rooms Savvas*. Small milk bar serving sheep's milk yoghurt from Lésvos, *loukoumádhes* and occasionally rice pudding.

Ta Mylarakia, by three restored windmills at Tambakhika, road to Vrondádhos (☎0271/40 412). Good food and atmospheric outdoor seating make reservations advisable in summer.

Ouzeri Theodhosiou, junction Egéou and Neoríon. The genuine article, with a large, reasonable menu, though it's best to wait until the ferries which dock immediately opposite have departed. Dinner only.

Drinking, nightlife and entertainment

Iviskos. Tasteful café that's the most popular daylight hangout on the quay, with a range of juices, coffees and alcoholic drinks.

To Loukoumi, alley off Aplotariás 27/c. Old warehouse refitted as a café (8am–2pm), ouzerí (8pm–2am) and occasional events centre. Well executed and worth checking out.

Metropolis, Egéou 92. Currently the best bar in terms of music, decor and crowd.

Omírio, south side of the central park. Cultural centre and events hall well worth stopping at: there are frequently changing exhibitions, and foreign musicians often come here after Athens concerts to perform in the large auditorium.

Beaches around Khíos Town

Khíos Town itself has no beaches worth mentioning; the closest decent one is at **KARFÁS**, 7km south past the airport and served by frequent blue buses. Once there you can **rent bikes** at Rabbit, or **cars** at MG, both uphill from the bus stop. Most of the Khiot tourist industry is based here, to the considerable detriment of the 500-metre-long beach itself, sandy only at the south end. The main bright spot is a unique **pension**, *Markos' Place* (☎0271/31 990; April–Nov, other times by arrangement; ③), installed in the former pilgrims' cells at the **Monastery of Áyios Yeóryios and Áyios Pandelímon**, on the hillside south of the bay. Markos Kostalas, who leases the premises from Thymianá municipality, has created a unique environment much loved by special-activity groups. Guests are lodged in the former pilgrims' cells, with a kitchen available; individuals are more than welcome (there are several single "cells"), though advance reservations are strongly suggested. At the south end of the beach, *O Karfas* (locally known as *Yiamos* after the proprietor) is a fair bet for reasonable and abundant **food**, including vegetables from their own plot. The slightly more expensive *Karatzas* mid-beach is rated second, though the seaview **hotel** upstairs (☎0271/31 180; ③) is the only one here still geared to non-package-tour custom. However, the best food of all is to be had at *O Dholomas*, 3km back towards town at Kondári, on a side road between the municipal swimming pool and the *Morning Star Hotel*.

Some 2km further along the coast from Karfás, **AYÍA ERMIÓNI** is less a beach than a fishing anchorage surrounded by a handful of tavernas and apartments to rent. The actual beach is at **Mégas Limniónas**, a few hundred metres further, even smaller than Kárfas but more scenic, especially at its south end where low cliffs provide a backdrop. *Taverna Angyra* is about the best and most popular eating place hereabouts. Both Ayía Ermióni and Mégas Limniónas are served by extensions of the blue bus route to either Karfás or Thymianá, the nearest inland village.

The coast road loops up to Thymianá, from where you can (with your own transport only) continue 3km south towards Kalimassiá to the turning for **Ayía Fotiní**, a 700-metre pebble beach with exceptionally clean water. There's no shade, however, unless you count shadows from the numerous blocks of rooms under construction behind the main road; a few **tavernas** cluster around the parking area where the side road meets the sea. The last settlement on this coast, 5km beyond Kalimassiá and served by long-distance bus, is beachless **KATARÁKTIS**, remarkable mainly for its pleasant water-front of balconied houses. The choicest among the tavernas here is *O Tsambos*.

Southern Khíos

The olive-covered, gently rolling countryside in the south of the island is also home to the **mastic bush**, *Pistacia lentisca*, for centuries used as a base for paints, cosmetics and chewable jelly beans which became a somewhat addictive staple in the Ottoman harems. Indeed, the interruption of the flow of mastic from Khíos to Istanbul by the revolt of spring 1822 was one of the root causes of the brutal Ottoman reaction.

The wealth engendered by the mastic trade supported twenty *mastikhokhoriá* (mastic villages) from the time the Genoese set up a monopoly in the substance during the fourteenth and fifteenth centuries, but the end of imperial Turkey, and the industrial revolution with its petroleum-based products, knocked the bottom out of the mastic market. Now it's just a curiosity, to be chewed – try the sweetened *Elma* brand gum – or drunk as a liqueur called *mastíkha*, though it has had medicinal applications since ancient times. These days, the *mastikhokhoriá* live mainly off their tangerines, apricots and olives.

The towns themselves, the only settlements on Khíos spared by the Ottomans in 1822, are architecturally unique, laid out by the Genoese but retaining a distinct Middle-Eastern feel.

The mastic villages

ARMÓLIA, 20km from town, is the first, smallest and least imposing of the mastic villages. Its main virtue is its pottery industry – the best shops are the last two on the right, driving southwest. **PYRGÍ**, 5km further south, is perhaps the liveliest of the communities, its houses elaborately embossed with *xistá*, geometric patterns cut into the plaster and then outlined with paint. In autumn, strings of tomatoes hung to dry from balconies add a splash of colour. On the northeast corner of the central square the twelfth-century Byzantine church of **Áyii Apóstoli** (Tues–Thurs & Sat 10am–1pm), embellished with much later frescoes, is tucked under an arcade. The giant **Cathedral of the Assumption** on the square itself boasts a *témblon* in an odd folk style dating from 1642, and an equally bizarre carved figure peeking out from the base of the pulpit. Pyrgí has a handful of **rooms**, many of them bookable through the Women's Agricultural and Tourist Cooperative (☎0271/72 496; ③). In the medieval core you'll find a bank, a post office, a minuscule OTE stall on the platía and a few souvláki grills (but no real tavernas). **OLÝMBI**, 7km further west along the bus route serving Armólia and Pyrgí, is the least visited of the mastic villages, but not devoid of interest. The characteristic tower-keep, which at Pyrgí stands half-inhabited away from the modernized main square, here looms bang in the middle of the platía, its ground floor occupied by two kafenía.

MESTÁ, 11km west of Pyrgí, has a more sombre feel and is considered the finest example of the genre. From its main square, dominated by the **Church of Taxiárkhis** (the largest on the island), a bewildering maze of cool, shady lanes leads off in all directions. But most streets end in blind alleys, except the critical half-dozen leading to as many gates; the northeast one still has an iron grate. If you'd like to stay, there are half a dozen **rooms** in restored traditional dwellings managed by Dhimitris Pipidhis (☎0271/76 319; ③); those run by the Floradhi (☎0271/76 455; ③) and Yialouri (☎0271/76 234; ②) households are somewhat less costly. Of the two **tavernas** on the main platía, *O Morias sta Mesta* is renowned for its tasty rural specialities, including pickled *krítamo* (rock samphire) and the locally produced raisin wine: heavy, semisweet and sherry-like. However, *Mesaionas* – whose tables share the square here – has perhaps the more helpful proprietor. One or the other place will be open in spring or autumn; there's even a **bar** or two in season, but Mestá remains just the right side of twee as most people here still work the land.

The south coast

One drawback to staying in Mestá is the dearth of good beaches nearby; the closest candidate is at **Merikoúnda**, 4km west of Mestá. Reached by an improved seven-kilometre side road starting between Olýmbi and Pyrgí, the little beach of **Káto Faná** is popular with Greek summer campers, who blithely disregard signs forbidding the practice; there are no facilities. A vaunted Apollo temple in the vicinity amounts to scattered masonry around a medieval chapel, located by the roadside some 400m above the shore.

Pyrgí is actually closest to the two major beach resorts in this corner of the island. The nearest, 6km distant, is **EMBORIÓS**, an almost landlocked harbour with three passable **tavernas** (*Porto Emborios* having the edge); there's a scanty, British-excavated acropolis on the hill to the northeast, vaguely signposted 1km along the road to Kómi. For swimming, follow the road to its end at an oversubscribed car park and the beach of **Mávra Vólia**, then continue by flagstoned walkway over the headland to two more dramatic pebble (part nudist) strands of red and black volcanic stones, twice the length and backed by impressive cliffs.

If you want golden sand you'll have to go to **KÓMI**, 3km northeast, also accessible from Armólia via Kalamotí; there are just a few tavernas (most reliable of these being the *Bella Mare*) and summer apartments behind the pedestrianized beachfront. The bus service, is fairly good in season, often following a loop route through Pyrgí and Emboriós. **Lílikas**, 2km east, has quieter pebble coves.

Central Khíos

The portion of Khíos extending west from Khíos Town, matches the south in terms of interesting **monuments**, and the road network makes touring under your own power an easy matter. There are also several **beaches** on the far shore of the island which, though not the best on Khíos, are fine for a dip at the end of the day.

The Kámbos

The **Kámbos**, a vast fertile plain carpeted with citrus groves, extends southwest from Khíos Town almost as far as the village of Khalkió. The district was originally settled by the Genoese during the fourteenth century, and remained a preserve of the local aristocracy until 1822. Exploring it by bicycle or motorbike is apt to be less frustrating than going by car, since the web of poorly marked lanes sandwiched between high walls guarantee disorientation and frequent backtracking; behind the walls you catch fleeting glimpses of ornate old mansions built from locally quarried sandstone. Courtyards are paved in pebbles or alternating light and dark tiles, and most still contain a *mánganos*, or water-wheel, once used to draw water up from wells up to 30m deep.

Many of the sumptuous three-storey dwellings, constructed in a hybrid Italo-Turco-Greek style, have languished in ruins since 1881, but a few have been converted for use as unique accommodation. Most famous of these is the *Villa Argenti*, ancestral home of the Italo-Greek counts Argenti de Scio; it was sold in 1996, however, and is currently shut. For now, stay at the well-marked and publicized *Hotel Perivoli* (☎0271/31 513, fax 32 042; ⑨), just 100m north of *Villa Argenti* (blue urban buses bound for Thymianá pass just 200m to the east). The rooms, no two alike, have fireplaces and (in most cases) en-suite baths and sofas. For **eating**, head for nearby Neokhóri where *O Kipos ton Oneiron* has a wide range of mezédhes and attractive marble decor.

Not strictly speaking in Kámbos, but most easily reached from it en route to the *mastikhokhoriá*, is an outstanding rural Byzantine monument. The thirteenth-century **church of Panayía Krína**, isolated amidst orchards and woods, is well worth the challenge of the maze of dirt tracks beyond Vavíli village, 9km from town. It's usually closed for snail's-pace restoration, but a peek through the apse window will give you a fair idea of the finely frescoed interior, sufficiently lit by a twelve-windowed drum. The alternating brick and stonework of the exterior alone justifies the trip here, though architectural harmony is marred by the later addition of a clumsy lantern over the narthex.

Néa Moní

Almost exactly in the middle of the island, the **monastery of Néa Moní** was founded by the Byzantine Emperor Constantine Monomakhos (The Dueller) IX in 1042, on the spot where a wonder-working icon had been discovered. It ranks among the most beautiful and important monuments on any of the Greek islands; the mosaics, together with those of Dháfni and Óssios Loukás on the mainland, are among the finest surviving art of their age in Greece, and the setting – high in still partly forested mountains 15km west of the port – is no less memorable.

Once a powerful and independent community of six hundred monks, Néa Moní was pillaged in 1822 and most of its residents put to the sword; since then many of its outbuildings have languished in ruins. The 1881 tremor caused comprehensive damage (skilfully repaired), while exactly a century later a forest fire threatened to engulf the place until the resident icon was paraded along the perimeter wall, miraculously repelling the flames. Today the monastery, with its giant refectory and vaulted water cisterns, is inhabited by just two elderly, frail nuns and a couple of lay workers.

Bus excursions are provided by the KTEL on Tuesday and Friday mornings; otherwise come by motorbike, or **walk** from Karyés, 7km northeast, to which there is a regular blue-bus service. Taxis from town, however, are not prohibitive, at about 5000dr round-trip per carload, including a wait while you look around.

Just inside the **main gate** (daily 8am–1pm & 4–8pm) stands a chapel/charnel house containing the bones of those who met their death here in 1822; axe-clefts in children's skulls attest to the savagery of the attackers. The katholikón, with the cupola resting on an octagonal drum, is of a design seen elsewhere only in Cyprus; the frescoes in the exonarthex are badly damaged by holes allegedly left by Turkish bullets, but the **mosaics** are another matter. The narthex contains portrayals of the *Saints of Khios* sandwiched between *Christ Washing the Disciples' Feet* and *Judas' Betrayal*, missing the kiss, which has unfortunately been smudged out. In the dome of the sanctuary, which once contained a complete life-cycle of Christ, only the *Baptism*, part of the *Crucifixion*, the *Descent from the Cross*, the *Resurrection* and the *Evangelists Mark and John* survived the earthquake.

The west coast

With your own transport, you can proceed 5km west of Néa Moní to **AVGÓNYMA**, a cluster of dwellings on a knoll overlooking the coast; the name means "Clutch of Eggs", an apt description when it is viewed from the ridge above. Since the 1980s, the place has been almost totally restored as a summer haven by descendants of the original villagers, though the permanent population is just seven. A returned Greek-American family runs an excellent, reasonable **taverna**, *O Pyrgos*, in an arcaded mansion on the main square; they also rent a few rooms (☎0271/42 175; ③), though the classiest **accommodation** option here is *Spitakia*, a complex of small restored houses for up to five people (☎0271/20 513; fax 43 052; ⑤).

A paved side road continues another 4km north to **ANÁVATOS**, whose empty, dun-coloured dwellings, soaring above pistachio orchards, are almost indistinguishable from the 300-metre-high bluff on which they're built. During the 1822 insurrection, some four hundred inhabitants and refugees threw themselves over this cliff rather than surrender to the besieging Ottomans, and it's still a preferred suicide leap. Anávatos can now only muster five souls, and, given a lack of reliable facilities and the eerie atmosphere, it's no place to be stranded at dusk.

West of Avgónima, the main road descends 6km to the coast in well-graded loops, also giving access to the northwest of Khíos (see below). Turning right (north) at the junction leads first to the beach at **Elínda**, alluring from afar but rocky and murky up close; it's better to continue towards more secluded coves to either side of Metókhi, or below **SIDHIROÚNDA**, the only village hereabouts, which enjoys a spectacular hilltop setting overlooking the coast.

All along this coast, as far southwest as Liménas Mestón, are round **watchtowers** erected by the Genoese to look out for pirates – the first swimmable cove you reach by turning left from the junction has the name **Kastélla**. A sparse weekday-only bus service resumes 9km south of the junction at **LITHÍ**, a friendly village of whitewashed buildings perched on a wooded ledge overlooking the sea. There are tavernas and kafenía near the bus stop, but the only places to stay are at recently prettified **Paralía Lithíou** 2km below, a weekend target of Khiot townies for the sake of its large but windswept beach. You may stay at *Kyra Dhespina* (☎0271/73 373; ③), but **eat** next door at *Ta Tria Adhelfia*; both are open most of the year.

Some 5km south of Lithí, the valley-bottom village of **VÉSSA** is an unsung gem, more open and less casbah-like than Mestá or Pyrgí, but still homogeneous. Its honey-coloured buildings are arrayed in a vast grid punctuated by numerous belfries; there's a simple taverna (*Snack Bar Evanemos*) installed in a tower-mansion on the main road, and you can stay at an old inn, *To Petrino* (☎0271/25 016; ④). Your last chance for a swim near Véssa is provided by a series of secluded sandy bays along the 16-kilometre road west to Liménas Mestón; only that of **Ayía Iríni** has a taverna, and all suffer from exposure to northerly winds.

Northern Khíos

Northern Khíos never really recovered from the 1822 massacre, and the desolation left by fires in 1981 and 1987 will further dampen inquisitive spirits. Since early this century the villages have languished all but deserted much of the year, which means that bus services are correspondingly sparse. About one-third of the former population now lives in Khíos Town, venturing out here only on the dates of major festivals or to tend grapes and olives, for at most four months of the year. Others, based in Athens or the US, visit their ancestral homes for just a few intensive weeks at mid-summer, when marriages are arranged between local families.

The road to Kardhámyla

Blue city buses run north from Khíos Town up to **VRONDÁDHOS**, an elongated coastal suburb that's a favourite residence of the island's many seafarers. Homer is reputed to have lived and taught here, and in terraced parkland just above the little fishing port you can visit his purported lectern, more probably an ancient altar of Cybele. Accordingly many of the buses out here are labelled "Dhasalópetra". Some 15km out of town, just past the tiny bayside hamlet of Pandoukiós, a side road leads to stony **Áyios Isídhoros** cove, home to the rather inconveniently located island **campsite**, *Chios Camping* (☎0271/74 111), though the site itself is shaded and faces Inoússes islet across the water.

Travelling by bus, **LANGÁDHA** is probably the first point on the eastern coast road where you'd be tempted to alight. Set at the mouth of a deep valley, this attractive little harbour settlement looks across its bay to a pine grove, and beyond to Turkey. There are a couple of rooms outfits, but most night-time visitors come for the sake of the excellent **seafood** at *Tou Koupelou*, better known as *Stelios*'s, on the quay; the remainder of the esplanade has been taken over by patisseries, bars and cafés. There is no proper beach anywhere nearby; **Dhelfíni** bay just north is an off-limits naval base.

Just beyond Langádha an important side road leads 5km up and inland to **PITYOÚS**, an oasis in a mountain pass presided over by a tower-keep; continuing 4km more brings you to a junction allowing quick access to the west of the island and the Volissós area (see p.661).

Kardhámyla and around

Most traffic proceeds to **ÁNO** and **KÁTO KARDHÁMYLA**, the latter 37km out of the main town. Positioned at opposite edges of a fertile plain rimmed by mountains, they initially come as welcome, green relief from Homer's crags. Káto, better known as **MÁRMARO**, is the larger, indeed the island's second town, with a bank, post office, OTE branch and filling station. However, there is little to attract a casual visitor: the port, mercilessly exposed to the *meltémi*, is strictly businesslike, and there are few tourist facilities. An exception is *Hotel Kardamyla* (☎0272/23 353; ⑤), co-managed with Khíos Town's *Hotel Kyma*. It has the bay's only pebble beach, and its **restaurant** is a reliable source of lunch if you're touring.

For better swimming head west 5km to **Nagós**, a gravel-shore bay at the foot of an oasis. The lush greenery is nourished by active springs up at a bend in the road, enclosed in a sort of grotto overawed by tall cliffs. The place name is a corruption of *naós*, after a large Poseidon temple that once stood near the springs, but centuries of orchard-tending, antiquities-pilfering and organized excavations after 1912 mean that nothing remains visible. Down at the shore the swimming is good, if a bit chilly, and there are two tavernas and one **rooms** place (☎0272/23 540; ③). Your only chance of relative solitude in July or August lies fifteen minutes' walk west at **Yióssonas**. This is a much longer beach, but sheltered, rockier and with no facilities.

Northwestern villages

Few outsiders venture beyond Yióssonas; on rare occasions an afternoon bus covers the distance between Mármaro and Kambiá village, 20km west. Along the way, **AMÁDHES** and **VÍKI** are attractive enough villages at the base of 1297-metre **Pilinéo**, the island's summit, easiest climbed from Amádhes. **KAMBIÁ**, overlooking a ravine dotted with chapels, has very much an end-of-the-line feel, despite the recent paving of the onward road south through Spartoúnda and Kipouriés to its union with the trans-island road to Volissós.

From Spartoúnda, a dirt road leads 8km west to another paved circuit taking in the far northwest of the island. Turning north through Khálandhra, you have a choice at Afrodhíssa: straight and downhill to the spa of **AYIÁZMATA**, with its tumbledown pier, seaweed-strewn beach and ugly new spa; or, better, turn left onto what approximates a coastal road for this part of the island. **KOUROÚNIA**, 6km from Afrodhíssia, is beautifully arranged in two separate neighbourhoods, looking out from thick forest cover. After 10km more, you reach **ÁYIO GÁLA**, where a disproportionate number of old ladies in headscarves hobble about. The place's claim to fame is a **grotto-church** complex, built into a palisade at the bottom of the village. Except on the August 23 festival date, you'll need to find Petros the key-keeper, who lives beside a eucalyptus tree at the top of the stairs leading down to the grotto. The larger of two churches occupies the mouth of the cave system; it's originally fifteenth century but has had an unfortunate pink exterior paint job that makes it look like a recent villa. Inside, however, a fantastically intricate *témblon* vies for your attention with a tinier, older chapel, built entirely within the rear of the cavern. Its frescoes are badly smudged, except for a wonderfully mysterious and mournful Virgin holding a knowing Child.

Volissós and around

VOLISSÓS, 42km from Khíos Town by the most direct road (45km via the easier Avgónyma route), was once the most important of the northwestern villages, and its old stone houses still lie appealingly beneath the crumbling hilltop Byzantine fort. The Genoese improved the towers, and near the top of the village is an utterly spurious "House of Homer" signpost, also Genoese. Volissós can seem depressing at first, with the bulk of its 250 remaining, mostly elderly, permanent inhabitants living in newer constructions around the main square – opinions improve with longer acquaintance.

Grouped around the platía you'll find a **post office** (but no bank), two shops and three mediocre **tavernas**; far better ones are found up in Pýrgos district, where *Pyrgos* (aka *Vasilis*) and the vegetarian *Kafenio E*, run by Nikos Koungoulios, are your options; reservations (☎0274/21 480) are advised for *Kafenio E*. A filling station operates 2.5km out of town, the only one hereabouts; you should plan on overnighting since the **bus** only comes out here on Sundays on a day-trip basis, and on Monday, Wednesday and Friday in the afternoon. This should cause no dismay, since the area has the best beaches on Khíos, and some of the most interesting **accommodation** on the island. Some sixteen old houses, most in Pýrgos, have been meticulously restored by Stella Tsakiri and Argyris Angelou (☎0274/21 421, fax 21 521; ④) and usually accommodate two people – all have terraces, fully equipped kitchens and features such as tree trunks upholding sleeping lofts. Larger families or groups should try for the three equally impressive units managed by Elysian Holidays (☎0274/21 128, fax 21 013; ④), very high up near the castle.

LIMNIÁ, the port of Volissós, lies 2km south, with kaïki skippers coming and going from Psará (mid-June to mid-Sept, Mon, Wed & Fri mid-morning). The best **tavernas** here are the long-established *Ta Limnia* on the jetty for *mayireftá*, and summer only *To Limanaki* at the rear of the cove. At Limniá you're not far from the fabled beaches either. A 1500-metre walk southeast over the headland brings you to **Managrós**, a seemingly endless sand-and-pebble beach; nearest **lodgings** are the bungalows of *Marvina Alvertou* (☎0274/21 335; ③). More intimate, sandy **Lefkáthia** lies just a ten-minute stroll along the cement drive threading over the headland north of the harbour; amenities are limited to a seasonal snack bar on the sand, and Ioannis Zorbas' apartments (☎0274/21 436; ④), beautifully set in a garden where the concrete track joins an asphalt road down from Volissós. This heads towards **Límnos** (not to be confused with Limniá), the next protected cove 400m east of Lefkáthia, with a seasonal psistariá operating behind the sand, and the *Latini Apartments*, graced with multiple stone terraces (☎0274/21 461; ④).

Ayía Markélla, 5km further west of Límnos, stars in many local postcards; it's a long, stunning beach fronting the monastery of Khíos's patron saint, the latter not especially interesting or useful for outsiders. Its cells are reserved for Greek pilgrims, while in an interesting variation on the expulsion of the money-changers from the temple, only religious souvenirs are allowed to be sold in the holy precincts, while all manner of plastic junk is on offer just outside. There's a snack bar as well, and around July 22 – the island's biggest festival – local "No Camping" signs are not enforced. The dirt road past the monastery grounds is passable to any vehicle, emerging up on the paved road between Melaniós and Volissós.

Satellite islands: Psará and Inoússes

There's a single settlement, with beaches and an isolated rural monastery, on both of Khíos's satellite isles, but each is surprisingly different from the other, and of course from their large neighbour. **Inoússes**, the nearer and smaller islet, has a daily kaïkia service from Khíos Town in season; **Psará** has less regular services subject to weather conditions (in theory minimum 3 weekly), and is too remote to be done justice on a day trip.

Psará

The birthplace of revolutionary war hero Admiral Kanaris, **Psará** devoted its merchant fleets – the third largest in 1820s Greece after Ídhra and Spétses – to the cause of independence, and paid dearly for it. Vexed beyond endurance, the Turks landed overwhelming forces in 1824, to stamp out this nest of resistance. Perhaps 3000 of the 30,000 inhabitants escaped in small boats which were rescued by a French fleet, but the majority retreated to a hilltop powder magazine and blew it (and themselves) up rather than surrender. The nationalist poet Solomos immortalized the incident in famous stanzas:

> *On the Black Ridge of Psará,*
> *Glory walks alone.*
> *She meditates on her heroes*
> *And wears in her hair a wreath*
> *Made from a few dry weeds*
> *Left on the barren ground.*

Today the year-round population barely exceeds four hundred, and it's a sad, stark place, never having really recovered from the holocaust; the Turks burned whatever houses and vegetation the blast had missed. The only positive recent development was a decade-long revitalization project instigated by a French-Greek descendant of Kanaris and a Greek team. The port was improved, mains electricity and pure water provided, a secondary school opened, and cultural links between France and the island established, though so far this has not been reflected in increased tourist numbers.

Arrival can be something of an ordeal: the regular small ferry from Khíos Town takes up to four hours to cover the 57 nautical miles of habitually rough sea. Use the port of Limniá to cross in at least one direction if you can; this route takes half the time at just over half the price.

Since few buildings in the east-facing harbour community predate this century, it's a strange hotchpotch of ecclesiastical and secular architecture that greets the eye on disembarking. There's a distinctly southern feel, more like the Dodecanese or the Cyclades, and some peculiar churches, no two alike in style.

If you **stay overnight**, there's a choice between a handful of fairly basic rooms and three large outfits: *Khakhaoulis Studios* (☎0274/61 233; ④) and *Apartments Restalia* (☎0274/61 000; ④), both a bit stark but with balconies and kitchens, or the EOT *xenónas* (☎0274/61 293; ③) in a restored prison. For **eating**, the best and cheapest place by far is the EOT-run *Spitalia*, housed in a restored medieval hospital at the north edge of the port. A **post office**, bakery and shop complete the list of amenities; there is no bank.

Psará's **beaches** are decent, improving the further northeast you walk from the port. You quickly pass Káto Yialós, Katsoúni and Lazarétta with its off-putting power station, before reaching **Lákka** ("narrow ravine"), fifteen minutes along, apparently named after its grooved rock formations in which you may have to shelter; much of this coast is windswept, with a heavy swell offshore. **Límnos**, 25 minutes out along the coastal path, is big and pretty, but there's no reliable taverna here, or indeed at any of the other beaches. The only other thing to do on Psará is to walk north across the island to the **Monastery of the Kímisis**; uninhabited since the 1970s; this comes to life only during the first week of August when its revered icon is carried in ceremonial procession to town, and then back again on August 6.

Inoússes

Inoússes has a permanent population of about three hundred – less than half its prewar figure – and a very different history from Psará. For generations this medium-sized islet has provided the Aegean with many of her wealthiest shipping families: the richest Greek shipowner in the world, Kostas Lemos, was born here, and virtually every street or square on Inoússes is named for one member or other of the numerous Pateras clan. This helps explain the large villas and visiting summer yachts in an otherwise sleepy Greek backwater – as well as a sporadically open **Maritime Museum** near the quay, endowed by various shipping magnates. At the west end of the quay, the bigwigs have also funded a large nautical academy.

Only on Sundays can you make an inexpensive **day-trip** to Inoússes from Khíos with the locals' ferry *Inousses*; on other days of the week this arrives at 3pm, returning early the next morning. On weekdays during the tourist season you must participate in the pricey excursions offered from Khíos, with return tickets running up to three times the cost of the regular ferry.

Two church-tipped islets, each privately owned, guard the unusually well-protected harbour; the **town** of Inoússes is surprisingly large, draped over hillsides enclosing a ravine. Despite the wealthy reputation, its appearance is unpretentious, the houses displaying a mix of vernacular and modest Neoclassical style. There is just one, fairly comfortable **hotel**, the *Thalassoporos* (☎0272/51 475; ④), on the main easterly hillside lane. **Eating out** is similarly limited to a simple ouzerí just below the nautical academy. It's best to come equipped with picnic materials, or be prepared to patronize one of the three shops (one on the waterfront, two up the hill). Beside the museum is a **post office** and a **bank**, with the **OTE** a few paces further west.

The rest of this tranquil island, at least the southern slope, is surprisingly green and well tended; there are no springs, so water comes from a mix of fresh and brackish wells, with a reservoir in the offing. The sea is extremely clean and calm on the sheltered southerly shore; among its beaches, choose from **Zepága**, **Biláli** or **Kástro**, five, twenty and thirty minutes' walk west of the port respectively. More secluded **Farkeró** lies 25 minutes east: first along a cement drive ending at a seaside chapel, then by path past pine groves and over a ridge. As on Psará, there are no reliable facilities at any of the beaches.

At the end of the westerly road, beyond Kástro, stands the somewhat macabre convent of **Evangelizmoú**, endowed by the Pateras family. Inside reposes the mummified body of the lately canonized daughter, Irini, whose prayers to die of cancer in place of her terminally ill father Panagos were answered early in the 1960s on account of her virtue and piety; he's entombed here also, having outlived Irini by some years. The abbess, presides over some twenty nuns; only women are allowed admission, and even then casual visits are not encouraged.

Lésvos (Mytilíni)

Lésvos, the third largest Greek island after Crete and Évvia, is not only the birthplace of Sappho, but also of Aesop, Arion and – more recently – the Greek primitive artist Theophilos, the Nobel laureate poet Odysseus Elytis and the novelist Stratis Myrivilis. Despite these **artistic associations**, Lésvos may not at first strike the visitor as particularly interesting or beautiful; much of the landscape is rocky, volcanic terrain, dotted with thermal springs and alternating with vast grain fields, salt pans or even near-desert. But there are also oak and pine forests as well as vast olive groves, some of these over five hundred years old. With its balmy climate and suggestive contours, the island tends to grow on you with prolonged acquaintance.

Lovers of medieval and Ottoman **architecture** certainly won't be disappointed. Castles survive at the main town of Mytilíni, at Mólyvos, Eressós and near Ándissa; most of these date from the late fourteenth century, when Lésvos was given as a dowry to a Genoese prince of the Gateluzzi clan following his marriage to the niece of one of

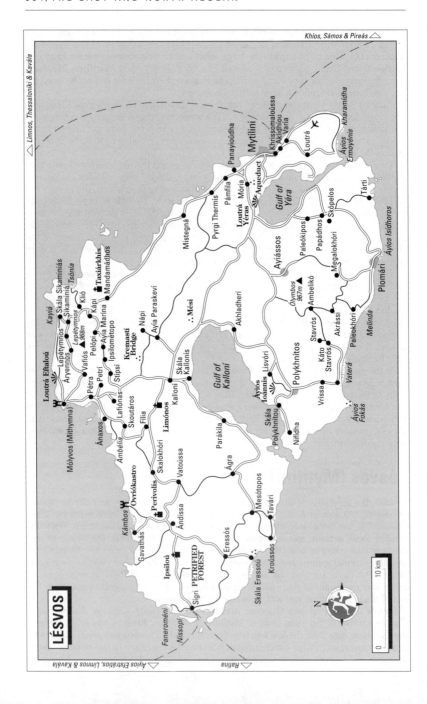

LÉSVOS

the last Byzantine emperors. Apart from Crete and Évvia, Lésvos was the only Greek island where Turks settled significantly in rural villages (they usually stuck to the safety of towns), which explains the odd Ottoman bridge, shed-like mosque or crumbling minaret often found in the middle of nowhere. Again, unusually for the Aegean islands, Ottoman reforms of the eighteenth century encouraged the emergence of a Greek Orthodox land- and industry-owning aristocracy, who built rambling mansions and tower-houses, a few of which survive.

Social and economic idiosyncrasies persist: anyone who has attended one of the lengthy village *paniyíria*, with music for hours on end and tables in the streets groaning with food and drink, will not be surprised to learn that Lésvos has the highest alcoholism rate in Greece. Breeding livestock, especially horses, is disproportionately important, and traffic jams caused by mounts instead of parked cars are not unheard of – signs reading "Forbidden to Tether Animals Here" are still part of the picture.

Historically, the olive plantations, oúzo distilleries, animal husbandry and fishing industry supported those who chose not to emigrate, but with these enterprises relatively depressed, mass-market **tourism** has made considerable inroads. However, there are still few large hotels outside the capital and Mólyvos, rooms still just outnumber villa-type accommodation, and the first official campsites only opened in 1990. Tourist numbers have in fact dropped in recent years, the result of stalled plans to expand the airport, unrealistic hotel pricing, and the dropping of the island from several tour operators' programs.

Public **transport** tends to radiate out from the harbour for the benefit of working locals, not daytripping tourists. Carrying out bus excursions from Mytilíni is next to impossible anyway, owing to the size of the island – about 70km by 45km at its widest points – and the poor state of many roads. Furthermore, the topography is complicated by the two deeply indented gulfs of Kalloní and Yéra, with no bridges at their mouths, which means that going from A to B involves an obligatory change of bus at either the port capital, on the east shore, or the town of Kalloní, in the middle of the island. It's best to decide on a base and stay there for a few days, exploring its immediate surroundings on foot or by rented vehicle.

Mytilíni Town

MYTILÍNI, the port and capital, sprawls between and around two bays divided by a fortified promontory, and in Greek fashion sometimes doubles as the name of the island. On the promontory sits the Byzantine-Genoese-Ottoman **fortress** (Tues–Sun 8.30am–3pm; 600dr), comprising ruined structures from all these eras and an Ottoman inscription above a Byzantine double-headed eagle at the south gate. Further inland, the town skyline is dominated in turn by the Germanic spire of **Áyios Theodhóros** and the mammary dome of **Áyios Therápon**, together expressions of the post-Baroque taste of the nineteenth-century Ottoman Greek bourgeoisie. They stand more or less at opposite ends of the **bazaar**, whose main street, Ermoú, links the town centre with the little-used north harbour of Páno Skála. On its way there Ermoú passes half a dozen well-stocked but expensive antique shops near the roofless **Yeni Tzami**. Between Ermoú and the castle lies a maze of atmospheric lanes lined with grandiose Belle Epoque mansions and elderly vernacular houses.

The excellent **Archeological Museum** (Tues–Sun 8.30am–3pm; 600dr) is housed partly in the mansion of a large estate just behind the ferry dock. Among the well-labelled and well-lit exhibits are a complete set of mosaics from a Hellenistic dwelling, rather droll terracotta figurines, votive offerings from a sanctuary of Demeter and Kore excavated in the castle, and Neolithic finds from present-day Thermí. A specially built annexe at the rear contains stone-cut inscriptions of various edicts and treaties, and – more interesting than you'd think – *stelae* featuring *nekródhipna* or portrayals of funerary meals. Yet another annexe 150m up the hill is not yet operational.

There's also a **Byzantine Art Museum** just behind Áyios Therápon, containing various icons (Mon–Sat 10am–1pm; 200dr), including one by Theophilos (see below). The small **Folk Art Museum** (Mon–Fri 9am–1pm; 300dr) on the quay next to the blue city-bus stop, is not worth the admission and can be skipped without regret.

Practicalities

There's no bus link with the **airport**, and a shared taxi for the 7km into Mytilíni is the usual method; Olympic Airways is southwest of the main harbour at Kavétsou 44. As on Khíos, there are two **bus stations**: the *astykó* (blue bus) service departing from the middle of the quay, the *iperastikó* (standard KTEL) buses leaving from a small station near Platía Konstandinopóleos at the southern end of the harbour. If you're intent on getting over to Ayvalík in **Turkey**, book tickets through either Dimakis Tours at Koundouriótou 73 (☎0251/27 865) or Mytilana Travel at no. 69 (☎0251/41 318). NEL has its own agency at no. 47 (☎0251/28 480), while G&A ferries are handled by Andonis Pikoulos at no. 73a (☎0251/27 000).

Car rental is best arranged through reputable chain franchises like Payless (Koundouriótou 49; ☎0251/43 555); Budget, next door (☎0251/25 846); Thrifty at no. 69 (☎0251/41 464) or Just at no. 47 (☎0251/43 080) – though it's generally cheaper to rent at the resort of your choice. Other amenities include the **OTE** and **post office**, next to each other on Vournázon, behind the central park, and three **banks** with cash dispensers: the Ethniki (National), Alpha Pisteos (Credit) – both on Koundouriótou – and the Emboriki (Commercial), on Ermoú. Before leaving town, you might stop at the jointly housed **tourist police/EOT office** (daily 8.30am–8pm; ☎0251/22 776), behind the customs building, in order to get hold of their excellent town and island maps, plus other brochures. If they're shut, try the **EOT** regional headquarters 300m away at Aristárkhou 6 (Mon–Fri 8am–2.30pm).

ACCOMMODATION

Finding **accommodation** can be difficult: the waterfront hotels are noisy and exorbitant, with few single rooms to speak of. If you need to stay, it's best to hunt for rooms between the castle and Ermoú. Yeoryíou Tertséti street in particular has two possibilities: the friendly *Pelayia Koumniotou* at no. 6 (☎0251/20 643; ②), or the fancier *Vetsikas/Dhiethnes* at no. 1 (☎0251/24 968; ③), whose rooms are en suite.

Past the Yeni Tzami, two quieter establishments between the north harbour and fortress are advertised – *Salina's Garden Rooms*, behind the Yeni Tzami at Fokéas 7 (☎0251/42 073; ③), co-managed with the *Thalia Rooms* across the street (☎0251/24 640; ③). *Zoumbouli Rooms*, facing the water on Navmakhías Ellís (☎0251/29 081; ③), are en suite, and may get more noise from traffic and the bar below. The bougainvillea-clad Neoclassical *Hotel Rex* at Katsakoúli 3, behind the Archeological Museum (☎0251/28 523; ③), looks inviting from the outside, but the en-suite rooms (no singles) are gloomy and a bit overpriced. For Belle Epoque character you're better off in the far south of town, at the *Villa 1900*, a restored mansion with period furnishings and ceiling murals, at P Vostáni 24 (☎0251/43 437; ⑤), where you may be able to bargain the price down a little.

EATING, DRINKING AND NIGHTLIFE

Dining options in Mytilíni are somewhat limited. The obvious, if blatantly touristy, venue for a seafood blow-out is the line of four **fish tavernas** on the southerly quay known as Fanári; all are comparable in terms of price and food. Stumbling off a ferry at dawn, revive yourself with *patsás* at *Averof*, next to the Alpha Credit Bank on Koundouróti. Clockwise around the quay at Koundouriótou 56, the *Asteria* (no sign) is a safe option for meat-and-

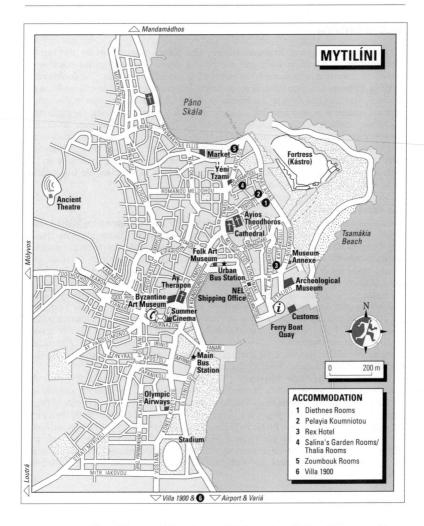

veg oven casseroles. A last surviving example of a dying breed is the *Krystal* ouzerí, on Koudouriótou between the Ionian Bank and the Bank of Greece, whose cavernous, wood-floored interior is lined with mirrors, bench seats and gaming tables.

If you're stuck here involuntarily, awaiting a dawn-departing ferry, some consolation can be derived from the town's decent **nightlife** and **entertainment**. *Hott Spott* is a fairly accurate self-description of the bar at Koundouriótou 63, near the NEL agency; *Cafe Iguana*, on the ground floor of the ex-*Hotel Bretannia* on the west quay is another popular watering hole. More formal live events form the heart of the Lesviakó Kalokéri, held in the castle from mid-July to mid-September, while the summer **cinema** Pallas is between the post office and the park on Vournázon.

Around Mytilíni

Beyond the airport and Krátigos village, the paved road becomes dirt up to **Kharamídha**, 14km from town and the closest decent beach (the fee-entry town "beach" at Tsamákia is mediocre); the eastern bay has a few tavernas. The double cove at **Áyios Ermoyénis**, 4km west, is more scenic but crowded at weekends, and has no facilities. The latter is directly accessible from Mytilíni via Loutrá village. For other pleasant immersions near Mytilíni, make for **Loutrá Yéras**, 8km along the main road to Kalloní. These public baths (daily: summer 8am–7pm; winter 10am–6pm; 200dr) are just the thing if you've spent a sleepless night on a ferry, with three ornate spouts that feed just-above-body-temperature water into a marble-lined pool in a vaulted chamber; there are separate facilities for each sex. A snack-bar/café operates seasonally on the roof of the bath house overlooking the gulf, and there is even an old **inn** nearby (☎0251/21 643; ②) for hydro-cure fanatics.

The Variá museums

The most rewarding single targets near Mytilíni are a pair of museums at **VARIÁ**, 3km south of town (half-hourly buses). The **Theophilos Museum** (Tues–Sun 9am–1pm & 4.30–8pm; 250dr) honours the painter, born here in 1873, with four rooms of wonderful, little-known compositions specifically commissioned by his patron Thériade (see below) in the several years leading up to his death in 1934; virtually the only familiar piece is likely to be *Erotokritos and Arethousa* in Room 3. A wealth of detail is evident in elegiac scenes of fishing, reaping, olive-picking and baking from the pastoral Lésvos which Theophilos obviously knew best; there are droll touches also, such as a cat slinking off with a fish in *The Fishmongers*. In classical scenes – *Sappho and Alkaeos*, a landscape series of Egypt, Asia Minor and the Holy Land, and historical episodes from wars historical and contemporary – Theophilos was clearly on shakier ground. *Abyssinians Hunting an Italian Horseman*, for instance, is clearly fantastic, being nothing more than Native Americans chasing down a Conquistador.

The adjacent **Thériade Museum** (Tues–Sun 9am–2pm & 5–8pm; 500dr) is the brainchild of another native son, Stratis Eleftheriades. Leaving the island at an early age for Paris, he gallicized his name to Thériade and went on to become a renowned avantgarde art publisher, convincing some of the leading artists of the twentieth century to participate in his ventures. The displays consist of lithographs, engravings, wood-block prints and watercolours by the likes of Mirò, Chagall, Picasso, Léger, Rouault and Villon, either annotated by the painters themselves or commissioned as illustrations for the works of prominent poets and authors – an astonishing collection for a relatively remote Aegean island.

Southern Lésvos

The southernmost portion of the island is indented by two great inlets, the gulfs of **Kalloní** and **Yéra** – the first curving in a northeasterly direction, the other northwesterly, thus creating a fan-shaped peninsula at the heart of which looms 968-metre Mount Ólymbos. Both shallow gulfs are in turn almost landlocked by virtue of very narrow outlets to the open sea.

Plomári and around

Due south of Mount Ólymbos, at the edge of the "fan", **PLOMÁRI** is the only sizeable coastal settlement in the south, and indeed the second largest on Lésvos, whose famous oúzo is produced at several nearby distilleries. Despite a lack of good beaches within walking distance, it's besieged in summer by hordes of Scandinavian tourists, but you can usually find a **room** (they are prominently signposted) at the edge of the old, charmingly dilapidated town, or (better) 1km west in Ammoudhélli suburb, which has a small gravel beach. Two specific outfits above Platía Beniamín include *Pension Lida* (☎0252/32 620; ③) and *Pension Kamara* (☎0252/31 901; ③). Rustling up a decent meal may present more difficulties, with the dinner-only *Platanos* taverna at the central plane tree often unbearably busy, and nothing special at that. Best of a usually mediocre bunch on the waterfront is *To Margaritari*, within sight of the bus stop, about the only place open reliably for lunch. Ammoudhélli can offer *To Ammoudhélli*, a seafood ouzerí perched over the water, and *Mama Katerina* on the opposite side of the road.

You'll probably do no worse at **Áyios Isídhoros**, 3km east, which is where most tourists actually stay; try the adjacent *Iy Mouria* or *Mama Papas* (sic), where the road turns inland to cross the creek draining to the long, popular pebble beach. Another beach is 6km west of Plomári at **Melínda**, an idyllic strand guarded by monoliths, where *Maria's* (☎0252/93 239; ③) taverna/rooms can be heartily recommended: it's an endearingly ramshackle place with good food at very reasonable prices. Even more unspoiled (thanks partly to the dreadful 7km side road in), **Tárti**, some 22km in total from Plomári, is a 400-metre bay where Lésvos hoteliers and restaurant owners take their holidays. Of the three **tavernas**, the one closest to road's end is by far the best and cheapest; **rooms** also line the final stretch of road should you want to stay.

The bus into Plomári travels via the pretty villages of Paleókipos and Skópelos (as well as Áyios Isídhoros), but if you have your own two-wheeler you can take a slight short cut by using the daytime-only ferry (no cars carried) between Skála Loutrón and Pérama across the neck of the Yéra Gulf. The road north from Plomári to Ayiássos has paving and public transport only up to Megalokhóri.

Ayiássos

AYIÁSSOS, nestled in a remote, wooded valley under the crest of Mount Ólymbos, is the most beautiful hill town on Lésvos – the ranks of traditional houses lining the narrow, cobbled streets are all protected by law. On the usual, northerly approach, there's no clue of the enormous village until you see huge ranks of parked cars at the southern edge of town (where the bus also leaves you).

Don't be put off by the endless ranks of wooden and ceramic kitsch souvenirs, aimed mostly at Greeks, but continue past the central **Church of the Panayía Vrefokratoússa**, built in the twelfth century to house an icon supposedly painted by the Evangelist Luke, to the old bazaar, with its kafenía, yoghurt shops and butchers' stalls. In certain kafenía bands of *santoúri*, clarinet, lap-drum and violin play on weekend afternoons, accompanying inebriated dancers on the cobbles outside. With such a venerable icon as a focus, the local August 15 *paniyíri* is one of the liveliest in Greece, let alone Lésvos.

The best **restaurants** are *Dhouladhelli*, on your left as you enter the village from the extreme south (bus stop) end, or *Dhayielles*, further along. At either of these spots you can eat for a fraction of the prices asked at the coastal resorts. There are a very few **rooms** available; ask at the *Anatoli* grill, between the two aforementioned restaurants.

Vaterá – and spas en route

A different bus route from Mytilíni leads to Vaterá beach via the inland villages of Polykhnítos and more attractive Vríssa. If you're after a hot bath, the small, domed spahouse 1500m east of Polyknítos has been well restored by an EU programme (Mon–Sat 7–11.30am & 4–7pm, Sun 7–11.30am; token admission); alternatively there are those at **Áyios Ioánnis** (token admission), fairly well signposted 2km below the village of Lisvóri. Flanking the chapel are two vaulted-chamber pools, though the water is odoriferous, iron-stained and best enjoyed on a cool evening.

VATERÁ itself is a huge, seven-kilometre-long sand beach, backed by vegetated hills; the swimming is delightfully calm and clean. The west end of this strip has several accommodation options, the nicest of the **hotels** clustered here being the Greek-and American-run *Vatera Beach* (☎0252/61 212, fax 61 164; ④). It also has a good attached restaurant with shoreline tables from where you can gaze on the cape of Áyios Fokás 3km to the west, where only foundations remain of a **temple of Dionysus** and a superimposed early Christian basilica. The **campsite** (*Dhionysos*) at Vaterá lies slightly inland from the portion of the beach east of the T-junction, where studio/villa units predominate. Here several more **tavernas** line the shore road, though none is especially brilliant and one (*Zouros*) is definitely to be avoided. If you intend to stay here you'll probably want your own transport, as the closest shops are 4km away at Vríssa, and the bus appears only a few times daily.

To the east, an intermittently paved road leads via Stavrós and hidden Ambelikó to either Ayiássos or Plomári within ninety minutes. When leaving the area going north towards Kalloní, the short cut via the coast guard base at **Akhladherí** is well worth using and is well paved despite tentative depiction on local maps.

Western Lésvos

The main road west of Loutrá Yéra is surprisingly devoid of settlement, with little to stop for before Kalloní other than the traces of an ancient **Aphrodite temple** at Mési (Messon), 1km north of the main road, and signposted just east of the Akhladherí turn-off. At the site (Tues–Sun 8.30am–3pm; free) just eleventh-century BC foundations and a few column stumps remain, plus the ruins of a fourteenth-century Genoese-built basilica; it was once virtually on the sea but a nearby stream has silted things up in the intervening millennia. All told, it's not worth a special trip, but certainly make the short detour if passing by – and brace yourself for the manically voluble caretaker.

KALLONÍ itself is an unembellished agricultural and market town more or less in the middle of the island, but you may spend some time here since it's the intersection of most bus routes. Some 3km south lies **SKÁLA KALLONÍS**, a principally Dutch and English package resort with a long, if coarse, beach on the lake-like gulf. Of the handful of restaurants, only the *Orange* merits a mention, though the bakery between the square and harbour does a good range of pies and croissants. **Cycle rental** – ideal for the flat terrain hereabouts – is the resort's main distinction; the other is its role as a **bird-watching** centre, attracting hundreds of twitchers for the spring nesting season in the adjacent salt marshes.

Inland monasteries and villages

West of Kalloní, the road winds 4km uphill to the **Monastery of Limónos**, founded in 1527 by the monk Ignatios. It is a huge complex, with just a handful of monks and lay workers to maintain three storeys of cells ringing the giant courtyard, adorned with strutting peacocks and huge urns with potted plants. Beside, behind and above are respectively an old-age home, a lunatic asylum and a hostel for pilgrims. The katholikón, with its carved-wood ceiling and archways, is built in Asia-Minor style and is traditionally off-limits to women; a sacred spring flows from below the west foundation wall. A former abbot established a **museum** (daily 9am–3pm, some evenings; 300dr) on two floors of the rear wing; the ground-floor ecclesiastical collection is good enough, but you should prevail upon the warden (easier done in large groups) to open the upper, ethnographic hall. The first room is a re-created Lesvian *salóni*, while the next is crammed with an indiscriminate mix of kitsch and priceless objects – Ottoman copper trays to badly stuffed egrets by way of brightly painted trunks – donated since 1980 by surrounding villages. An overflow of farm implements is stashed in a corner storeroom below, next to a chamber where giant *pithária* (urns) for grain and olive oil are embedded in the floor.

Beyond, the road west passes through Fília, where you can turn off for a time-saving short cut to Skoutáros and the north of Lésvos. Most traffic continues through to the tiered village of **SKALOKHÓRI**, its houses at the head of a valley facing the sea and the sunset, and **VATOÚSSA**, a landlocked and beautiful western settlement.

Some 8km beyond Vatoússa, a short track leads down to the sixteenth-century **Monastery of Perivolís** (daily 8am–7pm; pull on the bell rope for admission), built in the midst of a riverside orchard (*perivóli*). You should appear well before sunset, as only natural light is available to view the fine if faded frescoes in the narthex. In an apocalyptic panel worthy of Bosch, the *Earth and sea yield up their dead*, the whore of Babylon rides her chimaera and assorted sea-monsters disgorge their victims. On the north side you see a highly unusual iconography of *Abraham, the Virgin, and the penitent thief of calvary in paradise*. Further interest is lent by a humanized icon of Christ, under glass at the *témblon*.

ÁNDISSA, 3km further on, nestles under the west's only pine grove; at the edge of the village a sign implores you to "Come Visit Our Square", and that's not a bad idea, for the sake of its three enormous plane trees which shade several cafés and tavernas. Directly below Ándissa, a paved road leads 6km north to the fishing hamlet of **GAVATHÁS**, with a narrow, partly protected beach and a few places to eat and stay – such as the *Hotel Restaurant Paradise* (☎0253/56 376; ③). A dirt side track leads to the huge wave-battered beach of **Kámbos**, one headland east; you can keep going in the same direction, following signs pointing to "Ancient Andissa". They actually lead you to **Ovriókastro**, the most derelict of the island's Genoese castles, evocatively placed on a promontory within sight of Mólyvos.

Just beyond modern Ándissa there's an important junction. Keeping straight leads you past the still-functioning **Monastery of Ipsiloú**, founded in 1101 atop an extinct volcano and still home to four monks. The katholikón, tucked in one corner of a large, irregular courtyard, has a fine wood-lattice ceiling but had its frescoes repainted to detrimental effect in 1992; more intriguing are portions of Iznik tile stuck in the facade, and the handsome double gateway. Upstairs you can visit a fairly rich museum of ecclesiastical treasure (in theory 9am–3pm; small donation). Ipsiloú's patron saint is John the Theologian, a frequent dedication for monasteries overlooking apocalyptic landscapes like the surrounding parched, boulder-strewn hills.

Signposted just west is the turning for one of the main concentrations of specimens from Lésvos' rather overrated **petrified forest**, indicated by forest service placards which also warn of severe penalties for pilfering souvenir chunks. For once contemporary Greek arsonists cannot be blamed for the state of the trees, created by the combined action of volcanic ash and hot springs some fifteen to twenty million years ago. The other main cluster is south of Sígri (see below), but locals seem amazed that anyone would want to trudge though the barren countryside in search of them; upon arrival you may agree, since the mostly horizontal, two-to-three-metre-long sequoia chunks aren't exactly one of the world's wonders. If you're curious, there are a fair number of petrified logs strewn about the courtyard of Ipsiloú.

Sígri

SÍGRI, near the western tip of Lésvos, has an appropriately end-of-the-line feel accentuated by the recent local tourism slump. The bay here is guarded both by a Turkish **castle** and the long island of Nissopí, which protects the place somewhat from prevailing winds; accordingly it's an important NATO naval base, with the few weekly NEL ferries to Rafína, Áyios Efstrátios and Límnos obliged to dodge numbers of battleships anchored here. The eighteenth-century castle sports the sultan's monogram over the entrance, something rarely seen outside Istanbul, and a token of the high regard in which this productive island was held. A vaguely Turkish-looking church is in fact a converted **mosque**, while the town itself presents a drab mix of old and cement dwellings. The town **beach**, south of the castle headland, is narrow and hemmed in by the road; the far better beach of **Faneroméni** is 3.5km north by coastal dirt track from the northern outskirts of town, plus another 2km south, just below the fifteen-kilometre dirt track to Eressós; neither beach has any facilities.

If you want to **stay**, there's the *Hotel Nisiopi* (☎0253/54 316; ④), and a handful of **rooms**, including *Nelly's Rooms and Apartments* (☎0253/54 230; ③) looking right at the castle. Among very few **tavernas**, *Galazio Kyma* – the white building with blue trim, opposite the jetty – gets first pick of the fishermen's catch and can offer unbeatably fresh seafood.

Skála Eressoú

Most visitors to western Lésvos park themselves at the resort of **SKÁLA ERESSOÚ**, accessible via the southerly turning between Ándissa and Ipsiloú. The beach here, given additional character by an islet within easy swimming distance, runs a close second to Vaterá's, and consequently the place is beginning to rival Plomári and Mólyvos in visitor numbers – they form an odd mix of Brits, Scandinavians, Greek families, neo-hippies and lesbians (of whom, more below). Behind stretches the largest and most attractive agricultural plain on Lésvos, a welcome green contrast to the volcanic ridges above.

There's not much to Skála – just a roughly rectangular grid of perhaps five streets by eight, angling up to the oldest cottages on the slope of Vígla hill. The waterfront pedestrian zone (officially Papanikolí) is divided by a café-lined round platía mid-waterfront dominated by a bust of Theoprastus – the renowned botanist who hailed from **ancient Eressos**. This was not, as you might suppose, on the site of the modern inland village, but atop Vígla hill at the east end of the beach; some of the remaining citadel wall is still visible from a distance. Once on top the ruins prove even scantier, but it's worth the scramble up for the views – you can discern the ancient jetty submerged beyond the modern fishing anchorage.

Another famous reputed native of ancient Eressos was **Sappho**, and there are usually appreciable numbers of gay women here paying homage, particularly at the one hotel (*Antiopi*) devoted to their exclusive use, and in the clothing-optional zone of the beach west of the river mouth. In the river itself are about a hundred terrapins who have learned to come ashore for feeding and finger-nippings, so beware. Ancient Eressós endured into the Byzantine era, whose main legacy is the **Basilica of Áyios Andhréas** behind the modern church, merely foundations and an unhappily covered floor mosaic; the nearby museum of local odds and ends is even less compelling.

Skála has countless **rooms** and **apartments**, but ones near the sea fill early in the day or are block-booked by tour companies; in peak season often the best and quietest you can hope for is something inland overlooking a garden or fields. Late in the day it's wise to entrust the search to an agency, such as *Krenelos* (☎0253/53 246), just off the round "square"; you pay a small commission but it saves trudging about for vacancies. There are few bona fide **hotels**; longest established of these, well placed on the front if potentially noisy, is *Sappho the Eressia* (☎0253/53 233; ③).

Most **tavernas**, with elevated wooden dining platforms, crowd the beach; worthy ones, both on the eastern walkway, are *Iy Gorgona*, with friendly service and a large menu of Greek standards, and the British-run *Bennett's* at the far end of things opposite the islet. Inland, on the way to the museum, the *Aphrodite Home Cooking* taverna lives up to its name, with fair portions and comfortable garden seating. Back on the front, Canadian-run *Yamas* is the place for pancake breakfasts, veggie burgers, wholemeal bread and decadent chocolate desserts; they also function as an Anglophone bar at night. *Sympathy*, a few doors down, is coolly musical, with a mostly Greek-bohemian clientele. The gay women's contingent currently favours *Dhekati Mousa/Tenth Muse*, on the Theophrastos platía; a summer **cinema** further inland rounds up the nightlife.

Monastery on Nissyros

Orthodox priest

Venetian houses in the old harbour, Réthymnon

Windmill at sunset, Páros

View of Kástro and Khóra, Astypálea

Tomatoes drying, Khíos

Paleokhóra, Crete

Ferry at Foúrni

Church in Kástro, Síkinos

Café terrace, Kós

EITAN SIMANOR

CHARLES BOWMAN

Platía Ippokrátous, Rhodes Town

Shipwreck Bay, Zákynthos

MARC S. DUBIN

MARC S. DUBIN

Flagstone colours, Yialós, Sými Island

Kaïki-building, Pátmos, Dodecanese

Skála has an adjacent **post office** and **OTE**, a coin-op **laundry** near the church, and a cash dispenser booth on the seafront.

If you're returning to the main island crossroads at Kallóní, you can complete a loop from Eressós along the western shore of the Gulf of Kallóní via the hill villages of Mesótopos and Ágra; this route is currently all paved except for the first 11km out of Eressós, which should be asphalted by 1999.

Northern Lésvos

The main road north of Kallóní winds up a ridge and then down the other side into increasingly attractive country, stippled with poplars and blanketed by olive groves. Long before you can discern any other architectural detail, the silhouette of Mólyvos castle indicates your approach to the oldest established tourist spot on Lésvos.

Mólyvos (Míthymna)

MÓLYVOS (officially Míthymna), 61km from Mytilíni, is arguably the most beautiful village on Lésvos. Its tiers of sturdy, red-tiled houses, some standing defensively with their rear walls to the sea, mount the slopes between the picturesque harbour and the **Genoese castle** (Tues–Sun 8.30am–3pm; 500dr), which provides interesting rambles around its perimeter walls and views of Turkey across the straits. Closer examination reveals a score of weathered Turkish fountains along flower-fragrant, cobbled alleyways, a reflection of the fact that before 1923 Muslims constituted 35 percent of the local population and owned most of the finest mansions. You can try to gain admission to the Greek-built **Krallis** and **Yiannakos mansions**, or the municipal art gallery occupying the former residence of local author Argyris Eftaliotis, which hosts changing exhibits. The small **archeological museum** (Tues–Sun 8.30am–3pm; free) in the basement of the town hall, features finds from the ancient town, including blue Roman beads to ward off the evil eye (belief in this affliction is age-old and pan-Mediterranean). Archival photos depict the Greek conquest of the island in November 1912. Barely excavated **ancient Mithymna** to the northwest is of essentially specialist interest, though a necropolis has been unearthed next to the bus stop.

Modern dwellings and hotels have been sensibly banned from the preserved municipal core – the powerful Athenian watchdog group "Friends of Molyvos" has seen to that – but this has inevitably sapped all the authentic life from the upper bazaar; just one lonely tailor still plies his trade amongst the redundant souvenir shops. Having been cast as an upmarket resort, there are few phallic postcards or other tacky accoutrements in Mólyvos, but still constant reminders that you are strolling through a stage-set, however tasteful, for mass tourism.

PRACTICALITIES

The **town beach** is mediocre – though it improves somewhat as you head towards the southern end and a clothing-optional zone. Advertised **boat excursions** to bays as remote as Ánaxos and Tsónia (see pp.674 and pp.675) seem a frank admission of this failing; there are also six to eight daily **minibus shuttles** in season, linking all points between Ánaxos and Eftaloú.

The main sea-level thoroughfare, straight past the tourist office, heads towards the harbour; along it stands a number of bona fide **hotels**. These include *Adonis* (☎0253/71 866, fax 71 636; ④), comfortable enough though used as a brothel in winter, and the durable *Sea Horse* (☎0253/71 320; ④) down at the fishing harbour, fine if you're not interested in making an early night of it in season. For rooms, good choices to seek out include *Villa Ioanna* (☎0253/71 234; ③), an older house with painted ceilings; the modern studio units of Khryssí Bourdhadonaki (☎0253/72 193; ③), towards Ayía Kyriakí;

those of Panayiotis Baxevanellis (☎0253/71 558; ③), with a preponderance of double beds and a common kitchen; and the quiet, simple rooms of Varvara Kelesi (☎0253/71 460; ②), way up by the castle. Otherwise, rooms can be reserved through the municipal **tourist office** by the bus stop (daily: summer 8am–3pm & 6.30–8.30pm; spring & autumn 8.30am–3pm). The official **campsite**, *Camping Methymna*, lies 2km northeast of town on the Eftaloú road.

The sea view **tavernas** along the lower market lane of 17-Noemvríou are all much of a muchness, where you pay primarily for the view; it's far better to head down to the fishing port, where *The Captain's Table* combines the virtues of fresh seafood, meat grills and vegetarian mezédhes. The Irish-run *Galley*, hidden away by the little church, offers more westernized fare such as tomato-herb soup. Many consider the five-kilometre trip east to Vafiós worth it to patronize either *Taverna Vafios* or *Taverna Ilias*, especially the latter with its wonderful bread and bulk wine – avoid all fried dishes at either place and you'll be happier. Also highly recommended is *Iy Eftalou*, 4km northeast near the eponymous spa (see below), where the food and tree-shaded setting are splendid. For dessert, try the pudding-and-cake shop *El Greko* on the lower market lane, where the proprietor is a wonderful raconteur (in several languages).

Midsummer sees a short **festival** of music and theatre up in the castle. Night-owls are well catered for with a selection of **music bars**: the lively *Music Bazaar* and more sedate, retro *Skala* near the harbour; disco-ish *Congas Bar* below the shore road, and *Gatelouzi Piano Bar* near the Olive Press Hotel, a more genteel branch of state-of-the-art outdoor disco *Gatelouzi*, 3km towards Pétra, the place to be seen on a Saturday night. There's also an excellent, first-run summer **cinema** next to the taxi rank. Around the tourist office you'll find an automatic money-changing machine beside the National Bank, and numerous **motorbike** and **car rental** places. The main **post office** is near the top of the upper commercial street, with a seasonal branch on the shore road Mikhaíl Goútou.

Pétra and Ánaxos

Since there are political and practical limits to the expansion of Mólyvos, many package companies are now shifting their emphasis towards **PÉTRA**, 5km due south and marginally less busy. The town is beginning to sprawl untidily behind its broad sand beach and seafront square, and diners on the square regularly get sprayed by the exhaust fumes from buses, but the core of old stone houses, many with Levantine-style balconies overhanging the street, remains. Pétra takes its name from the giant rock monolith located some distance inland and enhanced by the eighteenth-century church of the **Panayía Glykofiloússa**, reached up over a hundred steps. Other local attractions include the sixteenth-century church of **Áyios Nikólaos**, with three phases of well preserved frescoes, and the intricately decorated **Vareltzídhena** mansion (Tues–Sun 8.30am–3pm; free guided tour).

There are a few small **hotels**, and a Women's Agricultural Tourism Cooperative (☎0253/41 238 or 41 340, fax 41 309), formed by Pétra's women in 1984 to offer something more unusual for visitors. In addition to operating an excellent, inexpensive **restaurant** on the square (which also serves as a tourist office, crafts shop and general information centre), they arrange **rooms** (②) in one of about 25 affiliated premises where advance reservations are usually needed. Aside from the cooperative's eatery, **tavernas** (like those behind the north beach) lack distinction, and you're better off either at the *Pittakos* ouzerí (dinner only) 100m south of the square, the old-fashioned *O Rigas* hidden in the back streets, or the *Grill Bar* right on the platía, ideal for a quick *souvláki* or octopus tentacle. At **Avláki**, 1.5km southwest en route to Ánaxos, there's an excellent, signposted eponymous taverna behind a tiny beach – well worth the trip out.

ÁNAXOS, 3km south of Pétra, is a jerry-built resort fringing by far the cleanest beach in the area: a kilometre of sand cluttered with sunbeds, pedaloes and not especially memorable snack bars. The blocks of **rooms** behind are fairly well monopolized by tour companies, and anyway you'd be plagued by mosquitoes from the river mouth. From anywhere along here you enjoy beautiful sunsets between and beyond three off-shore islets.

Around Mount Lepétymnos

East of Mólyvos, the villages of **Mount Lepétymnos**, marked by tufts of poplars, offer a day or two of rewarding exploration. The first stop, though not exactly up the hill, might be **Loutrá Eftaloú**, some rustic (and painfully hot) **thermal baths** 5km along the road passing the campsite. These are housed in an attractive, recently restored domed structure (always open; 200dr). Take a candle for nocturnal visits, and use it like a Swedish sauna – dashes out of the side door into the sea make subsequent immersion in the 44° water bearable. Nearby, there are a considerable number of luxury hotels and bungalow complexes, some surprisingly reasonable – the *Panselinos* (☎0253/71 904; ⑤) gets good marks.

The main road around the mountain first heads 5km east to **VAFIÓS**, with its two aforementioned **tavernas**, before curling north around the base of the peaks. Paving of this stretch should be complete by mid-1998, but twice-daily bus service back towards Mytilíni does not resume until Áryennos, 6km before the exquisite hill village of **SYKAMINIÁ** (Sykamiá), birthplace of the novelist Stratis Myrivilis. Below the "Plaza of the Workers' First of May", with its two traditional kafenía and views north to Turkey, one of the imposing basalt-built houses is marked as his childhood home. A marked trail shortcuts the twisting road down to **SKÁLA SYKAMINIÁS**, easily the most picturesque fishing port on Lésvos. Myrivilis used it as the setting for his best-known book, *The Mermaid Madonna*, and the tiny rock-top chapel at the end of the jetty will be instantly recognizable to anyone who has read the novel.

On a practical level, Skála has a few **pensions**, such as the central *Gorgona* (☎0253/55 301; ③), and four **tavernas**, the best and longest-lived of these being *Iy Skamnia* (aka *Iy Mouria*), with seating under the mulberry tree in which Myrivilis used to sleep on hot summer nights. In addition to good seafood, you can try the late-summer speciality of *kolokitholoúloudha yemistá* (stuffed squash blossoms). The only local beach, however, is the pebble strand of **Kayiá** 1.5km east, so Skála is perhaps better as a lunch stop rather than a base. A fairly rough, roller-coaster track follows the coast west back to Mólyvos.

Continuing east from upper Sykaminiá, you soon come to **KLIÓ**, whose single main street (marked "*kentrikí agorá*") leads down to a platía with a plane tree, fountain, kafenía and views across to Turkey. The village is set attractively on a slope, down which a six-kilometre dirt road, marked in English or Greek and better than maps suggest, descends to **Tsónia** beach. Here, 600m of beautiful pink volcanic sand has just a single taverna and another café at the fishing-anchorage end, and two new rooms places at the beach end.

South of Klió, the route forks at **KÁPI**, from where you can complete a loop of the mountain by bearing west along a mostly paved road. **PELÓPI** is the ancestral village of the unsuccessful 1988 US presidential candidate Michael Dukakis, and sports a former mosque now used as a warehouse on the main square. **IPSILOMÉTOPO**, the next village along, is punctuated by a minaret (but no mosque) and hosts revels on July 17, the feast of Ayía Marína. By the time you reach sprawling **STÍPSI**, you're almost back to the main Kalloní–Mólyvos road; there's a sporadic bus service out again, as well as a large **taverna** at the edge of town where busloads of tourists descend for "Greek Nights". There are also **rooms** to let, so Stípsi makes a good base for rambles along Lepétymnos' steadily dwindling network of trails; in recent years donkey-trekking has become more popular than walking, and you'll see outfitters advertising throughout the north of the island.

The main highway south from Klió and Kápi leads back to the capital through **MAN-DAMÁDHOS**. This attractive inland village is famous for its pottery, including the Ali-Baba style *pithária* (olive-oil urns) seen throughout Lésvos, but more so for the "black" icon of the Archangel Michael, whose enormous **monastery** (daily: summer 6am–10pm; winter 6.30am–7pm) in a valley just northeast, is the powerful focus of a thriving cult, and a popular venue for baptisms. The image – in legend made from a mixture of mud and the blood of monks slaughtered in a massacre – is really more idol than icon, both in its lumpy three-dimensionality and in the manner of veneration which seems a hangover from pagan times. First there was the custom of the coin wish, whereby you pressed a coin to the Archangel's forehead – if it stuck, your wish would be granted. Owing to wear and tear on the image, the practice is now forbidden, with supplicants referred to an alternative icon by the main entrance.

It is further believed that while carrying out his various errands on behalf of the faithful, the Archangel wears through more footwear than Imelda Marcos. Accordingly the icon was until recently surrounded not by the usual *támmata* (votive medallions) but by piles of miniature gold and silver shoes. The ecclesiastical authorities, embarrassed by these "primitive" practices, removed all the little shoes in 1986. Since then, a token substitute has re-appeared: several pairs of tin slippers which can be filled with money and left in front of the icon. Just why his devotees should want to encourage these perpetual peripatetics is unclear, since in Greek folklore the Archangel Michael is also the one who fetches the souls of the dying, and modern Greek attitudes towards death are as bleak as those of their pagan ancestors.

Límnos

Límnos is a prosperous agricultural island whose remoteness and peculiar ferry schedules have until now protected it from the worst excesses of the holiday trade. Most summer visitors are Greek, and as a foreign traveller, you're still likely to find yourself an object of curiosity and hospitality, though the islanders are becoming increasingly used to numbers of German and British visitors. Accommodation tends to be comfortable and pricey, with a strong bias towards self-catering units.

Among young Greek males, Límnos has a dire reputation, largely due to its unpopularity as an army posting; there is a conspicuous **military** presence, with the islanders making a good living off the soldiers and family members coming to visit. In recent years, the island has been the focus of disputes between the Greek and Turkish governments; Turkey has a long-standing demand that Límnos should be demilitarized and Turkish aircraft regularly overfly the island, serving to worsen already tense Greek–Turkish relations.

The bays of Bourniá and Moúdhros, the latter one of the largest natural harbours in the Aegean, almost divide Límnos in two. The west of the island is dramatically bare and hilly, with abundant volcanic rock put to good use as street cobbles and house masonry. Like most volcanic islands, Límnos produces excellent **wine** from westerly vineyards – a dry white of denomination quality – and some of the best retsina in Greece. The east is low-lying and speckled with marshes popular with duck-hunters, where it's not occupied by cattle, combine harvesters and vast cornfields.

Despite popular slander to that effect, Límnos is not flat, barren or treeless; much of the countryside consists of rolling hills, well vegetated except on their heights, and with substantial clumps of almond, myrtle, oak, poplar and mulberry trees. The island is, however, extremely dry, with irrigation water pumped from deep wells, and a limited number of potable springs. Yet various terrapin-haunted creeks bring sand to several long, sandy **beaches** around the coast, where it's easy to find a stretch to yourself – though there's no escaping the stingless jellyfish which periodically pour out of the

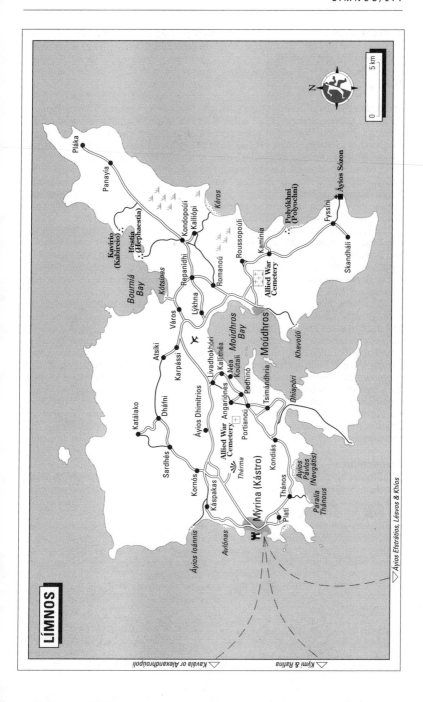

Dardanelles and die here in the shallows. On the plus side, beaches shelve gently, making them ideal for children, and they warm up early in summer, with no cool currents except near the river mouths.

Mýrina

MÝRINA (also called Kástro), the capital and port on the west coast, has the atmosphere of a provincial market town rather than of a resort. With five thousand inhabitants, it's pleasantly low-key, if not especially picturesque, apart from a core neighbourhood of old stone houses dating from the Ottoman occupation and the ornate Neoclassical mansions at Romeïkos Yialós. Few explicitly Turkish monuments have survived, though a fountain at the harbour end of Kýdha retains its inscription and is still highly prized for its drinking water. Most other things of interest line Kýdha/Karatzá, the main shopping street stretching from the harbour to **Romeïkós Yialós**, the beach and esplanade to the north of the castle, or Garoufalídhou, its perpendicular offshoot, roughly halfway along.

The originally Byzantine **castle** (access unrestricted), on a headland between the ferry dock and Romeïkós Yialós, is quite ruined despite later additions by the Genoese and Ottomans, but warrants a climb at sunset for views over the town, the entire west coast and – in exceptional conditions – over to Mount Áthos, 35 nautical miles west.

The **Archeological Museum** (Tues–Sun 8.30am–3pm; 600dr) occupies an old mansion behind Romeïkós Yialós, not far from the site of Bronze-Age Myrina in the suburb of Ríkha Nerá. Finds are assiduously labelled in Greek, Italian and English, and the entire premises are exemplary in terms of presentation – the obvious drawback being that the best items have been spirited away to Athens, leaving a collection that's essentially of specialist interest. The south ground-floor gallery is mainly devoted to pottery from Polyókhni (Polychni), the north wing contains more of the same plus items from ancient Myrina, while upstairs are galleries of post-Bronze-Age artefacts from Kavírio (Kabireio) and Ifestía (Hephaestia). The star upper-storey exhibits are votive lamps in the shape of **sirens**, found in an Archaic sanctuary at Hephaestia. Rather less vicious than Homer's creatures, they are identified more invitingly as the "muses of the underworld, creatures of superhuman wisdom, incarnations of a nostalgia for paradise". Another entire room is devoted to metalwork, of which the most impressive are gold jewellery and bronze objects, both practical (cheese graters) and whimsical (a snail).

Practicalities

The **airport** is 22km east of Mýrina, almost at the exact geographic centre of the island, sharing a runway with an enormous air-force base. Límnos is one of the few remaining destinations with a shuttle bus to and from the Olympic town terminal. **Ferries** dock at the southern end of the town, in the shadow of the castle.

The **bus station** is on Platía Eleftheríou Venizélou, at the north end of Kýdha. One look at the sparse schedules (only a single daily afternoon departure to most points, slightly more frequently to Kondiás and Moúdhros) will convince you of the need to **rent a vehicle**. Cars, motorbikes and bicycles can be had from either Myrina Rent a Car (☎0254/24 476), Petridou Tours (☎0254/22 039), Holiday (☎0254/24 357) or Auto Europe (☎0254/23 777); rates for bikes are only slightly above the island norm, but cars are expensive. A motorbike is generally enough to explore the coast and the interior, as there are few steep gradients but many perilously narrow village streets.

All three **banks**, two of them just off Kýdha flanking the **OTE**, have cash dispensers; the **post office** and Olympic airlines terminal are adjacent to each other on Garoufalídhou, with a laundry across the way by the Hotel Paris.

ACCOMMODATION

Despite Límnos' upmarket reputation, you may still be met off the boat with offers of a **room**. Otherwise, try the *Hotel Lemnos* (☎0254/22 153, fax 23 329; ④), by the harbour and available through Sunvil; the secluded *Apollo Pavillion* (☎ & fax 0254/23 712) on Frínis, a cul-de-sac about halfway along Garoufalídhou, with pricey hostel-type facilities in the basement (②) or large studios on the upper floors (③); or the quiet *Hotel Ifestos* in Andhróni district (☎0254/24 960, fax 23 623; ④) also available through Sunvil.

Romeïkós Yialós has several **pensions** housed in its restored houses, though all are affected by evening noise from the bars below; best value of the bunch is *Kosmos* at no. 21 (☎0254/22 050; ④). One block inland at Sakhtoúri 7, the *Pension Romeïkos Yialos* (☎0254; 23 787; ④) in a stone mansion is quieter. Just north of Romaïkós Yialós, the areas of Ríkha Nerá and Áyios Pandelímonas are likely bets for **self-catering units**; the best positioned are the hilltop *Afroditi Apartments* at Áyios Pandelímonas (☎0254/23 489; ⑤), again bookable through Sunvil. Finally, the *Akti Myrina* (☎0254/22 310, fax 22 352; winter ☎01/41 37 907) is a self-contained luxury complex of 110 wood-and-stone bungalows at the north end of Romeïkós Yialós, with all conceivable diversions and comforts. It's ferociously expensive – £180/$290 double half-board minimum in July – but costs considerably less if booked through a British tour operator.

There's no official campsite on Límnos, though Greek caravanners and campers tend to congregate at the north end of Platí beach (see below).

EATING AND DRINKING

About halfway along Kýdha, *O Platanos* serves traditional oven food on an atmospheric little square under two plane trees, while *Avra*, on the quay next to the port police, makes a good choice for a pre-ferry meal or an evening grill. **Seafood** is excellent on Límnos due to its proximity to the Dardanelles and seasonal fish migrations; accordingly there are no less than six tavernas arrayed around the little fishing port. There's little to distinguish their prices or menus, though *O Glaros* at the far end is considered the best – and works out slightly more expensive.

Not too surprisingly given the twee setting, the restaurants and bars along Romeïkós Yialós are pretty poor value except for a drink in sight of the castle – the northernmost bar often has live music. The tree-shaded tables of *Iy Tzitzífies* on the next bay north are a better option for beachfront dining.

Western Límnos

As town **beaches** go, Romeïkós Yialós is not at all bad, but if you're looking for more pristine conditions, head 3km north past *Akti Myrina* to **Avlónas**, unspoiled except for the *Porto Marina* luxury complex flanking it on the south. Some 6km from town you work your way through **KÁSPAKAS**, its north-facing houses in pretty, tiled tiers, before plunging down to **Áyios Ioánnis**. Here, the island's most unusual taverna features seating in the shade of a volcanic outcrop, with sandy coves beckoning beyond the fishing anchorage. If it's shut, *Taverna Iliovasilemata* to the south is good and friendly.

PLATÝ, 2km southeast of Mýrina, is a village of considerable architectural character, home also to three eating places. Best of these, 100m south of the pair on the main square, is the *Zimbabwe*, where the quality of the food (and the prices) belie its humble appearance. The long sandy **beach**, 700m below, is popular and usually jellyfish-free; except for the unsightly luxury compound at the south end, the area is still resolutely rural, with sheep wondering about at dawn and dusk. In the middle of the beach, the low-rise *Plati Beach Hotel* (☎0254/24 301, fax 23 583; ③) has an enviable position but is often full of package clients; there are basic rooms available at *Tzimis*

Taverna (☎0254/24 142; ③). More expensive, both for rooms and food, there's the poolside bar/restaurant attached to the tastefully landscaped *Villa Afroditi* (☎0254/23 141, fax 25 031; winter ☎01/96 41 910; ⑥), which has what could be the best buffet breakfast in Greece.

THÁNOS, roughly 2km to the southeast, seems a bigger version of Platý village, with a few tavernas and rooms in evidence; **Paralía Thánous**, a rough track ride below the village, is perhaps the most scenic of the southwestern beaches, with two tavernas, one (*O Nikos*) renting studio-apartments (☎0254/22 787; ③). Beyond Thános, the road curls over to the enormous beach at **Nevgátis** (Áyios Pávlos), flanked by weird volcanic crags on the west and reckoned to be the island's best. Despite this, there's only a seasonal drinks stall on the sand, and a taverna across the road.

Some 3km further along (11km from Mýrina), **KONDIÁS** is the island's third largest settlement, cradled between two hills tufted with Limnos's only pine forest. Stone-built, red-tiled houses combine with the setting to make Kondiás the most attractive inland village, though facilities are limited to a few noisy **rooms** above one of two kafenía. **Eating** is better at the two simple tavernas of **Dhiapóri**, 2km east, the shore annexe of Kondiás; the beach is unappealing, with the main interest lent by the narrow isthmus dividing the bays of Kondiás and Moúdhros.

Eastern Límnos

The shores of **Moúdhros bay**, glimpsed south of the trans-island road, are muddy and best avoided. The bay itself enjoyed considerable importance during World War I, when it served as the staging area for the unsuccessful Gallipoli campaign, and later saw the Ottoman surrender aboard the British warship HMS Agamemnon on October 30, 1918. The port of **MOÚDHROS**, the second largest town on Límnos, is a dreary place, with only a wonderfully kitsch, two-belfried church to recommend it. The closest decent beach is at **Khavoúli**, 4km south by dirt track and still far from the open sea. Yet there are three **hotels** here, including *To Kyma* (☎0254/71 333; ⑤), whose moderately priced restaurant is well placed for a lunch break when if you're visiting the archeological sites and beaches of eastern Límnos.

About 300m along the Roussopoúli road, you unexpectedly pass an **Allied military cemetery** (unlocked) maintained by the Commonwealth War Graves Commission, its neat lawns and rows of white headstones incongruous in such parched surroundings. In 1915, Moúdhros Bay was the principal base for the disastrous Gallipoli campaign. Of the 36,000 Allied dead, 887 are buried here, with 348 more at another graveyard near Portianoú – mainly battle casualties who died after having been evacuated to the base hospital at Moúdhros.

Indications of the most advanced Neolithic civilization in the Aegean have been unearthed at **Polyókhni (Polyochni)**, 3km from the gully-hidden village of **KAMÍNIA** (7km east of Moúdhros; two simple grill-tavernas). Since the 1930s, Italian excavations have uncovered four layers of settlement, the oldest from late in the fourth millennium BC, pre-dating Troy on the Turkish coast opposite; the town met a sudden, violent end from war or earthquake in about 2100 BC. The actual **ruins** (daily 9.30am–5.30pm; free) are of essentially specialist interest, though a *bouleuterion* (assembly hall) with bench seating, a mansion and the landward fortifications are labelled. During August and September the Italian excavators are about, and may be free to show you around the place. The site occupies a bluff overlooking a long, narrow rock-and-sand beach flanked by stream valleys.

Ifestía and Kavírio, the other significant ancient sites on Límnos, are reached via the village of Kondopoúli, 7km northeast of Moúdhros. Both sites are rather remote, and only feasible to visit if you have your own transport. Ifestía (Hephaestia), 4km from Kondopoúli by rough, signposted track, has little to offer non-specialists. **Kavírio**

(Kabireio), on the opposite shore of Tigáni Bay and accessed by the same road serving a new luxury complex, is more evocative. The ruins (daily 9.30am–3.30pm; free) are those of a sanctuary connected with the cult of the Samothracian Kabiroi (see p.683), though the site here is probably older. Little survives other than the ground plan, but the setting is undeniably impressive. Eleven column stumps stake out a stoa, behind eight spots marked as column bases in the telestirio or shrine where the cult mysteries took place. More engaging, perhaps, is a nearby sea-grotto identified as the Homeric **Spiliá toú Filoktíti**, where the Trojan war hero Philoctetes was abandoned by his comrades-in-arms until his stinking, gangrenous leg had healed. Landward access to the cave is via steps leading down from the caretaker's shelter.

The beach at **Kéros**, 2.5km by dirt road below **KALLIÓPI** (two snack bar/tavernas), is the best in this part of the island. A 1500-metre stretch of sand with dunes and shallow water, it attracts a number of Greek tourists and Germans with camper vans and windsurfers; a small drinks/snack bar operates near the parking area.

On the other side of Kondopoúli, reached via Repanídhi village, the pleasant if somewhat hard-packed beach of **Kótsinas** is set in the protected western limb of Bourniá Bay. The nearby anchorage offers a pair of tavernas and, up on a hill overlooking the jetty, a corroded, sword-brandishing statue of Maroula, a Genoese-era heroine who delayed the Ottoman conquest by a few years, and a large church of **Zoödhókhou Piyís** (the lifegiving spring). This is nothing extraordinary, but beside it 62 steps lead down through an illuminated tunnel in the rock to the brackish spring in question, oozing into a cool, vaulted chamber.

Áyios Efstrátios (Aï Strátis)

Áyios Efstrátios is without doubt one of the quietest and most isolated islands in the Aegean. Historically, the only outsiders to stay here were compelled to do so – it served as a place of exile for political prisoners under both the Metaxas regime of the 1930s and the various right-wing governments that followed the Civil War. It's still unusual for travellers to show up on the island, and, if you do, you're sure to be asked why you've come.

You may initially ask yourself the same question, for **ÁYIOS EFSTRÁTIOS** village – the only habitation on the island – is one of the ugliest in Greece. Devastation caused by an earthquake in 1967 which killed half the population, was compounded by the reconstruction plan: the contract went to a company with junta connections, who prevented the survivors from returning to their old homes and used army bulldozers to raze even those that could have been repaired. From the hillside, some two dozen structures of the old village overlook its replacement, whose grim rows of prefabs constitute a sad monument to the corruption of the junta years. If you're curious, there's a photograph of the village taken before the earthquake in the kafenío by the port.

Architecture apart, Áyios Efstrátios still functions as a very traditional fishing and farming community, with the prefabs set at the mouth of a wooded stream valley draining to the harbour beach. Tourist amenities consist of just two very basic **tavernas** and a single **pension** in one of the surviving old houses, which is likely to be full in the summer, so call in advance (☎0254/93 202; ②). Nobody will object, however, if you **camp** at the far end of the town beach.

As you walk away from the village – there are few cars and no real roads – things improve rapidly. The landscape, dry hills and valleys scattered with a surprising number of oak trees, is deserted apart from wild rabbits, sheep, an occasional shepherd, and some good beaches where you can camp in isolation. **Alonítsi**, on the north coast – a ninety-minute walk from the village following a track up the north side of the valley – is a two-kilometre stretch of sand with rolling breakers and views across to Límnos.

South of the village, there's a series of greyish sand beaches, most with wells and drinkable water, although with few proper paths in this part of the island, getting to them can be something of a scramble. **Lidharío**, at the end of an attractive wooded valley, is the first worthwhile beach, but again it's a ninety-minute walk, unless you can persuade a fisherman to take you by boat. Some of the caves around the coast are home to the rare Mediterranean monk seal, but you're unlikely to see one.

Ferries between Límnos and Kavála to Rafína call at Áyios Efstrátios every two or three days throughout the year; in summer a small Límnos-based ferry, the Aiolis, calls twice a week. Despite recent harbour improvements, this is still a very exposed anchorage, and in bad weather you could end up stranded here far longer than you bargained for. If an indefinite stay does not appeal, it's best to visit from Límnos on the day-trip offered by the Aiolis (usually Sun).

Samothráki (Samothrace)

After Thíra, **Samothráki** has the most dramatic profile of all the Greek islands. Originally colonized by immigrants from Thrace, Anatolia and Lésvos, it rises abruptly from the sea in a dark mass of granite, culminating in 1611-metre Mount Fengári. Seafarers have always been guided by its imposing outline, and in legend its summit provided a vantage point for Poseidon to watch over the siege of Troy. The forbidding coastline provides no natural anchorage, and landing is still very much subject to the vagaries of the notoriously bad local weather. Yet despite these difficulties, for over a millennium pilgrims journeyed to the island to visit the **Sanctuary of the Great Gods** and to be initiated into its mysteries. The Sanctuary remains the outstanding attraction of the island, which, too remote for most tourists (except during July and August), combines earthy simplicity with natural grandeur.

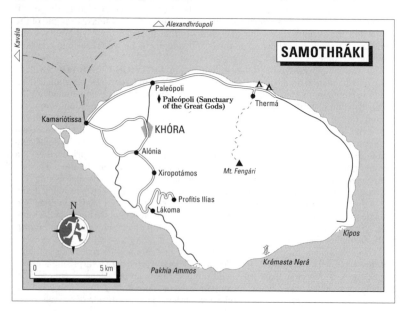

Kamariótissa and Khóra

Ferries and hydrofoils dock at the somewhat shabby and uninteresting port of **KAMARIÓTISSA**, where you're unlikely to want to stay long. There are nonetheless three hotels behind the tree-lined seafront and various rooms for rent in the maze of streets behind. As on most islands with a short season, accommodation is pricey for what you get, and bargaining is usually unproductive, especially in midsummer. Turning left as you step ashore, the first – and cheapest – hotel is the spartan *Kyma* (☎0551/41 263; ②); rooms overlooking the water can get noise from the *barákia* which constitute Samothráki's main **nightlife**. Calmer, but ridiculously pricey, is the *Niki Beach* (☎0551/41 545; ⑤) at the far north end of the quay. The seafront is also lined with **tavernas**, but the best one – *Orizontas*, with quick-served *mayireftá* and bulk wine – is slightly inland on the Khóra road.

Motorbikes and **cars** are in short supply, so it's worth grabbing one immediately on disembarkation – or reserving a bike in advance from Khanou Brothers (☎0551/41 511) or a car from Niki Tours (☎0551/41 465). The latter is also the Olympic Airways and main ferry/hydrofoil **agent**. As with lodging, rented transport is expensive by island standards, but if you've the means go for a car, as island roads are dangerously windswept for those on bikes. Note that there is only one **fuel pump** on the entire island, 1km above the port en route to Khóra. Kamariótissa also has a **bank** (no cash dispenser) but no post office.

Buses six times daily in season (but only twice weekly in winter) along the north coast to Thermá via Palaeópoli (the site of the Sanctuary) or Karyótes, or directly inland seven times daily to **KHÓRA**, the largest village and island capital. Far larger than implied by the portion visible from the sea, its attractive, whitewashed Thracian-style houses lie around a hollow in the western flanks of Mount Fengári, dominated by the Genoese Gateluzzi fort, of which little survives other than the gateway. Khóra has no reliable short-term **accommodation**, though asking for unadvertised rooms in the various kafenía along the winding commercial street may be productive. On the atmospheric, irregularly shaped platía, the *Iy Platia* ouzerí and the more down-to-earth *To Kastro* taverna between them provide the best (and not vastly overpriced) **suppers** on the island, with such delicacies as stuffed squid and *mýdhia saganáki*. Away from the square is the pleasant breakfast and evening **bar** *To Stenaki*, offering real coffee and a mix of good Greek and foreign music. There have been mutterings of moving the administrative capital down to Kamariótissa, but until further notice the island's **post office**, **OTE** branch and **tourist police** (☎0551/41 203) are found here.

The Sanctuary of the Great Gods

A wide but rough track leads north from Khóra to the hamlet of Paleópoli (see p.684), and, in a stony ravine between it and the plunging northeastern ridge of Mount Fengári, lie the remains of the **Sanctuary of the Great Gods**. From the late Bronze Age to the early Byzantine era, the mysteries and sacrifices of the cult of the Great Gods were performed on Samothráki, indeed in ancient Thracian dialect until the second century BC. The island was the spiritual focus of the northern Aegean, and its importance in the ancient world was comparable (although certainly secondary) to that of the Mysteries of Eleusis.

The religion of the Great Gods revolved around a hierarchy of ancient Thracian fertility figures: the Great Mother Axieros, a subordinate male deity known as Kadmilos, and the potent and ominous twin demons the *Kabiroi*, originally the local heroes Dardanos and Aeton. When the Aeolian colonists arrived (traditionally c 700 BC) they simply syncretized the resident deities with their own – the Great Mother became

Cybele, her consort Hermes, and the *Kabiroi* were fused interchangeably with the *Dioskouroi* Castor and Pollux, patrons of seafarers. Around the nucleus of a sacred precinct the newcomers made the beginnings of what is now the Sanctuary.

Despite their long observance, the mysteries of the cult were never explicitly recorded, since ancient writers feared incurring the wrath of the *Kabiroi* (who could brew up sudden, deadly storms), but it has been established that two levels of initiation were involved. Both ceremonies, in direct opposition to the elitism of Eleusis, were open to all, including women and slaves. The lower level of initiation or *myesis* may, as is speculated at Eleusis, have involved a ritual simulation of the life, death and rebirth cycle; in any case, it's known that it ended with joyous feasting and it can be conjectured, since so many clay torches have been found, that it took place at night. The higher level of initiation or *epopteia* carried the unusual requirement of a moral standard (the connection of theology with morality so strong in the later Judeo-Christian tradition was rarely made by the early Greeks). This second level involved a full confession followed by absolution and baptism in bull's blood.

The site

The **site** (Tues–Sun 8.30am–3pm; 600dr) is well labelled, simple to grasp and strongly evokes its proud past. It's a good idea to visit the **museum** first (open same hours as site; 600dr), with exhibits spanning all eras of habitation, from the Archaic to the Byzantine. Highlights among these include a frieze of dancing girls from the propylon of the temenos, entablatures from different parts of the Sanctuary, and Roman votive offerings such as coloured glass vials from the necropolis of the ancient town east of the Sanctuary.

The **Anaktoron** or hall of initiation for the first level of the mysteries, dates in its present form from Roman times. Its inner sanctum was marked by a warning *stele* (now in the museum) and at the southeast corner you can make out the **Priestly Quarters**, an antechamber where candidates for initiation donned white gowns. Next to it is the **Arsinoeion**, the largest circular ancient building known in Greece, used for libations and sacrifices. Within its rotunda are the walls of a double precinct (fourth century BC) where a rock altar, the earliest preserved ruin on the site, has been uncovered. A little further south, on the same side of the path, you come to the **Temenos**, a rectangular area open to the sky where the feasting probably took place, and, edging its rear corner, the conspicuous **Hieron**. Five columns and an architrave of the facade of this large Doric edifice (which hosted the higher level of initiation) have been erected; dating in part from the fourth century BC, it was heavily restored in Roman times. The stone steps have been replaced by modern blocks, but Roman benches for spectators remain in situ, along with the sacred stones where confession was heard.

To the west of the path you can just discern the outline of the **theatre**, while just above it, tucked under the ridge is the **Nymphaeum (Fountain) of Nike**, famous for the exquisitely sculpted marble centrepiece – the *Winged Victory of Samothrace* – which once stood breasting the wind at the prow of a marble ship. It was discovered in 1863 by the French and carried off to the Louvre, with a copy belatedly forwarded to the local museum. Due west of the theatre, occupying a high terrace, are remains of the main **stoa**; immediately north of this is an elaborate medieval fortification made entirely of antique material.

The rest of the island

The only accommodation near the site itself is in the tiny hamlet of **PALEÓPOLI**, where the old and basic *Xenia Hotel* (☎0551/41 166; ③) tries hard to compete with the *Kastro Hotel* (☎0551/41 001; ⑤), which comes with pool and restaurant; there are also some basic but en-suite **rooms** (③) down on the seashore below the *Kastro*. Four kilometres east, near Karyótes, is the much smaller *Elektra* (π0551/98 243; ④), though despite the family feel here, the lack of a restaurant means you may prefer to be nearer the action – such as it is – in Thermá (Loutrá), a further 2km east.

With its running streams, giant plane trees and namesake hot springs, **THERMÁ** is one of the better places to stay on Samothráki, although it's packed in late July and August, mainly with an odd mixture of German hippies and elderly Greeks here to take the waters. These are dispersed in three facilities: the sterile, junta-era main **baths** (daily 8am–1pm & 5–7pm; 400dr); the *psarováthres* or "fish ponds", a trio of pleasantly rustic open-air pools with a wooden sun-shade; and a small cottage with a very hot pool (keys from the warden of the main baths). The latter two facilities are reached by a dirt road starting above and to the right as you face the "improved" spa. The low waterfalls and rock pools of **Gría Váthra** are signposted 1500m up the paved side road leading east from the main Thermá access drive.

Thermá is a rather dispersed place, with a small jetty under construction to hopefully receive hydrofoils in calm weather. **Accommodation** includes the *Kaviros Hotel* (π0551/98 277, fax 98 278; ⑤), just east of the "centre", and – further dowhill, 700m from the beach – the *Mariva Bungalows* (π0551/98 258; ③). None of the four **tavernas** in "central" Thermá is very inspired, a possible result (or cause) of a predominance in self-catering rooms; *Paradhisos* has the best setting and charges accordingly. Near the *Mariva Bungalows*, *Iphestos* is lively and popular; try the roast goat or chicken. At the bus stop, *Kafenio Ta Therma* doubles as the nightspot for Greek and foreign hippies; about halfway along the track to Gría Váthra, *Shelter Pub* occupies the old schoolhouse.

Beyond Thérma, on the wooded coastline, are two municipal **campsites**: the first, 1500m from the village, although large, has no facilities except toilets, while the second, 3km from the village, is more expensive but has hot water, electricity, a small shop, restaurant and bar. The bus from Kamariótissa usually passes both sites.

Beaches on Samothráki's north shore are uniformly pebbly and exposed, but it's still worth continuing along the road east from Thermá. At **Cape Foniás** there's a Gateluzzi watchtower, and 45 minutes' walk inland along the stream, there are waterfalls and cold pools much more impressive than at Gría Váthra. The road surface ends at Foniás, but you can bump along the dirt road beyond to its end, 15km from Thermá at **Kípos** beach, a long strand facing the Turkish-held island of Ímvros. There's a rock overhang for shelter at one end, a spring, shower and summer drinks *kantína*, but no food available.

From the warmer south flank of the island, you've fine views out to sea, as well as looming Ímvros, now officially Gökçeada. Up to three daily buses go as far as **PROFÍTIS ILÍAS**, an attractive hill village with good tavernas but no place to stay, via Lákoma. From the latter a wide, eight-kilometre dirt track, passable for cars, leads east to **Pakhiá Ámmos**, an 800-metre sandy beach with a taverna-rooms place (π0551/94 235; ③) at the west end. The nearest (meagre) supplies are at Lákoma, but this doesn't deter big summer crowds who also arrive by excursion kaïkia. These also continue east to **Vátos**, a secluded (nudist) beach also accessible by land, the **Kremastá Nerá** coastal waterfalls, and finally Kípos beach (see above).

Thássos

Just 12km from the mainland, **Thássos** has long been a popular resort island for northern Greeks, and since the early 1990s has attracted a cosmopolitan variety of foreign tourists, drawn by the fame of French School excavations here. Accordingly, it's far from unspoiled, but there is only one mega-resort complex, so enclaves of bars and discos haven't completely swamped ordinary Greek rural life. Besides marble and olives, beekeeping, fruit and nuts are important products. Beehives often line the roadsides, and local honey or candied walnuts can be purchased everywhere. *Tsípouro* rather than

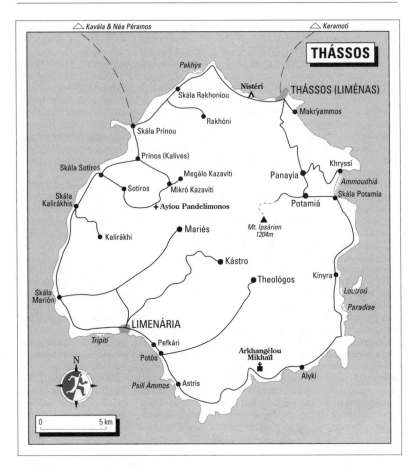

Kavála & Néa Péramos — Keramotí

THÁSSOS

Pakhýs

Nistéri

THÁSSOS (LIMÉNAS)

Skála Rakhoníou

Makrýammos

Rakhóni

Skála Prínou

Prínos (Kalíves)

Khryssí

Skála Sotíros

Megálo Kazavíti

Panayía

Ammoudhiá

Sotíros

Mikró Kazavíti

Skála Potamía

Skála
Kalirákhis

Ayíou Pandelímonos

Potamiá

Kalirákhi

Mariés

Mt. Ipsárion
1204m

Kástro

Kínyra

Theológos

Loutroú

Skála
Marión

Paradise

LIMENÁRIA

Tripití

Pefkári

Arkhangélou
Mikhaíl

Potós

Alyki

N

Psilí Ámmos   Astrís

0   5 km

wine is the main local tipple; pear extract, onions or spices like cinnamon or anise are
added to homemade batches.

Inhabited since the Stone Age, Thássos was settled by Parians in the seventh
century BC, attracted by gold deposits between modern Liména and Kínyra. Buoyed
by revenues from these, and from silver mines under Thassian control on the mainland
opposite, the ancient city-state here became the seat of a medium-sized seafaring
empire. Commercial acumen did not spell military invincibility however; the Persians
under Darius swept the Thasian fleets from the seas in 492 BC, and in 462 Athens permanently deprived Thássos of its autonomy after a three-year siege. The main port continued to thrive into Roman times, but lapsed into Byzantine and medieval obscurity.

Thássos is just small enough to circumnavigate in one full day on a rented motorbike
or car, which would give you an idea where you'd want to base yourself. The KTEL will
do the driving for you – albeit with little chance for stopping – some six times daily. **Car
rental** is dominated by Potos Care Rental (☎0593/23 969), with branches in all main
resorts, or Rent-a-Car Thassos (☎0593/22 535), also widely represented.

Liménas

LIMÉNAS (also known as Limín or Thássos), is the island's capital, though not the only port. Kavála-based ferries stop down the coast at Skála Prínou, with a KTEL bus always on hand to meet arrivals. The town, though largely modern, is partly redeemed by its pretty fishing harbour and the substantial remains of the ancient city which appear above and below the streets.

With its mineral wealth and safe harbour, **ancient Thássos** prospered from Classical to Roman times. The largest excavated area is the **agora**, a little way back from the fishing harbour. The site (free) is fenced but not always locked, and is best seen towards dusk. Prominent are two Roman *stoas* but you can also make out shops, monuments, passageways and sanctuaries from the remodelled Classical city. At the far end of the site (away from the sea) a fifth-century BC passageway leads through to an elaborate sanctuary of Artemis, a good stretch of Roman road and a few seats of the *odeion*. The archeological museum is shut until 1999 for extensive expansion, the new wings designed to accommodate a huge backlog of finds.

From a temple of Dionysos behind the fishing port, a path curls up to a **Hellenistic theatre**, fabulously positioned above a broad sweep of sea. It's currently out of bounds for excavations, though summer drama performances will be re-instituted in the future. On the same corner of the headland as the theatre, you can still see the old-fashioned kaḯkia being built, and gaze across to the uninhabited islet of Thassopoúla. It's possible to **rent boats** from the fishing harbour, self-skippered or not, to take you there and elsewhere.

From just before the theatre, the trail winds on to the acropolis, where a **Venetian-Byzantine-Genoese fort** arose between the thirteenth and fifteenth centuries constructed from recycled masonry of an Apollo temple which stood here. You can continue, following the remains of a massive circuit of fifth-century **walls** to a high terrace supporting the foundations of the **Athena Polyoukhos** (Athena Patroness of the City) temple, with Cyclopean walls. An artificial cavity in the rock outcrop just beyond was a **shrine of Pan**, shown in faint relief playing his pipes. From behind the summit, a rock-hewn **stairway** provided a discrete escape route to the Gate of Parmenon, the only gate to have retained its lintel; it's named from an ancient inscription ("Parmenon Made Me") on a nearby wall slab. From here a track, then a paved lane descend through the southerly neighbourhoods of the modern town, for a satisfying one-hour circuit.

Practicalities

Given the package-resort ethos, cuisine is not Liménas' strong point, and is generally overpriced. The picturesque **tavernas** at the old harbour are predictably touristy, and greasy fast food is all too abundant. A dependable favourite serving *mayireftá* is *Iy Piyi*, up at the south corner of the main square, next to the natural sunken spring of the name. Carnivores should head for *Vasilis's Grill*, on a pedestrian lane north of the square. A more recent entry on the scene is the eminently reasonable *Iy Stoa* ouzerí, on the waterfront near the Hotel Alkyon. Finally, *Orestis*, at the northwest corner of the square near *Iy Piyi*, serves the best ice cream on the island. By contrast, there's plenty of choice in local **bars**. *Full Moon* and the co-managed *Anonymous Cafe* near the *Hotel Amfipolis* are the Anglophile watering-holes; *Platia Cafe Bar* on yet another corner of the basilica square, has good music; while *Marina's Bar* near the *Hotel Alkyon* is the best waterfront nightspot, with a mainly Greek clientele.

Mountain- and motor-bikes can be had from Billy's Bikes (☎0593/22 490) or Thomai Tsipou (☎0593/22 815). The KTEL is on the front, virtually opposite the ferry mooring; the service is good, with regular daily buses to Panayía and Skála Potamiás,

Limenária via Potós, Theológos, Kínyra and Alykí. Thassos Tours (☎0593/23 250), at the east end of the waterfront, is the agent for Olympic Airways (closest airport at Khryssoúpoli on the mainland). The Ethniki/National and Emboriki/Commercial **banks** have cash dispensers.

ACCOMMODATION

At first glance Liménas – plagued with vehicle traffic and often noisy bars – seems an unlikely resort, with few **hotels** enjoying much in the way of calm or views. Despite this, there are some worthy finds; if none from the list below suits, there's also a zone in the southwest of town with a few relatively quiet rooms (②). The closest **campsite** to town is the good one at Nistéri cove, 2.5km west.

Akropolis (☎0593/22 488). Occupying a fine traditional house with flagstone floors, though it can get traffic noise; worth a try at slow times. ③.

Alkyon (☎0593/22 148, fax 25 662). Certainly the quietest of the harbour hotels; English tea and breakfast, plus friendly, voluble management make it a home from home for independent British travellers. Open most of the year; ask also about their cottage in Sotíros and beach villa at Astrís. ③.

Amfipolis (☎0593/23 101, fax 22 110). Housed in a folly, this is the town's most exclusive outfit – and you pay dearly for the privilege, though a package booking may yield some savings over rack rates. ⑥.

Athanasia (☎0593/23 247). Giant and eccentrically furnished rooms with balconies; take the lane inland from behind the *Xenia Hotel* to reach it. Run by a friendly fisherman, this place takes the overflow from the *Alkyon*. ③.

Dionysos (☎0593/22 198). Smallish, en-suite hotel just east of the central square, but quiet despite its location. ③.

Lena (☎0593/22 933). Good-value hotel near the post office, with English-speaking management; no packages. ③.

Mirioni (☎0593/23 256, fax 22 132). Excellent value, well run and allergic to package companies: enough said. It's co-managed with the more comfortable *Victoria* (④) next door, with which it shares a common breakfast room. ③.

Around the coast

Whether you plan to circumnavigate the island clockwise, or in the opposite direction, plan on a lunch stop at **Alykí**, roughly a third of the way along in the sequence described below.

Panayía, Potamiá and Mount Ipsárion

The first beach east of Liménas, **Makrýammos**, is an expensive playground for package tourists, so it's best to carry on to **PANAYÍA**, the attractive hillside village overlooking Potamiá Bay. It's a large, thriving place where life revolves around the central square with its large plane trees, fountain and slate-roofed houses. Top **accommodation** choice is the *Hotel Thassos Inn* (☎0593/61 612, fax 61 027; ④), up in the Tris Piyés district near the Kímisis church, with fine views over the rooftops. Second choice, slightly lower down, is the vine-shrouded *Hotel Theo* (☎0593/61 284; ④), more old fashioned but with a nice ground-floor bar. Down on the main road, beside the municipal car park, the newish, clean *Pension Stathmos* (☎0593/61 666; ④) is the quietest of several nearby, with stunning views out the back. There's reasonable **food** at *Iy Thea*, a view-terrace psistariá at the southeast edge of town en route to Potamiá.

POTAMIÁ, much lower down in the river valley, is far less prepossessing and thus little visited, though it has a lively winter carnival. It also offers the **Polygnotos Vayis Museum** (Tues–Sat 9am–1pm, summer also 6–9pm, Sun 10am–2pm; free), devoted to the locally born sculptor; though Vayis emigrated to America when young, he bequeathed most of his works to the Greek state. Potamiá also marks the start of the commonest route up to the 1204-metre summit of **Mount Ipsárion**. Follow the bull-dozer track to the big spring near the head of the valley extending west of the village (last water here), where you'll see the first red-painted arrows on trees. Beyond this point, cairns mark the correct turnings in a modern track system; forty minutes above the spring, take an older, wide track, which ends ten minutes later at a gulch and the current trailhead. The path is steep, strenuous and unmaintained, and you'll be depen-dent on cairns and painted arrows. Go early in the day or season, and allow for three-and-a-half hours up from Potamiá, and nearly as much for the descent.

Skála Potamiás and Khryssí Ammoudhiá

The onward road from Potamiá is lined with *dhomátia-* and apartment-type accommo-dation. Just before reaching the coast at **SKÁLA POTAMIÁS** at the southern end of the bay, the road splits: the right fork leads to Skála itself and some fairly uninspired tavernas; the left-hand option brings you to sand dunes extending all the way to the far end. An honourable exception amongst the **tavernas** is *Flor International* (no sign), at the corner where the bus turns around; the best places to **stay** would be either above the square amongst the vegetation – try *Hera* (☎0593/61 467; ③) – or north along the shore towards the sandy beach, in rooms to either side of the *Arion* (☎0593/61 486; ④) and *Anna* (☎0593/61 070; ④) hotels, themselves often booked by tours. The *Hotel Delfini*, quietly placed 100m back from the road (☎0593/61 462; ③), is also recom-mended. The north end of this beach is called **KHRYSSÍ AMMOUDHIÁ**, merely another cluster of tavernas, hotels and a campsite; a separate road (no bus service) descends the 5km from Panayía. Once there, you can choose between the self-catering *Villa Khrysafis* (☎0593/61 979; ⑤), or the elderly, twin premises of the *Phedra* (☎0593/61 471; ③) or *Golden Sand* hotels (☎0593/61 474; ③). The *Golden Beach* **camp-site** (☎0593/61 472) is the only official one on this side of the island.

Kínyra and Alykí

The tiny hamlet of **KÍNYRA**, some 24km south of Liménas, is overlooked by depressing burned zone and endowed with a poor beach, a couple of grocery stores and several small **hotels**. Those not block-booked include *Villa Athina* (☎0593/41 214; ②), whose top-floor rooms see the water over the olive trees, and the welcoming *Pension Marina* (☎0593/31 384; ②). There are few independent tavernas – try asking for half board from your hosts. Kínyra is convenient for the superior beaches of **Loutroú** (1km south) and **Paradise** (3km along), officially Makrýammos Kinýron. The latter ranks as most scenic of all Thassian beaches, with still-forested cliffs inland and a namesake islet offshore beyond the extensive shallows, with much cleaner water than at Khyrssí Ammoudhiá.

The south-facing coast of Thássos has the balance of the island's best beaches. **ALYKÍ** hamlet, 35km from Liménas, faces a perfect double bay which almost pinches off a headland. Alone of Thassian seaside settlements, it retains its original architecture as the presence of extensive antiquities here has led to a ban on local development. The ruins include an ancient temple to an unknown deity, and two exquisite early Christian basilicas out on the headland, with a few columns re-erected. The sand-and-pebble west bay, with its four tavernas, gets oversubscribed in peak season, though you can always get away to the less crowded east cove, or snorkel off the marble formations on the headland's far side. Among the **tavernas**, *O Glaros* up on the north hillside is the old-est and considered the best by island regulars. The *Koala Café* down on the sand pro-vides a semblance of **nightlife**, and there are a half-a-dozen **rooms** establishments, beginning beside *O Glaros* and trailing out along the main highway.

Arkhangélou Mikhaïl to Potós

Some 5km west of Alykí, the **convent of Arkhangélou Mikhaïl** (open reasonable daylight hours) clings spectacularly to a cliff on the seaward side of the road. Though founded in the twelfth century above the spot where a spring had gushed forth, it has been hideously renovated by the nuns resident here since 1974. A dependency of Filothéou on Mount Áthos (see p.390), its prize relic is a purported nail from the Crucifixion.

At the extreme south tip of Thássos, 9km further west, **ASTRÍS** (Astrídha) can muster two medium-sized hotels, a few rooms and a good beach. Just 1km west is another beach, **Psilí Ámmos**, with watersports on offer. After Liménas, **POTÓS** is the island's prime package venue, and is very densely built up. However, the kilometre-long beach to the south is still unspoiled, and on the semi-pedestrianized seafront, the original taverna *Iy Mouria* remains one of the cheaper and better places; next door, *Michael's Place* has great ice cream. There are plenty of rental outlets for cars, scooters and mountain bikes, including the headquarters of Potos Rent a Car; Potós is also the southernmost port for the summer hydrofoils which call at all west-coast resorts. **Pefkári** with its manicured beach, 1km west, is essentially an annexe of Potós, with high-rent resort complexes, but there are also more modest **accommodation** options such as *Prasino Veloudho* (☎0593/52 001, fax 51 232; ③).

Limenária and the west coast

LIMENÁRIA, the island's second town, was built to house German mining executives brought in by the Ottomans at the turn of the century. Their remaining mansions, scattered on the slopes above the harbour, lend some character, and the municipality has made a stab at prettifying the waterfront, but it remains one of the least attractive spots on Thássos, handy mainly for its **banks** and **post office**. At the east end of the quay, in some 1960s blocks, are a cluster of very basic **hotels** such as the *Menel* (☎0593/51 396; ③), with mostly Greek clientele. There are also plenty of **rooms** on offer, and a **campsite** between Limenária and Pefkári: the *Pefkari* (☎0593/51 190; June–Sept). For **eating** out, the *Pelikanos* restaurant (supper only) is noted for its soups among other dishes. The closest good beach is unsignposted **Trypití**, a couple of kilometres west – turn left into the pines at the start of a curve right. All development is well inland from the broad, 800-metre long strand, though there are umbrellas and chaise longues for rent.

Continuing clockwise from Limenária to Thássos town, there's progressively less to stop off for. The various *skáles* such as Skála Kalirákhis and Skála Sotíros are bleak, straggly and windy. **SKÁLA MARIÓN**, 13km from Limenária, is the exception that proves the rule: an attractive little bay, with fishing boats hauled up on the sandy foreshore, and the admittedly modern low-rise village arrayed in a U-shape all around. There are **rooms** available, a few tavernas, and most importantly two fine beaches to either side. **SKÁLA PRÍNOU** has little to recommend it, other than ferry connections to Kavála. Buses are usually timed to coincide with the ferries, but if you want to stay, there are several **hotels**, numerous **rooms**, quayside **tavernas** and an EOT **campsite** (☎0593/71 171; June–Sept) 1km south of the ferry dock. **SKÁLA RAKHONÍOU**, between here and Liménas, has more accommodation (including the *Perseus* campsite) and fish restaurants, as well as proximity to **Pakhýs** beach, 9km short of Liménas, and by far the best strand on the northwest coast. Narrow dirt tracks lead past various tavernas through surviving pines to the sand, partly shaded in the morning.

The interior

Few people get around to exploring inland Thássos – with the post-fire scrub barely waist-high, it's not always rewarding – but there are several worthwhile excursions to or around the hill villages besides the aforementioned trek up Mount Ipsárion from Potamiá.

From Potós you can head 10km up a good road to **THEOLÓGOS**, founded in the sixteenth century by refugees from Constantinople, which was the island's capital under the Ottomans (the last Muslims only departed after 1923). Its houses, most with oversized chimneys and slate roofs, straggle in long tiers to either side of the main street, surrounded by generous kitchen gardens or walled courtyards. Several **tavernas** advertise themselves on the approach road; of these, *Psistaria Lambiris* is longest established, and about the only one open for lunch. Most, such as *Kleoniki/Tou Iatrou* near the bus stop, are at their best in the evening when the *souvles* loaded with goat and suckling pig start turning. A few basic **rooms** are available (though none are signposted) – the baker on the square has rooms near the *Psistaria Lambiris*.

Despite apparent proximity on the map, there's no straightforward way from Theológos to **KÁSTRO**, the most naturally protected of the anti-pirate redoubts; especially with a car, it's best to descend to Potós and head up a rough, 17-kilometre dirt track from Limenária. Thirty ancient houses and a church surround a rocky pinnacle, fortified by the Byzantines and the Genoese, which has a sheer drop on three sides. Summer occupation by shepherds is becoming the rule after total abandonment in the last century, when mining jobs at Limenária proved irresistible, but there's only one kafenío on the ground floor of the former school, one telephone therein, far more sheep than people, and no mains electricity.

From Skála Marión an unmarked but paved road (slipping under the main highway bridge to the north) proceeds 11km inland to attractive **MARIÉS** at the top of a wooded stream valley; of two **tavernas** here, the well-signed one to the right is more of a going concern. From Skála Sotíros, a steep road heads 3.5km up to **SOTÍROS**, the only interior village with an unobstructed view of sunset over the Aegean and thus popular with foreigners who've bought up about half of the houses for restoration. On the ridge opposite are exploratory shafts left by the miners, whose ruined lodge looms above the church. On the plane-shaded square below the old fountain, *O Platanos* **taverna** is congenially run and there's good bulk wine.

From Prínos (Kalíves) on the coast road, you've a six-kilometre journey inland to the Kazavíti villages, shrouded in greenery that escaped the fires; they're signposted and mapped officially as Megálo and Mikró Prínos but still universally known by their Ottoman name. **MIKRÓ KAZAVÍTI** offers the simple grill-taverna *Paradhisos*, and the start of the track south for the **convent of Ayíou Pandelímona**. **MEGÁLO KAZAVÍTI**, 1km beyond, is the architectural showcase of the island, a fact not lost on the numerous outsiders who have summer homes here; on the magnificent platía are two fairly pricey **tavernas**. Some 4km up from its *skála*, **RAKHÓNI** is well set at the head of its denuded valley, paired with the small village of Áyios Yeóryios across the way. The road up to the square has plenty of simple **tavernas**.

travel details

To simplify the lists that follow we've excluded a regular sailing of the G&A company, which once a week runs a ferry in each direction (exact day changes according to season), linking Alexandhroúpoli with Límnos, Lésvos, Khíos, Sámos, Pátmos, Kálymnos, Kós and Rhodes; in peak season Ikaría, Léros and Sitía (Crete) are also included. Each one-way trip takes 26–36hr depending on the number of stops. We've also omitted the weekly DANE sailing of the *Patmos* between Rhodes, Kós, Sámos and Thessaloníki (22hr for the full run, usually at the weekend).

Sámos (Vathý) 4–7 weekly to Ikaría, Náxos, Páros, Sýros Pireás (14hr); 2–3 weekly to Khíos and Foúrni; 1–2 weekly to, Mýkonos and Tínos.

Sámos (Karlóvassi) As for Vathý, plus 2 weekly kaïki departures, usually early Mon and Thurs afternoon, to Foúrni.

Sámos (Pythagório) 1–2 weekly to Foúrni, Ikaría, Pátmos; 1–2 weekly (usually Wed and Sun afternoon) to Agathónissi, Lipsí, Pátmos, Léros, Kálymnos, with onward connections to all other Dodecanese (see p.630). Also expensive excursion kaïkia daily in season to Pátmos.

Ikaría 3–7 weekly to Sámos (both northern ports), Páros and Pireás (at least 3 weekly services via Évdhilos year-round); 3–4 weekly to Náxos and Sýros; 3 kaïkia weekly, from Áyios Kírykos, to Foúrni; 2–3 weekly to Khíos, Foúrni, Pátmos; 1–2 weekly to Mýkonos and Tínos.

Foúrni 4–5 weekly ferries, to Sámos (northern ports), Páros and Pireás; smaller ferries twice weekly to Sámos (Pythagório or Vathý), Ikaría, Pátmos, Khíos; morning kaïki to Ikaría, Mon, Wed, Fri, on weekends only by demand; twice weekly (usually Mon and Thur) morning kaïki to Karlóvassi (Sámos).

Khíos 5–9 weekly to Pireás (10hr) and Lésvos (3hr 30min); 1–2 weekly to Límnos (10hr); 2–3 weekly small ferries to Sámos (5hr); 1–2 weekly to Foúrni and Pátmos. Daily afternoon kaïki to Inoússes except Sunday morning; 3 weekly small ferries from Khíos Town to Psará (4hr), 2 weekly kaïkia on different days, mid-June to early September only, from Limní to Psará (2hr).

Psará 1 weekly direct to Pireás (8hr) and Lésvos (Mytilíni).

Lésvos 5–16 weekly from Mytilíni to Pireás (12hr direct, 13hr 30min via Khíos or Psará); 5–10 weekly to Khíos (3hr 30min); 4–8 weekly to Límnos (6hr from Mytilíni, 5hr from Sígri); 2 weekly to Thessaloníki (14hr); 1–2 weekly to Áyios Efstrátios (4hr) from Sígri only; 1–3 weekly to Kavála (12hr from Mytilíni, 10hr from Sígri); 1 weekly to Rafína (8hr from Sígri); 1 weekly to Psará (4hr); 1 weekly to Vólos, Sýros, Ándhros (July–Aug only).

Límnos 3–5 weekly to Kavála and Lésvos (Mytilíni or Sígri); 2–4 weekly to Áyios Efstrátios and Rafína; 1–3 weekly to Thessaloníki, Pireás, Khíos. Also a small local ferry to Áyios Efstrátios 3 times weekly.

Áyios Efstrátios 3–4 weekly to Límnos; 2–3 weekly to Rafína and Kavála; 1–2 weekly to Lésvos (Sígri).

Samothráki 2–3 daily ferries to/from Alexandhroúpoli (2hr 15min) in season, dropping to 5–6 weekly out of season. Also 2 weekly spring or autumn, up to 5 weekly in peak season, to Kavála (and thence other North Aegean islands).

Thássos 8–10 ferries daily, depending on season, between Kavála and Skála Prínou (1hr 15min; 7.30am–9.30pm, 6am–8pm to Kavála from the island); 10 daily between Keramotí and Liménas (45min; 7am–10pm, 6am–8.30pm from

Thássos). Except for extremely unreliable excursion kaïkia to Samothráki, no direct connections with any other island, you must travel via Kavála.

Hydrofoils

Just one company, Sámos Hydrofoils, operates in the **east Aegean**. Based on Sámos itself, this offers nearly daily early morning service from Vathý and Pythagório to Pátmos, Léros, Kálymnos and Kós (in the Dodecanese), returning in the late afternoon; 3–5 times weekly Lipsí is included; Ikaría is called at 2 times weekly, with Foúrni and Agathónissi served once weekly. Complementary service is provided by Dodecanese Hydrofoils (see p.630), based in Kálymnos and Rhodes, which go northbound in the morning and head south in the afternoon.

Thássos is served by hydrofoils from Kavála, which depart for Liménas 8–15 times daily from 7am–9pm (6am–8pm from Thássos); in summer there are also 2–4 daily departures from Kavála to the west-coast resorts of Skála Kalirákhon, Skála Marión, Limenária and Potós.

Samothráki is served by hydrofoil from Alexandhroúpoli from mid-May to mid-June and in September, once daily in the morning (1hr 30min); from mid-June through August another company kicks in with two more departures, usually afternoon, three days a week. One of these may continue on to Límnos, replacing a defunct ferry link from Samothráki.

International Hydrofoils

Service once daily (in theory), mid-June to mid-Sept, between Vathý (Sámos) and Kuşadası (Turkey). Fares are currently much the same as for a conventional ferry (see section below) if you bargain.

International ferries

Vathý (Sámos)–Kuşadasi (Turkey) At least 1 daily, late April to late October; otherwise a Turkish boat only by demand in winter, usually Fri or Sat. Morning Greek boat (passengers only), afternoon Turkish boats (usually 2 in season taking 2 cars apiece). Rates are £29/US$43 one way including taxes on both the Greek and Turkish sides, £33/$55 return; no day return rate. Small cars £30/$45 one way. Journey time 1hr 30min.

Also regular (2–3 weekly) services in season from **Pythagório**.

Khíos–Çeşme (Turkey) 2–12 boats weekly, depending on season. Thursday night and Saturday morning services tend to run year-round. Rates are £31/$49 one-way, £40/$64 return (no day return fare), including Greek taxes; no Turkish taxes. Small cars £42/$67 each way. Journey time 45min.

Mytilíni (Lésvos)–Ayvalik (Turkey) 5–9 weekly in season; winter link unreliable. Rates are similar to Khíos. Journey time 1hr 30min.

Flights

Khíos–Athens (4–5 daily; 50min)

Lésvos–Athens (3–5 daily; 45min)

Lésvos–Khíos (2 weekly; 25 min)

Lésvos–Thessaloníki (9 weekly; 1hr 10min–2hr)

Límnos–Athens (2–3 daily; 1hr)

Límnos–Lésvos (1 daily; 40min)

Límnos–Thessaloníki (1 daily; 50min)

Sámos–Athens (3–4 daily; 1hr)

Sámos–Thessaloníki (2 weekly; 1hr 40min)

CHAPTER ELEVEN

THE SPORADES AND ÉVVIA

The three northern **Sporades**, Skiáthos, Skópelos and Alónissos, are scattered (as their Greek name suggests) just off the mainland, their mountainous terrain betraying their origin as extensions of Mount Pelion in Thessaly. They are archetypal holiday islands, with a wide selection of good beaches, transparent waters and thick, pine forests. They're all very busy in season, with Skiáthos attracting by far the most package tours.

Skiáthos has the best beaches, and is still the busiest island in the group, though these days **Skópelos** gets very crowded, too. **Alónissos** is the quietest of the three, and has the wildest scenery, so it's really more for nature lovers than night owls. **Skýros**, further southeast, retains more of its traditional culture than the other three islands, though development is now well under way. The main town doesn't yet feel like a resort, but its main street is not without its fast food and souvenir shops. Unlike the other three islands, the best beaches are those close to the main town. To the south, the huge island of **Évvia** (or Euboea) runs for 150km alongside the mainland. It is one of the most attractive Greek islands, with a forested mountain spine and long stretches of rugged, largely undeveloped coast. Perhaps because it lacks any impressive ruins or real island feel due to its proximity to the mainland, Évvia is explored by few foreign tourists, though Athenians visit the island in force and have erected holiday homes around half a dozen of its major resorts.

The Sporades are well connected by bus and ferry both with Athens (via Áyios Konstandínos or Kými), Thessaloniki and Vólos, and it's easy to island-hop in the northern group. The only ferry connection to Skýros is from Kými, plus a Flying Dolphin

---

ACCOMMODATION PRICE CODES

Throughout the book we've used the following **price codes** to denote the cheapest available room in high season; all are prices for a double room, except for category ①, which represents per person rates. Out of season, rates can drop by up to fifty percent, especially if you are staying for three or more nights. Single rooms, where available, cost around seventy percent of the price of a double.

Rented private rooms on the islands usually fall into the ② or ③ categories, depending on their location and facilities, and the season; a few in the ④ category are more like plush self-catering apartments. They are not generally available from late October through to the beginning of April, when only hotels tend to remain open.

① 1400–2000dr	④ 8000–12,000dr
② 4000–6000dr	⑤ 12,000–16,000dr
③ 6000–8000dr	⑥ 16,000dr and upwards

For more accommodation details, see pp.39–42.

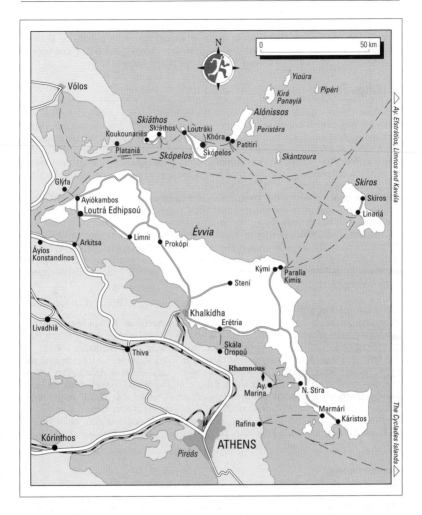

hydrofoil service in summer from Vólos via the other Sporades. Évvia is linked to the mainland by a bridge at its capital Khalkídha, and by a series of shuttle-ferries. Both Skiáthos and Skýros have airports.

Skiáthos

The commercialization of **Skiáthos** is legendary among foreigners and Greeks: it's a close fourth to that of Corfu, Mýkonos and Rhodes. But if you've some time to spare, or a gregarious nature, you might still break your journey here to sample the best, if most overcrowded, **beaches** in the Sporades. Along the south and southeast coasts, the road serves an almost unbroken line of villas, hotels and restaurants, and although this doesn't take away the island's natural beauty, it makes it difficult to find anything unspoiled or particularly Greek about it all. As almost the entire population lives in Skiáthos Town, a little walking soon pays off. However, camping outside official sites is strongly discouraged, since summer turns the dry pine-needles to tinder.

Skiáthos Town

Skiáthos Town, where the ferries dock, looks great from a distance, but as you approach, tourist development becomes very apparent, especially to the east side of the port and around Alexándhrou Papadhiamándi Street, where most of the services, the tackier shops, "English" pubs and eateries are located. But tucked into the alleys on the western, older side of town, it is still possible to find some pockets of charm: older houses, gardens and flowers galore. Skiáthos boasts some good restaurants and nightclubs, and can be fun, in a crowded, boisterous way.

The few sights comprise the **Papadhiamánti museum** (Tues–Sun 9.30am–1pm & 5–8pm; free) – housed in the nineteenth-century home of one of Greece's best-known novelists – and two antique shops, *Archipelago* two blocks in from the waterfront, and the enduring *Galerie Varsakis* (open usual shop hours), on Platía Trión Ierarkhón near the fishing port. The latter has one of the best **folklore displays** in Greece, and many of the older items would do the Benaki Museum proud; the proprietor neither expects, nor wants, to sell the more expensive of these, which include antique textiles, handicrafts and jewellery.

Arrival, transport and other facilities

Buses and **taxis** ply from the area around the **ferry harbour**. To Koukounariés, the bus is the cheapest option (280dr); it runs at least hourly in summer (every fifteen minutes at peak times), the last bus returning at 3am. Sharing a taxi is another option.

A large number of competing **rental outlets** in town, most on the front behind the ferry harbour, offer bicycles, mopeds, motorbikes, cars and motorboats. The lowest priced, small cars go for around 12,000dr a day, motorboats for 15,000dr a day; fuel and insurance are extra. Several travel agents organize "round the island" **mule trips** (5200dr a day), and there's **horse riding** at the *Pinewood Riding Club* (no phone) at Koukounariés. Most other facilities are on Alexándhrou Papadhiamándi, including the **OTE, post office, banks** and the Mare Nostrum travel agency, which will change your travellers' cheques without a commission.

Accommodation

Much of the island's accommodation is in Skiáthos Town. The few reasonably priced **hotels** or **pensions** are heavily booked in season, though you can usually find a room, albeit slightly more expensively than on most islands. At other times, supply exceeds demand and you can find very cheap **rooms** with a little bargaining. Try for locations in the older quarters to the west. There is no official accommodation bureau but there are several tourist agencies; lodgings in the flatlands to the north as they tend to be noisy. For an honest and helpful approach, try the *Mare Nostrum* at Papadhiamándi 21 (☎0427/21 463/4). Another option is Adonis Stamelos's rooms just outside town at Megáli Ammos (☎0427/22 962; ④). Good, small hotels include the *Bourtzi* (☎0427/22 694; ⑤) and *Pothos* (☎0427/21 304; ⑤), both immaculate with delightful gardens, and the *Orza Pension* (☎0427/22 430; ⑤), a remodelled house overlooking the sea on the west side of the port. Other fine options are the *Alkyon Hotel*, on the seafront at the commercial port end (☎0427/22 981; ⑥), or the *Meltemi Hotel*, on the front near the taxi rank (☎0427/22 493; ⑥).

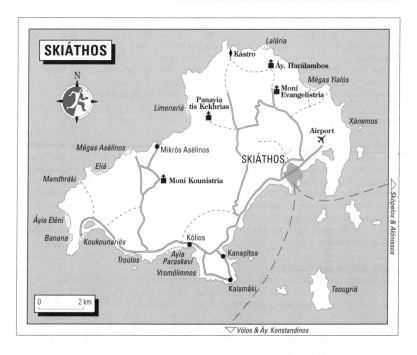

SKIÁTHOS

Laláría
Kástro
Áy. Harálambos
Mégas Yialós
Moní
Evangelístria
Panayía
tis Kekhrias
Limenariá
Xánemos
Airport
Mégas Asélinos
Mikrós Asélinos
SKIÁTHOS
Eliá
Mandhráki
Moní Kounístria
Áyia Eléni
Banana
Koukounariés
Kólios
Troúlos
Ayía
Paraskeví
Kanapítsa
Vromólimnos
Kalamáki
Tsougriá

Skópelos & Alónissos

0   2 km

▽ *Vólos & Áy. Konstandínos*

The island has four official **campsites** – at Koliós, Koukounariés, Asélinos and Xanémos beach. Koliós is by far the best, but Koukounariés and Asélinos are fairly decent too. Xanémos beach is 3km northeast of Skiáthos Town, right next to the airport runway, and, apart from being within walking distance of the town, has little to recommend it.

Eating, drinking and nightlife

You're spoiled for choice for **eating places**, but nothing is particularly cheap apart from the few burger/*gyros* joints. One of the best of the cheaper tavernas is *Zorba's*, opposite the taxi rank, while *Mesogeia*, above and to the west of Plátia Trión Ierarkhón, has excellent moussaka and home-cooked dishes. The English-run *Lemon Tree Restaurant* behind the National Bank, with its vegetarian food and *tapas*, now has a nearby rival, the *Daskalio Cafe Bar*, to the right of the police station, whose laid-back British owners serve excellent curries. For more elegant dining, head for *Agnantio*, at the start of the road to Evangelístria, for superlative Greek cuisine and views; *The Windmill* at the top of the hill above Áyios Nikólaos, for nouvelle cuisine and views; and *Desperado*, on the east waterfront, for great Mexican food. Back on the west side, above the flat rocks where people sunbathe, *Tarsanas* is a converted boatbuilders' yard with a picturesque veranda – the best place in town for an evening drink as the harbour lights come on.

Nightlife centres on the clubs on or near Polytekhníou. The best places are *Borzoi*, the oldest club on the island, *Stones* and the *Apothiki Music Hall* for Greek music and a good atmosphere, while on the seafront *BBC* pulses till dawn. In the bars in the back streets around Polytekniou you can hear a wider range of music; places like the *Banana* are pop-oriented and popular among British beer drinkers, the old and much loved

Kentavros plays jazz and blues, *Adagio* has classical music in the evenings, and stalwart *Admiral Benbow* belts out vintage Sixties soul. On the east shore, the chic *Remezzo* with its maritime motifs, is a perennial favourite. Skiáthos's new outdoor cinema *Refresh Paradiso*, on the ring road, shows new releases in their original language.

The little offshore Boúrtzi fortress has been transformed into an outdoor theatre for a six-week-long summer **festival** of music (Greek pop and classical) and drama, called *Óneiro tou Kyma* (Dream on the Wave), from the novel by Papadhiamándis.

Around the island

Other than using the buses or the various rental outlets in town (for which see above), you could also get your bearings on a **boat trip** around the island. These cost about 4000dr per person and leave at around 10am. Or try a boat trip to the islet of Tsougriá (opposite Skiáthos Town), where there's a good beach and a taverna. Boats leave from the fishing harbour beyond the Boúrtzi, and not the yacht anchorage to the north of the ferry harbour; east-coast boats leave from the quay area in front of the bus station.

If you're interested in seeing more of Skiáthos on foot, the locally produced guide to **walks** (by Rita and Dietrich Harkort; available in larger tourist shops) has detailed instructions and maps for trails all over the island.

Monasteries and Kástro

The **Evangelístria Monastery** (daily 8am–noon & 4–8pm) is more than an hour on foot out of Skiáthos Town. Founded in the late eighteenth century, it is exceptionally beautiful, even beyond the grandeur of isolation you find in all Greek monasteries. The Greek flag was raised here in 1807, and heroes of the War of Independence such as Kolokotronis pledged their oaths to fight for freedom here. To reach the monastery, walk 500m out of the centre of town on the road towards the airport until, at the point where the asphalt veers to the right, you take a prominently signposted tarmac track that veers left; be careful to stick to the tarmac and not to wander off onto the dirt roads.

Beyond Evangelístria, a mule track continues to the abandoned **Áyios Kharálambos monastery**, from where it's possible to walk across the island to the ruined capital of Kástro (see below) along another dirt road; this takes about two hours. To reach Kástro from Skiáthos Town, it's quicker to take the direct road, though in all it's still a hard five-to six-kilometre uphill slog; the turning is signposted on the road behind town, some distance beyond the turning for Evangelístria. You'll find it much easier if you do the walk in reverse. Just take a round the island kaïki ride and get off at the beach below Kástro. Another option is to ride a motorbike up the hill and then explore on foot.

Just over halfway between Evangelístria and Kástro, a well-used dirt track (signposted) turns left and heads towards the abandoned fifteenth-century monastery of **Panayía tís Kekhriás**, three hours' walk from town. It's said to be the oldest on the island and has a colony of bats inside. It's a beautiful walk (or organized donkey-ride), and there are two pebbly beaches below, one with a welcoming stream that provides a cool shower. Ignoring this excursion, the paved road continues to within a thirty-minute walk of **Kástro** – a spectacular spot, built on a windswept headland. In the past, the entrance was only accessible by a drawbridge, which has been replaced by a flight of steps. The village was built in the sixteenth century, when the people of the island moved here for security from pirate raids. It was abandoned three hundred years later in 1830, following independence from Turkey, when the population moved back to build the modern town on the site of ancient Skiáthos. The ruins are largely overgrown, and only three churches survive intact, the largest still retaining some original frescoes. From outside the gates, a path leads down the rocks to a good pebble **beach**; with a stream running down from the hills and a daytime café (with slightly overpriced food and drinks), it makes a good place to camp. For an apparently inaccessible spot though, it does attract a surprising number of people. All the island excursion boats call here, and even when they've gone, there's little chance of having the ruins or beach to yourself.

Finally, the seventeenth-century **Kounístra monastery**, can be reached by turning right off the paved road that runs up the island from Tróulos, the last beach before Koukounariés, to the beach at Asélinos. It's a very pretty spot, with a beautiful carved icon screen, splendid icons, a grape arbour and a taverna.

The beaches

The real business of Skiáthos is **beaches**. There are reputed to be more than sixty of them, but that's hardly enough to soak up the numbers of summer visitors: at the height of the season, the local population of five thousand can be swamped by up to fifty thousand visitors. The beaches on the northeast coast aren't easily accessible unless you pay for an excursion kaïki: reaching them on foot requires treks more arduous than those described above. The bus, though, runs along the entire south coast, and from strategic points along the way you can easily reach a good number of beaches. The prevailing summer *meltémi* wind blows from the north, so the beaches on the south coast are usually better protected. Most of the popular beaches have at least a drinks/snacks stall; those at Vromólimnos, Asélinos and Tróulos have proper tavernas.

The beaches before the **Kalamáki peninsula** (where English and rich Greeks have their villas) are unexciting, but on the promontory itself are the highly-rated **Ayía Paraskeví** and **Vromólimnos beaches**, flanked by the campsite and Kanapítsa hamlet; Vromólimnos offers windsurfing and waterskiing. For scuba enthusiasts, there is the *Dolphin Diving Centre* (☎0427/22 520) at the *Nostos* hotel, on the eastern side of the Kalamáki peninsula.

Just before Tróulos you can turn right up a paved road, which runs 4km north to **Mégas Asélinos**, a very good beach with a campsite and a reasonable taverna. A daily bus and excursion boats stop here, so it's crowded in season. A fork in the paved road leads to Kounístra monastery (see above) and continues to **Mikrós Asélinos**, just east of its larger neighbour and somewhat quieter.

The bus only goes as far as **KOUKOUNARIÉS**, a busy resort, though the three beaches are excellent if you don't mind the crowds. There's a majestic sandy bay of clear, gradually deepening water, backed by acres of pines, which despite its popularity it merits at least one visit if only to assess the claim that it's the best beach in Greece. The road runs behind a small lake at the back of the pine trees, and features a string of **hotels**, **rooms** and **restaurants**, as well as a good campsite. Here, the *Strofilia* apartments which sleep four (☎0427/49 251; ⑤) are particularly nicely furnished. Jet-skis, motorboats, windsurfing and waterskiing are all available off the beach.

Banana Beach (also known as Krassá), the third cove on the far side of Poúnda headland, is the trendiest of the island's nudist beaches. For the less adventurous, the turning for **Ayía Eléni**, 1km from the road, is a pleasant beach with a drinks kiosk. Further north, **Mandhráki** and **Eliá** beaches have similar facilities, and are accessible by bus.

The famed **Lalária beach**, on the northern stretch of coast, can be reached by "taxi-boats" from the town. Covered with smooth white stones, it's beautiful, with steep cliffs rising behind it; the swimming is excellent, but beware of the undertow. The island's three natural grottos – Skotiní, Glazía and Khalkiní – are nearby, and are included in many of the "round-the-island" trips. Southwest of Kástro are the greyish sands of **Mégas Yialós**, one of the less crowded beaches, and **Xánemos**, another nudist beach; both suffer from airport noise.

The only real way to get away from the crowds is to persuade a boat owner to take you out to one of Skiáthos' **islets**. Tsougriá, in particular, has three beaches, with a taverna on the main one.

Skópelos

Bigger, more rugged and better cultivated than Skiáthos, **Skópelos** is almost as busy, but its concessions to tourism are lower key and in better taste than in Skiáthos. Most of the larger beaches have sunbeds, umbrellas and some watersports, but smaller, secluded coves do exist. Inland, it is a well-watered place, growing olives, plums, pears and almonds. **Glóssa** and **Skópelos**, its two main towns, are also among the prettiest in the Sporades, clambering uphill along paved steps, their houses distinguished by attractive wooden balconies and grey slate roofs. A number of **nationalities** have occupied the island at various stages of its history, among them the Romans, Persians, Venetians, French and, of course, the Turks. The Turkish admiral, Barbarossa (Redbeard), had the entire population of the island slaughtered in the sixteenth century.

Loutráki, Glóssa and the west

Most boats call at both ends of Skópelos, stopping first at the small port of **LOUTRÁKI** with its narrow pebble beach, small hotels and rooms for rent. The village has been spoiled a little by development at either end, but it's not a bad place to stay if you're after peace and quiet; try *O Stelios* (④), a simple pension next to the *Flisvos* taverna, the *Pension Valentina* (☎0424/33 694; ④), or the *Avra* (☎0424/33 550; ⑤). Though most of the quayside tavernas don't offer value for money, there are exceptions: the café/shop in the platía by the harbour is shaded by beautiful chestnut trees and sells a highly recommended, home-made retsina; the *Flisvos* is a friendly place with decent pasta dishes, and the small ouzeri is good.

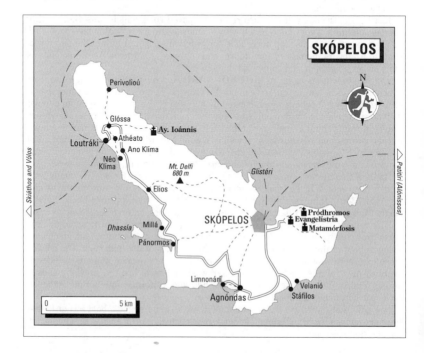

High above Loutráki, **GLÓSSA** would be perhaps a preferable base if it had more places to stay. It is a sizeable and quite beautiful, totally Greek town, with several kafenía, a taverna and a few rooms to let, some of which are hot and musty, with erratic water pressure. *Kostas and Nina's* place (☎0424/33 686; ②) has simple, clean rooms, some with a view; they also rent out studios longer term, or you could stay at the *Selinounda apartments* (☎0424/33 570; ④) on the road between Loutráki and Glóssa. There's one taverna, *To Agnandi*, which is a lively and authentic place to eat, and full most evenings. Incidentally, it's a good idea to accept offers of a taxi ride up to Glóssa from Loutráki; it's a stiff walk up even if you know the path short cuts, and taxi drivers will know if there are any vacancies. If it's really high season, though, and even Glóssa is packed, two nearby villages, Athéato and Paleó Klíma have rooms, while Élios on the coast below has two big hotels, bungalows and rooms.

Ninety minutes' walk from Glóssa, up to the north coast, will bring you to a **beach** the locals call **Perivolioú**. The walk itself is worthwhile, passing a **monastery** next to a stone cairn containing masses of human bones and skulls. There's also a huge hollow oak tree here, in the heart of which is a small tank of drinking water. The beach, when you get there, is nothing out of the ordinary, but there's spring water for drinking and a cave for shade.

East of Glóssa, a dirt road leads to the splendidly sited monastery of **Áyios Ioánnis Kastrí**, perched on the top of a rock high above a small sandy cove where you can swim. A new unsightly house nearby has spoiled the isolation somewhat, but the walk from Glóssa (again, about ninety minutes) is beautiful and peaceful, with hawks and nightingales for company.

Skópelos Town

If you stay on the ferry beyond Loutráki – probably the best plan – you reach **SKÓPELOS TOWN**, sloping down one corner of a huge, almost circular bay. The best way to arrive is by sea, with the town revealed slowly as the boat rounds the final headland. Though more and more people seem to have discovered Skópelos Town, the locals are making a tremendous effort to keep it from going the way of Skiáthos. The harbour area is practically wall-to-wall tavernas and cafés, but the shops and eateries in the back alleys tend to be imaginative and tasteful, with wooden, hand-painted name signs; the two real eyesores date from the junta years. Spread below the oddly whitewashed ruins of a Venetian **Kástro**, are an enormous number of churches – 123 reputedly, though some are small enough to be mistaken for houses and most are locked except for their annual festival day. Other sights include a **folklore museum** and photography exhibitions in summer.

Outside town, perched on the slopes opposite the quay, are two convents: **Evangelístria** (daily 8am–1pm & 4–7pm), which is within view of the town, and **Pródhromos** (daily 8am–1pm & 5–8pm). The monastery of **Metamórfosis**, also on this promontory, was abandoned in 1980 but is now being restored by the monks and is open to visitors. Access is simplest by following an old road behind the line of hotels along the bay to Evangelístria (an hour's walk). From there it's an extra half hour's scramble over mule tracks to Pródhromos, the remotest and most beautiful of the three. Ignore the new road that goes part way – it's longer, and misses most of the beauty of the walk.

Practicalities

The **ferry quay** is at the western end of a long promenade, lined with an array of boutiques, bars, stores and restaurants. To get to the **bus station**, turn left where the quay meets the main road, and follow the sea until you pass the children's swings and the second períptero; at the point where the road divides around a car park. Opposite the bus station entrance, a short road leads into a maze of lanes and signposts to the **post office**. There are banks about 50m from the quay.

In the main body of the town there are dozens of **rooms** for rent. Alternatively, there are three pleasant small hotels: *Andromache* (inquire at Madro Travel ☎0424/22 145; ④), in a quiet old house near the post office; relaxed and casual *Kyr Sotos* (☎0424/22 549; ④) also near the post office; and the clean, if basic *Lina Guest House* on the front (☎0424/22 637; ④). For larger, more **expensive hotels** higher up from the port, you're unlikely to find a space without having booked through a tour operator, but if you fancy the likes of the cosy *Elli* (☎0424/22 943; ⑤) on the east side of town, the modern *Aperitton* (☎0424/22 256; ⑤) on the ring road above the town, or the neo-rustic *Dionysos* (☎0424/23 210; ⑥), also on the ring road – each with a pool – ask about vacancies at Madro Travel (see above) on the quay; they're also the local Flying Dolphin agents.

There's a wide variety of **places to eat**, ranging from the acceptable to the truly excellent. Those at the near end of the harbour, like *Angelos-Ta Kymata*, *Molos* and *Klimataria*, all offer decent meals, while *Spyros* in the middle has been a reliable favourite for years. *To Aktaion* is also a good bet, with exceptionally pleasant staff and large, delicious and reasonably priced portions. Two *souvláki* places, both named *O Platanos*, compete for the distinction of having the best *yíros*. It's also worth heading a couple of kilometres towards Stáfilos to the *Terpsis* taverna for their stuffed-chicken speciality. And for a gourmet treat, the *Perivoli* is the place; you must make a reservation. It is located near "Souvlaki Square" – above the waterfront to the east of town.

Nightlife in Skópelos is on the increase, but is more of the late-night bar than the nightclub variety. That said, *Labikos*, *Kirki*, *Ano Kato* and *Kounos* on the back streets behind the waterfront, are popular in season, The *bouzouki* joint *Meintani* is housed in an old olive press near Souvlaki Square, while the *Skopelitissa* and *Anatoli* on top of the Kástro play Greek music till the early hours. Among the bars, look out for *Vengera*, in a restored house that compares favourably with the town's folk art museum.

Around the rest of the island

Buses cover the island's one paved road between Skópelos Town and Loutráki via Glóssa (around 6 times daily 7am–10.30pm), stopping at the paths to all the main beaches and villages. **Stáfylos**, 4km south of town, is the closest beach, though rather small and rocky. It's getting increasingly crowded, but the *Terpsis* taverna, which rents **rooms**, is a very pleasant spot shaded by a vast pine tree.

There's a very prominent "No Camping" sign at Stáfilos, but if you walk five minutes around the coast north to **Velanió**, there's spring water and a campsite near the beach. Here the pines and surf always draw a small, summer (often nudist) community.

Further around the coast to the west, the tiny horseshoe-shaped harbour of **AGNÓNDAS** (with its fish tavernas and rooms) is the start of a fifteen-minute path (2km by road) or half-hourly kaïkia trip to **LIMNONÁRI**, 100m of fine sand set in a closed, rocky bay.

PÁNORMOS is very much a full-blown, commercial resort, with rooms, tavernas, a campsite, yacht anchorage and watersports. The beach here is gravelly and steeply shelving, but there are small secluded bays close by. The thirty-room *Panormos Beach Hotel* (☎0424/22 711; ⑤) has a beautiful garden, fine views, and is lovingly looked after; beyond it the *Adrina Beach* (☎0424/23 373; ⑤) is one of the most attractive and most expensive hotels, in the Sporades. Slightly further on at **MILIÁ**, there is a tremendous, 1500m sweep of tiny pebbles beneath a bank of pines, facing the islet of Dhassía. There's one taverna and the *Kefalonitis Studios* (☎0424/23 998; ④) in this languid setting; nudist swimming is possible at a lovely five-hundred-metre-long beach a little way north. The shore beyond is indented with many tiny coves, ranging from individual- to family-size.

Further north, **ÉLIOS**, 9km short of Glóssa, is a medium-sized, fairly new resort settled by residents of the earthquake-damaged villages above it, with nothing special to offer besides a pleasant beach. Beyond here, the refurbished village of Paleó Klíma marks the start of a beautiful forty-minute **trail** to Glóssa, via the empty hamlet of Áyii Anáryiri and the oldest village on the island, **Athéato**.

West of Skópelos Town, various jeep tracks and old paths wind through olive and plum groves toward **Mount Dhélfi** and the Vathiá forest, or skirt the base of the mountain northeast to Revíthi hill with its fountains and churches, and the site of **Karyá**, with its *sendoúkia*: ancient rock-cut tombs which may be early Christian. To the northwest of Skópelos Town, **Glystéri** is a small pebble beach with no shade, whose taverna is much frequented by locals on Sundays. A fork off the Glystéri and Mount Dhélfi tracks can – in theory – be followed across the island to Pánormos within ninety minutes; it's a pleasant walk though the route isn't always obvious.

Alónissos and some minor islets

The most remote of the Sporades, **Alónissos** is also, at first sight, the least attractive. It has an unfortunate recent history. The vineyards were wiped out by disease in 1950 and the Khóra was damaged by an earthquake in 1965. Although its houses were mostly repairable, lack of water combined with corruption and the social control policies of

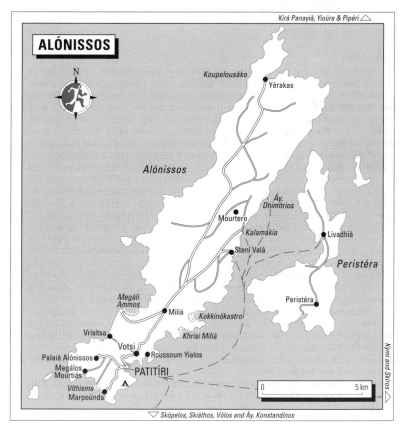

the new junta were instrumental in the transfer of virtually the entire population down to the previously unimportant anchorage of Patitíri. The result is a little soulless, but what charm may be lacking in the built environment on the coast is made up for by the hospitality of the islanders.

Patitíri and the old town

PATITÍRI is not a good introduction to the island, but it's trying hard to rectify that. The port, a pretty cove flanked by pine trees, is marred by the rows of flat-roofed concrete buildings rising up behind it. Nevertheless, the line of near-identical bars and restaurants that run along the waterfront is not unappealling. Alónissos attracts fewer visitors than Skíathos or Skópelos; most of those who do come stay in Patitíri, and from mid-July to the end of August it can get very crowded. It's easy, though, to pick up connections here for beaches and the old town, and there are several good hotels to choose from.

PALEÁ ALÓNISSOS is a fine but steep fifty-minute walk via a donkey track – signposted on the left just outside Patitíri. Alternatively, there's a frequent bus service in the mornings and afternoons. Although some houses are still derelict, much of the village has been painstakingly restored, mainly by the English and Germans who bought the properties at knock-down rates. Only a few local families continue to live here, which gives the village a rather odd and un-Greek atmosphere, but it is picturesque, and the views make the trip worthwhile.

Practicalities

All the important facilities are in Patitíri; the **OTE** (becoming obsolete as there are so many cardphones in town) is on the seafront and **buses** and **taxis** congregate next door. The **post office** is on the Khóra road, while kaïka leave from the quay beside the *Pension Flisvos* (see below). You can rent a moped, motorbike an even a car (check with Ikos Travel below) at reasonable prices. The roads between Patitíri, Stení Vála and the northernmost point on the island are paved, and the dirt roads down to the beaches in good condition: not half as dangerous as the twisting, busy roads on Skíathos and Skópelos. A couple of the rental places on the waterfront also rent out motorboats and dinghies.

Rooms are easy to find here, as you'll probably be approached with offers as you get off the ferry, sometimes by older women wearing traditional blue and white costumes. For low-cost rooms try *Eleni Athanasiou* (☎0424/65 240; ③), the *Ioulieta* pension (☎0424/65 463; ④), and *Pantheon* (☎0424/65 139; ④). *Liadromia* (☎0424/65 521; ④), above the port; *Niirides* (☎0424/65 643; ⑤), studio apartments with pool; and *Paradise* (☎0424/65 160; ④), on the promontory east of the port with a pool overlooking the sea, are the best in the higher price range. The local room-owners' association (☎0424/65 577), on the front, can also find you a room in Patitíri or nearby Vótsi. Ikos Travel, the Flying Dolphin agent (☎0424/65 320), can do bookings for a limited number of rooms and apartments in the old town, though accommodation here is in short supply so expect to pay well over the odds, particularly in season. Otherwise, ask around; few people put up "room for rent" signs, but try the simple and clean *Fadasia House* (☎0424/65 186; ④), at the entrance to the Khóra.

The **restaurants** along the front of Patitíri are reasonably priced, but the food is nothing special. The best place for breakfast is the *To Korali*; in the evenings, try the friendly *Pension Flisvos*. For the best meal in Patitíri go two blocks up from the petrol station on the waterfront to *To Kamaki*, a wonderful ouzerí with a amazing selection of seafood. Up in the old town, *Astrofengia* has the tastiest food, and *Paraport* at the Kástro the most spectacular views.

Nightlife is low key. The best of the seafront bars is *Pub Dennis*, whose ice-cream concoctions are divine, though both *En Plo* and *La Vie* are popular. Club-wise, *Borio* and *Enigma* are fairly European, while *Rembetika*, on the road to the old town, specializes in Greek music.

The island's beaches

Alónissos has some of the cleanest water in the Aegean, but it's lacking in sand beaches. There's only one really sandy beach on the island (Výthizma), the rest varying from rough to fine pebbles. There's no bus, but kaïkia run half-hourly from Patitíri north to Khrissí Miliá, Kokkinókastro, Steni Vála, Kalamákia and Áyios Dhimítrios, and south around the coast to Marpoúnda, Výthizma and Megálos Mourtiás. Kaïkia also sail occasionally to Livádhia and Peristéra islet.

At Patitíri there's decent swimming from the rocks around the promontory to the north; pick your way along a hewn-out path past the hotels and you're there (ladder provided). To the north, above the headlands, Patitíri merges into two adjoining settlements, **Roussoúm Yialós** and **Vótsi**. For better beaches, you'll have to get in a boat or on a bike.

Khrissí Miliá, the first good beach, has pine trees down to the sand and a taverna; there are a couple of new hotels on the hillside above, and it can get crowded in summer. At **Kokkinókastro**, over the hill to the north, excavations have revealed the site of ancient Ikos and evidence of the oldest known prehistoric habitation in the Aegean. There's nothing much to see, but it's a beautiful spot with a good red pebble beach, and, in July and August, a daytime bar.

THE MEDITERRANEAN MONK SEAL

The **Mediterranean monk seal** has the dubious distinction of being the European mammal most in danger of extinction. Fewer than eight hundred survive worldwide, the majority around the Portuguese Atlantic island of Madeira. A large colony off the coast of the West African state of Mauritania was decimated early in 1997: an estimated two hundred seals died, possibly poisoned by algae. Small numbers survive in the Ionian and Aegean seas; the largest population here, of around thirty seals, lives around the deserted islands north of Alónissos.

Monk seals can travel up to 200km a day in search of food, but they usually return to the same places to rear their **pups**. They have one pup every two years, and the small population is very vulnerable to disturbance. Originally, the pups would have been reared on sandy beaches, but with increasing disturbance by man, they have retreated to isolated sea caves, particularly around the coast of the remote islet of Pipéri.

Unfortunately, the seals compete with fishermen for limited stocks of fish, and, in the overfished Aegean, often destroy nets full of fish. Until recently it was common for seals to be killed by fishermen. This occasionally still happens, but in an attempt to protect the seals, the seas around the northern Sporades have been declared a **marine wildlife reserve**: fishing is restricted in the area north of Alónissos and prohibited within 5km of Pipéri. On Alónissos, the conservation effort and reserve have won a great deal of local support, mainly through the efforts of the Hellenic Society for the Protection of the Monk Seal (HSPMS), based at Steni Vála. The measures have won particular support from local fishermen, as tighter restrictions on larger, industrial-scale fishing boats from other parts of Greece should help preserve fish stocks, and benefit the fishermen financially.

Despite this, the government has made no serious efforts to enforce the restrictions, and boats from outside the area continue to fish around Pipéri. There are also government plans to reduce the prohibited area around Pipéri to 500m. On a more positive note, the HSPMS, in collaboration with the Pieterburen Seal Creche in Holland, has reared several abandoned seal pups, all of which have been successfully released in the seas north of Alónissos.

For the moment, your chances of actually seeing a seal are remote, unless you plan to spend a few weeks on a boat in the area. It's recommended that you shouldn't visit Pipéri or approach sea caves on other islands which might be used by seals, or try to persuade boat owners to do so.

STENÍ VÁLA, opposite the island of Peristéra, a haven for the yachts and flotillas that comb the Sporades, has almost become a proper village, with two shops, several houses, a bar, rooms and four tavernas, one of which stays open more or less throughout the year. There's a campsite (☎0424/65 258) in an olive grove by the harbour, a long pebble beach — Glýfa, where boats are repaired — and some stony beaches within reasonable walking distance in either direction. **KALAMÁKIA**, to the north, also has a couple of tavernas, and a few rooms.

If you want real solitude, **Áyios Dhimítrios**, **Megaliámmos**, and **Yérakas** (an old shepherds' village at the northernmost point) are possibilities. However, before committing yourself to a Robinson Crusoe existence, take one of the round-the-island trips available, and return the next day with enough food for your stay: there are no stores outside the port and Stení Vála. In the opposite direction from Patitíri, **Marpoúnda** features a large hotel and bungalow complex and a rather small beach. It's better to turn left after the campsite towards **Megálos Mourtiás**, a pebble beach with several tavernas linked by dirt track with Palaiá Alónissos, 200m above. **Výthizma**, the lovely beach just before Megálos Mourtiás, can only be reached by boat, the path here having been washed out. Further north, visible from Palaiá Alónissos, **Vrisítsa** is tucked into its own finger-like inlet. There's sand and a taverna, but little else.

Beyond Alónissos: some minor islets

Northeast of Alónissos, half-a-dozen tiny **islets** speckle the Aegean. Virtually none of these has any permanent population, or a ferry service, and the only way you can reach them – at least Peristéra, Kyrá Panayiá and Yioúra – is by excursion kaïki (ask at Ikos Travel), weather permitting. No boats are allowed to take you to the other, more remote islets, as they are protected areas within the Sporades National Marine Park. But though it is possible to be left for a night or more on any of the closer islands, when acting out your desert-island fantasies, be sure to bring more supplies than you need: if the weather worsens you'll be marooned until such time as small craft can reach you.

Peristéra is the closest islet to Alónissos, to which it was once actually joined, but subsidence (a common phenomenon in the area) created the narrow straits between the two. It is graced with some sandy beaches and there is rarely anyone around, though some Alónissans do come over for short periods to tend the olive groves, and in season there are regular evening "barbecue boats" from the main island. As on Alónissos, a few unofficial campers are tolerated, but there is only one spot, known locally as "Barbecue Bay", where campfires are allowed.

Kyrá Panayiá (also known as Pelagós) is the next islet out and is equally fertile. It's owned by the Meyístis Láuras monastery of Mount Áthos and there are two monasteries here, one still inhabited. Boats call at a beach on the south shore, one of many such sandy stretches and coves around the island. There's no permanent population other than the wild goats.

Nearby **Yioúra** boasts a stalactite cave reputed to be that of Polyphemus, the Cyclops who imprisoned Odysseus, but you won't be able to check its credentials. No one is allowed within 500m of the island, since, like Pipéri, it lies inside the restricted zone of the Marine Park.

Pipéri, near Yioúra, is a sea-bird and monk-seal refuge, and permission from a ministry of the environment representative (in Alónissos) is required for visits by specialists; non-scientists are not allowed. Tiny, northernmost **Psathoúra** is dominated by its powerful modern lighthouse, although here, as around many of these islands, there's a submerged ancient town, brought low by the endemic subsidence. Roughly halfway between Alónissos and Skýros, green **Skántzoura**, with a single empty monastery and a few seasonal shepherds, is a smaller version of Kyrá Panayiá.

Skýros

Despite its proximity to Athens, **Skýros** remained a very traditional and idiosyncratic island until recently. Any impetus for change had been neutralized by the lack of economic opportunity (and even secondary schooling), forcing the younger Skyrians to live in Athens and leaving behind a conservative gerontocracy. A high school has at last been provided, and the island has been somewhat "discovered" in the past decade. It's now the haunt of continental Europeans, chic Athenians and British, many of whom check into the "New Age" Skýros Centre, to "rethink the form and direction of their lives".

Meanwhile, Skýros still ranks as one of the most interesting places in the Aegean. It has a long tradition of painted **pottery** and ornate **woodcarving**, and a *salonáki skyrianí* (handmade set of chairs) is still considered an appropriate partial dowry for any young Greek woman. A very few old men still wear the vaguely Cretan traditional costume of

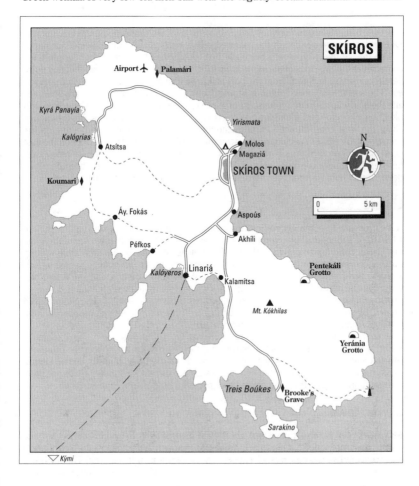

SKÍROS

Airport ✈ ● Palamári

Kyrá Panayía

Kalógrias
● Atsítsa

Yirismata

▲ ● Molos
● Magaziá

SKÍROS TOWN

N

Koumari ♦

● Áy. Fokás

0   5 km

● Aspoús

● Péfkos

● Akhíli

Kalóyeros Linariá

● Kalamítsa

**Pentekáli
Grotto**
◒

▲
Mt. Kókhilas

**Yeránia
Grotto**
◒

Treis Boúkes ● **Brooke's
Grave**

Sarakíno

▽ *Kými*

GOAT DANCES AND WILD PONIES

Skýros has some particularly lively, even outrageous festivals. The *Apokriatiká* (pre-Lenten) carnival here is structured around the famous **goat dance**, performed by masked revellers in the village streets. The foremost character in this is the Yéros, a menacing figure concealed by a goatskin mask and weighed down by garlands of sheep bells. Accompanying him are Korélles and Kyriés (who are transvestites, as only the men participate) and Frangi (maskers in "Western" garb). For further details, read Joy Koulentianou's *The Goat Dance of Skyros*, available in Athens and occasionally on the island.

The other big annual event takes place near Magaziá beach on August 15, when children race domesticated members of the **wild pony** herd, native to Skýros and said to be related to the Shetland pony (if so, it must be very distantly). They are thought, perhaps, to be the diminutive horses depicted in the Parthenon frieze, and at any time of the year you might find some of the tame individuals tethered and grazing near Skýros Town.

---

cap, vest, baggy trousers, leggings and *trokhádhia* (Skýrian sandals), but this is dying out. Likewise, old women still wear the favoured yellow scarves and long embroidered skirts.

The theory that Skýros was originally two islands seems doubtful, but certainly the character of the two parts of the island is very different. The north has a greener and more gentle landscape, and away from the port and town it retains much of its original pine forest. The sparsely inhabited south is mountainous, rocky and barren; there are few trees and the landscape is more reminiscent of the Cyclades than the Sporades. Compared with Skiáthos, Skópelos and Alónissos, Skýros isn't a great place for beaches. Most **beaches** along the west coast attract a certain amount of sea-borne rubbish, and, although the scenery is sometimes spectacular, the swimming isn't that good. The beaches on the east coast are all close to Skýros Town, and the best option is probably to stay here rather than heading for somewhere more isolated. The beaches at the north end have been commandeered by the big air force base there, which otherwise keeps a low profile.

Linariá

After crossing a seemingly endless expanse of sea, the boat docks at the tiny port of **LINARIÁ**, a functional place on the island's west coast. Most buildings are in the modern Greek-concrete-box style, and while it's a pleasant place to wile away time waiting for the ferry, there's little to keep you. Once here, try out the *mezedhopolío* next to *Kalí Kardhia* taverna, which has a wide selection of delectable dishes, and the *Kavos* bar, open day and night. In high season, kaïkia ply from Linariá to the Pentekáli and Ylania **grottos**, and to the islet of **Sarakino**, which has a cave and some of the Skyrian wild ponies. There's a reasonable sandy **beach** called Kalóyeros a few minutes' walk along the main road from Linariá, where you can camp.

A tarmac road connects Linariá to Skýros town, 10km away, and then continues round past the airport to Atsítsa, where the Skyros Centre has a branch; **buses** to **Skýros** and **Magaziá**, on the coast below, leave from the quay. Midway up the Linariá to Skýros-town route, a side road links Ahíli with Kalamítsa. Most other roads are passable by moped, apart from the direct track between Skýros town and Atsítsa.

Skýros Town

SKÝROS TOWN (also known as *Khorió*), with its decidedly Cycladic architecture, sits on the landward side of a high rock rising precipitously from the coast. According to legend, King Lycomedes pushed Theseus to his death from its summit. The town has a workaday atmosphere; it doesn't feel like a resort and isn't especially picturesque.

The older and more intriguing parts of town are higher up, climbing towards the **Kástro**, a mainly Byzantine building, built on the site of the ancient **acropolis**. There are few traces of the acropolis, although remains of the classical city walls survive below on the seaward side of the rock. The kástro is open to visitors; to reach its upper parts you pass through a rather private-looking gateway into the monastery, then through an attractive shaded courtyard and up a whitewashed tunnel. There's little to see at the top, apart from a few churches in various states of ruin, but there are great views over the town and the island, and the climb up takes you through the quieter and more picturesque part of town, with glimpses into traditionally decorated houses. With their gleaming copper pots, porcelain plates and antique embroideries decorating the hearth, these dwellings are a matter of intense pride among the islanders, who are often found seated in their doorways on tiny carved chairs.

At the northern end of town is the striking and splendidly incongruous **Memorial to Rupert Brooke**. It takes the form of a bronze statue of "Immortal Poetry" and its nakedness caused a scandal among the townspeople when it was first erected. Brooke, who visited the south of the island very briefly in April 1915, died shortly after of blood poisoning on a French hospital ship anchored offshore and was buried in an olive grove above the bay of Trís Boúkes. (The site can be reached on foot from Kalamítsa, by kaïki, or, less romantically, by taxi.) Brooke, who became something of a local hero, despite his limited acquaintance with Skýros, was adopted by Kitchener and later Churchill as the paragon of patriotic youth, in the face of his forthright socialist and internationalist views.

Just below the Brooke statue are two museums. The **Archeological Museum** (Tues–Sat 9am–3.30pm, Sun 9.30am–2.30pm; 500dr) has a modest collection of pottery and statues from excavations on the island, and a reconstruction of a traditional Skýros house interior. The privately-run **Faltaits Museum** (daily 10am–1pm & 5.30pm–8pm; free), in a nineteenth-century house built over one of the bastions of the ancient walls, is more interesting, with a collection of domestic items, costumes, embroideries, porcelain and rare books.

Practicalities

The **bus** from Linariá leaves you by the school; just below the main platía; the **OTE**, **post office** and **bank** are all nearby. Skyros Travel (☎0222/91 123 or 91 600), on the main street above the platía, can provide **information** and advice and can find a room or hotel; in high season it's a good idea to telephone them in advance. There are a few **moped** and **motorbike** rental places in the area around the platía.

You'll probably be met off the bus with offers of **rooms**, which it's as well to accept. If you'd like to stay in a traditional Skyrian house, those of *Anna Stergiou* (☎0222/91 657; ③) and *Maria Mavroyiorgi* (☎0222/91 440; ③) are both clean and cosy. Or you could try the pleasant *Nefeli* hotel (☎0222/91 964; ⑥) on the main road before the platía. There's a picturesque **campsite** nearer the beach, at the bottom of the steps below the archeological museum, with basic amenities but a good bar and a friendly management.

The platía and the main street running by it are the centre of village life, with a couple of noisy pubs and a wide choice of kafenía, tavernas and fast-food places. There are few outstanding **places to eat**; most are overpriced, or serve undistinguished food. *O Glaros*, just below the platía, is an exception: many of the local people eat here. It's a very basic taverna with a limited menu, but the owners are friendly and the food is good and reasonably priced. *Maryetis* has the best grilled fish and meat, *Sisyphos* has vegetarian specialities, and the *Sweets Workshop* does some wonderful cakes. For a special occasion, try *Kristina's* restaurant below the taxi rank (signposted); its Australian owner has an imaginative menu which has great desserts.

The town's **nightlife** is mostly bar-based until very late, when the few clubs get going. The most popular **bars** are *Renaissance*, *Kalypso* which plays jazz and blues, and

Rodon, also known for its good music. Later on, *Iy Stasis* is one of the most popular places. The best clubs include the *Skyropoula* and *Mylos*. Some bars also serve good breakfasts; here the favourite is *Anemos*, followed by *Kalypso* which has genuine Danish pastries.

Magaziá and Mólos and nearby beaches

A path leads down past the archeological museum towards the small coastal village of **MAGAZIÁ**, coming out by the official campsite (see p.709). From Magaziá, an 800-metre-long sandy beach stretches to the adjacent village of **MÓLOS**. In recent years, a sprawl of new development between the road and the beach has more or less joined the two villages together. Despite this, the beach is good, and there are lots of **rooms** down here for the young crowd that uses the beach's watersports and volleyball facilities. The Skyrian style *Katsarelia* at Magaziá (☎0222/91 446; ③), *Stamatis Marmaris* (☎0222/91 672; ③) beyond Mólos, and *Manolis Balotis* (☎0222/91 386; ③) near the campsite, are all excellent choices. A more up-market option is the *Paliopyrgos* hotel (☎0222/91 014; ⑤), 200m from the beach with a wonderful view. The beachfront **tavernas** compare favourably with those in town: the *Green Corner* opposite the campsite has delicious, cheap food to make up for its slow service, while the *Koufari* ouzeri near the *Xenia Hotel*, has excellent food for higher prices. At Mólos try the *Maryetis* garden restaurant and the ouzerí at *Balabani's Mill*, both at the end of the beach. It's worth sampling lobster in Skýros: it's a local speciality.

For quieter beaches, take the road past Mólos, or better, try the excellent and undeveloped (unofficial nudist) beach, *Papa tou Houma*, directly below the kástro. The path down to the beach is 150m beyond the *Skyropoula* disco, and isn't obvious from above. However, following the road south of here, the beaches are disappointing until **Aspoús**, which has a couple of tavernas and rooms to rent. Further south, **Akhíli**, had one of the best beaches on the island until the construction of its new marina. Southeast of Akhíli, the coast is rocky and inaccessible, although you can take a kaïki trip down to the bay of **Trís Boúkes**, passing some picturesque sea caves on the way.

Around the rest of the island

In summer, the whimsical bus service visits the more popular beaches. But if you want to branch out on your own, hire a moped. Roads, tracks and footpaths diverge from the main circle road, leading inward and seaward. Among the most interesting places to head for is **Palamári**, the neglected site of an early Bronze-Age settlement and a spectacular beach. Turn right after the road has begun to descend to the airport plain.

For a taste of the wooded interior, a hike on the dirt track from Skýros Town to **ATSÍTSA** is well worth the effort; it takes three to four hours, and is too rough for a moped. Atsítsa is an attractive bay with pine trees down to the sea (tapped by the Skyrian retsina industry), and an increasing number of rooms, in addition to the Skyros Centre buildings. The beach here is rocky and isn't great for swimming, but there are small sandy beaches fifteen and twenty minutes' walk to the north at **Kalógrias** and **Kyrá Panayiá**, though they are nothing out of the ordinary.

Elsewhere in the coniferous north, **Áyios Fokás** and **Péfkos** bays are easiest reached by a turning from the paved road near Linariá, while access from Atsítsa is via a reasonable dirt road. Both are in the process of being discovered by villa companies, but they have few rooms. Though quite primitive, Áyios Fokás has a very basic, excellent taverna; Péfkos has one too (both are only open in high season, as are all the other tavernas away from Liniariá, Skýros Town, Magaziá and Mólos). The bay is beautiful, and the beach reasonable but not that clean – the beaches around Skýros Town are much better for swimming.

As for exploring the great southern mountain of **Kókhilas**, this is best attempted only if you have a four-wheel drive vehicle, as the road is poor. A good road runs south of Kalamítsa to the naval base at Trís Boúkes (where Rupert Brooke is buried), which makes getting to the southern beaches easier. Kalamítsa, just south of Liniariá, lacks character, but the *Mouries* taverna between it and Liniariá is worth a stop, as is the remote beach half way to Trís Boúkes, which has no facilities.

Évvia (Euboea)

Évvia is the second-largest Greek island (after Crete), and seems more like an extension of the mainland to which it was in fact once joined. At **Khalkídha**, the gateway to the island, the curious old drawbridge has only a forty-metre channel to span, the island reputedly having been split from Attica and Thessaly by a blow from Poseidon's trident (earthquakes and subsidence being the more pedestrian explanations). Besides the new suspension bridge bypassing Khalkídha and linking Évvia to the mainland, there are ferry crossings at no fewer than seven points along its length, and the south of the island is closer to Athens than it is to northern Évvia.

Nevertheless, Évvia *is* an island, in places a very beautiful one. But it has an idiosyncratic history and demography, and an enduringly strange feel that has kept it out of the mainstream of tourism. A marked **Albanian influence** in the south, and scattered Lombard and Venetian watchtowers give it a distinctive flavour. Indeed, the island was the longest-surviving southerly outpost of the Ottoman Turks, who had a keen appreciation of the island's wealth, as did the Venetians and Lombards before them. The last **Ottoman garrison** was not evicted until 1833, hanging on in defiance of the peace settlement that awarded Évvia to the new Greek state. Substantial Turkish communities, renowned for their alleged brutality, remained until 1923.

Economically, Évvia has always been prized. By Greek standards, it's exceptionally **fertile**, producing everything from grain, corn and cotton to kitchen vegetables and livestock. The classical name "Euboea" means "rich in cattle," but nowadays cows are few and far between; its kid and lamb, however, are highly rated, as is the local retsina. Because of the collapse of much of its mining industry, parts of the island are actively seeking foreign tourism. For the moment, however, Greeks predominate, especially in the north around the spa of **Loutrá Edhipsoú**. In July and August, Évvia can seem merely a beach annexe for much of Thessaly and Athens.

In the rolling countryside of the **north**, grain-combines whirl on the sloping haymeadows between olive groves and pine forest. This is the most conventionally scenic part of the island, echoing the beauty of the smaller Sporades. The **northeast coast** is rugged and largely inaccessible, its few sandy beaches surf-pounded and often plagued by flotsam and jetsam; the **southwest** is gentler and more sheltered, though much disfigured by industrial operations. The **centre** of the island, between Khalkídha and the easterly port of Kými, is mountainous and dramatic, while the far **southeast** is mostly dry and very isolated.

Public **transport** consists of seasonal hydrofoils along the protected southwest coast from Khalkídha upwards, and passable bus services along the main roads to Káristos in the southeast, and Loutrá Edhipsoú in the northwest. Otherwise, explorations are best conducted by rented car; any two-wheeler will make little impact on the enormous distances involved.

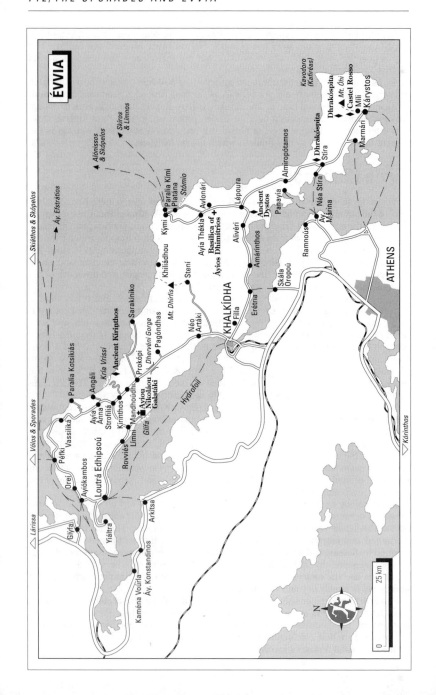

Khalkídha

The heavily industrialized island-capital of **KHALKÍDHA** (the ancient *Chalkis*, an appellation still used) is the largest town on Évvia, with a population of 50,000. A shipyard, rail sidings and cement works make it a dire place, apart from the old Ottoman quarter, **Kástro**, south of Venizélou Street, and the area around the Turkish fortress on the mainland. Hardly a trace remains of Khalkídha's once-thriving Jewish community, whose presence here dates back around 2500 years.

The entrance to the kástro – on the right as you head inland from the old Euripos bridge – is marked by the handsome fifteenth-century **mosque**, nominally a museum of Byzantine artefacts, but permanently locked. Beyond lie the remains of Karababa, the seventeenth-century Ottoman fortress, an arcaded Turkish aqueduct and the unique basilican **church of Ayía Paraskeví** (shut except during services). The church is an odd structure, converted by the Crusaders during the fourteenth century into a Gothic cathedral. In the opposite direction, in the new town, an **archeological museum**, Venizélou 13 (daily except Mon 8.30am–3pm; 500dr), has a good display of prehistoric, Hellenic and Roman finds from all over the island. The waterside overlooks the **Évripos**, the narrow channel dividing Évvia from the mainland, whose strange currents have baffled scientists for centuries. You can stand on the bridge that spans the narrowest point and watch the water swirling by like a river. Every few hours the current changes and the "tide" reverses. Aristotle is said to have thrown himself into the waters in despair at his inability to understand what was happening, so if you're puzzled you're in good company; there is still no entirely satisfactory explanation.

Practicalities

For most visitors, though, such activities are strictly time-fillers, with much the best view of the place to be had from the bus, train or hydrofoil on the way out. **Trains** arrive on the mainland-side of the channel, beneath the old fortress; given numerous, quick rail links with Athens, there's no conceivable reason to stay overnight. Most other services of interest lie within sight of the old Évripos bridge. The **hydrofoil** terminal sits just northeast, on the mainland side of the channel. The **bus station** is 400m from the bridge along Kótsou, then 50m right; no schedules are posted, but you should get a connection for any corner of the island as long as you show up by 2pm. The **OTE** is on Venizélou, near the museum, and cardphones are ubiquitous.

Options for **eating out** range from the restaurants lining the waterfront, where Athenians flock on Sundays to feast on Khalkídha's superior seafood, to a handful of acceptable grills serving adequate lunches in the immediate vicinity of the bus station.

Khalkídha to Kými

The coast road heading east out of Khalkídha is an exceptionally misleading introduction to the interior of Évvia. The industrial zone gives way to nondescript hamlets, which are succeeded between Erétria and Amárinthos by sequestered colonies of Athenian second homes and rather bleak beaches and large hotels frequented by British and German package-tour companies. There are some intriguing **Frankish towers** at Fýlla, worth a detour inland from Vasilikó if you have a car, and some easy connections to Athens, but little else.

Modern **ERÉTRIA** is a rather dreary resort laid out on a grid plan; for non-package travellers its main asset is a well-advertised ferry service across to Skála Oropoú in Attica. The site of **ancient Erétria** is more distinguished, though much of it lies under the town. A few scanty remains are dotted around the town centre, most conspicuously an **agora** and a **Temple of Apollo**, but more interesting are the excavations in the northwest corner, behind the excellent small museum (Tues– Sun 8.30am–3.15pm; 500dr), opened in 1991 in collaboration with the Swiss School of Archeology. Here a **theatre** has been uncovered; steps from the orchestra descend to an underground vault used for sudden entrances and exits. Beyond the theatre are the ruins of a **gymnasium** and a **sanctuary**. The museum guard will be happy to unlock the fourth-century BC **House of Mosaics**, five minutes' walk from the museum.

Just before Alivéri, an enormous modern power plant and a virtually intact medieval castle seem incongruously juxtaposed, and more Fýlla-type towers look down from nearby hills; thereafter, the route heads inland. Beyond Lépoura, where the road branches north and south, the scenery improves drastically. Take the north fork towards Kými, and cross some of the most peaceful countryside in Greece.

Twelve kilometres north of Lépoura, at Kháni Avlonaríou, stands the Romanesque thirteenth- or fourteenth-century **Basilica of Áyios Dhimítrios**, Évvia's largest and finest (ask for the key at the café next door). **AVLONÁRI** proper, 2km east, is dominated by a hill that commands most of the island's centre. At its crown is a huge Lombard or Venetian tower, rearing above the Neoclassical and vernacular houses that tier the lower slopes. This is the first place you'd probably choose to break a journey from Khalkídha, if you have your own vehicle; there's a single taverna below the platía, though no accommodation.

This part of Évvia is particularly well endowed with Byzantine chapels, since Avlonári was an archiepiscopal see from the sixth century onwards. Back on the road to Kými, a left fork just north of Kháni Avlonaríou (the bus goes this way) leads past the hamlet of Ayía Thékla, where a small, shed-like **chapel** of that saint, probably slightly later than Áyios Dhimítrios, hides in a lush vale below the modern church. Inside, enough fresco fragments remain with their large-eyed faces to suggest what has been lost over time. The right fork leads towards the coast and takes you past Oxílithos, with its somewhat more elaborate chapels of **Áyios Nikólaos** and **Ayía Ánna**, both at least a hundred years older than Áyios Dhimítrios.

The road hits the coast at the fine beach of **Stómio** (known also as just Paralía, or "Beach"), some 1500m of sand closing off the mouth of a river, which is deep, swimmable and often cleaner than the sea. To the north and east you glimpse the capes enclosing the broad bay of Kými. Up on the road, there are a couple of cafés and a small pension; most facilities, however, are further round the coast at **PLATÁNA**, where another river is flanked by a line of older houses, many with rooms or flats to rent.

Despite its name, the extremely functional port of **PARALÍA KÝMIS** has no real beach, and is not a particularly congenial place to be stuck overnight waiting for a ferry or hydrofoil to the Sporades or Límnos. The most substantial and traditional **taverna** is *Spanos/To Egeo*, at the south end of the front; there are just two **hotels**, *Coralli* (☎0222/22 212; ④) and *Beis* (☎0222/22 604; ④).

Most travellers get to **KÝMI** (the main ferry port to Skýros) by bus, which takes the inland route via Ayía Thékla. The upper part of town is built on a green ridge overlooking both the sea and Paralía Kými, 4km below. At the bottom of town, on the harbour-bound road, you can visit the **Folklore Museum**, which has an improbably large collection of costumes, household and agricultural implements, and old photos recording the doings of Kýmians both locally and in the USA, where there's a huge community. Among the emigrants was Dr George Papanikolaou, deviser of the "Pap" cervical smear test, and there's a statue honouring him up in the upper-town platía, where you might ask about **rooms**. There are some good **tavernas** like *To Balkoni*, on the main road towards the shore, with its superb view, where you can sample the products of the local vineyards.

To get up into the rugged country west of Kými, you must negotiate jeep tracks through the forest, or return to Khalkídha for the bus service up to **STENÍ**, a large and beautiful village at the foot of Mount Dhírfys. The village has a few cheap psistariés and two **hotels**, the *Dirfys* (☎0228/51 217; ③) and the *Steni* (☎0228/51 221; ③). It's a good area for hiking, most notably up the peaks of Dhírfys and Xirovoúni, and beyond to the isolated beach hamlets of Khiliádhou and Ayía Iríni, though you'll need a specialist hiking guide to do this (see "Books", p.832).

Southeast Évvia

The extension of Évvia southeast of Lépoura, so narrow that you can sometimes glimpse the sea on both sides, has a flavour very distinct from the rest of the island. Often bleak and windswept, it forms a geological unit with neighbouring Ándhros, with shared slates and marble. Ethnically, the south has much in common with that northernmost Cyclade: both were heavily settled by Albanian immigrants from the early fifteenth century onwards, and Arvanítika – a **medieval dialect** of Albanian – was until recently the first language of the remoter villages here. Even non-Arvanítika speakers often betray their ancestry by their startlingly fair colouring and aquiline features. For a place so close to Athens, the south is often surprisingly untouched by modernity; some of the houses have yet to lose their original slate roofs. Many lack electricity, and the few fields on the steep slopes are far more often worked by donkeys and horses than by farm machinery.

Immediately southeast of Lépoura, most maps persist in showing the lake of Dhístos in bright blue. In fact, the lake area has been almost totally drained and reclaimed as rich farmland, much to the detriment of the migratory birds who used to stop off here, and to the annoyance of Greek and foreign environmentalists who would prefer that they still did so. Atop the almost perfectly conical hill in the centre of the flat basin are the sparse fifth-century BC ruins of **ancient Dystos**, and a subsequent medieval citadel, hard to explore because the surroundings are so swampy.

Beyond the Dhístos plain, the main road continues along the mountainous spine of the island to Káristos at the southern end of the paved road system and bus line. If you have your own transport, it's worth stopping off at **STÝRA**, above which are a cluster of **Dhrakóspita** (Dragon Houses), signposted at the north edge of the village and reached by track, then trail. They are so named because only mythological beings were thought capable of shifting into place their enormous masonry blocks. Their origins and uses have yet to be definitively established. The most convincing theory suggests that they are sixth-century BC temples built by immigrants or slaves from Asia Minor working in the nearby marble and slate quarries.

The shore annexe of **NÉA STÝRA**, 5km downhill from the hill village, is a fairly standard package resort, worth knowing about only for its handy ferry connection to Ayía Marína (which gives access to ancient Rhamnous) on the Attic peninsula. Much the same can be said for **MARMÁRI**, 19km south, except in this case the ferry link is with Rafína. The road between Marmári and Kárystos has been messed up considerably in the lengthy process of constructing a superhighway through the island, a project whose end is not in sight.

Kárystos and around

At first sight **KÁRYSTOS** is a rather boring grid (courtesy of nineteenth-century Bavarian town-planners), which ends abruptly to east and west and is studded with modern buildings. King Otho liked the site so much that he contemplated transferring the Greek capital here, and there are still some graceful Neoclassical buildings dating from that period. Kárystos improves with prolonged acquaintance, though you're unlikely to stay for more than a few days. What it can offer is the superb (if often windy) beach of **Psilí Ámmos** to the west, and a lively, genuine working-port atmosphere. Only one plot of fenced-in foundations, in the central bazaar, bears out the town's ancient provenance, and the oldest obvious structure is the fourteenth-century Venetian **Bourtzi** (permanently locked) on the waterfront. This small tower is all that remains of once-extensive fortifications. Every evening the shore road is blocked with a gate at this point to allow an undisturbed promenade by the locals.

PRACTICALITIES
Rafína-based **ferries** and **hydrofoils** also serve Kárystos; **buses** arrive inland, above the central platía and below the National Bank, near a tiny combination grill/ticket office labelled KTEL. This has information on the extremely infrequent (once daily at best) departures to the remote villages of the Kavodóro (Kafiréas) cape to the east. Additional information on the August wine festival and sightseeing in the region is provided by the friendly office in the restored Town Hall.

Finding affordable **accommodation** can be a problem. The best bet in the middle range is the *Karystion* (☎0224/22 391; ④), in the park beyond the Bourtzi on the shore road, followed by the big *Galaxy* (☎0224/22 600; ④) on the west side of the waterfront, and the *Als*, just inland at mid-esplanade (☎0224/22 202; ③), which can be pretty noisy. Another strategy is to follow up signs in restaurant windows advertising **rooms** inland.

By contrast, you're spoilt for choice when **eating out**, as Kárystos must have more restaurants than the rest of Évvia put together. Among the best choices are the *Kavo Doros*, a friendly and reasonable taverna on Párodos Sakhtoúri just behind the front, which serves oven food; *Ta Kalamia*, at the west end of the esplanade by the start of Psilí Ámmos beach is a cheap, filling and popular lunchtime option; while the English-speaking *Ta Ovreika*, in the old Jewish quarter, Sakhtoúri 114, has both Greek and imaginative international cuisine.

AROUND KÁRYSTOS
The obvious excursion from Kárystos is inland towards **Mount Ókhi** (1399m) Évvia's highest peak after Dhírfys and Xirovoúni. **MÝLI**, a fair-sized village around a spring-fed oasis, 3km straight inland, makes a good first stop, with its few tavernas. Otherwise, the medieval castle of **Castel Rosso** beckons above, a twenty-minute climb up from the main church (longer in the frequent, howling gales). Inside the castle is a total ruin, except for an Orthodox **Chapel of Profítis Ilías** built over the Venetians' water cistern, but the sweeping views over the sea and the town make the trip worthwhile.

Behind, the ridges of Ókhi are as lunar and inhospitable as the broad plain around Káristos is fertile. From Míli, it's a three-hour-plus hike up the largely bare slopes, mostly by a path cutting across the new road, strewn with unfinished granite columns, abandoned almost two thousand years ago. The path passes a little-used alpine-club shelter (fed by spring water) and yet another *dhrakóspito*, even more impressive than the three smaller ones at Stýra. Built of enormous schist slabs, seemingly sprouting from the mountain, this one is popularly supposed to be haunted.

From Khalkídha to Límni

The main road due north from Khalkídha crosses a few kilometres of flat farmland and salt marsh on either side of the refugee settlement of Néa Artáki, after which it climbs steeply through forested hills and the **Dhervéni gorge**, gateway to the north of Évvia.

The village of **PROKÓPI** lies beyond the narrows, in a valley defined by the rich and beautiful woods that make it famous. A counterpoint, in the village itself, is the ugly 1960s pilgrimage church of **St John the Russian**, which holds the saint's relics. The "Russian" was actually a Ukrainian soldier, captured by the Turks in the early eighteenth century and taken to Turkey where he died. According to locals, his mummified body began to sponsor miracles, and the saint's relics were brought here by Orthodox Greeks from Cappadocian Prokópi (today Ürgüp) in the 1923 population exchange –

Évvian Prokópi is still referred to by the locals as Ahmétaga, the name of the old
Turkish fiefdom here that was bought by an English nobleman, Edward Noel, a cousin
of Lord Byron's, right after the War of Independence. His descendants now run summer courses in various crafts, based in the manor house.

Following a shady, stream-fed glen for the 8km north of Prokópi, you suddenly
emerge at Mandoúdhi, much the biggest village in the north of the island, though now
squarely in the doldrums following the collapse of the local magnesite industry; ignore
signs or depictions on certain maps of a beach at Paralía Mandoúdhi, which is nothing
more than abandoned quarries and crushing plants. The closest serviceable beach is
at **Paralía Kírinthos**, better known as **Krýa Vrýssi** (take a right-hand turning off the
main road, 3km beyond Mandoúdhi). At the coast, a river and an inlet bracket a small
beach, with the headland south of the river supporting the extremely sparse remains of
ancient Kirinthos. The hamlet of Kirinthos, just past Mandoúdhi, has some visitors,
owing to the craft school there.

Back on the main road, a fork at Strofiliá, 8km north of Mandoúdhi, offers a choice
of routes: continue north to the coastal resorts that curl round the end of the island (see
below), east to Pýli and then south to some unspoiled beaches on the way to Cape
Sarakíniko, or head west for Límni.

Límni

If you're hunting for a place to stay, **LÍMNI**, on the west coast 19km from Strofiliá, is
by far the most practical and attractive base north of Khalkídha. The largely
Neoclassical, tile-roofed town, built from the wealth engendered by nineteenth-century
shipping prowess, is the most appealing on the island, with serviceable beaches and a
famous convent nearby. A small **folk art museum** features pottery, coins and sculpture fragments, as well as local costumes, fabrics and furniture.

There is a regular **hydrofoil** service to Khalkídha and the Sporades, and buses from
Khalkídha stop at the north side of the quay. Límni has an **OTE**, a **post office** and **two
banks**, all inland just off the main through-road inito town from Strofiliá.

As yet, Límni gets few package tours, and accommodation is usually available in its
rooms or hotels, except during August. At the extreme south, quieter, end of the waterfront, the *Limni* (☎0227/31 316; ③) is good value, with singles and doubles; the *Plaza*
beside the bus stop, (☎0227/31 235; ③), is a bit more reasonable, but has no singles
and gets some noise from nocturnal revels outside. The *Pyrofanis* (☎0227/31 640), an
ouzerí beyond the *Plaza*, rents some **rooms** upstairs (⑤) and apartments (④) north of
town. The best **place to eat** in terms of setting, menu and popularity is *O Platanos*
(under the enormous quayside plane tree). Other local favourites are *Kallitsis* inland
from the waterfront, and *Lambros* and *O David* on the way to Katounia beach to the
south of town.

Around Límni

There are no recommendable beaches in Límni itself, though if you continue 2.5km
northwest from the town you reach the gravel strand of **Kokhýli**, with a basic but leafy
campsite out on the cape, 500m beyond mid-beach. Here there are some congenial
places to stay, most notably *Denis House* (☎0227/31 787; ④) and the more luxurious
Ostria (☎0227/32 247; ⑥) which has a pool.

ROVVIÉS, some 14km west of Límni, doesn't stand out, but with its medieval tower,
rooms, hotels, grid of weekenders' apartments and services, it's the last place of any
sort along the scenic coast road to Loutrá Edhipsoú.

The outstanding excursion from Límni is 7km south (under your own steam) to the
Convent of Ayíou Nikoláou Galatáki, superbly set on the wooded slopes of Mount
Kandhíli, overlooking the north Evvian Gulf. To get there, veer up and left at the

unsigned fork off the coast road; there's no formal scheme for visiting, but don't show up in the early afternoon or around sunset as the gates will be shut. Though much rebuilt since its original Byzantine foundation atop a Poseidon temple, the convent retains a thirteenth-century tower built to guard against pirates, and a crypt. One of a dozen or so nuns will show you frescoes in the katholikón dating from the principal sixteenth-century renovation. Especially vivid, on the right of the narthex, is the *Entry of the Righteous into Paradise*; the righteous ascend a perilous ladder, being crowned by angels and received by Christ while the wicked miss the rungs and fall into the maw of Leviathian.

Below Ayíou Nikoláou Galatáki, and easily combined with it to make a full half-day outing, are the pebble-and-sand beaches of **Glyfá**, arguably the best on Évvia's south-west-facing coast. There are several in succession, leading up to the very base of Mount Kandhíli, some reachable by paths, the last few only by boat. The shore is remarkably clean, considering the number of summer campers who pitch tents here for weeks on end; a single roadside spring, 2km before the coast, is the only facility in the whole zone.

Northern coastal resorts

Returning to the junction at Strofiliá, take the main road north for 8km to **AYÍA ÁNNA** (locally and universally elided to *Ayiánna*), which has long enjoyed the unofficial status of Évvia's most **folkloric village**, by virtue of traditional costumes worn by the older women, and an assiduous local ethnographer, Dimitris Settas, who died in 1989. The place itself is nothing extraordinary, and most passers-by are interested in the prominently marked turnoff for **Angáli beach**, 5km east. This is billed as the area's best, and it's sandy enough, but like this entire coast it's exposed and can get garbage-strewn, the low hills behind lending little drama. A frontage road, set back 200m or so, is lined by a few kilometres of anonymous villas and apartments, with the "village" at the north end.

Ten kilometres north of Ayía Ánna, a side road heads downhill for 6km, past the village of Kotsikiá, to **Paralía Kotsikiás**. The small cove with its taverna and rooms serves primarily as a fishing-boat anchorage, and its tiny, seaweed-strewn beach is of little interest. **Psaropoúli beach**, 2km below Vassiliká village (13km north of the Kotsikiá turnoff), is more useable in its three-kilometre length, but like Ayía Ánna it is scruffy and shadeless, with a smattering of rooms, self-catering units and tavernas not imparting much sense of community. **Elliniká**, the next signposted beach, lies only 800m below its namesake village inland; it's far smaller than Angáli or Psaropoúli, but cleaner and certainly the most picturesque spot on this coast, with a church-capped islet offshore as a target to swim to. The approach driveway has a very limited number of facilities: a minimarket, one taverna and a few studios.

Beyond Elliniká, the road (and bus line) skirts the northern tip of Évvia to curl southwest towards **PÉFKI**, a seaside resort mobbed with Greeks in summer, which straggles for some two kilometres along a mediocre beach. The best **restaurants**, near the north end of this strip, include *Ouzeri Ta Thalassina* and *Psitopolio O Thomas*, while *Zakharoplastio O Peristeras* proffers decadent desserts. **Accommodation** is the usual Évvian mix of self-catering units and a few seaside hotels such as *Galini* (☎0226/41 208; ④) and *Myrtia* (☎0226/41 202; ④), all resolutely pitched at mainlanders; the **campsite**, *Camping Pefki*, is 2km north of town behind the beach, rather pricey and geared to people with caravans.

The next resort (14km southwest), **OREÍ**, is a low-key fishing village, whose cafés are favoured by those in the know as the best places to watch the sun set. It has a fine statue of a Hellenistic bull, hauled up from the sea in 1965, and is also the last **hydrofoil stop** en route to Vólos and the Sporades. Some 7km further along the coast, **AYIÓKAMBOS** has a frequent ferry connection to Glyfá on the mainland opposite, from where there are buses to Vólos. Ayiókambos is surprisingly pleasant considering its port function, with a patch of beach, two or three tavernas and a few rooms for rent.

The trans-island bus route ends 14km south of Ayiókambos at **LOUTRÁ EDHIP-SOÚ**, which attracts older Greeks (filling more than a hundred creaky hotels and pensions) who come to bathe at the **spas** renowned since antiquity for curing everything from gallstones to depression. There are less regimented **hot springs** at **Yiáltra**, 15km west around the head of Edhipsós bay, where the water boils up on the rocky beach, warming the shallows to comfortable bath temperature. From Loutrá Edhipsoú, the coast road heads southeast to Límni.

travel details

Alkyon Tours (in cooperation with Nomicos ferry lines), and the competing Goutos Lines, provide expensive **conventional ferry** services out of Vólos, Áyios Konstandínos and Kými, with fares almost double those on Cyclades or Dodecanese lines. On the plus side, Alkyon maintain an Athens office (Akadhimías 97; ☎01/38 43 220) for purchase of ferry, Flying Icarus and combined bus-and-ferry tickets. Between April and October, Flying Dolphin and Flying Icarus **hydrofoils** operate between various mainland ports and the Sporades. These are pricier than the ferries but cut journey times virtually in half.

SKIÁTHOS, SKÓPELOS AND ALÓNISSOS
Ferries

Áyios Konstandínos to: Skiáthos (14 weekly; 3hr); Skópelos (10 weekly; 5hr, 6 continuing to Alónissos, 6hr).

Kými to: Alónissos (1 weekly; 3hr) and Skópelos (4 weekly; 3hr 30min).

Vólos to: Skiáthos (3–4 daily; 3hr) and Skópelos (3–4 daily; 4hr); Alónissos (at least daily; 5hr; this is the most consistent service out of season, and is always the cheapest).

Flying Dolphins (April–Oct only)

Áyios Konstandínos to: Skiáthos, Glóssa, Skópelos and Alónissos (April, May and early Oct 1–3 daily; June–Sept 3–5 daily).

Néos Marmarás (Khalkidhikí): to: Skiáthos, Skópelos, Alónissos (June–Aug 3 weekly).

Plataniás (Pílion) to: Skiáthos, Skópelos and Alónissos (June–Aug 1 daily).

Thessaloníki to: Skiáthos, Glóssa, Skópelos and Alónissos (June–Aug daily).

Tríkeri (Pílion) to: Vólos (June–mid-Oct daily); Skiáthos (June–mid-Sept 1 daily); Skiáthos, Skópelos and Alónissos (April–Oct daily).

Vólos to: Skiáthos, Glóssa and Skópelos (April, May and Oct 2 daily; June–Sept 4 daily); at least 2 daily (April–Oct) continue from Skópelos to Alónissos.

Flights
Athens to Skiáthos (3 daily; 40min).

SKÝROS
Ferries

Skýros is served by conventional ferry, the *Lykomides*, from **Kými** (2hr). Services are at least twice daily mid-June to mid-Sept (usually at around noon and 5pm), once daily (5pm) the rest of the year; ☎0222/22 020 for current information. There is a connecting bus service for the afternoon boat, from the Liossíon 260 terminal in Athens (departs 12.30pm).

Flying Dolphins
A weekly **hydrofoil** (June–Aug; Wed) links Skýros with Skiáthos, Skópelos and Alónissos.

Flights
Athens to: Skýros (mid June–Oct; 5 weekly; Nov–June 2 weekly).

ÉVVIA
Buses
Athens (Liossíon 260 terminal) to: Khalkídha (every 30min 7.45am–9pm; 1hr 40min); Kými (4–5 daily; 3hr 40min).

Khalkídha to: Kárystos (1–2 daily; 3hr); Límni (4 daily; 1hr 30min); Loutrá Edhipsoú (4 daily; 3hr); Kými (4 daily; 1 hr 45 min).

Trains

Athens (Laríssis station) to: Khalkídha (18 daily; 1hr 25min).

Ferries

Arkítsa to: Loutrá Edhipsoú (12 daily 6.45am–11pm; 50min).

Ayía Marína: to: Néa Stýra (summer 12–20 daily; 50min); Panayía (summer 3–4 daily; 50min).

Glýfa to: Ayiókambos (8 daily; 30min).

Rafína: to Kárystos (Mon–Thurs 4 daily, Tues–Thurs 2 daily, Fri, Sat & Sun 5 daily; 1hr); Marmári (4 daily; 1hr).

Skála Oropoú to: Erétria (hourly 5am–10pm; 25min).

Flying Dolphins

Khalkídha to: Límni, Loutrá Edhipsoú, Oreí, Skiáthos and Skópelos (May to mid-Oct 5 weekly; usually late afternoon).

Oreí to: Vólos, Skópelos and Alónissos (June to mid-Sept daily); Skiáthos (June to mid-Oct 2 daily).

Ilio Line Hydrofoils

Rafína to: Kárystos (mid-June to late Sept 4 weekly).

Tínos/Mýkonos (Cyclades) to: Kárystos (mid-June to late Sept 3 weekly).

Connecting buses from Athens run to Rafína (every 30min; 1hr 30min), Ayía Marína (5 daily; 1hr 15min) and Skála Oropoú (hourly; duration) all from the Mavromatéon terminal, and to Arkítsa and Glýfa from the Liossíon 260 terminal.

CHAPTER TWELVE

THE IONIAN ISLANDS

T he six **Ionian** islands, shepherding their satellites down the west coast of the mainland, float on the haze of the Adriatic, their green, even lush, silhouettes coming as a shock to those more used to the stark outlines of the Aegean. The fertility is a direct result of the heavy rains which sweep over the archipelago – and especially Corfu – from October to March, so if you visit in the off-season, come prepared.

The islands were the Homeric realm of Odysseus, centred on Ithaca (modern Itháki) and here alone of all modern Greek territory the Ottomans never held sway. After the fall of Byzantium, possession passed to the **Venetians** and the islands became a keystone in that city state's maritime empire from 1386 until its collapse in 1797. Most of the population must have remained immune to the establishment of Italian as the official language and the arrival of Roman Catholicism, but Venetian influence remains evident in the architecture of the island capitals, despite damage from a series of earthquakes.

On Corfu, the Venetian legacy is mixed with that of the **British**, who imposed a military "protectorate" over the Ionian islands at the close of the Napoleonic Wars, before ceding the archipelago to Greece in 1864. There is, however, no question of the islanders' essential Greekness: the poet Dioníssios Solómou, author of the National Anthem, hailed from the Ionians, as did Nikos Mantzelos, who provided the music, and the first Greek president, Ioannis Kapodistrias.

Today, **tourism** is the dominating influence, especially on **Corfu** (Kérkyra), which was one of the first Greek islands established on the package-holiday circuit. Its east coast is one of the few stretches in Greece with development to match the Spanish *costas*, and in summer even its distinguished old capital, Kérkyra Town, wilts beneath the onslaught. However, the island is large enough to retain some of its charms and is perhaps the most scenically beautiful of the group. Parts of **Zákynthos** (Zante) –

ACCOMMODATION PRICE CODES

Throughout the book we've used the following **price codes** to denote the cheapest available room in high season; all are prices for a double room, except for category ①, which represents per person rates. Out of season, rates can drop by up to fifty percent, especially if you are staying for three or more nights. Single rooms, where available, cost around seventy percent of the price of a double.

Rented private rooms on the islands usually fall into the ② or ③ categories, depending on their location and facilities, and the season; a few in the ④ category are more like plush self-catering apartments. They are not generally available from late October through to the beginning of April, when only hotels tend to remain open.

① 1400–2000dr	④ 8000–12,000dr
② 4000–6000dr	⑤ 12,000–16,000dr
③ 6000–8000dr	⑥ 16000dr and upwards

For more accommodation details, see pp.39–42.

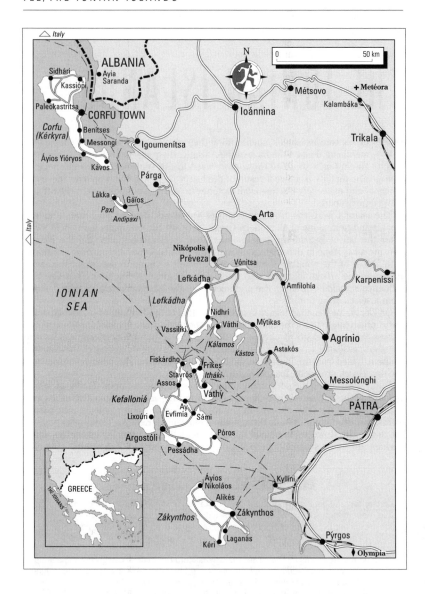

which with Corfu has the Ionians' best beaches – seem to be going along the same tourist path, following the introduction of charter flights from northern Europe, but elsewhere the pace and scale of development is a lot less intense. Little **Páxi** is a bit too tricky to reach and lacks the water to support a large-scale hotel, while **Lefkádha** – which is connected to the mainland by a causeway and "boat bridge" – has, so far at least, quite a low-key straggle of ports and only two major resorts. Perhaps the most

The islands of **Kýthira** and **Andikýthira**, isolated at the foot of the Peloponnese, are historically part of the Ionian islands. However, at some 200km from the nearest other Ionians, and with no ferry connections to the northerly Ionians, they are most easily reached from **Yíthio** or **Neápoli** and are thus covered in Chapter Two.

Similarly, the islet of **Kálamos**, Lefkádha's most distant satellite, is inaccessible from the islands and covered therefore in Chapter Four.

rewarding duo for island-hopping are **Kefalloniá** and **Itháki**, the former with a series of "real towns" and a life in large part independent of tourism, the latter, Odysseus's rugged capital, protected by an absence of sand. The Ionian islands' claims to Homeric significance are manifested in the countless bars, restaurants and streets named after characters in the Odyssey including the "nimble-witted" hero himself, Penelope, Nausica, Calypso and Cyclops.

Corfu (Kérkyra)

Between the heel of Italy and the west coast of mainland Greece, green, mountainous **Corfu (Kérkyra)** was one of the first Greek islands to attract mass tourism in the 1960s. Indiscriminate exploitation turned parts into eyesores, but much is still uninhabited olive groves, mountain or woodland. The majority of package holidays are based in the most developed resorts, but unspoiled terrain is often only a few minutes' walk away.

Corfu is thought to have been the model for Prospero and Miranda's place of exile in Shakespeare's *The Tempest*, and was certainly known to writers like Spenser, Milton and, – more recently – Lear, Miller, and Gerald and Lawrence Durrell. Lawrence Durrell's *Prospero's Cell* evokes the island's "delectable landscape", still evident in some of the best beaches in the whole archipelago.

Kérkyra Town

The capital, **Kérkyra Town** (or Corfu Town), was renovated for an EU summit in 1994, and is now one of the most elegant island capitals in the whole of Greece. Although many of its finest buildings were destroyed by Nazi bombers in the World War II, its two massive forts, the sixteenth century church of Áyios Spirídonhas, and buildings dating from French and British administrations remain intact. As the island's sole port of entry by ferry or plane, Corfu is packed in summer.

Arrivals, information and services

Ferries from Italy dock at the New Port (Néo Limáni) west of the Néo Froúrio (New Fort); those connecting to the mainland (Igoumenítsa, Párga and Pátra) dock further west on the seafront. The Old Port (Paléo Limáni), east of the New Port, is used for day excursions and ferries to Paxí. There are ferry offices at both ports; ferries to Italy or south towards Pátra become very busy in summer and booking is advisable. The port police (☎0661/32 655) can advise on services.

The **airport** is 2km south of the city centre. There are no airport buses, although local **blue buses** #5 and #6 can be flagged at the junction where the airport approach meets the main road (500m). It's a forty minute walk on flat terrain into town (right at the junction then follow the sea road). **Taxis** charge around 2000dr (but agree the fare in advance) or phone (☎0661/33 811) for a radio cab.

The **tourist office** (Mon–Fri 8am–2pm; ☎0661/37 520) on the corner of Vouleftón and Mantzárou has accommodation and transport details. The **OTE** at is Mantzárou 3

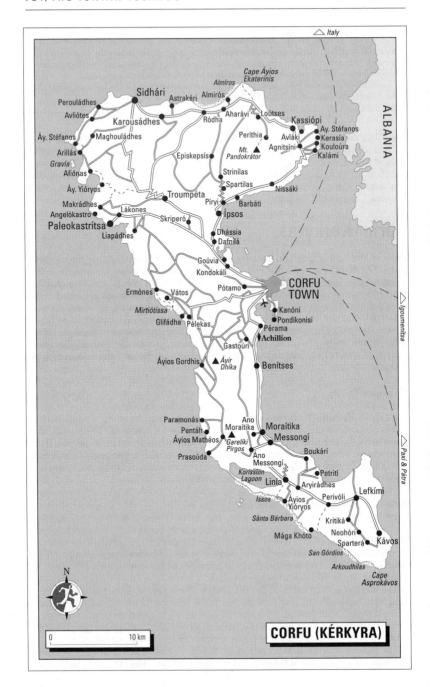

△ Italy

ALBANIA

Cape Áyios
Ekaterínis

Almíros

Sidhári

Astrakéri   Almirós

Perouládhes

Avliótes

Karousádhes   Ródha   Aharávi   Loútses   Kassiópi

Áy. Stéfanos   Maghouládhes   Perithia   Avláki   Ay. Stéfanos
                                                    Agnitsíni   Kerasía
Arillás   Mt.   Kouloúra
Gravía   Episkepsís   Pandokrátor   Kalámi
Afiónas
        Áy. Yióryos   Strinilas
                        Spartilas   Nissáki
Makrádhes   Píryi   Barbáti
Angelókastro   Lákones   Troumpéta   Ípsos
Paleokastrítsa   Skriperó
        Liapádhes   Dhássia
                            Dafnilá

                Goúvia
                Kondokáli

        Ermónes   Vátos   Pótamo   CORFU
                                        TOWN   △ Igoumenítsa

    Mirtiótissa   Kanóni
    Glifádha   Pélekas   Pondikonísi
                            Pérama
                Gastoúri   Achíllion

    Áyios Gordhís   ▲ Áyir   Benítses
                    Dhíka

    Paramonás   Áno
        Pentáh   Moraítika   Moraítika
    Áyios Mathéos   ▲   Messongí   △ Paxí & Pátra
                    Garelíki
        Prasoúda   Pírgos   Boukári
                    Áno
                    Messongí   Petrití
                Korission
                Lagoon   Linía   Aryirádhes
                    Issos   Perivóli   Lefkími
                        Áyios
                        Yióryos
            Sánta Bárbara   Kritiká
        Mága Khóto   Neohóri
                        Spárterá   Kávos
                San Górdios
                    Arkoudhílas   Cape
                                Asprokávos

N

0   10 km

CORFU (KÉRKYRA)

(daily 6am–midnight; ☎0661/45 699) and the **post office** is on the corner of Alexándhras and Zafiropoúlou (Mon–Fri 7.30am–8pm).

Transport

Corfu's **bus** service radiates from the capital. There are **two** terminals; the island-wide service is based on Avramíou, and the suburban system, which also serves nearby resorts such as Benítses and Ípsos, is based in Platía San Rocco (Platía G. Theotóki). Services stop around 6pm, and are scant on Sundays. Avramíou also serves Athens and Thessaloníki, and sells combined bus/ferry tickets. Major **ferry** lines have franchises on Ethníkis Antistásseos opposite the New Port: Minoan/Strintzis (☎0661/25 000 or 25 332), Anek (☎0661/32 664) and Adriatica (☎0661/38 089).

Cars can also be rented from international agencies at the airport; try Avis, Ethníkis Antistásseos 42 (☎0661/24 404), Budget, Venízelou 22 (☎0661/49 100; airport ☎0661/44 017) or Hertz (☎0661/33 547). Among local companies, Sunrise, Ethníkis Antistásseos 14, in the New Port (☎0661/44 325) rents out cars and **bikes**.

Accommodation

Accommodation in Corfu is busy all year round, and expensive. Room owners meet mainland and international ferries, and taxi drivers will often know of decent rooms. Budget travellers might best head straight for the **campsite** (☎0661/91 202) 2km north at Kondokáli – or, even further out, the superior campsite with cheap bungalows at **Dhássia** (see p.729). Most hotels are in the old town, or on the seafront.

Arcadian, Kapodhistríou 44 (☎0661/37 670). Mid-range hotel in a central setting. Street noise can be a problem. ③.

Astron, Dónzelot 15 (☎0661/39 505). A basic but reliable travellers' favourite for decades. Open year round. ④.

Atlantis, Xenofóndos Stratígou 48 (☎0661/35 560). Large and spacious air-conditioned hotel. Open year round. ③.

Bella Venezia, Zambéli 4 (☎0661/46 500). Smart and very good value: just behind the *Cavalieri*, with all the *Cavalieri*'s comforts, but cheaper. Open year round. ⑤.

Cavalieri, Kapodhistríou 4 (☎0661/39 041 or 39 336). Smart and friendly, with great views and a roof bar open to the public. Open year round. ⑥.

Europa, Yitsiáli 10 (☎0661/39 304). Small family hotel one block back from the Igoumenítsa ferry quay. ④.

Hermes, Markóra 14 (☎0661/39 268). A favourite with budget travellers. Overlooks the noisy market. Open year round. ②.

Kypros, Ayíon Patéron 13 (☎0661/40 675). Basic, but one of the best bets in the town; it's very central, so be prepared for noise. ③.

Olympic, Ioníou Voulís 4 (☎0661/30 532). Big international-style hotel with large and comfortable en-suite rooms. Open year round. ④.

The Town

Corfu Town comprises a number of distinct areas. The **Campiello**, the oldest, sits on the hill above the old port, while the streets running between the Campiello and Velisáriou are what remains of the town's **Jewish Quarter**. These districts form the core of the old town, and their tall, narrow alleys conceal some of Corfu's most beautiful architecture. **Mandoúki**, beyond the Old Port, is the commercial and dormitory area for the port, and is worth exploring as a living quarter of the city, away from the tourism racket. The town's **commercial area** lies inland from the **Spianádha** (Esplanade), roughly between G (Georgíou) Theotóki, Alexandhrás and Kapodhistríou streets, with shops and boutiques around Voulgaréous and G Theotóki and off Platía Theotóki. Tucked behind Platía San Rocco and Odhós Theotóki is the old **morning market** which sells fish and farm produce.

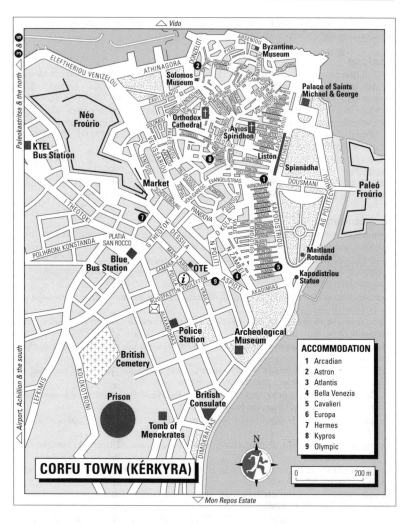

△ *Vido*

ELEFTHERIOU VENIZELOU

ARSENIOU

Byzantine Museum

ATHINAGORA

DONZELOT

PIERI

CAMPIELLO

Solomos Museum

ZAVITSIANOU

Palace of Saints Michael & George

Néo Froúrio

■ **KTEL Bus Station**

Orthodox Cathedral

Áyios Spiridhon

Listón

Spianádha

Market

EVANGELISTRIAS

PANDOVA

WINDMANN

DOUSMANI

Paleó Froúrio

I. THEOTOKI

G. THEOTOKI

DESSILA

PLATIA SAN ROCCO

POLIHRONI KONSTANDA

AS. POLITECHNOU

KAPODISTRIOU

Blue Bus Station

SAMARA

i

◆**OTE**

VOULETON

THALIA

RIZOSPASTON

AKADIMIAS

Maitland Rotunda

Kapodistriou Statue

ALEXANDRAS

Police Station

Archeological Museum

LEFKIMIS

KOLOKOTRONI

British Cemetery

Prison

Tomb of Menekrates

British Consulate

DIMOKRATIAS

ACCOMMODATION

1 Arcadian
2 Astron
3 Atlantis
4 Bella Venezia
5 Cavalieri
6 Europa
7 Hermes
8 Kypros
9 Olympic

CORFU TOWN (KÉRKYRA)

N

0   200 m

▽ *Mon Repos Estate*

The most obvious sights are the forts, the **Paleó Froúrio** and **Néo Froúrio**, whose designations (*paleó* – "old", *néo* – "new") are a little misleading, since what you see of the older structure was begun by the Byzantines in the mid-twelfth century, just a hundred years before the Venetians began work on the newer citadel. They have both been modified and damaged by various occupiers and besiegers since, the last contribution being the Neoclassical shrine of **St George**, built by the British in the middle of Paleó Froúrio during the 1840s. Looming above the old port, the Néo Froúrio (daily 9am–9pm; 400dr), is the more interesting of the two. The entrance, at the back of the fort, gives onto cellars, dungeons, and battlements, with excellent views over town and bay; there's a small gallery and café at the summit. The Paleó

Froúrio (daily 9am–9pm; 800dr) is rather dull in comparison but hosts daily son et lumière shows.

Just west of the Paleó Froúrio, the **Listón**, an arcaded street built during the French occupation by the architect of the Rue de Rivoli in Paris, and the green **Spianádha** (Esplanade) it overlooks, are the focus of town life. At the south end of the Spianádha, the **Maitland Rotunda** was built to honour the first British High Commissioner of Corfu and the Ionian islands. The neighbouring statue of Ioannis Kapodistrias celebrates the local hero and statesman (1776–1831) who led the diplomatic efforts for independence and was made Greece's first president in 1827. At the far northern end of the Listón, the nineteenth-century **Palace of SS Michael and George**, a solidly British edifice built as the residence of their High Commissioner (one of the last of whom was the future British Prime Minister William Gladstone), and later used as a palace by the Greek monarchy. The former state rooms house the **Sino-Japanese Museum** (Tues–Sat 8.30am–3pm, Sun 9.30am–2.30pm; 500dr) is a must for aficionados of Oriental culture. Amassed by Corfiot diplomat Gregorios Manos (1850–1929), it includes Noh theatre masks, woodcuts, wood and brass statuettes, samurai weapons, and art works from Thailand, Korea and Tibet. Opened in 1996, the adjoining **Modern Art Museum** (same hours and price) holds a small collection of contemporary Greek art. It's an interesting diversion, as are the gardens and café-bar secreted behind the palace.

In a nearby back street off Arseníou, five minutes' from the palace, is the **museum** (Mon–Fri 5–8pm; 200dr) dedicated to modern Greece's most famous poet, **Dionissios Solómous**. Born on Zákynthos, Solomos was author of the poem *Hýmnos yiá Élefthería (Hymn to Liberty)*, which was to become the Greek national anthem. He studied at Corfu's Ionian Academy, and lived in a house on this site for much of his life.

Up a short flight of steps on Arseníou, the **Byzantine Museum** (Tues–Sun 9am–3pm; 200dr) is housed in the restored church of the Panayía Andivouniótissa. It houses sculptures and sections of mosaic floors from Paleópolis and church frescoes. There are also some pre-Christian artefacts, and a collection of icons dating from the fifteenth to nineteenth centuries. Just to the southwest is Corfu's **Cathedral**, packed with icons, including a fine sixteenth-century painting of *St George slaying the dragon* by the Cretan artist Michael Damaskinos.

A block behind the Listón, down Odhós Spirídhonas, is the **church of Áyios Spirídhon**, whose maroon-domed campanile dominates the town. Here you will find the silver-encrusted coffin of the island's patron saint, **Spirídhon** – Spiros in the diminutive – after whom about half the male population is named. Four times a year (Palm Sunday and the following Saturday, August 11, and the first Sunday in November), to the accompaniment of much celebration and feasting, the relics are paraded through the streets of Kérkyra. Each of the days commemorates a miraculous deliverance of the island credited to the saint – twice from plague during the seventeenth century, from a famine of the sixteenth century and (a more blessed release than either of those for any Greek) from the Turks in the eighteenth century.

Corfu Town's **Archeological Museum** (Tues–Sun 9am–3pm; 800dr, free on Sun), just south round the coast, is the best in the archipelago. The most impressive exhibit is a massive (17m) gorgon pediment excavated from the Doric temple of Artemis at Paleópolis; this dominates an entire room, the gorgon flanked by panthers and mythical battle scenes. The museum also has fragments of Neolithic weapons and cookware, and coins and pots from the Corinthian era.

Just south of Platía San Rocco and signposted on the corner of Methodíou and Kolokotróni, the **British Cemetery** features some elaborate civic and military memorials. It's a quiet green space away from the madness of San Rocco, and in spring and early summer is alive with dozens of species of orchids and other exotic blooms.

The outskirts

Each of the following sights on the outskirts of the city is easily seen in a morning or afternoon, and best visited from the town rather than outlying resorts.

Around the bay from the Rotunda and Archeological Museum, tucked behind Mon Repos beach, the **Mon Repos** estate (8am–8pm; free) contains the most accessible archeological remains on the island. Thick woodland conceals two **Doric temples**, dedicated to Hera and Artemis. The Neoclassical Mon Repos **villa**, built by British High Commissioner Frederic Adam in 1824 and handed over to Greece in 1864, was the birthplace of Prince Philip and is due to be opened to the public in the near future.

The most famous excursion from Corfu Town is to the islets of **Vlakhérna** and **Pondikoníssi**, 2km south of town. A dedicated bus (#2) leaves San Rocco square every half hour, or it is a pleasant walk of under an hour. Reached by a short causeway, the tiny white convent of Vlakhérna is one of the most photographed images on Corfu. Pondikoníssi ("Mouse Island") can be reached by a short boat trip from the dock (500dr). Tufted with greenery and a small chapel, Vlakhérna is identified in legend with a ship from Odysseus's fleet, petrified by Poseidon in revenge for the blinding of his son Polyphemus, the Homeric echoes somewhat marred by the thronging masses and low flying aircraft from the nearby runway. A quieter destination is **Vido**, the wooded island visible from the old port, reached from there by hourly shuttle kaïki.

Four kilometres further to the south, past the resort sprawl of Peramá, is a rather more bizarre attraction: the **Achillion** (daily 9am–3pm; 700dr), a palace built in a (fortunately) unique blend of Teutonic and Neoclassical styles in 1890 by Elizabeth, Empress of Austria. Henry Miller considered it "the worst piece of gimcrackery" that he'd ever laid eyes on and thought it "would make an excellent museum for surrealistic art". The house and collection are small and, like the gardens, mostly roped off from visitors.

Eating and drinking

Most **restaurants** are around the old town, with some hard-to-find places favoured by locals concealed in the Campiello. Restaurants on main thoroughfares tend to be indifferent, though the *Averof*, in the old port behind Zavitsiánou, is a Corfu institution, offering above-par taverna cuisine. Below the Palace of SS Michael and George, the *Faliráki* is reasonably priced for its setting and has an imaginative menu. The *Orestes*, on Xenophóntos Stratígou in Mandoúki, is probably the best seafood restaurant in town. The *Pizzeria*, on Guildford Street, has a wide range of pizzas with a pleasing choice for vegetarians, as does *Quattro Stagione*, off the north side of N Theotóki. One of the smartest joints in town is the *Rex*, on Zavitsiánou behind the Listón, and no one staying in Corfu Town should miss the *Venetian Well Bistro*, on Platía Kremásti, a tiny square a few alleys to the south of the cathedral.

Nightlife

Corfu Town has plenty to offer in the way of **bars** and nightlife. On the Listón, avoid the mark-ups at the *Magnet* and follow the locals to *Koklia*, *Aegli* or *Olympia*, or drink in one of the hotels: the *Cavalieri* rooftop bar can be heaven at night. For local atmosphere, try *Dirty Dick's*, on the corner of Arseníou and Zavitsiánou, or the expat hangout *Mermaid*, on Agíon Pantón off the Listón, which will give you a different spin on island culture.

Corfu's self-proclaimed **disco** strip lies a few kilometres north of town, en route to Kondokáli. Here, at the (unofficial) *Hard Rock Café*, the *Hippodrome* disco complex (the town's biggest, with its own pool), and the bizarrely decorated *Apokalypsis* and *Coco Flash*, party animals dress up for wild and fairly expensive nights out. In some clubs, women travelling without male partners should beware *kamákia* – slang for

Greek males "spearfishing" for foreign women. Corfu Town's two **cinemas** – the Pallas on G Theotóki and the Orfeus on the corner of Akadimiás and Aspióti – tend to wind business down in high summer, but both often show English-language films.

The northeast and the north coast

The northeast, at least beyond the immediate suburbs, is the most typically Greek part of Corfu – it's mountainous, with a rocky coastline chopped into pebbly bays and coves, above wonderfully clear seas. Green **buses** between Corfu Town and Kassiópi serve all resorts, along with some blue suburban buses to Dhássia and Ípsos.

Corfu Town to Ípsos

The landscape between Corfu Town and Kondokáli is an industrial wasteland, and things don't improve much at **KONDOKÁLI** itself, a small village overrun by holiday developments. The old town consists of a short street with a number of bars and traditional psistariés, the best of which are *Gerekos* and *Takis*, and an international restaurant, *Flags*.

Neighbouring **GOÚVIA** is also Corfu's largest yachting marina. The village boasts a couple of small **hotels**, notably the *Hotel Aspa* (☎0661/91 303; ④), and some **rooms** – try Maria Lignou (☎0661/91 348; ④) or Yorgos Mavronas (☎0661/91 297 or 90 297; ④). There are a number of decent **restaurants**, including *The Captain's Table* and *Aries Taverna*, and a couple of pizzerias, *Bonito* and *Palladium*. The very narrow shingle **beach**, barely five metres wide in parts, shelves into sand; given the sea traffic the water quality is doubtful. Goúvia is the turn-off point for the **Danília Village** "Corfu Experience" (10am–3pm & 6pm–midnight), about 2km inland. It's an earnest attempt to encapsulate Greek village architecture and culture – a slick operation supposed to look like nineteenth-century Corfu, with workshops and a museum, and evening entertainment set around a reproduction village.

Two kilometres beyond Goúvia the coastline begins to improve at **DHÁSSIA** and **DHAFNILÁ**, set in two small wooded bays with pebbly beaches. Two large and expensive **hotels**, the *Dasía Chandris* (☎0661/33 871; ⑥) and *Corfu Chandris* (☎0661/97 100; ⑥), dominate Dhássia, with extensive grounds, pools and beach facilities. The more reasonable *Hotel Amalia* (☎0661/93 523; ⑤) has pleasant en-suite rooms and its own pool and garden. **Rooms** are scarce, although Spiros Rengis's minimarket has a few (☎0661/90 282; ③). Dhássia does, however, have the best **campsite** on the island, *Dionysus Camping Village* (☎0661/91 417, fax 91 760); tents are pitched under terraced olive trees. *Dionysus* also has simple bungalow huts, a pool, shop, bar and restaurant, and the friendly, multilingual owners offer a ten percent discount to Rough Guide readers.

ÍPSOS, 2km north of Dhássia, can't really be recommended to anyone but hardened bar-hoppers. There isn't room to swing a cat on the thin pebble beach, right beside the busy coast road, and the resort is pretty tacky. Most **accommodation** is pre-booked by package companies, although Ípsos Travel (☎0661/93 661) can offer rooms. *Corfu Camping Ípsos* (☎0661/93 579) has a bar and restaurant, and offers standing tents. Ípsos is also the base for the island's major **diving centre**, *Waterhoppers* (☎0661/93 876). **Eating** on the main drag is dominated by fast food, though a more traditional meal and a quieter setting can be found in the *Akrogiali* and *Asteria* tavernas, by the marina to the south of the strip.

North to Áyios Stéfanos

Ípsos has now engulfed the neighbouring hamlet of Pýryi, which is the main point of access for the villages and routes leading up to **Mount Pandokrátor**; the road, signposted Spartílas, is 200km beyond the junction in Pýryi. A popular base for walkers is the village of **STRINÍLAS**, 16km from Pýryi. Accommodation is basic but easy to come by: the *Elm Tree Taverna*, a long-time favourite with walkers, can direct you to rooms. In summer the main routes are busy, but there are quieter walks taking in the handsome Venetian village of Episkepsís, 5km northwest of Strinílas – anyone interested in walking the Pandokrátor paths is advised to get the **map** of the mountain by island-based cartographer Stephan Jaskulowski.

The coast road beyond Ípsos mounts the slopes of Pandokrátor towards **BARBÁTI**, 4km further on. Here you'll find the best beach on this coast and ample facilities; it's a favourite with families, and much **accommodation** is pre-booked in advance. There are some rooms – *Paradise* (☎0663/91 320; ③) and *Roula Geranou* (☎0663/92 397; ③).

The mountainside becomes steeper and the road higher beyond Barbáti, and the population thins drastically. **NISSÁKI** is a rather spread-out village with a number of coves, the first and last accessible by road, the rest only by track – one dominated by the gigantic, expensive and rather soulless *Nissaki Beach Hotel* (☎0663/91 232; ⑥). There are a couple of shops and a bakery, and a few travel and **accommodation agencies**. The British-owned Falcon Holidays (☎0663/91 318) rents out apartments above the first beach, a tiny, white-pebble cove with a trio of fine tavernas.

The two places no one visiting this coast should miss are Kalámi and neighbouring Kouloúra: the first for its Durrell connection, the latter for its exquisite bay (though neither has a beach worth mentioning). **KALÁMI** is on the way to being spoiled, but the village is still small; you can imagine how it would have been in the year Lawrence Durrell spent here on the eve of World War II. The **White House**, where Durrell wrote *Prospero's Cell*, is now split in two: the ground floor is an excellent taverna; the upper floor is let through CV Travel (see p.6). The owner of the *White House*, Tassos Athineos (☎0663/91 251), has rooms, and Yannis Vlachos (☎ and fax 0663/91 077) has rooms, apartments and studios in the bay, as do Sunshine Travel (☎0663/91 170) and Kalámi Tourism Services (☎0663/91 062, fax 91 369). The **restaurant** at the White House is recommended, as is *Matella's*, the *Kalami Beach Taverna* and *Pepe's*, which is on the beach.

The tiny harbour of **KOULOÚRA** has managed to keep its charm intact, set at the edge of an unspoiled bay with nothing to distract from the pine trees and kaïkia. The fine **taverna** here has to be the most idyllic setting for a meal in the whole of Corfu.

Around the coast to Akharávi

Two kilometres beyond Kouloúra down a shady lane, the large pebble cove of **Kerasiá** shelters the family-run *Kerasia Beach Taverna*. The most attractive resort on this stretch of coast, 3km down a lane from Agnitsíni on the main road, is **ÁYIOS STÉFANOS**. Most **accommodation** here is upmarket, and the village has yet to succumb to any serious development; so far only the *Kokhyli* pizzeria has rooms and apartments (☎0663/81 522). Recommended are the *Garini* and *Kaporelli* **tavernas**, and the *Eucalyptus* over by the village's small beach.

A thirty-minute walk from the coastguard station above Áyios Stéfanos, along a rough track, is the beach of **Avláki**, a pebble bay that provides lively conditions for the **windsurfers** who visit the beach's windsurf club. There are two **tavernas**, the *Barbaro* and *Avlaki*, and some **rooms** a few hundred yards back from the beach – *Mortzoukos* (☎0663/81 196; ④), and *Tsirimiagos*, ☎0663/81 522; ④).

Further round the coast is **KASSIÓPI**, a fishing village that's been transformed into a major party resort. Emperor Tiberius had a villa here, and the village's sixteenth-century church is believed to be on the site of a temple of Zeus, once visited by Nero. Little evidence of Kassiópi's past survives, apart from an abandoned Angevin *kástro* on the headland – most visitors come for the nightlife and the five pebbly beaches. Most **accommodation** in Kassiópi is through village agencies; the largest, Travel Corner (☎0663/81 220, fax 81 108), is a good place to start. An independent alternative, the smart *Kastro* café-pension, overlooks the beach behind the castle (☎0663/81 045; ④), and *Theofilos* (☎0663/81 261; ②) offers bargain rooms on Kalamíonas beach. Anglicized cuisine and fast food dominate **eating** in Kassiópi, but for something more traditional, head for the *Three Brothers* taverna on the harbour, or the neighbouring *Porto* fish restaurant. At night, Kassiópi rocks to the cacophony of its music and video bars: flashest is the gleaming hi-tech *Eclipse*, closely followed by the *Baron*, *Angelos* and *Jasmine*, all within falling-over distance of the small town square. The *Axis Club* boasts imported British DJs, and frolics sometimes extend onto the beach until dawn.

The coastline beyond Kassiópi is overgrown and marshy, until little-used **Almyrós Beach**, one of the longest on the island. It is also the least developed beach, with only a few apartment buildings under construction at the hamlet of **Almyrós**. Cape Áyios Ekaterínis, to the east, is backed by the **Antinióti lagoon**, smaller than Korissíon but still a haven for birds and twitchers. With its wide main road, **AKHARÁVI**, the next stop west on the main coast road, resembles an American Midwest truck stop, but the village proper is tucked behind this in a quiet crescent of old tavernas, bars and shops. Akharávi makes a quieter beach alternative to the southerly strands, and should also be considered by those seeking alternative routes up onto **Mount Pandokrátor**. Roads to small hamlets such as Áyios Martínos and Lafkí continue onto the mountain, and even a stroll up from the back of Akharávi will find you on the upper slopes in under an hour. **Accommodation** isn't easy to find, but a good place to start is Castaway Travel (☎0663/63 541, fax 63 376). There are a number of **restaurants** on Akharávi's main drag; go for the *Pump House* steak and pasta joint, the traditional tavernas *Chris's* and *George's*, or the *Young Tree*, which specializes in Corfiot dishes such as *sofríto* and *pastitsáda*. The bar-restaurants tend to get quite rowdy at night, although the light and airy *Captain's Bar* is a pleasant watering hole. For a quieter drink, head for the leafy awning of the friendly *Vevaiotis* kafenío in the old village.

Ródha, Sidhári and Avliótes

Just to the west, **RÓDHA** has tipped over into overdevelopment, and can't be recommended. Its central crossroads have all the charm of a service station, and the beach is rocky in parts and swampy to the west. "Old Ródha" is a small warren of alleys between the main road and the seafront, where you'll find the best **restaurants** and **bars**: the *Taverna Agra* is the oldest in Ródha and is the best place for fish, and the *Rodha Star Taverna* and *New Harbour* are also good. For bars, try *Nikos* near the *Agra* and the upmarket bar-club *Skouna*. For **accommodation**, the large *Hotel Afroditi* (☎0663/63 147, fax 63 125; ④) has decently priced en-suite rooms with sea views. Both the Anglo-Greek NSK UK Travel (☎0663/63 471, fax 63 274) and Yuko Travel on the main drag (☎0663/63 810; ③) rent rooms and handle car rental.

The next notable resort, **SIDHÁRI**, is expanding rapidly; it has a small but pretty town square, with a bandstand set in a small garden, but this is lost in a welter of bars, boutiques and snack joints. The beach is sandy but not terribly clean, and many people tend to head just west to the curious coves, walled by wind-carved sandstone cliffs. However, the main reason to visit Sidhári is to reach the **Dhiapóndia islands**; day trips to Mathráki, Othoní and Eríkoussa (see p.737) leave weekday mornings around 9am; unless you catch the 5.30am Sidhári bus from Corfu Town, your only option is to stay the night. The boats are run by Nearchos Seacruises (☎0663/95 248) and cost around 3000dr return per person. The best sources of **rooms** are Kostas Fakiolas at the *Scorpion* café-bar at the west of town (☎0663/95 046; ②) and Nikolaos Korakianitis's minimarket on the main road (☎0663/95 058; ③). The biggest accommodation agency is run by young tycoon Philip Vlasseros, whose Vlasseros Travel (☎0663/95 695) also handles car rental, excursions and horse riding. Sidhári's **campsite**, *Dolphin Camping* (☎0663/31 846), is some way inland from the junction at the western end of town. Most **restaurants** are pitched at those looking for a great night out rather than a quiet meal in a taverna. The *Olympic* is the oldest taverna here; also recommended are the

Diamond and *Sea Breeze* tavernas. There are no quiet bars in Sidhári, and two **nightclubs** vie for your custom, the *Remezzo* and its younger rival, *Ecstasy*.

The Sidhári bus usually continues to **AVLIÓTES**, a handsome hill town with bars and tavernas but few concessions to tourism. Avliótes is noteworthy for two reasons, however: its accessibility to the quiet beaches below the quiet village of Perouládhes, just over a kilometre away, and the fact that **Áyios Stéfanos** (see p.733) is under thirty minute's walk from here, downhill through lovely olive groves.

Paleokastrítsa and the northwest coast

The northwest conceals some of the island's most dramatic coastal scenery; the interior, violent mountainscapes jutting out of the verdant countryside. The area's honeypot attraction, **Paleokastrítsa**, is the single most picturesque resort on Corfu, but is suffering from its popularity. Further down the west coast, the terrain opens out to reveal long sandy beaches, such as delightful **Myrtiótissa** and the backpackers' haven of **Áyios Górdhis**. Public transport to the west coast is difficult: virtually all buses ply routes from Corfu Town to single destinations, and rarely link resorts.

Paleokastrítsa

PALEOKASTRÍTSA, a small village surrounded by dramatic hills and cliffs, has been identified as the Homeric city of Scheria, where Odysseus was washed ashore and escorted by Nausica to the palace of her father Alcinous, King of the Phaeacians. It's a stunning site though, as you would expect, one that's long been engulfed by tourism. The focal point of the village is the car park on the seafront, which backs onto the largest and least attractive of three **beaches**, home to sea taxis and kaïkia. The second beach, to the right and signed by flags for Mike's Ski Club, is stony with clear water, and the best of the three is a small unspoiled strand reached along the path by the *Astakos Taverna*. Protected by cliffs, it's undeveloped apart from the German-run Korfu-Diving Centre (☎0663/41 604) at the end of the cove. From the beach in front of the main car park, **boat trips** (around 2000dr) leave for the blue grottoes, a trip worth taking for the spectacular coastal views. Boats also serve as a taxi service to three neighbouring beaches, Áyia Triánda, Platakía and Alípa, which all have snack bars.

On the rocky bluff above the village, the **Theotókos Monastery** (7am–1pm & 3–8pm; free, although donations invited) is believed to have been established in the thirteenth century. There's also a museum, resplendent with icons, jewelled bibles and other impediment of Greek Orthodox ritual, though the highlight is the gardens, with spectacular coastal views. Paleokastrítsa's ruined castle, the **Angelokástro**, is around 6km up the coast; only approachable by path from the hamlet of Kriní, it has stunning, almost circular views of the surrounding sea and land.

Unfortunately, perhaps due to the pressure of commerce in such a small space, there's a rather aggressive air about tourism here. **Accommodation** is at a premium, and you may be expected to commit yourself for three to seven days in some places. A good **hotel** is the small, family-run *Odysseus* (☎0663/41 209, fax 41 342; ⑤) on the road into town, and the modern *Akrotiri Beach* (☎0663/41 237, fax 41 277; ⑥) is friendly and unpretentious for such a large and expensive hotel, and accessible on foot. There are good-value **rooms** for rent above Alípa Beach on the road down into Paleokastrítsa: try Andreas Loulis at the *Dolphin Snackbar* (☎0663/41 035; ③), Spiros and Theodora Michalas (☎0663/41 485; ③), or George Bakiras at the *Green House* (☎0663/41 311; ③). Above the village, past Nikos' Bikes, the friendly Korina family also have rooms (☎0663/44 0641; ④). *Paleokastritsa Camping* (☎0663/41 204, fax 41 104), is just off the main road into town, a ten-minute walk from the centre.

There isn't a huge choice of **restaurants** in the centre of Paleokastrítsa. The *Astakos Taverna* and *Corner Grill* are two traditional places, while *Il Pirata* offers a variety of

Italian and Greek dishes, including local fish and seafood, and the seafront *Smurfs* has good seafood menu. Also recommended are the very smart *St Georges on the Rock*, and the restaurant of the *Odysseus Hotel*. **Nightlife** hangouts include the restaurant-bars in the centre, and those straggling up the hill towards Lákones. By the Lákones turning is Paleokastrítsa's one nightclub, *The Paleo Club*, a small disco-bar with a garden.

Áyios Yéoryios and Áyios Stéfanos

Like many of the west coast resorts, **ÁYIOS YÉORYIOS**, 6km north of Paleokastrítsa, isn't actually based around a village. The resort has developed in response to the popularity of its large sandy bay, and it's a major **windsurfing** centre, busy even in low season. There are a couple of good **hotels** – the *Alkyon Beach* (0663/96 222; ④) and the *Chrisi Akti* (0663/96 207; ⑤) – and some rooms.

The most northerly of the west coast's resorts, **ÁYIOS STÉFANOS** is a low-key family resort, a quiet base from which to explore the northwest and the Diapóntia islands, visible on the horizon. Day trips to Mathráki, Othoní and Eríkoussa (see p.737) run every Thursday in season, and cost around 3000dr per person. Áyios Stéfanos's oldest **hotel**, the *Nafsika* (☎0663/51 051, fax 51 112; ②) has a large restaurant, a favourite with villagers, and gardens with a pool and bar, and in recent years, has been joined by the upmarket *Thomas Bay* (☎0663/51 787, fax 51 553; ③) and *Romanza* hotels (☎0661/22 873, fax 41 878; ⑤). For those on a budget, Peli's and Maria's gift shop offers bargain **rooms** (☎0663/51 424; ②), and the *Restaurant Evnios* (☎0663/51 766; ③) and *Hotel Olga* (☎0663/71 252; ②) have apartments above the village. A number of travel agencies handle accommodation, among them San Stefano (☎0663/51 157) and Mouzakitis Travel in the centre. Besides the *Nafsika*, good options for **eating** include the *Golden Beach Taverna*, and the *Waves Taverna*, on the beach. The *O Manthos* taverna serves Corfiot specialities like *sofríto* and *pastitsáda*. For **nightlife**, there's a couple of lively music bars, the *Condor* and the *Athens*, plus the small *Enigma* nightclub.

Central and southern Corfu

Two natural features divide the centre and south of Corfu. The first is the **Plain of Rópa**, whose fertile landscape backs on to some of the best beaches on this coast. Settlements and development stop a little to the south of Paleokastrítsa and only resume around **Ermónes** and **Pélekas** – a quick bus ride across the island from Corfu Town. Down to the south, a second dividing point is the **Korissíon lagoon**, the sandy plains and dunes that skirt this natural feature being great places for botanists and ornithologists. Beyond, a single road trails the interior, with sporadic side roads to resorts on either coast. The landscape here is flat, an undistinguished backdrop for a series of relatively undefiled beaches and, in the far south, **Kávos**, Corfu's big youth resort.

Ermónes to the Korísson Lagoon: the west coast

ERMÓNES, south of Paleokastrítsa, is one of the busiest resorts on the island, its lush green bay backed by the mountains above the Rópa River. The resort is dominated by the upmarket *Ermones Beach* **hotel** (☎0661/94 241; ⑥), which provides guests with a funicular railway down to the beach. More reasonable accommodation can be found at the *Pension Katerina* (③) and *Georgio's Villas* (③). Head for *George's* **taverna** above the beach for some of the best Greek food here: the *mezédhes* are often a meal in themselves. Just inland is the Corfu Golf and Country Club (☎0661/94 220), the only golf club in the archipelago, and said to be the finest in the Mediterranean.

The nearby small village of **VÁTOS** has a couple of tavernas, a disco and rooms, and is on the Glyfádha bus route from Corfu Town. Spiros Kousounis, owner of the *Olympic Restaurant and Grill* (☎0661/94 318; ④) has rooms and apartments, as does

Prokopios Himarios (☎0661/94 503; ④), next to the Doukakis café-minimarket. The Mirtiótissa **path** is signposted just beyond the extremely handy, if basic, *Vatos Camping* (☎0661/94 393).

Far preferable to the gravely sand of Ermónes are the sandy beaches just south of the resort, at Myrtiótissa and Glyfádha. In *Prospero's Cell*, Lawrence Durrell described **Myrtiótissa** as "perhaps the loveliest beach in the world"; until recently a well-guarded secret, the place hasn't been entirely swamped, but it's best visited at either end of the day or out of high season. Above the beach is the tiny whitewashed **Myrtiótissa Monastery**, dedicated to Our Lady of the Myrtles.

The sandy bay of **GLYFÁDHA**, walled in by cliffs, is dominated by the *Louis Grand* (☎0661/94 140, fax 94 146; ⑥), a large and expensive **hotel** in spacious grounds. There's another hotel at the far north end of the beach, the *Glifada Beach* (☎0661/94 258; ④) whose owners, the Megas family, also have a fine taverna. Most of the other accommodation is block-booked – it's a very popular family beach – but the *Gorgona* pool bar and *Restaurant Michaelis* might have rooms. Nightlife centres on two music bars, the *Kikiriko* and *Aloha*.

PÉLEKAS, inland and 2km south of Glyfádha, has long been popular for its views – the **Kaiser's Throne** viewing tower, along the road to Glyfádha, was Wilhelm II's favourite spot on the island. New developments are beginning to swamp the town, but there are still some good **hotels** here, including the elegant, upmarket *Pelekas* (☎0661/94 230; ⑥) and the friendlier, budget *Nicos* (☎0661/94 486; ④), as well as rooms at the *Alexandros* taverna (☎0661/94 215; ③). Among the **tavernas**, the *Alexandros* and *Roula's Grill House* are highly recommended. Pélekas's sandy **beach** is reached down a short path, where *Maria's Place* is an excellent family-run **taverna/rooms** place (☎0661/94 601; ③) with fish caught daily by the owner's husband.

Around 7km south of Pélekas, **ÁYIOS GÓRDHIS** is one of the key play beaches on the island, largely because of the activities organized by the startling **Pink Palace** complex (☎0661/53 101) which dominates the resort. It has pools, games courts, restaurants, a shop and a disco. Backpackers cram into communal rooms for up to ten (smaller rooms and singles are also available) for 5000dr a night, including breakfast and evening meal. Other accommodation is available on the beach, notably at the quieter *Michael's Place* taverna (☎0661/53 041; ③); the neighbouring *Alex-in-the-Garden* **restaurant** is also a favourite.

Inland from the resort is the south's largest prominence, the humpback of **Áyii Dhéka** (576m), reached by path from the hamlet of Áno Garoúna – it is the island's second largest mountain after Pandokrátor. The lower slopes are wooded, and it's possible to glimpse buzzards wheeling on thermals over the higher slopes.

Around 5km south by road from Áyios Górdhis, the fishing hamlet of **PENDÁTI** is still untouched by tourism. There is no accommodation here, but *Angela's* café and minimarket and the *Strofi* grill cater to villagers and the few tourists who stray by. Another 4km on, **PARAMONÁS** affords excellent views over the coastline, and has only a few businesses geared to tourism: the *Paramonás Bridge* restaurant (☎0663/75 761; ③) has **rooms** and **apartments** to rent, as does the *Areti Studios* (☎0661/75 838; ④) on the road in from Pentáti.

The town of **ÁYIOS MATHÉOS**, 3km inland, is still chiefly an agricultural centre, although a number of kafenía and tavernas offer a warm if bemused welcome to passers-by: head for the *Mouria* snack bar-grill, or the modern *Steki*, which maintains the tradition of spiriting tasty mezédhes onto your table unasked. On the other side of Mount Áyios Mathéos, 2km by road, is the **Gardhíki Pýrgos**, the ruins of a thirteenth-century castle built in this unlikely lowland setting by the Despots of Epirus. The road continues on to the northernmost tip of the beach on the sea edge of the **Korissíon lagoon**, which is most easily reached by walking from the village of Linía (on the Kávos bus route) via Íssos Beach; other, longer routes trail around the north end of the lagoon from Ano Messóngi and Hlomotianá. Over 5km long and 1km wide at its centre, Korissíon is home to turtles, tortoises, lizards, and numerous indigenous and migratory birds.

Benítses to Petríti: the east coast

South of Corfu Town, there's nothing to recommend before **BENÍTSES**, whose old town at the north end is reverting to a quiet bougainvillaea-splashed Greek village. There's really little to see here, beyond the ruins of a Roman bathhouse at the back of the village, and the tiny **Shell Museum**, part-exhibit, part-shop. **Rooms** are plentiful: try Bargain Travel (☎0661/72 137, fax 72 031; ②) and All Tourist (☎0661/72 223; ②). With the decline in visitors, however, some **hotels** are almost as cheap. The *Corfu Maris* (☎0661/72 035; ③), on the beach at the southern end of town, has modern en-suite rooms with balconies and views, while the friendly *Hotel Benitsa* and neighbouring *Agis* in the centre (both ☎0661/39 269; ③) offer quiet rooms set back from the main road. Benítses has its fair share of decent if not particularly cheap **tavernas**, notably *La Mer de Corfu* and the Corfiot specialist *Spiros*, as well as the plush *Marabou*. The **bars** at the southern end of town are fairly lively, despite new rules controlling all-night partying, and the *Stadium* **nightclub** still opens occasionally. If you're looking for a quiet drink head for the north end of the village, away from the traffic.

MORAÍTIKA's main street is an ugly strip of bars, restaurants and shops, but its beach is the best between Corfu Town and Kávos. Reasonable beach-side **hotels** include the *Margarita Beach* (☎0661/76 267; ④) and the *Three Stars* (☎0661/92 457; ④). There are **rooms** between the main road and beach, and up above the main road: try Alekos Bostis (☎0661/75 637; ③) or Kostas Vlachos (☎0661/55 350; ③). Much of the main drag is dominated by souvenir shops and minimarkets, as well as a range of **bars**, including the village's oldest, *Charlie's*, which opened in 1939. *Islands* **restaurant** is recommended for its mix of vegetarian, Greek and international food, as is the unfortunately named beach restaurant *Crabs*, where the seafood and special salads are excellent. The village proper, **ÁNO MORAÍTIKA**, is signposted a few minutes' hike up the steep lanes inland, and is virtually unspoiled. Its tiny houses and alleys are practically drowning in bougainvillea, among which you'll find two **tavernas**: the *Village Taverna* and the *Bella Vista*, which has a basic menu but justifies its name with a lovely garden, sea views and breezes.

Barely a hundred metres on from the Moraítika seafront, **MESSÓNGI** is disappointing: parts of the resort are sadly moribund. The sandy beach is dominated by the vast *Messonghi Beach* **hotel** complex (☎0661/76 684, fax 75 334; ⑥), one of the plushest on the island. Both the cheaper *Hotel Gemini* (☎0661/75 221, fax 75 213; ⑤) and *Pantheon Hall* (☎0661/75 802, fax 75 801; ③) have pools and gardens, and en-suite rooms with balconies. Half a kilometre inland from Messóngi, the *Sea Horse* **campsite** (☎0661/75 364) is a trek from the beach, but is one of the best on the island, with a pool, restaurant and shops, pitches shaded by olive trees and modern cabins (①). Despite several closures, Messóngi still has a number of good **restaurants**: notably the *Memories* taverna, which specializes in Corfiot dishes and serves its own barrel wine, and the upmarket *Castello*. An alternative is to head for the beach-side *Almond Tree* and *Sparos* tavernas a short walk south on the road to Boukári.

The quiet road from Messóngi to **BOUKÁRI** follows the seashore for about 3km, often only a few feet above it. Boukári itself comprises little more than a handful of tavernas, a shop and a few small, family-run hotels; the *Boukari Beach* is the best of the **tavernas**. The very friendly Vlachopoulos family who run the taverna also manage two small hotels nearby, the *Boukari Beach* and *Penelopi* (☎0661/51 269; ④), as well as good rooms attached to the taverna (②). Boukári is out of the way, but an idyllic little strip of unspoiled coast for anyone fleeing the crowds elsewhere on the island, and inland from here is the unspoiled wooded region around **Aryirádhes**, rarely visited by tourists and a perfect place for quiet walks.

Back on the coastline, the village of **PETRÍTI** fronts onto a small but busy dirt-track harbour, but is mercifully free of noise and commerce; its beach is rock, mud and sand, set among low olive-covered hills. The *Pension Egrypos* (☎0661/51 949; ④) has **rooms** and a **taverna**. At the harbour, three tavernas serve the trickle of sea traffic: the smart *Limnopoula* guarded by caged parrots, and the more basic but friendly *Dimitris* and *Stamatis*. Some way back from the village, near the hamlet of Vassilátika, is the elegant *Regina* **hotel**, with gardens and pool (☎0661/52 132, fax 52 135; ②).

Southern Corfu

Across the island on the west coast, the beach at **ÁYIOS YÉORYIOS** spreads as far south as Mága Khóro Point, and north to encircle the edge of the Korission lagoon, around 12km of uninterrupted sand. The village itself, however, is an unprepossessing sprawl. British package operators have arrived in force, with bars competing to present bingo, quizzes and video nights. The *Golden Sands* (☎0661/51 225; ⑤) has a pool, open-air restaurant and gardens, but the best **hotel** bargain is the smaller *Blue Sea* (☎0661/51 624, fax 51 172; ③). The most likely place to head for good **rooms** is at the southern end of the strip: the *Barbayiannis* taverna-bar (☎0661/52 110; ③). Besides the *Barbayiannis*, Áyios Yióryios has a number of good **restaurants**: *La Perla's* which serves Greek and north European food in a walled garden; the *Napoleon* psistariá; and the *Florida Cove*, with its beachcomber theme. **Nightlife** centres around music and pool bars like the *Gold Hart* and *Traxx*, although the best bar in Áyios Yióryios is the sea-edge *Panorama*, which has views as far south as Paxí.

A few minutes' walk north of Áyios Yéoryios, **Íssos** is by far the best and quietest beach in the area; the dunes north of Íssos are an unofficial nude bathing area. Facilities around Íssos are sparse: one **taverna**, the *Rousellis Grill* (which sometimes has rooms) a few hundred metres from the beach on the lane leading to Linía on the main road, and the *Friends* snack bar in Linía itself. An English-run **windsurfing school** operates on the beach.

Anyone interested in how a Greek town works away from the bustle of tourism shouldn't miss **LEFKÍMI**, on the island's east coast. The second largest town after Corfu, it's the administrative centre of the south of the island, and has some fine architecture, including two striking churches: **Áyios Theodóros**, on a mound above a small square, and **Áyios Arsénios**, with a vast orange dome that can be seen for miles. There are some **rooms** at the *Cheeky Face* taverna (☎0661/22 627; ②) and the *Maria Madalena* apartments (☎0661/22 386; ②), both by the bridge over the canal that carries the Chimáros River through town. A few **bars** and **restaurants** sit on the edge of the canal – try the *River* psistariá. Away from the centre, the *Hermes* bar has a leafy garden, and there are a number of other good local places where tourists are rare enough to guarantee you a friendly welcome, including the *Mersedes* and *Pacific* bars, and, notably, the *Kavouras* and *Fontana* tavernas.

There are no ambiguities in **KÁVOS**, directly south of Lefkími: either you like 24-hour drinking, clubbing, bungee-jumping, go-karts, video bars named after British sit-coms and chips with almost everything, or you should avoid the resort altogether. Kávos stretches over 2km of decent sandy beach, with watersports galore. This is very much package-tour territory; if you want independent **accommodation**, try Britannia Travel (☎0661/61 400) and Island Holidays (☎0661/23 439), and the nearest to genuine Greek **food** you'll find is at the *Two Brothers* psistariá, at the south end of town. *Future* is still the biggest **club**, with imported north European DJs, followed by *Whispers*. Favourite **bars** include *JCs*, *Jungle*, *The Face* and *Net*.

Beyond the limits of Kávos, where few visitors stray, a path leaving the road south to the hamlet of Sparterá heads through unspoiled countryside; after around thirty minutes of walking it reaches the cliffs of **Cape Asprokávos** and the crumbling **monastery of Arkoudhílas**. The cape looks out over the straits to Paxí, and down over deserted **Arkoudhílas beach**, which can be reached from Sp̣parterá, 5km by road but only 3km by the signed path from Kávos. Even wilder is **San Górdhios beach**, 3km further on from Spartéra, one of the least visited on the island.

Corfu's satellite islands

Corfu's three inhabited satellite islands, **Eríkoussa**, **Othoní** and **Mathráki**, in the quintet of **Dhiapondía islands**, are 20km off the northwest coast. Some travel agencies in the northern resorts offer **day trips** to Eríkoussa only, often with a barbecue thrown in – fine if you're happy to spend the day on the beach. A trip taking in all three islands from Sidhári or Áyios Stéfanos is excellent value: the islands are between thirty and sixty minutes apart by boat, and most trips allow you an hour on each (longer on sandy Eríkoussa).

Locals use daytrip boats between the islands, so it's possible to pay your way between them. There is also a twice-weekly **ferry** from Corfu Town, the *Alexandros II*, which brings cars and goods to the islands, but given that it has to sail halfway round Corfu first, it's the slowest way to proceed.

Mathráki

Hilly, densely forested and with a long empty beach, beautiful **Mathráki** is the least inhabited of the three islands. The beach begins at the edge of the tiny harbour, and extends south for 3km of fine, dark-red sand, a nesting site for the endangered **loggerhead turtle** (see p.751). It's important therefore not to camp anywhere near the beach – and not to make any noise there at night.

A single road rises from the harbour into the interior and the scattered village of **KÁTO MATHRÁKI**, where just one friendly taverna-kafenío-shop overlooks the beach and Corfu. The views are magnificent, as is the sense of isolation. However, construction work above the beach suggests Mathráki is expecting visitors, and islander Tassos Kassimis (☎0663/71 700; ②) already rents **rooms**. The road continues to the village of **Áno Mathráki**, with its single, old-fashioned kafenío next to the church, but this is beyond walking distance on a day visit.

Othoní

Six kilometres north, **Othoní** is the largest, and at first sight the least inviting of Corfu's satellite islands. The island has a handful of good tavernas and rooms for rent in its port, **ÁMMOS**, but the reception from islanders who aren't in the tourism trade is rather cool. Ámmos has two beaches, both pebbly, one in its harbour. The village kafenío serves as a very basic shop, and there's one smart **restaurant**, *La Locanda dei Sogni*, which also has **rooms** (☎0663/71 640; ④) – though these tend to be pre-booked by Italian visitors. Three tavernas, *New York*, *Mikros*, and tiny *Rainbow*, offer decent but fairly limited menus; the owner of the *New York* also offers rooms for rent (☎0663/71 581; ③). The island's interior is dramatic, and a path up out of the village leads through rocky, tree-covered hills to the central hamlet, **Khorió**, after a thirty-minute walk. Khório, like other inland villages, is heavily depopulated – only about sixty people still live on the island through the winter – but it's very attractive, and the architecture is completely traditional.

Eríkoussa

East of Othoní, **Eríkoussa** is the most popular destination for daytrippers. It's invariably hyped as a "desert island" trip, although this is a desert island with a medium-sized hotel, rooms, tavernas and a year-round community. In high season, it gets very busy: Eríkoussa has a large diaspora living in America and elsewhere who return to family homes in their droves in summer, so you may find your *yia sou* or *kaliméra* returned in a Brooklyn accent.

Eríkoussa has an excellent golden sandy beach right by the harbour, with great swimming, and another, quieter, beach reached by a path across the wooded island interior. The island's cult following keeps its one **hotel**, the *Erikoussa* (☎0663/71 555; ③), busy through the season; rooms are en suite with balconies and views. Simpler rooms are available from the *Anemomilos* **taverna** (☎0663/71 647; ③). If you're hoping to stay, phoning ahead is essential, as is taking anything you might not be able to buy – the only shop is a snack bar selling basic groceries.

Paxí (Paxos) and Andípaxi

Verdant, hilly and still largely unspoiled, **Paxí (Paxos)** is the smallest of the main Ionian islands. Barely 12km by 4km, it has no sandy beaches, no historical sites, only two hotels and a serious water shortage, yet is so popular it is best avoided in high season. Despite haphazard ferry connections with Corfu, Igoumenítsa and Párga, it still draws vast crowds, who can make its three harbour villages rather cliquey. It's also popular with yachting flotillas, whose spending habits have brought the island an upmarket reputation, and made it the most expensive place to visit in the Ionian islands (with the possible exception of Fiskárdho on Kefalloniá). There is only one – rather remote – official campsite (there are pockets of unauthorized camping) and most accommodation is blockbooked by travel companies, though there are local tour operators whose holiday deals are often a fraction of the price. The capital, **Gáios**, is quite cosmopolitan, with delis and boutiques, but northerly **Lákka** and tiny **Longós** are where hardcore Paxophiles head.

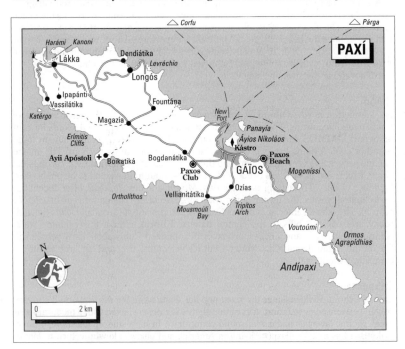

Gáïos

Most visitors arrive at **GÁÏOS**, or at the new port, 1km to the north. Gáïos is a pleasant town built around a small square on the seafront overlooking two islands, Áyios Nikoláos and Panayía. Room owners usually meet ferries, although it's advisable to phone ahead: try Gáïos Travel (☎0661/32 033), run by the friendly, English-speaking Ioannis Arvanatakis, and Paxos Tourist Enterprises (☎0661/31 675), both situated on the seafront. Paxí's two seasonal **hotels** are both near Gáïos: the *Paxos Beach Hotel* (☎0661/31 211; ⑨) which has smart en-suite bungalows on a hillside above a pebbly beach 2km south of town, and the fairly luxurious *Paxos Club Hotel* (☎0661/32 450, fax 32 097; ⑨), 2km inland from Gáïos.

Gáïos boasts a number of decent **tavernas**, the best of them being *Carcoleggio's*, 1.5km out of town towards Bogdanátika. The menu and wine list are limited, and opening hours unpredictable, but it fills up with islanders who flock for its *souvláki*. Also recommended are the *Blue Grotto*, *Spiro's*, *Dodo's*, and the *Gaïos Grill*, just off the west side of the town square. Of the pricey joints running down one side of the square, the *Volcano* is the best; the kafenía by the ferry ramp and at the bottom of the square is a much better bargain. The *Phenix* (sic) disco out by the New Port opens sporadically and has a terrace for sub-lunar fun. The island's one (basic) **campsite** is at Mogoníssi, 45 minutes' walk south (there's no bus), with a taverna above an imported sand beach.

Inland are some of the island's oldest settlements, such as Oziás and Vellianitátika, in prime walking country, but with few if any facilities. Noel Rochford's book, *Landscapes of Paxos* (Sunflower), lists dozens of walks, and cartographers Elizabeth and Ian Bleasdale's *Paxos Walking Map* is on sale in most travel agencies.

The rest of the island

Paxí's one main road runs along the spine of the island, with a turning at the former capital Magazía, leading down to the tiny port of Longós. The main road continues to Lákka, the island's funkiest resort, set in a breathtaking horseshoe bay. Two buses ply the road between Gáïos and Lákka six times a day, diverting on alternate trips to swing through Longós. The Gáïos–Lákka bus (45min) affords panoramic views, and the route is an excellent walk of under three hours (one way). A taxi between the two costs around 2000dr.

Approached from the south, **LÁKKA** is an unprepossessing jumble of buildings, but once in its maze of alleys and neo-Venetian buildings, or on the quay with views of distant Corfu, you do get a sense of its charm. Lákka's two **beaches**, Harámi and Kanóni, are the best on the island, although there have been complaints in high season of pollution from the yachts that cram the bay. Kanóni is a favourite with campers, but has no facilities. **Accommodation** is plentiful (except in high season) from the island's two biggest agencies: Planos Holidays (☎0661/31 744, fax 31 010) or Routsis (☎0661/31 807, fax 31 161), both on the seafront. The latter runs two bargain rooming houses, *Ilios* and *Lefcothea*. There's an embarrassment of good tavernas: the long running family taverna *Souris*, the friendly *Butterfly*, the *Nautilus*, which has the best view of any Paxiot restaurant, the hip *Ubu*, or the exotic *Rosa di Paxos* for a splurge. There's a similar wealth of bars: the lively *Harbour Lights*, the seafront *Romantica* cocktail bar, *Serano's* in the square, or Spiro Petrou's friendly kafenío – the hub of village life. Lákka is also best-sited for **walking**: up onto either promontory, to the lighthouse or Vassilátika, or to Longós and beyond. One of the finest walks – if combined with a bus or taxi back – is an early evening visit to the **Erimítis** cliffs, near the hamlet of Boikátika: on clear afternoons, the cliffs change colour at twilight like a seagoing Ayers Rock.

LONGÓS is the prettiest village on the island, and perfectly sited for morning sun and idyllic alfresco breakfasts. The village is dominated by the upmarket villa crowd, but the Planos office here (☎0661/31 530) is the best place to look for accommodation.

It has some of the island's best restaurants: the *Nassos*, with a wide variety of fish and seafood, the seafront *Vassilis*, where you have to squeeze in for the island bus when it rumbles by, and *Kakarantzas*. The hip jazz dive *Piano Bar* on the front, which drew crowds from all over the island, closed in 1996, but is rumoured to be reopening elsewhere in the village.

Longós has a small, scruffy beach, with sulphur springs favoured by local grannies, but most people swim off Levrékhio beach in the next bay south, which gets the occasional camper. (Islanders are touchy about camping for fear of fires; it's politic to ask at the beach taverna if it's acceptable to camp.) Longós is at the bottom of a steep winding hill, making **walking** a chore, but the short circle around neighbouring **Dendiátika** provides excellent views, and the walk to **Fontána** and **Magazía** can be done to coincide with a bus back to Longós.

Andípaxi

A mile south of Paxí, its tiny sibling **Andípaxi** has no accommodation and no facilities beyond a couple of beach tavernas open during the day in season. The sandy, bluewater coves have been compared with the Caribbean, but you'll have to share them with kaïkia and sea taxis from all three villages, plus larger craft from Corfu (boats from Paxí will also take you to its sea stacks and caves, the most dramatic in the Ionian islands). The trick is to head south away from the pleasure-craft moorings, although path widening has made even the quieter bays more accessible. Paths lead inland to connect the handful of homes and the southerly lighthouse, but there are no beaches of any size on Andípaxi's western coastline. In low season, there's also the risk of bad weather keeping pleasure craft in port and stranding you here.

Lefkádha (Lefkas)

Lefkádha is an oddity. Connected to the mainland by a long causeway through lagoons, it barely feels like an island – and historically in fact it isn't. It is separated from the mainland by a canal cut by Corinthian colonists in the seventh century BC, which has been redredged (after silting up) on various occasions since, and today is spanned by a thirty-metre boat-drawbridge built in 1986. Lefkádha was long an important strategic base, and approaching the causeway you pass a series of fortresses, climaxing in the fourteenth-century castle of **Santa Maura** – the Venetian name for the island. These defences were too close to the mainland to avoid an Ottoman tenure, which began in 1479, but the Venetians wrested back control a couple of centuries later. They were in turn overthrown by Napoleon in 1797 and then the British took over as Ionian protectors in 1810. It wasn't until 1864 that Lefkádha, like the rest of the Ionian archipelago, was reunited with Greece.

At first glance Lefkádha is not overwhelmingly attractive, although it is a substantial improvement on the mainland just opposite. The whiteness of its rock strata – *lefkás* means "white" – is often brutally exposed by road cuts and quarries, and the highest ridge is bare except for ugly military and telecom installations. With the marshes and sumpy inlets on the east coast, mosquitoes can be a midsummer problem. On the other hand, the island is a fertile place, supporting cypresses, olive groves and vineyards, particularly on the western slopes, and life in the mountain villages remains relatively untouched, with the older women still wearing traditional local dress – two skirts (one forming a bustle), a dark headscarf and a rigid bodice.

Lefkádha has been the home of various literati, including two prominent Greek poets, Angelos Sikelianos and Aristotelis Valaoritis, and the short-story writer Lefcadio Hearn, son of American missionaries. Support for the arts continues in the form of a

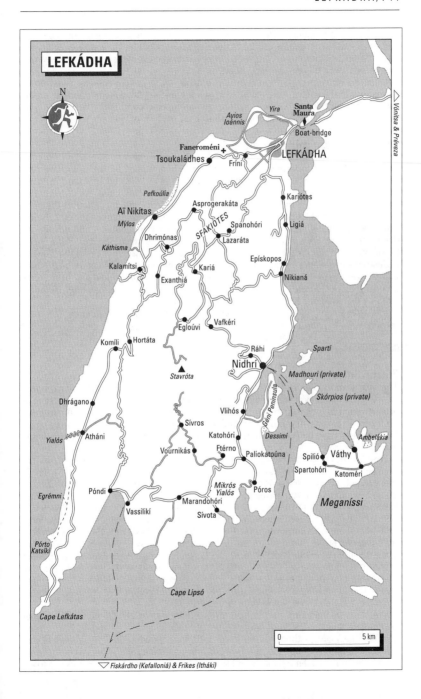

LEFKÁDHA

N

Santa
Maura

Yíra

Áyios
Ioánnis

Boat-bridge

Faneroméni

Tsoukaládhes

Fríni

LEFKÁDHA

Kariótes

Pefkoúlia

Asprogerakáta

Aï Nikítas

Mýlos

Spanohóri

Ligiá

Dhrimónas

Lazaráta

Káthisma

Epískopos

Kalamítsi

Kariá

Nikianá

Exanthiá

Vafkéri

Egloúvi

Komíli

Hortáta

Ráhi

Spartí

Nidhrí

Madhoúri (private)

Stavróta

Skórpios (private)

Dhrágano

Vlihós

Dessimí

Ambelákia

Yialós

Atháni

Sívros

Katohóri

Vournikás

Ftérno

Paliokatoúna

Spilió

Váthy

Spartohóri

Katoméri

Póndi

Mikrós
Yialós

Póros

Egrémni

Marandohóri

Vassilikí

Sívota

Meganíssi

Pórto
Katsíki

Cape Lipsó

Cape Lefkátas

0   5 km

Vónitsa & Préveza

Géni Peninsula

SFAKIÓTES

well-attended international **festival** of theatre and folk-dancing lasting nearly the whole of August, with most events staged in the Santa Maura castle. On a smaller scale, frequent village celebrations accompanied by *bouzouki* and clarinet ensure that the strong local wine flows well into the early hours.

Lefkádha remains relatively undeveloped, with just two major resorts: **Vassilikí**, in its vast bay in the south, claims to be Europe's biggest windsurf centre; **Nidrhí**, on the east coast, overlooks the island's picturesque archipelago, and is the launching point for the barely inhabited island of **Meganíssi**.

Lefkádha Town and around

Lefkádha Town sits at the island's northernmost tip, hard by the causeway. Like other southerly capitals, it was hit by the earthquakes of 1948 and 1953, and the town was devastated, with the exception of a few **Italianate churches**. As a precaution against further quakes, little was rebuilt above two storeys, and most houses built second storeys of wood, giving the western dormitory area an unintentionally quaint look. The town is small – you can cross it on foot in under ten minutes – and despite the destruction still very attractive, especially around the main square, Platía Áyios Spiridónas, and the arcaded high street of Ioánnou Melá. Much of Lefkádha Town is pedestrian-only, mainly because of the narrowness of its lanes. The centre boasts over half a dozen richly-decorated private family churches, usually locked and best visited around services. Many contain gems from the Ionian School of painting, including work by its founder, Zakynthian Panayiotis Doxaras.

The alleys off Spiridónas also conceal a small **folklore museum** (Mon–Fri 9am–9pm; 200dr) and a museum/shop dedicated to antique phonographs. To the north of town, Odhós Pfanoroménis houses an **archeological museum** (Tues–Sun 9am–1pm; free).

Practicalities

The **bus station** is on Odhós Dimítri Golémi opposite the small yacht marina. It now has services to almost every village on the island, and Nidrhí, Vassilikí and west coast beaches such as Kathísma have extensive daily services. **Car** and **motorbike** rental is useful for exploring; try EuroHire, Golémi 5 (☎0645/267 76), near the bus station. Most resorts have bicycle hire outlets, although you'll need stamina to do any more than local touring.

Hotels are actually dwindling in Lefkádha Town, and currently number just six. The smarter hotels, like the stylish seafront *Nirikos*, Ayías Mávras (☎0645/24 132, fax 23 756; ④) and the cosy *Santa Maura*, Spirídhon Viánta 2 (☎0645/22 342, fax 26 253; ⑤) are in busy areas, but are glazed against the noise and heat. The *Lefkas*, Pétrou Filípa Panáyou 2 (☎0645/23 916, fax 24 579; ⑥) and *Xenia*, Panagoú 2 (☎0645/24 762, fax 25 129; ⑤) are both large international hotels. The *Patron*, Platía Áyios Spiridónas (☎0645/22 359; ③) is a bargain, as is the *Byzantio*, Dörpfeld 40 (☎0645/22 629; ③): both are small and basic, and in very busy and noisy areas of town. There are basic **rooms** in the dormitory area west of Dörpfeld: the Lefkádha Room Owners Association, based in Nidhrí (Odhós Megálo Vlachí 8; ☎0645/92 701) can help, or try the *Pinepolis Rooms* (☎0645/24 175; ③) in Odhós Pinépolis, off the seafront two short blocks from the pontoon bridge. Lefkádha Town's campsite has closed, although there are decent sites at Karyótes and Epískopos, a few kilometres to the south.

The best **restaurants** are hidden in the backstreets: the *Reganto* taverna, on Dhimarkoú Venióti is the local favourite, but opening hours can be erratic. If it's closed, head for the *Lighthouse*, in its own small garden on Filarmoníkis. The *Romantika* on Mitropóleos has nightly performances of Lefkadhan *kantáthes*, while the smartest place in town is the *Adriatica*, Faneroménis and Merarkhías, where people tend to dress up to eat.

Of the **bars** in the main square, the *Thalassina* ouzerí is the cheapest, with occasional evening entertainment from buskers, jugglers and even fire-eaters. Further from the action the best is the *Cafe Karfakis*, on Ioánnou Melás, an old-style kafenío with splendid mezédhes. The most stylish bar is the hard-to-find *Vengera*, on Odhós Maxáïra, signposted a block down from the bus station, set in a shady garden and with a hip music policy. The town's **cinema**, *Eleni*, beyond the Archeological Museum on Pfaneroménis, is the only outdoor cinema in the archipelago; programmes change daily.

Around Lefkádha Town

The town has a decent and fairly large pebble beach across the lagoon at **Yíra**, a forty-minute walk from the top of Dörpfeld, either across the bridge or along Sikeliánou. In season there's also a bus (hourly 9am–4pm) from the bus station. Roughly 4km long, the beach is often virtually deserted even in high season; there's a **taverna** at either end, and at the western end a couple of **bars** in the renovated windmills, as well as the trendy *Club Milos*.

The uninhabited **Faneroméni monastery** (daily 8am–2pm & 4–8pm; free) is reached by any of the west-coast buses, or on foot from town (30min) through the hamlet of Fríni. There's a small museum, a chapel, and an ox's yoke and hammer, used when Nazi occupiers forbade the use of bells. There are wonderful views over the town and lagoon from the Fríni road.

The island's **interior**, best reached by bus or car from Lefkádha Town, offers mountainscapes of Alpine prospect and excellent walking between villages only a few kilometres apart. **KARYÁ** is its centre, with a hotel, the *Karia Village Hotel* (☎0645/51 030; ④), tucked away above the village, and some rooms: try Haritini Vlachou (☎0645/41 634; ③), the Kakiousis family (☎0645/61 136; ③), Olga Lazari (☎0645/61 547; ③) or Michael Chalikias (☎0645/61 026; ③). The leafy town square has a popular taverna, *La Platania*, and off it the smarter *O Rousos*. Kariá is the centre of the island's lace and weaving industry, with a fascinating small **museum** set in a lacemaker's home. The historic villages of **Vakféri** and **Engloúvi** are within striking distance, with the west coast hamlets of **Dhrimónas** and **Exanthía** a hike over the hills.

The east coast to Vassilikí

Lefkádha's east coast is the most accessible and the most developed part of the island. Apart from the campsites at Kariótes (*La Pissina* ☎0645/71 103) and Epískopos (*Episcopos Beach*, ☎0645/71 388), there's little point stopping before the small fishing ports of **LIYIÁ** which has some rooms and the hotel *Konaki* (☎0645 711 267; ④), or **NIKIANÁ**, where you'll find the hotels *Pegasos* (☎0645/71 766, fax 25 290; ⑥), and the smarter but considerably cheaper *Ionion* (☎0645/71 720; ④). Nikianá also has a trio of fine tavernas, notably the *Pantazis*, which also has rooms to let. Beaches here tend to be pebbly and small.

Most package travellers will find themselves in **NIDHRÍ**, the coast's biggest resort with ferry connections to Meganíssi and myriad **boat trips** around the nearby satellite islands. The German archeologist Wilhelm Dörpfeld believed Nidhrí, rather than Itháki, to be the site of Odysseus's capital, and did indeed find Bronze-Age tombs on the plain nearby. His theory identifying ancient Ithaca with Lefkádha fell into disfavour after his death in 1940, although his obsessive attempts to give the island some status over its neighbour are honoured by a statue on Nidhrí's quay. Dörpfeld's tomb is tucked away at Ayía Kiriakí on the opposite side of the bay, near the house in which he once lived, visible just above the chapel and lighthouse on the far side of the water.

Nidrhí is the prettiest resort on this coast, with some good pebble beaches and a lovely setting, but the centre is an ugly strip with heavy traffic. The best place to stay is the

Hotel Gorgona (☎0645/92 268, fax 92 558; ③), set in a lush garden away from the traffic a minute along the Ráhi road, which leads to Nidhrí's very own **waterfall**, a forty-five minute walk inland. There are also rooms in the centre – try Emilios Gazis (☎0645/92 703; ③) and Athanasios Konidaris (☎0645/92 749; ④). The town's focus is the Ákti Aristotéli Onássi quay, where most of the rather ritzy **restaurants** and **bars** are found. The *Barrel* and *Il Sappore* restaurants are recommended, as is the *Agra* on the beach. Nightlife centres around bars like *No Name* and *Byblos*, and the late-night *Sail Inn Club*.

Nidrhí sits at the mouth of a deep inlet stretching to the next village, somnolent **VLIKHÓS**, with a few good tavernas and mooring for yachts. Over the Géni peninsula across the inlet is the large **Dhessími Bay**, home to two adjacent campsites: *Santa Maura Camping* (☎0645/95 007, fax 26 087), and *Dessimi Beach Camping* (☎0645/95 374), right on the beach but often packed with outsized mobile homes.

The coast road beyond Vlikhós turns inland and climbs the foothills of Mount Stavróta, through the hamlets of Katohóri and Paliokatoúna to **Póros**, a quiet village with few facilities. Just south of here is the increasingly busy beach resort of **MAKRÝS YIALÓS**. It boasts a handful of **tavernas**, a few rooms at *Oceanis Studios* (☎and fax 0654/95 095; ④), plus the upmarket *Poros Beach Camping* (☎0654/23 203) which has bungalows (⑥), shops and a pool. Try the *Mermaid* taverna back from the beach.

Along the main road, walkers and drivers are recommended to take the panoramic detour to quiet **Voúrnika** and **Sývros** (the Lefkádha–Vasilíki bus also visits), which both have tavernas and some private rooms. It's around 14km to the next resort, the fjord-like inlet of **SÝVOTA**, 2km down a steep hill (bus twice daily). There's no beach except for a remote cove, but some fine fish tavernas: the *Ionion* is the most popular, but the *Delfinia* and *Kavos* are also good. Thomas Skliros (☎0645/31 151; ③) at the furthest supermarket, has a few **rooms**, and there's a basic unofficial campsite by the bus stop at the edge of the village.

Beyond the Syvóta turn, the mountain road dips down towards Kontaraína, almost a suburb of **VASSILIKÍ**, the island's premiere watersports resort. Winds in the huge bay draw vast numbers of windsurfers, with light morning breezes for learners and tough afternoon blasts for advanced surfers. Booking your **accommodation** ahead is mandatory in high season. The *Paradise* (☎0645/32 156; ②), a basic but friendly hotel overlooking the small rocky beach beyond the ferry dock, is the best bargain. Also good-value for its class is the neighbouring upmarket *Hotel Apollo* (☎0645/31 122, fax 31 142; ⑤). In the centre of town, the two main hotels are the smart and reasonably-priced *Vassiliki Bay Hotel* (☎0645/23 567, fax 22 131; ④), and the *Hotel Lefkátas* (☎0645/31 801, fax 31 804, ④), a large, modern building overlooking the busiest road in town. Rooms and apartments are available along the beach road to Póndi: *Billy's House* (☎0645/31 418), *Christina Politi's Rooms* (☎0645/31 440) and the *Samba Pension* (☎0645/31 555) are smart and purpose-built, though not particularly cheap. The largest of the three beach windsurf centres, Club Vassiliki, offers all-in **windsurf tuition** and accommodation deals. Vassilikí's only **campsite**, the large *Camping Vassiliki Beach* (☎0645/31 308, fax 31 458), is about 500m along the beach road; it has its own restaurant, bar and shop.

Vassilikí's pretty quayside is lined with tavernas and bars, notably the *Dolphin Psistaria*, the glitzier *Restaurant Miramare*, and the *Penguin*. One of the cheapest places to drink on the entire island is the no-name kafenío next to the bakery. Fliers sometimes advertise **raves** on the beach at Pórto Katsíki.

The beach at Vassilikí is stony and poor, but improves 1km on at tiny **PÓNDI**; most non-windsurfers however, use the daily kaïki trips to nearby Agiofíli or around Cape Lefkátas to the superior beaches at Pórto Katsíki and Egrémni on the sandy west coast. There's little accommodation at Póndi, but great views of the bay and plain behind, particularly from the terrace of the *Ponti Beach Hotel* (☎0645/31 572, fax 31 576; ④), which is very popular with holidaying Greeks, and has a restaurant and bar open to non-residents.

The west coast

Tsoukaládhes, just 6km from Lefkádha, is developing a roadside tourism business, but better beaches lie a short distance to the south, so there's very little reason to stay here. Four kilometres on, the road plunges down to the sand-and-pebble **Pefkoúlia beach**, one of the longest on the island, with a taverna, *Oinilos*, that has rooms at the north end, and unofficial camping down at the other end, about 3km away.

Jammed into a gorge between Pefkoúlia and the next beach, Mylos, is **AÏ NIKÍTAS**, the prettiest resort on Lefkádha, a jumble of lanes and small wooden buildings. The back of the village is a dust-blown car park, which detracts from the appeal of the pleasant, if basic, *O Aï Nikitas* **campsite** (☎0645/97 301), set in terraced olive groves. The most attractive **accommodation** is in the *Pension Ostria* (☎0645/97 483; ⑤), a beautiful blue and white building above the village decorated in a mix of beachcomber and ecclesiastical styles. Other options are in the alleys that run off the main drag; the best bets are the *Pansion Aphrodite* (☎0645/97 372; ④), the small *Hotel Selene* (☎0645/97 369; ④), and quieter *Olive Tree* (☎0645/97 453; ④). Best tavernas include the *Sapfo* and the *Agnantia*.

Sea taxis (1000dr one way) ply between Aï Nikítas and **Mýlos** beach, or it's a 45-minute walk (or bus ride) to the most popular beach on the coast, **Káthizma**, a shadeless kilometre of fine sand. There are two tavernas: the barn-like *Kathisma Beach*, and the *Sunset*, which has **rooms** (☎0645/24 142; ④). Beyond Káthisma, hairpin bends climb the flank of Stavróta towards the tiny village of **KALAMÍTSI**, where Spiro Karelis (☎0645/99 214; ②) and Spiro Verginis (☎0645/99 411; ②) have rooms. *Hermes* (☎0645/99 417; ③), the *Blue and White House* (☎0645/99 269; ③) and *Deili Rooms and Studios* (☎0645/99 456; ④) have larger rooms and apartments. There are also three good tavernas: the *Paradeisos* in its own garden with fountain, the more basic *Ionio* and, just north of the village, the aptly titled *Panorama View*. Three kilometres down a rough track is the village's quiet sandy beach.

South of Kalamítsi, past the hamlets of Khortáta and Komíli, the landscape becomes almost primeval. At 38km from Lefkádha Town, **ATHÁNI** is Lefkádha's most remote resort, with a couple of good tavernas which both have rooms: the *Panorama* (☎0645/33 291; ②) and *O Alekos* (☎0656/33 484; ③).

The road continues 14km to barren **Cape Lefkátas**, which drops abruptly 75 metres into the sea. Byron's Childe Harold sailed past this point, and "saw the evening star above, Leucadia's far projecting rock of woe: And hail'd the last resort of fruitless love". The fruitless love is a reference to Sappho, who in accordance with the ancient legend that you could cure yourself of unrequited love by leaping into these waters, leaped – and died. In her honour the locals termed the place *Kávos tis Kyrás* ("lady's cape"), and her act was imitated by the lovelorn youths of Lefkádha for centuries afterwards. And not just by the lovelorn, for the act (known as *katapontismós*) was performed annually by scapegoats – always a criminal or a lunatic – selected by priests from the Apollo temple whose sparse ruins lie close by. Feathers and even live birds were attached to the victims to slow their descent and boats waiting below took the chosen one, dead or alive, away to some place where the evil banished with them could do no further harm. The rite continued into the Roman era, when it degenerated into little more than a fashionable stunt by decadent youth. These days, Greek hang-gliders hold a tournament from the cliffs every July.

Lefkádha's satellites

Lefkádha has four satellite islands clustered off its east coast, although only one, **Meganíssi**, the largest and most interesting, is accessible. **Skórpios**, owned by the Onassis family, fields armed guards to deter visitors, **Madhourí**, owned by the family of poet Nanos Valaoritis, is private and similarly off-limits, while tiny **Spartí** is a large scrub-covered rock. Day trips from Nidhrí skirt all three islands, and some stop to allow swimming in coves.

Meganíssi

MEGANÍSSI, twenty minutes by frequent daily ferries from Nidrhí, is a large island with few facilities but a magical, if bleak landscape, a situation that's made it a favourite with island aficionados. Ferries stop first below **SPARTOKHÓRI**, an immaculate village with whitewashed buildings and an abundance of bougainvillea. The locals – many returned émigrés from Australia – live from farming and fishing and are genuinely welcoming. You arrive at a jetty on a pebble beach with a few tavernas and a primitive but free (for a night or two only) campsite provided by the *Star Taverna* (☎0645/51 107, fax 51 186). The village proper boasts three restaurants: a pizza place called the *Tropicana*, which can direct you to **rooms** (☎0645/51 425; ③), the *Rooftop Cafe*, and the traditional taverna *Lafkis*.

The attractive inland village of **KATOMÉRI** is an hour's walk through magnificent country. It has the island's one **hotel**, the *Meganisi*, a comfortable place with a restaurant (☎0645/51 240, fax 51 639; ③), and a few bars. Ten minutes' walk downhill is the main port of **VATHÝ**, with some accommodation (*Different Studios*: ☎0645/22 170; ③) and the island's best restaurants, notably the waterside taverna, *Porto Vathi*, which Lefkádhans flock to on ferries for Sunday lunch. After the high-season madness of Nidrhí, Meganíssi's unspoiled landscape is a tonic, and it's easy to organize a **day trip** from Nidrhí, getting off at Spartokhóri, walking to Katoméri for lunch at the *Meganisi*, and catching a ferry back from Váthy. Paths lead from Katoméri to remote beaches, including popular **Ambelákia**, but these aren't accessible on a day trip.

Kefaloniá

Kefaloniá is the largest of the Ionian islands – a place that has real towns as well as resorts. Like its neighbours, Kefaloniá was overrun by Italians and Germans in World War II; the "handover" after Italy's capitulation in 1943 led to the massacre of 5000 Italian troops on the island by invading German forces. These events form a key passage in Louis de Bernière's novel, *Captain Corelli's Mandolin*, a tragi-comic epic of life on the island from before the war to the present day.

Until the late 1980s, the island paid scant regard to tourism; perhaps this was in part a feeling that it could not easily be marketed. Virtually all of its towns and villages were levelled in the 1953 earthquake, and these masterpieces of Venetian architecture had been the one touch of elegance in a severe, mountainous landscape. A more likely explanation, however, for the island's late emergence on the Greek tourist scene is the Kefallonians' legendary reputation for insular pride and stubbornness.

Having decided on the advantages of an easily exploitable industry, however, Kefaloniá is at present in the midst of a tourism boom. Long favoured by Italians, it has begun attracting British package companies, for whom a new airport terminal has been constructed, while virtually every decent beach has been endowed with restaurants. There are definite attractions here, with some beaches as good as any in the Ionian islands, and a fine (if pricey) local wine, the dry white *Rombola*. Moreover, the island seems able to soak up a lot of people without feeling at all crowded, and the magnificent scenery can speak for itself, the escarpments culminating in the 1632-metre bulk of **Mount Énos**, declared a national park to protect the fir trees (*Abies cephalonica*) named after the island.

Kefaloniá airport is 11km south of town; there are no airport buses, so you'll have to resort to a taxi. The **bus** system is basic but expanding, and with a little legwork it can be used to get you almost anywhere on the island. Key routes connect Argostóli with Sámi, Fiskárdho, Skála and Póros. There's a useful connection from Sámi to the tiny resort of **Ayía Evfimía**, which attracts many package travellers. Using a moped, take care as the terrain is very rough in places – almost half the roads are unsurfaced – and the gradients can sometimes be a bit challenging for underpowered machines. The island has a plethora of **ferry** connections, principally from Fiskárdho to Lefkádha and Itháki, and from Sámi to Lefkádha, Itháki and the mainland, as well as links to Zákynthos, Kýllíni and Pátra.

Sámi and around

Most boats dock at the large, and not very characterful, port and town of **SÁMI**, built and later rebuilt near the south end of the Ithaki straits, more or less on the site of ancient Sámi. This was the capital of the island in Homeric times, when Kefalloniá was part of Ithaca's maritime kingdom: today the administrative hierarchy is reversed, Itháki being considered the backwater. With ferries to most points of the Ionian islands, and several companies introducing direct links to Italy – and one even to Pireas, Sámos and Turkey – the town is clearly preparing itself for a burgeoning future. Two kilometres beyond ancient Sámi, is a fine pebble beach, **Andisámi**.

The town has two smart **hotels**: the beachside *Sami Beach* (☎0674/22 802, fax 22 846; ⑥), and the quieter *Pericles* (☎0674/22 780, fax 22 787; ⑤) 500m back from the quay, which has extensive grounds, two pools and sports facilities. The best mid-range bet is the *Melissani* (☎0674/22 064; ④), behind the seafront; others in the category include the seafront *Ionion* (☎0674/22 035; ④) and *Athina* (☎0674/23 066; ④). The *Kyma* (☎0674/22 064; ③) on Platía Kyproú is very basic and old-fashioned. Both *periptera* on the quay offer rooms, as do a variety of private homes a few blocks back from the front. Sámi's one **campsite**, *Camping Karavomilos Beach* (☎0674/22 480, fax 22 932), has over 300 spaces, a taverna, shop and bar, and opens onto the beach.

Sámi doesn't have a great many **tavernas** beyond those on the seafront; visitors tend to go to the smart *Adonis Restaurant*, but the best bet is to follow the Greeks themselves to *Delfinia*, which produces succulent fresh fish and meat dishes, as well as a variety of vegetarian options. The *Riviera* is the favourite **bar** in the evenings, while the best place for a snack breakfast is *Captain Jimmy's*.

The Drogharáti and Melissáni caves

The one good reason to stay in Sámi is its proximity to the Drogharáti and Melissáni caves; the former 5km out of town towards Argostóli, the latter 3km north towards Áyia Evfimía. A very impressive stalagmite-bedecked chamber, **Drogharáti** (April–Oct daily 8am–6pm; 800dr) was previously used for concerts thanks to its marvellous acoustics – Maria Callas once sang here. **Melissáni** (same hours and price) is partly submerged in brackish water which, amazingly, emerges from an underground fault which leads the whole way under the island to a point near Argostóli. At this point, known as Katovóthres, the sea gushes endlessly into a subterranean channel – and, until the 1953 earthquake disrupted it – the current was used to drive seamills. That the water, now as then, still ends up in the cave has been shown with fluorescent tracer dye.

Ayía Evfimía

AYÍA EVFIMÍA, 9km north of Sámi, is a friendly little fishing harbour popular with package operators, yet with no major developments. Its two drawbacks are its beaches – the largest, Paradise Beach, is around 20m of shingle, although there are other coves to the south – and its poor connections (daily buses to Sámi and Fiskárdho, weekly to Ássos, a ferry to Itháki). **Accommodation** here is good at two small, smart **hotels**: *Pilaros* (☎0674/61 210; ④) and *Moustakis* (☎0674/61 030; ④). The *Dendrinos* **taverna**

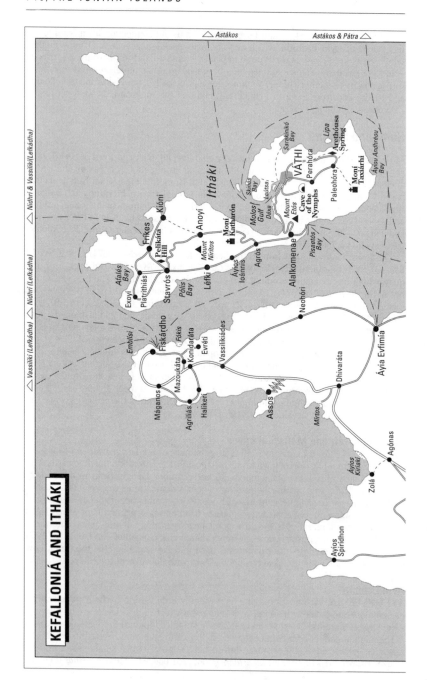

KEFALLONIÁ AND ITHÁKI

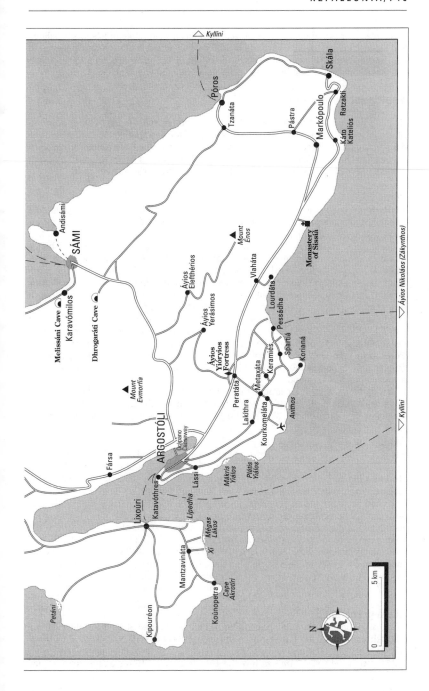

is the place for island cuisine; the *Pergola* also has a wide range of island specialities and standard Greek dishes. Hipsters head for the *Cafe Triton* at night, philhellenes to the *Asteria* kafenío, which doubles as the town barber's. The *Strawberry* zakharoplastío is the place for a decadent breakfast.

Southeast Kefalloniá

Heading directly **southeast from Sámi** by public transport is impossible; to get to **Skála** or **Póros** you need to take one bus to Argostóli and another on from there; five daily run to Skála, three to Póros. With your own vehicle, the back route from Sámi to Póros is an attractive option. It's eighty percent dirt track but negotiable with a decent moped; the road is signposted to the left just before the Dhrogaráti cave.

Póros

PÓROS was one of the island's earliest developed resorts, and shows it. Its small huddle of hotels and apartment blocks is almost unique on Kefalloniá, and not enhanced by a scruffy seafront and thin, pebbly beach.

Póros does, however, have a regular ferry link to **Kyllíni** on the mainland, a better link than the only alternative, remote **Astakós**. Póros is actually two bays: the first, where most tourists are based, and the actual harbour, a few minutes over the headland. There's plenty of rooms, apartments and a few **hotels**. The *Pension Astir* (☎0674/72 443; ③) has good-value en-suite rooms on the seafront, while the elegant new *Odysseus Palace* in the centre of town (☎0674/72 036, fax 72 148; ⑥), has offered good discounts in recent summers. Among **travel agents**, Poros Travel on the front (☎0674/72 476 or 72 284) offers a range of accommodation, as well as services such as car rental and ferry bookings. The seafront has the majority of the **restaurants**, and Póros's one nightclub, *J&A's*, overlooking the beach. At night, however, the old port is quieter and has more atmosphere, with tavernas such as *Tzivas* and the *Dionysus* which are strong on local seafood.

A rough road twists 12km around the rocky coastline from Póros to Skála at the southern extremity of the island. It's a lovely, isolated route, with scarcely a building on the way, save for a small chapel, 3km short of Skála, next to the ruins of a **Roman temple**.

Skála

SKÁLA is also developing as a resort, but in total contrast to Póros it's a low-rise development set among handsome pines above a few kilometres of good sandy beach. A **Roman villa** and some mosaics were excavated here in the 1950s, near the site of the Golden Beach Palace rooms, and are open daily to the public.

Its faithful return crowd keep Skála busy until well after Póros has closed for the season, and accommodation can be hard to find. Dennis Zapantis has studios and apartments at *Dionysus Rooms* (☎0671/83 283; ③), a block south of the high street, and rooms can be found at the *Golden Beach Palace* (☎0671/83 327; ③) above the beach. The more upmarket *Tara Beach Hotel* (☎0671/83 250, fax 83 344; ⑤) has rooms and individual bungalows in lush gardens on the edge of the beach. Skála boasts a number of good **restaurants**: the *Pines*, the *Flamingo*, and, on the beach, the *Paspalis* and *Sunset*. Drinkers head for *The Loft* cocktail **bar** and the beach-side *Pikiona* music bar.

Skála to Lourdháta

Some of the finest sandy beaches on the island are just beyond Skála below the village of Ratzákli, and around the growing micro-resort of **KÁTO KATELIÓS** which already has a hotel, the smart *Odyssia* (☎0671/81 614; ⑤), and some self-contained **apartments** available through the stylish *Arbouro* **taverna** (☎0671/81 192). However, the coast around

LOGGERHEAD TURTLES

The Ionian islands harbour the Mediterranean's main concentration of **loggerhead sea turtles** (*Caretta caretta*). These creatures, which lay their eggs at night on sandy coves, are under direct threat from the tourist industry in Greece. Each year, many turtles are injured by motorboats, their nests are destroyed by bikes ridden on the beaches, and the newly hatched young die entangled in deckchairs and umbrellas left out at night on the sand. The turtles are easily frightened by noise and lights, too, which makes them uneasy cohabitants with freelance campers and late-night discos.

The Greek government has passed **laws** designed to protect the loggerheads, including restrictions on camping at some beaches, but local economic interests tend to prefer a beach full of bodies to a sea full of turtles.

On Kefalloniá, the turtles' principal nesting ground is just west of Skála. Other important locations include Zákynthos, although numbers have dwindled to half their former strength in recent years, and now only about 800 remain. **Nesting grounds** are concentrated around the fourteen-kilometre bay of Laganás, but Greek marine zoologists striving to protect and study the turtles are in angry dispute with locals and the burgeoning tourist industry. Ultimately, the turtles' main hope of survival may rest in their being appreciated as a unique tourist attraction in their own right.

While capitalists and environmentalists are still at, well, loggerheads, the **World Wildlife Fund** has issued guidelines for visitors:

1. Don't use the beaches of Laganás and Yérakas between sunset and sunrise.
2. Don't stick umbrellas in the sand in the marked nesting zones.
3. Take your rubbish away with you – it can obstruct the turtles.
4. Don't use lights near the beach at night – they can disturb the turtles, sometimes with fatal consequences.
5. Don't take any vehicle onto the protected beaches.
6. Don't dig up turtle nests – it's illegal.
7. Don't pick up the hatchlings or carry them to the water, as it's vital to their development that they reach the sea on their own.
8. Don't use speedboats in Laganás Bay – a 9kph speed limit is in force for vessels in the bay.

Káto Kateliós is also Kefalloniá's key breeding ground for the **loggerhead turtle** (see above). Camping is discouraged and would, anyway, strand you miles from any facilities.

At the inland village of **MARKÓPOULO**, claimed by some to be the birthplace of homophonous explorer Marco Polo, the **Assumption of the Virgin festival** (August 15) is celebrated in unique style at the local church with small, harmless snakes with cross-like markings on their heads. Each year, so everyone hopes, they converge on the site to be grasped to the bosoms of the faithful; a few, in fact, are kept by the priests for those years when they don't naturally arrive. The celebrants are an interesting mix of locals and gypsies – some of whom come over from the mainland for the occasion. It's quite a spectacle.

The coastline is largely inaccessible until the village of **VLAKHÁTA**, which has some rooms – *Maria Studios* (☎0671/31 055) – and a good taverna, the *Dionysus*, but you're better off continuing to **LOURDHÁTA**, 2km to the south. It has a fine 1km shingle beach and a couple of **tavernas** on a tiny plane-shaded village square – the *New World* and the *Diamond* – as well as the smarter *Spiros* steak and grill house above. *Adonis* (☎0671/31 206; ②) and *Ramona* (☎0671/31 032; ③) have **rooms** just outside the village on the approach road, while the one **hotel**, the *Lara* (☎0671/31 157, fax 31 156; ⑤), by the beach, has en-suite rooms with sea views.

Argostóli and around

ARGOSTÓLI, Kefalloniá's capital, is a large and thriving town, virtually a city, with a marvellous site on a bay within a bay. The stone bridge, connecting the two sides of the bay, was initially constructed by the British in 1813. A small obelisk remains, but the plaque commemorating "the glory of the British Empire" has disappeared. The town was totally rebuilt after the earthquake but has an enjoyable street life that remains defiantly Greek, especially during the evening volta around Platía Metaxá – the nerve centre of town.

The **Korgialenío History and Folklore Museum** (Tues–Sun 8.30am–2pm; 500dr), on Ilía Zervoú behind the Municipal Theatre, has a rich collection of local cultural artefacts, including photographs taken before and after the 1953 quakes. The **Archeological Museum** (Tues–Sun 8.30am–2pm; 500dr), on nearby R. Vergóti, has two large rooms of pottery, jewellery, funerary relics and statuary, as well as a small Pan figure, once priapic but now bluntly detumescent, from a shrine found at the Melissáni lake.

Practicalities

Argostóli's shiny new **Kefallonía airport** lies 11km south of town. There are no airport buses, and suburban bus services are so infrequent that a taxi (around 3500dr) is the only dependable connection. Those arriving in Argostóli by bus from Sámi or elsewhere will wind up at the brand-new KTEL **bus station**, a minute from the Drapano causeway and close to the main square, **Platía Metaxá**. Argostóli's friendly **tourist office** (Mon–Fri 8am–2pm; open till 10pm in August; ☎0671/22 248 or 24 466) is on Metaxá at the north end of the seafront, next to the port authority and has information about rooms, and can advise on transport and other resorts around the island.

Hotels around Platía Metaxá stay open year round, but tend to be pricey: the best bet here is the *Mirabel* (☎0671/25 381, fax 25 384; ④). A good mid-range option away from the square is the *Mouikis*, Výronos 3 (☎0671/23 454; ④); and a decent budget hotel is the friendly *Parthenon*, Zakýnthou 4 (☎0671/22 246; ②), tucked behind the Mouikis. In a working town with a large permanent population, **private rooms** aren't too plentiful. Some of the best bargains can be found through waterfront tavernas, such as the *Kalafatis* (☎0671/22 627; ②), nearest to the Dhrápano bridge on the Metaxá waterfront, the *Tzivras* (☎0671/22 628; ②) on Vandorou, just off the centre of the waterfront, or Spiro Rouhotas' taverna (☎0671/23 941; ②), opposite the Lixoúri ferry ramp. A number of travel agencies also offer rooms, apartments and villas: try Ionian Options (☎0671/22 054) on 21-1 Máiou, by the Lixoúri ferry, or Filoxenos Travel (☎0671/23 055) on R Vergóti. The town's one **campsite**, *Argostoli Camping* (☎0671/23 487), lies 2km north of the centre, just beyond the Katovóthres sea mills; there's only an infrequent bus service in high season, so you'll probably have to walk.

The waterfront *Tzivras* or *Kalafatis* **tavernas** are the place to try Kefallonián cuisine; the *Captain's Table* just off the platía is worth a splurge and to hear Kefallonián *kantathes*. Local posers hang out at the *Da Cappo* café-bar, the *Flonitiko* café and the *Koukos* club-bar, on Vassiléos Yeoryíou off the square. The quay bars, particularly the kafenío by the Dhrápano bridge, are quiet, cheap and have the best views.

South of Argostóli: beaches and Áyios Yeóryos

Many package travellers will find themselves staying in **LÁSSI**, a short bus ride or twenty-minute walk from town. Lássi sprawls unattractively along a busy four-lane highway, but it does have good sandy beaches, particularly at **Makrýs Yiálos** and **Platýs Yiálos**, although they're right under the airport flight path. **Beaches** such as **Ávythos** are well worth seeking out, although if you're walking beyond

Kourkomeláta there is a real if occasional risk of being attacked by farm dogs, particularly during the hunting season (Sept 25–Feb 28). There is very little accommodation in the region, and precious few shops or bars. **Pessádha** has a regular ferry link with Zákynthos in summer, but little else.

With a moped, the best inland excursion is to **ÁYIOS YEÓRYOS**, the medieval Venetian capital of the island. The old town here supported a population of 15,000 until its destruction by an earthquake in the seventeenth century: substantial ruins of its **castle** (Tues–Sun 8.30am–3pm), churches and houses can be visited on the hill above the modern village of Peratata. Byron lived for a few months in the nearby village of Metaxáta and was impressed by the view from the summit in 1823; sadly, as at Messolóngi, the house where he stayed no longer exists. Two kilometres south of Áyios Yeóryos is a fine collection of religious icons and frescoes kept in a restored church that was part of the nunnery of Áyios Andréas.

Mount Énos

At 15km from a point halfway along the Argostóli–Sámi road, **Mount Énos** isn't really a walking option, but roads nearly reach the official 1632-metre summit. The mountain has been declared a national park, to protect the *Abies cephallonica* firs (named after the island) which clad the slopes. There are absolutely no facilities on or up to the mountain, but the views from the highest point in the Ionian islands out over its neighbours and the mainland are wonderful. In low season, watch the weather, which can deteriorate with terrifying speed.

Lixoúri

Hourly ferries (every two hours at weekends) ply between the capital and **LIXOÚRI** throughout the day. The town was flattened by earthquakes, and hasn't risen much above two storeys since. It's a little drab, but has good restaurants, quiet hotels, and is favoured by those who want to explore the eerie quakescapes left in the south and the barren north of the peninsula. The bargain **hotel** is the *Giardino* (☎0671/92 505, fax 92 525; ②), four blocks back from the front. There are also two decent beach hotels just south of town: the *Poseidon* (☎0671/92 518; ④) and *Summery* (☎0671/91 771, fax 91 062; ⑤). Two agencies offer accommodation in town: A. D. Travel (☎0671/93 142) a few blocks from the quay, and Perdikis Travel (☎0671/91 097, fax 92 503) on the quay. Among the tavernas, *Akrogiali* on the seafront draws admirers from all over the island. Nearby *Antoni's* mixes traditional dishes with steaks and European food, while *Maria's* is a good basic family taverna.

Lixoúri's nearest beach is **Lípedha**, a 2km walk south. Like the **Xí** and **Mégas Lákkos** beaches (served by bus from Lixoúri) it has rich red sand and is backed by low cliffs. Those with transport can also strike out for the monastery at **Kipouréon**, and north to the spectacular beach at **Petáni**.

The west coast and the road north

The journey between Argostóli and Fiskárdho, by regular bus or hire vehicle, is the most spectacular ride in the archipelago. Leaving town, the road rises into the Evmorfía foothills and, beyond Agónas, clings to nearly sheer cliffs as it heads for Dhivaráta, the stop for **Mýrtos Beach**. It's a 4km hike down on foot (you can also drive down), with just one taverna on the beach, but from above or below, this is the most dramatic beach in the Ionian islands – a splendid strip of pure white sand and pebbles.

Six kilometres on is the turning for the atmospheric village of **ÁSSOS**, clinging to a small isthmus between the island and a huge hill crowned by a ruined fort.

Accommodation is scarce – villagers invariably send you to Andreas Roukis's rooms
(☎0674/51 523; ③). Ássos has a small pebble beach, and a couple of tavernas, notably
the *Nefeli Garden* and the *Platanis Grill*, on a plane-shaded village square backed by the
shells of mansions ruined in the quake. It can get a little claustrophobic, but there's
nowhere else like it in the Ionian islands.

Fiskárdho

FISKÁRDHO, on the northernmost tip of the island, sits on a bed of limestone that
buffered it against the worst of the quakes. Two **lighthouses**, Venetian and Victorian,
guard the bay, and the ruins on the headland are believed to be from a twelfth-century
chapel begun by Norman invader Robert Guiscard, who gave the place his name. The
nineteenth-century harbour frontage is intact, nowadays occupied by smart restaurants
and chic boutiques.

The island's premier resort, Fiskárdho is very busy through to the end of October,
with accommodation at a premium. Bargain rooms are *Regina's* (no phone; ②) at the
back of the village. *Theodora's Café Bar* has rooms in whitewashed houses along the
quay (☎0674/41 297 or 41 310; ③), and the Koria handicraft shop has rooms on the
seafront (☎0674/41 270; ④). A quieter option is the *Nitsa Rooms* (☎0674/41 327; ④) in
the alley to the side of Nikos's bike rental on the quay, set in an exquisite garden. At
the top of the price range, *Fiskardhona* (☎0674/41 436; ⑤), opposite the post office, and
Philoxenia (☎0674/41 319; ⑤), next to Nikos's bike rental, offer rooms in renovated traditional island homes in the village. There's a wealth of good restaurants: the *Tassia* has
a vast range of seafood, and the *Captain's Table* serves succulent Greek and Kefallonián
fare. *Sirenes* is the favoured bar, although the seafront kafenía's mezédhes are the finest
to be had anywhere. There are two good pebble beaches – **Émblisi** 1km back out of
town, **Fókis** just to the south – and a nature trail on the northern headland. Daily **ferries** connect Fiskárdho to Itháki and Lefkádha in season.

Itháki

Rugged **Itháki**, Odysseus's legendary homeland, has had no substantial archeological
discoveries but it fits Homer's description to perfection: "There are no tracks, nor
grasslands . . . it is a rocky severe island, unsuited for horses, but not so wretched,
despite its small size. It is good for goats." In C Cavafy's splendid poem *Ithaca*, the
island is symbolized as a journey to life:

> *When you set out on the voyage to Ithaca*
> *Pray that your journey may be long*
> *full of adventures, full of knowledge.*

Despite the romance of its name, and its proximity to Corfu, very little tourist development has arrived to spoil the place. This is doubtless accounted for in part by a
dearth of beaches, though the island is good walking country, with a handful of small
fishing villages and various pebbly coves to swim from. In the north, apart from the
ubiquitous drone of mopeds, the most common sounds are sheep bells jangling and
cocks (a symbol of Odysseus) crowing.

Its beaches are minor, mainly pebble with sandy seabeds, but relatively clean and
safe; the real attractions are the interior and sites from the **Odyssey**. Some package
travellers will find themselves flying into Kefalloniá and being bussed to Fiskárdho (sit
on the left for the bus ride of your life), for a short ferry crossing to **Fríkes** or the premier resort **Kióni**. Most visitors will arrive at **Váthy**, the capital.

Váthy

Ferries from Pátra, Kefalloniá, Astakós, Corfu and Italy land at the main port and
capital of **VÁTHY** (Itháki Town), a bay within a bay so deep that few realize the mountains out "at sea" are actually the north of the island. This snug town has only a few
streets and little traffic, and boasts the most idyllic seafront setting of all the Ionian capitals. Like its southerly neighbours, it was damaged by the 1953 earthquake, but some
fine examples of pre-quake architecture remain here and in the northern port of **Kióni**.
Váthy has a small **archeological museum** on Odhos Kalliníko (Tues–Sun
8.30am–2pm; free) a short block back from the quay. There are banks, a post office,
police and a medical centre in town.

Váthy's two basic but decent **hotels** bookend the seafront: the *Odysseus* (☎0674/32
381; ④) is to the right of the ferry dock, the *Mentor* (☎0674/32 433, fax 32 293; ④) to its
left. Room owners meet ferries until the last knockings of the season, but you can also
call ahead to Vassili Vlassopoulou (☎0674/32 119; ②), whose rooms are in pleasant gardens by the church above the quay. Also within easy access are those owned by Sotiris
Maroulis at Odhós Odysseus 29, near the Perakhóra road (☎0674/28 300; ③). The
town's two travel agents, Polyctor Tours (☎0674/33 120, fax 33 130) and Delas Tours
(☎0674/321 104, fax 33 031) on the quay have accommodation throughout the island.

Even though it's tiny, Váthy has a wealth of **tavernas** and **bars**. Many locals head off
south around the bay with a torch towards *Gregory's*, popular for its lamb and fish, and
the more traditional *Tziribis* and *Vlachos*. In town, *O Nikos* is an excellent taverna that
fills early. The *Sirenes Ithaki Yacht Club* is upmarket with a nautical theme, while the
no-relation *Ithaki Yacht Club* on the front looks private but is actually a bar open to all.
Otherwise, head for the town's ancient kafenío one street back from the front.

There are two reasonable pebble **beaches** within fifteen minutes' walk of Váthy:
Dhéxa, over the hill above the ferry quay, and tiny **Loútsa**, opposite it around the bay.
Better beaches at Sarakinikó and Skinós to the south are an hour's trek by rough track
leaving the opposite side of the bay. In season, daily kaïkia ply between the quay and
remote coves.

Odysseus sites

Three of the main **Odysseus** sights are just within walking distance of Váthy: the
Arethoúsa Spring, the Cave of the Nymphs and ancient Alalkomenae, although the last
is best approached by **bus** or **taxi** (no more than 5000dr).

The Arethoúsa Spring

The walk to the **Arethoúsa Spring** – allegedly the place where Eumaeus, Odysseus's
faithful swineherd, brought his pigs to drink – is a three-hour round trip along a track
signposted next to the seafront OTE. The unspoiled landscape and sea views are magnificent, but the walk crosses slippery inclines and might best be avoided if you're nervous of heights. The route is shadeless, so take a hat and plenty of water.

Near the top of the lane leading to the spring path, a signpost points up to what is
said to have been the **Cave of Eumaeus**. The route to the spring continues for a few
hundred metres, and then branches off onto a narrow footpath through gorse-covered
steep cliffs. Parts of the final downhill track involve scrambling across rock fields (follow the splashes of green paint), and care should be taken around the small but ver-
tiginous ravine that houses the **spring**. The spring is sited at the head of a small ravine
below a crag known as **Korax** (the raven), which matches Homer's description of the
meeting between Odysseus and Eumaeus. In summer it's just a dribble of water.

The spring is a dead end – the only way out is back the way you came. If weather and time allow, there is a small cove for swimming a short scramble down from the spring. If you're uneasy about the gradients involved, it's still worth continuing along the track that runs above it, which loops round and heads back into the village of **Perakhóra** above Váthy, which has views as far as Lefkádha to the north. On the way, you'll pass **Paleokhóra**, the ruined medieval capital abandoned centuries ago, but with vestiges of houses fortified against pirate attacks and some churches still with Byzantine frescoes.

The Cave of the Nymphs

The **Cave of the Nymphs** (Marmarospíli), is about 2.5km up a rough but navigable road signposted on the brow of the hill above Déxa beach. The cave is atmospheric, but it's underwhelming compared to the caverns of neighbouring Kefalloniá, and these days is illuminated by coloured lights. The claim that this is the *Odyssey's* Cave of the Nymphs, where the returning Odysseus concealed the gifts given to him by King Alcinous, is enhanced by the proximity of Déxa beach, although there is some evidence that the "true" cave was above the beach, and was unwittingly demolished during quarrying many years ago.

Alalkomenae and Pisaetós

Alalkomenae, Heinrich Schliemann's much-vaunted "Castle of Odysseus", is signposted on the Váthy–Pisaetos road, on the saddle between Dhéxa and Pisaetós, with views over both sides of the island. The actual site, however, some 300m up hill, is little more than foundations spread about in the gorse. Schliemann's excavations unearthed a Mycenean burial chamber and domestic items such as vases, figurines and utensils (displayed in the archeological museum), but the ruins actually date from three centuries after Homer. In fact, the most likely contender for the site of Odysseus' castle is above the village of Stavrós (see below).

The road (though not buses) continues to the harbour of **Pisaetós**, about 2km below, with a large pebble beach that's good for swimming and popular with local rod-and-line fishermen. A couple of tavernas here largely serve the ferries from Fiskárdho, Sámi and Áyia Evfimía on Kefalloniá.

Northern Itháki

The main road out of Váthy continues across the isthmus and takes a spectacular route to the northern half of Itháki, serving the villages of **Léfki**, **Stavrós**, **Fríkes** and **Kióni**. There are three evenly spaced daily **buses**, though the north of Itháki is excellent moped country; the close proximity of the settlements, small coves and Homeric interest also make it good rambling country. Once a day a kaḯki also visits the last two of those communities – a cheap and scenic ride used by locals and tourists alike to meet the mainline ferries in Váthy. As with the rest of Itháki there is only a limited amount of accommodation.

Stavrós and around

STAVRÓS, the second largest town on the island, is a steep 2km above the nearest beach (Pólis Bay). It's a pleasant enough town nonetheless, with kafenía edging a small square that's dominated by a rather fierce statue of Odysseus and a tiny **museum** (Tues–Sun 9am–3pm) displaying local archeological finds. Stavrós's Homeric site is on the side of **Pelikáta Hill**, where remains of roads, walls and other structures have been suggested as the possible site of Odysseus's castle. Stavrós is useful as a base if both Fríkes and Kióni are full up, and is an obvious stopping-off point for exploring the northern hamlets and the road up to the medieval village of Anóyi (see below). Both Polyctor and Delas handle **accommodation** in Stavrós, and a number of the town's traditional tavernas, including the *Petra* (☎0674/31 596), offer rooms.

A scenic mountain road leads 5km southeast from Stavrós to **ANOYÍ**, whose name translates roughly as "upper land". Once the second most important settlement on the island, it is almost deserted today. The centre of the village is dominated by a freestanding Venetian campanile, built to serve the (usually locked) church of the **Panayía**; inquire at the kafenío about access to the church, whose Byzantine frescoes have been heavily restored following centuries of earthquake damage. On the outskirts of the village are the foundations of a ruined **medieval prison**, and in the surrounding countryside are some extremely strange rock formations, the biggest being the eight-metre-high Arakles (Heracles) rock, just east of the village. The **monastery of Katharón**, 3km further south along the road, has stunning views down over Váthy and the south of the island, and houses an icon of the *Panayía* – Virgin Mary – discovered by peasants clearing scrubland in the area. Byron is said to have stayed here in 1823, during his final voyage to Messolóngi. The monastery celebrates its festival on September 8 with services, processions and music.

Three roads leave Stavrós heading north: one, to the right, heads 2km down to Fríkes, while the main road, to the left, loops around the hill village of **Exoyí**, and on to **Platríthias**. On the outskirts of Platríthias, Mycenean remains establish that the area was inhabited at the time of Homer. A track leads down to **Afáles**, the largest bay on the entire island, with an unspoiled and little-visited pebble beach. The landscape around here, thickly forested in parts and dotted with vineyards, is excellent walking terrain.

Fríkes

At first sight, tiny **FRÍKES** doesn't appear to have much going for it. Wedged in a valley between two steep hills, it was only settled in the sixteenth century, and emigration in the nineteenth century almost emptied the place – as few as two hundred people live here today – but the protected harbour is a natural year-round port. Consequently, Fríkes stays open for tourism far later in the season than neighbouring Kióni, and has a better range of tavernas. There are no beaches in the village, but plenty of good, if small, pebble strands a short walk away towards Kióni. When the ferries and their cargoes have departed, Fríkes falls quiet and this is its real charm: a downbeat but cool place to lie low.

Fríkes' one **hotel** is the smart but pricey *Nostos* (☎0674/31 644, fax 31 716; ⑥). Kiki Travel (☎0674/31 726) has **rooms** and other accommodation, and the Polyctor Travel office (☎0674/31 771) offers accommodation in and around the village, as well as handling ferry tickets. Phoning ahead is advisable, but if you turn up here without a reservation, both the *Ulysses* taverna-kafenío on the front and the neighbouring souvenir shop have rooms as well. Fríkes has a wealth of good seafront **tavernas**, notably the *Symposium*, the *Kirki Grill* and the nearby *Penelope*.

Kióni

KIÓNI sits at a dead end 5km southeast of Fríkes. On the same geological base as the northern tip of Kefalloniá, it avoided the very worst of the 1953 earthquakes, and so retains some fine examples of pre-twentieth-century architecture. It's an extremely pretty village, wrapped around a tiny harbour, and tourism here is dominated by British blue-chip travel companies and visiting yachts.

The bay has a small **beach**, 1km along its south side, a sand and pebble strand below a summer-only snack bar. Better pebble beaches can be found within walking distance towards Fríkes. While the best **accommodation** has been snaffled by the Brits, some local businesses have rooms and apartments to let, among them *Apostolis* (☎0674/31 072),

Dellaportas (☎0674/31 481, fax 31 090) and *Kioni Vacations* (☎0674/31 668). A quieter option, a short walk uphill on the main road in the hamlet of Rákhi, are the rooms and studios run by Captain Theofilos Karatzis and his family (☎0674/31 679; ④), which have panoramic views. Alternatively, seek out the very helpful Yioryos Moraitis (☎0674/31 464, fax 31 702), whose boat rental company has access to accommodation in Kióni.

Kióni is poorly served for **restaurants**, with just two waterfront tavernas – the traditional *Avra* and the *Kioni* pizzeria – and the upmarket *Calypso* restaurant back in the village. Village facilities stretch to two well-stocked shops, a post office, and a couple of bars and cafes. Back up the hill towards the hamlet of Rákhi there's also the small, bunker-like *Kioni* cocktail bar and nightclub.

Zákynthos (Zante)

Zákynthos, most southerly of the six core Ionian islands, currently teeters between underdevelopment and indiscriminate commercialization. Much of the island is still green and unspoiled, but the sheer intensity of business in some resorts is threatening to spill over into the quieter parts.

The island has three distinct zones: the barren, mountainous north-west; the fertile central plain; and the eastern and southern coasts which house the resorts. The big resort – the biggest in the whole Ionian – is **Laganás**, on Laganás Bay in the south, a 24-hour party venue that doesn't give up from Easter until the last flight home in October. There are smaller, quieter resorts north and south of the capital, and the southerly Vassilikós peninsula has the best countryside and beaches, including exquisite **Yérakas**.

Although half-built apartment blocks are spreading through the central plain, this is where the quieter island begins: farms and vineyards, ancient villages, and the ruins of Venetian buildings levelled in the earthquakes. The island still produces fine wines, such as the white *Popolaro*, as well as sugar-shock inducing *mandoláto* nougat, whose honey-sweetened form is best. Zákynthos is also the birthplace of *kantádhes*, the hybrid of Cretan folk song and Italian opera ballad that can be heard in tavernas in Zákynthos Town and elsewhere. It is also one of the key breeding sites of the endangered **loggerhead sea turtle**, which breeds in Laganás Bay. The loggerhead (see p.751) is the subject of a continuing dispute between tourism businesses and environmentalists, has caused an international political scandal and even provoked a bomb attack against the environmentalists.

Zákynthos Town

The town, like the island, is known as both **ZÁKYNTHOS** and Zante. This former "Venice of the East" (*Zante, Fior di Levante*, "Flower of the Levant", in an Italian jingle), rebuilt on the old plan, has bravely tried to recreate some of its style, though reinforced concrete can only do so much.

The town stretches the length of a wide and busy harbour, bookended by the grand **Platía Solómou** square at the north, and the church of **Áyios Dhionýsios**, patron saint of the island, at the south. The square is named after the island's most famous son, the poet Dioníssios Solomoú, the father of modernism in Greek literature, who was responsible for establishing demotic Greek (as opposed to the elitist *katharevoúsa* dialect) as a literary idiom. He is also the author of the national anthem. There's a small **museum** devoted to his life and work in nearby Platía Ayíou Márkou (Mon–Sat 9am–noon; free) which shares its collection with the museum on Corfu (see p.727), where Solomoú spent most of his life. Platía Solomoú is also home to the town's **library**, which has a small collection of pre- and post-quake photography, and the

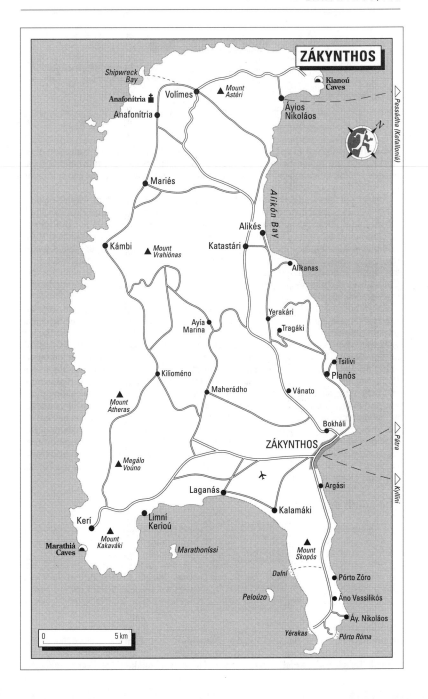

BOAT TRIPS

At least six pleasure craft offer **day trips** around the island from the quay in Zákynthos Town for 2000–3000dr. All take in sights such as the blue-water grottoes of the **Kianoú Caves** at Cape Skinári, and moor in To Naváyio, **Shipwreck Cove**, and the **Cape Kéri** caves. Shop around for the trip with the most stops, as eight hours bobbing round the coast can become a bore. Check also that the operators actually take you into the caves.

Byzantine Museum (Tues–Sun 8.30am–3pm; 400dr), notable for its collection of art works from the Ionian School, the region's post-Renaissance art movement, spear-headed by Zakynthian painter Panayiotis Doxaras. The movement was given impetus by Cretan refugees, unable to practise under Turkish rule.

Apart from the small **Zákynthos Museum** (Tues–Sun 8.30am–3pm; 400dr) – a mod-est collection of local historical artefacts next to the Solomoú Museum – the town's only other notable attraction is its massive **kástro**, brooding over the hamlet of **Bokháli** on its bluff above the town. The ruined Venetian fort (daily 8am–4pm; 400dr) has vestiges of dungeons, armouries and fortifications, and stunning views in all directions. Below the kástro walls, Bokháli has a couple of good though expensive tavernas, some host-ing nightly *kantáthes*, although Zakynthian driving habits make the thirty-minute walk from town a definite no-no after dark. The ugly new **amphitheatre** on the road out of town sometimes hosts concerts.

Zákynthos is a working town with few concessions to tourism, although there are hotels and restaurants aplenty, and it's the only place to stay if you want to see the island by public transport. Of the central hotels, the *Egli*, on Loútzi (☎0695/28 317; ③) is the bar-gain, tucked in beside the top-range and very expensive *Strada Marina* (☎0695/42 761, fax 28 733; ⑥). There are quieter hotels in the Repara district beyond Platía Solomoú: try either the *Reparo*, Dioníssiou Róma/Voultsou (☎0695/23 578; ④) or *Bitzaro*, Dhionysíou Róma (☎0695/23 644; ④), both near the scruffy municipal lido. The smart **restaurants** and bars of the seafront and Platía Ayíou Márkou are bedevilled by traffic, although the seafront *Village Inn* should be checked out for its bizarre gothic-Polynesian decor and the miniature jungle at the rear. First stop though, should be the friendly *Arekia* beyond the lido, which offers succulent taverna staples and nightly *kantádhes*. The neighbouring *Alivizos* also specializes in island cuisine and music. When the bored teens get off their bikes, they go **clubbing**, to bars like *Base* on Márkou, which plays anything from Miles Davis to Philip Glass, or the *Jazz Café*, on Tertséti which, despite plundering the London jazz club's logo, is actually a techno bar with DJ and 200dr cover.

The south and west

The road heading southeast from Zákynthos passes through **ARGÁSI**, the busiest resort on this coast, but with a beach barely a few feet wide in parts. It might, however, make a base for exploring the Vassilikós peninsula; there are rooms at the *Pension Vaso* (☎0695/44 599; ③) and *Andro* (☎0695/22 190; ③) on the main road in the centre of the village, and the seafront boasts some smart hotels: the *Locanda* (☎0695/45 386; ④) and the *Iliessa Beach* (☎0695/45 345; ④). Beyond a few indigenous tavernas, restaurant culture here is summed up, surreally, by an English caff that advertises a "Greek night" every Saturday.

Áno Vassilikó

At the southern tip of the island is **Áno Vassilikó**, where there are a few rooms with access to a sandy beach, and a great taverna/rooms hideaway at **Pórto Zóro** (also signed "Beach with Rocks and Flowers"). The expanding *Vasilikos Beach* (☎0695/24

114; ⑤) hotel/beach complex at **Áyios Nikólaos** has a good beach, with an embryonic hamlet and some rooms in the moon-like landscape behind it. Isolated Áyios Nikólaos lures day trippers from Argási, Kalamáki and Laganás with a **free bus** service in season.

Bulldozers are inventing new beaches, such as **Banana**, as quickly as their drivers can hack through the woods between the main road and the sea. The island's star is **Yérakas**, a sublime crescent of golden sand which is also a key loggerhead turtle breeding ground, and which is therefore off-limits between dusk and dawn. There's little here beyond two tavernas back from the beach and some pleasant, if remote, cabin accommodation at *Liuba Apartments* (☎0695/35 372; ⑤). The beach does draw crowds, but the 6am bus out of Zákynthos Town should secure you a few hours of Yérakas to yourself. Compared with Yérakas, **Pórto Róma**, on the east coast, is a disappointment, a small sand and pebble bay with a taverna and bar, some rooms on the approach road, and occasional hardy campers.

Laganás and Kalamáki

The vast majority of the 350,000 people or so who visit Zákynthos each year find themselves in **LAGANÁS**. The 9km beach in the bay is good, if trampled, and there are entertainments from watersports to ballooning, and even an occasional funfair. Beachfront bars and restaurants stretch for over a kilometre; the bars and restaurants on the main drag another kilometre inland. Some stay open around the clock; others just play music at deafening volume until dawn. The competing video and music bars can make Laganás at night resemble the set of *Bladerunner*, but that's how its predominantly English visitors like it. If this is your bag, there's no place better; if it isn't, flee. **Accommodation** is mostly block-booked by package companies. There's a basic campsite on the southern edge of town, where there are also quietish private rooms, and some bargain hotels – try the *Alexandros* (☎0695/51 580; ④) or *Galaxy* (☎0695/51 175; ④).

Neighbouring **KALAMÁKI** has a better beach than Laganás, and is altogether quieter, although both resorts suffer from airport noise. There are a number of good hotels, notably the *Crystal Beach* (☎0695/42 788, fax 42 917; ⑤), and the friendly Zakyta travel agency (☎0695/27 080) can also arrange accommodation. The two *Stanis* tavernas have extensive menus of Greek and international dishes, although the beachside version is geared more to lunches and its sibling more to evening meals. Alternatives include *Jools' Diner* and the *Merlis*. **Nightlife** centres around bars like *All Satros*, and the *Byzantio Club* on the hillside above the village, which has a garden with breathtaking views.

Kerí

The village of **KERÍ** is hidden in a fold above the cliffs at the island's southernmost tip. The village retains a number of pre-quake, Venetian buildings, including the church of the **Panayía Kerioú** – the Virgin is said to have saved the island from marauding pirates by hiding it in a sea mist. Kerí is also famous for a geological quirk, a series of small tar pools mentioned by both Pliny and Herodotus, but these have mysteriously dried up in recent years. A rough path leaving the southern end of the village leads 1km on to the lighthouse, with spectacular views of the sea, sea arches and stacks.

Makherádho, Kilioméno and Kámbi

The bus system does not reach the wild western side of the island, but a hire car or sturdy motorbike will get you there. **MAKHERÁDHO** boasts impressive pre-earthquake architecture set in beautiful arable uplands, surrounded by olive and fruit groves. The church of **Ayía Mávra** has an impressive free-standing campanile, and inside a splendid carved iconostasis and icons by Zákynthian painter Nikolaos Latsis. The town's major festival – one of the biggest on the island – is the saint's day, which falls on the first Sunday in June. The other notable church in town, that of the Panayía, commands breathtaking views over the central plain.

KILIOMÉNO is the best place to see surviving pre-earthquake domestic architecture, in the form of the island's traditional two-storey houses. The town was originally named after its church **Áyios Nikólaos**, whose impressive campanile, begun over a hundred years ago, still lacks a capped roof.

The road from Kilioméno climbs to the tiny clifftop hamlet of **KÁMBI**, destination for numerous coach trips to catch the sunset over the sea. The village contains a small **folk museum**, with a collection of domestic and agricultural artefacts, and local crafts such as embroidery. Its cliff-top **taverna** has extraordinary views over the 300-metre-high cliffs and western horizon. On an incline above the village there's an imposing concrete cross, constructed in memory of islanders killed here in the war, either by Nationalist soldiers or Nazis. The tiny village of **Mariés**, 5km to the north and set in a wooded green valley, has the only coastal access on this side of Zákynthos, a 7km track leading down to the rocky inlet of **Stenítis Bay** where there's a taverna and yacht dock.

The north

North and west from Zákynthos Town, the roads thread their way through luxuriantly fertile farmland, punctuated with tumulus-like hills. **Tsilívi**, 5km north of the capital, is the first beach resort here, just below the hamlet of **PLANÓS**. Unfortunately, this part of the coastline suffers from occasional oil pollution, with nothing but the winter storms to clear it. There's a good, basic **campsite**, *Zante Camping* (☎0695/24 754), beyond Planós, and some rooms – try *Gregory's* (☎0695/61 853; ③) or *Dolphin* (☎0695/27 425; ③) – but most visitors here are on package deals.

Alykón bay

Ormós Alikón, 12km north of Tsilívi, is a large sandy bay with lively surf and two of the area's largest resorts. **ALÍKANAS** is a small but expanding village, much of its accommodation being overseas villa rentals and **ALYKÉS**, named after the spooky salt pans behind the village, has the best beach north of the capital. There are **rooms** on the beach (try the *Golden Dolphin* taverna), and a couple of **hotels** set back from the village but with sea views – the *Ionian Star* (☎0695/83 416; ④) and the *Montreal* (☎0695/83 241; ⑤). Alykés is the last true resort on this coast, and the one where the bus service gives out. **Koróni**, 4km north, has sulphur springs flowing into the sea – follow the smell – which provide the odd sensation of swimming in a mix of cool and warm water.

Áyios Nikólaos, 6km, is a small working port serving daily ferries to and from Pessádha on Kefalloniá. From here another good trip is a ride by **kaïki** (1000dr) to the extreme northern tip of the island, where the **Kianoú (Blue) Caves** are some of the more realistically named of the many contenders in Greece. They're terrific for snorkelling, and when you go for a dip here your skin will appear bright blue. The road snakes onwards through a landscape of gorse bushes and dry-stone walls until it ends at the lighthouse of **Cape Skináni**. With one cafeteria, and a view of the mountainous expanse of Kefalloniá, it's a good spot for unofficial camping.

Volímes, Katastári and Ayía Marina

The northern towns and villages are accessible only to those with cars or sturdy motorbikes, although there are guided coach tours from the resorts, and none are really geared to tourism. **VOLÍMES** is the centre of the island's embroidery industry – with your own transport, you could make it to the **Anafonítria monastery**, 3km south, thought to have been the cell of the island's patron saint, Dhionysios, whose festivals are celebrated on August 24 and December 17. A track leads on to the cliffs overlooking **Shipwreck Bay** (To Navágio), with hair-raising views down to the shipwreck below. In the other direction from Volímes, the road leads 10km to Cape Skinari, where a lighthouse and kafenío overlook the rocky northern headland and the Kiánou blue sea caves. Two kilometres inland from Alíkes, **KATASTÁRI** is the largest settlement after the capital. Although it's unprepared for tourism, it's the place to see Zákynthian life as it's lived away from the tourism racket.

AYÍA MARÍNA, a few kilometres south of Katastári, has a church with an impressive Baroque altar screen, and a belfry that's being rebuilt from the remnants left after the 1953 earthquake. Like most Zákynthos churches, the belltower is detached, in Venetian fashion. Just above Ayía Marína is the *Parthenonas* taverna rightly boasting one of the best views on the island. From here you can see the whole of the central plain from beyond Alykés in the north to Laganás Bay in the south.

travel details

Corfu (Kérkyra)

There are three daily **flights** between Corfu and Athens (45min), and one to Thessaloníki (1hr). Roughly hourly (5am–10pm) **ferries** run between Corfu and Igoumenítsa (1–2hr). Additionally, most ferries between Italy (Brindisi, Bari, Otranto) and Greece stop at Corfu; stopover is free if specified in advance. The high-speed catamaran service between Brindisi, Corfu, Paxí and Lefkádha has been suspended.

Eríkoussa, Mathráki and Othoní

A **car ferry**, the *Alexandros II*, runs from Corfu Town to all the islands twice weekly (Tues & Sat, 6.30am). The ferry leaves from near the BP station on the seafront, midway between the Old and New Ports. Star Travel (☎0661/36 355) on the seafront has tickets and information, and also runs a seasonal excursion to the islands, although the Corfu connection involves sailing halfway round the island. Quicker access, favoured by islanders without vehicles, is via daily excursions from **Sidhári** run by Nearchos Seacruises (☎0663/95 248).

Paxí

Ferry connections to Paxí are haphazard: there is a weekly Monday morning **ferry** from Corfu through the year, and in season a ferry service (daily except Sun) from the Old Port of Corfu Town, leaving the quay below the Astron Hotel. At least one

of the following should be sailing at either 2pm or 5pm: the *Pegasus*, *Dolphin*, *Paxos Star*, or the *Anna Maria*. Check with Corfu's port police (☎0661/32 655) or a Paxíot travel company, as services change every year.

Lefkádha

5 **buses** daily to and from Athens (7hr), and 4 buses daily (3 on Sun) to and from Préveza (30min), passing Áktio airport (30min). At least 5 **ferries** daily in season from Nidrhí to Meganíssi; daily seasonal connections from Nidrhí to Kefalloniá (Fiskárdho and Sámi) and Itháki (Fríkes). The **hydrofoil** service linking Lefkádha with Paxí and Corfu has been suspended.

Kefalloniá

1 daily **flight** to and from Athens (45min).

Daily **ferries** from **Sámi** to Pátra (5hr); Astakós (2hr); Váthy (Itháki; 30min); Vassilikí (Lefkádha; 3hr). Also ferries from **Póros** to Kyllíni (2 daily; 1hr 30min); Zákynthos Town (1 daily; 2hr 30min); **Fiskárdho** to: Fríkes (Itháki; 1 daily; 1hr); Nidrhí (Lefkádha; 1 daily; 1hr 30min); Pisaetós (Itháki; 1 daily; 1hr); Vassilikí (Lefkádha; 4 daily; 2hr); **Argostóli** to: Kyllíni (2 daily; 2hr 30min); Lixoúri (12 daily, 8 on Sun; 30min); **Ayía Evfimía** to: Pisaetós (Itháki; 1 daily; 30min); Váthy (Itháki 1 daily; 1hr); **Pessádha** to: Áyios Nikoláos (Zákynthos; 2 daily; 1hr 30min).

Itháki (Ithaca)

Seasonal ferries from: **Fríkes** to: Fiskárdho (Kefalloniá; 1 daily; 1hr); Nidhrí (Lefkádha; 1 daily; 2hr); Vassilikí (Lefkádha; 1 daily; 1hr).

Pisaetós to: Fiskárdho (Kefalloniá; 1 daily; 1hr); Sámi (Kefalloniá; 3 daily; 1hr 30min); Ayía Evfimía (Kefalloniá; 1 daily; 30min).

Váthy to: Sámi (Kefalloniá; 4 daily; 1hr); Astakós (2 daily; 1hr 30min); Pátra (2 daily; 5hr). **Off season**, there is one daily service on each route, weather permitting.

Zákynthos

Seasonal ferries from: **Zákynthos Town** to: Kyllíni (5 daily; 1hr 30min); Pátra (daily; 3hr).

Áyios Nikoláos to: Pessádha (Kefalloniá; 2 daily May–Sept; 1hr 30min).

PART FOUR

THE

CONTEXTS

THE HISTORICAL FRAMEWORK

This section is intended just to lend some perspective to travels in Greece, and is heavily weighted towards the era of the modern, post-independence nation – especially the twentieth century. More detailed accounts of particular periods (Mycenae, Minoan Crete, Classical Athens, Byzantine Mystra, etc) are to be found in relevant sections of the guide.

NEOLITHIC, MINOAN AND MYCENAEAN AGES

Other than the solitary discovery of a fossilized Neanderthal skull near Thessaloníki, the earliest **evidence of human settlement** in Greece is to be found at Néa Nikomedhía, near Véria. Here, traces of large, rectangular houses dated to around 6000 BC have been excavated.

It seems that people originally came to this land in the eastern Mediterranean in fits and starts, predominantly from Anatolia. These **proto-Greeks** settled in essentially peaceful farming communities, made pottery and worshipped earth/fertility goddesses – clay statuettes of which are still found on the sites of old settlements. This simple way of life eventually disappeared, as people started to tap the land's resources for profit and to compete and trade.

MINOANS AND MYCENAEANS

The years between around **2000** and **1100 BC** were a period of fluctuating regional dominance, based at first upon sea power, with vast **royal palaces** serving as centres of administration. Particularly important were those at **Knossos** in Crete, and **Mycenae**, **Tiryns** and **Argos** in the Peloponnese.

Crete monopolized the eastern Mediterranean trade routes for an era subsequently called the **Minoan Age**, with the palace at Knossos surviving two earthquakes and a massive volcanic eruption on the island of Thíra (Santoríni), at some undefinable point between 1500 and 1450 BC. The most obvious examples of Minoan culture can be seen in frescoes, in jewellery and in pottery, the distinctive red-and-white design on a dark background marking the peak period of Minoan achievement. When Knossos finally succumbed to disaster, natural or otherwise, around 1400 BC, it was the flourishing centre of **Mycenae** that assumed the leading role (and gave its name to the civilization of this period), until it in turn collapsed around 1200 BC.

This is a period whose history and remains are bound up with its **legends**, recounted most famously by Homer. Knossos was the home of King Minos, while the palaces of Mycenae and Pylos were the respective bases of Agamemnon and Nestor; Menelaus and Odysseus hailed from Sparta and Ithaca. The Homeric and other legends relating to them almost certainly reflect the prevalence of violence, revenge and **war** as increasing facts of life, instigated and aggravated by trade rivalry. The increasing scale of conflict and militarization is exemplified in the massive fortifications – dubbed Cyclopean by later ages – that were built around many of the palaces.

The Greece of these years was by no means a united nation – as the Homeric legend reflects – and its people were divided into what were in effect a series of splinter groups, defined in large part by sea and mountain barriers and by access to **pasture**. Settlements flourished according to their proximity to and prowess on the sea and the fertility of their land; most were self-sufficient, specializing in the production of particular items for **trade**. Olives, for example, were associated with the region of Attica, and minerals with the island of Mílos.

THE DORIAN AND CLASSICAL ERAS

The Mycenaean-era Greek states had also to cope with and assimilate periodic influxes of new peoples and trade. The traditional view of the collapse of the Mycenaean civilization has it that a northern "barbarian" people, the **Dorians**, "invaded" from the north, devastating the existing palace culture and opening a "dark age" era. These days, archeologists see the influx more in terms of shifting trade patterns, though undoubtedly there was major disruption of the palace cultures and their sea powers during the eleventh century.

Two other trends are salient to the period: the almost total supplanting of the mother goddesses by **male deities** (a process begun under the Mycenaeans), and the appearance of an **alphabet** still recognizable by modern Greeks, which replaced the so-called "Linear A" and "Linear B" Minoan/Mycenaean scripts.

CITY-STATES: SPARTA AND ATHENS

The ninth century BC ushered in the beginnings of the Greek **city-state** (polis). Citizens – rather than just kings or aristocrats – became involved in government and took part in community activities and organized industry and leisure. Colonial ventures increased, as did commercial dealings, and a consequent rise in the import trade was gradually to create a new class of manufacturers.

The city-state was the life of the people who dwelt within it and each state retained both its independence and a distinctive style, with the result that the sporadic attempts to unite in a league against an enemy without were always pragmatic and temporary. The two most powerful states to emerge were Athens and Sparta, who were to exercise a rivalry over the next five centuries.

Sparta was associated with the Dorians, who had settled in large numbers on the fertile Eurotas (Évrotas) river plain. The society of Sparta and its environs was based on a highly militaristic ethos, accentuated by the need to defend the exposed and fertile land on which it stood. Rather than build intricate fortifications, the people of Sparta relied upon military prowess and a system of laws decreed by the (semi-legendary) **Lycurgus**. Males were subjected to military instruction between the ages

of seven and thirty. Weak babies were known periodically to "disappear". Girls too had to perform athletic feats of sprinting and wrestling, and even dwellings were more like barracks than houses.

Athens, the fulcrum of the state of Attica, was dynamic and exciting by contrast. Home to the administrations of **Solon** and **Pericles**, the dramatic talents of Sophocles and Aristophanes, the oratory of the hisotrian Thucydides and Demosthenes, and the philosophical power of Socrates and Plato, it made up in cultural achievement what it lacked in Spartan virtue. Yet Sparta did not deserve all the military glory. The Athens of the sixth and fifth centuries BC, the so-called **Classical period** in Greek history, played the major part in repelling the armies of the Persian king Xerxes at Marathon (490 BC) and Salamis (480 BC), campaigns later described by Aeschylus in *The Persians*.

Athens also gave rise to a tradition of **democracy** (*demokratia*), literally "control by the people" – although at this stage "the people" did not include either women or slaves. In Athens there were three organs of government. The Areopagus, composed of the city elders, had a steadily decreasing authority and ended up dealing solely with murder cases. Then there was the Council of Five Hundred (men), elected annually by ballot to prepare the business of the Assembly and to attend to matters of urgency. The Assembly gave every free man a political voice; it had sole responsibility for law-making and provided an arena for the discussion of important issues. It was a genuinely enfranchised council of citizens.

This was a period of intense creativity, particularly in Athens, whose actions and pretensions were fast becoming imperial in all but name. Each city-state had its **acropolis**, or high town, where religious activity was focused. In Athens, Pericles endowed the acropolis with a complex of buildings, whose climax was the temple of the Parthenon. Meanwhile, the era saw the tragedies of Sophocles performed, and the philosophies of Socrates and Plato expounded.

Religion at this stage was polytheistic, ordering all under the aegis of Zeus. In the countryside the proliferation of names and of sanctuary finds suggests a preference for the slightly more mundane Demeter and Dionysus.

THE PELOPONNESIAN WAR

The power struggles between Athens and Sparta, allied with various networks of city- states, eventually culminated in the **Peloponnesian War** of 431–404 BC. After these conflicts, superbly recorded by Thucydides and nominally won by Sparta, the city-state ceased to function so effectively.

This was in part due to drained resources and political apathy, but to a greater degree a consequence of the increasingly commercial and complex pressures on everyday life. Trade, originally spurred by the invention of **coinage** in the sixth century BC, continued to expand; a revitalized Athens, for example, was exporting wine, oil and manufactured goods, getting corn in return from the Black Sea and Egypt.

The amount of time each man had to devote to the affairs of government decreased, and a position in political life became a professional job rather than a natural assumption. Democracy had changed, while in philosophy there was a shift from the idealists and mystics of the sixth and fifth centuries BC to the Cynics, Stoics and Epicureans – followers, respectively, of Diogenes, Zeno and Epicurus.

HELLENISTIC AND ROMAN GREECE

The most important factor in the decline of the city-states was meanwhile developing outside their sphere, in the kingdom of Macedonia.

THE MACEDONIAN EMPIRE

Based at the Macedonian capital of Pella, **Philip II** (359–336 BC) was forging a strong military and unitary force, extending his territories into Thrace and finally establishing control over Athens and southern Greece. His son, **Alexander the Great**, in a brief but glorious thirteen-year reign, extended these gains into Persia and Egypt and parts of modern India and Afghanistan.

This unwieldy empire splintered almost immediately upon Alexander's death in 323 BC, to be divided into the three Macedonian dynasties of **Hellenistic Greece**: the Antigonids in Macedonia, the Seleucids in Syria and Persia, and the Ptolemies in Egypt. Each were in turn conquered and absorbed by the new Roman Empire, the Ptolemies – under their queen Cleopatra – last of all.

ROMAN GREECE

Mainland Greece was subdued by the Romans over some seventy years of campaigns, from 215 to 146. Once in control, however, **Rome** allowed considerable autonomy to the old territories of the city-states. Greek remained the official language of the eastern Mediterranean and its traditions and culture coexisted fairly peacefully with that of the overlords during the next three centuries.

In central Greece both **Athens** and **Corinth** remained important cities but the emphasis was shifting north – particularly to towns, such as **Salonica** (Thessaloníki), along the new Via Egnatia, a military and civil road engineered between Rome and Byzantium via the port of Brundisium (modern Brindisi).

THE BYZANTINE EMPIRE AND MEDIEVAL GREECE

The shift of emphasis to the north was given even greater impetus by the decline of the Roman Empire and its apportioning into eastern and western empires. In the year 330 AD the Emperor Constantine moved his capital to the Greek city of Byzantium and here emerged Constantinople (modern Istanbul), the "new Rome" and spiritual and political capital of the **Byzantine Empire**.

While the last western Roman emperor was deposed by barbarian Goths in 476, this oriental portion was to be the dominant Mediterranean power for some 700 years; only in 1453 did it collapse completely.

CHRISTIANITY

Christianity had been introduced under Constantine, and by the end of the fourth century was the official state religion, its liturgies (still in use in the Greek Orthodox church), creed and New Testament all written in Greek. A distinction must be drawn, though, between perceptions of Greek as a language and culture and as a concept. The Byzantine Empire styled itself Roman, or *Romios*, rather than Hellenic, and moved to eradicate all remaining symbols of pagan Greece. The Delphic Oracle was forcibly closed, and the Olympic Games discontinued, at the end of the fourth century.

The seventh century saw **Constantinople** besieged by Persians, and later Arabs, but the Byzantine Empire survived, losing only Egypt, the least "Greek" of its territories. From the ninth to the early eleventh centuries it enjoyed an archetypal "golden age", in culture, confidence and security. Tied up in the Orthodox Byzantine faith was a sense of spiritual superiority, and the emperors saw Constantinople as a "new Jerusalem" for their "chosen people". It was the beginning of a diplomatic and ecclesiastical conflict with the Catholic west that was to have disastrous consequences over the next five centuries. In the meantime the eastern and western patriarchs mutually excommunicated each other.

From the seventh through to the eleventh centuries **Byzantine Greece**, certainly in the south and centre, became something of a provincial backwater. Administration was absurdly top-heavy and imperial taxation led to semi-autonomous provinces ruled by military generals, whose lands were usually acquired from bankrupted peasants. This alienation of the poor provided a force for change, with a floating populace ready to turn towards or cooperate with the empire's enemies if terms were an improvement.

Waves of **Slavic raiders** needed no encouragement to sweep down from the north Balkans throughout this period. At the same time other tribal groups moved down more peaceably from **central Europe** and were absorbed with little difficulty. According to one theory, the nomadic **Vlachs** from Romania eventually settled in the Píndhos Mountains, and later, from the thirteenth century onwards, immigrants from **Albania** repopulated the islands of Spétses, Ídhra, Ándhros and Évvia, as well as parts of Attica and the Peloponnese.

THE CRUSADES: FRANKISH AND VENETIAN RULE

From the early years of the eleventh century, less welcome and less assimilable Western forces began to appear. The **Normans** landed first at Corfu in 1085, and returned again to the mainland with papal sanction a decade later on their way to liberate Jerusalem.

These were only a precursor, though, for the forces that were to descend en route for the **Fourth Crusade** of 1204, when Venetians, Franks and Germans turned their armies directly on Byzantium and sacked and occupied Constantinople. These Latin princes and their followers, intent on new lands and kingdoms,

settled in to divide up the best part of the Empire. All that remained of Byzantium were four small peripheral kingdoms or **despotates**: the most powerful in Nicaea in Asia Minor, less significant ones at Trebizond on the Black Sea, and (in present-day Greece) in Epirus and around Mystra in the Peloponnese (known in these times as the Morea).

There followed two extraordinarily involved centuries of manipulation and struggle between Franks, Venetians, Genoese, Catalans and Turks. The Paleologos dynasty at Nicaea recovered the city of Constantinople in 1261, but little of its former territory and power. Instead, the focus of Byzantium shifted to the Peloponnese, where the autonomous **Despotate of Mystra**, ruled by members of the imperial family, eventually succeeded in wresting most of the peninsula from Frankish hands. At the same time this despotate underwent an intense cultural renaissance, strongly evoked in the churches and shells of cities seen today at Mystra and Monemvassía.

TURKISH OCCUPATION

Within a generation of driving out the Franks, the Byzantine Greeks faced a much stronger threat in the expanding empire of the **Ottoman Turks**. Torn apart by internal struggles between their own ruling dynasties, the **Palaeologi** and **Cantacuzenes**, and unaided by the Catholic west, they were to prove no match for the Turks. On Tuesday, May 29, 1453, a date still solemnly commemorated by the Orthodox church, Constantinople fell to besieging Muslim Turks.

Mystra was to follow within seven years, and Trebizond within nine, by which time virtually all of the old Byzantine Empire lay under Ottoman domination. Only the **Ionian islands** and the **Cyclades**, which remained Venetian, and a few scattered and remote enclaves – like the Máni in the Peloponnese, Sfákia in Crete and Soúli in Epirus – were able to resist the Turkish advance.

OTTOMAN RULE

Under what Greeks refer to as the "Dark Ages" of **Ottoman rule**, the lands of present-day Greece passed into rural provincialism, taking refuge in a self-protective mode of village life that has only recently been disrupted. Taxes and discipline, sporadically backed up by the genocide of dissenting communities, were inflicted by the Turkish Porte, but estates passed into the hands of local chieftains who often had considerable independence.

Greek identity, meanwhile, was preserved through the offices of the **Orthodox church** which, despite instances of enforced conversion, the sultans allowed to continue. The **monasteries**, often secretly, organized schools and became the trustees of Byzantine culture, though this had gone into stagnation after the fall of Constantinople and Mystra, whose scholars and artists emigrated west, adding impetus to the Renaissance.

As Ottoman administration became more and more decentralized and inefficient, individual Greeks rose to local positions of considerable influence, and a number of communities achieved a degree of autonomy. Ambelákia village in Thessaly, for example, established an industrial cooperative system to export dyed cloth to Europe, paying only direct taxes to the sultan. And on the Albanian repopulated islands of the Argo-Saronic, a **Greek merchant fleet** came into being in the eighteenth century, permitted to trade throughout the Mediterranean. Greeks, too, were becoming organized overseas in the sizeable expatriate colonies of central Europe, which often had affiliations with the semi-autonomous village clusters of Zagória (in Epirus) and Mount Pílion.

THE STRUGGLE FOR INDEPENDENCE

Opposition to Turkish rule was becoming widespread, exemplified most obviously by the **Klephts** (brigands) of the mountains. It was not until the nineteenth century, however, that a resistance movement could muster sufficient support and firepower to prove a real challenge to the Turks. In 1770 a Russian-backed uprising had been easily and brutally suppressed, but fifty years later the position was different.

In Epirus the Turks were over-extended, subduing the expansionist campaigns of local ruler **Ali Pasha**. The French Revolution had given impetus to the confidence of "freedom movements", and the Greek fighters were given financial and ideological underpinnings by the Filikí Etería, or "Friendly Society", a secret group recruited among the exiled merchants and intellectuals of central Europe.

This somewhat motley coalition of Klephts and theorists launched their insurrection at the monastery of **Ayía Lávra** near Kalávryta in the Peloponnese, where on March 25, 1821, the Greek banner was openly raised by the local bishop, Yermanos.

THE WAR OF INDEPENDENCE

To describe in detail the course of the **War of Independence** is to provoke unnecessary confusion, since much of the rebellion consisted of local and fragmentary guerilla campaigns. What is important to understand is that Greeks, though fighting for liberation from the Turks, were not fighting as and for a nation. Motives differed enormously: landowners assumed their role was to lead and sought to retain and reinforce their traditional privileges, while the peasantry saw the struggle as a means towards land redistribution.

Outside Greece, prestige and publicity for the insurrection was promoted by the arrival of a thousand or so European **Philhellenes**, almost half of them German, though the most important was the English poet, **Lord Byron**, who died while training Greek forces at Messolóngi in April 1824.

Though it was the Greek guerilla leaders, above all **Theodhoros Kolokotronis**, "the old man of the Morea", who brought about the most significant military victories of the war, the death of Byron had an immensely important effect on public opinion in the West. Aid for the Greek struggle had come neither from Orthodox Russia, nor from the Western powers of France and Britain, ravaged by the Napoleonic Wars. But by 1827, when Messolóngi fell again to the Turks, these three powers finally agreed to seek autonomy for certain parts of Greece and sent a combined fleet to put pressure on the sultan's Egyptian army, then ransacking and massacring in the Peloponnese. Events took over, and an accidental naval battle in **Navarino Bay** resulted in the destruction of almost the entire Turkish-Egyptian fleet. The following spring Russia itself declared war on the Turks and the sultan was forced to accept the existence of an autonomous Greece.

In 1830 Greek independence was confirmed by the Western powers and **borders** were drawn. These included just 800,000 of the 6 million Greeks living within the Ottoman empire, and the Greek territories which were for the most part the poorest of the Classical and Byzantine lands, comprising Attica, the Peloponnese and the islands of the Argo-Saronic and Cyclades. The rich agricultural belt of Thessaly, Epirus in the West, and Macedonia in the north, remained in Turkish hands. Meanwhile, the Ionian islands were controlled by a British Protectorate and the Dodecanese by the Ottomans (and subsequently by the new Italian nation).

THE EMERGING STATE

Modern Greece began as a republic and **Ioannis Capodistrias**, its first president, concentrated his efforts on building a viable central authority and government in the face of diverse protagonists from the independence struggle. Almost inevitably he was assassinated – in 1831, by two chieftains from the ever-disruptive Máni – and perhaps equally inevitably the great Western powers stepped in. They created a monarchy, gave limited aid, and set on the throne a Bavarian prince, **Otho**.

The new king proved an autocratic and insensitive ruler, bringing in fellow Germans to fill official posts and ignoring all claims by the landless peasantry for redistribution of the old estates. In 1862 he was eventually forced from the country by a popular revolt, and the Europeans produced a new prince, this time from Denmark, with Britain ceding the Ionian islands to bolster support. **George I**, in fact, proved more capable: he built the first railways and roads, introduced limited land reforms in the Peloponnese, and oversaw the first expansion of the Greek borders.

THE MEGÁLI IDHÉA AND WAR

From the very beginning, the unquestioned motive force of Greek foreign policy was the **Megáli Idhéa** (Great Idea) of liberating Greek populations outside the country and incorporating the old territories of Byzantium into the kingdom. In 1878 **Thessaly**, along with southern Epirus, was ceded to Greece by the Turks.

Less illustriously, the Greeks failed in 1897 to achieve *énosis* (union) with **Crete** by attacking Turkish forces on the mainland, and in the process virtually bankrupted the state. The island was, however, placed under a High Commissioner, appointed by the Great Powers, and in 1913 became a part of Greece.

It was from Crete, also, that the most distinguished Greek statesman emerged. **Eleftherios Venizelos**, having led a civilian campaign for his island's liberation, was elected as Greek Prime Minister in 1910. Two years later he organized an alliance of Balkan powers to fight the **Balkan Wars** (1912–13), campaigns that saw the Turks virtually driven from Europe. With Greek borders extended to include the northeast Aegean, northern Thessaly, central Epirus and parts of Macedonia, the Megáli Idhéa was approaching reality. At the same time Venizelos proved himself a shrewd manipulator of domestic public opinion by revising the constitution and introducing a series of liberal social reforms.

Division, however, was to appear with the outbreak of **World War I**. Venizelos urged Greek entry on the British side, seeing in the conflict possibilities for the "liberation" of Greeks in Thrace and Asia Minor, but the new king, Constantine I, who was married to a sister of the German Kaiser, imposed a policy of neutrality. Eventually Venizelos set up a revolutionary government in Thessaloníki, and in 1917 Greek troops entered the war to join the French, British and Serbians in the **Macedonian campaign**. On the capitulation of Bulgaria and Ottoman Turkey, the Greeks occupied **Thrace**, and Venizelos presented demands at Versailles for the predominantly Greek region of Smyrna on the Asia Minor coast.

This was the beginning of one of the most disastrous episodes in modern Greek history. Venizelos was authorized to move forces into Smyrna in 1919, but by then Allied support had evaporated and in Turkey itself a new nationalist movement was taking power under Mustafa Kemal, or **Atatürk** as he came to be known. In 1920 Venizelos lost the elections and monarchist factions took over, their aspirations unmitigated by the Cretan's skill in foreign diplomacy. Greek forces were ordered to advance upon Ankara in an attempt to bring Atatürk to terms.

This so-called **Anatolian campaign** ignominiously collapsed in summer 1922 when Turkish troops forced the Greeks back to the coast and a hurried evacuation from **Smyrna**. As they left Smyrna, the Turks moved in and systematically massacred whatever remained of the Armenian and Greek populations before burning most of the city to the ground.

THE EXCHANGE OF POPULATIONS

There was now no alternative but for Greece to accept Atatürk's own terms, formalized by the Treaty of Lausanne in 1923, which ordered the

exchange of religious minorities in each country. Turkey was to accept 390,000 Muslims resident on Greek soil. Greece, mobilized almost continuously for the last decade and with a population of under five million, was faced with the resettlement of over 1,300,000 Christian refugees. The Megáli Idhéa had ceased to be a viable blueprint.

Changes, inevitably, were intense and far-reaching. The great agricultural estates of Thessaly were finally redistributed, both to Greek tenants and refugee farmers, and huge shanty towns grew into new quarters around Athens, Pireás and other cities, a spur to the country's then almost nonexistent industry.

Politically, too, reaction was swift. A group of army officers assembled after the retreat from Smyrna, "invited" King Constantine to abdicate, and executed five of his ministers. Democracy was nominally restored with the proclamation of a republic, but for much of the next decade changes in government were brought about by factions within the armed forces. Meanwhile, among the urban refugee population, unions were being formed and the Greek Communist Party (KKE) was established.

By 1936 the Communist Party had enough democratic support to hold the balance of power in parliament, and would have done so had not the army and the by then restored king decided otherwise. King George (Yiorgos) II had been returned by a plebiscite held – and almost certainly manipulated – the previous year, and so presided over an increasingly factionalized parliament.

THE METAXAS DICTATORSHIP

In April 1936 George II appointed **General John Metaxas** as prime minister, despite the latter's support from only six elected deputies. Immediately a series of KKE-organized strikes broke out and the king, ignoring attempts to form a broad liberal coalition, dissolved parliament without setting a date for new elections. It was a blatantly unconstitutional move and opened the way for five years of ruthless and at times absurd dictatorship.

Metaxas averted a general strike with military force and proceeded to set up a state based on **fascist** models of the age. Left-wing and trade union opponents were imprisoned or forced into exile, a state youth movement and secret police set up, and rigid censorship,

extending even to passages of Thucydides, imposed. It was, however, at least a Greek dictatorship, and though Metaxas was sympathetic to Nazi organization he completely opposed German or Italian domination.

WORLD WAR II AND THE GREEK CIVIL WAR

The Italians tried to provoke the Greeks into **World War II** by surreptitiously torpedoing the Greek cruiser *Elli* in Tínos harbour on August 15, 1940, but they met with no response. However, when Mussolini occupied Albania and sent an ultimatum on October 28, 1940, demanding passage for his troops through Greece, Metaxas responded to the Italian foreign minister with the apocryphal one-word answer **"ókhi"** (no). (In fact, his response, in the mutually understood French, was "C'est la guerre".) The date marked the entry of Greece into the war, and the gesture is still celebrated as a national holiday.

OCCUPATION AND RESISTANCE

Fighting as a nation in a sudden unity of crisis, the Greeks drove Italian forces from the country and took control of the long-coveted and predominantly Greek-populated northern Epirus (the south of Albania). However, the Greek army frittered away their strength in the snowy mountains of northern Epirus rather than consolidate their gains or defend the Macedonian frontier, and coordination with the British never materialized.

In April of the following year Nazi mechanized columns swept through Yugoslavia and across the Greek mainland, effectively reversing the only Axis defeat to date, and by the end of May 1941, airborne and seaborne **German invasion** forces had completed the occupation of Crete and the other islands. Metaxas had died before their arrival, while King George and his new self-appointed ministers fled into exile in Cairo; few Greeks, of any political persuasion, were sad to see them go.

The joint Italian-German-Bulgarian Axis **occupation** of Greece was among the bitterest experiences of the European war. Nearly half a million Greek civilians starved to death as all available food was requisitioned to feed occupying armies, and entire villages throughout the mainland and especially on Crete were burned at the least hint of resistance activity.

In the north the Bulgarians desecrated ancient sites and churches in a bid to annex "Slavic" Macedonia.

Primarily in the north, too, the Nazis supervised the deportation to concentration camps of virtually the entire **Greek-Jewish population**. This was at the time a sizeable community. Thessaloníki – where the former UN and Austrian president Kurt Waldheim worked for Nazi intelligence – contained the largest Jewish population of any Balkan city, and there were significant populations in all the Greek mainland towns and on many of the islands.

With a quisling government in Athens – and an unpopular, discredited Royalist group in Cairo – the focus of Greek political and military action over the next four years passed largely to the **EAM**, or National Liberation Front. By 1943 it was in virtual control of most areas of the country, working with the British on tactical operations, with its own army (**ELAS**), navy, and both civil and secret police forces. On the whole it commanded popular support, and it offered an obvious framework for the resumption of postwar government.

However, most of its membership was communist, and the British Prime Minister, **Churchill**, was determined to reinstate the monarchy. Even with two years of the war to run, it became obvious that there could be no peaceable post-liberation regime other than an EAM-dominated republic. Accordingly, in August 1943, representatives from each of the main resistance movements (including two noncommunist groups) flew from a makeshift airstrip in Thessaly to ask for guarantees from the "government" in Cairo that the king would not return unless a plebiscite had first voted in his favour. Neither the Greek nor British authorities would consider the proposal and the one possibility of averting civil war was lost.

The EAM contingent returned divided, as perhaps the British had intended, and a conflict broke out between those who favoured taking peaceful control of any government imposed after liberation, and the hard-line Stalinist ideologues, who believed such a situation should not be allowed to develop.

In October 1943, with fears of an imminent British landing force and takeover, ELAS launched a full-scale attack upon its Greek rivals; by the following February, when a ceasefire was arranged, they had wiped out all but the EDES, a right-wing grouping suspected of collaboration with the Germans. At the same time other forces were at work, with both British and Americans infiltrating units into Greece in order to prevent the establishment of a communist government when the Germans began withdrawing their forces.

CIVIL WAR

In fact, as the Germans began to leave in October 1944, most of the EAM leadership agreed to join a British-sponsored "official" **interim government**. It quickly proved a tactical error, however. With ninety percent of the countryside under their control, the communists were given only one-third representation. The king showed no sign of renouncing his claims, and, in November, Allied forces ordered ELAS to disarm. On December 3 all pretences of civility or neutrality were dropped; the police fired on a communist demonstration in Athens, and fighting broke out between ELAS and **British troops**, in the so-called **Dhekemvrianá** battle of Athens.

A truce of sorts was negotiated at Várkiza the following spring, but the agreement was never implemented. The army, police and civil service remained in right-wing hands and while collaborationists were often allowed to retain their positions, left-wing sympathizers, many of whom were not communists, were systematically excluded. The elections of 1946 were won by the right-wing parties, followed by a plebiscite in favour of the king's return. By 1947 guerilla activity had again reached the scale of a full **civil war**.

In the interim, King George had died and been succeeded by his brother Paul (with his consort Frederika), while the **Americans** had taken over the British role, and begun putting into action the cold-war **Truman doctrine**. In 1947 they took virtual control of Greece, their first significant postwar experiment in anti-communist intervention. Massive economic and military aid was given to a client Greek government, with a prime minister whose documents had to be countersigned by the American Mission in order to become valid.

In the mountains US "military advisers" supervised **campaigns against ELAS**, and there were mass arrests, court-martials and imprisonments – a kind of "White Terror" – lasting until 1951. Over three thousand executions were recorded, including a number of Jehovah's

Witnesses, "a sect proved to be under communist domination", according to US Ambassador Grady.

In the autumn of 1949, with the Yugoslav-Greek border closed after Tito's rift with Stalin, the last ELAS guerillas finally admitted defeat, retreating into Albania from their strongholds on Mount Grámmos. Atrocities had been committed on both sides, including, from the left, widescale destruction of monasteries, and the dubious evacuation of children from "combat areas" (as told in Nicholas Gage's virulently anti-communist book *Eleni*). Such errors, as well as the hopelessness of fighting an American-backed army, undoubtedly lost ELAS much support.

RECONSTRUCTION AMERICAN STYLE 1950–67

It was a demoralized, shattered Greece that emerged into the Western political orbit of the 1950s. It was also perforce American-dominated, enlisted into the Korean War in 1950 and NATO the following year. In domestic politics, the US Embassy – still giving the orders – foisted a winner-take-all electoral system, which was to ensure victory for the right over the next twelve years. All leftist activity was banned; those individuals who were not herded into political "re-education" camps or dispatched by firing squads, legal or vigilante, went into exile throughout Eastern Europe, to return only after 1974.

The American-backed, highly conservative **"Greek Rally"** party, led by General Papagos, won the first decisive post-civil war elections in 1952. After the general's death, the party's leadership was taken over – and to an extent liberalized – by **Constantine Karamanlis**. Under his rule, stability of a kind was established and some economic advances registered, particularly after the revival of Greece's traditional German markets. However, the 1950s was also a decade that saw wholesale **depopulation** of the villages as migrants sought work in Australia, America and Western Europe, or the larger Greek cities.

The main crisis in foreign policy throughout this period was **Cyprus**, where a long terrorist campaign was waged by Greeks opposing British rule, and there was sporadic threat of a new Greek-Turkish war. A temporary and unworkable solution was forced on the island by Britain in 1960, granting independence without the possibility of self-determination or union with Greece. Much of the traditional Greek-British goodwill was destroyed by the issue, with Britain seen to be acting with regard only for its two military bases (over which, incidentally, it still retains sovereignty).

By 1961, unemployment, the Cyprus issue and the imposition of US nuclear bases on Greek soil were changing the political climate, and when Karamanlis was again elected there was strong suspicion of a fraud arranged by the king and army. Strikes became frequent in industry and even agriculture, and King Paul and autocratic, fascist-inclined Queen Frederika were openly attacked in parliament and at protest demonstrations. The far right grew uneasy about **"communist resurgence"** and, losing confidence in their own electoral influence, arranged the assassination of left-wing deputy **Grigoris Lambrakis** in Thessaloníki in May 1963. (The assassination, and its subsequent cover-up, is the subject of Vassilis Vassilikos's thriller *Z*, filmed by Costa-Gavras.) It was against this volatile background that Karamanlis resigned, lost the subsequent elections and left the country.

The new government – the first controlled from outside the Greek right since 1935 – was formed by **George Papandreou's** Centre Union Party, and had a decisive majority of nearly fifty seats. It was to last, however, for under two years as conservative forces rallied to thwart its progress. In this the chief protagonists were the army officers and their constitutional Commander-in-Chief, the new king, 23-year-old **Constantine II**.

Since power in Greece depended on a pliant military as well as a network of political appointees, Papandreou's most urgent task in order to govern securely and effectively was to reform the armed forces. His first Minister of Defence proved incapable of the task and, while he was investigating the right-wing plot that was thought to have rigged the 1961 election, "evidence" was produced of a leftist conspiracy connected with Papandreou's son Andreas (himself a minister in the government). The allegations grew to a crisis and George Papandreou decided to assume the defence portfolio himself, a move for which the king refused to give the necessary sanction. He then resigned in order to gain approval at the polls but the king would not order fresh elections, instead persuading members of the Centre Union – chief among them **Constantine Mitsotakis** – to defect and organize a coalition government. Punctuated by strikes, resignations and mass demonstrations, this lasted for a year and a half until new elections were eventually set for May 28, 1967. They failed to take place.

THE COLONELS' JUNTA 1967–74

It was a foregone conclusion that Papandreou's party would win popular support in the polls against the discredited coalition partners. And it was equally certain that there would be some sort of anti-democratic action to try and prevent them from taking power. Disturbed by the party's leftward shift, King Constantine was said to have briefed senior generals for a coup d'état, to take place ten days before the elections. However, he was caught by surprise, as was nearly everyone else, by the **coup** of April 21, 1967, staged by a group of "unknown" colonels. It was, in the words of Andreas Papandreou, "the first successful CIA military putsch on the European continent".

The **Colonels' Junta**, having taken control of the means of power, was sworn in by the king and survived the half-hearted counter-coup which he subsequently attempted to organize. It was an overtly **fascist regime**, absurdly styling itself as the true "Revival of Greek Orthodoxy" against Western "corrupting influences", though in reality its ideology was nothing more than warmed-up dogma from the Metaxas era.

All political activity was banned: trade unions were forbidden to recruit or meet; the press was so heavily censored that many papers stopped printing, and thousands of "communists" were arrested, imprisoned, and often tortured. Among the persecuted were both Papandreos, the composer Mikis Theodorakis (deemed "unfit to stand trial" after three months in custody) and Amalia Fleming (widow of Alexander Fleming). The best known Greek actress, Melina Mercouri, was stripped of her citizenship in absentia, and thousands of prominent Greeks joined her in exile. Culturally, the colonels put an end to popular music (closing down most of the Pláka rembétika clubs) and inflicted ludicrous censorship on literature and the theatre, including (as under Metaxas) a ban on production of the Classical tragedies.

The colonels lasted for seven years, opposed (especially after the first year) by the majority of the Greek people, excluded from the European community, but propped up and given massive aid by US presidents **Lyndon Johnson** and **Richard Nixon**. To them and the CIA the junta's Greece was not an unsuitable client state: human rights considerations were considered unimportant; orders were placed for sophisticated military technology and foreign investment on terms highly unfavourable to Greece was open to multinational corporations. It was a fairly routine scenario for the exploitation of an underdeveloped nation.

Opposition was voiced from the beginning by exiled Greeks in London, the United States and Western Europe, but only in 1973 did demonstrations break out openly in Greece. On November 17 the students of Athens **Polytechnic** began an occupation of their buildings. The ruling clique lost its nerve; armoured vehicles stormed the Polytechnic gates and a still-undetermined number of students were killed. Martial law was tightened and junta chief **Colonel Papadopoulos** was replaced by the even more noxious and reactionary **General Ioannides**, head of the secret police.

THE RETURN TO CIVILIAN RULE 1975–81

The end of the ordeal, however, came within a year as the dictatorship embarked on a disastrous political adventure in **Cyprus**. By attempting to topple the Makarios government and impose *énosis* (union) on the island, they provoked a Turkish invasion and occupation of forty percent of Cypriot territory. The army finally mutinied and **Constantine Karamanlis** was invited to return from Paris to again take office. He swiftly negotiated a ceasefire (but no solution) in Cyprus, withdrew temporarily from NATO, and warned that US bases would have to be removed except where they specifically served Greek interest.

In November 1974 Karamanlis and his Néa Dhimokratía (New Democracy) party was rewarded by a sizeable majority in **elections**, with a centrist and socialist opposition. The latter was comprised by PASOK, a new party led by Andreas Papandreou.

The election of Néa Dhimokratía was in every sense a safe conservative option but to Karamanlis's enduring credit it oversaw an effective and firm return to democratic stability, even legitimizing the KKE (Communist Party) for the first time in its history. Karamanlis also held a **referendum on the monarchy** – in which 59 percent of Greeks rejected the return of Constantine – and instituted in its place a French-style presidency, which he himself occupied from 1980 to 1985 (and has done so again from 1990). Economically there were limited advances although these were more than offset by inflationary defence spending (the result of renewed tension with Turkey), hastily negotiated entrance into the EU, and the decision to let the drachma float after decades of its being artificially fixed at 30 to the US dollar.

Crucially, though, Karamanlis failed to deliver on vital reforms in bureaucracy, social welfare and education; and though the worst figures of the junta were brought to trial, the face of Greek political life and administration was little changed. By 1981 inflation was hovering around 25 percent, and it was estimated that tax evasion was depriving the state of one-third of its annual budget. In foreign policy the US bases remained and it was felt that Greece, back in NATO, was still acting as little more than an American satellite. The traditional right was demonstrably inadequate to the task at hand.

PASOK 1981–89

Change – **allayí** – was the watchword of the election campaign which swept Andreas Papandreou's Panhellenic Socialist Movement, better known by the acronym **PASOK**, to power on October 18, 1981.

The victory meant a chance for Papandreou to form the first socialist government in Greek history and break a near fifty-year monopoly of authoritarian right-wing rule. With so much at stake the campaign had been passionate even by Greek standards, and PASOK's victory was greeted with euphoria both by the generation whose political voice had been silenced by defeat in the Civil War and by a large proportion of the young. They were hopes which perhaps ran naively and dangerously high.

The victory, at least, was conclusive. PASOK won 174 of the 300 parliamentary seats and the Communist KKE returned another thirteen deputies, one of whom was the composer Mikis Theodorakis. Néa Dhimokratía moved into unaccustomed opposition. There appeared to be no obstacle to the implementation of a radical **socialist programme**: devolution of power to local authorities, the socialization of industry

(though it was never clear how this was to be different from nationalization), improvement of the social services, a purge of bureaucratic inefficiency and malpractice, the end of bribery and corruption as a way of life, an independent and dignified foreign policy following expulsion of US bases, and withdrawal from NATO and the European Community.

A change of style was promised, too, replacing the country's long traditions of authoritarianism and bureaucracy with openness and dialogue. Even more radically, where Greek political parties had long been composed of the personal followers of charismatic leaders, PASOK was to be a party of ideology and principle, dependent on no single individual member. Or so, at least, some of the youthful PASOK political enthusiasts thought.

The new era started with a bang. The wartime resistance was officially recognized; hitherto they hadn't been allowed to take part in any celebrations, wreath-layings or other ceremonies. Peasant women were granted pensions for the first time – 3000 drachmas a month, the same as their outraged husbands – and wages were indexed to the cost of living. In addition, civil marriage was introduced, family law reformed in favour of wives and mothers, and equal rights legislation was put on the statute book.

These popular **reformist moves** seemed to mark a break with the past, and the atmosphere had indeed changed. Greeks no longer lowered their voices to discuss politics in public places or wrapped their opposition newspaper in the respectably conservative *Kathimerini*. At first there were real fears that the climate would be too much for the military and they would once again intervene to choke a dangerous experiment in democracy, especially when Andreas Papandreou assumed the defence portfolio himself in a move strongly reminiscent of his father's attempt to remove the king's appointee in 1965. But he went out of his way to soothe **military susceptibilities**, increasing their salaries, buying new weaponry, and being super-fastidious in his attendance at military functions.

THE END OF THE HONEYMOON

Nothing if not a populist, **Papandreou** promised a bonanza he must have known, as a skilled and experienced economist, he could not deliver. As a result he pleased nobody on the **economic** front.

He could not fairly be blamed for the inherited lack of investment, low productivity, deficiency in managerial and labour skills and other chronic problems besetting the Greek economy. On the other hand, he certainly aggravated the situation in the early days of his first government by allowing his supporters to indulge in violently anti-capitalist rhetoric, and by the prosecution and humiliation of the Tsatsos family (owners of one of Greece's few modern and profitable businesses – cement, in this case) for the illegal export of capital, something of which every Greek with any savings is guilty. These were cheap victories and were not backed by any programme of public investment, while the only "socializations" were of hopelessly lame-duck companies.

Faced with this sluggish economy, and burdened with the additional charges of (marginally) improved social benefits and wage indexing, Papandreou's government had also to cope with the effects of **world recession**, which always hit Greece with a delayed effect compared with its more advanced European partners. **Shipping**, the country's main foreign-currency earner, was devastated. Remittances from emigré workers fell off as they joined the lines of the unemployed in their host countries, and tourism receipts diminished under the dual impact of recession and Reagan's warning to Americans to stay away from insecure and terrorist-prone Athens airport.

With huge quantities of imported goods continuing to be sucked into the country in the absence of domestic production, the **foreign debt** topped £10 billion in 1986, with inflation at 25 percent and the balance of payments deficit approaching £1 billion. Greece also began to experience the social strains of **unemployment** for the first time. Not that it didn't exist before, but it had always been concealed as under-employment by the family and the rural structure of the economy – as well as by the absence of statistics.

The result of all this was that Papandreou had to eat his words. A modest spending spree, joy at the defeat of the right, the popularity of his Greece-for-the-Greeks foreign policy, and some much needed reforms saw him through into a **second term**, with an electoral victory in June 1985 scarcely less triumphant than the first. But the complacent and, frankly, dishonest slogan was "Vote PASOK for Even Better Days".

By October they had imposed a two-year wage freeze and import restrictions, abolished the wage-indexing scheme and devalued the drachma by fifteen percent. Papandreou's fat was pulled out of the fire by none other than that former bogeyman, the **European Community**, which offered a huge two-part loan on condition that an IMF-style **austerity programme** was maintained.

The political fallout of such a classic right-wing deflation, accompanied by shameless soliciting for foreign investment, was the alienation of the Communists and most of PASOK's own political constituency. Increasingly autocratic – ironic given the early ideals of PASOK as a new kind of party – Papandreou's response to **dissent** was to fire recalcitrant trade-union leaders and expel some 300 members of his own party. Assailed by strikes, the government appeared to have lost direction completely. In local elections in October 1986 it lost a lot of ground to Néa Dhimokratía, including the mayoralties of the three major cities. Athens, Thessaloníki and Pátra.

Papandreou assured the nation that he had taken the message to heart but all that followed was a minor government reshuffle and a panicky attempt to undo the ill-feeling caused by an incredible freeing of **rent controls** at a time when all wage-earners were feeling the pinch badly. Early in 1987 he went further and sacked all the remaining PASOK veterans in his cabinet, including his son, though it is said, probably correctly, that this was a palliative to public opinion. The new cabinet was so un-Socialist that even the right-wing press called it **"centrist"**.

Similar about-faces took place in **foreign policy**. The initial anti-US, anti-NATO and anti-EC rhetoric was immensely popular, and understandable for a people shamelessly bullied by bigger powers for the past 150 years. There was some high-profile nose-thumbing, like refusing to join EC partners in condemning Jaruzelski's Polish regime, or the Soviet downing of a Korean airliner, or Syrian involvement in terrorist bomb-planting. There were some forgettable embarrassments, too, like suggesting Gaddafi's Libya provided a suitable model for alternative socialist development, and the Mitterrand-Gaddafi-Papandreou "summit" in Crete, which an infuriated Mitterrand felt he had been inveigled into on false pretences.

WOMEN'S RIGHTS IN GREECE

Women's right to vote wasn't universally achieved in Greece until 1956 and, until the mid 1970s, adultery was still a punishable offence, with cases regularly brought to court. The socialist party, PASOK, was elected for terms of government in 1981 and 1985 with a strong theoretical programme for **women's rights**, and their women's council review committees, set up in the early, heady days, effected a landmark reform with the 1983 **Family Law**. This prohibited dowry and stipulated equal legal status and shared property rights between husband and wife.

Subsequently, however, the PASOK governments did little to follow through on **practical issues**, like improved child care, health and family planning. Contraception is not available as part of the skeletal Greek public health service, leaving many women to fall back on abortions – only recently made legal under certain conditions, but running (as for many years past) to an estimated 70–80,000 a year.

By far the largest organization is the **Union of Greek Women**. Founded in 1976, this espouses an independent feminist line and is responsible for numerous consciousness-raising activities across the country, though it remains too closely linked to PASOK for comfort. As a perfect metaphor for this, Margaret Papandreou felt compelled to resign from the Union following her well-publicized divorce from ex-Premier Andreas, leaving it without her effective and vocal leadership. Other, more autonomous groups, have been responsible for setting up advice and support networks, highlighting women's issues within trade unions, and campaigning for changes in media representation.

None of this is easy in a country as polarized as Greece. In many rural areas women rely heavily on traditional extended families for security, and are unlikely to be much affected by legislative reforms or city politics. Yet Greek men of all classes and backgrounds are slowly becoming used to the notion of women in positions of power and responsibility, and taking a substantial share in child-rearing – both postures utterly unthinkable two decades ago, and arguably one of the few positive legacies with which PASOK can at least in part be credited.

Much was made of a strategic opening to the Arab world. Yasser Arafat, for example, was the first "head of state" to be received in Athens under the PASOK government. Given Greece's geographical position and historical ties, it was an imaginative and appropriate policy. But if Arab investment was hoped for, it never materialized.

In stark contrast to his early promises and rhetoric, the "realistic" policies that Papandreou pursued were far more conciliatory towards his big Western brothers. This was best exemplified by the fact that **US bases** remained in Greece, largely due to the fear that snubbing NATO would lead to Greece being exposed to Turkish aggression, still the only issue that unites the main parties to any degree. As for the once-reviled **European Community**, Greece had become an established beneficiary and its leader was hardly about to bite the hand that feeds.

SCANDAL

Even as late as mid-1988, despite the many betrayals of Papandreou, despite his failure to clean up the public services and do away with the system of patronage and corruption, and despite a level of popular displeasure that brought a million striking, demonstrating workers into the streets (February 1987), it seemed unlikely that PASOK would be toppled in the following year's **elections**.

This was due mainly to the lack of a credible alternative. Constantine Mitsotakis, a bitter personal enemy of Papandreou since 1965, when his defection had brought down his father's government and set in train the events that culminated in the junta, was an unconvincing and unlikeable character at the helm of Néa Dhimokratía. Meanwhile, the liberal centre had disappeared and the main communist party, KKE, appeared trapped in a Stalinist time warp under the leadership of Kharilaos Florakis. Only the Ellenikí Aristerá (Greek Left), formerly the European wing of the KKE, seemed to offer any sensible alternative programme, and they had a precariously small following.

So PASOK could have been in a position to win a third term by default, when a combination of spectacular **own goals**, plus perhaps a general shift to the Right influenced by the cataclysmic events in Eastern Europe, conspired against them.

First came the extraordinary cavortings of the Prime Minister himself. Towards the end of 1988, the seventy-year-old Papandreou was flown to Britain for open-heart surgery. He took the occasion, with fear of death presumably rocking his judgement, to make public a year-long liaison with a 34-year-old Olympic Airways hostess, **Dimitra "Mimi" Liani**. The international news pictures of an old man shuffling about after a young blonde, to the public humiliation of Margaret, his American-born wife, and his family, were not popular (Papandreou has since divorced Margaret and married Mimi). His integrity was further questioned when he missed several important public engagements – including a ceremony commemorating the victims of the 1987 Kalamáta earthquake – and was pictured out with Mimi, reliving his youth in nightspots.

The real damage, however, was done by **economic scandals**. It came to light that a PASOK minister had passed off Yugoslav corn as Greek in a sale to the EC. Then, far more seriously, it emerged that a self-made con man, **Yiorgos Koskotas**, director of the **Bank of Crete**, had embezzled £120m (US$190m) of deposits and, worse still, slipped though the authorities' fingers and sought asylum in the US. Certain PASOK ministers and even Papandreou himself were implicated in the scandal. Further damage was done by allegations of illegal **arms dealings** by still more government ministers.

United in disgust at this corruption, the other Left parties – KKE and Ellinikí Aristerá – formed a coalition, the **Synaspismós**, taking still more support from PASOK.

THREE BITES AT THE CHERRY

In this climate of disaffection, an inconclusive result to the **June 1989 election** was no real surprise. What was less predictable, however, was the formation of a bizarre **"kathàrsis" coalition** of conservatives and communists, united in the avowed intent of cleansing PASOK's increasingly Augean stables.

That this coalition emerged was basically down to Papandreou. The Synaspismós would have formed a government with PASOK but set one condition for doing so – that Papandreou should step down as Prime Minister – and the old man would have none of it. In the deal finally cobbled together between the left and Néa Dhimokratía, Mitsotakis was denied the premiership, too, having to make way for his compromise party colleague, **Tzanetakis**.

During the three months that the coalition lasted, the kathàrsis turned out to be largely a question of burying the knife as deeply as possible into the ailing body of PASOK. Andreas Papandreou and three other ministers were officially accused of involvement in the Koskotas affair – though there was no time to set up their **trial** before the Greek people returned once again to the polls. In any case, the chief witness and protagonist in the affair, Koskotas himself, was still imprisoned in America, awaiting extradition proceedings.

Contrary to the Right's hope that publicly accusing Papandreou and his cohorts of criminal behaviour would pave the way for a Néa Dhimokratía victory, PASOK actually made a slight recovery in the **November 1989 elections**, though the result was still inconclusive. This time the Left resolutely refused to do deals with anyone and the result was a consensus caretaker government under the neutral aegis of an academic called Zolotas, who was pushed into the Prime Minister's office, somewhat unwillingly it seemed, from Athens University. His only mandate was to see that the country didn't go off the rails completely while preparations were made for yet more elections.

These took place in **April 1990** with the same captains at the command of their ships and with the Synaspismós having completed its about-turn to the extent that in the five single-seat constituencies (the other 295 seats are drawn from multiple-seat constituencies in a complicated system of reinforced proportional representation), they supported independent candidates jointly with PASOK. Greek communists are good at about-turns, though; after all, composer Mikis Theodorakis, musical torch-bearer of the Left during the dark years of the junta, and formerly a KKE MP, was by now standing for Néa Dhimokratía.

On the night, Néa Dhimokratía scraped home with a majority of one, later doubled with the defection of a centrist, and **Mitsotakis** finally got to achieve his dream of becoming Prime Minister. The only other memorable feature of the election was the first parliamentary representation for a party of the Turkish minority in Thrace, and for the ecologists – a focus for many disaffected PASOK voters.

A RETURN TO THE RIGHT: MITSOTAKIS

On assuming power, Mitsotakis followed a course of **austerity measures** to try and revive the chronically ill economy. Little headway was made, though given the world recession, it was hardly surprising. Greece still has **inflation** up towards twenty percent and a growing **unemployment** problem.

The latter has been exacerbated, since 1990, by the arrival of thousands of impoverished **Albanians**. They have formed something of an underclass, especially those who aren't ethnically Greek, and are prey to vilification for all manner of ills. They have also led to the first real immigration measures in a country whose population is more used to being on the other side of such laws.

Other conservative measures introduced by Mitsotakis included laws to combat strikes and **terrorism**. The terrorist issue had been a perennial source of worry for Greeks since the appearance in the mid-1980s of a group called **17 Novemvriou** (the date of the Colonels' attack on the Polytechnic in 1973). They have killed a number of industrialists and attacked buildings of military attachés and airlines in Athens, so far without any police arrests. It hardly seemed likely that Mitsotakis's laws, however, were the solution. They stipulated that statements by the group could no longer be published, and led to one or two newspaper editors being jailed for a few days for defiance – much to everyone's embarrassment.

The **anti-strike laws** threatened severe penalties but were equally ineffectual, as breakdowns in public transport, electricity and rubbish collection all too frequently illustrated.

As for the **Koskotas scandal**, the villain of the piece was eventually extradited and gave evidence for the prosecution against Papandreou and various of his ministers. The trial was televised and proved as popular as any soap opera, as indeed it should have been, given the twists of high drama – which included one of the defendants, Koutsoyiorgas, dying in court of a heart attack in front of the cameras. The case against Papandreou gradually petered out and he was officially acquitted in early

1992. The two other surviving ministers, Tsovolas and Petsos, were convicted and given short prison sentences.

The great showpiece trial thus went with a whimper rather than a bang, and did nothing to enhance Mitsotakis's position. If anything, it served to increase sympathy for Papandreou, who was felt to have been unfairly victimized. The real villain of the piece, Koskotas, was eventually convicted of major **fraud** and is now serving a lengthy sentence.

THE MACEDONIAN QUESTION

Increasingly unpopular because of the desperate austerity measures, and perceived as ineffective and out of his depth on the international scene, the last thing Mitsotakis needed was a major **foreign policy** headache. That is exactly what he got when, in 1991, one of the breakaway republics of the former Yugoslavia named itself Macedonia, thereby injuring Greek national pride and sparking off vehement protests at home and abroad. Diplomatically, the Greeks fought tooth and nail against the use of the name, but their position became increasingly isolated, and by 1993 the new country had gained official recognition, from both the EU and the UN – albeit under the convoluted title of the Former Yugoslav Republic of Macedonia (FYROM).

Salt was rubbed into Greek wounds when the FYROM started using the Star of Veryína as a national symbol on their new flag. Greece still refuses to call its northerly neighbour Macedonia, instead referring to it as Ta Skópia after the capital – and you can't go far in Greece these days without coming across officially placed protestations that "Macedonia was, is, and always will be Greek and only Greek!" Strong words.

THE PENDULUM SWINGS BACK

In effect, the Macedonian problem more or less directly led to Mitsotakis's **political demise**. In the early summer of 1993 his ambitious young Foreign Minister, **Andonis Samaras**, disaffected with his leader, jumped on the bandwagon of resurgent Greek nationalism to set up his own party, **Politikí Ánixi** (Political Spring), after leaving Néa Dhímokratía. His platform, still right-wing, was largely based on action over Macedonia, and during the summer of 1993 more ND MPs broke ranks, making Politikí Ánixi a force to be reckoned with. When parliament was called upon to approve severe new budget proposals, it became clear that the government lacked support, and early elections were called for October 1993. Mitsotakis had also been plagued for nearly a year by accusations of phone-tapping, and had been linked with a nasty and complicated contracts scandal centred around a national company, AGET.

Many of ND's disillusioned supporters reverted directly to PASOK, and **Papandreou** romped to election victory.

THE MORNING AFTER

And so, a frail-looking Papandreou, now well into his seventies, became Prime Minister for the third time. He soon realized that the honeymoon was going to be neither as sweet nor as long as it had been in the 80s.

PASOK immediately fulfilled two of its pre-election promises by removing restrictions on the reporting of statements by terrorist groups and renationalizing the Athens city bus company. The new government also set about improving the health system, and began to set the wheels in motion for Mitsotakis to be tried for his alleged misdemeanours, although the charges were mysteriously dropped in early 1995, prompting allegations of under-the-table dealings between Papandreou and his old rival.

The government's main source of unpopularity continued to be **the economy**, because of the ongoing austerity measures. There was increasing tension with Albania as refugees poured across the border in ever greater numbers, and several ethnic Greek activists went on trial in Tirana for subversive activities. Meanwhile, the dispute over the **Macedonian question** provided no diplomatic victories, and the trade embargo imposed by Greece in late 1993 merely incurred trouble with the European Court of Justice.

Both main parties received a slap in the face when their support was substantially decreased in the **Euroelections** of summer 1994. The principal gains were made by Politkí Ánixi, who doubled their share of the vote, and the two left-wing parties – Synaspismós virtually rose from the dead to secure two seats, as did the KKE. The following spring, presidential elections were held, and Papandreou contrived a deal with Samarás to get Kostís Stefanopoulos,

a respected lawyer and ex-leader of the defunct DIANA (Democratic Renewal – another ND offshoot) elected by consensus.

Throughout 1995, a **scandal** raged about bad conditions and corruption in Koridhalós jail in Athens, home to the surviving junta officers, and Koskotas, among others. This culminated in the head warden being arrested, when a large stash of guns, ammunition and drugs were discovered in the office. In November, relations thawed somewhat with "Macedonia", Greece opening the mutual border for trade and tourism again, in exchange for some changes in the wording of the new republic's constitution, and the removal of the star of Verýina from its flag, though dispute over the name still exists.

THE END OF AN ERA

By late 1995, Papandreou was a very sick man, and when he suffered severe lung and kidney infections he was rushed to Onassis hospital, and only survived through being hooked up to a life-support system. The country was in effect rudderless for two months, until the old demagogue finally faced up to his own mortality, and signed a letter **resigning** as Prime Minister in mid-January 1996. The "palace clique" of Mimi Liani and cohorts was beaten off in the parliamentary replacement vote and **Kostas Simitis**, a colourless but respected technocrat, was chosen as leader, although his official position as PASOK party leader was not confirmed until a vote later in the year, after more infighting with Papendreou's men. Old Andreas finally succumbed to his illness on June 22, 1996, prompting a moving display of national mourning, befitting the country's dominant politician of the late twentieth century.

Simitis had already encountered some severe domestic criticism over his handling of the tense face-off with Turkey over the uninhabited island of **Ímia**. Eventually he had bowed to US pressure and ordered a shame-faced withdrawal of Greek troops, conceding disputed status to the tiny islet. However, a more human interpretation is that he realized it just wasn't worth having a war about. In any case, Simitis cleverly rode the wave of pro-PASOK sympathy caused by Papandreou's death, and called general elections a year early in September 1996. Consequently, PASOK secured a comfortable victory by several percentage points over ND. The KKE and Synaspismós also secured seats in parliament, as did the new DIKKI party, which had been formed a year earlier by ex-PASOK minister Tsovólas. The big surprise was the collapse in support for Politikí Ánixi, who fared so badly that Samarás didn't even gain a seat for himself. Evert resigned as ND leader, being succeeded by Karamanlis' nephew Kostas, who is attempting to regain the central ground.

THE CURRENT SITUATION

For the time being, Simitis's position seems secure, although his first full-term has not been without its problems, mainly arising from the economic squeeze caused by continuing **austerity measures**. In December 1996, the farmers staged a dramatic protest, closing off the country's main road and rail arteries for several weeks, before dismantling the blockades in time for people to travel for the Christmas holidays. Much of 1997 saw the teachers or students (or both) on strike over proposed educational reforms.

Simitis, by nature far more pro-European than his maverick predecessor, is showing no signs of being deflected from the unenvious task of getting the Greek economy in sufficiently good shape to meet the criteria for **monetary union**. Indeed, he has met with some success, and the fact that inflation is down in single figures for the first time in ages, is testament to his ability as an accountant, for which he has received credit from friends and enemies alike.

In September 1997, Greece received a timely boost to national morale and economic prospects, when the 2004 **Olympic games** were awarded to Athens. Simitis sensibly warned against people just treating it as an excuse for unbridled money-making projects, and it is to be hoped that more substantial and long-lasting benefits will arise. At least Athenian residents and visitors alike can look forward with a greater degree of confidence to the completion of both the metro, and the new airport at Spata.

THE GREEK MINORITIES

The principal Greek minorities – Vlachs, Sarakatsáni, Turks, Jews, Slavophones, Catholics and Gypsies – are little known, even within Greece. Indeed, to meet Vlachs or Sarakatsáni who remain true to their roots you'll have to get to some fairly remote parts of Epirus. Greco-Turks are another matter, with a sizeable (and recently problematic) community living, as they have done for centuries, in Thrace. The Jews of Greece, as so often, tell the saddest history, having been annihilated by the Nazi occupiers during the latter stages of World War II. Slavophones are officially a taboo subject, and the Catholics restricted to the Cylcades, while the Gypsies are admired – from a distance – only for their musicality.

THE VLACHS AND SARAKATSÁNI

The **Vlachs'** homeland is in the remote vastness of the **Píndhos Mountains** in northwestern Greece near the Albanian frontier. Traditionally they were transhumant shepherds, although some have long led a more settled existence in Métsovo and a score of villages around. As the town grew in prosperity, the Vlachs traded their sheep products further and further afield. Local merchants established themselves in Constantinople, Vienna, Venice and elsewhere, expanding into other lines of business: Vlachs played a major role in Balkan mule-back haulage and the hotel trade – specifically *caravanserais* where mule convoys halted.

They are an ancient, close-knit community with a strong sense of identity, like their rival shepherd clan, the *Sarakatsáni* (see p.787), whom they despise as "tent-dwellers" and who, in turn, just as passionately despise them for living in houses. Unlike the Sarakatsánsi, however, their mother tongue is not Greek, but Vlach, a Romance language, which even today is full of words that anyone with a little Latin can easily recognize: *loop* for wolf, *mulier* for women, *pene* for bread. When the Italians invaded Greece in World War II, Vlach soldiers were often used as interpreters. Incidentally, the Vlachs prefer to call themselves *Roumaní* (Arouman) and their language *Roumaniká*; the word *vlákhos* in Greek can mean "yokel" or "bumpkin".

It used to be thought that the Vlachs were descendants of Roman legionaries stationed in the provinces of Illyria and Dacia, who over the centuries had wandered up and down through the Balkans in search of grazing for their sheep. Those who finally settled in northern Greece were trapped there by the creation of modern frontiers upon the disintegration of the Austro-Hungarian and Ottoman empires. Because of these supposed Romanian connections and enduring Greek anxieties about the Slavophile separatist tendencies of the peoples of northern Greece (see below), the Vlachs have been objects of suspicion to the modern state. To their chagrin many villages with Slav-sounding names were officially renamed during the Metaxas dictatorship of the 1930s (though in fact many of these names seem to stem from other Slavic invaders), and Vlach school children forbidden to use their mother tongue.

There is, however, a more recent, better supported theory about their origins, which argues that the Greek Vlachs at least are of Greek descent and have always inhabited these same regions of the Píndhos Mountains; during Roman times the Romans found it convenient to train local people as highway guards for the high passes on the old Roman road, the Via Egnatia, which connected Constantinople with the Adriatic. Thus the Vlachs learned Latin through their association with the Romans and preserved it in distorted form because of the isolation of their homeland and the exclusive nature of their pastoral way of life.

Sadly, though probably inevitably, the Vlachs' unique traditions are in danger of extinction. Only fifty or so years back, a prosperous Vlach family might have 10,000 sheep, and when they set off on the annual migration from their lowland winter pastures to the mountains it was like a small army on the march, two or three complete generations together with all their animals and belongings. Nowadays few flocks number more than 250 ewes, and the annual migration takes place in lorries – though a few veterans still do it on foot. Hundreds of Vlachs have sold their flocks and moved to the towns or emigrated. There are depressingly few young men among the remaining shepherds. The hardships of their life are too many and the economic returns too small.

The **Sarakatsáni**, celebrated in Patrick Leigh Fermor's *Roumeli* and J. K. Campbell's *Honour, Family and Patronage* (see p.829), by contrast appear to be indigenous, and speak an archaic form of Greek. The distinctive costumes and reed tents which Leigh Fermor described are now a thing of the past, to be pulled out only for feast days and ethnographic theme-parks, but traces of their former life style persist. Until a few decades ago they were true transhumants, moving between winter quarters well below the snowline and summer pastures in the mountains. After World War II the government required them to establish permanent winter dwellings, but they still return each summer to the heights, where they pasture their sheep on land rented from the village councils – often made up of their hereditary adversaries, the Vlachs.

JEWS AND TURKS

Jews and **Turks** in Greece are, for historical reasons, conveniently considered together. Since the decline of the Ottoman empire, these two Greek minorities have often suffered similar fates as isolated groups in a non-assimilating culture. Yet it seems that enclaves of each will endure for the forseeable future.

ORIGINS AND SETTLEMENTS

The **Greek Jewish community** is one of the oldest established in Europe, dating back to the early Hellenistic period when Jews were already settled at Rhodes, Corinth, Athens, Thebes, Salonika, Véria, Delos, Crete and Sparta. During the Roman and Byzantine eras, the Jews were termed *Romaniote* and urban colonies flourished throughout the Balkans. In Greece these additionally included, by the twelfth to fourteenth centuries, Corfu, Zákynthos, Pátra, Khalkídha, Lárissa and, most importantly, Ioánnina.

The most numerically significant Jewish communities in Greece, however, date back to shortly after the taking of Constantinople by the **Ottomans**. In 1493 Sultan Beyazit II invited Spanish and Portuguese Jews expelled from those countries to settle in the Ottoman empire. The great influx of **Sephardim** (Ladino-speak-

ing Jews) soon swamped many of the original Romaniot centres, particularly Kós, Rhodes, Véria and Salonika, and within two centuries, Ladino – a mix of medieval Spanish and Portuguese with Turkish, Hebrew and Arabic augments – had largely supplanted Greek as the lingua franca of Balkan Jewry, with Italian and Hungarian refugee Jews nearly as numerous as the Romaniotes. However, *Ladinismo* (the medieval Iberian Jewish culture) never penetrated the Romaniote enclaves of Ioánnina and Khalkídha, which remain Greek-speaking to this day. Moreover, the Greek- and non-Greek-speaking Jews differed in religious observance as well as language, resulting in numerous small synagogues being founded in each town for each group – and little intermarriage between the sects.

Ottoman officials and their families fanned out across the Balkans to consolidate imperial administration, thus sowing the seeds of the numerous **Muslim communities** in present-day Bulgaria, Albania, Yugoslavia and Greece. The Ottoman authorities often appointed Jews as civil servants and tax collectors; one, Joseph Nasi, became governor of the Cyclades in 1566, but dared not show his face there, ruling instead through a representative.

As a result of this and other episodes, especially on Crete, Jews became identified with the ruling hierarchy in the eyes of the Orthodox Christian population, and at the outset of the 1821 **War of Independence** the Jewish quarters of Pátra, Trípoli, Athens and virtually all others within the confines of the nascent Greek state, were put to the sword along with the Muslim population. Survivors of the various massacres fled north, to the territories that remained under Ottoman control. Within the new Greek kingdom, a small community of Ashkenazi Jews arrived in Athens, along with the Bavarian king Otho, during the 1830s.

UNDER THE GREEK STATE

The **expansion** of the Greek nation thereafter resulted in the decline of both the Greek-Jewish and Greek-Turkish populations. New annexations or conquests (Thessaly in 1878, Epirus, Macedonia, the northeast Aegean and Crete in 1913) provoked a wave of forced or nervous Judaeo-Turkish migration to the other side of the receding Ottoman frontier. While Jews were never forbidden to stay in newly occupied territory, rarely were they explicitly welcomed, although the Romaniote communities in Ioánnina and Khalkídha were understandably pro-Greek. During the latter half of the nineteenth century – long after such incidents had peaked in Western Europe – there were repeated outbreaks of anti-Semitic riots whenever Jewish communities were falsely accused of murdering Christian children in order to obtain blood thought necessary for ritual use.

The Turks – or more correctly, Muslims, since "Turk" was a generic term for any Muslim, including Albanians, and ethnic Greeks who had converted to Islam for economic advantage – were subject to various expulsion orders. Between 1913 and 1923 the **Muslims of Crete**, mostly converted islanders, were forced to choose between apostasy to Christianity or exile, if they hadn't emigrated voluntarily between 1898 and 1913. (The newly Orthodox can today often be distinguished by their ostentatiously Christian surnames, such as Stavroulakis, Khristakis, and so on.) Those who opted to stand by their faith were summarily deposited in the closest Turkish-Muslim settlements on Greek islands just over the Ottoman border; Kós Town, the nearby village of Platáni, and Rhodes Town were three of the more convenient ones.

When the Italians formally annexed the **Dodecanese** after World War I, the **Muslims** were allowed to remain and were thus rendered exempt from any of the provisions of the 1923 Treaty of Lausanne (which stipulated the wholescale exchange of "Turk" and "Greek" populations in the wake of the Asia Minor war). Additionally, the Jewish communities of Kós and Rhodes flourished, as there was little or no anti-Semitism under Italian Fascist rule. In **Rhodes** there had been a long tradition of cooperation between the Muslim and the Jewish communities. In Ottoman days Jews were the only *millet* (subject ethnic group) allowed out after the city gates were closed at dusk, and since 1948 Muslim and Jewish leaders have consulted on how best to counter government strategies to deprive each of their rights and property. The dilapidated refugee village of Kritiká ("the Cretans") still huddles by the seaside on the way to the airport, and walking through Rhodes's old town it's easy to spot dwindling numbers of Turkish names on the signboards of various sandalmakers, kafenía, and kebab stands. Those

Turks who live in the old town itself, however, have in some cases been there since the sixteenth century and will proudly tell you that they have every right to be considered native Rhodians. Notwithstanding, numbers diminish through emigration to Turkey every year, with those leaving denied any right of return.

In **Kós**, Cretan Muslims settled both in the port town – where they remain active in the antique and shoemaking trade – and at Platáni, which still has a mixed Greek Orthodox and "Turkish" population. However numbers have dropped by two-thirds, and the Turkish-language primary school forcibly closed, since the first major Cyprus crisis of 1964.

During the early 1900s, the same era as the Cretan deportations, the status of mainland Jews and Turks in the path of Greek nationalism was more ambiguous. Even after the respective 1878 and 1913 acquisitions of **Thessaly**, **Epirus** and **Macedonia**, Muslim villages continued to exist in these regions. The Tsamídhes, an Albanian-speaking, nominally Muslim tribe localized in Epirus and Thesprotía, were left alone until World War II, when they made the grievous error of siding with the invading Axis armies; they were hunted down and expelled forthwith first by the National Army and later guerrilla bands.

Thessaloníki in the late nineteenth and early twentieth century was one of the largest Jewish towns in the world. Jews made up roughly half the population, and dominated the sailing, shipping and chandlery trades, such that the harbour ceased operations on Saturday but functioned on Sunday. In addition there were numerous Dönme or Ma'min, Jews who had chosen to follow the "false messiah" Sabbatai Zvi into Islam in the 1670s but maintained certain aspects of Jewish worship in secret. As provided for by the Treaty of Lausanne, the authorities insisted on the departure of the Dönme along with other Turkic Muslims. The 20,000 Dönme (Turkish for "renegades", after Zvi's conversion to Islam) insisted that they were "really" Jews, but to no avail. Indeed as early as 1913, with a rapid influx of Greek Orthodox into the conquered city, Thessaloníki had already begun to lose its strong Hebraic character; the fire of 1917, emigration to Palestine, the arrival of Greek Orthodox refugees from Anatolia after 1923, and the arrival of the Nazis effectively brought an era to a close.

The same period, around the time of World War I, also saw the end of Muslim (and minute Jewish) enclaves on the islands of **Thássos**, **Samothráki**, **Límnos**, **Lésvos** and **Khíos**, where it is claimed the "Turks" themselves destroyed the fine Turkish bath before departing. On **Sámos** there is a special, tiny Jewish cemetery with the graves of two brothers – apparently Ashkenazi merchants who died between the World Wars; otherwise there had not been a significant Jewish community here since Byzantine times, and Muslims were uniquely forbidden to settle here after the seventeenth century.

Western Thrace, the area between the Néstos and Évros rivers, was always home to large numbers of Muslims, and it remained their last bastion after the 1919–1922 Asia Minor War. The **Treaty of Lausanne** (1923) confirmed the right of this minority to remain in situ, in return for a continued Greek Orthodox presence in Istanbul (still known to Greeks as *Konstandinoúpoli*), the Prince's Islands and on the islands of Tenedos and Imvros.

Over the years the Turks have repeatedly abrogated the terms of the pact by repressive measures and reduced the Turkish Greek Orthodox population to three percent of pre-1923 levels. The Greeks have acted comparatively leniently, and today Muslims still make up a third of the population of Greek Thrace, being highly visible in the main towns of **Alexandhroúpoli**, **Komotiní** and **Xánthi**. Muslims control much of the tobacco culture hereabouts and the baggy-trousered women can frequently be glimpsed from the trains which pass through their fields.

The loyalty of these Thracian "Turks" to the Greek state was amply demonstrated during **World War II**, when they resisted the invading Bulgarians and Nazis side-by-side with their Christian compatriots. In return the two occupying forces harassed and deported to death camps many local Muslims. During the 1946–49 Civil War Thracian Muslims again suffered at the hands of ELAS, who found the deep-seated conservatism of these villagers exasperating, and laboured under the misconception that all local Muslims were traitors.

Only the **Pomaks**, a non-Turkic Muslim group of about 40,000 centred around Ekhínos, north of Xánthi, collaborated to any extent with the Bulgarians, probably on the basis of ethnic affinity. The Pomaks as a group were probably Slavic Bogomil heretics forcibly converted to Islam in the sixteenth century; they speak a degenerate dialect of Bulgarian with generous mixtures of Greek and Turkish. The authorities still keep them on a tight rein; Pomaks require a travel permit to leave their immediate area of residence around Ekhínos, and visitors require a permit for their villages, too. Pomaks are occasionally found living outside Thrace, particularly near certain mines in Viotía, the mainland region opposite Évvia, where their skills as sappers and tunnellers are required; apparently they have also prompted the reopening of the mosque in nearby Khalkídha for their regular use.

Until recently, the Orthodox and "Turkish" Thracian communities lived in a fairly easy (if distant) relationship with each other, but during the early 1990s a series of ugly intercommunal incidents and official prosecution of Turkish political leaders cast doubt on the carefully cultivated international image of Greece's toleration of its minorities. It has, in fact, always been true that treatment of these Muslims functions as a barometer of relations at a more general level between Greece and Turkey, and as a quid pro quo for perceived maltreatment of the remaining Greek Orthodox in Turkey.

But it is the **Jews** rather than the Muslims who have suffered the greatest catastrophes during and since **World War II**. Jews who chanced to live in the Italian zone of occupation were initially no worse off than their compatriots, but after Italy's capitulation in September 1943 and the German assumption of control, conditions deteriorated drastically. Eighty-five percent of a Jewish population of around 80,000 was rounded up by the Nazis in the spring of 1944, never to return. The Bulgarian occupation forces tended to substitute Greek Jews for Bulgarian ones on the death trains as part of their "Bulgarization" programme, thus earning an unjustified reputation for clemency.

Greek Christians often went to extraordinary lengths to protect their persecuted countrymen, overshadowing the few instances of sordid betrayal; in this respect the Greek record is rather better than many western European countries, France for example. The mayor and bishop of Zákynthos and the bishop of Khalkídha put themselves at risk to save the local Jewish communities, virtually ordering their Christian neighbours to hide and feed them; as a result nearly all of them survived. In Athens, the police chief and the archbishop arranged for the issue of false identity cards and baptismal certificates, which again saved huge numbers of Jews. In Athens, Tríkala, Lárissa and Vólos especially, where the rabbi was active in the resistance to occupation, Jews were warned in good time of what fate the Germans had in store for them, and took to the hills to join the partisans. Romaniote Jews, indistinguishable from their Orthodox neighbours in appearance and tongue, fared best, but the Ladino-speaking Jews of northern Greece, with their distinctive surnames and customs, were easy targets for the Nazis. It must also be said that certain portions of the Greek business community in **Thessaloníki** benefited greatly from the expulsion of the Jews, and needed little encouragement to help themselves to the contents of the abandoned Jewish shops. Jewish sensibilities were further offended in the postwar era when the German desecration of the huge Jewish cemetery was completed by the construction of the University of Thessaloníki and expansion of the fairgrounds.

The paltry number of **survivors** returning from the death camps to Greece was insufficient to form the nucleus of a revival in most provincial towns, and moving to Athens or **emigration** to Israel were often a preferable alternative to living with ghosts. Currently barely 6000 Jews remain in Greece. In Thessaloníki there are around a thousand Sephardim, who generally keep a low profile aside from the Molho family's famous bookstore. Lárissa retains about three hundred Sephardim, who are still disproportionately important in the clothing trade. However young Jewish women outnumber their male counterparts, so intermarriage with Orthodox men is now a pattern. Small Romaniot communities of a hundred persons or less continue to exist in Khalkídha, Ioánnina, Corfu, Tríkala and Vólos. The Kós, Khaniá, and Rhodes congregations were virtually wiped out, and today only about forty Jews – many of these from the mainland – live in Rhodes town. Here, the Platía ton Evreón Martirón (Square of the Jewish Martyrs), at the edge of the former Jewish quarter, commemorates over 1800 Jews of Kós and Rhodes deported by the Germans. About 3000 of today's Greek Jews live in Athens, which is also home to the **Jewish Museum of Greece** (see p.92).

SLAVOPHONES

Despite a population exchange between Greece and Bulgaria in 1918, and the flight of many **Slavophones** abroad after 1948, there remain approximately 40,000 individuals in Greece whose at-home language is some approximation of Macedonian. They dwell in a ribbon along the northern frontier, from Préspa to the Thracian frontier at the Néstos River. If Greeks can seem unreasonable on the question of "Turks", they become positively apoplectic at the mention of any Slavic minority; successive governments of whatever political stripe have indicated that any official recognition of such is out of the question, and counter any activism to the contrary with arrests or unofficial harassment. This position becomes slightly more understandable when such a population is viewed as a potential fifth column for a theoretically expansionist FYROM (Former Yugoslav Republic of Macedonia). Slavophones in Greece did not have their position in Greece made any more tenable during the Civil War, when at various times – until such were suppressed as an expression of "bourgeois nationalism" – communist statements contained references to "self-determination for Macedonian peoples", which could be construed to mean dismembering northern Greece and joining parts of it to a hypothetical Macedonian state. In the event, the victorious central government leaned hard on everybody unlucky enough to be dwelling in a northern border zone, regardless of political hue; in some places villages were evacuated, in others Greek-speaking colonists of "healthy national character" were imported to dilute the Slavophone population, along with other discriminatory measures. These had their desired effect, inasmuch as many Slavophones emigrated to Yugoslavia, Canada, America and Australia, where some have become part of the increasingly vocal pro-Macedonian lobby. Since the 1980s there has been some improvement in terms of increased material prosperity, but don't look for Slavic-language schools or public song performances any time soon.

CATHOLICS

The **Catholics** of the Cyclades, numbering no more than 12,000, are a legacy of Venetian settlement in the Aegean following the piratical Fourth Crusade in 1204. Today they live principally on the islands of Sýros and Tínos, with much tinier enclaves on Thíra, Náxos and in Athens, and a large expatriate community in Montreal. Often Italianate last names (Dellaroka) or given names (Leonardho, Frangisko) distinguish them from their neighbours. Descended from once-powerful feudal lords, they are today insignificant in civic as well as numerical terms, though they have always attracted suspicion as being less than "100% Greek"; in 1994 a civil servant on Náxos was promoted out of harm's way after making an outrageous public pronouncement about "Papist fifth-columnists in our midst."

GYPSIES

The **Gypsies** first came to the Balkans in about the eleventh century, probably a low-ranking caste from Rajasthan on the Indian subcontinent, and were soon well enough established to figure in Byzantine chronicles of the 1300s. Nazi policy towards them was even harsher than towards the Jews: they were sent directly to extermination facilities, reckoned not even worth a month of slave labour. Given their elusive, anti-authoritarian nature, no one knows exactly how many Gypsies there are in Greece at present; 150,000, of which ninety percent are nominally Greek Orthodox and the rest Muslim, seems a good guess. They are concentrated on the mainland, especially Thessaly, and in the Athenian neighbourhoods of Kolonós and Ayía Varvára, though they maintain a transient presence on all of the larger islands, and families are a common sight on the ferry-boats. Driving outsized trucks fitted with loud-hailers, Gypsy vendors are a common sight across the country, peddling plastic garden furniture, cheap carpets, house plants, basketry, watermelons and other produce – rather a comedown from their traditional livelihoods of metal smithing, bear training, shadow-puppeteering and horse dealing, which it seems their

Rajasthani ancestors also engaged in. Marginalized by centuries of nationalism and industrial advance, they are in Greece – as elsewhere in central Europe – undereducated, increasingly reliant on begging and generally despised by the majority population.

But an echo of the past survives in such events the **zoöemboropaniyíri** (animal-trading festival), a movable feast, which begins at Peloponnesian Stymfalía around September 14 (the Raising of the Cross), drifts west in stages to meet another party coming from Káto Akhaïa, and then travelling jointly to Nafpaktós, where the fair finishes on October 26, the feast of Áyios Dhimítrios. Rural tools and spit-roasted meat amongst tatty synthetic goods characterize this as a harvest fair, with gypsies figuring prominently both as livestock dealers and evening musicians.

Gypsies are finally (if often grudgingly) being properly credited with disproportionate prominence in the ranks of Greek mainland instrumental **musicians**, among them the *sandoúri* player Aristidhis Moskhos, the late clarinettist Vassilis Soukas, the late crooner Manolis Angelopoulos, the protest guitarist Kostas Hatzis, and the *laïko* star Eleni Vitali. Indeed virtually all of the now-settled clans of mainland clarinettists were originally of Gypsy origin, and for every personality like Vitali who makes no bones about their background, there is another who still feels he or she must conceal it. Incidentally, it is worth emphasizing that Gypsies are not necessarily more talented musically than their host culture; it's just that for many centuries, excluded from bazaar guilds or even fixed residence, they had few other choices of profession. Until recently in many northern towns, there was a designated kafenío in the marketplace which acted as an "employment exchange" for Gypsy musicians between engagements. For more on Greek music in general, see p.812.

250 YEARS OF ARCHEOLOGY

Archeology until the second half of the nineteenth century was a very hit-and-miss affair. The early students of antiquity went to Greece to draw and make plaster casts of the great masterpieces of Classical sculpture. Unfortunately, a number soon found it more convenient or more profitable to remove objects wholesale, and might be better described as looters than scholars or archeologists.

EARLY EXCAVATIONS

The British **Society of Dilettanti** was one of the earliest promoters of Greek culture, financing expeditions to draw and publish antiquities. Founded in the 1730s as a club for young aristocrats who had completed the Grand Tour and fancied themselves arbiters of taste, the Society's main qualification for membership (according to most critics) was habitual drunkenness. Its leading spirit was Sir Frances Dashwood, a notorious rake who founded the infamous Hellfire Club. Nevertheless, the Society was the first body organized to sponsor systematic research into Greek antiquities, though it was initially most interested in Italy. Greece, then a backwater of the Ottoman Empire, was not a regular part of the Grand Tour and only the most intrepid adventurers undertook so hazardous a trip.

In the 1740s, two young artists, **James Stuart** and **Nicholas Revett**, formed a plan to produce a scholarly record of the ancient Greek buildings. With the support of the society they spent three years in Greece, principally Athens, drawing and measuring the surviving antiquities. The first volume of *The Antiquities of Athens* appeared in 1762, becoming an instant success. The publication of their exquisite illustrations gave an enormous fillip to the study of Greek sculpture and architecture, which became the fashionable craze among the educated classes; many European Neoclassical town and country houses date from this period.

The Society financed a number of further expeditions to study Greek antiquities, including one to Asia Minor in 1812. The expedition was to be based in Smyrna, but while waiting in Athens for a ship to Turkey, the party employed themselves in excavations at **Eleusis**, where they uncovered the Temple of Demeter. It was the first archeological excavation made on behalf of the Society, and one of the first in Greece. After extensive explorations in Asia Minor, the participants returned via Attica, where they excavated the Temple of Nemesis at **Rhamnous** and examined the Temple of Apollo at **Sounion**.

Several other antiquarians of the age were less interested in discoveries for their own sake. A French count, **Choiseul-Gouffier**, removed part of the **Parthenon frieze** in 1787 and his example prompted **Lord Elgin** to detach much of the rest in 1801. These were essentially acts of looting – "Bonaparte has not got such things from all his thefts in Italy", boasted Elgin – and their legality was suspect even at the time.

Other discoveries of the period were more ambiguous. In 1811, a party of English and German travellers, including the architect C.R. Cockerell, uncovered the **Temple of Aphaia** on **Aegina** (Áyina) and shipped away the pediments. They auctioned off the marbles for £6000 to Prince Ludwig of Bavaria, and inspired by this success, returned to Greece for further finds. This time they struck lucky with 23 slabs from the **Temple of Apollo Epicurius** at **Bassae**, for which the British Museum laid out a further £15,000. These were huge sums for the time and highly profitable exercises, but they were also pioneering archeology for the period. Besides, removing the finds was hardly surprising: Greece, after all, was not yet a state and had no public museum; antiquities discovered were sold by their finders – if they recognized their value.

THE NEW NATION

The **Greek War of Independence** (1821–28) and the establishment of a modern Greek nation changed all of this – and provided a major impetus to archeology. Nationhood brought an increased pride in Greece's Classical heritage, nowhere more so than in **Athens**, which succeeded Náfplio as the nation's capital in 1834 largely on the basis of its ancient monuments and past.

As a result of the selection of Prince Otho of Bavaria as the first king of modern Greece in 1832, the **Germans**, whose education system laid great stress on Classical learning, were in the forefront of archeological activity.

One of the dominant Teutonic figures during the early years of the new state was **Ludwig Ross**. Arriving in Greece as a student in 1832, he was on hand to show the new king around the antiquities of Athens when Otho was considering making the town his capital. Ross was appointed deputy keeper of antiquities to the court, and in 1834 began supervising the excavation and restoration of the **Acropolis**. The work of dismantling the accretion of Byzantine, Frankish and Turkish fortifications began the following year. The graceful Temple of Athena Nike, which had furnished many of the blocks for the fortifications, was rebuilt, and Ross's architect, Leo von Klenze, began the reconstruction of the **Parthenon**.

The Greeks themselves had begun to focus on their ancient past when the first stirrings of the independence movement were felt. In 1813 the **Philomuse Society** was formed, which aimed to uncover and collect antiquities, publish books and assist students and foreign philhellenes. In 1829 an orphanage on the island of Éyina, built by Kapodistrias, the first President of Greece, became the first Greek **archeological museum**.

In 1837 the **Greek Archeological Society** was founded "for the discovery, recovery and restoration of antiquities in Greece". Its moving spirit was **Kyriakos Pittakis**, a remarkable figure who during the War of Independence had used his knowledge of ancient literature to discover the Clepsydra spring on the Acropolis – solving the problem of lack of water during the Turkish siege. In the first four years of its existence, the Archeological Society sponsored excavations in Athens at the **Theatre of Dionysus**, the **Tower of the Winds**, the **Propylaia** and the **Erechtheion**. Pittakis also played a major role in the attempt to convince Greeks of the importance of their heritage; antiquities were still being looted or burned for lime.

THE GREAT GERMANS: CURTIUS AND SCHLIEMANN

Although King Otho was deposed in 1862 in favour of a Danish princeling, Germans remained in the forefront of Greek archeology in the 1870s. Two men dominated the scene, Heinrich Schliemann and Ernst Curtius.

Ernst Curtius was a traditionally Classical scholar. He had come to Athens originally as tutor to King Otho's family and in 1874 returned to Greece to negotiate the **excavations of Olympia**, one of the richest of Greek sanctuaries and site of the most famous of the ancient panhellenic games. The reigning German Kaiser Wilhelm I intended that the excavation would proclaim to the world the cultural and intellectual pre-eminence of his empire. Curtius took steps to set up a **German Archeological Institute** in Athens and negotiated the **Olympia Convention**, under the terms of which the Germans were to pay for and have total control of the dig; all finds were to remain in Greece, though the excavators could make copies and casts; and all finds were to be published simultaneously in Greek and German.

This was an enormously important agreement, which almost certainly prevented the treasure of Olympia and Mycenae following that of Troy to a German museum. But the Europeans were still in very acquisitive mode: French consuls, for example, had been instructed to purchase any "available" local antiquities in Greece and Asia Minor, and had picked up the Louvre's great treasures, the Venus de Milo and Winged Victory of Samothrace, in 1820 and 1863 respectively.

At **Olympia**, digging began in 1875 on a site buried beneath many feet of river mud, silt and sand. Only one corner of the Temple of Zeus was initially visible, but within months the excavators had turned up statues from the east pediment. Over forty magnificent sculptures, as well as terracottas, statue bases and a rich collection of bronzes were uncovered, together with more than 400 inscriptions. The laying bare of this huge complex was a triumph for official German archeology.

While Curtius was digging at Olympia, a man who represented everything that was anathema to orthodox Classical scholarship was standing archeology on its head. **Heinrich Schliemann's** beginnings were not auspicious for one who aspired to dig for ancient cities. The son of a drunken German pastor, he left school at fourteen and spent the next five years as a grocer's assistant. En route to seeking his fortune in Venezuela, he was left for dead on the Dutch coast after a shipwreck. Later, working as a bookkeeper in Amsterdam, he began to study languages. His phenomenal memory enabled him to master four by the age of 21. Following a six-week study of Russian, Schliemann was sent to St Petersburg as a trading agent and had amassed a fortune by the time he was 30. In 1851 he visited California, opened a bank during the Gold Rush and made another fortune.

His financial position secure for life, Schliemann was almost ready to tackle his life's ambition – the search for **Troy** and the vindication of his lifelong belief in the truth of Homer's tales of prehistoric cities and heroes. By this time he spoke no less than seventeen languages, and had excavated on the island of **Ithaca**, writing a book which earned him a doctorate from the University of Rostock.

Although most of the archeological establishment, led by Curtius, was unremittingly hostile to the millionaire amateur, Schliemann sunk his first trench at the hill called Hisarlık, in northwest Turkey, in 1870; excavation proper began in 1871. In his haste to find the city of Priam and Hector and to convince the world of his success, Schliemann dug a huge trench straight through the mound, destroying a mass of important evidence, but he was able nevertheless to identify nine cities, one atop the next. In May of 1873 he discovered the so-called **Treasure of Priam**, a stash of gold and precious jewellery and vessels. It convinced many that the German had indeed found Troy, although others contended that Schliemann, desperate for academic recognition, assembled it from other sources. The finds disappeared from Berlin at the end of World War II, but in 1994 archeologists discovered that artefacts held by some museums in Russia originated in Troy and announced plans to put the Treasure of Priam on display – probably in St Petersburg – in the near future.

Three years later Schliemann turned his attentions to **Mycenae**, again inspired by Homer, again following a hunch. Alone among contemporary scholars, he sought and found the legendary graves of Mycenean kings inside the existing Cyclopean wall of the citadel rather than outside, unearthing in the process the magnificent treasures that today form the basis of the prehistoric collection in the National Archeological Museum in Athens.

He dug again at Troy in 1882, assisted by a young architect, Wilhelm Dörpfeld, who was destined to become one of the great archeologists of the next century (though his claim for Lefkádha as ancient Ithaca never found popular acceptance). In 1884 Schliemann returned to Greece to excavate another famous prehistoric citadel, this time at **Tiryns**.

Almost single-handedly, and in the face of continuing academic hostility, Schliemann had revolutionized archeology and pushed back the knowledge of Greek history and civilization a thousand years. Although some of his results have been shown to have been deliberately falsified in the sacrifice of truth to beauty, his achievement remains enormous.

The last two decades of the nineteenth century saw the discovery of other important Classical sites. Excavation began at **Epidaurus** in 1881 under the Greek archeologist **Panayotis Kavvadias**, who made it his life's work. Meanwhile at **Delphi**, the French, after gaining the permission to transfer the inhabitants of the village to a new town and demolishing the now-vacant village, began digging at the sanctuary of Apollo. Their excavations began in 1892, proved fruitful and continued non-stop for the next eleven years; they have gone on sporadically ever since.

EVANS AND KNOSSOS

The beginning of the twentieth century saw the domination of Greek archeology by an Englishman, **Sir Arthur Evans**. An egotistical maverick like Schliemann, he too was independently wealthy, with a brilliantly successful career behind him when he started his great work and recovered for Greek history another millennium. Evans excavated the **Palace of Minos** at **Knossos** on Crete, discovering one of the oldest and most sophisticated of Mediterranean societies.

The son of a distinguished antiquarian and collector, Evans read history at Oxford, failed to get a fellowship and began to travel. His chief interest was in the Balkans, where he was special correspondent for the *Manchester Guardian* in the uprising in Bosnia. He took enormous risks in the war-torn country, filing brilliant dispatches and still finding time for exploration and excavation.

In 1884, at the age of 33, Evans was appointed curator of the Ashmolean Museum in Oxford. He travelled whenever he could, and it was in 1893, while in Athens, that his attention was drawn to **Crete**. Evans, though very short-sighted, had almost microscopic close vision. In a vendor's stall he came upon some small drilled stones with tiny engravings in a hitherto unknown language; he was told they came from Crete. He had seen Schliemann's finds from Mycenae, and had been fascinated by this prehistoric culture. Crete, the crossroads of the Mediterranean, seemed a good place to look for more.

Evans visited Crete in 1894 and headed for the legendary site of **Knossos**, where a Cretan had already done some impromptu digging, revealing massive walls and a storeroom filled with jars. Evans bought a share of the site and five years later, after the Turks had been forced off the island, returned to purchase the rest of the land. Excavations began in March 1899 and within a few days evidence of a great complex building was revealed, along with artefacts which indicated an astonishing cultural sophistication. The huge team of excavation workers unearthed elegant courtyards and verandahs, colourful wall paintings, pottery and jewellery and sealstones – the wealth of a civilization which dominated the eastern Mediterranean 3500 years ago.

Evans continued to excavate at Knossos for the next thirty years, during which time he established, on the basis of changes in the pottery styles, the system of dating that remains in use today for classifying Greek prehistory: Early, Middle and Late Minoan (Mycenean on the mainland). He published his account of the excavation in a massive six-volume work, *The Palace of Minos*, which was published between 1921 and 1936. Like Schliemann, Evans attracted criticism and controversy for his methods – most notably his decision to reconstruct parts of the palace – and many of his interpretations of what he found. Nevertheless, his discoveries and his dedication put him near to the pinnacle of Greek archeology.

INTO THE TWENTIETH CENTURY: THE FOREIGN INSTITUTES

In 1924 Evans gave to the **British School of Archeology** the site of Knossos, along with the Villa Ariadne (his residence there) and all other lands within his possession on Crete. At the time the British School was one of several foreign archeological institutes in Greece; founded in 1886, it had been preceded by the **French School**, the **German Institute** and the **American School**.

Greek archeology owes much to the work and relative wealth of these foreign schools and others that would follow. They have been responsible for the excavation of many of the most famous sites in Greece: the **Heraion on Sámos** (German), the sacred island of **Delos** (French), sites on **Kós** and in **southern Crete** (Italian), **Corinth** and the **Athenian Agora** (American), to name but a few. Life as a resident foreigner in Greece at the beginning of the century was not for the weak-spirited (one unfortunate member of the American School was shot and killed by bandits while on a trip to visit sites in the Peloponnese), but there were compensations in unlimited access to antiquities in an unspoiled countryside.

The years between the two world wars saw an expansion of excavation and scholarship, most markedly concerning the **prehistoric civilizations**. Having been shown by Schliemann and Evans what to look for, a new generation of archeologists was uncovering numerous prehistoric sites on the mainland and Crete, and its members were spending proportionately more time studying and interpreting their finds. Digs in the 1920s and 1930s had much smaller labour forces (there were just 55 workmen under Wace at Mycenae, as compared with hundreds in the early days of Schliemann's or Evans's excavations) and they were supervised by higher numbers of trained archeologists. Though perhaps not as spectacular as their predecessors, these scholars would prove just as pioneering as they established the history and clarified the chronology of the newly discovered civilizations.

One of the giants of this generation was **Alan Wace**, who while Director of the British School of Archeology from 1913–23 conducted excavations at Mycenae and established a chronological sequence from the nine great **tholos** tombs on the site. This led Wace to propose a new chronology for prehistoric Greece, and put him in direct conflict with Arthur Evans. Evans believed that the mainland citadels had been ruled by Cretan overlords, whereas Wace was convinced of an independent Mycenaean cultural and political development. Evans was by this time a powerful member of the British School Managing Committee, and his published attacks on Wace's claims, combined with the younger archeologist's less than tactful reactions to Evans's dominating personality, resulted in the abrupt halt of the British excavations at

Mycenae in 1923 and the no less sudden termination of Wace's job. Wace was pressured to leave Greece, and it was not until 1939 that he returned. In the interval his theories gained growing support from the archeological community, and are today universally accepted.

Classical archeology was not forgotten in the flush of excitement over the Mycenaeans and Minoans. The period between the wars saw the continuation of excavation at most established sites, and many new discoveries, among them the sanctuary of Asclepius and its elegant Roman buildings on **Kós**, excavated by the Italians from 1935 to 1943, and the Classical Greek city of **Olynthos**, in northern Greece, which was dug by the American School from 1928 to 1934. After the wholesale removal of houses and apartment blocks that had occupied the site, the American School also began excavations in the **Athenian Agora**, the ancient marketplace, in 1931, culminating in the complete restoration of the Stoa of Attalos.

The advent of **World War II** and the invasion of Greece first by the Italians and then the Germans called a halt to most archeological work, although the Germans set to work again at **Olympia**, supposedly due to Hitler's personal interest.

A few Allied nation archeologists also remained in Greece, principal among them **Gorham Stevens** and **Eugene Vanderpool**, of the American School, both of whom did charitable work. Back in America and Britain, meanwhile, archeologists were in demand for the intelligence arm of the war effort, both for their intimate knowledge of the Greek terrain and their linguistic abilities, which proved invaluable in decoding enemy messages.

POSTWAR EXCAVATIONS

Archeological work was greatly restricted in the years after World War II, and in the shadow of the Greek Civil War. A few monuments and museums were restored and reopened but it was not until 1948 that excavations were resumed with a Greek clearance of the Sanctuary of Artemis at **Brauron** in Attica. In 1952 the American School resumed its activities with a dig at **Lerna** in the Peloponnese. Greek archeologists began work at the Macedonian

site of **Pella**, the **Necromanteion of Ephyra**, and, in a joint venture with the French, at the Minoan site of **Kato Zakros** on Crete.

These and many other excavations – including renewed work on the major sites – were relatively minor operations in comparison to earlier digs. This reflected a modified approach to archeology, which laid less stress on discoveries than on documentation. Instead of digging large tracts of a site, archeologists concentrated on small sections, establishing chronologies through meticulous **analysis** of data. Which is not to say that there were no **finds**. At Mycenae, in 1951, a second circle of graves was unearthed; at Pireás (Piraeus), a burst sewer in 1959 revealed four superb Classical bronzes; and a dig at the Kerameikos cemetery site in Athens in 1966 found 4000 potsherds used as ballots for ostracism. Important work has also been undertaken on **restorations** – in particular the **theatres** of the Athens Acropolis, Dodona and Epidaurus, which are used in summer festivals.

The two great postwar excavations, however, have been as exciting as any in the past. At **Akrotiri** on the island of **Thíra** (Santorini), **Spiros Marinatos** revealed, in 1967, a Minoan-era site that had been buried by volcanic explosion around 1550 BC. The buildings were two and three storeys high and superbly frescoed.

A decade later came an even more dramatic find at **Veryína**, in northern Greece. Here, **Manolis Andronikos** found a series of royal tombs dating from the fourth century BC. Unusually, these had escaped plundering by ancient grave robbers and contained an astonishing hoard of exquisite gold treasures. Piecing together clues – the hurriedness of the tomb's construction, an ivory head, gilded leg armour – Andronikos showed this to have been the tomb of **Philip II of Macedon**, father of **Alexander the Great**. Subsequent forensic examination of the body supported historical accounts of Philip's limp and blindness.

It was an astonishing and highly emotive find, as the artefacts and frescoed walls showed the sophistication and Hellenism of ancient Macedonian culture. With the background of an emerging Macedonian state on Greece's northern border, archeology had come head-to-head with politics.

MYTHOLOGY, AN A TO Z

While all ancient cultures had their **myths**, it is those from ancient Greece that have had the greatest influence on Western civilization. The Trojan War, the wanderings of Odysseus, the adventures of Heracles – these stories and many more have inspired some of the finest literature, music and art.

Homer and **Hesiod** were the first poets to write down some of the stories in around 800 BC, but they had existed for many years, perpetuated by word of mouth. With the enactment of the myths in the rituals of their religious festivals and ceremonies, along with their representation in the designs on their pots and the performances of the stories at the theatre and drama competitions, Greek myth and culture became inextricably blended.

Many versions of the myths exist, some of which are contradictory and confusing. Below is a summary of the principal **gods** and **heroes**. For further reading Robert Graves' *The Greek Myths* is a good handbook although perhaps a bit dry and academic, Pierre Grimal's *Dictionary of Classical Mythology* is a very good reference, but perhaps the best starting point and a way into feeling how the myths might have been told is to read Homer's epics *The Iliad* and *The Odyssey.*

Agamemnon see Atreus; Trojan War

Aphrodite When Cronos castrated Uranus (see below) and threw his testicles into the sea, the water spumed and foamed and produced Aphrodite, which means "born from sea foam". Her girdle made people fall in love with the wearer, but her famed adultery with Ares ended in tears when she found herself ensnared in the nets that Hephaestus (see p.799), her husband, had made to expose her infidelity. She restored her virginity, but later had an affair with Hermes which produced the double-sexed offspring – Hermaphroditus. She particularly favoured the mortal Paris.

Apollo was the illegitimate son of Zeus and Leto. His twin sister Artemis was goddess of the moon and he was the god of the sun. His first noteworthy deed was to kill the Python snake that terrorised the land around Delphi, a city with which he had a great affinity. He established his shrine there, and through the priestess and the oracle, gave prophesies to those who wished to know the future. A god of outstanding beauty, he represents the arts of music and poetry and was often depicted with a lyre, which was a gift to him from Hermes. He was not unlucky in love, but was famously spurned by Daphne (see p.798).

Ares, the god of war and the son of Zeus and Hera, was usually attended by his demon henchmen Deimos (Fear) and Phobos (Terror). His violence, however, did not necessarily render him all-victorious – he was more than once outwitted by Athena and Heracles. As adulterous as the other gods, he was exposed in flagrante delicto with Aphrodite by her husband Hephaestus. The animals associated with Ares – the dog and the vulture – illuminate his character.

Argonauts, see Jason and the Argonauts

Ariadne, see Theseus, Ariadne and the Minotaur

Artemis, Apollo's twin, was the goddess of hunting and of the moon. She was the protecting deity for the Amazons – the tribe of warrior women who were independent of men – and was always described as a virgin with perpetual youth. She killed the huntsman Orion who tried to rape her, and instigated the death of Actaeon who had seen her bathe naked by changing him into a stag and setting his own hounds upon him.

Athena did not have a conventional birth – she sprang out of the head of Zeus ready for battle with armour, helmet and spear. Athena stayed a virgin and so her son Ericthonius was born in an equally unlikely way – he grew from her cast off garments that had been soaked with Hephaestus' semen. She was the protectress of Athens, and was regarded as the goddess of reason and wisdom. She discovered olive oil, helped to build the Argo and looked after her favourite mortals, particularly Odysseus.

Atlas, see Heracles

Atreus (house of) A dynasty of revenge, murder, incest and tragedy. Atreus hated his younger brother Thyestes, and when their separate claims for kingship of Mycenae were voiced, the gods marked out Atreus for the task.

Atreus banished Thyestes, but when he learned that his wife had had an affair with him, Atreus feigned forgiveness and recalled him from exile. He then had Thyestes' sons murdered, cut up, cooked and fed to Thyestes. When Thyestes had finished eating, Atreus showed him the heads of his children, making it clear to him the true nature of the meal. He again banished Thyestes, who took refuge at Sicyon and, sanctioned by the gods, fathered Aegisthus by his daughter, Pelopia. Pelopia then married Atreus, her uncle, and Aegisthus (who did not know who his real father was) was brought up and cared for by Atreus. When Aegisthus came of age, Atreus instructed him to kill Thyestes, but Aegisthus found out the truth, returned to Mycenae and killed Atreus. Atreus' two sons were Agamemnon and Menelaus. Agamemnon paid for his father's crimes by dying at the hands of his wife Clytemnestra (who had committed adultery with Aegisthus while he Agamemnon was fighting at Troy). She ensnared him in a net while he took a bath and stabbed him to death. She in turn was killed by her son Orestes, who was absolved of matricide by Athena.

Bacchus, see Dionysos

Centaurs and Lapiths The Centaurs were monstrous beings with the heads and torsos of men and the lower bodies of horses. They lived a debauched life feeding on raw flesh and enjoying the pleasures of wine. There are many tales of Centaurs battling with Heracles on his journey to complete the twelve labours, but the most famous story is of the fight that broke out between them and the Lapiths, a race of heroes and warriors who were the descendants of the river god Pineus (the Piniós flows near Olympus). Pirithous, a Lapith who shared the same father as the Centaurs, invited them all to his wedding. At the feast the Centaurs tried to abduct the women, including the bride. A bloody brawl followed, of which the Lapiths were the victors.

Cronos The Titan Cronos was the youngest son of Gaia and Uranus, who seized power of the heavens by castrating his father. Once on the throne, Cronos lived in fear of the prediction that one of his offspring would one day overthrow him, and so swallowed all of his children except Zeus (see p.803) – Zeus's mother Rhea had substituted a stone for the bundle that Cronos thought was his baby. Cronos and his

Titan brothers were defeated in a vicious battle by Zeus and his Olympian supporters.

Daphne The nymph Daphne was one of the daughters of the river god Pineus. Apollo took a fancy to her and chased her through the woods to have his way, but just as he caught up with her, she prayed to her father to save her. He took pity and turned her into a laurel tree, and she became rooted to the spot. Apollo loved her even as a tree and made the laurel sacred, dedicating wreathes of its leaves as a sign of honour. Her name, to this day, is the Greek word for the laurel tree.

Demeter was the goddess of agriculture and corn, and she exercised her power when she made the whole Earth sterile, in protest against her daughter Persephone's abduction by Hades. She was greatly revered all over Greece, particularly where wheat was grown. She invented the mill and was highly respected at religious festivals associated with fertility and growth.

Dionysos, also known as Bacchus, was the god of wine and mystic ecstasy. He was the son of Zeus and because he was ripped from his mother's womb at six months, Zeus sewed him up in his thigh for the remaining three. As a young boy he was disguised as girl to hide him from Hera, and his feminine demeanour – long hair and dresses – stayed with him. He rode in a chariot drawn by panthers and draped in ivy and vines and was followed by a coterie of minor gods. He instituted the Bacchanalia where the people, but mostly the women (see Maenads), were inspired into frenzy and ecstasy. He rescued Ariadne from Náxos, and became associated with theatre, revelry and celebration.

Eurydice, see Orpheus and Eurydice

Golden Fleece, see Jason and the Argonauts

Hades' name means "the invisible", because in the battle with Cronos and the Titans he concealed himself by wearing the magic helmet given to him by the Cyclops. The helmet makes other appearances in Greek mythology (see Perseus p.802). He drew by lot the realm of the Underworld. To refer to him as Hades was thought to bring about his awesome anger, so the Greeks called him by his surname Pluto, which means "the rich" and alludes to the wealth that lies hidden underground. His wife was Demeter's daughter, Persephone (see p.803).

Helen was the daughter of Zeus, who came as a swan to her mother Leda. She was believed to be the most beautiful woman in the world. Her husband Menelaus, king of Sparta, entertained the Trojans Paris and Aeneas and was foolish enough to leave them in her hospitality; Paris abducted her. Some say she went willingly, impressed by his beauty and wealth, others say she was raped. In either event her departure from Sparta was the cause for the Trojan War (see p.803).

Hera was Zeus's sister and wife and the most powerful of the goddesses – she wreaked her vengeance and jealousy on any who Zeus seduced and the offspring of most of his encounters (see Io). Zeus punished her heavily for her anger against Heracles by suspending her from her wrists from Mount Olympus, and weighing her ankles down with anvils. Despite her portrayal as jealous, vindictive and irascible, she was the protecting deity of wives.

Heracles was the superhero of the ancient world. His mother was the mortal Alcmene, and his father Zeus. Jealous Hera sent two snakes to kill Heracles while he was still in his cradle, which he duly strangled; all good preparation for his twelve labours.

The labours were commanded by King Eurystheus, although it's not clear why Heracles was compelled to perform them. Nevertheless, the tasks took him to the fringes of the known world, even involving his supporting it on his shoulders while Atlas took a break to lend him a hand in his final task. The tasks were: to kill the Nemean lion; to kill the many-headed Hydra monster; to bring back the wild boar Erymanthus alive; to hunt the Keryneian hind that was sacred to Artemis; to kill the man-eating birds at the lake of Stymphaleia; to clean the stables of King Augias; to bring back the untameable Cretan bull alive; to capture the flesh-eating horses of Diomedes; to fetch the girdle of the Amazon warrior queen; to fetch the herds of Geryon from beyond the edge of the ocean; to fetch Cerberus the guard dog of hell from the underworld; and finally to fetch the golden apples from the garden of the Hesperides.

The twelve labours proved that Heracles had the right stuff to be a god, and his death was as dramatic as his life. Deianeira his wife gave him a garment that she thought had magic powers and would protect him from being unfaithful to her. When he put it on, it burned into his flesh and slowly and painfully killed him. The cloth had been drenched in the poisonous blood of the Centaur Nessus whom Heracles had killed when he had tried to rape Deianeira.

Hephaestus was the god of fire and a master craftsman. In his forges and workshops on volcanic Límnos (where the Cyclops worked for him) he fashioned everything from jewellery to armour. He was made lame from the injuries he sustained when Zeus threw him from Olympus (a fall that lasted a full day) because he had defended Hera in a quarrel. He was very ugly, but was married to Aphrodite (see p.797), the most beautiful of the goddesses.

Hermes was the son of Zeus and Maia, the daughter of Atlas. He showed his mettle by stealing Apollo's cattle while still a baby, and then set to inventing the lyre (by stretching the guts of a cow over a tortoise shell) and producing a flute from hollow reeds. He exchanged them both with Apollo (see p.797) for his cattle, the golden staff which Apollo had used to control the herd, and the secrets of the art of prophecy. He was the god of commerce and travel, often depicted wearing winged shoes, a wide-brimmed hat and carrying the staff which showed his position as the divine messenger.

Hippolytus and Phaedra Hippolytus, son of the hero Theseus and the Amazon Hippolyta was an accomplished hunter who revered Artemis and scorned Aphrodite. Aphrodite sought to teach him a lesson and conspired for Phaedra, the new wife of Theseus, to fall in love with the young man. When spurned by Hippolytus she feared he might reveal her advances and so accused him of rape. When Theseus heard this, he called upon Poseidon to kill his son and Hippolytus was flung from his chariot and torn apart by his horses. Phaedra in shame and remorse hanged herself.

Io was only one of the many mortals Zeus singled out for carnal satisfaction. Having had his way he chose to conceal his misdemeanour by turning her into a cow, denying to Hera (see above) that he had ever touched the beast. Hera demanded her as a present, and placed her under the watchful eyes (he had a hundred of them) of Argos the guard. She then proceeded to torment the poor cow by sending a stinging gadfly to goad her on her travels and drive her insane. She made for the sea, first to the Ionian gulf, which was named after her, and then crossed the straits into Asia at the Bosphorus – literally the Cow Crossing. Before settling in Egypt, she wandered all over Asia, even bumping into Prometheus, who was chained for a few centuries to the Caucasus mountain range.

Jason and the Argonauts Jason, a great Greek hero, was set an almost impossible task by his step-uncle Pelias to win the power that was his by birthright. He had to sail to the ends of the earth and bring back the Golden Fleece. He assembled his crew, which reads like a who's who of heroes of the Ancient Greek world, and commissioned a ship, called the Argo after its maker Argos, which was built with the help of Athena – its prow had the remarkable power of speech and prophecy. A long journey full of stories and surprises followed. Some of the crew didn't complete the voyage, including Heracles who missed the boat when it set sail because he was searching for his favourite, Hylas – the beautiful boy who had been abducted by the Nymphs. The prophet Phineus gave Jason directions and advice in return for him killing the Harpies that were plaguing him – he told Jason how to deal with the moving rocks and reefs that might smash his ship. Armed with this knowledge, Jason and the Argonauts reached their destination. On arrival in Colchis, however, the King Aeetes would not hand over the Golden Fleece until Jason had completed various labours. The king's daughter, the witch Medea (see below), fell in love with Jason and helped him with her magic powers. They stole the fleece and fled, pursued by Aeetes. Medea stalled her father by tearing up her brother Apsyrtus and casting his body parts into the sea; Aeetes had to slow down to collect the pieces. Zeus was greatly angered by this heinous crime and the Argo spoke to the crew telling them that they would have to purify themselves at Circe's island. After many more adventures and wanderings through treacherous seas, the crew arrived at Corinth where Jason dedicated the Golden Fleece to Poseidon.

Judgement of Paris The goddess Eris (Strife) began a quarrel between Athena, Hera and Aphrodite, by throwing a golden apple between them and saying that it belonged to whoever was the most beautiful. All the gods were too frightened to judge the contest, so Hermes took them to the top of Mount Ida for Paris, the son of Priam of Troy to decide. Each used bribery to win his favour: Athena offered him wisdom and victory in combat, Hera the kingdom of Asia, but Aphrodite, the winner of the contest, offered him the love of Helen of Sparta.

Lapiths, see Centaurs and Lapiths

Maenads The Maenads were the possessed female followers of Dionysos (see p.798). They wore scanty clothes, had wreaths of ivy around their heads and played upon tambourines or flutes in their procession. They had power over wild animals, and their hysteria led their imagination to dizzy heights so that they believed they drank milk or honey from fresh water springs. In their orgiastic ecstasies and frenzies they tore limb from limb those who offended them, did not believe or who spied upon their rites – including Orpheus (see p.801).

Medea exacted gruesome revenge on any who stood against her. She persuaded the daughters of Pelias (see Jason above) to cut their father up and put him in a boiling cauldron having convinced them that if they did so she could rejuvenate him. His body parts, to their extreme disappointment, did not come back together. Acastus, Pelias' son, banished her and Jason as a punishment. She went with Jason to Corinth, where he abandoned her to marry Creusa the daughter of Creon, who banished her. In revenge, Medea orchestrated a gruesome death for Creusa, with her young sons instrumental in the deed, and then murdered them.

Minotaur, see Theseus, Ariadne and the Minotaur

Mount Olympus, see Zeus

Muses The muses were the result of nine nights of lovemaking between Mnemosyne (Memory) and Zeus. They were primarily singers and were the inspiration for music (to which they gave their name), but also had power over thought in all its forms: persuasion, eloquence, knowledge, history, mathematics and astronomy. Apollo conducted their singing around the Hippocrene fountain on Mount Helicon.

Nymphs There were various subspecies of nymph: Meliads were the nymphs of the ash trees; Naiads lived in the springs and streams; Dryads were tree nymphs; Oreads were the mountain nymphs; and the Alseids lived in the groves. They were thought to be the daughters of Zeus and attended the great goddesses, particularly Artemis. Like the fairies of folk stories, they often occur in tales of love (see Daphne).

Odysseus Our word odyssey derives from Odysseus' ten-year journey home, which was no less fraught with danger, adventure and grief than the ten-year war against the Trojans which preceded it. Shipwrecked, tried and tested by the gods, held against his will by bewitching women, almost drawn to death by the hypnotic Sirens, witnessing his comrades devoured by the giant one-eyed Cyclops and all the time missing and desiring his faithful wife Penelope, Odysseus proved himself to be a great and scheming hero. At the end of his long and arduous journey he arrived at his palace on Ithaca to find suitors surrounding his wife. He contrived a cunning trap and killed them all with his bow. Penelope hardly recognized him; so long had he been away, that she had to test his identity by questioning him about their marriage bed. Odysseus answered correctly having made the bed himself from the olive tree that grew on the site of the palace and around which he had built his home.

Oedipus was a man cursed. The oracle said that Laius should not father any children, for if he did one would kill him. When Oedipus was born Laius abandoned the baby, piercing his ankles with a nail and tying them together: this is how Oedipus got his name which means "swollen foot". But the baby was discovered and brought up at the court of the neighbouring king, Polybus, at Corinth. The Delphic Oracle revealed to the adult Oedipus that he would kill his father and marry his mother. When he heard this news he resolved not to return home to Corinth, but making his journey he met with Laius, who was himself on the road to consult the oracle as to how to rid Thebes of the Sphinx. Because the road was narrow, Laius ordered Oedipus to get out of the way, and when one of the guards pushed him, Oedipus drew his sword in anger and, not knowing that Laius was his father, killed him and his entourage. He then made his way to the Thebes, where Laius had been king, and solved the riddle of the Sphinx, thus putting a stop to the plague. As a reward and in thanks, he was crowned king and offered Laius' widow Jocasta (his mother) in marriage.

Plague then fell upon Thebes, because of the crimes of patricide and incest at the heart of the city. The Delphic Oracle instructed Oedipus to expel the murderer of Laius, and in his ignorance he cursed the murderer and banished him. The seer and prophet Teiresias then revealed the full nature of the crime to Jocasta and Oedipus; she hanged herself and he put out his own eyes. He left the city as a vagabond accompanied by his daughter Antigone, and only at his death was granted peace. Attica, the country that received his dead body, was blessed.

Orpheus and Eurydice Orpheus was the greatest musician and was given his lyre by Apollo himself. He sang so beautifully that the animals would stop what they were doing and the trees would uproot themselves to come closer to him to listen. Even the rocks and stones were moved by his songs. He enlisted in the crew of Argonauts and sang for them to row their oars in time. On his return from the Argo's voyage he married the nymph Eurydice. She was bitten by a snake on the banks of the river Pineus and died, and Orpheus was so distraught that he went to the Underworld to bring her back. His wish to restore her to life was granted by Hades on the condition that during the return journey to the Earth, he would not look back at her. As he approached daylight his mind became plagued with doubts and, turning around to see if she was behind him, he lost her forever. He preached that Apollo was the greatest god, much to the anger of Dionysos, who set the Maenads on him. They tore him apart and cast his head, still singing, into the river Hebrus. It was finally washed up on the shores of the island of Lésvos.

Pan The god of shepherds and flocks, Pan was the son of Hermes and a Nymph and, with his beard, horns, hairy body and cloven hooves, was said to be so ugly that his own mother ran from him in fear. He had an insatiable libido, energetically pursuing both sexes. Apollo learned the art of prophecy from Pan and hunters looked to him for guidance. He enjoyed the cool woodland shade and streams of Arcadia and relished his afternoon naps so much that he wreaked havoc if he was disturbed.

Pandora, see Prometheus

Pegasus, see Poseidon

Penelope, see Odysseus

Persephone was out picking flowers one day when the Earth opened up and swallowed her; she had been abducted by Hades (see p.798). Her mother Demeter was distraught and when she found out the truth, she left Olympus in protest and made the Earth sterile so that it grew no crops. Zeus ordered Hades to return Persephone, but because she had eaten a magic pomegranate she was bound to him. The compromise was that she should be allowed to return to Earth for two thirds of the year and to reside with Hades for the remaining third. So Demeter divided the year into seasons and saw to it that while Persephone was with Hades the Earth would be sterile and in winter, but that while Demeter was on Earth the ground would be fertile for spring, summer and autumn.

Perseus A son of Zeus, and believed to be a direct ancestor of Heracles, Perseus was cast out to sea in a trunk with his mother Danae, because his grandfather feared that he would one day kill him. Danae and Perseus were washed up on an island, where they were discovered by a fisherman who looked after them. When Perseus came of age, the king of the island demanded that he bring back the head of Medusa the Gorgon, whose gaze could turn people to stone. Perseus acquired some special aids to perform the task – Hades' helmet, which made him invisible, and winged sandals to fly through the air – and had the divine assistance of Athena and Hermes. He cut off Medusa's head by looking at her reflection in Athena's polished shield. On his return flight he saw and fell in love with Andromeda, who was being offered as a sacrifice. He rescued her and returned home to find his mother had been raped by the King. He held up the gorgon's head, turned the king to stone and then presented the head as a gift to Athena, who placed it in the middle of her shield. Perseus went on to participate in the king of Larissa's celebratory games; he competed in the discus-throwing competition but his throw went off course and killed his grandfather, who was a spectator.

Phaedra, see Hippolytus and Phaedra

Poseidon In the battle with Cronos and the Titans, Poseidon, the brother of Zeus, was given the trident by the Cyclops which he used to shake both sea and land. He was awarded, by lot, the realm of the sea and lived in the salty deep. He produced some strange offspring, including the Cyclops Polyphemus who had it in for Odysseus (see p.801), and even had union with the gorgon Medusa – which resulted in the winged horse Pegasus. He quarrelled frequently with the other gods, competing with them for power over some of the major cities including Athens, Corinth and Argos, but his great hatred was for the Trojans who had double-crossed him by not paying him for helping them to build their city.

Prometheus For someone whose name means "forethought", Prometheus showed a distinct lack of it. In his desire to help mankind, he stole fire from the heavens and was immediately punished by Zeus who bound him in chains, tied him to the mountains and then sent an eagle to perpetually peck at his liver. Zeus then dealt with mankind by sending Pandora to Prometheus' brother Epimetheus, whose name means "afterthought". Her curiosity about the contents of his box got the better of her and, peeping inside, she unleashed all the evils and one good (hope) on the world. Prometheus gave some useful advice to Heracles when he passed by on one of his labours and Heracles repaid him by setting him free.

Theseus, Ariadne and the Minotaur
Theseus' father, Aegeus of Athens, sent him as a child away from Athens for his own safety. At sixteen the hero returned, in full strength and with the weapons that his father had set aside for him. Theseus was destined for a life of action, comparable to Heracles', and his greatest adventure was to kill the Minotaur on Crete. As a tribute from Athens, King Minos was owed six men and six women every nine years for sacrifice to the Minotaur – a gruesome beast, half-man half-bull, born from the bestial copulation of the queen Pasiphae with the huge bull sent by Poseidon. The Minotaur was kept in the labyrinth at Crete. Ariadne, Minos's daughter, contrived to help Theseus kill the Minotaur, having fallen in love with him. She gave him a ball of thread so that he would not lose his way in the labyrinth and then accompanied him in his flight from the island, only to be abandoned later on the island of Náxos. Dionysos saw her there weeping on the shore and took pity on her; he married her and took her to the land of the gods. Theseus, meanwhile, on his return to Athens forgot to hoist the white sails as a sig-

nal to his father that he was alive and Aegeus thinking that his son had been killed by the Minotaur threw himself into the sea which took his name: the Aegean.

Titans The Titans were the six male children of Uranus and Gaia. Their six sisters, who helped them father numerous gods, were called the Titanides. Cronos was the youngest Titan, and after he had overthrown his father he helped his brothers to power. The Titans lost their grip when they were toppled by the upstart Olympians, led by Zeus, in the giant battle called the Titanomachia.

Trojan War When Menelaus of Sparta realized that the Trojan Paris had made off with his wife, he called on his brother Agamemnon of Mycenae. Together they roused the might of Greece to get her back. With just about every Greek hero (Ajax, Achilles, Troilus, Hector, Paris, Odysseus, Priam, Diomedes, Aeneas) making an appearance in this epic, the story of the Trojan war is arguably the greatest tale from the ancient world. Homer's *Iliad* dealt with only one aspect of it, the wrath of Achilles. The ten-year war, fought over a woman and which sent many heroes' souls down to Hades, was finally won by the trickery of the Greeks, who used a huge wooden horse left ostensibly as a gift to the Trojans to smuggle an armed platoon inside the city walls. The cunning plan was thought to be the work of Odysseus (see p.801), who, like many of the surviving heroes, had a less than easy journey home.

Sirens, see Odysseus

Uranus was the personification of the sky and by his conjugation with Gaia (Earth) fathered many children including Cronos and the Titans (see above). Gaia became so exhausted by her husband's continuing advances that she sought protection from her sons. Her youngest son Cronos was the only one to assist – he cut off Uranus's testicles with a sickle and threw them into the sea.

Zeus was the supreme deity, king of gods and men, but he did not get to this position without a struggle. His father, the Titan Cronos, seized power of the heavens by castrating Uranus the sky god, and lived in fear that one of his offspring would one day overthrow him, and so swallowed all of his children except Zeus, whose mother, Rhea, came to the rescue and hid him in a cave on the island of Crete. When he came of age, Zeus poisoned Cronos so that he vomited up all Zeus's siblings and with their help, and the assistance of the Cyclops, cast Cronos and the Titans from Mount Olympus, the home of the gods. The Cyclops gave Zeus the thunderbolt as a weapon to use in the battle and it became his symbol of power. He used his position to make laws, control the gods and men and to get his way with whomever he fancied. The myths are littered with the tales of his infidelities, libidinous desires and the deeds of his children who include Heracles, Perseus and Helen (see p.788 and p.800).

Mark Espiner

WILDLIFE

For anyone who has first seen Greece at the height of summer with its brown parched hillsides and desert-like ambience, the richness of the wildlife – in particular the flora – may come as a surprise. As winter changes to spring, the countryside (and urban waste ground) transforms itself from green to a mosaic of coloured flowers, which attract a plethora of insect life, followed by birds. Isolated areas, whether true islands or remote mountains such as Olympus, have had many thousands of years to develop their own individual species. Overall, Greece has around 6000 species of native flowering plants, nearly four times that of Britain but in the same land area. Many are unique to Greece, and make up about one third of Europe's endemic plants.

SOME BACKGROUND

In early antiquity Greece was thickly forested: Aleppo and Calabrian pines grew in coastal regions, giving way to fir or lack pine up in the hills and low mountains. But this **native woodland** contracted rapidly as human activities expanded. By classical times, a pattern had been set of forest clearance, followed by agriculture, abandonment to scrub and then a resumption of cultivation or grazing. Huge quantities of timber were consumed in the production of charcoal, pottery and metal smelting, and for ships and construction work. Small patches of virgin woodland have remained, mostly in the north and northeast, but even these are under threat from the loggers and arsonists.

Modern Greek **farming** often lacks the rigid efficiency of northern European agriculture. Many peasant farmers still cultivate little patches of land, and even city dwellers travel at weekends to collect food plants from the countryside. Wild greens are gathered, to be cooked like spinach, under the generic term *khórta*. Grape hyacinth bulbs are boiled as a vegetable. The buds and young shoots of capers, and the fruit of wild figs, carobs, plums, strawberry trees, cherries and sweet chestnuts are harvested. Emergent snails are collected after wet weather. The more resilient forms of wildlife can coexist with these land-uses, but for many Greeks only those species that have practical uses are regarded as having any value.

Despite an often negative attitude to wildlife, Greece was probably the first place in the world where it was an object of study. Theophrastus (372–287 BC) was the first recorded **botanist** and a systematic collector of general information on plants, while his contemporary, Aristotle, studied the animal world. During the first century AD the distinguished physician Dioscorides compiled a herbal that remained a standard work for over a thousand years.

Since the 1970s, tourist developments have ribboned out along coastlines, sweeping away both agriculture and wildlife havens as they do so. These expanding resorts increase local employment, often attracting inland workers to the coast; the generation that would have been shepherds and graziers on remote hillsides, now work in bars and tavernas for the tourist. Consequently, the pressure of domestic animal grazing, particularly in the larger islands, has been significantly reduced and allows the regeneration of tree seedlings. Crete, for example, now has more woodland than at any time in the last five centuries.

FLOWERS

Whereas in temperate northern Europe, plants flower from spring through into the autumn, the arid summers of Greece confine the main **flowering period** to the spring, to a climatic window when the days are bright, the temperatures are not too high and the ground water supply still adequate. **Spring** starts in the southeast, in Rhodes in early March, and then travels progressively westwards and northwards. Rhodes, Kárpathos and eastern Crete are at their best in March, western Crete in early April, the Peloponnese and eastern Aegean mid-April to late April, and the Ionian in early May, though cold dry winters can cause several weeks' delay. In the higher mountains the floral spring is held back until the chronological summer, with the alpine zones of central and western Crete in full flower in June, while mainland mountain blooms emerge in July.

The delicate flowers of early spring – orchids, fritillaries, anemones, cyclamen, tulips and small bulbs, are replaced as the season progresses by more robust shrubs, tall perennials and abundant annuals, but many of these close down completely for the fierce **summer**. A few tough plants, like shrubby thyme and savory, continue to flower through the heat and act as magnets for butterflies.

Once the worst heat is over, and the first showers of **autumn** arrive, so does a second spring, on a much smaller scale but no less welcome after the brown drabness of summer. Squills, autumn cyclamen, crocus in varying shades, pink or lilac colchicum, yellow sternbergia and other small bulbs all come into bloom, while the seeds start to germinate for the following year's crop of annuals. By the new year early spring bulbs and orchids are flowering in the south.

SEASHORE

Plants on the **beach** tend to be hardy species growing in a difficult environment where fresh water is scarce. Feathery tamarisk trees are adept at surviving this habitat, and consequently are often planted to provide shade. On hot nights you may see or feel them dribbling away surplus saltwater from their branches.

Sand dunes in the southern and eastern islands may have the low gnarled trees of the prickly **juniper**. These provide shelter for a variety of colourful small plants like pink campions, yellow restharrow, white stocks, blue alkanet and violet sea-lavender. The flat sandy areas or slacks behind the dunes can be home to a variety of plants, where they have not been illegally ploughed for cultivation. Open stretches of beach sand usually have fewer plants, particularly nowadays in resort areas where the bulldozed "spring cleaning" of the beach removes the local flora along with the winter's rubbish.

FRESHWATER

Large areas of **freshwater** are scarce, particularly in the warmer south. Many watercourses dry up completely in the hot season, and what seem to be summer dry river courses are often simply flood-beds, which fill irregularly at times of torrential rain. Consequently, there are few true aquatic plants compared with much of Europe. However, species that survive periodic drying-out can flourish, such as the giant reed or **calamus**, a bamboo-like grass reaching up to 6m in height and often cut for use as canes. It often grows in company with the shrubby, pink-flowered and very poisonous oleander.

CULTIVATED LAND

Arable fields can be rich with colourful weeds: scarlet poppies, blue bugloss, yellow or white daisies, wild peas, gladioli, tulips and grape hyacinths. Small **meadows** can be equally colourful, with slower-growing plants such as orchids in extraordinary quantities. The rather dull violet flowers of the mandrake conceal its celebrated history as a narcotic and surgical anaesthetic. In the absence of herbicides, olive groves can have an extensive underflora. In the presence of herbicides there is usually a yellow carpet of the introduced weedkiller-resistant *Oxalis pes-caprae*, which now occurs in sufficient quantity to show up in satellite photographs.

LOWER HILLSIDES

The rocky earth makes cultivation on some hillsides difficult and impractical. Agriculture is often abandoned and areas regenerate to a rich mixture of shrubs and perennials – **garigue** biome. With time, a few good wet winters, and in the absence of grazing, some shrubs develop into small trees, intermixed with tough climbers – the much denser **maquis** vegetation. The colour yellow often predominates in early spring, with brooms, gorse, Jerusalem sage and the three-metre giant fennel, followed by the pink and white of large rockroses – *Cistus* spp. An abundance of the latter is often indicative of an earlier fire, since they flourish in the cleared areas. Strawberry trees are also resistant to fire; they flower in winter or early spring, producing an orange-red edible (though disappointingly insipid) fruit in the autumn. The Judas tree flowers on bare wood in spring, making a blaze of pink against the green hillsides.

A third vegetation type is **phrygana** – smaller, frequently aromatic or spiny shrubs, often with a narrow strip of bare ground between each hedgehog-like bush. Many **aromatic herbs** such as lavender, rosemary, savory, sage and thyme are natives to these areas, intermixed with other less tasty plants such as the toxic euphorbias and the spiny burnet or wire-netting bush.

Nearly 160 species of **orchid** are believed to occur in Greece; their complexity blurs species' boundaries and keeps botanists in a state of taxonomic flux. In particular, the *Ophrys* bee and spider orchids have adapted, through their subtleties of lip colour and false scents, to seduce small male wasps. These insects mistake the flowers for a potential mate, and unintentionally assist the plant's pollination. Other orchids mimic the colours and scents of honey-producing plants, to lure bees. Though all species are officially protected, many are still picked for decoration – in particular the giant *Barlia* orchid – and fill vases in homes, cafés, tavernas and even on graves.

Irises have a particular elegance and charm. The blue-to-violet winter iris, as its name suggests, is the first to appear, followed by the small blue *gynandriris*. The flowers of the latter open after midday and into the night, to wither by the following morning. The widow iris is sombre-coloured in funeral shades of black and green, while the taller, white *Iris albicans*, the holy flower of Islam, is a relic of Turkish occupation. On the limestone peaks of Sámos, *Iris suavolens* has short stems, but huge yellow and brown flowers.

MOUNTAINS AND GORGES

The higher **mountains** of Greece have winter snow cover, and cooler weather for much of the year, so the flowering is consequently later than at lower altitudes. The **limestone peaks** of the mainland, and of islands such as Corfu, Kefalloniá, Crete, Rhodes, Sámos and Thássos, hold rich collections of attractive rock plants, flowers whose nearest relatives may be from the Balkan Alps or from the Turkish mountains. Gorges are another spectacular habitat, particularly rich in Crete. Their inaccessible cliffs act as refuges for plants that cannot survive the grazing, competition, or more extreme climates of open areas. Many of Greece's endemic plants – bellflowers, knapweeds and *Dianthus*

spp. in particular – are confined to cliffs, gorges or mountains.

Much of the surviving **original woodland** is in mountain areas. In the south, the woodland includes cypress, Greek fir and pine, with oak and flowering ash. The cypress is native to the south and east Aegean, but in its columnar form it has been planted everywhere with a Mediterranean climate. It is sometimes said that the slim trees are the male and the broader, spreading form are female, but female cones on the thin trees prove this wrong. Further north there are also juniper and yew, with beech, hornbeam, maple, chestnut and poplar. The cooler shade of woodland provides a haven for plants which cannot survive full exposure to the Greek summer. Such species are the wonderful red, pink or white peonies and the scarlet martagon lily, along with helleborine and birds-nest orchids, and numerous ferns.

With altitude, the forest thins out to scattered individual conifers and kermes oak, before finally reaching a limit at around 1500–2000m. Above this treeline are summer meadows, and then bare rock. If not severely grazed, these habitats are home to many low-growing, gnarled, but often splendidly floriferous plants, such as aubrieta, alyssum, storksbill, prickly thrift, dwarf rose, saxifrage and viola.

BIRDS

Migratory species, which have wintered in East Africa, move north in spring through the eastern Mediterranean, from mid-March to mid-May, or later, depending on the season and the weather. Some stop to breed in Greece, others move on into the rest of Europe. The southern islands can be the first landfall after a long sea crossing, and smaller birds recuperate for a few days before moving on north. Larger birds such as storks and ibis often fly very high, and binoculars are needed to spot them as they pass over. In autumn the birds return, but usually in more scattered numbers. Although some species, such as quail, are shot, there is nothing like the wholesale slaughter that takes place in some other Mediterranean countries.

Swallows, and their relatives the martins, are constantly hawking through the air to catch insects, as are the larger and noisier swifts. Warblers are numerous, with the Sardinian warbler often conspicuous because of its black head, bright red eye, and bold habits; the

Rüppell's warbler is considerably rarer. Other small insect eaters include stonechats, flycatchers and woodchat shrikes.

Lesser kestrels are brighter, noisier versions of the common kestrel, and often appear undisturbed by the presence of humans. At night, the tiny Scops owl has a very distinct, repeated single note call, very like the sonar beep of a submarine. Larger **raptors** occur in remoter areas, particularly around mountain gorges and cliffs. Buzzards are perhaps the most abundant, and mistaken by optimistic birdwatchers for the rarer, shyer eagles. Griffon vultures are unmistakable, soaring on broad, straight-edged wings, whereas the lammergeier is a state-of-the-art flying machine with narrow, swept wings, seen over mountain tops by the lucky few.

Also to be seen in the mountains are ravens, and smaller, colourful birds such as alpine choughs, common choughs, black-and-white wheatears, wallcreepers and the blue rock thrush. In lowland areas, hoopoes are a startling combination of pink, black and white, particularly obvious when they fly. The much shyer golden oriole has an attractive song but is rarely seen for more than a few moments before hiding its brilliant colours among the olive trees. Rollers are bright blue and chestnut, while multicoloured flocks of slim and elegant bee-eaters fill the air with their soft calls as they hunt insects. Brightest of all is the kingfisher, more commonly seen sea-fishing than in northern Europe.

In those areas of **wetland** that remain undrained and undisturbed, birds flourish. In saltmarshes, coastal lagoons, estuaries and freshwater, herons and egrets, ducks, osprey, glossy ibis and spoonbills, black storks, white storks, pelicans, cormorants and many waders can be seen feeding. Greater flamingos sometimes occur, as lone individuals or small flocks, particularly in salt pans in the eastern Aegean.

MAMMALS

Greece's small **mammal** population ranges from small rodents and shrews to hedgehogs, hares and squirrels (a very dark form of the red). Rats are particularly common in Corfu. Medium-sized mammals include badgers and foxes, but one of the commonest is the fast-moving, ferret-like, stone (or beech) marten, named for its habit of decorating stones with its droppings to mark territory.

In the mainland mountains, mainly in the north, are the shy **chamois** and **wild boar**, with even shyer predators like lynx, wolves and brown bear. In the White Mountains of Crete an endemic ibex, known to Cretan hunters as agrimi or kri-kri, is occasionally seen running wild or, more rarely, as a steak. Once in danger of extinction, a colony of them was established on the offshore island of Dhía, where they exterminated the rare local flora.

The extremely rare Mediterranean **monk seal** also breeds on some stretches of remote coast in the east Aegean and Sporades; the small world population is now highly endangered since losing many individuals – and most of its main breeding ground – to a toxic algal bloom off Morocco. If spotted, these seals should be treated with deference; they cannot tolerate human disturbance, and on present trends are unlikely to survive much beyond the millennium.

REPTILES AND AMPHIBIANS

Reptiles flourish in the hot dry summers of Greece and there are many species, the commonest being **lizards**. Most of these are small, slim, agile and wary, rarely staying around for closer inspection. They're usually brown to grey, with subtle patterns of spots, streaks and stripes though in adult males the undersides are sometimes brilliant orange, green or blue. The more robust green lizards, with long whip tails, are up to 50cm or more in length, but equally shy and fast-moving unless distracted by territorial disputes with each other.

On some islands, mainly in the central and eastern Aegean, lives the angular, iguana-like **agama**, sometimes called the Rhodes dragon. Occasionally reaching a robust 30cm in length, their skin is rough and grey to brown with indistinct patterning. Unlike other lizards, they will often stop to study you, before finally disappearing into a wall or under a rock.

Geckoes are large-eyed nocturnal lizards, up to 15cm long, with short tails and often rough skins. Their spreading toes have claws and ingenious adhesive pads, allowing them to walk up house walls and onto ceilings in their search for insects. Groups of them lie in wait near bright lights that attract their prey, and small ones living indoors can have very pale, almost transparent skins. Not always popular locally – the Greek name means "defiler" after their outisized faeces – they should be left alone to eat mosquitoes and other bugs. The **chameleon** is a rare, slow-moving and swivel-eyed inhabitant of eastern Crete and some eastern Aegean islands such as Sámos. Although essentially green, it has the ability to adjust its coloration to match the surroundings.

Once collected for the pet trade, **tortoises** can be found on much of the mainland, and some islands, though not on Crete. Usually it is their noisy progress through vegetation on sunny or wooded hills that first signals their presence. They spend their often long lives grazing the vegetation and can reach lengths of 30cm. **Terrapins** are more streamlined, freshwater tortoises which love to bask on waterside mud by streams or ponds, including on many islands. They are usually shy and nervous, and are often only seen as they disappear underwater. They are scavengers and will eat anything, including fingers if handled.

Sea turtles occur mostly in the Ionian, but also in the Aegean. The least rare are the loggerhead turtles (*Caretta caretta*), which nest on Zákinthos and Kefalloniá and occasionally in Crete. Their nesting grounds are disappearing under tourist resorts, and they are a protected endangered species (see p.751).

Snakes are abundant in Greece and many islands; most are shy and non-venomous. Several species, including the Ottoman and nose-horned **vipers**, do have a poisonous bite, though they are not usually aggressive. They are adder-like and often have a very distinct, dark zigzag stripe down the back. They are only likely to bite if a hand is put in the crevice of a wall or a rock-face where one of them is resting, or if they are attacked. Unfortunately, the locals in some areas attempt to kill any snake they see, and thus greatly increase the probability of their being bitten. Most snakes are not only completely harmless to humans, but beneficial in that they keep down populations of pests such as rats and mice. There are also three species of legless lizards – slow-worm, glass lizard and legless skink – all equally harmless, which suffer because they are mistaken for snakes. The general principle should be to leave them alone, and they will do the same for you.

Snakebites cause very few deaths in Europe. Many snakes will bite under stress, whether they are venomous or not. If a bite injects venom, then swelling will normally occur within 1–30 minutes. If it does, get medical attention. Keep the bitten part still, and keep all body movements as gentle as possible. Do not cut or suck the wound, but if medical attention is not nearby then bind the limb firmly to slow the blood circulation but not so tightly as to stop the blood flow. Many reptiles can harbour *Salmonella* bacteria, so should be handled cautiously and preferably not at all. This applies particularly to tortoises.

Frogs and **toads** are the commonest amphibians in most of Greece, particularly in the spring breeding season. The green toad has green marbling over a pinkish or mud-coloured background, and a cricket-like trill. Frogs prefer the wettest places, and the robust marsh frog particularly revels in artificial water storage ponds, where the concrete sides magnify their croaking impressively. **Tree frogs** are tiny jewels, usually emerald green, with huge and strident voices at night. They rest by day in trees and shrubs, and can sometimes be found in quantity plastered onto the leaves of waterside oleanders.

Newts, complete with lacy external gills, can be seen in a few alpine tarns of the north mainland; search for **salamanders** in ponds at breeding time, under stones and in moist crevices outside the breeding season. The orange-on-black fire salamander is often found promenading in the mountains after rain.

INSECTS

Greece teems with **insects**. Some pester, like flies and mosquitoes, but most are harmless to humans. The huge, slow-flying, glossy black carpenter bee may cause alarm by its size and noise, but is rarely a problem.

Grasshoppers and **crickets** swarm through open areas of vegetation in summer, with several larger species that are carnivorous on the smaller and can bite strongly if handled. Larger still is the grey-brown locust, which flies noisily before crash-landing into trees and shrubs. The high-pitched and endlessly repeated chirp of house crickets can drive to distraction, as can the summer whirring of cicadas on the trunks of trees. The latter insects are giant relatives of the aphids that cluster on roses.

From spring through to autumn Greece is full of **butterflies**, particularly in late spring and early summer. There are three swallowtail species, named for the drawn-out corners of the hind-wings, in shades of cream and yellow, with black and blue markings. Their smaller relatives, the festoons, lack the tails, but add red spots to the palette. The rarer, robust brown and orange pasha is unrelated but is Europe's largest butterfly. In autumn the black and orange plain tiger or African monarch may appear, sometimes in large quantities. In areas of deciduous woodland, look high up and you may see fast-flying large tortoiseshells, while lower down, southern white admirals skim and glide through clearings between the trees. Some of the smallest but most beautiful butterflies are the blues. Their subtle, camouflaging grey and black undersides make them vanish from view when they land and fold their wings.

Some of the Greek **hawkmoths** are equally spectacular, particularly the green and pink oleander hawkmoth. Their large caterpillars can be recognized by their tail horn. The hummingbird hawkmoth, like its namesake, hovers at flowers to feed, supported by a blur of fast-moving wings. Tiger moths, with their black and white forewings and startling bright orange hind-wings, are the "butterflies" that occur in huge quantity in sheltered sites in the Dodecanese islands such as Rhodes and Níssyros. The giant peacock moth is Europe's largest, up to 15 cm across. A mixture of grey, black and brown, with big eye-spots, it is usually only seen during the day while resting on tree trunks.

Other insects include the camouflaged praying mantids, holding their powerful forelegs in a position of supplication until another insect comes within reach. The females are voracious, and notorious for eating the males during sex. Ant-lion adults resemble a fluttery dragonfly, but their young are huge jawed and build pits in the sand to trap ants. Hemispherical carob beetles collect balls of dung and push them

---

FLORA AND FAUNA FIELD GUIDES

FLOWERS

Hellmut Baumann, *Greek Wild Flowers and plant lore in ancient Greece* (Herbert Press, UK). Crammed with fascinating ethnobotany, plus good colour photographs.

Blamey and Grey-Wilson *Mediterranean Wild Flowers* (HarperCollins, UK). Comprehensive field guide, with coloured drawings.

Lance Chilton, *Plant check-lists* (Marengo Publications, UK). Plant and wildlife lists for a number of Greek islands and resorts.

Pierre Delforge *Orchids of Britain and Europe* (HarperCollins, UK). A comprehensive guide, with recent taxonomy.

Oleg Polunin *Flowers of Greece and the Balkans* (Oxford University Press, UK). An older field guide, but with colour photographs.

BIRDS

Richard Brooks *Birding in Lesbos* (Brookside Publishing, UK). Includes a list of birdwatching sites, with detailed maps, plus an annotated species-by-species bird list with much useful information.

Handrinos and Akriotis *Birds of Greece* (A&C Black, UK). A comprehensive guide that includes island birdlife.

Heinzel, Fitter and Parslow *Collins Guide to the Birds of Britain and Europe* (Collins, UK/Stephen Green Press, US). Though covering most of Europe, these two field guides have the best coverage of Greek birds.

Petersen, Mountfort and Hollom *Field Guide to the Birds of Britain and Europe* (Collins, UK/Stephen Green Press, US).

MAMMALS

Corbet and Ovenden *Collins Guide to the Mammals of Europe* (Collins, UK/Stephen Green Press, US). The best field guide on its subject.

REPTILES

Arnold, Burton and Ovenden *Collins Guide to the Reptiles and Amphibians of Britain and Europe* (Collins, UK/Stephen Green Press, US). A useful guide though excluding the Dodecanese and east Aegean islands.

INSECTS

Michael Chinery *Collins Guide to the Insects of Britain and Western Europe* (Collins, UK/Stephen Green Press, US). Although Greece is outside the geographical scope of the guide, it will provide general identifications for most insects seen.

Higgins and Riley *A Field Guide to the Butterflies of Britain and Europe* (Collins, UK/Stephen Green Press, US). A thorough and detailed field guide that illustrates nearly all species seen in Greece.

around with their back legs, while the huge long-horn beetles of the southern Ionian islands munch their way through tree trunks. Longhorns are named for their absurdly extended, whip-like antennae. Cockroaches of varying species live in buildings, particularly hotels, restaurants and bakeries, attracted by warmth and food scraps.

Corfu is famous for its extraordinary **fireflies**, which flutter in quantities across meadows and marshes on May nights, speckling the darkness with bursts of cold light to attract partners. Look carefully in nearby hedges, and you may spot the less flashy, more sedentary glow-worm.

Centipedes are not often seen, but the fast-moving 20cm *Scolipendra* should be treated with respect since they can give very painful bites. Other non-vertebrates of interest include the land crabs, which are found in the south and east. They need water to breed, but can cause surprise when found walking on remote hillsides. There are plenty of genuine marine creatures to be seen, particularly in shallow seawater sheltered by rocks – sea cucumbers, sea butterflies, octopus, starfish and sea urchins.

Lance Chilton

MUSIC

Music is central to Greek culture; even the most indifferent visitor will be aware of its ubiquitous presence in vehicles, tavernas, ferryboats and other public spaces. Like most aspects of Greece, it's an amalgamation of native and Oriental styles, with occasional contributions from the West. In fact, Western music made little impression until recent decades, when aesthetic disputes arose between adherents of folk- or *laïki*-derived styles and those spurning ethnic roots in favour of jazz/cabaret, symphonic and rock idioms – a reflection of the modernizing-versus-traditionalism debates raging in the nation at large.

Many older songs, invariably in Eastern-flavoured minor scales, have direct precedents in the forms and styles of both **Byzantine religious chant** and that of the **Ottoman Empire**, though some of the more nationalistically minded claim their partial descent from now-lost melodies of ancient Greece. Almost all native Greek instruments are near-duplicates of ones used throughout the Islamic world, though it's an open question as to whether the Byzantines, Arabs or Persians first constructed particular instruments. To this broadly Middle Eastern base Slavs, Albanians and Italians have added their share, resulting in an extraordinarily varied repertoire of traditional and modern pieces.

BYZANTINE SACRED MUSIC

Sacred **Byzantine chant** forms the bedrock from which much later Greek secular music sprung. Despite its canonical constancy, and prohibition on instrumentation, it is by no means a museum tradition. Some of the finest liturgical chanting can be heard on Mount Áthos in northern Greece, but only men can visit, by special arrangement (see p. 000). More conveniently, tenor **Lycourgos Angelopoulos** and his excellent choir – the best group currently active – used to chant every Sunday at Ayía Iríni church in Athens's flower market, and may once again do so when its restoration is complete. Greeks get tetchy with foreign critics who fail to give Byzantine music its due, but they are partly to blame themselves; there are a lot of mediocre Greek-originated recordings about – groups headed by Costas Zorbas and Khristodhoulos Khalaris being particularly forgettable – while quality musicians go unrecorded. The great Constantinopolitan *psáltis* (chanter) Thrasyvoulos Stanitsas, who moved to Athens in 1964, has no extant discography, while all of the Angelopoulos recordings in print have been brought out on French labels. Overseas record stores, unsure of whether to stock Byzantine music as "ethnic" or "sacred", often end up not stocking it at all, or only by special order.

DISCOGRAPHIES

BYZANTINE DISCOGRAPHY

Lycourgos Angelopoulos and Choir
Liturgie Byzantine: Ensemble Lycourgos
Angelopoulos en Concert (CD, *Le Chant du
Monde/Harmonia Mundi* LDX 274971); *The
Divine Liturgy of St John Chrysostom* (CD,
Opus OPS 30–78) and *Ioannis Koukouzelis,
Le Maïstor Byzantin: Mathimata* (CD, Jade
JAD C129) are the three French pressings of
this accomplished group currently available;
to the country's detriment, there is nothing
now in print in Greece.

REGIONAL FOLK MUSIC

The most promising times to hear regional folk
music are at the numerous **summer festivals** –
as well as larger cultural programmes – when
musicians (often based in Athens or other city
clubs in winter) tour the islands and villages.
However, it's as well to know that during the
1967–74 junta a marked decline in this type of
music began, with the result that traditional
instrumentation is now often replaced with
something more appropriate to rock concerts.
The musicians, who are deprived of – or actively scorn – the oral transmission of technique
from older master players, are not what they
could be.

CRETE, KÁSSOS, KHÁLKI AND
KÁRPATHOS

This arc of southern islands is one of the most
promising areas in Greece for hearing live music
at any season of the year. The dominant instrument here is the **lýra**, a three-stringed fiddle
directly related to the Turkish *kemençe*. This is
played not on the shoulder but balanced on the
thigh, often with tiny bells attached to the bow,
which the musician can jiggle for rhythmical
accent. The strings are metal, and since the
centre string is just a drone, the player impro-
vises only on the outer two. Usually the *lýra* is
backed up by one or more **laoúta**, more elongated than the Turkish/Arab *oud* and not unlike
the medieval lute. These are rarely used to their
full potential – a *laoúto* solo is an uncommon
treat – but a good player will find the harmon-
ics and overtones of a virtuoso *lýra* piece, at the
same time coaxing a pleasing, chime-like tone
from his instrument.

In several places in the southern Aegean,
notably northern Kárpathos, a primitive bagpipe, the **askómandra** or **tsamboúna**, joins
the *lýra* and *laoúto*. During the colonels' dictatorship the playing of the bagpipe in the
Cyclades was banned lest tourists think the
Greeks "too primitive" – though hopefully, all
concerned have recovered from any sense of
cultural inferiority. If you remember
Kazantzakis's classic novel (or the movie), Zorba
himself played a **sandoúri**, or hammer dul-
cimer, for recreation, but it was actually little
known until after 1923 on other islands, being
introduced by Asia Minor refugees. Today,
accomplished players are few and in *Kritikí*
(Cretan music), *nisiotiká* (island songs) and *rembétika* (see below), the instrument has been rel-
egated to a supporting role. On older Cretan
recordings you may hear solos on the *voúlgari*, a
stringed instrument, essentially a small *saz*
(Turkish long-necked, fretted lute), which has
now all but died out. Modern Cretan artists to
look out for on recordings include **Kostas
Moundakis**, the late acknowledged *lýra* master, the late **Nikos Xylouris**, justifiably dubbed
"The Nightingale of Crete" for his fine voice,
and his brother Andonis who performs under
the name **Psarandonis**.

OTHER AEGEAN ISLANDS

On most of the Aegean islands, and particularly
the Cyclades, you'll find the *lýra* replaced by a
more familiar-looking **violí**, essentially a
Western violin. Backing was provided until
recently by *laoúto* or *sandoúri*, though these
days you're more likely to be confronted (or
affronted) by a bass-guitar-and-drum rhythm
section. Hilltop shepherds used to pass the time
fashioning a reed-wailer known as the
karamoúza, made from two goat horns, though
this too has all but disappeared.

Unlike on Crete, where you can often catch
the best music in special clubs or *kéndra*,
Aegean island performances tend to be sponta-
neous and less specialized; festivals and saints'
days in village squares offer the most promising
opportunities. The melodies, like much folk
music the world over, rely heavily on the penta-
tonic scale. Lyrics, especially on the smaller
islands, touch on the perils of the sea, exile and
– in a society where long periods of separation
and arranged marriage were the norm – thwart-

ed love. Though in the past three decades the **Konitopoulos** clan from Náxos, especially Irini Konitopoulou-Legaki, has become synonymous with this music, both live and recorded, older stars like the sisters **Anna** and **Emilia Khatzidhaki** and **Effi Sarri** offer a warmer, more innocent delivery.

IONIAN ISLANDS

Alone of all modern Greek territory, the Ionian islands – except for Lefkádha – never saw Turkish occupation and have a predominantly Western musical tradition. The indigenous song-form is Italian both in name, **kantádhes**, and instrumentation (guitar and mandolin); it's most often heard these days on **Lefkádha** and **Zákynthos**.

THE PELOPONNESE, CENTRAL GREECE AND EPIRUS

Many of the folk lyrics of the Peloponnese, central and western Greece hark back to events of the years of Turkish occupation and to the War of Independence; others, in a lighter tone, refer to aspects of pastoral life (sheep, elopements, fetching water from the well and so on). All this is lumped together as **paleá dhimotiká**, folk ballads. The essential instrumentation consists of the *klaríno* (clarinet), which reached Greece during the 1830s, introduced either by Gypsies or by members of King Otto's Bavarian entourage. Backing was traditionally provided by a *koumpanía* consisting of *kithára* (guitar), *laoúto*, *laoutokithára* (a hybrid in stringing and tuning), and *violí*, with *toumberléki* (lap drum) or *défi* (tambourine) for rhythm. Stalwart vocalists to look for on old recordings include **Yiorgos Papasidheris** and **Yioryia Mittaki**, the latter actually of Arvanitic (Albanian-speaking) origin, as well as **Roza Eskenazy** and **Rita Abatzi** (see under "Rémbetika", p.814). Among instrumentalists, the violinist **Yiorgos Koros**, and clarinetists **Yiannis Saleas** and the late **Vassilis Soukas** are especially remarkable – the latter two examples of the Gypsy or Gypsy-descended musicians who virtually dominate instrumental music on mainland Greece.

The music of **Epirus** (*Ípiros*) still exhibits strong connections with that of northern Epirus (now falling within neighbouring Albania) and the Former Yugoslav Republic of Macedonia, particularly in the polyphonic pieces sung by both men and women. They tend to fall into three basic categories, which are also found further south: **mirolóyia** or laments (the instrumental counterpart is called a *skáros*); drinking songs or **tis távlas**; and various danceable melodies (see below), common to the entire mainland and many of the islands. Most famous of the Epirot clarinettists are members of the numerous Khalkias clan, including the late, great **Tassos Khalkias** and a younger, very distant relative, **Petros Loukas Khalkias**.

Many mainland pieces are danceable, divided by rhythm into such categories as *kalamatianó* (a line dance), *tsámiko*, *khasaposérviko* or *syrtó*, the quintessential circle dance of Greece. Those that are not include the slow, stately *kleftikó*, similar to the *rizítiko* of Crete, both of which relate, baldly or in metaphor, incidents or attitudes from the years of Ottoman rule and the rebellions for freedom.

Since the *paleá dhimotiká* are strongly associated with national identity, it's not surprising that they were for many years pressed into political service. During election campaigns each party's local storefront headquarters or sound trucks blasted out continuous *paleá dhimotiká* (plus *andártika* – see p.821 – by the Left), interspersed with political harangues. Since 1989, however, this practice has been (officially) banned.

MACEDONIA AND THRACE

Thrace and **Macedonia** remained Ottoman territory until early this century, with a bewilderingly mixed population, so music here – often shriller and less lyrical than in the south – has a more generically Balkan feel. Meriting a special mention are the brass bands, introduced last century by Ottoman military musicians, peculiar to the area around Flórina. The north has also remained, owing to the huge influx of Anatolian refugees after 1923, a rich treasure-trove for collectors and ethnomusicologists seeking to document the fast vanishing old music of Asia Minor. *Kálanda* (carols), carnival dances, wedding processionals and table songs abound. Incidentally, amongst the Pomaks and other local Muslims, the main festival and wedding season in Thrace runs from autumn through spring, the opposite of elsewhere; summer is reserved for tending the precious local tobacco crop.

REGIONAL FOLK DISCOGRAPHY

*Songs of... (Society for the Dissemination of National Music, Greece). A thirty-plus strong series of field recordings from the 1950s through 1970s, each covering traditional music of one region or type. All LPs contain lyrics in English and are easily available in Athens in LP, cassette or CD form, especially at the Musicological Museum. Best to date are *Thrace 1* (SDNM 106); *Epirus 1* (SDNM 111); *Peloponnese* (SDNM 113); *Mytilene and Chios* (SDNM 110); *Mytilene and Asia Minor* (SDNM 125); *Rhodes, Khalki and Symi* (SDNM 104); and *Kassos and Karpathos* (SDNM 103).

*Various *Dhimotiki Paradhosi: Morias* (CD, Minos 7 24383 49042 4). Good, inexpensive anthology of Peloponnesian standards featuring Yiorgos Papasidheris on many tracks.

Various *Grèce – Chants polyphoniques et musique d'Epiré* (Ocora, France; cassette only, 4558631). One of the best recordings from Epirus. *Klaríno*, frame drums and bells for the dances, polyphonic vocals on the ballads and laments.

*Various *Paniyiria sta Khoria mas* (CD, Minos 7 24348 00112 2). Another good general anthology of non-electrified, pre-1960s material.

*Various *Takoutsia, Musiciens de Zagori: Inédit – Grèce – Epiré* (Inédit/Auvidis, France). Drinking songs, dance tunes and dirges performed by one of the last working clans of Epirot Gypsy musicians.

*Khronis Aïdhonidhis *T'Aïdhonia tis Anatolis: Songs of Thrace and Asia Minor* (Minos 847/848, Greece). One of the best and most accessible collections available, featuring Thrace's top folk singer, plus accompaniment by Ross Daly and several solos by versatile Yiorgos Dalaras. Aïdhonis sings alone on the equally good *Tragoudhia keh Skopi tis Thrakis/Songs and Tunes of Thrace* (Crete University Press 7/8).

*Avthentika Nisiotika tou Peninda (Lyra CD 0168). Good Cretan and Pontic material from the 1950s, with the Dodecanese also represented, from the collection of the late Ted Petrides, musician and dance master.

*Banda tis Florinas (CD, Ano Kato 2008, Thessaloníki). Wonderfully twisted brass-band music unique to central and western Macedonia, verging into ethnic-jazz territory somewhere between klezmer and New Orleans. Recommended for demolishing stereotypes about Greek music.

*Roza Eskenazi and Rita Ambatzi *Se Dhimotika Tragoudhia/In Folk Songs* (CD, Minos 4 802167 29). Incredible verve, showing the versatility of these two normally associated with rembétika.

*Kastellorizo (Syrtos 561) and ***Tradgoudhia keh Skopi tis Kalymnou** (Syrtos 564) Studio productions of Kalymniote musician Manolis Karpathios; the Kálymnos disc is harsh but compelling.

The Thracian **kaváli**, or end-blown flute, is identical to the Turkish and Bulgarian article (and similar to the disappearing *floyéra* of the south mainland); so too is the northern bagpipe, or **gáïda**. The **zournás**, a screechy, double-reed oboe similar to the Islamic world's *shenai*, is much in evidence at weddings or festivals, together with the deep-toned **daoúli** drum, as a typically Muslim or Orthodox Gypsy ensemble. Other percussion instruments like the *daïrés* or tambourine and the *darboúka*, the local version of the *toumberléki*, make for some sharply demarcated dance rhythms such as the *zonarádhikos*. The *klaríno* is present here as well, as are two types of *lýres*, but perhaps the most characteristic melodic instrument of Thrace is the **oúti** or oud, whose popularity received a boost after refugee players arrived. Noteworthy performers – both still alive and active – include oudist **Nikos Saragoudhas** and golden-voiced singer **Khronis Aïdhonidhis**.

REMBÉTIKA

Rembétika began as the music of the Greek urban dispossessed – criminals, refugees, drug-users, defiers of social norms. It has existed in some form in Greece and Constantinople since at least the turn of the century, perhaps a little before. But it is as difficult to define or get to the origins of as jazz or blues, with which it shares similarities in spirit and circumstance. The themes of the earliest recorded songs – illicit or frustrated love, drug addiction, police oppression, disease and death – and the tone of the delivery – resignation to the singer's lot, coupled with defiance of authority – will be familiar to Westerners. But even the word "*rembétika*" is of uncertain derivation, the most likely one being *harabati*, an Ottoman Turkish word meaning, approximately, "privileged drunkard", and searches for the birth of *rem-*

*Tassos Khalkias** (CD, EMI 74321 318232). #4 of the long out-of-print "Great Solos" series, this re-released CD features the master clarinettist at his most heartfelt.

Petros Loukas Khalkias *Dhromi tis Psykhis* (CD, Papingo/BMG-Ariola 74321 318232) and *Miroloyia keh Yirizmata* (LP and CD, Lyra 4717). Technically impeccable updating of the clarinet tradition, but with traditional backing *koumpanía* of *laoúto*, *vióli* and percussion; the Papingo disc is more orchestrated and easier to find.

Irini Konitopoulou-Legaki *Athanata Nisiotika 1* (Tzina-Astir 1020). A 1978 warhorse, beloved of bus drivers across the islands, though the Konitopoulos family hails from Náxos.

Yiorgos Konitopoulos and Clan *Thalassa keh Paradhosi* (EMI 14C 064 71253). Standard taverna or party fare throughout the islands; slicker than *Athanata Nisiotika* but no worse for it.

Lesvos Aiolis (CD, Crete University Press 9/10). Songs and dances from the most Anatolian-influenced of the east Aegean islands.

Thanassis Moraitis *Arvanitic Songs* (FM-Pella 652). Re-issued 1988 recording of a concert sung in *arvanítika* – the medieval dialect of Albanian spoken by thousands around Attica, Évvia and the Argo-Saronic. Varied, and better than many such ethnographic reconstructions.

Yannis Parios *Ta Nisiotika Vol 1* (CD, Minos 430/431) and Vol 2 (CD, Minos 1017/1018).

Parios sparked a renewal of interest in *nisiotikó* –traditional island music – with the first of these two discs done a decade apart, each accompanied by members of the Konitopoulos clan. Maybe not the most "authentic" versions, but easy on the ear, and both went platinum – Volume 1 with sales of nearly a million.

Domna Samiou *Seryiani me tin Domna Samiou* (LP, Sirios 86003/CD, Minos 7243 4 89781 27). Fine 1986 session with the inveterate collector, singer and revivalist – arguably her best since the 1973 *Ekhe Yia Panayia* (LP/CD EMI Columbia 14C 062 70115). Her more recent *Domna Samiou* (CD, Minerva CD 213) may be easier to find, and features several Tassos Khalkias clarinet solos.

Seryiani sta Nisia Mas (MBI 10371/10372). Excellent compilation of various pre-1960s *nisiótika* hits and artists. Highlight of Volume 1 is Emilia Hatzidhaki's rendition of *Bratsera*.

Aristeidhis Vasilaris *Floyera* (FM 678). Third issue of FM Records' 12-volume series profiling Greek folk instruments in turn. Excellent documentation, including interview with Vasilaris.

Savina Yiannatou *Anixi sti Saloniki/Spring in Salonika* (LP/CD, Lyra 4765). Recreations of Ladino Sephardic songs, the latest of several such efforts, with Middle Eastern instrumental backing; Savina's voice can take some getting used to, however. The CD has four extra cuts and full notes.

bétika must be conducted in the Asia Minor of the last years of the Ottoman empire as well as in Greece proper.

Most outsiders equate Greek music with the **bouzoúki**, a long-necked, fretted, three-stringed lute derived, like the Turkish *saz* and *baglamás*, from the Byzantine *tanbur*. Early in this century, however, only a small proportion of Greek mainland musicians used it. At the same time, across the Aegean in Smyrna and Constantinople, musical cafés, owned and staffed almost entirely by Greeks, Jews and Armenians before 1923, had become popular. Groups usually featured a violinist, a *sandoúri* player and a female vocalist, who usually jingled castanets and danced on stage. The metrically free, improvisational singing style was known as *café-amanés* or just **amanés** (plural *amanédhes*), after both the setting and the frequent repetition of the exclamation *aman aman*

(alas, alas), used both for its sense and to fill time while the performers searched their imaginations for more explicit lyrics.

Despite the sparse instrumentation, this was an elegant, riveting performance style requiring considerable skill, harking back to similar vocalization in Central Asia. Some of its greatest exponents included **Andonis "Dalgas"** (Wave) **Dhiamantidhis**, so nicknamed for the undulations in his voice; **Roza Eskenazi**, a Jew who grew up in Constantinople; her contemporary **Rita Abatzi**, from Smyrna; **Marika Papagika**, from the island of Kós, who emigrated to America where she made her career; **Agapios Tomboulis**, a tanbur and oud player of Armenian background; and **Dhimitris "Salonikiyé" Semsis**, a master fiddler from Strumitsa in northern Macedonia. The cross section of origins for these performers gives a good idea of the range of cosmopolitan influences brought to bear in the formative years of *rembétika*.

The 1923 **exchange of populations** was a key event in the history of *rembétika*, resulting in the influx to Greece of over a million Asia Minor Greeks, many of whom settled in shanty towns around Athens, Pireás and Thessaloníki. The musicians, like most of the other refugees, were, in comparison to the Greeks of the host country, extremely sophisticated; many were highly educated, could read and compose music, and had even been unionized in the towns of Asia Minor. Typical of these were **Panayiotis Toundas**, a Smyrniote composer who after arrival in Athens eventually became head of the Greek division of first Odeon and then Columbia Records, succeeding Semsis in that capacity, and **Vangelis Papazoglou**, another composer who failed to survive World War II. It was galling for them to initially live on the periphery of the new society in poverty and degradation; most had lost all they had in the hasty evacuation, and many ordinary refugees, from inland Anatolia, could speak only Turkish. In their misery they sought relief in another long-standing Ottoman institution, the *tekés* or hashish den.

In the **tekédhes** of Pireás, Athens and Thessaloníki, a few men would sit on the floor around a charcoal brazier, passing around a *nargilés* (hookah) filled with hashish. One of them might improvise a tune on the *baglamás* or the *bouzoúki* and begin to sing. The words, either his own or those of the other *dervíses* ("dervishes" – several rembetic terms were a burlesque of those of mystical Islamic tradition), would be heavily laced with insider's argot, in the manner of the Harlem jive of the same era. As the *taxími* (long, studied introduction) was completed, one of the smokers might rise and begin to dance a **zeïbékiko**, named after the *zeybeks*, a warrior caste of western Anatolia. It would be a slow, intense, introverted performance following an unusual metre (9/8), not for the benefit of others but for himself.

By the early 1930s, several important male musicians had emerged from the *tekés* culture: the beguiling voiced **Stratos Payioumtzis**, Anestis Delias (aka **Artemis**), who was to die during the World War II occupation, the only *rembétis* to actually succumb to drug addiction;

Yiorgos Tsoros, better known as **Batis**, an indifferent musician but generous and engaging; and **Markos Vamvakaris**, the most famous of this quartet. Though an indisputable master of the *bouzoúki*, he protested that his voice, ruined perhaps from too much hash-smoking, was no good for singing. But he soon bowed to encouragement and his gravelly, unmistakable sound set the standard for male vocals over the next decade. His only close peer as an instrumentalist was **Ioannis Papaioannou,** with whom he occasionally played, whose sometime vocalist **Rena Dalia** recorded a few famous cuts in Turkish – a practice which stopped altogether after the 1950s, with the dying off of the audience that understood such lyrics, and the first Cyprus crises.

This "Golden Age" of *rembétika* – as indeed it was, despite the unhappy lives of many performers, and necessarily limited audience – was short lived. The association of the music with a drug-laced underworld would prove its undoing. After the imposition of the Metaxas dictatorship in 1936, harder-core musicians, with their uncompromising lyrics and lifestyles, were blackballed by the recording industry; anti-hashish laws were systematically enforced, and police harassment of the *tekédhes* was stepped up. Even possession of a *bouzoúki* or *baglamás* became a criminal offence, and several of the big names did time in jail. Others went to Thessaloníki, where the police chief Vassilis Mouskoundis was a big fan of the music and allowed its practitioners to smoke in private.

For a while, such persecution – and the official encouragement of tangos and frothy Italianate love songs, which always had a much wider public – failed to dim the enthusiasm of the **mánges** (roughly translatable as "wide boys" or "hep cats") who frequented the hash dens. Beatings or prison terms were taken in their stride; time behind bars could be used, as it always had been around the Aegean, to make *skaptó* (dug-out) instruments. A *baglamás* could easily be fashioned from a gourd cut in half or even a tortoise shell (the sound box), a piece of wood (the neck), catgut (frets), and wire for strings. Jail songs were composed and became popular in the underworld. The excerpt below, loosely translated from the 1930s argot, is a typical, much-recorded sample:

ly Lakhanádhes ("The Pickpockets")
Down in Lemonádhika there was a ruckus.
They caught two pickpockets who acted
innocent.
They took 'em to the slammer in handcuffs
They'll get a beating if they don't cough up
the loot.
Don't beat us, coppers, you know very well.
This is our job, and don't ask for bribes.
We lift purses and wallets so we can
Have a regular rest in jail.
                                    Vangelis Papazoglou

Moreover, the *rembétes* suffered from the disapproval of the puritanical Left as well as the puritanical Right; the growing Communist Party of the 1930s considered the music and its habitués hopelessly decadent and apolitical. An anecdote relates that when Vamvakaris was about to join the leftist resistance army ELAS in 1944, he was admonished not to sing his own material "lest it corrupt the heroic proletariat". The Left preferred *andártika* (Soviet-style revolutionary anthems), though **Sotiria Bellou**, a *rembétissa* (female rembetic musician) and active communist whose career began late in the 1940s, was a conspicuous exception.

Bellou was one of several important female vocalists to accompany **Vassilis Tsitsanis**, the most significant composer and *bouzoúki* player to emerge after Vamvakaris; the others were **Marika Ninou** and **Ioanna Yiorgakopoulou**, the latter also a composer in her own right. From Tríkala in Thessaly, Tsitsanis abandoned law studies to cut his first record in 1936 for Odeon, directed by rembetic composer **Spyros Peristeris**. The war interrupted his – and everyone else's – recording career from late 1940 until late 1945; when it, and the Civil War that followed, ended, a huge backlog of songs composed during the occupation awaited the studios. The traumatic decade between 1939 and 1948 had erased the fashion for *mastouriaká* or songs about getting stoned; more than ever, audiences instead craved vaguely Neapolitan melodies and words about love. Tsitsanis was happy to oblige, and for the first time *rembétika* enjoyed something like a mass following, but his love lyrics were anything but insipid, and the demoralization of the war years prompted him

to also compose darker works, most famous of these *Synnefiazmeni Kyriakí:*

Cloudy Sunday, you seem like my heart.
Which is always overcast, Christ and Holy
Virgin!
You're a day like the one I lost my joy.
Cloudy Sunday, you make my heart bleed.
When I see you rainy, I can't rest easy.
You blacken my life and I sigh deeply.

Although Tsitsanis performed almost up to his death in 1984 – his funeral in Athens was attended by nearly a quarter of a million people – 1953 effectively marked the end of the original rembetic style. In that year, Manolis Khiotis added a fourth string to the *bouzoúki*, allowing it to be tuned tonally rather than modally; electrical amplification to reach larger audiences, maudlin lyrics and over-orchestration were not long in following. Performances in huge, barn-like clubs, also called *bouzoúkia*, became debased and vulgarized. Virtuoso *bouzoúki* players, assisted by kewpie-doll-type female vocalists, became immensely rich: the so-called *arkhondorembétes* like Khiotis and **Yiorgos Zambetas**. The clubs themselves were clip-joints where Athenians paid large sums to break plates and watch dancing whose flashy steps and gyrations were a travesty of the simple dignity and precise, synchronized footwork of old.

Ironically, the original *rembétika* material was rescued from oblivion by the colonels' junta. Along with dozens of other features of Greek culture, *rembétika* verses were banned. The younger generation coming of age under the dictatorship took a closer look at the forbidden fruit and derived solace, and deeper meanings, from the nominally apolitical lyrics. When the junta fell in 1974 – even a little before – there was an outpouring of re-issued recordings of the old masters. Initially these were merely 33rpm pressings of the original 78s, with no re-editing or liner notes, but the industry – prompted in part by demand overseas – has lately resorted to higher production values, though little in the way of startlingly new finds.

Over the next decade live *rembétika* also enjoyed a revival, beginning with a clandestine 1979 club near the old Fix brewery in Athens,

REMBÉTIKA DISCOGRAPHY

Early rembétika – anthologies

Authentic USA Rembetika, Vols. 1–4 (CD, Lyra 4644 and 4635-4637). The title is a wild misnomer, unless original 78s were released first in the USA, as these feature all the usual suspects, already well established in Greece. Volume 4 is devoted to songs about tuberculosis, the scourge of Greece until the 1950s.

*Amanedhes (LP, Margo 8222/CD, Minos 724383443529). Includes some early cuts made in Istanbul, with Gypsy clarinettists appearing on several tracks.

*The Greek Archives (CD, FM Records, Greece). Recent and luxuriously packaged; the material, uneven but generally worthy, is arranged in two series, each disc devoted to a song type or featured artist. Passing muster so far from the first series are #1 (*Rembetico Song in America 1920–1940*, Archives 627); #6 (*Women of the Rembetico Song*, Archives 632); #7 (*Unknown Smyrna 1922–1940*, Archives 633); #8 (*Armenians, Jews, Turks & Gipsies* [NB as portrayed, not performing], Archives 634); and #9 (*Constantinople in Old Recordings*, Archives 635). From the second, unnumbered batch, *Anthology of Rémbetiko* [sic] *Songs 1933–1940* (FM 654), *Anthology of Smyrnean Songs 1920–1938* (FM 658) and *Songs of the Sea* (FM661) are wonderful.

*Greek Oriental: Smyrneic-Rembetic Songs and Dances (LP/CD, Polylyric 9033, US). Superb collection spanning the 1920s to early 1930s, with Roza, Rita, Marika Papagika and Dhimitris Semsis. Good sleeve notes; the CD version has six extra tracks.

*Greek Oriental Rembétika 1911–37 (Arhoolie, US). A worthwhile compilation, with Roza

Eskenazi, Andonis Dalgas, and many more. Includes Roza's *Why I Smoke Cocaine*.

*Historic Urban Folk Songs from Greece (Rounder CD 1079, US/Direct Distribution, UK). The above-cited artists, plus many more on terrific selections, mostly from the 1930s.

*Lost Homelands: The Smyrnaic Song in Greece, 1928–1933 (CD, Heritage HT27). Lots of Dalgas, the great rivals Rita Abatzi and Roza Eskenazi, plus instrumental improvisations; as usual for this label, top sound quality and good notes.

*Iy Megali tou Rembetikou (LP, Margo/CD, Minos; Greece). A collection of over twenty albums, but only the first ten are worth it, and available on CD. The best are #1 (*Early Performers*, CD Minos 4 80193 25), #3 (*Vassilis Tsitsanis*, LP Margo 8150), #4 (*Ioannis Papaioannou*, LP Margo 8152), #7 (*Stratos Payoumtzis*, LP Margo 8217), #8 (*Kostas Roukounas*, CD Minos 4 80267 29) and #9 (*Spyros Peristeris* composer, mostly Markos Vamvakris playing, LP Margo 8219).

*Rembétika in Pireaus 1933–1937 (Heritage CDs HT 26 and 30). The gang that played – and smoked – together, in top form: Markos, Batis, Stratos and Artemis, plus lesser-known figures.

*Iy Rembetiki Istoria (LP, EMI Regal 14C 034 70364-70380/CD, Minos). Six-volume series which was among the first material re-issued after the junta fell, and still a good start to a collection. #1, #2 and #4 are Smyrneïc/Asia Minor songs; #5 is the weakest disc.

*Smyrneïka 1927–1935 (MBI 10557). Duplicates parts of the Polylyric and Rounder discs; worth snagging in Greece only if you can't find the other two.

---

whose street credentials were validated when it was raided and closed by the police. Today, however, the fashion has long since peaked, and only a bare handful of clubs and bands remain from the dozens which made their appearance between 1978 and 1986.

LAÏKO: SON OF REMBETIKA

The modification of the *bouzoúki* gave rise to the dominant urban style of the 1960s and 1970s: **laïko**, roughly translatable as "popular" music, and subdivided into *elafrolaïkó* (light pop) and *laïkodhimotikó* (so-called urban

folk). As apolitical and escapist as its predecessor, *laïko* infuriated the clandestine Left but remained immensely popular among the masses. Prominent stars and composers included the late **Stratos Dhionysiou, Dhimitris Mitropanos, Apostolos Kaldaras**, and the late **Manolis Angelopoulos**. The mid-1970s to the present has seen a new generation arise, including **Khristos Nikolopoulos, Eleni Vitali, Makis Khristodoulopoulos** and the versatile female stars **Haris Alexiou, Glykeria** and **Dhimitra Galani**, whose range – like that of Yiorgos Dalaras – extends to cov-

Early rembétika – single artists

*Rita Abatzi 1933–1938 (CD, Heritage HT 36). With outstanding accompanists and notes, this has the edge on *Rita Ambatzi I* (Minos 7 24348 040923 3), part of the Arkheio series in Greece. The only discs so far devoted exclusively to this refugee Smyrnean, with a huskier, more textured voice than her peer Roza Eskenazi.

*Dalgas Andonios Dhiamandidhis 1928–1933 (Heritage CD HT 34). The best disc devoted entirely to the gifted *amanés* artist; *Periorizmena Antitypa ya Syllektes* (LP, Lyra 4621, Greece) is a second choice. Dalgas also appears on *Great Voices of Constantinople* (Rounder CD1113), trading tracks with the great Turkish vocalist Hafiz Burhan, though the title is misleading as all the Dalgas cuts were recorded in Athens.

Anestis Dhelias 1912–1944 (Lyra 4642, Greece). Mostly *mastouriaká* (hash songs) by the man known as Artemis, performed by the Gang of Four; search bargain bins in Greece.

*Roza Eskenazi 1933–1936 (CD, Heritage HT35). Superb renditions with her usual sidemen Semsis, Tomboulis, plus Lambros on *kanonáki*; extremely varied selection of standards and rare gems make this the best of several collections available.

*Marika Papagika *Greek Popular and Rebetic Music in New York 1918–1929* (CD, Alma Criolla, Berkeley California, ACCD802). Her best work, with husband Gus backing on *sandoúri*; includes a superb, rare duet with Marika Kastrouni.

*Vangelis Papazoglou 1897–1943 (CD, Lyra 4713-14). Double album of his compositions from the 1920s and 1930s, sung by most of the top stars of the era, including Stellakis, Roza Eskenazi, Kostas Roukounas and Rita Abatzi. Marred by poor sound quality, but several versions of his classic *Iy Lakhanadhes*.

Later and contemporary rembétika

*Sotiriou Bellou 1946–1956 (LP, Margo 8163/CD, Minos 4 80217 24). Virtually the only disc under her name without the electric backing of later years; includes the original of the classic *Ta Kavourakia*. #5 in *Iy Megali tou Rembetikou* series.

Marika Ninou *Stou Tzimi tou Khondrou/At Jimmy the Fat's* (LP, Venus-Tzina1053). Poor sound quality since it was a clandestine wire recording, but still a classic. Ninou performs live with Tsitsanis in the early 1950s, including two cuts in Turkish.

*Marika Ninou/Vassilis Tsitsanis (LP, Philips 7116 819/CD, Philips 6483004). Not as soulful as the Venus disc, but a far better sound and more than adequate renditions of their favourites, including *Synnefiazmeni Kyriaki* and the gut-wrenching *Yennithika*.

Vasilis Tsitsanis *Yia Panta 1937–1940* vols 1 and 2 (LP, EMI-HMV 401026, 401027 Greece); 1938–1955 (LP, EMI 70193). First vinyl discs of two multi-volume series; mostly Stratos on vocals.

*Vassilis Tsitsanis 1936–1946 (CD 1124, Rounder US/Direct UK). A fine first disc to begin a Tsitsanis collection; again mostly male singers, but includes his reputed first recording, a *mastouriaká* with Yioryia Mittaki, and good notes.

*Ioanna Yiorgakopoulou *Iy Rembetissa* (CD, EMI 4 80014 29). First and best of four identically titled albums featuring this unjustly neglected singer-composer.

*Stavros Xarhakos *Rembetiko* (CD, CBS 70245). Soundtrack to the namesake film, available as a double LP or, in shorter form, on one CD. Virtually the only "original" rembétika to be composed in the last forty years, with lyrics by poet Nikos Gatsos.

---

ers of folk songs and participation in the most contemporary ventures imaginable (see below).

Any summary of *laïko* singers would be incomplete without **Yiorgos (George) Dalaras**, a musical phenomenon in Greece since he made his 1968 vinyl debut with the folk-rock composer Manos Loïzos. Born in 1952, the son of a Pireás *rembétika* player, Dalaras has featured on over sixty records, spanning the range of Greek music from Anatolian and *dhimotiká* material, the works of Theodhorakis, Hatzidhakis and Markopoulos, and – more

recently – collaborations with the flamenco guitarist Paco de Lucia and American blues star Al Di Meola.

Something of a national institution, Dalaras has always – even during the junta years – remained a fierce supporter of popular struggles, with benefit concerts for various worthy causes. In his commitment to quality musicianship. he has scrupulously avoided the banalities of the *bouzoúki* pop scene. In Greece, his concerts pack 80,000 at a time into football stadiums – rather more than the football teams themselves – and produce rivers of tears.

LAÏKO DISCOGRAPHY

*Haris Alexiou From a huge discography, start with *Ta Tragoudhia tis Haroulas* (LP/CD, Minos 349) and the more recent *Dhi'Evkhon* (LP/CD, Philips 512869).

*Yiorgos Dalaras *Latin* (Minos 671/672). A 1987 team-up with Al Di Meola, for which Dalaras taught himself enough Spanish to sing passably; nearly half a million copies sold. *Mikra Asia* (Minos 154) was his first hit record in 1972, and has worn well.

*The Dance of Heaven's Ghosts (EMI 7243 8 55644 20, UK). Well-balanced compilation of the most accessible (and slick) *laïko*, with samples of Haris Alexiou, Yiannis Parios, Eleni Vitali and others.

*Kostas Hatzis and Haris Alexiou *Iy Alexiou Tragoudhaei Hadzis* (CD, Minos 1002/1003). Hatzis by himself is disappointing; but with Alexiou, singing in Greek or (on two cuts) Romany, it's Greek flamenco.

ÉNTEKHNO AND NÉO KÝMA MUSIC

One meaning of *éntekhno* in Greek is "art" composition, where instruments and melodic elements of authentic folk or rembetic music are juxtaposed in ways never heard in their natural environment. In this sense it remains rooted in popular tradition, and its most famous exemplars, exact contemporaries Mikis Theodhorakis and Manos Hatzidhakis, began working in the late 1950s. **Theodhorakis'** international reputation is perhaps a bit inflated, due to his overplayed and over-covered 1965 soundtrack for *Zorba the Greek*; indeed soon after this he shunned Byzantine/folk/rembetic influence completely in favour of quasi-classical, overtly political symphonic works and film soundtracks dictated by his Communist affiliation. (In 1989, he suddenly shifted right to serve as a Minister Without Portfolio in a *Néa Dhimokratía* government, before quitting politics altogether in disgust). Perhaps his most accessible work remains his 1964 settings of poetry by Odysseas Elytis, his 1966 and 1974 sessions with the *Khorodhia Trikalon* (the Trikala Choir) and numerous recordings with vocalist **Maria Farandouri**.

Hatzidhakis, who died in June 1994, mostly steered clear of political statements;

instead he launched, during the 1980s, his own record label Sirios to provide a forum for various non-mainstream musicians. Like Theodorakis, his own compositional weakness was a tendency towards quasi-symphonic, highly arranged instrumentation; like his peer, he was haunted by soundtracks composed for various movies starring Melina Mercouri, most notably *Never on Sunday* (1960). A soundtrack – in this case for *Ta Kokkina Fanaria/The Red Lanterns* (1963) proved the big break for **Stavros Xarkhakos**, who followed this up twenty years later with best-selling music for the film *Rembetiko*; indeed *éntekhno* seems ideally suited for the genre. Xarkhakos' exact contemporary, **Yiannis Markopoulos**, also did the all-but-obligatory soundtrack (*Who Pays the Ferryman*, 1978) but otherwise is perhaps the most interesting and consistently Greek-sounding of these four composers to emerge from the 1960s, not least in the range of quality artists – **Xylouris, Dalaras, Tania Tsanaklidhou, Kharalambos Garganourakis** – whom he has persuaded to sing for him.

A related offshot, **néo kýma** (New Wave) music emerged in small Athenian clubs during the early 1960s. It was essentially a blend of watered-down *éntekhno* with French *chanson*

ÉNTEKHNO AND NÉO KÝMA DISCOGRAPHY

*Khristodhoulos Khalaris *Dhrossoulites* (CD, Minos 7243 480179 25). Still his most riveting work, with lyrics by Nikos Gatsos and vocals by Khrysanthos and Dhimitra Galani.

*Yannis Markopoulos *Thitia* (LP/CD, EMI 14C062 70123) with Manos Eleftheriou and Tania Tsanaklidhou and the best selling *Seryiani ston Kosmo* (LP, Minos 350) with Yiorgos Dalaras are commonly reckoned his best outings. *Anexartita* (CD Minos EMI 7243 834897 25) is an excellent 1975 date with top vocalists on each track, plus Markopoulos live with the original version of his wrenching *Iy Elladha*.

*Mikis Theodhorakis *To Axion Esti* (LP/CD, Columbia). The setting of Elytis, with Grigoris Bithikotsis on vocals. The four 1974 sessions with the Khorodhia Trikalon may still be around on CD (Olympic 1099-1102).

and Bob Dylan-ish ballads. Like *rembétika* venues, most of the *néo kýma* boites were closed down during the 1967–74 military junta, and failed to revive thereafter.

Instead, during the late 1970s, the Communist Party attempted to "raise the consciousness of the masses" by updating *andártika* from the 1940s as the preferred popular music, lacing it with elements of Latin American *nuevo canción* and Kurt Weill, but to no avail; *laïko* was too deeply rooted, and songs with heavy messages remained a minority taste. In different guises, this is a repeated tale in Greece: a self-appointed Westernized cultural elite unsuccessfully attempting, by fiat, to banish "low-class" oriental habits.

THE GUITARIST-COMPOSERS

One of the first significant musicians to challenge the supremacy of the *bouzoúki* was Thessaloníki-born **Dhionysis Savvopoulos**, who appeared on the scene in 1966 with a maniacal, rasping voice and elliptical, angst-ridden lyrics, his persona rounded out by shoulder-length hair and outsized glasses. Stylistically, his early work is impossible to pigeonhole: equal parts twisted Macedonian folk, Bob Dylan, and Frank Zappa at his jazziest would be a rough approximation. Because his material was not overtly political, Savvopoulos was one of the few "protest" artists able to per-

form under the junta, and became something of a consolation and password to the generation coming of age under it. Despite a modest discography compared to the *éntekhno* composers, it's difficult to overestimate his effect on subsequent artists. Credit (or blame) for much Greek rock and fusion jazz can be laid at Savvopoulos' door; during his brief tenure as head of Lyra records, and later as an independent producer, he gave breaks to numerous younger artists.

Among Savvopoulos' protégés and spiritual heirs, the first was **Nikos Xydhakis**, whose landmark 1978 pressing, *Iy Ekdhikisi tis Yiftias* (The Revenge of Gypsydom) really expressed a backlash of *laïko* culture (*laïko*, in Greek, can mean "common" or "low-class" as well as "popular") against the pretentiousness of some recent *éntekhno* and "politically correct" music. The spirited, defiant lyrics – with Savvopoulos singing the opening track – and highly rhythmic melodies were both homage to and send-up of the *laïko* music beloved by truck-drivers, Gypsy or otherwise. Both artists have gone on to pursue successful independent careers, Xydhakis in the somewhat repetitive mode that *laïko* fans dismiss as *koultouriárika* ("culture stuff"), not quite as high-brow as *éntekhno* but too eclectic or arty to be really rootsy. In 1987, Xydhakis collaborated with Ross Daly (see below) and vocalist **Eleftheria Arvanitaki** on *Konda sti Dhoxa*

THE GUITARIST-COMPOSERS DISCOGRAPHY

****Sokratis Malamas** *Kyklos* (LP, Lyra 4744) embodies his latest style; the earlier *Tis Meras keh tis Nykhtas* (LP, Lyra 4654) is more in the mode of Papazoglou.

Notis Mavroudhis and Nikos Houliaras *Ekdhromi* (LP, Zodiac 88002). Rare, guitar-voice duo: one side contains haunting versions of Epirot folk songs, the other original pieces. Worth scouring the flea market for.

****Nikos Papazoglou** *Kharatsi* (LP, Lyra 3369) mixes his rock and introspective styles; the 1990 offering *Synerga* (LP, Lyra 4559, Greece) is gentler, even mystical.

****Dhionysis Savvopoulos** Though not his first disc, the 1970 *Ballos* (LP, Lyra 3573) established his position irrevocably; *Dheka Hronia Kommatia* (LP, Lyra 3715/CD, Lyra 0081) is a retrospective anthology of the artist's first (some say best) decade; yet

Trapezakia Exo (LP, Lyra 3360/CD, Lyra 0041), with *Eleftheria Arvanitaki*, is a personal favourite.

****Nikos Xydhakis and Eleftheria Arvanitaki** *Konda sti Dhoxa mia Stigmi* (Lyra, Greece/CD Lyra 0039). One of the best Greek discs of the late 1980s, with haunting Xydhakis arrangements and compositions; their 1991 follow-up *Tenedos* (LP, Lyra 4590) was less even but had the wonderful single *Tsigaro Ego sto Stoma mou dhen Evala Oute Ena*.

****Nikos Xydhakis and Friends** *Iy Ekdhikisi tis Yiftias* (LP, Lyra 3308/CD, Lyra 0019. Groundbreaking recording of the late 1970s, still much loved (and sold) in Greece; its follow-up *Ta Dhithen* (LP, Lyra 3320/CD, Lyra 0019) with Manolis Rassoulis is nearly its equal, containing the single *Iy Manges Dhen Yparkhoun Pia* covered by Haris Alexiou.

mia Stigmi, a particularly successful blend of folk, Byzantine and Asia Minor styles.

A Thessalonian like Savvopoulous, **Nikos Papazoglou** is a more varied songwriter than Xydhakis, effortlessly filling stadiums on his tours. His material, also based on *laïki* and folk, often has a harder electric-rock edge, though his 1990 *Synerga* can match Xydhakis for introspection and orientalism. A younger singer to look out for is **Sokratis Malamas**, who started out with Papazoglou but whose mature style is more orchestrated.

Other guitarist-songwriters who broke out of the *bouzoúki* mould in the mid-1960s, most still with active careers, are the Gypsy protest singer **Kostas Hatzis**, **Notis Mavroudhis** (often heard in Athens classical concert halls as well) and **Arletta**. Such a list makes it clear that Greece has an established tradition of guitar playing independent of any Latin American influences.

CONTEMPORARY MUSIC

With the stranglehold of the *bouzoúki* broken, the way was clear by the 1980s for even more radical experiments – some keeping faith with Greek traditions, others unabashedly Westernized. Out of northern Greece came **Khimerini Kolymvites**, a group of architects led by Aryiris Bakirtzis, whose eponymous first album has acquired enduring cult status in the years since its 1981 release. Mainland *laïko*,

folk and even a few stray island influences meld with rich, drunken harmonies drawn out on both bowed and plucked strings.

Other composers of the decade included **Thanos Mikroutsikos**, briefly Minister of Culture after the death of Melina Mercouri, who despite his high-brow *éntekhno* leanings has worked with Alexiou, Galani and Dalaras. **Lina Nikolakopoulou**, together with her frequent collaborator **Stamatis Kraounakis** made a splash in 1985 with *Kykloforo keh Oploforo*, a thoughtful, if somewhat slick, exploration of the boundaries between rock, jazz-cabaret and *éntekhno*. She also co-composed, with Mikroutsikos, the bestselling *Krataiei Khronia Avti iy Kolonia*, and its huge hit single *Mia Pista apo Fosforo*.

BYZANTINE, ANATOLIAN AND FOLK REVIVAL GROUPS

Another Greek approach in the late 1970s and early 1980s was to combine **folk** and **Byzantine traditions**. Long before his unfortunate ventures into speculative Byzantine song, instrument maker and arranger **Khristodhoulos Khalaris** followed up a version of the Cretan epic *Erotokritos*, featuring Nikos Xylouris and Tania Tsanaklidhou, with the riveting *Dhrossoulites* that introduced **Khrysanthos**, a male singer with a distinctive high-register voice, on alternate tracks with Dhimitra Galani.

Ottoman – rather than Byzantine – Constantinople was the inspiration of **Vosporos**, a group coordinated in Istanbul from 1986 to 1992 by **Nikiforos Metaxas** to explore Ottoman classical, devotional and popular music. Their specific appeal and pertinence to Grecophiles was demonstrated by their first album, subtitled "Greek Composers of The City" (ie Constantinople) and showcasing the contribution of Greek and other non-Turkish musicians to the Ottoman courtly tradition. Since then the group has been reconstituted as **Fanari tis Anatolis**, in which Greek vocalist Vassiliki Papayeoryiou and Turkish singer Melda Kurt alternate varied Greek material with Anatolian folk lyrics or mystical Aleví ballads.

Ross Daly, whose interests and style overlap somewhat with Vosporos, also merits catching on disc or live – in Athens clubs or on tour. English-born but Irish by background, Daly plays a dozen traditional instruments and has absorbed influences not only from Crete, where

---

CONTEMPORARY MUSIC DISCOGRAPHY

***Khimerini Kolymvites** (self-produced, 1981). First and best of four discs by a group of architects from Thessaloníki and Kavála, with surreal lyrics and rich melodies.

***Stamatis Kraounakis and Lina Nikolakopoulou** *Kykloforo keh Oploforo* (LP, Polydor 827589). The most successful of their several collaborations.

***Thanos Mikroutsikos, Lina Nikolakopoulou, Haris Alexiou** *Krataei Khronia Avti iy Kolonia* (Minos 852). Uneven 1990 effort, but Haris is wonderful as ever; the single *Mia Pista apo Fosforo* caught on across the Aegean, with a Turkish cover version by Sezen Aksu.

BYZANTINE, ANATOLIAN AND FOLK REVIVAL GROUPS DISCOGRAPHY

*Dhynameis tou Egeou *Anatoliko Parathiro* (CD, Sirios 89004). Last and best recording from five folk revivalists now working independently.

*Ross Daly *Selected Works* (CD, BMG Ariola 70205 or Riente 01, Germany). The best place to start, a compilation from many earlier, out-of-print albums (a chronic problem with Daly's work). Other goodies, still available, include *Ross Daly* (LP, RCA-BMG 70184), *Khori* (LP/CD RCA-BMG 70194) and *An-Ki* (RCA-BMG 27021), with Iranian percussionist Jamshid Chemirani.

*Vosporos *Greek Composers of Constantinople* (LP/CD, EMI 064 1701421). First, 1987 exploration of the medieval Constantinopolitan dimension of Greek music; also notable is *Live at the Palas Theatre* (LP, Lyra-Om 51/52). Since 1994, balanced vocals in Greek and Turkish have become pre-eminent, without a loss of instrumental virtuosity and innovation; it's hard to choose between *Ellinika keh Asikika* (CD, MBI 10608-2) and *Valkania Oneira/Balkan Dreams* (CD, MBI 10645).

he was long resident, but from throughout the Near East. Alone or with a group, he has recorded strikingly contemporary interpretations of traditional pieces, as well as original compositions.

A handful of other groups have attempted to rework folk music, from the islands and Smyrna. The first of these was the late-1980s band **Dhynameis tou Egeou**, who – impeded by some ill-advised use of bells, sitar and Egyptian *ney* – never realized their full potential. Its individual members Nikos Grapsas, Khristos Tsiamoulis, Mikhalis Klapakis, Petros Tambouris

and Yiannis Zevgolis have now been freed to accompany musicians such as Khronis Aïdhonidhis. **Domna Samiou**, a sort of musical equivalent to the Dora Stratou dance group, has led more rigorously authentic, floating groups since the late 1960s. Still active in her 70s, Domna sings both well known and obscure material in various corners of the country and attracts like-minded musicians dedicated to the preservation of traditional music.

Marc Dubin,
with contributions by George Pissalides

BOOKS

Where separate editions exist in the UK and USA, publishers are detailed below in the form UK publisher; US publisher, unless the publisher is the same in both countries. Where books are published in one country – or Athens – only, this follows the publisher's name.

O/p signifies an out-of-print but still highly recommended book; the recommended Greek-specialist book dealers often have stocks of these. University Press is abbreviated as UP.

TRAVEL AND GENERAL ACCOUNTS

MODERN ACCOUNTS

Kevin Andrews *The Flight of Ikaros* (Penguin o/p). Intense and compelling account of an educated, sensitive archeologist loose in the backcountry during the aftermath of the Civil War.

Gerald Durrell *My Family and Other Animals* (Penguin). Sparkling, very funny anecdotes of Durrell's childhood on Corfu – and his passion for the island's fauna: toads, tortoises, bats, scorpions, the lot.

Lawrence Durrell *Prospero's Cell* (Faber & Faber; Penguin o/p); *Reflections on a Marine Venus* (Faber & Faber/Penguin); *The Greek Islands* (Faber & Faber/Penguin, the former o/p). The elder Durrell lived before the Second World war with Gerald and the family on Corfu, the subject of *Prospero's Cell*. *Marine Venus* recounts Lawrence's 1945–47 experiences and impressions of Rhodes and other Dodecanese islands. *Greek Islands* is a lyrical but rather dated and occasionally bilious guide to the archipelagos.

John Gill *Stars over Paxos* (Pavilion, UK). The author of the *Rough Guide to Corfu* muses on life in the Ionian islands.

Sheelagh Kanneli *Earth and Water: A Marriage in Kalamata* (Efstathiadhis, Athens). A classic account of that rare thing – a foreign woman integrating successfully into provincial Greek society. Rich in period detail of pre-tourism and pre-earthquake Kalamáta.

Patrick Leigh Fermor *Roumeli* (Penguin); *Mani* (Penguin; Peter Smith). Leigh Fermor is an aficionado of the vanishing minorities, relict communities and disappearing customs of rural Greece. These two books, written in the late 1950s and early 1960s, are not so much travelogues as scholarship interspersed with strange and hilarious yarns. Though overwritten in parts, they remain among the best books written on any aspect of modern Greece.

Peter Levi *The Hill of Kronos* (Harvill, o/p; Dutton, o/p). Beautifully observed landscape, monuments and eventually politics as Levi describes how he is drawn into resistance to the colonels' junta. *A Bottle in the Shade: Journeys in the Peloponnese* (Sinclair Stevenson, UK) describes his return, three decades later, to his old haunts, and proves less engaged and more ruminant.

Henry Miller *The Colossus of Maroussi* (Minerva, o/p; New Directions). Corfu and the soul of Greece in 1939, with Miller, completely in his element, at his most inspired.

James Pettifer *The Greeks: the Land and People since the War* (Penguin; Viking). A useful, if spottily edited introduction to contemporary Greece – and its recent past. Pettifer charts the state of the nation's politics, food, family life, religion, tourism, and other topics.

Patricia Storace *Dinner with Persephone* (Granta; Pantheon). A New-York poet, resident for a year in Athens (with forays to the provinces) puts the country's psyche on the couch, while avoiding the same position with various predatory males. Storace has a sly sense of humour, and in showing how permeated – and imprisoned – Greece is by its imagined past, gets it right 95 percent of the time. Excellent.

Sarah Wheeler *An Island Apart* (Abacus, UK). Entertaining chronicle of a five-month ramble through Évvia, one of the least-visited islands.

Wheeler has a sure touch with Greek culture and an open approach to nuns, goatherds or academics; the sole quibble is her success in making Évvia seem more interesting than it really is.

OLDER ACCOUNTS

James Theodore Bent *Aegean Islands: The Cyclades, or Life Among Insular Greeks* (o/p). Originally published in 1881, this remains the best account of island customs and folklore; it's also a highly readable, droll account of a year's Aegean travel, including a particularly violent Cycladic winter.

Robert Byron *The Station* (Century, UK, o/p). Travels on Mount Áthos in the 1930s, by one of the pioneering scholars of Byzantine art and architecture.

Nikos Kazantzakis *Travels in Greece: Journey to the Morea* (Bruno Cassirer, UK, o/p). Slightly stilted translation of the Cretan novelist's journey around the Peloponnese, and his increasing alienation from 1930s Greece. Easy to find in specialist shops.

Edward Lear *Journals of a Landscape Painter in Greece and Albania* (Century, o/p). Highly entertaining journals of two journeys through Greece and Albania in autumn 1848 and spring 1849, by the famous landscape painter and author of *The Book of Nonsense*. Further doses of Lear, *The Corfu Years* and *The Cretan Journal*, have been published by Denise Harvey in Athens.

Sidney Loch *Athos, The Holy Mountain* (Molho, Thessaloníki, Greece). A resident of Ouranópoli, on the periphery of Mount Áthos, from 1924 to 1954, Loch recounts the legends surrounding the various monasteries, as gleaned from his years of walking through the monastic republic.

Richard Stoneman, ed *A Literary Companion to Travel in Greece* (Getty Centre for the History of Art and the Humanities, US). Ancient and medieval authors, plus Grand Tourists – good for dipping into.

Terence Spencer *Fair Greece, Sad Relic: Literary Philhellenism from Shakespeare to Byron* (Denise Harvey, Athens, available in UK; Scholarly Press). Greece – and incipient philhellenism – from the fall of Constantinople to the War of Independence, as conveyed by English poets, essayists and travellers.

THE CLASSICS

Many of the classics make excellent companion reading for a trip around Greece – especially the historians **Thucydides** and **Herodotus**. Reading **Homer**'s *Odyssey* when you're battling with or resigning yourself to the vagaries of island ferries puts your own plight into perspective. One slightly less well known Roman source, especially recommended for travels around the Peloponnese, is **Pausanias**'s fourth-century AD *Guide to Greece*, annotated by Peter Levi in its Penguin edition with notes on modern identifications of sites mentioned.

Most of the standard undergraduate staples are part of the **Penguin Classic** paperback series. **Routledge** also has a huge, steadily expanding backlist of Classical Studies, though many titles are expensive and quite specialized; paperback editions are indicated.

Homer *The Iliad; The Odyssey*. The first concerns itself, semi-factually, with the late Bronze Age siege of the Achaeans against Troy in Asia Minor; the second recounts the delayed return home, via seemingly every corner of the Mediterranean, of the hero Odysseus. For a verse rendition, Richard Lattimore's translation (University of Chicago, *Iliad*; HarperCollins, *Odyssey*) has yet to be bettered; for prose, the best choices are by the father-and-son team of E.V. Rieu (*Iliad*, Penguin) and D.C.H. Rieu (*Odyssey*, Penguin).

Herodotus *The Histories* (Penguin), or A.D. Godley, tr (Cambridge UP). Revered as the father of systematic history and anthropology, this fifth-century BC Anatolian writer chronicled both the causes and campaigns of the Persian Wars, as well as the contemporary, assorted tribes and nations inhabiting Asia Minor.

Ovid *Metamorphoses*, A.D. Melville, tr (Oxford UP). Though collected by a first-century AD Roman writer, this remains one of the most accessible renditions of the more piquant Greek myths, involving transformations as divine blessing or curse.

Pausanias *The Guide to Greece* (Penguin, 2 vols). Essentially the first-ever guidebook, intended for Roman pilgrims to the holy sites of the Greek mainland; invaluable for later archeologists in assessing damage or change to temples over the intervening centuries, or (in some cases) locating them at all.

Plutarch *The Age of Alexander; On Sparta; The Rise and Fall of Athens.* (Penguin). Another ancient author, writing perhaps with benefit of hindsight – but with the detriment of shaky sources and much conjecture.

Thucydides *History of the Peloponnesian War* (Penguin). Bleak month-by-month account of the conflict, by a cashiered Athenian officer whose affiliation and dim view of human nature usually didn't get in the way of his objectivity; see the review of George Cawkwell's book for a revisionist view.

Xenophon *The History of My Times* (Penguin). Thucydides stopped his coverage of the Peloponnesian War in 411 BC; this work continues events until 362 BC.

ANCIENT HISTORY & INTERPRETATION OF THE CLASSICS

A.R. Burn *History of Greece* (Penguin). Probably the best general introduction to ancient Greece, though for fuller and more interesting analysis you'll do better with one or other of the following more specialized titles.

George Cawkwell *Thucydides and the Peloponnesian War* (Routledge). New, revisionist overview of Thucydides' work and relations with main personalities of the war, challenging previous assumptions of his infallibility.

M.I. Finley *The World of Odysseus* (Penguin). Good on the interrelation of Mycenaean myth and fact.

Simon Hornblower *The Greek World 479–323 BC* (Routledge). An erudite survey of ancient Greece at its zenith, from the end of the Persian Wars to the death of Alexander, which has become a standard university paperback text.

Robin Lane Fox *Alexander the Great* (Penguin). An absorbing study, which mixes historical scholarship with imaginative psychological detail.

Michael Grant and John Hazel *Who's Who in Classical Mythology* (Routledge). Gazetteer of over 1200 mythological personalities, together with historical and geographical background.

Pierre Grimal, ed *Dictionary of Classical Mythology* (Penguin). Though translated from the French, considered to still have the edge on the more recent Grant/Hazel title.

John Kenyon Davies *Democracy and Classical Greece* (Fontana; Harvard UP).

Established and accessible account of the Classical period and its political developments.

Oswyn Murray *Early Greece* (Fontana; Harvard UP). The Greek story from the Mycenaeans and Minoans through to the beginning of the Classical period.

Robin Osborne *Greece in the Making 1200–479 BC* (Routledge). Well illustrated paperback on the rise of the city-state.

F.W. Walbank *The Hellenistic World* (Fontana; Harvard UP). Greece under the sway of the Macedonian and Roman empires.

ANCIENT RELIGION

Harry Brewster *River Gods of Greece* (I.B. Tauris; St Martin's). Most ancient rivers had a deity associated with them; here are the cults and legends.

Walter Burkert *Greek Religion* (Blackwell; Harvard UP, o/p). Ancient religion, that is; a thorough discussion of rites, cults and deities in the translated German landmark text.

Matthew Dillon *Pilgrims and Pilgrimage in Ancient Greece* (Routledge). Pricey hardback exploring not only the main sanctuaries such as Delphi, but also minor oracles, the role of women and children, and secular festivities attending the rites.

Nano Marinatos and Robin Hagg *Greek Sanctuaries: New Approaches* (Routledge). Form and function of the temples, in the light of recent scholarship.

R. Gordon Wasson, Albert Hoffmann, Carl Ruck *The Road to Eleusis: Unveiling the Secret of the Mysteries* (Harcourt Brace, o/p). Well-argued monograph expounding the theory that the Eleusinian mysteries were at least in part a psychedelic trip, courtesy of grain-ergot fungus. Guaranteed to outrage conventional classicists.

FOOD AND WINE

Andrew Dalby *Siren Feasts* (Routledge). Subtitled "A history of food and gastronomy in Greece", this analysis of Classical and Byzantine texts demonstrates just how little Greek cuisine has changed in three millennia; also excellent on the introduction and etymology of common vegetables and herbs.

James Davidson *Courtesans and Fishcakes* (HarperCollins, UK). Not just a compendium of quirks – though attitudes and insults about consumption and consummation there are a-plenty – but wine, women and seafood in ancient Athens, placed in their social context.

Miles Lambert-Gócs *The Wines of Greece* (Faber & Faber). Comprehensive survey of the emerging and improving wines of Greece, with plenty of historical background; unfortunately few of these grace middle-of-the-road taverna tables as yet.

ARCHEOLOGY AND ART

John Beckwith *Early Christian and Byzantine Art* (Yale UP). Illustrated study placing Byzantine art within a wider context.

William R. Biers *Archeology of Greece: An Introduction* (Cornell UP). A recently revised and excellent standard text.

John Boardman *Greek Art* (Thames & Hudson, UK). A very good concise introduction: part of the "World of Art" series.

Chris Hellier *Monasteries of Greece* (Tauris Parke; St Martin's Press). Magnificently photographed survey of the surviving, active monasteries and their treasures, with insightful accompanying essays.

Reynold Higgins *Minoan and Mycenaean Art* (Thames & Hudson). A clear, well-illustrated round-up.

Sinclair Hood *The Arts in Prehistoric Greece* (Penguin; Yale UP). Sound introduction to the subject.

Roger Ling *Classical Greece* (Phaidon, UK). Another useful illustrated introduction.

Colin Renfrew *The Cycladic Spirit* (Thames & Hudson; Abrams). A fine, illustrated study of the meaning and purpose of Cycladic artefacts.

Gisela Richter *A Handbook of Greek Art* (Phaidon; Da Capo). Exhaustive survey of the visual arts of ancient Greece.

Suzanne Slesin et al *Greek Style* (Thames & Hudson; Crown). Stunning and stylish interiors from Corfu, Rhodes and Sérifos, among other spots.

R.R.R. Smith *Hellenistic Sculpture* (Thames & Hudson). Modern reappraisal of the art of Greece under Alexander and his successors.

David Talbot Rice *Art of the Byzantine Era* (Thames & Hudson). Talbot Rice was, with Robert Byron, one of the pioneering scholars in the "rediscovery" of Byzantine art; this is an accessible illustrated study.

Peter Warren *The Aegean Civilizations* (Phaidon, o/p; P. Bedrick Books, o/p). Illustrated account of the Minoan and Mycenaean cultures.

BYZANTINE, MEDIEVAL AND OTTOMAN HISTORY

Archbishop Kallistos (Timothy) Ware *The Orthodox Church* (Penguin). Good introduction to what is effectively the established religion of Greece, by the Orthodox archbishop resident in Oxford.

Averil Cameron *The Mediterranean World in Late Antiquity, AD 395–600* (Routledge). Essentially the early Byzantine years.

Nicholas Cheetham *Medieval Greece* (Yale UP, o/p in US). General survey of the period and its infinite convolutions in Greece, with Frankish, Catalan, Venetian, Byzantine and Ottoman struggles for power.

John Julius Norwich *Byzantium: The Early Centuries*; *Byzantium: the Apogee* and *Byzantium: The Decline* (all Penguin; Viking-Knopf). Perhaps the main surprise for first-time travellers to Greece is the fascination of Byzantine monuments, above all at Mystra. This is an astonishingly detailed yet readable trilogy.

Michael Psellus *Fourteen Byzantine Rulers* (Penguin). A fascinating contemporary source, detailing the stormy but brilliant period from 976 to 1078.

Steven Runciman *The Fall of Constantinople, 1453* (Canto-Cambridge UP) is the standard account of the event; *The Great Church in Captivity* (Cambridge UP) follows the vicissitudes of the Orthodox Patriarchate in Constantinople up to the War of Independence. *Byzantine Style and Civilization* (Penguin, o/p in US) and *Mistra* (Thames & Hudson, o/p in US) are more slanted towards art, culture and monuments.

MODERN GREECE

Timothy Boatswain and Colin Nicolson *A Traveller's History of Greece* (Windrush Press; Interlink). Slightly dated (coverage ceases in early 1990s), but a well-written overview of the important Greek periods and personalities.

Richard Clogg *A Concise History of Greece* (Cambridge UP). A remarkably clear and well-illustrated account of Greece, from the decline of Byzantium to 1991, with the emphasis on recent decades; there are numerous maps and lengthy feature captions to the artwork.

Douglas Dakin *The Unification of Greece, 1770–1923* (Ernest Benn, o/p; St Martin's Press, o/p). Benchmark account of the foundation of the Greek state and the struggle to extend its boundaries.

Oriana Falacci *A Man* (Arrow; Pocket Books, o/p). Account of the junta years, relating the author's involvement with Alekos Panagoulis, the anarchist who attempted to assassinate Colonel Papadopoulos in 1968. Issued ostensibly as a "novel" in response to threats by those who were implicated in Panagoulis' own murder in 1975.

John S. Koliopoulos *Brigands with a Cause* (Oxford UP). History of the brigandage in newly independent Greece and its significance in the struggle for the recovery of territory from Turkey in the nineteenth century.

H.A. Lidderdale, trs and ed *The Memoirs of General Makiryannis, 1797–1864* (Oxford UP, o/p). The "Peasant General", one of the few honest and self-sacrificing protagonists of the Greek uprising, taught himself to write at age 32 to set down this apologia of his conduct, in vivid demotic Greek. Heartbreaking in its portrayal of the incipient schisms, linguistic and otherwise, that tore the country apart until recently.

Michael Llewellyn Smith *Ionian Vision, Greece in Asia Minor, 1919–22* (Allen Lane, o/p; St Martin's Press, o/p). Standard work by the current UK ambassador to Greece, on the disastrous Anatolian campaign, which led to the exchange of populations between Greece and Turkey.

Yiannis Roubatis *Tangled Webs: The US in Greece 1947–67* (Pella Publishing, US). Chronicles growing American involvement in Greece during the lead-up to the military coup.

C.M. Woodhouse *Modern Greece, A Short History* (Faber & Faber). Woodhouse was active in the Greek Resistance during World War II. Writing from a more right-wing perspective than Clogg, this history (spanning from the foundation of Constantinople in 324 to the present), is briefer and a bit drier, but scrupulous with facts. *The Rise and Fall of the Greek Colonels* (Granada, o/p; Watts), recounts the (horror) story of the dictatorship.

WORLD WAR II AND ITS AFTERMATH

Nicholas Gage *Eleni* (Collins Harvill/ Ballantine). Controversial account by a Greek-born *New York Times* correspondent who returns to Epirus to avenge the death of his mother, condemned by an ELAS tribunal in 1948. Superb descriptions of village life, but blinkered political "history" – the basis of an utterly forgettable 1985 movie. The book inspired a response by a left-wing writer, **Vassilis Kavathas**, whose family had been decimated by the Right, entitled *Iy Alli Eleni* (The Other Eleni), not as yet translated into English.

Edmund Keeley *The Salonika Bay Murder* (Princeton UP). The assassination in 1948 of a CBS correspondent, apparently by minions of the Royalist government, was a major incident. This analysis fingers the colluding Greek and US intelligence services.

Kati Marton *The Polk Conspiracy* (Times Books, US). Another treatment of the Polk case, written as a gripping early Cold War whodunnit, and reaching a similar conclusion.

Mark Mazower *Inside Hitler's Greece: The Experience of Occupation 1941–44* (Yale UP). Somewhat choppily organized, but the standard of scholarship is high and the photos alone justify the price. Demonstrates how the complete demoralization of the country and the incompetence of conventional politicians led to the rise of ELAS and the onset of civil war.

George Psychoundakis *The Cretan Runner* (John Murray, o/p; Transatlantic Arts, o/p; Efstathiadis, Athens). Narrative of the invasion of Crete and subsequent resistance, by a participant who was a guide and message-runner for all the British protagonists – including Patrick Leigh Fermor, the translator of the book.

Marion Sarafis and Martin Eve *Background to Contemporary Greece, V. 1 & 2* (Merlin, UK). Papers and panel discussion from a late 1980s conference on the Civil War, with former belligerents confronting each other across podiums. Left-wing bias, but Sarafis herself – widow of an ELAS general – is impressive, especially in Volume 1.

Adrian Seligman *War in the Islands* (Allan Sutton, UK). Collected oral histories of a little-known Allied unit: a flotilla of caiques organized to raid the Axis-held Aegean islands. *Boy's Own* stuff, with service-jargon-laced prose, but lots of fine period photos and detail.

Michael Ward *Greek Assignments: SOE 1943–UNSCOB 1948* (Lycabettus Press, Athens). The author, British consul in Thessaloniki from 1971 to 1983, parachuted into the Píndhos as a guerrilla and walked the width of the country; most amazing is how the Germans controlled only the towns, leaving the countryside to the Resistance. While assigned to discourage other British servicemen from doing so, he married a Greek and later returned to observe the Civil War.

C.M. Woodhouse *The Struggle for Greece, 1941–49* (Hart-Davis, o/p; Beekman). A masterly and by no means uncritical account of this crucial decade, explaining how Greece emerged without a Communist government.

ETHNOGRAPHY

J.K. Campbell *Honour, Family and Patronage* (Oxford UP). A classic study of a Sarakatsáni community in the Píndhos mountains, with much wider applicability to rural Greece.

Costis Copsides *The Jews of Thessaloniki through the Postcards (sic) 1886–1917* (self-published, Thessaloniki). Jewish personalities, business and monuments, and the pre-fire city in general, as seen by Jewish postcard publishers.

Rae Dalven *The Jews of Ioannina* (Lycabettus Press, Greece, available in the UK/US). History and culture of the thriving pre-Holocaust community, related by a poet and translator of Cavafy (see "Modern Greek Poetry", below), herself an Epirot Jew.

Juliet du Boulay *Portrait of a Greek Mountain Village* (Oxford UP, o/p in UK). An account of the village of Ambéli, on Évvia, during the 1960s. The habits and customs of an all-but-vanished way of life are observed and evoked in an absorbing narrative.

James Faubion *Modern Greek Lessons* (Princeton UP). Much the same ground as Storace's work, but covered rather more academically (occasionally preciously) by another long-term resident of Athens, and with an excellent chapter on homosexuality in Greece.

Gail Holst-Warhaft *Road to Rembétika: Songs of Love, Sorrow and Hashish* (Denise Harvey, Greece, available in the UK). The most

intriguing Greek urban musical style of this century, evocatively traced by a Cornell University musicologist. Be sure to get the most recent edition available, as the discography is regularly updated.

Anastasia Karakasidou *Fields of Wheat, Hills of Blood* (University of Chicago, US). Excellent but controversial work on the Slavophone minority of northern Greece (see box pp.344–345), declined for publication by Cambridge UP.

John Cuthbert Lawson *Modern Greek Folklore and Ancient Greek Religion: A Study in Survivals* (University Books, New York; o/p). This is to Greece what *The Golden Bough* is to the world at large; well worth scouring libraries and antiquarian dealers for.

Peter Mackridge and Eleni Yannakakis *Ourselves and Others: Development of a Greek Macedonian Identity since 1912* (Berg, UK). Less provocative than the Karakasidou volume, but covers much the same ground.

Clay Perry *Vanishing Greece* (Conran Octopus; Abbeville Press). Well captioned photos depict the threatened landscapes and relict ways of life in rural Greece; now in paperback.

Nikos Stavroulakis *Salonika: Jews and Dervishes* (Talos Press, Athens, available in the US). Monograph by the former curator of the Jewish Museum of Greece, lavishly illustrated with old photos, of two of Thessaloníki's most distinctive communities – which have vanished only this century.

T.J. Winnifrith *The Vlachs: The History of a Balkan People* (Duckworth; St Martin's Press). Rather heavy going hotchpotch on the existing Vlach communities in Greece and the rest of the Balkans, but the only study easily available.

MODERN GREEK LITERATURE

Roderick Beaton *An Introduction to Modern Greek Literature* (Oxford UP). Chronological survey of fiction and poetry from independence to 1821, with a useful discussion on the "Language Question".

FICTION

Maro Douka *Fool's Gold* (Kedros, Athens*; Roundhouse, Oxford, UK). Describes an upper-class young woman's involvement, and subsequent disillusionment, with the clandestine resistance to the junta.

Eugenia Fakinou *The Seventh Garment* (Serpent's Tail). Greek history, from the War of Independence to the colonels' junta, as told through the life stories (interspersed in counterpoint) of three generations of women; it's a rather more successful experiment than Fakinou's *Astradeni* (Kedros, Athens*), in which a young girl – whose slightly irritating narrative voice is adopted throughout – leaves the island of Sými, with all its traditional values, for Athens.

Stratis Haviaras *When the Tree Sings* (Picador/Simon & Schuster, both o/p) and *The Heroic Age* (Penguin, o/p). Two-part, faintly disguised autobiography about coming of age in Greece in the 1940s, by the former poetry curator of Harvard University library. Written in English because Haviaras felt his experiences too keenly to set them down in Greek.

Nikos Kazantzakis *Zorba the Greek*; *Christ Recrucified* (published in the US as *The Greek Passion*); *Report to Greco*; *Freedom or Death* (*Captain Mihalis* in the US); *The Fratricides* (all Faber & Faber; Touchstone). The most accessible (and Greece-related) of the numerous novels by the Cretan master. Even with inadequate translation, their strength – especially that of *Report to Greco* – shines through.

Artemis Leontis, ed *Greece: A Traveller's Literary Companion* (Whereabouts Press, San Francisco, US). An overdue idea, brilliantly executed: various regions of the country as portrayed in (very) short fiction or essays by modern Greek writers. A recommended antidote to the often condescending Grand Tourist accounts.

Stratis Myrivilis *Life in the Tomb* (Quartet; New England UP). A harrowing and unorthodox war memoir, based on the author's experience on the Macedonian front during 1917–18, well translated by Peter Bien. Completing a kind of trilogy are two later novels, set on the north coast of Lésvos, Myrivilis's homeland: *The Mermaid Madonna* and *The Schoolmistress with the Golden Eyes* (Efstathiadis, Athens, Greece). Translations of these are not so good, and tend to be heavily abridged.

Alexandros Papadiamantis *The Murderess* (Writers & Readers). Landmark turn-of-the-century novel set on the island of Skíathos, in which an old woman, appalled by the fate that awaits them in adulthood, concludes that little girls are better off dead. Also available is a collection of

Papadiamantis short stories, *Tales from a Greek Island* (Johns Hopkins UP).

Dido Sotiriou *Farewell Anatolia* (Kedros, Greece*). A classic since its initial appearance in 1962 (it is now in its 56th Greek printing), this epic chronicles the traumatic end of Greek life in Asia Minor, from World War I to the catastrophe of 1922, as narrated by a fictionalized version of the author's father.

Stratis Tsirkas *Drifting Cities* (Kedros*). Set by turns in the Jerusalem, Cairo and Alexandria of World War II, this unflinchingly honest and humane epic of a Greek army hero secretly working for the Leftist resistance got the author denounced by the Communist Party.

Vassilis Vassilikos *Z* (Four Walls Eight Windows). A novel based closely enough on events – the 1963 political assassination of Gregoris Lambrakis in Thessaloníki – to be banned under the colonels' junta, and brilliantly filmed by Costa-Gavras in 1968.

Yiorgos Yatromanolakis *The History of a Vendetta* (Dedalus/Hippocrene). Greek magic realism as the tales of two families unravel from a murder in a small Cretan village.

Alki Zei *Achilles' Fiancée* (Kedros, Greece*). A recent bestseller, following the woman of the title from the German occupation to the Civil War, exile as a leftist in Tashkent and Paris, and a return to Greece after the junta's fall.

* These books are part of a highly recommended "Modern Greek Writers" series, currently numbering nearly thirty titles, issued by the Athenian company Kedros Publishers.

MODERN GREEK POETRY

With two Nobel laureates in recent years – George Seferis and Odysseus Elytis – modern Greece has an extraordinarily intense and dynamic poetic tradition. Translations of all of the following are excellent.

C.P. Cavafy *Collected Poems* (Chatto & Windus/Princeton UP). The complete works, translated by Edmund Keeley and Philip Sherrard, of perhaps the most accessible modern Greek poet, resident for most of his life in Alexandria. For some, *The Complete Poems of Cavafy* (Harcourt Brace Jovanovich), translated by Rae Dalven, is a superior version.

Odysseus Elytis *The Axion Esti* (Anvil Press; Pittsburgh UP); *Selected Poems* (Anvil Press;

Viking Penguin, o/p); *The Sovereign Sun* (Bloodaxe Books; Temple UP, Philadelphia, o/p). The major works in good English versions.

Modern Greek Poetry (Efstathiadis, Athens). Decent anthology of translations, predominantly of Seferis and Elytis.

Yannis Ritsos *Exile and Return, Selected Poems 1967–1974* (Anvil Press; Ecco Press). A fine volume of Greece's foremost Leftist poet, from the junta era when he was internally exiled on Sámos.

George Seferis *Collected Poems, 1924–1955* (Anvil Press, o/p; Princeton UP, o/p). Virtually the complete works of the Nobel laureate, with Greek and English verses on facing pages. More recent, but lacking the facing Greek text, is *Complete Poems* (Anvil Press/Princeton UP).

GREECE IN FOREIGN FICTION

Louis de Bernières *Captain Corelli's Mandolin* (Minerva; Random House). Set on Kefalloniá during the World War II occupation, this is a brilliant tragicomedy by an author best known for his South American extravaganzas. It has won praise from Greek intellectuals despite its disparagement of ELAS – quite an achievement.

John Fowles *The Magus* (Vintage; Dell). Fowles's biggest and best novel: a tale of mystery and manipulation – plus Greek island life – inspired by his stay on Spétses as a teacher, in the 1950s.

Olivia Manning *The Balkan Trilogy, vol. 3: Friends and Heroes* (Mandarin, UK). In which Guy and Harriet Pringle escape from Bucharest to Athens, in its last months before the invasion of 1941. Wonderfully observed and moving.

Mary Renault *The King Must Die, The Last of the Wine, The Mask of Apollo* (Sceptre; Random House) and others (all Penguin except *Masks*). Mary Renault's imaginative reconstructions are more than the adolescent's reading they're often taken for, with impeccable research and tight writing. The trio above retell, respectively, the myth of Theseus, the life of a pupil of Socrates, and that of a fourth-century BC actor. The life of Alexander the Great is told in *Fire from Heaven, The Persian Boy* and *Funeral Games*, available separately or in one economical volume (all Penguin).

Evelyn Waugh *Officers and Gentleman* (Penguin). This volume of the wartime trilogy includes an account of the Battle for Crete and subsequent evacuation.

SPECIFIC GUIDES

ARCHEOLOGY

A.R. and Mary Burn *The Living Past of Greece: A Time Traveller's Tour of Historic and Prehistoric Places* (Herbert Press; HarperCollins). Unusual in extent, this covers sites from Minoan through to Byzantine and Frankish, with good clear plans and lively text.

Paul Hetherington *Byzantine and Medieval Greece: Churches, Castles and Art* (John Murray). Gazetteer of all major mainland sites, though frustratingly misses the islands. Readable, authoritative and with useful plans.

Evi Melas (ed) *Temples and Sanctuaries of Ancient Greece: A Companion Guide* (Thames & Hudson, o/p). Excellent collection of essays on the main sites, written by archeologists who have worked at them.

Alexander Paradissis *Fortresses and Castles of Greece* (Efstathiadis, Athens). Three extremely prolix volumes, widely available in Greek bookshops.

REGIONAL GUIDES

Marc Dubin *The Rough Guide to Rhodes, the Dodecanese and the East Aegean* (Penguin). Exhaustive coverage of the islands described in Chapters Nine and Ten of this book, by a part-time resident of Sámos.

John Fisher and Geoff Garvey *The Rough Guide to Crete* (Penguin). An expanded and practical guide to the island by two Cretaphiles, who contributed the Crete chapter this book.

Peter Greenhalgh and Edward Eliopoulos *Deep Into Mani* (Faber & Faber, o/p). A former member of the wartime Resistance revisits the Máni 40 years after first hiding there, and 25 years after Patrick Leigh Fermor's work, in the company of a British scholar. The result is a superb guide to the region and excellent arm-chair reading.

Lycabettus Press Guides (Athens, Greece). This series takes in many of the more popular islands and certain mainland highlights; most, despite long intervals between revisions, pay their way both in interest and usefulness – in particular those on Páros, Kós, Pátmos, Náfplio, Ídhra, and the travels of St Paul.

Nikos Stavroulakis *Jewish Sites and Synagogues of Greece* (Talos Press, Athens). Lavishly illustrated alphabetical gazetteer of all Jewish monuments in Greece, with town plans and full histories of the communities that created them. A few have been demolished since publication, however.

RAILWAYS

Michael Ward *The Railways of Greece: Their Inception and Development* (self-published, Athens; order on ☎30/1/72 13 894). A history of operations, plus extensive locomotive catalogues and diagrams.

YACHTING

H.M. Denham *The Aegean* and *The Ionian Islands to the Anatolian Coast* (John Murray, UK, o/p). Long the standard references if you were out yachting; still found in secondhand book shops.

Rod Heikell *Greek Waters Pilot* (Imray, Laurie, Norrie and Wilson, UK). Rather better than the preceding, which it has superseded.

HIKING

Marc Dubin *Trekking in Greece* (Lonely Planet). An excellent walkers' guide, expanding on the hikes covered in this book and adding others, both around the mainland and on the islands. Includes day-hikes and longer treks, plus extensive preparatory and background

---

BOOKSHOPS

Athens has a number of excellent bookshops, at which many of the recommendations above should be available (at fifty percent mark-up for foreign-published titles): see p.121 for addresses. In **London**, the Hellenic Bookservice, 91 Fortess Rd, Kentish Town, London NW5 1AG (☎0171/267 9499), and Zeno's Greek Bookshop, 6 Denmark St, WC2H 8LP (☎0171/836 2522), are knowledgeable and well-stocked specialist dealers in new, secondhand and out-of-print books on all aspects of Greece.

---

information. Look for a new version with a UK publisher in 1999.

Lance Chilton *Various Walking Pamphlets* (Marengo Publications, UK). Small but thorough guides to the best walks at various mainland and island charter resorts, accompanied by three-colour maps. Areas covered to date include: Áyios Yeóryios, Corfu; Yeoryioúpolis and Plakiás, Crete; Stoúpa, Peloponnese; Líndhos, Rhodes; and Kokkári, Sámos. In specialist UK shops or by mail order; catalogue from 17 Bernard Crescent, Hunstanton PE36 6ER, ☎ & fax 01485/532710.

Tim Salmon *The Mountains of Greece: A Walker's Guide* (Cicerone Press; Hunter). The emphasis in this highly practical walkers' handbook updated in 1993, is more specifically on the mainland mountains. The highlight is a superb traverse, roughly following the Píndhos crest, from Delphi to Albania.

LANGUAGE

So many Greeks have lived or worked abroad in America, Australia and, to a much lesser extent, Britain, that you will find someone who speaks English in the tiniest island village. Add to that the thousands attending language schools or working in the tourist industry – English is the lingua franca of most resorts, with German second – and it is easy to see how so many visitors come back having learned only half a dozen restaurant words between them.

You can certainly get by this way, but it isn't very satisfying, and the willingness and ability to say even a few words will transform your sta-

tus from that of dumb *tourístas* to the honourable one of *ksénos*, a word which can mean foreigner, traveller and guest all rolled into one.

LEARNING BASIC GREEK

Greek is not an easy language for English speakers but it is a very beautiful one, and even a brief acquaintance will give you some idea of the debt owed to it by Western European languages.

On top of the usual difficulties of learning a new language, Greek presents the additional problem of an entirely separate **alphabet**. Despite initial appearances, this is in practice fairly easily mastered – a skill that will help enormously if you are going to get around independently (see the alphabet box on p.835). In addition, certain combinations of letters have unexpected results. This book's transliteration system should help you make intelligible noises but you have to remember that the correct **stress** (marked throughout the book with an acute accent) is crucial. With the right sounds but the wrong stress people will either fail to understand you, or else understand something quite different from what you intended.

Greek **grammar** is more complicated still: nouns are divided into three genders, all with different case endings in the singular and in the plural, and all adjectives and articles have to agree with these in gender, number and case. (All adjectives are arbitrarily cited in the neuter

LANGUAGE-LEARNING MATERIALS

TEACH-YOURSELF GREEK COURSES

Breakthrough Greece (Pan Macmillan; book and two cassettes). Excellent, basic teach-yourself course – completely outclasses the competition.

Greek Language and People (BBC Publications, UK; book and cassette available). More limited in scope but good for acquiring the essentials, and the confidence to try them.

Anne Farmakides A Manual of Modern Greek (Yale/McGill; 3 vols). If you have the discipline and motivation, this is one of the best for learning proper, grammatical Greek; indeed, mastery of just the first volume will get you a long way.

PHRASEBOOKS

The Rough Guide to Greek (Penguin, UK/US). Practical and easy-to-use, the Rough Guide phrase-

books allow you to speak the way you would in your own language. Feature boxes fill you in on dos and don'ts and cultural know-how.

DICTIONARIES

The Oxford Dictionary of Modern Greek (Oxford University Press, UK/US). A bit bulky, but generally considered the best Greek–English, English–Greek dictionary.

Collins Pocket Greek Dictionary (HarperCollins, UK/US). Very nearly as complete as the Oxford and probably better value for the money.

Oxford Learner's Dictionary (Oxford University Press, UK/US). If you're planning a prolonged stay, this pricey two-volume set is unbeatable for usage and vocabulary. There's also a more portable one-volume Learner's Pocket Dictionary.

form in the following lists.) Verbs are even worse. To begin with at least, the best thing is simply to say what you know the way you know it, and never mind the niceties. "Eat meat hungry" should get a result, however grammatically incorrect. If you worry about your mistakes, you'll never say anything.

KATHAREVOUSSA, DHIMOTIKI AND DIALECTS

Greek may seem complicated enough in itself, but its impossibilities are multiplied when you consider that for the last century there has been an ongoing dispute between two versions of the language: **katharévoussa** and **dhimotikí**.

When Greece first achieved independence in the nineteenth century, its people were almost universally illiterate, and the language they spoke – **dhimotikí**, "demotic" or "popular" Greek – had undergone enormous change since the days of the Byzantine Empire and Classical times. The vocabulary had assimilated countless borrowings from the languages of the various invaders and conquerors, from the Turks, Venetians, Albanians and Slavs.

The finance and inspiration for the new Greek state, and its early leaders, came largely from the diaspora – Greek families who had been living in the sophisticated cities of Central and Eastern Europe, or in Russia. With their European notions about the grandeur of Greece's past, and lofty conception of Hellenism, they set about obliterating the memory of subjugation to foreigners in every possible field. And what better way to start than by purging the language of its foreign accretions and reviving its Classical purity.

They accordingly set about creating what was in effect a new form of the language, **katharévoussa** (literally "cleansed" Greek). The complexities of Classical grammar and syntax were reinstated, and Classical words, long out of use, were reintroduced. To the country's great detriment, *katharévoussa* became the language of the schools and the prestigious professions, government, business, the law, newspapers and academia. Everyone aspiring to membership in the elite strove to master it, and to speak it – even though there was no absolute and defined idea of how many of the words should be pronounced.

The *katharévoussa/dhimotikí* debate has been a highly contentious issue through most of this century. Writers – from Sikelianos and Seferis to Kazantzakis and Ritsos – have all championed the demotic in their literature. Meanwhile, crackpot right-wing governments forcibly (re-)instated katharévoussa at every opportunity. Most recently, the **colonels' junta** of 1967–1974 reversed a decision of the previous government to teach in dhimotikí in the schools, bringing back katharévoussa, even on sweet wrappers, as part of their ragbag of notions about racial purity and heroic ages.

Dhimotikí returned once more after the fall of the colonels and now seems here to stay. It is used in schools, on radio and TV, in newspapers (with the exception of the extreme right-wing *Estia*) and in most official business. The only institutions which refuse to bring themselves up to date are the church and the legal professions – so beware rental contracts.

This is not to suggest that there is any less confusion. The Metaxas dictatorship of the 1930s changed scores of village names from Slavic to Classical forms and these official **place names** still hold sway on most road signs and maps – even though the local people may use the dhimotikí form. Thus you will see "Leonídhion" or "Spétsai" written, while everyone actually says Leonídhi or Spétses.

DIALECTS AND MINORITY LANGUAGES

If the lack of any standard Greek were not enough, Greece still offers a rich field of linguistic diversity, both in its dialects and minority languages. Ancient **dialects** are alive and well in many a remote area, and some of them are quite incomprehensible to outsiders. The dialect of Sfákia in Crete is one such. Tsakónika (spoken in the east-central Peloponnese) is another, while the dialect of the Sarakatsáni shepherds is said to be the oldest, a direct descendant of the language of the Dorian settlers.

The language of the Sarakatsáni's traditional rivals, the **Vlachs**, on the other hand, is not Greek at all, but a derivative of early Latin, with strong affinities to Romanian. In the Yugoslav and Bulgarian frontier regions you can still hear Slavic **Macedonian** spoken, while small numbers of Sephardic Jews in the north speak **Ladino**, a medieval form of Spanish. Until a few decades ago **Arvanitika** – a dialect of medieval Albanian – was the first language of many villages of inland Attica, southern Évvia, northern Ándhros, and much of the Argo-Saronic area; it is still widely spoken among the older generation. Lately the clock has been turned back as throngs of Albanian refugees circulate in Athens and other parts of the country. In Thrace there is also a substantial **Turkish**-speaking population, as well as some speakers of **Pomak** (a relative of Bulgarian with a large Greco-Turk vocabulary).

THE GREEK ALPHABET: TRANSLITERATION

Set out below is the Greek alphabet, the system of transliteration used in this book, and a brief aid to pronunciation.

Greek	Transliteration	Pronounced
Α, α	a	a as in father
Β, β	v	v as in vet
Γ, γ	y/g	y as in yes except before consonants or α, o or οι when its a breathy g as in gap.
Δ, δ	dh	th as in then
Ε, ε	e	e as in get
Z, ζ	z	z sound
Η, η	i	i as in ski
Θ, θ	th	th as in theme
Ι, ι	i	i as in ski
Κ, κ	k	k sound
Λ, λ	l	l sound
Μ, μ	m	m sound
Ν, ν	n	n sound
Ξ, ξ	x	x and in box
O, o	o	o as in toad
Π, π	p	p sound
Ρ, ρ	r	rolled r sound
Σ, σ, ς	s	s sound, except z before μ
Τ, τ	t	t sound
Υ, υ	i	i as in ski
Φ, φ	f	f sound
Χ, χ	kh	harsh h sound, like ch in loch
Ψ, ψ	ps	ps as in lips
Ω, ω	o	o as in toad, indistinguishable from o

Combinations and dipthongs

ΑΙ, αι	e	e as in get
ΑΥ, αυ	av/af	av or af depending on following consonant
ΕΙ, ει	i	long i, as in ι or η
ΟΙ, οι	i	long i, as in ι or η
ΕΥ, ευ	ev/ef	ev or ef, depending on following consonant
ΟΥ, ου	ou	ou as in tourist
ΓΓ, γγ	ng	ng as in angle; always medial
ΓΚ, γκ	g/ng	g as in goat at the beginning of a word, ng in the middle
ΜΠ, μπ	b/mb	b at the beginning of a word, mb in the middle
ΝΤ, ντ	d/nd	d at the beginning of a word, nd in the middle
ΤΣ, τσ	ts	ts as in hits
ΤΖ, τζ	tz	j as in jam

Note: An umlaut over one of two adjacent vowels means they're pronounced separately; it often functions as the primary stress in this book. Thus kaïki is "ky-ee-key" not "cake-key", and Aóös is pronounced "Ah-ohs" not "Ah-oos".

GREEK WORDS AND PHRASES

Essentials

Yes	*Néh*	Yesterday	*Khthés*	Big	*Megálo*
Certainly	*Málista*	Now	*Tóra*	Small	*Mikró*
No	*Ókhi*	Later	*Argótera*	More	*Perisótero*
Please	*Parakaló*	Open	*Anikhtó*	Less	*Ligótero*
Okay, agreed	*Endáxi*	Closed	*Klistó*	A little	*Lígo*
Thank you		Day	*Méra*	A lot	*Polý*
(very much)	*Efkharistó (polý)*	Night	*Níkhta*	Cheap	*Ftinó*
I (don't)		In the morning	*Tó proï*	Expensive	*Akrivó*
understand	*(Dhen) Katalavéno*	In the afternoon	*Tó apóyevma*	Hot	*Zestó*
Excuse me,	*Parakaló, mípos*	In the evening	*Tó vrádhi*	Cold	*Krýo*
do you speak	*miláteh angliká?*	Here	*Edhó*	With	*Mazí*
English?		There	*Ekí*	Without	*Horís*
Sorry/		This one	*Aftó*	Quickly	*Grígora*
excuse me	*Signómi*	That one	*Ekíno*	Slowly	*Sigá*
Today	*Símera*	Good	*Kaló*	Mr/Mrs	*Kýrios/Kyría*
Tomorrow	*Ávrio*	Bad	*Kakó*	Miss	*Dhespinís*

Other Needs

To eat/drink	*Trógo/Píno*	Stamps	*Gramatosímata*	Toilet	*Toualéta*
Bakery	*Foúrnos, psomádhiko*	Petrol station	*Venzinádhiko*	Police	*Astynomía*
Pharmacy	*Farmakío*	Bank	*Trápeza*	Doctor	*Iatrós*
Post office	*Takhydhromío*	Money	*Leftá/Khrímata*	Hospital	*Nosokomío*

Requests and Questions

To ask a question, it's simplest to start with parakaló, then name the thing you want in an interrogative tone.

Where is the bakery?	*Parakaló, o foúrnos?*	How many?	*Póssi* or *pósses?*
Can you show me		How much?	*Póso?*
the road to . . . ?	*Parakaló, o dhrómos yiá . . . ?*	When?	*Póteh?*
We'd like a room	*Parakaló, éna dhomátio yiá*	Why?	*Yatí?*
for two	*dhýo átoma?*	At what time . . . ?	*Ti óra . . . ?*
May I have a kilo		What is/Which is . . . ?	*Ti íneh/pió íneh . . . ?*
of oranges?	*Parakaló, éna kiló portokália?*	How much (does it cost)?	*Póso káni?*
Where?	*Poú?*	What time does it open?	*Tí óra aníyi?*
How?	*Pós?*	What time does it close?	*Tí óra klíni?*

Talking to People

Greek makes the distinction between the informal (*esí*) and formal (*esís*) second person, as French does with *tu* and *vous*. Young people, older people and country people nearly always use *esí* even with total strangers. In any event, no one will be too bothered if you get it wrong. By far the most common greeting, on meeting and parting, is *yiá sou/yiá sas* – literally "health to you".

Hello	*Khérete*	My name is . . .	*Meh léneh . . .*
Good morning	*Kalí méra*	Speak slower, please	*Parakaló, miláte pió sigá*
Good evening	*Kalí spéra*	How do you say it	
Good night	*Kalí níkhta*	in Greek?	*Pos léyeteh stá Eliniká?*
Goodbye	*Adío*	I don't know	*Dhen xéro*
How are you?	*Ti kánis/Ti káneteh?*	See you tomorrow	*Thá sé dhó ávrio*
I'm fine	*Kalá ímeh*	See you soon	*Kalí andhámosi*
And you?	*Keh esís?*	Let's go	*Pámeh*
What's your name?	*Pos se léneh?*	Please help me	*Parakaló, ná mé voithísteh*

Greek's Greek

There are numerous words and phrases which you will hear constantly, even if you rarely have the chance to use them. These are a few of the most common.

Éla!	Come (literally) but also Speak to me! You don't say! etc.	*Po-po-po!*	Expression of dismay or concern, like French "O la la!"
Orísteh?	What can I do for you?	*Pedhí moú*	My boy/girl, sonny, friend, etc.
Léyeteh!	Standard phone response	*Maláka(s)*	Literally "wanker", but often used
Ti néa?	What's new?		(don't try it!) as an informal
Ti yíneteh?	What's going on (here)?		address.
Étsi k'étsi	So-so	*Sígá sigá*	Take your time, slow down
Ópa!	Whoops! Watch it!	*Kaló taxídhi*	Bon voyage

Accommodation

Hotel	*Xenodhokhío*	hot water	*zestó neró*
Inn	*Xenónas*	Cold water	*krýo neró*
Youth hostel	*Xenónas neótitos*	Can I see it?	*Boró ná tó dhó?*
A room . . .	*Éna dhomátio . . .*	Can we camp here?	*Boroúmeh na váloumeh*
for one/two/three people	*yiá éna/dhýo/tría átoma*		*ti skiní edhó?*
for one/two/three nights	*yiá mía/dhýo/trís vradhiés*	Campsite	*Kamping/Kataskínosi*
with a double bed	*méh megálo kreváti*	Tent	*Skiní*
with a shower	*méh doús*		

On the Move

Aeroplane	*Aeropláno*	Where are you going?	*Pou pas?*
Bus	*Leoforío*	I'm going to . . .	*Páo sto . . .*
Car	*Aftokínito*	I want to get off at . . .	*Thélo na katévo sto . . .*
Motorbike, moped	*Mihanáki, papáki*	The road to . . .	*O dhrómos ya . . .*
Taxi	*Taksí*	Near	*Kondá*
Ship	*Plío/Vapóri/Karávi*	Far	*Makriá*
Bicycle	*Podhílato*	Left	*Aristerá*
Hitching	*Otostóp*	Right	*Dheksiá*
On foot	*Meh ta pódhia*	Straight ahead	*Katefthía*
Trail	*Monopáti*	A ticket to . . .	*Éna isistírio ya . . .*
Bus station	*Praktorío leoforíon*	A return ticket	*Éna isistírio me epistrofí*
Bus stop	*Stási*	Beach	*Paralía*
Harbour	*Limáni*	Cave	*Spiliá*
What time does it leave?	*Ti óra févyi?*	Centre (of town)	*Kéndro*
What time does it arrive?	*Ti óra ftháni?*	Church	*Eklissía*
How many kilometres?	*Pósa hiliómetra?*	Sea	*Thálassa*
How many hours?	*Pósses óres?*	Village	*Horió*

Numbers

1	*énos/éna/mía*	12	*dhódheka*	90	*enenínda*
2	*dhýo*	13	*dhekatrís*	100	*ekató*
3	*trís/tría*	14	*dhekatésseres*	150	*ekatón penínda*
4	*tésseres/téssera*	20	*íkosi*	200	*dhiakóssies/ia*
5	*pénde*	21	*íkosiéna*	500	*pendakóssies/ia*
6	*éxi*	30	*triánda*	1000	*khílies/hilia*
7	*eftá*	40	*saránda*	2000	*dhío khiliádhes*
8	*okhtó*	50	*penínda*	1,000,000	*éna ekatomírio*
9	*enyá*	60	*exínda*	first	*próto*
10	*dhéka*	70	*evdhomínda*	second	*dhéftero*
11	*éndheka*	80	*ogdhónda*	third	*tríto*

The time and days of the week

Sunday	*Kyriakí*	What time is it?	*Ti óra íneh?*
Monday	*Dheftéra*	One/two/three o'clock	*Mía óra, dhýo/trís (óres)*
Tuesday	*Tríti*	Twenty minutes to four	*Tésseres pará íkosi*
Wednesday	*Tetárti*	Five minutes past seven	*Eftá keh pénde*
Thursday	*Pémpti*	Half past eleven	*Éndheka keh misí*
Friday	*Paraskeví*	Half-hour	*Misí óra*
Saturday	*Sávato*	Quarter-hour	*Éna tétarto*

A GLOSSARY OF WORDS AND TERMS

ACROPOLIS Ancient, fortified hilltop.

AGORA Market and meeting place of an ancient Greek city.

AMPHORA Tall, narrow-necked jar for oil or wine.

ÁNO Upper; as in upper town or village.

APSE Polygonal or curved recess at the altar end of a church.

ARCHAIC PERIOD Late Iron Age period, from around 750 BC to the start of the Classical period in the fifth century BC.

ARKHONDIKÓ A stone mansion in the villages of the Zagóri.

ASTYKÓ (Intra) city, municipal, local; adjective applied to phone calls and bus services.

ATRIUM Open, inner courtyard of a house.

ÁYIOS/AYÍA/ÁYII Saint or holy (m/f/plural). Common place name prefix (abbreviated Ag or Ay), often spelled AGIOS or AGHIOS.

BASILICA Colonnaded, "hall-" or "barn-" type church, most common in northern Greece.

BEMA Rostrum for oratory (and later the chancel) of a church.

BOULEUTERION Auditorium for meetings of an ancient town's deliberative council.

BYZANTINE EMPIRE Created by the division of the Roman Empire in 395 AD, this, the eastern half, was ruled from Constantinople (modern Istanbul). In Greece, Byzantine culture peaked twice: in the eleventh century, and again at Mystra in the early fifteenth century.

CAPITAL The top, often ornamented, of a column.

CELLA Sacred room of a temple, housing the cult image.

CLASSICAL PERIOD Essentially from the end of the Persian Wars in the fifth century BC until the unification of Greece under Philip II of Macedon (338 BC).

CORINTHIAN Decorative columns, festooned with acanthus florettes.

DHIMARKHÍO Town hall.

DHOMÁTIA Rooms for rent in private houses.

DORIAN Northern civilization that displaced and succeeded the Mycenaeans and Minoans through most of Greece around 1100 BC.

DORIC Primitive columns, dating from the Dorian period.

ENTABLATURE The horizontal linking structure atop the columns of an ancient temple.

EPARKHÍA Greek Orthodox diocese, also the smallest subdivision of a modern province.

EXONARTHEX The outer vestibule or entrance hall of a church.

FORUM Market and meeting place of a Roman-era city.

FRÁKHTES Dry-stone walls, on islands.

FRIEZE Band of sculptures around a temple. Doric friezes consist of various tableaux of figures (METOPES) interspersed with grooved panels (TRIGLYPHS); Ionic ones have continuous bands of figures.

FROÚRIO Medieval castle.

GARSONIÉRA/ES Studio self-catering apartment/s.

GEOMETRIC PERIOD Post-Mycenaean Iron Age era named for the style of its pottery; begins in the early eleventh century BC with the arrival of Dorian peoples. By the eighth century BC, with the development of representational styles, it becomes known as the ARCHAIC period.

HELLENISTIC PERIOD The last and most unified "Greek empire", created in the wake of Alexander the Great's Macedonian empire and finally collapsing with the fall of Corinth to the Romans in 146 BC.

HEROÖN Shrine or sanctuary, usually of a demigod or mortal; war memorials.

IERÓN Literally, "sacred" – the space between the altar screen and the apse of a church, reserved for a priest.

IKONOSTÁSI Screen between the nave of a church and the altar, supporting at least three icons.

IONIC Elaborate, decorative development of the older DORIC order; Ionic temple columns are slimmer with deeper "fluted" edges, spiral-shaped capitals, and ornamental bases. CORINTHIAN capitals are a still more decorative development, with acanthus florettes.

IPERASTYKÓ Inter-city, long-distance – as in phone calls and bus services.

JANISSARY Member of the Turkish Imperial Guard, often forcibly recruited in childhood from the local population.

KAFENÍO Coffee house or café; in a small village the centre of communal life and probably serving as the bus stop, too.

KAÏKÍ (plural KAÏKIA) Caique, or medium-sized boat, traditionally wooden and used for transporting cargo and passengers; now refers mainly to island excursion boats.

KALDERÍMI Cobbled mule- and footpaths.

KÁMBOS Fertile agricultural plateau, usually near a river mouth.

KÁSTRO Any fortified hill (or a castle), but most usually the oldest, highest, walled-in part of an island KHÓRA.

KATHOLIKÓN Central chapel of a monastery.

KÁTO Lower; as in lower town or village.

KENTRIKÍ PLATÍA Central square.

KHOKHLÁKI Pebble mosaic.

KHÓRA Main town of an island or region; literally it means "the place". An island khóra may also be known by the same name as the island.

KOUROS Nude statue of an idealized young man, usually portrayed with one foot slightly forward of the other.

MACEDONIAN EMPIRE Empire created by Philip II in the mid-fourth century BC.

MEGARON Principal hall or throne room of a Mycenaean palace.

MELTÉMI North wind that blows across the Aegean in summer, starting softly from near the mainland and hitting the Cyclades, the Dodecanese and Crete full on.

METOPE see FRIEZE

MINOAN Crete's great Bronze Age civilization, which dominated the Aegean from about 2500 to 1400 BC.

MONÍ Formal term for a monastery or convent.

MOREÁS Medieval term for the Peloponnese; the outline of the peninsula was likened to the leaf of a mulberry tree, *moreá* in Greek

MYCENAEAN Mainland civilization centred on Mycenae and the Argolid from about 1700 to 1100 BC.

NAOS The inner sanctum of an ancient temple; also, any Orthodox Christian shrine.

NARTHEX Vestibule or church entrance hall.

NEOLITHIC Earliest era of settlement in Greece, characterized by the use of stone tools and weapons together with basic agriculture. Divided arbitrarily into Early (c 6000 BC), Middle (c 5000 BC) and Late (c 3000 BC).

NÉOS, NÉA, NÉO "New" – a common part of a town or village name.

NOMÓS Modern Greek province – there are more than fifty of them. Village bus services are organized according to their borders.

ODEION Small amphitheatre, used for musical performances, minor dramatic productions, or councils.

ORCHESTRA Circular area in a theatre where the chorus would sing and dance.

PALAESTRA Gymnasium for athletics and wrestling practice.

PALEÓS, PALEÁ, PALEÓ "Old" – again common in town and village names.

PANAYÍA Virgin Mary.

PANIYÍRI Festival or feast – the local celebration of a holy day.

PANDOKRÁTOR Literally "The Almighty"; generally refers to the stern portrayal of Christ in Majesty frescoed or in mosaic in the dome of many Byzantine churches.

PARALÍA Beach or seafront promenade.

PEDIMENT Triangular, sculpted gable below the roof of a temple.

PENDENTIVE Any of four triangular sections of vaulting with concave sides, positioned at a corner of a rectangular space to support a circular or polygonal dome; often adorned with frescoes of the four evangelists.

PERÍPTERO Street kiosk.

PERISTEREÓNES Pigeon towers.

PERISTYLE Gallery of columns around a temple or other building.

PINAKOTHIKI Picture gallery.

PYRGOS Tower or bastion.

PITHOS (plural PITHOI) Large ceramic jar for storing oil, grain etc. Very common in Minoan palaces and used in almost identical form in modern Greek homes.

PLATÍA Square, plaza.

PROPYLAION Portico or entrance to an ancient building; often used in the plural, propylaia.

SQUINCH Small concavity across a corner of a columnless interior space, which supports a superstructure such as a dome.

SKÁLA The port of an inland island settlement, nowadays often larger and more important than its namesake, but always younger since built after the disappearance of piracy.

STELE Upright stone slab or column, usually inscribed; an ancient tombstone.

STOA Colonnaded walkway in Classical-era marketplace.

TAVERNA Restaurant; see "Eating and Drinking" in Basics, p.43, for details of the different types of specialist eating places.

TÉMBLON Wooden altar screen of an Orthodox church, usually ornately carved and painted and studded with icons.

TEMENOS Sacred precinct, often used to refer to the sanctuary itself.

THEATRAL AREA Open area found in most of the Minoan palaces with seat-like steps around. Probably a type of theatre or ritual area, though this is not conclusively proven.

THOLOS Conical or beehive-shaped building, especially a Mycenaean tomb.

TRIGLYPH see FRIEZE

TYMPANUM The recessed space, flat or carved in relief, inside a pediment.

VOLTA Promenade.

ACRONYMS

ANEK Anonymí Navtikí Etería Krítis (Shipping Co of Crete, Ltd), which runs most ferries between Pireás and Crete, plus many to Italy.

EAM National Liberation Front, the political force behind ELAS.

ELAS Popular Liberation Army, the main resistance group during World War II and the basis of the communist army in the Civil War.

EK Fascist party (Ethnikó Kómma), consisting mostly of adherents to the imprisoned junta colonel, Papadopoulos.

ELTA The postal service.

EOS Greek Mountaineering Federation, based in Athens.

EOT Ellinikós Organismós Tourismoú, the National Tourist Organization.

FYROM Former Yugoslav Republic of Macedonia.

KKE Communist Party, unreconstructed.

KTEL National syndicate of bus companies. The term is also used to refer to bus stations.

ND Conservative (Néa Dhimokratía) party.

NEL Navtikí Etería Lésvou (Lesvian Shipping Co), which runs most of the northeast Aegean ferries.

OSE Railway corporation.

OTE Telephone company.

PASOK Socialist party (Pan-Hellenic Socialist Movement).

SEO Greek Mountaineering Club, based in Thessaloníki.

INDEX

Stay in touch with us!

ROUGH*NEWS* is Rough Guides' free newsletter.
In three issues a year we give you news, travel
issues, music reviews, readers' letters and the
latest dispatches from authors on the road.

I would like to receive ROUGH*NEWS*: please put me on your free mailing list.

NAME . . . .

ADDRESS . . . .

Please clip or photocopy and send to: Rough Guides, 1 Mercer Street, London WC2H 9QJ, England
or Rough Guides, 375 Hudson Street, New York, NY 10014, USA.

the perfect getaway vehicle

low-price holiday car rental.

rent a car from holiday autos and you'll give yourself real freedom to explore your holiday destination. with great-value, fully-inclusive rates in over 4,000 locations worldwide, wherever you're escaping to, we're there to make sure you get excellent prices and superb service.

what's more, you can book now with complete confidence. our £5 undercut* ensures that you are guaranteed the best value for money in holiday destinations right around the globe.

drive away with a great deal, call holiday autos now on **0990 300 400** and quote ref RG.

holiday autos miles ahead

*in the unlikely event that you should see a cheaper like for like pre-paid rental rate offered by any other independent uk car rental company before or after booking but prior to departure, holiday autos will undercut that price by a full £5. we truly believe we cannot be beaten on price.